P9-ELV-720

MYTH, LEGEND, AND CUSTOM
IN THE OLD TESTAMENT

170324

THEODOR H. GASTER

Myth, Legend, and Custom in the Old Testament

A comparative study
with chapters from Sir James G. Frazer's
Folklore in the Old Testament

1817

HARPER & ROW, PUBLISHERS

NEW YORK AND EVANSTON

Folklore in the Old Testament (3 vols.) by Sir James G. Frazer was published by Macmillan & Company, London, 1918.

MYTH, LEGEND, AND CUSTOM IN THE OLD TESTAMENT. *Copyright © 1969 by Theodor H. Gaster. Printed in the United States of America. All rights reserved. No part of this book may be used or reproduced in any manner whatsoever without written permission except in the case of brief quotations embodied in critical articles and reviews. For information address Harper & Row, Publishers, Incorporated, 49 East 33rd Street, New York, N.Y. 10016.*

FIRST EDITION

LIBRARY OF CONGRESS CATALOG CARD NUMBER: 69–17018

D-T

221.6

G

Contents*

THE PENTATEUCH

GENESIS

In the Beginning

Adam and Eve

The Garden of Eden

* ▲ indicates passages incorporated from Sir James G. Frazer's *Folklore in the Old Testament.*

"If Cain be avenged sevenfold"

The Sons of God and the Daughters of Man

32. "Sons of God"   79
    properties conveyed through sexual intercourse
    the mortal span

The Deluge

▲ 33–45. Deluge stories around the world   82
    46. The mountain of deliverance   128
    47. The dispatch of the birds   129
    48. The rainbow   130

The Tower of Babel

▲ 49. Scaling heaven   132
▲ 50. The confusion of tongues   135
    51. Babel   138

The Patriarchs

ABRAHAM

    52. Abraham and Melchizedek   139
▲ 53. "Cutting" a covenant   140
    54. Seeing the fourth generation   156

SODOM AND GOMORRAH

    55. Entertaining angels unawares   156
        the submerged city
        itinerant strangers as gods in disguise
    56. Blinding for impiety   158
    57. Taboo on looking back   159
    58. The pillar of salt   160

    59. The proposed sacrifice of Isaac   161

JACOB

    60. Twin culture-heroes   163
        hostile twins

The Exodus

FORMER PROPHETS

JEREMIAH

Zephaniah

Zechariah

Malachi

THE HOLY WRITINGS

PSALMS

PROVERBS

Preface

This book is an attempt to gather into one place all that can be derived from Comparative Folklore and mythology for the interpretation of the Old Testament. It grew out of the publishers' invitation to me to prepare an updated edition of Sir James G. Frazer's *Folklore in the Old Testament* on the lines of what I had previously tried to do for his *Golden Bough*. Very soon after I set to work, however, it became increasingly apparent that, to produce a work of any real use, I should have to go beyond that specification. For Frazer's book is, in fact, simply a collection of disjointed disquisitions on various points of folklore, which either take the Old Testament as their point of departure or try to wind up with it. In no sense does it offer complete coverage of the field, and more is left out than is put in. Moreover, although these essays may be invaluable in themselves, their connection with the Bible is often tenuous and sometimes even depends on false philology.

What I have done, then, is to go through the Old Testament from cover to cover and pick out, verse by verse, anything on which Comparative Folklore or mythology may throw light. In this effort, I have kept my sights not only on elucidating the overt sense of the text but also on recovering by the aid of such material the undercurrents of thought and the subliminal elements of the writers' minds; for it is obvious that in order fully to appreciate any work of art, attention must be paid not only to what the author expresses but also to what has—albeit subconsciously—impressed itself upon him. In other words, the background of a picture is just as important as the foreground.

The enormous amount of material that had to be digested has made it necessary for me to be terse, rather than discursive. I have not gone in for literary frills, since this is designed primarily as a work of reference. At the same time, I have made a special point of including ample references to the more elusive monographs and articles which have appeared on any particular theme in learned periodicals published since 1900. In this respect, the reader's attention is directed to the heading "Literature" at the top of certain sections of the notes. Because titles are cited recognizably in the notes, it has not seemed necessary to overburden the book with a separate bibliography.

What is here assembled covers not only stories and myths but also customs

xxi

and popular concepts. These last are often enshrined in the words and expressions used in the original Hebrew, and in such cases I have had perforce
to get a little philological. I have, however, always consulted the convenience
of the man who wants to eat the meal without bothering too much about the
recipe or the cooking, and I have therefore tried always to separate the kitchen
from the dining room—which means that I have relegated purely technical
matter to the notes, which the lay reader can skip.

The work is based on a card file, now running to more than 17,000 items,
which I have been assembling for the past thirty-five years. I do not claim
that everything here presented is of equal significance or even relevance. Like
my great predecessor, I have found it hard at times to avoid flying off at a
tangent; popular usages and concepts are so closely interwoven that one has
often to bring in purely secondary and tangential material in order to unravel
what comes as a tangled complex. Nor do I claim for a moment that all of the
interpretations of Scriptural passages here offered are equally valid or that all
of them are definitive. Many are simply suggestions. I hope, however, that—
as is so often the case with Frazer's work—even when theories and deductions
are rejected, the actual collection of material may still prove useful to students in other contexts.

I should like also to forestall, right here at the start, the oft-expressed
objection that bringing cargo from the seven seas may be a pleasant pastime
for treasure-seekers, but is not a sound procedure for a scientific expedition.
A lot of people these days look down their noses at the Frazerian method of
comprehensive comparison on the grounds that it jumbles together material
drawn from different climes and centuries. In the present case, it is claimed,
it is methodologically frail to institute parallels between Biblical beliefs and
practices and those of peoples who lived (or live) much later and in quite
other environments. To this it may be rejoined that, unless specifically stated,
such comparisons are never intended to imply direct cultural contacts or
borrowings, but merely to illustrate patterns of thought and feeling, to show
the variety with which certain basic notions have been expressed in different
times and places, and to suggest, on the strength of cumulative analogues,
the true (or original) significance of things which may now be seen only in
a distorting mirror. In precisely the same way, *semantic* parallels between
diverse languages are no less valid and instructive because those languages
themselves are unrelated. Indeed, in both cases the diversity enhances, rather
than diminishes, the significance of the comparison. Moreover, in *interpreting*
any one or other particular custom I have generally used the control of
context, choosing that explanation which best accords with the acknowledged
tenor and meaning of other usages with which it is ceremonially associated.
True, some of the explanations may even then be incorrect, but this seems
a calculated risk worth taking, for while, on the one hand, some things in the

Old Testament may thus become distorted, on the other hand, some may otherwise be missed.

Finally, where does Frazer come in? My original commission was to edit him, and I am afraid that, instead, I have smothered him. For one thing, I have, with a few exceptions, reserved for a future volume all matter dealing with legal institutions (e.g., ultimogeniture). For another, I have cut out the whole of his lengthy disquisition on the worship of trees and stones, as now merely repeating what may readily be found in any number of standard works on Comparative Religion. Let me say, then, that apart from this I have here retained what I could, and have marked it dutifully and piously with the notations ▲ and ▼ at the beginnings and ends of the relevant sections of the text. In the notes the sign ▲ is placed at the beginning only. Moreover, in such cases I have enclosed my own additions, both in the text and in the notes, between square brackets. The reader may be assured, therefore, that Frazer is indeed here, and I would add only that even in the parts which he did not write he is likewise here in a very real sense. However much his methods and conclusions may be decried today as imperfect and outmoded, the fact remains that nobody who works in this general field and who can now command a wider view and a better perspective can fail to recognize that he does so largely by standing on the master's shoulders.

*   *   *

I have had no help from colleagues in preparing this book, and have indeed been constrained, over these long years, to plow a lonely furrow. The field is not yet sufficiently cultivated, and the ground is still very hard. Perhaps the reader will make allowances for this fact.

On the other hand, I would here record with deep gratitude the generous and ready assistance which I have received over the years from the Simon R. Guggenheim and Lucius N. Littauer Foundations and from Columbia University's Council for Research in the Social Sciences. My warmest thanks are due also to Miss Eleanor Jordan, of Harper & Row, who spent laborious days and endless care in knocking a difficult manuscript into shape. She has made me appreciate more keenly what Elijah must have felt in the wilderness when those succoring ravens at last hovered into sight.

T.H.G.

Introduction

The folklore of the Old Testament consists of stories, songs, customs, institutions, and idioms. It is the residue of what Israel inherited from her pagan ancestors or adopted and adapted from her neighbors.

I. MYTH AND STORY

Major elements of this heritage are *myth* and *story,* but these are usually modified or recast to suit the outlook and taste of a later age. The ancient landmarks are not dishonored, but new building changes their aspect and the surrounding scene.

Myth in Genesis

In the earlier chapters of the Book of Genesis the traditional stories are retold, as often as not, in order to exemplify the current situation of man or some general and continuing principle. Thus, the time-hallowed myth of the wind which swept the primordial waters becomes a paradigm of how the creative spirit brings order out of chaos, while that of the expulsion of the first man and woman from Paradise for eating the fruit of knowledge is retold to illustrate man's constant sacrifice of innocence to intellect.

Myth in the Prophets

The prophets, too, employ the ancient myths in a special way. The primary function of an Old Testament prophet was to trace and expound the continuing plan and purpose of God in passing events. This involved recognizing characteristic traits of his operations, and to do so the prophets drew upon *mythological* as well as historical precedents. Thus, the defeat of Israel's enemies and oppressors could be regarded as a repetition, on the stage of events, of his mythological discomfiture of the primeval Dragon; while the eventual restoration of the monarchy could be portrayed by applying to David the ancient myth of the king or hero who, like Arthur or Barbarossa, had not really died but would someday return to his people in their hour of need.

Ancient Near Eastern parallels

A hundred years ago, most of such mythological allusions would have passed unnoticed. Today, however, thanks to the rediscovery through archaeological exploration of so much of Mesopotamian, Canaanite, Hittite, and Egyptian literature, it is possible at long last to recognize that, for all its distinctive qualities, the Old Testament is in fact saturated with the popular lore of the Ancient Near East. The notion, for instance, that water preceded all things (§2) likewise occurs in Babylonian and Egyptian mythology, both of which likewise attest the creation of man from clay (§§8, 315). Similarly the story of the Faery Garden (Eden) finds a parallel among the Sumerians; and that of the forbidden dalliance of the Sons of God with the daughters of men (§32) revolves around a theme which recurs in a Hittite legend. Again, the narrative of the Deluge (§33) is found in substantially the same form— including such details as the construction of the ark and the dispatch of the birds—in the far older Babylonian Epic of Gilgamesh. That this legend was indeed current in divers parts of the Ancient Near East is evidenced by the fact that fragments of Hittite and Hurrian (Horite) versions have actually been recovered and that a portion of the Babylonian recension has actually turned up in the ruins of the Palestinian city of Megiddo. Take, likewise, the tale of the rivalry between Jacob and Esau (§60). The contest between the more or less civilized man and his savage and shaggy antagonist appears earlier in the same Babylonian myth; while the familiar tale of Joseph and Potiphar's wife finds a parallel in an Egyptian folktale of the thirteenth century B.C. (§76). So too, the exposure of the infant Moses in the bulrushes reproduces, with appropriate change of scene, an earlier legend associated with Sargon, king of Agade (§78).

Mythological figures

It is likewise from Ancient Near Eastern sources that we at last learn the true character of several mythological figures mentioned allusively in the Old Testament. It is now apparent, for instance, that the familiar *cherub* was not —as formerly supposed—a nightgowned angel, but simply the equivalent of the Mesopotamian *karibu,* a form of griffin, so that the cherub who guards the entrance to Eden is but a variant of fairy tale's Dragon Who Guards the Treasure; and that on which the Lord rides (Ps. 18:10) of the Garuda bird of the Indic Vishnu and of otherworldly mounts in other cultures (§19). Similarly, behind the statement, in the story of Cain and Abel (Gen. 4:7), that "Sin croucheth at the door" we can now recognize an allusion to the demonic "Croucher" of Mesopotamian popular belief (§23), and behind the various references to Resheph, formerly rendered as a common noun meaning "flame," the Canaanite plague-god of that name (§§103, 242, 269, 298, 338). Leviathan, the monster vanquished primordially by Yahweh and destined to be vanquished again at the end of the present era (Isa. 27:1), is now seen to be but a Hebraization of Leviathan vanquished by Baal in an earlier Canaanite myth from Ras Shamra-Ugarit (§§186, 295); while the broad theme of the Conquest of the Dragon—probably reflecting the seasonal subjugation of floods—has its counterparts in Sumerian, Babylonian, and Hittite myths, as well as many parallels in European folktale and custom.

Other characters of ancient myth similarly make their appearance in the Old Testament. The members of the heavenly court, for example, are still designated as *bᵉnê elōhîm*, or *bᵉnê El*, "sons of God," as in the Ugaritic texts (§§**32, 291, 318**); the Babylonian *lilith*, or demonic hag, is classed among the demons who inhabit desolate places (§**190**); Kôshar, the Canaanite god of minstrelsy, is mentioned as the archetype of the musician (§**217**); the Lord of Hell bears the ancient Sumerian name of "King of Terrors" (§**304**); and the virtuous Daniel of the Ugaritic *Poem of Aqhat* is cited by the prophet Ezekiel as the legendary paragon of righteousness (§**210**).

Mythological allusions

Near Eastern sources also enable us to detect mythological allusions which are not fully spelled out and which would otherwise elude us. In Isaiah's "Daystar (KJV: Lucifer), son of the morning," for example, and in Ezekiel's "fallen paragon" we may now recognize figures who have in fact several congenors in ancient mythology (§§**180, 213**); while the "pleasant plantings" which Isaiah excoriates as a heathen abomination can now be identified as the equivalent of the familiar "gardens of Adonis"—seedboxes ritually watered and made to germinate as a symbol of the resurrection of the dead or discomfited spirit of vegetation (§**184**). The bound "Fool" (Heb.: *Kᵉsîl*) of Job 38:31 now reveals himself as a form of Orion (§**300**); while an allusion to the widespread legend of the phoenix is recognized by some scholars in another passage of the same book (§**312**).

A peculiarly fascinating instance of the way in which Ancient Near Eastern sources may throw light on the origins of a Biblical story is afforded by the tale of how the first woman was created from the rib of the first man and named Eve, "mother of all the living." This, it would now seem, was motivated simply by the fact that in Sumerian cuneiform script the two signs NIN.TI could be read alternatively as "Lady of the Rib" or as "Lady of Life." The Hebrew compiler, who had such a cuneiform original before him, was therefore prompted to incorporate two alternative interpretations of that name (§**11,a**).

Mythological vocabulary

Sometimes ancient myths (and usages) survive only in a chance word or phrase, as when *we* speak of Cupid or the Muses, or employ such terms as *martial, jovial, protean, tawdry,* and *melancholy*. The vocabulary of the Old Testament is full of such relics. Take, for instance, the familiar description of the Promised Land as one *flowing with milk and honey*. This expression comes straight out of ancient legends about the Earthly Paradise, for that is one of the characteristic features of that blessed realm.[1] Conversely, the several references to "the gates of Death" (Ps. 9:13; Job 38:17), or of Sheol (Isa. 38:10), echo traditional portrayals of the netherworld as a subterranean or otherworldly city. So too, when Isaiah denounces Babylon as "one who has been playing Rahab" (Isa. 14:4), he is alluding to the well-known myth of the arrogant and blustering Dragon who was so called; and of the same order is the designation of Egypt by that name (Isa. 30:7; Ps. 87:4). Again, in the Song of Songs (8:6), the pangs of love are styled "fiery *reshephs* (RSV: flashes of fire)," whereby they are compared to the assaults of the ancient Canaanite plague-god, just as we might speak of *Cupid's darts.*

Occasionally, to be sure, the allusions are not quite so patent, and the recognition of them cannot go beyond a suspicion or guess. Who is to say, for example, whether the Book of Job's description of disease as "the firstborn of Death" (18:13) is simply an *ad hoc* poetic image or an echo of ancient mythology? Similarly, when the dance of the Shulammite is likened, in the Song of Songs (7:1), to "the dance of Mahanaim," the words may possibly allude to some variant of the tale recounted in Genesis 32:1–2 (§**71**), wherein the Phantom Host there associated with that place were portrayed, as in parallel stories elsewhere, as a troupe of celestial dancers (e.g., in Greek mythology, the rout of Artemis). Such a mythological allusion is possible, but it is by no means certain, and scarcely transcends the bounds of conjecture.

Mythological clichés

Popular stories have their characteristic phrases, tenaciously preserved through centuries of retelling. "Fee, fi, fo, fum," for example, is an integral element of *Jack and the Beanstalk,* and "Grandma, what big eyes you have!" of *Little Red Riding Hood.* A mere reference to such phrases is sufficient to evoke the entire tale. So, in the poetry of the Old Testament, there is evidence of a standard mythological vocabulary, drawn from traditional pagan prototypes.

The primeval Dragon is "smitten" (Isa. 51:9 [LXX]; Ps. 68:21; Job 26:12) or "roared at" (Isa. 50:2; Ps. 104:7), as in the Canaanite texts from Ras Shamra-Ugarit; the contumacious Rahab is "stilled" or "given his quietus" (Isa. 14:4; 30:7; Job 38:11);[2] the abode of God is in "the far recesses of the north" (Isa. 14:13; Ps. 48:2), as likewise in the Ugaritic myths; the members of the heavenly court are "sons of God" (Gen. 6:2, 4; Pss. 29:1; 89:6; Job 1:6; 2:1; 38:7), as in Canaanite and Akkadian; Yahweh "chariots upon the clouds" (Isa. 19:1; Ps. 104:3), as does Baal; and Leviathan is described as "the fleeing serpent"[3] and "the twisted serpent" (Isa. 27:1; Job 26:13)— precisely the same epithets as are used in an Ugaritic text to define that fell monster.

Parallels among primitive peoples

But "not from eastern windows only." Many of the stories related in the Old Testament are by no means peculiar to the Ancient Near East, but are simply particular forms of tales current elsewhere in the world.

The story of the Earthly Paradise, for instance, is found alike in the Ancient

Near East, Classical, and primitive cultures, and contains the same details of the special food forbidden to mortals and of the central river (or fountain) which is the primary source of earth's waters and which is diffused by four streams flowing to the four quarters (§§12–16). Similarly, if we dismiss as secondary the detail of her formation from the rib of Adam (see above), Eve would have been in the Garden from the beginning, and she thus becomes simply a Hebrew version of the seductive Fairy Mistress, a fairly ubiquitous figure in folktales of the Earthly Paradise or the Enchanted Realm (§§11,b, 321). Again, legends of a primeval deluge which destroyed the first race of men and from which only one or a few specially pious persons were spared, though often severely localized, are a feature of almost all primitive mythologies, and usually include the incident of deliverance in an ark or special vessel and the grounding of it on a high mountain (§§33–45). So too the Tower of Babel finds analogues in several primitive stories revolving around the theme of men's impious attempt to scale heaven, and the confusion visited upon them (§49).

Nor are these the only examples. Likewise familiar to all students of Comparative Folklore are the tale of the man who, like Abraham, entertains angels unawares (§55); of the city which, like Sodom and Gomorrah, is submerged or destroyed through the impiety or inhospitality of its inhabitants (§55,a); of the man or woman transformed, like Lot's wife, into a pillar of salt (sometimes, into stone) as a punishment for disobedience (§58); of the twin culture-heroes who, like Jacob and Esau, quarrel while still in the womb (§60); of the Phantom Host which appears on a dark or stormy night, even as the host of angels or otherworldly beings appeared to Jacob at Maḥanaim (§71); of the coat dipped, like Joseph's, in the blood of a wild beast, to feign that its owner had met his death by ravin (§75); of the rejected siren who brings false charges, like Potiphar's wife, against the object of her passion (§76); of the hero exposed, like Moses, at birth (§78); of the miraculous parting of waters (§86); of the rash vow whereby, like Jephthah, a man is obliged to sacrifice his own offspring (§115); of the "Uriah Letter" (§140); the Judgment of Solomon (§150), and the Ascension of Elijah (§159); of the king who, like David, will posthumously return to his people (§§205,a 227); and of the man, like Jonah, swallowed by a fish but subsequently disgorged intact (§236).

It is worth pointing out, however, that in citing such parallels from *primitive* cultures special caution is necessary, for many of them may in fact be nothing but "playbacks" of the Biblical stories picked up from Christian missionaries and then elaborated or garbled. Thus, when a tale from Tahiti tells of a first woman named Ivi created from the rib of the first man,[4] it is not difficult to recognize the Scriptural Eve masquerading in native garb. Similarly, when we are told in a story from the island of St. Cristoval that the first woman was fashioned out of *red* clay,[5] it is easy to detect the influence of a popular piece of Biblical exegesis, which connects the name Adam and the *adamah,* or "earth," whence he was taken, with the Hebrew word *adôm,* "red." This is the kind of thing that a missionary might very well have absorbed in his seminary days and then passed on in his retelling of the Scriptural narrative, only to have it served up by the natives to a later generation of eager anthropologists!

Localization of myths

Storytellers often lend added interest to their tales by giving them a local setting familiar to their listeners; and this device appears also in the Old Testament. Thus, the mythical Earthly Paradise is located (not without a strain on geography) somewhere in Mesopotamia (§13), and two of the four mythical rivers which issue from it are identified with the Tigris and Euphrates (§14). Similarly, the mythical tower reared to heaven (§49) is equated with the great stepped temple (*ziggurat*) of Babylon; and the concomitant motif of the confusion of tongues—well-attested elsewhere—serves fancifully to explain the name of that city, i.e., Babel-Babble (§51). Again, the widespread tale of the submerged city is located at Gomorrah, on the shores of the Dead Sea, simply because the name Gomorrah suggests a Semitic word meaning "flood, submerge" (§55,b); and the story of the traveler who has to wrestle with the spirit of a stream before he can cross it is located, on the same principle, at the Ford of Jabbok, simply because that name suggests the Hebrew word *'abaq,* "wrestle" (§72). The celestial army—a variant of the European Phantom Host—is encountered by Jacob at Maḥanaim, because Maḥanaim can be interpreted to mean "twin camps" (§71)! In the same way too, the "red man" (Heb.: *'adôm*), who is the antagonist of the hero in many folktales relating to the rivalry of culture twins, is identified with Edom, the eponymous hero of the Edomites (§62).

Telltale names

Another device for enhancing popular interest is to give the characters of a story arbitrary or invented names significant of their roles. One recalls at once Aristophanes' Lysistrata, "Madame de Mobilisation," who seeks to "bring the boys back home" from the Peloponnesian War, as well as Shakespeare's Doll Tearsheet or Constable Goodman Dull, and Sheridan's redoubtable Mrs. Malaprop. In precisely the same way, in the Old Testament stories, Solomon's leman is called Delilah, or "Coquette," and the contumacious Dragon whom Yahweh subdues is Rahab, "Sir Bluster," or Leviathan, "Wriggly." By the same token too, Cain wanders to the quite fictitious land of Nod, a name which itself means "wandering."

Reinterpretation

In course of time, the original purport of a story often comes to be forgotten, and the traditional details are then reinterpreted in accordance with the understanding of later generations. There are several examples of this in the Old Testament.

The story of Cain and Abel, for instance, revolved originally around the rivalry of the smith and the herdsman, for that is what the names themselves really denote. For the Scriptural writer, however, it is simply a didactic, moral tale about the first murder, and its several traditional elements, such as the wandering and marking of the smith—originally designed to indicate the characteristic trait of his occupation and his sacrosanct status—have taken on an entirely different complexion (§§22, 24). The ceremony of walking around a city or area as a symbol of establishing title to it—a ceremony attested in several parts of the world—has lost its significance for the Biblical historian and become but a triumphal march around the beleaguered Jericho (§104). The ancient notion that the human body consists of *twelve* essential parts is likewise lost to the author of the gruesome tale in the Book of Judges (ch. 19) concerning the ravished wife who was dissected into twelve pieces; to him this is motivated only by the desire of her husband to send a portion of her, as a grim warning, to each of the twelve tribes of Israel (§118)! In somewhat similar fashion, the original meaning of the acts performed by Elijah in his celebrated confrontation with the prophets of Baal on Mt. Carmel no longer comes through in the Scriptural narrative. The twelve stones which he erected on the spot, and which really represented a familiar feature of rain-making rites, are interpreted as twelve slabs used to reconstitute the wrecked altar of Yahweh—one for each of the tribes of Israel! Similarly, the loud cries uttered in that same ceremony are taken to be invocations to Baal, whereas Comparative Folklore suggests that they were originally imitations of thunder in a magical procedure (§158).

Myth as propaganda

Sometimes, too, a deliberately polemical note is introduced in these reinterpretations of pagan usages. Thus, the ceremony of passing children through fire in order to "sain" them against evil powers—a ceremony which is likewise well-attested elsewhere—is represented as a form of human sacrifice (§199).

Nowhere, perhaps, is this form of transmutation more in evidence than in the story of Esther, which appears to have originated as a tale told in the harems about the shrewdness of a woman in frustrating a jealous intrigue at the Persian court. In the Biblical version, however, it has become the foiling of a plot against the Jews, and the story has been so reshaped as to explain at the same time the characteristic features of a local festival (*Purim*).

Political use of myth

The adaptation of the ancient tales may also be determined by *political* considerations. Thus, the traditional story of the Rival Twins is taken, as we have seen, to symbolize the relations between Israel and her eastern rival, Edom

(§60); while the "hero" of the time-hallowed legend of the divine paragon who was ousted from Paradise for his overweening pride is paradigmatically identified by the prophet Ezekiel with the proud king of Tyre, destined for a fall (§213). So, too, in Psalms 47:3 and 98:1–3, the mythical monsters whom, in the old myth, the storm-god defeated in order to acquire or assert his kingship, are converted into hostile nations whom Yahweh subdues in order to evince his sovereignty and achieve salvation for his people; and when Joel speaks (2:20) of God's eventually removing "the northerner" from the territory of his people, he is transmuting the mythological figure of the demon from the north into a specific political foe of Israel (§233).

An especially instructive example of this process is afforded by the brief (and probably truncated) story of the cursing of Canaan in Genesis 9:20–27. Canaan is excoriated because his father Ham looked upon Noah's nakedness. The original version of this tale evidently revolved around the belief—paralleled elsewhere—that one must not look upon a kinsman's genitals lest one cast the evil eye on his procreative powers. (This belief seems, indeed, to underlie the express commandments in Leviticus 18:6–7). Now, in terms of the story itself, there is, to be sure, nothing odd (as critics have supposed) in the fact that Ham's son, rather than himself, is cursed. The point is simply that because Noah had been made to suffer indignity from his son, so Ham, who perpetrated the offense, will suffer indignity from *his*, for Canaan will be condemned to be the slave of his brothers. But this old story is given a political complexion: it signifies the subjugation of the Canaanites by the Israelites and the Philistines, and Cain is made a son of Ham because, when the story was written, the land was largely a vassal of Egypt, who was regarded as a son of Ham (cf. Gen. 10:6).

Aetiological myths

Another way of accommodating general stories to a local scene is to use them *aetiologically*—that is, as explanations of familiar names or of current customs and institutions. Thus, when Jacob wrestles with the mysterious antagonist, the scene is laid near a place called Penuel, the name of which is taken to mean Face-of-God, on the grounds that the hero there beheld the face of a divine being (god), yet survived. Similarly, when the adversary maims him in the ischiac nerve—a detail which recurs in parallel stories elsewhere—this serves to account for the fact that the Israelites refrain from eating the ischiac nerve of animals (§72).

A particularly interesting example of this process occurs in the story of Jephthah's daughter, told in the Book of Judges. When she learns that she has been doomed to be sacrificed, as the result of her father's rash vow, she begs to be allowed to go with her companions and roam upon the hills for two months. In commemoration of this, adds the Biblical storyteller, "Israelite maidens go to bewail the daughter of Jephthah for four days every year." Here a popular folktale has been used to explain the widespread custom of bewailing the crops or the vanished spirit of fertility at seasonal ceremonies (§115).

Suppression

There are also cases in which details of the older stories have been deliberately *suppressed* in order to accommodate the whole to a new outlook. In many cultures, for instance, the separation of heaven from earth is the subject of a distinct myth. Thus, in the Mesopotamian Epic of Creation (*Enuma Elish*), it is said to be accomplished by Marduk's splitting the vanquished Tiamat lengthwise, "like an oyster," and then using the upper part of her body to constitute the firmament, and the lower the bedrock of the earth; while the Hittite *Story of Ullikummi* refers to a cleaver by which the sundering was effected. There are likewise Egyptian myths on the subject, and in several primitive cultures the separation is represented as the forced severance of Father Sky and Mother Earth when they were locked in conjugal embrace. The compiler of Genesis, however, eschews these mythological fancies, because they are out of keeping with his own monotheistic outlook: heaven is parted from earth solely by the fiat of God (§5). Again, in the story of Cain and Abel, the *débat* between the smith (Cain) and the herdsman (Abel), which was part and parcel of the original tale and which is, in fact, a characteristic element of this entire genre, has been excised as irrelevant to the new complexion given it by the Biblical writer. Indeed, in this case, the excision is made quite blatantly by the simple expedient of leaving a gap in the text (§22)!

In the same way too, in the story of the dalliance of the sons of God with the daughters of men (Gen. 6:1–4), the fate of the former (elaborated, to be sure, in later pseudepigraphic and rabbinic literature) is omitted from the Biblical version, because it was alien to the compiler's purpose in retelling the tale: he wanted simply to account for the limitation of human life to a maximum of one hundred and twenty years (§32)!

A further instance of this process appears in the narrative of the Deluge. In general, this hews close to the earlier versions in the Babylonian Epic of Gilgamesh and in the *Story of Atraḫasis*.[6] Yet, one important detail is missing: the eventual translation of the hero to the Blessed Isle, where he enjoys immortality. To the Israelite writer, no one could be immortal, and the inclusion of such a patently mythological detail would impair the moral import which he was seeking to give to the ancient tale.

II. THE ROLE OF MYTH IN THE OLD TESTAMENT

Thus far we have been discussing the bearing of specific ancient and primitive myths upon specific passages of the Old Testament. But this raises the larger question: What is the role of myth *per se* in the Old Testament in general— that is, in the articulation of Israel's peculiar genius and message or, in theological terms, in the process of divine revelation? It is to this that we must now address ourselves.

In the first place, then, it should be recognized that myth is not (as often supposed) simply something ancient and archaic, subsequently superseded by logical and philosophical forms of discourse. Myth, or *mythopoeia,* is an independent and autonomous faculty of the mind which may operate at any time and in any age, alongside of intellection and speculation. Its characteristic is that it envisages and expresses things in terms of their impact, not of their essence; it is impressionistic, not analytic, and it finds its expression in poetry and art rather than in science. Its concern is with experience, not with categorization; it articulates a present, existential situation in general, continuous terms, translating the punctual into the durative, the real into the ideal.

From this it follows that the individual's relation to myth is necessarily one of *involvement.* Myth depicts his own situation by means of a particularizing story, but in the final analysis he is a participant, not merely an auditor or spectator.

Coming now to the myths and stories of the Old Testament, the essential thing about them is that they are paradigms of the continuing human situation; we are involved in them. Adam and Eve, characters in an ancient tale, are at the same time Man and Woman in general; we are all expelled from our Edens and sacrifice our happiness to the ambitions of our intellects. All of us metaphorically flee our Egypts, receive our relevation, and trek through our deserts to a promised land which only our children or our children's children may eventually enjoy. In every generation God fights the Dragon, and David fells Goliath. We all wrestle with angels through a dark night.

Not infrequently the real lesson of such a myth strikes home only when the light of Comparative Folklore is shed upon it; and this holds good not only for ancient stories but also for ancient institutions and usages. The whole process of ritual ablutions, for example, gains added meaning and pertinence when it is realized that to the Scriptural writers bathing in "living waters" meant immersion in the primal, uncontaminated essence of existence, and not simply the removal of impurity. So too, the primitive practice of carrying one's god around in a chest (ark) is more than a piece of crude hocus-pocus; it is an expression, in unsophisticated terms, of the necessity of the divine presence in the wilderness of our lives. Or again, the tinkling bells on the robes of the high priest, which protected him from death when he entered the holy of holies, are more than a primitive apotropaic device to scare demons: they are a reminder of the ambivalent nature of the divine and otherworldly, which alarms as well as attracts.

All of this is not mere allegorization, for it is not something read in later on the basis of more sophisticated philosophies. These implications are inherent in the myths and usages from the beginning. Behind the concept of demons lies the feeling which inspires it, the existential situation which this archaic idiom articulates. A bride, for instance, who veils her face as a disguise from evil spirits is simply a girl scared of the hazards of marriage; and when a family welcomes the ghosts of its ancestors at a seasonal festival, what is really implied is the lively sense that the past is involved in the present and that we are haunted by our memories and traditions.

Things which *we* can express today by rational and speculative categories were articulated by our remote forebears in impressionistic images, and it is these images that inform myths. *We* might say, for example, that an apprehension of Natural Law involves the ability of men to transcend their diurnal experiences, and of the transcendent to be concentrated and objectified in the immediate. But these are abstract—almost metaphysical—terms which had not been developed at the time the bulk of the Old Testament was written. For a Biblical writer, the same truth will be expressed by saying that for the Law of God to be received by men, man must go up the mountain, and God come down. *We* can say, if we adopt a teleological view of history, that the obscurities which envelop human existence will eventually yield to the progress of science and insight. Malachi, borrowing an image from ancient iconography, says that in the Last Days the sun of righteousness will arise with healing in its wings. *We* can say that tyranny, obfuscation, and evil will eventually be eliminated by a clearer understanding of the real principle of the universe and the ground of existence. Isaiah says that in the end the Lord, with his strong and grim sword, will smite Leviathan, the crooked serpent, the primeval marplot, who may be temporarily chained, but who has yet to be slain.

Even God does not escape this more primitive mode of articulation; it is, indeed, the price of his revelation. *We* can speak of the Absolute, the Principle of Nature, the Cosmic Ground, the dynamics of history, and the ultimate referent of experience, and when we speak of these things in terms of a *being,* we are indulging in deliberate *personification*—that is, we are applying to what we can envisage as concepts the characteristics and attributes of a distinct category, that of personality. But to the writers of the Old Testament, no such transference (or *metaphor*) was involved; there were no *two* entities arbitrarily identified with each other. The Absolute, the Principle of Nature, the dynamics of history, and so forth were *persons*—beings, not ideas—and man apprehended them not by intellectual subscription to a concept but through social relationship with a Being. The God who led the Israelites out of Egypt by his strong hand and outstretched arm *was* indeed the dynamic of history, but he was that as a person, not a personification. The wind is the breath of God; the thunder is his voice. These are not just literary images or conceits; wind and thunder are here parts of a person, not impersonal forces.

Comparative Folklore helps us to recover this primitive stance, to envisage the world by other than dialectic definitions. It retrieves a lost dimension of experience. It has become customary of late to call this approach by the name of *mythopoeia.* I should prefer to call it poetry. It is, as Cassirer pointed out, the stuff of the affective, as distinct from the intellectual, side of the mind, and equally determines meaning and significance. It must be recognized, however, that these two sides of the mind are not watertight compartments; they tend continually to overflow into each other. The immediacy and urgency of myth and ritual inevitably recede as men's developing powers of detached analysis provide an alternative to sympathetic involvement; and when that happens, the survival of traditional forms comes to depend more on their esthetic appeal than on their functional efficacy. Ritual turns into art, and myth is increasingly replaced by philosophy or science. Conversely, however, art and philosophy continue to draw on myth and ritual. The Old Testament stands in the stream of this development. Mythic modes of expression become literary *metaphors,* and survive only vestigially, as when *we* speak of Cupid or the Muses.

This raises a delicate problem, for in the case of ancient texts it is often exceedingly difficult, if not impossible, to determine whether a metaphor is live or dead—that is, whether the underlying myth is still a matter of popular belief or whether that original belief has evaporated into a mere verbal conceit. We know, for instance, that disease and bodily affliction were anciently regarded as the assaults of demons; yet, when Saul declares (II Sam. 1:9), "Cramp (or, Agony) has seized me," is Cramp (or Agony) to be spelled, so to speak, with a capital letter, or is the expression merely an idiomatic relic, as when *we* speak of a heart *seizure?* Similarly, when Resheph is said (Hab. 3:5) to attend upon Yahweh, or when the pangs of love are described as "fiery *re-shephs"* (Song of Songs 8:6), do the writers really have in mind the figure of the Canaanite plague-god of that name, or is this simply a case of metonymy? This is a problem which I will not even attempt to resolve, but it must at least be mentioned.

Myth, as an expression of existential experience, is thus the natural language of Religion. It is, in fact, what transmutes historical data into religious truth. The Exodus from Egypt is a historical datum; it becomes a matter of religion only when myth has portrayed it in paradigmatic terms. The Crucifixion is likewise a historical datum, but what, for a Christian, distinguishes the agony of Jesus from that of the two thieves is the factor of *salvation*—that is, the introduction into the story of that mythic element which expresses the hearer's own situation and concern. To be sure, such symbolic significance, issuing as it does out of the hearer's own experience, is necessarily variable, even though the actual story line may remain constant. Thus, the particular Egypt from which men escape today may not be that one from which the Israelites departed, and in our own day and age the Dragon may be Automation or what not. Accordingly, it is not to be supposed that when ancient mythological stories are used in the Old Testament they were necessarily interpreted by the Scriptural writers within their primal frame of reference. To name but one significant point of difference, mythological characters (like demons and dragons) which originally represented independent powers in a world not yet regarded as a systematic cosmos have somehow to be subsumed to the overarching authority of Yahweh and to be depicted as elements within the economy of his dispensation. But it is just this plasticity which gives the old myths their continuing validity and relevance, and which makes the mythic mode of expression the supreme vehicle for the living Word of God. In many and divers ways has God spoken to our fathers . . . and still speaks.

III. CUSTOM AND BELIEF

Light on popular beliefs

It is not only by supplying *literary* parallels that Comparative Folklore throws light on the Biblical narratives and, indeed, on the Old Testament in general. No less significant is the contribution which it makes by clarifying particular belief entertained by many peoples in order to account for megaliths (§100). the earlier inhabitants of the Holy Land were *giants* links up at once with a belief entertained by many peoples in order to account for megaliths (§100). The statement, in the Book of Samuel, that Agag, the king of the Amalekites, when brought before the prophet, came "with limping gait (EV: delicately),'' hypocritically chanting a dirge, stands in an arresting light when it is observed that a limping dance was (and still is) a characteristic feature of mourning ceremonies in the Near East (§129). The epithet, "baldpate," hurled by the urchins at the prophet Elisha, acquires added force when it is related to the widespread belief that a hairless man is impotent (§164). The fact that both Jacob and Moses incorporate predictions of the future into their farewell speeches is elucidated by the well-attested ancient notion that a dying man has the gift of prophecy (§74). So too, when Abel's blood cries out from the ground, the idea becomes fully intelligible only when the narrative is aligned with the worldwide belief that the blood is the seat of the *élan vitale* and thus a substitute for the outraged ghost (§25).

The entire story of Jacob's encounter with the "unco" being at the Ford of Jabbok is revealed by Comparative Folklore to be a pastiche of familiar popular notions. The mysterious antagonist is simply the personified current of the stream; he must vanish ere daybreak, in accordance with a belief which prevails everywhere concerning witches, elves, fairies, nixes, and nocturnal spirits. His name must remain undivulged, because the name is an essential part of the identity, so that knowledge of it can furnish control over a person; *nomina omina sunt* (§72).

The world and man

There are likewise many parallels in the Old Testament to beliefs entertained elsewhere concerning the features of the world and the nature and destiny of man.

The firmament is portrayed as a metal strip (Heb.: *raqî'ᵃ;* §4). Heaven and earth alike rest on pillars (§309). Misconduct, especially on the part of the king, can impair the fertility of the soil (§§144, 198). Fire can purge a man from evil spirits (§199). The sun is portrayed by the prophet Malachi as winged—a concept which also finds expression in Ancient Near Eastern art (§248). The wind flits across the primeval deep like a bird (Heb.: $m^e rah eph$-eth: §3).

The blood is the seat of life (§§9, 25). The heart or soul can leave a man temporarily in moments of stress; it can be *ex-cited* out of him (§336), and deception is called "stealing the heart" (§69). Conversely, the soul can be prevented from escaping by being bound to the body by fillets (§208).

Leprosy or similar disfigurement of the skin is a punishment for impiety (§93); so is blindness (§56). A man's strength or essential self can lie in his hair (§§117, 164), and the hair is therefore shorn when he suffers legal disgrace (§139) or, in rites of mourning, when he participates in that diminution of the corporate life which is entailed by the death of a kinsman (§135). Life itself can be portrayed as a thread, snapped at death (§§218, 311); and Death binds men in his toils (§§253, 286). At the moment of demise, a man's soul may be said to take wing like a bird (§274); and the ghosts of women who die in childbirth haunt the uplands seeking their babes (§205).

Common ideas about *animals* also find parallels in the Old Testament. The serpent, for instance, is shrewd and wily (§18). Certain beasts, like Balaam's ass, can "flair" ghosts or other invisible beings (§99). The stork is renowned for its kindliness to its young, and is therefore called *hasîdah,* "the kindly."

Traces of *popular medicine* may also be recognized by the comparative method. Thus, when Reuben supplies his temporarily barren mother with mandrakes as an aid to further conception, his action can be explained by the persistent popular tradition that the mandrake is an aphrodisiac (§67); while when the lovesick maiden in the Song of Songs begs to be "stayed" with apples (or quinces), she is drawing on an equally widespread belief that the fruits in question are an antidote to the effects of powerful emotion or to irregular movements of the heart (§333).

To folk medicine likewise belongs the action of David's counselors in placing the beauteous virgin Abishag in his bed to warm him in his old age. This action, we are told expressly, had no sexual implications. It is elucidated immediately by the popular belief that the aura of the young can rejuvenate the ageing—a belief which, as late as the eighteenth century, prompted certain superannuated English gentlemen (including members of the cloth) to rent accommodation in girls' boarding schools (§147)!

To the realm of popular usages belong also several references to *magical* procedures, such as waving (§166) and whispering (§171), the employment of *new* implements (§166), the use of bells (§91) and of salt (§211) to forefend evil spirits, and the practice of divination at crossroads (§212,a).

Sometimes, to be sure, it is difficult to distinguish between folk medicine and magic, as when the bones of a holy man are said to resuscitate an adjacent corpse (§168), or when a prophet "stretches himself out" upon a dead or moribund boy to revive him (§157).

There are also sundry references to standard types of *taboo*. In addition to the ban on divulging names, to which we have already referred, there is the curse implicit on taking a census. Here we have the familiar proscription of *counting:* to know the number of anything can be as perilous as knowing its name, for it can equally enable one to control its identity (§146). No less widespread is the taboo involved in the story of how Lot's wife was forbidden to look back on leaving Sodom (§57).

Lastly, among standard *ritual procedures* mentioned in the Old Testament and illumined by Comparative Folklore it will suffice to cite the references to animal and even human scapegoats (§194), to the necessity of silence in the presence of a god (§241), to the custom of accompanying offerings with salt, and to that of circuiting the altar in worship—this last originally a method of warding off evil spirits (§257).

IV. FOLKLORE AND LITERARY GENRES

It is not only on the *content* of Old Testament literature but also on its *form* that Comparative Folklore throws interesting new light.

It has been observed increasingly in recent years that there is often a close connection between forms of literature and traditional patterns of ritual or public ceremony. An outstanding example is the development of drama out of the program of seasonal festivals,[7] and scholars have suggested that a ritual background may likewise be detected in divers hymns of the Indic Rig Veda,[8] in the Scandinavian Elder Edda,[9] in some of the odes of the classic Chinese *Book of Songs*,[10] and in the English Mummers' Play.[11] In the same way, several of the literary *genres* of the Old Testament seem to have been conditioned by the exigencies of ritual or cultic ceremonies for which they were originally designed.

Dirges

Dirges, for example, are usually composed in a halting, or scazonic, meter.[12] Whereas a normal Hebrew verse—there are, of course, variations—usually consists in two half lines of parallel sense, each containing *three* accentual beats (e.g., *A snáre have ye béen to Mizpáh, / a nét outspréad on Tabór:* Hos. 5:1), in dirges the last beat of the second half is cut off, to produce a distinctly *limping* effect (e.g., *Outdoórs they líe on the gróund, / my yóung men and óld; / My yóuths and máidens áll / fáll by the swórd:* Lam. 2:21). Now, it so happens that a characteristic feature of Near Eastern funerals is a lamentation chanted while the mourners circle around the bier *with a curious limping step*. It is not difficult to see, therefore, that the peculiar meter must have been designed originally to "mark the pace" in this ceremony, even though it subsequently came to survive simply as a literary convention.

Funeral dirges were (and still are) customarily intoned by female relatives of the deceased or by professional wailing women. This in turn led to the literary convention of putting laments over fallen cities into the mouth of an imaginary female inhabitant. Threnodies of this type have indeed come down to us from ancient Mesopotamia (where they hark back to Sumerian times), and it is to this ritual origin that we may now trace the characteristic style of the Biblical Book of Lamentations, much of which is similarly put into the mouth of a mourning "daughter of Zion."

Psalms of asylum

Likewise rooted in popular custom is the literary form of certain psalms (e.g., Pss. 7, 17, 26), in which a suppliant beseeches the favorable judgment of God against men who are laying charges against him. These psalms are characterized by a more or less standard structure and by the presence, in a more or less stereotyped sequence, of certain clichés. They usually begin with the statement that the suppliant is seeking *refuge* in Yahweh. They then appeal to him specifically as a *judge* (or a "prober of hearts"), and—in juridical language—identify the suppliant with the "righteous" or innocent party, and his accusers or opponents with the "wicked," or guilty. The latter are said to be *pursuing* (i.e., persecuting) him, and to be setting traps and ambushes for him. The Psalmist protests his innocence, sometimes exonerating himself of specific offenses, and on one occasion (Ps. 7:3) contenting himself with the blanket formula, "I have not done *this*," i.e., so-and-so, evidently to be filled in as required. Again in legal terms, Yahweh is sometimes besought to find the Psalmist's antagonists *guilty* and to make them *pay indemnity* (Heb.: *ha'ashîmēm*).

Such compositions were evidently conditioned in the first place by the Ancient Near Eastern practice of providing asylum at shrines and altars for men pursued by vendettas. They became the temporary guests of the resident deity and could therefore claim the protection of their host, in accordance with the established convention of bedouin society. The practice of adjudicating disputes beside the altar is mentioned specifically in the Old Testament itself in connection with Solomon's dedication of the Temple (I Kings 8:31–32), and one recalls that both Adonijah and Joab fled to the altar to escape the royal wrath. The formal procedure evidently involved the recitation under oath of a "negative confession," protesting innocence of specific charges (§313). If the suppliant lied, the god himself would exact retribution, but if he was indeed guiltless, he might in this way escape an unjust and peremptory fate.

Some of these Biblical "psalms of asylum" seem, indeed, to have been adapted from compositions in use at pagan sanctuaries, for it is significant that when they mention the name of Yahweh, that name often overloads the meter, suggesting that it is a later insertion.[13]

Kingship psalms

In the same way, too, psalms which begin with the words, *The Lord has become king* (EV: The Lord reigneth) are now generally recognized to have been patterned after a traditional style of hymn composed for the annual enthronement of the deity at the New Year festival. To the Hebrews the ceremony was, in all likelihood, no longer a living thing, but the style survived as a literary convention.

A good example of this type is Psalm 93, which boldly transfers to Yahweh the mythic exploits attributed to Baal in the Canaanite myths from Ras Shamra: he subdues sea and river, ensconces himself as king in "the height," and occupies a glorious palace (§276).

Hallelujah

The familiar *Hallelujah* at the beginning or end of a psalm is likewise the relic of an ancient popular usage. The Hebrew word *hallel,* which came to mean "praise," is really an onomatopoeic word (like *yell, howl,* etc.) expressive of inarticulate shouting or screaming. Now, among primitive peoples, the earliest form of prayer—as, in fact, of song in general—consists precisely in such ecstatic ejaculations. It is, for instance, by the frantic chanting of meaningless syllables that certain Australian aborigines seek to produce rainfall;[14] while the Yamana of Tierra del Fuego have been observed to perform their ritual dances to such inarticulate cries as

ha ma la, ha ma la, ha ma la, ha ma la,
O la la la la, la la la la la

and their neighbors, the Selk'nam perform in the same way.[15] So too among the Veddas of Ceylon a common prayer is the equally meaningless

tan tandinanan tandinana
tanan tandina tandinana[16]

and similar chants are intoned in the Peyote cult of the North American Arapaho.[17] In pre-Islamic usage, such shouting, accompanied by a skipping march (*ṭawāf*) around the altar, was indeed known as *taḥlīl.* It survives in the modern *dhikr,* or wild shriek, and its counterpart may be heard at any "hot gospel" rally.

Out of this inarticulate ejaculation there develops in time the *invocation* of the holy name, e.g., *ya Allah, iō Bacche,* etc.—a development illustrated, on a more profane level, by the substitution of *"Jesus!"*, *Madonna mia,* or *sacre nom de Dieu* for the original *oh, ah, ouch,* in modern swearing.[18]

This in turn produces the *elaborated invocation,* in which the name is tricked out with laudatory epithets, e.g., *Allah akbar* (Allah is mighty), *Holy, holy, holy, is the Lord of Hosts,* etc. This is the ancient Arabic *takbīr* ("aggrandizement") or *tasbīḥ* ("laudation") and the Greek *epiklēsis*. A good Biblical example is Exodus 34:6–7 (which really represents what Moses cried out to God, rather than vice versa, as commonly supposed): *Yahweh, Yahweh, a god compassionate and gracious, long-suffering and of abundant kindness and fidelity* (or, *truth*), etc.

Finally comes the stage where the epithets are validated by lengthier descriptions of the god's deeds, exploits and qualities; this yields the full-fledged *hymn.*

Taunt-songs

Again, it was a common custom in antiquity to open hostilities with an exchange of taunts and boasts between the opposing armies or their commanders. It is thus that Marduk and Tiamat preface their combat in the Babylonian Epic of Creation (*Enuma Elish*), and in the Old Testament, David and Goliath follow suit, each boasting the prowess of his god, much in the manner of the "My-dad-can-lick-your-dad" of brawling schoolchildren today. The practice is by no means confined to the Orient. The Welsh thought that such invective (*glam dichen*) could actually inflict physical damage on an opponent, and a crossfire of "taunt (*nith*)-songs" is a recognized method of settling disputes among the inhabitants of Greenland. Among the Arabs this produced a special genre of martial poetry, known as *hijâ*-verse, and literary specimens of this may be found in the Old Testament in the bellicose little Song of Lamech (Gen. 4:23–24) and in the utterances of Balaam, the seer commissioned by the king of Moab to "curse" the invading Israelites (§§**31, 98**).

Ballad

Lastly, there is the *ballad*. A ballad—as the very name implies—is primarily a song accompanying a dance, and its literary structure is determined by that fact. Leading characteristics of the ballad are therefore: (a) a *refrain,* designed to permit the various sections of the dancers each to utter the crucial exclamation, and (b) constant *repetition of keywords,* often tricked out with elaborations or "incremental supplements,"[19] matching the constant return of the dancers to their original positions and the constant elaboration of steps and movements. Often, too, an important word is repeated with emphasis at the end of a verse or stanza, like a final crashing chord of the accompanying music. Other characteristic features are an initial appeal to the audience to "listen," and a rapid, almost jerky transition (or "leap") from incident to incident, chiming with the rapid transitions in the dance. In short, a ballad is choreography in words—at least in its pristine form.

All of these features appear in the Biblical Song of Deborah (§**109**), which may therefore be regarded as a specimen of this genre:

1. The song is put into the mouth of the woman Deborah herself, and she is expressly bidden (v. 12) to bestir herself and sing.

2. There is an opening invocation (v. 3) to "hearken" and "give ear," as in the English ballads of *Richard of Almaigne* ("Sitteth all stille, ant herkneth to me"), *King Edward the First* ("A-stounde herkneth to my song"), *The Heir of Linne* ("Lithe and listen, gentlemen, / To sing a song I will beginne"), *Jemmy Dawson* ("Come, listen to my mournful tale, / Ye tender hearts and lovers dear"), *The Birth of Saint George* ("Listen, lords, in bower and hall, / I sing," etc.) and *George Barnwell* ("All youths of fair England . . . / to my song give ear"). Moreover, that this form is indeed ancient is shown by its presence in the Canaanite *Hymeneal of Nikkal and Yariḫ* from Ras Shamra-Ugarit ("Hearken, ye songstresses"), the Hittite *Myth of the Kingdom of Heaven* ("Let the mighty gods now hearken"), and the Biblical *Song of Lamech* ("Adah and Zillah, hear my voice, / Womenfolk of Lamech, give ear to what I say").

3. A refrain, "Bless ye the Lord," appears at the end of verses 2 and 9, and it has been suggested[20] that it was meant to be repeated also, as a kind of antiphon, elsewhere in the song.

4. Certain keywords are constantly repeated, with characteristic "incremental elaboration," e.g.:

> v. 4: The skies *also dripped,*
> the clouds also *dripped water.*[21]
>
> v. 7: *They ceased from law and order,*[22]
> in Israel *they ceased,*
> until I, Deborah, *arose,*
> *arose, a mother in Israel.*
>
> v. 13: *Then marched* a mere remnant against stalwarts,
> the army of the Lord *marched* for me . . . .
>
> v. 19: Came *kings, they fought;*
> then *fought the kings* of Canaan.
>
> v. 21: *The brook of Kishon* swept them away,
> *the brook* . . . .[23]
> *the brook Kishon.*
>
> v. 23: They came not *to the help of the Lord,*
> *to the help of the Lord* amid the warriors.
>
> v. 24: *Blessed above women* be Jael,
> among women in the tent be she *blessed!*
>
> v. 27: *Between her feet he crouched, he fell* . . .
> *between her feet he crouched, he fell;*
> *where he crouched, there fell he* subdued.

5. The important word *Israel* is repeated emphatically—a kind of ringing cry (almost like "Texas! Texas!" at a ball game) at the end of clauses or stanzas, in verses 2, 3, 5, 7, 8, 9, and 11, and the word *warriors* in verses 13 and 23.[24]

6. Incidents are linked rapidly and almost mechanically by the constant repetition of the word, *then* (verses 8, 11, 13, 19, 22).

7. Likewise characteristic of the ballad are the introductory clauses giving the setting in time:

> v. 2: When men loosed all restraint(?) in Israel.
> v. 4: When thou didst go forth, O Lord, from Seir;
>   when thou didst march from the territory of Edom.
> v. 6: In the days of Shamgar, the son of 'Anat,
>   in the days of Jael . . . .

This recalls the typical opening of many an English and Scottish ballad, e.g., *The Tournament of Tottenham* ("It befel in Tottenham, on a dire day"); *Fair Rosamond* ("Whenas King Henry ruled this land, / The second of that name"); and *The Brave Lord of Willoughby* ("The fifteenth of July, / with glistening spear and shield, / A famous fight in Flanders / was foughten in the field").

8. Then there is the rhetorical question, designed to enhance suspense and to give the dancers an opportunity for a resounding burst of song by way of reply. Admittedly, this is not evident in our present Hebrew text, but without altering a single letter and by simply redividing the consonants of the first word (viz., *mî qôl* for *mi-qôl*), it may be readily elicited from a clause in verse 11 which has thus far baffled commentators:

> *What is this noise of people huzzah-ing*[25]
> *between the water-troughs?*
> *Why, they are recounting there*
> *the triumphant acts of the Lord!*

This again recalls a similar device in the English and Scottish ballads, e.g., " 'Who have we here?' Lord Bodwell said," in *The Murder of the King of Scots,* or the more poetic, "Ye highlands, ye highlands, / Oh, where have ye been? / They hae slain the Earl of Murray / and hae laid him in the green."

9. Lastly, the virtually onomatopoeic words of verse 22:

> *'az hal*ᵉ*mū 'iqbê sūsîm*[26]
> *dah*ᵃ*rôt dah*ᵃ*rôt 'abbirāw*

which may be rendered approximately,

> *Then hammered the hoofs of his horses;*
> *stamp, stamp, stamp went his stallions,*

may likewise have been accompanied by a vigorous stamping of feet on the part of the dancers.

The whole song, then, may be put into the category of the song-with-dance (i.e., *ballad*), wherewith, as we are told expressly in the Old Testament itself, women welcomed their menfolk when they returned victorious from battle. It

thus provides an excellent example of the manner in which popular custom
conditioned literary form.

Something of the same sort may be recognized also in the song which Moses
and the children of Israel are said to have sung after they had crossed the Sea
of Reeds dryshod (Exod. 15). Here too we have the same introductory phrase,
I will sing of the Lord, and the same repetition of crucial words, with "incremental supplements":

> v. 2: This is *my God,* and I will extol him,
>   *my father's god,* and I will exalt him;
> v. 4: Pharaoh's chariots and army
>   he hurled in the *sea;*
>   his picked captains sank
>   in the *Sea of Reeds;*
> v. 16: *Until thy people passed over, O Lord,*
>   *until this people whom thou hadst gotten passed over.*

There is likewise the same emphasis upon a cardinal word at the end of a
clause or stanza:

> v. 1: horse and mount he threw into the *sea;*
> v. 4: Pharaoh's chariots and army
>   he hurled in the *sea;*
> v. 8: The deeps congealed in the heart of the *sea;*
> v. 10: Thou didst blow with thy breath (wind);
>   then covered them the *sea;*
> v. 19 (perhaps an excerpt from another song):
>   When Pharaoh with his horses and chariots
>   entered the *sea;*
>   when with his horsemen
>   (he entered) the *sea,*
>   the Lord turned back on them
>   the waters of the *sea,*
>   but the Israelites walked on dry land
>   in the midst of the *sea.*

There is also the same type of rhetorical question:

> v. 11: Who is like thee 'mid the gods, O Lord,
>   who 'mid the holy ones (LXX) so majestic as thee . . . ?

And it is said expressly (v. 20) that at the same time Miriam and the womenfolk "went forth with timbrels and dance" and also sang.

A new look at the Minor Prophets

These, however, are not the only instances of the relation of literary forms
to popular usages. Comparative Folklore also makes an important contribution

to the understanding of the Minor Prophets by illuminating the cultic background against which they spoke.

If we line up the successive images and metaphors used by a minor prophet, these may often be found to coincide with the various elements of ritual ceremonies connected with pagan seasonal festivals. This suggests that the prophets were often delivering their messages in terms of satire upon such apostatic performances. Thus, when a prophet speaks of Yahweh's *pouring out his wrath like water* (Hos. 5:10), he may be taking a sly dig at the pagan ceremony of pouring water as a rain-charm (§221). Similarly, when he says that *Yahweh will search out Jerusalem with lamps* (Zeph. 1:12), he may be deriding the "heathen" custom of staging torchlight processions through the city in seasonal rites (§243). And when he warns his recalcitrant countrymen that Yahweh is about to *hold a banquet, and has already invited his guests* (Zeph. 1:7), he may be alluding pointedly to the fact that a standard feature of the cultic myths associated with pagan seasonal celebrations was the banquet tended by or to the god in order to re-cement his ties with his worshipers (§243). Other examples of such use of satire are given in the body of this work.

If this basic supposition is correct, an important conclusion follows for the literary analysis of the prophetic books. Instead of fragmentizing them and regarding them as compilations from different hands simply because they seem sometimes to pass too rapidly and inconsequentially from one theme to another, we may now rather try to fit the apparently disconnected pieces into a single over-all pattern of seasonal ceremonies, and thereby vindicate the unity of the whole. Thus, when the Book of Joel passes from a picture of devastation and mourning to a description of Yahweh's final war against the heathen and of the assize at which he will judge them, there is no need to assume that the themes are unrelated and that the several prophecies therefore proceed from different authors. For the fact is that the usual pattern of seasonal festivals is that an initial period of mortification and abstinence—symbolizing the eclipse of life at the close of the agricultural year—is followed by a mimetic battle between Old and New, Life and Death, Rain and Drought, Summer and Winter, or the like, which is mythologized as the defeat by the god of his contumacious opponents (e.g., the victory of Marduk over Tiamat and her allies in the Babylonian New Year myth, of the Hittite Weather-god over the Dragon in the cult-legend of the Feast of Purulli, and of Baal over Yam and Mot in the Canaanite poems from Ras Shamra). Then, in turn, comes the divine assembly at which the order of the world and the fates of men are determined for the incoming year. Joel, therefore, may have been preaching against the background of this consecutive program, and the seeming incoherence and inconsequence disappear (§231).

That there was, indeed, an undercurrent of such allusive satire in these prophetic utterances is seemingly indicated by the striking conclusion of the Book of Hosea (14:9)—a book in which the same pattern can be discerned:

> Whoever is wise will understand these things,
> whoever is discerning will know them.

These words may be read as a Hebrew equivalent of the familiar *Verbum sapienti sat* (A word to the wise).

V. THE SPOKEN WORD

Popular literature is *heard,* rather than *read,* and the influence of recitation is present everywhere in the Old Testament.

"Hear ye"

1. The reciter draws his audience by an introductory invitation to the crowd to listen, somewhat like the *oyez* of the town crier. So the prophets often begin with the cry, *Hear ye* or *Give ear.*

Cante-fable

2. To keep his audience awake and interested, a storyteller often punctuates his narrative, at appropriate places, with popular songs, in which all may join. This device is common to many cultures, and is characteristic especially of early Arabic romances (*sāj*). It is known technically as *cante-fable.* A good example in the Old Testament is the song put into the mouth of the Israelites after crossing the Sea of Reeds dryshod (Exod. 15). So too, when the prophet Jonah is ensconced in the belly of the "great fish," and the story comes to a logical and dramatic standstill until he is disgorged, he is represented as spending the intervening time chanting a prayer which consists largely of liturgical clichés paralleled in the Book of Psalms and elsewhere. This was evidently chanted by the audience; they were spending the "intermission," so to speak, intoning snatches from a Hebrew *Hymns Ancient and Modern!* Again, after telling the story of Cain and Abel, the narrator starts reciting the family tree of the former's descendants. This, to be sure, is tedious stuff for an audience which has gathered to hear a good story. But the storyteller knows how to relieve their boredom. When he comes to Lamech, Cain's descendant in the fifth generation, he suddenly interpolates a little war song chanted by a tribe named the Lamechites, and deftly foists it upon the ancient worthy (§**31**). So also, in the equally tedious account of the stages by which the Israelites crossed the wilderness in their exodus from Egypt, when the narrator gets to their halt at a place named Beër, and when he realizes that his audience is nodding or dozing, he rouses their flagging interest by introducing a popular song chanted annually when a new *beër,* or water pit, was dug.

Repetition of messages

3. When the story requires that a message be conveyed, it is often repeated *in extenso* (cf. Gen. 24:22–49). This device likewise characterizes the older

Sumerian, Akkadian, and Ugaritic epics, and it is found also in the Iliad and Odyssey, in the Kalevala (though there perhaps only through Linröth's editing), and elsewhere.[27] It originated, we may suggest, in the exigencies of *recitation:* the crowd of listeners was constantly swelling, and newcomers had to be kept abreast of the story. This was a way of doing so.

Oracles in verse

4. It is likewise, perhaps, to the factor of oral communication that we should attribute the convention of delivering oracles—and hence prophecies— in verse.[28] To be sure, in moments of enthusiasm speech is apt anyway to fall into cadences, as anyone who reads Cicero or listens to an inspired orator or an enraptured preacher can easily test. But in the case of oracles something else seems also to be involved. A man would often *send,* rather than *go,* to consult an oracle, and it was, of course, essential that the messenger should report the divine words *verbatim,* without distortion or error due to lapse of memory. In this situation, verse would have served as a mnemonic technique, and at the same time have guaranteed accuracy, for any involuntary garbling or deliberate falsification would have been readily betrayed (unless the messenger were exceptionally clever or skillful) by resultant defects of scansion. (This, of course, does not apply to oracles derived from omens, divination, or astrology, for these were interpretations of signs—commentaries, as it were, on actual phenomena—rather than communications of spontaneous outbursts. Nor does it apply to oracles which may have been written down on tablets. We are speaking only of those which had to be reported by word of mouth.)

Deictic expressions

5. Yet another evidence of the influence of recitation upon literary form and style is afforded by the use of the adverbs *there* and *thither* in contexts where they would be intelligible only if accompanied by a gesture on the part of the speaker. Job, for example, declares in a famous passage (1:21) that not only did he come naked from the womb but that he will also return *thither* in the same condition. Nobody, however, returns to his mother's womb, naked or otherwise; yet, the expression is clarified immediately once it is realized that the story was told *orally* and that at this point the narrator (like Job himself) must have *pointed to the earth* (§294). Similarly, when the prophet Habakkuk, portraying the advent of the Lord in terms of sunrise, remarks (3:4) that, although the first glow has indeed streaked the mountains, *"there* lies the hiding-place of his might," the phrase becomes intelligible and vivid only when one sees it as accompanied by a wave of the speaker's hand toward the region below the horizon, whence the full glory of the sun is yet to emerge.

Of the same order, too, is the expression, "May the Lord do thus and more to me," used so often in the swearing of oaths. This again is meaningless except in the context of *recitation,* when the narrator would have accompanied the words by drawing his finger across his throat, or the like.[29]

Distortion and modernization

Literature which is passed down by word of mouth naturally undergoes verbal changes in successive generations. Anyone who has studied the textual variants of traditional ballads, songs or stories will not need to be told that constant modernization of vocabulary is part and parcel of the process of transmission. We must expect the same sort of thing in the Old Testament; and indeed we find it. In Psalm 68:4, Yahweh is acclaimed as "he who rides across the deserts," the Hebrew for which is *rōkeb ba-ʿᵃrābôth.* This, however, is simply a misunderstanding and consequent modification of a very similar expression, *rōkeb ʿᵃrāPHôth,* "he that rides upon the clouds," which is a standard epithet of Baal in the Canaanite poems from Ras Shamra-Ugarit. It is not a mere textual corruption (as many modern scholars suppose),[30] but a popular distortion, of the same order as that which turned the *girasole* into the *Jerusalem* artichoke or the London tavern called the *El Infanta de Castille* into the *Elephant and Castle.*

Nor are such changes wrought only by the mouths of the "common folk"; learned editors and professional antiquarians also play their hands in the process. One recalls, for instance, what Bishop Percy did to the reliques of ancient English poetry, and how the meticulous Ritson pilloried him for such sacrilege; how Walter Scott occasionally prettified the Scottish ballads; and how Wilhelm Grimm modified and stylized the peasant language of the famous *Household Tales.* There is similar evidence of the "learned sock" in the Old Testament. To be sure, in some cases the archaic language of the traditional myths and stories is retained intact by dint of usage, just as the British still speak of "lords puisne" and we of the Capitol. Thus, the epithets which characterize Leviathan in Isaiah 27:1 and Job 26:13 are archaic and recur nowhere else in the Hebrew Scriptures; while in Ezekiel's parable of the Fallen Paragon (28:14) the word which describes the cherub with wings *outspanned* (viz., *mimšaḥ*) is likewise an archaic, not a current, term.[31]

On the other hand, however, there are clear evidences elsewhere of "Percyfication" on the part of ancient editors—changes due not to *oral* misunderstanding but to failure to interpret written words which happen to have grown obsolete. An instructive illustration of what took place in such later redaction of traditional material is afforded by comparing two versions of the same saying in the Book of Proverbs—a cumulative anthology of time-honored aphorisms. In 12:23 we are told that *a prudent man conceals (his) knowledge,* but in 13:16 that *a prudent man acts with knowledge.* Now, the point here is that what came later to be understood as the normal Hebrew word for *acts* (viz., *yaʿᵃśeh*) was really an archaic word (viz., **yaʿᵃśeh;* cf. Arabic *ʿ-sh-y*) meaning *conceals.* The one version, therefore, even though it misinterpreted it (or was it itself misunderstood even later), at least preserved the original term of the traditional proverb; the other, though it did *not* misinterpret it, "Percyfied" it, substituting the current term (Heb.: *k-s-h*).[32]

Similar modernization can be recognized elsewhere. David's lament for Saul and Jonathan, for example, contains in the present text the obscure lines:

> *Ye mountains of Gilboa,*
>   *be there no dew nor rain upon you,*
>   *ye fields of offerings* (Heb.: *śᵉdê tᵉrūmôth*)!

We now know, however, from a passage in one of the Ras Shamra poems, that this bizarre reading is simply a later editor's attempt to "correct" a very similar archaic expression (viz., *šeraʿ tᵉhômôth*) which really meant "neither upsurge of the deeps," and referred to the ancient belief that the earth is watered by the cosmic ocean in the form of rain from above and of the upwelling of springs from below.[33]

Take, again, Samson's famous riddle in Judges 14:14: *What is the eater out of which has come something to eat, the strong out of which has come something sweet?* The answer, as we know, was *a lion infested by bees carrying honey,* but it has been observed that in the original version the point evidently depended—as so often in riddles—on a play of words, an archaic Hebrew word for *honey* being identical in form with that for *lion,* while *the eater* was a common popular expression for a ravening beast (§117).

Another example of the same process may be detected in Psalm 82:7, where it is said of those who claimed to be gods and celestial beings that

> Nevertheless ye shall die like men,
>   and fall *like one of the princes.*

As most scholars have recognized, the word *princes* is here somewhat odd, for what the context demands is surely a reference to the myth of the "fallen angels." In later Hebrew, however, "princes" came indeed to be a common designation for angels, and it is therefore plain that it has here been substituted for some more archaic term. What that term was is anybody's guess. It may be suggested, perhaps, that it was *Nephilim,* a term for the primeval giants (associated with the fallen angels) in Genesis 6:4 and Numbers 13:33, for whatever that term may really have meant, it could have come to be derived fancifully from the Hebrew word *n-ph-l,* "fall," and this would provide a singularly effective play on words![34]

These examples, taken together with parallel phenomena in popular literature everywhere, should warn us, incidentally, against the prevalent tendency of Bible scholars to assume that a given work or passage must necessarily have been *composed* at a late date merely because it contains words or grammatical constructions of demonstrably late vintage. In the case of works which may have passed down orally, all that such evidence really indicates is the late date of the extant *redaction*.[35]

VI. FOLKLORE AND TEXTUAL CRITICISM

Another contribution which Comparative Folklore makes to the understanding of the Old Testament is that it sometimes enables us to vindicate the authenticity of the traditional text against arbitrary modern emendations.

Thus, in Deuteronomy 32:10 (§**103**), the unusual expression, "howling wilderness," has taxed the ingenuity of commentators, and the Hebrew words have therefore been variously "corrected." But Comparative Folklore reveals that among the bedouin the desert is popularly known as "the place of ululation" because the shrill winds which sweep across it are regarded as the howling or shrieking of demons.

Again, in Ezekiel 28:14 (§**213**), the paragon who is cast out of Paradise is said to have walked there originally *amid fiery stones* (Heb.: *'abnê esh*). Not so, say several modern scholars, deftly altering the Hebrew text: he walked *amid beings divine* (Heb.: *bᵉnê el*)! But Comparative Folklore shows that Paradise is often pictured as a place of precious stones, and a Mesopotamian lexical text actually specifies "fiery stone" as the name of a particular gem. The dulled radiance of the celestial jewels is thus restored.

In Psalm 68:22 (§**266,a**), Yahweh declares that he is able to retrieve men from Bashan and from the depths of the sea. The reference to Bashan, a region east of the Jordan, has puzzled Biblical scholars, and by clever manipulation of the Hebrew text (i.e., *mi-<ki>bshan <esh>* for the traditional *mi-Bashan*) the verse has therefore been made to assert that Yahweh rescues men *from the fiery furnace*. Comparative Folklore shows, however, that in the mythology of the Canaanites, Bashan and Sea (Yam) were the names of dragons which the god Baal was said to have subdued. Moreover, the archaic words for "capture" and "muzzle"—words actually used in the Canaanite myth—can indeed be recognized behind those traditionally rendered, "retrieve, bring back." Hence it becomes apparent that the Biblical poet was simply adapting a time-honored myth: what the verse really says is that Yahweh is able to make a captive of the Dragon and to muzzle Sir Sea in the depths.

In Ezekiel 24:17, eating the *bread of men* (Heb.: *leḥem 'anāshîm*) is described as a rite of mourning. This too has baffled modern exegetes, as it already baffled the translators of the ancient Aramaic and Latin Versions, and the phrase has therefore been emended, by the omission of but a single letter (viz., *leḥem 'ônîm*) to *bread of mourners*—an expression which actually occurs in Hosea 9:4. The fact is, however, that one of the purposes of funeral meals is to re-cement the ruptured ties of the community, and this is the basic meaning of the word rendered "men." Indeed, even at the present day, its exact equivalent (*awnâse, waniseh*) is a not uncommon term among Arabs for funeral meats![36]

In Amos 8:14 the recalcitrant Israelites are charged with swearing loyalty to false gods and with taking oaths by the formula, *As the way* (Heb.: *DeReK*) *of Beersheba lives!* This clearly makes no sense, and modern scholars have therefore emended the traditional text to read, *As thy (god) Dod* (Heb.: *DôDᵉKā*) *lives, O Beersheba*, on the assumption that Dod (literally, Beloved) was the name of a heathen deity. But our increased knowledge of ancient Canaanite religion now discloses that the Hebrew consonants traditionally vocalized as *DeReK*, "way," are really to be read *DôRᵉKā*, "thy pantheon," the word *dôr* being a standard name for the circle or family of the pagan gods![37]

In Hosea 6:11 (§221) the prophet threatens reprobate Israel in the words, *Yahweh has set a harvest for you!* Modern critics, unable to penetrate the meaning of these words, have blithely finagled them to read, *Yahweh has laid up abominations for thee!* But, apart from the fact that abominations are elsewhere always something perpetrated *against* Yahweh rather than *by* him, this facile emendation overlooks the point, which Comparative Folklore demonstrates, that the prophet is preaching against the background of pagan seasonal celebrations. His ringing cry to the harvesters that Yahweh has another kind of harvest in store for them is therefore singularly effective, particularly since it comes as the climax of his speech. Thus, in more senses than one, Comparative Folklore removes an abomination.

A final example is furnished by Hosea 8:6 (§228). In the traditional text this reads:

> *That calf of thine, O Samaria, is a stinking thing*
> . . . .
> *For out of Israel is he;*
> *a workman made him, and he is no god.*

The second line is notoriously difficult, and once again various emendations have been proposed. But once again Comparative Folklore clarifies what is otherwise obscure; for the fact is that, by mere redivision of the Hebrew consonants, the words rendered, *For out of Israel is he* can be read, *For who is (this) El the Bull*, and from texts discovered at Ras Shamra-Ugarit we now know that this was a common designation of the supreme god of the Canaanites.[38]

NOTES

INTRODUCTION

1. See: H. Usener, in Rhein. Mus. 57 (1902), 177–92; I. Guidi, in RB 12 (1903), 241 ff.; T. H. Gaster, Thespis[2], 222; Stith Thompson, *MI*, F 701.1.

2. The Hebrew word is *sh-b-th*. In Isa. 30:7 it lies concealed beneath the impossible reading, *Rahab hem shabeth*, which must be corrected to *Rahab ha-mashbath*. In Isa. 14:4 the concocted verb *marhēbah*, "she that plays the role of Rahab," was misunderstood by the early Jewish editors and therefore distorted to *madhēbah*, which, however, is barely translatable. The correct reading can be restored from the Greek (Septuagint) and Syriac versions, and from the Dead Sea Isaiah scroll.—In Job 38:11 the mythological allusion has again been lost by the displacement of a single letter: for *ū-phô' yāshîth bi-gᵉ'ôn gallêkā* read *ū-phô' yishbôth gᵉ'ôn gallêkā*.

3. This is simply the conventional rendering of Heb. *bārī*ᵃḥ,* but it is by no means certain; for other explanations, see: W. F. Albright, in BASOR 83 (1941) 39, n.3 ("ancient, primeval"); T. H. Gaster, in JRAS 1944.47, n.49 ("sinister"); C. Rabin, in JTS 47 (1946), 38–41.

4. Cf. J. G. Frazer, FOT, ed. min., 5.

5. C. E. Fox, The Threshold of the Pacific (1924), 238.

6. For translations, cf. ANET 43–44 (Sumerian); 93 ff. (Akkadian); 104 ff.

7. See: Gilbert Murray, in Jane Harrison's Themis (1912), 314 ff.; Jane Harrison, Ancient Art and Ritual (1913); F. M. Cornford, The Origin of Attic Comedy[2], ed. T. H. Gaster (1961).

8. E.g., Rig Veda ix.112; cf. L. von Schroeder, Mysterium und Mythus (1903).

9. Bertha S. Phillpotts, The Elder Edda and Scandinavian Drama (1920).

10. B. Schindler, in Orient and Occident: Moses Gaster Anniversary Volume (1936), 498–52.

11. See: R. J. E. Tiddy, The Mummers' Play (1923).—A similar theory has been applied to the Italian *maggio* and *bruscello*: P. Toschi, Dal dramma liturgico alla rappresentazione sacra (1940); V. de Bartholomaeis, Le origini della poesia drammatica italiana (1924); S. Fontana, Il maggio (1929); G. Cocchiara, Le vastasate (1926). Cf. also: R. Stumpfl, Kultspiele der Germanen als Ursprung des mittelalterlichen Dramas (1956).

12. On this meter (called conventionally *qînah*), cf. K. Budde, in ZAW 2 (1882), 1–52; 3 (1883), 11.

13. E.g., Pss. 7:1, 4, 7, 9; 17:1, 14; 26:1, 6, 12.

14. A. C. Bouquet, Sacred Books of the World (Penguin 1954), 27–28.

15. M. Gusinde, Die Feuerland Indianer (1931–37), ii.115, 1139–40.

16. C. G. and B. Z. Seligmann, The Veddas (1911), 366.

17. B. Nettl, Music in Primitive Culture (1956), 23.—On this subject in general, cf. C. M. Bowra, Primitive Song (Mentor Books, 1964), 64 f.

18. A clear reference to such cries may be recognized in the Old Testament itself in Psalm 68:4, which should be rendered: *"Cast up a highway for him who rides across the deserts, (to the cry,) 'Yah is his name!'";* cf. Exod. 15:3.

19. Cf. F. Gummere, The Popular Ballad (reprint, 1959), 117 ff.; S. Mirsky, "The Origin of Anadiplosis in Hebrew Literature," in Tarbiz 28 (1959), 171–80 (Hebrew).

20. I. W. Slotki, in JTS 33 (1932), 341–54.

21. The repetition of the verb is deliberate, and no emendation is required.

22. An approximate rendering of Hebrew *pᵉrāzôn* (cf. Arabic *f-r-z;* Akkadian *parṣu*), the exact meaning of which is still unknown.

23. Hebrew, *qiddūmîm* (G. A. Smith: "spates"), the exact meaning of which is unknown. At all events, it is an "incremental addition," and hence should not be emended into a verbal form, e.g., *qiddᵉmam*, "confronted them," as in LXX.

24. In Psalm 68, the word *Elôhîm* ("God") is similarly repeated throughout at the beginning or end of clauses and stanzas; vv.2, 3, 4, 5, 6, 7, 8, 9, 10, 16, 17, 18, 19, 22, 25, 27, 29, 32, 33, 35, 36 (*bis*). If this is indeed a structural device, the recognition of it would invalidate Albright's view (in Mowinckel Festschrift, 1955.1–12) that the psalm is really but a string of disconnected *incipits* of ancient hymns.

25. With George Adam Smith, I take *mᵉhaṣᵉṣîm* to be onomatopoeic. For the sentiment, cf. Euripides, *Medea*, 67–69. As anyone knows, who has traveled in the East or in the Greek islands, the local fountain or washing place is always a center of chatter and gossip.

26. Reading, with most modern scholars, *sūsîm, dahᵃrôth* for the *sūs mi-dahᵃrôth* of the received text; *sūs-ma* (with archaic *-ma*) would also be possible.

27. Cf. Myth of Gilgamesh and Agga (ANET, 46), 48 (Sumerian); J. Friedrich, in OLz 1937.518, n.1 (Hittite); C. H. Gordon, Ugaritic Handbook (1947), 34 (Ugaritic). For instances in *Greek* literature, cf. Odyssey 3.115 f.; 5.306; Theognis 633; Sophocles, Ajax 433; Pindar, Nem. 7.153. For the device in Finnish rune-verses, cf. K. Krohn, Die folkloristische Arbeitsmethode (1926), 80. And who does not recall Humpty Dumpty's "I told them once, I told them twice;/ They would not listen to advice," and the Duchess' "I beat him once, I beat him twice,/ I beat him till he sneezes," in *Alice through the Looking-Glass*?

28. Note that in Herodotus, oracles are usually reproduced in Greek hexameters.

29. I Sam. 3:17; 14:44; 20:13; II Sam. 3:9; I Kings 2:23; II Kings 6:31, etc. A similar expression occurs in Arabic, e.g., Tabari, Annales, ed. M. J. de Goeje (1897–1901), i.852,2; ii.453,12.

30. So, for instance, rsv. But this strains the normal sense of the verb *sôlū*, "cast up a highway," which has then to be twisted to mean "Lift up a song." This ruins the point: the god who normally careers through the sandy tracts of the desert is to have a level highway prepared for his triumphant progress. For the sentiment, cf. Isa. 40:3.

31. Cf. Akkadian *mašāḫu;* Vulgate actually renders *extentus*.

32. Cf. I. Eitan, in JQR, N.S. 14 (1923), 46 f.

33. H. L. Ginsberg, in JBL 57 (1938), 209–13.

34. The same process may perhaps be recognized in Micah 1:11. The prophet is excoriating various cities of Judah by playing on their names. Concerning Beth ha-Eṣel he observes that *Lamentation has taken from you its* standing-place (Heb.: *'emdāthô*). Here, I suggest, the point lies in the fact that the name suggests an archaic word **eṣel* (akin to Arabic *aṣl*) meaning "firm root." This word may originally have stood in the text and have been replaced later by a more familiar term.

35. These *oral* modifications of archaic words and phrases must be sharply distinguished from cases in which ancient spellings in a *written* text baffled later scribes and were therefore "emended." Two arresting examples of the latter process are: (*a*) Ps. 68:19, *Thou hast asscended on high, hast led captives in thy train, hast received tributes among men*, where *among men* (Heb.: *bā-ādām*) is a "correction" of an archaic *bdm*, "from their hands"; (*b*) Ps. 16:3, *I will not pour their libations out of blood, nor take their names upon my lips*, where *out of blood* (Heb.: *mi-dam*) is again a "correc-

tion" of the same archaic *bdm*, "with (my) hands." Yet another illuminating example occurs in Balaam's oracle, Num. 24:23; see below, §98.

36. G. Schumacher, in MDPV 1904.75 f.; J. Morgenstern, Rites of Birth, Marriage and Death among the Semites (1966), 149.

37. F. Neuberg, in JNES 9 (1950), 215–17; cf. T. H. Gaster, in Orientalia 11 (1942), 60.

38. This interpretation is due to Tur Sinai.

THE
PENTATEUCH

Genesis

In the Beginning

1 Creation as shaping Gen. 1:1

To the Hebrews, as to most ancient peoples, creation was not a philosophical or metaphysical concept; it involved no question of the nature of existence or of the emergence of being from nonbeing. To create meant simply to give shape and form, and all the Hebrew words which are so rendered derive from the vocabulary of handicraft, and refer primarily to the paring of leather, the moulding of clay and the like.[1]

2 Primordial water 1:2

Two things have no shape or form: water and wind. These, therefore, were regarded as primordial—not, that is to say, as the actual substances out of which all else was brought into being, but as having preceded all other things in order of time. Moreover, since of all things (with the single exception of fire), they alone moved and "spoke," they were considered especially numinous and potent.

The primality of water[1] is an idea by no means exclusive to the Hebrews, nor—as some scholars have supposed—was it borrowed by them from the Babylonians and derived from the fact that the oldest Babylonian cities happen to have been built on lagoons. On the contrary, it is found all over the world, among peoples living in the most diverse geographical conditions. The Sumerians, for instance, describe the goddess of the sea (Nammu) as "the mother who gave birth to heaven and earth."[2] The Babylonian Epic of Creation (*Enuma Elish*) opens with a reference to the time when there was as yet nothing but ocean;[3] and another mythological poem from Mesopotamia says categorically that in the beginning "all lands were sea."[4] The Egyptians entertained the same notion:[5] a passage in the Book of the Dead has the god Atum threaten that "the earth will revert to floodwaters, as in the beginning."[6] Similarly, in Indic myth, Vishnu extracts the earth from a watery abyss[7] or, according to another account, there was originally only a primal ocean pervaded by the creator god Prajapati in the form of wind.[8] In the Iliad of Homer, Ocean and his consort Thetys are described as the creators of the gods and, indeed, of all things;[9] while in the Finnish Kalevala earth and heaven are said

3

to have come into being through the splitting of an egg dropped by a teal upon the knee of Ilmatar, a nymph who lived in the primordial deep.[10]

On the American continent, this belief in the primality of water is attested among the Achomawi,[11] Poma,[12] Maidu,[13] Miwok,[14] and Diegueno Indians of California,[15] among the Arapaho of Oklahoma,[16] the Crow of Montana[17] and the Creeks of Alabama;[18] while the Quiché of Mexico speak of a primeval ocean swept by Hurakan (hurricane), the mighty wind.[19] The Yoruba of the Sudan[20] and the Gabon of the Congo likewise speak of water as having preceded all things.[21]

Since it represented a substance which existed before corruptibility and contamination had come into the world, this primal water was credited with special virtues and properties.[22] Among the Babylonians it was esteemed the most potent of all vehicles of magic, and nothing could resist a spell in which it was employed or which was pronounced in the name of Ea, god of the primordial deep.[23] Tanks purporting to contain such water were a feature of Babylonian temples,[24] and magicians often described themselves as agents or emissaries of Ea.[25]

Water—because it seemed so often to be saying something—either in a roar or in a whisper—and because it could capture images (reflections)[26]— was also regarded as imbued with special wisdom. In the Odyssey, Proteus, genius of the ocean, is omniscient and reveals special knowledge to Menelaus at Pharos.[27] Nereus, son of Pontos (the Sea), likewise possesses special lore;[28] while his daughter Theonoe knows all things past and future.[29] Similarly, the Eskimo goddess Sedma, who lives in the depths of the sea, possesses a magical knowledge whereby she is instantly aware of any infringement of traditional taboos.[30] In ancient Mesopotamian folklore it was held that seven primeval sages who had taught mankind the arts of civilization had emerged in bygone days from the primal deep[31] or, alternatively, that a semi-pisciform god named Oannes (or Oes or Euadnes) rose daily from the Persian Gulf for the same purpose.[32] In the Book of Ecclesiasticus, in the Apocrypha of the Old Testament, the sea is said to have been one of the original abodes of Wisdom;[33] and it is not impossible that when the author of the Book of Job makes deep and sea declare that "Wisdom is not in me," he is protesting against similar ancient mythological concepts.[34]

3 Primordial wind   1:2, 6–8

Equally widespread is the belief in the primality of wind. The creator-god both of the Hindus and of the Quiché of Mexico sweeps the primal deep in this form, while in the ancient Phoenician cosmogony related by the mythographer Sanchuniathon mention is made of primordial wind.[1]

In the Bible this primal wind is described as the breath of God, just as thunder is his voice,[2] and lightning—according to the Book of Job[3]—his sneezings. In the same way, the strong east wind which parted the waters of the Sea of Reeds at the time of the exodus from Egypt is described in the poetic account of that event as the breath of Yahweh;[4] while in an Egyptian hymn from Hibeh the four winds are said to issue from the mouth of the god Amun[5]—a concept which finds a parallel in modern Chinese folklore.[6] The Indic Rig Veda likewise describes wind as the breath of Varuna.[7]

It is quite futile to dispute whether the words of the Biblical text should be rendered "breath of God," "spirit of God," or simply "mighty wind," for the whole point is that these things were not differentiated in the Hebrew mind.[8]

The wind is said to have "moved," "hovered," "swept," or "brooded" over the face of the waters. The Hebrew word so translated recurs only once in Scripture, and there it denotes the motion of an eagle protecting its eyrie.[9] It has therefore been suggested by some scholars that it is a relic of the concept —attested alike among the ancient Greeks[10] and the modern Polynesians— that the earth was hatched out of an egg.[11] The fact is, however, that the word has now turned up in the Canaanite poems discovered at Ras Shamra-Ugarit, and there it refers to the coasting of a bird in flight.[12] More probably, therefore, we should recognize in the Biblical term the faded reminiscence of a quite different mythological notion, namely, that of the *wind-bird*. Elsewhere in the Old Testament God is said to ride on the wings of the wind,[13] and in the Mesopotamian *Legend of Adapa* that hero breaks the wings of the south wind when it threatens to capsize his craft while he is out fishing.[14]

The notion of the wind-bird is, indeed, widespread in ancient and primitive cultures.[15] The Sumerians spoke of a winged demon of the storm named "Heavy Wind" (Im. Dugud) or "Flashing Wind" (Im. Gig);[16] the Teutons had their storm-bird Hraesvelgr,[17] and the Norsemen a demonic eagle of the winds called Thiassi, the flapping of whose wings caused thunder.[18] In India, the counterpart is the eagle Garuda,[19] and the belief is attested also among the Chinese,[20] Burmese,[21] Finns,[22] Shetland Islanders,[23] Tlingits, and Aztecs.[24] A myth current among the Athapascans of North America tells of a raven which hovered primordially over the waters and the clapping of whose wings was thunder;[25] while the Mixtecs know of two winds which swept the primal deep in the form of a bird and a serpent.[26] In the Russian *Tale of the Armament of Igor* the wind is asked why "with tireless wing" it kept hurling arrows at an army.[27]

To be sure, in the Biblical version, this concept survives only as an unconscious etymological relic, actually irreconcilable with the dominant idea that the wind is the breath of God.

4 The firmament   1:6–8

God stretched a reef or septum across the primordial waters to divide them into an upper and lower register. This septum, the canopy of the earth, is what we call the firmament.

The Hebrew word rendered "firmament"[1] means properly "a strip of hammered metal,"[2] and this too is a vestige of older folklore. In the Book of Job the sky is similarly portrayed as a molten surface (even a mirror) polished by

God's breath, i.e., by the winds which drive away the clouds that bestain it.[3] In Homer, heaven is made of brass,[4] and the same idea is attested also by the poet Pindar.[5] Alternatively, it is made of iron—a notion mentioned not only in the Odyssey[6] but also in Egyptian sources;[7] while in the Finnish Kalevala it is made by the divine smith Ilmarinen out of the finest steel.[8]

5   The separation of heaven and earth

In the Biblical version the sky is raised simply by the fiat of God. Here, however, the writer has suppressed or expurgated older and cruder mythological fancies. A Hittite myth of the second millennium B.C. refers to a magical cleaver which sundered heaven from earth;[1] and in the Babylonian Epic of Creation (*Enuma Elish*), heaven is the upper, and earth the lower half of the carcass of a vanquished monster slit lengthwise "like an oyster."[2] Even more common is the idea that the separation was effected by an inconsiderate god or goddess who forcibly parted Father Sky and Mother Earth when they were locked in conjugal embrace.[3] The Egyptians asserted, for example, that the god Shu (or, in other versions, Ptah, Sokaris, Osiris, Khnum, and Upuwast of Assiut) had insinuated himself between the encoupled Heaven and Earth, seized the female and raised her aloft to form the sky.[4] In Hindu myth, Indra thus parts Dyaus (Sky) and Prithivi (Earth);[5] while among the Maoris of New Zealand the tale is told that Sky (Rangi) and Earth (Papa) were violently sundered by one of their children, Tane-mahuta, aided by the divine marplot Tutenganahau.[6] Among the Bihors of India and in parts of West Africa the story runs that the severance was accomplished by an old woman wielding a knife;[7] and in Tahiti it is said to have been done by the god Rau using the plant *Dracontium polyphyllum*.[8] In Chinese folklore it was Tuangku who parted heaven from earth,[9] and in Pacific myths the feat is attributed to a serpent. Both Mohammed[10] and the Japanese classic *Nihongi* refer to a time when heaven and earth were still united.[11]

6   "God saw that it was good"   1 *passim*

> *After every major act of creation God looks upon his handiwork and "sees that it is good."*[1]

This phrase is more than a poetic flourish. It reflects the practice of Mesopotamian craftsmen of inspecting their products and formally pronouncing them satisfactory before releasing them from their workshops.[2] King Ashurbanipal thus approved one of the buildings which he erected at Nineveh,[3] and in the poem *Enuma Elish,* Ea (using the same term) "approves" his son Marduk immediately after the latter's birth.[4]

7   The primal upsurge   2:6

> *At first, the heavens sent no rain. The earth was moistened solely by a spout of waters which rose from underground.*

In many standard translations it is said that what ascended from the ground in primeval times was a *mist*,[1] but we now know that the Hebrew word is really a technical term (borrowed ultimately from Sumerian) meaning an upsurge of subterranean waters.[2] The notion recurs elsewhere in the Old Testament itself. Thus in the Scriptural story of the Flood we are informed explicitly that that calamity befell the earth because the "windows of heaven" (i.e., the celestial sluices) were opened at the same time as "the fountains of the deep burst forth";[3] and in the account of creation given in the eighth chapter of the Book of Proverbs, it is stated that at the same time as God condensed the clouds, he also fixed the fountains of the deep.[4] Even closer, however, to what is described in our present passage is the statement in an Old Babylonian creation myth that at first "all lands were sea, and in the midst of that sea was a spring which served as a pipe."[5]

The same conception is attested in later Semitic literature.[6] The Syrian church father Ephraim Syrus (306–73), commenting on the words of Genesis 49:25, "Blessings of heaven above, blessings of the deep which croucheth below," explains that the former are rain and dew, while the latter denote the rivers, which are fed from the subterranean ocean.[7] Similarly, Mas'udi, the Arab traveler and encyclopedist (d. 956), declares in his *Golden Meadows* that "according to some, the rivers are fed by a Great Deep of fresh water, quite distinct from the ocean";[8] and this idea obtains also in modern Palestinian Arab folklore.[9]

The Hittites had a similar notion, for in the remnants of their literature which have come down to us we hear of something called the *hwanhwessar* (or *hwanhwanar*) which appears to be a subterranean source of the earth's waters.[10] It is associated in one text with Ea, the Mesopotamian god of the nether waters,[11] and in another with the rivers,[12] while in the ritual for the New Year (Puruli) festival "the house of the *hwanhwanar*" is committed into the custody of the king—evidently as the steward of his country's fertility—and it is associated in some way with the alternative source of water flowing down (i.e., with the melting of the snows) from Mount Zaliyanu.[13]

To a Syrian or Palestinian writer the idea that the earth was at first watered by a subterranean spring rather than by rain might indeed have held a special appeal, for he could then see in that primordial condition the prototype of what in fact took place annually when the world order was, as it were, renewed at the beginning of the agricultural cycle in autumn. In many parts of the country, before the onset of the "early rains" at that season, the soil is watered only by springs which burst forth at the foot of the hills.[14]

Adam and Eve

▲ Attentive readers of the Bible can hardly fail to remark a striking discrepancy between the two accounts of the creation of man recorded in the first and second chapters of Genesis. In the first chapter, we read how, on the fifth day of creation, God created the fishes and the birds, all the creatures that live in the water or in the air; and how on the sixth day he created all terrestrial animals, and last of all man, whom he fashioned in his own image, both male and female. From this narrative we infer that man was the last to be created of all living beings on earth, and that the human beings consisted of a man and a woman, produced to all appearance simultaneously, and each of them reflecting in equal measure the glory of their divine original. But when we proceed to the second chapter, we learn with surprise that God created man first, the lower animals next, and woman last of all, fashioning her as a mere afterthought out of a rib which he abstracted from the man's body.

The flagrant contradiction between the two accounts is explained by modern scholars on the theory that they are derived from two different documents, which were afterwards somewhat clumsily combined into a single book. The account of the creation in the first chapter is derived from what is called the Priestly Document, which was composed by priestly writers during or after the Babylonian captivity; that in the second chapter from what is called the Jehovistic Document, written several hundred years earlier, probably in the ninth or eighth century before our era. The difference between the religious standpoints of the two writers is manifest. The later or priestly writer conceives God in an abstract form as withdrawn from human sight, and creating all things by a simple fiat. The earlier or Jehovistic writer conceives God in a very concrete form as acting and speaking like a man, modelling a human being out of clay, planting a garden, walking in it at the cool of the day, calling to the man and woman to come out from among the trees behind which they have hidden themselves, and making coats of skin to replace the too scanty garments of fig-leaves with which our abashed first parents sought to conceal their nakedness. ▼

8   Man formed from earth or clay   **2:7**

▲ Of the two narratives the earlier is not only the more picturesque but also the richer in folklore, retaining many features redolent of primitive simplicity

8

which have been affaced by the later writer. The author seems to have imagined that *God moulded the first man out of clay,* as a potter might do, and that having kneaded and patted the clay into the proper shape, the deity animated it by breathing into its mouth and nostrils. To the Hebrews, it may be added, this derivation of our species from the dust of the ground would have suggested itself the more naturally because, in their language, the word for "ground" (*adamah*) is similar to that for "man" (*adam*).

This fancy is, however, by no means confined to Scripture. The Mesopotamians too conceived man to have been fashioned in such manner.[1] [In a cuneiform text from Ashur, the earlier capital of Assyria, the goddess Aruru is said to have pinched him out of clay;[1a] and by virtue of this expertise it is the same goddess who likewise fashions the hero Enkidu in the Epic of Gilgamesh.[1b] In another myth the feat is attributed to the mother-goddess Mama (or Mami), man being created as a kind of robot for the service of the gods.[1c] Elsewhere, again, she is described as forming seven primeval males and seven primeval females out of clay.[1d] Ea (Zallamuru), god of wisdom and of the waters, is also said to have made man out of clay taken from the bed of the primordial ocean (*apsu*).[1e]] According to Berossus, a Babylonian priest of the third century B.C., whose account of creation has been preserved in a Greek version, Bel, the lord of heaven, ordered one of the minor gods to behead himself, whereupon the other gods caught the flowing blood, mixed it with earth and fashioned man out of the bloody paste.[2]

In Egyptian mythology, Knum, the potter god, is said to have moulded man on the wheel,[3] [and he was believed to repeat the experiment in the course of the generations. On bas-reliefs at Luxor depiciting the births of Queen Hatshepsut and of Amenhotep III, he is shown shaping two diminutive figures in the same manner;[3a] and in the celebrated *Admonitions of Ipuwer,* which describe conditions in Egypt during the unsettled days of the First Intermediary Period (2300–2050 B.C.), it is said that things are in such chaos that "Khnum can no longer fashion mortals."[3b] Similarly, in the *Instruction of Amen-em-opet,* composed (probably) in the sixth or seventh century B.C., man is described as "but clay and straw, with God as his builder."[3c]]

A similar legend was current among the Greeks. Prometheus is said to have moulded the first man out of clay mixed with the water of the River Panopeus in Phocis;[4] [while in one of the mimes of Herondas, a pander bringing charges against a man who has broken into his brothel observes tartly that "he ought to know what kind of fellow he is and *of what clay he is compounded.*"[4a]]

Stories of the same sort have been recorded among the savages and barbarians of today or yesterday.

Thus the Australian blacks in the neighbourhood of Melbourne said that Bunjie, the Creator, cut three large sheets of bark with his big knife. On one of these he placed some clay and worked it up with his knife into a proper consistence. He then laid a portion of the clay on one of the other pieces of bark and shaped it into a human form; first he made the feet, then the legs, then the

trunk, the arms, and the head. Thus he made a clay man on each of the two
pieces of bark; and being well pleased with his handiwork, he danced round
them for joy. Next he took stringy bark from the eucalyptus tree, made hair of
it, and stuck it on the heads of his clay men. Then he looked at them again, was
pleased with his work, and again danced round them for joy. He then lay down
on them, blew his breath hard into their mouths, their noses, and their navels;
and presently they stirred, spoke, and rose up as full-grown men.[5]

The Maoris of New Zealand say that a certain god, variously named Tu,
Tiki, and Tane, took red riverside clay, kneaded it with his own blood into a
likeness or image of himself, with eyes, legs, arms, and all complete, in fact,
an exact copy of the deity; and having perfected the model, he animated it by
breathing into its mouth and nostrils, whereupon the clay effigy at once came
to life and sneezed. "Of all these things," said a Maori, in relating the story
of man's creation, "the most important is the fact that the clay sneezed, foras-
much as that sign of the power of the gods remains with us even to this day in
order that we may be reminded of the great work Tu accomplished on the
altar of the Kauhanga-nui, and hence it is that when men sneeze the words
of Tu are repeated by those who are present"; for they say, "Sneeze, O spirit
of life." So like himself was the man whom the Maori Creator Tiki fashioned
that he called him *Tiki-ahua,* that is, Tiki's likeness.[6]

A very generally received tradition in Tahiti was that the first human pair
was made by Taaroa, the chief god. They say that after he had formed the
world he created man out of red earth, which was also the food of mankind
until bread-fruit was produced. Further, some say that one day Taaroa called
for the man by name, and when he came he made him fall asleep. As he
slept, the Creator took out one of his bones (*ivi*) and made of it a woman,
whom he gave to the man to be his wife, and the pair became the progenitors
of mankind. This narrative was taken down from the lips of the natives in the
early years of the mission to Tahiti. The missionary who records it observes:
"This always appeared to me a mere recital of the Mosaic account of creation,
which they had heard from some European, and I never placed any reliance on it, although they have repeatedly told me it was a tradition among
them before any foreigner arrived."[7]

In Nui, one of the Ellice Islands, they say that the god Aulialia made models
of a man and a woman out of earth, and when he raised them up they came
to life. He called the man Tepapa and the woman Tetata.[8]

The Pelew Islanders relate that a brother and sister made men out of clay
kneaded with the blood of various animals, and that the characters of these
first men and of their descendants were determined by the characters of the
animals whose blood had been mingled with the primordial clay; for instance,
men who have rat's blood in them are thieves, men who have serpent's blood in
them are sneaks, and men who have cock's blood in them are brave.[9]

According to a Melanesian legend, told in Mota, one of the Banks' Islands, the hero Qat moulded men of clay, the red clay from the marshy riverside at Vanua Lava. At first he made men and pigs just alike, but his brothers remonstrated with him, so he beat down the pigs to go on all fours and made man walk upright. Qat fashioned the first woman out of supple twigs, and when she smiled he knew she was a living woman.[10]

The natives of Malekula, one of the New Hebrides, give the name of Bokor to the great being who kneaded the first man and woman out of clay.[11]

The inhabitants of Noo-hoo-roa, in the Kei Islands, of New Guinea say that their ancestors were fashioned out of clay by the supreme god, Dooadlera, who breathed life into the clay figures.[12]

According to the Bare'e-speaking Torajas of Central Celebes there were at first no human beings on the earth. Then Ilai, the god of the upper world, and Indara, the goddess of the under world, resolved to make men. They committed the task to Ikombengi, who made two models, one of a man and the other of a woman, out of stone or, according to others, out of wood. When he had done his work, he set up his models by the side of the road which leads from the upper to the under world, so that all spirits passing by might see and criticize his workmanship. In the evening the gods talked it over, and agreed that the calves of the legs of the two figures were not round enough. So Ikombengi went to work again, and constructed another pair of models which he again submitted to the divine criticism. This time the gods observed that the figures were too pot-bellied, so Ikombengi produced a third pair of models, which the gods approved of, after the maker had made a slight change in the anatomy of the figures, transferring a portion of the male to the female figure. It now only remained to make the figures live. So Ilai returned to his celestial mansion to fetch eternal breath for the man and woman; but in the meantime the Creator himself, whether from thoughtlessness or haste, had allowed the common wind to blow on the figures, and they drew their breath and life from it. That is why the breath returns to the wind when a man dies.[13]

The Dayaks of Sakarran in Borneo say that the first man was made by two large birds. At first they tried to make men out of trees, but in vain. Then they hewed them out of rocks, but the figures could not speak. Then they moulded a man out of damp earth and infused into his veins the red gum of the kumpang-tree. After that they called to him and he answered; they cut him and blood flowed from his wounds, so they gave him the name of Tannah Kumpok or "moulded earth."[14] Some of the Sea Dayaks, however, are of a different opinion. They think that a certain goddess named Salampandai is the maker of men. He hammers them into shape out of clay, thus forming the bodies of children who are to be born into the world. There is an insect which makes a curious clinking noise at night, and when the Dayaks hear it, they say that it is the clink of Salampandai's hammer at her work. The story goes that she was commanded by the gods to make a man, and she made one of stone; but the figure could not speak and was therefore rejected. So she set to work again, and made a man of iron; but neither could he speak, so the gods would have none of him. The third time Salampandai made a man of clay, and he had the power of speech. Therefore the gods were pleased and said, "The man you have made will do well. Let him be the ancestor of the human race, and you must make others like him." So Salampandai set about fashioning human beings, and she is still fashioning them at her anvil, working away with her tools in unseen regions. There she hammers out the clay babies, and when one of them is finished she brings it to the gods, who ask the infant, "What would you like to handle and use?" If the child answers, "A sword," the gods pronounce it a male; but if the child replies, "Cotton and a spinning-wheel," they pronounce it a female. Thus they are born boys or girls, according to their own wishes.[15]

The natives of Nias, an island to the south-west of Sumatra, have a long poem descriptive of the creation, which they recite at the dances performed at the funeral of a chief. In this poem, which is arranged in couplets after the style of Hebrew poetry, the second verse repeating the idea of the first in somewhat different terms, we read how the supreme god, Luo Zaho, bathed at a celestial spring which reflected his figure in its clear water as in a mirror, and how, on seeing his image in the water, he took a handful of earth as large as an egg, and fashioned out of it a figure like one of those figures of ancestors which the people of Nias construct. Having made it, he put it in the scales and weighed it; he weighed also the wind, and having weighed it, he put it on the lips of the figure which he had made; so the figure spoke like a man or like a child, and God gave him the name of Sihai.[16, 16a]

The Bila-an, a wild tribe of Mindanao, one of the Philippine Islands, relate the creation of man as follows. They say that in the beginning there was a certain being named Melu, of a size so huge that no known thing can give any idea of it; he was white in colour, and had golden teeth, and he sat upon the clouds, occupying all the space above. Being of a very cleanly habit, he was constantly rubbing himself in order to preserve the whiteness of his skin unsullied. The scurf which he thus removed from his person he laid on one side, till it gathered in such a heap as to fidget him. To be rid of it he constructed the earth out of it, and being pleased with his work he resolved to make two beings like himself, only much smaller in size. He fashioned them accordingly in his own likeness out of the leavings of the scurf whereof he had moulded the earth, and these two were the first human beings. But while the Creator was still at work on them, and had finished one of them all but the nose, and the other all but the nose and one other part, Tau Dalom Tana came up to him and demanded to be allowed to make the noses. After a heated argument with the Creator, he got his way and made the noses, but in applying them to the faces of our first parents he unfortunately placed them upside down. So warm had been the discussion between the Creator and his assistant in regard to the noses, that the Creator quite forgot to finish the other part of the second figure, and went away to his place above the clouds, leaving the first man or the first woman (for we are not told which) imperfect; and Tau Dalom Tana also went away to his place below the earth. After that a heavy rain fell, and the two first of human kind nearly perished, for the rain ran off the tops of their heads into their upturned nostrils. Happily the Creator perceived their plight and coming down from the clouds to the rescue he took off their noses and replaced them right end up.[17]

The Bagobo, a pagan tribe of South-Eastern Mindanao, say that in the beginning a certain Diwata made the sea and the land, and planted trees of many sorts. Then he took two lumps of earth, shaped them like human figures, and spat on them; so they became man and woman. The old man was called Tuglay, and the old woman, Tuglibung. They married and lived together, and the old man made a great house and planted seeds of different kinds, which the old woman gave him.[18]

[The creation of man out of clay is duly mentioned in the Indian classic, *Satapatha Brahmana,* and likewise forms the theme of many modern folktales current in that country.[18a]]

The Kumi, who inhabit portions of Arakan and the Chittagong hill tracts in eastern India, told Captain Lewin the following story of the creation of man. God made the world and the trees and the creeping things first, and after that he made one man and one woman, forming their bodies of clay; but every night, when he had done his work, there came a great snake, which, while God was sleeping, devoured the two images. This happened twice or thrice, and God was at his wits' end, for he had to work all day, and could not finish the pair in less than twelve hours; besides, if he did not sleep, "he would be no good," as the native narrator observed with some show of probability. So, as I have said, God was at his wits' end. But at last he got up early one morning and first made a dog and put life into it; and that night, when he had finished the images, he set the dog to watch them, and when the snake came, the dog barked and frightened it away. That is why to this day, when a man is dying, the dogs begin to howl; but the Kumis think that God sleeps heavily nowadays, or that the snake is bolder, for men die in spite of the howling of the dogs. If God did not sleep, there would be neither sickness nor death; it is during the hours of his slumber that the snake comes and carries us off.[19]

A similar tale is told by the Khasis of Assam. In the beginning, they say, God created man and placed him on earth, but on returning to look at the work of his hands he found that the man had been destroyed by the evil spirit. This happened a second time, whereupon the deity created first a dog and then a man; and the dog kept watch and prevented the devil from destroying the man. Thus the work of the deity was preserved.[20]

The same story also crops up, with a slight varnish of Hindu mythology, among the Kurkus, an aboriginal tribe of the Central Provinces of India. According to them, Rāvana, the demon-king of Ceylon, observed that the Vindhyan and Satpura ranges were uninhabited, and he besought the great god Mahadeo to people them. So Mahadeo, by whom they mean Siva, sent a crow to find for him an anthill of red earth, and the bird discovered such an anthill among the mountains of Betul. Thereupon the god repaired to the spot, and taking a handful of the red earth he fashioned out of it two images, in the likeness of a man and a woman. But no sooner had he done so than two fiery horses, sent by Indra, rose from the earth and trampled the images to dust. For two days the Creator persisted in his attempts, but as often as the images were made they were dashed in pieces by the horses. At last the god made an image of a dog, and breathed into it the breath of life, and the animal kept off the fiery steeds of Indra. Thus the god was able to make the two images of man and woman undisturbed, and bestowing life upon them, he called them Mula and Mulai. These two became the ancestors of the Kurku tribe.[21]

A similar tale is told, with a curious variation, by the Mundas, a primitive tribe of Chota Nagpur. They say that the Sun-god, by name Singbonga, first fashioned two clay figures, one meant to represent a man and the other a woman. But before he could endow the figures with life, the horse, apprehensive of what in future he might endure at their hands, trampled them under its hoofs. In those days the horse had wings and could move about much faster than now. When the Sun-god found that the horse had destroyed his earthen figures of men, he first created a spider and then fashioned two more clay figures like those which the horse had demolished. Next he ordered the spider to guard the effigies against the horse. Accordingly the spider wove its web round the figures in such a way that the horse could not break them again. After that, the Sun-god imparted life to the two figures, which thus became the first human beings.[22]

The Cheremiss of Russia, a Finnish people, tell a story of the creation of man which recalls episodes in the Toradjan and Indian legends of the same event. They say that God moulded man's body of clay and then went up to heaven to fetch the soul, with which to animate it. In his absence he set the dog to guard the body. But while he was away the Devil drew near, and blowing a cold wind on the dog he seduced the animal by the bribe of a fur-coat to relax his guard. Thereupon the fiend spat on the clay body and beslavered it so foully, that when God came back he despaired of ever cleaning up the mess and saw himself reduced to the painful necessity of turning the body outside in. That is why a man's inside is now so dirty. And God cursed the dog the same day for his culpable neglect of duty.[23]

Turning now to Africa, we find the legend of the creation of mankind out of clay among the Shilluks of the White Nile, who ingeniously explain the different complexions of the various races by the differently coloured clays out of which they were fashioned. They say that the creator Juok moulded all men out of earth, and that while he was engaged in the work of creation he wandered about the world. In the land of the whites he found a pure white earth or sand, and out of it he shaped white men. Then he came to the land of Egypt and out of the mud of the Nile he made red or brown men. Lastly, he came to the land of the Shilluks and finding there black earth he created black men out of it. The way in which he modelled men was this. He took a lump of earth and said to himself, "I will make man, but he must be able to walk and run and go out into the fields, so I will give him two long legs, like the flamingo." Having done so, he thought again, "The man must be able to cultivate his millet, so I will give him two arms, one to hold the hoe, and the other to tear up the weeds." So he gave him two arms. Then he thought again, "The man must be able to see his millet, so I will give him two eyes." He did so accordingly. Next he thought to himself, "The man must be able to eat his millet, so I will give him a mouth." And a mouth he gave him accordingly. After that he thought within himself, "The man must be able to dance and speak and sing and shout, and for these purposes he must have a tongue." And a tongue he gave him accordingly. Lastly, the deity said to himself, "The man must be able to hear the noise of the dance and the speech of great men, and for that he needs two ears." So two ears he gave him, and sent him out into the world a perfect man.[24]

The Fans of West Africa say that God created man out of clay, at first in the shape of a lizard, which he put in a pool of water and left there for seven days. At the end of the seven days God cried, "Come forth," and a man came out of the pool instead of a lizard.[25]

The Ewe-speaking tribes of Togo-land, in West Africa, think that God still makes men out of clay. When a little of the water with which he moistens the clay remains over, he pours it on the ground, and out of that he makes the bad and disobedient people. When he wishes to make a good man he makes him out of good clay; but when he wishes to make a bad man, he employs only bad clay for the purpose. In the beginning God fashioned a man and set him on the earth; after that he fashioned a woman. The two looked at each other and began to laugh, whereupon God sent them into the world.[26]

[Among the Dogon of the French Sudan it is related that the high god Amma kneaded two balls of clay, out of which sprang the first human couple. (He had previously made his own mate in the same way.[26a]) Similarly the Yoruba say that man was made out of clay by the god Obatala and his wife Odudua, and then animated by the breath of the supreme deity, Olorun.[26b]]

The story of the creation of mankind out of clay occurs also in America, both among the Eskimo and the Indians, from Alaska to Paraguay. Thus the Eskimo of Point Barrow, in Alaska, tell of a time when there was no man in the land, till a certain spirit named á sĕ lu, who resided at Point Barrow, made a clay man, set him up on the shore to dry, breathed into him, and gave him life.[27] The Unaligmiut of Norton Sound relate how the Raven made the first woman out of clay, to be a companion to the first man; he fastened water-grass to the back of the head to be hair, flapped his wings over the clay figure, and it arose, a beautiful young woman.[28]

The Acagchemem Indians of California said that a powerful being called Chinigchinich created man out of clay which he found on the banks of a lake; male and female created he them, and the Indians of the present day are the descendants of the clay man and woman.[29]

According to the Maidu Indians of California the first man and woman were created by a mysterious personage named World-Initiate (*Kodom-yéponi*), who descended from the sky by a rope made of feathers. His body shone like the sun, but his face was hidden and never seen. One afternoon he took dark red earth, mixed it with water, and fashioned two figures, one of them a man and the other a woman. He laid the man on his right side and the woman on his left side, in his house. He lay thus and sweated all that afternoon and all that night. Early in the morning the woman began to tickle him in the side. He kept very still and did not laugh. By and by he arose, thrust a piece of pitch-wood into the ground, and fire burst out. The two people were very white. No one to-day is so white as they were. Their eyes were pink, their hair was black, their teeth shone brightly, and they were very handsome. It is said that World-Initiate did not finish the hands of the people, because he did not know how best to do it. The coyote, or prairie-wolf, who plays a great part in the myths of the Western Indians, saw the people and suggested that they ought to have hands like his. But World-Initiate said, "No, their hands shall be like mine." Then he finished them. When the coyote asked why their hands were to be like that, World-Initiate answered, "So that, if they are chased by bears, they can climb trees." The first man was called Kuksu, and the first woman was called Morning-Star Woman.[30]

The Kawakipais, or Diegueño Indians, who occupy the extreme south-western corner of California say that in the beginning there was no earth or solid land, nothing but salt water. But under the sea lived two brothers, of whom the elder was named Tcaipakomat. Both kept their eyes shut, for if they had not done so, the salt water would have blinded them. After a while the elder brother came up to the surface and looked about him, but he could see nothing but water. The younger brother also came up, but on the way to the surface he incautiously opened his eyes, and the salt water blinded him; so when he emerged he could see nothing at all, and therefore he sank back into the depths. Left alone on the face of the deep, the elder brother now under-took the task of creating a habitable earth out of the waste of waters. As the culmination of his word, he took a lump of light-colored clay, split it partly up, and made a man of it. Then he took a rib from the man and made out of it a woman, who was called Sinyaxau, or First Woman (from *siny,* "woman," and *axau*, "first"). From this couple the human race is descended.[31] [Similarly, the Kato of California say that the Thunder-god made man of earth and clay;[31a] while the Choctaws and Natchez assert that the Master of Breath formed him in the same way in a cave on Bending Hill, in Natchez territory.[31b, 31c]]

The Hopi or Moki Indians of Arizona similarly believe that in the beginning there was nothing but water everywhere, and that two deities, apparently goddesses, both named Huruing Wuhti, lived in houses in the ocean, one of them in the east, and the other in the west; and these two by their efforts caused dry land to appear in the midst of the water. Nevertheless the sun, on his daily passage across the newly created earth, noticed that there was no living being of any kind on the face of the ground, and he brought this radical defect to the notice of the two deities. Accordingly the divinities met in consultation, the eastern goddess passing over the sea on the rainbow as a bridge to visit her western colleague. Having laid their heads together they resolved to make a little bird; so the goddess of the east made a wren of clay, and together they chanted an incantation over it, so that the clay bird soon came to life. Then they sent out the wren to fly over the world and see whether he could discover any living being on the face of the earth; but on his return he reported that no such being existed anywhere. Afterwards the two deities created many sorts of birds and beasts in like manner, and sent them forth to inhabit the world. Last of all the two goddesses made up their mind to create man. Thereupon the eastern goddess took clay and moulded out of it first a woman and afterwards a man; and the clay man and woman were brought to life just as the birds and beasts had been so before them.[32]

The Pima Indians, another tribe of Arizona, allege that the Creator took clay into his hands, and mixing it with the sweat of his own body, kneaded the whole into a lump. Then he blew upon the lump till it began to live and move and became a man and a woman.[33]

A priest of the Natchez Indians in Louisiana told Du Pratz "that God had kneaded some clay, such as that which potters use, and had made it into a little man; and that after examining it, and finding it well formed, he blew upon his work, and forthwith that little man had life, grew, acted, walked, and found himself a man perfectly well shaped." As to the mode in which the first woman was created, the priest frankly confessed that he had no information, the ancient traditions of his tribe being silent as to any difference in the creation of the sexes; he thought it likely, however, that man and woman were made in the same way. So Du Pratz corrected his erroneous ideas by telling him the tale of Eve and the rib, and the grateful Indian promised to bruit it about among the old men of his tribe.[34]

The Michoacans of Mexico said that the great god Tucapacha first made man and woman out of clay, but that when the couple went to bathe in a river they absorbed so much water that the clay of which they were composed

all fell to pieces. To remedy this inconvenience the Creator applied himself
again to his task and moulded them afresh out of ashes, but the result was
again disappointing. At last, not to be baffled, he made them of metal. His
perseverance was rewarded. The man and woman were now perfectly water-
tight; they bathed in the river without falling in pieces, and by their union
they became the progenitors of mankind.[35]

[In Aztec mythology, the Tarascan deity Tocupacha made man and woman
out of clay;[35a] while in similar vein the *Popul Vuh* relates that the Creator
first made man out of moist earth, but his experiment proved a failure.]

According to a legend of the Peruvian Indians, which was told to a Spanish
priest in Cuzco about half a century after the conquest, it was in Tiahuanaco
that the human race was restored after the great flood which had destroyed
them all, except one man and woman. There in Tiahuanaco, which is about
seventy leagues from Cuzco, "the Creator began to raise up the people and
nations, that are in that region, making one of each nation of clay, and painting the dresses that each one was to wear. Those that were to wear their hair,
with hair; and those that were to be shorn, with hair cut; and to each nation
was given the language that was to be spoken, and the songs to be sung, and
the seeds and food that they were to sow. When the Creator had finished painting and making the said nations and figures of clay, he gave life and soul to
each one, as well men as women, and ordered that they should pass under
the earth. Thence each nation came up in the places to which he ordered
them to go."[36]

The Lengua Indians of Paraguay believe that the Creator, in the shape of a
beetle, inhabited a hole in the earth, and that he formed man and woman out
of the clay which he threw up from his subterranean abode. At first the two
were joined together, "like the Siamese twins," and in this very inconvenient
posture they were sent out into the world, where they contended, at great dis-
advantage, with a race of powerful beings whom the beetle had previously
created. So the man and woman besought the beetle to separate them. He
complied with their request and gave them the power to propagate their
species. So they became the parents of mankind. But the beetle, having created
the world, ceased to take any active part or interest in it.[37] We are reminded of
the fanciful account which Aristophanes, in the *Symposium* of Plato, gives of
the original condition of mankind; how man and woman at first were knit
together in one composite being, with two heads, four arms, and four legs,
till Zeus cleft them down the middle and so separated the sexes.[38]

[The Chaco of Paraguay say that Beetle made the first couple out of clay
thrown up from his hole. They were Siamese twins.[38a]]

It is to be observed that in a number of these stories the clay out of which
our first parents were moulded is said to have been red. The colour was probably intended to explain the redness of blood. Though the Jehovistic writer
in Genesis omits to mention the colour of the clay which God used in the

construction of Adam, we may perhaps, without being very rash, conjecture that it was red. For the Hebrew word for man in general is *adam,* the word for ground is *adamah,* and the word for red is *adom;* so that by a natural and almost necessary concatenation of causes we arrive at the conclusion that our first parent was modelled out of red earth. If any lingering doubt could remain in our mind on the subject, it would be dissipated by the observation that down to this day the soil of Palestine is of a dark reddish brown. ▼

9   Man animated by divine breath   2:7

The *rude clay,* we are told, *was animated by the breath of God.* This idea too is by no means exclusive to the Bible. In Hindu myth, the creator god Prajapati brings life to man in precisely the same way, thus imparting to him also his mental and spiritual faculties.[1] So too in ancient Greek belief, the clay figure moulded by Prometheus beside the waters of Panopeus was quickened by the breath of the goddess Athene.[2] Among the Yoruba of West Africa, the supreme god Olorun is said to have given life in this manner to the insensate clod kneaded by his agent, Obatala;[3] while the Creeks, Choctaws, and Seminole Indians of North America hold that man, previously moulded by his hands, was inspired with life by the high god, therefore designated "the Master of Breath" (*Esaugetuh Emisser*).[4] A variant on the theme, current among the Unaligmiut Eskimos of Norton Sound, asserts that primeval Raven fashioned both men and beasts out of mud and then fanned life into them with his wings.[5]

More is implied by such tales than the mere origin of respiration. Breath is everywhere a synonym for "self," a vehicle of the *élan vitale.* One thinks immediately of such familiar examples as the Hebrew *nephesh,*[6] the Sanskrit *atman,* the Greek *pneuma,* the Latin *anima,* and the Slavonic *duch* (whence Gypsy *duk*);[7] but the usage is common also in the speech of primitive peoples. Thus, the West Australian *waug* means both "breath" and "self," and the same is true of the Javanese *nawa,* and of the word *piuts* in the language of the Netela Indians of California.[8]

In popular custom the idea comes out especially in the practice of catching the last breath of a dying person so as to transmit his personality to the succeeding generation.[9] For this reason Joseph kisses the dying Jacob;[10] and in the pseudepigraphical Book of Jubilees it is said that Jacob himself printed no less than seven kisses on the mouth of his grandfather Abraham when the latter was *in articulo mortis.*[11] Similarly, in Vergil's *Aeneid,* when Dido, queen of Carthage, commits suicide upon the departure of Aeneas, her sister Anna rushes forward to the pyre, exclaiming:

> If the last breath yet linger on thy lips,
> Suffer me with my mouth to gather it;[12]

while Cicero speaks of mothers who were cruelly "withheld from the last embrace of their sons—mothers who prayed for nothing more than to be al-

lowed to catch with their mouths the last breath of their offspring."[13] The idea
is echoed also in English literature. Alexander Pope has Heloise cry out to
Abelard

> Suck my last breath and catch my flying soul,

while Shelley invokes Adonais:

> O let thy breath flow from thy dying soul
> Even to my mouth and heart, that I may suck![14]

Among the Seminoles of Florida, when a woman died in childbirth, the infant
was held over her face to receive her parting breath, the vehicle of her spirit;[15]
and only a century ago the superstition prevailed in Lancashire, England, that
a witch could not die unless an associate caught her last breath, and with it
her familiar spirit, with her mouth.[16]

In the Ancient Near East it was not only gods that were believed thus to
convey to men the essence of life. In the Tell el Amarna Letters (fourteenth
century B.C.) the pharaohs of Egypt—as punctual incarnations of deity—are
said similarly to transmit it to their subjects;[17] while in the Biblical Book of
Lamentations the king of Judah is described as "the breath of our nostrils."[18]

The breath of God was the source not only of physical vitality but also of
intelligence; it was what turned man not only into a living being but also into
homo sapiens. Says the Book of Job: *Surely it is the breath which is in man,
and the inspiration of the Almighty (Shaddai) that give him understanding.*[19]

Breath, however, is but one of the essential vehicles of life; another is
blood.[20] Accordingly, an alternative version of how man became a living
being speaks in terms not of inspiration by divine breath but of infusion of the
rude clay by divine blood.[21] A myth from Ashur, the earlier capital of Assyria,
tells, for instance, how the parliament of lesser gods suggested to their lord
Enlil that one of their number, a certain Lamga, be slain and man created
from his blood to do chores for them;[22] while in the so-called Epic of Creation
(*Enuma Elish*), man is fashioned out of the blood and bone of Kingu, a god
who has been executed for commanding an army against the authority of the
supreme deity.[23] A counterpart in Greek legend asserts that man sprang from
the blood of the slain Titans who had rebelled against the rule of Kronos,[24] or
from that of the vanquished Giants;[25] while the Emperor Julian reports a
popular tradition according to which "after Zeus had completed the ordering of
all things, the human race sprang from the drops of his blood which had
fallen."[26] Similarly, among the Maori of New Zealand the story runs that the
creator god Tibi mixed red clay with his own blood in order to form man.[27]
Lastly, even in the Koran, Allah is said to have "made man out of flowing
blood."[28]

10   Man made in the image of God   1:26–27; 5:1

The Biblical statement that *Man was created in the image and likeness of God* is simply another way of saying the same thing. But once again the thought is not the exclusive property of the Biblical writer. The *Teaching of Ani,* which appears to date toward the end of the Egyptian Empire, says categorically that "Man is the counterpart of God,"[1] and in the *Maxims of Khety,* which seem to have been composed during the time of the Middle Kingdom, human beings are described as "replicas of God, which issue from his limbs."[2] A fine twist is given to this idea, in the first century C.E., by the neo-Stoic philosopher, C. Masonius Rufus. "Of all earthly creatures," he declares, "man alone is wholly a replica of God, since he has qualities (*aretai,* virtues) analogous to His."[3]

11   Woman   2:21–23

(a)   Woman formed from man's rib

A recent theory provides a fascinating explanation of this story. In the cuneiform script of the Sumerians, it is pointed out, the same sign TI denotes both "life" and "rib." Hence, in a Sumerian story now lost, a female character called NIN.TI—that is, "Lady of TI"—could be interpreted either as "Lady of Life" or as "Lady of the Rib." The former interpretation, it is suggested, led to the designation of the first woman as *Eve,* for this represents the Hebrew *Ḥawwah,* which is connected with the word *ḥay,* "living." Eve, as the Scriptural writer says explicitly (3:20), received her name because she was "the mother of all living." The latter interpretation, on the other hand, led to the tale that she had been formed from the rib of the first man.[1]

It might seem at first sight that this ingenious theory stumbles against the objection that, as shown above (§8), the story of woman's creation from the rib of man is not in fact confined to the peoples of the Ancient Near East, but occurs also in many other parts of the world, e.g., in Polynesia, among the Karens of Burma, and among the Bedel Tartars of Siberia. Indeed, Frazer's parallels can be significantly augmented. The same story is told, for instance, by the Salinan Indians of California,[2] while the Yuki of the same state say that woman was made out of man's rib by the god Taikomol.[3] Similarly too the Serranos (likewise of California) assert that the first woman was fashioned by the god Pakrokitat out of a portion of man's body just above the right ribs.[4] An Arosi myth from the island of St. Cristoval in the Pacific Ocean affords an interesting variation on the theme. The god Haituibwari, we are told, came down upon Mt. Hoto and made woman out of red clay. He breathed on it in order to animate it, and then baked it. Subsequently man was created out of one of her ribs![5] Lastly, in a tale from Greenland, man is made out of earth, and woman out of his *thumb.*[6]

These, to be sure, are arresting parallels, but a word of caution is in order, for many modern anthropologists believe that such tales are really, as often as not, mere "playbacks" (adapted, of course, and distorted) of the Biblical account, heard from missionaries. Thus, such impressive authorities as J. A. Mason and A. L. Kroeber are convinced that the Salinan and Yuki myths adduced above are directly dependent on the Bible;[7] while in the story from St. Cristoval suspicion is immediately aroused by the telltale mention of *red* clay, since this might well reflect a missionary's introduction of the time-honored (but actually erroneous)[8] association of the name Adam and of the Hebrew word *adamah,* "earth," with *adôm,* "red," in his retelling of the Scriptural narrative.[9]

(b) The woman in Paradise

If, then, we disregard these primitive "parallels" and accept the theory that the story of Eve's creation from the rib of Adam originated simply in the ambiguity of Sumerian script, we shall have to regard it as a mere secondary accretion to an earlier tale featuring a Woman in Eden, and we are faced with the question: Who, in that earlier tale, was this Femme Fatale who tempted the first man and brought about his fall? Who, in other words, was the lady whom the Sumerians designated NIN.TI?

Comparative Folklore suggests an alluring answer: *she was none other than the Beautiful Fay or Fairy Mistress who appears ubiquitously in tales of journeys to the otherworld or to the Earthly Paradise.*[10] She is usually portrayed as dwelling on an enchanted island or in some similar domain and as giving succor to the hero on his travels. It is thus, for instance, that she appears, in the Babylonian Epic of Gilgamesh, in the character of Siduri, who endeavors to detain the hero on her faery island while he is wandering in search of immortality.[11] In the manner of all genuine folktales, she does not really possess a distinctive name, for we now know that Siduri is simply a Hurrian (Horite) word for "girl, lady."[12] She is simply the Femme Fatale of the Enchanted Isle, a kind of earthly paradise. Her Greek counterpart is the more familiar Calypso who likewise seeks to detain Odysseus and who—this is important—proffers him food.[13] The Fairy Mistress turns up again in Indic folktale. The twelfth story in Somadeva's famous Vampire Tales (*Vetalapancavimsati*) tells how the fairy princess Mrigankavati rises from an island of gold, enamors and seduces the prince Yasahkatu, and how he eventually leads her back to his kingdom, after breaking the spell which has been holding her imprisoned.[14]

Next we turn to Celtic romance. A common feature of the Irish *imram,* or tale of the journey to the otherworld, is the appearance of a siren who dwells in an earthly paradise and tries to seduce the hero by promising him immortality, or eternal youth, or freedom from care, or all these things together. In many versions she offers him magical fruit (e.g., an apple), consumption of which will prevent his return to the normal world.[15] Thus in the Imram of Malduin, that hero is subjected to the blandishments of a *fée* who tries to persuade him to remain on the faery Island of Maidens.[16] The same element appears also in the romances of Bran, Connla, Cuchulainn, and Teigue.[17] In the Arthurian cycle, the role of the Fairy Mistress is played by Morgan le Fay, about whom traditions varied.[18] According to Geoffrey of Monmouth—who is the earliest writer to mention her—she dwells in an island paradise along with her eight sisters and possesses magic herbs and simples.[19] Chrétien de Troyes, on the other hand, makes her the sister of Arthur and mistress of Guingamor, lord of Avalon.[20] These variations show that she was already a figure of traditional popular lore before the several literary accounts came to be written. She has further affinities in the fairy mistresses of such Celtic heroes as Lanval and Desiré.[21] According to Loomis, she is related to the Irish goddess Morrigan ("Queen"), the Welsh Modron, the Celtic Matrona,[22] in which case her name would have approximately the same meaning as Siduri.

The Fairy Mistress plays a similar role, again in the person of Morgan le Fay, in the tale of Ogier the Dane;[23] and she may be recognized also in the character of the Elf-queen, "lady of an unco land," who seduces Thomas the Rhymer in the famous English ballad.[24] An analogous figure appears also in a popular romance from Hawaii.[25] Moreover, the tradition of the seductive sylph in Paradise survived in another form in Jewish lore itself—namely, in the familiar legend of Lilith, allegedly the first wife of Adam.[26]

The Garden of Eden

The Biblical story of Paradise is a tapestry woven of ancient threads; all of its salient features recur in the traditional folklore of other peoples.[1]

12   The Earthly Paradise   2:8–3:24

The Earthly Paradise is at once the terrestial pleasance of the gods, the primeval home of man, and the eventual destination of the blessed dead. It stands for that original state of bliss to which, in this vale of tears, man longingly looks back, and which he hopes eventually to regain. It thus symbolizes both the remote memory and the distant hope of the human race.[2]

The concept of such a faery garden is virtually universal. Our earliest reference to it occurs in the literature of the Sumerians of Mesopotamia, and dates to the second millennium B.C.[3] It is there located at a place named Dilmun, apparently to be identified with the island of Bahrein in the Persian Gulf.[4] It is described as the "clear and radiant" dwelling of the gods, where "no raven croaked, no dove drooped its head, no beast ravined," and where there was neither old age nor sickness nor sorrow. It was fed by "the waters of abundance" which flowed from a source "whence issue all the streams of the earth." Situated where the sun rises, it was thither that Ziusudra, the Sumerian Noah, was eventually translated as a reward for his piety.[5] This, however, was not the only conception of the Earthly Paradise entertained by the ancient Mesopotamians, for the celebrated Epic of Gilgamesh tells of a pleasance (*ḫiṣṣu*) of the gods likewise situated at the place of sunrise and distinguished by the fact that its trees bore jewels.[6]

The Indians too knew of such a wondrous garden, called Nandana, in which the god Indra disported himself;[7] while in Somadeva's famous *Ocean of Story* the hero Guṇādhya is blessed with a glimpse of the magical pleasance of the gods, known as Devikṛiti.[8] The Buddhists likewise speak of the Happy Land (Sukhavati), "adorned with jewel trees, frequented by all manner of sweet-voiced birds," fed by delightful waters which run hot or cold to suit the pleasure of its inhabitants, and where the terrain is one unending stretch of green, unhemmed by black hills.[9]

For the Greeks there was, of course, the familiar Garden of the Hesperides,[10] described by Euripides as "God's quiet garden by the sea,"[11] and distinguished especially by its golden apples.

The ancient Canaanite poems discovered at Ras Shamra-Ugarit speak in similar vein of a "demesne of the gods," reached after a journey of "a thousand miles, ten thousand furlongs" and lying at the source of the earth's waters, at the place (i.e., the horizon) where the upper and nether oceans meet.[12]

Celtic romances know likewise of a distant Elysium, styled—like its more ancient Sumerian prototype—"the Land of the Living" (*Tir na mBéo*)[13] and sometimes, as in the *Serglige Cuchulain,* regarded as an island.[14] A similar Earthly Paradise, similarly styled (*jir lifanda manna*), appears in Norse literature;[15] while all readers of the English and Scottish ballads will recall the glowing descriptions of faery realms in such old favorites as *Sweet William's Ghost, Clerk Saunders,* and Ritson's *Dead Men's Song.*[16]

Christopher Columbus, setting out to discover the earthly paradise, was told that he might find it in the west, nestling amid the mountains of Paria, at a spot "whence flowed mighty streams over all the earth," or, alternatively, on the fabled island of Bimini, where a magical fountain restored youth and vigor to the aged and exhausted.[17] For long centuries the natives of Cuba, Yucatan, and Honduras had been setting forth in search of these rejuvenating waters, and if they never came back, their kinsmen at home averred that they had remained under the spell of the enchanted land.[18] It was, indeed, under the influence of such tales that both Ponce de Leon and De Soto embarked on their voyages of discovery.[19]

The Aztecs of Mexico sang, for their part, of Tlapallan, the land of the red sunrise, a region of extraordinary wealth and luxuriance, where their primal ancestors were believed to have dwelt;[20] and the Quichés told of Pan-paxil-pa-cayala, the Land between the Falling Waters, where "one could not count the fruits nor estimate the quantity of honey and food."[21]

13   The location of Paradise   2:8

(a) In the east

The Biblical writer *locates the Faery Garden in the east,*[1] and even attempts to give it a precise geographical situation. But we need not go off on a wild-goose chase; this trait is purely mythological and was part of the popular tradition which he inherited. It recurs in several of the sister versions. Thus, as we have seen, the Dilmun of the Sumerians lay near the rising sun. Similarly in the Egyptian Pyramid Texts, although the happy Field of Rushes is transferred to the heavens, it is located in the eastern quarter of them,[2] and it was only after the Sixth Dynasty that it was shifted, under the influence of Osirian doctrine, to the west.[3] Among the Iranians, the Region of the Blest (*Airyana vaêya*) was likewise situated in the east, beside the sources of the Oxus and Jaxartes rivers;[4] while Islamic folklore knew of such a realm atop a jacinth hill in the east.[5] It is on an eastern mountain too that the Majavoes of North America place paradise;[6] while the Aztecs assert that their faery land of Tlapallan is in the east, and they call the east wind "the wind of Paradise" (*Tlavocavitl*).[7] The ancient Mexicans held that deceased chieftains and other superior persons went to the eastern paradise of Huitzilopochtli and accompanied the sun on his daily journey.[8] Similarly, the Guarayos of Bolivia bury their dead facing the east, whither they are to go;[9] and the Japanese aver that the deceased inhabit an eastern island.[10]

(b) In the west

To be sure, under the influence of the idea that the dead sink with the setting sun, Paradise comes also to be located in the *west*. The Greeks, for example, said that the Fortunate Isles lay in the Western Ocean;[11] and the same belief obtains at the present day among the Australian aborigines,[12] the Tongans,[13] and the North American Iroquois.[14] The native tribes of Chile, too, say that the dead travel westward to Gulchemen, a place beyond the mountains;[15] and the Haitians that they go to Coaibai, a paradise in the western valleys.[16]

(On the abode of the gods in the *north*, see below, §263.)

(c) In the sky

Sometimes, too, on the strength of the idea that heaven is but a supernal duplicate of earth (see below, §272), Paradise is located in the sky, as for instance by the Egyptians.[17] Even then, however, the landscape is made to conform to the earthly pattern. Like its terrestrial counterpart, it lies at the confluence of two great streams—originally, of course, the upper and nether oceans—and this spot is identified with the point at which the Milky Way divides into two arms.[18] By the same process, the River which waters the Garden—called by the Egyptians the Celestial Nile[19] and by the Greeks the Celestial Eridanos—is seen in the Milky Way itself or in a constellation.[20]

14   The Waters of the Garden   2:10–14

(a) The "Confluence of the Two Streams"

The Faery Garden is not only the focus of men's dreams and hopes, but also the source of the earth's fertility—that is, of its waters. Hence it is commonly located in Ancient Near Eastern literature at the confluence of the celestial and subterranean oceans.[1] This is specifically mentioned, as we have seen, in Mesopotamian and Canaanite (Ugaritic) mythology. It is possible that the idea obtained also in Egypt, for in the famous Egyptian *Tale of the Shipwrecked Sailor,* a wondrous island—like those encountered by Sindbad— which has all the appearance of being an Isle of the Blest, is indeed situated at the junction of two streams.[2] This, however, cannot be pressed, for the expression may mean simply that waters swept it on either side, as is said, for instance, of Calypso's isle in the Odyssey.[3] More to the point, perhaps, is a celebrated passage in the Koran where Moses is made to declare that he will not rest until he has discovered "the junction of the two oceans" (*majma' al-baḥrain*).[4]

(b) The Paradisal River and the Four Streams

The Biblical writer eschews these traditional fancies. For him, the source of earth's waters is a single *river* which issues majestically out of the Garden and then divides into four tributaries. To be sure, he makes an attempt to give the latter a precise location, identifying two of them with the Tigris and Euphrates.[5] But, once again, this should not send us on a wild-goose chase. This detail is purely mythological and is part and parcel of the traditional picture of the Faery Garden. It occurs ubiquitously in the sister versions,[6] and all that is really meant is that the primal River fed the earth in all four directions. In precisely the same way, four streams were said to have issued from the Hindu paradise on Mt. Meru, and four streams likewise flowed from the Fountain of Arduisir in the Iranian Realm of the Blest. In Tibetan belief, four streams course from the root of Zampu, the tree of life, which grows on the sacred hill, Himavata.[7] The Chinese say that four life-giving streams flow from the Kwan-lun hills;[8] and the Slavs hold that four streams flow from under the magic stone Alatuir in the island paradise of Bonyan.[9] On the American continent, the idea is attested among the Sioux, Aztecs, and Mayas;[10] and it has also been recorded among the Polynesians.[11] In the Scandinavian Edda, four streams issue from the spring Hvergelmir in Asaheim, the home of the gods;[12] and there is perhaps also a trace of this notion in Homer's statement that four rivers issued from four springs outside the cave of Circe.[13] Furthermore, it has been suggested that the four rivers of Hades, familiar to all readers of Classical literature, may have been but an infernal counterpart of the paradisal streams.[14]

(c) The Paradisal Fountain

An alternative to the paradisal River was the *paradisal Fountain*. This, to be sure, is not mentioned in our present story, but it appears unequivocally in the graphic description of paradisal bliss given in Psalm 36:8–9:

> Thou dost give them to drink of the River of thy delights;[15]
> for with Thee is the Fountain of Life;

and the expression occurs several times—albeit in a metaphorical sense— in the Book of Proverbs.[16] This too has abundant parallels in folklore.[17] In the Koran, for example, we read of the wondrous paradisal fountains, Salsabil and Kauthar ("Abundance");[18] while the North American Indians knew, as we have seeen, of a Fountain of Youth and Vigor on the paradisal island of Bimini (or Boiuca).[19] A hula chant from Hawaii likewise makes mention of such a fountain;[20] while in Celtic belief it was held that in the midst of the island of Avalon flowed a rill from which sprang a fountain the waters of which gave life to the spirits of the departed.[21] An old French poem speaks in similar vein of a fountain of perpetual youth in the land of Cocagne; all who bathe in it are at once rejuvenated.[22] In Pseudo-Callisthenes' version of the Alexander legend, the hero goes in search of the Fountain of Immortality;[23] and it need scarcely be added that the Fountain of Youth, Beauty, or Immortality is a very common feature of European folktales.[24]

15   The land of gold and gems

A characteristic of Paradise in the folklore of many peoples is that it is *a land of gold and gems*.[1] Thus in the Mesopotamian Epic of Gilgamesh the trees of the Faery Garden bear fruit of carnelian and lapis lazuli,[2] while the prophet Ezekiel declares that the inhabitants of Eden "walk up and down amid flashing gems."[3] Meru, the divine mountain of Hindu belief, is golden,[4] and, according to the Mahabharata, there is a golden region on the sacred hill of Uttarakaru.[5] In one of Somadeva's Vampire Tales (*Vetalapanchavimsati*) there is an island of gold which rises miraculously from the ocean and which is really a faery otherworld.[6] In the scriptures of the "Happy Land" Buddhists of Japan it is stated that every part of the "Buddha-field" in that blessed realm (*Sukhavati*) contains jewels and gems, and that the trees yield gold, silver, beryl, crystal, coral, and emerald. When the Lord Buddha flies to heaven with his disciple Nanda, he sees lilies with stalks of lapis lazuli, and shoots of diamonds, as well as trees brilliant with golden gems.[7] In like fashion, the Greek poet Pindar describes the Isles of the Blest as a place where "flowers of gold are blazing, some on the shore from radiant trees, while others the water fostereth."[8] Horaisan, the Japanese "Land of Life," likewise has trees with roots of silver, trunks of gold, and fruits of rare jewels;[9] while in the Scandinavian Elder Edda the righteous are assured that they will dwell in golden heavenly halls.[10] Medieval Celtic descriptions of Paradise depict it as filled with objects made of crystal and glass;[11] and in the Scottish ballad of *Hin Etin* the elfin lover builds for his mistress in the otherworld a bower "made secure . . . Wi' carbuncle and stane."[12] Similarly, in the *Ballad of the Wee Wee Man,* Paradise includes a place

> Where the roof was o' the beaten gold,
> And the floor was o' the cristal a'.[13]

Jewish legend too speaks of a golden heaven.[14]

Against this background it seems possible that when the Biblical writer makes a point of saying that one of the tributaries of the paradisal River encompassed "the whole land of Havilah, where there is gold . . . as well as bdellium and onyx," he was trying—albeit grotesquely—to give precise local coloring to a time-hallowed mythological tradition.

16 The food of Paradise

(a) The garden is the earthly pleasance of the gods. It must therefore contain the equivalent of that special substance on which they habitually sustain their divine qualities of incorruptibility, deathlessness, and omniscience.

The notion of such special food is virtually ubiquitous in folklore.[1] Homer says explicitly that the élan vitale (*ichôr*) of the gods is sustained by heavenly fare: they do not eat bread or drink wine on Olympus, but feed only on nectar and ambrosia.[2] Thetis pours both into the nostrils of Patroclus to render him immune to corruption of the body,[3] and Apollo is ordered by Zeus to anoint the body of Sarpedon with ambrosia,[4] as Aphrodite anoints that of Hector, to the same end.[5] Demeter makes Demophon immortal by pouring ambrosia over him,[6] and Thetis does the same to Achilles.[7] Berenice[8] and Aeneas[9] too are immortalized in this way. Odysseus refuses the offer of Calypso to render him immortal and eternally young, and therefore declines the nectar and ambrosia proffered by her handmaids.[10] Tantalos steals nectar and ambrosia from the table of the gods in order to make himself deathless.[11] Aristotle, quoting Hesiod as his authority, defines mortals as those who do not partake of nectar and ambrosia,[12] and the latter is sometimes called specifically *athanasia,* "immortality," in Greek literature.[13]

Counterparts of nectar and ambrosia are the soma of the Hindus and the haoma juice of the Iranians. Similarly too, in the Celtic romance of Cuchulainn, nuts in Elysium confer immortality,[14] and food of immortality is given by a goddess to the hero Connla when he journeys to the abode of the blest.[15] So too in Norse mythology, the goddess Idhunn has in her keeping certain apples which rejuvenate aging gods,[16] and Irish lore tells of hazel nuts, food of the gods, which are to be found at the mouths of rivers. They are eaten, it is said, by salmon, and if the latter are then caught and consumed, the consumer acquires special wisdom and knowledge.[17]

Similar fancies were certainly entertained in the Ancient Near East.[18] In the Babylonian *Legend of Adapa* that hero is offered special "food of life" in heaven, and remains mortal only because he foolishly declines it.[19] So too in the Canaanite (Ugaritic) *Poem of Aqhat,* when the goddess Anat tries to coax that hero into surrendering to her the divine bow which, by mere chance, has come into his possession, she promises him—as it were, in the same breath —that he will dine with Baal and also enjoy immortality.[20]

The tasting of such food—"pie in the sky when you die"—was, in fact, what was held out as the ultimate reward of the righteous; thereby they too would become immortal. Thus in an inscription of the eighth century B.C. from the North Syrian kingdom of Sama'l, the wish is expressed that "the soul of [the deceased king] Panamuwa may eat and drink in company with Hadad (i.e., Baal),"[21] and in such pseudepigraphic classics as *The Book of Enoch,*[22] the *Testaments of the Twelve Patriarchs,*[23] and the *Life of Adam and Eve,*[24] as well as in later rabbinic literature,[25] vivid pictures are painted of these paradisal repasts. Aphraates, a Syrian writer of the fourth century C.E., furnishes a particularly glowing account. "The air," he says, "is pleasant and tranquil; a bright light shines; the trees bear fruit constantly, and their leaves never fall. They emit a sweet fragrance, and in their shade the souls of the departed eat and are never glutted."[26] Such feasts are often portrayed in Christian catacombs at Rome, the wine being poured by Peace and Charity.[27]

The Romans too knew of these celestial banquets. Augustus, says Horace, is destined to join Hercules himself as the heavenly table companion of the gods;[28] while the Emperor Julian mockingly portrays the shades of the Caesars at table immediately beneath the moon, in the uppermost zone of the atmosphere.[29]

In Hebrew tradition, such food is sometimes identified with *manna,* the mysterious substance supplied to the Israelites in the wilderness.[30] This is now believed to have been a gum exuded by one or more of the trees which grow there (see below, §88), but it was popularly supposed to be an effusion from heaven and to represent "the bread of angels."[31] Significant in this respect is the fact that it is said expressly to have tasted like honey, for among the Greeks the nectar of the gods was often identified as honeydew.[32]

(b) Such divine fare is obviously taboo to mortals, in accordance with the widespread idea that if you eat anyone's bread you establish communion and enter into kinship with him.[33] It is, as we have seen, by declining to do so that the Mesopotamian hero Adapa foregoes the chance of immortality. Similarly in the Canaanite (Ugaritic) *Poem of Baal,* that genius of rainfall and fertility is held prisoner in the netherworld through being enticed to descend thither and eat of food proferred by his rival Mot, god of death and sterility.[34] Arab folklore of the present day insists that one who eats of the food of the jinns (demons) must remain with them; and this is the theme of a popular tale current among the Mandaeans of Iraq and Iran.[35] Persephone, in the familiar Greek myth, is detained in Hades through imprudently tasting seven seeds of a pomegranate given to her by Pluto.[36] In Shinto myth, the primeval goddess Izanami, after her death, eats of the food of the "land of Yomi," and this prevents her husband Izanagi from bringing her back.[37] Similarly, when Ogier the Dane has been shipwrecked, through the wiles of Morgan le Fay, on a rock near Avalon, he falls into her power by eating an apple from the otherworld orchard which he finds there.[38] So too in Saxo Grammaticus' account of King Gotham's visit to the enchanted realm of Guthmund, some of his companions are prevented from escaping because they have partaken of food there, disregarding the express instructions of their guide, Thorkill.[39] In the same vein, a Norse ballad tells of a certain Sir Bosmer who was seduced by an elf-queen and prevented from returning to the world of men through quaffing a Lethean draught;[40] and it is probable that Tam Linn of the famous Scottish ballad met his doom by consuming faery meats.[41]

Sometimes, to be sure, though the underlying idea is the same, prudence prevails. The Finnish hero Wainamoinen, for instance, expressly refuses drink in the faery realm of Manala;[42] and in the folktales of the Sioux Indians the doughty Ahaketah shows similar discretion.[43] Swedish folklore contains several stories, purportedly true, of human midwives who attended the birth of trolls but cautiously refused to eat anything offered to them, and were therefore able to return.[44] A Jewish legend tells likewise of a professional circumciser (*mohel*) who discreetly declined his host's food when called to perform his office in the land of the demons (*mazzikin*).[45] From Picardy comes the tale of a man who went to rescue one of the Devil's three fair daughters but was expressly warned by her not to drink wine in her father's house;[46] while in a Gascon legend, when St. Peter sends a certain prince on a mission underground, he cautiously provides him with enough bread to prevent him from eating food there.[47] This in turn finds its counterpart in the celebrated English ballad of Thomas the Rhymer. Seduced by the queen of elfland, he rides away with her until he comes to a "garden green" the fruit of which he wishes to pluck for her:

> "O no, O no, true Thomas," she says,
>   "That fruit maun not be touched by thee,
> For a' the plagues that are in hell
>   Light on the fruit of this countrie.
>
> "But I have a loaf here in my lap,
>   Likewise a bottle of claret wine,
> And now, ere we go farther on,
>   We'll rest awhile, and ye may dine."[48]

In the same vein too The Banks Islanders related, in the nineteenth century, that a certain woman had once succeeded in returning safely from a visit to her dead brother in the netherworld because she had carefully restrained from eating anything while she was there;[49] while among the Zulus of South Africa the belief obtains that if the spirit of the dead touch food down below, it will never come back to the earth.[50] Conversely, the natives of New Caledonia, as well as the Melanesians and Kiwai Papuans, assert that the departed are deliberately tempted to eat the food of the nether regions in order to keep them imprisoned there.[51]

(c) Scattered around the world are several tales which parallel the Biblical story that the tasting of forbidden *fruit* "brought death into the world and all our woe."[52] Thus the Efe of Africa assert that God commanded the first human being, Ba-atsi (whom he kneaded out of loam, covered with skin, and then infused with blood), that his children might eat freely of all the trees of

the forest except the Tahu tree. One day, however, a pregnant woman became
seized with an irresistible desire to taste the forbidden fruit. She tried in turn
to persuade her husband to do so. At first he refused; eventually he yielded.
The moon reported their deed to God, who thereupon sent death among men.[53]

The Djaga of the same continent have a different version. The god Ruwa,
they say, led the first human being to a banana grove, but forbade them to eat
a certain kind of yam, called Ula (or Ukaho), planted in the center of it. A
stranger, however, visited the people and induced them to cook and eat it.
Ruwa's minister recognized the smell and reported the matter to his master.
Thereupon the god declared that he would break their bones and burst their
eyes until at last they should die.[54]

There are also Tongan, Singhalese, and North American Indian myths
which play on the same general theme.[55] It may be questioned, however,
whether all of these are genuine parallels to the Biblical narrative. Some at
least may well be mere "playbacks" of the Scriptural story, heard from missionaries and then elaborated, garbled, or adapted.

17   The Trees of Paradise 2:9

▲ With a few light but masterly strokes the Biblical writer depicts for
us the blissful life of our first parents in the happy garden which God had
created for their abode. There every tree that was pleasant to the sight and
good for food grew abundantly; there the animals lived at peace with man
and with each other; there man and woman knew no shame, because they knew
no ill: it was the age of innocence. But this glad time was short, the sunshine was soon clouded.

In this account everything hinges on the tree of the knowledge of good
and evil: it occupies, so to say, the centre of the stage in the great tragedy,
with the man and woman and the talking serpent grouped round it. But when
we look closer we perceive a second tree standing side by side with the other
in the midst of the garden. It is a very remarkable tree, for it is no less than the
tree of life, whose fruit confers immortality on all who eat of it. Yet in the
actual story of the fall this wonderful tree plays no part. Its fruit hangs there
on the boughs ready to be plucked; unlike the tree of knowledge, it is hedged
about by no divine prohibition, yet no one thinks it worth while to taste of the
luscious fruit and live for ever. The eyes of the actors are all turned on the
tree of knowledge; they appear not to see the tree of life. Only, when all
is over, does God bethink himself of the wondrous tree standing there neglected
with all its infinite possibilities, in the midst of the garden; and fearing lest
man, who has become like him in knowledge by eating of the one tree, should
become like him in immortality by eating of the other, he drives him from the
garden, and appoints cherubim, or griffins, and a self-revolving flaming sword
to guard the way to the tree of life.

It appears to be generally recognized that some confusion has crept into the account of the two trees, and that in the original story the tree of life did not play the purely passive and spectacular part assigned to it in the existing narrative. Accordingly, some have thought that there were originally two different stories of the fall, in one of which the tree of knowledge figured alone, and in the other the tree of life alone, and that the two stories have been unskillfully fused into a single narrative by an editor, who has preserved the one nearly intact, while he has clipped and pared the other almost past recognition. It may be so, but perhaps the solution of the problem is to be sought in another direction. The gist of the whole story of the fall appears to be an attempt to explain man's mortality, to set forth how death came into the world. It is true that man is not said to have been created immortal and to have lost his immortality through disobedience; but neither is he said to have been created mortal. Rather we are given to understand that the possibility alike of immortality and of mortality was open to him, and that it rested with him which he would choose; for the tree of life stood within his reach, its fruit was not forbidden to him, he had only to stretch out his hand, take of the fruit, and eating of it live for ever. Indeed, far from being prohibited to eat of the tree of life, man was implicitly permitted, if not encouraged, to partake of it by his Creator, who had told him expressly, that he might eat freely of every tree in the garden, with the single exception of the tree of the knowledge of good and evil. This suggests that the *forbidden* tree was really a tree of death, not of knowledge, and that the mere taste of its fruit sufficed to entail death on the eater. *Accordingly we may suppose that in the original story there were two trees, a tree of life and a tree of death; that it was open to man to eat of the one and live for ever, or to eat of the other and die; that God, out of good will to his creature, advised man to eat of the tree of life and warned him not to eat of the tree of death; and that man, misled by the serpent, ate of the wrong tree and so forfeited the immortality which his benevolent Creator had designed for him.*

[This, however, is but one possibility. Comparative Folklore and Religion suggest another. The essence of the story, as we have seen, is that the food of Paradise is taboo to mortals because it can convey to them qualities which are the characteristics and perquisites of divine beings. Now, the two essential qualities are: (a) incorruptibility, and (b) special knowledge, or even omniscience. The food might thus be conceived as the vehicle of either the one or the other. Accordingly, where it is identified as the fruit of a special tree, that tree might be either (a) the tree of immortality (life), or (b) the tree of knowledge; and the Biblical story might therefore represent a conflation of these originally alternative versions.] ▼

(a) The Tree of Life

The Hebrews were not the only people of the Ancient Near East to possess the notion of the Tree of Life.[1] An early Egyptian Pyramid text mentions such a tree on a distant island, in quest of which King Pheops sets out;[2] and a not uncommon scene on Egyptian reliefs depicts the Pharaoh standing beside a sacred tree (perhaps a persea) in the company of divine beings "who promise him countless years of life, reckon these upon the notched tallies of the palm branch, and inscribe his name upon the fruit."[3] There are also sundry references to a "tree of life" situated in the Egyptian Elysium, the so-called "Field of Peace" (*sḫt ḥtp*), the fruit of which is enjoyed by the righteous.[4]

The evidence from Mesopotamia is somewhat less certain, but perhaps still worth citing. A frequent scene in Assyrian reliefs is that of the king standing beside a tree in the company of griffinlike genii, who are either plucking or touching its leaves and who seem to be handing him a cone or somehow applying it to his person or his weapons.[5] It used to be thought that this scene represented the pollination of the date palm, but C. J. Gadd has pointed out that the tree is not in fact a palm, and has suggested that it is rather to be understood as "the source of magic virtue which the 'genii' take and transfer to the king, or which the king draws directly by touching the tree." He obtains life and strength "by identifying himself with the life of the tree."[6] Symbolic identification with a flourishing tree does not, to be sure, imply a belief in a mythological tree of life, but if Gadd's interpretation is, in general, on the right lines, there seems no reason why the tree should not indeed have been the tree of life, more especially since the expression "tree of life" (GIŠ.TI), admittedly of uncertain connotation, does indeed appear occasionally in cuneiform texts.[7]

The Tree of Life was likewise a feature of the Happy Land in Chinese Buddhism;[8] while in ancient Indic lore, the chief of five wondrous trees was *paridyata,* the forfeiture of whose benefits was the destined doom of the sinful.[9] Similarly too, in the Celtic paradise of Avalon grew a hazel tree which furnished both the gods and the blessed with life-giving nuts;[10] just as in later Jewish lore the righteous are said to be destined to enjoy the fruit of the Tree in the afterlife.[11]

(b) The Tree of the Knowledge of Good and Evil

Comparative Folklore also throws light on the true nature of the Tree of the Knowledge of Good and Evil.[12] As we have seen, the purpose of the trees in general was to convey to the divine inhabitants of Paradise those qualities of incorruptibility and special sapience with which they were credited. The knowledge of good and evil, therefore, is not—as all too often supposed —a specific branch of knowledge (e.g., sexual awareness),[13] nor is it knowledge of the distinction between good and evil (which Hebrew idiom would express quite differently);[14] it is knowledge *in toto,* such as the gods possess. The expression is to be construed as a *merism*—that is, a figure of speech in which contrasting parts are used to convey the notion of a whole, e.g., "officers and men" for "army," or "dollars and cents" for "cash."[15]

That this is the correct interpretation is shown also by the fact that it restores to the tale the same central theme as runs through all the earlier stories in the Book of Genesis, namely, that of God's jealous regard for his own prerogatives, against any encroachment by ambitious man. It is this theme that underlies the stories of the consorting of human women with divine beings (6:1–4) and of the building of the Tower of Babel. In both those cases man's present situation is represented as the punishment for aspiring to be like the gods. In the former, to prevent his absorbing immortality, his life-span is immediately curtailed; in the latter, to prevent his scaling heaven, he is scattered over the earth. So here, consideration of the folklore background enables us to recognize that the true theme of the story is a similar abortive attempt on the part of man to usurp divine status and quality—in this case, by feeding himself on that magical fare of Paradise consumption of which makes the gods what they are.

18 The Serpent   3:1–15

The Serpent is one of the cast of characters which the Biblical writer inherited from traditional stories about Paradise, but which he then transmogrified to suit his own purpose.

(a) The Serpent as guardian

Originally the Serpent would have been simply the guardian of the sacred trees or fountain, for this is a standard role of serpents (and of dragons, who are really but their first cousins) throughout world folklore.[1] We need think only of Ladon who guards the golden apples in the Greek Garden of the Hesperides,[2] or of the dragon who watched over Apollo's gold in Scythia;[3] or who guarded the wondrous rowan tree in the Celtic tale of Fraoch.[4] A serpent served also as a sentinel in the temple of Athene at Athens;[5] and in modern Hellenic lore there is likewise a guardian serpent on Mt. Argaios in Cappadocia.[6]

Alike in Norse and in Siberian *märchen* the serpent lies at the foot of the world-tree,[7] and serpents are frequently depicted on ancient Mesopotamian boundary stones and memorial deeds.[8] The serpent or dragon who guards the pot of gold is familiar, indeed, to every reader of European folktales, and is similarly a common figure in popular tales from Central Asia.[9] Aristeas, a Greek from the area of the Sea of Marmora, tells in a poem of various journeys which he took "in the spirit"; one of them led him to the one-eyed Armaspians among whom he found griffins guarding treasure.[10]

(b) The "subtil beast"

The serpent is described as "subtil," but this does not mean necessarily that he was evil or even sly. The same Hebrew word is used regularly in the Book of Proverbs as the opposite of "simple" or "stupid."[11] The serpent is credited with special sapience or intelligence for two reasons. First, he lives near water, and water, as we have seen (above, §2), was regarded as the seat of primordial wisdom. Second, since the serpent creeps into the earth and frequents tomb-stones, he is often deemed an embodiment of the sapient dead. This belief is attested in antiquity by both Ovid[12] and Plutarch,[13] but it is common also among modern primitive peoples. The Zulus, for example, consider serpents to be *amatongos,* or spirits of the deceased;[14] while in Indonesia the idea obtains that a certain "soul-substance" (distinct from the soul itself) animates the de-parted and causes them to come forth from the earth in the form of serpents.[15] Similar notions have been recorded among the Dyaks of Borneo[16] and in Japan,[17] while the Kaffirs hold that a python is the incarnation of a dead chief-tain,[18] and the Nandi of East Africa that if a serpent settles on a woman's bed, it is the spirit of an ancestor come to tell her that her next child will be deliv-ered safely.[19]

By virtue of such associations the serpent is considered not only wise but also mantic.[20] Serpents were kept in Greek temples so that oracles might be sought from them;[21] while among the Tami of New Guinea they are regularly consulted as being the prophetic spirits of ancestors.[22] A belief current both in ancient and in modern times is that if a man's ear be licked by a serpent, he will thereby acquire the gift of soothsaying.[23]

To the Biblical writer, however, the serpent is certainly sinister as well as shrewd, and this too echoes a popular tradition which is abundantly attested. The Arabs, for example, maintain that every serpent is a potential demon,[24] and Mohammed instructed his followers that serpents should be killed on sight.[25] The Hurons of Canada say that the serpent is the cause of all mal-adies,[26] and the aborigines of Victoria, Australia, that it brought death into the world.[27] Among the peasantry of Suffolk, England, sight of a serpent betokens death;[28] and both ancient Greek[29] and modern Arabic[30] folklore maintain that to dream of serpents is an omen of imminent hostility. This belief, it may be added, is current also among the Mrus of Aracan.[31]

The ambivalent character of the serpent is brought out arrestingly in the popular lore of Palestinian Arabs at the present day, where the male (called *'arbîd,* "malevolent") is regarded as ill-disposed and destructive, whereas the female (called *ḥayyeh*) is beneficial and guards shrines.[32]

(c) The cast skin

By reason of the fact that it constantly sloughs its skin the serpent is popu-larly deemed immortal, or thought at least to be continually rejuvenated.[33] A famous passage in the Babylonian Epic of Gilgamesh relates how that hero was told about a magical plant, called "Greybeard-grow-young," which grew at the bottom of a lake. He dived in and recovered it, but subsequently, when he went for a swim, a serpent sniffed the scent and stole it from his boat. The implication is, of course, that the serpent secured for itself what might else have fallen to man.[34] Similarly, in an inscription carved on an ancient Egyptian tomb there is a prayer that its inhabitant may enjoy "long years like the *n°y* and *sau*-serpents,"[35] and Plutarch tells us that of all animals on earth the serpent alone does not fear old age.[36] The Phoenician mythographer Sanchuniathon says likewise of the serpent that it is very long-lived and possesses the quality of sloughing its skin and assuming a second youth;"[37] while in Latin and Greek the same word is used for "slough of a serpent" and for "old age,"[38] and even today the Italians speak of "being older than a serpent" (*aver più anni d'un serpente*).

Nor is it only among ancient peoples that this belief is attested.

▲ The Wafipa and Wabende of East Africa say that one day God came down to earth, and addressing all living creatures said, "Who wishes not to die?" Unfortunately man and the other animals were asleep; only the serpent was awake and he promptly answered, "I do." That is why men and all other animals die. The serpent alone does not die of himself. He only dies if he is killed. Every year he changes his skin, and so renews his youth and his strength.[39]

In like manner the Dusuns of British North Borneo say that when the Creator had finshed making all things, he asked, "Who is able to cast off his skin? If any one can do so, he shall not die." The snake alone heard and answered, "I can." For that reason down to the present day the snake does not die unless he is killed by man. The Dusuns did not hear the Creator's question, or they also would have thrown off their skins, and there would have been no death.[40]

Similarly the Todjo-Toradjas of Central Celebes relate that once upon a time God summoned men and animals for the purpose of determining their lot. Among the various lots proposed by the deity was this, "We shall put off our old skin." Unfortunately mankind on this momentous occasion was represented by an old woman in her dotage, who did not hear the tempting proposal. But the animals which slough their skins, such as serpents and shrimps, heard it and closed with the offer.[41] Again, the natives of Vuatom, an island in the Bismarck Archipelago, say that a certain To Konokonomiange bade two lads fetch fire, promising that if they did so they should never die, but that, if they refused, their bodies would perish, though their shades or souls would survive. They would not hearken to him, so he cursed them, saying, "What! you would all have lived! Now you shall die, though your soul shall live. But the iguana (*Goniocephalus*) and the lizard (*Varanus indicus*) and the snake (*Enygrus*), they shall live, they shall cast their skin and they shall live for evermore." When the lads heard that, they wept, for bitterly they rued their folly in not going to fetch the fire for To Konokonomiange.[42]

The people of Nias, an island to the west of Sumatra say that, when the earth was created, a certain being was sent down from above to put the finishing touches to the work. He ought to have fasted, but, unable to withstand the pangs of hunger, he ate some bananas. The choice of food was very unfortunate, for had he only eaten river crabs, men would have cast their skins like crabs, and so, renewing their youth perpetually, would never have died. As it is, death has come upon us all through the eating of those bananas.[43] Another version of the Niasian story adds that "the serpents on the contrary ate the crabs, which in the opinion of the people of Nias cast their skins but do not die; therefore serpents also do not die but merely cast their skin."[44]

Thus not a few peoples appear to believe that the happy privilege of immortality, obtainable by the simple process of periodically shedding the skin, was once within reach of our species, but that through an unhappy chance it was transferred to certain of the lower creatures, such as serpents, crabs, lizards, and beetles. According to others, however, men were at one time actually in possession of this priceless boon, but forfeited it through the foolishness of an old woman. Thus the Melanesians of the Banks Islands and the New Hebrides say that at first men never died, but that when they advanced in life they cast their skins like snakes and crabs, and came out with youth renewed. After a time a woman, growing old, went to a stream to change her skin; according to some, she was the mother of the mythical or legendary hero Qat, according to others, she was Ul-ta-marama, Change-skin of the world. She threw off her old woman. Thus the Melanesians of the Banks' Islands and the New Hebrides stick. Then she went home, where she had left her child. But the child refused to recognize her, crying that its mother was an old woman, not like this young stranger. So to pacify the child she went after her cast integument and put it on. From that time mankind ceased to cast their skins and died.[45]

A similar story of the origin of death is told in the Shortlands Islands[46] and by the Kai, a Papuan tribe of north-eastern New Guinea. The Kai say that at first men did not die but renewed their youth. When their old brown skin grew wrinkled and ugly, they stepped into water, and stripping it off got a new, youthful white skin instead. In those days there lived an old grandmother with her grandchild. One day the old woman, weary of her advanced years, bathed in the river, cast off her withered old hide, and returned to the village, spick and span, in a fine new skin. Thus transformed, she climbed up the ladder and entered her house. But when her grandchild saw her, he wept and squalled, and refused to believe that she was his granny. All her efforts to reassure and pacify him proving vain, she at last went back in a rage to the river, fished her wizened old skin out of the water, put it on, and returned to the house a hideous old hag again. The child was glad to see his granny come back, but she said to him, "The locusts cast their skins, but ye men shall die from this day forward." And sure enough, they have done so ever since.[47]

Still farther away from the Banks Islands the very same story is repeated by the To Koolawi, a mountain tribe of Central Celebes. As reported by the Dutch missionaries who discovered it, the Celebes version of this widely diffused tale runs thus. In the olden time men had, like serpents and shrimps, the power of casting their skin, whereby they became young again. Now there was an old woman who had a grandchild. Once upon a time she went to the water to bathe, and thereupon laid aside her old skin and hung it up on a tree. With her youth quite restored she returned to the house. But her grandchild did not know her again, and would have nothing to do with his grandmother; he kept on saying, "You are not my grandmother; my grandmother was old, and you are young." Then the woman went back to the water and drew on her old skin again. But ever since that day men have lost the power of renewing their youth and must die.[48]

Another Melanesian tradition ascribes the introduction of death to purely economic causes. In the days when men changed their skins and lived for ever, the permanence of property in the same hands was found to be a great inconvenience; it bore very hard on the heirs, who were perpetually tantalized by the prospect of an inheritance to which it was legally and physically impossible that they should ever succeed. All this time Death had resided either in a shadowy underground region called Panoi or by the side of a volcanic vent in Santa Maria, it is not quite certain which; but now in answer to the popular demand he was induced to come abroad and show himself. He was treated to a handsome funeral of the usual sort; that is to say, he was laid out on a board and covered with a pall, a pig was killed, and the mourners enjoyed a funeral feast and divided the property of the deceased. Afterwards, on the fifth day, the conch shell was blown to drive away the ghost. In short, nothing was left undone to soothe and gratify the feelings of the departed. So Death returned down the road to the underground region from which he had emerged; and all mankind have since followed him thither.[49]

(d) The falsified message

Not impossibly then, the popular tradition on which the Biblical author built his own story revolved originally around the theme of how the serpent had managed to acquire for himself what had in fact been destined for man. And here Comparative Folklore suggests an alluring possibility, for that earlier story may have belonged to a type which we find in fact in many parts of the world and which tells how a benevolent God sent an envoy to man to inform him how he might obtain immortality but how that envoy cunningly falsified the message to his own advantage.

Thus the Namaquas, or Hottentots, say that once upon a time the Moon wished to send mankind a message of immortality, and the hare undertook to act as messenger. So the Moon charged him to go to men and say, "As I die and rise to life again, so shall you die and rise to life again." Accordingly the hare went to men, but either out of forgetfulness or malice he reversed the message and said, "As I die and do not rise to life again, so you shall also die and not rise to life again." Then he went back to the Moon, and she asked him what he had said. He told her, and when she heard how he had given the wrong message, she was so angry that she threw a stick at him which split his lip. That is why the hare's lip is still cloven. So the hare ran away and is still running to this day. Some people, however, say that before he fled he clawed the Moon's face, which still bears the marks of the scratching, as anybody may see for himself on a clear moonlight night.[50]

A similar tale, with some minor differences, is told by the Bushmen. According to them, the Moon formerly said to men, "As I die and come to life again, so shall ye do; when ye die, ye shall not die altogether but shall rise again." But one man would not believe the glad tidings of immortality, and he would not consent to hold his tongue. For his mother had died, he loudly lamented her, and nothing could persuade him that she would come to life again. A heated altercation ensued between him and the Moon on this painful subject. "Your mother's asleep," says the Moon. "She's dead," says the man, and at it they went again, hammer and tongs, till at last the Moon lost patience and struck the man on the face with her fist, cleaving his mouth with the blow. And as she did so, she cursed him saying, "His mouth shall be always like this, even when he is a hare. For a hare he shall be. He shall spring away, he shall come doubling back. The dogs shall chase him, and when they have caught him they shall tear him in pieces. He shall altogether die. And all men, when they die, shall die outright. For he would not agree with me, when I bid him not to weep for his mother, for she would live again. 'No,' says he to me, 'my mother will not live again.' Therefore he shall altogether become a hare. And the people, they shall altogether die, because he contradicted me flat when I told him that the people would do as I do, returning to life after they were dead." So a righteous retribution overtook the sceptic for his scepticism, for he was turned into a hare, and a hare he has been ever since. But still he has human flesh in his thigh, and that is why, when the Bushmen kill a hare, they will not eat that portion of the thigh, but cut it out, because it is human flesh. And still the Bushmen say, "It was on account of the hare that the Moon cursed us, so that we die altogether. If it had not been for him, we should have come to life again when we died. But he would not believe what the Moon told him, he contradicted her flat."[51] In this Bushman version of the story the hare is not the animal messenger of God to men, but a human sceptic who, for doubting the gospel of eternal life, is turned into a hare and involves the whole human race in the doom of mortality. This may be an older form of the story than the Hottentot version, in which the hare is a hare and nothing more.

The Nandi of British East Africa relate that when the first men lived upon the earth, a dog came to them one day and said, "All people will die like the Moon, but unlike the Moon you will not return to life again unless you give me some milk to drink out of your gourd and beer to drink through your straw. If you do this, I will arrange for you to go to the river when you die and to come to life again on the third day." But the people laughed at the dog, and gave him some milk and beer to drink off a stool. The dog was angry at not being served in the same vessels as a human being, and though he put his pride in his pocket and drank the milk and beer from the stool, he went away in high dudgeon, saying, "All people will die, and the Moon alone will return to life." That is why, when people die, they stay away, whereas when the Moon goes away she comes back again after three days' absence.[52] In this story nothing is said as to the personage who sent the dog with the message of immortality to men; but from the messenger's reference to the Moon and from a comparison with the parallel Hottentot story, we may reasonably infer that it was the Moon.

In some stories, however, *two* messengers are despatched, and the cause of death is said to have been the dilatoriness or misconduct of the one who bore the glad tidings of immortality. Thus, the Hottentots say that the Moon once sent an insect to men with this message: "Go thou to men and tell them, 'As I die, and dying live, so shall ye also die, and dying live.' " As he crawled along, the hare came leaping after him and stopping beside him asked the nature of his errand. The insect answered, "I am sent by the Moon to men, to tell them that as she dies, and dying lives, they also shall die, and dying live." The hare said, "As thou art an awkward runner, let me go." And away he tore with the message, while the insect came creeping slowly behind. When he came to men, the hare perverted the message which he had officiously taken upon himself to deliver, for he said, "I am sent by the Moon to tell you, 'As I die, and dying perish, in the same manner ye shall also die and come wholly to an end.' " Then the hare returned to the Moon, and told her what he had said to men. The Moon was very angry and reproached the hare, saying, "Darest thou tell the people a thing which I have not said?" With that she took a stick and hit him over the nose. That is why the hare's nose is slit down to this day.[53]

The same tale is told, with some slight variations, by the Tati Bushmen or Masarwas, who inhabit Bechuanaland, the Kalahari desert, and portions of Southern Rhodesia. The men of old time, they say, told this story. The Moon wished to send a message to the men of the early race, to tell them that as she died and came to life again, so they would die, and dying come to life again. So the Moon called the tortoise and said to him, "Go over to those men there, and give them this message from me. Tell them that as I dying live, so they dying will live again." Now the tortoise was very slow, and he kept repeating the message to himself, so as not to forget it. The Moon was very vexed with his slowness and with his forgetfulness; so she called the hare and said to her, "You are a swift runner. Take this message to the men over yonder: 'As I dying live again, so you will dying live again.' " So off the hare started, but in her great haste she forgot the message, and as she did not wish to show the Moon that she had forgotten, she delivered the message to men in this way, "As I dying live again, so you dying will die for ever." Such was the message delivered by the hare. In the meantime the tortoise had remembered the message, and he started off a second time. "This time," said he to himself, "I won't forget." He came to the place where the men were, and he delivered his message. When the men heard it they were very angry with the hare, who was sitting at some distance. She was nibbling the grass after her race. One of the men ran and lifted a stone and threw it at the hare. It struck her right in the mouth and cleft her upper lip; hence the lip has been cleft ever since. That is why every hare has a cleft upper lip to this day, and that is the end of the story.[54]

In a story told by the A-Louyi of the Upper Zambesi, the messengers of death and of life respectively are the chameleon and the hare. They say that Nyambe, whom they identify with the sun, used to dwell on earth with his wife Nasilele, whom they identify with the moon. But Nyambe retired to heaven from fear of men. Whenever he carved wood, men carved it also; when he made a wooden plate, so did they. After he had withdrawn to the sky, it happened that Nyambe's dog died. He loved the animal, and said, "Let the dog live." But his wife said, "No, I won't have it. He's a thief." Nyambe still persisted. "For my part," said he, "I love my dog." But his wife said, "Throw him out." So they threw him out. By and by Nyambe's mother-in-law died, and his wife said to him, "Let her live," just as Nyambe himself had said to her about his dog. But Nyambe answered, "No, let her die and be done with it. I said to you that my dog should live, and you refused. It is my wish that your mother should die for good and all." So die she did for good and all. After that the husband and wife sent two messengers, a chameleon and a hare, to men on the earth. To the chameleon they said, "When thou art come to men, say to them, 'Ye shall live'; but as for thee, O hare, when thou art come to men, say to them, 'Ye shall die once for all.'" The chameleon and the hare set off with their messages. Now the chameleon, as he went, kept constantly turning about, but the hare ran. So the hare arrived first, and said that men should die once for all. Having delivered his message, the hare returned. That is why, when men die, they die once for all.[55] From this Louyi legend it would appear that human mortality resulted from a domestic jar in heaven, the deity falling out with his wife over his dead dog and mother-in-law. From such seemingly trivial causes may flow such momentous consequences.

The Ekoi of Southern Nigeria, on the border of the Cameroons, attribute human mortality to the gross misconduct of a duck. It happened in this way. The sky-god Obassi Osaw one day thought to himself, "Men fear to die. They do not know that perhaps they may come to life again. I will tell them that sometimes such a thing may happen, then they will have less dread of death." So he stood up in his house in the sky, and called a frog and a duck before him. To the frog he said, "Go to earth and say to the people, 'When a man dies, it is the end of all things; he shall never live again.'" To the duck he said, "Go tell the earth folk that if a man dies he may come to life again." He then led them a little way and showed them the road, saying, "Take my message. Duck, you may go to the left hand. Frog, keep to the right." So the frog kept on to the right, and when he came to the earth he delivered his message of death to the first men he met, telling them that when they died it would be an end of them. In due time the duck also reached the earth, but happening to arrive at a place where the people were making palm oil, she fell to gobbling it up and forgot all about the message of immortality which the good god had charged her to deliver to mankind. That is why we are all mortal down to this day. We are bound to go by the message of the frog; we cannot go by the message of the duck, which never reached us.[56]

The story of the two messengers is related also by the Negroes of the Gold Coast, and in their version the two are a sheep and a goat. The following is the form in which the tale was told by a native to a Swiss missionary at Akropong. In the beginning, when sky and earth existed, but there were as yet no men on earth, there fell a great rain, and soon after it had ceased a great chain was let down from heaven to earth with seven men hanging on it. These men had been created by God, and they reached the earth by means of the chain. They brought fire with them and cooked their food at it. Not long afterwards God sent a goat from heaven to deliver the following message to the seven men, "There is something that is called Death; it will one day kill some of you; but though you die, you will not perish utterly, but you will come to me here in heaven." The goat went his way, but when he came near the town he lit on a bush which seemed to him good to eat; so he lingered there and began to browse. When God saw that the goat lingered by the way, he sent a sheep to deliver the same message. The sheep went, but did not say what God had commanded her to say; for she perverted the message and said, "When you once die, you perish, and have no place to go to." Afterwards the goat came and said, "God says, you will die, it is true, but that will not be the end of you, for you will come to me." But the men answered, "No, goat, God did not say that to you. What the sheep first reported, by that we shall abide."[57] In another version of the story, also told at Akropong, the parts of the goat and the sheep are inverted; it is the sheep that bears the good tidings and loiters by the way to browse, and it is the goat that bears the evil tidings, and is the first to deliver them. The story ends with the melancholy reflection that "if only the sheep had made good speed with her message, man would have died but returned after death; but the goat made better speed with the contrary message, so man returns no more."[58]

In an Ashanti version of the story the two messengers are also a sheep and a goat, and the perversion of the message of immortality is ascribed sometimes to the one animal and sometimes to the other. The Ashantis say that long ago men were happy, for God dwelt among them and talked with them face to face. However, these blissful days did not last for ever. One unlucky day it chanced that some women were pounding a mash with pestles in a mortar, while God stood by looking on. For some reason they were annoyed by the presence of the deity and told him to be off; and as he did not take himself off fast enough to please them, they beat him with their pestles. In a great huff God retired altogether from the world and left it to the direction of the fetishes; and still to this day people say, "Ah, if it had not been for that old woman, how happy we should be!" However, God was very good-natured, and even after he had gone up aloft, he sent a kind message by a goat to men on earth, saying, "There is something which they call Death. He will kill some of you. But even if you die, you will not perish completely. You will come to me in heaven." So off the goat set with this cheering intelligence. But before he came to the town, he saw a tempting bush by the wayside, and stopped to browse on it. When God looked down from heaven and saw the goat loitering by the way, he sent off a sheep with the same message to carry the joyful news to men without delay. But the sheep did not give the message aright. Far from it: she said, "God sends you word that you will die, and that will be an end of you." When the goat had finished his meal, he also trotted into the town and delivered his message, saying, "God sends you word that you will die, certainly, but that will not be the end of you, for you will go to him." But men said to the goat, "No, goat, that is not what God said. We believe that the message which the sheep brought us is the one which God sent to us." That unfortunate misunderstanding was the beginning of death among men.[59] However, in another Ashanti version of the tale the parts played by the sheep and goat are reversed. It is the sheep who brings the tidings of immortality from God to men, but the goat overruns him, and offers them death instead. In their innocence men accepted death with enthusiasm, not knowing what it was, and naturally they have died ever since.[60]

In a version of the story which is told by the Akamba of British East Africa the two gospel messengers are a chameleon and a thrush, whom God sent out together to find people who died one day and came to life the next, and to bear the glad tidings of immortality to men. So off they set, the chameleon leading the way, for in those days he was a very high and mighty person indeed. As they went along, what should they see but some people lying like dead by the wayside. The chameleon went up to them and said softly, *"Niwe, niwe, niwe."* But the thrush asked him testily what he was making that noise for. The chameleon mildly answered, "I am only calling the people who go forward and then come back," and he explained to the thrush that these seemingly dead folk would rise from the dead, just as he himself in walking lurches backward and forward before he takes a step. This argument from analogy, which might have satisfied a Butler, had no effect on the sceptical thrush. He derided the idea of the resurrection. Undeterred by this blatant infidelity the chameleon persisted in calling to the dead people, and sure enough they opened their eyes and listened to him. But the thrush rudely interrupted him and told the dead people that dead they were and dead they would remain, nothing could bring them to life. With that he flew away, and though the chameleon stayed behind and preached to the corpses, telling them that he had come from God on purpose to bring them to life again, and that they were not to believe the lies of that shallow sceptic the thrush, they turned a deaf ear to his message; not one of those dead corpses would so much as budge. So the chameleon returned crestfallen to God and reported the failure of his mission, telling him how, when he preached the glad tidings of resurrection to the corpses, the thrush had roared him down, so that the corpses could not hear a word he said. Thereupon God cross-questioned the thrush, who stated that the chameleon had so bungled the message that he, the thrush, felt it to be his imperative duty to interrupt him. The simple-minded deity believed the lying thrush, and being very angry with the honest chameleon he degraded him from his high position and made him walk very slow, lurching this way and that, as he does down to this very day. But the thrush he promoted to the office of wakening men from their slumber every morning, which he still does punctually at 2 A.M. before the note of any other bird is heard in the tropical forest.[61]

In all these versions of the story the message is sent from God to men, but in another version, reported from Togoland in West Africa, the message is despatched from men to God. They say that once upon a time men sent a dog to God to say that when they died they would like to come to life again. So off the dog trotted to deliver the message. But on the way he felt hungry and turned into a house, where a man was boiling magic herbs. So the dog sat down and thought to himself, "He is cooking food." Meantime the frog had set off to tell God that when men died they would prefer not to come to life again. Nobody had asked him to give that message; it was a piece of pure officiousness and impertinence on his part. However, away he tore. The dog, who still sat hopefully watching the hell-broth brewing, saw him hurrying past the door, but he thought to himself, "When I have had something to eat, I will soon catch froggy up." However, froggy came in first, and said to the deity, "When men die, they would prefer not to come to life again." After that, up comes the dog, and says he, "When men die, they would like to come to life again." God was naturally puzzled, and said to the dog, "I really do not understand these two messages. As I heard the frog's request first, I will comply with it. I will not do what you said." That is the reason why men die and do not come to life again. If the frog had only minded his own business instead of meddling with other people's, the dead would all have come to life again to this day. But frogs come to life again when it thunders at the beginning of the rainy season, after they have been dead all the dry season while the Harmattan wind was blowing. Then, while the rain falls and the thunder peals, you may hear them quacking in the marshes.[62] Thus we see that the frog had his own private ends to serve in distorting the message. He gained for himself the immortality of which he robbed mankind.

In Calabar a somewhat different version of the same widespread story is told. The messengers are a dog and a sheep, and they go backwards and forwards between God and men. They say that for a long time after the creation of the world there was no death in it. At last, however, a man sickened and died. So the people sent a dog to God to ask him what they should do with the dead man. The dog stayed so long away that the people grew tired of waiting and sent off a sheep to God with the same question. The sheep soon returned, and reported that God said, "Let the dead man be buried." So they buried him. Afterwards the dog returned also and reported that God said, "Put warm ashes on the dead man's belly, and he will rise again." However, the people told the dog that he came too late; the dead man was already buried according to the instructions of the sheep. That is why men are buried when they die. But as for the dog, he is driven from men and humiliated, because it is through his fault that we all die.[63]

In these stories the origin of death is ascribed to the blunder or wilful deceit of one of the two messengers. However, according to another version of the story, which is widely current among the Bantu tribes of Africa, death was caused, not by the fault of the messenger, but by the vacillation of God himself, who, after deciding to make men immortal, changed his mind and resolved to make or leave them mortal; and unluckily for mankind the second messenger, who bore the message of death, overran the first messenger, who bore the message of immortality. In this form of the tale the chameleon figures as the messenger of life, and the lizard as the messenger of death. Thus the Zulus say that in the beginning Unkulunkulu, that is, the Old Old One, sent the chameleon to men with a message, saying, "Go, chameleon, go and say, Let not men die." The chameleon set out, but it crawled very slowly and loitered by the way to eat the purple berries of the *ubukwebezane* shrub or of a mulberry tree; however, some people say that it climbed up a tree to bask in the sun, filled its belly with flies, and fell fast asleep. Meantime the Old Old One had thought better of it and sent a lizard post-haste after the chameleon with a very different message to men, for he said to the animal, "Lizard, when you have arrived, say, Let men die." So the lizard ran, passed the dawdling chameleon, and arriving first among men delivered his message of death, saying, "Let men die." Then he turned and went back to the Old Old One who had sent him. But after he was gone, the chameleon at last arrived among men with his joyful news of immortality, and he shouted, saying, "It is said, Let not men die!" But men answered, "Oh! we have heard the word of the lizard; it has told us the word, 'It is said, Let men die.' We cannot hear your word. Through the word of the lizard, men will die." And died they have ever since from that day to this. So the Zulus hate the lizard and kill it whenever they can, for they say, "This is the very piece of deformity which ran in the beginning to say that men should die." But others hate and hustle or kill the chameleon, saying, "That is the little thing which delayed to tell the people that they should not die. If he had only told us in time, we too should not have died; our ancestors also would have been still living; there would have been no diseases here on earth. It all comes from the delay of the chameleon."[64]

The same story is told in nearly the same form by other Bantu tribes such as the Bechuanas,[65] the Bastutos,[66] the Baronga,[67] the Ngoni,[68] and apparently by the Wa-Sania of British East Africa.[69] It is found, in a slightly altered form, even among the Hausas, who are not a Bantu people.[70] To this day the Baronga and the Ngoni owe the chameleon a grudge for having brought death into the world by its dilatoriness. Hence, when they find a chameleon slowly climbing on a tree, they tease it till it opens its mouth, whereupon they throw a pinch of tobacco on its tongue, and watch with delight the creature writhing and changing colour from orange to green, from green to black in the agony of death; for so they avenge the great wrong which the chameleon did to mankind.[71]

Sometimes, the motifs of the cast skin and the falsified message are combined. Thus the Gallas of East Africa attribute the mortality of man and the immortality of serpents to the mistake or malice of a certain bird which falsified the message of eternal life entrusted to him by God. The creature which did this great wrong to our species is a black or dark blue bird, with a white patch on each wing and a crest on its head. It perches on the tops of trees and utters a wailing note like the bleating of a sheep; hence the Gallas call it *holawaka* or "the sheep of God," and explain its apparent anguish by the following tale. Once upon a time God sent that bird to tell men that they should not die, but that when they grew old and weak they should slip off their skins and so renew their youth. In order to authenticate the message God gave the bird a crest to serve as the badge of his high office. Well, off the bird set to deliver the glad tidings of immortality to man, but he had not gone far before he fell in with a snake devouring carrion in the path. The bird looked longingly at the carrion and said to the snake, "Give me some of the meat and blood, and I will tell you God's message." "I don't want to hear it," said the snake tartly, and continued his meal. But the bird pressed him so to hear the message that the snake rather reluctantly consented. "The message," then said the bird, "is this. When men grow old they will die, but when you grow old you will cast your skin and renew your youth." That is why people grow old and die, but snakes crawl out of their old skins and renew their youth. But for this gross perversion of the message God punished the heedless or wicked bird with a painful internal malady, from which he suffers to this day; that is why he sits wailing on the tops of trees.[72]

Again, the Melanesians, who inhabit the coast of the Gazelle Peninsula in New Britain, say that To Kambinana, the Good Spirit, loved men and wished to make them immortal. So he called his brother To Korvuvu and said to him, "Go to men and take them the secret of immortality. Tell them to cast their skin every year. So will they be protected from death, for their life will be constantly renewed. But tell the serpents that they must thenceforth die." However, To Korvuvu acquitted himself badly of his task; for he commanded men to die, and betrayed to the serpents the secret of immortality. Since then all men have been mortal, but the serpents cast their skins every year and never die.[73]

A similar story of the origin of death is told in Annam. They say that Ngoc hoang sent a messenger from heaven to men to say that when they reached old age they should change their skins and live for ever, but that when serpents grew old they must die. The messenger came down to earth and said, rightly enough, "When man is old he shall cast his skin; but when serpents are old they shall die and be laid in coffins." So far so good. But unluckily there happened to be a brood of serpents within hearing, and when they learned the doom pronounced on their kind, they fell into a fury and said to the messenger, "You must say it over again and just the contrary, or we will bite you." That frightened the messenger, and he repeated his message, changing the words thus, "When the serpent is old he shall cast his skin; but when man is old he shall die and be laid in the coffin." That is why all creatures are now subject to death, except the serpent, who, when he is old, casts his skin and lives for ever.[74] ▼

19   The Cherubim   3:24

> *After the expulsion of Adam and Eve, God posted* cherubim *at the entrance to the Garden, to bar access to the Tree of Life (or Immortality).*

A cherub is not, as commonly supposed, a nightgowned angel, nor is he an amoretto. The word is identical with the Mesopotamian *karibu,* which denotes a winged monster—somewhat like a griffin—such as stood before the portals of Babylonian and Assyrian palaces, just as similar creatures stand before temples and palaces throughout Southeast Asia.[1] By the ninth century B.C. the cherub had already become a familiar figure in Syro-Palestinian art. At Tel Halaf, cherubim are portrayed beside a (stylized) tree,[2] and prancing cherubim are shown on a relief from Aleppo.[3] The cherub is likewise depicted on one of the celebrated ivories from Samaria.[4] Mythologically, he is but a Semitic form of that familiar figure whom we have already encountered—the Dragon who guards the treasure or the pot of gold. Analogous too in point of general motif are the "scorpion-men" who guard the mountain of sunrise in the Babylonian Epic of Gilgamesh;[5] while in the Indic Rig Veda the road to Paradise is watched by the demon Sarameya, accompanied by two broadnosed, four-eyed, speckled hounds.[6]

A less exalted, but more diverting counterpart of the cherubim may be recognized in the winged griffins which served as foot-scrapers before the door of Samuel Johnson's house while he was residing at Brighton, England![7]

20   The Revolving Sword   3:24

> *In addition to the cherubim God placed at the gate of Eden "a flaming sword which turned every way."*

The expression "flaming sword" occurs elsewhere in the Old Testament and means not a sword made of fire, but simply a flashing or glittering weapon.[1]

Nor, as is commonly imagined, was this sword wielded by the cherubim; it was something quite independent of them—an additional safeguard. The true parallel is afforded, therefore, by Celtic romances which tell of a revolving spiked portcullis at the entrance to the castle of the otherworld, which beheads, or slashes to pieces, any rash intruder.[2] Thus, in the romance entitled *Wigalois,* the hero comes to a marble gate before which runs a waterwheel on an iron track; the wheel is set with sharp swords and clubs.[3] Similarly, in the thirteenth-century French poem, *La Mule sans Frein,* Gawain arrives at a revolving castle, but when his mule rushes toward the gate, the portcullis descends and cuts his tail in half;[4] while in Chretien's *Iwain* both the knight and his steed receive similar treatment.[5] Analogous too, in a general way, is the incident in the Irish legend (*imram*) of the journey of Malduin and his companions to the otherworld: on a faery island they are confronted by a fiery revolving rampart.[6]

21   The role of man   2:15

To the authors of the Westminster Confession the prime duty of man is to know God and enjoy him forever. To Ecclesiastes (12:13) it is to fear him and keep his commandments. To the Buddhist, it is to achieve release from the shackles of selfhood. But the writer of our Biblical story walked in the groove of far older Mesopotamian thought. To him the first man was a "happy innocent" whose primary purpose was to serve as the gardener of Paradise—a notion which grew up, of course, in an agricultural society.

This conception of man's role in the world is constant in Mesopotamian myths of creation.[1] Thus, in the version preserved in the *Enuma Elish,* the sole function of the "mannikin" fashioned by order of Marduk is to perform chores (*dullu*) for the gods and to provide them with earthly abodes.[2] Similarly, in an earlier Babylonian tale, the goddess Mami moulds such a creature solely in order that he may "bear the yoke," i.e., do menial service;[3] while in a myth from Ashur, the ancient capital of Assyria, the company of the gods advise their divine overlords to create man so that he may "construct dwellings for the great gods . . . mark off boundaries . . . water the earth . . . raise plants."[4] A similar notion may possibly be detected also in a Babylonian ritual for the restoration of a temple. Since that ceremony was evidently regarded as marking a "new beginning," it was characterized by the recitation of an archetypal myth, describing the creation of various gods and goddesses of civilization and ultimately of man. Unfortunately, this text has come down to us in fragmentary condition, but the concluding line of the portion which remains has been restored by modern scholars to read: "(The god Ea) created mankind for the perform[ance of chores on behalf of the gods]."[5] Lastly, a Sumerian text from Nippur represents the purpose of man's creation as that of building temples for the gods.[6]

Our author's view is, then, that man was a laborer from the start, not (as is commonly supposed) that he acquired this status only in consequence of his fall. The punishment which God imposed on him was not that he should work the earth, but that thenceforth the earth would also yield "thorns and thistles," so that he would have to work amid constant frustration, "in the sweat of his brow." Moreover, the ground that he would be cultivating would no longer be the blessed faery garden. In precisely the same way, the punishment of woman was that childbirth—*her* normal role—would be attended with pain.

Cain and Abel

22   Behind the Biblical Story   4:1–16

To the modern reader, as to the Biblical writer, the story of Cain and Abel is the story of the first murder.[1] Behind it, however, lies an older and more primitive tale which has been skillfully adapted to a new purpose.

(a) Smith and herdsman

The character of the older tale is betrayed by the very names of the protagonists. Cain means "Smith," and Abel "Herdsman."[2] Its original purpose, therefore, was to account for the pariah status of the smith in a pastoral society. He is at once an outcast and a wanderer, but the very qualities which make him so endow him at the same time with a certain aura of mystery and awesomeness which render him sacrosanct and untouchable. To indicate this, he is sometimes marked or branded with a special sign.[3]

This peculiar status of the smith is attested from one end of the world to the other.[4] It derives partly from the fact that the smith is very often an alien and intruder; partly also it is a survival from the close of the Stone Age, when metal and iron were new-fangled substances held in awe.

The smith is an alien because he is often an itinerant tinker coming from the outside and possessed of a strange and potent technique superior to the prevailing level of culture and one against which even the time-honored gods and demons cannot stand up. Alternatively, he is the lingering relic of a vanquished race, enslaved and despised by his conquerors and their descendants. In either case, he is viewed with awe or with suspicion.[5] It is significant, for instance, that among those peoples of Africa that live in the areas of the Northern Congo and Upper Nile (as far as Abyssinia) and that belong to the Negroid stock the smith is almost invariably held in reverence, whereas among the pastoral tribes of Hamite stock he is just as invariably despised. It is, of course, the latter attitude that is reflected in the Biblical story.

To cite specific cases: among the Bari of the Upper Nile, the smith wanders homeless from hut to hut and is an outcast;[6] while among the Dinka he is excluded from the community and has to live in the forest.[7] Similarly, among the Tibbu, smiths are pariahs, and though they inspire a certain numinous awe, they are obliged to marry among themselves. The craft is passed on from father to son, since no one else is willing to practice it.[8] Again, the Tumal smiths of Somaliland, who also function as magicians, are a caste apart and are disdained;[9] and in the Rezaz area of Arabia (which lies opposite) they likewise rank as outcasts. Until recently most of them were Jews, because others avoided the profession.[10] The same is true of Abyssinia, where smith-craft is pursued mostly by the "Jewish" Falashas.[11] The Wa-Nobbos, a Hamite hunting tribe of East Africa, regard the smith as beyond the pale; he has no legal rights, and—what is especially significant for the story of Cain—may be put to death with impunity by his superiors.[12] Among the Masai, smelting and smithcraft are relegated to a special caste, who were originally foreigners. Encounter with a smith is believed to bring disaster, and "smith" (ol kononi) is itself a "dirty word."[13] The Qashgai of Iran likewise regard the smith as an outsider;[14] while in parts of the Hindu Kush area smiths form a segregated group, consisting of non-natives, for no native will adopt the forbidding craft;[15] and in Nepal smiths, carpenters, and turners are, by a combination of magical and economic considerations, alike virtual outcasts.[16]

As we have said, the abhorrence of the smith is but one of two possible reactions to his uncanny and numinous character. To round out the picture, therefore, it will be well to cite a few instances in which he enjoys esteem rather than suffers contempt. Among the Wajagga, a Hamitic Bantu people of Africa, the smith is treated with special reverence by virtue of his magical powers;[17] and among the Katanga smiths constitute a distinct secret society (bwanga).[18] In the Southern Congo they rank equal to shamans,[19] and among the Basoga and Baloholo their status is like that of chieftains;[20] while the Fan of West Africa use the same word for "blacksmith" and "priest."[21] In pre-Columbian America smiths exercised magico-religious functions.[22] The Yakuts of Siberia attribute to them the power to heal without the assistance of spirits;[23] while in Sugnan and other parts of the Pamir they are more highly respected than the official religious leaders (mullahs).[24] A Yakut proverb declares that "smiths and shamans are of the same breed."[25] Sanchuniathon, the ancient Phoenician antiquary, as quoted by Eusebius, says that the smith-god Chusôr (the Kôthar of the Ugaritic mythological poems) first invented magical spells —a role commonly attributed to Gypsy smiths and tinkers.[26]

The ambivalent status of the smith—now an object of respect, now of disdain—is admirably illustrated among the Buriats of Siberia, who recognize both benevolent "white smiths," under the patronage of a western god (tengri), and malevolent "black smiths," under that of an eastern one.[27]

The belief that iron and metal—the stock-in-trade of smiths—can avert demons is universal,[28] and it will suffice to cite a few representative instances:

In the pseudepigraphic *Testament of Solomon* a demon is scared by iron.[29] In an Aramaic magical incantation from Nippur (dating, probably, to the eighth or ninth century C.E.) the reciter wears iron armor and an iron head-piece to forefend—not to protect himself from—demons.[30] In England a red-hot iron poker is plunged into the churn to prevent witches from interfering with the making of butter.[31] Iron horseshoes, hung in a house or over its main door, are likewise apotropaic.[32] Arabs cry, "Iron! iron!" or "Iron, thou un-lucky one!" to defend themselves gainst a jinn, or spirit.[33] Hindus believe that demons flee from iron; they therefore carry a piece of iron when visiting the sick.[34] In German and Slavonic folklore, iron is waved in the air to ward off the demons of whirlwind.[35] Mohammed's mother had a piece of iron bound on her hand and throat at his birth;[36] and iron is placed on the bed of a woman in labor in Germany[37] and Italy.[38] The Torajas of the Celebes place a child on a piece of iron on the seventh day after birth.[39] Similarly, in Russian, Polish, Siberian, and Slovak popular usage, an iron knife is placed in the cradle to forefend the night-hag Nocritsa;[40] and in Sicily people touch iron to avert ill-omen after seeing a corpse or a funeral procession.[41] The Roman poet Ovid says explicitly that iron averts demons.[42]

Here too magical properties are ambivalent, and it should therefore be added that iron is sometimes regarded, *en revanche,* as the perquisite of demons and witches. Thus in a modern Greek tale an iron dervish eats a man.[43] In other Balkan tales a demon is made half of iron or is a wolf with an iron head.[44] In German tales the beldam Berchta is sometimes described as made of iron.[45]

Steel has the same character. In German folklore, steel knives avert demons;[46] and a steel knife or sword is placed beside a woman in childbirth both by Jews[47] and Armenians[48] of a more superstitious cast of mind. In Fin-land, steel under a pillow averts nightmare.[49] In Sweden, a woman carries something made of steel on her first outing after childbirth;[50] and in Denmark, a steel knife placed at the bottom of a boat affords protection against the mis-chievous river sprite, Nökhe.[51]

(b) The rivalry of professions

The Biblical writer did not know, or did not care, about the original purport of the story or the true character of Cain. To him it was simply the story of the first murder, and the protagonists are therefore represented as a "tiller of the ground" and a "keeper of sheep." Whether this change was his own innova-tion, or whether the story had come down to him in this form, we cannot tell, but in any case the change was in line with a well-established literary tradition, for tales of the rivalry between shepherd and farmer appear as early as the second millennium B.C. in the popular literature of the Sumerians.

One such tale, for instance, describes an altercation between Enten, the genius of cattle, and his brother Enmesh, the genius of crops, as to which of the two should be recognized as "steward of the divine estate" *par excellence.*

Each recites his merits and accomplishments. In the end, the supreme god Enlil chooses the former.[52]

Another tale revolving around the same theme relates how Dumuzi, the divine shepherd, and Enkimdu, the divine farmer, both sue for the hand of the goddess Inanna. Her brother Utu (the Sun) recommends the shepherd, but she herself prefers the farmer. The chagrined shepherd protests his superiority, and the farmer tries vainly to soothe him. Eventually, the rejected suitor intrudes upon the two lovers in the midst of their amours, but becomes abashed and withdraws. Thereupon, however, the goddess calls after him, telling him not to feel unduly hurt and declaring that he is welcome to pasture his flock in the fields which belong properly to the farmer.[53] The implication of this story, as Thorkild Jacobsen has pointed out, is that "putting the farmer before the shepherd is really a matter of personal choice only. . . . Actually, one is as good as the other, both are equally useful and necessary members of society; the produce of the one balances that of the other. Though there is rivalry between them, there should be no enmity."[54]

A third Sumerian tale treats of a quarrel between Laḫar, the god of cattle, and Ashnan, the goddess of grain, who have been created respectively to provide food and clothing for the gods and eventually also for men. Each extols his achievement and belittles the other's. Finally, the high gods Enlil and Enki decide the issue, but how we do not know, since the end of the text is still missing.[55]

Tales of this kind belong to a widespread literary and dramatic genre known as the *débat*.[56] The antagonists can also be rival metals, e.g., copper and silver, as in another Sumerian example,[57] or they can be Sea and Land, or such abstractions as Logos and Logina, as in the Sicilian mimes of Epicharmus, the older contemporary of Aeschylus;[58] or seasons, like Spring and Summer, as in the final scene of Shakespeare's *Love's Labour Lost* and as in many a European folkplay.[59] Or, again, they can be plants, like the date palm and the tamarisk in an early Mesopotamian fable,[60] or the pomegranate and the apple in Aesop;[61] or animals, as in other Mesopotamian texts,[62] or like the ant and the fly in Phaedrus,[63] or the fox and the panther in Babrius.[64] Lastly, as in our own Near Eastern examples, they can be members of rival trades or professions, as in the European Shrovetide pantomimes and as in the Jewish buffoon plays performed on the Feast of Purim.[65]

This opens up an interesting speculation. In all the examples we have mentioned—and, in fact, throughout this genre—the actual *débat* is of the essence of the tale. In the Biblical version, on the other hand, it is strangely absent. But it is just possible that it has been deliberately suppressed, as irrelevant to the writer's purpose, for in the traditional Hebrew text of Genesis 4:8 there is in fact a mystifying gap. *And Cain said unto Abel his brother* (we read) *. . . and it came to pass, when they were in the field, that Cain rose up against Abel his brother, and slew him.* What did Cain say? The Ancient Versions supply the words, *Let us go into the field,*[66] but is it not possible that this was simply a rough-and-ready attempt to get rid of the lacuna, and that what really stood in the original version was the substance of the *débat,* in which Abel extolled his achievements and thus aroused Cain's anger?

23 "Sin crouches at the door"   4:7

When Cain perceives that Abel's offering has been accepted, while his own has not, "his countenance falls." But God reassures him:

> *If thou wert acting well, would it not be lifted up?*
> *But if thou dost not act well. . . .*
> *Sin crouches at the door,*[1]
> *and his lust is fastened upon thee*
> *but thou shouldst master him.*

The phrase embodies an interesting tidbit of folklore. The "Croucher" (*Rabiṣu*) was a familiar figure of Mesopotamian demonology.[2] He is contrasted in one text with the two protective genii who, in the form of giant colossi, guarded the entrances of Babylonian and Assyrian palaces and mansions.[3] in another[4] he is said to "set the hair on end," as does the spirit which flits before the face of Job.[5] In the *Legend of Nergal and Ereshkigal* the netherworld demon Namtar (Fate) is said to be "the croucher" in that darkling realm.[6]

Another version of the idea that demons lie in wait at the entrances of houses may be found in the notion that the child-stealing beldam perches on the rooftop, to pounce on newborn babes—a belief which is not only mentioned explicitly in Mesopotamian sources[7] but which also underlies the Roman practice—mentioned by Pliny[8]—of shooting arrows over roofs to protect expectant mothers. Similarly too, in Syrian texts reference is made to a "demon of the roof" (*bar egara*) who pounces on men as they leave the house.[9]

24 The mark of Cain   4:15

The *mark of Cain* was not, as all too often supposed, a brand of shame, but rather a sign of protection, indicating that he was the inviolable ward of Yahweh. In the original version of the story, it signalized that the smith was sacrosanct.

Throughout antiquity, the special protégés and devotees of a god bore a distinctive mark or brand, like slaves.[1] Thus, in the Babylonian Epic of Gilgamesh the goddess Ninsun "adopts" the hero's companion Enkidu by placing a mark or tag (*endu*) on his neck;[2] and acolytes (*shirkê*) in Babylonian temples bore a sign, in the shape of a star, on their hands.[3] In Egypt sacral tattooing was widely practiced.[4] At the temple of Heracles near the Canobic mouth of the Nile fugitive slaves marked with sacral stigmata could not be reclaimed, for they were thus endenizened to the god.[5] In Roman Egypt, priests of Isis bore a crossmark on their brows.[6] The Hebrew prophet Ezekiel (9:4) likewise orders those who are faithful to Yahweh to wear a distinguishing mark on their brows. The Greek maenads are sometimes depicted on vases tattooed with pictures of fauns or snakes.[7] Such sacral tattooing was current among the Thracians in general[8] and is mentioned in the inscription of Pandaros at Epidaurus.[9] Ptolemy VI Physcon ordered the Jews of Alexandria to be signed with the mark of Dionysus;[10] and pilgrims to the temple of the Syrian Goddess at Hierapolis (Membij) similarly "stigmatized" themselves.[11] Devotees of Mithra were signed on the brow;[12] and initiants into the Mysteries were commonly sealed in the same way.[13] Christian baptism was commonly known as "sealing,"[14] and the rite bears that name also in the sacred literature of the Mandaeans of Iraq and Iran.[15] Jewish circumcision is also so designated.[16] In much the same spirit too the Ewe-speaking peoples of the Slave Coast tattoo themselves to indicate devotion to a particular deity or membership in a secret society.[17]

More directly illustrative of the mark of Cain is the fact that the nomadic smiths (Ṣleb) of the Sudan are distinguished to this day by a cross-shaped mark (ṣleb) on their brows![18]

This sacral marking and tattooing is, of course, merely an extension of the common ancient practice of branding slaves (and cattle) in token of ownership—a practice attested not only in Classical sources[19] but also in Egypt[20] and Babylon.[21] Indeed, a Babylonian expression for "to emancipate" was "to clean the brow."[22, 23]

In some parts of the world it was not only slaves and votaries but also criminals and offenders that were marked with a special sign.[24] In the Middle Ages and as late as the seventeenth century (especially in America), blasphemers, when convicted, were branded with the letter B;[25] while in England it was only in 1822 that Parliament formally abolished the custom of branding felons with an F on their left cheeks before admitting them to "benefit of clergy." Persons who brawled in church were similarly marked,[26] and by a law passed in 1547 a vagabond was to be "signed" with the letter Y, branded with a hot iron on his or her breast, and to be sent back to his or her native place to serve as a slave to its inhabitants.[27] Not impossibly, some similar usage was in the mind of the Biblical writer when he recast the more ancient tale.

24a   Excursus

> *In the foregoing exposition it has been suggested that the mark of Cain was the relic of an earlier story in which it represented the distinguishing sign of the sacrosanct smith (qayin). In light, however, of the notion that the blood or ghost of a murdered man haunts his assailant and demands vengeance, an alternative explanation, here given in Frazer's words, also becomes possible.*

▲ The mark of Cain [albeit transmogrified in the Biblical version,] may originally have represented a mode of disguising a homicide or of rendering him so repulsive or formidable in appearance that his victim's angry ghost would either fail to recognize him or be scared of haunting him.

Here again, the basic idea is admirably illustrated from ancient Greek practise. Plato tells us that according to a time-honored belief in Attica, the ghost of a man who had just been killed was angry with his slayer and troubled him, being enraged at the the sight of the homicide stalking freely about in his (the ghost's) old familiar haunts; hence it was needful for the homicide to depart from his country for a year until the wrath of the ghost had cooled down, nor might he return before sacrifices had been offered and ceremonies of purification performed. If the victim chanced to be a foreigner, the slayer had to shun the native land of the dead man as well as his own, and in going into banishment he had to follow a prescribed road;[1] for clearly it would never do to let him rove about the country with the angry ghost at his heels.

Again, we have seen that among the Akikuyu a murderer is believed to be tainted by a dangerous pollution (*thahu*) which he can communicate to other people by contact. That this pollution is connected with his victim's ghost appears from one of the ceremonies which are performed to expiate the deed. The elders of the village sacrifice a pig beside one of those sacred fig-trees which play a great part in the religious rites of the tribe. There they feast on the more succulent parts of the animal, but leave the fat, intestines, and some of the bones for the ghost, who is supposed to come that very night and devour them in the likeness of a wild cat; his hunger being thus stayed, he considerately refrains from returning to the village to trouble the inhabitants.[2]

Among the Bagesu of Mount Elgon, in British East Africa, when a man has been guilty of manslaughter and his victim was a member of the same clan and village, he must leave the village and find a new home elsewhere, even though he may settle the matter amicably with the relations of the deceased. Further, he must kill a goat, smear the contents of its stomach on his chest, and throw the remainder upon the roof of the house of the murdered man "to appease the ghost."[3] In this tribe very similar ceremonies of expiation are performed by a warrior who has slain a man in battle; and we may safely assume that the intention of the ceremonies is to appease the ghost of his victim. The warrior returns to his village, but he may not spend the first night in his own house, he must lodge in the house of a friend. In the evening he kills a goat or sheep, deposits the contents of the stomach in a pot, and smears them on his head, chest, and arms. If he has any children, they must be smeared in like manner. Having thus fortified himself and his progeny, the warrior proceeds boldly to his own house, daubs each door-post with the stuff, and throws the rest on the roof, probably for the benefit of the ghost who may be supposed to perch, if not to roost, there. For a whole day the slayer may not touch food with the hands which shed blood; he conveys the morsels to his mouth with two sticks cut for the purpose. On the second day he is free to return home and resume his ordinary life.[4]

So too among the Nilotic Kavirondo (another tribe of British East Africa), a murderer is separated from the members of his village and lives in a hut with an old woman, who attends to his wants, cooks for him, and also feeds him, because he may not touch his food with his hands. This separation lasts for three days, and on the fourth day a man, who is himself a murderer, or who has at some time killed a man in battle, takes the murderer to a stream, where he washes him all over. He then kills a goat, cooks the meat, and puts a piece of it on each of four sticks; after which he gives the four pieces to the murderer to eat in turn. Next he puts four balls of porridge on the sticks, and these also the murderer must swallow. Finally, the goat-skin is cut into strips, and one strip is put on the neck, and one strip round each of the wrists of the homicide. This ceremony is performed by the two men alone at the river. After the performance the murderer is free to return home. It is said that, until this ceremony is performed, the ghost cannot take its departure for the place of the dead, but hovers about the murderer.[5]

Among the Boloki of the Upper Congo, the fear of ghostly vengeance sits heavy on anyone who has slain a fellow townsman: to deceive the angry ghost, he mourns for his victim as though he were a brother, neglecting his toilet, shaving his head, fasting, and lamenting with torrents of crocodile tears.[6]

Finally, among the Omaha Indians of North America a murderer, whose life was spared by the kinsmen of his victim, had to observe certain stringent regulations for a period which varied from two to four years. He must walk barefoot, and he might eat no warm food, nor raise his voice, nor look around. He had to pull his robe about him and to keep it tied at the neck, even in warm weather; he might not let it hang loose or fly open. He might not move his hands about, but had to keep them close to his body. He might not comb his hair, nor allow it to be blown about by the wind. No one would eat with him, and only one of his kindred was allowed to remain with him in his tent. When the tribe went hunting, he was obliged to pitch his tent about a quarter of a mile from the rest of the people, "lest the ghost of his victim should raise a high wind which might cause damage."[7] The reason here alleged for banishing the murderer from the camp probably gives the key to all similar restrictions among primitive peoples: *the seclusion of manslayers from society is dictated by no moral aversion to their crime; it springs purely from dread of the ghost by which the homicide is supposed to be pursued and haunted.*

This fear of the wrathful ghost of the slain is probably at the root of many ancient customs observed in connexion with homicide; it may well have been one of the principal motives for inflicting capital punishment on murderers. For if such persons are dogged by a powerful and angry spirit, which makes them a danger to their fellows, society can obviously protect itself very simply by sacrificing the murderer to the ghost; in other words, by putting him to death. But then it becomes necessary to guard the executioners in their turn against the ghosts of their victims, and various precautions are adopted for this purpose. For example, among the Bakongo, of the Lower Congo, when a man has been executed for murder, his body is burnt to ashes. "By reducing the body to ashes they believe that they thereby destroy his spirit, and thus prevent the spirit from seeking revenge by bewitching his executioners."[8] At Porto Novo, on the coast of Guinea, the public executioner used to decorate the walls of his house with the jawbones of his victims in order to prevent their ghosts from troubling him at night.[9] At Issini, on the Gold Coast, executioners used to remain in seclusion for three days after doing their office; during that time they lived in a hut built for the purpose at a distance from the village. When the three days were over they proceeded to the place of execution, and there called thrice by name on the criminal whom they had put to death,[10] the invocation being probably supposed to protect them against the ghost of their victim.

Another mode of effecting the same purpose is to taste of the murderer's blood; this has been customary with executioners on the Lower Niger in West Africa, and among the Shans of Burma. The alleged intention of the custom is to prevent the executioner from being affected by a kind of homicidal madness or otherwise contracting a fatal illness;[11] but these effects are in all probability believed to be wrought by the ghost of the slain man, who has entered into and taken possession of the body of his slayer, and the motive for tasting of his blood is to bring about a reconcilement between them by establishing a blood covenant.[12] Among the Tupi Indians of Brazil a man who had publicly executed a prisoner had to fast and lie in his hammock for three days, without setting foot on the ground; further, he had to make incisions in his breast, arms, and other parts of his body, and a black powder was rubbed into the wounds, which left indelible scars so artistically arranged that they presented the appearance of a tight-fitting garment. It was believed that he would die if he did not observe these rules and draw blood from his own body after slaughtering the captive.[13] The former practice was probably designed to provide standing evidence that the executioner had given satisfaction to his victim and made his peace with him, while the latter may have been intended to satisfy the ghost's demand of blood for blood, or possibly to establish a blood covenant with him. Could any reasonable ghost ask for more?

This interpretation of the marks on the executioner's body is supported by a custom current among the Yabim, on the north-eastern coast of New Guinea. When the kinsmen of a murdered man have accepted a blood-wit instead of avenging his death, they take care to be marked with chalk on the forehead by the relatives of the murderer, "lest the ghost should trouble them for failing to avenge his death, and should carry off their pigs or loosen their teeth."[14] In this custom, to be sure, it is not the murderer but the kinsmen of his victim who are marked. The principle, however, is the same. The ghost of the murdered man naturally turns in fury on his heartless relatives who have not exacted blood for his blood. But just as he is about to swoop down on them to loosen their teeth, or steal their pigs, or make himself unpleasant in other ways, he is brought up short by the sight of the white mark on their black or coffee-coloured brows. It is the receipt for the payment in full of the blood-wit; it is the proof that his kinsfolk have exacted a pecuniary, though not a sanguinary, compensation for his murder; with this crumb of consolation he is bound to be satisfied, and to spare his family any molestation in future. The same mark might obviously be put for the same purpose on the murderer's brows to prove that he had paid in cash, or whatever may be the local equivalent for cash, for the deed he had done, and that the ghost therefore had no further claim upon him. Was the mark of Cain originally a mark of this sort? Was it a proof that he had paid the blood-wit? Was it a receipt for cash down?

On the theory which I have just indicated it is obvious that the mark of Cain could only be put on a homicide when his victim was a man of the same tribe or community as himself, since it is only to men of the same tribe or community that compensation for homicide is paid. But the ghost of slain enemies are certainly not less dreaded than the ghosts of slain friends; and if you cannot pacify them with a sum of money paid to their kinsfolk, what are you to do with them? Many plans have been adopted for the protection of warriors against the spirits of the men whom they have sent out of the world before their due time. Apparently one of these precautions is to disguise the slayer so that the ghost may not recognize him; another is to render his person in some way so formidable or so offensive that the spirit will not meddle with him.[15]

Among the Ba-Yaka, a Bantu people of the Congo Free State, "a man who has been killed in battle is supposed to send his soul to avenge his death on the person of the man who killed him; the latter, however, can escape the vengeance of the dead by wearing the red tail-feathers of the parrot in his hair, and painting his forehead red."[16] The Thonga of south-eastern Africa believe that a man who has killed an enemy in battle is exposed to great danger from his victim's ghost, who haunts him and may drive him mad. To protect himself from the wrath of the ghost, the slayer must remain in a state of taboo at the capital for several days, during which he may not go home to his wife, and must wear old clothes and eat with special spoons off special plates. In former times it was customary to tattoo such a man between the eyebrows, and to rub in medicines into the incisions, so as to raise pimples and to give him the appearance of a buffalo when it frowns.[17] Among the Basutos "warriors who have killed an enemy are purified. The chief has to wash them, sacrificing an ox in the presence of the whole army. They are also anointed with the gall of the animal, which prevents the ghost of the enemy from pursuing them any farther."[18]

Among the Wawanga, of the Elgon district in British East Africa, a man on returning from a raid, on which he has killed one of the enemy, may not enter his hut until he has taken cow's dung and rubbed it on the cheeks of the women and children of the village, and has purified himself by the sacrifice of a goat, from whose forehead he cuts a strip of skin and wears it round his right wrist for the next four days.[19] Among the Bantu tribes of Kavirondo, in British East Africa, when a man has killed a foe in battle he shaves his head on his return home, and his friends rub a medicine, which generally consists of cow's dung, over his body to prevent the spirit of the slain man from troubling him.[20] In these cases the cow's dung may serve either to wipe off the ghost or to disgust and repel him. Among the Ja-Luo, a Nilotic tribe of Kavirondo, the warrior who has slain a foe in battle shaves his head three days after his return from the fight; and before he enters his village he must hang a live fowl, head uppermost, round his neck; then the bird is decapitated and its head left hanging round his neck. Soon after his return a feast is made for the slain man, in order that his ghost may not haunt his slayer.[21]

Even when no mention is made of the ghosts of the slain by our authorities, we may still safely assume that the purificatory rites performed by or for warriors after bloodshed are intended to appease or repel or deceive these angry spirits. Thus among the Ngoni of British Central Africa, when a victorious army approaches the royal village, it halts by the bank of a stream, and all the warriors who have killed enemies smear their bodies and arms with white clay, but those who were not the first to dip their spears in the blood of the victims, but merely helped to despatch them, whiten their right arms only. That night the manslayers sleep in the open pen with the cattle, and do not venture near their own homes. In the early morning they wash off the white clay from their bodies in the river. The witch-doctor attends to give them a magic potion, and to smear their persons with a fresh coating of clay. This process is repeated on six successive days, till their purification is complete. Their heads are then shaved, and being pronounced clean they are free to return to their own homes.[22] Among the Borâna Gallas, when a war-party has returned to the village, the victors who have slain a foe are washed by the women with a mixture of fat and butter, and their faces are painted red and white.[23] Masai warriors, who have killed barbarians in a fight, paint the right half of their bodies red and the left half white.[24] Similarly a Nandi, who has slain a man of another tribe, paints one side of his body red, and the other side white; for four days after the slaughter he is deemed unclean and may not go home. He must build a small shelter by the river and live there; he may not associate with his wife or sweetheart, and he may only eat porridge, beef, and goat's flesh. At the end of the fourth day he must purify himself by drinking a strong purge made from the *segetet* tree, and by drinking goat's milk mixed with bullock's blood.[25] Among the Thompson Indians of British Columbia it used to be customary for men who had slain enemies to blacken their faces. If this precaution were neglected, it was believed that the spirits of their victims would blind them.[26] A band of Tinneh Indians, who had

massacred a helpless party of Eskimo at the Copper River, considered themselves to be thereby rendered unclean, and they observed accordingly a number of curious restrictions for a considerable time afterwards. Those who had
actually shed blood were strictly prohibited from cooking either for themselves or for others; they might not drink out of any dish nor smoke out of any
pipe but their own; they might eat no boiled flesh, but only flesh that was raw
or had been broiled at a fire or dried in the sun; and at every meal, before they
would taste a morsel, they had to paint their faces with red ochre from the
nose to the chin and across the cheeks almost to the ears.[27]

Among the Chinook Indians of Oregon and Washington a man who had
killed another had his face painted black with grease and charcoal, and wore
rings of cedar bark round his head, his ankles, knees, and wrists. After five
days the black paint was washed off his face and replaced by red. During these
five days he might not sleep nor even lie down; he might not look at a child
nor see people eating. At the end of his purification he hung his head-ring of
cedar bark on a tree, and the tree was then supposed to dry up.[28] Among the
Eskimo of Langton Bay the killing of an Indian and the killing of a whale
were considered to be equally glorious achievements. The man who had killed
an Indian was tattooed from the nose to the ears; the man who had killed a
whale was tattooed from the mouth to the ears. Both heroes had to refrain
from all work for five days, and from certain foods for a whole year; in particular, they might not eat the heads nor the intestines of animals.[29] Among
the Southern Massim of British New Guinea a warrior who has slain a man
remains secluded in his house for six days. During the first three days he may
eat only roasted food and must cook it for himself. Then he bathes and black-
ens his face for the remaining three days.[30] When a party of Arunta, in Central
Australia, are returning from a mission of vengeance, on which they have
taken the life of an enemy, they stand in fear of the ghost of their victim, who
is believed to pursue them in the likeness of a small bird, uttering a plaintive
cry. For some days after their return they will not speak of their deed, and
continue to paint themselves all over with powdered charcoal, and to decorate
their foreheads and noses with green twigs. Finally, they paint their bodies and
faces with bright colours, and become free to talk of the affair; but still of
nights they must lie awake listening for the plaintive cry of the bird in which
they fancy they hear the voice of their victim.[31]

In Fiji any one who had clubbed a human being to death in war was consecrated or tabooed. He was smeared red by the king with turmeric from the
roots of his hair to his heels. A hut was built, and in it he had to pass the next
three nights, during which he might not lie down, but must sleep as he sat.
Till the three nights had elapsed he might not change his garment, nor remove
the turmeric, nor enter a house in which there was a woman.[32] That these rules
were intended to protect the Fijian warrior from his victim's ghost is strongly
suggested, if not proved, by another Fijian custom. When these savages had
buried a man alive, as they often did, they used at nightfall to make a great

uproar by means of bamboos, trumpet-shells, and so forth, for the purpose of frightening away his ghost, lest he should attempt to return to his old home. And to render his house unattractive to him they dismantled it and clothed it with everything that to their thinking seemed most repulsive.[33] So the North American Indians used to run through the village with hideous yells, beating on the furniture, walls, and roofs of the huts to drive away the angry ghost of an enemy whom they had just tortured to death.[34] A similar custom is still observed in various parts of New Guinea and the Bismarck Archipelago.[35]

Elsewhere I have conjectured that mourning costume in general was originally a disguise adopted to protect the surviving relatives from the dreaded ghost of the recently departed.[36] Whether that be so or not, it is certain that the living do sometimes disguise themselves to escape the notice of the dead. Thus in the western districts of Timor, a large island of the Indian Archipelago, before the body of a man is coffined, his wives stand weeping over him, and their village gossips must also be present, "all with loosened hair in order to make themselves unrecognizable by the *nitu* (spirit) of the dead."[37] Again, among the Herero of South-West Africa, when a man is dying he will sometimes say to a person whom he does not like, "Whence do you come? I do not wish to see you here," and so saying he presses the fingers of his left hand together in such a way that the tip of the thumb protrudes between the fingers. "The person spoken to, now knows that the other has decided upon taking him away after his death, which means that he must die. In many cases, however, he can avoid this threatening danger of death. For this purpose he hastily leaves the place of the dying man, and looks for a doctor or magician (*ongana*) in order to have himself undressed, washed, and greased again, and dressed with other clothes. He is now quite at ease about the threatening of death caused by the deceased; for, says he, 'Now, our father does not know me.' He has no longer any reason to fear the dead."[38]

In like manner we may suppose that, when Cain had been marked by God, he was quite easy in his mind, believing that the ghost of his murdered brother would no longer recognize and trouble him. This explanation has the advantage of relieving the Biblical narrative from a manifest absurdity. For on the usual interpretation God affixed the mark to Cain in order to save him from human assailants, apparently forgetting that there was nobody to assail him, since the earth was as yet inhabited only by the murderer himself and his parents. Hence by assuming that the foe of whom the first murderer went in fear was a ghost instead of a living man, we avoid the irreverence of imputing to the deity a grave lapse of memory little in keeping with the divine omniscience. Here again, therefore, the comparative method approves itself a powerful *advocatus Dei*.

To all of the foregoing it may be objected, with some show of reason, that the ghost of the murdered Abel is nowhere alluded to in the Biblical narrative, according to which it was not the ghost, but the blood, of his victim which endangered the murderer by calling aloud from the ground for vengeance. It is true that the conception of blood thus endowed with a voice and with a thirst for vengeance differs from the conception of a ghost, being a simpler and possibly a more primitive idea; yet in practice it perhaps made little material difference to the manslayer whether he believed himself to be pursued by the bloody phantom or only by the dolorous voice of his victim's blood shrieking after him. Still it cannot be denied that in the Old Testament it is the actual blood, and not the ghost, of the murdered person which figures prominently in the references to manslaughter and to the retribution which should overtake the slayer. Thus in the Priestly Document we read, with regard to homicide, that "blood, it polluteth the land: and no expiation can be made for the land for the blood that is shed therein, but by the blood of him that shed it" (Num. 35:33). The notion seems to have been, that so long as the blood lay exposed to the air and had not run away or soaked into the ground, it continued to call aloud for vengeance on the murderer, but that its mouth could be stopped and its voice stifled by a handful of earth. Hence Job, looking for death and passionately appealing against the injustice of his fate, cries out in his agony, "O earth, cover not my blood, and let my cry have no *resting* place" (16:18). And in denouncing the wrath of God on Jerusalem for all the innocent blood shed in the city, the prophet Ezekiel exclaims, "Woe to the bloody city, to the caldron whose rust is therein, and whose rust is not gone out of it! bring it out piece by piece; no lot is fallen upon it. For her blood is in the midst of her; she set it upon the bare rock; she poured it not on the ground to cover it with dust; that it might cause fury to come up to take vengeance, I have set her blood upon the bare rock, that it should not be covered" (24:6–8). Here it is mentioned as a great aggravation alike of the guilt and of the danger of Jerusalem, that the blood shed in her midst still weltered in clotted pools, like rust, on her rocky surface instead of being mercifully covered with dust or allowed to soak into the ground; for so long as it lay there festering in the sun, the multitudinous voices of the slain would ascend up to heaven, clamouring in a doleful chorus for vengeance on their slayers.[39] The belief that unavenged human blood cries aloud from the ground is still held by the Arabs of Moab. A Bedouin of that country told a preaching friar that "the blood cries from the earth, and it continues to cry until the blood of an enemy has been shed."[40]

So scrupulous, indeed, were the ancient Hebrews about leaving blood of any sort exposed to the air, that the Levitical law (Lev. 17:13) commands the hunter or fowler to cover up with dust the blood of the beast or fowl which he has poured out on the ground. The precept may well embody a traditional usage based on an ancient belief that animals, like men, acknowledged the obligation of avenging the death of their kind on their murderer or his kinsfolk, and that consequently if their blood was left uncovered, it would cry aloud to all beasts or birds of the same sort to exact retribution from the guilty hunter or fowler who had spilt it on the ground. At all events similar notions as to the practice of blood revenge by animals and birds are common among savages in modern times,[41] and they may well have prevailed among the Semites in antiquity, though we need not suppose that they were consciously present to the mind of the author or editor of Leviticus. It would appear that in the opinion of some savages not only may the blood of animals cry to heaven for vengeance, but if its cry is not answered, the slayer of the beast may be compelled, like Cain, to roam an outlaw from land to land for the rest of his life. Thus in a legend of the Waboungou, a tribe of German East Africa, we hear of a skilful hunter who one day killed an elephant with his arrows. Thereupon a mysterious personage called the Great Sultan appeared to him and said, "The smell of spilt blood has reached even to me. That blood calls for vengeance. If you do not bring me the bones of the elephant, there can be no peace between us. I will tell all the Sultans to drive you from their countries, so that you will henceforth find no place where to build a hut." But the obstinate hunter refused to bring the bones of the elephant to the Great Sultan. Therefore the Sultan drove him from his kingdom, and the wretch went roving from land to land till the day of his death.[42]

* * *

We may smile at these quaint fancies of vengeful ghosts, shrieking gore, and Earth opening her mouth to drink blood or to vomit out her guilty inhabitants; nevertheless it is probable that these and many other notions equally unfounded have served a useful purpose in fortifying the respect for human life by the adventitious aid of superstitious terror. The venerable framework of society rests on many pillars, of which the most solid are nature, reason, and justice; yet at certain stages of its slow and laborious construction it could ill have dispensed with the frail prop of superstition. ▼

25 Abel's blood   4:10

Cain's crime is discovered when Abel's blood cries to God from the ground.

"The blood is the life," and is in this respect an alternative to the "spirit."[1] Abel's blood which cries from the ground is therefore the same thing as his spirit or ghost calling for vengeance.

Homer, for instance, speaks alternatively of the blood and of the soul as issuing from a mortal wound;[2] and Theophrastus assures us that the blood is the seat of the intelligence.[3] The ancient Germans, we are told, used to drink blood mixed with wine and honey in order to acquire additional *élan vitale*,[4] and a medieval chronicler relates of the Hungarians that they were wont to fortify themselves in battle by slashing the bodies of captives and sucking their blood, the idea being that they thus absorbed an extra "personality."[5] Nor, indeed, are such practices confined to ancient times. Even at the present day, a wounded Somali sucks his blood in order to regain his strength;[6] while among the Caribs a newborn boy is sprinkled with drops of his father's blood in order that the latter's courage and vitality may be transmitted to him.[7] Moreover, it is customary among huntsmen in Upper Austria to drink the blood of a newborn beast so as to gain what they call a resolute breast.[8]

Other qualities too can be thus imbibed. It is recorded, for example, that when the Count of Montmorency was put to death at Toulouse in 1632, the troops drank his blood in order to fill their veins with his intrepid valor;[9] and the natives are said to have done likewise when the Jesuit missionary, Jean de Brebeuf, was martyred by the Iroquois in 1648.[10]

The idea that the blood is the life comes out also in the superstition that witches and other workers of evil can be rendered innocuous if their blood is shed. There is an interesting allusion to this belief in Shakespeare's *Henry the Sixth* where Talbot says to La Pucelle:

> I'll have a bout with thee;
> Devil or devil's dam, I'll conjure thee;
> Blood will I draw on thee; thou art a witch.[11]

Similarly, in Cleveland's *Rebel Scot* occur the lines:

> Scots are like witches; do but whet your pen,
> Scratch till blood come, they'll not hurt you then.

The idea that the blood of a murdered man thus demands satisfaction is attested elsewhere in both the ancient and modern Near East. One of the cries uttered by Job in his anguish is that the earth will not cover his blood and that there will be no place in it but will echo its cry;[12] while when Judah the Maccabee and his followers inaugurated their revolt against Antiochus Epiphanes, they besought God to "hearken to the blood that cries unto Him."[13] Palestinian Arabs of the present day believe that as soon as a slain man's blood seeps into the ground, a special spirit arises, known as "the lier-in-wait" (*raṣad*). This spirit haunts the spot and can be heard every evening (or, according to another tradition, every Wednesday and Friday and on each anniversary of his death) repeating his last words, until satisfaction is exacted from his assailants. Should such a spirit trouble a passer-by, the latter must shout at it, "Spirit, go and revenge yourself on him who actually slew you!"[14] Nor, indeed, is it only in the Near East that this notion prevails.[15] The idea that blood speaks appears also in the German folktale of *Sweetheart Roland* and in the Norse folktale of *Mastermaid;* and it likewise informs one of the episodes of the Finnish Kalevala.[16]

The blood need not actually *speak;* it can also deliver its message simply by refusing to be stanched.[17] Later Jewish legend says, for instance, that the blood of the murdered priest Zechariah (cf. II Chron. 24:20–22; Matt. 23:35;

Luke 11:51) continued to bubble up and could be stayed only after Nebuzaradan had made a moving appeal to it.[18] So too the blood of the goat which Joseph's brethren slew in order to pretend that he had been killed by a wild beast (cf. Gen. 37:31) will go on flowing until the Messiah comes,[19] even as will that of Abel himself.[20]

Such blood, issuing from a corpse, can betray a murderer.[21] Matthew of Paris relates that after the death of Henry II of England at Chinon, when his brother Richard came to view the body, blood gushed from its nostrils "as if the spirit were indignant at the approach of him who was believed to be the murderer, so that the blood seemed to be crying to God."[22] The incident is incorporated, indeed, in Shakespeare's *Richard the Third,* where the Lady Anne exclaims at Henry's funeral:

> O gentlemen, see, see! Dead Henry's wounds
> Open their congeal'd mouths and bleed afresh![23]

Similarly, according to John Stow, when Henry VI's body was conveyed in an open coffin to burial, it bled both at St. Paul's and at Blackfriars.[24] Incidents of the same kind are also reported in legal annals. Thus, in Sir Simonds D'Ewes' account of the celebrated Babb murder at Kingston, Somerset, in 1613, it is said that the culprit was betrayed in this manner, and it was thus too that Philip Standsfield was apprehended for the slaying of his father in 1688.[25] In the time of King Christian II of Denmark, the identity of a murderer was likewise revealed when the victim's corpse bled as soon as the felon approached it;[26] and readers of the *Niebelungenlied* will recall that it was in this way that Krienhield fastened upon Hagen the murder of Siegfried.[27]

As both Orestes[28] and Lady Macbeth[29] discovered, the blood of a murdered man cannot be wiped out. But they were not alone in this discovery. The blood of David Rizzio, the Italian secretary of Mary Queen of Scots, who was done to death in 1565–66, is said still to stain the floor at Holyrood;[30] while the famous Zimmern Chronicle relates that the blood on the dagger which slew Graf von Sonnenberg in 1511 cannot be effaced.[31] In the chapel of the convent of the Carmelites at Paris it is still possible to see the drops of blood which flowed from eighty priests massacred during the French Revolution; and at Cothele, a mansion on the banks of the River Tamar, the blood of a warden treacherously slain by the lord of the manor in olden times remains visible to this day.[32] In Cornwall, England, blood-stained rapiers are left to rust, because it is taken for granted that they can never be cleaned.[33]

Because it cries for vengeance and blights the soil until such vengeance is exacted, blood must not be allowed to fall on the ground.[34] The Arab writer Ibn Hishām (d. A.D. 828) records a pre-Islamic tradition that, when this happens, the spirit of the deceased immediately roams around the spot, in the form of a demon (*ḥamat*), demanding drink.[35] This notion had, however, been flatly repudiated by Mohammed, though it is still held in Morocco that "blood always contains spirits (*jnūn*)."[36] Among the Igalwa of West Africa, we are told, "blood, even from a small cut in the finger or from a fit of nose-bleeding, is most carefully covered up and stamped out if it has fallen on the earth. Blood is the life, and life in Africa means a spirit; hence the liberated blood is the liberated spirit, and liberated spirits are always whipping into people who don't want them."[37] For the same reason, the aborigines of Australia scrupulously avoid letting any of the blood shed in the initiatory rite of circumcision fall on the ground,[38] while the Warika and Damaras (Hereros) of South West Africa[39] and the Caffres of Natal[40] insist that when an animal is slaughtered as little as possible of its blood must be spilled on the earth.

▲ The belief that the earth is a powerful divinity, who is defiled and offended by the shedding of human blood and must be appeased by sacrifice, prevails, or prevailed till lately, among some tribes of Upper Senegal, who exact expiation even for wounds which have merely caused blood to flow without loss of life. Thus at Laro, in the country of the Bobos, "the murderer paid two goats, a dog, and a cock to the chief of the village, who offered them in sacrifice to the Earth on a piece of wood stuck in the ground. Nothing was given to the family of the victim. All the villagers, including the chief, afterwards partook of the flesh of the sacrificial victims, the families of the murderer and his victim alone being excluded from the banquet. If it was an affair of assault and wounds, but blood had not been shed, no account was taken of it. But when blood had been spilt, the Earth was displeased at the sight, and therefore it was necessary to appease her by a sacrifice. The culprit gave a goat and a thousand cowries to the chief of the village, who sacrificed the goat to the Earth and divided the cowries among the elders of the village. The goat, after being offered to the Earth, was also divided among the village elders. But the injured party throughout the affair was totally forgotten and received nothing at all, and that, too, logically enough. For the intention was not to compensate the injured party for his wrong at the cost of the wrongdoer, but to appease the Earth, a great and redoubtable divinity, who was displeased at the sight of bloodshed.[41]

Among the Nounoumas, another tribe of Upper Senegal, the customs and beliefs in regard to bloodshed were similar. A murderer was banished for three years and had to pay a heavy fine in cowries and cattle, not as a blood-wit to the family of his victim, but to appease the Earth and the other local divinities, who had been offended by the sight of spilt blood. The ox or oxen were sacrificed to the angry Earth by a priest who bore the title of the Chief of the Earth, and the flesh, together with the cowries, was divided among the elders of the village, the family of the murdered man receiving nothing, or at most only a proportionate share of the meat and money.[42] ▼

In the Middle Ages, special precautions were taken to avoid shedding the blood of executed felons and for this reason stoning was commonly preferred as the means of carrying out capital sentences.[43] Sir Walter Scott informs us that when a certain Captain Christian was shot by order of the Manx Government after the Restoration in 1660, the place of execution was covered by blankets to prevent his blood from spilling on the ground.[44]

This, it may be added, is the real origin of the Biblical commandment (Gen. 3:4–6) against shedding blood.

26 The errant ghost

The demand for vengeance which a murdered man can raise through his blood can be raised also simply through his vagrant ghost. Alike in ancient Mesopotamia[1] and in ancient and modern Greece,[2] the spirits of those who have died by violence are regarded as potent demons, and among the aborigines of Australia no otherworldly being is more dreaded than the *ingna* or unexpiated ghost.[3] Similar notions have been recorded—to cite but a few instances—among the North American Iroquois,[4] the Karens of Burma,[5] and in Thailand,[6] while this is also a common theme of German folktales.[7] Such persons cannot lie peacefully in their graves.[8] Often, too, they constitute a special danger because they have not been duly buried, since the main purpose of burial rites is precisely to tuck the dead away comfortably so that they do not become a nuisance to the living—or, in broader terms, so that the past does not haunt and invade the present.[9]

27 The contagion of bloodshed 4:12

(a) The banishment of homicides

▲ [He who sheds blood incurs the miasma of his victim's spirit, and this is contagious. Accordingly, he becomes a kind of "Typhoid Mary" and, as we have seen, must be expelled from the community.

The point is brought out very clearly in the Biblical tale.] Cain is obliged to go into exile not because God has cursed him, but because the earth has done so. As the result of having swallowed his brother's blood, it has refused henceforth to yield him its produce. What is implicit is that a murderer poisons the source of life and therefore jeopardizes the supply of food not only for himself but also for others. He becomes a public menace, surrounded by a contagion which all men naturally shun, and as such he has to exclude himself from the community. He is plague-stricken and infected: his very touch may blight the earth.

An admirable illustration of this is afforded by a certain rule of ancient Greek law. In Attica, a homicide who had been banished and against whom during his absence a second charge had been brought, was allowed to return to plead in his defence; but he might not set foot on the land, he had to speak from a ship, and even the ship might not cast anchor or put out a gangplank.[1]

The judges avoided all contact with the culprit, for they judged the case sitting or standing on the shore.[2] Clearly the intention of this rule was to put the manslayer in quarantine, lest by touching Attic earth even indirectly he should blast it. For the same reason, if such a man, sailing the sea, had the misfortune to be cast away on the country where his crime had been perpetrated, he was allowed indeed to camp on the shore till a ship came to take him off, but he was expected to keep his feet in sea-water all the time,[3] evidently in order to counteract, or at least dilute, the poison which he was supposed to instil into the soil.

[It appears, indeed, to have been a general principle of Greek law until the time of Draco that slayers of their kinsmen or countrymen be banished, a rule particularly familiar from the stories of Orestes and Oedipus.[3a] Other taboos too were placed on manslaughter. In Athens, for instance, they might not be spoken to, if encountered,[3b] and the judges had to avoid physical contact with them when condemning them.[3c] In Cyrene, a manslayer who came to a temple as a suppliant had to be led to the altar in silence.[3d]

On the other hand, it should be observed that the contagion was often thought to be limited to the area or country in which the crime was committed.[3e] Adrastus the Phrygian, for example, did not defile neighboring Lydia,[3f] and there is evidence from inscriptions that at least in some cases exiled manslayers might find permanent refuge elsewhere and not have to wander indefinitely.[3g] Indeed, both Demosthenes and Plato say categorically that it is the "spirit" *of the immediate area* that has to be appeased.[3h]

As among the Greeks, so among the Canaanites a manslayer was banished. In the Ugaritic *Poem of Aqhat,* after the slaying of that youth, his father Daniel pronounces over a city that might be harboring the unknown murderer the curse that its inhabitants (who would thus share the blood-guilt) may collectively flee forever and be compelled to seek their only refuge as guests at shrines.[3i] Similarly, among the Arabs, the murderer of a kinsman is banished under the standard formula declaring him an outcast (*holi*);[3j] while in Morocco he is debarred from vegetable gardens and orchards, and may not even come near cattle, lest he spread his contagion to them.[3k]]

Such ancient quarantining of manslayers finds its counterpart in the seclusion still enforced on murderers by the savages of Dobu, an island off the southeastern extremity of New Guinea. On this subject a missionary, who resided there for seventeen years, writes as follows: "When the chief Gaganumore slew his brother (mother's sister's son) he was not allowed to return to his own village, but had to build a village of his own. He had to have a separate lime-gourd and spatula; a water-bottle and cup of his own; a special set of cooking pots; he had to get his drinking cocoanuts and fruit elsewhere; his fire had to be kept burning as long as possible, and if it went out it could not be relit from another fire, but by friction. If the chief were to break this tabu, his brother's blood would poison his blood so that his body would swell, and he would die a terrible death."[4]

In similar vein the Akikuyu of British East Africa believe that if a man who has killed another comes and sleeps at a village and eats with a family in their hut, the persons with whom he has eaten contract a dangerous pollution (*thahu*), which might prove fatal to them, were it not removed in time by a medicine-man. The very skin on which the homicide slept has absorbed the taint and might infect any one else who slept on it. So a medicine-man is called in to purify the hut and its inmates.[5] Similarly among the Moors of Morocco a manslayer "is considered in some degree unclean for the rest of his life. Poison oozes out from underneath his nails; hence anybody who drinks the water in which he has washed his hands will fall dangerously ill. The meat of an animal which he has killed is bad to eat, and so is any food which is partaken of in his company. If he comes to a place where people are digging a well, the water will at once run away. It is a common, although not universal, rule that he must not perform the sacrifice at the Great Feast with his own hands; and in some tribes, mostly Berber-speaking ones, there is a similar prohibition with reference to a person who has killed a dog, which is an unclean animal. All blood which has left the veins is unclean and haunted by *jnūn*" (jinns).[6]

(b) Bloodshed renders the soil barren

In the Biblical narrative, the blood of the murdered man is not the only inanimate object that is personified. If the blood is represented as crying aloud, the earth is represented as opening her mouth to receive it. To this personification of the earth Aeschylus offers a parallel, for he speaks of the ground drinking the blood of the murdered Agamemnon.[7] But in Genesis the attribution of personal qualities to the earth seems to be carried a step further, for we are told that the murderer was "cursed from the ground"; and that when he tilled it, the land would not yield him her strength, but that a wanderer and a vagabond should he be in the world. The implication apparently is that the earth, polluted by blood and offended by his crime, would refuse to allow the seed sown by the murderer to germinate and bear fruit.

[This idea appears repeatedly in the Old Testament itself.[7a] "Blood," says the Law of Moses, "pollutes the land, and no expiation can be made for the land . . . except by the blood of him who shed it."[7b] Similarly, in his great farewell song the law-giver declares that it is one of the graces of Yahweh, as the champion of Israel, that he "avenges the blood of his servants and achieves expiation for his people (and) his land."[7c] Again, in David's lament over Saul and Jonathan he prays that, in accordance with established beliefs, neither rain nor dew may fall on the mountains of Gilboa, where they were slain.[7d] In the Ugaritic *Poem of Aqhat,* the murder of that youth likewise entails drought, and is confirmed when the crops are seen to have been suddenly blighted.[7e]]

The ancient Greeks apparently entertained similar notions as to the effect of polluting earth by the shedding of human blood, or, at all events, the blood of kinsfolk; for tradition told how the matricide Alcmaeon, haunted by the ghost of his murdered mother Eriphyle, long wandered restlessly over the world, till at last he repaired to the oracle at Delphi, and the priestess told him, that "the only land whither the avenging spirit of Eriphyle would not dog him was the newest land, which the sea had uncovered since the pollution of his mother's blood had been incurred."[8] Following the directions of the oracle, he discovered at the mouth of the Achelous the small and barren Echinadian Islands which, by washing down the soil from its banks, the river was supposed to have created since the perpetration of his crime; and there he took up his abode.[9] According to one version of the legend, the murderer had found rest for a time in the bleak upland valley of Psophis, among the solemn Arcadian mountains, but even there the ground refused to yield its increase to the matricide, and he was forced, like Cain, to resume his weary wandering.[10]

[In the Eumenides of Aeschylus the goddess Athene warns the people not to incur blight or sterility through bloodshed;[10a] while Sophocles has Oedipus declare that, as the result of his having slain his father Laius, the whole land of Thebes is languishing under the curse of infertility.[10b] So too when Pelops slays Stymphalus, king of the Arcadians, the soil becomes barren.[10c] In Samothrace, says Livy, it was commonly supposed that "the earth became polluted by blood shed in homicide";[10d] while a modern legend current at Koropion, in Attica, asserts that when a peasant once shot a witch or vampire (*lamia*), no grass grew where her blood had dripped.[10e] A similar belief is reported also from the Faroe Islands.[10f]] ▼

28   The curse of wandering   4:12

Cain is condemned to be "a wanderer and a vagabond in the earth."

As we have seen, in the original story this was intended to account for the nomad status of the itinerant smith (*qayin,* Cain). Within the framework of the Biblical version, however, it takes on a different complexion.

"Nothing," says Homer, "is worse for mortals than wandering,"[1] but in ancient times the curse of wandering lay not only in homelessness but also in the hazards of travel upon roads unpoliced and unguarded. Indeed, in recognition of this ancient kings often made a point of mentioning in their triumphal inscriptions that they had brought security to the highways. Thus on an inscription at Medinet Habu, Ramses III (c. 1195.64 B.C.) boasts that in his reign "Egypt and the other lands are at peace. . . . A woman can go about at her will and as far as she pleases, with her veil lifted;"[2] while on a Phoenician stele of the ninth century B.C. discovered at Karatepe, in Cilicia, a certain King Azitiwadda of Adana declares that "in my days a woman can stroll in places which were previously feared, where (even) a man feared to go."[3] Similarly, in the Biblical Song of Deborah (Judg. 5), a sign of parlous times is that "caravans ceased, and wayfarers went by devious routes."[4]

Hence, when Cain complains to Yahweh, *My punishment is greater than I can bear . . . since every man that meets me will slay me,* he is referring not (as is commonly supposed) to potential avengers of Abel—for persons who chanced to meet him in foreign parts would in any case scarcely know of his crime—but to the peril of footpads to whom he would be inevitably exposed.

The curse of wandering was not infrequently invoked by the Romans on their enemies. Readers of the classics will at once recall Tibullus' dire imprecation that anyone who is

> Deaf to the Muses' voice, or barters love
> May through full three hundred cities roam;[5]

while in the same vein Ovid has Hypsipile invoke upon Medea the curse that

> When all the earth and sea she has traversed,
> She in her roaming may essay the skies,
> Helpless, forlorn, stain'd with her bloody crime![6]

29 The Land of Nod   4:16

Cain wanders to the land of Nod.

This is pure folklore. The Hebrew word *nôd* means "wandering," and there is no need to go looking for a country of that name.[1] The use of such symbolic names is, indeed, a hallmark of folktales. In the Old Testament itself we have Adam, meaning "Man"; Cain and Abel, meaning "Smith and Herdsman"; and Delilah, meaning "Coquette."[2] Similarly, in the Babylonian story of the Deluge, the mountain on which the ark rests is called Niṣir, "Preservation";[3] and in the Epic of Gilgamesh the Calypsolike siren on the remote island is named simply Siduri, a Hurrian (Horite) word for "lady, damsel."[4] In the Canaanite (Ugaritic) *Epic of K-r-t,* the witch who magically removes the king's sickness is Sh-'-t-q-t, "Remover";[5] while in Homer we have the seafaring names of the Phaeacians (e.g., Prymneus, "Helmsman," Nauteus, "Jack Tar")[6] and of the Nereids,[7] as well as such characters as Phemois Terpiades, "Reciter, son of Dulcet," the bard,[8] and Dolôn, "Trickster," the Trojan spy.[9]

European nursery tales give us Snowhite, Cinderella, Hans Dumm, and even Humpty Dumpty; while from America comes Johnny Appleseed.

The device is employed especially by dramatists. Thus, in the comedies of Aristophanes, the woman who leads a sex strike to "bring the boys home" from the Peloponnesian War is called Lysistrata, as if "Madame de Mobilisation"; while the old codger is Chremes (or Chremylos), "Grunter, Old Grouch," and the braggart politician is Paphlagaôn, "Mr. Windbag." In the same way, Shakespeare has his Doll Tearsheet and Constable Goodman Dull, and Sheridan the redoubtable Mrs. Malaprop. The cardboard figures of the English miracle plays, such as Everyman, and of the mummers' play (e.g.,

Bold Slasher) will also come to mind, not to speak of Bunyan's Christian and the like.[10]

It may be added that some of the ancient Near Eastern myths, such as the Ugaritic *Poem of Baal,* become fully intelligible only when the symbolic significance of proper names (e.g., Baal, "rain," and Môt, "sterility") is appreciated.

(Certain, or uncertain, scholars have objected that the explanation of "land of Nod" as purely symbolical involves the paradox that Cain ends his wanderings in the Land of Wandering.[11] What these pundits have not had the mother-wit to observe is that the paradox is deliberate and of the very essence of the tale, as the Biblical writer wants it to be understood: a haunted man, however much he may ostensibly settle down, nevertheless continues to live in a climate of restlessness!)

30 Other Interpretations

1. S. H. Hooke suggests (in *Folk-Lore* 50 [1939], 58–65) that our tale originated in the primitive rite of performing a human sacrifice for the fertility of the crops and of then banishing the officiant from the community for a short period, as being potentially defiled. Analogies to this latter practice are found in the Babylonian Akîtu (New Year) ceremonies and in the ritual for the Hebrew Day of Atonement described in Lev. 16. In both cases, the dispatcher of the scapegoat (or scape-ram) was sent away until the conclusion of the festival. This theory (partly anticipated by A. Brock-Utne, in ZAW 54 [1936], 202 ff.) leaves too much to later transmutation by the Biblical writer, for all of the supposed original elements are read into the narrative, rather than out of it. In the Scriptural version, the land is rendered barren, not fertile, by the slaying of Abel; and Cain is put away not merely temporarily, until the rites of the new life have been completed, but permanently.

2. P. Ehrenzweig (in ZAW 35 [1915], 4 ff.) sees a cardinal element of the original story in the statement (Gen. 4:17) that Cain built a city. The real point, he suggests, was that both of the brothers at first wanted to build that city jointly, but sought an oracle as to who should rule it. The oracle favored Abel, whereupon Cain slew him! This, of course, is simply reading the story of Romulus and Remus into the Biblical narrative. By the same method, any number of other well-known folktales could be read *into* the text, but this is imagination run riot, not exegesis. All the features of the tale which really demand explanation, i.e., the names of the two principal characters, the fact that one is a "keeper of sheep" and the other a "tiller of the soil," the marking of Cain and his wandering, are left out of account.

3. William Robertson Smith (*Kingship and Marriage in Early Arabia* [1885], 251), without going into the origin of the story as a whole, explains the mark of Cain as nothing other than "the *shart,* or tribal mark which every man in early Arabian society bore on his person, and without which the

ancient form of blood-feud, as the affair of a whole stock, however scattered, and not of near relatives alone, could hardly have been worked." "The *shart,*" he adds, "was in old times a tattooed mark by which men who had mutual obligations, i.e. men of the same stock, recognized one another." This, however, overlooks the fact that Cain is driven from his own territory, so that the mark has to protect him from strangers, not from his kinsmen. Besides, it ignores the evidence which we have adduced above for the practice of sacred tattooing and branding for quite other reasons.

The Song of Lamech

31 An ancient war cry   4:23–24

In listing the progeny of Cain the Biblical writer interrupts the tedious genealogical chain to observe that Cain's great-great-great grandson Lamech is said to have composed a piece of poetry for the benefit or edification of his two wives, Adah and Zillah. What he composed, however, were no polite album verses, but a bellicose little song designed to reassure them that the man they had married was no sissy and could take good care of himself—and of them. In the stately language of the King James Version, the song runs as follows:

> *Adah and Zillah, hear my voice,*
> *ye wives of Lamech, hearken unto my speech;*
> *for I have slain a man to my wounding,*
> *and a young man to my hurt.*
> *If Cain shall be avenged sevenfold,*
> *surely Lamech seventy and sevenfold!*

(a) Battle taunts

Scholars have long since suggested that this poem was not in fact composed by a man named Lamech, but was the traditional war cry of a tribe so called, and that it was artificially inserted here by the Biblical compiler because of the identity of names.

Such songs, in which the champions of either side proclaimed their own prowess and ridiculed their opponents—a prototype of the "My-dad-can-lick-your-dad" of American schoolchildren—were a regular preliminary of combat in ancient times. In the Babylonian epic *Enuma Elish,* when the god Marduk engages the hosts of Tiamat, he first recites a war chant inviting her to hand-to-hand encounter.[1] Similarly, in the Epic of Gilgamesh, when Enkidu challenges that hero to fight, he first threatens to "speak forcefully (*danniš*)" to him.[2] In the Canaanite (Ugaritic) *Poem of Baal,* there is a similar exchange between Baal and his antagonist Yam, in which the former accuses the latter of upstart conduct and invokes the curse that the "Lord of Hell" (Ḥorôn) may break his head and the goddess Ashtareth crack his skull.[3] David and Goliath initiate hostilities in the same way, each vaunting the prowess of his god.[4] This initial "vaunt"[5] seems also to be intended by the prophet Isaiah when he describes how

> Yahweh sallies forth like a soldier,
>   like a warrior with passion ablaze,
> raises his war-cry and shouts,
>   vaunts himself over his foes;[6]

while in the Book of Job, Eliphaz declares that the wicked

> stretches his hand against God,
>   makes boasts against the Almighty,
> charges at him full-tilt.[7]

Early Arabic literature knows of a special class of poems, called *hijâ,* consisting of taunting satire against enemies recited by professional bards (*sha'ir*) before battle;[8] and it has been suggested that when Balaam was summoned by the king of Moab to curse Israel, the intention was that he should recite such verses.[9] A vivid description of how the recital of these taunts is still a convention of warfare among bedouins is given by the late Mrs. E. A. Finn in her account of a fight between the Shifat and Lifta tribes in the present century:

> During this fight one of the enemy challenged the sheikh . . . to single combat. The mode of challenge was characteristic: "Come on, thou rider of a *kadeesh* (hack horse)"; thus offering affront both to the rider and to his valued mare. . . . The men, and more especially the women, encourage the combatants, during the actual fight, by improvised verses praising their favorite warriors and recounting their deeds of prowess.[10]

Among the Irish, hostilities were initiated by a ceremony known as *glam dichen*—that is, the pronouncement of a satiric curse by a poet. This, we are told, "was no mere expression of opinion, but a most potent weapon of war, which might blister an adversary's face or even cost him his life. . . . It was at one time accompanied with ritual action; it was uttered 'on one foot, one eye,' and was sometimes used by a group of poets as a grim and elaborate ceremony of malediction."[11] Such taunts appear, indeed, in the Celtic *Echtra Conlat* and in the *Voyage of Bran;* while an ancient Indic counterpart has been recognized in one of the hymns of the Rig Veda.[12]

In Norway, too, altercations between groups often commence with an exchange of "*nith* (quarrel)-songs," or invective in verse.[13] This is common also among the Eskimos:

> A not uncommon way of dealing with offenses is for the aggrieved party to challenge the offender to a satirical song contest. Challenger and challenged compose satirical songs about each other, which in due time they deliver, surrounded and supported by their friends. The man whose song receives the greater acclaim on the part of the audience wins, and temporarily gains in social prestige, while the position of his rival is correspondingly debased.[14]

The taunts are likewise a regular feature of the English Mummers' Play.[15] Thus, in the Michinhampton play, Black Knight informs his adversary Gallantyne that *I'll cut thee up in slices / in less than half an hour.*[16] In the Cornwall play, St. George says of the Dragon: *I'll clip his wings, he shall not fly; / I'll cut him down, or else I die.*[17] And in the Frodsham "Soul-caking" play, King George boasts: *Is there a man before me will stand, / I'll cut him down with my iron hand.* To which Turkish Knight retorts: *I'll cut thee, I will slash thee, and after that, I'll send thee to Turkey to be made mince pies of.*[18]

(b) Adah and Zillah

Against this background Lamech's song takes on a new meaning. Adah and Zillah, though ostensibly proper names (for which, indeed, there are good parallels in Semitic nomenclature), may have been chosen by the poet because they suggested common nouns of contrasting sense and thus constituted what is called a *merism*—that is, a figure of speech in which contrasting parts are used to convey the notion of a whole (see above, §17c). Adah can be interpreted from a Semitic word meaning "dawn,"[19] and Zillah from one meaning "shadow." They will thus signify respectively "maid of the dawn" and "maid of the dusk," and this would be simply the equivalent of our own "every blonde and brunette" or the like.[20] The Hebrew words usually rendered "wives of Lamech" will then mean simply "womenfolk of Lamech (the tribe)."

(c) "If Cain be avenged sevenfold"

Cain too will be no proper name but rather the common noun meaning "smith," and the reference will be to the smith's sacrosanct status (see above, §22).

The sense and spirit of the song may thus be rendered as follows:

> *Maid of dawn and maid of dusk,*
>   *this my utterance hear;*[21]
> *Womenfolk of Lamech's tribe,*
>   *to what I say give ear:*
> *If e'er a grown man scratch me,*
>   *behold, I lay him low;*
> *the same I do to merest boys*
>   *for but a single blow.*
> *If injury unto a smith*
>   *men sevenfold requite,*
> *sevenfold and seventy*
>   *is due a Lamechite!*

The Sons of God and the Daughters of Man

32 "Sons of God"**6:1–3**

When mankind began to multiply upon the earth, the "sons of God" took a fancy to beautiful human women and proceeded to consort with them. Yahweh, however, became disturbed by these capers. "My spirit," he declared, "is not going to abide permanently[1] in man." He therefore limited the span of human life to a maximum of one hundred and twenty years.

We now know from Canaanite texts that "sons of God" was the regular term among the pagans for the members of the pantheon.[2] This story, therefore, was adopted and adapted from earlier mythology, and its theme is *miscegenation between gods and men*.

(a) Properties conveyed through sexual intercourse

The story is based on the widespread notion that sexual intercourse can convey the qualities of the one partner to the other.[3] Hence, such intercourse between gods and mortal women, or between goddesses and mortal men, is discountenanced and taboo, lest the divine thus become human, and the human divine. It is the latter possibility, involving the acquisition of immortality, that alarms Yahweh, and he therefore deals promptly with the situation by arbitrarily limiting the span of human life.

Stories built around this theme appear elsewhere in ancient literature. A Hittite myth discovered at Boghazköy tells of a mortal named Hupasiyas who, at the bidding of a goddess, undertakes to fight a dragon, but only on condition that she will first sleep with him. When his mission has been accomplished, she immediately whisks him away to a distant mountaintop, where she builds a house for him. Instructing him not to open the shutters, lest he catch sight of his wife and children in the valley below and be filled with longing to return to them, she departs on an errand. In her absence, Hupasiyas disobeys her orders, and indeed beholds his family. When the goddess returns, she perceives from his persistent whining what has happened. Thereupon, in a burst of fury, she burns down the house, with the mortal inside it. The motif of this tale is clearly the same as that which underlies the Biblical narrative: the goddess fears lest the divine essence conveyed to Hupasiyas through her intercourse with him be in turn transmitted by him to his wife, and thence pass to mortals. It is for this reason that she withdraws him to an inaccessible spot and, when his family ties assert themselves, eventually destroys him.[4]

Similarly, in Greek myth, when Oechalia, the wife of Amphitryon, declares to him that Zeus has slept with her, he never lies with her again, evidently fearful of thus receiving the divine essence.[5] Indeed, it was commonly believed by the Greeks that if a mortal presumed to consort with a goddess, he had to be put to death. Plutarch tells us, for instance, that a certain Molus who had raped a nymph was later found beheaded.[6] So too, when Anchises, the father of Aeneas, is accosted by Aphrodite on Mount Ida, he is hesitant to consort with her on the grounds that "no man ever remains sound who consorts with immortal goddesses";[7] and Tityos, when he offers violence to Leto, is slain by the shafts of Apollo, and has also to suffer dire punishment in Hades.[8]

(To be sure, there are many stories in Greek mythology concerning Zeus' amours with mortal women, but it must be remembered that, in the form in which they have come down to us, these stories no longer retain their pristine complexion. What came later to be represented as mortal women, at a time when this type of myth was more a thing for the poet than for the pietist, were originally local goddesses or nymphs, and what came to be identified as Zeus was originally a local deity who enjoyed connubium with her. Thus it is only when the literary veneer is spread over them that many of these tales come to defy the ancient tabu on miscegenation between gods and mortals. Others again, both in Greece and elsewhere, are told for the express purpose of indicating that kings and heroes, supposedly born of such unions, have something of divinity in them and were not run-of-the-mill human beings.)

In northern Europe the love of a nymph or giantess was likewise thought to bring death or misfortune to a mortal;[9] and the same notion occurs in the English ballads of *Thomas the Rhymer, The Unquiet Grave, Sweet William's Ghost, Tam Linn,* and *Clerk Colvill.*[10] Similarly too the natives of New Caledonia believe that intercourse with an otherworld being is fatal,[11] and a legend to the same effect is still current in the highlands of Scotland. The Breton ballad *Le Sieur Nau* implies the same thing.[12]

(b) The mortal span

One hundred and twenty occurs elsewhere in the Old Testament as a conventional round number. Thus, the total weight of gold dishes in the Tabernacle is 120 shekels.[13] Both Hiram of Tyre and the Queen of Sheba send Solomon

120 talents of gold.[14] There are 120 priestly trumpeters at the dedication of the Temple.[15] Similarly, 120,000 followers of Zebah and Zalmuna are slain by the forces of Gideon.[16] Solomon offers 120,000 sheep at the dedication of the Temple.[17] One hundred and twenty thousand men from the tribes of Reuben, Gad, and Manasseh defect to David against Saul;[18] and Pekah, the son of Remaliah, slays 120,000 apostatic Judeans in a single day.[19] This round number is probably to be explained as thrice forty, i.e., as an hyperbolic exaggeration of what is elsewhere in the Bible the typical round number.[20]

As the conventional maximum span of human life, the figure may be illustrated from the case of Moses[21] and—if we reckon thirty years to a generation —from the formula, "to see the fourth generation" used in Scriptural and Phoenician blessings.[22] It is noteworthy also that at the end of the Book of Job (42:16), when all things are doubled unto him, he is said in the Greek (Septuagint) Version to have lived 240 years, though the traditional (Masoretic) text gives the number as *one* hundred and forty.[23]

The Deluge

The closest parallel to the Biblical story of the Flood, and undoubtedly the primary source of it, occurs in the Mesopotamian Epic of Gilgamesh, our fullest version of which is furnished by an Akkadian recension prepared, in the seventh century B.C., for the great library of King Ashurbanipal at Nineveh.[1] The story itself is, of course, far older;[2] indeed, we have fragments of versions dating as much as a thousand years earlier,[3] and we possess also portions of a Sumerian archetype.[4] Moreover, that the story enjoyed wide diffusion over the Near East, and was by no means confined to Babylonia, is apparent from the survival of translations (albeit fragmentary) into the languages of the Hittites and Hurrians, antedating the first millennium B.C. Portions of the poem have also been found recently in the ruins of the Palestinian city of Megiddo.

Gilgamesh, a king of Erech (cf. Gen. 10:10), sets out in search of the means of immortality. After sundry adventures, he is at last advised to betake himself to Utnapishtim, the Babylonian Noah, who lives on a distant island and is reputedly immortal. Voyaging thither at some hazard, he asks Utnapishtim for the precious secret. In reply, the ancient hero tells him that he possesses no such secret, but has been given immortality as a special and peculiar reward from the gods. By way of explanation, he relates the story of the Deluge.

"You know," says he, "the city of Shurrupak, which lies on the Euphrates. It is an old, old city, and once upon a time the gods themselves delighted to dwell in it. But they eventually grew displeased with it, and resolved to send a flood. Ea, the god of wisdom and subtlety, however, was privy to their counsel and revealed this decision to me by having the wind whistle a warning through the wattles of my hut. 'Take thought,' it warned, 'for your life and belongings. Build a ship thirty cubits long and thirty cubits wide. Put in it specimens of every living thing, provision it, and launch it on the waters.' 'But what am I to tell my townsfolk?' I asked. 'Tell them,' came the answer, 'that the high god Enlil has taken a dislike to you and will have nothing more to do with you, and that you have therefore decided to leave his domain and betake yourself to the sea, which belongs to your lord Ea, who will feed you on fish and fowl.'

"I did as I was bidden, drew up plans, built the ship and provisioned it. When all was ready, I caulked the outer side with bitumen and the inner side with asphalt. Then I brought my family and possessions aboard. The same evening, the louring clouds—those princes of darkness—sent a prodigious rain, and a storm blew up. I appointed a helmsman, and committed the craft to the waters. In the gray of the morning, a dense black cloud suddenly rolled up from the horizon, and all the gods began to let loose. Came Adad with his escorts and thundered; came Nergal and wrenched off the anchor; came Ninurta, bringing woe and disaster; came the Anunaki, flashing their lightning torches. Everything then turned black; you could not even see your neighbor. Even the gods in heaven were scared.

"For six days and nights, wind and flood raged. On the seventh day, however, the battling wind seemed to exhaust itself and, suddenly, it died down, and the flood abated. I surveyed the scene. Not a sound was to be heard. Everything, including mankind, had turned to mud and clay. I opened a hatch, and daylight fell upon my face. I began to weep, all the time looking around for signs of land. At last, on the twelfth day, some dozen patches of land were to be seen emerging from the waters, and eventually the ship grounded on Mount Niṣir. There it remained for a further six days.

"On the seventh day, I sent out a dove, but it came back, for it found no place to rest. Then I sent out a swallow, but it too came back. Finally, I sent out a raven. The raven, however, soon saw that the waters had receded; it found food, and started to caw and wallow in the mud; it never came back.

"Thereupon, I proceeded to unload and disembark, and set out a savory offering to the gods on the mountaintop. They smelled the savor and started to swarm around like flies. At length, the goddess Ishtar stepped forward and, held up her massive necklace, the same which the sky-god had anciently made for her adornment. 'Look at these jewels,' she cried. 'Just as I can never put them out of my mind, so I can never banish the thought of these terrible days we have witnessed. Now, however, let us all fall to the banquet—all that is, except Enlil, for the disaster was his idea!'

"Now, when Enlil saw that I had been spared alive, he grew very angry and demanded to know who had given me warning of what the gods had planned. Ninurta thereupon suggested that it could only have been Ea, for Ea has a reputation of knowing everything in advance and of being equal, with his shrewdness and cunning, to any emergency. At this, however, Ea himself broke in and started to upbraid Enlil for his unconscionable brutality. The guilty alone, he declared, and not the whole of mankind, should have been punished, and this could have been done by launching wild beasts or dispatching a plague against them, rather than by wholesale destruction. 'Moreover,' he added slyly, 'I didn't actually give away the secret. I merely sent Utnapishtim the same kind of hint as one might get from a dream. Abnormally intelligent as he is, he drew his own conclusions!'

"Enlil was persuaded by these words and, leading me back aboard, along with my wife, he conferred his blessing on us both, telling me that we should henceforth enjoy the status of divine beings. Since, however, such beings have no place in the normal world of men, we were to be transferred to this remote island, far out on the horizon, there to enjoy our bliss for ever."

The older recensions, of which only fragments survive, tell substantially the same story, though the hero is sometimes called Atraḫasis, or "Superwise," rather than Utnapishtim. Similar too is the far older Sumerian version, where the hero is named Ziusudra, "the long-lived" (the Sumerian equivalent of Utnapishtim), and where he is likewise warned by the wind sighing through the crevices of a wall, likewise ordered to build an ark which grounds on a mountain after seven days and nights, likewise offers sacrifices to the gods, and is likewise rendered immortal and translated to the paradisal land of Dilmun.

Curiously enough, this ancient Sumerian story has been preserved also in a late Greek version by Berosus, a Babylonian writer of the third century B.C., who compiled a *Story of Chaldaea* in three books. These, unfortunately, have perished, but the passage about the Flood has survived in an indirect quotation by Eusebius of Caesarea (264–338 C.E.) in his *Chronicles*. The story is essentially as related above, except that the second bird comes back with muddy claws (just as in the Bible it returns with a green leaf in its beak), and that the hero's companions in the ark are instructed by a divine voice from heaven to journey to Babylon and there renew civilization.[5] ▼

34 Egypt

An Egyptian story of a deluge is preserved in the so-called Book of the Dead.[1] The god Atum announces his intention of flooding wicked mankind with the waters of the primeval ocean (Nun). The flood starts at Henensu, or Herakleopolis, in Upper Egypt, and submerges the entire country. The only survivors are certain persons who have been rescued in "the boat of millions of years," i.e., the barque of the sun-god, with Temu himself. Temu seems to have sailed to the Island of Flame—but the text is mutilated.

▲ 35 Greece

Legends of a destructive deluge, in which the greater part of mankind perished, meet us also in the literature of ancient Greece.[1] As told by the mythographer Apollodorus, the story runs thus: "Deucalion was the son of Prometheus. He reigned as king in the country about Phthia and married Pyrrha, the daughter of Epimetheus and Pandora, the first woman fashioned by the gods. But when Zeus wished to destroy the men of the Bronze Age, Deucalion by the advice of Prometheus constructed a chest or ark, and having

stored in it what was needful he entered into it with his wife. But Zeus poured
a great rain from the sky upon the earth and washed down the greater part
of Greece, so that all men perished except a few, who flocked to the high
mountains near. Then the mountains in Thessaly were parted, and all the
world beyond the Isthmus and Peloponnese was overwhelmed. But Deucalion
in the ark, floating over the sea for nine days and as many nights, grounded
on Parnassus, and there, when the rains ceased, he disembarked and sacrificed
to Zeus, the God of Escape. And Zeus sent Hermes to him and allowed him
to choose what he would, and he chose men. And at the bidding of Zeus he
picked up stones and threw them over his head; and the stones which Deucalion threw became men, and the stones which Pyrrha threw became women.
That is why in Greek people are called *laoi* from *laas,* 'a stone.' "[2]

In this form the Greek legend is not older than about the middle of the
second century before our era, the time when Apollodorus wrote, but in substance it is much more ancient, for the story was told by Hellanicus, a Greek
historian of the fifth century B.C., who said that Deucalion's ark drifted not
to Parnassus but to Mount Othrys in Thessaly.[3] The other version has the
authority of Pindar, who wrote earlier than Hellanicus in the fifth century B.C.;
for the poet speaks of Deucalion and Pyrrha descending from Parnassus and
creating the human race afresh out of stones.[4] According to some, the first city
which they founded after the great flood was Opus, situated in the fertile
Locrian plain between the mountains and the Euboic Gulf. But Deucalion is
reported to have dwelt at Cynus, the port of Opus, distant a few miles across
the plain; and there his wife's tomb was shown to travellers down to the beginning of our era. Heer husband's dust is said to have rested at Athens.[5]

It is said also that an ancient city on Parnassus was overwhelmed by the
rains which caused the deluge, but the inhabitants, guided by the howling of
wolves, found their way to the peaks of the mountain, and when the flood had
subsided they descended and built a new city, which they called Lycorea or
Wolf-town in gratitude for the guidance of the wolves.[6] Lucian speaks of
Deucalion's ark, with the solitary survivors of the human race, grounding on
what was afterwards the site of Wolf-town, while as yet all the rest of the world
was submerged.[7] But according to another account, the mountain to which
Deucalion escaped was a peak in Argolis, which was afterwards called Nemea
from the cattle which cropped the greensward on its grassy slopes. There the
hero built an altar in honour of Zeus the Deliverer, who had delivered him
from the great flood.[8] The mountain on which he is said to have alighted is
probably the table-mountain, now called Phouka, whose broad flat top towers
high above the neighbouring hills and forms a conspicuous landmark viewed
from the plain of Argos.

The Megarians told how in Deucalion's flood Megarus, son of Zeus, escaped
by swimming to the top of Mount Gerania, being guided by the cries of some
cranes, which flew over the rising waters and from which the mountain after-

wards received its new name.[9] According to Aristotle, writing in the fourth century B.C., the ravages of the deluge in Deucalion's time were felt most sensibly "in ancient Hellas, which is the country about Dodona and the river Achelous, for that river has changed its bed in many places. In those days the land was inhabited by the Selli and the people who were then called Greeks (*Graikoi*) but are now named Hellenes."[10] Some people thought that the sanctuary of Zeus at Dodona was founded by Deucalion and Pyrrha, who dwelt among the Molossians of that country.[11]

Various places in Greece claimed the honour of having been associated in a particular manner with Deucalion and the great flood. Among the claimants, as might have been expected, were the Athenians, who, pluming themselves on the vast antiquity from which they had inhabited the land of Attica, had no mind to be left out in the cold when it came to a question of Deucalion and the deluge. They annexed him accordingly by the simple expedient of alleging that when the clouds gathered dark on Parnassus and the rain came down in torrents on Lycorea, where Deucalion reigned as king, he fled for safety to Athens, and on his arrival founded a sanctuary of Rainy Zeus, and offered thank-offerings for his escape.[12] In this brief form of the legend there is no mention of a ship, and we seem to be left to infer that the hero escaped on foot. Be that as it may, he is said to have founded the old sanctuary of Olympian Zeus and to have been buried in the city. Down to the second century of our era the local Athenian guides pointed with patriotic pride to the grave of the Greek Noah near the later and far statelier temple of Olympian Zeus, whose ruined columns, towering in solitary grandeur above the modern city, still attract the eye fom far, and bear silent but eloquent witness to the glories of ancient Greece.[13]

Nor was this all that the guides had to show in memory of the tremendous cataclysm. Within the great precinct overshadowed by the vast temple of Olympian Zeus they led the curious traveller to a smaller precinct of Olympian Earth, where they pointed to a cleft in the ground a cubit wide. Down that cleft, they assured him, the waters of the deluge ran away, and down it every year they threw cakes of wheaten meal kneaded with honey.[14]

Another place where the great flood was commemorated by a similar ceremony was Hierapolis on the Euphrates. There down to the second century of our era the ancient Semitic deities were worshipped in the old way under a transparent disguise imposed on them, like modern drapery on ancient statues, by the nominally Greek civilization which the conquests of Alexander had spread over the East. Chief among these aboriginal divinities was the great Syrian goddess Astarte, who to her Greek worshippers masqueraded under the name of Hera. Lucian has bequeathed to us a very valuable description of the sanctuary and the strange rites performed in it.[15] He tells us that according to the general opinion the sanctuary was founded by Deucalion, in whose time the great flood took place.

The people of Hierapolis tell a marvelous thing. They say that a great chasm opened in their country, and all the water of the flood ran away down it. "I have seen the chasm," he proceeds, "and a very small one it is under the temple. Whether it was large of old and has been reduced to its present size in course of time, I know not, but what I saw is undoubtedly small. In memory of this legend they perform the following ceremony; twice a year water is brought from the sea to the temple. It is brought not by the priests only, but by all Syria and Arabia, ay and from beyond the Euphrates many men go to the sea, and all of them bring water. The water is poured into the chasm, and though the chasm is small yet it receives a mighty deal of water. In doing this they say that they comply with the custom which Deucalion instituted in the sanctuary for a memorial at once of calamity and of mercy."[16]

In this late Greek version of the deluge legend the resemblances to the Babylonian version are sufficiently close; and a still nearer trait is supplied by Plutarch, who says that Deucalion let loose a dove from the ark in order to judge by its return or its flight whether the storm still continued or had abated.[17] In this form the Greek legend of the great flood was unquestionably coloured, if not moulded, by Semitic influence, whether the colours and the forms were imported from Israel or from Babylon.

But Hierapolis on the Euphrates was not the only place in Western Asia which Greek tradition associated with the deluge of Deucalion. There was, we are told, a certain Nannakos, king of Phrygia, who lived before the time of Deucalion, and, foreseeing the coming catastrophe, gathered his people into the sanctuaries, there to weep and pray. Hence "the age of Nannakos" became a proverbial expression for great antiquity or loud lamentations.[18] When the deluge had swept away the whole race of mankind, and the earth had dried up again, Zeus commanded Prometheus and Athena to fashion images of mud, and then summoning the winds he bade them breathe into the mud images and make them live. So the place was called Iconium after the images (*eikones*) which were made there.[19]

Though the deluge associated with the name of Deucalion was the most familiar and famous, it was not the only one recorded by Greek tradition. Learned men, indeed, distinguished three such great catastrophes. The first, we are told, took place in the time of Ogyges, the second in the time of Deucalion, and the third in the time of Dardanos.[20] Ogyges (or Ogygos), is said to have founded and reigned over Thebes in Boeotia,[21] which, according to the learned Varro, was the oldest city in Greece, having been built in ante-diluvian times before the earliest of all the floods.[22] So great was the devastation wrought in Attica by the flood that the country remained without kings from the time of Ogyges down to the reign of Cecrops.[23] If we may trust the description of a rhetorical poet, the whole earth was submerged by the deluge, even the lofty peaks of Thessaly were covered, and the snowy top of Parnassus itself was lashed by the snowy billows.[24]

If Ogyges was originally, as seems probable, a Boeotian rather than an Attic hero, the story of the deluge in his time may well have been suggested by the vicissitudes of the Copaic Lake which formerly occupied a large part of Central Boeotia.[25] For, having no outlet above ground, the lake depended for its drainage entirely on subterranean passages or chasms which the water had hollowed out for itself in the course of ages through the limestone rock, and according as these passages were clogged or cleared the level of the lake rose or fell. In no lake, perhaps, have the annual changes been more regular and marked than in the Copaic; for while in winter it was a reedy mere, the haunt of thousands of wild fowl, in summer it was a more or less marshy plain, where cattle browsed and crops were sown and reaped. So well recognized were the vicissitudes of the seasons that places on the bank of the lake such as Orchomenus, Lebadea, and Copae, had summer roads and winter roads by which they communicated with each other, the winter roads following the sides of the hills, while the summer roads struck across the plain. With the setting in of the heavy autumnal rains in November the lake began to rise and reached its greatest depth in February or March, by which time the mouths of the emissories were completely submerged and betrayed their existence only by swirls on the surface of the mere. Yet even then the lake presented to the eye anything but an unbroken sheet of water. Viewed from a height, such as the acropolis of Orchomenus, it appeared as an immense fen, of a vivid green colour, stretching away for miles and miles, overgrown with sedge, reeds, and canes, through which the river Cephisus or Melas might be seen sluggishly oozing, while here and there a gleam of sunlit water, especially towards the north-east corner of the mere, directed the eye to what looked like ponds in the vast green swamp. Bare grey mountains on the north and east, and the beautiful wooded slopes of Helicon on the south, bounded the fen. In spring the water began to sink. Isolated brown patches, where no reeds grew, were the first to show as islands in the mere; and as the season advanced they expanded more and more till they met. By the middle of summer great stretches, especially in the middle and at the edges, were bare. In the higher parts the fat alluvial soil left by the retiring waters was sown by the peasants and produced crops of corn, rice, and cotton; while the lower parts, overgrown by rank grass and weeds, were grazed by herds of cattle and swine. In the deepest places of all, the water often stagnated the whole summer, though there were years when it retreated even from these, leaving behind it only a bog or perhaps a stretch of white clayey soil, perfectly dry, which the summer heat seamed with a network of minute cracks and fissures. By the end of August the greater part of the basin was generally dry, though the water did not reach its lowest point till October. At that time what had lately been a fen was only a great brown expanse, broken here and there by a patch of green marsh, where reeds and other water-plants grew. In November the lake began to fill again fast.

Such was the ordinary annual cycle of changes in the Copaic Lake in modern times, and we have no reason to suppose that it was essentially different in antiquity. But at all times the water of the lake has been liable to be raised above or depressed below its customary level by unusually heavy or scanty rainfall in winter or by the accidental clogging or opening of the chasms. As we read in ancient authors of drowned cities on the margin of the lake, so a modern traveller tells of villagers forced to flee before the rising flood, and of vineyards and corn-fields seen under water.[26] One such inundation, more extensive and destructive than any of its predecessors, may have been associated ever after with the name of Ogyges.

The theory which would explain the great flood of Ogyges by an extraordinary inundation of the Copaic Lake, is to some extent supported by an Arcadian parallel. We have seen that in Greek legend the third great deluge was associated with the name of Dardanos. Now according to one account, Dardanos at first reigned as a king in Arcadia, but was driven out of the country by a great flood, which submerged the lowlands and rendered them for a long time unfit for cultivation. The inhabitants retreated to the mountains, and for a while made shift to live as best they might on such food as they could procure; but at last, concluding that the land left by the water was not sufficient to support them all, they resolved to part; some of them remained in the country with Dimas, son of Dardanos, for their king; while the rest emigrated under the leadership of Dardanos himself to the island of Samothrace.[27] According to a Greek tradition, which the Roman Varro accepted, the birthplace of Dardanos was Pheneus in north Arcadia.[28] The place is highly significant, for, if we except the Copaic area, no valley in Greece is known to have been from antiquity subject to inundations on so vast a scale and for such long periods as the valley of Pheneus. The natural conditions in the two regions are substantially alike. Both are basins in a limestone country without any outflow above ground: both receive the rain water which pours into them from the surrounding mountains: both are drained by subterranean channels which the water has worn or which earthquakes have opened through the rock; and whenever these outlets are silted up or otherwise closed, what at other times is a plain becomes converted for the time being into a lake. But with these substantial resemblances are combined some striking differences between the two landscapes. For while the Copaic basin is a vast stretch of level ground little above sea-level and bounded only by low cliffs or gentle slopes, the basin of Pheneus is a narrow upland valley closely shut in on every side by steep frowning mountains, their upper slopes clothed with dark pine woods and their lofty summits capped with snow for many months of the year. The river which drains the basin through an underground channel is the Ladon, the most romantically beautiful of all the rivers of Greece. When I was at the springs of the Ladon in 1895, I learned from a peasant on the spot that three years before, after a violent shock of earthquake, the water ceased to run for three hours, the chasm at the bottom of the pool was exposed, and fish were seen lying on the dry ground. After three hours the spring began to flow a little, and three days later there was a loud explosion, and the water burst forth in immense volume. Similar stoppages of the river have been reported both in ancient and modern times; and whenever the obstruction has been permanent, the valley of Pheneus has been occupied by a lake varying in extent and depth with the more or less complete stoppage of the subterranean outlet. According to Pliny there had been down to his day five changes in the condition of the valley from wet to dry and from dry to wet, all of them caused by earthquakes.[29] In Plutarch's time the flood rose so high that the whole valley was under water, which pious folk attributed to the somewhat belated wrath of Apollo at Hercules, who had stolen the god's prophetic tripod from Delphi and carried it off to Pheneus about a thousand years before.[30] However, later in the same century the waters had again subsided, for the Greek traveller Pausanias found the bottom of the valley to be dry land, and knew of the former existence of the lake only by tradition.[31] At the beginning of the nineteenth century the basin was a swampy plain, for the most part covered with fields of wheat or barley. But shortly after the expulsion of the Turks, through neglect of the precautions which the Turkish governor had taken to keep the mouth of the subterranean outlet open, the channel became blocked, the water, no longer able to escape, rose in its bed, and by 1830 it formed a deep lake about five miles long by five miles wide. And a broad lake of greenish-blue water it still was when I saw it in the autumn of 1895, with the pine-clad mountains descending steeply in rocky declivities or sheer precipices to the water's edge, except for a stretch of level ground on the north, where the luxuriant green of vineyards and maize-fields contrasted pleasingly with the blue of the lake and the sombre green of the pines. A few years later and the scene was changed. Looking down into the valley from a pass on a July afternoon, a more recent traveller beheld, instead of an expanse of sea-blue water, a blaze of golden corn with here and there a white point of light showing where a fustanella'd reaper was at his peaceful toil. The lake had disappeared, perhaps for ever; for we are told that measures have now been taken to keep the subterranean outlets permanently open, and so to preserve for the corn the ground which has been won from the water.[32]

In a valley which has thus suffered so many alternations between wet and dry, between a broad lake of sea-blue water and broad acres of yellow corn, the traditions of great floods cannot be lightly dismissed; on the contrary everything combines to confirm their probability. The story, therefore, that Dardanos, a native of Pheneus, was compelled to emigrate by a great inundation which swamped the lowlands, drowned the fields, and drove the inhabitants to the upper slopes of the mountains, may well rest on a solid foundation of fact. And the same may be true of the flood recorded by Pausanias, which rose and submerged the ancient city of Pheneus at the northern end of the lake.[33]

From his home in the highlands of Arcadia, the emigrant Dardanos is said to have made his way to the island of Samothrace.[34] According to one account, he floated thither on a raft;[35] but according to another version of the legend, the great flood overtook him, not in Arcadia, but in Samothrace, and he escaped on an inflated skin, drifting on the face of the waters till he landed on Mount Ida, where he founded Dardania or Troy.[36] Certainly, the natives of Samothrace, who were great sticklers for their antiquity, claimed to have had a deluge of their own before any other nation on earth. They said that the sea rose and covered a great part of the flat land in their island, and that the survivors retreated to the lofty mountains which still render Samothrace one of the most conspicuous features in the northern Aegean and are plainly visible in clear weather from Troy.[37] As the sea still pursued them in their retreat, they prayed to the gods to deliver them, and on being saved they set up landmarks of their salvation all round the island and built altars on which they continued to sacrifice down to later ages. And many centuries after the great flood fishermen still occasionally drew up in their nets the stone capitals of columns, which told of cities drowned in the depths of the sea. The causes which the Samothracians alleged for the inundation were very remarkable. The catastrophe happened, according to them, not through a heavy fall of rain, but through a sudden and extraordinary rising of the sea occasioned by the bursting of the barriers which till then had divided the Black Sea from the Mediterranean. At that time the enormous volume of water dammed up behind these barriers broke bounds, and cleaving for itself a passage through the opposing land created the straits which are now known as the Bosphorus and the Dardanelles, through which the waters of the Black Sea have ever since flowed into the Mediterranean. When the tremendous torrent first rushed through the new opening in the dam, it washed over a great part of the coast of Asia, as well as the flat lands of Samothrace.[38]

With the ancient Greek tradition of a great inundation, consequent on the sudden opening of the Bosphorus and the Dardanelles, we may compare a modern Turkish tradition, which has been recorded at Constantinople.

The Turks say that Iskender-Iulcarni, by whom they mean Alexander the Great, lived before Moses and conquered both the East and the West. In the course of his conquests he sent to demand tribute from Katifé, Queen of Smyrna, whose ruined castle bears her name (*Katifé-Calessi*) to this day. But the queen not only refused the demand but threatened, in very insulting language, to drown the king if he persisted in pressing it. Enraged at her reply, the conqueror resolved to punish the queen for her insolence by drowning her in a great flood. "I will open the Bosphorus," said he, "and make of it a strait." For that purpose he employed both Moslem and infidel workmen, from which we gather that, according to popular Turkish tradition, Mohammed must have lived, not only before Alexander the Great, but even before Moses. Calmly overlooking this slight chronological difficulty, the story proceeds to relate that the infidel workmen received only one-fifth of the pay

which rewarded the exertions of the true belivrs. So th canal was in process
of excavation. But when it was nearly completed, Iskender, for some unexplained reason, reversed the proportions of the pay, giving the true believers
only one-fifth of what he paid to the infidels. Consequently, the Moslems
withdrew in disgust, and the heathen were left alone to finish the canal. The
strait of Bosphorus was about to be opened, when the current of the Black
Sea swept away the frail remaining dyke and drowned the infidels who were at
work in the great trench. The inundation spread over Bithynia, the kingdom
of which Smyrna was the capital, and several cities of Africa. Queen Katifé
perished in the waters. The whole world would soon have been engulfed, if
ambassadors from every land had not implored Iskender-Iulcarni to save
mankind from the threatened catastrophe. So he commanded to pierce the
Strait of Gibraltar in order to let the water of the Mediterranean escape into
the ocean. When that new canal was opened, the drowned cities of Asia Minor
reappeared from the bed of the sea.

Ever since that flood a town of Asia Minor, situated some way inland from
Smyrna, has been known in the Turkish tongue by the name of Denizli, which
signifies "City on the Sea." But the towns of Africa remained beneath the
waves. To this day, on the coast of Africa, you can see the ruins of the cities
under water. The Black Sea used to cover the greater part of Mount Caucasus.
After the piercing of the Bosphorus the isthmus of the Crimea appeared. All
along the Asiatic coast of the Black Sea, to a distance of three hours from the
shore, you may find at a considerable height the places where ships used to be
moored.[39]

[The Greeks also entertained the idea that floods were divine visitations
upon human wickedness. In a vivid passage of the Iliad, Homer describes how,
when Zeus is angry with men for perverting justice, the whole earth becomes
embroiled in violent storm, the rivers rush in full spate, the streams pour
wildly from the mountains.[39a]] ▼

▲ 36 Europe

Apart from the ancient Greek stories of a great flood, it is remarkable that
very few popular traditions of a universal or widespread deluge have been
recorded in Europe. An Icelandic version of the tradition occurs in the
Younger Edda, the great collection of ancient Norse myths and legends which
was put together by Snorri Sturluson about 1222 A.D. We there read how the
god Bor had three divine sons, Odin, Wili, and We, and how these sons slew
the giant Ymir. From the wounds of the dying giant there gushed such a
stream of blood that it drowned all the other giants except one, named Bergel-
mir, who escaped with his wife in a boat, and from whom the later race of
giants is descended.[1]

A Welsh legend of the deluge runs thus. Once upon a time the lake of
Llion burst and flooded all lands, so that the whole human race was drowned,

all except Dwyfan and Dwyfach, who escaped in a mastless ship and re-peopled the land of Prydain (Britain). The ship also contained a male and female of every sort of living creature, so that after the deluge the animals were able to propagate their various kinds and restock the world.[2]

A Lithuanian story of a great flood is also reported. One day it chanced that the supreme god Pramzimas was looking out of a window of his heavenly house, and surveying the world from this coign of vantage he could see nothing but war and injustice among mankind. The sight so vexed his righteous soul that he sent two giants, Wandu and Wejas, down to the sinful earth to destroy it. Now the two giants were no other than Water and Wind, and they laid about them with such hearty good will, that after twenty nights and twenty days there was very little of the world left standing. The deity now looked out of the window again to see how things were progressing, and, as good luck would have it, he was eating nuts at the time. As he did so, he threw down the shells, and one of them happened to fall on the top of the highest moun-tain, where animals and a few pairs of human beings had sought refuge from the flood. The nutshell came, in the truest sense of the word, as a godsend; everybody clambered into it, and floated about on the surface of the far-spread-ing inundation. At this critical juncture the deity looked out of the window for the third time, and, his wrath being now abated, he gave orders for the wind to fall and the water to subside. So the remnant of mankind were saved, and they dispersed over the earth. Only a single couple remained on the spot, and from them the Lithuanians are descended. But they were old and naturally a good deal put out by their recent experience; so to comfort them God sent the rainbow, which advised them to jump over the bones of the earth nine times. The aged couple did as they were bid; nine times they jumped, and nine other couples sprang up in consequence, the ancestors of the nine Lithuanian tribes.[3]

A story of a great flood has also been recorded among the Voguls, a people of the Finnish or Ugrian stock, who inhabit the country both on the east and the west of the Ural Mountains, and who therefore belong both to Asia and Europe.[4] The story runs thus. After seven years of drought the Great Woman said to the Great Man, "It has rained elsewhere. How shall we save our-selves? The other giants are gathered in a village to take counsel. What shall we do?" The Great Man answered, "Let us cut a poplar in two, hollow it out, and make two boats. Then we shall weave a rope of willow roots five hundred fathoms long. We shall bury one end of it in the earth and fasten the other to the bow of our boats. Let every man with children embark in the boat with his family, and let them be covered in with a tarpaulin of cowhide, let victuals be made ready for seven days and seven nights and put under the tarpaulin. And let us place pots of melted butter in each boat." Having thus provided for their own safety, the two giants ran about the villages, urging the inhabitants to build boats and weave ropes. Some did not know how to set about it, and the giants showed them how it should be done. Others preferred to seek a

place of refuge, but they sought in vain, and the Great Man, to whom they
betook themselves because he was their elder, told them that he knew no place
of refuge large enough to hold them. "See," said he, "the holy water will soon
be on us; for two days we have heard the rumble of its waves. Let us embark
without delay." The earth was soon submerged, and the people who had not
built boats perished in the hot water. The same fate befell the owners of boats
whose ropes were too short, and likewise those who had not provided themselves with liquid butter wherewith to grease the rope as it ran out over the
gunwale. On the seventh day the water began to sink, and soon the survivors
set foot on dry ground. But there were neither trees nor plants on the face of
the earth; the animals had perished; even the fish had disappeared. The survivors were on the point of dying of hunger, when they prayed to the great
god Numi-târom to create anew fish, animals, trees, and plants, and their
prayer was heard.[5] ▼

▲ 37   India

No legend of a great flood is to be found in the Vedic hymns, the most
ancient literary monuments of India, which appear to have been composed at
various dates between 1500 and 1000 B.C., while the Aryans were still settled
in the Punjab and had not yet spread eastward into the valley of the Ganges.
But in the later Sanskrit literature a well-marked story of a deluge repeatedly
occurs in forms which combine a general resemblance with some variations
of detail. The first record of it meets us in the *Satapatha Brahmana,* an important prose treatise on sacred ritual, which is believed to have been written
not long before the rise of Buddhism, and therefore not later than the sixth
century B.C., at a time when the Aryans occupied the upper valley of the
Ganges as well as the valley of the Indus. As related in the *Satapatha
Brahmana,* the story runs as follows:[1]

"In the morning they brought to Manu water for washing, just as now also
they are wont to bring water for washing the hands. When he was washing
himself, a fish came into his hands. It spake to him the word, 'Rear me, I will
save thee!' 'Wherefrom wilt thou save me?' 'A flood will carry away all these
creatures: from that I will save thee!' 'How am I to rear thee?' It said, 'As
long as we are small, there is great destruction for us: fish devours fish. Thou
wilt first keep me in a jar. When I outgrow that, thou wilt dig a pit and keep
me in it. When I outgrow that, thou wilt take me down to the sea, for then I
shall be beyond destruction.' It soon became a *ghasha* (a large fish); for that
grows largest of all fish. Thereupon it said, 'In such and such a year that flood
will come. Thou shalt then attend to me by preparing a ship; and when the
flood has risen thou shalt enter into the ship, and I will save thee from it.'
After he had reared it in this way, he took it down to the sea. And in the
same year which the fish had indicated to him, he attended to the advice of
the fish by preparing a ship, and when the flood had risen, he entered into the

ship. The fish then swam up to him, and to its horn he tied the rope of the ship, and by that means he passed swiftly up to yonder northern mountain. It then said, 'I have saved thee. Fasten the ship to a tree; but let not the water cut thee off, whilst thou art on the mountain. As the water subsides, thou mayest gradually descend!' Accordingly he gradually descended, and hence that slope of the northern mountain is called 'Manu's descent.' The flood then swept away all these creatures, and Manu alone remained here.

"Being desirous of offspring, he engaged in worshipping and austerities. During this time he also performed a *pâka*-sacrifice: he offered up in the waters clarified butter, sour milk, whey, and curds. Thence a woman was produced in a year: becoming quite solid she rose; clarified butter gathered in her footprint. Mitra and Varuna met her. They said to her, 'Who art thou?' 'Manu's daughter,' she replied. 'Say thou art ours,' they said. 'No,' she said, 'I am the daughter of him who begat me.' They desired to have a share in her. She either agreed or did not agree, but passed by them. She came to Manu. Manu said to her, 'Who art thou?' 'Thy daughter,' she replied. 'How, illustrious one, art thou my daughter?' he asked. She replied, 'Those offerings of clarified butter, sour milk, whey, and curds, which thou madest in the waters, with them thou hast begotten me. I am the blessing: make use of me at the sacrifice! If thou wilt make use of me at the sacrifice, thou wilt become rich in offspring and cattle. Whatever blessing thou shalt invoke through me, all that shall be granted to thee!' He accordingly made use of her as the benediction in the middle of the sacrifice; for what is intermediate between the fore-offerings and the after-offerings, is the middle of the sacrifice. With her he went on worshipping and performing austerities, wishing for offspring. Through her he generated this race, which is this race of Manu; and whatever blessing he invoked through her, all that was granted to him."[2]

Stories of a primeval flood obtain also in modern Indian folklore. The Bhils, a wild jungle tribe of Central India, relate that once upon a time a pious man (*dhobi*), who used to wash his clothes in a river, was warned by a fish of the approach of a great deluge. The fish informed him that out of gratitude for his humanity in always feeding the fish, he had come to give him this warning, and to urge him to prepare a large box in which he might escape. The pious man accordingly made ready the box and embarked in it with his sister and a cock. After the deluge Rama sent out his messenger to inquire into the state of affairs. The messenger heard the crowing of the cock and so discovered the box. Thereupon Rama had the box brought before him, and asked the man who he was and how he had escaped. The man told his tale. Then Rama made him face in turn north, east, and west, and swear that the woman with him was his sister. The man stuck to it that she was indeed his sister. Rama next turned him to the south, whereupon the man contradicted his former statement and said that the woman was his wife. After that, Rama inquired of him who it was that told him to escape, and on learning that it was the fish, he at once caused the fish's tongue to be cut out for his pains; so that sort of fish has been tongueless ever since. Having executed this judgment on the fish for blabbing, Rama ordered the man to repeople the devastated world. Accordingly, the man married his sister and had by her seven sons and seven daughters.[3]

In this story the warning of the coming flood given by the fish to its human benefactor resembles the corresponding incident in the Sanskrit story of the flood too closely to be independent. It may be questioned whether the Bhils borrowed the story from the Aryan invaders or whether on the contrary the Aryans may not have learned it from the aborigines whom they encountered in their progress through the country. In favor of the latter view it may be pointed out that the story of the flood does not occur in the most ancient Sanskrit literature, but only appears in books written long after the settlement of the Aryans in India.

The Kamars, a small Dravidian tribe of the Raipur District and adjoining States, in the Central Provinces of India, tell the following story of a great flood. They say that in the beginning God created a man and woman, to whom in their old age were born two children, a boy and a girl. But God sent a deluge over the world in order to drown a jackal which had angered him. The old couple heard of the coming deluge, so they shut up their children in a hollow piece of wood with provision to last them till the flood should subside. Then they closed up the trunk, and the deluge came and lasted for twelve years. The old couple and all other living things on earth were drowned, but the trunk floated on the face of the waters. After twelve years God created two birds and sent them to see whether his enemy the jackal had been drowned. The birds flew over all the corners of the world, and they saw nothing but a log of wood floating on the surface of the water. They perched on it, and soon heard low and feeble voices coming from inside the log. It was the children saying to each other that they had only provisions for three days left. So the birds flew away and told God, who then caused the flood to subside, and taking out the children from the log of wood he heard their story. Thereupon he brought them up, and in due time they were married, and God gave the name of a different caste to every child who was born to them, and from them all the inhabitants of the world are descended.[4]

The Hós or Larka Kols, an aboriginal race who inhabit Singbhum, in south-western Bengal, say that after the world was first peopled mankind grew incestuous and paid no heed either to God or to their betters. So Sirma Thakoor, or Sing Bonga, the Creator, resolved to destroy them all, and he carried out his intention, some say by water, others say by fire. However, he spared sixteen people, and from them presumably the present race of mortals is descended.[5]

The Lepchas of Sikkim have a tradition of a great flood during which a couple escaped to the top of a mountain called Tendong, near Darjeeling.[6]

According to a native legend, Tibet was long ago almost totally inundated,

untii a deity of the name of Gya, whose chief temple is at Durgeedin, took
compassion on the survivors, drew off the waters through Bengal, and sent
teachers to civilize the wretched inhabitants, who were destined to repeople
the land, and who up to that time had been very little better than monkeys.[7]—
The Singphos of Assam relate that once upon a time mankind was destroyed
by a flood because they omitted to offer the proper sacrifices at the slaughter
of buffaloes and pigs. Only two men, Khun litang and Chu liyang, with their
wives, were saved, and being appointed by the gods to dwell on Singrabhum
hill, they became the progenitors of the present human race.[8]—The Lushais
of Assam have a legend that the king of the water demons fell in love with a
woman named Ngai-ti (Loved One), but she rejected his addresses and ran
away; so he pursued her, and surrounded the whole human race with water
on the top of a hill called Phun-lu-buk, which is said to be far away to the
north-east. As the water continued to rise, the people took Ngai-ti and threw
her into the flood, which thereupon receded. In flowing away, the water hollowed out the deep valleys and left standing the high mountains which we see
to this day; for down to the time of the great flood the earth had been level.[9]
Again, the Anals of Assam say that once upon a time the whole world was
flooded. All the people were drowned except one man and one woman, who
ran to the highest peak of the Leng hill, where they climbed up a high tree and
hid themselves among the branches. The tree grew near a large pond, which
was as clear as the eye of a crow. They spent the night perched on the tree,
and in the morning, what was their astonishment to find that they had been
changed into a tiger and a tigress! Seeing the sad plight of the world, the
Creator, whose name is Pathian, sent a man and a woman from a cave on a
hill to repeople the drowned world. But on emerging from the cave, the
couple were terrified at the sight of the huge tiger and tigress, and they said
to the Creator, "O Father, you have sent us to repeople the world, but we do
not think that we shall be able to carry out your intention, as the whole world
is under water, and the only spot on which we could make a place of rest is
occupied by two ferocious beasts, which are waiting to devour us; give us
strength to slay these animals." After that, they killed the tigers, and lived
happily, and begat many sons and daughters, and from them the drowned
world was repeopled.[10] ▼

▲ 38 Eastern Asia

The Chingpaws (or Singphos) of Upper Burma, like their brethren in
Assam, have a tradition of a great flood. They say that when the deluge came,
a man Pawpaw Nan-chaung and his sister Chang-hko saved themselves in a
large boat. They had with them nine cocks and nine needles. After some days
of rain and storm they threw overboard one cock and one needle to see whether
the waters were falling. But the cock did not crow and the needle was not
heard to strike bottom. They did the same thing day after day, but with no

better result, till at last on the ninth day the last cock crew and the last needle was heard to strike on a rock. Soon after the brother and sister were able to leave their boat, and they wandered about till they came to a cave inhabited by two elves or fairies (*nats*), a male and a female. The elves bade them stay and make themselves useful in clearing the jungle, tilling the ground, hewing wood, and drawing water. The brother and sister did so, and soon after the sister gave birth to a child. While the parents were away at work, the old elfin woman, who was a witch, used to mind the baby; and whenever the infant squalled, the horrid wretch would threaten, if it did not stop bawling, to make mince meat of it at a place where nine roads met. The poor child did not understand the dreadful threat and persisted in giving tongue, till one day the old witch in a fury snatched it up, hurried it to the meeting-place of nine roads, and there hewed it in pieces, and sprinkled the blood and strewed the bits all over the roads and the country round about. But some of the titbits she carried back to her cave and made into a savoury curry. Moreover, she put a block of wood into the baby's empty cradle. And when the mother came back from her work in the evening and asked for her child, the witch said, "It is asleep. Eat your rice." So the mother ate the rice and curry, and then went to the cradle, but in it she found nothing but a block of wood. When she asked the witch where the child was, the witch replied tartly, "You have eaten it." The poor mother fled from the house, and at the crossroads she wailed aloud and cried to the Great Spirit to give her back her child or avenge its death. The Great Spirit appeared to her and said, "I cannot piece your baby together again, but instead I will make you the mother of all nations of men." And then from one road there sprang up the Shans, from another the Chinese, from others the Burmese, and the Bengalees, and all the races of mankind; and the bereaved mother claimed them all as her children, because they all sprang from the scattered fragments of her murdered babe.[1]

The Bahnars, a primitive tribe of Cochin China, tell how once on a time the kite quarrelled with the crab, and pecked the crab's skull so hard that he made a hole in it, which may be seen down to this very day. To avenge this injury to his skull, the crab caused the sea and the rivers to swell till the waters reached the sky, and all living beings perished except two, a brother and a sister, who were saved in a huge chest. They took with them into the chest a pair of every sort of animal, shut the lid tight, and floated on the waters for seven days and seven nights. Then the brother heard a cock crowing outside, for the bird had been sent by the spirits to let our ancestors know that the flood had abated, and that they could come forth from the chest. So the brother let all the birds fly away, then he let loose the animals, and last of all he and his sister walked out on the dry land. They did not know how they were to live, for they had eaten up all the rice that was stored in the chest. However, a black ant brought them two grains of rice: the brother planted them, and next morning the plain was covered with a rich crop. So the brother and sister were saved.[2]

A legend of a deluge recorded by a French missionary among the Bannavs, one of the savage tribes which inhabit the mountains and tablelands between Cochin China, Laos, and Cambodia, relates that the father of the human race was saved from an immense inundation by means of a large chest in which he shut himself up; but of the origin or creator of this father they know nothing.[3] The tradition is probably only an abridged form of the deluge legend which, as we have just seen, is recorded by another French missionary among the Bahnars, who may be supposed to be the same with the Bannavs.

The Benua-Jakun, a primitive aboriginal tribe of the Malay Peninsula, in the State of Johore, say that the ground on which we stand is not solid, but is merely a skin covering an abyss of water. In ancient times Pirman, that is the deity, broke up this skin, so that the world was drowned and destroyed by a great flood. However, Pirman had created a man and a woman and put them in a ship of *pulai* wood, which was completely covered over and had no opening. In this ship the pair floated and tossed about for a time, till at last the vessel came to rest, and the man and woman, nibbling their way through its side, emerged on dry ground and beheld this our world stretching away on all sides to the horizon. At first all was very dark, for there was neither morning nor evening, because the sun had not yet been created. When it grew light, they saw seven small shrubs of rhododendron and seven clumps of the grass called *sambau*. They said one to another, "Alas, in what a sad plight are we, without either children or grandchildren!" But some time afterwards the woman conceived in the calves of her legs, and from her right calf came forth a male, and from her left calf came forth a female. That is why the offspring of the same womb may not marry. All mankind are the descendants of the two children of the first pair.[4]

In Kelantan, a district of the Malay Peninsula, they say that one day a feast was made for a circumcision, and all manner of beasts were pitted to fight against one another. There were fights between elephants, and fights between buffaloes, and fights between bullocks, and fights between goats; and at last there were fights between dogs and cats. And when the fights took place between dogs and cats, a great flood came down from the mountains, and overwhelmed the people that dwelt in the plains. And they were all drowned in that flood, save only some two or three menials who had been sent up into the hills to gather firewood. Then the sun, moon, and stars were extinguished, and there was a great darkness. And when light returned, there was no land but a great sea, and all the abodes of men had been overwhelmed.[5]

The legend of a great flood plays an important part in the traditionary lore of the Lolos, an aboriginal race who occupy the almost impregnable mountain fastnesses of Yunnan and other provinces of South-Western China, where they have succeeded in maintaining their independence against the encroachments of the Chinese. In primeval times, runs the story, men were wicked, and Tse-gu-dzih, a legendary patriarch who enjoys many of the attributes of divinity, sent down a messenger to them on earth, asking for some flesh and blood from a mortal. No one would give them except only one man, Du-mu by name. So Tse-gu-dzih in wrath locked the rain-gates, and the waters mounted to the sky. But Du-mu, who complied with the divine injunction, was saved, together with his four sons, in a log hollowed out of a *Pieris* tree; and with them in the log were likewise saved otters, wild ducks and lampreys. From his four sons are descended the civilized peoples who can write, such as the Chinese and the Lolos, whereas the ignorant races of the world are the descendants of the wooden figures whom Du-mu constructed after the deluge in order to repeople the drowned earth.[6]

The Kamchadales have a tradition of a great flood which covered the whole land in the early days of the world. A remnant of the people saved themselves on large rafts made of tree-trunks bound together; on these they loaded their property and provisions, and on these they drifted about, dropping stones tied to straps instead of anchors in order to prevent the flood from sweeping them away out to sea. When at last the water of the deluge sank, it left the people and their rafts stranded high and dry on the tops of the mountains.[7] ▼

▲ 39   Indonesia

The Bataks of Sumatra relate that, when the earth grew old and dirty, the Creator, whom they call Debata, sent a great flood to destroy every living thing. The last human pair had taken refuge on the top of the highest mountain, and the waters of the deluge had already reached to their knees, when the Lord of All repented of his resolution to make an end of mankind. So he took a clod of earth, kneaded it into shape, tied it to a thread, and laid it on the rising flood, and the last pair stepped on it and were saved. As the descendants of the couple multiplied, the clod increased in size till it became the earth which we all inhabit at this day.[1]

The natives of Nias, an island to the west of Sumatra, say that in days of old there was strife between the mountains of their country as to which of them was the highest. The strife vexed their great ancestor Balugu Luome-wona, and in his vexation he went to the window and said, "Ye mountains, I will cover you all!" So he took a golden comb and threw it into the sea, and it became a huge crab, which stopped up the sluices whereby the waters of the sea usually run away. The consequences of the stoppage were disastrous. The ocean rose higher and higher till only the tops of two or three mountains in Nias still stood above the heaving billows. All the people who with their cattle had escaped to these mountains were saved, and all the rest were drowned.[2]

The natives of Engano, another island to the west of Sumatra, have also their story of a great flood. Once on a time, they say, the tide rose so high that it overflowed the island and every living being was drowned, except one woman. She owed her preservation to the fortunate circumstance that, as she drifted along on the tide, her hair caught in a thorny tree, to which she was thus enabled to cling. When the flood sank, she came down from the tree, and saw with sorrow that she was left all alone in the world. Beginning to feel the pangs of hunger, she wandered inland in the search for food, but finding nothing to eat, she returned disconsolately to the beach, where she hoped to catch a fish. A fish, indeed, she saw; but when she tried to catch it, the creature glided into one of the corpses that were floating on the water or weltering on the shore. Not to be balked, the woman picked up a stone and struck the corpse a smart blow therewith. But the fish leaped from its hiding-place and made off in the direction of the interior. The woman followed, but hardly had she taken a few steps when, to her great surprise, she met a living man. When she asked him what he did there, seeing that she herself was the sole survivor of the flood, he answered that somebody had knocked on his dead body, and that in consequence he had returned to life. The woman now related to him her experiences, and together they resolved to try whether they could not restore all the other dead to life in like manner by knocking on their corpses with stones. No sooner said than done. The drowned men and women revived under the knocks, and thus was the island repeopled after the great flood.[3]

The Ibans or Sea Dyaks of Sarawak, in Borneo, are fond of telling a story which relates how the present race of men survived a great deluge, and how their ancestress discovered the art of making fire. The story runs thus. Once upon a time some Dyak women went to gather young bamboo shoots for food. Having got them, they walked through the jungle till they came to what they took to be a great fallen tree. So they sat down on it and began to pare the bamboo shoots, when to their astonishment the trunk of the tree exuded drops of blood at every cut of their knives. Just then up came some men, who saw at once that what the women were sitting on was not a tree but a gigantic boa-constrictor in a state of torpor. They soon killed the serpent, cut it up, and carried the flesh home to eat. While they were busy frying the pieces, strange noises were heard to issue from the frying-pan, and a torrential rain began to fall and never ceased falling till all the hills, except the highest, were submerged and the world was drowned, all because these wicked men had killed and fried the serpent. Men and animals all perished in the flood, except one woman, a dog, a rat, and a few small creatures, who fled to the top of a very high mountain. There, seeking shelter from the pouring rain, the woman noticed that the dog had found a warm place under a creeper; for the creeper was swaying to and fro in the wind and was warmed by rubbing against the trunk of the tree. She took the hint, and rubbing the creeper hard against a piece of wood she produced fire for the first time. That is how the art of making fire by means of the fire-drill was discovered after the great flood. Having no husband the woman took the fire-drill for her mate, and by its help she gave birth to a son called Simpang-impang, who, as his name implies, was but half a man, since he had only one arm, one leg, one eye, one ear, one cheek, half a body, and half a nose. These natural defects gave great offence to his playmates the animals, and at last he was able to supply them by striking a bargain with the Spirit of the Wind, who had carried off some rice which Simpang-impang had spread out to dry. At first, when Simpang-impang demanded compensation for this injury, the Spirit of the Wind flatly refused to pay him a farthing; but being vanquished in a series of contests with Simpang-impang, he finally consented, instead of paying him in gongs or other valuables, of which indeed he had none, to make a whole man of him by supplying him with the missing parts and members. Simpang-impang gladly accepted the proposal, and that is why mankind have been provided with the usual number of arms and legs ever since.[4]

Another Dyak version of the story relates how, when the flood began, a certain man called Trow made a boat out of a large wooden mortar, which had hitherto served for pounding rice. In this vessel he embarked with his wife, a dog, a pig, a fowl, a cat, and other live creatures, and so launched out on the deep. The crazy ship outrode the storm, and when the flood had subsided, Trow and his wife and the animals disembarked. How to repeople the earth after the destruction of nearly the entire human race was now the problem which confronted Trow; and in order to grapple with it he had recourse to polygamy, fashioning for himself new wives out of a stone, a log, and anything else that came to hand. So he soon had a large and flourishing family, who learned to till the ground and became the ancestors of various Dyak tribes.[5] The Ot-Danoms, a tribe of Dutch Borneo in the valley of the Barito, tell of a great deluge which drowned many people. Only one mountain peak rose above the water, and the few people who were able to escape to it in boats dwelt on it for three months, till the flood subsided and the dry land appeared once more.[6]

The Bare'e-speaking Toradjas of Central Celebes also tell of a flood which once covered the highest mountains, all but the summit of Mount Wawom Pebato, and in proof of their story they point to the sea-shells which are to be found on the tops of hills two thousand feet and more above the level of the sea. Nobody escaped the flood except a pregnant woman and a pregnant mouse, who saved themselves in a pig's trough and floated about, paddling with a pot-ladle instead of an oar, till the waters sank down and the earth again became habitable. Just then the woman, looking about for rice to sow, spied a sheaf of rice hanging from an uprooted tree, which drifted ashore on the spot where she was standing. With the help of the mouse, who climbed up the tree and brought down the sheaf, she was able to plant rice again. But before she fetched down the sheaf, the mouse stipulated that as a recompense for her services mice should thenceforth have the right to eat up part of the harvest. That is why the mice come every year to fetch the reward of their help from the fields of ripe rice; only they may not strip the fields too bare. As for the woman, she in due time gave birth to a son, whom she took, for want of another, to be her husband. By him she had a son and daughter, who became the ancestors of the present race of mankind.[7]

The Alfoors of Ceram, a large island between Celebes and New Guinea, relate that after a great flood, which overwhelmed the whole world, the mountain Noesake appeared above the sinking tide, its sides clothed with great trees, of which the leaves were shaped like the female organs of generation. Only three persons survived on the top of the mountain, but the sea-eagle brought them tidings that other mountain peaks had emerged from the waters. So the three persons went thither, and by means of the remarkable leaves of the trees they repeopled the world.[8]

The inhabitants of Rotti, a small island to the south-west of Timor, say that in former times the sea flooded the earth, so that all men and animals were drowned and all plants and herbs beaten down to the earth. Not a spot of dry ground was left. Even the high mountains were submerged, only the peak of Lakimola, in Bilba, still rose solitary over the waves. On that mountain a man and his wife and children had taken refuge. After some months the tide still came creeping up and up the mountain, and the man and his family were in great fear, for they thought it would soon reach them. So they prayed the sea to return to his old bed. The sea answered, "I will do so, if you give me an animal whose hairs I cannot count." The man thereupon heaved first a pig, then a goat, then a dog, and then a hen into the flood, but all in vain; the sea could number the hairs of every one of them, and it still came on. At last he threw in a cat: this was too much for the sea, it could not do the sum, and sank abashed accordingly. After that the osprey appeared and sprinkled some dry earth on the waters, and the man and his wife and children descended the mountain to seek a new home. Thereupon the Lord commanded the osprey to bring all kinds of seed to the man, such as maize, millet, rice, beans, pumpkins, and sesame, in order that he might sow them and live with his family on the produce. That is the reason why in Rotti, at the end of harvest, people set up a sheaf of rice on the open place of the village as an offering to Mount Lakimola.[9]

The Nages, in the centre of the East Indian island of Flores say that Dooy, the forefather of their tribe, was saved in a ship from the great flood. His grave is under a stone platform, which occupies the centre of the public square at Boa Wai, the tribal capital. The harvest festival, which is attended not only by the villagers but also by people from far and near, takes place round this grave of their great ancestor. On this occasion the civil chief of the tribe is gorgeously arrayed in golden jewellery, and on his head he wears the golden model of a ship with seven masts in memory of the escape of their great ancestor from the flood.[10]

Stories of a great flood are told also by some of the wild tribes of Mindanao, one of the Philippine Islands. One such tale is said to be current among the Atás of the Davao District, who are supposed to be descendants of an invading people that intermarried with the Negritoes and other aboriginal tribes. The greatest of all the spirits, it is said, is Manama, who made the first men from blades of grass, weaving them together until they assumed the human form. In this manner he created eight persons, male and female, who later became the ancestors of the Atás and all the neighbouring tribes. Long afterwards the water covered the whole earth, and all the Atás were drowned except two men and a woman. The waters carried them far away, and they would have perished if a great eagle had not come to their aid. The bird offered to carry them on its back to their homes. One of the men refused, but the other man and the woman accepted the offer and returned to Mapula.[11]

One of the tribes which inhabit the eastern coast of Formosa are the Ami. They are supposed to have been the last to arrive in this part of the island. These people possess the story of a great flood in several different versions. One of them, recorded at the village of Popkok relates how a brother and sister escaped in a wooden mortar from a destructive deluge, in which almost all living beings perished; how they landed on a high mountain, married, begat offspring, and founded the village of Popkok in a hollow of the hills, where they thought they would be secure against another deluge.[12]

[The Ifugas of Kiangau relate, in similar vein, that a brother and sister named Wigam and Bugan were the only survivors of a primeval flood which swept that area. They found refuge on Mount Amuyas.[12a]]

The primitive inhabitants of the Andaman Islands, in the Bay of Bengal, have a legend of a great flood, which may be related here, though their islands do not strictly belong to the Indian Archipelago. They say that some time after they had been created, men grew disobedient and regardless of the commands which the Creator had given them at their creation. So in anger he sent a great flood which covered the whole land, except perhaps Saddle Peak where the Creator himself resided. All living creatures, both men and animals, perished in the waters, all save two men and two women, who, having the good luck to be in a canoe at the time when the catastrophe occurred, contrived to escape with their lives. When at last the waters sank, the little company landed, but they found themselves in a sad plight, for all other living creatures were drowned. However, the Creator, whose name was Puluga, kindly helped them by creating animals and birds afresh for their use. But the difficulty remained of lighting a fire, for the flood had extinguished the flames on every hearth, and all things were of course very damp. Hereupon the ghost of one of their friends, who had been drowned in the deluge, opportunely came to the rescue. Seeing their distress he flew in the form of a kingfisher to the sky, where he found the Creator seated beside his fire. The bird made a dab at a burning brand, intending to carry it off in his beak to his fireless friends on earth, but in his haste or agitation he dropped it on the august person of the Creator himself, who, incensed at the indignity and smarting with pain, hurled the blazing brand at the bird. It missed the mark and whizzing past him dropped plump from the sky at the very spot where the four people were seated moaning and shivering. That is how mankind recovered the use of fire after the great flood. When they had warmed themselves and had leisure to reflect on what had happened, the four survivors began to murmur at the Creator for his destruction of all the rest of mankind; and their passion getting the better of them they even plotted to murder him. From this impious attempt they were, however, dissuaded by the Creator himself, who told them, in very plain language, that they had better not try, for he was as hard as wood, their arrows could make no impression on him, and if they dared so much as to lay a finger on him, he would have the blood of every mother's son and daughter of them. This dreadful threat had its effect: they submitted to their fate, and the mollified Creator condescended to explain to them, in milder terms, that men had brought the great flood on themselves by wilful disobedience to his commands, and that any repetition of the offence in future would be visited by him with condign punishment. That was the last time that the Creator ever appeared to men and conversed with them face to face; since then the Andaman Islanders have never seen him, but to this day they continue to do his will with fear and trembling.[13] ▼

▲ 40 New Guinea and Melanesia

In the Kabadi district of British New Guinea the natives have a tradition that once a time a certain man Lohero and his younger brother were angry with the people about them, and they put a human bone into a small stream. Soon the great waters came forth, forming a sea, flooding all the low land, and driving the people back to the mountains, till step by step they had to escape to the tops of the highest peaks. There they lived till the sea receded, when some of them descended to the lowlands, while others remained on the ridges and there built houses and formed plantations.[1]

The Valmans of Berlin Harbour, on the northern coast of New Guinea, tell how one day the wife of a very good man saw a great fish swimming to the bank. She called to her husband, but at first he could not see the fish. So his wife laughed at him and hid him behind a banana-tree, that he might peep at it through the leaves. When he did catch sight of it at last, he was horribly afraid, and sending for his family, a son and two daughters, he forbade them to catch and eat the fish. But the other people took bow and arrow and a cord, and they caught the fish and drew it to land. Though the good man warned them not to eat of the fish, they did it notwithstanding. When the good man saw that, he hastily drove a pair of animals of every sort up into the trees, and then he and his family climbed up into a coco-nut tree. Hardly had the wicked men consumed the fish than water burst from the ground with such violence that nobody had time to save himself. Men and animals were all drowned. When the water had mounted to the top of the highest tree, it sank as rapidly as it had risen. Then the good man came down from the tree with his family and laid out new plantations.[2]

The natives of the Mamberao River, in Dutch New Guinea, are reported to tell a story of a great flood, caused by the rising of the river, which overwhelmed Mount Vanessa, and from which only one man and his wife escaped, together with a pig, a cassowary, a kangaroo, and a pigeon. The man and his wife became the ancestors of the present race of men; the beasts and birds became the ancestors of the existing species. The bones of the drowned animals still lie on Mount Vanessa.[3]

The Fijians have a tradition of a great deluge, which they call Walavu-levu: some say that the flood was partial; others that it was universal. The way in which the catastrophe came about was this. The great god Ndengei had a monstrous bird called Turukawa, which used to wake him punctually by its cooing every morning. One day his two grandsons, whether by accident or design, shot the bird dead with their bows and arrows, and buried the carcase in order to conceal the crime. So the deity overslept himself, and being much annoyed at the disappearance of his favourite fowl, he sent out his messenger Uto to look for it everywhere. The search proved fruitless. The messenger reported that not a trace of the bird was to be found. But a second search was more successful, and laid the guilt of the murder at the door of the god's grandsons. To escape the rage of their incensed grandfather the young scapegraces fled to the mountains and there took refuge with a tribe of carpenters, who willingly undertook to build a stockade strong enough to keep Ndengei and all his catchpolls at bay. They were as good as their word, and for three months the god and his minions besieged the fortress in vain. At last, in despair of capturing the stockade by the regular operations of war, the baffled deity disbanded his army and meditated a surer revenge. At his command the dark clouds gathered and burst, pouring torrents of rain on the doomed earth. Towns, hills, and mountains were submerged one after the other; yet for long the rebels, secure in the height of their town, looked down with unconcern on the rising tide of waters. At last when the surges lapped their wooden walls and even washed through their fortress, they called for help to a god, who, according to one account, instructed them to form a float out of the fruit of the shaddock; according to others, he sent two canoes for their use, or taught them how to build a canoe for themselves and thus ensure their own safety. It was Rokoro, the god of carpenters, who with his foreman Rokola came to their rescue. The pair sailed about in two large double canoes, picking up the drowning people and keeping them on board till the flood subsided. Others, however, will have it that the survivors saved themselves in large bowls, in which they floated about. Whatever the minor variations may be in the Fijian legend, all agree that even the highest places were covered by the deluge, and that the remnant of the human race was saved in some kind of vessel, which was at last left high and dry by the receding tide on the island of Mbengha. The number of persons who thus survived the flood was eight. Two tribes were completely destroyed by the waters; one of them consisted entirely of women, the members of the other had tails like those of dogs. Because the survivors of the flood landed on their island, the natives of Mbengha claimed to rank highest of all the Fijians, and their chiefs always acted a conspicuous part in Fijian history: they styled themselves "Subject to heaven alone." It is said that formerly the Fijians always kept great canoes ready for use against another flood, and that the custom was only discontinued in modern times.[4]

The Melanesians of the New Hebrides say that their great legendary hero Qat disappeared from the world in a deluge. They show the very place from which he sailed away on his last voyage. It is a broad lake in the centre of the island of Gaua. In the days of Qat the ground now occupied by the lake was a spacious plain clothed with forest. Qat felled one of the tallest trees in the wood and proceeded to build himself a canoe out of the fallen trunk. While he was at work on it, his brothers would come and jeer at him, as he sat or stood there sweating away at his unfinished canoe in the shadow of the dense tropical forest. "How will you ever get that huge canoe through the thick woods to the sea?" they asked him mockingly. "Wait and see," was all he deigned to answer. When the canoe was finished, he gathered into it his wife and his brothers and all the living creatures of the island, down to the smallest ants, and shut himself and them into the vessel, which he provided with a covering. Then came a deluge of rain; the great hollow of the island was filled with water, which burst through the circle of the hills at the spot where the great waterfall of Gaua still descends seaward, with a thunderous roar, in a veil of spray. There the canoe swept on the rushing water through the barrier of the hills, and driving away out to sea was lost to view. The natives say that the hero Qat took away the best of everything with him when he thus vanished from sight, and still they look forward to his joyful return. When Bishop Patteson and his companions first landed on Mota, the happy natives took him for the long-lost Qat and his brethren. And some years afterwards, when a small trading vessel was one day seen standing in for the island of Gaua and making apparently for the channel down which the water of the great cascade flows to mingle with the sea, the old people on the island cried out joyfully that Qat was come again, and that his canoe knew her own way home. But alas! the ship was cast away on the reef, and Qat has not yet come home.[5]

A story of a great flood, like that which the natives of the New Hebrides tell, is related by the natives of Lifu, one of the Loyalty Islands, which lie to the south of the New Hebrides. The tale runs thus:

"An old man named Nol made a canoe inland; the natives laughed at him for making it so far from the sea, declaring that they would not help him to drag it to the coast; but he told them that it would not be necessary, for the sea would come to it. When it was finished the rain fell in torrents and flooded the island, drowning everybody. Nol's canoe was lifted by the waters and borne along by a current; it struck a high rock which was still out of the water, and split it in two. (These two rocks are still pointed out by the natives: they form the heads of a fine bay on the north side of the island.) The water then rushed into the sea and left Lifu 'high and dry.'

"This tradition may have reference to the time when Lifu, after the first lift, was a lagoon island like what the island of Uvea is now. If so, it shows that this island has been inhabited for a very long time."[6] ▼

▲ 41   Polynesia and Micronesia

Legends of a great flood in which a multitude of people perished are told by the natives of those groups of islands which under the general names of Polynesia and Micronesia are scattered widely over the Pacific. "The principal facts," we are told, "are the same in the traditions prevailing among the inhabitants of the different groups, although they differ in several minor particulars. In one group the accounts state, that in ancient times Taaroa, the principal god (according to their mythology, the creator of the world), being angry with men on account of their disobedience to his will, overturned the world into the sea, when the earth sank in the waters, excepting a few *aurus*, or projecting points, which, remaining above its surface, constituted the principal cluster of islands. The memorial preserved by the inhabitants of Eimeo states, that after the inundation of the land, when the water subsided, a man landed from a canoe near Tiataepua, in their island, and erected an altar, or *marae*, in honour of his god."[1]

In Tahiti the legend ran as follows. Tahiti was destroyed by the sea: no man, nor hog, nor fowl, nor dog survived. The groves of trees and the stones were carried away by the wind. They were destroyed, and the deep was over the land. But two persons, a husband and a wife, were saved. When the flood came, the wife took up her young chicken, her young dog, and her kitten; the husband took up his young pig. (These were all the animals formerly known to the natives; and as the term *fanaua*, "young," is both singular and plural, it may apply to one or more than one chicken, etc.). The husband proposed that they should take refuge on Mount Orofena, a high mountain in Tahiti, saying that it was lofty and would not be reached by the sea. But his wife said that the sea would reach to Mount Orofena, and that they had better go to Mount Pita-hiti, where they would be safe from the flood. So to Mount Pita-hiti they went; and she was right, for Orofena was overwhelmed by the sea, but Pita-hiti rose above the waste of waters and became their abode. There they watched ten nights, till the sea ebbed, and they saw the little heads of the mountains appearing above the waves. When the sea retired, the land remained without produce, without man, and the fish were putrid in the caves and holes of the rocks. They said, "Dig a hole for the fish in the sea." The wind also died away, and when all was calm, the stones and the trees began to fall from the heavens, to which they had been carried up by the wind. For all the trees of the land had been torn up and whirled aloft by the hurricane. The two looked about, and the woman said, "We two are safe from the sea, but death, or hurt, comes now in these stones that are falling. Where shall we abide?" So the two dug a hole, lined it with grass, and covered it over with stones and earth. Then they crept into the hole, and sitting there they heard with terror the roar and crash of the stones falling down from the sky. By and by the rain of stones abated, till only a few stones fell at intervals, and then they dropped one by one, and finally ceased altogether. The woman said, "Arise, go out, and see whether the stones are still falling." But her husband said, "Nay, I go not out, lest I die." A day and a night he waited, and in the morning he said, "The wind is truly dead, and the stones and the trunks of trees cease to fall, neither is there the sound of the stones." They went out, and like a small mountain was the heap of fallen stones and tree trunks. Of the land there remained the earth and the rocks, but the shrubs were destroyed by the sea. They descended from the mountain, and gazed with astonishment: there were no houses, nor coco-nuts, nor palm-trees, nor bread-fruit, nor hibiscus, nor grass: all was destroyed by the sea. The two dwelt together. The woman brought forth two children; one was a son, the other a daughter. They grieved that there was no food for their children. Again the mother brought forth, but still there was no food; then the breadfruit bore fruit, and the coco-nut, and every other kind of food. In three days the land was covered with food and in time it swarmed with men also, for from those two persons, the father and the mother, all the people are descended.[2]

In Raiatea, one of the Leeward Islands in the Tahitian group, tradition ran that shortly after the peopling of the world by the descendants of Taata, the sea-god Ruahatu was reposing among groves of coral in the depths of ocean when his repose was rudely interrupted. A fisherman paddling his canoe overhead, in ignorance or forgetfulness of the divine presence, let down his hooks among the branching corals at the bottom of the clear translucent water, and they became entangled in the hair of the sleeping god. With great difficulty the fisherman wrenched the hooks out of the ambrosial locks and began pulling them up hand-over-hand. But the god, enraged at being disturbed in his nap, came also bubbling up to the surface, and popping his head out of the water upbraided the fisherman for his impiety, and threatened in revenge to destroy the land. The affrighted fisherman prostrated himself before the sea-god, confessed his sin, and implored his forgiveness, beseeching that the judgment denounced might be averted, or at least that he himself might escape. Moved by his penitence and importunity, Ruahatu bade him return home for his wife and child and go with them to Toamarama, a small island situated within the reefs on the eastern side of Raiatea. There he was promised security amid the destruction of the surrounding islands. The man hastened home, and taking with him his wife and child he repaired to the little isle of refuge in the lagoon. Some say that he took with him also a friend, who was living under his roof, together with a dog, a pig, and a pair of fowls; so that the refugees numbered four souls, together with the only domesticated animals which were then known in the islands. They reached the harbour of refuge before the close of day, and as the sun set the waters of the ocean began to rise, and the inhabitants of the adjacent shore left their dwellings and fled to the mountains. All that night the waters rose, and next morning only the tops of the high mountains appeared above the widespread sea. Even these were at last covered, and all the inhabitants of the land perished. Afterwards the waters retired, the fisherman and his companions left their retreat, took up their abode on the mainland, and became the progenitors of the present inhabitants.[3]

The coral islet in which these forefathers of the race found refuge from the great flood is not more than two feet at the highest above the level of the sea, so that it is difficult to understand how it could have escaped the inundation, while the lofty mountains which tower up thousands of feet from the adjacent shore were submerged. This difficulty, however, presents no stumbling-block to the faith of the natives; they usually decline to discuss such sceptical doubts, and point triumphantly for confirmation of their story to the coral, shells, and other marine substances which are occasionally found near the surface of the ground on the tops of their highest mountains. These must, they insist, have been deposited there by the waters of the ocean when the islands were submerged.[4]

It is significant, as we shall see later on, that in these Tahitian legends the flood is ascribed solely to the rising of the sea, and not at all to heavy rain, which is not even mentioned. On this point William Ellis, to whom we owe the record of these legends, makes the following observations: "I have frequently conversed with the people on the subject, both in the northern and southern groups, but could never learn that they had any accounts of the windows of heaven having been opened, or the rain having descended. In the legend of Ruahatu, the Toamarama of Tahiti, and the Kai of Kahinarii in Hawaii, the inundation is ascribed to the rising of the waters of the sea. In each account, the anger of the god is considered as the cause of the inundation of the world, and the destruction of its inhabitants."[5]

When Ellis preached in the year 1822 to the natives of Hawaii on the subject of Noah's deluge, they told him of a similar legend which had been handed down among them. "They said they were informed by their fathers, that all the land had once been overflowed by the sea, except a small peak on the top of Mouna-Kea, where two human beings were preserved from the destruction that overtook the rest, but they said they had never before heard of a ship, or of Noah, having been always accustomed to call it *kai a Kahinárii* (sea of Kahinárii)."[6]

The Maoris of New Zealand have a long legend of the deluge. They say that when men multiplied on the earth and there were many great tribes, evil prevailed everywhere, the tribes quarrelled and made war on each other. The worship of the great god Tane, who had created man and woman, was neglected and his doctrines openly denied. Two great prophets, indeed, there were who taught the true doctrine concerning the separation of heaven and earth, but men scoffed at them, saying that they were false teachers and that heaven and earth had been from the beginning just as we see them now. The names of these two wise prophets were Para-whenua-mea and Tupu-nui-a-uta. They continued to preach till the tribes cursed them, saying, "You two can eat the words of your history as food for you, and you can eat the heads of the words of that history." That grieved the prophets, when men said the wicked words "Eat the heads," and they grew angry. So they took their stone axes and cut down trees, and dragged the trunks to the source of the Tohinga River, and bound them together with vines and ropes, and made a very wide raft. Moreover, they built a house on the raft, and put much food in it, fern-root, and sweet potatoes, and dogs. Then they recited incantations and prayed that rain might descend in such abundance as would convince men of the existence and power of the god Tane, and would teach them the need of worship for life and for peace. After that the two prophets embarked on the raft, along with two men called Tiu and Reti and a woman named Wai-puna-hau. But there were other women also on the raft. Now Tiu was the priest on the raft, and he prayed and uttered incantations for rain. So it rained in torrents for four or five days, and then the priest repeated incantations to make the rain cease, and it ceased. But still the flood rose; next day it reached the settlement, and on the following day the raft was lifted up by the waters, and floated down the River Tohinga. Great as a sea was now the inundation, and the raft drifted to and fro on the face of the waters. When they had tossed about for seven moons, the priest Tiu said to his companions, "We shall not die, we shall land on the earth"; and in the eighth month he said moreover, "The sea has become thin; the flood has begun to subside." The two prophets asked him, "By what do you know?" He answered, "By the signs of my staff." For he had kept his altar on one side of the deck, and there he performed his ceremonies, and repeated his incantations, and observed his staff. And he understood the signs of his staff, and he said again to his companions, "The blustering winds of the past moons have fallen, the winds of this month have died away, and the sea is calm." In the eighth month the raft no longer rolled as before; it now pitched as well as rolled, so the priest knew that the sea was shallow, and that they were drawing near to land. He said to his companions, "This is the moon in which we shall land on dry earth, for by the signs of my staff I know that the sea is becoming less deep." All the while they floated on the deep they repeated incantations and performed ceremonies in honour of the god Tane. At last they landed on dry earth at Hawaiki. They thought that they might find some of the inhabitants of the world still alive, and that the earth would look as it had looked before the flood. But all was changed. The earth was cracked and fissured in some places, and in others it had been turned upside down and confounded by reason of the flood. And not one soul was left alive in the world. They who came forth from the raft were the solitary survivors of all the tribes of the earth. When they landed, the first thing they did was to perform ceremonies and repeat incantations. They worshipped Tane, and the Heaven (Rangi), and Rehua, and all the gods; and as they worshipped them they offered them seaweed, a length of the priest's two thumbs for each god. Each god was worshipped in a different place, and for each there was an altar, where the incantations were recited. The altar was a root of grass, a shrub, a tree, or a flax-bush. These were the altars of the gods at that time; and now, if any of the people of the tribes go near to such altars, the food they have eaten in their stomachs will swell and kill them. The chief priest alone may go to such holy spots. If common folk were to go to these sacred places and afterwards cook food in their village, the food would kill all who ate it. It would be cursed by the sin of the people in desecrating the sanctity of the altars, and the punishment of the eaters would be death. When the persons who were saved on the raft had performed all the ceremonies needful for removing the taboo under which they laboured, they procured fire by friction at one of the sacred places. And with the fire the priest kindled bundles of grass, and he put a bundle of burning grass on each altar beside the piece destined for the god; and the priests presented the sea-weed to the gods as a thank-offering for the rescue of the people from the flood and for the preservation of their lives on the raft.[7]

Other Maori stories of a great flood associate the catastrophe with a certain legendary hero called Tawhaki. They say that once upon a time two of his brothers-in-law attacked and wounded him and left him for dead. But he recovered from his wounds and quitted the place where his wicked brothers-in-law lived. Away he went with all his own warriors and their families, and he built a fortified village upon the top of a very lofty mountain, where he could easily defend himself, and there they all dwelt secure. "Then he called aloud to the gods, his ancestors, for revenge, and they let the floods of heaven descend, and the earth was overwhelmed by the waters and all human beings perished, and the name given to that event was 'The overwhelming of the Mataaho,' and the whole of that race perished."[8] Some say that Tawhaki was a man, who went up to the top of a mountain, and, having there transfigured himself by putting off his earthly raiment and put on a garment of lightning, was worshipped as a god, and all the tribes chanted incantations and offered sacrifices to him. In his divine character he once, in a fit of anger, stamped on the floor of heaven, so that it cracked and the celestial waters burst through and flooded the earth.[9] Others say[10] that it was Tawhaki's mother who caused the deluge by weeping so copiously that her tears, falling on the earth, inundated it and drowned all men.[10a]

In Micronesia as well as Polynesia the story of a great flood has been recorded. The Pelew Islanders say[11] that once on a time a man went up into the sky, whence the gods with their shining eyes, which are the stars, look down every night upon the earth. The cunning fellow stole one of these bright eyes and brought it home with him, and all the money of the Pelew Islanders has been made out of that starry eye ever since. But the gods were very angry at the theft, and down they came to earth to reclaim their stolen property and to punish the thief. They disguised themselves in the likeness of ordinary men, and begged for food and lodging from door to door. But men were churlish and turned them away without a bite or a sup. Only one old woman received them kindly in her cottage, and set before them the best she had to eat and drink. So when they went away they warned the old woman to make a raft of bamboo ready against the next full moon, and when the night of the full moon came she was to lie down on the raft and sleep. She did as she was bidden. Now with the full moon came a dreadful storm and rain, and the sea rose higher and higher, and flooded the islands, rent the mountains, and destroyed the abodes of men; and people knew not how to save themselves, and they all perished in the rising flood. But the good old dame, fast asleep on the raft, was borne on the face of the waters and drifted till her hair caught in the boughs of a tree on the top of Mount Armlimui. There she lay, while the flood ebbed and the water sank lower and lower down the sides of the mountain. Then the gods came down from the sky to seek for the good old woman whom they had taken under their protection, but they found her dead. So they summoned one of their women-folk from heaven, and she entered into the dead body of the old woman and made her live. After that the gods begat five children by the resuscitated old wife, and having done so they left the earth and returned to heaven; the goddess who had kindly reanimated the corpse of the ancient dame also went back to her mansion in the sky. But the five children of the divine fathers and the human mother repeopled the Pelew Islands, and from them the present inhabitants are descended.[11a-b] ▼

▲ **42 Australia**

The Kurnai, an aboriginal Australian tribe of Gippsland, in Victoria, say that a long time ago there was a very great flood; all the country was under water, and all the black people were drowned except a man and two or three women, who took refuge in a mud island near Port Albert. The water was all round them. Just then the pelican came sailing by in his canoe, and seeing the distress of the poor people he went to help them. One of the women was so beautiful that he fell in love with her. When she would have stepped into the canoe, he said, "Not now, next time"; so that after he had ferried all the rest, one by one, across to the mainland, she was left to the last. Afraid of being alone with the ferryman, she did not wait his return on his last trip, but swam ashore and escaped. However, before quitting the island, she dressed up a log in her opossum rug and laid it beside the fire, so that it looked just like herself. When the pelican arrived to ferry her over, he called, "Come on, now." The log made no reply, so the pelican flew into a passion, and rushing up to what he took to be the woman, he lunged out with his foot at her and gave the log a tremendous kick. Naturally he only hurt his own foot, and what with the pain and the chagrin at the trick that had been played him, he was very angry indeed and began to paint himself white in order that he might fight the

husband of the impudent hussy who had so deceived him. He was still engaged
in these warlike preparations, and had only painted white one half of his black
body, when another pelican came up, and not knowing what to make of such
a strange creature, half white and half black, he pecked at him with his beak
and killed him. That is why pelicans are now black and white; before the flood
they were black all over.[1]

According to the aborigines about Lake Tyers, in Victoria, the way in which
the great flood came about was this. Once upon a time all the water in the
world was swallowed by a huge frog, and nobody else could get a drop to
drink. It was most inconvenient, especially for the fish, who flapped about and
gasped on the dry land. So the animals laid their heads together and came to
the conclusion that the only way of making the frog disgorge the waters was to
tickle his fancy so that he should laugh. Accordingly they gathered before him
and cut capers and played pranks that would have caused any ordinary person
to die of laughing. But the frog did not even smile. He sat there in gloomy
silence, with his great goggle eyes and his swollen cheeks, as grave as a judge.
As a last resort the eel stood up on its tail and wriggled and danced about,
twisting itself into the most ridiculous contortions. This was more than even
the frog could bear. His features relaxed, and he laughed till the tears ran down
his cheeks and the water poured out of his mouth. However, the animals had
now got more than they had bargained for, since the waters disgorged by the
frog swelled into a great flood in which many people perished. Indeed the whole
of mankind would have been drowned, if the pelican had not gone about in a
canoe picking up the survivors and so saving their lives.[2]

Another legend of a deluge current among the aborigines of Victoria relates
how, many long ages ago, the Creator Bunjil was very angry with the black
people because they did evil. So he caused the ocean to swell by urinating into
it, and in the rising flood all black people were drowned, except those whom
Bunjil loved and catching up from the water fixed as stars in the sky. Nevertheless one man and one woman escaped the deluge by climbing a high tree on
a mountain; so they lived and became the ancestors of the present human
race.[3] ▼

▲ 43   North America

[Stories of a primeval deluge are likewise to be found among many of the
Indian tribes of North America, though often, to be sure, they refer to local,
rather than worldwide, disasters.[1] Moreover, in the form in which they have
been recorded, not a few of them seem to betray the influence of the Bible.
This may be due either to contact with Christians or to subconscious coloration by missionary rapporteurs.]

The Papagos of south-western Arizona say that the first days of the world
were happy and peaceful. The sun was then nearer the earth than he is now:
his rays made all the seasons equable and clothing superfluous. Men and ani-

mals talked together: a common language united them in the bonds of brother-hood. But a terrible catastrophe put an end to those golden days. A great flood destroyed all flesh wherein was the breath of life: the hero Montezuma and his friend the coyote alone escaped. For before the waters began to rise, the coyote prophesied the coming of the flood, and Montezuma took warning, and hollowed out a boat for himself, and kept it ready on the top of Santa Rosa. The coyote also prepared an ark for himself; for he gnawed down a great cane by the river bank, entered it, and caulked it with gum. So when the waters rose, Montezuma and the coyote floated on them and were saved; and when the flood retired, the man and the animal met on dry land. Anxious to discover how much dry land was left, the man sent out the coyote to explore, and the animal reported that to the west, the south, and the east there was sea, but that to the north he could find no sea, though he had journeyed till he was weary. Meanwhile the Great Spirit, with the help of Montezuma, had restocked the earth with men and animals.[1a]

The Pimas, a neighbouring tribe, related to the Papagos, say that the earth and mankind were made by a certain Chiowotmahke, that is to say Earth-prophet. Now the Creator had a son called Szeukha, who, when the earth be-gan to be tolerably peopled, lived in the Gila valley. In the same valley there dwelt at that time a great prophet, whose name has been forgotten. One night, as the prophet slept, he was wakened by a noise at the door. When he opened, who should stand there but a great eagle? And the eagle said, "Arise, for be-hold, a deluge is at hand." But the prophet laughed the eagle to scorn, wrapt his robe about him, and slept again. Again, the eagle came and warned him, but again he would pay no heed. A third time the long-suffering bird warned the prophet that all the valley of the Gila would be laid waste with water, but still the foolish man turned a deaf ear to the warning. That same night came the flood, and next morning there was nothing alive to be seen but one man, if man indeed he was; for it was Szeukha, the son of the Creator, who had saved himself by floating on a ball of gum or resin. When the waters of the flood sank, he landed near the mouth of the Salt River and dwelt there in a cave on the mountain; the cave is there to this day, and so are the tools which Szeukha used when he lived in it. For some reason or other Szeukha was very angry with the great eagle, though that bird had warned the prophet to escape for his life from the flood. So with the help of a rope-ladder he climbed up the face of the cliff where the eagle resided, and finding him at home in his eyrie he killed him. In and about the nest he discovered the mangled and rotting bodies of a great multitude of people whom the eagle had carried off and devoured. These he raised to life and sent them away to repeople the earth.[2]

The Luiseño Indians of Southern California also tell of a great flood which covered all the high mountains and drowned most of the people. But a few were saved, who took refuge on a little knoll near Bonsall. The place was called Mora by the Spaniards, but the Indians call it Katuta. Only the knoll remained above water when all the rest of the country was inundated. The survivors stayed there till the flood went down. To this day you may see on the top of the little hill heaps of sea-shells and seaweed, and ashes, and stones set together, marking the spot where the Indians cooked their food. The shells are those of the shell-fish which they ate, and the ashes and stones are the remains of their fire-places. The writer who relates this tradition adds that "the hills near Del Mar and other places along the coast have many such heaps of sea-shells, of the species still found on the beaches, piled in quantities." The Luiseños still sing a Song of the Flood, in which mention is made of the knoll of Katuta.[3]

[The Choctaws of Mississippi, in what looks suspiciously like a distortion of the Biblical tale, relate that once upon a time a prophet was sent by the high god to foretell a flood. Nobody, however, took any notice. When the flood eventually came, the prophet took to a raft. After floating for several months, he caught sight of a black bird and signaled to it, but the bird simply cawed and flew away. Later he espied a bluish bird, and again signaled. This time the bird flapped its wings in response, moaned dolorously, and then guided the raft to where the sun was breaking through. Next morning, the prophet landed on an island filled with all kinds of animals. Among them was the black bird, whom he cursed, and the bluish bird, which he blessed. The former is the crow, whom the Choctaws abominate; the latter, the dove, whom they hold in honor.[3a]]

According to Du Pratz, the early French historian of Louisiana, the tradition of a great flood was current among the Natchez, an Indian tribe of the Lower Mississippi. He tells us that on this subject he questioned the guardian of the temple, in which the sacred and perpetual fire was kept with religious care. The guardian replied that "the ancient word taught all the red men that almost all men were destroyed by the waters except a very small number, who had saved themselves on a very high mountain; that he knew nothing more regarding this subject except that these few people had repeopled the earth."[4] Elsewhere he reports the tradition somewhat more fully as follows. "They said that a great rain fell on the earth so abundantly and during such a long time that it was completely covered except a very high mountain where some men saved themselves; that all fire being extinguished on the earth, a little bird named Coüy-oüy, which is entirely red (it is that which is called in Louisiana the cardinal-bird), brought it from heaven." The Cherokee Indians are said to have a tradition that the water once prevailed over the land until all mankind were drowned except a single family. The coming of the calamity was revealed by a dog to his master. For the sagacious animal went day after day to the banks of a river, where he stood gazing at the water and howling piteously. Being rebuked by his master and ordered home, the dog opened his mouth and warned the man of the danger in which he stood. "You must build a boat," said he, "and put in it all that you would save; for a great rain is coming that will flood the land." The animal concluded his prediction by informing his master that his salvation depended on throwing him, the dog, into the water; and for a sign of the truth of what he said he bade him look at the back of his neck. The man did so, and sure enough, the back of the dog's neck was raw and bare, the flesh and bone appearing. So the man believed, and following the directions of the faithful animal he and his family were saved, and from them the whole of the present population of the globe is lineally descended.[5]

The Montagnais of the Hudson Bay Territory have a tradition of a great flood which covered the world. God, being angry with the giants, commanded a man to build a large canoe. The man did so, and when he had embarked in it, the water rose on all sides, and the canoe with it, till no land was anywhere to be seen. Weary of beholding nothing but a heaving mass of water, the man threw an otter into the flood, and the animal dived and brought up a little earth. The man took the earth or mud in his hand and breathed on it, and at once it began to grow. So he laid it on the surface of the water and prevented it from sinking. As it continued to grow into an island, he desired to know whether it was large enough to support him. Accordingly he placed a reindeer upon it, but the animal soon made the circuit of the island and returned to him, from which he concluded that the island was not yet large enough. So he continued to blow on it till the mountains, the lakes, and the rivers were formed. Then he disembarked.[6]

The Hareskin Indians, another Tinneh tribe, say that a certain Kunyan, which means Wise Man, once upon a time resolved to build a great raft. When his sister, who was also his wife, asked him why he would build it, he said, "If there comes a flood, as I foresee, we shall take refuge on the raft." He told his plan to other men on the earth, but they laughed at him, saying, "If there is a flood, we shall take refuge on the trees." Nevertheless the Wise Man made a great raft, joining the logs together by ropes made of roots. All of a sudden there came a flood such that the like of it had never been seen before. The water seemed to gush forth on every side. Men climbed up in the trees, but the water rose after them, and all were drowned. But the Wise Man floated safely on his strong and well-corded raft. As he floated he thought of the future, and he gathered by twos all the herbivorous animals, and all the birds, and even all the beasts of prey he met with on his passage. "Come up on my raft," he said to them, "for soon there will be no more earth." Indeed, the earth disappeared under the water, and for a long time nobody thought of going to look for it. The first to plunge into the depth was the musk-rat, but he could find no bottom, and when he bobbed up on the surface again he was half drowned. "There is no earth!" said he. A second time he dived, and when he came up, he said, "I smelt the smell of the earth, but I could not reach it." Next it came to the turn of the beaver. He dived and remained a long time under water. At last he reappeared, floating on his back, breathless and unconscious. But in his paw he had a little mud, which he gave to the Wise Man. The Wise Man placed the mud on the water, breathed on it, and said, "I would there were an earth again!" At the same time he breathed on the handful of mud, and lo! it began to grow. He put a small bird on it, and the patch of mud grew still bigger. So he breathed, and breathed, and the mud grew and grew. Then the man put a fox on the floating island of mud, and the fox ran round it in a single day. Round and round the island ran the fox, and bigger and bigger grew the island. Six times did the fox make the circuit of the island, but when he made it for the seventh time, the land was complete even as it was before the flood. Then the Wise Man caused all the animals to disembark and landed them on the dry ground. Afterwards he himself disembarked with his wife and son, saying, "It is for us that this earth shall be repeopled." And repeopled it was, sure enough. Only one difficulty remained with which the Wise Man had to grapple. The floods were still out, and how to reduce them was the question. The bittern saw the difficulty and came to the rescue. He swallowed the whole of the water, and then lay like a log on the bank, with his belly swollen to a frightful size. This was more than the Wise Man had bargained for; if there had been too much water before, there was now too little. In his embarrassment the Wise Man had recourse to the plover. "The bittern," he said, "is lying yonder in the sun with his belly full of water. Pierce it." So the artful plover made up to the unsuspecting bittern. "My grandmother," said he, in a sympathizing tone, "has no doubt a pain in her stomach." And he passed his hand softly over the ailing part of the bittern as if to soothe it. But all of a sudden he put out his claws and clawed the swollen stomach of the bittern. Such a scratch he gave it! There was a gurgling, guggling sound, and out came the water from the stomach bubbling and foaming. It flowed away into rivers and lakes, and thus the world became habitable once more.[7]

Some Tinneh Indians affirm that the deluge was caused by a heavy fall of snow in the month of September. One old man alone foresaw the catastrophe and warned his fellows, but all in vain. "We will escape to the mountains," said they. But they were all drowned. Now the old man had built a canoe, and when the flood came, he sailed about in it, rescuing from the water all the animals he fell in with. Unable long to support this manner of life, he caused the beaver, the otter, the musk-rat, and the arctic duck to dive into the water in search of the drowned earth. Only the arctic duck came back with a little slime on its claws; and the man spread the slime on the water, caused it to grow by his breath, and for six days disembarked the animals upon it. After that, when the ground had grown to the size of a great island, he himself stepped ashore. Other Tinnehs say that the old man first sent forth a raven, which gorged itself on the floating corpses and came not back. Next he sent forth a turtle-dove, which flew twice round the world and returned. The third time she came back at evening, very tired, with a budding twig of fir in her mouth.[8] The influence of Christian teaching on this last version of the story is manifest.

The Tlingits of Alaska speak of a universal deluge, during which men were saved in a great floating ark which, when the water sank, grounded on a rock and split in two; and that, in their opinion, is the cause of the diversity of languages. The Tlingits represent one-half of the population, which was shut up in the ark, and all the remaining peoples of the earth represent the other half.[9] This last legend may be of Christian origin, for it exhibits a sort of blend of Noah's ark with the tower of Babel.

[A legend current among the Tsimshians of British Columbia says that the flood was sent by the god Laxha, who became annoyed by the noise created by boys at play.[9a]]

The Kaska Indians, a tribe of the Athapascan stock in the northern interior of British Columbia, have a tradition of a great flood which runs as follows:

"Once there came a great flood which covered the earth. Most of the people made rafts, and some escaped in canoes. Great darkness came on, and high winds which drove the vessels hither and thither. The people became separated. Some were driven far away. When the flood subsided, people landed wherever they found the nearest land. When the earth became dry, they lived in the places near where they had landed. People were now widely scattered over the world. They did not know where other people lived, and probably thought themselves the only survivors. Long afterwards, when in their wanderings they met people from another place, they spoke different languages, and could not understand one another. This is why there are now many different centres of population, many tribes, and many languages. Before the flood there was but one centre; for all the people lived together in one country, and spoke one language."[10]

Thus the Kaskan tradition combines the story of a great flood with an explanation of the origin of the diversity of tongues.

Legends of a great flood appear to have been current among the Indian tribes of the state of Washington.

"Do you see that high mountain over there?" said an old Indian to a mountaineer about the year 1860, as they were riding across the Cascade Mountains. "I do," was the reply. "Do you see that grove to the right?" the Indian next asked. "Yes," answered the white man. "Well," said the Indian, "a long time ago there was a flood, and all the country was overflowed. There was an old man and his family on a boat or raft, and he floated about, and the wind blew him to that mountain, where he touched bottom. He stayed there for some time, and then sent a crow to hunt for land, but it came back without finding any. After some time it brought a leaf from that grove, and the old man was glad, for he knew that the water was abating."[11]

When the earliest missionaries came among the Spokanas, Nez Perces, and Cayuses, who, with the Yakimas, used to inhabit the eastern part of Washington State, they found that these Indians had their own tradition of a great flood, in which one man and his wife were saved on a raft. Each of these three tribes, together with the Flathead tribes, had its own separate Ararat on which the survivors found refuge.[12]

In North America legends of a great flood are not confined to the Indian tribes; they are found also among the Eskimo and their kinsfolk the Greenlanders. Thus, a story current around Norton Sound relates that in the first days the earth was flooded, all but a very high mountain in the middle. The water came up from the sea and covered the whole land except the top of this mountain. Only a few animals escaped to the mountain and were saved; and a few people made a shift to survive by floating about in a boat and subsisting on the fish they caught till the water subsided. As the flood sank and the mountains emerged from the water, the people landed from the canoe on these heights, and gradually followed the retreating flood to the coast. The animals which had escaped to the mountains also descended and replenished the earth after their kinds.[13]

With regard to the Greenlanders, their historian Crantz tells us that "almost all heathen nations know something of Noah's Flood, and the first missionaries found also some pretty plain traditions among the Greenlanders; namely, that the world once overset, and all mankind, except one, were drowned; but some were turned into fiery spirits. The only man that escaped alive, afterwards smote the ground with his stick, and out sprang a woman, and these two repeopled the world. As a proof that the deluge once overflowed the whole earth, they say that many shells, and relics of fishes, have been found far within the land where men could never have lived, yea that bones of whales have been found upon a high mountain."[14] Similar evidence in support of the legend was adduced to the traveller C. F. Hall by the Innuits or Eskimo with whom he lived. He tells us that "they have a tradition of a deluge which they attribute to an unusually high tide. On one occasion when I was speaking with Tookoolito concerning her people, she said, 'Innuits all think this earth once covered with water.' I asked her why they thought so. She answered, 'Did you never see little stones, like clams and such things as live in the sea, away up on mountains?' "[15]

Another is reported by a different German missionary from the same region. He obtained it at the mission-station of Mkulwe, on the Saisi or Momba river, about twenty miles from where the river flows into Lake Rukwa. His informant professed to have had it from his grandfather, and stoutly asserted that it was a genuine old tradition of the country and not borrowed from foreigners. His statement was corroborated by another truth-loving native, who only differed from his fellow in opining that the African Noah sent out two doves instead of one. The story runs thus:

Long ago, the rivers came down in flood. God said to the two men, "Go into the ship. Also take into it seeds of all sorts and all animals, male and female." They did so. The flood rose high, it overtopped the mountains, the ship floated on it. All animals and all men died. When the water dried up, the man said, "Let us see. Perhaps the water is not yet dried up." He sent out a dove, she came back to the ship. He waited and sent out a hawk, but she did not return, because the water was dried up. The men went out of the ship, they also let out all animals and all seeds.[16] ▼

▲ 44   Central America and Mexico

The Indians about Panama "had some notion of Noah's flood, and said that when it happened one man escaped in a canoe with his wife and children, from whom all mankind afterwards proceeded and peopled the world."[1]

The Indians of Nicaragua believed that since its creation the world had been destroyed by a deluge, and that after its destruction the gods had created men and animals and all things afresh.[2]

"The Mexicans," says the Italian historian Clavigero, "with all other civilized nations, had a clear tradition, though somewhat corrupted by fable, of the creation of the world, of the universal deluge, of the confusion of tongues, and of the dispersion of the people; and had actually all these events represented in their pictures. They said, that when mankind were overwhelmed with the deluge, none were preserved but a man named Coxcox (to whom others give the name of Teocipactli), and a woman called Xochiquetzal, who saved themselves in a little bark, and having afterwards got to land upon a mountain called by them Colhuacan, had there a great many children; that these children were all born dumb, until a dove from a lofty tree imparted to them languages, but differing so much that they could not understand one another. The Tlascalans pretended that the men who survived the deluge were transformed into apes, but recovered speech and reason by degrees."[3]

In the Mexican manuscript known as the *Codex Chimalpopoca,* which contains a history of the kingdoms of Culhuacan and Mexico from the creation downwards, there is contained an account of the great flood. It runs thus. The world had existed for four hundred years, and two hundred years, and three score and sixteen years, when men were lost and drowned and turned into fishes. The sky drew near to the water; in a single day all was lost, and the day of Nahui-Xochitl or Fourth Flower consumed all our subsistence (all that there was of our flesh). And that year was the year of Ce-Calli or First House; and on the first day, the day of Nahui-Atl, all was lost. The mountains themselves were sunk under the water, and the water remained calm for fifty and two springs. But towards the end of the year Titlacahuan had warned the man Nata and his wife Nena, saying, "Brew no more wine, but hollow out a great cypress and enter therein when, in the month of Toçoztli, the water shall near the sky." Then they entered into it, and when Titlacahuan had shut the door of it, he said to him, "Thou shalt eat but one sheaf of maize, and thy wife but one also." But when they had finished, they came forth from there, and the water remained calm, for the log moved no more, and opening it they began to see the fishes. Then they lit fire by rubbing pieces of wood together, and they roasted fishes. But the gods Citlallinicue and Citlallo-tonac at once looked down and said, "O divine Lord, what fire is that they are making there? wherefore do they thus fill the heaven with smoke?" Straightway Titlacahuan Tetzcatlipoca came down, and he grumbled, saying, "What's that fire doing here?" With that he snatched up the fishes, split their tails, modelled their heads, and turned them into dogs.[4]

In Michoacan, a province of Mexico, the legend of a deluge was also preserved. The natives said that when the flood began to rise, a man named Tezpi, with his wife and children, entered into a great vessel, taking with them animals and seeds of diverse kinds sufficient to restock the world after the deluge. When the waters abated, the man sent forth a vulture, and the bird flew away, but finding corpses to batten on, it did not return. Then the man let fly other birds, but they also came not back. At last he sent forth a humming-bird, and it returned with a green bough in its beak.[5] In this story the messenger birds seem clearly to be reminiscences of the raven and the dove in the Noachian legend, of which the Indians may have heard through missionaries.

The Huichol Indians, who inhabit a mountainous region near Santa Catarina in Western Mexico, have also a legend of a deluge. By blood the tribe is related to the Aztecs, the creators of that semi-civilized empire of Mexico which until 1722 that the Spaniards succeeded in subduing them, and the Franciscan the Spanish invaders destroyed; but, secluded in their mountain fastnesses, the Huichols have always remained in a state of primitive barbarism. It was not missionaries, who followed the Spanish army into the mountains, built a few churches and converted the wild Indians to Christianity. But the conversion was hardly more than nominal. It is true that the Huichols observe the principal Christian festivals, which afford them welcome excuses for lounging, guzzling, and swilling, and they worship the saints as gods. But in their hearts they cling to their ancient beliefs, customs, and ceremonies: they jealously guard their country against the encroachments of the whites: not a single Catholic priest lives among them; and all the churches are in ruins.[6]

The Huichol story of the deluge runs thus. A Huichol was felling trees to clear a field for planting. But every morning he found, to his chagrin, that the trees which he had felled the day before had grown up again as tall as ever. It was very vexatious and he grew tired of labouring in vain. On the fifth day he determined to try once more and to go to the root of the matter. Soon there rose from the ground in the middle of the clearing an old woman with a staff in her hand. She was no other than Great-grandmother Nakawe, the goddess of earth, who makes every green thing to spring forth from the dark underworld. But the man did not know her. With her staff she pointed to the south, north, west, and east, above and below; and all the trees which the young man had felled immediately stood up again. Then he understood how it came to pass that in spite of all his endeavours the clearing was always covered with trees. So he said to the old woman angrily, "Is it you who are undoing my work all the time?" "Yes," she said, "because I wish to talk to you." Then she told him that he laboured in vain. "A great flood," said she, "is coming. It is not more than five days off. There will come a wind, very bitter, and as sharp as chile, which will make you cough. Make a box from the salate (fig) tree, as long as your body, and fit it with a good cover. Take with you five grains of corn of each colour, and five beans of each colour; also take the fire and five squash-stems to feed it, and take with you a black bitch." The man did as the woman told him. On the fifth day he had the box ready and placed in it the things she had told him to take with him. Then he entered the box with the black bitch; and the old woman put on the cover, and caulked every crack with glue, asking the man to point out any chinks. Having made the box thoroughly water-tight and air-tight, the old woman took her seat on the top of it, with a macaw perched on her shoulder. For five years the box floated on the face of the waters. The first year it floated to the south, the second year it floated to the north, the third year it floated to the west, the fourth year it floated to the east, and in the fifth year it rose upward on the flood, and all the world was filled with water. The next year the flood began to abate, and the box settled on a mountain near Santa Cantarina, where it may still be seen. When the box grounded on the mountain, the man took off the cover and saw that all the world was still under water. But the macaws and the parrots set to work with a will: they pecked at the mountains with their beaks till they had hollowed them out into valleys, down which the water all ran away and was separated into five seas. Then the land began to dry, and trees and grass sprang up. The old woman turned into wind and so vanished away. But the man resumed the work of clearing the field which had been interrupted by the flood. He lived with the bitch in a cave going forth to his labour in the morning and returning home in the evening. But the bitch stayed at home all the time. Every evening on his return the man found cakes baked ready against his coming, and he was curious to know who it was that baked them. When five days had passed, he hid himself behind some bushes near the cave to watch. He saw the bitch take off her skin, hang it up, and kneel down in the likeness of a woman to grind the corn for the cakes. Stealthily he drew near her from behind, snatched the skin away, and threw it on the fire. "Now you have burned my tunic!" cried the woman and began to whine like a dog. But he took water mixed with the flour she had prepared, and with the mixture he bathed her head. She felt refreshed and remained a woman ever after. The two had a large family, and their sons and daughters married. So was the world repeopled, and the inhabitants lived in caves.[7]

The Cora Indians, a tribe of nominal Christians whose country borders that of the Huichols on the west, tell a similar story of a great flood, in which the same incidents occur of the woodman who was warned of the coming flood by a woman, and who after the flood cohabited with a bitch transformed into a human wife. But in the Cora version of the legend the man is bidden to take into the ark with him the woodpecker, the sandpiper, and the parrot, as well as the bitch. He embarked at midnight when the flood began. When it subsided, he waited five days and then sent out the sandpiper to see if it were possible to walk on the ground. The bird flew back and cried, "Ee-wee-wee!" from which the man understood that the earth was still too wet. He waited five days more, and then sent out the woodpecker to see if the trees were hard and dry. The woodpecker thrust his beak deep into the tree, and waggled his head from side to side; but the wood was still so soft with the water that he could hardly pull his beak out again, and when at last with a violent tug he succeeded he lost his balance and fell to the ground. So when he returned to the ark he said, "Chu-ee, chu-ee!" The man took his meaning and waited five days more, after which he sent out the spotted sandpiper. By this time the mud was so dry that, when the sandpiper hopped about, his legs did not sink into it; so he came back and reported that all was well. Then the man ventured out of the ark, stepping very gingerly till he saw that the land was dry and flat.[8]

In another fragmentary version of the deluge story, as told by the Cora Indians, the survivors of the flood would seem to have escaped in a canoe. When the waters abated, God sent the vulture out of the canoe to see whether the earth was dry enough. But the vulture did not return, because he devoured the corpses of the drowned. So God was angry with the vulture, and cursed him, and made him black instead of white, as he had been before; only the tips of his wings he left white, that men might know what their colour had been before the flood. Next God commanded the ringdove to go out and see whether the earth was yet dry. The dove reported that the earth was dry, but that the rivers were in spate. So God ordered all the beasts to drink the rivers dry, and all the beasts and birds came and drank, save only the weeping dove (*Paloma llorona*), which would not come. Therefore she still goes every day to drink water at nightfall, because she is ashamed to be seen drinking by day; and all day long she weeps and wails.[9] In these Cora legends the incident of the birds, especially the vulture and the raven, seems clearly to reflect the influence of missionary teaching.

The Tarahumares, an Indian tribe who inhabit the mountains of Mexico farther to the north than the Huichols and Coras, say that they were once fighting among themselves, and Father God (*Tata Dios*) sent much rain, and all the people perished. After the flood God despatched three men and three women to repeople the earth. They planted corn of three kinds, soft corn, hard corn, and yellow corn, and these three sorts still grow in the country.[10] ▼

▲ 45   South America

At the time of their discovery the Indians of Brazil, in the neighbourhood of what was afterwards Rio de Janeiro, had a legend of a universal deluge in which only two brothers with their wives were saved. According to one account, the flood covered the whole earth and all men perished except the ancestors of those Indians, who escaped by climbing up into high trees,[1] others, however, thought that the survivors were saved in a canoe.[2]

The Caingangs, or Coroados, an Indian tribe of Rio Grande do Sul, the most southerly province of Brazil, have a tradition of a great flood which covered the whole earth inhabited by their forefathers. Only the top of the coastal range called Serra do Mar still appeared above the water. The members of three Indian tribes, namely the Caingangs, the Cayurucres, and the Cames, swam on the water of the flood toward the mountains, holding lighted torches between their teeth. But the Cayurucres and the Cames grew weary, they sank under the waves and were drowned, and their souls went to dwell in the heart of the mountain. However, the Caingangs and a few of the Curutons made shift to reach the mountain, and there they abode, some on the ground, and some on the branches of trees. Several days passed, and yet the water did not sink, and they had no food to eat. They looked for nothing but death, when they heard the song of the *saracuras,* a species of waterfowl, which flew to them with baskets of earth. This earth the birds threw into the water, which accordingly began slowly to sink. The people cried to the birds to hurry, so the birds called the ducks to their help, and working together they soon cleared enough room and to spare for all the people, except for such as had climbed up the trees: these latter were turned into monkeys. When the flood subsided, the Caingangs descended and settled at the foot of the mountain. The souls of the drowned Cayurucres and Cames contrived to burrow their way out from the bowels of the mountain in which they were imprisoned; and when they had crept forth they kindled a fire, and out of the ashes of the fire one of the Cayurucres moulded jaguars, and tapirs, and ant-bears, and bees, and animals of many other sorts, and he made them live and told them what they should eat. But one of the Cames imitated him by fashioning pumas, and poisonous snakes, and wasps, all in order that these creatures should fight the other animals which the Cayurucres had made, as they do to this day.[3]

The Pamarys, Abederys, and Kataushys, on the river Purus, relate that once upon a time people heard a rumbling above and below the ground. The sun and moon, also, turned red, blue, and yellow, and the wild beasts mingled fearlessly with men. A month later they heard a roar and saw darkness ascending from the earth to the sky, accompanied by thunder and heavy rain, which blotted out the day and the earth. Some people lost themselves, some died, without knowing why; for everything was in a dreadful state of confusion. The water rose very high, till the earth was sunk beneath the water and only the branches of the highest trees still stood out above the flood. Thither the people had fled for refuge, and there, perched among the boughs, they perished of cold and hunger; for all the time it was dark and the rain fell. Then only Uassu and his wife were saved. When they came down after the flood they could not find a single corpse, no, not so much as a heap of bleached bones. After that they had many children, and they said one to the other, "Go to, let us build our houses on the river, that when the water rises, we too may rise with it." But when they saw that the land was dry and solid, they thought no more about it. Yet the Pamarys build their houses on the river to this day.[4]

The Jibaros, an Indian tribe on the upper waters of the Amazon, in the territories of Peru and Ecuador, have also a tradition, more or less confused, of a great deluge which happened long ago. They say that a great cloud fell from heaven, which turned into rain and caused the death of all the inhabitants of the earth; only an old man and his two sons were saved, and it was they who repeopled the earth after the deluge, though how they contrived to do so without the assistance of a woman is a detail about which our authority does not deign to enlighten us. However that may be, one of the two sons who survived was cursed by his father, and the Jibaros are descended from him. The curse may be a reminiscence of the story of Noah and his sons recorded in Genesis, of which the Jibaros may have heard through missionaries. The difficulty of propagating the human species without the help of the female sex would seem to have struck the acuter minds among the Jibaros, for according to some of them the survivors of the deluge were a man and a woman, who took refuge in a cave on a high mountain, together with samples of all the various species of the animal kingdom. This version provides, with commendable foresight, for the restoration of animals as well as of men after the great flood. Yet another version of the story told by the Jibaros solves the problem of population in a more original manner. Nobody, they say, escaped the flood but two brothers, who found refuge in a mountain which, strange to tell, rose higher and higher with the rise of the waters. When the flood had subsided, the two brothers went out to search for food, and on their return to the hut what was their surprise to find victuals set forth ready for them! To clear up the mystery, one of the brothers hid himself, and from his place of concealment he saw two parrots with the faces of women enter the hut and prepare the meal. Darting out from his ambush he seized one of the birds and married it or her, and from this marriage sprang three boys and three girls, who became the ancestors of the Jibaros.[5]

The Arawaks of British Guiana believe that since its creation the world has been twice destroyed, once by fire and once by flood. Both destructions were brought on it by Aiomun Kondi, the great "Dweller on High," because of the wickedness of mankind. When the destruction by deluge was at hand, a pious and wise chief named Marerewana was informed of the coming flood and saved himself and his family in a large canoe. Fearing to drift away out to sea or far from the home of his fathers, he had made ready a long cable of bush-rope, with which he tied his bark to the trunk of a great tree. So when the waters subsided he found himself not far from his former abode.[6]

Legends of a great flood are current also among the Indians of the Orinoco.

On this subject Humboldt observes: "I cannot quit this first chain of the mountains of Encamarada without recalling a fact which was not unknown to Father Gili, and which was often mentioned to me during our stay among the missions of the Orinoco. The aborigines of these countries have preserved a belief that at the time of the great flood, while their fathers were forced to betake themselves to canoes in order to escape the general inundation, the waves of the sea broke against the rocks of Encamarada. This belief is not found isolated among a single people, the Tamanaques; it forms part of a system of historical traditions of which scattered notices are discovered among the Maypures of the great cataracts, among the Indians of the Rio Erevato, which falls into the Caura, and among almost all the tribes of the Upper Orinoco. When the Tamanaques are asked how the human race escaped this great cataclysm, 'the Age of Water,' as the Mexicans call it, they say that one man and one woman were saved on a high mountain called Tamanacu, situated on the banks of the Asiveru, and that on casting behind them, over their heads, the fruits of the Mauritia palm, they saw springing from the kernels of these fruits men and women, who repeopled the earth."[7] This they did in obedience to a voice which they heard speaking to them as they descended the mountain full of sorrow at the destruction of mankind by the flood. The fruits which the man threw became men, and the fruits which the woman threw became women.[8]

The Incas of Peru had also a tradition of a deluge. They said that the water rose above the highest mountains in the world, so that all people and all created things perished. No living thing escaped except a man and a woman, who floated in a box on the face of the waters and so were saved. When the flood subsided, the wind drifted the box with the two in it to Tiahuanacu, about seventy leagues from Cuzco.[9]

The Chiriguanos, a once powerful Indian tribe of southeastern Bolivia, tell the following story of a great flood. They say that a certain potent but malignant supernatural being, named Aguara-Tunpa, declared war against the true god Tunpaete, the Creator of the Chiriguanos. His motive for this declaration of war is unknown, but it is believed to have been pure spite or the spirit of contradiction. In order to vex the true god, Aguara-Tunpa set fire to all the prairies at the beginning or middle of autumn, so that along with the plants and trees all the animals perished on which in those days the Indians depended for their subsistence; for as yet they had not begun to cultivate maize and other cereals, as they do now. Thus deprived of food the Indians nearly died of hunger. However, they retreated before the flames to the banks of the rivers, and there, while the earth around still smoked from the great conflagration, they made shift to live on the fish which they caught in the water. Seeing his human prey likely to escape him, the baffled Aguara-Tunpa had recourse to another device in order to accomplish his infernal plot against mankind. He caused torrential rain to fall, hoping to drown the whole Chiriguano tribe in the water. He very nearly succeeded. But happily the Chiriguanos contrived to defeat his fell purpose. Acting on a hint given them by the true god Tunpaete, they looked out for a large mate leaf, placed on it two little babies, a boy and a girl, the children of one mother, and allowed the tiny ark with its precious inmates to float on the face of the water. Still the rain continued to descend in torrents; the floods rose and spread over the face of the earth to a great depth, and all the Chiriguanos were drowned; only the two babes on the leaf of mate were saved. At last, however, the rain ceased to fall, and the flood sank, leaving a great expanse of fetid mud behind. The children now emerged from the ark, for if they had stayed there, they would have perished of cold and hunger. Naturally the fish and other creatures that live in the water were not drowned in the great flood; on the contrary they thrived on it, and were now quite ready to serve as food for the two babes. But how were the infants to cook the fish which they caught? That was the rub, for of course all fire on earth had been extinguished by the deluge. However, a large toad came to the rescue of the two children. Before the flood had swamped the whole earth, that prudent creature had taken the precaution of secreting himself in a hole, taking with him in his mouth some live coals, which he contrived to keep alight all the time of the deluge by blowing on them with his breath. When he saw that the surface of the ground was dry again, he hopped out of his hole with the live coals in his mouth, and making straight for the two children he bestowed on them the gift of fire. Thus they were able to roast the fish they caught and so to warm their chilled bodies. In time they grew up, and from their union the whole tribe of the Chiriguanos is descended.[10]

The natives of Tierra del Fuego, in the extreme south of South America, tell a fantastic and obscure story of a great flood. They say that the sun was sunk in the sea, that the waters rose tumultuously, and that all the earth was submerged except a single very high mountain, on which a few people found refuge.[11] ▼

46   The mountain of deliverance   8:4

In all flood stories the heroes are rescued (obviously) by reaching high ground.[1] The mountain of deliverance is usually identified with some prominent local hill or elevation. Thus—to cite but a few representative instances—in the Classical versions it is Parnassus,[2] Etna,[3] Athos,[4] Nemea,[5] or Othrys.[6] In the Carib version from Orinoco it is Mt. Tamanacu.[7] Elsewhere on the American continent it is Carro Naztarny in the region of the Rio Grande, the peak of old Zuni in New Mexico, of Colhuacan on the Pacific coast, of Apola in Mixteca, and of Mt. Neba in the province of Guayami.[8] In the Hindu Mahabharata, Manu moors his ship on the highest point of the Himalayas.[9]

In the Biblical version the ark eventually comes to rest on "the mountains of Ararat." The latter is the ancient name of Armenia (Akkadian, Urartu), and the reason why this region is chosen is that Armenia and the Caucasus were popularly believed to be the end of the earth. The Hittites, for example, re-garded the Lullu, who dwelt there, as the "outlandish" people *par excellence*—numskulls from "back of the beyond."[10] Similarly, it was in that general area that the Greeks located the mythical Hyperboreans, the "folk beyond the north," who were virtually outside of civilization.[11] So too in Aeschylus' *Prometheus Bound,* the wastes of contiguous Scythia are described as the farthermost borne of the earth, untrodden and uninhabited.[12]

The Elburz mountains, which bound the area, were in turn depicted as part of the range which girded the earth and prevented its being flooded by the surrounding cosmic ocean.[13] In Arabic lore this range is known as the Qâf, or Circle;[14] and the Malayans still speak of the Caucasus as "the hills of Qâf" (*Bikut Qâf*).[15] The idea, however, is much more ancient: in the so-called Eridu Creation Story from Mesopotamia, the god Marduk is said to have consummated the formation of the earth by constructing a rampart or revet-ment (*tamlû;* cf. Hebrew *millô*) "over against the ocean,"[16] and both in the Biblical Book of Proverbs (26:10) and in Job (26:10)[17] the same action is attributed to Yahweh. The ark, bobbing along on the surface of the waters, is eventually jolted to a stop by this range.

The same tradition appears in the Babylonian narrative of the Deluge where the ark is said to ground on Mt. Niṣir,[18] an eminence which the Annals of Ashurnaṣirpal locate in the same general area.[19] Berosus too says that the ark rested "in the mountains of the Kurds," and adds that fragments of it were diligently collected in his day—as they have been throughout the centuries—for use as amulets! The ancient Aramaic translation (Targum) of Genesis likewise identifies Ararat with Kurdistan.[20]

47   The dispatch of the birds   8:6–12

The familiar incident of the dispatch of the raven and dove occurs, in slightly different form, in the more ancient Babylonian story of the Deluge:

> When the seventh day arrived
> I sent out a dove, and let it go.
> The dove departed, but came back to me.
> It came back because there was no resting-place.
>   Then I sent out a swallow, and let it go.
> The swallow departed, but came back to me.
> It came back because there was no resting-place.
>   Then I sent out a raven, and let it go.
> The raven departed,
> But when it found that the waters had ebbed,
> It ate and flitted around;
> It cawed, and it came not back.[1]

It will be observed that in this earlier version not only are there *three* distinct birds, as against the Bible's two, but also the roles of the dove and raven are reversed. Comparative Folklore suggests that this preserves a motif of the original folktale which the later Biblical variation has obscured.

In the first place, we have a number of Classical statements about ravens who guided travelers to their desired haven. Apollo, for instance, is said to have assumed the form of a raven in order to guide colonists from Thera to Cyrene;[2] and it was a white raven, sacred to that god, that pointed the way for the wandering Boeotians.[3] Similarly, according to Strabo,[4] two ravens led Alexander the Great to the Sea of Ammon.[5]

Second, there is evidence from various ages and climes that ravens used sometimes to be dispatched by mariners in order to ascertain the proximity of land.[6] Pliny tells us, for example, that the inhabitants of Ceylon (Taprobane) employed the bird in this way when they sailed to India;[7] and the ancient Norsemen are reputed to have used the same device.[8] In the original Semitic tale, therefore, the hero might well have been imagined to follow a time-honored nautical practice. There may, however, be even more to the matter than this. Widespread in world folklore is the belief that the raven possesses special prophetic powers.[9] A popular expression for it among the Arabs is "father of omens" (abu zayir), and the men of St. Kilda used to speak of a man's "having the foresight of a raven."[10] Usually, to be sure, the bird is regarded as portending death or ill-hap ("Quoth the raven: Nevermore"),[11] but sometimes it was indeed regarded in antiquity as lucky. Thus, a Babylonian soothsayer tells King Esarhaddon that "if a raven enters a house with its prey in its bill, this betokens riches to come";[12] and elsewhere in Mesopotamian literature it is styled "the helper of the gods."[13] As we shall see later, it is probably for that reason that ravens are specified as the birds which succoured the prophet Elijah into wilderness.[14]

Lastly, as regards the substitution of the dove for the raven in the Biblical narrative, a tradition recorded by Plutarch is perhaps not without interest: doves, he says, come home when a storm is brewing, but fly away when fair weather seems promised.[15]

48 The rainbow[1]   9:12–16

The rainbow does not appear in the older Babylonian story of the Deluge, and Comparative Folklore suggests an interesting possibility of how it may have got into the Biblical version.

Among many peoples the rainbow is regarded as the bow of the thundergod or of some legendary hero.[2] Thus, in ancient Indic belief, it was the bow (rehitam) of Indra; and the modern Hindus sometimes identify it as that of Rama.[3] Among the Iranians, it is the weapon of Rustam or Bahman[4] and is known also in popular lore as the Devil's Bow (keman e-seytan).[5] The pre-Islamic Arabs saw in it the bow of the divine warrior Qozaiḥi.[6] Finnish folklore says that it is the bow of Ukko,[7] the god of thunder, or of the hero Wäinämöinen;[8] and an analogous notion obtains also among the Siberians.[9]

Now, in some versions of the Flood story that disaster is said to have been occasioned not by the wickedness of men but by a rebellion of the gods, and it was customary alike in ancient and medieval times for a victorious warrior to hang his triumphant arms in a temple or church both as a token of his powers and as a warning to future upstarts.[10] Indeed, in as early a source as the Babylonian Epic of Creation, the god Marduk is said to have suspended his bow in heaven after vanquishing the rebellious Ti'amat and her cohorts[11] even as did Qozaiḥi in Arab legend.[12] Not impossibly, then, the bow in the Biblical story is simply a transmogrified reminiscence of such an earlier version.

Nor, indeed, need the bow itself have been originally the same phenomenon as is today recognized under that name. For the fact is that ancient peoples did not always so identify it. In Mesopotamia, for instance, the rainbow was regarded not as a bow but as a ring (marratu), only the upper half of which appeared above the horizon.[13] In Lithuanian myth, it was the girdle of the goddess Laima;[14] and in the Armenian version of Philo's Questions and Solutions regarding Genesis and Exodus, it is that of Ormazd.[15] On the other hand, what was known as the Bow was a star or constellation. In Mesopotamia this was the popular name of Sirius, considered to be the regnant constellation of the month of August (Ab).[16]

In Classical antiquity the rainbow is usually considered a sign of disaster.[17] Among certain primitive peoples, however, it does indeed appear, as in the Bible, as a symbol of divine benevolence. The Chibchas (Muyscas) of Colombo, for instance, relate that once upon a time, Chibchachun, the tutelary god of the Bogotans, offended by the wickedness of the people, sent a flood. The people thereupon appealed to the culture-hero Bocicha. The latter appeared as a rainbow, struck the mountain with his staff, and opened a conduit for waters. Chibchachum was driven underground.[18]

Similarly, the Bataks of Sumatra tell the tale that their high god, enraged at the incest of a certain wizard with his grandchild Si Dole, sent a drought for three years. When finally rain fell, Si Dole appeared in the form of a rainbow, as she has done ever since after rain, as a memorial of that event.[19]

The Tower of Babel

11:1–9

▲ Having accounted for the natural condition of men, the Biblical record next turns to their diffusion over the earth and to the differences in their forms of speech.

At first, we are told, all men spoke the same language. Later, when they migrated from their original home in the east, they came to the plain of Shinar and decided to build a city and a tower with its top in the heavens, seeking thereby to raise a permanent monument to themselves in case they should eventually be dispersed over the face of the earth. Yahweh, however, discountenanced their enterprise as an example of man's overweening ambition. He therefore came down and confused their language, so that they could no longer understand one another. Then he indeed dispersed them in all directions. ▼

▲ 49 Scaling heaven

Stories which bear a certain resemblance to the Biblical legend are reported from several parts of the world.[1] Thus, in Africa, the Ba-Luyi, a tribe of the Upper Zambesi, say that formerly their god Nyambe (whom they identify with the sun) used to dwell on earth, but that he afterwards ascended up to heaven on a spider's web. From his post up aloft he said to men, "Worship me." But men said, "Come, let us kill Nyambe." Alarmed at this impious threat, the deity fled to the sky, from which it would seem that he had temporarily descended. So men said, "Come, let us make masts to reach up to heaven." They set up masts and added more masts, joining them one to the other, and they clambered up them. But when they had climbed far up, the masts fell down, and all the men on the masts were killed by the fall.[2]

The Bambala of the Congo say "that the Wangongo once wanted to know what the moon was, so they started to go and see. They planted a big pole in the ground, and a man climbed up it with a second pole which he fastened to the end; to this a third was fixed, and so on. When their Tower of Babel had reached a considerable height, so high in fact that the whole population of the village was carrying poles up, the erection suddenly collapsed, and they fell victims to their ill-advised curiosity. Since that time no one has tried to find out what the moon is."[3]

The Kulwe, a Bantu tribe living near Lake Rukwe in Tanganyika, tell a similar tale. According to them, men one day said to each other, "Let us build high, let us reach the moon!" So they rammed a great tree into the earth, and fixed another tree on the top of it, and another on the top of that, and so on, till the trees fell down and the men were killed. But other men said, "Let us not give up this undertaking," and they piled trees one on the top of the other, till one day the trees again fell down and the men were killed. Then the people gave up trying to climb aloft to the moon.[4]

[The Njamwezi of Tanganyika tell a similar tale. The Valengo, a large family which lived in primeval times, decided one day to build a tower to heaven. For several months they worked assiduously on the project, until at last it seemed to be nearing completion. Thereupon they summoned all their sons and grandsons to witness the crowning moment. Suddenly, however, a storm burst from the sky and overturned the structure. The Valengo were killed to the last man; wherefore, when a family becomes extinct, the Njamwesi say, "It has died like the Valengo."[4a]]

The Ashanti have a tradition that God of old dwelt among men, but that, resenting an affront put on him by an old woman, he withdrew in high dudgeon to his mansion in the sky. Disconsolate at his departure, mankind resolved to seek and find him. For that purpose they collected all the porridge pestles they could find and piled them up, one on the top of the other. When the tower thus built had nearly reached the sky, they found to their dismay that the supply of pestles ran short. What were they to do? In this dilemma a wise man stood up and said, "The matter is quite simple. Take the lowest pestle of all, and put it on the top, and go on doing so till we arrive at God." The proposal was carried, but when they came to put it in practice, down fell the tower, as indeed you might have expected. However, others say that the collapse of the tower was caused by the white ants, which gnawed away the lowest of the pestles. In whichever way it happened, the communication with heaven was not completed, and men were never able to ascend up to God.[5]

The Anal clan of the Kuki tribe, in Assam, tell of an attempt made by a man to climb up into the sky, in order to recover his stolen property. The story is as follows. Once upon a time there was a very pious man who devoted much time to worshipping God, and he had a pet bitch. Envious of his noble qualities, the sun and moon resolved to rob him of his virtue. In pursuit of this nefarious design, they promised to give him their virtue, if only he would first entrust them with his. The unsuspecting saint fell into the trap, and the two celestial rogues made off with his virtue. Thus defrauded, the holy man ordered his dog to pursue and catch the thieves. The intelligent animal brought a long pole and climbed up it to reach the fugitives, and the saint swarmed up the pole behind his dumb friend. Unfortunately he ascended so slowly that, before he reached the sky, the white ants had eaten away the lower end of the pole, so he fell down and broke his neck. But the bitch was more agile; before the white ants had gnawed through the wood, she had got a footing in the sky, and there the faithful animal is to this day, chasing the sun and moon round and round the celestial vault. Sometimes she catches them, and when she does so, the sun or moon is darkened, which Europeans call an eclipse. At such times the Anals shout to the bitch, "Release! Release!" meaning, of course, that she is to let go the sun or moon.[6]

[Again, a story current among the Lepcha of Sikkim describes how their remote ancestors—notorious for their folly—once started building a tower to heaven. When it had reached an impressive height, the builders at the top called to those at the bottom for more stones. The latter, however, thought they were being told to cut away the foundations. They did so, and the structure collapsed, killing half of the tribe. The ruins are still shown.[6a]

A Hindu legend, preserved in the Brahmaṇas, relates that in ancient times the demons resolved to build a fire-altar which would reach the sky. Indra, however, pulled out a brick, and the edifice toppled. All of the builders except two were turned into spiders; the two became the hounds of Yama, god of death.[6b]]

A story of an attempt to build a tower that should reach up to the clouds is told also by the natives of Lifu, one of the Loyalty Islands. The tale runs as follows:

"Their forefathers assembled at a place to build, or rather erect, a scaffolding which should reach to the clouds. They had no idea of works in stone, hence their 'tower of Babel' was raised by tying stick to stick with native vines. They laboured on undaunted by the sad consequences of the discovery and stealing of yams underground; perhaps they anticipated a more agreeable issue to their explorations in the heavens. But, alas, for human expectations! before the top touched the clouds, the ground-posts became rotten, and the whole affair came down with a crash."[7]

In Mexico, it is told of the great pyramid of Cholula that once upon a time certain giants aspired to build out of clay and bitumen a tower which would reach to heaven, so that they might enjoy from the top of it the spectacle of the rising and setting sun. When, however, they had reared it as high as they could, the inhabitants of heaven, at the bidding of their overlord, came down to all four quarters of the earth, overthrew the structure by a thunderbolt, and scattered the builders in all directions. In this case, however, the mention of clay and bitumen strongly suggest that the tale is dependent on the Biblical narrative, for while these were the materials out of which the Tower of Babel was constructed, the latter seems never to have been used by the Mexican for such purpose, nor is it to be found anywhere near Cholula.[8]

*   *   *

[The story of the tower upreared to the sky is but a particular variation on a more general theme, viz., that of the impious attempt to scale heaven in order to challenge the authority of the supreme god or of other supernal powers.[8a] Three stories revolving around this theme indeed appear in the literature of the Ancient Near East.

The first is a Hittite myth, the extant version of which dates from the latter half of the second millennium B.C. Hahhimas, a kind of Jack Frost, having paralyzed the earth and captured all the gods who are dispatched against him, eventually challenges the supreme Weather-god with the threat, "I will ascend unto heaven." The Supreme God warns him, however, that even though he may seize and paralyze the limbs of all other beings, he will not be able to immobilize his (the Supreme God's) all-seeing and ever-watchful eyes, and will therefore meet his deserts. The text is unfortunately incomplete, but it would appear that in the end Hahhimas was indeed discomfited, for our myth is accompanied by rubrics for a ceremony in honor of the beneficent Sun-god and of the Spirit of Vegetation (Telipinu), who must therefore have succeeded in besting the monster and have themselves emerged triumphant.[8b]

A second Hittite myth embodying the same basic motif relates how the god Kumarbi, at odds with the reigning sovereign of heaven, engendered a monstrous creature, Ullikummi, who grew up miraculously in the form of a stone pillar and, mounted on the shoulder of a subaqueous giant, tried to rock the floor of heaven and topple the gods from their thrones. In this case too, however, the impious effort proved abortive, for the god Ea severed the monster from his support by means of a magic cleaver, and he crashed forthwith to his doom.[8c]

The third instance of our theme occurs in the Old Testament itself, for in Isaiah 14:12–15 the contumacious king of Babylon is likened to a certain Helal (E.V.: "Lucifer, Day Star"), son of Dawn, who aspired to scale heaven, to enthrone himself on the divine mountain, above the highest stars, and to assume the role of a supernal being,[8d] but who eventually fell and was "cut down."

The most familiar of all such stories, however, is the Greek myth of the twin giants Otos and Ephialtes who sought to challenge the authority of the gods by storming heaven and who piled Mt. Ossa upon Mt. Pelion in order to ascend thither. They too came to a sorry end at the hands of either Apollo or Artemis (there are different versions).[8e]] ▼

▲ 50 The confusion of tongues 11:6–9

Not only in the Old Testament, but also in the folklore of primitive peoples, the building of the tower to heaven is associated with a subsequent confusion of tongues.[1] Thus the Gherko Karens, who live in Burma, relate that they became separated from the Red Karens in the thirteenth generation after Adam, when the people decided to build a pagoda up to heaven, but were frustrated in that design by the wrath of God who came down, confounded their tongue, and caused one group to separate from the rest.

The Mikirs of Assam tell a similar tale concerning the mighty descendants of Ram who, tired of the mastery of earth, tried to conquer heaven by building a tower up to it, only to have their speech confounded and to be scattered to the corners of the world.[2]

In the same vein too the Toltecs of Mexico relate how certain men who had escaped a great cataclysm in a closed chest (*toptlipetlacali*) sought refuge from a possible second disaster by building a tower to heaven, only to have their tongue confused and to be dispersed to different parts of the world.[3]

To be sure, some of these stories seem to betray Biblical influence. Thus, in the Polynesian island of Tuamotu the legend runs that after a flood sent by the god Vatea to punish sinful men, the descendants of a certain pious Rata, who had been spared from the disaster by being instructed to build an "ark," attempted to erect at Maragai a temple which would reach heaven and enable them to see the god face to face. Vatea, however, destroyed the edifice and dispersed them, at the same time confusing their tongues. Originally all spoke one language; now they speak three languages.[4]

Not a few peoples, however, have attempted to explain the diversities of human speech without reference to a Tower of Babel or similar structures.

Thus the Greeks had a tradition that for many ages men lived at peace, without cities and without laws, speaking one language, and ruled by Zeus alone. At last Hermes introduced diversities of speech and divided mankind into separate nations. So discord first arose among mortals, and Zeus, offended at their quarrels, resigned the sovereignty and committed it to the hands of the Argive hero Phoroneus, the first king of men.[5]

The Wa-Sania of British East Africa say that of old all the tribes of the earth knew only one language, but that during a severe famine the people went mad and wandered in all directions, jabbering strange words, and so the different languages arose.[6] A different explanation of the diversities of language is given by the Kachcha Nagas, a hill tribe of Assam. According to them, at the creation all men were of one race, but they were destined soon afterwards to be broken up into different nations. The king of the men then on earth had a daughter named Sitoylê. She was wondrous fleet of foot, and loved to roam the jungle the livelong day, far from home, thereby causing much anxiety to her parents, who feared lest she should be devoured by wild beasts. One day her father conceived a plan for keeping her at home. He sent for a basket of linseed, and upsetting it on the ground he ordered his daughter to put the seeds back, one by one, into the basket, counting them as she did so. Then thinking that the task he had set her would occupy the maiden the whole day, he withdrew. But by sunset his daughter had counted all the seeds and put them back in the basket, and no sooner had she done so than away she hurried to the jungle. So when her parents returned, they could find no trace of their missing daughter. After searching for days and days, however, they at last came across a monster python lying gorged in the shade of the trees. All the men being assembled, they attacked the huge reptile with spear and sword. But even as they struck at the snake, their appearance changed, and they found themselves speaking various dialects. The men of the same speech now drew apart from the rest and formed a separate band, and the various bands thus created became the ancestors of the different nations now existing on earth.[7] But what became of the princess, whether she was restored to her sorrowing parents, or whether she had been swallowed by the python, the story does not relate.

The Kukis of Manipur, another hill race of Assam, account for the diversity of languages in their tribes by saying, that once on a time the three grandsons of a certain chief were all playing together in the house, when their father bade them catch a rat. But while they were busy hunting the animal, they were suddenly smitten with a confusion of tongues and could not understand each other, so the rat escaped. The eldest of the three sons now spoke the Lamyang language; the second spoke the Thado language; and as for the third, some say that he spoke the Waiphie language, but others think it was the Manipur tongue which he spoke. At all events the three lads became the ancestors of three distinct tribes.[8]

The Encounter Bay tribe of South Australia trace the origin of languages to an ill-tempered old woman, who died long ago. Her name was Wurruri, she lived towards the east, and generally walked about with a big stick in her hand to scatter the fires round which other people were sleeping. When at last she died, her people were so glad to be rid of her, that they sent messengers in all directions to announce the good news of her death. Men, women, and children accordingly assembled, not to mourn but to rejoice over the decease and to celebrate it by a cannibal banquet. The Raminjerar were the first who fell upon the corpse and commenced to devour the flesh; and no sooner did they do so than they began to speak intelligibly. The other tribes to the eastward, arriving later, ate the contents of the intestines, which caused them to speak a language slightly different. Last of all came the northern tribes, and having consumed the intestines and all that remained of the corpse, they spoke a language which differed still more from that of the Raminjerar.[9]

The Maidu Indians of California say that down to a certain time everybody spoke the same language. But once, when the people were having a burning, and everything was ready for the next day, suddenly in the night everybody began to speak in a different tongue, except that each husband and wife talked the same language. That night the Creator, whom they call Earth-Initiate, appeared to a certain man named Kuksu, told him what had happened, and instructed him how to proceed next day when the Babel of tongues would commence. Thus prepared, Kuksu summoned all the people together, for he could speak all the languages. He taught them the names of the different animals and so forth in their various dialects, showed them how to cook and to hunt, gave them their laws, and appointed the times for their dances and festivals. Then he called each tribe by name, and sent them off in different directions, telling them where they were to dwell.[10] Quiché of Guatemala told of a time, in the early ages of the world, when men lived together and spoke but one language, when they invoked as yet neither wood nor stone, and remembered naught but the word of the Creator, the Heart of heaven and of earth. However, as years went on the tribes multiplied, and leaving their old home came to a place called Tulan. It was there, according to Quiché tradition, that the language of the tribes changed and the diversity of tongues originated; the people ceased to understand each other's speech and dispersed to seek new homes in different parts of the world.[11] ▼

51   Babel

Just as the primitive stories often identify the mythical Tower with some prominent local landmark, so the Biblical writer identifies it with one in the plain of Shinar—that is, in Babylonia. This reflects a popular identification of it with one of the great stepped pyramids, or ziggurats, of that area, and such identification was no doubt suggested by the fact that these edifices were indeed regarded by the Babylonians as links between heaven and earth. Thus Esagila, the principal ziggurat of Babylon, shrine of its tutelary god Marduk, was styled "House of the Foundation of Heaven and Earth (*E-temen-an-ki*), and King Nabupolassar (625–605 B.C.), who restored it, says of it that "it has its base at the navel of the earth, and its top in heaven." Similarly, the ziggurat at Kish was known as "the lofty tower of the deities Zababa and Innana, the summit whereof is in heaven"; and that at Larsa as "the link between heaven and earth."[1] The notion survives curiously in the following modern description of a church:

> *Steeple that rises high,*
> *Bond between sun and sod,*
> *Link between earth and sky,*
> *Union of man with God.*[2]

The Biblical writer, however, is even more precise, for when he says (11:9) that the tower was named "Babble" because the Lord there made a babble (Heb.: *balal*) of men's tongues, he is simply playing—not without strain—on the name Babel, i.e., Babylon, which really means "Gate of God" (*bab ili*).[3] Evidently, then, he had Esagila specifically in mind.

The Patriarchs

ABRAHAM

52 Abraham and Melchizedek   14:18–20

Melchizedek, king of Salem and priest of El 'Elyon (RSV: God Most High), concludes a covenant with Abraham the Hebrew by the mutual consumption of bread and wine. In the same way, Isaac makes a pact with the Philistines over food and drink (Gen. 26:30), and, in the time of Joshua, the Israelites become pledged to the Gibeonites when they eat of the latter's provisions (Jos. 9:11–14). So too, the prophet Obadiah (7) describes confederates as "men of thy bread," and the Psalmist speaks (50:5) of men "who make a covenant over a meal."[1]

The underlying notion is that persons who have broken bread together and thus absorbed a common substance thereby enter into a mutual relationship.[2] Among bedouin Arabs such "com-panionship" is established if one take but a morsel of food or a few pinches of salt in another man's tent; this puts one temporarily under his protection.[3] In the same sense, Herodotus informs us that the Nasamonaeans used to conclude pacts between individuals by each drinking out of the other's hand.[4] In Madagascar, such pacts are still made by having the parties drink out of the same bowl; and in the Watubela and Luang-Sermata Islands, quarrels are composed in this manner.[5]

In the Papuan villages of Leti, Moa, and Lakor, treaties of friendship between neighboring communities are forged by eating common flesh and drinking common blood; while to the same end the Kumis of Southeast India kill and eat a goat together, smearing the blood over the parties. A more savage variant of this is the practice in the Timorlaut Islands of killing a slave and eating him jointly.[6]

The Mandaeans of Iraq and Iran periodically recement their social ties by sharing a ritual meal;[7] and this was also the reason why the ancient Greeks used to celebrate a family meal beside the tombs of their deceased relatives, and why it is sometimes portrayed on the gravestone.[8]

Melchizedek accompanies the proffering of food and drink by a solemn declaration that Abraham is thereby embraced within the sphere of El 'Elyon's numinous providence and protection [Heb.: *berakah*]: "Blessed [Heb.: *bāruk*] be Abram by El 'Elyon, owner [RSV: maker] of heaven and earth." So too Isaac declares to the high contracting party of the Philistines that they are thenceforth "blessed [*bāruk*] of Yahweh" (Gen. 26:29). The point of the declaration is that the local or family god was regarded among the ancient Semites as a member of the kindred group.[9] Accordingly, when members of different groups entered into a pact of commensality, their gods also were involved in the arrangement and had also to extend their protection to the "party of the second part." An interesting illustration of this is afforded by a passage in the Ugaritic (Canaanite) *Poem of Aqhat,* our extant copy of which dates to the fourteenth century B.C. When the thug Yatpan (really the murderer of her brother) extends his protection to the maiden Pughat, he proffers a goblet of wine and then declares "(Now) let our god be given to drink of the wine, even the god . . . who owns these domains."[10] Similarly, in Vergil's *Aeneid,* when the Carthaginians (i.e., Phoenicians) welcome Aeneas to her realm, their queen Dido fills a traditional goblet with wine and invokes Jupiter, Vergil's Roman equivalent for the Semitic god, who, men say, makes the laws for host and guest (*hospitibus nam te dare jura loquuntur*).[11]

▲ 53 "Cutting" a covenant   15:10 ff.

After quitting Babylonia, the land of his birth, Abraham is said to have migrated to Canaan and there to have received from God in person the assurance of the future grandeur and glory of his race. To confirm his promise the deity, we are told, condescended to enter into a regular covenant with the patriarch, observing all the legal formalities which were customary on such occasions among men. The narrative of this important transaction affords us an interesting glimpse into the means adopted by covenanters in primitive society for the purpose of creating a binding obligation on both sides.

God, we are told, commanded Abraham, saying to him, "Take me an heifer of three years old, and a she-goat of three years old, and a ram of three years old, and a turtledove, and a young pigeon." So Abraham took the heifer, the she-goat, and the ram, cut them in two, and laid each half of the animal over against the other; but the birds he did not divide. And when the birds of prey came down on the carcasses, Abraham drove them away. When the sun was going down, Abraham sank into a deep sleep, and a horror of great darkness fell upon him. And it came to pass that when the sun had set, and it was dark, behold a smoking furnace and a flaming torch passed between the pieces of the sacrificial victims, and God proclaimed his covenant with Abraham.

In this description the horror of great darkness which falls on Abraham at sunset is a premonition of the coming of God, who in the darkness of night passes between the pieces of the slaughtered animals in the likeness of a smoking furnace and a flaming torch. In doing so the deity only complied with the legal formalities required by ancient Hebrew law at the ratification of a covenant; for we know from Jeremiah that it was the custom of the contracting parties to cut a calf in twain and pass between the pieces.[1] That this was the regular form observed on such occasions is strongly suggested by the Hebrew phrase for making a covenant, which is literally to "cut a covenant,"[2] [and the same expression has now turned up in a cuneiform document from ancient Qatna (modern Mishrifé) in Syria, of the fourteenth century B.C.[2a]]. Moreover, the inference is confirmed by analogies in the language and ritual of the Greeks. They too spoke of *cutting* oaths in the sense of *swearing* them,[3] and of *cutting* a treaty instead of *making* one,[4] and such expressions (which have their counterpart also in Latin)[5] are undoubtedly derived from a custom of sacrificing victims and cutting them in pieces as a mode of adding solemnity to an oath or treaty. We are told, for instance, that when Agamemnon was about to lead the Achaeans to Troy, the soothsayer Calchas brought a boar into the market-place and divided it into two parts, one on the west, and one on the east. Then each man, with a drawn sword in his hand passed between the pieces of the animal, and the blade of his sword was smeared with the blood. Thus they swore enmity to Priam.[6]

[The same procedure was observed in Lithuania as late as the fourteenth century, for it is recorded that in 1351 King Kestutus of that country ratified a treaty with the king of Hungary by having his soldiers march between the severed head and the trunk of an ox.[6a]]

Ceremonies of a like kind are still observed at peace-making by savage tribes in Africa and India. Thus among the Kavirondo, of British East Africa, in making peace after a war, the vanquished side takes a dog and cuts it in halves. The delegates from each side then hold respectively the forequarters and the hindquarters of the divided dog, and swear peace and friendship over the half dog which they hold in their hands.[7] A similar ceremony is used to seal a covenant of peace among the Nandi, another tribe of the same region. They cut a dog in halves: the two halves are held by men representing the two sides who have been at war; and a third man says, "May the man who breaks this peace be killed like this dog."[8] Among the Bagesu, a Bantu tribe of Mount Elgon, in British East Africa, when two clans have been at war and wish to make peace, the representatives of the clans hold a dog, one by the head and the other by the hind legs, while a third man cuts the dog through with a large knife at one stroke. The body is then thrown away in the bush and left, and thereafter the members of the two clans may freely intermingle without any fear or trouble or danger.[9]

Among the Masai of East Africa, "in settling serious disputes by oath, each disputant takes hold of a goat or sheep, which is then cut in two. This is done in presence of witnesses, and the matter thus settled is not supposed to be re-opened."[10] In the Wachaga tribe of the same region, when two districts have resolved to form a solemn league and covenant of peace, the ceremony observed

at the ratification of the treaty is as follows. The warriors of the two districts
assemble and sit down crowded together in a circle on some piece of open
ground. A long rope is stretched round the assembly and its free ends are
knotted together on one side, so that the whole body of warriors from both
sides is enclosed within the rope. But before the knot is tied, the rope is moved
thrice or seven times round the circle and a kid is carried with it. Finally, on
the side of the circle where the ends are knotted together, the rope is passed
over the body of the kid, which is held stretched at full length by two men, so
that the rope and the kid form parallel lines, the rope being over the kid.
These motions of the rope and of the kid round the sitting warriors are carried
out by two uncircumcised and therefore childless lads; and the circumstance
is significant, because the lads symbolize that infertility or death without offspring which the Wachaga regard as the greatest of curses, and which they
commonly refer to the action of the higher powers. In most of their treaties
they imprecate this dreaded curse on perjurers, and on the contrary call down
the blessing of numerous progeny on him who shall keep his oath. In the
ceremony under discussion the employment of uncircumcised youths is intended not merely to symbolize the fate of the perjurer but to effect it by
sympathetic magic. For a similar reason the curses and the blessings are recited
by old men, because they are past the age of begetting children. The recitation
runs as follows, "If after the making of this covenant I do anything to harm
thee or devise devices against thee without giving thee warning, may I be split
in two like this rope and this kid!" Chorus, "Amen!" "May I split in two
like a boy who dies without begetting children!" Chorus, "Amen!" "May my
cattle perish, every one!" Chorus, "Amen!" "But if I do not that; if I be true
to thee, so may I fare well!" Chorus, "Amen!" "May my children be like the
bees in number!" Chorus, "Amen!" And so forth and so forth. When the
representatives of the two covenanting districts have sworn the oath, the rope
and the kid are cut in two at one stroke, and the spouting blood sprinkled on
the covenanters, while the old men in a comprehensive formula call down
curses and blessings impartially on both sides. Afterwards the flesh of the
goat is eaten by old men who are past the age of begetting children, and the
rope is divided between the two districts, each of which keeps its portion carefully. If epidemics should break out and be attributed by the diviners, who
interpret the will of the higher powers, to some breach of the treaty committed
wittingly or unwittingly by the inhabitants of the afflicted country, the rope
must be expiated or, as the native phrase goes, "cooled." For the magical
power with which the covenant invested the rope is now believed to be actively
engaged in avenging its violation. The expiation consists in sacrificing a lamb
and smearing its blood and dung on the rope, while the following words are
spoken: "Those people have done wrong without knowing it. Rope, to-day
I expiate thee, that thou mayst harm them no more! Be expiated! Be expiated!
Be expiated!" The persons who have committed the breach of faith are expiated

by a medicine-man, who sprinkles them with a magical mixture compounded out of the blood of tortoises, rock-badgers, and antelopes, together with portions of certain plants, the whole being administered by means of a bunch of herbs of definite sorts and accompanied by appropriate words.[11]

Somewhat different, though conforming to the same general type, are the ceremonies observed at peace-making among some tribes of South Africa. Thus, in the Barolong tribe, when the chief wished to make a covenant of peace with another chief who had fled to him for protection, he took the paunch of a large ox, and bored a hole through it, and the two chiefs crawled through the hole, the one after the other, in order to intimate by this ceremony that their tribes would thenceforth be one.[12] Similarly among the Bechuanas "in making a public covenant or agreement with one another, two chiefs *tshwaragana moshwang;* that is to say, an animal is slaughtered, and some of the contents of its stomach are laid hold of by both covenanting parties, their hands meeting together and laying hold of each other, while covered over with the contents of the sacrificed animal's stomach. This would seem to be the most solemn form of public agreement known in the country."[13]

Equivalent ceremonies are observed at peace-making among some of the hill tribes of Assam. Thus the Nagas "have several ways of taking an oath. The commonest and most sacred is for the two parties to the oath to lay hold of a dog or fowl, one by its head the other by its tail or feet, whilst the animal or bird is cut in two with a *dâo,* emblematic of the perjurer's fate."[14] According to another authority, the most sacred oath is for each party to take a fowl, one by the head and the other by the legs, and in this manner to pull it asunder, intimating that treachery or breach of agreement would merit the same treatment."[15] Other Naga tribes of Assam have a somewhat different way of settling disputes. "A representative of each of the litigant parties holds an end of a cane basket inside which a cat, alive, is placed, and at a signal a third man hacks the cat in two, and both sides then cut it up with their daos, taking care to stain the weapon with blood. On the occasion when I saw this ceremony I was told that the ceremony was a form of peace-making or treaty, and that therefore the slaughter of the cat bound them in a kind of covenant."[16]

[Sometimes, too, the ceremony is performed in cases where the intention is simply to forge a union rather than to compose a quarrel. In Iran, for instance, it is customary for a bridal party to pass between the severed heads and carcasses of five sheep.[16a]]

*   *   *

Why should the parties to a covenant or an oath ratify it by killing an animal, cutting it in pieces, standing on the pieces or passing between them, and smearing the blood on their persons? Two different theories have been suggested. The one may be called the *retributive* theory and the other the *sacramental* or purificatory. According to the former, the killing and cutting up of the victim is symbolic of the retribution which will overtake the man who breaks the covenant or violates the oath; he, like the animal, will perish by a violent death.[16b] This certainly appears to be the interpretation put upon the ceremony by some of the peoples who observe it. Thus the Wachaga say, "May I split in two like this rope and this kid!" and in cutting a dog in two the Nandi say, "May the man who breaks this peace be killed like this dog."

A similar ceremony, accompanied by similar imprecations, used to solemnize the making of peace among the Awome, a people of the Niger delta who are better known to Europeans as New Calabars. When two towns or subtribes grew weary of fighting, they would send to the ancient village of Ke, situated near the coast, to the east of the Sombreiro River, where there was a fetish or ju-ju called Ke-ni Opu-So. On such occasions the fetish priest was invited to come and preside over the ratification of peace between the belligerents. Accordingly he came in his canoe decked with young palm leaves, and arranged with the former foes to meet on an appointed day and swear to the covenant. When the day came, the people gathered together, and the inhabitants of Ke also came, bringing with them the necessary offerings, which consisted of a sheep, a length of black or dark blue cloth, gunpowder, and grass or grass seed. Over these offerings the old enemies swore peace and friendship, the priest first saying, "To-day we Ke people bring peace to your town. From now on neither of you may have evil mind against the other." With these words he drew forward the sheep and cleft it in two, saying, "Should either town fight again, may it be cleft asunder like this sheep." Then, lifting up the piece of dark cloth, he said, "As this cloth is dark, so may the offending town be darkened." Next, setting fire to the gunpowder, he said, "As this powder is burnt, so may fire burn the guilty town." Lastly, holding out the grass, he said, "Should either town fight again, may that town be covered with grass." On account of the services which the people of Ke rendered as peace-makers, an ancient law of Calabar forbade any other town to wage war on Ke under pain of banishment to be inflicted on the transgressors by all the other members of the tribe in concert.[17] In these Calabar rites the retributive intention of cleaving the sheep in two is expressed without ambiguity, and it is corroborated by the imprecations by which the other symbolic ceremonies are accompanied.

The same explanation is given of the similar rite among the Nagas, and is confirmed by the variations in the form of the oath, which seem best explained as signifying the retribution that will befall the perjurer. The retributive theory can be also supported by evidence drawn from classical antiquity. Thus when the Romans and the Albans made a treaty, which, according to Livy, was the most ancient treaty on record, the representative of the Roman people prayed to Jupiter, saying, "If the Roman people shall knowingly and of set purpose depart from the terms of this treaty, then smite thou them, O Jupiter, on that day, as I smite this boar-pig to-day." So saying, he smote and killed the pig with a flint knife.[18] Again, we read in Homer that at the making of a truce between the Greeks and the Trojans, lambs were slaughtered, and while they lay gasping out their life on the ground, Agamemnon poured a libation of wine, and as he did so, both Greeks and Trojans prayed that whichever side violated their oath, their brains might be dashed out, even as the wine was poured on the ground.[19]

The retributive intention of the sacrifice in such cases comes out very clearly in an Akkadian inscription, which records the solemn oath of fealty taken by Mati'-ilu, king of Arpad (751 B.C.) to Ashur-nirari, king of Assyria. Part of the inscription runs thus: "This he-goat has not been brought up from its flock for sacrifice, neither for sickness nor for slaughter, but it has been brought up that Mati'-ilu may swear fealty by it to Ashur-nirari, king of Assyria. If Mati'-ilu sins against his oath, just as this he-goat has ben brought up from his flock, so that he returns not to his flock and sets himself no more at the head of his flock, so shall Mati'-ilu be brought up from his land, with his sons, his daughters, . . . and the people of his land, and he shall not return to his land, neither set himself at the head of his land. This head is not the head of the he-goat, it is the head of Mati'-ilu, it is the head of his sons, of his nobles, of the people of his land. If Mati'-ilu breaks this oath, as the head of this he-goat is cut off, so shall the head of Mati'-ilu be cut off. This right foot is not the right foot of the he-goat, it is the right hand of Mati'-ilu, the right hand of his sons, of his nobles, of the people of his land. If Mati'-ilu [breaks this covenant], just as the right foot [of this he-goat] is torn off [so shall the right hand of Mati'-ilu, the right hand of] his sons [of his nobles, and of the people of his land], be torn off." Here there is a long gap in the inscription. We may conjecture that in the missing portion the dismemberment of the victim was further described, and that as each limb was lopped off, the sacrificer proclaimed that it was not the limb of the goat that was severed, but the limb of Mati'-ilu, of his sons, his daughters, his nobles, and the people of his land, if they should prove traitors to their liege lord, the king of Assyria.[20]

[Rites of the same kind are described also in Babylonian records in connection with the swearing of oaths in general: an animal is cut up, and the man swearing the oath invokes a similar fate on himself, should he break his word.[20a] So too in a Hittite ritual for composing a domestic quarrel, a sheep and a pig are cut up, and the pieces thrown into a hole; and they are described explicitly as substitutes for the human parties involved.[20b]]

Similar sacrifices, accompanied and interpreted by similar imprecations, likewise meet us in the ritual of barbarous peoples at the present time. Thus on the island of Nias, by way of ratifying a solemn oath or covenant, a man will cut the throat of a sucking-pig, while at the same time he calls down on his own head a like death if he forswears himself or breaks his engagement.[21] In the island of Timor a common form of giving evidence on oath is this: the witness takes a fowl in one hand and a sword in the other, and says, "Lord God, who art in heaven and on earth, look upon me! If I bear false witness to harm my fellow-men, may I be punished! This day I make my oath, and if I am not speaking the truth, may my head be cut off like the head of this fowl!" So saying, he chops off the bird's head on a wooden block.[22] Among the Battas of Sumatra when chiefs are assembled to make peace or enter into a solemn covenant, a pig or a cow is brought forth, and the chiefs stand round it, each with his spear in his hand. Then the gongs are beaten, and the oldest or most respected chief cuts the animal's throat with his knife; afterwards the beast's body is opened, and the still palpitating heart torn out and chopped into as many bits as there are chiefs present. Each chief thereupon puts his morsel on a spit, roasts or warms it at a fire, and holding it up says, "If ever I break my oath, may I be slain like this beast that lies bleeding before me, and may I be eaten as its heart is now eaten." So saying he swallows the morsel. When all the chiefs have observed this rite, the still reeking carcass is divided among the people present and serves them for a feast.[23]

The Malagasy had a solemn form of swearing allegiance to a new sovereign, which was called "spearing the calf." A young bullock was killed and dismembered, the head and tail being cut off and reversed in their position at each end of the animal, while the hind-feet and the fore-feet were similarly transposed; moreover the carcass was cut open, and a spear thrust into the bowels. Then a number of the chiefs or other principal men who were to be sworn, took hold of the spear, as many as could conveniently grasp it, and standing round the mangled animal listened, while the senior judge pronounced the oath, calling down many terrible curses on all who should perjure themselves, and winding up with these words, "If any of you ever retract, if any of you ever refuse allegiance to the sovereign appointed to reign, whether all has been specifically named or not, whether present or absent, great or small, old or young, male or female, newly brought to life or still unborn, whether holding the spear or not holding it, behold this glittering spear! behold this young bullock! and let the perjurer be as this bullock; let him be speared of god; let him not be favoured in any thing, but let him be wholly accursed!"[24]

Among the Gallas of East Africa, when a man is accused of a crime, a common form of clearing himself from the accusation is this. A cock and a rusty knife are handed to him; he kills the bird, cuts it limb from limb, then hacks the body in pieces till he has made mince meat of it down to the last feather, which he throws away with an imprecation, praying that, if he is guilty, it may be done unto him as he has done unto the fowl.[25] Among the Akikuyu of East Africa the most solemn form of oath is administered by beating a goat to death with a stone and imprecating at the same time a like fate on all who should forswear themselves. The ceremony may only be performed by an elder of a particular clan. C. W. Hobley has described how the oath was administered to the tribe on a particular occasion, when the head chief desired to bind his people to the discharge of certain obligations which they had of late neglected. "A male goat of not less than two or three colours had its four legs tied together in a bunch by means of a green withy, a number of twigs of certain plants were gathered and then packed in between the legs and the body of the animal. . . . These preparations being complete all the participators in the oath moved to the windward of the animal—all except the elder who conducted the ceremony. The elder in question then took a large stone and beat the legs of the animal until he considered they were broken, all the time calling out that any who broke the oath would have their legs broken in a similar way. He then enumerated the obligations which it was essential they should fulfil. Next he hammered the spine of the animal, and finally beat in the skull with a stone, continually haranguing the assembly and condemning them to a similar fate if they broke the oath by omitting to fulfil the duties he enumerated. It is considered very deadly to stand down wind from the goat while this ceremony is going on. The assembled crowd then marched off chanting, and about half a mile down the road another speckled male goat had been slaughtered and the blood and contents of the stomach were spread on the path; each member of the assembly had to tread in this with his bare feet, and on every one who did this the oath was considered binding. The second goat was killed by its stomach being opened. Neither of the sacrificial animals was eaten but left in the bush to be devoured by hyenas.[26]

Again, among the Chins, who inhabit the hills on the borders of Assam and Burma, when two tribes take an oath of friendship, they meet and produce a tame bison. The wise men of each village pour liquors over it and mutter to their respective spirits to note the agreement which is now to be made over blood. The chiefs of either side each take a spear and standing on opposite sides of the bison drive their spears into its heart. If guns and not spears are used, the two chiefs simultaneously fire into the animal's brain or heart. As the bison falls its throat is cut and the blood collected in bowls; the tail of the animal is then cut off and dipped in the blood, and with it the chiefs and elders of the two parties daub the blood on each other's faces, whilst the wise men mutter, "May the party who breaks this agreement die even as this animal has died, and may he be buried outside the village and his spirit never rest; may his family also die and may every bad fortune attend his village."[27]

In the old days, when the Karens of Burma desired to make peace with their enemies, the representatives of the two sides met and proceeded as follows. Filings made from a sword, a spear, a musket barrel, and a stone were mixed in a cup of water with the blood of a dog, a hog, and a fowl, which were killed for the purpose. This mixture of blood, water, and filings was called the "peace-making water." Next the skull of the slaughtered dog was chopped in two, and the representative of one side took the lower jaw of the animal and hung it by a string round his neck, while the representative of the other hung the dog's skull, including the upper jaw, round his neck in like manner. Thereafter the representatives solemnly promised that their people would thenceforth live at peace with each other, and in confirmation of the promise they drank the "peace-making water," and having drunk it they said, "Now that we have made peace, if any one breaks the engagement, if he does not act truly, but goes to war again and stirs up the feud again, may the spear eat his breast, the musket his bowels, the sword his head; may the dog devour him, may the hog devour him, may the stone devour him!"[28] Here the sword, the spear, the musket, and the stone, as well as the slain dog, hog, and fowl, are supposed to assist in bringing down vengeance on the perjurer, who has imbibed portions of them all in the "peace-making water."

In these examples the retributive virtue ascribed to the sacrifice is rendered unmistakable by the accompanying words: the slaughter of the animal symbolizes the slaughter of the perjurer, or rather it is a piece of imitative magic designed to bring down on the transgressor the death which he deserves. A retributive effect is also ascribed to the slaughter of an animal in the following instances, though in them apparently the efficient cause is believed to be the ghost of the slain animal rather than the magical virtue of the ceremony. Thus the Kayans or Bahaus of Central Borneo swear in ordinary cases on the tooth of a royal tiger; but in serious cases they put a dog slowly to death by stabbing it repeatedly with a sword, while the man who takes the oath smears his body with the streaming blood. They believe that if he forswears himself the ghost of the dog will haunt, bite, and kill him.[29] Similarly, among the Ossetes of the Caucasus, a man who swears will sometimes cut off a cat's head or hang a dog, praying that if he swears falsely or breaks his oath, the cat or dog may bite or scratch him.[30] Here again it seems obvious that it is the ghost of the hanged dog or decapitated cat which is charged with the duty of avenging perjury.[31]

*　　　　　*　　　　　*

But it may be questioned whether the retributive function of the sacrifice suffices to explain the remarkable feature in the Hebrew and Greek rite which consists in passing between the pieces of the slain animal or standing upon them. Accordingly Robertson Smith suggested what we may call the sacramental or purificatory interpretation of the rite. He supposed that "the parties stood between the pieces, as a symbol that they were taken within the mystical life of the victim,"[32] and in confirmation of this view he pointed to the use of the very same rite in other cases to which the idea of punishment or retribution appears to be inapplicable, but of which some at least can be explained as modes of ceremonial purification. Thus in Boeotia a form of public purification was to cut a dog in two and pass between the pieces.[33] A similar rite was observed at purifying a Macedonian army. A dog was cut in two: the head and fore part were placed on the right, the hinder part, with the entrails, was placed on the left, and the troops in arms marched between the pieces. On the conclusion of the rite the army used to divide into two and engage in a sham fight.[34] Again, it is said that when Peleus sacked Iolcus, he slew the king's wife Astydamia, cut her in pieces, and caused the army to march between the pieces into the city.[35] The ceremony was probably regarded as a form of purification to which a high degree of solemnity was imparted by the use of a human victim. This interpretation is confirmed by the ritual which the Albanians of the Caucasus observed at the temple of the Moon; from time to time they used to sacrifice a sacred slave by stabbing him with a spear, after which the body was carried to a certain place and all the people stepped on it as a purificatory rite.[36] Among the Basutos of South Africa a form of ceremonial purification is this. They slaughter an animal, pierce it through and through, and then cause the person who is to be purified to pass through the hole in the carcass.[37] We have seen that among the Barolong of South Africa a similar rite is observed at making a covenant: the covenanters force themselves through a hole in the stomach of the slaughtered animal. Together, these South African customs suggest that the passage between the pieces of a sacrificial victim is a substitute for passing through the carcass itself.

The purificatory, or better, perhaps, the protective, interpretation of such rites is strongly confirmed by the practice of the Arabs of Moab, who still observe similar ceremonies in times of public calamity, such as drought or epidemic, and explain them as intended to deliver the people from the evil which afflicts or threatens them. If, for example, the tribe is suffering from the ravages of cholera, the sheikh will stand up in the middle of the camp and cry out, "Redeem yourselves, O people, redeem yourselves!" Thereupon every family takes a sheep, sacrifices it, and, having divided it in two, hangs the pieces under the tent or on two posts in front of the door. All the members of the family then pass between the two pieces of the victim; children too young to walk are carried by their parents. Often they pass several times between the bleeding fragments of the sheep, because these are thought to possess the virtue of driving away the evil or the jinn who would injure the tribe. A similar remedy is resorted to in seasons of drought, when the pastures are withered and the cattle dying for lack of rain. The sacrifice is regarded as a ransom for man and beast. The Arabs say, "This is our ransom, for us and for our flocks." Questioned as to the mode in which the ceremony produces this salutary effect, they say that the sacrifice meets and combats the calamity. The epidemic or drought, or whatever it may be, is conceived as a wind blowing across the plains and sweeping all before it, till it encounters the sacrifice which, like a lion, bestrides the path. A terrific combat ensues; the disease or drought is beaten and retires discomfited, while the victorious sacrifice remains in possession of the field.[38] Here certainly there is no idea of retribution: neither symbolically nor magically is the death of the sheep supposed to entail the death of the people who pass between the joints of mutton; on the contrary, it is believed to save their lives by protecting them against the evil which, in one way or another, threatens their existence.

In like circumstances a precisely similar custom is observed and similarly explained by the Chins, who inhabit the hill country bordering on Assam and

Burma. Among these people, "when a person believes that he is followed by an enraged spirit, such as the spirit of cholera, it is a common practice to cut a dog in half without severing the entrails and to place the fore-quarters on one side of the road and the hind-quarters on the other side and connected by the intestines stretched across the road; this is to appease the spirit and to dissuade him from following any further."[39] So strictly do the Chins personify cholera as a dangerous spirit, that when a party of them visited Rangoon in time of the epidemic, they carried their swords drawn, wherever they went, to scare away the demon, and they spent the day hiding under bushes that he might not find them.[40] Similar means of averting a plague or pestilence used to be employed by the Koryaks of north-eastern Siberia. They slaughtered a dog, wound the guts about two posts, and passed under them.[41] No doubt they also thought in this way to give the slip to the spirit of disease, who would find an insurmountable barrier in dog's guts. Again, women after childbirth are commonly supposed to be unclean and to be exposed to the attacks of malignant supernatural beings. Hence among the gipsies of Transylvania, when a woman in such circumstances leaves her bed of sickness, she is made to pass between the pieces of a cock which has been cut in two, if her child is a boy, but between the pieces of a hen, if her child is a girl; after which the cock is eaten by men, or the hen by women.[42]

In all these cases the passage between the severed pieces of the animal is clearly protective, not retributive, in intention: the flesh and blood of the victim are thought somehow or other to present an obstacle to the powers of evil, and so to prevent them from pursuing and injuring the person who has passed through the narrow way. All such ceremonies may therefore be called purificatory in the wide sense of the word, since they purify or deliver the sufferer from malignant influences.

Returning to the point from which we started, we may now ask whether the ancient Hebrew form of making a covenant, by passing between the severed pieces of a sacrificial victim, was retributive or purificatory in its intention; in other words, was it a symbolic mode of imprecating death on the perjurer? or was it a magical mode of purifying the covenanters from evil influences and so guarding them against certain dangers to which both parties alike were exposed? The other instances which I have cited of passing between the severed pieces of a sacrificial victim seem to support the purificatory or protective explanation of the Hebrew rite; for while none of them require the retributive interpretation, some positively exclude it; and on the other hand some are only explicable on the purificatory or protective hypothesis, which is in fact expressly alleged by certain of the peoples, such as the Arabs and the Chins, who observe the custom. Certainly, in any attempt to explain the ancient Hebrew rite, much weight must be given to the analogy of the modern Arab ceremony; for the two customs are identical in form, and the peoples who practise or have practised them are both members of the Semitic family, speaking kindred

Semitic languages and inhabiting the same country; since the land of Moab, where the Arabs still observe the ancient custom, formed part of the land of Israel, where Abraham of old sojourned and covenanted with God in like manner. The inference seems almost inevitable, that the ancient Hebrew and the modern Arab rite are both derived from a common Semitic original, the purificatory or protective intention of which is still clearly borne in mind by the Arabs of Moab.

One question still remains to be asked. In what did the purificatory or protective virtue of such an act consist? why should the passage between the pieces of a slaughtered animal be thought to protect a man against danger? Robertson Smith's answer is given in what may be called the sacramental interpretation of the custom. He supposed that the persons who stood or passed between the pieces of the victim were thought to be thereby united with the animal and with each other by the bond of a common blood; in fact, he held that such a covenant is only a variant of the widespread custom known as the blood covenant, in which the covenanters artificially create a tie of consanguinity between themselves by actually mixing a little of their own blood.[43] On this hypothesis the only material difference between the two forms of covenant is, that the blood of an animal is substituted in the one for the human blood of the covenanters themselves in the other. Much is to be said for this theory. In the first place, as we saw, the South African evidence clearly points to the conclusion that the passage between the severed pieces of a sacrificial victim is merely a substitute for the passage through the carcass of the animal. This conclusion is confirmed by observing that the Chins, in cutting the sacrificial dog in two, do not absolutely divide it, but keep the forequarters connected with the hind-quarters by the string of the animal's guts, under which the people pass; and the same appears, though less clearly, to have been the practice of the Koryaks. The retention of the string of guts as a bond uniting the otherwise severed halves of the victim seems clearly to be an attempt to combine the theoretical unity of the slain animal with the practical convenience of dividing it, so as to admit of the passage of people through its carcass. But what could be the sense of thus putting people, as it were, into the body of the animal unless it were for the purpose of investing them with some qualities which the animal is believed to possess, and which, it is assumed, can be transferred to anybody who physically identifies himself with the animal by actually entering into it?

That this is indeed the conception at the base of the rite is suggested by the analogy of a custom observed by the Patagonian Indians. Among these people, "in some cases when a child is born, a cow or mare is killed, the stomach taken out and cut open, and into this receptacle while still warm the child is laid. Upon the remainder of the animal the tribe feast. . . . A variation of the foregoing birth-ceremony is yet more savage. If a boy is born, his tribe catch a mare or a colt—if the father be rich and a great man among his people, the former; if not, the latter—a lasso is placed round each leg, a couple round the neck, and a couple round the body. The tribe distribute themselves at the various ends of these lassos and take hold. The animal being thus supported cannot fall. The father of the child now advances and cuts the mare or colt open from the neck downwards, the heart, etc., is torn out, and the baby placed in the cavity. The desire is to keep the animal quivering until the child is put inside. By this means they believe that they ensure the child's becoming a fine horseman in the future."[44] The custom and the reason alleged for it are both significant. If you wish to make a child a good horseman, these Indians argue, the best possible way is to identify him at birth with a horse by putting him into the body of a living mare or colt; surrounded by the flesh and blood of the animal he will be one with it corporeally, he will have the hunting seat of a Centaur, whose human body is actually of a piece with the body of his horse. In short, the placing of the child in the body of the mare or colt is neither more nor less than a piece of sympathetic magic intended to endue a human being with equine properties.

On the same principle, as Robertson Smith pointed out,[45] we can explain the Scythian form of covenant by treading on the hide of a slaughtered ox. All who put their right feet on the hide thereby made themselves one with the animal and with each other, so that all were united by a tie of common blood which ensured their fidelity to each other. For the placing of one foot on the hide was probably an abridged form of wrapping up the man completely in it; as a worshipper at the shrine of the Syrian goddess at Hierapolis used to kneel on the skin of the sheep he had sacrificed, and drawing the sheep's head and trotters over his own head and shoulders prayed, as a sheep, to the goddess to accept his sacrifice of a sheep.[46]

This interpretation is strikingly confirmed by an African parallel. Among the Wachaga of East Africa it is customary for lads to receive what may be called their war-baptism two years after they have been circumcised. They assemble with their fathers and all the grown men at the chief's village. Two oxen and two goats are killed, and their blood is caught in an ox-hide, which is held by several men. The lads strip themselves and go in long rows four times round the blood-filled hide. Then they stand in a row. An old man makes a small cut in each of their lower arms. Thereupon each boy, stepping up to the blood-filled hide, allows some drops of blood from his arm to fall into it, takes up a handful of the mixed blood, swallows it, and puts on his clothes. Then they crouch down round the chief, and after many speeches each lad receives a war-name from his father or, if his father is dead, from an old man who acts in place of his father. Next the chief harangues them, declaring that they are no longer children but soldiers, and instructing them in their new duties. He also gives them all a common scutcheon for their shields, which marks them out as belonging to one and the same company.[47] Here the lads who are to fight shoulder to shoulder in the same company knit themselves together by a double bond of blood, their own and the blood of the sacrificed animals, which are mixed together in the ox-hide and drunk together from the hide by each of the future warriors.

Thus if my analysis of the Covenant of Abraham is correct, the rite is composed of two distinct but correlated elements, namely, first, the cutting of the victim in two, and, second, the passing of the covenanters between the pieces. Of these two elements the first is to be explained by the retributive, and the second by the sacramental theory. The two theories are complementary to each other, and together furnish a complete explanation of the rite.

Before leaving the subject of Abraham's covenant, it may be well to return for a little to the practice of the Arabs of Moab. The name which they give to the sacrifice in question is *fedu,* and the term is defined as "the immolation of a victim sacrificed generally in the face of Allah to deliver man or beast from some malady or impending destruction."[48] In short, the sacrifice appears to be a ransom offered to God for the people or their flocks: it is a substitute which the deity deigns to accept instead of human and animal life. Hence the words with which the sheikh commands the offering: "Redeem yourselves, O people! Redeem yourselves!" Hence, too, the saying of the Arabs that the sacrifice is a ransom for themselves and their flocks.[49]

This vicarious theory of sacrifice as a substitute offered for the life of a man or animal appears to be widely spread, not only among the Arabs of Moab, but among the fellaheen or peasantry of Palestine generally. The term, *fedu* is commonly applied to the vicarious sacrifice of an animal in a general sense, without any necessary implication that the sacrificer cuts the victim in two and passes between the pieces. The following definition of *fedu* was given to Professor Curtiss by Derwish Hatib, of Der Atiyeh, in the Syrian Desert, who is a lecturer and leads the service in the mosque of his village: "*Fedu* means that it redeems the other, in place of the other, substitute for the other. Something is going to happen to a man, and the sacrifice is a substitute for him. It prevents disease, sufferings, robbery and enmity."[50] Again, a Moslem at Nebk in the Syrian Desert told Professor Curtiss that "the *fedu* is commonly for the future to ward off evil. When they lay the foundation of a house, they slaughter with the idea that (*Khuddr*) St. George, will preserve the workmen. Every house must be redeemed. If not redeemed by the sacrifice of some animal, it must be redeemed by a human life."[51] Similarly, an orthodox Moslem, servant of a shrine at Homs, informed Professor Curtiss that he was familiar with the *fedu*. He said, "In moving from house to house, or in occupying a new building; the first night he sleeps in the house he kills the *fedu*. The object is the bursting forth of blood unto the face of God. It is for himself and family, a redemption. It keeps off disease and the jinn."[52] To the same effect the minister of the "Chair" on the mountainside of Zebedani said, "When a man finishes a house, he makes a sacrifice on the doorstep. It is redemption for the building. Every house must have its death, a man, woman, child, or animal. God has appointed a *fedu* for every building through sacrifice. If God has accepted the sacrifice he has redeemed the house."[53]

These statements clearly prove that the *fedu* or sacrifice of an animal at occupying a new house is vicarious: it is a substitute for the human life, which otherwise God or a saint would require at the hands of the occupants. Similarly the sacrifice which in some parts of Syria is still offered for a child appears to be regarded as a substitute accepted by God or a saint for the life of the child. Thus, speaking of the custom of sacrificing for children, one of the Ismailiyeh of northern Syria said, "When they make a sacrifice for a child they slaughter the victim in the courtyard where he lives, and put a few drops of blood on his forehead and on his nose, to indicate that the sacrifice is on his behalf. The breaking forth of blood is *fedu*. It redeems the child. They vow to the saint that blood shall flow for the child if he redeems it." The sacrifice offered for a son is usually a goat or a sheep, but if the family is poor, a cock will be accepted for a baby boy, and a hen for a baby girl.[54]

Thus it appears that the essence of all these sacrifices consists in its vicarious character: the animal is a substitute for the man. The principle of substitution in sacrifice is brought out with unmistakable clearness in a custom observed by Indian Moslems at the largest mosque in Baghdad, to which they go on pilgrimage: "They vow that if a man who is ill begins to recover he shall go to the shrine. He is stripped to the waist. Then two men lift a lamb or a kid above his head, and bathe his face, shoulders, and the upper part of his body with the blood. While the butcher kills the animal the sheikh repeats the first sura of the Koran. They also wrap him in the skin of the animal."[55] Here the pouring of the animal's blood on the man, and the wrapping of him in the skin, are very instructive. In order to perfect the substitution of the animal for the man, the ritual requires that the man should as far as possible be identified with the animal, being drenched with its blood and clothed with its skin. How could the pretended identification be represented more graphically?

The same principle of substitution is still followed in Syria not only in the relation of man to God, but in the relation of man to man. "In the neighbourhood of Nablus it is customary, when a reconciliation has been made between the murderer and the avenger of blood, for the murderer to kill a goat or a sheep. He then kneels before the avenger with a red handkerchief tied about his neck. Some of the blood of the animal slain is put on the palms of his hands. The avenger draws his sword and intimates that he could take his life from him, but that he gives it back to him."[56] Here the identification of the man with the animal is carried out by smearing him with the blood of the slaughtered sheep or goat, and tying a red handkerchief round his neck to simulate the severance of his head from his body.

We can now fully understand the sacrificial ritual at the temple of the great Syrian goddess in antiquity, in accordance with which the worshipper clothed himself in the skin of the sheep which he offered to the deity. The life of the sheep was a substitute for his own, and to perfect the substitution he pretended to be a sheep.

Now, too, we can understand why in certain solemn sacrifices, to avert or mitigate calamity, the sacrificer cuts the victim in two and passes between the parts. The passage between the parts, as we saw, is probably a modification of an older practice of passing through the carcass; and that in its turn can hardly have any other meaning than that the man identifies himself with the animal into whose body he forces himself, and that he offers it to the higher powers as a substitute for himself. The principle of vicarious sacrifice, which has played so great a part in the history of religion, could hardly be carried out more perspicuously than in these savage and bloody rites.

*   *   *

[Another possible explanation of the ceremony which we have been discussing is suggested by the presence in sundry Danish folktales and ballads of the motif that cutting a person's body in half and walking between the parts can procure immunity from harm or bewitchment.[56a] Thus, in the folksong of Asmund Freydegaever a beldam bids a hero cut her in twain and walk between the parts so that she may thereby be free from attack and hurt. He does the former, but not the latter, and she falls dead.[56b] Similarly, in the legend of Starkard, a weary giant bids the young Hader decapitate him and walk between the head and the rump "so that he might gain immunity against all weapons." Hader, however, runs away after the beheading for fear that the giant might fall upon him in vengeance.[56c]

Conversely, but harking back to the same idea, in the legend of Dietrich of Bern, a female giant is so skilled in magic that even after being slain the portions of her body come together again, and she is unscathed. At the third thrust, however, Dietrich makes a point of walking through the severed parts, whereupon she is finally dead.[56d] So too in th ballad of King Diderik of Loven, the hero slays a dragon and walks through its severed parts. This destroys its remaining strength and prevents its revival.[56e]

These examples may perhaps permit the inference that the peculiar ceremony which we have been discussing was intended as a symbol not of retribution for a violated oath but of protection for the contracting parties to an agreement or treaty.

Yet, even this does not exhaust the possible interpretations. Still another explanation is suggested by the widespread custom of cutting an object in two and giving one half to each party, when they pledge themselves to one another. This signifies that each is responsible for one half of the agreement and that the maintenance of it depends on their mutual cooperation. Thus, in the Polynesian island of Leti, Moa, and Lakor, quarrels are composed by the parties' eating together at a feast and then splitting a stick in two, each keeping a piece.[56f] Similarly, the Kei Islands make peace by ceremonially cutting a *kalapa*-leaf in twain; each party then takes home one piece of it. This is called *kalduke,* which means virtually the same thing as "split token" in English usage.[56g] Of the same tenor too was a practice widely observed of old among lovers in Britain: a silver ninepenny-piece (called a "commendation ninepence") was broken in half, each retaining one part.[56h]

*   *   *

The animals which Abraham cut in half consisted, besides a turtledove and a young pigeon, of a *three-year-old* heifer and a *three-year-old* goat. A three-year-old beast means simply a full-grown beast; the expression actually recurs elsewhere in the Bible.[56i] In the same way, in Greek, a friend whom one has had for three years is an old and trusted friend.[56j]

It may be observed in this connection that, according to the Greek (Septuagint) version of I Samuel 1:24, what Hannah brought to the sanctuary at Shiloh when she dedicated the infant Samuel to the service of Yahweh was a three-year-old bull, not three bulls, as the traditional Hebrew text has it.[56k] Three-year-old heifers are mentioned also in the Talmud as sacrificial beasts;[56l] and they are similarly specified in a Hittite ritual.[56m] ▼

54   Seeing the fourth generation

The promise to Abraham that his descendants "shall return hither in the fourth generation" embodies a tidbit of Hebrew folklore to the effect that the fourth generation is the last which might possibly be considered as part of the near future, and the last which a man might expect to see in his lifetime— and then only by the exceptional grace of God. Yahweh, we are told, extends his punishment of the wicked only to the fourth generation, but bestows his steadfast love upon the pious unto the thousandth.[1] Job is finally rewarded by living to see "his sons and his son's sons, four generations";[2] and so too in an inscription from Nerab, of the seventh century B.C., the hope is expressed that "on the day of my death my mouth shall not have been stopped from speaking articulate words, and I shall see with my eyes offspring of the fourth generation."[3]

Four generations were evidently reckoned to a century. By Classical times, however, life expectancy had increased, and the number was conventionally reduced to three.[4]

SODOM AND GOMORRAH   18:16—19:29

55   Entertaining angels unawares   18:1–32

The stories of how both Abraham and Lot entertain angels unawares are but Hebrew versions of the widespread folktale of *Hospitality Rewarded* (Q 45.1). This type of tale exists in two main forms:

1. A god or saint visits a city in disguise. He is given hospitality by an indigent or childless person (often a couple), subsequently reveals his identity, and rewards his benefactor(s) by (a) material wealth, or (b) inexhaustible replenishment of their victuals (see below, §165) or (c) the granting of special wishes, or (d) the promise of a son and heir.[1] This, with the last-named benefit, is the form preserved in the story of Abraham. The classic parallel is the tale, told by Ovid and Hyginus, of how Jupiter, Neptune, and Mercury (i.e., *three* visitors, as in the Biblical narrative!), while traveling through Boeotia, came in disguise to Hyrieus (or Hyreus), a childless peasant (or, as others say, a prince) of Tanagra, and, in return for his hospitality, granted him the boon of a son, who was in fact Orion.[2]

2. In the other form, the reward of the poor but charitable host(s) is accompanied by the punishment of his (or their) rich but niggardly neighbors, who have unanimously cold-shouldered the stranger: their city sinks into the ground (F 944) or their houses catch fire. This is the form which underlies the story relating to Lot, although, as we shall see, the Biblical writer has introduced certain changes.

(a) The submerged city

Parallels to this form are legion. When, says Pausanias, the goddess Demeter came in disguise to Argolis, she was hospitably received by the couple Athera and Mysios, but turned away by Kolontas. Thereupon she decreed that the latter would be "burned along with his house."[3] Buddhist legend relates similarly that once, when a wandering saint (*arhat*) visited the city of Holaolakia, everyone rebuffed him except one man. The city was therefore destroyed, but that man was spared.[4] The same story is told also in Germany about the visit of an itinerant dwarf to a hamlet on the shores of Lake Thun.[5] According to the version embodied in Hölty's poem, *Töffel und Käthe,* only a pious couple who received him were spared from a flood which subsequently engulfed their niggardly neighbors.[6] In the same vein, a story current in the North Riding district of Yorkshire, England, relates that when two itinerant saints once arrived at the town of Simmerwater, in the parish of Asgarth, they were rebuffed by everyone except a poor cottager. In consequence, the city was submerged, but he alone was spared.[7] The same story, it may be added, is told also about Lough in the Belvidere area[8] and about Brecknockmere (Llangorse Pool) in Wales.[9] From Rome comes the tale of how everyone except one poor woman once refused hospitality to a holy man who appeared as a beggar; all their houses caved in, but hers stood.[10] Similar tales are told also concerning the famous village of Lourdes in Gascony,[11] and—outside Europe—in the popular lore of Nyasaland, Africa.[12]

There are, of course, slight variations from place to place. Sometimes, for instance, the offense of which the submerged city is guilty is not specifically inhospitality but simply general wickedness.[13] It is such indiscriminate turpitude, for example, that is said to have caused the submersion of Is in Brittany[14] and of Birket Ram, near Banias, in Syria.[15]

To be sure, in neither of the two Biblical stories is the city's sin defined as inhospitality. In the Abraham version, it is general "outrage,"[16] and in the Lot version it is "sodomy."[17] But the original drift comes through clearly enough in the juxtaposition in each case of the destruction of the city with the visit of the angels and their hospitable reception by the two central characters. Moreover, that the Hebrews indeed knew of a version of the tale in which the offense was niggardliness or inhospitality is clear from Ezekiel 16:49 f., where it is said in so many words that Sodom was destroyed because its affluent inhabitants refused to "succour (*lit.* grasp the hand of) the poor and needy."

(b) Itinerant strangers as gods in disguise

The notion that itinerant strangers may be gods in disguise reappears in many other cultures.[18] In the Odyssey, for instance, when Antinous, the chief suitor of Penelope, hurls a stool at Odysseus after the latter has returned home unrecognized, he is warned that one should not cast out a hapless wanderer "for maybe he is a god from heaven." Gods, it is added, often wander through cities in the guise of strangers in order to see for themselves the *hybris* of men on the one hand, and their decency of conduct on the other.[19] So too it is related in the Acts of the Apostles that when Paul, coming as a stranger, cured a cripple at Lystra, the people exclaimed "in the speech (popular idiom?) of Lycaonia: 'Gods are come down to us in the likeness of men.' "[20] And when, on the island of Melita, he shook a viper from his hand without suffering harm, they "said that he was a god."[21]

56   Blinding for impiety   19:11

The *blinding* of the wicked men of Sodom is another feature of the story on which Comparative Folklore and Religion shed light, for the fact is that loss of sight was very commonly regarded in antiquity as the punishment for sacrilege, impiety, or gross misconduct.[1] Thus, in the Canaanite (Ugaritic) *Poem of Aqhat* a curse is invoked on the city of Abelim that its inhabitants may be collectively blinded by Baal in retribution for the murder of that hero.[2] A Babylonian text likewise invokes Shamash—both as god of justice and as dazzling sun—to make a miscreant blind;[3] while early South Arabian inscriptions sometimes contain the formula, "May he who alters this become blind!"[4] Similarly, in a Hittite ritual dealing with disloyal persons, not only are they to be symbolically "unmanned" by being dressed in female garments, but they are also to be blinded.[5] So too one of the curses called down upon the disobedient in the Great Commination of Deuteronomy 28 is that they be deprived of their sight (v. 28), and this is likewise the punishment which Elisha invokes upon the servants of the king of Syria who are tracking him down (II Kings 6:18).

In Greek and Roman literature, blinding is frequently mentioned as the usual punishment for infamy. Apuleius, in his *Metamorphoses,* preserves a characteristic form of commination: "May the Syrian Goddess, mistress and mother of all, and holy Sabazius, and Bellona and the Idaean Mother and Queen Venus with her Adonis render thee blind."[6] Aegyptus is said to have been struck blind for forcing entry into the temple of Poseidon at Mantinea.[7] Teiresias lost his sight when he saw Athene naked taking a bath;[8] and this latter idea survived in later European folklore in the belief that "peeping Toms" who gained unlawful sight of Berchta, the Wild Hunt, the Devil, or the Witches' Dance (often through a keyhole) would be instantly blinded.[9] The idea even passed into Christian hagiography: the mother of St. Genovese of Paris, we are told, once boxed her ears for going to church, and was immediately blinded.[10]

57   Taboo on looking back   19:17, 26

Another feature of the story on which folklore casts interesting light is the taboo imposed upon Lot and his family not to look back when they depart from Sodom.

Within the dramatic context of the story this means, of course, that they must set their faces hopefully toward the future, not nostalgically toward the past. This, however, is simply a clever "literary" twist to an element of the older folktale which really had its origin in magic and in religious convention, for it is a common rule in ancient rituals that one must not turn one's gaze backward.[1] Thus, in a Hittite ritual for the exorcism of demons, the witch is instructed to depart, at the end of her ministrations, "without turning round";[2] and in a Babylonian charm to relieve sickness the patient is given the warning that he must return home with his gaze fixed ahead.[3] In Vedic times, this rule applied also in Hindu funeral ceremonies,[4] just as in the Odyssey it obtains in the case of offerings to the dead.[5] In the famous incident wherein Odysseus throws back Ino's scarf, he is said to do so without looking back,[6] and both Aeschylus and Sophocles tell us that purificatory rites (especially propitiations of the Furies) required that the performer do not turn round.[7] When servants attacked the infant Heracles and were caught and burned, his mother Alcmene instructed her handmaid to toss the ashes off a cliff and then return home without looking back;[8] and a scholiast on Theocritus informs us that people were not permitted to look to the rear during the monthly offerings to Hecate at the crossroads or during the rites of Apollo in the Valley of Tempe.[9] Lucian informs us that after purifying a client a magician had to march him home without looking behind him;[10] and Jamblichus asserts that when people left home on a journey they were told not to look back, since the Furies might be behind them[11]—an idea which finds a counterpart in later German popular usage.[12] At the Lemuria, or Feast of Ghosts, the Romans would not look backward,[13] and when they made offerings to the shades they observed the same rule.[14] Persons who gathered herbs or other ingredients for medical or magical purposes had likewise to refrain from looking behind them;[15] it is said, in fact, that Medea herself observed this rule,[16] and it is still standard practice among charm-mongers both in Mesopotamia and at Mecca.[17] Finally, an English story relates that seven clergymen once tried to exorcize a prankish ghost by transforming it into a colt. A boy was then told to lead it to the brink of Cranmere Pool, untie the halter, and himself return without looking back. He disobeyed; so the colt kicked out his eye, and then disappeared in a ball of fire.[18]

The motif of not looking back is reflected also in several well-known myths and legends (C 961.1). Orpheus was not permitted to look back when he led Eurydice out of Hades;[19] nor was the Japanese hero Izanagi when he went to bring Izanami out of the realm of the dead (Yomi).[20] Aeneas too was ordered to depart from Hades without looking back;[21] and in medieval legend this rule was imposed on heroes who made journeys to Paradise.[22]

58   The pillar of salt   19:26

What happened to Lot's wife for breaking this taboo has happened also to several other characters in popular tales.[1] It is told in Sicily, for example, that when St. Vito, at the command of God, was departing with Crescenzia from the city of Mazara, he told her not to look back, but she did and was turned to a pillar of salt.[2] Similarly, in a Moravian ballad of the same general tenor as the English *The Maid and the Palmer,* a girl who looks back when she is told not to is turned to a pillar of salt,[3] and parallel tales are reported from Germany and Bulgaria.[4]

Sometimes, to be sure, the miscreant is turned to stone, rather than salt; but the idea is basically the same.[5] Thus, an excellent parallel to the Biblical narrative is afforded by an Indian tale which relates that a saint (*arhat*) was once doing penance in the woodlands of Pettan. One of his disciples went to the city to beg alms. Everyone, except the wife of a shepherd, maltreated him. Thereupon the saint resolved to punish the city by submerging it; but he first told the woman to depart, ordering her not to turn back. She disobeyed, and was turned then and there to stone.[6] In the same vein, a tale from Rome has it that the region of Castello was formerly a city, or rather a very beautiful district, but once upon a time a voice came to an old woman who lived there telling her to depart at once, but to take care not to look back, no matter what noise she might hear. The woman set out, carrying her hen and her chickens in a basket on her head. Suddenly, however, she heard a loud noise, and turned back. Thereupon she became a pillar of white stone, which can still be seen.[7]

Even more elaborate, but embracing the same motif, is an Italian legend from Sassari. Some five hours' distance from Alghero, in the general area of Nurra, it is said, lies the so-called "Pool of Baracis," where there was once a city of the same name. The city was deluged as a punishment for its wickedness, the waters subsequently rising and flowing together to form the present pool. What happened was that Jesus Christ, disguised as a pilgrim, came begging to that city, but nobody gave him anything. At last he met a little old woman, who lived on the outskirts. She invited him into her home, bidding him wait till her bread was baked, so that they might eat it together. Christ thereupon turned the little rolls which she had put into the oven into big loaves. Then he told her to flee with her son, but not to turn back, no matter what noise she might hear. No sooner had the woman finished baking the bread than she set out for Monteforte, with her basket on her head and the baby in her arms. But when she got to Montegirato, there was a storm at sea, and the waters were flooding the country. Terrified by the pounding of the waves and by the desperate and heart-rending cries of the poor wretches who were drowning, she could not resist turning back to see what was happening. At once she was turned to stone and stayed rooted where she was.[8]

The Italians have other stories of the same character. In Sicily, for instance, old Giufa took it into his head to sow the Tyrrhenian sea. God finally allowed him to do so, on condition that he would not turn back. His hat blew off, so he turned back to retrieve it. You can guess what happened: he and his oxen were turned to stone.[9]

Sometimes, of course, people have been turned to stone for other reasons than just looking back. In Cagliari, for instance, they tell of a woman who burst out laughing during religious ceremonies at the Feast of St. Antine (Constantine). That could not be tolerated. There and then she was turned into a monolith, and that monolith is still standing near the church of the saint in the region of Sedilo.[10] The same thing, they say, happened once, on a somewhat larger scale, in the parish of Burian, Cornwall (England). If you go there, you can see a circle of nineteen upright stones, called Dance-Maine, or Merry Maidens. The name tells the tale: they were a group of girls who were turned to stone for dancing on the sabbath day.[11]

As in so many other cases, the Biblical writer has tried to give "a local habitation and a name" to a purely mythical tale. So he identifies the submerged city with Gomorrah, on the banks of the Dead Sea, simply because that name suggests a Semitic word gh-m-r meaning "submerge."[12] One may compare Simmertown, i.e., sous-mer town (or submerge-town) in the English story we have quoted.

59 The proposed sacrifice of Isaac 22:1–18

Abraham's fidelity is tested by God. He is commanded to sacrifice his only son Isaac upon Mt. Moriah. He travels thither for three days. At the moment when he is about to slay the lad, a messenger (angel) of the Lord calls from heaven and bids him desist. Abraham catches

*sight of a ram entangled in a neighboring thicket. The ram is sub-
stituted.*

There are interesting parallels to this tale (S 263.2.1) in Classical literature.—In order to obtain favorable winds for his army as they sail from Aulis
against Troy, Agamemnon is commanded to sacrifice his daughter Iphigenia.
At the critical moment, however, the maiden is spared by the intervention of
Artemis, who substitutes a doe.[1]—During a severe plague in Lacedaemon, an
oracle orders the annual sacrifice of a high-born origin. Helena, a potential
victim, is rescued in the nick of time, when an eagle seizes the sacrificial
sword and transfers it to a heifer.[2]—Similarly, during a plague at Falerii, the
maiden Valeria Luperca is rescued from intended sacrifice when an eagle
seizes the sacrificial weapon and places it upon a heifer.[3]

*   *   *   22:17

*As a reward for his piety, Abraham is promised that his offspring will be
innumerable as the stars of heaven and as the sand on the seashore.*

Stars and sand are regular symbols of multitude not only in the Old Testament (Gen. 26:14; Exod. 32:13; Nahum 3:16) but also in the literature of
the Egyptians, Mesopotamians, Arabs, Greeks, and Romans:

EGYPTIAN. *Stars:* Ramses II "erected monuments numerous as the stars of
heaven": Obeliscus Flaminius. He desires "years like sand, jubilees like
stars": Pap. Turin, P.R. 20.1.9.

Sand: Pap. Harris, 4.4; 29.12; Pap. Anastasi, 1.21, 9; Sethe, Urkunden,
iv.687; Mariette, Dendereh i.48a.

Cf. H. Grapow, Die bildlichen Ausdrücke des Aegyptischen (1924), 35,
59–60.

MESOPOTAMIAN. *Stars:* Ashurbanipal, Annals, i.88; TCL 3 iii.164; *AKA* 358
iii.43; *KAH* 13, r. iii.8–9.

Passages are collected by M. Held in JCS 15 (1961), 24. Cf. also K. Tallquist, in Hakedem 1.9.

ARABIC. See I Goldziher, in ZA 7.294 f.

GREEK AND ROMAN. *Stars:* Plato, Euthyd. 294 B; Callimachus, Del. 175;
Theocritus 30.27; Plautus, Poen. 430; Catullus, 7.7; 61.12; Ovid, Amores
ii.10.13.—Passages are collected in Headlam-Knox, Herodas (1922), ad i.33.

Sand: Iliad 2.800; 9.385; Pindar, Pyth., 9.84; Callimachus, Artemis 253.

JACOB

*Jacob and Esau, the ancestors respectively of the Israelites and the
Edomites, are said to have been* twins.

60   Twin culture-heroes   25:21–26

This conforms to a common folklore pattern, for many peoples throughout the world tell (or have told) stories about primeval twins or heroic pairs from whom they, or they and their nearest neighbors, derive their cultural and ethnic origins.[1] Such stories have various motivations. They may reflect: (a) an original blending of two strains in a given population; (b) the split of a common parent stock into two different groups; (c) the dual structure of a given society, or the co-existence in a given area of two different types of inhabitants, e.g., herdsmen and agriculturalists; (d) the foundation of two neighboring cities by the same people, or the subservience of both to the same government. Or, again, they may express simply the inbuilt duality—the yin-yang—of nature.

The parade example of such twin culture-heroes is, of course, Romulus and Remus,[2] but these founders of Rome by no means stand alone. The Tha-thun of Burma, for instance, trace their descent to the twins Titha-Kumma and Dyaza-Kumma, and the Peguans (Talaings) of the same area to a pair named Thama and Wimila.[3] In Assam, the Ahom kingdom is derived traditionally from the twins Khunlun and Khunlai, who are said to have come out of the sky.[4] In Panope, in the Caroline Islands, civilization is traced to the twin heroes, Olo-sipa and Ola-sapa.[5] The Koita of New Guinea recognize as their founding fathers the twins Kirimaikalu and Kirimaika.[6] The Baikari Caribs of Brazil speak of Keri and Kame;[7] and the Dahomey of Honsu and Honsi.[8]

Legends of twin culture-heroes are especially common among the North American Indians. It will suffice to mention only: Ioskeha and Tawiskara, among the Iroquois;[9] Menabozho and Chokanipok, among the Algonquins; Tobadizini and Nayenezkani, among the Navaho; Pensanto and Onkoito, among the Maidu; and Kanizyslak and Nemokois, among the Kwakiutl.[10]

South America too contributes its quotient. The Yunkas of Peru have their Pachakamak and Wichama; the Tupis of Brazil their Tamendonaéra and Arikuté; the Guamachucos their Apocatequil and Piguerao; and the Yurakaré of Bolivia their Tiri and Karu.[11]

The hostile twins   21:22

The twins are often portrayed as *rivals*. Mainly, of course, this reflects the traditional hostility between two neighboring peoples or between two elements of the same people. It is also influenced, however, by a widespread belief that two children cannot be begotten at the same time by a human father, so that in the case of twins one of them must be of divine origin and therefore superior, or else of demonic origin and therefore inferior, to the other.[12] Thus, in the case of the Iroquois culture-twins, Ioskeha is said to be good, and Tawiskara evil.[13] Among the Hurons, one of the twins is designated "Good Creator" (Hahgwediju), and the other "Bad Creator" (Hahgwedaetgah).[14]

Among the Melanesians, Tagaro is useful, and his twin Suge-matua is useless.[15] Among the Ainu of Japan, Shi-acha is the "rough uncle,"[16] and Mi-acha the "good uncle"; and in the Gwelle Peninsula we have Tokumbinana, the clever twin, and his stupid brother, Tokovoruru.[17]

Jacob and Esau "struggle" while still in their mother's womb.

To point up the fact that the traditional hostility between neighbors or groups is something in the very order of nature, and not merely the outcome of particular circumstances, the twins are sometimes said to have quarreled even before they were born.[18] Proitus and Acrisius, the twin sons of Abas, king of Argos, who subsequently contend for their father's realm (the equivalent of the birthright in our Biblical tale), are said in Greek legend to have tussled in the womb;[19] and a similar story is told about Flint and Sapling, the twin heroes of the Iroquois.[20] Moreover, it is not without significance that in the dialect of the Syrian and Palestinian Arabs, the cognate of the Hebrew word conventionally rendered *struggled* is actually used of *siblings who follow one another immediately in order of birth,* as well as of persons habitually engaged in quarrels.[21]

61   The hairy man   25:25

The contrasting characters of the twins or pair of heroes is sometimes expressed in *physical* terms. The one is strong, and the other weak,[1] or, as in the lore of the New Hebrideans, the one is fair and the other dark.[2] One way of bringing out this contrast is to represent the inferior member of the pair as closer to an animal, possessed of a hairy pelt.[3] Esau is therefore described by the Biblical writer as hairy from birth. Similarly in the Babylonian Epic of Gilgamesh—where, if they are not physically twins, they nevertheless represent the same basic idea—the hero's companion Enkidu is described expressly as "hairy," the same Semitic word being employed as is applied by the Biblical writer to Esau.[4] The same characterization appears also in a Hungarian folktale[5] and in the story of Eisenhans in the Grimm collection.[6] Indeed, shagginess is almost everywhere the hallmark of the primitive man;[7] he is the prototype at once of the beatnik and of the "hairy-chested he-man."

62   The sinister redhead

But Esau is not only hairy at birth; he is also "ruddy," and this trait too reflects popular lore, for the belief is widespread that redheads are sinister and dangerous.[1] In Roumania, for example, a red-haired man (*roscovan*) is thought to cast the evil eye[2] and is known as a "child of Judas";[3] while in the Balkans generally redheads are deemed vampires.[4] Similarly, in modern Greece the very expression "redhead" is commonly avoided.[5] Proverbs from the Toscana in Italy warn against red-haired persons;[6] and in French folklore, people are advised to keep a distance of at least thirty paces from a red-polled man or a bearded woman.[7] In the same vein too, a familiar German proverb declares that *Rotes Haar und Edsenholz / Wachst auf keinem guten Boden;*[8] while in England the red-haired man is often credited with demonic qualities.[9]

There is frequent reference to this belief in European literature. Fulco of Jerusalem, for example, was a redhead, and in mentioning this fact William of Tyre finds it necessary to add that "contrary to the general rule applying to this color, he was affable, benign and kindhearted."[10] So too, in the Teutonic *Didriks Saga,* the traitor Sifki is depicted as red-haired;[11] and in Christian art, the same is true of Judas Iscariot—a tradition to which Shakespeare himself bears witness.[12]

The Hebrew word for "ruddy" is *admôni* (formed from *adôm,* "red"), and that for "hairy" is *sa^{c}ir.* The Biblical writer therefore uses these traits of the traditional tale to account for the name Edom and to explain why it was also known as Se^{c}ir.[13] Modern scholars have concluded from this that the ruddiness and hairiness of Esau are a mere "etiological legend"—a "just-so story"—invented for this express purpose. Such a view, however, completely misprizes the Biblical writer's art and technique. For him—and the point bears stressing—etiology was a process not of *invention* but of *application.* The ruddiness and hairiness of the "inferior" twin were part and parcel of the original folktale; all he did was to give to these traditional traits a clever, topical twist.

▲ 63   Jacob steals the blessing   27:1–40

Two points in the familiar story of how Jacob stole the paternal blessing from his brother Esau invite special attention: first, the displacement of the elder by the younger son; second, the means by which the displacement was effected. The younger son pretended to be his elder brother by dressing in his elder brother's clothes and by wearing kidskins on his hands and neck for the purpose of imitating the hairiness of his elder brother's skin; and to this pretence he was instigated by his mother, who actively assisted him in the make-believe by putting his elder brother's garments on his body and the kidskins on his hands and neck. In this way Jacob, the younger son, succeeded in diverting to himself the paternal blessing which was intended for his elder brother, and thus served himself heir to his father. It seems possible that in this story there may be preserved the reminiscence of a legal ceremony whereby a younger son was substituted for his elder brother as rightful heir to the paternal inheritance.

(a) Sacrificial skins in ritual

Among the Gallas of East Africa it is customary for childless couples to adopt children; and so close is the tie formed by adoption that even if the couple should afterwards have offspring of their own, the adopted child retains all the rights of the firstborn. In order to transfer a child from its real to its adoptive parents, the following ceremony is performed. The child, who is commonly about three years old, is taken from its mother and led or carried away into a wood. There the father formally relinquishes all claim to it, by declaring that thenceforth the child is dead to him. Then an ox is killed, its blood is smeared on the child's forehead, a portion of its fat is put round the child's neck, and with a portion of its skin the childs' hands are covered.[1] The resemblance of this ceremony to Jacob's subterfuge is obvious: in both cases the hands and neck of the person concerned are covered with the skin or fat of a slain animal. But the meaning of the ceremony is not yet apparent. Perhaps we may discover it by examining some similar rites observed on various occasions by tribes of East Africa.

Among these it is a common practice to sacrifice an animal, usually a goat or a sheep, skin it, cut the skin into strips, and place the strips round the wrists or on the fingers of persons who are supposed in one way or other to benefit thereby; it may be that they are rid of sickness or rendered immune against it, or that they are purified from ceremonial pollution, or that they are invested with mysterious powers.[2] Thus, among the Akamba, when a child is born, a goat is killed and skinned, three strips are cut from the skin, and placed on the wrists of the child, the mother, and the father respectively.[3] Among the Akikuyu, on a like occasion, a sheep is slaughtered, and a strip of skin, taken from one of its fore-feet, is fastened as a bracelet on the infant's wrist, to remove the ill-luck or ceremonial pollution (*thahu*) which is supposed to attach to new-born children.[4] Again, a similar custom is observed by the Akikuyu at the curious rite of "being born again" or "born of a goat" as the natives call it, which every Kikuyu child had formerly to undergo before circumcision. The age at which the ceremony is performed varies with the ability of the father to provide the goat or sheep which is required for the due observance of the rite; but it seems that the new birth generally takes place when a child is about ten years or younger. If the child's father or mother is dead, a man or woman acts as proxy on the occasion, and in such a case the woman is thenceforth regarded by the child as its own mother. A goat or sheep is killed in the afternoon and the stomach and intestines are reserved. The ceremony takes place at evening in a hut; none but women are allowed to be present. A circular piece of the goat-skin or sheep-skin is passed over one shoulder and under the other arm of the child who is to be born again; and the animal's stomach is similarly passed over the child's other shoulder and under its other arm. The mother, or the woman who acts as mother, sits on a hide on the floor with the child between her knees. The goat's or sheep's gut is passed round her and brought in front of the child. She groans as if in labour, another woman cuts the gut as if it were the navel-string, and the child imitates the cry of a new-born infant. Until a lad has thus been born again in mimicry, he may not assist at the disposal of his father's body after death, nor help to carry him out into the wilds to die. Formerly the ceremony of the new birth was combined with the ceremony of circumcision; but the two are now kept separate.

Such is the curious custom of the new birth, as it is, or used to be practised by the Akikuyu, and as it was described to Mr. and Mrs. Routledge[5] by natives who had freed themselves from tradition and come under the influence of Christianity. Yet great reluctance was shown to speak about the subject, and neither persuasion nor bribery availed to procure leave for the English inquirers to witness the ceremony. The general meaning of this custom seems plain enough and indeed is sufficiently declared in the alternative title which the Akikuyu give to it, namely, "to be born of a goat." It consists essentially in a pretence that the mother is a she-goat and that she has given birth to a kid. This explains why the child is enveloped in the stomach and skin of a goat, and why the goat's guts are passed round both mother and child. So far as the mother is concerned, this assimilation to an animal comes out perhaps more clearly in an independent account which C. W. Hobley has given of the ceremony; though in his description the animal which the mother mimics is a sheep and not a goat. The name of the ceremony, he tells us, is *Ku-chiaruo ringi,* the literal translation of which is "to be born again." He further informs us that the Akikuyu are divided into two guilds, the Kikuyu and the Masai, and that the ceremony of being born again differs somewhat as it is observed by each. When the parents of the child belong to the Masai guild, the rite is celebrated as follows. "About eight days after the birth of the child, be it male or female, the father of the infant kills a male sheep and takes the meat to the house of the mother, who eats it assisted by her neighbours as long as they belong to the Masai guild. At the conclusion of the feast the mother is adorned with the skin from the left fore-leg and shoulder of the sheep, the piece of skin being fastened from her left wrist to left shoulder; she wears this for four days, and it is then taken off and thrown on to her bed and stays there till it disappears. The mother and child have their heads shaved on the day this ceremony takes place; it has no connection with the naming of the child which is done on the day of its birth."[6] Here the intention seems to be to assimilate the mother to a sheep; this is done by giving her sheep's flesh to eat and investing her with the skin of the animal, which is left lying on the bed where, eight days before, she gave birth to the child. For it is to be observed that in this form of the ritual the simulation of the new birth follows the real birth at an interval of only a few days.

But if the parents belong to the Kikuyu guild, the ritual of the new birth is as follows in the south of the Kikuyu country. "The day after the birth a male sheep is killed and some of the fat of the sheep is cooked in a pot and given to the mother and infant to drink. It was not specifically stated that this had a direct connection with the rite referred to, but the description commenced with a mention of this. When the child reaches the age of from three to six years the father kills a male sheep, and three days later the novice is adorned with part of the skin and the skin of the big stomach. These skins are fastened on the right shoulder of a boy or on the left shoulder of a girl. The skin used for a boy has, however, the left shoulder and leg cut out of it, and that for a girl has the right shoulder and leg cut away. The child wears these for three days, and on the fourth day the father cohabits with the mother of the child. There is, however, one important point, and that is that before the child is decorated with the sheep-skin it has to go and lie alongside its mother on her bed and cry out like a newly born infant. Only after this ceremony has been performed is the child eligible for circumcision. A few days after circumcision the child returns to sleep on a bed in its mother's hut, but the father has to kill a sheep before he can return, and the child has to drink some of the blood, the father also has to cohabit with the mother upon the occasion."[7]

In this form of the ritual the ceremony of the new birth is deferred until several years after the real birth. But the essence of the rite appears to be the same: it is a pretence that the mother is a sheep, and that she has given birth to a lamb. However, we must note the inconsistency of using, for the purpose of this legal fiction, a ram instead of a ewe.

Having described the ceremony of the new birth in the two forms in which it is observed by the two guilds of the Akikuyu, Hobley proceeds to describe another Kikuyu ceremony, which is similar in form to the rite of the new birth and is designated by a similar, though not identical, name (*Ku-chiaruo kungi* instead of *Ku-chiaruo ringi*). It is a ceremony of adoption and is said to resemble the Swahili rite called *ndugu Kuchanjiana*. "If a person has no brothers or parents he will probably try to obtain the protection of some wealthy man and his family. If such a man agrees to adopt him, he will take a male sheep and slaughter it, and the suppliant takes another one. The elders are assembled and slaughter these sheep, and strips of the skin (*rukwaru*) from the right foot and from the chest of each sheep are tied round each person's hand, each is decorated with strips of skin from the sheep of the other party. The poor man is then considered as the son of the wealthy one, and when the occasion arises the latter pays out livestock to buy a wife for his adopted son."[8] In this ceremony there can hardly be any pretence of a new birth, since both the performers are males; but on the analogy of the preceding customs it seems fair to suppose that the two parties, the adopting father and the adopted son, pretend to be sheep.

Further, a similar ritual is observed before the Kikuyu ceremony of circumcision. On the morning of the day which precedes the rite of circumcision, a he-goat is killed by being strangled; it is then skinned, and the skin having been cut into strips, a strip of the skin is fastened round the right wrist and carried over the back of the hand of each male candidate, after which the second finger of the candidate's hand is inserted through a slit in the strip of skin.[9]

A similar custom is observed by the Washamba, another tribe of East

Africa. Before the rite of circumcision is performed, they sacrifice a goat to an ancestral spirit, and cut wristlets from its skin for the boys who are to be circumcised, as well as for their parents and kinsfolk. In sacrificing the goat the father of the boy prays to the ancestor, saying, "We are come to tell thee that our son is to be circumcised to-day. Guard the child and be gracious, be not wrathful! We bring thee a goat."[10] Here, by binding strips of the skin on their own bodies, the members of the family seem to identify themselves with the goat which they offer to the ancestral ghost.

Among the Wachaga of Mount Kilimanjaro, about two months after circumcision the lads assemble at the chief's village, where the sorcerers or medicine-men are also gathered together. Goats are killed and the newly circumcised lads cut thongs from the hides and insert the middle fingers of their right hands through slits in the thongs. Meantime the sorcerers compound a medicine out of the contents of the stomachs of the goats, mixed with water and magical stuffs. This mixture the chief sprinkles on the lads, perhaps to complete the magical or sacramental identification of the lads with the animal. Next day the father of each lad makes a feast for his relations. A goat is killed, and every guest gets a piece of the goat's skin, which he puts round the middle finger of his right hand.[11]

We may compare a ceremony observed among the Bworana Gallas when lads attain their majority. The ceremony is called *ada* or forehead, but this is explained by a word *jara,* which means circumcision. On these occasions the young men, on whose behalf the rite is celebrated, assemble with their parents and elder relatives in a hut built for the purpose. A bullock is there sacrificed, and every person present dips a finger into the blood, which is allowed to flow over the ground; the men dab the blood on their foreheads, and the women on their windpipes. Further, the women smear themselves with fat taken from the sacrificial victim, and wear narrow strips of its hide round their necks till the next day. The flesh of the bullock furnishes a banquet.[12]

A similar use of sacrificial skins is made at marriage in some of these African tribes. Thus among the Wawanga of the Elgon District, in British East Africa, a part of the marriage ceremony is this. A he-goat is killed, and a long strip of skin is cut from its belly. The bridegroom's father, or some other elderly male relative, then slits the skin up lengthwise and passes it over the bride's head, so that it hangs down over her chest, while he says, "Now I have put this skin over your head; if you leave us for any other man, may this skin repudiate you, and may you become barren."[13] Again, among the Theraka, a tribe who live on both sides of the Tana River in British East Africa and closely resemble the Akikuyu in appearance and language, when a husband brings his bride to his village, he kills a goat and carries it before the girl into the hut; according to others, the goat is laid before the door of the hut and the girl must jump over it. A strip of the goat's skin is then put on the bride's wrist.[14] Again, among the Wa-giriama, a Bantu tribe of British East Africa, on the day after marriage the husband kills a goat, and cutting off a piece of skin from its forehead makes it into an amulet and gives it to his wife, who wears it on her left arm. The flesh of the goat is eaten by the persons present.[15]

Among the Nandi of British East Africa, on the marriage day a goat, specially selected as a strong, healthy animal from the flock, is anointed and then killed by being strangled. Its entrails are extracted and omens drawn from their condition. Afterwards the animal is skinned, and while the women roast and eat the meat, the skin is rapidly dressed and given to the bride to wear. Moreover, a ring and a bracelet are made out of the skin; the ring is put on the middle finger of the bridegroom's right hand, and the bracelet is put on the bride's left wrist.[16]

Again, rings made from the skin of a sacrificed goat are placed on the fingers of persons who form a covenant of friendship with each other. The custom appears to be common among the tribes of British East Africa. Thus, among the Wachaga "friendships are formed by the *Kiskong'o* ceremony, which consists in taking the skin from the head of a goat, making a slit in it, and putting it upon the middle finger in the form of a ring."[17] Similarly, among the Akamba, the exchange of rings made out of the skin of a sacrificial victim, which has been eaten in common, cements the bond of friendship.[18]

Among the Akikuyu a similar, but somewhat more elaborate, ceremony is observed when a man leaves his own district and formally joins another. He and the representative of the district to which he is about to attach himself each provide a sheep or, if they are well off, an ox. The animal is killed, "and from the belly of each a strip is cut, and also a piece of skin from a leg of each animal. Blood from each of the two animals is put into one leaf and the contents of the two bellies into another leaf. The elders (*ki-á-ma*) slit the two pieces of skin from the leg and the two strips from the belly, and make four wristlets; the two coming from the beast of one party are placed on the right arm of the other party, and *vice versa*. The elders then take the two leaves containing blood, and both parties to the transaction extend their hands; the elders pour a little blood into all the four palms, and this is passed from the palms of the one person to those of the other. All round are called to see that the blood is mingled, and hear the proclamation that the two are now of one blood."[19] This last example is instructive, since it shows clearly that the intention of the rite is to make the two contracting parties of one blood; hence we seem bound to explain on the same principle the custom of encircling their wrists with strips of skin taken from the same animals which furnished the blood for the ceremony.

We have seen that the same custom of wearing wristlets made from the skin of a sacrificial victim is observed by the Wachaga of Mount Kilimanjaro when they sacrifice a goat to an ancestral spirit at circumcision. The ritual varies somewhat according as the spirit is an ancestor in the paternal or the maternal line. If he is a paternal ancestor, the strip of skin is worn on the middle finger of the right hand; if he is a maternal ancestor, it is worn on the middle finger of the left hand. If the sacrifice was offered to an undefined ancestor on the father's side, the strip is worn on the big toe of the right foot; if it was offered to an undefined ancestor on the mother's side, it is worn on the big toe of the left foot.[20] Again, among the Wachaga, on the eighth day after a death, a goat is sacrificed to the ancestral spirits, and rings made from the skin of its head are given to all the surviving female relations to wear. This is believed to avert all evil consequences of the death.[21]

Again, similar sacrificial customs are observed in cases of sickness. For example, among the Wawanga it sometimes happens that a sick man in a state of delirium calls out the name of a departed relative. When he does so, the sickness is at once set down at the door of the ghost, and steps are taken to deal effectually with him. A poor old man is bribed to engage in the dangerous task of digging up the corpse, after which the bones are burnt over a nest of red ants, and the ashes swept into a basket and thrown into a river. Sometimes the mode of giving his quietus to the ghost is slightly different. Instead of digging up his bones, his relatives drive a stake into the head of the grave, and, to make assurance doubly sure, pour boiling water down after it. Having thus disposed of the ghost in a satisfactory manner, they kill a black ram, rub dung from the stomach of the animal on their chests, and tie strips of its skin round their right wrists. Further, the head of the family, in which the sickness occurred, binds a strip of the skin round the second finger of his right hand, and the sick man himself fastens a strip round his neck.[22] In this case we cannot regard the sacrifice of the black ram as intended to soothe and propitiate the ghost who had just had a stake thrust through his head and boiling water poured on his bones. Rather we must suppose that the sacrifice is due to a lingering suspicion that even these strong measures may not be wholly effectual in disarming him; so to be on the safe side the sick man and his friends fortify themselves against ghostly assaults by the skin of a sacrificial victim, which serves them as an amulet.[23]

Further, the custom of wearing portions of the skins of sacrificial victims is commonly observed among these East African tribes at expiatory ceremonies. Among the Wachaga, for example, if a husband has beaten his wife and she comes back to him, he cuts off a goat's ear and makes rings out of it, which they put on each other's fingers. Until he has done this, she may neither cook for him nor eat with him.[24] Again, like many other peoples, the Wachaga look upon a smith with superstitious awe as a being invested with mysterious powers, which elevate him above the level of common men. This atmosphere of wonder and mystery extends also to the instruments of his craft, and particularly to his hammer, which is supposed to be endowed with magical or spiritual virtue. Hence he must be very careful how he handles the hammer in presence of other people, lest he should endanger their lives by its miraculous influence. For example, if he merely points at a man with the hammer, they believe that the man will die, unless a solemn ceremony is performed to expiate the injury. Hence a goat is killed, and two rings are made out of its skin. One of the rings is put on the middle finger of the smith's right hand, the other is put on the corresponding finger of the man whose life he has jeopardized, and expiatory formulas are recited. A similar atonement must be made if the smith has pointed at any one with the tongs, or has chanced to hit any one with the slag of his iron. Again, when he is hammering a piece of iron for somebody, and the head of the hammer flies off, the smith says to the owner of the iron, who commonly sits by watching the operation, "The chief wants you. I must keep your iron and cannot work it until you have given him satisfaction." So the owner of the iron must bring a goat, and they kill the animal and eat its flesh together. Next they cut rings out of the skin of the goat's head and place the rings on each other's fingers with mutual good wishes and blessings. Moreover, another ring, made out of the goat's skin, is put on the handle of the hammer; and with the hammer thus decorated, or rather guarded against the powers of evil, the smith resumes and completes his task of hammering the iron into the desired shape.[25]

Again, among the Wachaga on the eastern side of Mount Kilimanjaro, it is a custom that a newly married woman may not drink the milk of a cow belonging to her husband which has just calved, unless she makes the following expiation. Her husband kills a goat or an ox and cuts off one of the forelegs together with the breast. These pieces are put on the young wife's head and she is sent way to her own people, with the words, "Go home (to your mother's people). Do not quarrel with your husband. May your cows give plenty of milk, may your goats cast good kids, may your beans not be eaten by mice, nor your corn by birds. When you go to market, may you be well received and find a chance of cheating. But be careful not to cheat so as to be found out and be taken to law." With these good wishes the young wife is sent away to her parents, who receive her solemnly, take the flesh from her head, and lay it on the ground. Then they take the leg of the goat or ox and cut out of the skin a ring large enough to be pushed over the woman's left hand. There they fasten it, and then push four small morsels of flesh between the ring and her hand. These pieces she must eat, a fifth piece, which they afterwards push through, she allows to fall on the ground. Finally her mother's people utter good wishes like those which her husband's people uttered when they sent her with the goat's flesh and skin to her old home. That ends the ceremony, and after it is over, the young wife is free to drink the milk of the cow at her husband's house.[26] The exact meaning of this ceremony in all its details is no longer understood even by the natives themselves, and we can hardly hope to divine it; but the general intention appears to be to expiate the breach of a taboo which forbade a young wive to partake of the milk of a cow that had just calved on her husband's farm. As we shall see later on, the drinking of milk among these East African tribes is hedged round by many curious restrictions, the object of which is to guard, not the drinker of the milk, but the cow, against certain evil consequences believed to flow from contact of the fluid with tabooed persons or things. In the present case we may conjecture that if the young wife were to drink of the cow's milk without first performing the ceremony of expiation, she would be supposed thereby to endanger the cow's milk and perhaps even its life.

Expiatory ceremonies involving the use of the skin of a sacrificial victim are performed by the Akikuyu on a variety of occasions. For example, if two men, who have been circumcised at the same time, fight each other and blood is spilt, ceremonial pollution is incurred, and a medicine-man must be called in to remove it. He kills a sheep, and the elders put a strip of its skin on the wrist of each of the two men. This removes the pollution and reconciles the adversaries.[27] Again, among the Akikuyu, the wives of smiths usually wear armlets of twisted iron. If a man enters the hut of a smith and cohabits with a woman so decorated, a state of ceremonial pollution is incurred, which can only be expiated by another smith, who kills a sheep, and, cutting strips from its skin, puts them on the wrists of the man, his wife, and any children she may have. The bracelet is placed on the left wrist of a woman, on the right wrist of a man.[28] Again, in the same tribe, if the side pole of a bedstead breaks, the person lying on the bed incurs a state of ceremonial pollution. A sheep must be killed, and a bracelet made from its skin must be placed on the arm of the person whose bed gave way; otherwise he or she might die.[29] Again, among the Akikuyu, if a man strikes another who is herding sheep or cattle, so that blood is drawn, the flock or herd is thereby brought into a state of ceremonial pollution. The offender must give a sheep, and the elders kill it, and place a strip of its skin on the wrist of the culprit.[30] Again, when a Kikuyu child has been circumcised, and leaves the village for the first time after the ceremony, if it should happen that in the evening the goats and sheep return from pasture and enter the village before the child has come back, then that child is ceremonially unclean, and may not return to the village till the usual ceremony of expiation has been performed. His father must kill a sheep, and place a strip of its skin on his child's arm. Till that is done the child may not return to the village, but must sleep at a neighbouring village, where some of the boys live who went through the ceremony of circumcision along with him.[31] Again, if a Kikuyu man or woman has been bitten by a hyena or a dog, he or she is unclean, and must be purified in the usual way by a medicine-man, who kills a sheep and puts a strip of its skin on the patient's wrist.[32] Further, if a Kikuyu man strikes a woman who is with child, so that she miscarries, the culprit must bring two sheep, which are killed and eaten, the one by the villagers and the elders, the other by the woman and visitors. Moreover, bracelets are made out of the skin of the first of these sheep and placed on the wrists of all persons present who are nearly related either to the offender or to the woman.[33]

Expiatory ceremonies of the same kind are performed by the Wawanga, in the Elgon District of British East Africa. For example, if a stranger forces his way into a hut, and in doing so his skin cloak falls to the ground, or if he be bleeding from a fight, and his blood drips on the floor, one of the inmates of the hut will fall sick, unless proper measures are taken to prevent it. The offender must produce a goat. The animal is killed, and the skin, having been removed from its chest and belly, is cut into strips; these strips are stirred round in the contents of the goat's stomach, and every person in the hut puts one of them round his right wrist. If any person in the hut should have fallen sick before this precaution was taken, the strip of skin is tied round his neck, and he rubs some of the goat's dung on his chest. Half of the goat is eaten by the occupants of the hut, and the other half by the stranger in his own village. The same procedure is resorted to by the Wawanga in case the artificial tail which a woman wears has been torn off her, or she should be guilty of the gross impropriety of entering a hut without that appendage. Indeed, the Wawanga believe that a woman may cause her husband's death simply by walking abroad without her tail. To avert the catastrophe the husband demands a goat from her people, and eats it in company with his wife, who further ties a strip of skin from the goat's belly round her neck and rubs some of the contents of its stomach on her chest. This saves her husband's life. Again, a man of this tribe, returning from a raid on which he has killed one of the enemy, may not enter his own hut till he has purified himself by the sacrifice of a goat; and he must wear a strip of skin taken from the goat's forehead for the next four days.[34] Once more, the Wawanga, like many other savages, believe that a woman who has given birth to twins is in a very parlous state, and a variety of purificatory ceremonies must be performed before she can leave the hut; otherwise there is no saying what might not happen to her. Among other things they catch a mole and kill it by driving a wooden spike into the back of its neck. Then the animal's belly is split open and the contents of the stomach removed and rubbed on the chests of the mother and the twins. Next, the animal's skin is cut up, and strips of it are tied round the right wrist of each of the twins, and round the mother's neck. They are worn for five days, after which the mother goes to the river, washes, and throws the pieces of skin into the water. The mole's flesh is buried in a hole under the verandah of the hut, before the door, and a pot, with a hole knocked in the bottom, is placed upside down over it.[35] Among the Bantu tribes of Kavirondo, at the northeastern corner of Lake Victoria Nyanza, it is a rule that only very near relations are allowed to penetrate beyond the first of the two fireplaces which are found, one behind the other, in every hut. Any person who transgresses this rule must kill a goat, and all the occupants of the hut wear small pieces of the skin and smear a little of the dung on their chests.[36]

Lastly, it may be noticed that a similar use of sacrificial skins is made by some of these East African tribes at certain solemn festivals which are held by them at long intervals determined by the length of the age grades into which the whole population is divided. For example, the Nandi are divided into seven such age grades, and the festivals in question are held at intervals of seven and a half years. At each of these festivals the government of the country is transferred from the men of one age grade to the men of the age grade next below it in point of seniority. The chief medicine-man attends, and the proceedings open with the slaughter of a white bullock, which is purchased by the young warriors for the occasion. After the meat has been eaten by the old men, each of the young men makes a small ring out of the hide and puts it on one of the fingers of his right hand. Afterwards the transference of power from the older to the younger men is formally effected, the seniors doffing their warriors' skins and donning the fur garments of old men.[37] At the corresponding ceremony among the Akikuyu, which is held at intervals of about fifteen years, every person puts a strip of skin from a male goat round his wrist before he returns home.[38]

On a general survey of the foregoing customs we may conclude that the intention of investing a person with a portion of a sacrificial skin is to protect him against some actual or threatened evil, so that the skin serves the purpose of an amulet. This interpretation probably covers even the cases in which the custom is observed at the ratification of a covenant, since the two covenanters thereby guard against the danger which they apprehend from a breach of contract. Similarly, the strange rite of the new birth, or birth from a goat, which the Akikuyu used to observe as a preliminary to circumcision, may be supposed to protect the performers from some evil which would otherwise befall them. As to the mode in which the desired object is effected by this particular means, we may conjecture that by wearing a portion of the animal's skin the man identifies himself with the sacrificial victim, which thus acts as a sort of buffer against the assaults of the evil powers, whether it be that these powers are persuaded or cajoled into taking the beast for the man, or that the blood, flesh, and skin of the victim are thought to be endowed with a certain magical virtue which keeps malignant beings at bay. This identification of the man with the animal comes out most clearly in the Kikuyu rite of the new birth, in which mother and child pretend to be a she-goat and her newborn kid. Arguing from it, we may suppose that in every case the attachment of a piece of sacrificial skin to a person is only an abridged way of wrapping him up in the whole skin for the purpose of identifying him with the beast.

With these rites we may compare a ceremony performed by certain clans in south-eastern Madagascar for the sake of averting the ill-luck with which a child born under an evil destiny is supposed to be threatened. An ox is sacrificed, and its blood rubbed on the brow and behind the ears of the infant. Moreover, a sort of hoop or large ring is made with a thong cut from the victim's hide, and through this hoop the mother passes with the child in her arms.[39] The custom of passing through a hoop or other narrow opening in order to give the slip to some actual or threatened calamity is widespread in the world;[40] but a special significance attaches to the practice when the aperture is formed by the skin of a sacrificial victim. Like the rite of passing between the pieces of a slaughtered animal,[41] the act of passing through a ring of its hide may perhaps be interpreted as an abridged form of entering into the victim's body in order to be identified with it and so to enjoy the protection of its sacred character.

(b) The new birth

The quaint story of the Diverted Blessing, with its implication of fraud and treachery practised by a designing mother and a crafty son on a doting husband and father, wears another and a far more respectable aspect, if we suppose that the discreditable colour it displays has been imported into it by the narrator, who failed to understand the true nature of the transaction which he described. That transaction, if I am right, was neither more nor less than a legal fiction that Jacob was born again as a goat for the purpose of ranking as the elder instead of the younger son of his mother. We have seen that among the Akikuyu of East Africa, a tribe possibly of Arabian, if not of Semitic, descent, a similar fiction of birth from a goat or a sheep appears to play an important part in the social and religious life of the people. It will be some confirmation of our hypothesis if we can show that the pretence of a new birth, either from a woman or from an animal, has been resorted to by other peoples in cases in which, for one reason or another, it has been deemed desirable that a man should, as it were, strip himself of his old personality and, assuming a new one, make a fresh start in life. In short, at an early stage in the history of law the legal fiction of a new birth has often been employed for the purpose of effecting and marking a change of status. The following instances may serve to illustrate this general proposition.

In the first place, then, the fiction of a new birth has been made use of, not unnaturally, in cases of adoption for the sake of converting the adopted child into the real child of his adopting mother. Thus the Sicilian historian Diodorus informs us that when Herakles was raised to the rank of the gods, his divine father Zeus persuaded his wife Hera to adopt the bastard as her own true-born son, and this the complacent goddess did by getting into bed, clasping Herakles to her body, and letting him fall through her garments to the ground in imitation of a real birth; and the historian adds that in his own day the barbarians followed the same procedure in adopting a son.[42] During the Middle Ages a similar form of adoption appears to have been observed in Spain and other parts of Europe. The adopted child was taken under the mantle of his adopting father or mother; sometimes he was passed through the folds of the flowing garment. Hence adopted children were called "mantle children."[43]

Among the pastoral Bahima of Central Atrica, "when a man inherits children of a deceased brother, he takes the children and places them one by one in the lap of his chief wife, who receives them and embraces them and thus accepts them as her own children. Her husband afterwards brings a thong, which he uses for tying the legs of restive cows during milking and binds it round her waist in the manner a midwife binds a woman after childbirth. After this ceremony the children grow up with the family and are counted as part of it."[44] In this ceremony we may detect the simulation of childbirth both in the placing of the children on the woman's lap and in the tying of a thong round her waist after the manner of midwives, who do the same for women in actual childbed.

Further, the pretence of a new birth has been enacted for the benefit of persons who have erroneously been supposed to have died, and for whom in their absence funeral rites have been performed for the purpose of laying their wandering ghosts, who might otherwise haunt and trouble the survivors. The return of such persons to the bosom of their family is embarrassing, since on the principles of imitative magic or make-believe they are theoretically dead, though practically alive. The problem thus created was solved in ancient Greece and ancient India by the legal fiction of a new birth; the returned wanderer had solemnly to pretend to come to life by being born again of a woman before he might mix freely with living folk. Till that pretence had been enacted, the ancient Greeks treated such persons as unclean, refused to associate with them, and excluded them from all participation in religious rites; in particular, they strictly forbade them to enter the sanctuary of the Furies. Before they were restored to the privileges of civil life, they had to be passed through the bosom of a woman's robe, to be washed by a nurse, wrapped in swaddling clothes, and suckled at the breast. Some people thought that the custom originated with a certain Aristinus, for whom in his absence funeral rites had been performed. On his return home, finding himself shunned by all as an outcast, he applied to the Delphic oracle for advice, and was directed by the god to perform the rite of the new birth. Other people, however, with great probability believed that the rite was older than the time of Aristinus and had been handed down from remote antiquity.[45] In ancient India, under the like circumstances, the supposed dead man had to pass the first night after his return in a tub filled with a mixture of fat and water. When he stepped into the tub, his father or next of kin pronounced over him a certain verse, after which he was supposed to have attained to the stage of an embryo in the womb. In that character he sat silent in the tub, with clenched fists, while over him were performed all the sacraments that were regularly celebrated for a woman with child. Next morning he got out of the tub, at the back, and went through all the other sacraments he had formerly partaken of from his youth upwards; in particular he married a wife or espoused his old one over again with due solemnity.[46] This ancient custom appears to be not altogether obsolete in India even at the present day. In Kumaon a person supposed to be dying is carried out of the house, and the ceremony of the remission of sins is performed over him by his next of kin. But should he afterwards recover, he must go through all the ceremonies previously performed by him from his birth upwards, such as putting on the sacred thread and marrying wives, though he sometimes marries his old wives over again.[47]

But in ancient India the rite of the new birth was also enacted for a different and far more august purpose. A Brahmin householder who performed the regular half-monthly sacrifices was supposed thereby to become himself a god for the time being,[48] and in order to effect this transition from the human to the divine, from the mortal to the immortal, it was necessary for him to be born again. For this purpose he was sprinkled with water as a symbol of seed. He feigned to be an embryo and as such was shut up in a special hut representing the womb. Under his robe he wore a belt, and over it the skin of a black antelope; the belt stood for the navel-string, and the robe and the black antelope skin typified the inner and outer membranes (the amnion and chorion) in which an embryo is wrapped. He might not scratch himself with his nails or a stick, because he was an embryo, and were an embryo scratched with nails or a stick, it would die. If he moved about in the hut, it was because a child moves about in the womb. If he kept his fists clenched, it was because an unborn babe does the same. If in bathing he put off the black antelope skin but retained his robe, it was because the child is born with the amnion but not with the chorion. By these observances he acquired, besides his old natural and mortal body, a new and glorified body, invested with superhuman powers and encircled with an aureole of fire. Thus by a new birth, a regeneration of his carnal nature, the man became a god.[49]

Thus we see that the ceremony of the new birth may serve different purposes, according as it is employed to raise a supposed dead man to life or to elevate a living man to the rank of a deity. In modern India it has been, and indeed still is, occasionally performed as an expiatory rite to atone for some breach of ancestral custom. The train of thought which has prompted this use of the ceremony is obvious enough. The sinner who has been born again becomes thereby a new man and ceases to be responsible for the sins committed by him in his former state of existence; the process of regeneration is at the same time a process of purification, the old nature has been put off and an entirely new one put on. For example, among the Korkus, an aboriginal tribe of the Munda or Kolarian stock in the Central Provinces of India, social offences of an ordinary kind are punished by the tribal council, which inflicts the usual penalties, but "in very serious cases, such as intercourse with a low caste, it causes the offender to be born again. He is placed inside a large earthen pot which is sealed up, and when taken out of this he is said to be born again from his mother's womb. He is then buried in sand and comes out as a fresh incarnation from the earth, placed in a grass hut which is fired, and from within which he runs out as it is burning, immersed in water, and finally has a tuft cut from his scalp-lock and is fined two and a half rupees."[50] Here the ceremony of the new birth seems clearly intended to relieve the culprit from all responsibility for his former acts by converting him into an entirely new person. With what show of reason could he be held to account for an offence committed by somebody else before he was born?

Far more elaborate and costly is the ceremony of the new birth when the sinner who is to be regenerated is a person of high birth or exalted dignity. In the eighteenth century "when the unfortunate Raghu-Náth-Ráya or Ragoba, sent two Brahmins as ambassadors to England, they went by sea as far as Suez, but they came back by the way of Persia, and of course crossed the Indus. On their return they were treated as outcasts, because they conceived it hardly possible for them to travel through countries inhabited by *Mlec'h'has* or impure tribes, and live according to the rules laid down in their sacred books: it was also alleged, that they had crossed the Attaca. Numerous meetings were held in consequence of this, and learned Brahmins were convened from all parts. The influence and authority of Raghu-Náth-Ráya could not save his embassadors. However, the holy assembly decreed, that in consideration of their universal good character, and of the motive of their travelling to distant countries, which was solely to promote the good of their country, they might be regenerated and have the sacerdotal ordination renewed. For the purpose of regeneration, it is directed to make an image of pure gold of the female power of nature; in the shape either of a woman or of a cow. In this statue the person to be regenerated is enclosed and dragged through the usual channel. As a statue of pure gold and of proper dimensions would be too expensive, it is sufficient to make an image of the sacred *Yoni,* through which the person to be regenerated is to pass. Raghu-Náth-Ráya had one made of pure gold and of proper dimensions: his ambassadors were regenerated, and the usual ceremonies of ordination having been performed, and immense presents bestowed on the Brahmins, they were re-admitted into the communion of the faithful."[51] Again, "it is on record that the Tanjore Nayakar, having betrayed Madura and suffered for it, was told by his Brahman advisers that he had better be born again. So a colossal cow was cast in bronze, and the Nayakar shut up inside. The wife of his Brahmin guru [teacher] acted as nurse, received him in her arms, rocked him on her knees, and caressed him on her breast, and he tried to cry like a baby."[52]

In India the fiction of a new birth has further been employed for the purpose of raising a man of low caste into a social rank higher than the one to which his first or real birth had consigned him. For example, the Maharajahs of Travancore belong to the Sudra caste, the lowest of the four great Indian castes, but they appear regularly to exalt themselves to a level with the Brahmins, the highest caste, by being born again either from a large golden cow or from a large golden lotus-flower. Hence the ceremony is called *Hiranya Garbham,* "the golden womb," or *Patma Garbha Dānam,* "the lotus womb-gift," according as the effigy, from which the Maharajah emerged new-born, represented a cow or a lotus-flower. When James Forbes was at Travancore, the image through which the potentate passed was that of a cow made of pure gold; and after his passage through it the image was broken up and distributed among the Brahmans. But when the ceremony was performed by the Rajah Martanda Vurmah in July 1854, the image was cast in the form of a lotus-flower and was estimated to have cost about £6000. Inside the golden vessel had been placed a small quantity of the consecrated mixture, composed of the five products of the cow (milk, curd, butter, urine, and dung); which suggests that the proper rebirth for the Maharajah is rather from the sacred cow than from the sacred lotus. After entering the vessel, His Highness remained within it for the prescribed time, while the officiating priests repeated prayers appropriate to the occasion.[53] . . . .

From later notices of the ceremony we may infer that the Maharajahs have since reverted to the other, and perhaps more orthodox, form of the new birth, namely the birth from a cow. Thus in the year 1869 it was announced that "another not less curious ceremony, called *Ernjagherpum,* will take place next year, whereat His Highness (the Maharajah of Travancore) will go through a golden cow, which thereupon will also become the property of the priests."[54] Again, we read that "the Maharaja of Travancore, a Native State in the extreme South of India, has just completed the second and last of the costly ceremonies known as 'going through the golden cow,' which he has to perform in order to rank more or less on the same footing as a Brahmin—his original caste being that of Sudra. The first of these ceremonies is known as *Thula-purusha danam*—Sanskrit *Thula,* scales; *purusha,* man; and *danam,* gift of a religious character. The ceremony consists in the Maharaja entering the scales against an equal weight of gold coins, which are afterwards distributed among Brahmins. . . . The second ceremony is known as the *Hirannya garbham*—Sanskrit *hirannya,* gold; and *garbham,* womb—and constitutes the process known as going through the golden cow. A large golden vessel is constructed, ten feet in height and eight feet in circumference. This vessel is half filled with water, mixed with the various products of the cow, and Brahmins perform the prescribed rites over it. The Maharaja next enters the vessel by means of a specially constructed ornamental ladder. The cover is then put on, and the Raja immerses himself five times in the contained fluid, while the Brahmins keep up a chanted accompaniment of prayers and Vedic hymns. This portion of the ceremony lasts about ten minutes, after which time the Maharaja emerges from the vessel and prostrates himself before the image of the diety of the Travancore kings. The high priest now places the crown of Travancore on the Raja's head, and after this he is considered to have rendered himself holy by having passed through the golden cow. The previous ceremony of being weighed against gold simply fitted him for performing the more exalted and more costly ceremony of going through the golden cow. The cost of these curious ceremonies is very great; for quite apart from the actual value of the gold, much expenditure is incurred in feasting the vast concourse of Brahmins who assemble in Trevandrum on these occasions. From time immemorial, however, the Rajas of Travancore have performed these ceremonies, and any omission on their part to do so would be regarded as an offense against the traditions of the country, which is a very stronghold of Hindu superstition."[55]

If none could be born again save such as can afford to provide a colossal cow of pure gold for the ceremony, it seems obvious that the chances of regeneration for the human race generally would be but slender, and that practically none but the rich could enter into the realms of bliss through this singular aperture. Fortunately, however, the expedient of employing a real cow instead of a golden image places the rite of the new birth within the reach even of the poor and lowly, and thus opens to multitudes a gate of paradise which otherwise would have been barred and bolted against them. Indeed we may with some probability conjecture, that birth from a live cow was the original form of the ceremony, and that the substitution of a golden image for the real animal was merely a sop thrown to the pride of Rajahs and other persons of high degree, who would have esteemed it a blot on their scutcheon to be born in vulgar fashion, like common folk, from a common cow. Be that as it may, certain it is that in some parts of India a real live cow still serves as the instrument of the new birth. Thus in the Himalayan districts of the North-Western Provinces "the ceremony of being born again from the cow's mouth (*gomukhaprasava*) takes place when the horoscope foretells some crime on the part of the native or some deadly calamity to him. The child is clothed in scarlet and tied on a new sieve, which is passed between the hind legs of a cow forward through the fore-legs to the mouth and again in the reverse direction, signifying the new birth. The usual worship, aspersion, etc., takes place, and the father smells his son as the cow smells her calf."[56] Here, though it is necessarily impossible to carry out the simulation of birth completely by passing the child through the body of the living cow, the next best thing is done by passing it backwards and forwards between the cow's legs; thus the infant is assimiliated to a calf, and the father acts the part of its dam by smelling his offspring as a cow smells hers. Similarly in Southern India, when a man has for grave cause been expelled from his caste, he may be restored to it after passing several times under the belly of a cow.[57] Though the writer who reports this custom does not describe it as a ceremony of rebirth, we may reasonably regard it as such in the light of the foregoing evidence. A further extenuation of the original ceremony may perhaps be seen in the practice of placing an unlucky child in a basket before a good milch cow with a calf and allowing the cow to lick the child, "by which operation the noxious qualities which the child has derived from its birth are removed."[58]

To return now to the point from which we started, I conjecture that the story of the deception practiced by Jacob on his father Isaac contains a reminiscence of an ancient legal ceremony of new birth from a goat, which it was deemed necessary or desirable to observe whenever a younger son was advanced to the rights of the firstborn at the expense of his still living brother; just as in India to this day a man pretends to be born again from a cow when he desires to be promoted to a higher caste or to be restored to the one which he has forfeited through his misfortune or misconduct. But among the Hebrews, as among the Akikuyu, the quaint ceremony may have dwindled into a simple custom of killing a goat and placing pieces of its skin on the person who was supposed to be born again as a goat. In this degenerate form, if my conjecture is well founded, the ancient rite has been reported and misunderstood by the Biblical narrator. ▼

*   *   *

[A blessing (Hebrew, *b*ᵉ*rakah*) is not simply a benediction; it is the special quality, power, or grace which resides in a person or thing. A father transmits this quality to his firstborn, and a leader to his successor (e.g., Moses to Joshua). The reception of it is vital to success.[58a] Says Ben Sira:

> The blessing of a father establishes the houses of the children;
> but the curse of the mother roots out the foundations,[58b]

and the sentiment is echoed in the Scottish proverb:

> A father's blessing bigs the town;
> A mother's curse can ding it down.[58c]

Especially effective is the blessing pronounced by a dying man. The chief of the Ohaverero, for example, customarily blesses his people before he dies,[58d] just as Moses blessed Israel; and a similar usage is recorded among the Arabs.[58e]

Conversely, the curse of a father or leader spells doom. Homer tells us that the "Furies (Erinyes) always follow the firstborn,"[58f] and Plato that the curse of parents is stronger than all others.[58g] The Nandi of East Africa say likewise that a father's curse is the "most serious";[58h] while among the Mpongwe of Gabon, "there is nothing which a young person so much deprecates as the curse of an aged person, and especially that of a revered father."[58i]

Westermarck suggests that the special potency of the father's blessing or curse derives from the days when he was invested with sacerdotal functions.[58j]]

64 Jacob at Bethel   28:11–19

▲ (a) Dreams of the gods

As critics have seen, the story of Jacob's dream was probably told to explain the immemorial sanctity of Bethel, which may well have been revered by the aboriginal inhabitants of Canaan long before the Hebrews invaded and conquered the land. The belief that the gods revealed themselves and declared their will to mankind in dreams was widespread in antiquity; and accordingly people resorted to temples and other sacred spots for the purpose of sleeping there and holding converse with the higher powers in visions of the night, for they naturally supposed that the deities or the deified spirits of the dead would be most likely to manifest themselves in places specially dedicated to their worship. For example, at Oropus in Attica there was a sanctuary of the dead soothsayer Amphiaraus, where inquirers used to sacrifice rams to him and to other divine beings, whose names were inscribed on the altar; and having offered the sacrifice they spread the skins of the rams on the ground and slept on them, expecting revelations in dreams.[1] The oracle appears to have been chiefly frequented by sick people who sought a release from their sufferings, and, when they had found it, testified their gratitude by dropping gold or silver coins into the sacred spring.[2]

There was a similar dormitory for the use of patients who came to consult the Good Physician in the great sanctuary of Aesculapius near Epidaurus. Patients who had slept there and had been healed of their infirmities through the revelations accorded to them in dreams, used to commemorate the cures on tablets, which were set up in the holy place as eloquent testimonies to the restorative powers of the god and to the saving faith of those who put their trust in him. The sacred precinct was crowded with such tablets in antiquity, and some of them have been discovered in modern times.[3]

Again, on the wild ironbound coast of Laconia, where the great range of Taygetus descends in naked crags to the sea, there was an oracular shrine, where a goddess revealed their hearts' desires to mortals in dreams. Different opinions prevailed as to who the goddess was. The Greek traveller Pausanias, who visited the place, though that she was Ino, a marine goddess; but he acknowledged that he could not see the image in the temple for the multitude of garlands with which it was covered, probably by worshippers who thus expressed their thanks for the revelations vouchsafed to them in sleep. The vicinity of the sea, with the solemn lullaby of its waves, might plead in favour of Ino's claim to be the patroness of the shrine. Others, however, held that she was Pasiphae in the character of the Moon; and they may have supported their opinion, before they retired at nightfall to the sacred dormitory, by pointing to the silvery orb in the sky and her shimmering reflection on the moonlit water. Be that as it may, the highest magistrates of Sparta appear to have frequented this sequestered spot for the sake of the divine counsels which they expected to receive in slumber, and it is said that at a momentous crisis of Spartan history one of them here dreamed an ominous dream.[4]

Ancient Italy as well as Greece had its oracular seats, where anxious mortals sought for advice and comfort from the gods or deified men in dreams. Thus the soothsayer Calchas was worshipped at Drium in Apulia, and persons who wished to inquire of him sacrificed a black ram and slept on the skin.[5] Another ancient and revered Italian oracle was that of Faunus, and the mode of consulting him was similar. The inquirer sacrificed a sheep, spread out its skin on the ground, and sleeping on it received an answer in a dream. If the seat of the oracle was, as there is reason to think, in a sacred grove beside the cascade at Tibur, the solemn shade of the trees and the roar of the tumbling waters might well inspire the pilgrim with religious awe and mingle with his dreams.[6] The little circular shrine, which still overhangs the waterfall, may have been the very spot where the rustic god was believed to whisper in the ears of his slumbering votaries.

(b) The heavenly ladder

Far different from these oracular seats in the fair landscapes of Greece and Italy was the desolate stony hollow among the barren hills, where Jacob slept and saw the vision of angels ascending and descending the ladder that led from earth to heaven. The belief in such a ladder, used by divine beings or the souls of the dead, meets us in other parts of the world. Thus, speaking of the gods of West Africa, Miss Kingsley tells us that "in almost all the series of native traditions there, you will find accounts of a time when there was direct intercourse between the gods or spirits that live in the sky, and men. That intercourse is always said to have been cut off by some human error; for example, the Fernando Po people say that once upon a time there was no trouble or serious disturbance upon earth because there was a ladder, made like the one you get palm-nuts with, 'only long, long'; and this ladder reached from earth to heaven so the gods could go up and down it and attend personally to mundane affairs. But one day a cripple boy started to go up the ladder, and he had got a long way up when his mother saw him, and went up in pursuit. The gods, horrified at the prospect of having boys and women invading heaven, threw down the ladder, and have since left humanity severely alone."[7]

The Bare'e-speaking Toradjas of Central Celebes say that in the olden time, when all men lived together, sky and earth were connected with each other by a creeper. One day a handsome young man, of celestial origin, whom they call Mr. Sun (*Lasaeo*), appeared on earth, riding a white buffalo. He found a girl at work in the fields, and falling in love with the damsel he took her to wife. They lived together for a time, and Mr. Sun taught people to till the ground and supplied them with buffaloes. But one day it chanced that the child, which Mr. Sun had by his wife, misbehaved in the house and so offended his father that, in disgust at mankind, he returned to heaven by the creeper. His wife attempted to clamber up it after him, but he cut the creeper through, so that it and his wife together fell down to earth and were turned to stone. They may be seen to this day in the form of a limestone hill not far from the river Wimbi. The hill is shaped like a coil of rope and bears the name of the Creeper Hill (*Tamoengkoe mBaloegai*).[8] Further, in Toradja stories we hear of a certain Rolled-up Rattan, by which mortals can ascend from earth to heaven. It is a thorny creeper growing about a fig-tree and adding every year a fresh coil round the bole. Any person who would use it must first waken it from sleep by shattering seven cudgels on its tough fibres. That rouses the creeper from its slumber; it shakes itself, takes a betel-nut, and asks the person what he wants. When he begs to be carried up to the sky, the creeper directs him to seat himself either on its thorns or on its upper end, taking with him seven bamboo vessels full of water to serve as ballast. As the creeper rises in the air, it heels over to right or left, whereupon the passenger pours out some water, and the creeper rights itself accordingly. Arrived at the vault of heaven, the creeper shoots through a hole in the firmament, and, grappling fast by its thorns to the celestial floor, waits patiently till the passenger has done his business up aloft and is ready to return to earth. In this way to hero of the tale makes his way to the upper regions and executes his purpose there, whatever it is, whether it be to recover a stolen necklace, to storm and pillage a heavenly village, or to have a dead man restored to life by the heavenly smith.[9]

The Bataks of Sumatra say that at the middle of the earth there was formerly a rock, of which the top reached up to heaven, and by which certain privileged beings, such as heroes and priests, could mount up to the sky. In heaven there grew a great fig-tree (*waringin*) which sent down its roots to meet the rock, thus enabling mortals to swarm up it to the mansions on high. But one day a man out of spite cut down the tree, or perhaps rather severed its roots, because his wife, who had come down from heaven, returned thither and left him forlorn.[10] Again, "a Mazovian legend tells how a certain pilgrim, on his way to worship at the Holy Sepulchre, became lost in a rocky place from which he could not for a long time extricate himself. At last he saw hanging in the air a ladder made of birds' feathers. Up this he clambered for three months, at the end of which he reached the Garden of Paradise, and entered among groves of gold and silver and gem-bearing trees, all of which were familiar with the past, the present, and the future."[11]

Different from these imaginary ladders are the real ladders which some people set up to facilitate the descent of gods or spirits from heaven to earth. For example, the natives of Timorlaut, Babar, and the Leti Islands in the Indian Archipelago worship the sun as the chief male god, who fertilizes the earth, regarded as a goddess, every year at the beginning of the rainy season. For this beneficent purpose the deity descends into a sacred fig-tree (*waringin*), and to enable him to alight on the ground the people place under the tree a ladder with seven rungs, the rails of which are decorated with the carved figures of two cocks, as if to announce the arrival of the god of day by their shrill clarion.[12] When the Toradjas of Central Celebes are offering sacrifices to the gods at the dedication of a new house, they set up two stalks of plants, adorned with seven strips of white cotton or barkcloth, to serve the gods as ladders whereby they may descend to partake of the rice, tobacco, betel, and palm-wine provided for them.[13] Among the Dyaks of Dusun, in Southern Borneo, when a medicine-man is called into a house to heal a sick person, an altar with offerings is set up in the middle of the room, and from it a light ladder, made of reeds, is stretched to the ridge of the roof. In response to an invocation the spirits alight on the roof, and descending the ladder enter into the medicine-man, who, thus possessed by them, dances wildly about and then sucks the sickness out of the patient's body.[14]

Again, some peoples both in ancient and modern times have imagined that the souls of the dead pass up from earth to heaven by means of a ladder, and they have even placed miniature ladders in the graves in order to enable the ghosts to swarm up them to the abode of bliss. Thus in the Pyramid Texts, which are amongst the oldest literature of the world, mention is often made of a ladder up which dead Egyptian kings climbed to the sky; in many Egyptian graves there has been found a ladder, which may have been intended to enable the ghost to scramble up out of the grave, perhaps even to ascend up to heaven, like the kings of old.[15]

The Mangars, a fighting tribe of Nepal, are careful to provide their dead with ladders up which they may climb to the celestial mansions. "Two bits of wood, about three feet long, are set up on either side of the grave. In the one are cut nine steps or notches forming a ladder for the spirit of the dead to ascend to heaven; on the other every one present at the funeral cuts a notch to show that he has been there. As the maternal uncle steps out of the grave, he bids a solemn farewell to the dead and calls upon him to ascend to heaven by the ladder that stands ready for him."[16]

It is, or used to be, a popular belief in Russia, that "the soul had to rise from the grave, and therefore certain aids to climbing were buried with the corpse. Among these were plaited thongs of leather and small ladders. One of the most interesting specimens of survival to be found among the customs of the Russian peasantry is connected with this idea. Even at the present day, when many of them have forgotten the origin of the custom, they still, in some districts, make little ladders of dough, and have them baked for the benefit of the dead. In the Government of Voroneje a ladder of this sort, about three feet high, is set up at the time when a coffin is being carried to the grave; in some other places similar pieces of dough are baked in behalf of departed relatives on the fortieth day after their death, or long pies marked crosswise with bars are taken to church on Ascension Day and divided between the priest and the poor. In some villages these pies, which are known as *Lyesenki* or 'ladderlings,' have seven bars or rungs, in reference to the Seven Heavens. The peasants fling them down from the belfry, and accept their condition after their fall as an omen of their own probable fate after death."[17] From the Russians the belief and the custom have been borrowed by the Cheremiss. They imagine that the abode of bliss is somewhere up aloft, and to enable a dead man to mount up to it, they obligingly place a small ladder in the coffin or supply him with the article on the fortieth day after burial.[18] The Besisi and Jakun, two pagan tribes of the Malay Penninsula, provide their dead with soul-ladders (*tangga sĕmangat*), which are plain upright or inclined sticks, whereby the soul of the deceased can leave the grave at pleasure.[19]

(c) The sacred stone   28:18

The idea of a stone tenanted by a god or other powerful spirit was not peculiar to ancient Israel; it has been shared by many peoples in many lands. The Arabs in antiquity worshipped stones,[20] and even under Islam the Black Stone at Mecca continues to occupy a principal place in their devotions at the central shrine of their religion.[21] We are told that in olden time all the Greeks worshipped unwrought stones instead of images. In the market-place of Pharae, in Achaia, there were thirty square stones, to each of which the people gave the name of a god.[22] At Megara there was a stone in the shape of a pyramid, which was called Apollo Carinus;[23] on coins of the city it is represented as an obelisk standing between two dolphins.[24] Near Gythium in Laconia there was an unwrought stone which went by the name of Zeus Cappotas; legend ran that the matricide Orestes had been cured of his madness by sitting on it.[25] In a temple of Hercules at Olmones in Boeotia the god was represented, not by an image, but in the old fashion by an unwrought stone.[26] The inhabitants of Thespiae, in Boeotia, honoured Love above all the gods; and the great sculptors Lysippus and Praxiteles wrought for the city glorious images of the amorous deity in bronze and marble. Yet beside these works of refined Greek art the people paid their devotions to an uncouth idol of the god in the shape of a rough stone.[27] The Aenianes of Thessaly worshipped a stone, sacrificing to it and covering it with the fat of victims. They explained its sanctity by a story, that in days of old one of their kings had slain another king in single combat by hurling this stone at him.[28]

The worship of rude stones has been practiced all over the world, nowhere perhaps more systematically than in Melanesia. Thus, for example, in the Banks Islands and the Northern New Hebrides the spirits to whom food is offered are almost always connected with stones on which the offerings are made. Certain of these stones have been sacred to some spirit from ancient times, and the knowledge of the proper way of propitiating the spirit has been handed down, generation after generation, to the particular man who is now the fortunate possessor of it. "But any man may find a stone for himself, the shape of which strikes his fancy, or some other object, an octopus in his hole, a shark, a snake, an eel, which seems to him something unusual, and there-fore connected with a spirit. He gets money and scatters it about the stone, or on the place where he has seen the object of his fancy; then he goes home to sleep. He dreams that some one takes him to a place and shews him the pigs or money he is to have because of his connexion with the thing that he has found. This thing in the Banks Islands becomes his *tano-oloolo,* the place of his offering, the object in regard to which offering is made to get pigs or money. His neighbours begin to know that he has it, and that his increasing wealth has its origin there; they come to him, therefore, and obtain through him the good offices of the spirit he has come to know. He hands down the knowledge of this to his son or nephew. If a man is sick he gives another who is known to have a stone of power—the spirit connected with which it is suggested that he has offended—a short string of money, and a bit of the pepper root, *gea,* that is used for kava; the sick man is said to *oloolo* to the possessor of the stone. The latter takes the things offered to his sacred place and throws them down, saying, 'Let So-and-So recover.' When the sick man recovers he pays a fee. If a man desires to get the benefit of the stone, or whatever it is, known to another, with a view to increase of money, pigs, or food, or success in fighting, the possessor of the stone will take him to his sacred place, where probably there are many stones, each good for its own purpose. The applicant will supply money, perhaps a hundred strings a few inches long. The introducer will shew him one stone and say, 'This is a big yam,' and the worshipper puts money down. Of another he says it is a boar, of another that it is a pig with tusks, and money is put down. The notion is that the spirit, *vui,* attached to the stone likes the money, which is allowed to remain upon or by the stone. In case the *oloolo,* the sacrifice, succeeds, the man benefited pays the man to whom the stones and spirits belong."[29]

From this instructive account we learn that in these islands a regular sanctuary may originate in the fancy of a man who, having noticed a peculiar-looking stone and dreamed about it, concludes that the stone must contain a powerful spirit, who can help him, and whom he and his descendants henceforth propitiate with offerings. Further, we see how such a sanctuary, as it rises in reputation, may attract more and more worshippers, and so grow wealthy through the offerings which the gratitude or the cupidity of the devotees may lead them to deposit at the shrine. Have we not here a Melanesian counterpart of the history of Bethel?

Again, speaking of the natives of Aneityum, one of the Southern New Hebrides, Dr. George Turner tells us that "smooth stones apparently picked up out of the bed of the river were regarded as representatives of certain gods, and wherever the stone was, there the god was supposed to be. One resembling a fish would be prayed to as the fisherman's god. Another, resembling a yam, would be the yam god.[30] A third, round like a bread-fruit, the bread-fruit god, and so on.

Again, describing the religion of Futuna, an island of the New Hebrides, another missionary writes, "Some gods worshipped by the natives inhabited trees and stones, and thus their religion descended to fetishism. Further, they possessed sacred or magical stones, to make the fruits of the earth grow. The stones resembled in form the yams, or fruits, over which their magic influence was used. The stones for causing bread-fruit to grow were almost exactly like the fruit; but in others the resemblance between the stones and the objects represented was fanciful. These stones were very numerous, and common people as well as chiefs possessed them. Some were used for catching fish; others were love-charms to help the possessor in obtaining a wife or husband; others were used in war to give a steady aim in throwing the spear, or in warding off blows of enemies. The sorcerers used them in making disease, and the sacred men in causing drought, hurricanes, rain, etc."[31]

The natives of the Torres Straits Islands used to worship round painted stones, which they believed could help them in fishing or procure them a fair wind, and so forth.[32] For example, some of these stones were supposed to give success in turtle-fishing; accordingly their assistance was invoked and offerings made to them.

In one of the Samoan Islands the god Turia had his shrine in a very smooth stone, which was kept in a sacred grove. The priest was careful to weed all round about, and covered the stone with branches to keep the god warm. When prayers were offered on account of war, drought, famine, or epidemic, the branches were carefully renewed. Nobody dared to touch the stone, lest a poisonous and deadly influence should radiate from it on the transgressor.[33] In another Samoan village two oblong smooth stones, standing on a platform, were believed to be the parents of Saato, a god who controlled the rain. When the chiefs and people were ready to go off for weeks to the bush for the sport of pigeon-catching, they laid offerings of cooked taro and fish on the stones, accompanying them with prayers for fine weather and no rain. Any one who refused an offering to the stones was frowned upon; and if rain fell, he was blamed and punished for bringing down the wrath of the fine-weather god and spoiling the sport of the season. Moreover, in time of scarcity, when people were on their way to search for wild yams, they would give a yam to the two stones as a thank-offering, supposing that these gods caused the yams to grow, and that they could lead them to the best places for finding such edible roots. Any person casually passing by with a basket of food would also stop and lay a morsel on the stones. When such offerings were eaten in the night by dogs or rats, the people thought that the god became temporarily incarnate in these animals in order to consume the victuals.[34]

In Bowditch Island, South Pacific, the great native god was called Tui Tokelau, or king of Tokelau. He was thought to be embodied in a stone, which was kept carefully wrapt up in fine mats, and never seen by any one but the king, and that only once a year, when the decayed mats were stripped off and thrown away. In time of sickness fine mats were brought as offerings and rolled round the sacred stone, which thus became busked up to a prodigious size; but as the idol stood exposed to the weather under the open sky, the mats soon rotted. No one dared to appropriate what had been offered to the god; so the old mats, as they were taken off, were heaped in a place by themselves and left to decay. Once a year, about the month of May, a great festival was

held there in honour of the god. It lasted a whole month. All work was laid
aside. The people assembled from the islands of the group and feasted and
danced, praying for life, health, and a plentiful supply of coco-nuts.[35] In
Nikunau, an island of the Gilbert Group in the South Pacific, the gods and
goddesses were represented by sandstone slabs or pillars. If the stone slab
represented a goddess it was not set up erect, but laid down on the ground, the
natives thinking that it would be cruel to make the divine lady stand so long.[36]
The worship of stones appears to be common among the Naga tribes of Assam.
For instance, on a ridge near the Sema village of Champini, there may be
seen a large solitary stone, about nine feet long by two feet wide; one end of
the stone is split off and lies close by. The place is surrounded by a circle of
trees. The stone is the god Puzzi, but he is dead, because Tukko, the god of
the Angamis, a neighbouring hill tribe, came and fought him, knocked him
down, and cut his head off.[37]

There is hardly a village in Northern India which has not its sacred stone.
Very often the stone is not appropriated to any one deity in particular, but
represents the aggregate of the local divinities who have the affairs of the community under their charge.[38] In Chhattisgar, for example, a division of the
Central Provinces, the village god, Thakur Deo, is represented by a collection
of oddly shaped stones, which usually lie on a platform under a shady tree. In
the Drug subdivision the sacred stones are shaped like two-legged stools.
Every village worships Thakur Deo twice a year, in the months of Paus and
Chaitra, and on these occasions they sacrifice goats and fowls to him and
have a feast.[39] Among the tribes of the Hindu Kush, "in every village in which
Shins are in the majority, there is a large stone which is still more or less the
object of reverence. Each village has its own name for this stone, but an oath
taken or an engagement made over it, is often held more binding than where
the Koran is used. In several villages goats are still annually sacrificed beside
the stone, which is sprinkled with blood, and in other places the practice has
only lately been discontinued."[40]

The Miao-kia of Southern China revere certain natural stones of more
or less geometrical shape. These they enclose in little wooden shrines roofed
with tiles or thatch, and from time to time they offer sacrifices before them.
Like the Chinese, they also burn sticks of incense before oddly shaped rocks
or boulders.[41] The Ingouch tribe of the Caucasus regard certain rocks as
sacred and offer costly sacrifices to them, especially at funerals.[42] The king
of Karagwe, in Central Africa, to the west of Lake Victoria Nyanza, used to
set beer and grain before a large stone on the hillside, hoping to be favoured
with better crops for doing so, although in conversation with Speke he admitted that the stone could not eat the food or indeed make any use of it.[43]
In Busoga, a district of Central Africa, to the north of Lake Victoria Nyanza,
"each piece of rock and large stone is said to have its spirit, which is always
active in a district either for good or for evil."[44] The Menkieras of the French

Sudan, to the south of the Niger, offer sacrifices to rocks and stones. For example, at Sapo the village chief owns a great stone at the door of his house. Any man who cannot procure a wife, or whose wife is childless, will offer a fowl to the stone, hoping that the stone will provide him with a wife or child. If his wishes are granted, the man will present another fowl to the stone as a thank-offering.[45]

The Huron Indians of Canada worshipped certain rocks, to which they offered tobacco. Of these the most celebrated was one called Tsanhohi Arasta, that is, the abode of Tsanhohi, which was a kind of bird of prey. It seems to have stood on the bank of a river, perhaps the St. Lawrence, down which the Indians paddled on their way to Quebec. There, it was said, on the summit of a great crag there dwelt a demon, who could make their voyage prosperous. So in passing they used to stop paddling and offer him tobacco, depositing it in one of the clefts of the rock, and praying, "O demon, who dost inhabit this place, here is some tobacco which I offer to you. Help us, save us from shipwreck, defend us from our enemies, cause us to do good business and to return safe and sound to our village."[46] The great oracle of the Mandan Indians was a thick porous stone some twenty feet in circumference, whose miraculous utterances were believed with implicit confidence by these simple savages.[47] The Minnetarees, another Indian tribe of the Missouri, revered the same or a similar oracular stone, and consulted it in like manner.[48]

In some mountain districts of Norway down to the end of the eighteenth century the peasants used to keep round stones, which they washed every Thursday evening, and, smearing them with butter or some other grease before the fire, laid them on fresh straw in the seat of honour. Moreover, at certain seasons of the year they steeped the stones in ale, believing that they would bring luck and comfort to the house.[49]

This Norwegian custom of smearing the stones with butter reminds us of the story that Jacob poured oil on the stone which he set up to commemorate his vision at Bethel. The legend is the best proof of the sanctity of the stone, and probably points to an ancient custom of anointing the sacred stone at the sanctuary. Certainly the practice of anointing holy stones has been wide-spread. At Delphi, near the grave of Neoptolemus, there was a small stone on which oil was poured every day; and at every festival unspun wool was spread on it.[50] Among the ancient Greeks, according to Theophrastus, it was characteristic of the superstitious man that when he saw smooth stones at crossroads he would pour oil on them from a flask, and then falling on his knees worship them before going his way.[51] Similarly Lucian mentions a Roman named Rutillianus, who, as often as he spied an anointed or crowned stone, went down on his knees before it, and after worshipping the dumb deity remained standing in prayer beside it for a long time.[52] Elsewhere, the same sceptical writer refers scornfully to the oiled and wreathed stones which were supposed to give oracles.[53] Speaking of the blind idolatry of his heathen days, the Christian writer Arnobius says, "If ever I perceived an anointed stone, greasy with oil, I used to adore it, as if there were some indwelling power in it, I flattered it, spoke to it, I demanded benefits from the senseless block."[54] At the present day the peasants of Kuklia in Cyprus still anoint, or anointed till lately, the great corner-stones of the ruined temple of the Paphian Aphrodite.[55] In doing so it may well be that they keep up a custom handed down from antiquity.

The Waralis, a tribe who inhabit the jungles of Northern Konkan, in the Bombay Presidency, worship Waghia, the lord of tigers, in the form of a shapeless stone smeared with red lead and clarified butter. They give him chickens and goats, break coco-nuts on his head, and pour oil on him. In return for these attentions he preserves them from tigers, gives them good crops, and keeps disease from them.[56] And generally in the Bombay Presidency, particularly in the Konkan districts, fetish stones are worshipped by the ignorant and superstitious for the purpose of averting evil or curing disease. In every village such stones are to be seen. The villagers call each of them by the name of some god or spirit, of whom they stand in great fear, believing that he has control over all demons or ghosts. When an epidemic prevails in a village people offer food, such as fowls, goats, and coco-nuts, to the fetish stones.[57] For example, at Poona there is such a sacred stone which is coloured red and oiled.[58] Among the Bedars or Baydarus of Southern India the spirits of men who die unmarried are supposed to become *Virika* or heroes, and to their memory small temples and images are erected, where offerings of cloth, rice, and the like are made to their ghosts. "If this be neglected, they appear in dreams, and threaten those who are neglectful of their duty. These temples consist of a heap or cairn of stones, in which the roof of a small cavity is supported by two or three flags; and the image is a rude shapeless stone, which is occasionally oiled, as in this country all other images are."[59] Among the Todas of the Neilgherry Hills, in Southern India, the sacred buffaloes migrate from place to place in the hills at certain seasons of the year. At the sacred dairies there are stones on which milk is poured and butter rubbed before the migration begins. For example, at Modr there are four such stones, and they are rounded and worn quite smooth, probably through the frequent repetition of the ceremony.[60]

In the Kei Islands, to the south-west of New Guinea, every householder keeps a black stone at the head of his sleeping-place; and when he goes out to war or on a voyage or on business, he anoints the stone with oil to secure success.[61] "Although the Malagasy have no temples they have sacred places, where certain sacrifices are offered, and which may be considered as a kind of altar. Of these, the headstones of their tombs, rude undressed slabs of blue granite or basalt, are the most prominent, being, as already mentioned, anointed with the blood and fat of the animals killed both at funerals and on other occasions, especially at the New Year's festival. In numerous places, other stones may be seen anointed in a similar way. Some of these are in the bed of streams, being thus honoured to propitiate the spirits supposed to dwell in the water or around it. Other stones are anointed by women who wish to obtain children."[62] Thus with regard to the Betsileo, a tribe in central Madagascar, we are told that "in many parts of the country are large stones, which strike the eye of every traveller, owing to the fact that they present the appearance of having been greased all over, or at any rate of having had fat or oil poured on the top. This has given rise to a belief among strangers that these stones were gods worshipped by the Betsileo. I think it can scarcely be said that they were reverenced or treated as divinities, but that they were connected with superstitious beliefs there can be no shadow of a doubt. There are two kinds of single stones in the country looked upon thus superstitiously by the people. One kind, called *vàtobétròka,* is resorted to by women who have had no children. They carry with them a little fat or oil with which they anoint the stone, at the same time apostrophising it, they promise that if they have a child, they will return and re-anoint it with more oil. These same stones are also resorted to by traders, who promise that if their wares are sold at a good price and quickly, they will return to the stone and either anoint it with oil, or bury a piece of silver at its base. These stones are sometimes natural but curious formations, and sometimes, but more rarely, very ancient memorials of the dead."[63] At Ambatondrazaka, in Madagascar, there is one of these venerable stones, which gives its name to the town; for Ambatond-razaka means "The Town of the Stone of Razaka." This Razaka is said to have been a man or a woman who died long ago. The stone is partly buried in the earth, but so much of it as is visible is of oblong shape, standing about a foot above the ground, and enclosed within a rough circle of masonry. It is customary to anoint the stone with grease and oil, and to sprinkle it with the blood of sacrificial victims.[64] At a certain spot in a mountain pass, which is particularly difficult for cattle, every man of the Akamba tribe, in British East Africa, stops and anoints a particular rock with butter or fat.[65] ▼

▲ 65 Jacob at the Well

When, upon meeting her at the well, Jacob kissed his pretty cousin Rachel, he burst into tears. Biblical commentators are a little puzzled to explain why. They suppose that his tears flowed for joy at the happy termination of his journey, and they account for this mode of manifesting pleasure by the greater sensibility of Oriental peoples, or by the less degree of control which they exercise over the expression of their feelings. The explanation perhaps contains a measure of truth; but the commentators have apparently failed to notice that among not a few races weeping is a conventional mode of greeting strangers or friends, especially after a long absence, and that as such it is often a simple formality attended with hardly more emotion than our custom of shaking hands or raising the hat.

One of the peoples among whom this etiquette was rigorously required of all who had any claim to good breeding, were the Maoris of New Zealand. "The affectionate disposition of the people," we are told, "appears [especially] in the departure and return of friends. Should a friend be going a short voyage to Port Jackson, or Van Dieman's Land, a great display of outward feeling is made: it commences with a kind of ogling glance, then a whimper, and an affectionate exclamation; then a tear begins to glisten in the eye; a wry face is drawn; then they will shuffle nearer to the individual, and at length cling round his neck. They then begin to cry outright, and to use the flint about the face and arms; and, at last, to roar most outrageously, and almost to smother with kisses, tears, and blood, the poor fellow who is anxious to escape all this. On the return of friends, or when visited by them from a distance, the same scene, only more universally, is gone through; and it is difficult to keep your own tears from falling at the melancholy sight they present, and the miserable howlings and discordant noises which they make. There is much of the cant of affection in all this; for they can keep within a short distance of the person over whom they know they must weep, till they have prepared themselves by thinking, and have worked themselves up to the proper pitch; when, with a rush of pretended eagerness, they grasp their victim (for that is the best term to use), and commence at once to operate upon their own bodies, and upon his patience. There is one thing worthy of observation, that, as they can command tears to appear, upon all occasions, at a moment's warning, so they can cease crying when told to do so, or when it becomes inconvenient to continue it longer. I was once much amused at a scene of this kind, which happened at a village called Kaikohi, about ten miles from the Waimate. Half-a-dozen of their friends and relations had returned, after an absence of six months, from a visit to the Thames. They were all busily engaged in the usual routine of crying; when two of the women of the village, suddenly, at a signal one from the other, dried up their tears, closed the sluices of their affection, and very innocently said to the assembly: 'We have not finished crying yet: we will go and put the food in the oven, cook it, and make the baskets for it, and then we will come and finish crying; perhaps we shall not have done when the food is ready; and if not, we can cry again at night.' All this, in a canting, whining tone of voice, was concluded with a 'Shan't it be so? he! shan't it be so? he!' I spoke to them about their hypocrisy, when they knew they did not care, so much as the value of a potato, whether they should ever see those persons again, over whom they had been crying. The answer I received was, 'Ha! a New Zealander's love is all outside: it is in his eyes, and his mouth.' "[1] Again, we read that "emotion characterised the meeting of New Zealanders, but parting was generally un-attended by any outward display. At meeting men and women pressed their noses together, during which, in a low lachrymose whine, they repeated amidst showers of tears circumstances which had occurred mutually interesting since they last met. Silent grief is unknown among them. When the parties meeting are near relatives and have been long absent, the pressing of noses and crying were continued for half an hour; when the meeting was between accidental acquaintances, it was merely nose to nose and away. This salutation is called *hongi*, and is defined as a smelling. Like the Eastern custom of eating salt, it destroyed hostility between enemies. During the *hongi* the lips never met, there was no kissing."[2]

Similarly, among the aborigines of the Andaman Islands "relatives, after an absence of a few weeks or months, testify their joy at meeting by sitting with their arms round each other's necks, and weeping and howling in a manner which would lead a stranger to suppose that some great sorrow had befallen them; and, in point of fact, there is no difference observable between their demonstrations of joy and those of grief at the death of one of their number. The crying chorus is started by women, but the men speedily chime in, and groups of three or four may thus be seen weeping in concert until, from sheer exhaustion, they are compelled to desist."[3] Among the people of Mungeli Tahsil, in the Bilaspur district of India, "it is an invariable practice when relatives come together who have not met for a long while, for the womenfolk to weep and wail loudly. A son has been away for months and returns to his parents' house. He will first go and touch the feet of his father and mother. When he has been seated, the mother and sisters come to him and each in turn, placing both hands on his shoulders, weeps loudly and in a wailing tone narrates anything special that has taken place in his absence."[4] Among the Chauhans of the Central Provinces in India etiquette requires that women should weep whenever they meet relatives from a distance. "In such cases when two women see each other they cry together, each placing her head on the other's shoulder and her hands at her sides. While they cry they change the position of their heads two or three times, and each addresses the other according to their relationship, as mother, sister, and so on. Or if any member of the family has recently died, they call upon him or her, exclaiming 'O my mother! O my sister! O my father! Why did not I, unfortunate one, die instead of thee?' A woman when weeping with a man holds to his sides and rests her head against his breast. The man exclaims at intervals, 'Stop crying, do not cry.' When two women are weeping together it is a point of etiquette that the elder should stop first and then beg her companion to do so, but if it is doubtful which is the elder, they sometimes go on crying for an hour at a time, exciting the younger spectators to mirth, until at length some elder steps forward and tells one of them to stop."[5]

The custom of shedding floods of tears as a sign of welcome seems to have been common among the Indian tribes of both South and North America.[6] So too among the Tupis of Brazil, who inhabited the country in the neighborhood of Rio de Janerio, etiquette required that when a stranger entered the hut where he expected to receive hospitality, he should seat himself in the hammock of his host and remain there for some time in pensive silence. Then the women of the house would approach, and sitting down on the ground about the hammock, they would cover their faces with their hands, burst into tears, and bid the stranger welcome, weeping and paying him compliments in the same breath. While these demonstrations were proceeding, the stranger on his part was expected to weep in sympathy, or if he could not command real tears, the least he could do was to heave deep sighs and to look as lugubrious as possible. When these formalities, exacted by the Tupi code of good manners, had been duly complied with, the host, who had hitherto remained an apparently indifferent and unconcerned spectator, would approach his guest and enter into conversation with him.[7] The Lenguas, an Indian tribe of the Chaco, "employ among themselves a singular form of politeness when they see again any one after some time of absence. It consists in this: the two Indians shed some tears before they utter a word to each other; to act otherwise would be an insult, or at least a proof that the visit was not welcome."[8]

In the sixteenth century the Spanish explorer, Cabeça de Vaca, describes a similar custom observed by two tribes of Indians who inhabited an island off what seems to be now the coast of Texas. "On the island," he says, "there dwell two peoples speaking different languages, of whom the one are called and Capoques and the other Han. They have a custom that when they know each other and see each other from time to time, they weep for half an hour before they speak to one another. Then the one who receives the visit rises first and gives all he possesses to the other, who accepts it and soon afterwards goes away; sometimes even, after the gift has been accepted, they go away without speaking a word.[9]

Nicolas Perrot, who lived among the Indians for many years in the latter part of the seventeenth century, describes how a party of Sioux, visiting a village of their friends the Ottawas, "had no sooner arrived than they began, in accordance with custom, to weep over all whom they met, in order to signify to them the sensible joy they felt at having found them."[10] Indeed, the Frenchman himself was more than once made the object, or rather the victim, of the like doleful demonstrations. Being sent by the governor of New France to treat with the Indian tribes beyond the Mississippi, he took up his quarters on the banks of that river, and there received an embassy from the Ayeos, the neighbors and allies of the Sioux, whose village lay some days to the westward, and who wished to enter into friendly relations with the French. A French historian has described the meeting of these Indian ambassadors with poor Perrot. They wept over him till the tears ran down their bodies; they beslobbered him with the filth which exuded from their mouths and their noses, smearing it on his head, his face, and his clothes, till he was almost turned sick by their caresses, while all the time they shrieked and howled most lamentably. At last the present of a few knives and awls had the effect of checking these noisy effusions; but having no interpreter with them, they were quite unable to make themselves intelligible, and so had to return the way they came without effecting their purpose. A few days later four other Indians arrived, one of whom spoke a language understood by the French. He explained that their village was nine leagues up the river, and he invited the French to visit it. The invitation was accepted. At the approach of the strangers the women fled to the woods and the mountains, weeping and stretching out their arms to the sun. However, twenty of the chief men appeared, offered Perrot the pipe of peace, and carried him on a buffalo's skin into the chief's hut. Having deposited him there, they and the chief proceeded to weep over him in the usual way, bedewing his head with the moisture which dripped from their eyes, their mouths, and their noses. When that indispensable ceremony was over, they dried their eyes and their noses, and offered him the pipe of peace once more. "Never in the world," adds the French historian, "were seen such people for weeping; their meetings are accompanied by tears, and their partings are equally tearful."[11]

Disgusting as such forms of salutation may seem to us, it is not impossible that the application of all these exudations to the person of the stranger was not a mere accident, the effect of uncontrollable emotion, but that it may have been seriously intended to form a corporeal as well as a spiritual union with him by joining parts of their body to his. At least this is suggested by similar ceremonies elsewhere, in which effusions of spittle are apparently employed to this end. Thus, among the Chubras, the scavengers of the Punjab, when a new candidate is admitted to their lowly order, the following procedure is observed. "Over a rectangular pit is put a *chárpái,* and beneath it the candidate is seated in the pit, while the Chuhrás sit on the *chárpái.* Each bathes in turn, clearing his nose and spitting, so that all the water, etc., falls on to the man in the pit. He is then allowed to come out and seated on the *chárpái.* After this all the Chuhrás wash his body and eat with him, and then ask him to adopt their profession." In explanation of this ceremony we are told that "Chuhrás think that the dirt of their own bodies purifies others, and they so remove it with their own hands. If a man follows their occupation but does not undergo the ordeal described above, they do not treat him as a Chuhrá or effect any relationship with him."[12] On this explanation it may be observed that, while ideas of purification no doubt differ widely in different peoples, it is difficult to believe that a very high degree of ceremonial cleanliness can be regarded as indispensable to any man who would engage in the business of scavenging and sweeping the streets. It seems more probable that the process of bedewing the candidate with the dirty water, spittle, and nasal excretion of other scavengers is intended not so much to purge him from all uncleanness as, on the contrary, to dirty him with the dirt of his future colleagues, and, by sinking him to their level, to make him one with them.

Certainly spittle has been employed as a bond of union by other peoples besides these Indian scavengers. For example, among the Baluba, a tribe of the Belgian Congo, a ceremony performed at initiating a candidate into the secret order of sorcerers is as follows. A new pot is produced, containing beer, flour, and two kinds of bark. Each sorcerer then spits into the pot, and the candidate must swallow the contents of the pot without wincing or pulling a wry face. When he has gulped it down, the grand master addresses him, saying, "You have drunk something of ourselves. Know that henceforth you will be powerless to injure us by your charms, since after our death we should be able to take vengeance and to come and seize you." So saying he breaks the pot.[13] Here the notion is that spittle, being part of a man, confers on the spitter a magical power over him who has swallowed it. Hence it is natural that as a part of the person, spittle should be used like blood to form the cement of a binding covenant. It is so used, for example, by the Wachaga of East Africa. When two persons of that tribe wish to make a solemn agreement which will be obligatory on both parties, they sit down on a hide with a vessel of milk or beer between them. Each of them then utters the oath, waving a stick in a circle over the liquid. Having done so, each of them takes a mouthful of the milk or beer and spits it into the mouth of the other, or they both spit the mouthful back into the vessel, and then drink the contents of the vessel together. They believe that should either of them forswear himself, the liquid which he has swallowed will kill him. If the matter is pressing and there is no time for these formalities, the two covenanters will simply spit into each other's mouths, and this answers the purpose of giving a guarantee of good faith equally well. In whichever form the covenant is concluded, the spittle which passes from the body of the one convenanter into the body of the other is conceived as the magical substance which ensures the fulfillment of the agreement.[14] The Nandi of British East Africa similarly make use of spittle in ratifying agreements and imparting blessings. Thus in concluding a covenant of peace or arranging a marriage, both parties spit to make sure that the pact will be kept; and when a man has sold cattle, grain, or household utensils, he spits to show that the sale is complete. Again, old people and warriors often spit on children when they greet them; and a dying father, uncle, or elder will spit in a boy's hand when the lad comes to bid him farewell, and the grateful youth will rub the dying man's spittle on his face.[15] Similarly, among the Masai of British East Africa, when small children salute very old men, the greybeards spit on them, saying, "May God give you long life and grey hairs like mine."[16] Among the Suk, another tribe of British East Africa, before a man shakes hands with you he spits on his hands.[17] "Not only amongst the Masai, but in the allied Nandi and Suk peoples, to spit at a person is a very great compliment. The earlier travellers in Masailand were astonished, when making friendship with old Masai chiefs and head-men, to be constantly spat at. When I entered the Uganda Protectorate and met the Masai of the Rift Valley for the first time, every man, before extending his hand to me, would spit on the palm."[18] At Orango, in the Bissagos

Archipelago, when two men wish to make friends, they spit into each other's hands,[19] probably as a guarantee of mutual confidence and good faith, since in so doing each of them, on the principles of sympathetic magic, places himself at the mercy of the other by entrusting him with a vital portion of himself. ▼

66   Jacob's marriage   29:15–27

In the present version of the tale the substitution of Leah for Rachel is explained on the basis that traditional custom forbade a younger daughter to be married before her elder sister, and this usage certainly obtains in many parts of the world.[1] It is attested, for instance, in ancient Iceland[2] and it is observed to this day in Indonesia[3] and among the Zulus of Africa.[4] Not impossibly, however, the Biblical writer has simply rationalized in terms of contemporary custom an older folktale revolving around the practice known to folklorists as the False Bride.

"It is," says Westermarck in his classic *History of Human Marriage,*[5] "a common custom among Slavonic, Teutonic and Romance peoples, as also among the Esthonians, that when the bridegroom or his representative comes to fetch the bride from her home, a false bride is substituted for the real one, another woman, frequently an ugly old one, or a little girl, or even a man being palmed off on him as his bride. In Brittany, the substitutes are first a little girl, then the mistress of the house, and lastly the grandmother. In the Samerberg district of Bavaria a bearded man in woman's clothes personates the bride, in Esthonia, the bride's brother or some other young man. Sometimes the substitution takes place already at the betrothal, and sometimes only at the wedding feast. The custom is not restricted to Europe. Among the Beni-Amer in Northeast Africa, when women with a camel are sent to fetch the bride, her people often substitute a false bride for the true one, and it is only when the procession is well outside the village that the substitute reveals herself and runs back laughing."[6]

Underlying this custom is the belief that the false bride will protect the true one against demons and against the evil eye and, as they say in Western Bohemia, "carry the bad luck from the true bride out of the house."[7] This explanation is supported by a Javanese custom of placing two wooden effigies, one of a man and the other of a woman, at the foot of the bridal bed. Called Lorobonyhoyo, or youth and maiden, they are designed to foil the demons who hover around to pounce on the newlyweds.[8]

It has been suggested that this custom likewise underlies the story told by Ovid of how Mars tried to bring Minerva to his bed by soliciting the intervention of the old crone Anna Perenna only to discover, when he lifted the bridal veil at the wedding, that the old crone had outwitted him by substituting herself![9] It should be added that stories of the False Bride are by no means infrequent in world folklore,[10] and that the reverse obtains in the widespread custom (*jus primae noctis*) of resorting to a substitute bridegroom on the wedding night, in order to divert demonic mischief.[11]

67   Reuben and the mandrakes   30:14–18

Because of the resemblance of its root to the human form, the mandrake is almost universally credited with magical powers.[1] Dioscorides, the Greek physician, calls it "Circe's plant" (*kirkeion*),[2] and among modern Arabs it is known as the "apple of the jinns" and is used in concocting philtres.[3] Theophrastus says that it is an antidote against spells and enchantments,[4] and Josephus records the popular belief that it expels demons.[5] Indeed, it has been suggested that the drug named *moly* which Hermes supplied to Odysseus in order to counteract the magic potions brewed by Circe[6] was really the mandrake.[7]

The plant is used especially, as in our Biblical narrative, as an aphrodisiac and as an antidote to barrenness. It is thus mentioned, for example, by the Greek comic dramatist Alexis (4th cent. B.C.),[8] and Aphrodite, the goddess of love, was sometimes styled, "Our Lady of the Mandrake."[9] The Hebrew word rendered "mandrake" is indeed connected with a verbal root meaning "to love"[10] and has its English counterpart in the popular term, "love-apple." In the Song of Songs (7:14), when the maiden invites her lover to enjoy her favors, she adds to her inducements the statement that she has stored up for him fragrant mandrakes. In Jewish folklore, the mandrake was long believed to relieve barrenness;[11] while in Germany and some other parts of Europe it was customary to place mandrakes under a bridal bed.[12] Nor, indeed, was it only upon human beings that this plant was believed to work: a medieval bestiary records the superstition that the male elephant stimulates desire in its mate by eating mandrakes and also feeding them to her.[13]

68   The theft of the teraphîm   31:34

There has been a good deal of speculation—often fantastic—concerning the precise character of the *teraphîm,* conventionally rendered "household gods."[1] However, the point of the narrative has at last been clarified by a cuneiform document from the Mesopotamian city of Nuzu. This document, dated to around 1400 B.C., comes from the very clime and environment in which the Biblical story plays and indicates that, according to local usage, a man who laid claim to the prime portion of an estate had to be in possession of the household gods or actually hold them in his hands.[2] Rachel's purpose was, therefore, to secure this right for Jacob.

The lesson of the story is profound: only he who cherishes and retains the family traditions can rank as the true heir of its property and destiny. The point is brought out significantly, in another context, in the words which Hector addresses to his brother Aeneas, when the latter flees from burning Troy:

To thee doth Troy commend her household gods;
Now take them as companions of thy fate.[3]

69 Stealing the heart 31:20, 26

When Jacob outwits Laban by stealing the household gods (teraphîm), *he is said in the original Hebrew to have* stolen *the latter's*
heart.

The expression preserves an interesting piece of folklore. In ancient times
the heart was considered, as it still is among primitive peoples, the seat not
only of the emotions but also of the mental processes.[1] Alike among the
Hebrews and the Babylonians, for example, a common expression for "to
think" was "to say in the heart."[2] The heart was thus symbolic of the total
self, and in moments, such as sleep or trance, when a man had temporarily
lost consciousness, the heart was believed temporarily to have departed from
him.[3] It could even be enticed out of him by magic or by the action of
demons.[4] To *steal the heart* meant, therefore, more than to bemuse the
emotions; it meant to gain complete control over a person's self-direction. In
the Egyptian Pyramid Texts mention is made of a class of demons called
"stealers of the heart" who were thought to divest the dead of consciousness.[5]

Conversely, the Hebrew expression, *to guard* (RSV: *keep*) *the heart,* used in
Proverbs 4:23, meant to preserve the total self from bewitchment.[6]

▲ 70 The covenant at the cairn 31:46–49

*Jacob and Laban conclude a convenant by erecting a cairn and
swearing an oath of mutual fidelity upon it. Subsequently they share
a meal, sitting on the stones.*[1]

The eating of food upon the stones was probably intended to ratify the
covenant. How it was supposed to do so may perhaps be gathered from a
Norse custom described by the old Danish historian, Saxo Grammaticus. He
tells us that "the ancients, when they were to choose a king, were wont to
stand on stones planted in the ground, and to proclaim their votes, in order
to foreshadow from the steadfastness of the stones that the deed would be
lasting."[2] In fact, the stability of the stones may have been thought to pass
into the person who stood upon them and so to confirm his oath. Thus we
read of a certain mythical Rajah of Java, who bore the title of Rajah Sela
Perwata, "which in the common language is the same as Wátu Gúnung, a name
conferred upon him from his having rested on a mountain like a stone, and
obtained his strength and power thereby, without other aid or assistance."[3]
At a Brahman marriage in India the bridegroom leads the bride thrice round
the fire, and each time he does so he makes her tread with her right foot on a
millstone, saying, "Tread on this stone; like a stone be firm. Overcome the
enemies; tread the foes down."[4] This ancient rite, prescribed by the ritual

books of the Aryans in Northern India, has been adopted in Southern India outside the limits of the Brahman caste. The married couple "go round the sacred fire, and the bridegroom takes up in his hands the right foot of the bride, and places it on a millstone seven times. This is known as *saptapadi* (seven feet), and is the essential and binding portion of the marriage ceremony. The bride is exhorted to be as fixed in constancy as the stone on which her foot has been thus placed."[5] Similarly at initiation a Brahman boy is made to tread with his right foot on a stone, while the words are repeated, "Tread on this stone; like a stone be firm. Destroy those who seek to do thee harm; overcome thy enemies."[6] Among the Kookies of Northern Cachar at marriage "the young couple place a foot each upon a large stone in the centre of the village, and the Ghalim [headman] sprinkles them with water, and pronounces an exhortation to general virtue and conjugal fidelity, together with a blessing and the expression of hopes regarding numerous progeny."[7] In the Kallan caste of Madura, Trichinopoly, and Tanjore, patterns are drawn with rice-flour on a bride's back at marriage, her husband's sister decorates a grinding-stone in the same way, invokes blessings on the woman, and expresses the hope that she may have a male child as strong as a stone.[8] In Madagascar it is believed that you can guard against the instability of earthly bliss by burying a stone under the main post or under the threshold of your house.[9]

On the same principle we can explain the custom of swearing with one foot or with both feet planted on a stone. The idea seems to be that the solid enduring quality of the stone will somehow pass into the swearer and so ensure that the oath will be kept.[10] Thus there was a stone at Athens on which the nine archons stood when they swore to rule justly and according to the laws.[11] A little to the west of St. Columba's tomb in Iona "lie the black stones, which are so called, not from their colour, for that is grey, but from the effects that tradition says ensued upon perjury, if any one became guilty of it after swearing on these stones in the usual manner; for an oath made on them was decisive in all controversies. Mac-Donald, King of the Isles, delivered the rights of their lands to his vassals in the isles and continent, with uplifted hands and bended knees, on the black stones; and in this posture, before many witnesses, he solemnly swore that he would never recall those rights which he then granted: and this was instead of his great seal. Hence it is that when one was certain of what he affirmed, he said positively, I have freedom to swear this matter upon the black stones."[12] Again, in the island of Fladda, another of the Hebrides, there was formerly a round blue stone on which people swore decisive oaths.[13] At the old parish church of Lairg, in Sutherlandshire, there used to be built into an adjoining wall a stone called the Plighting Stone. "It was known far and wide as a medium—one might almost say, as a sacred medium—for the making of bargains, the pledging of faith, and the plighting of troth. By grasping hands through this stone, the parties to an agreement of any kind bound themselves with the inviolability of a solemn oath."[14]

Similar customs are observed by rude races in Africa and India. When two Bogos of Eastern Africa, on the border of Abyssinia, have a dispute, they will sometimes settle it at a certain stone, which one of them mounts. His adversary calls down the most dreadful curses on him if he forswears himself, and to every curse the man on the stone answers "Amen!"[15] Among the Akamba of British East Africa solemn oaths are made before an object called a *kithito,* which is believed to be endowed with a mysterious power of killing perjurers. In front of the object are placed seven stones, and the man who makes oath stands so that his heels rest on two of them.[16] At Naimu, a village of the Tangkhuls of Assam, there is a heap of peculiarly shaped stones upon which the people swear solemn oaths.[17] At Ghosegong, in the Garo hills of Assam, there is a stone on which the natives swear their most solemn oaths. In doing so they first salute it, then with their hands joined and uplifted, and their eyes steadfastly fixed on the hills, they call on Mahadeva to witness to the truth of what they affirm. After that they again touch the stone with all the appearance of the utmost fear, and bow their heads to it, calling again on Mahadeva. And while they are making their declaration they look steadfastly to the hills and keep their right hand on the stone.[18] The Garos also swear on meteoric stones, saying, "May Goera (the god of lightning) kill me with one of these if I have told a lie."[19] In this case, however, the use of the stone is retributive rather than confirmatory; it is designed, not so much to give to the oath the stability of the stone, as to call down the vengeance of the lightning-god on the perjurer. The same was perhaps the intention of a Samoan oath. When suspected thieves swore to their innocence in the presence of chiefs, they "laid a handful of grass on the stone, or whatever it was, which was supposed to be the representative of the village god, and, laying their hand on it, would say, "In the presence of our chiefs now assembled, I lay my hand on the stone. If I stole the thing may I speedily die."[20]

In this last case, and perhaps in some of the others, the stone appears to be conceived as instinct with a divine life which enables it to hear the oath, to judge of its truth, and to punish perjury. Oaths sworn upon stones thus definitely conceived as divine are clearly religious in character, since they involve an appeal to a supernatural power who visits transgressors with his anger. But in some of the preceding instances the stone is apparently supposed to act purely through the physical properties of weight, solidity, and inertia; accordingly in these cases the oath, or whatever the ceremony may be, is purely magical in character. The man absorbs the valuable properties of the stone just as he might absorb electrical force from a battery; he is, so to say, petrified by the stone in the one case just as he is electrified by the electricity in the other. The religious and the magical aspects of the oath on a stone need not be mutually exclusive in the minds of the swearers. Vagueness and confusion are characteristic of primitive thought, and must always be allowed for in our attempts to resolve that strange compound into its elements.

These two different strains of thought, the religious and the magical, seem both to enter into the Biblical account of the covenant made by Jacob and Laban on the cairn. For on the one hand the parties to the covenant apparently attribute life and consciousness to the stones by solemnly calling them to witness their agreement,[21] just as Joshua called on the great stone under the oak to be a witness, because the stone had heard all the words that the Lord spake unto Israel.[22] Thus conceived, the cairn, or the pillar which stood in the midst of it, was a sort of Janus-figure with heads facing both ways for the purpose of keeping a sharp eye on both the parties to the covenant. And on the other hand the act of eating food together on the cairn, if I am right, is best explained as an attempt to establish a sympathetic bond of union between the covenanters by partaking of a common meal, while at the same time they strengthened and tightened the bond by absorbing into their system the strength and solidity of the stones on which they were seated.

The custom of erecting cairns as witnesses is apparently not extinct in Syria even now. One of the most famous shrines of the country is that of Aaron on Mount Hor. The prophet's tomb on the mountain is visited by pilgrims, who pray the saint to intercede for the recovery of sick friends, and pile up heaps of stones as witnesses (*meshhad*) of the vows they make on behalf of the sufferers.[23] ▼

71   Jacob at Maḥanaim: The Furious Host   32:1–2

Jacob went on his way, and certain "messengers from the otherworld" (RSV: *"the angels of God"*)[1] *encountered him. When Jacob saw them, he said, "Why, this is the Otherworld Army* (RSV: *the army of God*)!" *So he called the place Maḥanaim* [*from the Hebrew word,* maḥaneh, *"army, camp"*].

What Jacob saw was simply a form of the familiar Phantom Host, which is commonly believed to ride across the heavens in stormy weather.[2] In European folklore, to be sure, it is more commonly portrayed as a Wild Hunt,[3] but frequently also as an army of old soldiers who "never die but simply fade away." In Spain, for instance, it was known anciently as the *exercito antiguo*[4] or *huesta antigua,*[5] the latter name having now been transmogrified into that of a single nocturnal spirit, Estantigua. Similarly, it was a popular belief in Brittany, Savoy, and Scotland that Arthur and his men rode abroad and could be seen on windswept nights;[6] indeed, as late as the nineteenth century they were said to be sighted regularly around Cadbury Castle, in Somerset. Pliny records an analogous superstition among the Cimbri concerning a phantom army,[7] and Dionysius of Halicarnassus speaks of the same fancy among the Romans.[8] When the rainy season begins in November, around the Feast of St. George, the Palestinian Arabs say, in like fashion, that the saint is driving his horses across the sky.[9]

History records several instances of this army's having been "seen" before

crucial battles. It is said, for example, to have appeared at the siege of Byzantium by Philip II,[10] and near Worms in 1098,[11] while older readers
will remember the "angels of Mons" in World War I. To the same general
sphere of ideas belongs also the popular belief recorded by Pausanias that the
neighing of ghostly horses and the clash and din of ghostly warriors could
still be heard nightly at Marathon.[12]

Belief in the Phantom Host appears also in other forms. Among the Greeks,
for example, it seems to have been identified alternatively with the train of
departed spirits which followed in the wake of Hecate,[13] or again, with a
celestial rout of bacchanals accompanying Artemis or Dionysus.[14] This last
is particularly interesting to us, since in the Song of Songs (6:13) the gyrations of the maiden in the dance are fancifully likened to "the dance of
Maḥanaim," which may perhaps reflect an alternative tradition in which the
otherworld beings popularly associated with the name of that place were
represented as a troupe of celestial dancers.[15]

72   Jacob at the ford of Jabbok   32:23–33

▲ (a) The mysterious adversary

After parting from Laban at the cairn, Jacob, with his wives and children, his flocks and his herds, pursued his way southward. From the breezy,
wooded heights of the mountains of Gilead he now plunged down into the
profound ravine of the Jabbok thousands of feet below. The descent occupies
several hours, and the traveller who accomplishes it feels that, on reaching the
bottom of the deep glen, he has passed into a different climate. From the
pine-woods and chilly winds of the high uplands he descends first in about an
hour's time to the balmy atmosphere of the village of Burmeh, embowered
in fruit-trees, shrubs, and flowers, where the clear, cold water of a fine fountain will slake his thirst at the noonday rest. Still continuing the descent, he
goes steeply down another two thousand feet to find himself breathing a hot-
house air amid luxuriant semi-tropical vegetation in the depths of the great
lyn of the Jabbok. The gorge is, in the highest degree, wild and picturesque.
On either hand the cliffs rise almost perpendicularly to a great height; you
look up the precipices or steep declivities to the skyline far above. At the bottom of this mighty chasm the Jabbok flows with a powerful current, its blue-
grey water fringed and hidden, even at a short distance, by a dense jungle of
tall oleanders, whose crimson blossoms add a glow of colour to the glen in
early summer. The Blue River, for such is its modern name, runs fast and
strong. Even in ordinary times the water reaches to the horses' girths, and
sometimes the stream is quite unfordable, the flood washing grass and bushes
high up the banks on either hand. On the opposite or southern side the ascent
from the ford is again exceedingly steep. The path winds up and up; the
traveller must dismount and lead his horse. It was up that long ascent that

Jacob, lingering alone by the ford in the gloaming, watched the camels labouring, and heard the cries of the drivers growing fainter and fainter above him, till sight and sound of them alike were lost in the darkness and the distance.

The scene may help us to understand the strange adventure which befell Jacob at the passage of the river. He had sent his wives, his handmaids, and his children, riding on camels, across the river, and all his flocks and herds had preceded or followed them. So he remained alone at the ford. It was night, probably a moonlight summer night; for it is unlikely that with such a long train he would have attempted to ford the river in the dark or in the winter when the current would run fast and deep. Be that as it may, in the moonlight or in the dark, beside the rushing river, a man wrestled with him all night long, till morning flushed the wooded crests of the ravine high above the struggling pair in the shadows below. The stranger looked up and saw the light and said, "Let me go, for the day breaketh." So Jupiter tore himself from the arms of the fond Alcmena before the peep of dawn;[1] so the ghost of Hamlet's father faded at cockcrow; so Mephistopheles in the prison warned Faust, with the hammering of the gallows in his ears, to hurry, for the day— Gretchen's last day—was breaking. But Jacob clung to the man and said, "I will not let thee go, except thou bless me." The stranger asked him his name, and when Jacob told it he said, "Thy name shall be called no more Jacob, but Israel: for thou hast striven with God and with men, and hast prevailed." But when Jacob inquired of him, "Tell me, I pray thee, thy name," the man refused to mention it, and having given the blessing which Jacob had extorted, he vanished. So Jacob called the name of the place Peniel, that is, the Face of God; "For," said he, "I have seen God face to face, and my life is preserved." Soon afterwards the sun rose and shone on Jacob, and as it did so he limped; for in the struggle his adversary had touched him on the hollow of the thigh. "Therefore the children of Israel eat not the sinew of the hip which is upon the hollow of the thigh, unto this day: because he touched the hollow of Jacob's thigh in the sinew of the hip."

The story is obscure, and it is probable that some of its original features have been slurred over by the compilers of Genesis because they savoured of heathendom. Hence any explanation of it must be to a great extent conjectural. But taking it in connexion with the natural features of the place where the scene of the story is laid, and with the other legends of a similar character which I shall adduce, we may perhaps, suppose that Jacob's mysterious adversary was the spirit of the river, and that the struggle was purposely sought by Jacob for the sake of obtaining his blessing. This would explain why he sent on his long train of women, servants, and animals, and waited alone in the darkness by the ford. He might calculate that the shy river-god, scared by the trampling and splashing of so great a caravan through the water, would lurk in a deep pool or a brake of oleanders at a safe distance, and that when all had passed and silence again reigned, except for the usual monotonous swish of the current, curiosity would lead him to venture out from his lair and inspect the ford, the scene of all this hubbub and disturbance. Then the subtle Jacob, lying in wait, would pounce out and grapple with him until he had obtained the coveted blessing. It was thus that Menelaus caught the shy sea-god Proteus sleeping at high noon among the seals on the yellow sands, and compelled him reluctantly to say his sooth.[2] It was thus that Peleus caught the sea-goddess Thetis and won her, a Grecian Undine, for his wife.[3] In both these Greek legends the supple, slippery water-spirit writhes in the grip of his or her captor, slipping through his hands again and again, and shifting his or her shape from lion to serpent, from serpent to water, and so forth, in the effort to escape; not till he is at the end of all his shifts and sees no hope of evading his determined adversary does he at last consent to grant the wished-for boon. So, too, when Hercules wrestled with the river-god Achelous for the possession of the fair Deianira, the water-sprite turned himself first into a serpent and then into a bull in order to give the brawny hero the slip; but all in vain.[4]

These parallels suggest that in the original form of the tale Jacob's adversary may in like manner have shifted his shape to evade his importunate suitor.

The view that Jacob's adversary at the ford of the Jabbok was the river-god himself may perhaps be confirmed by the observation that it has been a common practice with many peoples to propitiate the fickle and dangerous spirits of the water at fords. Hesiod says that when you are about to ford a river you should look at the running water and pray and wash your hands; for he who wades through a stream with unwashed hands incurs the wrath of the gods.[5] When the Spartan king Cleomenes, intending to invade Argolis, came with his army to the banks of the Erasinus, he sacrificed to the river, but the omens were unfavourable to his crossing. Thereupon the king remarked that he admired the patriotism of the river-god in not betraying his people, but that he would invade Argolis in spite of him. With that he led his men to the seashore, sacrificed a bull to the sea, and transported his army in ships to the enemy's country.[6] When the Persian host under Xerxes came to the river Strymon in Thrace, the Magians sacrificed white horses and performed other strange ceremonies before they crossed the stream.[7] Lucullus, at the head of a Roman army, sacrificed a bull to the Euphrates at his passage of the river.[8] "On the river-bank, the Peruvians would scoop up a handful of water and drink it, praying the river-deity to let them cross or to give them fish, and they threw maize into the stream as a propitiatory offering; even to this day the Indians of the Cordilleras perform the ceremonial sip before they will pass a river on foot or horseback."[9] Old Welsh people "always spat thrice on the ground before crossing water after dark, to avert the evil influences of spirits and witches."[10]

A Zulu story relates how a man named Ulangalasenzantsi went to fetch his children, taking ten oxen with him. His way was barred by ten swollen rivers, to each of which he sacrificed an ox, whereupon the river divided and allowed him to pass through. As to this we are told that "when a river has been safely crossed, it is the custom in some parts [of South Africa] to throw a stone into its waters, and to praise the *itongo*. . . . When Dingan's army was going against Umzilikazi, on reaching the banks of the Ubulinganto, they saluted it, and having strewed animal charcoal (*umsizi*) on the water, the soldiers were made to drink it. The object of this was to deprecate some evil power destructive to life, which was supposed to be possessed by the river. It is a custom which cannot fail to recall what is recorded of Moses under somewhat different circumstances.[11] There can be little doubt that Ulangalasenzantsi threw the oxen into the rivers as a sacrifice to the *amatongo* (ancestral spirits), or more probably to river-gods."[12] From another writer we learn that Kafirs spit on the stones which they throw into the water at crossing a river. He tells us that "the natives in olden days were in the habit of either sacrificing some animal or offering some grain to appease ancestral spirits living in the river. The bushmen used to offer up some game they had killed, or in the absence of that would offer up an arrow. It is very doubtful whether the natives have any fully formed conception of what we call a river-spirit; it seems more probable, on the whole, that they imagined some ancestral spirit to be living in the river, or that some fabulous animal had its home in the water.[13]

When the Masai of East Africa cross a stream they throw a handful of grass into the water as an offering; for grass, the source of life to their cattle, plays an important part in Masai superstition and ritual.[14] Among the Baganda of Central Africa, before a traveller forded any river, he would ask the spirit of the river to give him a safe crossing, and would throw a few coffee-berries as an offering into the water.[15] At certain spots on the rivers Nakiza and Sezibwa, in Uganda, there was a heap of grass and sticks on either bank, and every person who crossed the river threw a little grass or some sticks on the one heap before crossing, and on the other heap after crossing; this was his offering to the spirit of the river for a safe passage through the water. From time to time more costly offerings were made at these heaps; the worshipper would bring beer, or an animal, or a fowl, or some bark-cloth, tie the offering to the heap, and leave it there, after praying to the spirit. The worship of each of these rivers was cared for by a priest, but there was no temple.[16]

When Speake and his companions were ferried over the Nile near the Karuna Falls, a party of Banyoro, travelling with them, sacrificed two kids, one on either side of the river, flaying them with one long cut each down their breasts and bellies. The slaughtered animals were then laid, spread-eagle fashion, on their backs upon grass and twigs, and the travellers stepped over them, that their journey might be prosperous. The place of sacrifice was chosen under the directions of the wizard of the falls.[17]

The Ituri river, one of the upper tributaries of the Congo, forms the dividing-line between the grass land and the great forest. "When my canoe had almost crossed the clear, rapid waters, a hundred and fifty yards wide," reports a modern traveller, "I noticed on the opposite bank two miniature houses built close to the edge and resembling in every feature the huts of the villagers. The old chief was loth to explain the object of these houses, but at length I was told that they were erected for the shade of his predecessor, who was told that he must recompense them for their labours by guarding the passage of those crossing the river. From that time, whenever a caravan was seen to approach the bank, a little food would be carried down to the ghost-houses, as a warning that the shade's protection was needed for the caravan about to cross."[18] Among the Ibos of the Awka district, in Southern Nigeria, when a corpse is being carried to the grave and the bearers have to cross water, a she-goat and a hen are sacrificed to the river.[19]

The Badagas, a tribe of the Neilgherry Hills in Southern India, believe in a deity named Gangamma, "who is supposed to be present at every stream, and especially so at the Koondé and Pykaré rivers, into which it was formerly the practice for every owner of cattle, which had to cross them at their height, to throw a quarter of a rupee, because their cattle used frequently to be carried away by the current and destroyed. It is enumerated amongst the great sins of every deceased Badaga, at his funeral, that he had crossed a stream without paying due adoration to Gangamma."

Among the Mahafaly and Sakalava of southern Madagascar certain chiefs are forbidden to cross certain rivers, while others are bound to go and salute all the rivers of the country.[21] In Cayor, a district of Senegal, it is believed that the king would inevitably die within the year if he were to cross a river or an arm of the sea.[22] A certain famous chief of the Angoni, in British Central Africa, was cremated near a river; and even now, when the Angoni cross the stream, they greet it with the deep-throated manly salutation which they accord only to royalty.[23] And when the Angoni ferry over any river in a canoe they make a general confession of any sins of infidelity of which they may have been guilty towards their consorts, apparently from a notion that otherwise they might be drowned in the river.[24] The Toradjas of Central Celebes believe that water-spirits, in the shape of snakes, inhabit the deep pools and rapids of rivers. Men have to be on their guard against these dangerous beings. Hence when a Toradja is about to make a voyage down a river, he will often call out from the bank, "I am not going to-day, I will go to-morrow." The spirits hear the announcement, and if there should be amongst them one who is lying in wait for the voyager, he will imagine that the voyage has been postponed and will defer his attack accordingly till the following day. Meantime the cunning Toradja will drop quietly down the river, laughing in his sleeve at the simplicity of the water-sprite whom he has bilked.[25]

Nor are the spirits of rivers the only water-divinities which bold men have dared to fight or punish. When a storm swept away the first bridge by which Xerxes spanned the Hellespont for the passage of his army, the king in a rage sentenced the straits to receive three hundred lashes and to be fettered with chains. And as the executioners plied their whips on the surface of the water, they said, "O bitter water, thy master inflicts this punishment on thee because thou hast wronged him who did no wrong to thee. But King Xerxes will cross thee, willy nilly. And it serves thee right that no man sacrifices to thee, because thou art a treacherous and a briny river."[26] The ancient Celts are said to have waded into the billows as they rolled in upon the shore, hewing and stabbing them with swords and spears, as if they could wound or frighten the ocean itself.[27] Irish legend tells of a certain Tuirbe Tragmar who, standing "on Telach Bela (the Hill of the Axe), would hurl a cast of his axe in the face of the floodtide, so that he forbade the sea, which then would not come over the axe."[28] The Toradjas of Central Celebes relate that one of their tribes, which is proverbial for stupidity, once came down to the sea-shore when the tide was out. Immediately they built a hut on the beach below high-water mark. When the tide rose and threatened to wash away the hut, they regarded it as a monster trying to devour them, and sought to appease it by throwing their whole stock of rice into the waves. As the tide still continued to advance, they next hurled their swords, spears, and chopping-knives into the sea, apparently with the intention of wounding or frightening the dangerous creature and so compelling him to retreat.[29] Once on a time, when a party of Arafoos, a tribe of mountaineers on the northern coast of Dutch New Guinea, were disporting themselves in the surf, three of them were swept out to sea by a refluent wave and drowned. To avenge the death their friends fired on the inrolling billows for hours with guns and bows and arrows.[30] Such personifications of the water as a personal being who can be cowed or overcome by physical violence, may help to explain the weird story of Jacob's adventure at the ford of the Jabbok.

[It should be observed also that the general theme of the wrestling of a man with an angel or demon likewise occurs in European folktales. A Hungarian story tells how a man struggled with a demon and released him only upon the granting of a request.[30a] Similarly, in a tale from Bosnia, a man fights with a vampire all night and lets him go only at cockcrow.[30b]]

(b) The shrinking sinew

The tradition that a certain sinew in Jacob's thigh was strained in the struggle with his nocturnal adversary is clearly an attempt to explain why the Hebrews would not eat the corresponding sinew in animals. Both the tradition and the custom have their parallels among some tribes of North American Indians, who regularly cut out and throw away the hamstrings of the deer they kill.[31] The Cherokee Indians assign two reasons for the practice. One is that "this tendon, when severed, draws up into the flesh; ergo, any one who should unfortunately partake of the hamstring would find his limbs drawn up in the same manner."[32] The other reason is that if, instead of cutting out the hamstring and throwing it away the hunter were to eat it, he would thereafter easily grow tired in travelling.[33] Both reasons assume the principle of sympathetic magic, though they apply it differently. The one supposes that, if you eat a sinew which shrinks, the corresponding sinew in your own body will shrink likewise. The other seems to assume that if you destroy the sinew without which the deer cannot walk, you yourself will be incapacitated from walking in precisely the same way. Both reasons are thoroughly in keeping with savage philosophy. Either of them would suffice to account for the Hebrew taboo. On this theory the narrative in Genesis supplies a religious sanction for a rule which was originally based on sympathetic magic alone.

[It should, however, be observed also that the thigh was commonly regarded in antiquity as the seat of procreation.[33a] Note, too that in Greek mythology, Dionysus is said to have been born from the thigh of Zeus.[33b] Accordingly, a man who is smitten seriously in the thigh is likely, by ancient ideas, to have been prevented from begetting progeny; as a symbol of discomfiture, this would therefore be the physical complement to the surrender of his *berakah* ("blessing") and the disclosure of his name.

Other features of the story may likewise be illustrated from Comparative Folklore. Thus, the idea that *demons, being "princes of darkness," lose their power at daybreak and must then depart* was widespread in the Ancient Near East.—An Egyptian incantation against the child-stealing witch, dating from the sixteenth century B.C., warns her to be gone since daylight is approaching.[33c] So too in Babylonian charms against the analogous Lamashtu,[33d] as well as in other spells against evil spirits in general.[33e]—A Canaanite magical plague of the eighth century B.C., designed to forefend the ravages of Lilith, cautions her to be gone when the sun rose.[33f]

Later Greek magical texts make the same point. Demons are warned to "flee and run away quickly, since the sun is rising,"[33g] or to "fly away before dawn";[33h] and the notion that evil spirits fear daybreak turns up frequently in late Greek and Latin writers.[33i]

In modern European folklore, water-spirits must be back in the water before dawn,[33j] while fairies must depart, and ogres become powerless, at cockcrow.[33k] Then, too, ghosts are laid [33l] and the Wild Hunt returns.[33m]

Again, the condition for release which Jacob imposes on his vanquished antagonist is that the latter will confer blessing (Heb. *b-r-k*) upon him and disclose his name (vv. 26–27).—The *blessing* which is here implied is more than mere verbal benediction; it is conferment of a numinous quality, or spe-

cial superhuman "nature," inherent in gods and demons and by them bestowed on men and objects which they favour.[33n] It is his meed of this quality
that a dying father passes on to his heir, and it is this that Jacob wrests from
Esau. Accordingly, Jacob's demand upon his opponent is a demand for the
surrender of his special powers.

Then there is the element of the disclosure of the *name*. The point here is
that in primitive thought, a man's name is not merely an appellation, but denotes what he is to the world outside of himself—that is, his "outer" as distinguished from his "inner" being.[33o] To know a person's name is, therefore,
a good step toward controlling his identity. For this reason, it is customary
in many parts of the world not to divulge a child's name before it has been
baptized or subjected to similar protective rites.[33p] For the same reason, too,
it is common practice to change a man's name in time of grave illness in order
thereby to change his identity and foil hovering demons. This is attested, for
instance, among the Arabs,[33q] the Jews,[33r] the Mongols,[33s] and the Baholoho
of Africa.[33t]

In light of the foregoing observations, it is apparent that, like so many
other traditional tales in Genesis, this one too has been doctored by the Biblical writer to accommodate it to later Israelitic religious ideas. In the first
place, as Frazer has shown, the story belongs *au fond* to a type in which a
human traveller wrestles with the superhuman spirit of a river or brook. Here,
however, that spirit is reduced to a mere man, however mysterious he may
be (vv. 24–25). Second, in the original story, the human being must physically have discomfited his divine opponent, thus scoring an outright victory
over him, for otherwise there would be no point in the latter's immediate plea
for release, nor would the human being have been in a position to pose demands (v. 26). In the Biblical version, however, it is the mysterious adversary
who, inconsistently, maims Jacob, rather than vice-versa (vv. 25, 31)—an
inconsistency which has indeed been remarked by many modern scholars.[33u] ▼

73 Guardian angels   48:16

In a stage of civilization in which there is as yet not knowledge of natural
properties or organic structures, the power which anything exerts or the
effect which it produces is attributed to external manipulation. The manipula-
tors are what we call gods or demons, and they have control not only of
phenomena but also of events. The latter include the vicissitudes of individual
lives. Accordingly, besides the great gods who have charge of universal or
cosmic things, each man has also his own god or "familiar spirit" who determines his general destiny; and even when civilization advances, this primitive
notion tends to persist as a matter of traditional folklore.

Such a personal god was known to the Mesopotamians as "the guardian of
a man's welfare" (*maṣṣar šulmi*), and the recipient of his good offices re-

garded himself as his spiritual son (*mâr ili*).[1] In monotheistic systems, these gods came, of course, to be subordinate to the single deity who ruled all things, and they were then considered his messengers or "angels." The notion was, to be sure, more a matter of popular fancy than of formal religious dogma, and it is in this guise that it is represented, for instance, alike in the Jewish Talmud,[2] in Jesus' warning not to "despise any of these little ones, since their angels always behold the face of my Father,"[3] and in early patristic writings.[4]

The idea was, however, by no means confined to the Semitic world. The Greek comic dramatist Menander (342–241 B.C.) declares in similar fashion that "as soon as a man is born, a familiar spirit (*daimōn*) stands before him to serve as his kindly guide through life";[5] and Horace asserts that every human being has a natal "genius" which regulates his star, is the god of his human nature, and is manifest in his face, now bright and now gloomy.[6] Brutus, it is related, saw a vision of his own fatal "genius" before his defeat at the battle of Philippi in 42 B.C.,[7] and an Egyptian astrologer warned Mark Antony to keep away from Octavius because "thy familiar is in fear of his."[8] The native genius of a woman was identified as her personal Juno.[9] It would appear, however, that among the Greeks and Romans the idea originated "not from the people, but from the philosophers."[10]

In Teutonic folklore, the spirit is said to be assigned at birth and to accompany an individual through life, protecting him from hurt and harm.[11] Analogous ideas are widespread throughout Europe,[12] while the Armenians hold that the natal genius trims a baby's nails and brings a smile to its lips when it plays with him. When the child is old enough, however, the spirit returns to heaven.[13]

Medieval hagiology likewise attests this belief. St. Francisca, for example, had a guardian spirit which in her youth took the form of a young boy, and later of an adult angel;[14] and Calmet tells of a Cistercian monk whose familiar prepared his chamber for him whenever he returned from a journey.[15] A common salutation among French peasants as late as the nineteenth century was *Bonjour à vous et à votre compagnie,* i.e., your guardian angel.[16]

Sometimes the spirit is associated in popular belief with the physical concomitants of birth. The Kaboos of Sumatra, for instance, identify it with the umbilical cord and the placenta; and the Bettaks of the same island say that every person has two such familiars; one, called the *kaka,* located in the sperm when he was conceived, and the other, called the *agi,* in the afterbirth.[17]

Sometimes too the notion is given a moral twist by the assumption that every man has two familiars, one motivating his good instincts, the other, his bad ones. This idea is familiar especially in Jewish popular tradition, appearing already in the Dead Sea Scrolls;[18] but it is likewise well attested in Roman literature.[19]

Nor, finally, have modern theologians been averse to using this belief for homiletic purposes. It will suffice to mention Swedenbourg's dictum that "every man has an associate spirit."

74 Jacob's last words 49

On his deathbed Jacob calls together his sons and tells them what will befall them in days to come.[1] His final address is thus more than a parting blessing. Like that of Moses, who similarly predicts the future of the tribes of Israel,[2] it reflects a widespread popular belief that the dying are prescient.[3] Gradually relinquishing the limitations of mortality, they become increasingly detached from the punctual and momentary and increasingly sensitive to that eternal continuum in which past, present, and future blend and blur. Consequently, that which is yet to come is as immediate to them as that which now is, and they are able to describe it. "At the advent of death," says Xenophon, "men become more divine, and hence can foresee the future."[4] Or, as Aristotle puts it, "A man's soul (*psyche*) is never more active than when he is at the point of death."[5]

In the Iliad, the dying Patroclus predicts the death of Hector at the hands of Achilles,[6] and the dying Hector that of Achilles himself.[7] Similarly, in Sophocles' *Women of Trachis,* the dying Heracles summons Alcmene so that she may learn from his last words "the things I now know by divine inspiration";[8] while Vergil puts into the mouth of the expiring Orodes the dire prediction that his slayer will soon meet retribution.[9] Socrates too is said by Plato to have made predictions during his last moments, feeling that "on the point of death, I am now in that condition in which men are most wont to prophesy."[10] From Poseidonius comes the story that a dying Rhodian once predicted that six of his companions would follow him to the grave in a certain order, and the prophecy came true.[11] So too it is related that when the Indian Calamus ascended the pyre at his execution, Alexander the Great bade him state his last wish. "No matter," was the reply. "The day after tomorrow I shall be seeing you again." Two days later Alexander died.[12]

Apocryphal writings of the early centuries of our era, such as the celebrated *Ascension of Moses* and the *Ascension of Isaiah,* likewise revolve around this idea;[13] and it is attested also in Arabic folklore.[14] Nor, indeed, is it absent from English literature. In Shakespeare's *King Richard the Second,* John of Gaunt declares roundly,

> Methinks I am a prophet new inspired,
> And thus expiring do foretell of him;[15]

while in *The Merchant of Venice,* Nerissa comforts Portia with the assurance that "Your father was ever virtuous, and holy men at their death have good inspirations."[16] Byron speaks likewise of "Death's prophetic ear,"[17] and the belief (which is recorded from Lancashire as late as the nineteenth century)[18] is mentioned frequently in Charles Reade's *The Cloister on the Hearth.*[19] It appears also in several German folktales,[20] and in Schiller's *Wilhelm Tell,* Attinghausen has a vision of the future before he dies.[21]

JOSEPH

The story of Joseph consists very largely in three familiar tales, which have been fancifully and artificially clustered around him.

75   The bloodstained coat[1]   37:3

Joseph receives a special kind of coat or tunic from his father. This, together with his boastful dreams of glory, incites the envy of his brethren, who decide to make away with him. At first they cast him into a dry pit, but later, when a caravan of traders passes by, they retrieve him and sell him into slavery. To account for his disappearance, they dip his distinctive garment into the blood of a slain goat, and then produce it to his father as evidence that he has been ravined by wild beasts.

Readers of the *Arabian Nights* will at once recognize in this the same theme as there occurs in the tale of Kemerezzeman and Budour.[2] Kemerezzeman and the beautiful Budour have been miraculously bedded together by jinns in a distant place. Kemerezzeman, however, virtuously declines to enjoy his bedmate. Both are wafted back to their homes. Kemerezzeman goes into a decline pining for Budour, while she herself is held under constraint by her father. At length, her half-brother Merzewan sets out to locate the handsome youth. He finds him, but his doting father will not let him go. So Merzewan arranges a feigned hunting expedition. He and Kemerezzeman kill their camel and a horse, dip Kemerezzeman's clothes in their blood, and leave them on the wayside so that Kemerezzeman's father may discover them and suppose that his son has been ravined by a lion.

Later in the story the same motif is repeated: Amyed and Asaad, the two sons of Kemerezzeman, receive sexual overtures from each other's mothers, Heyat en-Nufus and Budour. When they decline, the women accuse them of attempted rape. Their father orders his treasurer to take them into the desert and kill them, and to bring back two vials of blood as proof that the deed has been done. At the critical moment, however, the treasurer's horse bolts, and he runs after it, only to be faced by a lion. Amyed slays the lion. The treasurer then dips the lad's clothes in its blood and also fills two vials with it, which he duly brings back to Kemerezzeman as "proof" that the sentence of death has been carried out.

This, however, is not the only parallel that Comparative Folklore affords. The same stratagem figures also in the Turkish tales of Jefā and Sefā and of the Handsome Water-carrier in the Billur Köschk collection,[3] and, to show how widespread is the motif, it need be mentioned only that it is attested likewise in the folklore of modern Iceland[4] on the one hand and of the Ainus of Japan on the other.[5]

Recognition by means of a garment is in itself a common motif in folktales. Two examples from Classical myth must suffice. The first is the familiar recognition of Orestes by his sister Electra.[6] The second is the story of Hippothous:[7]

Alope, daughter of King Cercyon, is seduced by Poseidon and clandestinely bears a son, Hippothous. Clad in a rich robe, the child is exposed on a mountain. A shepherd finds and tends him. A second shepherd, attracted by the robe and suspecting that the child may be of noble birth, offers to take over. The two nearly come to blows, but finally appeal to King Cercyon. He orders the robe to be produced, and recognizes it as part of his daughter's clothing. Her guilt is thus revealed.

Joseph's distinctive garment is identified traditionally as a "coat of many colors." It seems a pity to strip him of so decorative and familiar a vesture, but, like several other elements of popular Bible lore (e.g., the nightgowned cherubim of Paradise, the horns on Moses' brow, and the "whale" that swallowed Jonah), this one too disappears under the searching light of a more exact scholarship. What Joseph received from his father is described in the original Hebrew as a "coat of *pasîm*"—a garment which is said in the story of Amnon and Tamar (II Sam. 13:18–19) to have been worn by the latter and to have been customarily affected by the princesses of the blood royal. Now, *pasîm* is the plural of a word *pas,* which normally means "length, extension." Literally, therefore, the garment was a "coat of lengths."[8] The Greek Septuagint and some of the other ancient translators took this to mean a garment made out of various lengths of different materials—that is, a kind of quilted or patchwork tunic,[9] and it is from this interpretation that the familiar "coat of many colors" is derived. What was really intended, however, was a coat which was extra long and extended to the ankles, like the skirted *tunica talaris* worn by Catholic priests.[10] It is not difficult to see how such a garment might have struck Joseph's brethren as somewhat "sissified" and effeminate, and have made of him a kind of Little Lord Fauntleroy; while at the same time it could not fail to arouse their envy, just because it was characteristic of royalty.

Closely interwoven with this motif is, of course, that of the abandonment of Joseph in the pit. Here, in point of fact, two elements are combined. The first is that of the expulsion of a younger brother from the household on account of his sinister dreams.[11] This has an exact parallel in a Balkan folktale[12] and is also found elsewhere in European popular lore.[13] The second is that of the casting of the victim into a pit.[14] Here again a story in the Arabian Nights affords an arresting parallel:[15]

Hasib Kerimeddin (we read) was once working alongside of some wood-cutters when he discovered a cistern filled with honey. With their aid, he extricated it and sold it at the market. Fearful, however, that he would take all the profits for himself, they led him back to the cistern and, telling him to remove whatever honey might still remain in it, they abandoned him there, reporting to his father that he had been killed by a wolf.

Another version of this story appears in the aforementioned Turkish collection of Billur Köschk;[16] while a famous Peruvian myth tells, in similar vein, how the children of the sun, jealous of their youngest brother, shut him up in a hole in the ground, whence, however, he later emerged, winged, as Manco Capac, the founding father of the Incas.[17]

76 Potiphar's wife[1]   39:7-20

Joseph winds up at the court of the Pharaoh in Egypt. The wife of Potiphar, the captain of the guard, becomes enamored of him and tries to seduce him. When he rebuffs her, she falsely accuses him to her husband, producing in "evidence" his garment, which she snatches off him when he flees her advances. Joseph is imprisoned.

The lady has her sisters everywhere, so that comparable stories are told in many parts of the world. Curiously enough, the earliest known parallel comes from Egypt where the Biblical story plays. A papyrus of the thirteenth century B.C. relates the tale of two brothers, an elder named Anpu (Anubis) and a younger named Bata. The former is married; the latter is not. Bata lives in Anpu's house and works for him. One day, when he comes from the field carrying grain, Anpu's wife attempts to seduce him. "Wild like a leopard," he indignantly repels her. Thereupon she takes fat and grease, makes herself vomit, neglects her toilet and lies down terribly sick. When Anpu returns home and asks her what is wrong, she accuses Bata of having tried to rape her. Anpu sets out after him, but Bata is able eventually, under oath, to convince him of his innocence—he even chops off his penis to make the defense persuasive!—and the two brothers are reconciled.[2]

There are several versions of the tale in Classical literature. The most familiar is, of course, that of the guilty passion of Phaedra for Hippolytus. When he refused her advances, she "cleft open the doors of her bedchamber, rent her garments, and falsely charged him with assault."[3] Of the same tenor, too, is the legend of Anteia (alias Stheneboea) and Bellerophon. Rebuffed by him, she accused him falsely of having attempted to seduce her.[4] A third version relates how Astydameia, the wife of Acastus, fell in love with Peleus and revenged herself for his indifference by falsely denouncing him to her husband.[5] Lastly, the story was told of Biadice, the wife of Cretheus, that she had become enamored of her nephew Phrixus who, when he repulsed her overtures, found himself falsely accused.[6]

A story in the Indic Jatāka tells how the stepmother of Prince Paduma leveled charges against him for the same reason, and persuaded the king to put him to death.[7] Similarly, the cadre of the Sindbad cycle, in the medieval Tales of the Seven Masters, is the story of a prince falsely accused by his stepmother, whose advances he has repelled.

Persian[8] and Chinese[9] versions of the tale are also known, and it likewise appears as an incident in the Armenian epic, The Daredevils of Sassoun.[10] A somewhat more sophisticated variant may be found in Boccaccio's Decameron,[11] and a story of the same purport is reported as current among North American Indians.[12]

In the Thousand and One Nights the tale is told in reverse: a Jewish cadi, leaving home on a business trip, entrusts the care of his wife to his brother. The latter attempts to seduce her. Denied her favors, he subsequently accuses her to her husband of having committed adultery.[13]

Not impossibly, a far older version is to be recognized in a Canaanite myth (preserved only in a Hittite version) which relates how the goddess Asherath complained to her husband Elkunirša (i.e., *El qôneh 'areṣ,* "the God who owns the earth"; cf. Gen. 14:19) that Baal had attempted to lie with her, when he had in fact repulsed her.[14]

▲ 77 Joseph's cup   44:2, 5

When his brethren came to Egypt to procure corn during the famine, and were about to set out on their homeward journey to Palestine, Joseph caused his silver drinking-cup to be hidden in the mouth of Benjamin's sack. Then when the men were gone out of the city and were not yet far off, he sent his steward after them to tax them with theft in having stolen his cup. A search was accordingly made in the sacks, and the missing cup was found in Benjamin's sack. The steward reproached the brethren with their ingratitude to his master, who had treated them hospitably, and whose kindness they had repaid by robbing him of the precious goblet. "Wherefore have ye rewarded evil for good?" he asked. "Is not this it in which my lord drinketh, and whereby he indeed divineth? ye have done evil in so doing." And when the brethren were brought back and confronted with Joseph, he repeated these reproaches, saying, "What deed is this that ye have done? know ye not that such a man as I can indeed divine?" Hence we may infer that Joseph piqued himself in particular on his power of detecting a thief by means of his divining cup.

The use of a cup in divination has been not uncommon both in ancient and modern times, though the particular mode of employing it for that purpose has not always been the same. Thus in the life of the Neoplatonic philospher Isidorus we read that the sage fell in with a sacred woman, who possessed a divine talent of a remarkable kind. She used to pour clean water into a crystal cup, and from the appearances in the water she predicted the things that should come to pass.[1] Such predictions from appearance in water formed a special brand of divination, on which the Greeks bestowed the name of *hydromantia.*

How Joseph used his magic cup for the detection of a thief or for other purposes of divination we do not know, but we may conjecture that he was supposed to draw his inferences from figures which appeared to him in the water. Certainly this mode of divination is still practised in Egypt, and it may have been in vogue in that conservative country from remote antiquity. Its modern name is the Magic Mirror. "A pure innocent boy (not more than twelve years of age) is directed to look into a cup filled with water and inscribed with texts, while under his cap is stuck a paper, also with writing on it, so as to hang over his forehead; he is also fumigated with incense, while sentences are murmured by the conjuror. After a little time, when the boy is asked what he sees, he says that he sees persons moving in the water, as if in a mirror. The conjuror orders the boy to lay certain commands on the spirit, as for instance to set up a tent, or to bring coffee and pipes. All this is done at once. The conjuror asks the inquisitive spectators to name any person whom they wish to appear on the scene, and some name is mentioned, no matter whether the person is living or dead. The boy commands the spirit to bring him. In a few seconds he is present, and the boy proceeds to describe him. The description, however, according to our own observation, is always quite wide of the mark. The boy excuses himself by saying that the person brought before him will not come right into the middle, and always remains half in the shade; but at other times he sees the persons really and in motion. When a theft is committed the magic mirror is also sometimes questioned, as we ourselves were witnesses on one occasion. (This is called *darb el mandel.*) The accusations of the boy fell upon a person who was afterwards proved to be quite innocent, but whom the boy, as it appeared, designedly charged with the crime out of malevolence. For this reason such experiments, formerly much in vogue, were strictly prohibited by the government, though they are still practised."[2]

Similar modes of divination have been practised in other parts of the world. Thus, in Scandinavia people used to go to a diviner on a Thursday evening in order to see in a pail of water the face of the thief who had robbed them.[3] This latter oracle has been described more fully by another writer. The natives of Tahiti, he tells us, "had also recourse to several kinds of divination, for discovering the perpetrators of acts of injury, especially theft. Among these was a kind of water ordeal. It resembled in a great degree the *wai haruru* of the Hawaiians. When the parties who had been robbed wished to use this method of discovering the thief, they sent for a priest, who, on being informed of the circumstances connected with the theft, offered prayers to his demon. He now directed a hole to be dug in the floor of the house, and filled with water; then, taking a young plantain in his hand, he stood over the hole, and offered his prayers to the god, whom he invoked, and who, if propitious, was supposed to conduct the spirit of the thief to the house, and place it over the water. The image of the spirit, which they imagined resembled the person of the man, was, according to their account, reflected in the water, and being perceived by the priest, he named the individual, or the parties, who had committed the theft, stating that the god had shewn him the image in the water."[4]

When Sir Frank Swettenham had been robbed in the Malay Peninsula, he was introduced to an Arab, who asserted that he would be able to tell him all about the robbery, provided he might fast in solitude for three days in an empty house, but that without such a preparation he could not see what he sought. "He told me that after his vigil, fast, and prayer, he would lay in his hand a small piece of paper on which there would be some writing; into this he would pour a little water, and in that extemporised mirror he would see a vision of the whole transaction. He declared that, after gazing intently into this divining-glass, the inquirer first recognised the figure of a little old man; that having duly saluted this *Jin,* it was only necessary to ask him to conjure up the scene of the robbery, when all the details would be re-enacted in the liquid glass under the eyes of the gazer, who would there and then describe all that he saw."[5] Some diviners in South-Eastern New Guinea profess to descry the face of a culprit in a pool of water into which coco-nut oil has been squeezed.[6] Among the Mossi, a nation of the French Sudan, in the upper valley of the Niger, the royal pages, who are boys under puberty, are bound to observe strict continence. Once a year their chastity is tested as follows. Each page must look at his reflection in a calabash of water, and from the appearance of the reflection it is judged whether he has been chaste or not. In former days, before the French occupation of the country, any page thus convicted of unchastity was executed on the spot. Every year the faithfulness of the king's wives was tested by a similar ordeal, and all who were found guilty were put to death.[7] Among the Eskimos, when a man has gone out to sea and has not returned in due time, a wizard will undertake to ascertain by means of the magic mirror whether the missing man is alive or dead. For this purpose he lifts up the head of the nearest relation of the missing man with a stick; a tub of water stands under, and in this mirror the wizard professes to behold the image of the absent mariner either overset in his canoe or sitting upright and rowing. Thus he is able either to comfort the anxious relatives with an assurance of the safety of their friend or to confirm their worst fears by the tidings of his death.[8]

An early Christian writer has let us into the secret of the tricks to which ancient oracle-mongers resorted for the purpose of gratifying their dupes with a vision of the gods in water. They had a closed chamber built, the roof of which was painted blue. In the middle of the floor they set a vessel full of water which, reflecting the blue roof, presented the appearance of the sky. The vessel was made of stone, but it had a glass bottom, and beneath it was an opening into a secret chamber under the floor, where the confederates of the prophet assembled and played the parts which he assigned to them immediately under the oracular chasm. Meantime the inquirers of the oracle, gazing into the water, beheld, as they thought, a miraculous vision, and accordingly believed implicitly all that the prophet told them.[9]

But the magic mirror is not the only form of divination in which the material instrument employed for the discovery of truth is a vessel of water. An Indian mode of detecting a thief is to inscribe the names of all the suspected persons on separate balls of paste or wax, and then to throw the balls into a vessel of water. It is believed that the ball which contains the name of the thief will float on the surface, and that all the others will sink to the bottom.[10] In Europe young people used to resort to many forms of divination on Midsummer Eve in order to ascertain their fortune in love. Thus in Dorsetshire a girl on going to bed would write the letters of the alphabet on scraps of paper and drop them in a basin of water with the letters downwards; and next morning she would expect to find the first letter of her future husband's name turned up, but all the other letters still turned down.[11] In Shropshire a girl will sometimes write the initials of several young men of her acquaintance on bits of paper, wrap a little ball of bread in each paper, and put the small packets in a glass of water; the young man whose initials first rise to the surface will win her hand.[12]

Sometimes the fates are ascertained by dropping substances of one kind or another in a vessel of water and judging of the issue by the position or configuration which the substance assumes in the water. Thus among the Bahima or Banyankole, a pastoral tribe of Uganda, a medicine-man would sometimes take a pot of water and cast certain herbs into it, which caused a froth to rise; then he dropped four coffee-berries into the water, marked the positions which they took up, and inferred the wishes of the gods according to the direction in which the berries pointed or the side which they turned up in floating.[13] Among the Garos of Assam a priest will sometimes divine by means of a cup of water and some grains of uncooked rice. Holding the cup of water in his left hand, he drops the rice into it, grain by grain, calling out the name of a spirit as each grain falls. The spirit who chances to be named at the moment when two grains, floating in the water, collide with each other, is the one who must be propitiated.[14] In Scotland a tea-stalk floating on the surface of a teacup was supposed to betoken a stranger. "It was taken from the cup and tested with the teeth whether soft or hard. If soft, the stranger was a female; if hard, a male. It was then put on the back of the left hand and struck three times with the back of the right. The left hand was then held up and slightly shaken. If the tea-stalk fell off, the stranger was not to arrive; if it stuck, the stranger would arrive."[15] In the Highlands of Scotland the art of divining by the tea-leaves or sediment in a tea-cup was carried out in still greater detail. Even yet, we are told, young women resort in numbers to fortune-tellers of this class, who, for the simple reward of the tea, spell out to them most excellent matches. The prediction is made from the arrangement of the sediment or tea-leaves in the cup after the last of the liquid has been made to wash the sides of the cup in the *deiseal* or right-hand-turn direction and then poured out.[16] In England similar prophecies are hazarded from tea-leaves and coffee-grounds left at the bottom of cups.[17] So in Macedonia people divine by coffee. "One solitary bubble in the centre of the cup betokens that the person holding it possesses one staunch and faithful friend. If there are several bubbles forming a ring close to the edge of the cup, they signify that he is fickle in his affections, and that his heart is divided between several objects of worship. The grounds of coffee are likewise observed and variously explained according to the forms which they assume: if they spread round the cup in the shape of rivulets and streams money is prognosticated, and so forth."[18]

In Europe a favourite mode of divination is practised by pouring molten lead or wax into a vessel of water and watching the forms which the substance assumes as it cools in the water. This way of prying into the future has been resorted to in Lithuania, Sweden, Scotland, and Ireland.[19] Again, in Ireland a certain disease called *esane* was supposed to be sent by the fairies, and in order to prognosticate its course or prescribe for its treatment diviners used to inspect coals which they had dropped into a pot of clean water.[20]

In one or other of these ways Joseph may be supposed to have divined by means of his silver cup. ▼

77a   One hundred years and ten   50:26

Joseph lives one hundred and ten years. This is an *Egyptian* touch, for no less than twenty-seven ancient Egyptian texts mention one hundred and ten years as the ideal mortal span, whereas the Israelites set it at one hundred and twenty years (see above, §32a).[1]

Exodus

Moses

▲ With the life of Joseph the partiarchal age of Israel may be said to end. A brilliant series of biographical sketches, vivid in colouring and masterly in the delineation of character, has described the march of the patriarchs from the banks of the Euphrates to the banks of the Nile. There the historian leaves them for a time. The curtain descends on the first act of the drama, and when it rises again on the same scene, some four hundred years are supposed to have elapsed, and the patriarchal family has expanded into a nation. From this point the national history begins, and the first commanding figure in it is that of Moses, the great leader and lawgiver, who is said to have delivered his people from bondage in Egypt, to have guided them in their wanderings across the Arabian desert, to have moulded their institutions, and finally to have died within sight of the Promised Land, which he was not to enter. In the story of his exploits, as in that of so many national heroes, later ages unquestionably embroidered the sober tissue of fact with the gay threads of fancy; yet the change thus wrought in the web has not been so great as to disguise the main strands beyond recognition. We can still trace the limbs of the man under the gorgeous drapery of the magician who confronted Pharaoh and wrought plagues on all the land of Egypt; we can still perceive the human features through the nimbus of supernatural glory which shone on the features of the saint and prophet as he descended from the mountain, where he had conversed with God and had received from the divine hands a new code of law for his people. It is indeed remarkable that, though Moses stands so much nearer than the partriarchs to the border line of history, the element of the marvellous and the miraculous enters much more deeply into his story than into theirs. While from time to time they are said to have communed with the deity, either face to face or in visions, not one of them is represented as a worker of those signs and wonders which occur so frequently in the career of Moses. We see them moving as men among men, attending to the common business and sharing the common joys and sorrows of humanity. Moses, on the other hand, from the beginning to the end of his life is represented as set apart for a great mission and moving accordingly on a higher plane than ordinary mortals, with hardly any traces of those frailties which are incidental to all men, and which, touched in by a delicate brush add so much life-like colour to the portraits of the patriarchs. ▼

[The few details which the Bible gives about the personal life of Moses represent him as the typical hero of national legend, who comes into the world and departs from it in an aura of mystery. He is exposed in infancy beside a river and rescued by a princess, and at the close of his career he disappears on a hilltop. His "call" is authenticated by three miraculous signs, and he is equipped with a wonder-working rod which divides a sea or lake, makes the bitter waters sweet, and produces a stream from a rock. These traits are abundantly paralleled elsewhere in folk literature.]

▲ 78 Moses in the bulrushes   Exod. 2:1–11

[In order, apparently, to enhance the wonder of a hero's career, popular story loves to relate how he was exposed at birth[1] and rescued from imminent death only by what might seem to vulgar eyes an accident, but what was really the hand of Fate interposed to preserve him for his high destiny. Moreover, it is sometimes specified, as in the Biblical tale, that his rescuer or foster-mother was a princess.[1a]

Thus, of the legendary Semiramis, queen of Assyria, daughter of the goddess Derceto by a mortal man, it is told that she was exposed in infancy upon a rock and rescued only by kindly doves who nurtured her.[1b]—A somewhat similar story is narrated by the Greek writer Aelian concerning Gilgamesh, the celebrated Mesopotamian hero. His mother, the daughter of King Senechoros of Babylon, though confined by her father within the citadel, was gotten with child by an unknown lover. Her guardians, dreading the king's anger at their lack of vigilance, cast the new-born babe from the parapet of the castle wall; but an eagle which had been circling overhead swooped down, broke the child's fall, and, bearing it on its back, deposited it gently in a garden. The gardener took it home and reared it as his own.[1c]—Similarly, in Greek legend, Aegisthus, the murderer of Agamemnon, is said to have been the fruit of incestuous intercourse between Pelopia and her father Thyestes. When he was born, his mother exposed him, but shepherds discovered him and gave him to a she-goat to suckle.[1d]

So too, after an oracle had declared that he would someday slay his father, Oedipus was ordered exposed on the slopes of Mount Cithaeron. The herdsman, however, to whom he had been committed, passed him on to another, a servant of King Polybus of Corinth, who in turn carried him to the queen. The latter, having no son of her own, adopted the foundling and passed him off as her natural offspring. Reared at a foreign court, Oedipus grew up to fulfill the oracle by slaying his true father, Laius, whom he encountered while he was driving his chariot in a narrow pass of the Phocian mountains.[1e]

Paris of Troy is likewise said to have been abandoned on Mount Ida after his birth, to have been nursed there for five days by a she-bear, and subsequently to have been reared in secret by one of Priam's servants.[1f]—In the same way too, the twins Amphion and Zethus, begotten by Zeus upon Antiope, were exposed at birth and eventually rescued by a neatherd;[1g] and similar stories are related concerning Heleus, Iamos, and Atalanta.[1h]

In Japanese mythology, the tale of the exposed child is told of the ancient hero Hiruko;[1i] in Britain of Arthur, and in Wales of Llew Llangwyffes.[1j]

A real historical personage who is said to have been exposed in infancy is Cyrus, the first king of Persia. His father, Cambyses, runs the story, had ordered his grand vizier to remove the child and put it to death in order to prevent the fulfilment of a prophetic dream that the lad, the offspring of a foreign mother, would someday dominate Asia and thus eclipse his (Cambyses') own dynasty. The vizier, however, turned the child over to a herdsman, whose wife happened just to have given birth to a still-born babe. When her husband entered the house, carrying a handsome baby boy, adorned with fine raiment and jewels of gold, her heart went out to it, and she entreated him to give her the live child, but to take her dead child, dress it in the clothes and trinkets of the royal infant, and to expose the little corpse, thus bedecked, in a lonely place among the mountains. "Thus," said she, "our own child will receive a royal funeral, and we shall save the life of the princely infant." So when their dead child, wrapt in regal finery, had lain stark and cold on the mountains for three days, the herdsman reported to the grand vizier that his commands had been obeyed, and the vizier sent some of his trustiest guards, and they brought him word of what they had seen, and how they had buried the infant. Thus the young prince Cyrus grew up in the wild mountains as the putative son of the king's herdsman.[2]

Moses is not only exposed at birth, but also drawn out of the *waters*. This too has abundant parallels both in mythology and in folklore. Stories of this type are told particularly about the founders of dynasties and kingdoms, whose parentage and upbringing have long been forgotten.

A peculiarly arresting example is the legend of Sargon of Agade, the first Semitic king to reign over Babylonia (c. 2300 B.C.). A redoubtable conqueror and an active builder, he achieved great renown, but apparently did not know the name of his own father. A text discovered in the remains of the royal library at Nineveh, but copied from a far older original, tells the story as follows:

Sargon, the mighty king, king of Agade, am I.
My mother was a nun (?); my father I knew not.
My father's kinsmen lived in the hills.
My city was Azupiranu, on the banks of the Euphrates.
When my mother, the nun (?), had conceived me, she bore me in secret.
She put me in a basket of rushes, with bitumen sealed me in.
Then she cast me into the river, but the river did not overwhelm me.
The river bore me up, and carried me to a drawer of water, one Akki.

As he dipped his ewer, Akki hauled me out.
He [adopted me and] reared me as his own son.
He set me to tending his garden.
While I was so engaged, the goddess Ishtar granted me her love
I came to reign over the kingdom for four and . . . years.
The black-headed people I ruled and gov[erned].[3]

It is by no means impossible that the Biblical writer was acquainted with this earlier story, and modeled his own narrative upon it. On the other hand, both the Mesopotamian and the Hebrew tales may equally well be regarded as independent offshoots from the common root of popular imagination; and this view is supported by the occurrence of a parallel legend in the great Indian epic, the *Mahabharata,* since it is hardly likely that the authors of that work knew anything of Semitic traditions. The poet relates how the king's daughter Kunti or Pritha was beloved by the Sun-god and bore him a son "beautiful as a celestial," "clad in armour, adorned with brilliant golden ear-rings, endued with leonine eyes and bovine shoulders." But ashamed of her frailty, and dreading the anger of her royal father and mother, the princess, "in consultation with her nurse, placed her child in a waterproof basket, covered all over with sheets, made of wicker-work, smooth, comfortable and furnished with a beautiful pillow. And with tearful eyes she consigned it to (the waters of) the river Asva." Having done so, she returned to the palace, heavy at heart, lest her angry sire should learn her secret. But the basket containing the babe floated down the river till it came to the Ganges and was washed ashore at the city of Champa in the Suta territory. There it chanced that a man of the Suta tribe and his wife, walking on the bank of the river, saw the basket, drew it from the water, and on opening it beheld a baby boy "(beautiful) as the morning sun, clad in a golden armour, and with a beautiful face adorned with brilliant ear-rings." Now the pair were childless, and when the man looked upon the fair infant, he said to his wife, "Surely, considering that I have no son, the gods have sent this child to me." So they adopted him, and brought him up, and he became a mighty archer, and his name was Karna. But his royal mother had news of him through her spies.[4]

A similar story is told of the exposure and upbringing of Trakhan, the famous sixteenth-century king of Gilgit, a town situated at a height of about five thousand feet above the sea in the very heart of the snowy Himalayas. His father Tra-Trakhan had married a woman of a wealthy family at Darel. Being passionately devoted to polo, the king was in the habit of going over to Darel every week to play his favourite game with the seven brothers of his wife. One day, so keen were they all on the sport, they agreed to play on condition that the winner should put the losers to death. The contest was long and skilful, but at last the king won the match, and agreeably to the compact he, like a true sportsman, put his seven brothers-in-law to death. When he came home, no doubt in high spirits, and told the queen the result of the match, with its painful but necessary sequel, she was so far from sharing in his glee that she actually resented the murder, or rather the execution, of her seven brothers and resolved to avenge it. So she put arsenic in the king's food, which soon laid him out, and the queen reigned in his stead. Now it so happened that at the time she was with child by the king, and about a month afterwards gave birth to a son and called his name Trakhan. But so deeply did she mourn the death of her brothers, that she could not bear to look on the child of their murderer; hence she locked the infant in a wooden box and secretly threw it into the river. The current swept the box down the river as far as Hodar, a village in the Chilas District. Now it chanced that, as it floated by, two poor brothers were gathering sticks on the bank; and, thinking that the chest might contain treasure, one of them plunged into the water and drew it ashore. In order not to excite the covetousness of others by a display of the expected treasure, they hid the chest in a bundle of faggots and carried it home. There they opened it, and what was their surprise to discover in it a lovely babe still alive. Their mother brought up the little foundling with every care; and it seemed as if the infant brought a blessing to the house, for whereas they had been poor before, they now grew richer and richer, and set down their prosperity to the windfall of the child in the chest. When the boy was twelve years old, he conceived a great longing to go to Gilgit, of which he had heard much. So he went with his two foster-brothers, but on the way they stayed for a few days at a place called Baldas on the top of a hill. Now his mother was still queen of Gilgit, but she had fallen very ill, and as there was none to succeed her in Gilgit the people were searching for a king to come from elsewhere and reign over them. One morning, while things were in this state and all minds were in suspense, it chanced that the village cocks crew, but instead of saying as usual "Cock-a-doodle-do" they said *"Beldas tham bayi,"* which being interpreted means, "There is a king at Baldas." So men were at once sent to bring down any stranger they might find there. The messengers found the three brothers and brought them before the queen. As Trakhan was handsome and stately, the queen addressed herself to him, and in course of conversation elicited from him his story. To her surprise and joy she learned that this goodly boy was her own lost son, whom on a rash impulse of grief and resentment she had cast into the river. So she embraced him and proclaimed him the rightful heir to the kingdom of Gilgit.[5]

[Nor are such tales confined to the Orient. Readers of Classical literature will recall at once the Greek legend of the god Dionysus, son of Semele by Zeus. Semele's father Cadmus, it is related, had mother and child shut up in a chest and cast adrift upon the waves. Semele perished under the ordeal, but the infant was retrieved and nursed by her sister, Ino.[5a]—Similar too is the tale of Perseus, begotten by Zeus upon Danae in a golden shower. Perseus too was shut up in a chest, along with his mother, and thrown into the sea. The chest drifted to the island of Seriphios, where it was caught by a fisherman in a net.

On opening it and beholding the mother and her child, he was touched with compassion, took them to his home, and brought up the boy as his own son.[5b] —Pelias and Nereus, twin sons of Tyro by Poseidon, were likewise found— according to one version of the story—floating down the Enipeus in a wooden ark.[5c]

Among the Greeks and Romans, as among the Orientals, the story was told especially about the founders of dynasties or kingdoms.

An excellent example is the legend of Telephus, begotten by Heracles upon Auge, daughter of King Aleus of Tegea. According to one account, Auge's angry and incredulous father ordered mother and child to be put into a chest and cast into the sea. The chest, however, drifted to the mouth of the River Caicus, in Mysia, where it was found by Teuthras, king of that country. Teuthras married Auge and brought up Telephus as his own son.[5d]

Again, according to Roman tradition, the founder of the Eternal City himself was exposed in infancy on the banks of the River Tiber, and might have perished but for the providential interposition of a she-wolf and a woodpecker.[5e]

A story of similar character was told, centuries later, about T'u Küeh, the founder of the Turkish nation, who is said to have been exposed in early childhood in a swamp, but to have been saved therefrom and nourished by a she-wolf, whom he subsequently married.[5f]—A legend of the same kind is related also by the Zains of India concerning their ancient prince, Aghaṭa. Born by a slave-girl to a priest of the court, Aghaṭa had been foredestined to be king. Thereupon the reigning sovereign, Sughaṭita ordered him slain, but the two soldiers commissioned to carry out this order deposited the child instead beside a well. There he was discovered by a gardener and his wife, who realized his special character by the lustre which enveloped him and by the fact that all nature bloomed in his presence.[5g]—In like vein, Iranian popular lore tells how a child born to Humai, daughter of Behmen-dirag-dast, was exposed in a chest on the Euphrates because he had been foredestined to greatness. Like his congeners in the sister tales, he was eventually rescued by a fuller.[5h]

So popular, indeed, was the motif of the child drawn out of the water that it sometimes entered into ordinary "household tales," without being attached to heroic characters of history. Thus, a popular Greek tale, known as that of the Tzizinaena, tells of a poor girl who prayed to St. Michael that her expected child would grow up to be famous and prosperous. The saint assured her that he would live to dispossess a local grandee named Marcianos. On hearing of this, Marcianos had the child put in a chest (or, in other versions, a sack) and cast adrift, but it was retrieved by a fisherman (or shepherd) and survived to fulfill the prophecy. (The story exists also in Coptic and Ethiopic versions.)[5i]

Lastly, there are some curious twists on the old story. A medieval Jewish legend, for example, says that Joshua, the successor of Moses, was cast into the waters in infancy, but rescued by a fish, which swallowed him. The fish was caught and served at a royal banquet. When it was slit open, out sprang our hero, thereafter to become the protégé of the royal household.[5j]—Again, a tale included in *The Golden Legend* relates that the mother of Judas Iscariot cast him in infancy upon the waters through fear of a prophecy that he would bring woe upon the world. The sea carried him to an island named Scariot, where the queen nursed him in secret. Eventually he escaped to Jerusalem, where he entered the service of Pontius Pilate. One day, Pontius sent him to steal apples from a neighbor's orchard. It so happened, however, that the orchard belonged to Judas' true father. The latter, who did not recognize his own son, caught him and berated him. Pilate, however, rewarded the youth by giving him all the man's property and, to boot, the man's wife. Judas thus became the paramour of his own mother! (This is, of course, simply an adaptation and elaboration of the Oedipus legend.)[5k]

The story of the hero retrieved in infancy from a river may perhaps reflect the primitive notion that charismatic men draw their special qualities from water, the primordial, uncontaminated element, which is the primal source of power and wisdom (see above, §2).—In Southeastern Asia, for example, kings are often said for this reason to have been born of water nymphs;[51] and similar claims are made for more than one hero of ancient Greek legend.[5m]—In Indonesia, the kings of San-fo-ta'i are known as "sperm of water nymph (*long tsin*)."[5n]—The Emperor of Palaung Pagan of China was born, it is said, of the union of the water nymph Thusandi and Prince Thurya; while the king of Palenbang was the offspring of King Sowran and the daughter of the submarine sovereign.[5o]—In ancient Mesopotamia, Ea, god of the waters, imparted "know-how" (Sumerian, IGI.GAL, "insight") to new kings;[5p] a formula to that effect is employed by the kings of Lagash,[5q] and the same thing is said also by Lugalzagisi of Uruk[5r] and by Hammurapi.[5s]—In Egypt, the new pharaoh was baptized by the deities of the four quarters of the earth;[5t] and in Israel, both the pretender Adonijah and Solomon himself were installed beside water.[5u]

The basic notion of the special power of water appears in European popular lore. In a Basque legend, a hero who has subdued a dragon cannot kill him until the princess whom he has thus rescued throws magical water in his face and thereby gives him extra strength.[5v] Similarly, in a Russian tale, a hero named Gol insists that the princess fortify him for a like feat with "water of heroes."[5w]]

*   *   *

This, however, is but one possible explanation of the story. Another is that it reflects an old custom of testing the legitimacy of children by throwing them into the water and leaving them to swim or sink, the infants which swam being accepted as legitimate and those which sank being rejected as bastards.[6] In the light of this conjecture it may be significant that in several of these stories the birth of the child is represented as supernatural, which in this connexion cynics are apt to regard as a delicate synonym for illegitimate. Thus in Greek legend the child Perseus and the child Telephus were fathered upon the god Zeus and the hero Hercules respectively; in Roman legend the twins Romulus and Remus were gotten on their virgin mother by the god Mars; and in the Indian epic the princess ascribed the birth of her infant to the embrace of the Sun-god. In the Babylonian story, on the other hand, King Sargon, less fortunate or more honest than his Greek, Roman, and Indian compeers, frankly confessed that his father was unknown. The Biblical narrative of the birth of Moses drops no hint that his legitimacy was doubtful; but when we remember that his father Amram married his paternal aunt, that Moses was the offspring of the marriage,[7] and that later Jewish law condemned all such marriages as incestuous,[8] we may perhaps, without being uncharitable, suspect that in the original form of the story the mother of Moses had a more particular reason for exposing her babe on the water than a general command of Pharaoh to cast all male children of the Hebrews into the river.[9] Be that as it may, it appears that the water ordeal has been resorted to by peoples far apart for the purpose of deciding whether an infant is legitimate or not, and therefore whether it is to be saved or destroyed. Thus the Celts are said to have submitted the question of the legitimacy of their offspring to the judgment of the Rhine; they threw the infants into the water, and if the babes were bastards the pure and stern river drowned them, but if they were true-born, it graciously bore them up on its surface and wafted them gently ashore to the arms of their trembling mothers.[10] Similarly in Central Africa the explorer Speke was told "about Ururi, a province of Unyoro, under the jurisdiction of Kiméziri, a noted governor, who covers his children with bead ornaments, and throws them into the N'yanza, to prove their identity as his own true offspring; for should they sink, it stands to reason some other person must be their father; but should they float, then he recovers them."[11] ▼

79   Moses at Horeb   3:1–5

(a) The Burning Bush

It has been suggested that this story was based on the phenomenon of volcanic steam seen from a distance rising over shrub on a mountain.[1] (This, however, should not be taken to imply that the Biblical narrative had its origin in an historical occurrence, it merely explains how, in general, tales of this type may have arisen.)[2] On the other hand, however, it should be borne in mind that in ancient times the appearance of an "automatic fire" was always regarded as a prime form of divine manifestation (see below, §258, b).

An arresting parallel to the Biblical story is recorded in the annals of Christian saints. On March 24, 1400—so the legend runs—the Virgin Mary was revealed at Chalons, France, in a burning bush the blaze of which could be seen for miles, but which afterward remained green.[3]

(b) The removal of shoes

The custom of *removing shoes at holy places* is mentioned again in the story of Joshua's encounter with the captain of the angelic army at Jericho,[4] and is well attested also in other cultures.

On a Sumerian seal from the third millennium B.C.[5] and again on a seal of Gudea of Lagash[6] a worshiper is shown standing barefoot before his god. The Phoenicians are said to have removed their linen stockings upon entering holy areas,[7] and in their cult of "Heracles" at Gades, in Spain, they went unshod.[8] In Greece, the same usage obtained at Ialysos[9] and in the sacred precinct of Despoina at Lycosauca,[10] and it is also enjoined in the ritual ordinances at Eresos.[11] Participants in the Mysteries likewise performed the rites barefoot[12] —a practice ridiculed by Aristophanes.[13] In the later Attiscult, the devotees went without shoes,[14] although this may have been specifically a rite of mourning. In times of drought the Romans performed a barefoot dance called *nudipedalia*.[15] The custom survived in the Catholic Church, where participants in processions often walk barefoot.[16] Similarly, as is well known, shoes are removed on entering mosques or Buddhist temples.

Various explanations of this usage have been proposed.[17] According to one theory,[18] its purpose was to ensure that all knots were untied, i.e., all impediments removed which might impair converse with deity. According to another,[19] the object of going barefoot was to absorb more easily the magical power of the earth. This, however, conflicts with the widespread notion that sacred or numinous persons must *not* touch the earth with their feet, lest their peculiar quality be drained away by it.[20]

A third view is that ritual barefootedness is an attenuated relic of ritual nudity which is well attested in both ancient and modern usage. Thus, Sumarian votaries are depicted on plaques from Lagash, Ur, and Nippur,[21] as also on a vase from Uruk[22] and in clay from Khafaje,[23] standing nude before their gods. The practice was likewise quite common among the Greeks and Romans;[24] while the pre-Islamic Arabs often performed the ṭawāf, or ritual circumambulation of the altar *in puris naturalibus*,[25] and prayer too was often offered in the nude.[26] Even today Palestinian Arab women sometimes strip when invoking *welis*[27] or when conducting the plowing ritual to induce rainfall.[28]

Such ritual nudity may be explained in two different ways. On the one hand, it may have been designed to protect sacred and "divine" places and objects from contamination by human frailty. In that case, the practice would hang together with the common provision, in later times, that suppliants or pilgrims wear new or special raiment.[29] On the other hand, its purpose may have been to expose the human body more directly to the "aura" of the sacred and divine.

Yet a third explanation, however, is also possible, for the fact is that in some parts of the world shoes are removed as a gesture of respect to indicate loss of dignity before a superior, i.e., a curtailment of selfhood. Thus, in India, low-caste Hindus remove their shoes and turbans when passing through high-caste streets;[30] while it is recorded that in Mexico, everyone was required to put off his shoes in the presence of Montezuma, the Aztec king.[31]

Going unshod was a standard gesture of mourning, alike in the Semitic and the Classical worlds. When Yahweh bade the prophet Ezekiel not to mourn for his wife, he told him specifically to keep his shoes on;[32] and when David departed in mourning from Jerusalem, following the insurrection of Absalom, he went weeping and barefoot.[33] To this day, Jewish mourners doff their shoes or sit in felt slippers.[34] Syrian women go barefoot from the house where a death has occurred to the threshing floor where the funeral exercises take place;[35] while the Mandaeans of Iraq and Iran use the expression "unshod" (*bihifia*) to denote a state of mourning.[36] Similarly, in Greek tradition, the women who accompanied Demeter in her mourning for the abducted Persephone went barefoot.[37] Aphrodite mourned unshod for Adonis,[38] and Antinoe for Aetacon.[39] Likewise in Rome, the nobles who removed the ashes of Augustus walked barefoot,[40] and this was a common practice in funeral corteges.[41]

80   The three proofs of Moses' commission[1]   3:13—4:17

Before sending him on his mission, God supplies Moses with three signs of authentication: his staff turns into a serpent and then resumes its normal shape; his hand becomes leprous and then recovers; and he converts water to blood (Exod. 4:1–9).

All of these signs recur elsewhere in the Biblical saga. When Moses and Aaron first appear before Pharaoh, Aaron throws down his staff and it turns into a serpent.[2] When Miriam, the sister of Moses, objects to his taking an Ethiopian wife, she becomes a leper, but is subsequently allowed to recover.[3] And when Moses wishes initially to demonstrate God's power to Pharaoh, he turns the rivers of Egypt to blood.[4] We may take it, therefore, that the three tokens of authentication were drawn from the repertory of standard miracles familiar in the popular lore of the day. But there is, perhaps, more to the matter than this. It is a common feature of folktales all over the world that a hero has to qualify for his mission by performing a set of seemingly impossible *tasks*. He has, for instance, to find berries in winter, to wash black wool white, to skin a stone, to bind the waves of the sea, and so forth.[5] It may therefore be suggested that it was a threefold test of this kind that popular fancy originally associated with the selection and appointment of the Israelite leader. Subsequently, however, the real point of the story came to be forgotten, and the miraculous feats performed by Moses were represented as tokens of authentication graciously vouchsafed to him by Yahweh.

81   The rod of Moses

[The *rod of Moses* is the equivalent of the familiar magician's wand,[1] the primary purpose of which is to transmit its possessor's special "power" to the object upon which he desires to exercise it.[2] Such wands are abundantly attested in ancient literature; a few reresentative examples will suffice.

In the Old Testament itself, the angel who appears to Gideon touches the latter's sacrifice with the tip of his wand, and flame arises;[3] while the prophet Hosea makes reference to the pagan practice of consulting wands for oracles.[4]

In the Canaanite (Ugaritic) Epic of Keret, a witch expels the king's sickness by touching him with a wand.[5]

In Greek lore, Athene transforms Odysseus from beggar to prince by tapping him with a wand.[6] Hermes can overpower men's senses by touching them with a wand[7] said—in one version—to have been given to him by Apollo.[8] Circe changes Odysseus' companions to swine by touching them with her wand.[9] The soothsayer Teresias carries a wand;[10] and wands figure among the mantic paraphernalia of Cassandra.[11] They are mentioned also in late Greek magical prescriptions,[12] as also in Hindu texts.[13]

The feats accomplished by Moses' rod likewise belong to the common repertoire of folklore.[14] Thus, the dividing of the Sea of Reeds by the use of this instrument finds a parallel in a Kaffir legend which tells how a chieftain, fleeing from his enemies, caused the waters of Lake Tanganyika to part by rousing his staff over them.[15] A similar feat is attributed in Irish legend to a Christian saint.[16]

Equally familiar to students of folklore is the motif of obtaining water from a rock, or a spring from the earth, by striking either with a rod.[17] Rhea, wishing to procure water in which to bathe the newborn Zeus, struck the mountain with a rod, and a stream gushed forth.[18] Poseidon struck with his trident the place where he had lain with Amymone, daughter of Danaos, and this gave rise to the Fountain of Lerna.[19] Dionysus struck the earth near Pylos with his thysus, and the River Dionysios came into being.[20] Atalanta, suffering thirst while on a hunt, struck a rock near Zarax, and a spring, thereafter known as Kryphanta, welled up.[21]

The feat is attributed also to several Christian saints, e.g., to St. Gertrude (5th cent.) at Vaux-en-Dieulet;[22] to St. Fursy (c. 650) at Lagny-en-Brie; to St. Lupus at Châlons (7th cent.);[23] to St. Frimatus (1103) at Vitré, in Brittany;[24] to St. Francis of Paula (1416–1507) at a rock in Calabria;[25] to St. Usrus at Busscia;[26] to St. Pharoildis, at Bruay;[27] to St. James of Terentaise, at Puppini;[28] to St. Julian, first bishop of Mans;[29] and to St. Dunstan.[30]]

▲ With this story of the magical production of water from the rock we may compare also a legend told by the Bare'e-speaking Toradjas of Central Celebes.

They say that an ancient hero named Dori, the son of the first man Lasaeo, came on his travels with two slaves to a certain place, where he lodged for the night in a house. Now Dori was meanly clad, but his slaves wore fine clothes. So the people of the house took the slaves for noblemen, and their master they took for a slave. Therefore they gave Dori no water to wash his hands with, and no palm-wine to drink. Thereupon Dori went out and struck the rock with the butt end of his spear, making a hole in the rock, from which water gushed out. When Dori had washed his hands with the water, he struck another rock with his spear, and from the hole so made palm-wine flowed forth. Having drunk the wine, the hero closed up the hole; but the hole from which the water flowed may be seen to this day. After that the people perceived that Dori was a great man.[31]

Analogous too is a German legend which tells how a man obtained *wine* from a stem by striking it.[32] ▼

82   The incident at the inn   4:25–26

The whole point of this story is lost in the conventional English versions through faulty translation of Zipporah's words. In the original, these read, *You are a* ḥatan *of bloodshed,* and since the Hebrew word *ḥatan* normally means "bridegroom," they are usually rendered, *You are a bloody bridegroom,* though what that means nobody seems able to explain satisfactorily.[1] The fact is, however, that this is really an ancient tale, in which this crucial term was employed in a more primitive sense. What that sense was comes out from the fact that in Arabic, the cognate term *ḥatana* means "circumcise," and derivatives from it are then used by extension to denote "one related by ties of tribal circumstances."[2] What Zipporah did, therefore, with admirable presence of mind, was to forge *ad hoc* a bond of kinship with the mysterious stranger, whereby Moses would be rendered immune from assault!

Thus interpreted, her procedure finds striking illustration in the practice of the Australian aborigines whereby the blood of one newly circumcised is immediately applied to other members of the tribe in order to establish covenant with them.[3] Similarly too, when the Urabuna (in the central part of Australia) initiate a lad by the rite of circumcision, they touch the stomachs of his elder brothers with his severed foreskin.[4]

83   The death of Moses   [Deut. 34]

Moses dies on a mountain; so does Aaron.[1]

Among modern bedouin it is a common custom to bury distinguished persons on mountains, so that their spirits may look down upon the tribal camps.[2] So too the ancient Norsemen interred their dead on hills,[3] and in the Eddas the expression "to die into the hill" is used for burial in barrows.[4] The Comanches and Arapahos of North America likewise lay their dead to rest on mountains,[5] as do also the Caribs and Patagonians.[6]

There may, however, be more to the Biblical legend than this, for the fact is that in many parts of the world the belief obtains that at death men ascend a mountain, to be in converse with the gods.[7] An ancient Mesopotamian euphemism for sudden or violent death was "to reach one's mountain";[8] while among the inhabitants of the D'Entrecasteaux Group of New Guinea it is held to this day that the dead climb the spirit-mountain, Bwebeso.[9] In Tahiti, the abode of the departed is said to be on a mountain on the western side of Riautua;[10] and in Madagascar they go to a mountain in the north.[11] Similar ideas prevail in the Shortland Islands[12] and among the Dayaks of Borneo.[13] Bondei ghosts journey to Mt. Mlinga,[14] and Chinese folklore locates the realm of the dead on the Kuen-lun hills.[15] In Western Java, they ascend to the summit of Gunung Danka.[16] A common Slavonic notion is that they go up a glass hill;[17] while in the Scottish Highlands, the hills are said to be lit by a mysterious fire whenever a great man dies.[18]

Related to this is the idea that great national heroes lie in the mountains ready to return in the hour of their people's need.[19] The idea is most familiar to students of folklore from the case of Kaiser Friedrich Barbarossa of Prussia, who is said to be biding his time in the Kyffhauser Mountains,[20] but the legend is also told of such worthies as Merlin, Fionn, Bruce, King Marko, and Holger the Dane, and appears also in Armenian,[21] Iranian,[22] Indian,[23] and Korean folklore.[24] Here again, a notion submerged in the Biblical version rises to the surface in later popular lore, for the Samaritans indeed believe that Moses will return at the end of the present age to usher in the restoration of his people's fortune and the Kingdom of God on earth.[25]

The Exodus

84 The "finger of God" 8:19

When the plague of gnats (lice) fell upon the Egyptians, the magicians said to Pharaoh, This is the finger of God.

The more correct translation would be, *This is the finger of a god,* for the expression reproduces a common notion of Ancient Near Eastern folklore.[1] Alike in Egyptian itself[2] and in Akkadian,[3] plague or similar affliction was known popularly as "the hand of a god," while a Canaanite letter discovered at Ras Shamra-Ugarit speaks of "the hand(s) of the gods being here like death."[4] Among the Sumerians "Hand of God" was the name of a demon.[5]

It is often asserted that an analogous expression, "Finger of (the goddess) Asherah," occurs in a letter from Ta'anach, of the fifteenth century B.C., but this interpretation is due to a misreading of the cuneiform text, which speaks of the expert (*ummanu*), i.e., wizard, of Asherah, rather than of her finger (*ubânu*).[6]

In Luke 11:20, Jesus says, "It is by the finger of God that I cast out demons." A. Deissmann has connected this statement with our passage, and then also with a reference in Greek charms from Egypt to exorcizing demons "by the finger of the god."[7] But the latter surely refers to the well-known amuletic figure of Horus the Younger (Harpocrates), with his finger to his lips.[8] However, images of two fingers alone were indeed a not uncommon talisman in Egypt.[9]

85 The escorting angel 14:19–20

On their journey out of Egypt the Israelites are escorted by an "angel of the Lord" who goes in front of them.

Here again we have an element of popular lore, for the notion of such a guiding and guarding spirit can be illustrated from later Nabataean, Palmyrene, and Safaitic inscriptions, where mention is made of a deity named Shi'a

Alqum (ha-qum), "accompanier of the People," whose function was evidently to escort and protect caravans.[1]

Angel interposes mist

When the Egyptians were pressing hard upon the Israelites, the angel changed his position from vanguard to rearguard and interposed a cloud between the two hosts.

The Hittites believed likewise that armies were escorted by a god named Yarris who had the power of hiding warriors in moments of peril,[2] and in the Iliad, gods and goddesses throw a mist around their protégés to protect them from their foes in battle. Aphrodite thus shields Paris from attack by Menelaus;[3] Athene thus screens Achilles,[4] and Apollo Agenor.[5] Similarly, in more recent folklore, the Serbian *vîly, or* guardian spirit, is thought to screen heroes in combat by shrouding them in cloud or mist.[6]

▲ 86   The Passage through the Sea of Reeds   14:21–31

Finding the children of Israel useful in the capacity of bondsmen, Pharaoh long refused to let them depart; but at last his resolution was broken by a series of plagues and calamities which Moses, the great champion of Israel, called down with the divine assistance on the land and people of Egypt. So, turning their backs gladly on the country where they had endured oppression for so many years, the Israelites marched eastwards towards the Red Sea. But hardly were they gone when Pharaoh repented of having let them go, and pursued after them with a mighty host of chariots and horsemen to drag them back to the bondage from which they had just escaped. He came up with the long train of fugitives on the shore of the Red Sea. The Israelites were in a perilous situation. Behind them was the enemy and in front was the sea. Which way were they to turn? A contest between the helpless and unarmed multitude on the one side and the disciplined army on the other could only end in a massacre, and to plunge into the waves appeared to be certain death. However, Moses did not hesitate. At the bidding of God he stretched out his hand over the sea, and the waters parted, leaving a broad highway in their midst, on which the children of Israel marched dryshod to the farther shore, the billows standing as it were petrified into walls of translucent blue crystal on the right hand and on the left. The Egyptians followed them along the lane of yellow sand; but when the Israelites had reached the other bank, and their enemies were yet in the midst of the waters, Moses stretched out his hand once more over the sea, and at once the blue walls broke into sheets of curling foam, which rushing together with a thunderous roar overwhelmed the Egyptians beneath the waves; men and horses and chariots all sank like stones into the depths, not one of them escaped. Thus did the Lord deliver the Israelites and smite their enemies.[1]

There are well-authenticated instances of similar passages over which later generations have thrown a similar veil of mystery and romance. After narrating the march of his people through the Red Sea, which according to him opened a way for them miraculously on being struck by the rod of Moses, the Jewish historian Josephus compared an incident in the history of Alexander the Great. When it was God's will, he tells us, that the Persian Empire should fall before the invader, the Pamphylian Sea drew back and allowed Alexander and his host to march through its bed.[2] Nor was the Jewish historian singular in his opinion of the miraculous interposition of the divinity in favour of the Macedonian conqueror. Many Greek historians shared his view, and the Greek comic poet Menander alluded to the passage of Alexander through the sea in terms which a Jew might have applied to the passage of Israel through the Red Sea.[3] It is true that Arrian, the historian of Alexander the Great, so far diminishes the marvel as to explain the drying up of the sea by a sudden change of wind from south to north, but this change of wind itself he attributes to an act of Providence.[4] Now if we had only these vague reports of Alexander's exploit to go upon, they might have been dismissed by a sceptical historian as purely fabulous. Nevertheless we know from more sober and precise narratives that, stripped of the supernatural halo with which the lovers of the marvellous invested it, the feat was really performed. What happened was this. On his expedition against Darius and his host, Alexander had arrived with his army at Phaselis in Lycia. Here he had the choice of two routes by which to pursue his march eastward. Immediately to the north of the city the mountains, a branch of the great Taurus range, descended steeply to the sea, leaving at their foot a narrow strip of beach which, in calm weather or with a north wind blowing, was bare and passable by travellers, but which, with a south wind driving the waves on the shore, was deep under water. This was the direct road to Pamphylia. Another road lay through the mountains, but it was long, circuitous, and so steep that it went by the name of the Ladder. Alexander resolved to divide his forces, and sending a portion of them by the long road over the mountains he proceded himself with a detachment by the shore road. The decision was a bold one, for it chanced that the weather was stormy, and the waves, sweeping over the narrow beach, broke in foam against the foot of the cliffs. All day long the soldiers waded through the water up to their waists, but at evening they emerged, dripping and weary, on dry land at the farther end of the pass.[5] Such was the exploit which rumour exaggerated into a passage like that of Moses and the Israelites through the Red Sea. In his own letters the conqueror mentioned his march along the beach without, apparently, making any allusion to the dangers and difficulties by which it had been beset;[6] and a late historian affirms that the wind, providentially veering from south to north, rendered the march along the beach easy and rapid.[7] Yet it is difficult to suppose that in Alexander's adventurous career this particular feat should have attained so high a degree of renown if it had not been attended by an unusual measure of hardship and peril. We may acquiesce then in the romantic, yet probably true, tale of the hero and his soldiers wading waist-deep all day through the water, with an angry sea on the one side and the frowning cliffs above them on the other.

With this daring deed of the Macedonian king may be compared an exploit of the Romans in the second Carthaginian war. The centre of the Carthaginian power in Spain was the city of New Carthage, situated on a nearly landlocked bay and naturally defended by the sea on two sides and by a lagoon on the third. On his arrival in Spain as commander-in-chief of the Roman armies, Scipio the Elder resolved to take the enemy's capital by storm, but before delivering the assault he carefully reconnoitred the situation of the city. The lagoon, which protected it on the west, was connected with the sea by an artificial channel, through which the tide flowed and ebbed daily. From fishermen the Roman general learned that the lagoon was fordable at ebb-tide, being no deeper than a man's waist in some places and his knees in others. Having ascertained this, he laid his plans accordingly, and in a speech to the army publicly announced that the sea-god Neptune had appeared to him in a dream and promised to lend him such assistance in the attack as should be manifest to the whole army. The announcement, accompanied by a seasonable offer of golden crowns to those who should be the first to mount the walls, was received by the army with enthusiasm. Next morning, therefore, the storming parties, preceded by men with ladders, advanced with great spirit against the walls, the trumpets sounding the charge. The ladders were planted, the Romans swarmed up them, and engaged in hand-to-hand conflict with the defenders on the battlements. But though the assault was pressed with great gallantry, it failed. The ladders were overturned and the assailants overwhelmed under showers of beams and missiles of all kinds hurled on them from the top of the wall. So the Roman trumpets sounded the retire, and the survivors fell sullenly back. By this time the day was wearing on to noon, the hour when, as Scipio had learned from the fishermen, the tide would begin to ebb in the lagoon. In anticipation of the moment he stationed five hundred men with ladders on the edge of the lagoon, and ordered fresh troops, provided with more ladders than before, to renew the attack on the land side. Again, the trumpets sounded the charge, again the Romans advanced, planted the ladders, and swarmed up them. And now, while the whole attention of the besieged was engaged in repelling this fresh assault, the tide in the lagoon began to ebb, and, reinforced by a strong north wind, was soon running like a mill-race through the channel out to sea. Scipio gave the word: the five hundred men, preceded by the guides, plunged boldly into the flood, and struggled, splashing and floundering, through the water to the farther shore. The rest of the army watched their advance with enthusiasm, remembering the promise of Neptune to their general, and believing that the sea-god himself was opening a passage through the deep for the Roman arms and leading the storming-party in person. Fired with this belief they locked their shields together and rushed at the gates to hew them down with axes and cleavers. Meantime the five hundred had made their way through the lagoon to dry land, planted their ladders, and climbed the walls, which they found deserted, all the defenders being engaged in repelling the attack elsewhere. So, advancing unresisted through the streets, they opened the gates to their comrades, who were battering them from without. Thus the assailants obtained possession of the city, and the resistance of the defenders soon turned into a massacre.[8]

[The phenomenon has also been attested in more recent times. In 1495, for example, and again in 1645, a strong wind drove back the waters of the Rhône into the Lake of Geneva for a distance of about a quarter of a league. "It looked," says the record, "like a wall of water"—words strikingly reminiscent of those used in the Scriptural narrative (Exod. 14:22). "The inhabitants should go down on dry ground between the bridges and pass from one bank to the other." So too, in 1738 when the Russians were fighting the Turks, they were able to enter the Crimea at the Isthmus of Perekop only because a strong wind suddenly blew upon the waters of the Putrid Sea, at the northwest corner of the Sea of Azov, causing them to recede and permit passage. It is related also by an eyewitness that on one occasion the waters of Lake Menzaleh at the entrance to the Suez Canal were driven back by the east wind as much as seven miles![8a]]

The Wafipas, an African tribe on the shores of Lake Tanganyika, relate a story of one of their kings which bears some resemblance to the story of the passage of Israel through the Red Sea. Being threatened with death by his enemies the Watwakis and by some of his own tribe, who were hostile to him, the king fled before them, but his flight was arrested by the waters of the great lake. Then he sacrificed a sheep, dipped his staff in the blood of the victim, and struck the surface of the water with the blood-stained staff. The lake immediately opened a passage for him, and through it he escaped from his pursuers.[9] The Bayas of the French Congo, on the borders of the Cameroons, have a similar tradition. They say that in the old days they were unacquainted with the art of working iron, and sent to another tribe at a distance to learn the secret. Their messengers had to cross the river Kadei, and attempted to do so in a bark canoe, but the frail vessel capsized. So they had recourse to magic; the river, mastered by their spells, divided in two, of which one part flowed back to its source, so that the messengers were able to traverse its bed without wetting their feet.[10] ▼

87   The Song at the Sea   15

> *The crossing of the Sea of Reeds is related first in prose (Exod. 14);*
> *then in a rousing song (Exod. 15:1–17).*

The insertion of songs into prose narratives—as again in the case of Deborah's song of victory in the fifth chapter of the Book of Judges, and of the psalm supposedly sung by Jonah in the belly of the "great fish"—had a practical motive. In ancient times, as still among bedouin, the majority of people could not read. Traditional tales and sages were known to them principally through recitation, and the insertion at appropriate intervals of well-known songs in which all could join was a ready way of reliving tedium and of securing "audience participation," as well, perhaps of preventing strain on the reciter's voice. Such songs would have served also to mark logical pauses in the sequence of narratives, though they need not originally have had any connection with them.

This type of composition is known to students of folklore as the cante-fable, and is attested among peoples of widely different cultures.[1] Basuto folktales, for instance, usually include portions in verse, which are chanted;[2] while it is common practice among African Negroes, when they listen to a traditional tale, to intone certain passages in rhythm.[3] The Ainu of Japan follows the same pattern;[4] so do the Eskimos of North America.[5] Among modern Arabs, this is the regular way in which traditional romances are recited in public, and ancient Arabic sages are usually composed in a mixture of prose and verse.[6] The device is likewise not unknown to European folktales.[7] On the other hand, in parts of India the process is the other way about, prose being inserted into stories originally composed in verse.[8]

The song portrays the event in terms of traditional mythology: Yahweh repeats in a moment of history that which, according to time-honored myth, he did in primordial times.[9] The action of the east wind upon the waters is represented as the blast of his breath (v. 10; cf. ch. 14:21). He assumes the role of the ancient warrior-god (v. 3),[10] defeating the contumacious genius of the sea—the role played in the lore of Babylon by Marduk and in that of Canaan by Baal.[11] By virtue of his victory he acquires eternal kingship (v. 18), precisely as do Marduk[12] and Baal.[13] Like them too, he is installed in a new palace built by his own hands (v. 17),[14] and upreared in what is described as "the mountain of his inheritance (landed estate)"—the very term used in the Canaanite (Ugaritic) poem to characterize the site of Baal's new palace.[15]

The song employs pastoral metaphors, and is therefore the product of the later settled life, not of the earlier desert days. Yahweh guides his people like sheep (v. 13),[16] leads them as a shepherd leads his flock to water (v. 12),[17] and brings them, as sheep are brought into the fold at dusk,[18] into his "holy habitation," which, by a significant play on words, is characterized at the same time as his "pasture."[19]

87a Sweetening bitter waters   15:23–26

On their journey through the wilderness the Israelites come to a place named Marah (i.e., Bitter), where the waters are so bitter that they cannot be drunk. At Yahweh's indication, Moses throws a twig into them and they become sweet.

The incident is illustrated by an Indian practice of purifying marshy waters by rubbing the powder of a nut called *Strychnus potatorum* on the sides of vessels from which they are poured; this causes the impurities to sink to the bottom. In Egypt, bitter almonds are used to the same end, while in the sandy Landes of Bordeaux, where the water is often contaminated by albuminous matter, chips of oak are thrown into it. The tannin which these contain neutralizes the albumen and causes the coagulates to subside from the surface.[1]

In the same sense too, an ancient Greek tradition relates that turbid waters at the spring of Neda, on Mt. Lycaeus, were rendered limpid when a branch was thrown into them.[2]

88   Manna—the "Bread of Angels"   16:13–25

In the morning there was a layer of dew all over the camp, and when that layer of dew had lifted, behold, upon the face of the wilderness there was a fine flakelike thing, fine as hoarfrost on the ground. When the Israelites saw it, they said to one another, "It is—what [man]?" for they did not know what it was. But Moses said to them, "It is the food which Jehovah has given you to eat". . . . The Israelites called it manna [man]; it was like coriander seed, and the taste of it was like wafers made with honey.

(Cf. Num. 11:7–9: The manna was like coriander seed, and its appearance was like bdellium . . . and the taste of it was like the taste of cakes baked with oil. When the dew fell upon the camp at night, the manna fell with it.)

(a) It is now generally recognized that the mysterious substance which the Israelites called *manna* was probably the exudation of the three *Tamarix gallica mannifera*, which in fact grows in the Sinai Peninsula. This exudation is produced mainly through the action of insects, during a six- to ten-week period which reaches its high point in June.[1]

The phenomenon was known also to Greek and Latin writers, who likened the substance to dew.[2] It seems likewise to have been the substance which is described in the Scandinavian Edda[3] to have been shed like dew from the world-tree Yggdrasill, and which was called "honey-fall" (*hunâng fall*).[4]

(b) In Hebrew popular lore, this substance was thought to fall directly from heaven and to be the food of the celestial beings—which must have gone back, of course, to pre-Israelitic paganism. Thus, in Psalm 78:24–25 it is described as "the grain of heaven" and as "the food of angels," and it is similarly portrayed in Psalm 105:40 and in the apocryphal Wisdom of Solomon 16:20.

This too has interesting parallels in Classical belief. "Honeydew" is said by both Hesiod[5] and Aristotle[6] to come from heaven, while Columella declares explicitly that it springs "from the morning dew."[7] Similarly too, in the Indic Rig Veda,[8] honey (*madhu*, mead) is poured from the clouds; while in the Finnish Kalevala,[9] a bee is bidden fetch it from heaven.

W. H. Roscher has shown[10] that honeydew is the substance called by the Greeks *ambrosia* and *nectar* and held to be the food of the gods.[11] Conceived as something to eat, it was called ambrosia ("food of immortality"), while as a liquid it was known as nectar, though the two names tend to be used interchangeably.

(c) In *Wisdom of Solomon* 16:20, the curious detail is added that this "bread of angels" had "the virtue of every pleasant savour" and was "agreeable to every taste," and later Rabbinic legend elaborates this in the statement that manna had for every man the taste of that food which he most relished.[12] An interesting parallel to this occurs in the Celtic Curaig Imram[13] where the same is said of the faery food tasted by the companions of Mailduin on their voyage to the otherworld.

▲ 89   The ox that gores   21:28–32

In the Book of the Covenant, the oldest code of laws embodied in the Pentateuch, it is laid down that "if an ox gore a man or a woman, that they die, the ox shall be surely stoned, and his flesh shall not be eaten; but the owner of the ox shall be quit. But if the ox were wont to gore in time past, and it hath been testified to his owner, and he hath not kept him in, but that he hath killed a man or a woman; the ox shall be stoned, and his owner also shall be put to death."[1] In the much later Priestly Code the rule regulating the punishment of homicidal animals is stated more comprehensively as part of the general law of blood-revenge which was revealed by God to Noah after the great flood: "And surely your blood, the blood of your lives, will I require; at the hand of every beast will I require it; and at the hand of man, even at the hand of every man's brother, will I require the life of man. Whoso sheddeth man's blood, by man shall his blood be shed."[2]

The principle of blood-revenge has been carried out in the same rigorous manner by savage tribes; indeed some of them have pushed the principle of retaliation yet further by destroying even inanimate objects which have accidentally caused the death of human beings. For example, Kukis of Chittagong, in North-Eastern India, "like all savage people, are of a most vindictive disposition; blood must always be shed for blood; if a tiger even kills any of them, near a village, the whole tribe is up in arms, and goes in pursuit of the animal; when, if he is killed, the family of the deceased gives a feast of his flesh, in revenge of his having killed their relation. And should the tribe fail to destroy the tiger, in this first general pursuit of him, the family of the deceased must still continue the chace; for until they have killed either this, or some other tiger, and have given a feast of his flesh, they are in disgrace in the village, and not associated with by the rest of the inhabitants. In like manner, if a tiger destroys one of a hunting party, or of a party of warriors on an hostile excursion, neither the one nor the other (whatever their success may have been) can return to the village, without being disgraced, unless they kill the tiger. A more striking instance still of this revengeful spirit of retaliation is, that if a man should happen to be killed by an accidental fall from a tree, all his relations assemble, and cut it down; and however large it may be, they reduce it to chips, which they scatter in the winds, for having, as they say, been the cause of the death of their brother."[3]

In the Malay code of Malacca there is a section dealing with vicious buffaloes and cattle, and herein it is ordained that "if the animal be tied in the forest, in a place where people are not in the habit of passing, and there gore anybody to death, it shall be put to death."[4] Among the Bare'e-speaking Toradjas of Central Celebes "blood-revenge extends to animals: a buffalo that has killed a man must be put to death."[5] This is natural enough, for "the Toradja conceives an animal to differ from a man only in outward appearance. The animal cannot speak, because its beak or snout is different from the mouth of a man; the animal runs on all fours, because its hands (fore-paws) are different from human hands; but the inmost nature of the animal is the same as that of a man. If a crocodile kills somebody, the family of the victim may thereupon kill a crocodile, that is to say, the murderer or some member of his family; but if more crocodiles than men are killed, then the right of revenge reverts to the crocodiles, and they are sure to exercise their right on somebody or other. If a dog does not receive his share of the game, he will refuse next time to join in the hunt, because he feels himself aggrieved. The Toradja is much more sensible than we are of the rights of animals; in particular he deems it highly dangerous to make fun of a beast. He would utter a lively protest and predict heavy storms and floods of rain if, for instance, he saw anybody dress up an ape in human clothes. And nobody can laugh at a cat or dog with impunity."[6] Among the Bogos, a tribe on the northern outskirts of Abyssinia, a bull, or a cow, or any head of cattle that kills a human being is put to death.[7]

At the entrance of a Bayaka village, in the valley of the Congo, Torday saw a roughly constructed gallows, on which hung a dead dog. He learned that as a notorious thief, who had been in the habit of making predatory raids among the fowls, the animal had been strung up to serve as a public example.[8]

Among the Arabs of Arabia Petraea, when an animal has killed a man, its owner must drive it away, crying after it "Scabby, scabby!" He may never afterwards recover possession of the beast, under pain of being compelled to pay the bloodwit for the homicide committed by the brute. Should the death have been caused by a sheep or a goat in a flock, as by sending a heavy stone hurtling down a steep slope, but the particular animal which set the stone rolling be unknown, then the whole flock must be driven away with the cry, "Away from us, ye scabby ones!"[9]

Similar principles of retributive justice were recognized in antiquity by other nations than the Israelites. In the *Avesta,* the ancient lawbook of the Iranians, it is laid down that if "the mad dog, or the dog that bites without barking, smite a sheep or wound a man, the dog shall pay for it as for wilful murder. If the dog shall smite a sheep or wound a man, they shall cut off his right ear. If he shall smite another sheep or wound another man, they shall cut off his left ear. If he shall smite a third sheep or wound a third man, they shall cut off his right foot. If he shall smite a fourth sheep or wound a fourth man, they shall cut off his left foot. If he shall for the fifth time smite a sheep or wound a man, they shall cut off his tail. Therefore they shall tie him to the post; by the two sides of the collar they shall tie him. If they shall not do so, and the mad dog, or the dog that bites without barking, smite a sheep or wound a man, he shall pay for it as for wilful murder."[10] It will be generally admitted that in this enactment the old Persian lawgiver treats a worrying dog with great forbearance; for he gives him no less than five distinct chances of reforming his character before he exacts from the irreclaimable culprit the extreme penalty of the law.

At Athens, the very heart of ancient civilization in its finest efflorescence, there was a court specially set apart for the trial of animals and of lifeless objects which had injured or killed human beings. The court sat in the town-hall (*prytaneum*), and the judges were no less than the titular king of all Attica and the four titular kings of the separate Attic tribes. As the town-hall was in all probability the oldest political centre in Athens, if we except the fortress of the Acropolis, whose precipitous crags and frowning battlements rose immediately behind the law-court, and as the titular tribal kings represented the old tribal kings who bore sway for ages before the inhabitants of Attica overthrew the monarchical and adopted the republican form of government, we are justified in assuming that the court held in this venerable building, and presided over by these august judges, was of extreme antiquity; and the conclusion is confirmed by the nature of the cases which here came up for judgment, since to find complete parallels to them we have had to go to the rude justice of savage tribes in the wilds of India, Africa, and Celebes. The offenders who were here placed at the bar were not men and women, but animals and implements or missiles of stone, wood, or iron which had fallen upon and cracked somebody's crown, when the hand which had hurled them was unknown.[11] To ridicule the Athenian passion for sitting on juries, the comic poet Aristophanes has described in one of his plays a crazy old juryman trying a dog, with all legal formalities, for stealing and eating a cheese.[12] Perhaps the idea of the famous scene, which was copied by Racine in his only comedy, *Les Plaideurs,* may have occurred to the Athenian poet as he whiled away an idle hour among the spectators in the court-house, watching with suppressed amusement the trial of a canine, bovine, or asinine prisoner at the bar charged with maliciously and feloniously biting, goring, kicking, or otherwise assaulting a burgess of Athens.

Strangely enough the great philosopher of idealism, Plato himself, cast the mantle of his authority over these quaint relics of a barbarous jurisprudence by proposing to incorporate them in the laws of that ideal state which he projected towards the end of his life. Yet it must be confessed that, when he came to compose *The Laws,* the tremulous hand of the aged artist had lost much of its cunning, and that, large as is the canvas on which his latest picture is painted, its colours pale beside the visionary glories of *The Republic.* Few books bear more visibly impressed upon them the traces of faded imaginative splendour and of a genius declined into the vale of years. In this his latest work the sun of Plato shines dimly through the clouds that have gathered thick about its setting. The passage, in which the philosopher proposed to establish a legal procedure modelled on that of the Athenian town-hall, runs as follows: "If a beast of burden or any other animal shall kill any one, except it be while the animal is competing in one of the public games, the relations of the deceased shall prosecute the animal for murder; the judges shall be such overseers of the public lands as the kinsman of the deceased may appoint; and the animal, if found guilty, shall be put to death and cast beyond the boundaries of the country. But if any lifeless object, with the exception of a thunderbolt or any such missile hurled by the hand of God, shall deprive a man of life either by falling on him or through the man's falling on it, the next of kin to the deceased shall, making expiation for himself and all his kin, appoint his nearest neighbour as judge; and the thing, if found guilty, shall be cast beyond the boundaries, as hath been provided in the case of the animals."[13]

Nor were animals at Rome always exempted from the last severity of the law. An ancient statute or custom, which tradition ascribed to the royal legislator and reformer Numa, directed that if any man ploughed up a boundary stone, not only he himself but the oxen which had aided and abetted him in the commission of the sacrilege should be sacred to the God of Boundaries;[14] in other words, both the man and his beasts were placed outside the pale of the law, and anybody might slay them with impunity.[15]

Such ideas and the practices based on them have not been limited to savage tribes and the civilized peoples of pagan antiquity. On the continent of Europe down to comparatively recent times the lower animals were in all respects considered amenable to the laws. Domestic animals were tried in the common criminal courts, and their punishment on conviction was death; wild animals fell under the jurisdiction of the ecclesiastical courts, and the penalty they suffered was banishment or death by exorcism and excommunication. Nor was that penalty by any means a light one, if it be true that St. Patrick exorcized the reptiles of Ireland into the sea or turned them into stones,[16] and that St. Bernard, by excommunicating the flies that buzzed about him, laid them all out dead on the floor of the church.[17] The prerogative of trying domestic animals was built, as on a rock, upon the Hebrew law in the Book of the Covenant. In every case advocates were assigned to defend the animals, and the whole proceedings, trial, sentence, and execution, were carried out with the strictest regard for the forms of justice and the majesty of the law. The researches of French antiquaries have brought to light the records of ninety-two processes which were tried in French courts from the twelfth to the eighteenth century. The last victim to suffer in that country was a cow, which underwent the extreme penalty of the law in the year of our Lord one thousand seven hundred and forty. On the other hand, the title of the ecclesiastical authorities to exercise jurisdiction over wild animals and vermin, such as rats, locusts, caterpillars, and the like, was not altogether, at least at first sight, so perfectly clear and unambiguous on Scriptural grounds, and it had accordingly to be deduced from Holy Writ by a chain of reasoning in which the following appear to have formed the most adamantine links. As God cursed the serpent for beguiling Eve; as David cursed Mount Gilboa on account of the deaths of Saul and Jonathan; and as our Saviour cursed the fig-tree for not bearing figs in the off season; so it clearly follows that the Church has full power and authority to exorcize, excommunicate, anathematize, execrate, curse, and damn the whole animate and inanimate creation without any exception whatsoever. It is true that some learned canonists, puffed up with the conceit of mere human learning and of philosophy falsely so called, presumed to cavil at a line of argument which to plain men must appear irrefragable. They alleged that authority to try and punish offences implies a contract, pact, or stipulation between the supreme power which administers the law and the subjects which submit to it, that the lower animals, being devoid of intelligence, had never entered into any such contract, pact, or stipulation, and that consequently they could not legally be punished for acts which they had committed in ignorance of the law. They urged, further, that the Church could not with any show of justice ban those creatures which she refused to baptize; and they laid great stress on the precedent furnished by the Archangel Michael, who in contending with Satan for possession of the body of Moses, did not bring any railing accusation against the Old Serpent, but left it to the Lord to rebuke him. However, such quibbles and chicane, savouring strongly of rationalism, were of no avail against the solid strength of Scriptural authority and traditional usage on which the Church rested her jurisdiction. The mode in which she exercised it was generally as follows.

When the inhabitants of a district suffered from the incursions or the excessive exuberance of noxious animals or insects, they laid a complaint against the said animals or insects in the proper ecclesiastical court, and the court appointed experts to survey and report upon the damage that had been wrought. An advocate was next appointed to defend the animals and show cause why they should not be summoned. They were then cited three several times, and not appearing to answer for themselves, judgment was given against them by default. The court after that served a notice on the animals, warning them to leave the district within a specified time under pain of adjuration; and if they did not take their departure on or before the date appointed, the exorcism was solemnly pronounced. However, the courts seem to have been extremely reluctant to push matters to extremity by proclaiming the ban, and they resorted to every shift and expedient for evading or at least deferring the painful necessity. The motive for this long delay in launching the ecclesiastical thunder may have been a tender regard for the feelings of the creatures who were to be blasted by it; though some sceptics pretended that the real reason was a fear lest the animals should pay no heed to the interdict, and, instead of withering away after the anathema, should rather be fruitful and multiply under it, as was alleged to have happened in some cases. That such unnatural multiplication of vermin under excommunication had actually taken place the advocates of the ecclesiastical courts were not prepared to deny, but they attributed it, with every show of reason, to the wiles of the Tempter, who, as we know from the case of Job, is permitted to perambulate the earth to the great annoyance and distress of mankind.

Nor again, could the curse be reasonably expected to operate for the benefit of parishioners whose tithes were in arrear. Hence one of the lights of the law on this subject laid it down as a first principle that the best way of driving off locusts is to pay tithes, and he supported this salutary doctrine by the high authority of the prophet Malachi,[18] who represents the deity as remonstrating in the strongest terms with the Israelites on their delay in the payment of his tithes, painting in the most alluring colours the blessings which he would shower down on them, if only they would pay up, and pledging his word that, on receipt of the arrears, he would destroy the locusts that were devouring the crops. The urgency of this appeal to the pockets as well as to the piety of his worshippers is suggestive of the low ebb to which the temple funds were reduced in the days of the prophet. His stirring exhortation may have furnished the text of eloquent sermons preached under similar circumstances from many a pulpit in the Middle Ages.[19]

If Satan thus afflicted animals in the Old World, it could not reasonably be expected that he would spare them in the New. Accordingly we read without surprise that in New England "a dog was strangely afflicted at Salem, upon which those who had the spectral sight declared that a brother of the justices afflicted the poor animal, by riding upon it invisibly. The man made his escape, but the dog was very unjustly hanged. Another dog was accused of afflicting others, who fell into fits the moment it looked upon them, and it also was killed."[20]

In Savoy it is said that animals sometimes appeared in the witness-box as well as in the dock, their testimony being legally valid in certain well-defined cases. If a man's house was broken into between sunset and sunrise, and the owner killed the intruder, the act was considered a justifiable homicide. But it was deemed just possible that a wicked man, who lived all alone, might decoy another into spending the evening with him, and then, after murdering him, might give it out that his victim was a burglar, whom he had slain in self-defence. To guard against this contingency, and to ensure the conviction of the murderer, the law sagaciously provided that when anybody was killed under such circumstances, the solitary householder should not be held innocent, unless he produced a dog, cat, or cock, an inmate of his house, which had witnessed the homicide and could from personal knowledge attest the innocence of its master. The householder was compelled to make his declaration of innocence before the animal, and if the beast or bird did not contradict him, he was considered to be guiltless, the law taking it for granted that the Deity would directly interpose and open the mouth of the cat, dog, or cock, just as he once opened the mouth of Balaam's ass, rather than allow a murderer to escape from justice.[21]

In modern Europe, as in ancient Greece, it would seem that even inanimate objects have sometimes been punished for their misdeeds. After the revocation of the edict of Nantes, in 1685, the Protestant chapel at La Rochelle was condemned to be demolished, but the bell, perhaps out of regard for its value, was spared. However, to expiate the crime of having rung heretics to prayers, it was sentenced to be first whipped, and then buried and disinterred, by way of symbolizing its new birth at passing into Catholic hands. Thereafter it was catechized, and obliged to recant and promise that it would never again relapse into sin. Having made this ample and honourable amends, the bell was reconciled, baptized, and given, or rather sold, to the parish of St. Bartholomew. But when the governor sent in the bill for the bell to the parish authorities, they declined to settle it, alleging that the bell, as a recent convert to Catholicism, desired to take advantage of a law lately passed by the king, which allowed all new converts a delay of three years in paying their debts.[22]

In English law a relic of the same ancient mode of thought survived till near the middle of the nineteenth century in the doctrine and practice of deodand.[23] It was a rule of the common law that not only a beast that killed a man, but any inanimate object that caused his death, such as a cart-wheel which ran over him, or a tree that fell upon him, was *deodand* or given to God, in consequence of which it was forfeited to the king and sold for the benefit of the poor. Hence in all indictments for homicide the instrument of death used to be valued by the grand jury, in order that its money value might be made over to the king or his grantee for pious uses. Thus in practice all deodands came to be looked on as mere forfeitures to the king. Regarded in that light they were very unpopular, and in later times the juries, with the connivance of the judges, used to mitigate the forfeitures by finding only some trifling thing, or part of a thing, to have been the occasion of the death. It was not till the year 1846 that this curious survival of primitive barbarism was finally abolished by statute.

[Provisions concerning "the ox that gores" are to be found also in earlier Mesopotamian codes of law.[23a] Thus, in the *Code of Eshnunna* (18th cent. B.C.), it is laid down that if one man's ox gores another's to death, the price of both is to be divided equally between their respective owners. (This accords with the Hebrew law, Exod. 21:35.) On the other hand, if an ox which is known to be a habitual gorer causes a man's death after its owner has been warned but has neglected to take precautions, that owner must pay an indemnity of one-third of a mina of silver, or, if the victim be a slave, of fifteen shekels. The same provision is made also in case of death caused by the bite of a rabied dog whose owner has been warned without avail.[23b]—In the *Code of Hammurapi* (1726 B.C.), approximately the same rule is prescribed in the case of death from a habitual gorer: the forewarned but negligent owner must pay an indemnity of one-half—or, if the victim be a slave, one-third—of a mina of silver. A preceding clause lays down, however, that if an ox gore a man to death while it is walking along a road, no liability is incurred, presumably because its owner would then have been exercising all reasonable care and not just letting it run loose.[23c]

It will be observed that in neither of these earlier systems is there any question of *punishing* the offending beast. This, therefore, puts a question mark against Frazer's suggestion that the Hebrew law is a relic of ancient usage embodying that principle. If he is right, the Hebrew rule would have been a peculiar atavistic survival of what had in fact been discarded centuries before in the sister systems.—It should be observed also that while, in the Hebrew legislation as elsewhere, stoning was indeed a method of executing criminals,[23d] in this case it may well have served a purely utilitarian purpose: obviously, one could not risk getting sufficiently close to a habitual gorer as to be able to dispatch it in the normal way by slitting its throat! The further provision against eating its flesh would then be nothing other than the normal Hebrew prohibition against eating of any animal that had not actually been slaughtered.] ▼

▲ 90   **Not to seethe a kid in its mother's milk**   23:19

A modern reader is naturally startled when among the solemn commandments professedly given by God to Israel he finds the precept, "Thou shalt not seethe a kid in its mother's milk." [This commandment occurs three times in the Pentateuch,[1] and since, in two of these instances, it is expressly connected with the presentation of firstfruits,] it has been supposed that it may have been directed originally against some pagan rite or practise which the lawgiver reprobated and desired to suppress.[2] [A measure of support for this theory is derived from the fact that in a Canaanite text of the thirteenth century B.C., the act of seething a kid in milk is indeed mentioned as part of a ritual celebration;[2a]] while a member of the Jewish Karaite sect, writing at a far later date, records that "there was a custom among the ancient heathen, who, when they had gathered all the crops, used to boil a kid in its mother's milk, and then, as a magical rite, sprinkle the milk on trees, fields, gardens, and orchards, believing that in this way they would render them more fruitful the following year."[3] So far as this explanation assumes a superstition to lie at the root of the prohibition, it may well be correct; and accordingly it may be worth while to inquire whether analogous prohibitions, with the reasons for them, can be discovered among rude pastoral tribes in modern times, for on the face of it the rule is likely to be observed rather by people who depend on their flocks and herds than by such as subsist on the produce of their fields and gardens.

Now, among pastoral tribes in Africa at the present day there appears to be a widespread and deeply rooted aversion to boil the milk of their cattle, the aversion being founded on a belief that a cow whose milk has been boiled will yield no more milk, and that the animal may even die of the injury thereby done to it. For example, the milk and butter of cows form a large part of the diet of the Moslem natives of Sierra Leone and the neighbourhood; but "they never boil the milk, for fear of causing the cow to become dry, nor will they sell milk to any one who should practise it. The Bulloms entertain a similar prejudice respecting oranges, and will not sell them to those who throw the skins into the fire, 'lest it occasion the unripe fruit to fall off.' "[4] Thus it appears that with these people the objection to boil milk is based on the principle of sympathetic magic. Even after the milk has been drawn from the cow it is supposed to remain in such vital connexion with the animal that any injury done to the milk will be sympathetically felt by the cow. Hence to boil the milk in a pot is like boiling it in the cow's udders; it is to dry up the fluid at its source. This explanation is confirmed by the beliefs of the Moslems of Morocco, though with them the prohibition to boil a cow's milk is limited to a certain time after the birth of the calf. They think that "if milk boils over into the fire the cow will have a diseased udder, or it will give no milk, or its milk will be poor in cream; and if biestings happen to fall into the fire, the cow or the calf will probably die. Among the Ait Wäryâgäl the biestings must not be boiled after the third day and until forty days have passed after the birth of the calf; if they were boiled during this period, the calf would die or the milk of the cow would give only a small quantity of butter."[5] Here the prohibition to boil milk is not absolute but is limited to a certain time after the birth of the calf, during which the cow may be thought to stand in a closer relation of sympathy than ever afterwards both to her calf and to her milk. The limitation of the rule is therefore significant and rather confirms than invalidates the explanation of the prohibition here suggested. A further confirmation is supplied by the superstition as to the effect on the cow of allowing its milk to fall into the fire; if such an accident should happen at ordinary times, the cow or its milk is believed to suffer, but if it should happen shortly after the birth of its calf, when the thick curdy milk bears the special English name of biestings, the cow or the calf is expected to die. Clearly the notion is that if at such a critical time the biestings were to fall into the fire, it is much the same thing as if the cow or the calf were to fall into the fire and to be burnt to death. So close is the sympathetic bond then supposed to be between the cow, her calf, and her milk.

The train of thought may be illustrated by a parallel superstition of the Toradjas in Central Celebes. These people make much use of palm-wine, and the lees of the wine form an excellent yeast in the baking of bread. But some Toradjas refuse to part with the lees of the wine for that purpose to Europeans, because they fear that the palm-tree from which the wine was extracted would soon yield no more wine and would dry up, if the lees were brought into contact with the heat of the fire in the process of baking.[6] This reluctance to subject the lees of palm-wine to the heat of fire lest the palm-tree from which the wine was drawn should thereby be desiccated, is exactly parallel to the reluctance of African tribes to subject milk to the heat of fire lest the cow from which the milk was extracted should dry up or actually perish.

The objection to boil milk for fear of injuring the cows is shared by pastoral tribes of Central and Eastern Africa. When Speke and Grant were on their memorable journey from Zanzibar to the source of the Nile, they passed through the district of Ukuni, which lies to the south of the Victoria Nyanza. The king of the country lived at the village of Nunda and "owned three hundred milch cows, yet every day there was a difficulty about purchasing milk, and we were obliged to boil it that it might keep, for fear we should have none the following day. This practice the natives objected to, saying, 'The cows will stop their milk if you do so.' "[7] Similarly Speke tells us that he received milk from some Wahuma (Bahima) women whom he had treated for ophthalmia, but he adds, "The milk, however, I could not boil excepting in secrecy, else they would have stopped their donations on the plea that this process would be an incantation or bewitchment, from which their cattle would fall sick and dry up."[8]

Among the Masai of East Africa, who are, or used to be, a purely pastoral tribe depending for their sustenance on their herds of cattle, to boil milk "is a heinous offence, and would be accounted a sufficient reason for massacring a caravan. It is believed that the cattle would cease to give milk."[9] Similarly the Baganda, of Central Africa, believed that to boil milk would cause the cow's milk to cease, and among them no one was ever normally permitted to boil milk.[10]

Among the Bahima or Banyankole, a pastoral tribe of Central Africa, both the rule and the exception are similar. "Milk must not be boiled for food, as the boiling would endanger the health of the herd and might cause some of the cows to die. For ceremonial use it is boiled when the umbilical cord falls from a calf, and the milk which has been sacred becomes common. Milk from any cow that has newly calved is taboo for several days, until the umbilical cord falls from the calf; during this time some member of the family is set apart to drink the milk, but he must then be careful to touch no milk from any other cow."[11] So, too, among the Thonga, a Bantu tribe of South-Eastern Africa, "the milk of the first week after a cow has calved is taboo. It must not be mixed with other cows' milk, because the umbilical cord of the calf has not yet fallen. It can, however, be boiled and consumed by children as they do not count! After that milk is never boiled: not that there is any taboo to fear, but it is not customary. Natives do not give any clear reason for these milk taboos."[12]

To return to the Bahima of Central Africa, they even say that "if a European puts his milk into tea it will kill the cow which gave the milk."[13] The same prohibition to boil milk is observed, probably for the same reason, by the Southern Gallas of the same region,[14] the Nandi of British East Africa,[15] and the Wagogo, the Wamegi, and the Wahumba, three tribes of what till lately was German East Africa.[16] And among the tribes of the Anglo-Egyptian Sudan "the majority of the Hadendoa will not cook milk, and in this the Artega and the Ashraf resemble them."[17]

Relics of a similar belief in a sympathetic relation between a cow and the milk that has been drawn from her are reported to exist among some of the more backward peoples of Europe down to the present time. Among the Esthonians, when the first fresh milk of a cow after calving is to be boiled, a silver ring and a small saucer are laid under the kettle before the milk is poured into it. This is done "in order that the cow's udder may remain healthy, and that the milk may not be bad." Further, the Esthonians believe that "if, in boiling, the milk boils over into the fire, the cow's dugs will be diseased."[18] Bulgarian peasants in like manner think that "when the milk, in boiling, runs over into the fire, the cow's supply of milk is diminished and may even cease entirely."[19] In these latter cases, though no scruple seems to be felt about boiling milk, there is a strong objection to burning it by letting it fall into the fire, because the burning of the milk is supposed to harm the cow from which the milk was extracted, either by injuring her dugs or by checking the flow of her milk. A like train of thought may explain the Eskimo rule that no water should be boiled inside a house during the salmon fishery, because "it is bad for the fishery."[20]

A similar fear of tampering with the principal source of subsistence may well have dictated the old Hebrew commandment, "Thou shalt not seethe a kid in its mother's milk." On this theory an objection will be felt to seething or boiling a kid in any milk, because the she-goat from which the milk had been drawn would be injured by the process, whether she was the dam of the boiled kid or not. The reason why the mother's milk is specially mentioned may have been either because as a matter of convenience the mother's milk was more likely to be used than any other for that purpose, or because the injury to the she-goat in such a case was deemed to be even more certain than in any other. For being linked to the boiling pot by a double bond of sympathy, since the kid, as well as the milk, had come from her bowels, the mother goat was twice as likely as any other goat to lose her milk or to be killed outright by the heat and ebullition.

Again it is a rule with many cattle-keeping tribes of Africa that milk may not be drunk by women during menstruation, and in every case the motive for the prohibition appears to be a fear lest, by virtue of sympathetic magic, the women should exert a baneful influence on the cows from which the milk was extracted. Thus with regard to the tribes of the Anglo-Egyptian Sudan we are told that "no menstruous woman drinks milk lest the animal from which it was drawn should suffer, and the Bedawib say that any infringement of this rule would render sterile both the woman and the animal from which the milk was taken; nor may a menstruous woman drink *semn* (butter)."[21] Among the Banyoro of Central Africa "during menstruation the wives of wealthy cattle owners were given milk to drink from old cows which were not expected to have calves again; wives of men with only a limited number of cows were prohibited from drinking milk at all and had to live on vegetable food during the time of their indisposition, because their condition was considered harmful to the cows, should they drink milk. After living on a vegetable diet a woman fasted at least twelve hours before she ventured to drink milk again." Moreover, all the time of her monthly period a woman took care not to touch any milk-vessels.[22] The milk of the old cow, on which a rich woman at such seasons was allowed to subsist, had to be kept separate from the common stock of milk and reserved for the patient alone.[23] Among the Bahima of the same region the customs are similar. A menstruous woman may neither drink milk nor handle the milk-vessels; she eats vegetables and drinks beer all the time of her sickness, unless her husband happens to be a rich man, who may give her the milk of an old cow that is past the age of bearing. "Should a woman continue to drink milk during her indisposition it is thought she would injure the cows, especially their generative powers."[24] So, too, at a Bahima girl's first menstruation her father provides her with milk from an old cow, and she may not drink the milk of other cows or handle any milk-vessels for fear of thereby harming the cattle. The condition attached by the Banyoro and Bahima to the drinking of milk by menstruous women is significant; the cow from which the milk is drawn must be past the age of bearing a calf, and as she will soon lose her milk in any case, it does not matter much if she loses it a little sooner through the pollution of her milk by the menstruous woman. Among the Baganda, also, no menstruous woman

might come into contact with any milk-vessel or drink milk till she had recovered from her sickness.[25] Though the reason for the prohibition is not
mentioned, we may safely assume that it was the same belief in the noxious
influence which women at such times are thought to exercise on milch cows.

Among the Kafir tribes of South Africa in like manner milk is forbidden to
women at menstruation; should they drink it the people believe that the cattle
would die.[26] Not only a Kafir girl at her first menstruation but the maidens
who wait on her are forbidden to drink milk, lest the cattle should die; the
period of seclusion and taboo to which the damsels must submit on this occasion may last from one to two weeks.[27] Among the Thonga, about Delagoa
Bay, not only is a menstruous woman forbidden to drink the milk of cows,
she may not even approach the cattle kraal or look at the animals.[28] If a
Kafir woman infringes the rule by drinking milk during her monthly period,
her husband may be fined from one to three head of cattle, which are paid to
the chief. Formerly this time of abstinence from milk lasted for seven or eight
days a month.[29] Further, among the Kafirs menstruous women are forbidden
to cross those parts of the kraal which are frequented by the cattle; for if a
drop of their blood were to fall on the path, "any oxen passing over it would
run great risk of dying from disease." Hence women have to make circuitous
paths from one hut to another, going round the back of the huts in order to
avoid the forbidden ground. The tracks which they use may be seen at every
kraal. But there is no such restriction on the walks of women who are past
child-bearing, because they have ceased to be a source of danger.[30] Among
the Kaniyans of Cochin, in Southern India, a woman at menstruation may
neither drink milk nor milk a cow.[31]

The disabilities thus imposed on women at menstruation are perhaps dictated by a fear lest the cows whose milk they drink should yield milk mingled
with blood. Such a fear is widespread among the pastoral tribes of Central
Africa.[32] The same fear may explain the Zulu custom which forbids a wounded
man to drink milk until he has performed a certain ceremony.[33] Similarly
among the Nandi of British East Africa persons who have been wounded or
are suffering from boils or ulcers may not drink fresh milk,[34] probably from
a like regard for the welfare of the herd. This fear of injuring the cows through
the infection of blood may perhaps also explain a Bechuana custom of removing all wounded persons to a distance from their towns and villages.[35]

Women in childbed and for some time after it are believed by many savages
to be a source of dangerous infection, on which account it is customary to
isolate them like lepers from the rest of the community.[36] Hence it is not
surprising to find that among the Thonga a woman may not drink any milk
from the birth of her child till the infant has been formally presented to the
moon, which takes place usually in the third month after her delivery. Afterwards she is allowed to drink only the milk of cows which have calved many
times.[37] Among the Banyoro "a woman at childbirth may drink milk, but, if

the child is a boy, she is given the milk from a cow that has lost her calf; whereas, if the child is a girl, she is free to drink the milk from any cow."[38] The restriction thus imposed on a woman who has given birth to a male child points to a fear that she might injure ordinary cows if she were suffered to drink their milk. The same fear is apparently entertained in a high degree by the Nandi, whenever a woman has given birth to twins. For among them "the birth of twins is looked upon as an inauspicious event, and the mother is considered unclean for the rest of her life. She is given her own cow and may not touch the milk or blood of any other animal. She may enter nobody's house until she has sprinkled a calabash full of water on the ground, and she may never cross the threshold of a cattle kraal again."[39] If a mother of twins even approaches the cattle-pen, the Nandi believe that the animals will die.[40] The Suk, another tribe of British East Africa, seem to entertain a like dread of pregnant women, for among them a woman during her pregnancy lives on the milk of a cow set apart for her use. The animal must never have suffered from any sickness, and no one else may drink its milk at the same time.[41] Banyoro herdsmen believe that the entrance of a nursing mother into their houses or kraals is in some way harmful to the cows, though in what the harm is supposed to consist has not been ascertained.[42] Perhaps the notion may be that the milk in the woman's breasts is so much milk abstracted from the udders of the cows.

The pollution of death is also with some people a bar to the drinking of milk. Thus, in the Rowadjeh and Djaafere tribes of Arabs, near Esne in Egypt, "if any person of the family die, the women stain their hands and feet blue with indigo; which demonstration of their grief they suffer to remain for eight days, all that time abstaining from milk, and not allowing any vessel containing it to be brought into the house; for they say that the whiteness of the milk but ill accords with the sable gloom of their minds."[43] Among the Dinka the near relatives of a dead man may not touch milk during the first few days after the death, that is, during the time that they sleep near the grave.[44] With the Banyoro of Central Africa mourning lasted from two to six months, and all that time the mourners were forbidden to drink milk, the relatives and friends of the deceased meanwhile providing them with oxen to eat and beer to drink.[45] Some of the tribes of British East Africa expose their dead to be devoured by hyenas, and among them the persons who have handled the corpse and carried it out to its last resting-place, there to await the wild beasts, are subject to various taboos; in particular they are forbidden to drink milk. For example, among the Nandi the men who have discharged this office bathe in a river, anoint their bodies with fat, partially shave their heads, and live in the hut of the deceased for four days, during which time they may not be seen by a boy or a female. Further, they may not touch food with their hands, but must eat with the help of a potsherd or chip of a gourd, and they may not drink milk.[46] Among the Akikuyu of the same region the relative who has exposed a corpse returns to the house of the deceased, but he may not enter the village by the gate; he must break a way for himself through the village fence. The reason for this singular mode of entrance is not mentioned, but we may conjecture that the motive for adopting it is a wish to throw the ghost off the scent, who might pursue his relative back to the house through the familiar gateway, but is brought short up at the hole in the fence. Having reached the house, the man who has discharged the last duty to the dead must live alone in it for eight days. Food is set down for him by his kinsfolk in front of the door. It consists exclusively of vegetables, for flesh and especially milk he is forbidden to partake of. When eight days have passed, an old woman comes and shaves the hair of his head, for which service she receives a goat. After that he breaks out through the village fence, probably with the fear of the ghost still before his eyes or behind his back, and betakes himself to the elders and medicine-men, who are assembled outside of the village. They sacrifice a goat and besmear him from head to foot with the contents of the animal's stomach. A medicine-man gives him a particular beverage to drink, and having quaffed it the man is clean once more; he may now enter the village in the usual way by the gate, and he is again free to drink milk.[47] When a death has taken place in a Zulu village, no milk is drunk nor are the cattle allowed to be milked on that day.[48] And with regard to the Kafirs of South Africa in general we are told that after a death "the people in the kraal are all unclean. They may not drink milk, nor may they transact any business with other kraals, until the doctor has cleansed them. Those who touched the dead body are specially unclean, and so is every implement which was used to make the grave with, or the dead body touched. Those who touched the dead body, or the dead man's things, have to wash in running water. A doctor is called in, and he offers a sacrifice to cleanse the cows, the milk, and the people; yet for several months the people are not allowed to sell any oxen. The doctor takes some medicine and mixes it with milk, making all the people drink the decoction; this is done at a spot far away from the kraal."[49] An earlier authority on the Kafirs of South Africa tells us that with them no person ceremonially unclean may drink milk, and that among such persons are a widow and a widower, the widow being unclean for a month and the widower for half a month after the death of husband or wife respectively.[50] Similarly among the Todas of Southern India, who are a purely pastoral people, a widower and a widow are forbidden to drink milk for a period which may extend for many months.[51] In the Konkan, a province of the Bombay Presidency, the use of milk is prohibited during the period of mourning.[52]

No satisfactory motive is assigned for the common prohibition thus laid on mourners to partake of milk; for the reason alleged by Arab women in Egypt, that the whiteness of the milk would not comport with the blackness of their sorrow, is clearly a fanciful afterthought. In the light of the evidence which has come before us, we may conjecture that in all cases the original motive was a fear lest the cows might die, if their milk were drunk by a man or woman who was thus deeply tainted with the pollution and infection of death.

Among the Akamba and Akikuyu of British East Africa intercourse between the human sexes is strictly forbidden so long as the cattle are at pasture, that is, from the time when the herds are driven out in the morning till the time when they are driven home in the evening.[53] This remarkable prohibition, first reported by a German observer some thirty years ago, might appear to an educated European to be founded on a simple sense of decency and a calculation of practical utility; but any such interpretation would totally misread the working of the native African mind. Subsequent inquiries proved that, as I had conjectured,[54] the intercourse of the human sexes is supposed to be in some way injurious to the cattle while they are at grass. An investigation was instituted by C. W. Hobley, and he found that "this custom still exists and is still strictly followed, but it refers only to the people left in the kraal, and does not apply to the herdsmen; if the people in the kraal infringed this prohibition it is believed that the cattle would die off, and also that the children would sicken: no explanation was offered as to why the herdsmen were exempt."[55] Among the Akamba in particular it is believed that "if a man cohabits with a married woman in the woods while the cattle are out grazing, it brings *makwa* [a curse] upon the cattle and they will die. The woman, however, is generally afraid of evil falling on the precious cattle, and confesses. The cattle are then taken out of their kraal, medicine is placed on the ground at the gate, and they are then driven back over the medicine, and this lifts the curse. The woman also has to be ceremonially purified by an elder."[56] Moreover, for eight days after the periodical festival which the Akikuyu hold for the purpose of securing God's blessing on their flocks and herds, no commerce is permitted between the human sexes. They think that any breach of continence in these eight days would be followed by a mortality among the flocks.[57]

The belief that the cohabitation of men with women is, under certain circumstances, injurious to the cattle, may explain why the most sacred dairymen of the pastoral Todas must avoid women altogether.[58] An idea of the same sort may underlie the Dinka custom [mentioned above] which entrusts the milking of cows to boys and girls under puberty, and the Kafir custom which restricts the use of fresh milk to young people and very old people; all other persons, that is, all adults in the prime of life, may use only curdled milk.[59] "In the south of Africa, it is only the children who drink milk in a sweet state; it is generally left to get sour in large earthen pans, or in bottles of quagga-skin. After two or three days the whey is carefully separated from the congealed mass, and in its stead they add a little sweet milk or cream, to allay the sourness of the curds."[60] Among the Ovambo of South-West Africa "milk is drunk quite fresh only by small children, probably never by grown persons."[61] Among the Baganda of Central Africa "milk was drunk curdled or clotted; no grown-up person cared to drink it fresh; it was, however, given fresh to young children and infants."[62] The Akikuyu of British East Africa make much use of the milk both of cows and goats, but only children drink it fresh.[63] Among the Bechuanas "there are two months in the year, at the cow-calving time, which is generally about the month of October, when none but the uncircumcised are permitted to use the milk of cows that have calved."[64] As the uncircumcised would usually be under puberty, it seems likely that this Bechuana rule is based on the idea that the intercourse of the human sexes may injuriously affect a cow in the critical time when she has lately dropped her calf. We have seen that in other tribes the first milk of a cow after calving may not be used in the ordinary way, but is either made over to boys or children, or is reserved for the use of one particular person who may drink no other milk. Similar precautions are taken by the Badagas of Southern India to guard the first milk of a cow after calving from abuses which might conceivably endanger the health of the animal.[65]

Perhaps the practice of eating milk in the form of sour curds, which prevails among the pastoral tribes of Africa,[66] may spring not altogether from a preference for curds, but partly at least from a superstitious notion that the sympathetic bond between the cow and its milk is weakened or severed when the milk has been turned into curds or buttermilk, and that accordingly you run less risk of sympathetically hurting the cow when you eat curds than when you drink fresh milk. Such an idea at all events might explain why in some tribes the drinking of fresh milk is confined to children and old people, that is, to the classes who are physically unable to endanger the supply of the precious fluid by sexual commerce. The Bahima seem to suppose that the sympathetic bond between the milk and the cow is severed when the milk is converted into butter; for, whereas they will not sell the milk lest it should fall into the hands of persons who might injure the cows by drinking it, they never had any objection to parting with butter.[67] The Bahima, it is to be observed, use butter chiefly as an unguent to anoint their bodies, though at times they also eat it.[68] But the butter which a man applies to himself externally is probably not conceived to form so close a link between him and the animal as the milk which he takes internally; hence any improper use he may make of butter is less likely, on the principles of sympathetic magic, to injure the cow than an improper use of her milk, and accordingly it is less needful to guard against the abuse of butter than against the abuse of milk. Among the Todas the milk of the sacred herd may be freely consumed by the most holy dairymen, but what they leave over must be converted into clarified butter (nei) before it is sold; it may not be drunk by the profane in its original form as it came from the cow.[69] From all this it appears that any process which converts milk into another substance, such as curds, butter, or cheese, may be regarded, though it need not necessarily be regarded, as snapping, or at all events weakening, the link which binds the milk to the cow, and, therefore, as enabling the milk in its new form to be used by the profane without injury to the cattle.[70] Among tribes which hold such views the operations of the dairy aim, so to say, at disenchanting the milk for the benefit of the cow, at breaking the tie which binds the two together, lest it should drag the animal down to death.

The theory that a cow remains in direct physical sympathy with her milk, even after she has parted with it, is carried out by some pastoral tribes to the length of forbidding the milk to be brought into contact either with flesh or with vegetables, because any such contact is believed to injure the cow from which the milk was drawn. Thus the Masai are at the utmost pains to keep milk from touching flesh, because it is a general opinion among them that such contact would set up a disease in the udders of the cow which had yielded the milk, and that no more milk could be extracted from the animal. Hence they can seldom be induced, and then only most reluctantly, to sell their milk, lest the purchaser should make their cows ill by allowing it to touch flesh. For the same reason they will not suffer milk to be kept in a pot in which flesh has been cooked, nor flesh to be put in a vessel which has contained milk, and consequently they have two different sets of pots set apart for the two purposes.[71] The belief and practice of the Bahima are similar. Once when a German officer, encamped in their country, offered them one of his cooking-pots in exchange for one of their milk-pots, they refused to accept it, alleging that if milk were poured into a pot in which flesh had been boiled, the cow that had yielded the milk would die.[72]

But it is not merely in a pot that milk and flesh may not come into contact with each other; they may not meet in a man's stomach, because contact there would be equally dangerous to the cow whose milk was thus contaminated. Hence pastoral tribes who subsist on the milk and flesh of their cattle are careful not to eat beef and milk at the same time; they allow a considerable interval to elapse between a meal of beef and a meal of milk, and they sometimes even employ an emetic or purgative in order to clear their stomach entirely of the one food before it receives the other. For example, "the food of the Masai consists exclusively of meat and milk, but it is considered a great offence to partake of milk (which is never allowed to be boiled) and meat at the same time, so that for ten days the Masai lives exclusively on milk, and then ten days solely on meat.[73]

If a Masai should be tempted to eat beef and drink milk on the same day, he endeavours to avert the ill consequences of the act by tickling his throat with a stalk of grass so as to produce vomiting before he passes from the one article of diet to the other.[74] Similarly the Washamba of German East Africa never drink milk and eat meat at the same meal; they believe that if they did so, it would infallibly cause the death of the cow from which the milk was obtained. Hence many of them are unwilling to dispose of the milk of their cows to Europeans, for fear that the ignorant or thoughtless purchaser might kill the animals by mixing their milk with flesh meat in his stomach.[75] Again, among the Bahima there is a firm belief that cows would sicken should milk and meat or vegetable meet in the stomach."[76] So, too, the pastoral Banyoro abstain from drinking milk for about twelve hours after a meal of meat and beer; they say that such a period of abstinence is necessary, because "food eaten indiscriminately will cause sickness among the cattle."[77] Among the Nandi of British East Africa "meat and milk may not be taken together. If milk is drunk, no meat may be eaten for twenty-four hours. Boiled meat in soup must be eaten first, after which roast meat may be taken. When meat has been eaten, no milk may be drunk for twelve hours, and then only after some salt and water has been swallowed. If no salt, which is obtained from the salt-licks, is near at hand, blood may be drunk instead. If anybody breaks the rule he is soundly flogged."[78] Among the pastoral Suk of British East Africa it is forbidden to partake of milk and meat on the same day.[79]

Similar, though somewhat less stringent, rules about the separation of flesh and milk are observed by Orthodox Jews to this day. One who has eaten flesh or broth ought not to taste cheese or anything made of milk for an hour afterwards; strait-laced people extend the period of abstinence to six hours. Moreover, flesh and milk are carefully kept apart. There are separate sets of vessels for them, each bearing a special mark, and a vessel used to hold milk may not be used to hold flesh. Two sets of knives are also kept, one for cutting flesh, the other for cutting cheese and fish. Moreover, flesh and milk are not cooked in the oven together nor placed on the table at the same time; even the table-cloths on which they are set ought to be different. If a family is too poor to have two table-cloths, they should at least wash their solitary table-cloth before putting milk on it after meat.[80]

But the contamination of milk with meat is not the only danger against which the pastoral tribes of Africa, in the interest of their cattle, seek to guard themselves by rules of diet. They are equally solicitous not to suffer milk to be contaminated by vegetables; hence they abstain from drinking milk and eating vegetables at the same time, because they believe that the mixture of the two things in their stomachs would somehow be harmful to the herd. Thus among the pastoral Bahima, of Ankole, "various kinds of vegetables, such as peas, beans, and sweet potatoes, may not be eaten by any member of the clans unless he fasts from milk for some hours after a meal of vegetables. Should a man be forced by hunger to eat vegetables, he must fast some time after eating them; by preference he will eat plantains, but even then he must fast ten or twelve hours before he again drinks milk. To drink milk while vegetable food is still in the stomach is believed to endanger the health of the cows."[81] So the Bairo of Ankole, "who eat sweet potatoes and ground-nuts, are not allowed to drink milk, as it would then injure the cattle."[82]

Among the Banyoro "the middle classes who keep cows and also cultivate are most careful in their diet not to eat vegetables and to drink milk near together. Persons who drink milk in the morning do not eat other food until the evening, and those who drink milk in the evening eat no vegetables until the next day. Sweet potatoes and beans are the vegetables they avoid most of all, and each person, after eating such food, is careful to abstain from drinking milk for a period of two days. This precaution is taken to prevent milk from coming into contact with either meat or vegetables in the stomach; it is believed that food eaten indiscriminately will cause sickness among the cattle."[83]

Among the Baganda "no person was allowed to eat beans or sugar-cane, or to drink beer, or to smoke Indian hemp, and at the same time to drink milk; the person who drank milk fasted for several hours before he might eat or drink the tabooed foods, and he might not drink milk for a similar period after partaking of such food."[84]

The primitive who believes that he himself can be magically injured through the secretions of his body naturally applies the same theory to his cattle and takes the same sort of steps to safeguard them as to safeguard himself. If this view is right, the superstitious restrictions imposed on the use of milk which have come before us are analogous to the superstitious precautions which the savage adopts with regard to the disposal of his shorn hair, clipped nails, and other severed parts of his person. In their essence they are not religious but magical. Yet in time such taboos might easily receive a religious interpretation. For while the logical distinction between magic and religion is sharp as a knife-edge, there is no such acute and rigid line of cleavage between them historically. With the vagueness characteristic of primitive thought the two are constantly fusing with each other, like two streams, one of blue and one of yellow water, which meet and blend into a river that is neither wholly yellow nor wholly blue. But the historical confusion of magic and religion no more dispenses the philosophic student of human thought from the need of resolving the compound into its constituent parts than the occurrence of most chemical elements in combination dispenses the analytical chemist from the need of separating and distinguishing them. The mind has its chemistry as well as the body. Its elements may be more subtle and mercurial, yet even here a fine instrument will seize and mark distinctions which might elude a coarser handling.

If the distinctions drawn between Hebrew and African usages in respect to the boiling of milk, the regulation of a mixed diet of milk and flesh, and between animals as clean and unclean, or edible and inedible be well founded, they tend to prove that the Hebrew usages in all these matters took their rise in the pastoral stage of society, and accordingly they confirm the native tradition of the Israelites that their ancestors were nomadic herdsmen, roaming with their flocks and herds from pasture to pasture, for many ages before their descendants, swarming across the fords of the Jordan from the grassy uplands of Moab, settled down to the stationary life of husbandmen and vine-dressers in the fat land of Palestine. ▼

▲ 91   The golden bells   28:33–35

Why should the priest in his violet robe, with the fringe of gay pome-granates dangling at his heels, fear to die if the golden bells were not heard to jingle, both when he went into, and when he came forth from the holy place? The most probable answer seems to be that the chiming of the holy bells was thought to drive away the envious and wicked spirits who lurked about the door of the sanctuary, ready to pounce on and carry off the richly apparelled minister as he stepped across the threshold in the discharge of his sacred office. At least this view, which has found favour with some modern scholars,[1] is strongly supported by analogy; for it has been a common opinion, from the days of antiquity onwards, that demons and ghosts can be put to flight by the sound of metal, whether it be the musical jingle of little bells, the deep-mouthed clangor of great bells, the shrill clash of cymbals, the booming of gongs, or the simple clink and clank of plates of bronze or iron knocked together or struck with hammers or sticks. Hence in rites of exorcism it has often been customary for the celebrant either to ring a bell which he holds in his hand, or to wear attached to some part of his person a whole nest of bells, which jingle at every movement he makes.[2]

Lucian tells us that spectres fled at the sound of bronze and iron, and he contrasts the repulsion which the clank of these metals exerted on spirits with the attraction which the chink of silver money wielded over women of a certain class.[3] At Rome, when the ghosts of the dead had paid their annual visit to the old home in the month of May, and had been entertained with a frugal repast of black beans, the householder used to show them the door, bidding them, "Ghosts of my fathers, go forth!" and emphasizing his request or command by the clash of bronze.[4]

Nor did such notions expire with expiring paganism. They survived in full force under Christianity into the Middle Ages and long afterwards. The learned Christian scholiast, John Tzetzes, tells us that the clash of bronze was just as effective to ban apparitions as the barking of a dog,[5] a proposition which few reasonable men will be inclined to dispute.

In Christian times, however, the sound deemed above all others abhorrent to the ears of fiends and goblins has been the sweet and solemn music of church bells. The first Provincial Council of Cologne laid it down as an opin-ion of the fathers that at the sound of the bells summoning Christians to prayer demons are terrified and depart, and the spirits of the storm, the powers of the air, are laid low.[6] Again, the service book known as the Roman Pontifical recognizes the virtue of a church bell, wherever its sound is heard, to drive far off the powers of evil, the gibbering and mowing spectres of the dead, and all the spirits of the storm.[7] A great canonist of the thirteenth century, Durandus, in his once famous and popular treatise on the divine offices, tells us that "bells are rung in processions that demons may fear and flee. For when they hear the trumpets of the church militant, that is, the bells, they are afraid, as any tyrant is afraid when he hears in his land the trumpets of a powerful king, his foe. And that, too, is the reason why, at the sight of a storm rising, the Church rings its bells, in order that the demons, hearing the trumpets of the eternal king, that is, the bells, may be terrified and flee away and abstain from stirring up the tempest."[8] On this subject the English antiquary, Francis Grose, the friend of the poet Burns,[9] writes as follows: "The passing-bell was anciently rung for two purposes: one, to bespeak the prayers of all good Christians for a soul just departing; the other, to drive away the evil spirits who stood at the bed's foot, and about the house, ready to seize their prey, or at least to molest and terrify the soul in its passage: but by the ringing of that bell (for Durandus informs us, evil spirits are much afraid of bells), they were kept aloof; and the soul, like a hunted hare, gained the start, or had what is by sportsmen called Law. Hence, perhaps, exclusive of the additional labour, was occasioned the high price demanded for tolling the greatest bell of the church; for that being louder, the evil spirits must go farther off, to be clear of its sound, by which the poor soul got so much more the start of them: besides, being heard farther off, it would likewise procure the dying man a greater number of prayers. This dislike of spirits to bells is mentioned in the *Golden Legend,* by W. de Worde. 'It is said, the evill spirytes that ben in the regyon of th' ayre, doubte moche when they here the belles rongen: and this is the cause why the belles ben rongen whan it thondreth, and whan grete tempeste and outrages of wether happen, to the ende that the feindes and wycked spirytes should be abashed and flee, and cease of the movynge of tempeste.' "[10]

Of the two reasons which Grose assigns for the ringing of the Passing Bell we may surmise that the intention of driving away evil spirits was the primary and original one, and that the intention of bespeaking the prayers of all good Christians for the soul just about to take its flight was secondary and derivative. In any case the ringing of the bell seems formerly to have regularly begun while the sufferer was still in life, but when his end was visibly near.[11] Thus in his *Anatomie of Abuses* Stubbes tells of the dreadful end of a profane swearer down in Lincolnshire: "At the last, the people perceiving his ende to approche, caused the bell to toll; who, hearing the bell to toll for him, rushed up in his bed very vehemently, saying, 'God's bloud, he shall not have me yet'; with that his bloud gushed out, some at his toes endes, some at his fingers endes, some at hys wristes, some at his nose and mouth, some at one joynt of his body, some at another, never ceasing till all the bloud in his body was streamed forth. And thus ended this bloudy swearer his mortal life."[12] Again, when Lady Catherine Grey was dying a captive in the Tower, the Governor of the fortress, perceiving that his prisoner was about to be released from his charge, without any royal warrant, said to Mr. Bokeham, "Were it not best to send to the church, that the bell may be rung?" And she, feeling her end to be near, entered into prayer, saying, "O Lord! into thy hands I commend my soul: Lord Jesus, receive my spirit!"[13] Thus for her, as for many, the sound of the Passing Bell was the *Nunc dimittis*. A writer in the first half of the eighteenth century, speaking of the dying Christian who has subdued his passions, says that, "if his senses hold out so long, he can hear even his passing-bell without disturbance."[14]

That the real purpose of the Passing Bell was to dispel maleficent beings hovering invisible in the air rather than to advertise persons at a distance and invite their prayers, is strongly suggested by the apparently primitive form in which the old custom has here and there been kept up down to modern times. Thus in some parts of the Eifel Mountains, a district of Rhenish Prussia, when a sick person was at the point of death, the friends used to ring a small hand-bell, called a Benedictus bell, "in order to keep the evil spirits away from the dying man."[15] Again, at Neusohl, in northern Hungary, it is said to have been usual to ring a small hand-bell softly when a dying man was near his end, "in order that the parting soul, lured away by death, may still linger for a few moments on earth near its stiffening body." When death had taken place, the bell was rung a little farther off, then farther and farther from the body, then out at the door, and once round the house "in order to accompany the soul on its parting way." After that, word was sent to the sexton that the bell of the village church might begin to toll.[16] A similar custom is said to have prevailed in the Böhmerwald mountains, which divide Bohemia from Bavaria.[17] The motive assigned for it—the wish to detain the parting soul for a few moments by the sweet sound of the bell—is too sentimental to be primitive; the true original motive was doubtless, as in the case of the similar custom in the Eifel Mountains, to banish the demons that might carry off the poor soul at the critical moment. Only when the little bell has performed this kindly office, tinkling for the soul at its setting out, does the big bell in the steeple begin to toll, that its sonorous tones may follow, like guardian angels, the fugitive on its long journey to the spirit land.

Throughout the Middle Ages and down to modern times the sound of church bells was also in great request for the purpose of routing witches and wizards, who gathered unseen in the air to play their wicked pranks on man and beast. There were certain days of the year which these wretches set apart more particularly for their unhallowed assemblies or Sabbaths, as they were called, and on such days accordingly the church bells were specially rung, sometimes the whole night long, because it was under cover of darkness that witches and warlocks were busiest at their infernal tasks. For example, in France witches were thought to scour the air most particularly on the night of St. Agatha, the fifth of February; hence the bells of the parish churches used to be set ringing that night to drive them away, and the same custom is said to have been observed in some parts of Spain.[18] Again, one of the most witching times of the whole year was Midsummer Eve; and accordingly at Rottenburg in Swabia the church bells rang all that night from nine o'clock till break of day, while honest folk made fast their shutters, and stopped up even chinks and crannies, lest the dreadful beings should insinuate themselves into the houses.[19] Other witches' Sabbaths used to be held at Twelfth Night and the famous Walpurgis Night, the eve of May Day, and on these days it used to be customary in various parts of Europe to expel the baleful, though invisible, crew by making a prodigious racket, to which the ringing of hand-bells and the cracking of whips contributed their share.[20]

But though witches and wizards chose certain seasons of the year above all others for the celebration of their unholy revels, there was no night on which they might not be encountered abroad on their errands of mischief by belated wayfarers, none on which they might not attempt to force their way into the houses of honest folk who were quiet, but by no means safe, in bed. Something, therefore, had to be done to protect peaceable citizens from these nocturnal alarms. For this purpose the watchmen, who patrolled the streets for the repression of common crime, were charged with the additional duty of exorcizing the dreaded powers of the air and of darkness, which went about like roaring lions seeking what they might devour. To accomplish this object the night watchman wielded spiritual weapons of two different sorts but of equal power; he rang a bell, and he chanted a blessing, and if the sleepers in the neighbourhood were roused and exasperated by the jingle of the one, they were perhaps soothed and comforted by the drone of the other, remembering, as they sank back to sleep, that it was only, in the words of Milton,[21]

> the bellman's drowsy charm
> To bless the doors from nightly harm.

The benediction which thus broke the stillness of night was usually cast in a poetical form of such unparalleled atrocity that a bellman's verses have been proverbial ever since.[22] Their general tenor may be gathered from the lines which Herrick puts in the mouth of one of those public guardians, from whose nightly orisons the poet, like Milton himself, must have often suffered:

> From noise of scare-fires rest ye free,
> From murders Benedicitie;
> From all mischances that may fright
> Your pleasing slumbers in the night;
> Mercie secure ye all, and keep
> The goblin from ye, while ye sleep.
> Past one aclock and almost two,
> My masters all, "Good day to you."[23]

We have seen that according to mediaeval authors church bells used to be rung in thunderstorms for the purpose of driving away the evil spirits who were supposed to be causing the tempest. To the same effect an old German writer of the sixteenth century, who under the assumed name of Naogeorgus composed a satirical poem on the superstitions and abuses of the Catholic Church, has recorded that

> If that the thunder chaunce to rore, and stormie tempest shake,
> A wonder is it for to see the wretches howe they quake,
> Howe that no fayth at all they have, nor trust in any things,
> The clarke doth all the belles forthwith at once in steeple ring:
> With wondrous sound and deeper farre, than he was woont before,
> Till in the loftie heavens darke, the thunder bray no more.
> For in these christned belles they thinke, doth lie such powre and might,
> As able is the tempest great, and storme to vanquish quight.
> I sawe my self at Numburg once, a town in Toring coast,
> A bell that with this title bolde, hir self did prowdly boast,
> "By name I Mary called am, with sound I put to flight
> The thunder crackes, and hurtfull stormes, and every wicked spright."
> Such things whenas these belles can do, no wonder certainlie
> It is, if that the Papistes to their tolling alwayes flie,
> When haile, or any raging storme, or tempest comes in sight,
> Or thunder boltes, or lightning fierce that every place doth smight.[24]

In the Middle Ages, we are told, all over Germany the church bells used to be rung during thunderstorms; and the sexton received a special due in corn from the parishioners for his exertions in pulling the bell-rope in these emergencies. These dues were paid in some places as late as the middle of the nineteenth century.[25] For example, at Jubar in the Altmark, whenever a thunderstorm burst, the sexton was bound to ring the church bell, and he received from every farmer five "thunder-sheaves" of corn for the pains he had been at to rescue the crops from destruction.[26] Writing as to the custom in Swabia about the middle of the nineteenth century, a German author tells us that "in most Catholic parishes, especially in Upper Swabia, the bells are rung in a thunderstorm to drive away hail and prevent damage by lightning. Many churches have special bells for the purpose; for instance, the monastery of Weingarten, near Altdorf, has the so-called 'holy Blood-bell,' which is rung during a thunderstorm. In Wurmlingen they ring the bell on Mount Remigius, and if they only do it soon enough, no lightning strikes any place in the district. However, the neighbouring villages, for example Jesingen, are often discontented at the ringing of the bell, for they believe that with the thunderstorm the rain is also driven away."[27] With regard to the town of Constance, in particular we read that, when a thunderstorm broke, the bells of all the parish churches not only in the city but in the neighbourhood were set a-ringing; and as they had been consecrated, many persons believed that the sound of them furnished complete protection against injury by lightning. Indeed, in their zeal not a few people assisted the sexton to pull the bell-ropes, tugging at them with all their might to make the bells swing high. And though some of these volunteers, we are informed, were struck dead by lightning in the very act of ringing the peal, this did not prevent others from doing the same. Even children on such occasions rang little hand-bells made of lead or other metals, which were adorned with figures of saints and had been blessed at the church of Maria Loretto in Steiermerk or at Einsiedeln.[28] Under certain feudal tenures the vassals were bound to ring the church bells on various occasions, but particularly during thunderstorms.[29]

The bells were solemnly consecrated and popularly supposed to be baptized by the priests; certainly they received names and were washed, blessed, and sprinkled with holy oil "to drive away and repel evil spirits."[30] Inscriptions engraved on church bells often refer to the power which they were supposed to possess of dispelling storms of thunder, lightning, and hail; some boldly claim such powers for the bells themselves, others more modestly pray for deliverance from these calamities; for instance, a bell at Haslen bears in Latin the words, "From lightning, hail, and tempest, Lord Jesus Christ deliver us!"[31] Speaking of St. Wenefride's Well, in Flintshire, the traveller and antiquary Pennant in the eighteenth century tells us that "a bell belonging to the church was also christened in honour of her. I cannot learn the names of the gossips, who, as usual, were doubtless rich persons. On the ceremony they all laid hold of the rope; bestowed a name on the bell; and the priest, sprinkling it with holy water, baptised it in the name of the Father, etc.; he then clothed it with a fine garment. After this the gossips gave a grand feast, and made great presents, which the priest received in behalf of the bell. Thus blessed, it was endowed with great powers; allayed (on being rung) all storms; diverted the thunderbolt; drove away evil spirits. These consecrated bells were always inscribed. The inscription on that in question ran thus:

'Sancta Wenefreda, Deo hoc commendare memento,
Ut pietate tua nos servet ab hoste cruento.'

And a little lower was another address:

'Protege prece pia quos convoco, Virgo Maria.' "[32]

However, the learned Jesuit Father, Martin Delrio, who published an elaborate work on magic early in the seventeenth century, indignantly denied that bells were baptized, though he fully admitted that they were named after saints, blessed, and anointed by ecclesiastical authority. That the ringing of church bells laid a wholesome restraint on evil spirits, and either averted or allayed the tempests wrought by these enemies of mankind, was, in the opinion of the learned Jesuit, a fact of daily experience too patent to be denied; but he traced these happy results purely to the consecration or benediction of the bells, and not at all to their shape or to the nature of the metal of which they were founded. He spurned as a pagan superstition the notion that the sound of brass sufficed of itself to put demons to flight, and he ridiculed the idea that a church bell lost all its miraculous virtue when it was named—he will not allow us to say baptized—by the priest's concubine.[33] Bacon condescended to mention the belief that "great ringing of bells in populous cities hath chased away thunder, and also dissipated pestilent air"; but he suggested a physical explanation of the supposed fact by adding, "All which may be also from the concussion of the air, and not from the sound."[34]

While all holy bells no doubt possesed in an exactly equal degree the marvellous property of putting demons and witches to flight, and thereby of preventing the ravages of thunder and lightning, some bells were more celebrated than others for the active exertion of their beneficent powers. Such, for instance, was St. Adelm's Bell at Malmesbury Abbey and the great bell of the Abbey of St. Germains in Paris, which were regularly rung to drive away thunder and lightning.[35] In old St. Paul's Cathedral there was a special endowment for "ringing the hallowed belle in great tempestes and lighteninges."[36] However, the feats of European bells in this respect have been thrown into the shade by the bells of Caloto in South America; though probably the superior fame of the bells of Caloto is to be ascribed, not so much to any intrinsic superiority of their own, as to the extraordinary frequency of thunderstorms in that region of the Andes, which has afforded the bells of the city more frequent opportunities for distinguishing themselves than fall to the lot of ordinary church bells.

The great discovery that it is possible to silence thunder and extinguish the thunderbolt by the simple process of ringing a bell, has not been confined to the Christian nations of Europe and their descendants in the New World; it has been shared by some at least of the pagan savages of Africa. "The Teso people," we are informed, "make use of bells to exorcise the storm fiend; a person who has been injured by a flash or in the resulting fire wears bells round the ankles for weeks afterwards. Whenever rain threatens, and rain in Uganda almost always comes in company with thunder and lightning, this person will parade the village for an hour, with the jingling bells upon his legs and a wand of papyrus in his hand, attended by as many of his family as may happen to be at hand and not employed in necessary duties. Any one killed outright by lightning is not buried in the house according to the usual custom, but is carried to a distance and interred beside a stream in some belt of forest. Upon the grave are put all the pots and other household utensils owned by the dead person, and at the door of the hut upon which the stroke fell, now of course a smoking ruin, is planted a sacrifice of hoes which is left for some days. It is interesting to note the efficacy attributed to bells and running water, as in some old European superstitions."[37] As it seems improbable that the Bateso learned these practices from the missionaries, we may perhaps give them the undivided credit of having invented for themselves the custom of exorcizing the storm-fiend by bells and mollifying him by presents of pots and hoes laid on the scene of his devastation and the grave of his victim.

The Chinese also resort to the use of gongs, which for practical purposes may be regarded as equivalent to bells, with a view of combating the ill effects of thunder; but the circumstances under which they do so are peculiar. When a person has been attacked by smallpox, and the pustules have come out, but before the end of the seventh day, whenever it thunders, some member of the family is deputed to beat on a gong or drum, which is kept in readiness for the emergency. The beater has the assistance of another member of the family to inform him when the thunder has ceased, for the operator himself makes far too much noise to be able to distinguish between the peals of thunder and the crash of his gong or the roll of his drum. The object, we are told, of this gong-ing or drumming is to prevent the pustules of the smallpox from breaking or bursting; but the explanations which the Chinese give of the way in which this result is effected by the beating of a gong or a drum can hardly be regarded as satisfactory.[38] On the analogy of the European theory we may conjecture that originally the bursting of the pustules was supposed to be brought about by the demon of thunder, who could be driven away by the banging of a gong or the rub-a-dub of a drum.

But while savages seem quite able of themselves to hit on the device of scar-ing evil spirits by loud noises, there is evidence to show that they are also ready to adopt from Europeans any practices which, in their opinion, are likely to serve the same purpose. An instance of such borrowing is recorded by two missionaries, who laboured among the natives of Port Moresby, in British New Guinea. "One night during a thunderstorm," they say, "we heard a terrible noise in the village;—the natives were beating their drums and shouting lustily in order to drive away the storm-spirits. By the time their drumming and vociferation ceased, the storm *had* passed away, and the villagers were well satisfied. One Sabbath night, in a similar way, they expelled the sickness-pro-ducing spirits who had occasioned the death of several natives! When the church bell was first used, the natives thanked Mr. Lawes for having—as they averred—driven away numerous bands of ghosts from the interior. In like man-ner they were delighted at the bark of a fine dog domesticated at the mission house (the dingo cannot bark), as they felt certain that all the ghosts would now be compelled to rush back to the interior. Unfortunately, the ghosts got used to the bell and the dog! So the young men had to go about at night—often hiding in terror behind trees and bushes—well armed with bows and arrows, to shoot down these obnoxious spirits."[39]

Some of the Pueblo Indians of Arizona exorcize witches by the sound of bells; but probably they borrowed the practice from the old Spanish mission-aries, for before the coming of Europeans the use of all metals, except gold and silver, and hence the making of bells, was unknown among the aborigines of America. An American officer has described one of these scenes of exorcism as he witnessed it at a village of the Moki, perched, like many Pueblo villages, on the crest of a high tableland overlooking the fruitful grounds in the valley below:

"The Moki have an implicit belief in witches and witchcraft, and the air about them is peopled with maleficent spirits. Those who live at Oraybe exorcise the malign influences with the chanting of hymns and ringing of bells. While with General Crook at that isolated and scarcely-known town, in the fall of 1874, by good luck I had an opportunity of witnessing this strange mode of incantation. The whole village seeemd to have assembled, and after shouting in a loud and defiant tone a hymn or litany of musical sound, emphasised by an energetic ringing of a bell, advanced rapidly, in single file, down the trail leading from the crest of the precipice to the peach orchards below. The performers, some of the most important of whom were women, pranced around the boundaries of the orchard, pausing for a brief space of time at the corners, all the while singing in a high key and getting the worth of their money out of the bell. At a signal from the leader a rush was made for the trees, from which, in less than an hour, the last of the delicious peaches breaking down the branches were pulled and carried by the squaws and children to the village above."[40] The motive for thus dancing round the orchard, to the loud chanting of hymns and the energetic ringing of a bell, was no doubt to scare away the witches, who were supposed to be perched among the boughs of the peach-trees, battening on the luscious fruit.

The use of bells and gongs for the purpose of exorcism has been equally familar to many peoples who need not have borrowed either the instruments or the application of them from the Christian nations of Europe. In China "the chief instrument for the production of exorcising noise is the gong. This well-known circular plate of brass is actually a characteristic feature of China, resounding throughout the empire every day, especially in summer, when a rise in the death-rate induces an increase in devil-expelling activity. Clashing of cymbals of brass, and rattling of drums of wood and leather, intensify its useful effects. Very often small groups of men and even women are beating on gongs, cymbals, and drums for a succession of hours. No protest is heard from their neighbours, no complaint that they disturb their night's rest; such savage music then must either sound agreeable to Chinese ears, or be heard with gratitude as a meritorious work, gratuitously performed by benevolent folks who have at heart the private and public weal and health."[41] In Southern China these solemn and public ceremonies of exorcism take place chiefly during the heat of summer, when cholera is rampant and its ravages are popularly attributed to the malice of demons hovering unseen in the air. To drive these noxious beings from house and home is the object of the ceremonies. The whole affair is arranged by a committee, and the expenses are defrayed by subscription, the local mandarins generally heading the list of subscribers with goodly sums. The actual business of banishing the devils is carried out by processions of men and boys, who parade the streets and beat the bounds in the most literal sense, striking at the invisible foes with swords and axes, and stunning them with the clangour of gongs, the jangle of bells, the popping of crackers, the volleys of matchlocks, and the detonation of blunderbusses.[42]

In Annam the exorcizer, in the act of banning the demons of sickness from a private house, strums a lute and jingles a chain of copper bells attached to his big toe, while his assistants accompany him on stringed instruments and drums. However, the chime of the bells is understood by the hearers to proceed from the neck of an animal on which a deity is galloping to the aid of the principal performer.[43] Bells play a great part in the religious rites of Burma. Every large pagoda has dozens of them, and the people seem to be much attached to their sweet and sonorous music. At the present day their use is said to be, not so much to drive away evil spirits, as to announce to the guardian spirits that the praises of Buddha have been chanted; hence at the conclusion of his devotions the worshipper proclaims the discharge of his pious duty by three strokes on a bell.[44] However, we may conjecture that this interpretation is one of those afterthoughts by which an advanced religion justifies and hallows the retention of an old barbaric rite that was originally instituted for a less refined and beautiful purpose. Perhaps in Europe also the ringing of church bells the sound of which has endeared itself to so many pious hearts by its own intrinsic sweetness and its tender associations, was practised to banish demons from the house of prayer before it came to be regarded as a simple means of summoning worshippers to their devotions in the holy place.

Among ruder peoples of Asia, however, the use of bells in exorcism, pure and simple, has lingered down to modern times. At a funeral ceremony observed by night among the Michemis, a Tibetan tribe near the northern frontier of Assam, a priest, fantastically bedecked with tiger's teeth, many-coloured plumes, bells and shells, executed a wild dance for the purpose of exorcizing the evil spirits, while the bells jingled and the shells clattered about his person.[45] Among the Kirantis, a tribe of the Central Himalayas, who bury their dead on hill-tops, "the priest must attend the funeral, and as he moves along with the corpse to the grave he from time to time strikes a copper vessel with a stick, and, invoking the soul of the deceased, desires it to go in peace, and join the souls that went before it."[46] This beating of a copper vessel at the funeral may have been intended, either to hasten the departure of the ghost to his own place, or to drive away the demons who might molest his passage. It may have been for one or other of these purposes that in antiquity, when a Spartan king died, the women used to go about the streets of the city beating a kettle.[47] Among the Bantu tribes of Kavirondo, in Central Africa, when a woman has separated from her husband and gone back to her own people, she deems it nevertheless her duty on his death to mourn for him in his village. For that purpose "she fastens a cattle bell to her waist at the back, collects her friends, and the party proceeds to the village at a trot, the bell clanking in a melancholy manner the whole way."[48] Here, again, the sound of the bell may be intended to keep the husband's ghost at a safe distance, or perhaps to direct his attention to the dutifulness of his widow in sorrowing for his death. In the south-eastern districts of Dutch Borneo it is customary with the Dyaks to sound gongs day and night so long as a corpse remains in the house. The melancholy music begins as soon as a dying man has breathed his last. The tune is played on four gongs of different tones, which are beaten alternately at regular intervals of about two seconds. Hour after hour, day after day the melody is kept up; and we are told that nothing, not even the Passing Bell of Catholic Europe, is more weird and affecting to a listener than the solemn notes of these death-gongs sounding monotonously and dying away over the broad rivers of Borneo.[49]

Though we are not informed why the Dyaks in this part of Borneo beat the gongs continuously after a death, we may conjecture that the intention is to keep off evil spirits rather than simply to announce the bereavement to friends at a distance; for if the object was merely to convey the intelligence of the decease to the neighbourhood, why sound the gongs continuously day and night so long as the body remains in the house? On the other hand we know that in Borneo the sound of metal instruments is sometimes employed expressly for the purpose of exorcizing demons. An English traveller in North Borneo describes how on one occasion he lodged in a large house of the Dusuns, which was inhabited by about a hundred men with their families: "As night came on they struck up a strange kind of music on metal tambourines. A mysterious rhythm and tune was apparent in it, and when I asked if this was *main-main* (*i.e.* larking), they said no, but that a man was sick, and they must play all night to keep away evil spirits."[50] Again, the Dusuns of North Borneo solemnly expel all evil spirits from their villages once a year, and in the expulsion gongs are beaten and bells rung to hasten the departure of the demons. While the men beat gongs and drums, the women go in procession from house to house, dancing and singing to the measured clash of brass castanets, which they hold in their hands, and to the jingle of little brass bells, of which bunches are fastened to their wrists. Having driven the demons from the houses, the women chase or lead them down to the bank of the river, where a raft has been prepared to convey them beyond the territories of the village. Figures of men, women, animals, and birds, made of sago-palm leaf, adorn the raft, and to render it still more attractive offerings of food and cloth and cooking pots are deposited on the planks. When the spiritual passengers are all aboard, the moorings are loosed, and the bark floats away down stream, till it rounds the farthest reach of the river and disappears from sight in the forest. Thus the demons are sent away on a long voyage to return, it is fondly hoped, no more.[51]

The Patâri priest in Mirzapur and many classes of ascetics throughout India carry bells and rattles made of iron, which they shake as they walk for the purpose of scaring demons. With a like intent, apparently, a special class of devil priests among the Gonds, known as Ojhyâls, always wear bells.[52] It seems probable that a similar motive everywhere underlies the custom of attaching bells to various parts of the person, particularly to the ankles, wrists, and neck, either on special occasions or for long periods of time: originally, we may suppose, the tinkle of the bells was thought to protect the wearer against the assaults of bogies. It is for this purpose that small bells are very commonly worn by children in the southern provinces of China and more sparingly by children in the northern provinces;[53] and silver ornaments, with small bells hanging from them, are worn by Neapolitan women on their dresses as amulets to guard them against the Evil Eye.[54] The Yezidis, who have a robust faith in the devil, perform at the conclusion of one of their pilgrimage festivals a ceremony which may be supposed to keep that ravening wolf from the fold of the faithful. An old man is stripped and dressed in the skin of a goat, while a string of small bells is hung round his neck. Thus arrayed, he crawls round the assembled pilgrims emitting sounds which are intended to mimic the bleating of a he-goat. The ceremony is believed to sanctify the assembly,[55] but we may conjecture that it does so by encircling believers with a spiritual fence which the arch enemy is unable to surmount. With a like intention, probably, a Badaga priest in Southern India ties bells to his legs before he essays to walk barefoot across the glowing embers of a fire-pit at a solemn ceremony which is apparently designed to secure a blessing on the crops.[56]

In Africa bells are much used by the natives for the purpose of putting evil spirits to flight, and we need not suppose that the custom has always or even generally been borrowed by them from Europeans, since the blacks have believed in spirits and have been acquainted with the metals, particularly with iron, from time immemorial. For example, the Yoruba-speaking people of the Slave Coast believe that there are certain wicked spirits called *abikus,* which haunt the forests and waste places and, suffering much from hunger, are very desirous of taking up their abode in human bodies. For that purpose they watch for the moment of conception and insinuate themselves into the embryos in the wombs of women. When such children are born, they peak and pine, because the hungry demons within them are consuming the better part of the nourishment destined for the support of the real infant. To rid the poor babe of its troublesome occupant, a mother will offer a sacrifice of food to the demon, and while he is devouring it, she avails herself of his distraction to attach small bells and iron rings to her child's ankles and iron chains to its neck. The jingling of the iron and the tinkling of the bells are thought to keep the demons at a distance; hence many children are to be seen with their feet weighed down by iron ornaments.[57] Among the Baganda and Banyoro of Central Africa young children learning to walk used to have small bells attached to their feet, and the reason alleged for the custom was that the bells helped the child to walk or strengthened its legs;[58] but perhaps the original motive was to deliver the little one at this critical time from the unwelcome attentions of evil spirits. With the same intention, possibly, among the Baganda parents of twins wore bells at their ankles during the long and elaborate ceremonies which the superstitious beliefs of their country imposed upon husband and wife in such cases; and special drums, one for the father and another for the mother, were beaten continually both by day and by night.[59]

Among the Bogos, to the north of Abyssinia, when a woman has been brought to bed, her female friends kindle a fire at the door of the house, and the mother with her infant walks slowly round it, while a great noise is made with bells and palm-branches for the purpose, we are told, of frightening away the evil spirits.[60] It is said that the Gonds of India "always beat a brass dish at a birth so that the noise may penetrate the child's ears, and this will remove any obstruction there may be to its hearing."[61] The reason here assigned for the custom is not likely to be the original one; more probably the noise of the beaten brass was primarily intended, like the sound of bells among the Bogos, to protect the mother and her newborn babe against the assaults of demons. So in Greek legend the Curetes are said to have danced round the infant Zeus, clashing their spears against their shields, to drown the child's squalls, lest they should attract the attention of his unnatural father Cronus, who was in the habit of devouring his offspring as soon as they were born.[62] We may surmise that this Greek legend embodies a reminiscence of an old custom observed for the purpose of protecting babies against the many causes of infantile mortality which primitive man explains by the agency of malevolent and dangerous spirits. To be more explicit, we may conjecture that in former times, when a Greek child was born, the father and his friends were wont to arm themselves with spear or sword and shield and to execute a war dance round the child, clashing their spears or swords against their shields, partly in order to drown the cries of the infant, lest they should attract the attention of the prowling spirits, but partly also to frighten way the demons by the din; while in order to complete the discomfiture of the invisible foes they brandished their weapons, cutting and thrusting vigorously with them in the empty air. At least this conjecture is supported by the following analogies.

A Spanish priest, writing towards the beginning of the eighteenth century, has described as follows the practices observed by the Tagalogs of the Philippine Islands at the birth of a child. "The *patianak,* which some call goblin (if it be not fiction, dream, or their imagination), is the genius or devil who is accustomed to annoy them. . . . To him they attribute the ill result of childbirth, and say that to do them damage, or to cause them to go astray, he places himself in a tree, or hides in any place near the house of the woman who is in childbirth, and there sings after the manner of those who go wandering, etc. To hinder the evil work of the *patianak,* they make themselves naked, and arm themselves with cuirass, bolo, lance, and other arms, and in this manner place themselves on the ridgepole of the roof, and also under the house, where they give many blows and thrusts with the bolo, and make many gestures and motions ordered to the same intent."[63] According to another version, the husband and his friends arm themselves with sword, shield, and spear, and thus equipped hew and slash furiously in the air, both on the roof of the house and underneath it (the houses being raised above the ground on poles), for the purpose of frightening and driving away the dangerous spirit who would injure the mother and child.[64] These armed men, repelling the demon from the newborn babe by cut and thrust of their weapons, appear to be the savage counterpart of the ancient Greek Curetes.

Similar beliefs concerning the dangers to which infants are exposed from spiritual enemies have led the wild Kachins of Burma to adopt very similar precautions, for the sake of guarding a mother and her offspring. "At the instant of birth the midwife says 'the child is named so-and-so.' If she does not do this, some malignant *nat* or spirit will give the child a name first, and so cause it to pine away and die. If mother and child do well, there is general drinking and eating, and the happy father is chaffed. If, however, childbirth is attended with much labour, then it is evident that *nats* are at work and a *tumsa* or seer is called into requisition. This man goes to another house in the village and consults the bamboos (*chippawt*) to discover whether it is the house-*nat* who is averse, or whether a jungle *nat* has come and driven the guardian *nat* away. These jungle *nats* are termed *sawn*, and are the spirits of those who have died in childbirth or by violent deaths. They naturally wish for companions, and so enter the house and seize the woman and child. If the bamboo declares that it is the house-*nat* who is angry, he is propitiated by offerings of spirits or by sacrifice in the ordinary manner. If, however, it appears that a *sawn* has taken possession, then prompt action is necessary. Guns are fired all round the house and along the paths leading into the village, arrows are shot under the floor of the house, *dhas* [swords or large knives] and torches are brandished over the body of the woman, and finally old rags, chillies, and other materials likely to produce a sufficiently noisome smell are piled under the raised flooring and set fire to, thereby scaring away any but the most obstinate and pertinacious spirits."[65]

When a Kalmuk woman is in travail, her husband stretches a net round the tent, and runs to and fro beating the air with a club and crying, "Devil avaunt!" until the child is born: this he does in order to keep the foul fiend at bay.[66] Among the Nogais, a tribe of Tartars, "when a boy is born, everybody goes to the door of the house with kettles. They make a great noise, saying that they do so in order to put the devil to flight, and that he will have no more power over the spirit of that child."[67] In Boni or Bone, a princedom of Southern Celebes, when a woman is in hard labour, the men "sometimes raise a shout or fire a gun in order, by so doing, to drive away the evil spirits who are hindering the birth"; and at the birth of a prince, as soon as the infant has been separated from the afterbirth, all the metal instruments used for expelling demons are struck and clashed "in order to drive way the evil spirits."[68] For the same purpose drums are beaten in the Aru islands, to the south-west of New Guinea, when a delivery is unduly delayed.[69] The spirit of a certain stream, which flows into Burton Gulf, on Lake Tanganyika, is believed by the natives of the neighbourhood to be very unfriendly to women with child, whom he prevents from bringing forth. When a woman believes herself to be suffering from his machinations, she orders sacrifices to be offered and certain ceremonies to be performed. All the inhabitants of the village assemble, beat drums near the hut where the patient is confined, and shout and dance "to drive away the evil spirit."[70] Among the Singhalese of Ceylon, when a birth has taken place, "the cries of the babe are drowned by those of the nurse, lest the spirits of the forest become aware of its presence and inflict injury on it."[71] So the ancient Romans believed that a woman after childbirth was particularly liable to be attacked by the forest god Silvanus, who made his way into the house by night on purpose to vex and harry her. Hence during the night three men used to go round the thresholds of the house, armed respectively with an axe, a pestle, and a besom; at every threshold they stopped, and while the first two men smote it with the axe and the pestle, the third man swept it with his broom. In this way they thought to protect the mother from the attacks of the woodland deity.[72]

But from this digression we must return to the use of bells as a means of re-pelling the assaults of ghosts and demons. Among the Sunars, who are the goldsmiths and silversmiths of the Central Provinces in India, children and young girls wear hollow anklets with tinkling bells inside; but when a married woman has had several children, she leaves off wearing the hollow anklet and wears a solid one instead. "It is now said that the reason why girls wear sound-ing anklets is that their whereabouts may be known, and they may be prevented from getting into mischief in dark corners. But the real reason was probably that they served as spirit scarers."[73] Among the Nandi of British East Africa, when a girl is about to be circumcised, she receives from her sweethearts and admirers the loan of large bells, which they usually wear on their legs, but which for this solemn occasion they temporarily transfer to the damsel. A popular girl will frequently receive as many as ten or twenty bells, and she wears them all when the painful operation is performed upon her. As soon as it is over, she stands up and shakes the bells above her head, then goes to meet her lover, and gives him back the borrowed bells.[74] If we knew why Nandi warriors regularly wear bells on their legs, we should probably know why girls wear the very same bells at circumcision. In the absence of positive information we may surmise that they are regarded as amulets, which protect both sexes against the supernatural dangers to which each, in virtue of its special func-tions, is either permanently or temporarily exposed.

In the Congo region the natives fear that demons may enter their bodies through the mouth when they are in the act of drinking; hence on these occas-sions they make use of various contrivances in order to keep these dangerous beings at a distance, and one of the devices is to ring a bell before every draught of liquid. A chief has been observed to drink ten pots of beer at a sit-ting in this fashion, shaking his magic bell every time before he raised the beaker to his lips, while by way of additional precaution a boy brandished the chief's spear in front of that dignitary to prevent the demons from insinuating themselves into his stomach with the beer.[75] In this region, also, bells which have been enchanted by the fetish-man are worn as amulets, which can avert fever, bullets, and locusts, and can render the wearer invisible.[76] Among the Bkerewe, who inhabit Ukerewe, the largest island in Lake Victoria Nyanza, it is customary to fasten a bell immediately over the door of every house, and every person on entering the dwelling is careful to ring the bell by knocking his head against it, not, as in Europe, to warn the inmates of his arrival, but to ward off evil spirits and to dispel the enchantments of sorcerers.[77] In West Africa the jangling of bells helps to swell the general uproar which accompanies the periodic banishment of bogies from the haunts of men.[78]

To be sure, from a few of the examples which have been cited it appears that sometimes the sound of bells is supposed, not so much to repel evil spirits, as to attract the attention of good or guardian spirits,[79] but on the whole the attractive force of these musical instruments in primitive ritual is far less conspicuous than the repulsive. The use of bells for the purpose of attraction rather than of repulsion may correspond to that more advanced stage of religious consciousness when the fear of evil is outweighed by trust in the good, when the desire of pious hearts is not so much to flee from the Devil as to draw near to God whether it be that the priest in his violet robe, as he crossed the threshold of the sanctuary, was believed to repel the assaults of demons or to attract the attention of the deity by the chime and jingle of the golden bells, the practices and beliefs collected in this chapter may serve to illustrate and perhaps to explain the ancient Hebrew custom from which we started. ▼

Leviticus

Comparative Folklore illustrates several particulars of the laws and rituals enjoined in the Book of Leviticus. Cases in point are: the procedure for the ordination of priests (ch. 8); the manifestation of the so-called "glory of the Lord" (9:6, 23); the descent of automatic fire on the altar (9:24); the dietary laws (ch. 11); the annual ritual of the scapegoat and of the collective communal confession and purgation (ch. 16); and the enactments concerning the observance of the Passover (ch. 23). Each of these incorporates traditional magical notions, although there is, of course, no telling that the latter were anything more than atavistic survivals.

The folklore background of Biblical laws and institutions is reserved for a future volume. In the meanwhile, the curious reader may be referred to the more general treatments of the scapegoat and Passover rituals in my *Festivals of the Jewish Year* (1954), and in my *Passover* (1949), and of the dietary laws in my *Holy and Profane* (1955). Some of the other topics mentioned above are touched upon in the following sections of the present book:

anointment (ch. 8, *passim*)	§284
automatic fire (9:24)	§158
banishment of scapegoat to a "solitary land" (16:22)	§194
bathing (16:4)	§§2, 148
"the blood is the life" (17:14; 19:26)	§25
children offered to Moloch (20:2)	§199
conduct affects fertility (28:3–5, 14–20)	§§144, 198
disfigurement in mourning (10:6; 19:28; 21:10)	§135
lepers (13:45–46)	§194
sevenfold retribution for sins (26:27)	§31

Numbers

If an Israelite suspected his wife of infidelity, he might bring her before the priest for trial by the "waters of ordeal." After preliminary ceremonies, the priest poured some holy water into an earthen vessel and mingled with it a small quantity of dust taken from the floor of the tabernacle. Then, when the woman's hair had been loosed, he handed her the concoction to drink, at the same time administering a curse (the words of which were written on a document subsequently dipped into the water) to the effect that if she were guilty, this would cause her "thigh to fall away" and "her belly to swell." Otherwise she would be proven innocent.

This is the only example in Scripture of trial by ordeal and, although the stratum of the Pentateuch in which it is embedded is the relatively late Priestly Code,[1] there can be little doubt that it represents a genuinely ancient practise, since this form of jurisdiction is in fact commonplace in early and primitive law[2] [and can be illustrated also from Assyrian usage[2a]].

In many parts of Africa, it has been, and perhaps still is, customary to submit criminal charges, particularly accusations of witchcraft, to the test of poison: the accused, and sometimes the accusers also, are compelled to swallow a poisoned draught, and according to the result a verdict of guilty or not guilty is returned. As a rule, a man is declared innocent if he vomits up the poison, but guilty if he either retains it or evacuates it by purging. Death from the effect of the poison is regarded as a sure sign of guilt, but often it is not awaited by the crowd of spectators, who, as soon as it appears that the supposed culprit cannot eject the poison in the approved fashion, rush on him and despatch him with every symptom of rage and every refinement of cruelty.[3]

In presenting the evidence it will be convenient to follow the geographical order, beginning with the west coast, where the poison ordeal has prevailed from Senegal in the north to Angola in the south, spreading also far into the interior along the great valleys of the Niger and Congo.

The Balantes are a tribe of pagan Negroes now settled on the left bank of the river Casamance in Senegal, not far from Sedhiou. Their religion is a system of fetishism, and they stand in great fear of witches and wizards. Accusations of witchcraft are extremely common. A branch of a tree or a bunch of flowers placed by night outside a hut is enough to draw down on the owner a charge of witchcraft, and he is forced to purge himself from the dark suspicion by appealing to the poison ordeal. Not that his accuser is exempt from danger; if it appears that his charge is baseless, he in his turn may have to drain the poisoned cup or be sold as a slave for the benefit of his intended victim. Every person who is accused of witchcraft must repair on a certain day, under the escort of the notables, to the place appointed for the ordeal. Any refusal to comply with this obligation, any attempt to evade it, are crimes which society punishes by burning the culprit alive. Arrived at the seat of judgment the accused receives a cup of poison from the official whose duty it is to conduct the ordeal. The poison is brewed by pounding in a mortar the bark of a certain tree, which the Balantes call *mansone* or *bourdane*. Having drained the cup in the presence of the notables, the accused hastens to a neighbouring spring, where he gulps a great quantity of water, while his friends souse his whole body with water drawn from the fountain. His eyes are now staring, his mouth gaping, sweat bursts in beads from every part of his skin. If he can vomit up the poison, he is acquitted and suffers no other ill consequences than a few days' indisposition; if despite all his efforts he is unable to rid himself of the morbid matter, he falls into convulsions, and within twenty or twenty-five minutes after drinking the draught he drops to the earth like a stone. Succumbing to the effects of the poison, the poor wretch is of course set down as a witch or wizard who has richly deserved his or her fate; and his goods, if he has any, are divided among the notables of his village. This arrangement naturally leads to the frequent detection, or at least accusation, of sorcery. However, the rigour of the law is mercifully tempered by an appeal to the pity or the pocket of the official whose duty it is to brew and administer the poison; for he proportions the strength, or rather the weakness, of the dose to the value of the considerations he has received from the accused or his friends. For this purpose he, or rather she (for the poisoner is generally an old woman), pays a series of domiciliary visits in the village where the patient resides on whom she is shortly to operate; and entering into communication with his kinsfolk she supplies them with good advice or, what they appreciate still more, a powerful antidote, according to the liberality with which they reward these friendly advances. Thus mercy seasons justice.[4]

The course of justice, or rather of injustice, is similar among the Bagnouns, another tribe of Negroes on the Casamance River, who are reputed to have been in former days the most powerful people of this region. Faith in witchcraft is with them, as with practically all African peoples, an article of their creed, and accusations of practising that black art are promulgated under the shadow of night by a personage known as Mumbo Jumbo, who parades the village at unseasonable hours, his face hidden by a mask and his body disguised with a mantle of leaves. All whom he denounces as witches or wizards must demonstrate their innocence or guilt, as the case may be, by an appeal to the poison ordeal.[5]

The same ordeal is resorted to, though in a milder form, by the Sereres, a people of mixed origin who inhabit the coast of Senegambia from Cape

Verd on the north to the Gambia River on the south. Resisting alike the allurements and the menaces of Mohammedan missionaries, the Sereres have remained faithful to their own special form of paganism. They adore two gods, one of whom, named Takhar, presides over justice. His priests are old men recruited in certain families and charged with the lucrative business of judging all cases of theft and witchcraft. In the discharge of his judicial functions the priest contrives to discover the theft by playing on the superstitious fears of the thief, and to detect the witchcraft by administering the usual dose of poison to the suspected witch. But the brew which he compounds for the latter purpose is seldom strong enough to prove fatal; the deaths which ensue from it, we read, are just frequent enough to maintain in the minds of the vulgar a wholesome fear of the divinity.[6]

Among the Landamas, or Landoomans, and the Naloos, two pagan tribes, who inhabit the neighbourhood of the Rio Nuñez in Senegal, there exists a secret society whose grand master bears the title of Simo. He lives in the woods and is never seen by the uninitiated. Whoever is suspected of sorcery is forthwith delivered to the Simo, who acts as chief magistrate. The accused is questioned, and if he confesses, he is condemned to pay a fine; if, on the other hand, he maintains his innocence, he is compelled to drink a liquor made with the bark of a tree which gives to water a beautiful red colour. The accused and the accuser are obliged to swallow the same medicine, or rather poison; they must drink it fasting and entirely naked, except that the accused is allowed a white pagne, which he wraps round his loins. The liquor is poured into a small calabash, and the accuser and accused are forced to take an equal quantity, until, unable to swallow more, they expel it or die. If the poison is expelled by vomiting, the accused is innocent and then he has a right to reparation; if it passes downwards, he is deemed not absolutely innocent; and if it should not pass at all at the time, he is judged to be guilty.[7]

The poison ordeal is found in a variety of forms among some tribes of Upper Senegal or the French Sudan; for example, it occurs among the Mossi, a pagan people of mixed blood formed by the fusion of conquering invaders with subject aborigines, who occupy a vast plain in the great bend of the Niger, a little to the north of the Gold Coast. Thus at Dembo, in the district of Yatenga, when any young person died unexpectedly, it was customary to make the whole population swear by the Earth that they had not killed him or her by sorcery, and to attest their innocence they had to drink a draught of water mixed with a red powder, which was supposed to kill the guilty. The nature of this red powder is not mentioned, but we may conjecture that it was prepared from the pounded bark of the so-called sass or sassy wood (*Erythrophleum guineense*), which furnishes the poison employed in the ordeal over a great part of Africa. In other villages of the same district the draught which the accused must drink in order to refute a charge of witchcraft was tinctured, not with the red powder, but with earth taken from the sacrificial places. This is like the Hebrew custom of mixing the bitter water with dust from the sanctuary. All who refused to purge themselves by the ordeal were put to death. At Kabayoro, a Mossi village in the canton of Koumbili, when a man or woman fell sick without any manifest cause, they laid the sickness at the door of a witch or wizard; and should the patient die, they washed the hands of the corpse in water and compelled the suspected sorcerer to drink the potion, protesting his innocence and imprecating death on his own head if he lied. If he were guilty, the corpse-tinctured water was supposed to kill him; but if he were innocent, it did him no harm.[8]

In this last form of the ordeal the fatal effect of the draught is clearly attributed, not to a vegetable poison, but to the deadly influence which the corpse is believed to exert over the murderer. Among the tribes in this district of the French Sudan the ordeal by drinking water mixed with sacred earth is apparently common. In every case the earth employed for this purpose seems to be drawn from the place where sacrifices are offered to Earth, a great divinity in these parts, and frequently the oath is administered by the priest, who bears the title of Chief of the Earth. For example, at Pissié, a village of the Kassounas-Fras tribe, whenever any person died suddenly, and his death was, as usual, ascribed to witchcraft, the chief of the village, who was also the priest of Earth, compelled all the adults of that particular ward, men and women, to come forth from their houses and attend him to the place where sacrifices were offered to Earth in the middle of the village. There he took earth from the holy spot, and putting it in water obliged all to swallow the draught and to swear their innocence under pain of being killed by the divinity. Sometimes, we are told, the guilty wretch who denied his crime was slain by the Earth, to whose divinity he had falsely appealed.[9] Similarly at Saveloo, a village of the Bouras, an aboriginal and primitive tribe of the Gold Coast, when a death occurred and the relations of the deceased were of opinion that he had been taken off by sorcery, the chief of the village forced both the accuser and the accused to drink a potion containing dust and earth which had been taken from the sacrificial place of the deified Earth. As they drank they swore, praying that the draught might kill them if they forswore themselves. One of the two was believed always to fall a victim to the deadly power of the holy dust and earth in his belly; and the chief of the village thereupon confiscated or, as the natives put it, "collected," the personal property of the supposed culprit and seized his children as slaves.[10] Among the Dagaris and Zangas, two heathen tribes whose territories lie partly in the French Sudan and partly in the British Gold Coast, the ordeal and oath were similar; and among them, it is said, the belly of the guilty person, who had drunk the water and forsworn himself, would sometimes swell up, so that he died. In such cases the deified Earth was believed to have punished him for his crime.[11] We may compare the effect of the bitter water in the Hebrew ordeal, which was thought to cause the belly of the adulteress to swell and her thigh to fall away.[12]

Amongst the free Negroes of Liberia, to the south of Sierra Leone, the poison ordeal is still in vogue, though it is said to be disappearing among the Kru people of this region in consequence of the frequent intercourse which the Kru men, as sailors and traders, maintain with Europeans. The poison is prepared from the bark of the *Erythrophleum guineense,* a tall forest tree which grows commonly in West Africa. In popular language the decoction is known as sassy-wood, the adjective *sass* being allegedly a native word for "bad." If the accused vomits up the poison, he is deemed innocent; if he dies under its influence, he is guilty; if he neither voids the poison nor dies, he is given an emetic to relieve him and is advised to quit the village and find a home elsewhere. Among the Grebo people of Liberia there exists a secret society called Kwi-iru for the detection and punishment of witches and wizards, and the persons whom members of the society denounce are obliged to clear themselves of the charge of witchcraft by submitting to the poison ordeal in presence of the assembled people. An officer of the society pounds the bark in a mortar, pours water on it, and having decanted the poisonous liquor into a wooden bowl, he prays to God that if the accused be innocent, he may vomit the poison, but that if he be guilty, it may kill him. The suspected wizard or witch then drains the draught, and according to its effect he or she is deemed to have been rightly or wrongly accused.[13]

The Neyaux of the Ivory Coast believe that no man dies naturally, and that all deaths are the result of witchcraft. Those who inhabit the house of the suspected witch are obliged, under orders of the soothsayer, to drink a decoction prepared from the red bark of a tree which the natives call *boduru.* Having swallowed it, they must run till the poison takes effect; if they are innocent, it is rejected by the stomach; if they are guilty, they die in agony and convulsions.[14]

On the Gold Coast the wood which furnishes the poison for the ordeal is called *odum.* The accused either drinks a decoction of the wood or chews a piece of the wood and afterwards drinks a bowl of water. The poison acts both as an emetic and as a purge: if the accused vomits it up, he is acquitted; if he does not, his guilt is established. Women accused of adultery, for example, have to drink a brew of this poison in presence of a priest; the draught is believed to have power to burst the belly of an adulteress. Fear of the consequences, it is said, often leads unfaithful wives to confess their guilt.[15]

At Aneho, on the coast of Togoland, there is a certain fetish named Nanyo, who is appealed to in all cases of death which are suspected to be due to poison. If the accused denies his guilt, he must drink the fetish water. The priest makes him sit down on a stool and digs a small hole in the ground before him. Next he snips off some locks of the suspected prisoner's hair, pares his nails, and buries the clippings of the hair and the parings of the nails in the hole, together with a small fetish object which he has brought forth from the fetish hut. Having filled up the hole, the priest next touches all the joints of the accused person's body with a fetish stick, telling him that in these places he will experience the first ill effects of his crime, if he forswears himself. Then he hands a calabash of fetish water to the accused, who takes it in his left hand and drinks thrice out of it. This ends the ceremony, and all go home. If after drinking the water the man dies within seven days, he is supposed to have been killed by the fetish. The priests carry his body out of the village and deposit it on a scaffold, where it remains exposed to wind and weather. In the swampy districts about Degbenu the bleaching skeletons of many such victims of the ordeal may be seen.[16]

On the Slave Coast, as on the Gold Coast, the most common ordeal is, or rather used to be, the drinking of a decoction of *odum* wood. The custom prevailed both among the Ewe-speaking and the Yoruba-speaking peoples of this region. The potion is, as usual, prepared by a priest, who thus has it in his power to kill or save the accused according to the strength or weakness of the dose which he infuses into the liquor. If the poison is not at once rejected by the stomach, it kills the drinker, and the fetish is considered to have declared his guilt by slaying him. A guilty man dares not undergo the ordeal, but the innocent submit to it without fear, and indeed frequently demand it in order to prove their innocence; hence it is the guiltless who ordinarily perish.[17]

In Benin, so firm was the faith of the people in the justice of the ordeal that in the consciousness of innocence they appealed to it voluntarily; sometimes they vomited up the poison and escaped, sometimes they retained it and perished. When the accused person vomited, his vomit was examined to see whether "the evil thing had come out."[18]

In Southern Nigeria, particularly among the tribes about Calabar, no death was considered natural except through extreme old age, so that in the case of sickness or death it was supposed that some one or other was practising witchcraft or wizardry against the life of the sufferer. This dreaded power is called *ifot*. On a death occurring, the juju [that is, fetish] man might be asked to discover the guilty party, which he was never at a loss to do, and those he denounced were subjected to the ordeal of the poison bean, the *Physostigma venenosum* of botanists. It is administered in every way in which poison is given, and is held to be a test of the possession or nonpossession of the *ifot*. When the accused vomits the poison draught, *ifot* is not found in the individual, and he is consequently innocent of the crime with which he is charged; but if his stomach does not reject it, he dies, which is conclusive proof of his guilt.[19]

Among the Kagoro, a war-like tribe of Northern Nigeria, the poison ordeal is also in vogue. The poison is extracted from the pith of a tree, which is pounded and soaked in water. Having drunk the poisoned draught, the accused has to walk round the empty calabash; if he vomits, he is as usual deemed innocent, but if he fails to eject the poison, he dies the same day. A powerful man can submit to the ordeal by deputy in the shape of a fowl, which drinks the poison for him.[20]

The Negroes of the Cross River, in the Cameroons, believe that a sorcerer has in his body, near his heart, an evil spirit in the shape of an owl, which can quit his body at night and suck the blood of men or women, thus causing their death. When a man is accused of keeping such a foul fiend in his body, he is compelled to submit to the poison ordeal in the presence of the whole village. The poison is prepared from the Calabar bean, which grows wild in the district. If within three hours of drinking the draught he vomits up both the bean and the water in which it has previously been steeped, he is declared innocent; in the interval he sits before the house under strict guard. Sometimes the poison proves fatal in two hours.[21]

The Bayas, who inhabit the right bank of the Kadeï river in French Congo, on the borders of the Cameroons, cannot understand how any but old people can die from natural causes. All other deaths they imagine to be due to spells cast on the deceased persons by women. Accordingly when a man in the prime of life has died, all his womenkind and especially his wives, are assembled and obliged to submit to the poison ordeal. The poison consists of an infusion of a certain bark called *banda* in water. As usual, innocence is demonstrated by vomiting up the poison, and guilt is proved by dying of it. The body of the culprit is opened by the medicine-man, and the source of the witch's magical power is supposed to be found within it in the form of a bird.[22]

The poison ordeal also obtains, or used to obtain, among the Fans of the Gaboon.[23] The poison used for this purpose is obtained sometimes from the bark of the *Erythrophleum micranthum* tree. A person is seldom required to drink more than half a pint of the decoction. If it acts freely as a diuretic it is a mark of innocence; but if as a narcotic, and produces dizziness or vertigo, it is a sure sign of guilt. Small sticks are laid down at the distance of eighteen inches or two feet apart, and the suspected person, after he has swallowed the draught, is required to walk over them. If he has no vertigo, he steps over them easily and naturally; but, on the other hand, if his brain is affected, he imagines they rise up before him like great logs, and in his awkward effort to step over them, he is very apt to reel and fall to the ground. In some cases this draught is taken by proxy; and if a man is found guilty, he is either put to death or heavily fined and banished from the country.[24]

Nowhere, perhaps, in Africa has this barbarous method of detecting an imaginary crime been applied more extensively or with greater rigour than among the tribes which inhabit the vast valley of the Congo River and its tributaries. Towards the end of the sixteenth century and at the beginning of the seventeenth century an English seaman, a native of Leigh, in Essex, spent eighteen years in Portuguese West Africa, and he has described the poison ordeal as it was practised in Loango, the province which is bounded on the south by the lower course of the Congo:

"When any man is suspected for an offence, he is carried before the king, or before Mani Bomma, who is a judge under the king. And if he denies matters, not to be proved except by their oath, then this suspected person swears thus: They have a kind of root which they call *Imbando;* this root is very strong, and is scraped into water. The virtue of this root is, that if they put too much into the water, the person that drinketh it cannot void urine: and so it strikes up into the brain, as if he was drunk, and he falls down as if he was dead. And those that fall are counted guilty, and are punished. In this country none on any account dieth, but they kill another for him: for they believe they die not their own natural death, but that some other hath bewitched them to death. And all those are brought in by the friends of the dead whom they suspect; so that there many times come five hundred men and women to take the drink, made of the foresaid root *Imbando.* They are brought all to the high-street or market-place, and there the master of the *Imbando* sits with his water, and gives every one a cup of water by one measure; and they are command to walk in a certain place till they make water, and then they are free. But he that cannot urine presently falls down, and all the people, great and small, fall upon him with their knives, and beat and cut him to pieces. But I think the witch that gives the water is partial, and gives to him whose death is desired the strongest water, but no man of the bye-standers can perceive it. This is done in the town of Longo, almost every week throughout the year."[25]

To this day trial by ordeal survives among the tribes of the Congo. The ordeals are various, but the most popular and widespread of all is the poison ordeal, which is reported to prevail throughout nearly the whole extent of the Congo State. Like the other ordeals, it is resorted to on a great variety of occasions, at judicial trials, funerals, religious assemblies, lunar incantations, and so forth, whenever justice or injustice demands the detection and punishment of a real or imaginary criminal. In this region, as in many other parts of Africa, sickness and death, public calamities and private misfortunes are regularly attributed to the machinations of sorcerers, and the assistance of the medicine-man or witch-doctor (*nganga*) is invoked to find a remedy for the evil or to bring the wrongdoer to justice. Sometimes the person whom the medicine-man denounces as the witch or wizard is put to death or otherwise punished without any further formalities; but generally the accused, who energetically denies his guilt, is given an opportunity of clearing his character by drinking poison, and strong in the conviction of his innocence the suspected wizard submits to the ordeal. Throughout a considerable part of the Congo the poison employed for this purpose is called by the natives *nkassa,* whence among Europeans the ordeal goes by the name of *cassa* or *casca.* The potion is prepared and administered by the medicine-man in presence of a crowd who have assembled to witness the trial. If the accused dies on the spot, he is naturally regarded as guilty of the witchcraft laid to his charge; if he escapes with his life, his character as an honest man and no wizard is established. Should the supposed culprit be a man of property or conscious

of guilt, he will often, in the interval between the accusation and the trial,
seek out the medicine-man and induce him by convincing arguments, or a
sufficient bribe, to mix the dose so that it shall not be mortal. The draught
is generally prepared either from the root of a plant belonging to the genus
Strychnos, or from the bark of a tree; but sometimes it is made from the juice
of a euphorbia or a decoction of boiled ants. The root or bark is scraped into
water, which is thereupon boiled; the strength or weakness of the dose
naturally varies with the amount of poison infused into the water. In different
parts of the Congo valley the poison employed in the ordeal goes by different
names. Thus in the Lower Congo it is called *muavi,* among the Upotos it is
named *bundi,* and among the Azandes it goes by the name of *dawa.* Among the
Bangalas one poison known as *nka* or *mbonde* is prepared by scraping the
red root of a shrub of the genus *Strychnos;* the powder thus produced is
infused into cold water, and the potion is then drunk by the accused, who is
supposed to die infallibly if he is guilty, but merely to suffer from indisposition
if he is innocent. The first effect of the drug is to produce a state resembling
intoxication. Some people accused of witchcraft offer voluntarily to drink the
poison in order to demonstrate their innocence. Among the Bangalas there is
another ordeal of the same sort known by the name of *mokungu.* The poison
is a juice extracted from the bark of a tree called *mukungu,* which grows commonly in the forests, and perhaps belongs to the family of acacias. This ordeal
is generally reserved for women, who do not drink the juice, but are obliged
to drop a little of it under the eyelid of one of their eyes. If the woman is
guilty, the eye bursts; if she is innocent, she takes no harm. Slave women who
have lost one eye in this way are not uncommon in Bangala villages. In some
tribes the accused may procure a proxy in the person of a slave or a friend
to drink the poison for him; a friend will readily perform this good office,
confiding in the other's innocence and his own immunity. If the accused
should fail to eject the poison, without dying from the effect of it, he is put
to death with every refinement of cruelty and barbarity. In the country of
the Azandes the ordeal assumes a milder form. The poison (*dawa*) is usually
administered in the first instance to fowls in order to discover the criminal,
who, on being detected, must undergo the ordeal in his own person or pay
the forfeit. Among the Abarambos, for example, the poison is given by the
chief to three fowls, and a ritual dance follows, until the effect of the drug upon
the birds becomes apparent. If one only of the fowls succumbs, there has been
no witchcraft; but if two or three perish, it is a clear case of sorcery.[26]

Among the Ababua, a tribe of the Upper Congo, deaths are regularly attributed to the magical arts of witches or wizards, who have cast a spell on the
deceased or caused an evil spirit (*likundu*) to enter into his body. Hence when
a chief dies, a medicine-man is called in to detect the criminal or criminals.
All the wives of the dead man are obliged to undergo the ordeal by swallowing
a poison extracted from the root of a plant. Those who fall down under the

influence of the drug are killed and eaten. When an ordinary freeman or freewoman dies, the medicine-man accuses some one in the village of having caused the death, and the accused has to submit to the poison ordeal in the usual way. If he passes through it unscathed, his innocence is demonstrated, and he receives from the medicine-man a slave by way of compensation. When the acused has died or been killed, the corpse is often opened in order to detect the magical substance or evil spirit (*likundu*), by which the witch or wizard wrought his foul enchantments. The substance or spirit is commonly produced in the shape of a rounded body containing a dark liquid; it is probably the gall-bladder. Such judicial murders are frequent among the Ababua.[27] They ascribe every accident and misfortune, however trivial or natural its cause, to the malice of an ill-wisher or sorcerer. Sickness, death, the ravages of a storm, the burning of a hut, are all indifferently traced to the same fatal agency. Accordingly the suspected sorcerer is compelled to submit to one of several ordeals according to the gravity of the charge. One of these ordeals is the drinking of an infusion of poisonous herbs. If the accused is innocent he will vomit up the poison; but if he is guilty he dies, and his expiring agonies are greeted with shouts of approval and delight.[28]

Further, the poison ordeal is in vogue among the tribes who occupy the valleys of the great tributaries which flow into the Congo from the south. Thus among the Bambala, a Bantu tribe inhabiting the tract of country between the Inzia (Saie) and Kwilu rivers, the ordeal is resorted to in cases of alleged witchcraft, parricide, or minor offences.[29]

Similar beliefs and practices in regard to the poison ordeal prevail among two neighbouring Bantu tribes, the Ba-Yaka and the Ba-hauna.[30] They occur also among the Bangongo, a tribe which inhabits the angle between the Lubudi and Sankuru rivers, and belongs, like the Bambala, to the Bushongo or, as it is called by Europeans, the Bakuba nation. In this tribe, when any one dies a natural death without any apparent cause, the death is set down to the maleficence of a demon acting through the agency of a person who is possessed, consciously or unconsciously, by the evil spirit. The brother of the deceased commonly accuses one of the villagers, generally an old man or old woman, of having in this way killed his departed relative; and a witch-doctor, who bears the title of *Miseke,* is summoned to administer the poison ordeal to the accused. The poison is extracted from a plant called *ephumi,* and is kept for the purpose of the ordeal in a miniature hut of straw, about two feet high, in the middle of the principal street. A cup of the poison being presented to the accused, he says, "If I have killed So-and-so, if I have killed So-and-so, if I have killed So-and-so, may you kill me," smiting his hands together thrice, "but if I am innocent, prove it." He then runs towards the forest, pursued by all the villagers, the friends of the deceased crying, "You have killed So-and-so, and you will die," while his friends, on the contrary, encourage him by shouting, "Prove that you are innocent! Prove that you are innocent!" The witch-doctor (*Miseke*) runs by the side of the fugitive, striking him on the head with a child's bell, and saying continually, *"Ephumi, ephumi, kill the moloki!"* that is, "Poison, poison, kill the man possessed of the devil," for in this tribe it appears that the name *moloki* is applied, not so much to the demon himself, as to the person of whom he has taken possession. If the accused is seized with a fit of vomiting, he is considered innocent, and his accuser must pay him several thousands of cowries as damages. If he cannot rid himself of the poison by vomiting, he dies, and his guilt is thought to be fully demonstrated.[31]

Among the Bashilange, a tribe which borders on the Bakuba or Bushongo nation, when two persons have quarrelled and one of them refuses to accept the decision of a third whom they have chosen to arbitrate between them, the arbitrator may order the recalcitrant party to undergo an ordeal by drinking the infusion of a certain bark. The draught is prepared by a medicine-man in the presence of the arbitrator, but no drowned fly may float on the surface of the liquid, and no menstruous woman may ever have been in the house where the potion is compounded.[32] Among the tribes of the Kasai river and its affluents, which flow into the Congo from the south, an important place is occupied by the Balunda. Sickness, misfortune, and death are set down by them, not to natural causes, but to the machinations of an enemy, and to discover the culprit the services of a soothsayer are called in. Sometimes he accuses a person of having done the mischief, and then the accused has to prove his innocence, if he can, by drinking *m'bambu,* which is a decoction of the bitter bark of the *Erythrophleum.*[33]

Southward of the vast region of the Congo and its tributaries, the poison ordeal, with all its attendant superstitions and iniquities, is or was till lately rampant in Angola. Among the Songos, in the interior of Angola, disputes about property are referred to the Soba or chief of the town, but if the litigants refuse to accept his decision, they have recourse to the poison ordeal. In this tribe the poison is usually drunk, not by the suitors themselves, but by their children or their dogs, who act as proxies for their parents or owners respectively. The poison is administered weak, so that death seldom results from it. The person whose child or dog first vomits the dose wins his case; but if before that happens, one of the champions, whether child or dog, collapses under the influence of the drug, the party whom he or she represents is cast in the suit.[34]

Among the tribes which inhabit the western regions of Africa from Angola southward the practice of the poison ordeal has not, so far as I am aware, been recorded; among the Herero, the chief Bantu tribe of South-West Africa, it is definitely said to be unknown.[35] Indeed, throughout the whole southern extremity of the continent, from Angola and the Zambesi on the north to the Cape of Good Hope on the south, the poison ordeal has been seldom described, from which we may perhaps infer that it has been little practised.

However, it was formerly in vogue among the Zulus of Natal at the time when they were governed by the tyrant Chaka in the early part of the nineteenth century. In those days, whenever a person had died and been buried, his or her relations regularly had recourse to a diviner in order to discover the man who, through the agency of an evil spirit, had caused the death of their friend. Having consulted his magical instrument, which might be a horn of oil or a pot of boiling water, the diviner denounced somebody as the culprit, often fastening the guilt on a man or woman whom he knew to be at enmity with the family of the deceased. The person thus accused was at once taken into custody, and next morning before sunrise he had to swallow a mixture made from the bark of the *moave* tree and certain powders, the whole being made up in three balls, each of the size of a lemon. Before taking the poison he was stripped naked, lest he should conceal anything that might counteract the effect of the drug, and he knelt with his hands crossed before the man who administered the dose. While the accused was engaged in swallowing the poison, his relations and the kinsfolk of the deceased continued to beat the ground with sticks, while one of them cried out, "If this man or woman has communicated with evil spirits, may the *moave* burst him!" to which all responded in chorus, "Burst him!" Then the first speaker went on, "If this man or woman who has been the death of So-and-so, has been falsely accused, and has not communicated with evil spirits, then may the *moave* spare him!" to which all answered, "Spare him!" These prayers and responses they kept repeating till the accused vomited, which, we are told, happened only through the roguery of the man in charge of the ordeal, who had been bribed by the relations of the supposed culprit to diminish the dose.[36]

Among the Bawenda, a Bantu tribe which inhabits the north-eastern corner of the Transvaal, between the Limpopo and Levuvu rivers, no case of death or illness occurs without some living person being suspected or accused of having caused it by sorcery; for in the opinion of the Bawenda, as of many other savages, nobody dies a natural death. Hence when any such misfortune has befallen them, the family of the sick or of the dead engage a witch-doctor to detect and bring to justice the witch or wizard (*moloi*), who is supposed to be the author of the calamity. If the witch-doctor lays the blame on two persons, and it cannot be determined by ordinary methods which of the two is in fact the criminal, recourse is had to the poison ordeal. Both of them are given a strongly poisonous potion to drink, and the one who is intoxicated thereby is clearly the guilty party and suffers the penalty of his crime by being clubbed to death.[37]

Farther to the north, among the tribes of Sofala and Manica, in Portuguese East Africa, the poison ordeal seems to be resorted to only in cases of suspected sorcery or cannibalism. A man accused of injuring or killing another by spells or magic must undergo the ordeal. The poison is concocted and administered by the *nganga* or witch-doctor, on whose ill or good will the life of the accused depends. The poison is extracted from pieces of the bark of the *Erythrophleum,* which are ground to a coarse powder and placed in a small calabash of water. The blood of a fowl is added to the mixture, and the draught is heated by red-hot pieces of quartz crystal dropped into the water. If the accused vomits the drug, he is innocent and safe; if he does not, he dies a painful death, while the bystanders heap all sorts of indignities and insults on him, as he lies writhing in agony on the ground. The supposed culprit is detected by the witch-doctor, who dances about arrayed in the skins of animals and with a sort of tiara of reedbuck horns upon his head. In the course of this dance he draws out suspected persons from the throng of spectators, till he at last pounces on the doomed man.[38]

Passing still northward we come to the Zambesi. A well-informed writer has put it on record that "on the Zambesi the poison ordeal is a great institution. When a death has occurred in a village through an accident with a lion or a crocodile, the diviner is called in to smell out the sorcerer. When suspicion is fixed on a person he has to undergo the poison ordeal, the theory of which is this: people use magic so as to eat human flesh without being detected. By magic they change themselves into crocodiles or lions, and lie in wait for the person they wish to eat; having eaten the person, they change themselves back into human beings again by magic. Now, it is supposed that if a person has human flesh in his stomach the poison will work inwardly and kill the person, for it combines with the human flesh he has eaten. If, however, he has eaten no human flesh the poison will be vomited up.[39]

Among the Bantu tribes of British Central Africa the poison ordeal is, or rather was not confined to cases of witchcraft; it is a regular form of judicial procedure for the discovery of crime, such as theft or other offences. And the intervention of the witch-doctor is not necessary to put the ordeal in operation. Anybody who feels himself under a cloud of suspicion may demand it in order to clear his character. So firm is the belief of the natives in the powerlessness of the poison to harm the innocent, that none except consciencestricken criminals ever seem to shrink from the trial.[40] Sometimes the poison is taken by proxy, being administered to a dog or a fowl, instead of to the accused man or woman, and according as the animal or bird survives or perishes, so is the accused innocent or guilty. To indicate or to establish the relationship between the two, each dog or fowl is tethered by a string to the person whom it represents.[41]

The use of the poison ordeal is familiar also to the Bantu tribes of German East Africa. Thus in the district of Mkulwe or Mkurue, to the south of Lake Rukwa, when the sickness of a chief, or the death of important people in rapid succession, is traced by the medicine-man to witchcraft, that powerful personage requires that every inhabitant of the village shall prove his innocence or guilt by drinking a decoction of the poisonous *moavi* (*mwavi*) bark. As usual, innocence is proved by vomiting up the poison, and guilt by retaining it in the stomach and dying from its effect. The use of the ordeal is now forbidden under heavy penalties, but it is still sometimes resorted to in secret, and most of the natives retain their faith in its infallibility. When the young wives of old men are suspected of adultery, they are allowed to clear their character by a milder form of the ordeal. A piece of the bark is thrown into boiling water, and the accused must twice dip both hands slowly into the seething fluid. If she is scalded, she is guilty and must name her paramour, who is obliged to pay a heavy fine, while as a rule the woman escapes with nothing worse than scalded hands.[42]

The poison ordeal is also in vogue among the Wanyamwesi, a large tribe who occupy an extensive country of German East Africa to the south of the Lake Victoria Nyanza. Sometimes the medicine-man (*mganga*) administers the poison in the first instance to a hen, which appears as proxy for the defendant. But if all parties are not satisfied with the result of the experiment on the fowl, there is no help for it but the defendant must swallow the poison in his own person.[43] Among the Wagogo, another tribe of the same region, whose country lies to the eastward of that of the Wanyamwesi, the custom of the poison ordeal was similar, and in light cases it was similarly permissible to administer the poison to a fowl instead of to the accused.[44] Among the Wahehe, who occupy the country to the east of the Wagogo, the ordeal was again similar, and similarly in lighter cases the poison might be administered to a dog or a fowl instead of to the accused.[45]

Among the Wanika of British East Africa, who include a number of tribes or sub-tribes inhabiting the country a little way inland from the sea in the south-eastern part of the territory, murder and sorcery are capital crimes, and if the evidence is inadequate or conflicting, a decision is obtained by recourse to an ordeal. One of the ordeals in use consists in compelling the accused to eat a piece of poisoned bread; if he escapes uninjured, he is deemed innocent, otherwise he is pronounced guilty and punished accordingly.[46] Among the Wawanga of the Elgon District, in British East Africa, when two persons have a dispute which they cannot settle peaceably between themselves, a medicine-man will sometimes administer a potion to both of them, and the one who falls down insensible after drinking the stuff loses his case and often his life, being belaboured by the winner with sticks, which complete the work begun by the draught. If both parties fall down impartially, it is judged that the medicine or charm has failed to work. Though we are not told, we may infer that poison is one of the ingredients in the potion. This is a general form of trial for all offences, and the results which it yields are presumably in every case equally satisfactory.[47]

The poison ordeal is also in use among the Basoga, a Bantu people who admit a district on the northern shore of Lake Victoria Nyanza. It is commonly resorted to in cases of doubt and difficulty. Accuser and accused drink a liquid prepared from the *madudu,* a narcotic plant. Or they may depute the disagreeable task to their slaves, who swallow the potion for them. The final appeal, however, is said to be to the chief.[48]

Among the Baganda, a powerful Bantu nation, whose country adjoins that of the Basoga on the west, the poison ordeal was resorted to in cases where neither of two disputants could prove himself to be in the right, or where one of them was dissatisfied with the judgment given by the king. The poison was administered by a priest attached to the temple of the war-god Kibuka. It bore the native name of *madudu* and was obtained by boiling the fruit of the datura plant.[49]

Among the Banyoro, another powerful Bantu nation, whose territory adjoins that of their rivals the Baganda on the west, the poison ordeal was similar. As among many other African tribes, the poison was sometimes administered to two fowls, which acted as proxies for the human litigants.[50]

The Wawira, who inhabit the open grass-lands and dense forests to the west of the southern end of Lake Albert Nyanza, believe that death is always caused by sorcery. Suspicion generally falls on the wives of a deceased man; hence on the death of a husband the widows commonly take to flight. If the suspected witch is apprehended, she must clear herself by the poison ordeal or perish in the attempt. As ordinarily happens, to vomit up the poison is a proof of innocence; to retain it is at once a demonstration of guilt and a cause of death.[51]

Many different ordeals were in use among the tribes of Madagascar, but of them all the poison ordeal was the most famous. The poison was derived from the kernel of the fruit of the tagena tree (*Tanghinia venenifera* or *veneneflua*), a small and handsome tree which grows in the warmer parts of the island. Used in small quantities, an extract of the nut acts like an emetic; but in larger doses it is a virulent poison. It was employed chiefly for the detection of infamous crimes, such as witchcraft and treason, when ordinary evidence could not be obtained. The people believed that some supernatural power, a sort of "searcher of hearts," inhered in the fruit, which entered into the suspected person and either proved his innocence or established his guilt. A portion of two kernels was rubbed down in water or in the juice of a banana, and the accused had to drink the infusion, having previously eaten a little rice and swallowed three small pieces of fowl's skin. After a few minutes tepid water was administered to him to cause vomiting, and if he succeeded in throwing up the three pieces of fowl's skin uninjured, he was deemed innocent. The people retained a firm faith in the supernatural virtue of the ordeal, and often, strong in the consciousness of their innocence, demanded of the authorities to have the poison administered to them for the purpose of clearing their character from every shadow of suspicion. Sometimes the inhabitants of whole villages drank the poison, and the consequent mortality was very great. It was computed that about one-tenth of the population took the poison in the course of their lives, and that upwards of three thousand perished by it every year.[52]

When a person was accused of sorcery and had to undergo the ordeal, he was taken out of doors and his head was covered with a mat, after which he was led to the house where the ordeal was to take place. Then the official who presided at the trial prayed to the deity named Raimanamango, who was supposed to reside in the egg-shaped fruit of the tangena tree. He said: "Hear, hear, hear, and hearken well, O thou Raimanamango, searcher, trier, or test; thou art a round egg made by God. Though thou hast no eyes, yet thou seest; though thou hast no ears, yet thou hearest; though thou hast no mouth, yet thou answerest: therefore hear and hearken well, O Raimanamango!" Next, the presiding official solemnly cursed the accused if he should be found guilty of sorcery, saying, "If thou findest that he has the root of sorcery, or the trunk of sorcery, or the leaves of sorcery, then kill him immediately, kill him instantly, let him die forthwith, tear his flesh, wring or twist his bowels, tear them into pieces. For thou, Raimanamango, art God, who wilt not permit sorcerers, that murder people, to live; therefore, if thou findest that he is guilty of sorcery, kill him." Next he cursed the accused if he should have a secret charm or antidote to counteract the effect of the poison, saying, "Now though he flatters himself secure while confiding in these, suffer not thyself, O Tangena, to be conquered by them, for thou art God; therefore, if he is a sorcerer, kill him quickly, kill him immediately, let him die forthwith; kill him without delay, burst him and tear his flesh, and tear his arms into pieces; break his heart, burst his bowels. Oh kill him instantly, kill him in a moment," and so forth. And to provide for the case of the accused proving to be innocent, the god was prayed to as follows: "Therefore, if he be innocent, let him live quickly, preserve his heart without delay; let him greatly rejoice, let him dance and run about merrily, like one who has drunk cold water; let him become like cold water, which is refreshing; let flesh return to him, if thou findest that he has no sorcery or witchcraft to kill persons with. Now, take care then, and forget not to return back through the same door through which I made thee enter into him." The curses which preceded the drinking of the poisoned draught in this Malagasy ordeal may be compared with the curses pronounced by the priest in administering the bitter water of the Hebrew ordeal. When a member of a family fell ill, all the slaves in the household had often to submit to the ordeal, since they were suspected of causing the sickness by witchcraft. Should the sovereign himself be indisposed, not only his slaves but all persons in personal attendance on him might be compelled to attest their loyalty and innocence by drinking the poison.[53] Accuser and accused often deputed the painful duty of drinking the poison to two fowls or two dogs, which acted as their proxies; and the guilt or innocence of the principal was decided according to the vomit of his four-footed or feathered deputy.[54]

The poison ordeal has been practised in India from time immemorial.[55]

The ancient Indian lawbook which passes under the name of Vishnu, but which in its final form can hardly be earlier than about the year 200 A.D.,[56] recognizes and describes the ordeals by the balance, by fire, by water, by poison, and by sacred libation, that is, by drinking water in which the images of gods have been dipped.[57] The rules which the code lays down for the administration of the poison ordeal are as follows:

"All (other) sorts of poison must be avoided (in administering this ordeal), except poison from the *Sriṅga* tree, which grows on the Himalayas. (Of that) the judge must give seven grains, mixed with clarified butter, to the defendant. If the poison is digested easily, without violent symptoms, he shall recognise him as innocent, and dismiss him at the end of the day." And while the judge administered the poison to the defendant, he was to recite the following prayer: "On account of thy venomous and dangerous nature thou art destruction to all living creatures; thou, O poison, knowest what mortals do not comprehend. This man being arraigned in a cause, desires to be cleared from guilt. Therefore mayest thou deliver him lawfully from this perplexity."[58] But the poison ordeal might not be administered to lepers, bilious persons, and Brahmans, nor might recourse be had to it during the rainy season.[59]

And in regard to the administration of the ordeal by sacred libation, the same code lays down the following rules:

"Having invoked terrible deities (such as Durgâ, the Âdityas or others, the defendant) must drink three handfuls of water in which (images of) those deities have been bathed, uttering at the same time the words, 'I have not done this,' with his face turned towards the deity (in question). He to whom (any calamity) happens within a fortnight or three weeks (such as an illness, or fire, or the death of a relative, or a heavy visitation by the king), should be known to be guilty; otherwise (if nothing adverse happens to him), he is freed from the charge. A just king should honour (with presents of clothes, ornaments, etc.) one who has cleared himself from guilt by an ordeal."[60]

This account of the poison ordeal, as it was practised in antiquity, is supplemented by other ancient authorities. Thus according to the lawgiver Nârada, the poison was to be administered by a Brahman fasting, with his face turned to the north or east, and the quantity of poison in the dose should vary with the season. In the cold season the amount should be seven barleycorns, in the hot season five, in the rainy season four, and in autumn three,[61] which seems to imply that in the opinion of the ancients the virulence of the poison varied with the season, so that at certain times of the year a smaller dose sufficed to produce the same effect which at other times could only be brought about by a larger. According to the lawgiver Kâtyâyana, the poison should be given in the forenoon in a cool place, mixed with thirty times as much clarified butter, well pounded. Nârada prescribed that the person who had drunk the poison should sit down in the shade and be watched for the rest of the day, without being allowed to eat food.[62] The lawgiver Pitâmaha recommended that in order to prevent fraud the accused should be carefully guarded for three or five days before the ordeal, lest he should take drugs or practise charms and enchantments which might counteract and annul the effect of the poison.[63] According to one account, which claimed the authority of the lawgiver Nârada, the effect of the full dose of poison was only to be observed in the space of time during which the judge could clap his hands five hundred times; while the rule that the accused was to be kept under observation for the rest of the day applied only to cases in which smaller quantities of the poison had been administered.[64] The symptoms produced by the drinking of the poison are thus described in the *Vishatantra:* "The first attack of the poison causes the erection of the hair (on the body), (then follow) sweat and dryness of the mouth, after that arise (frequent) changes of colour, and trembling of the body. Then the fifth attack causes the immobility of the eyes, loss of speech, and hiccoughing. The sixth, hard breathing and loss of consciousness, and the seventh, the death of the person."[65] According to Yâjnavalkya, the person who was about to undergo the ordeal prayed to the poison as follows: "O poison, thou art Brahman's son, firm in the duty of (making known the) truth, save me."[66] The administrator of the ordeal addresses the poison in the following terms: "Poison, thou art a maleficent substance, created to destroy guilty or impure creatures; thou wert vomited by the great serpent Bashooky to cause the guilty giants to perish. Here is a person accused of an offence of which he professes to be innocent. If he is really not guilty, strip thyself of thy maleficent properties in his favour, and become nectar for him." And according to the same authority the proof of innocence consists in surviving the drinking of the poison for three days.[67]

All the ancient lawgivers seem to agree in prescribing the poison of the *sriṅga* as the proper one for use in the ordeal, though two of them, namely Kâtyâyana and Pitâmaha, permitted the employment of the *vatsanâbha* also for that purpose.[68] The *sriṅga* is said to be the root of one of the poisonous Himalayan species of *Aconitum,* generally referred to as *Aconitum ferox,* which is found in the Himalayas to a considerable height. The venom resides in the root, and is as dangerous when applied to a wound as when taken internally. Hence all along the Himalayas, before the introduction of firearms, the poison used to be smeared on arrows; and the wild tribes of the Brahmaputra valley, such as the Abors, Daphlas, and Akas, employed it in war as well as in hunting tigers. The natives believe that even the exhalation of the plant has power to poison the air, and the Gurkhas allege that by means of it they could so infect the rivers and springs that no enemy would be able to penetrate into their country.[69]

The practice of the poison ordeal appears to be based on a theory that the poison is an animated and intelligent being, who, on entering the stomach of the accused person, readily detects the symptoms of his guilt or innocence and kills or spares him accordingly. This personification of the poison is plainly assumed in the prayers which are addressed to it in India, Madagascar, and some parts of Africa, and it is further indicated by the ceremonies which sometimes accompany the act of procuring the poisonous bark from the tree. The same ascription of superhuman knowledge to the poison comes out also in the belief that, when the drug does not kill the drinker, it confers on him the power of divination, in virtue of which he is able to detect and expose the guilty witch or wizard. On the same theory we can perhaps explain why persons who undergo the ordeal are commonly regarded as innocent if they vomit the poison, but guilty if they either retain it or discharge it by evacuation of the bowels. As an intelligent being, the poison is apparently supposed to quit the body of the accused as soon as, by ocular inspection of the man or woman's interior, he is satisfied of his or her innocence, and in that case he takes his departure by the same door by which he entered the body, namely by the mouth, thus retracing his steps and thereby acknowledging that his services as an executioner were not wanted. But should he on the contrary discover in the culprit's stomach the clear evidence of guilt, which is supposed to exist there in a material shape, he either remains in the person of the criminal for the purpose of killing him or her, or quits it by a different channel from that by which he effected his entrance, thus implicitly passing sentence of condemnation on the accused, since he has failed to pronounce an acquittal by retracing his steps.

While this is perhaps the general theory of the poison ordeal, it seems in some cases to be either combined or confused with a notion that in vomiting the poison the culprit simultaneously rids himself of his guilt, which comes out of him in a material form and can be discovered in his vomit. That apparently is why sometimes the evil principle or evil spirit is exhorted to come out from the accused, and why sometimes the vomit of the alleged witch or wizard is scrutinized for evidence of his or her guilt.

It must apparently remain doubtful whether the bitter water of the Hebrew ordeal contained any poisonous ingredients or derived its supposed virtues purely from the dust of the sanctuary, with which it was mixed, and from the curses which were pronounced over it and washed off into it. If it was really, as seems probable, innocuous in itself and deleterious only through the superstitious fears which it excited in the mind of the guilty woman who drank it, the imaginary powers which it was supposed to acquire from the dust of the sanctuary may be compared with the imaginary powers which in Africa and India the water of the ordeal has sometimes been thought to acquire either from the sacred earth with which it is mixed or from the images of the gods which have been dipped in it. In all such cases superstition comes to the aid of morality, and supplies the material vehicle of justice with that punitive force which on purely physical principles is lacking.

Whatever may have been the actual composition of the bitter water, there can be no doubt that the ceremony of washing off the written curses into it, and then giving the water to the accused woman to drink, was a superstition pure and simple, which could not possibly produce **the** supposed effect on an adulteress, while it left a faithful wife unharmed. The notion, that the magical influence of a written charm, whether for good or evil, can be communicated to any person by making him or her drink the water into which the characters have been washed off, is widespread among superstitious people at the present time and has no doubt been so since the days of antiquity. In Senegambia a native Mohammedan doctor will write passages of the Koran in Arabic characters on a wooden board, wash off the characters in water, and then give the infusion to the patient to drink, who thus absorbs the blessed influence of the holy words through the vehicle of the dirty water.[70] In Morocco a person who desires to secure the love of another, will buy of a priest a love-charm written on paper, soak the paper in water, and give the water to be drunk by the unsuspecting object of his or her affection, who is expected to conceive a passion accordingly for the charmer.[71] In North Africa a doctor will write his magical formula on a cake of barley or on onion peel, and give his patient the cake or the peel to eat. Sometimes he will write the words on the bottom of a plate, efface the writing, and then cause the sufferer to eat out of the plate. Eggs are often employed for the same purpose. The prescription, or rather the spell, is scrawled on the shell of an egg; the egg is then boiled and eaten by the sick person, who is supposed to benefit by the magical virtue thus infused into his body.[72] Similarly in Egypt the most approved mode of charming away sickness or disease is to write certain passages of the Koran on the inner surface of an earthenware cup or bowl, then to pour in some water, stir it until the writing is quite washed off, and finally to let the patient gulp down the water, to which the sacred words, with all their beneficent power, have been transferred by this simple process.[73] Among the descendants of Arab immigrants in South-Eastern Madagascar, when a person was ill, it used to be custom to write prayers in Arabic characters on a piece of paper, steep the paper in water, and give the water to the patient to drink.[74] To eat a paper on which a charm has been written is a common cure for disease in Tibet; and a more refined, yet equally effective, way of ensuring the same happy result is to reflect the writing on a mirror, wash the mirror, and give the washings to the sufferer to imbibe.[75] So in China spells "are used as cures for sick persons, by being either written on leaves which are then infused in some liquid, or inscribed on paper, burned, and the ashes thrown into drink, which the patient has to swallow."[76] In Annam the priests are in possession of diverse cabalistic signs, which they similarly employ, according to circumstances, for the cure of diverse diseases. For example, if a man suffers from colic, accompanied by inflammation of the bowels, the priest will paint the corresponding signs in red letters on yellow paper, burn the paper, and throw the ashes into a bowl of cold water, which he will give the patient to drink. In the case of other diseases the paper will be red and the signs black, but the manner and the efficacity of the cure will be identical.[77] In Japan it is said to have been customary in some cases to cause an accused person to drink water in which a paper, inscribed with certain peculiar characters, had been steeped, and it was believed that the water thus tinctured would torment the culprit in his inward parts till he confessed his guilt.[78]

With these parallels before us we can fully understand, even if we cannot entirely believe, the powerful accession of force which the bitter water of the Hebrews was supposed to receive from the curses pronounced over it and washed into it by the officiating priest. ▼

93   Leprosy as punishment   13:10

Miriam and Aaron malign Moses for having married an Ethiopian woman. Yahweh punishes Miriam with "leprosy," which is cured only by intercession by Moses.

The disease with which Miriam was afflicted was, in all probability, not *leprosy*—that is, Hansen's disease—proper, but a similar cutaneous infection known as *vitiligo*.[1]

Leprosy, scabs, blotches, pimples and other disfigurements of the skin are very commonly regarded in popular lore as punishments for violating taboos or for lying and spreading slander.

In ancient Egypt, leprosy (or something like it) was believed to be visited upon those who drank the milk of the pig,[2] which was deemed an unclean animal;[3] and the same notion prevails to this day among the peasantry of Northern Arcadia, in Greece.[4] On the island of Wetar, between New Guinea and the Celebes, leprosy is considered to be the consequence of eating the totem animal;[5] while the Wa-Hehe of Tanganyika[6] and the Nyganja-speaking tribes of Mozambique and Nyasaland[7] hold that this offense brings scabs. The Omaha Indians think likewise that anyone who feeds on elk—the totem animal—becomes leprous;[8] and the Bush Negroes of Surinam entertain a similar belief about the consumption of the *capiai*—a piglike beast.[9] Among the Chasas of Orissa it is supposed that the infliction of injury on the totem animal entails this retribution.[10]

Moral offenses too are thus requited. In the *Choephoroe* of Aeschylus, Orestes observes that leprosy is visited by the Furies on anyone who refuses to avenge the murder of a kinsman.[11] Lying, in particular, raises blisters on the tongue.[12] In one of Theocritus' *Idylls* a goatherd tosses the compliment to his beloved that he runs no risk of such affliction in singing her praises;[13] while on the other hand, Horace reproaches the fickle Barine that he would not be at all surprised if her teeth and finger-nails became blackened as the condign punishment for her taradiddles.[14] Ovid, somewhat more cynical in such matters, alludes to the same belief only to discredit it on the grounds that perfidious minxes never seem to break out in spots.[15] The ancient Irish believed similarly that "blotches showed themselves on the faces of Bretons who gave unjust judgments";[16] and in a Jewish folktale a frustrated brother-in-law who falsely accuses a woman of adultery becomes leprous.[17]

In the case of Miriam there is added point in the story inasmuch as the Ethiopian woman was a Negro.[18] The lawgiver's sister, in seeking to impose a color bar, is made to demonstrate her own "whiteness" in unexpectedly drastic fashion!

94 The soul as shadow 14:9

The Israelites begin to lose heart in the wilderness. Joshua and Caleb try to reassure them, advising them that the Promised Land is an earthly paradise, "flowing with milk and honey" and that the inhabitants are by no means as invincible as they may seem. "We shall eat them up," they declare. "Their shadow is departed from them."

The word *shadow,* i.e., shade, is here interpreted to mean "defense" or "protection." Comparative Folklore suggests, however, that this is really an allusion to the popular belief that a man's shadow is an index of his life, and that the departure of it indicates imminent death. On this belief, see fully below, §302.

95 The Blossoming Rod 17:16–26

The story of the Blossoming Rod is a favorite in many parts of the world.[1] An excellent Classical parallel is the tale of how Heracles once deposited his club beside a pillar at Troezen. Immediately the pillar put forth blossoms. It was still shown in the time of Pausanias.[2]

Christian hagiography likewise knows several parallels. In 253, it is related, a certain Desiderius was designated by God as the chosen successor of the bishop of Langres. Since he could not be identified, a delegation was sent to Rome to seek counsel. On the return journey it met a laborer of that name driving a cart. He dismounted and stuck his staff into the ground. At once it blossomed.[3] Somewhat similarly, in the fifth century, St. Orans was offered the bishopric of Auch, which he at first declined. His staff, however, rooted itself in solid rock and then blossomed, revealing that he was indeed chosen of God.[4] The same story, it may be added, was told also concerning the election of Paul of Reims to the see of Trois-Châteaux.[5]

The motif appears also in several European folk tales, but not always as a sign of divine election.[6]

96 The Covenant of Salt 18:19

The use of salt in the making of covenants is mentioned again in II Chron. 13:5: "Ought you not to know that the Lord God of Israel gave the kingship for ever to David and his sons by a covenant of salt?"

Three explanations of this usage have been suggested:

(*a*) Salt is a token of incorruptibility (see §211), and therefore symbolizes that the covenant is meant to remain inviolable forever.

(*b*) Eating another man's salt implies entering into a covenant with him by the method of commensality (see §52). This was a common practice among

the Arabs, who indeed signify such pacts by the expression, "There is salt between us."[1] Indeed, according to Burton, some tribes require a renewal of such
bonds every twenty-four hours, since otherwise, as they put it, "the salt is not
in our stomachs."[2]

(c) Eating a man's salt implies entry into his service. Our own word, salary
(cf. Latin, sal, "salt") derives from this usage.[3]

Among the Phoenicians, the gods Misor (Uprightness) and Sydyk (Recti-
tude) were said to have been the discoverers of salt. This tradition probably
had reference to the fact that they were regarded as especially concerned with
the faithful maintenance of covenants.[4]

97   The Song at the Well   21:17–18

RSV: Spring up, O well—Sing to it!—
         the well which the princes dug,
         which the nobles of the people delved,
         with the scepter and with their staves.[1]

Like that of Lamech (above, §31), this little song had originally no connection with the circumstances to which it is now related. It was really a traditional chant associated with the digging of wells.[2] The waters were thought to
be controlled by an indwelling spirit (Arabic, weli), who was bidden bring
them to the surface.[3] Nilus tells us of an analogous practice among the
bedouins: when they were in need of water, they danced beside a spring and
sang to it;[4] while the Moslem writer Qazwini relates that "when the wells at
Ilabistan (in Persia) failed, a feast was held at the source, with music and
dancing, to induce it to flow again."[5] So too, Arabs of modern Palestine sometimes ask pardon of a well before drawing water from it.[6]

The digging of the well is often ceremoniously inaugurated by the sheikh or
headman, and it is to this, undoubtedly, that the words of our song refer. According to the famous traveler, Alois Musil, it is the custom of the Arabs in the
Wady eth-Thamad—the very region in which the Biblical incident plays—to
scoop out pits in the gravel of the dry torrent bed. In these water is gathered.
"Such water-pits," he informs us, "are called bīr, biyâr. Since they are regularly filled up [with gravel] by the winter rains, they have to be freshly dug
each spring. Each tent possesses its own bīr; those of the heads of families or
clans are restored with special care, and although the chiefs seldom work with
their own hands, it is always said, 'Sheikh N. dug this well.' "[7] Very similar is
the usage which prevails at Jarsalmer, in India, where the prince goes annually
in state to the spring of Gharsisar to perform the sacred act of cleansing it
from accumulated mud and sand; first he takes out a handful, than all follow
his example.[8]

The action of the chief is, of course, part of his general role as steward of
his people's water supply.[9] In the Hittite ritual for the annual festival of Puruli,
the "house of the nether upsurge," i.e., the subterranean waters, is formally

given into the custody of the king,[10] while in an inscription of Ramses II it is said that the waters of the netherworld pay heed to him by virtue of the fact that he dug a well.[11] To the same circle of ideas belongs also the practice of the Greenlanders, whereby when a new spring is opened, the angekok, or ceremonial "patriarch," must be the first to drink of it, in order to rid it of harmful spirits.[12]

98   Balaam   22—24

(a) Professional cursing

Among ancient and primitive peoples, a curse is more than a mere wish for evil; it is a means of conveying it by word or act.[1] Curses have to be pronounced in the name—that is, on the authority—of a god or demon or other-worldly being, since their potency lies precisely in the fact that they mobilize against a man forces which are normally beyond human control or resistance and which can be countered only by more powerful beings of the same order.

Curses are considered to work more effectively if they are uttered by some-one who is habitually en rapport with superior beings and who is versed in the appropriate techniques. Among the Maori of New Zealand, for example, the curse spoken by a priest is deemed ineluctable;[2] while the Gallas of Ethiopia stand in especial dread of one invoked by a wizard.[3]

For this reason it was customary in ancient warfare to engage professional sorcerers to curse the enemy before battle was joined, such execrations being regarded as themselves the equivalent of weapons. This, for instance, was common usage among the Babylonians, and so dangerous did they consider the curse that the king himself would not run the risk of pronouncing it, in case he did anything amiss; instead, a royal eunuch bearing his name and wearing his robes substituted for him.[4] Similarly, it is recorded by Josephus that in the civil war between Hyrcanus II and Aristobulus II (69–63 B.C.), the pious Onias, who enjoyed a reputation as a miracle-monger, was summoned by the former to place curses on the latter and on his followers.[5] The usage was especially common among the Arabs. The partisans of Mohammed, we are told, invited a poet to curse the foe before the famous battle of Bedr;[6] and it was, in general, the practice of bedouin warriors to recruit the services of a kahin, or soothsayer, in similar situations.[7]

(Not impossibly, it is such a professional excoriator, rather than some other-worldly being, that is really meant by the "messenger (EV: angel) of Yahweh" who, in Judges 5:23, is said to have pronounced a curse on the inhabitants of Meroz for not coming to the aid of Deborah and Borak against Zabin, king of Canaan.)

(b) Augur consulted before battle

But it was not only such professional cursers that were called upon before battle. Equally important was it to ascertain the will of the gods and the destined outcome of the encounter. The professional curser had therefore to function also as an *augur*. It is well known, for example, that the Romans rarely (if ever) went into battle without first "taking the omens," but the usage is in fact far older. In a letter from the Amorite city of Mari, dating around 1700 B.C., it is related that King Hammurapi, before attacking Shabazun, sent a seer (*barū*) in the van of his troops "to gather omens."[8] A similar practice is attested also among the Hittities[9] and readers of the Iliad will recall at once the analogous role of the seer Calchas.[10] In the Old Testament itself, the king of Israel consults the prophets of Yahweh before engaging the Syrians at Ramoth-gilead,[11] and the officers of Hezekiah, king of Judah, repair to Isaiah to seek the will of the Lord concerning the threat posed by Assyria.[12] Similarly too, in ancient Irish warfare, the services of a professional magician, known as "the analyzer of song" (*teinm-laighda*) were often enlisted before the commencement of hostilities;[13] while among the bedouin of Arabia, the soothsayer (*'aqîd*) frequently ranks as the virtual commander of an army when it is mounting an attack.[14]

The omens were taken from observation of heavenly bodies, from the flight of birds, and from the characteristics and movements of animals which might appear upon the scene.[15]

(c) Balaam as a typical soothsayer

Both by the actions which he performs and by the epithets which are applied to him Balaam is stamped as just such a combined curser and augur.[16] He is summoned by Balak, king of Moab, precisely on account of his reputation in this field (Num. 22:6). He can speak only as the medium of an elohim, or otherworldly being (22:35; 24:13).

He seeks oracles at sacred places situated on hilltops (22:41; 23:14), and his revelation comes at night (22:20).

He orders seven altars to be erected at each spot and seven bullocks and rams to be offered (23:13, 14, 29). He orders his employer Balak to wait beside the altars while he himself "takes a walk" (Heb. *h-l-k*) in search of the oracle (23:3, 15–16; 24:1). The latter comes as the result of an "encounter" (Heb.: *q-r-h*) with the elohim, or otherworldly being (23:3–4). Furthermore, he is described as "one whose eyes are opened" (24:4, 16) and also by another epithet which means either the same thing or else "one whose sight (lit. eye) is unblemished" (24:3, 15). Lastly, he is said to "give counsel" as well as to prophesy to his master (24:14).

All of this can be abundantly illustrated from Comparative Folklore and Religion.

An elevated spot is, of course, an obvious choice for observation of heavenly bodies, and therefore a necessity for astrological divination. Roman augurs likewise favored the arx for the practice of their art[17] and likewise experienced their general revelations at night.[18] What is especially interesting here, however, is that one of the high places to which Balaam repairs is named expressly "the

Field of the Watchers" (23:14). Originally, no doubt, this meant simply "look-out spot, belvedere," but it may be suggested that the Biblical writer picked this particular place because the word "watchers" (Heb.: *ṣôphîm*) also con-veyed the notion of "astrological observers," as in the expression "watchers of the skies"—*ṣophê shamêm*—used by the Phoenician historiographer, Sanc-huniathon.[19] Mesopotamian texts use the analogous verb *naṣāru* and the noun *maṣṣartu* in the same sense,[20] and it is therefore significant, in support of our suggestion, that when the prophet Habakkuk watches for the oracle of Yahweh, his action is likewise described by the Hebrew word *ṣ-ph-h* and he is said to post himself upon a *maṣṣor*—the equivalent of the Mesopotamian *maṣṣartu* (Hab. 2:1).[21]

Again the erection of the seven altars and the sacrifice of the seven bullocks and rams chime perfectly with the familiar use of the number seven in magical procedures.[22] Elisha, for example, orders the leprous Naaman to bathe seven times in the Jordan (II Kings 5:10, 14), just as modern European witches sometimes enjoin the sick to dip their shirts seven times into south-running water.[23] Elijah orders his servant to scan the skies seven times for signs of rain (I Kings 18:43); and Joshua's men circuit Jericho seven times on the seventh day (Josh. 6:4, 15). In a charm contained in the famous London Magical Papyrus, the name of the goddess Aphrodite must be repeated seven times on seven days,[24] and a Demotic spell prescribes the use of seven new bricks or palmsticks, seven clean loaves, seven lumps of salt, and the repetition of a formula seven times.[25] Similarly, in the Talmud, a magical recipe demands the use of seven twigs from seven trees, seven nails from seven bridges, etc.;[26,27] while an Aramaic spell from Nippur exorcizes the Devil by "sealing" him with seven seals.[28]

The action of "taking a walk" (*h-l-k*) in order to receive an oracle can be illustrated from the parallel use of exactly the same term in exactly the same sense in Mesopotamian texts;[29] while the statement that the oracle is vouch-safed in an "encounter" with the god is strikingly illuminated by the fact that precisely the same word (*q-r-y*) is employed in South Arabian inscriptions to denote the oracular appearance of a deity beside the ritual "stone of circum-ambulation" (*q-y-f, m-q-f*).[30] It is likewise found in the same technical sense elsewhere in the Old Testament itself.[31]

Lastly, when Balaam says to Balak (24:14), *Come, let me advise you what this people will do to yours hereafter,* his words can be illuminated by the fact that among the Arabs one of the technical terms for the augur called in by the sheikh or king, especially before embarking on military adventures, was indeed "adviser" (*wa'iz*).[32]

In the ancient poetic "redes" incorporated in the narrative, Balaam is styled, as we have said, "the man with open eyes." To the redactor this meant no more than that he had clear vision or was a clairvoyant (cf. 23:21), and it is in this sense that the expression indeed recurs in the Book of Psalms (119:18) and in the Mandaean description of a seer as a "revealer, whose

eyes are opened."[33] Exactly parallel too would be the Akkadian term *igigallu*
(from Sumerian IGI.GAL), "large eye," used of a man with insight. Hammurapi, for instance, claims that Ea, the lord of wisdom, endowed him with
this quality, and the gods Marduk and Nabu are credited with it.[34] It may be
suggested, however, that originally "one with open eyes" was a technical epithet
of diviners, and referred more specifically to the characteristic glazed stare
of clairvoyants and of persons in a trance.[35] In the Fiji Islands, for example,
diviners, when in trance, roll their eyes and then look around with a vacant
stare.[36] Similarly, in the Sandwich Islands, the shaman is said to operate in a
state of convulsion, with "strained and terrified eyes";[37] while wide-open eyes
characterized ecstatics at *zikrs* in Gaza witnessed by A. H. Sayce.[38] Pliny tells
us that persons who slept, like hares, with their eyes open were said in ancient
Greece to "corybantize," in reference to the stare characteristic of the Cory-
bantic devotees of Dionysus when in a state of rapture.[39]

The other epithet which is applied to Balaam in the poetic "redes" is somewhat more obscure; he is called "the man who is *shetūm* of eye," but what
shetūm means is not known for certain. According to one interpretation
(adopted by the King James Version), it denotes simply "open"; but another
view is that the Hebrew consonants should be differently vocalized (viz., *she-
tam*) to yield the sense "he who is of unblemished eye (i.e., sight)." In that
case, we may recognize once more a standard traditional description of seers
and soothsayers. The expression would be the counterpart of the words "he
who is of unblemished mouth (i.e., speech)" used alike in Canaanite[40] and
Mesopotamian[41] texts.

(d) Balaam's oracles

The form of Balaam's oracles likewise depicts his role as a typical soothsayer.

1. *He resorts to astrology.* This comes out in the famous words (24:17):

> *I see it, but not now*
> *behold it, but not nigh;*
> *A star has stepped out of Jacob,*
> *and a rod has risen out of Israel.*
> *It will crush the brow of Moab,*
> *and break down all the sons of Sheth.*

Traditionally, the "star" has been taken to be a figurative expression for the
future deliverer and restorer of Israel;[42] it is in this sense, for instance, that
it is interpreted in the Dead Sea Scrolls,[43] and it was in accordance with this
view that Bar Kosibah, the leader of the Second Jewish Revolt against the
Romans, in A.D. 125, was known popularly as Bar Cocheba, "son of the star."
In our opinion, however, the whole prophecy has been misunderstood. It really
depends on the ancient notion that everything on earth has its counterpart in

heaven. In accordance with this idea the Mesopotamians developed an elaborate celestial geography.[44] The north, or right side of the sky was characterized as the land of Akkad; the south, or left side, as Elam; the west, or upper reaches, as Amurru or Syria; the east, or lower reaches, as Subartu or Gutium.[45] Accordingly, a phenomenon appearing in any one of these quarters betokened the fate or fortune of the corresponding quarter on earth. What Balaam means, then, is that a comet, wandering star, or even meteor has appeared in the quarter of the heavens representing Israel and is heading toward the outskirts of that which answers to Moab, where it will eventually "strike."

(The terms used are, in fact, technical expressions drawn from astronomy; they can be paralleled in the reports of Mesopotamian stargazers and diviners. Thus, the word [d-r-k] rendered "has stepped forth" [or "has taken its course"; RSV: lamely, "shall come forth"] is the equivalent of the Akkadian *etēqu*, "pass, travel," regularly used of the assumed movements of heavenly bodies.[46] That rendered "has risen" [Heb. *qām*]—literally, "has taken its stand"—corresponds to the technical Akkadian *nazāzu*, "stand," used of a star or constellation in the ascendant, or at its zenith;[47] while that rendered "nigh" [q-r-b] answers to a term employed in Babylonian and Assyrian texts to denote specifically the imminent approach of a heavenly body to another zone.[48])

Thus interpreted, the prophecy finds a striking counterpart in an inscription of the Egyptian pharaoh Thothmes III: "There came a star, (and) inasmuch as it came from the south of them, it was something which had never been seen before. No one could stand."[49] There are also several Hittite parallels.[50]

Comets, of course, were always regarded in antiquity as omens of disaster.[51] When, in 524 B.C., a comet appeared traveling eastward toward the Milky Way, a Chinese official declared that it was a broom which would sweep away the old and bring in the new, and that the feudal princes would suffer from calamities by fire.[52] The Dead Sea Scroll of the War of the Sons of Light and Darkness[53] and the Sibylline Oracles[54] alike predict them as a sign of the Last Days. The Romans thought they forbode the death of princes.[55] A comet appeared, for instance, before the assassination of Julius Caesar.[56] Nero was scared when a comet was seen.[57] Halley's comet preceded the death of the Emperor Macrinus in A.D. 218, and of Attila in A.D. 451. A comet and shooting stars appeared likewise before the battle of Pharsalus.[58]

The belief persisted into medieval and later ages.[59] A comet heralded the Norman conquest of Britain in 1066.[60] Disasters suffered by the Christians at the hands of the Turks in 1456 were popularly attributed to the appearance of a comet;[61] and a comet accompanied the great earthquake at Lima, Peru, in 1746.[62]

The idea is well expressed in Shakespeare's *Julius Caesar:*[63]

> When beggars die there are no comets seen;
> The heavens themselves blaze forth the death of princes;

while in similar vein, Milton declares that

> Satan stood
> Unterrifi'd and like a comet burned
> That . . . .
> from his horrid[a] hair
> Shakes pestilence and war.[64]

Elizabeth I of England, it is recorded, was warned not to look on the comet of October 10, 1580. She, however, defied this advice and ordered the windows to be thrown open, to show her complete reliance on Divine Providence and her belief that comets were not supernatural.[65] Nevertheless, it was only when Halley's comet was "fixed" in 1682 that the fear of comets was appreciably dispelled in civilized countries.

2. *Balaam also draws his oracles from the appearance of wild animals.*[66] Unfortunately, this has been obscured in the traditional versions, owing to corruption of the text. Scholars have long recognized, however, that the words (24:23) usually rendered

> *Alas, who shall live when God does this?*
> *(Or, Oh, who can survive when God has doomed him?)*[67]
> *But ships shall come from the direction of Kittim (Cyprus)*
> *and shall afflict Asshur and Eber,*
> *and he also shall come to destruction*

can be so rendered only by torturing syntax. On the other hand, by simple redistribution of the Hebrew letters and by a very slight emendation, the following sense can be extracted:[68]

> *Howling beasts ('iyyim)*[69] *come hieing*[70] *from the Northland,*[71]
> *and yowling beasts (ṣiyyim)*[72] *from the far reaches of the West,*[73]
> *but even as I look, they have passed by;*[74]
> *so too shall this one disappear!*

This reconstruction has the further point to commend it that the word rendered Northland—strictly, the land of Sama'l, in North Syria—also means *the left side,* and omens from this direction—as our own word "sinister" attests—were commonly regarded as boding disaster.[75] A Mesopotamian text, for example, says specifically that foxes coming from that direction are ominous.[76] A similar belief is mentioned in the Talmud;[77] while in Arabic folklore, *bariḥ* "coming from the left," was a term applied to a noxious beast.[78]

3. *Double-entendre.* Lastly, in the manner characteristic of ancient oracles,

[a] I.e., bristling; cf. Latin *horridus.*

Balaam often conveys the real purport of his words by means of *double-entendre*. Thus, in the "astrological" prophecy which we have discussed above, the word rendered "rod" can also mean "comet" or "meteor,"[79] and that rendered "brow" (or "fringes, sidelocks") can also mean "outskirts," as regularly in the Canaanite texts from Ras Shamra-Ugarit; while the expression, "sons of Sheth"—which really denotes the Shutu, a bedouin people[80]—suggests at once the Hebrew word *š'eth*, "pride, hauteur,"[81] and that conventionally translated "break down" is really an iterative form of a verb meaning "bow down," so that this final phrase implies at the same time that the star (or comet, or meteor) *will bow down all the haughty.*[82]

Similarly, when he excoriates the Kenites—a wandering tribe of smiths (cf. Heb.: *Qayin;* above, §22), he does so by an ominous play on their names—a device which, we shall see, was also employed by Isaiah and Micah (see below, §237). Unfortunately, this does not come out in the conventional rendering, which runs as follows (RSV):

> *Enduring is your dwelling place*
> *and your nest is set in the rock;*
> *Nevertheless Kain (i.e., Kenites) shall be wasted.*
> *How long shall Asshur take you captive?*

The point is, however, that the word for "nest" viz., *ken,* is a pun on the name *Kain* (Kenite);[83] while that rendered "shall be wasted" really means "shall be for burning," so that the sense is that the smith (*kain*) who now mans the forge shall someday himself be the fuel for someone else's! Lastly, the concluding line could also be rendered, *Even as I look (ashūr),*[84] *they are setting thee aflame,* continuing the same picture.[85]

99 Balaam's ass

When Balaam goes to curse Israel, Tahweh sends an angel to obstruct his path. Three times Balaam's ass sees the angel and shies, though his master does not see him.

The belief that animals can descry spirits is virtually universal.[1]—In the Odyssey, when the goddess Athene appears to Odysseus, the dogs of the swineherd Eumaios perceive her presence, though the hero's son Telemachos does not.[2]—On the race course at Olympia, says Pausanias, there was an altar at which the horses regularly shied, because they saw the ghost of a hero who was buried nearby.[3]—Certain dogs, declares Pliny, had the faculty of seeing fauns invisible to men.[4]—A story told in the Poetic Edda relates that dogs would not attack Othin when he appeared in the form of the wanderer Grimir, because they penetrated the disguise.[5]—Russian folklore asserts that a hunter's hound bristles and barks at the approach of a wood-spirit (*leshy*), though to the hunter himself the spirit appears to be an ordinary peasant.[6]—In

Bulgaria, it is believed that dogs flair ghosts;[7] and in Iceland that horses can see the *mori,* a kind of second self which accompanies individuals.[8]—The Masai of East Africa[9] and the Khonds of India[10] maintain that cattle can discern ghosts; and this belief is widely attested also throughout Europe[11] and in China.[12] In Morocco, dogs are said to howl at night because they see Death or a jinn;[13] and alike in Welsh[14] and Jewish[15] folklore, they do so when the spirit or angel of Death is at hand.

An arresting parallel to the Biblical narrative is provided by an Italian folktale from Acireale:

Between Aci Castello and San Filipo, there is an ancient oak, haunted by spirits who prevent anyone from passing. A man who once found himself at the spot around midnight and who wanted at all costs to forge ahead, was knocked so violently against the walls on either side of the road that he died. Another, who likewise reached the place at midnight, with his donkey, was forced to turn back. And a laborer who came by one day with a cartload of hay saw the rear-axle of his vehicle buckle and the oxen stop in a fit of terror. He had to take to his heels, leaving everything on the roadside.[16]

Deuteronomy

100 Aborigines as giants

Deut. 2:10–11, 20–21

The early inhabitants of Moab and Ammon are portrayed as *giants*. So are those of Canaan. The spies dispatched by Moses thus describe them.[1] Og, king of Bashan, is said to be the last of the giants and to have a giant's bed.[2] The original name of Hebron, viz., City of Arba' is interpreted as that of a primitive giant.[3] The race of giants, we are told, was eliminated by Joshua, and survived only in the Philistine cities of Gaza, Gath, and Ashdod.[4] Four of them (including Goliath) are mentioned later in the time of David.[5]

The notion that the aborigines of a country were giants is widespread in folklore. It is inspired by the presence of megaliths in a place or area.[6] Thus, the fellahin in Egypt attribute the pyramids to gigantic jinns,[7] and French peasants call large boulders "stones of Gargantua."[8] Antioch, in Syria, where huge monuments abound, is said to have been peopled originally by giants;[9] and in modern Greece large ruins are popularly regarded as the work of prehistoric "Hellenic" titans.[10] Similar beliefs are recorded by several medieval Arab geographers and antiquaries,[11] and still obtain among bedouin,[12] as they do also, for example, in the Celtic folklore of Wales.[13]

Another reason for this belief is the discovery of oversized skeletons and fossils—really those of prehistoric mastodons. This was a common notion in Classical antiquity,[14] and is widely attested also in later European, Asian, and American lore.[15] To cite but one representative instance, huge fossil bones found at Punto S. Elena, in Ecuador, gave rise to the legend that the area was once peopled by giants.[16] Indeed, it is a common belief that early man in general was of gigantic stature;[17] in Jewish lore, Adam himself is sometimes portrayed as a giant.[18]

In Hebrew, the primeval giants are called generically *Rephaîm*[19] and *'Anaqîm*.[20] These were probably the names of historical ancient peoples, for the former may be associated with the designation "man of Rapha, Raphaite" borne by a certain King Daniel in the Ugaritic *Poem of Aqhat*,[21] and the latter with the *Iy'nk*, a Palestinian people mentioned in Egyptian execration texts of the eighteenth or nineteenth century B.C.[22] The use of both names as ordinary common nouns meaning "giants" finds a parallel in the development of the Teutonic terms *hün* and *iötunn* from the Huns and Jutes, and of the Slovene *obor* from the Avars. Of the same order too is the Slavonic *tchud*, which originally meant Finn.[23]

The Moabites are said to have called these ancient giants *Emîm,* and the Amorites, *Zamzumîm.* These were probably inventions (or popular distortions of historic names)[24] designed to identify the aborigines as eerie spirits or "bogey-men" haunting ruins and desolate places, for the former was evidently associated with the Hebrew word, *êmah,* "terror," and the latter with the onomatopoeic Arabic *zamzama,* "zoom, murmur," and—even more significantly—*zizim,* "the low voice of a jinn (otherwise called an *'azîf*) heard at night in the desert."[25]

▲ 101   Boring a servant's ear[1]   15:12–17

The Deuteronomic law enacted that when a purchased Hebrew slave had served his master for six years, he should be set free in the seventh year; but if he refused to accept his liberty because he loved his master and his master's house, then it was provided that his master should take an awl and thrust it through the slave's ear into the door, after which the slave should serve him forever. In the early code known as the Book of the Covenant, which is preserved in the Book of Exodus, a similar provision is made in somewhat different terms as follows:[2] "But if the slave shall plainly say, I love my master, my wife and my children; I will not go free: then his master shall bring him into the presence of the (household) gods[2a] and shall bring him to the door or to the door-post; and his master shall bore his ear through with an awl; and he (the slave) shall serve him for ever." The difference between the two versions should be carefully noted: in Deuteronomy, the slave's ear is to be pinned to the door, whereas in Exodus it is prescribed only that it be bored with an awl at the door.

The exact meaning of the ceremony remains obscure in spite of the efforts of the commentators to elucidate it.[3] Its general purport appears to be rightly given by Driver: "The ear, as the organ of hearing, is naturally that of obedience as well; and its attachment to the door of the house would signify the perpetual attachment of the slave to that particular household."[3a]

The Hebrew custom may be compared with one observed by the Ewe Negroes of Togoland in West Africa when they desire to prevent a slave from running away from them. For that purpose the master brings the slave before a fetish named Nanyo. There the priest pares the nails of the slave's fingers and toes, shears some of the hair of his head, and buries the parings of the nails and the shorn hair, along with a fetish mark, in the earth. After that the slave gives a promise that he will not run away, and to confirm him in this good resolution the priest administers to him a draught of fetish water, which is believed to possess the virtue of killing the man out of hand if he were to break his pledged word by deserting his master.[4] Here the deposition of the severed hair and nails with the fetish seems clearly intended to give the fetish the means of injuring the slave by working magic on these portions of his person; for it is a common article of the magical creed that a man can be harmed sympathetically through any harm done to his cut nails and hair.[5] On this principle the hair and nails deposited with the fetish serve as a surety or bail for the slave, that he will not run away. Exactly in the same way among the Nandi of British East Africa, "to ensure a prisoner not attempting to escape the captor shaves his head and keeps the hair, thus placing him at the mercy of his magic."[6] In the light of these African customs we may conjecture that among the Hebrews the intention of pinning a servant's ear to the doorpost either of his master's house or of the sanctuary was to give his master or the deity complete magical control over the man by means of his blood which adhered to the doorpost. We have seen that there is some doubt whether the ceremony was performed at the door of the master's house or at the door of the sanctuary, the form of the commandment in Deuteronomy favouring the former interpretation, and the form of the commandment in the older Book of the Covenant favouring the latter interpretation. The parallelism of the Ewe custom, so far as it goes, supports the view that the piercing of the servant's ear was done not at the master's house but at the sanctuary; for among the Ewe Negroes the slave is similarly taken to the shrine of the fetish, and it is the fetish priest, and not the man's master, who performs the ceremony of cutting the hair and nails and administering the draught which is supposed to act as a fresh and binding pledge of the slave's fidelity. On the strength of this analogy we may surmise that among the Hebrews the boring of a servant's ear was originally performed as a solemn religious or magical rite at the sanctuary, even though in later days it may have degenerated into a simple domestic ceremony performed by the master at his own house and interpreted in a purely symbolical sense.

Among other tribes of West Africa the mutilation of an ear is actually performed as a means of ensuring the permanent attachment of a slave to his master, but in this case, curiously enough, it is the ear, not of the slave, but of the master that is mutilated. We read that "among the Wolofs, as among all the peoples of Senegambia and even among the Moors on the right bank of the river, there is observed a strange custom which at first seems very surprising. A slave who wishes to escape from a master whom he dislikes, chooses in his own mind some one whose captive he wishes to become and cuts off a piece of his ear. If he cannot make his way to the master whom he desires, he contents himself with cutting the ear of the man's child or even of his horse, and from that moment his old owner has not the least right over him; the slave becomes the property of him whose blood he has shed. The moral intention of the custom is plain enough; the captive seems thus to say that he prefers to expose himself to the just wrath of him whom he has offended rather than remain at the mercy of a bad and capricious master; and as his new owner has a right of reselling him to his old master for a variable price, called 'the price of blood,' we can understand that the captive is bound to behave well, lest he should revert to the possession of him from whom he wished to flee."[7]

The explanation which the writer offers of the custom appears accommodated rather to European than to African ideas. More probably, perhaps, the shedding of his new master's blood is supposed either to establish a blood relationship between the slave and his proprietor or to give the slave at all events a certain magical control over his master by means of the blood which he has drawn from him. On this latter interpretation the ceremony is to some extent the converse of the Hebrew rite. The Hebrew law contemplates the case of a master who desires to prevent his slave from running away, and for that purpose draws blood from the slave's ear as a guarantee of his fidelity; the African rule contemplates the case of a slave who desires to prevent his master from giving him up, and for that purpose draws blood from his master's ear as a guarantee of his protection. But in each case the ear pierced is that of the party to the covenant whose loyalty the other party has some reason to distrust, and whom accordingly he seeks to bind by a tie of blood.

To this interpretation of the Wolof custom it may be objected that the cutting of a horse's ear is permitted as a substitute in cases where the slave cannot cut the ear either of his new master or of his master's child. How, it may pertinently be asked, can you establish a blood relationship with a man by spilling the blood of his horse? To this it may perhaps be answered that though the horse's blood could hardly be thought to establish a blood relationship with the owner, it might possibly be supposed to give the slave a magical control over him, which would answer the same purpose of securing him against the caprice and tyranny of his master; since the field over which magical influence can be exerted to a man's prejudice is commonly held to be a very wide one, embracing his personal possessions as well as the severed parts of his body.[8]

If this explanation of the Wolof custom should be thought too subtle, a simpler and perhaps more probable one is suggested by a parallel usage of the Bare'e-speaking Toradjas of Central Celebes. Among these people, we are informed, slaves used to possess a remarkable privilege which ensured them against ill-usage at the hands of their masters. When a slave was not well treated, he would abandon his master and seek refuge in the house of another, where he damaged or destroyed some article of property. His old master soon followed him thither and demanded his surrender. But his new master refused to give up the runaway till he had received compensation from the old master for the damage or destruction wrought by the slave; and this compensation usually consisted in a buffalo. Thus it was to a master's interest to treat his slaves leniently, since he could be obliged to pay for any damages to the doing of which his severity might goad them. But if a slave was resolved never to return to his old master, on reaching the house of the man into whose service he desired to enter, he did not content himself with damaging or destroying a single article of property, but laid about him with such indiscriminate violence that he soon ran up a bill for damages amounting to five buffaloes or even more. So heavy a bill his old master seldom thought it worth his while to discharge for the sake of getting back on his hands an unwilling slave, who might play him the same trick another day. Accordingly, the slave's old master acquiesced in the loss of his services, and his new master accepted those services as a compensation for the ravages which the servant had committed in his house. However, we are told that the surest measure which a slave could adopt for the purpose of establishing himself irretrievably in the house of a new master was to cut off a lock of hair from a member of the family, generally one of the master's children, and to throw it on the fire before the person from whom the hair was abstracted could put himself on his guard or thwart the intention of his assailant. This act of aggression, if successfully perpetrated, was deemed so deep an insult that no compensation could wipe it out; and the slave therefore remained permanently with his new master.[9]

Here the cutting of a lock of hair from some member of the new master's family appears to be the equivalent of the Wolof practice of cutting the ear either of the new master himself or of one of his children, and the effect of the act in both cases is precisely the same, namely, to render the return of the slave to his old master impossible. But though in Senegambia and Celebes these modes of transferring a slave permanently to a new master are described as if they rested on a purely economic consideration of injury done to property or honour, we may suspect that at bottom both are magical, the blood of the ear in the one case and the hair of the head in the other forming the real guarantee on which the slave relies for security of tenure in his new home, since by means of the blood or the hair he can work magic on his master, and thus through the influence of fear can restrain him from exercising his rights of ownership in an arbitrary or cruel manner. However, this explanation is open to the objection that the slave does not preserve the lock of hair, as we should expect him to do, but on the contrary destroys it by throwing it on the fire. If this objection is not fatal to the theory, we must apparently conclude that savage man, like his civilized brother, does not invariably regulate his actions in conformity with the laws of an inflexible logic.

The suspicion of a magical basis underlying both these primitive forms of conveyancing is confirmed, so far as the Toradjas of Celebes are concerned, by the explanation which some of them give of a custom observed at the ear-marking of cattle. It is their practice to cut off a piece from one or both ears of every buffalo calf at birth, and the pieces of ears are dried and hung from the roof. Asked why they keep these fragments of their buffaloes, most of the people can give no reason at all; but "some say that it is to prevent the buffaloes from straying (a part of the animal, to wit the tip of the ear, attracts the whole buffalo)."[10] This explanation of the practice is probably the true one; certainly it fits exactly into that system of sympathetic magic which at a certain stage of evolution has moulded man's thought and cast the fluid material of custom into many quaint and curious shapes. If that is so, we may conclude, with a fair degree of probability, that the process which a modern Toradja adopts to prevent his buffalo from straying is essentially of the same sort as the process which an ancient Hebrew adopted to prevent his servant from running away: in both we may detect an old magical rite which was thought to give a master as firm a hold on his man and on his beast as if he actually held both of them by the ear.

Thus it appears that according to the laws of primitive logic you can ensure your control of a man by the simple process of cutting his ear and drawing a few drops of his blood, and this conception may well explain the rite prescribed in the Book of Exodus. It may likewise illustrate an otherwise obscure passage in Psalm 40:6, where the psalmist, addressing the deity, declares, "Ears hast thou dug (or pierced) for me." Perhaps by this declaration the worshipper desires to express his absolute submission to the divine will, employing for that purpose a metaphor borrowed from the proceeding by which in ordinary life a master bound a servant to himself by a tie of the closest and most enduring nature. [Indeed, in much the same way, the Middle Assyrian Code of Laws (§40) provides that a man who meets a harlot on the street and does not apprehend her is to receive fifty lashes, be stripped, and compelled to do the king's service for one month. In token of his servitude, he is to have his ears pierced and then pinned back by means of a string passed through them.[10a] In the Deuteronomic version, on the other hand, where the slave's ear is not merely bored but nailed to the door, the meaning of the ceremony lies not so much in the act of mutilation as in that of symbolic attachment.] ▼

102   Cultic transvestitism   22:5

The interchange of garments between the sexes is condemned by the Mosaic Law as an "abomination" (Heb.: *tô'ēbah*). Since this term is commonly employed in Scripture to characterize heathen practices,[1] it is probable that what is here prohibited is not transvestitism in general but rather a specific cultic usage, such as in fact finds parallels in many ancient and primitive cultures.[2]

To start with examples drawn from antiquity: on the island of Cos, says Plutarch, priests of Hercules dressed as women;[3] while at Rome, men who participated in the vernal mysteries of that god did likewise.[4] So too in the cult of Dionysus, males often adopted feminine costume,[5] just as at the annual festival of Oschophoria boys were attired as girls,[6] and at the Skirophoria, men were garbed like women.[7] The same practice is attested also in connection with the cult of Leukippos in Crete;[8] and Lucian tells us that the emasculated devotees of the Syrian Goddess at Hierapolis were supplied with women's garb by persons into whose houses they cast their severed parts.[9] (In exactly the same way, the eunuch priests of the goddess Hudigamma in modern India affect feminine attire.[10]) Lastly, Tacitus relates that the priest of the Nahanarvals, an ancient German tribe, was customarily arrayed like a woman.[11]

The practice finds an echo in myth, for it is on this basis that we should probably account for the legends that Dionysus himself was given women's clothes by the goddess Rhea at Cybela,[12] that the Lydian Hercules served the queen Omphale in the guise of a woman,[13] and that the Phrygian Attis assumed feminine raiment.[14]

Turning now to modern primitive peoples, the following examples may be cited. Among the Sea Dyaks of Borneo,[15] as also among the Bugis of the South Celebes,[16] priests are frequently dressed like women, and the same holds good for several Indian tribes of North America.[17] In the Pelew Islands, men chosen by the goddess to serve her as priests assume the role of women and wear women's clothes.[18] Zulu priests don female raiment during rain-making ceremonies, petticoats simulating clouds.[19] In the Congo, there is a sacrificial priest named Grandmother, who dresses and acts like a woman;[20] while on Duke of York Island, the head of the *dukduk* secret societies is similarly styled Old Woman and is appropriately attired.[21] Among the Kod-yaks,[22] the Chukchis of North East Asia,[23] and on the isle of Rambree, off the coast of Arcan,[24] shamans and vagabond "conjurers" are also so costumed. In India, males attached to the sect of the Vallabha deem it an act of piety to assimilate themselves to women, alike in dress as in behavior,[25] and the same custom is reported also among effeminate men in Madagascar.[26]

Sometimes, however, it is women who adopt masculine costume on ceremonial occasions. This is reported, for instance, as common usage among one of the secret societies of the Pangwe;[27] while in Uganda, the female "medium," when speaking as the mouthpiece of the god Mukasa, adjusts her clothing in masculine fashion.[28]

A survival of cultic transvestitism may be recognized in the custom whereby, in the Frei- and Kelleramt of Switzerland, boys and girls exchange clothing on the Monday after Shrove Sunday;[29] and some folklorists have even traced to the same ritual origin the common practice whereby men and women facetiously don one another's headgear at fairs and galas!

The origin of the custom is disputed. According to some scholars, it is a method of assimilating the worshiper to the person of the deity[30] (though it is difficult then to explain why the devotees of the male Hercules affected feminine attire). According to others, it is a form of disguise, designed to foil demons and similar noxious spirits.[31] Probably, as Frazer has observed,[32] there is no single origin for all the examples of this practice; in some, the former idea comes into play; in others, the latter. It has also been suggested that, in cases where men wear women's clothes in the performance of magical rites, this reflects the widespread belief that magic (especially when it aims at promoting fertility) is primarily the province of the female sex, and that—at least in some instances—the usage may go back to a time when priesthood

was in the hands of women.[33] It should be borne in mind also that transvestitism is a well-known symptom of sexual abnormality,[34] and that such
abnormality is frequently associated with religious psychosis.

103   Moses' farewell song   **32**

In a long poem which purports to have been chanted by Moses shortly
before his death, Israel is chided and threatened for its ingratitude and infidelity to Yahweh. A graphic picture is painted of how it became his "peculiar people":

                                                                              7–14

Ask your father, and he will tell you,
  your elders, and they will declare unto you:
When the Most High ('Elyôn) doled out the nations,
  parcelled out the human race,
he fixed the bounds of peoples
  by the number of the gods.[1]
Then (this) people of his became Yahweh's share,
  Jacob his allotted estate.
He found him in a desert land,
  in the howling waste of a wilderness;
he fended him, tended him,
  kept him as the apple of his eye.
Like an eagle which watches(?) its nest,
  which flutters over its young,
which spreads its wings to catch them,
  and carries them on its plumes,
(so) Yahweh alone did lead him,
  and no alien god was with him.
He sent him riding forth
  over the heights of the earth;
fed him on the produce of the fields,
  suckled him on honey from rocks
and on oil from granite crags,
  on curds from cattle and milk from sheep,
on fat from lambs and rams,
  from bulls of Bashán and from goats,
and on the finest of wheat.
  Foaming wine did you drink
—the blood of the grape!

(a) These verses are cited explicitly as part of an ancient story. We may
therefore see in them the relic of a pre-Israelitic myth harking back to a time

when 'Elyôn, "the One-on-high" (EV: the Most High), was regarded as the supreme god, and Yahweh as a subordinate member of the pantheon.

'Elyôn is mentioned as a Canaanite deity on an inscription of the sixth century B.C. discovered at Sujin, near Aleppo,[2] and again in the Phoenician theogony recorded by Sanchuniathon.[3] In Genesis 14:28 Melchizedek, king of Salem, is described as his priest. The name was later appropriated as a title of Yahweh.[4] In Psalm 82:6—another relic of pagan mythology[5]—the supernal gods are styled "sons of 'Elyôn,"[6] and some scholars would recognize the same epithet in a fragmentary passage of a text from Ras Shamra-Ugarit.[7] It survives also in the Talmud as an appellation of the angels;[8] while Luke declares that the merciful and compassionate among men will rank in the eyes of God as equal to "the sons of the Most High."[9]

The notion that the earth was primevally parceled out among the gods finds a parallel in the Babylonian Epic of Creation, where, after his victory over the monster Tiamat and his installation as their king, Marduk is said to have divided the six hundred gods into equal celestial and terrestrial companies, to have allotted them their several "portions," and to have determined "the ways of the earth."[10] In later times, the distribution was said to have been made among the *angels,* who thus became the "princes" or tutelary patrons of the various lands. Says the Book of Ecclesiasticus: "The Lord appointed (angelic) princes for all lands, but Israel became his own portion."[11] The notion reflects, of course, the manner in which ancient emperors assigned the administration of their various provinces to subordinate officers.

(**b**) For the rest, our passage alludes to the familiar tale of the child who is exposed at birth on a mountain or in some other inhospitable place, but is eventually found and succored by divine intervention or by a friendly beast or bird. We need think only of the exposure of Zeus or Dionysus in Classical myth, although other examples occur all over the world.[12]

Seen in this light, the reference to the feeding of Israel on *honey* and curd has special point, for this was the characteristic food of newborn babes. It was thus that Zeus,[13] Dionysus,[14] and Iamos[15] were nurtured, and we are told in the Odyssey that the abandoned daughters of Pandareos were similarly succored by Aphrodite who, as in our Biblical passage, also supplied them with "delicious wine."[16] Indian[17] and Teutonic[18] sources attest the same usage; while it is significant that, according to Tertullian, the reason why, in the Coptic Church, neophytes are given milk and honey at baptism is that "they may eat like the newborn."[19] So too, in pagan charms, honey is often mentioned as an agent of regeneration.[20]

It is likewise against the background of the time-honored myth that we may best appreciate why, in the immediately following verses, Yahweh is likened to a protective *eagle,* for in several stories of the Exposed Child succor is brought by this or some similar bird. Achaemenes of Persia, for example, abandoned in infancy, was said to have been sheltered from the glaring sun by the wings of a friendly eagle;[21] and, again in Iranian legend, Zal, the son of Sam, exposed on the Elburz mountains, was picked up and nurtured by the wondrous bird Simurgh.[22] So too, when Ptolemy I Soter was exposed as a child on the order of his father Lagos, he was sheltered by an eagle.[23]

A variation on the same theme is the story that the child was miraculously caught by the king of the birds when thrown from a tower. This is told by Aelian about the Babylonian hero Gilgamos (i.e., Gilgamesh)[24] and by Pausanias about Aristomenes, the hero of the Messenians.[25]

(c) Our passage contains other interesting tidbits of folklore. Thus, the description of the desert, in which the infant Israel was exposed, as a *howling waste* reflects a common bedouin belief that the shrill winds and other eerie sounds which infest it are the shrieks of demons.[26] Indeed, a popular Arabic designation of the wilderness is "Howl-land";[27] and it is significant that the ancient Aramaic Version (Targum) renders the expression in our text by the words, "a place where demons and spirits howl."[28]

(d) So too, in the statement that Yahweh kept Israel *as the apple of his eye*—even as a son is told, in the Book of Proverbs, to keep his father's precepts[29]—a piece of popular lore may be detected. The Hebrew word rendered "apple" means properly *mannikin,* and this reflects the widespread idea that a diminutive human figure may be seen in the pupil of the eye.[30] Both the Arabs[31] and the Iranians[32] speak similarly of the "little man" in the eye, and a German popular expression for the pupil is *das Männlein im Auge.*[33] Socrates once asked Alcibiades whether a man's image could be seen in his eye, and Alcibiades replied in the affirmative.[34] The Macusi of former British Guiana believe that a mannikin in the eye reports to little people who live in the head all that passes on earth.[35]

Alternatively, the pupil is called "the baby." This, for instance, is likewise a common designation among the Arabs (*bubu*) and the Iranians (*kak*), as also in Syriac (*bab^etha*) and in the Old Testament itself (Zech. 2:12). The Germans speak of it as *das Kindlein;* the Spaniards as *la niña del ojo;* and the ancient Greeks called it "the girl" (*korē*). This can be traced, in fact, as far back as the Old Kingdom of Egypt, for in the Pyramid Texts (e.g., No. 93) the pupil is called similarly "the maiden in the eye."[36]

Among many peoples the belief prevails that the mannikin fades shortly before death, and such fading is therefore taken to presage imminent demise.[37]

The mannikin represents the soul, commonly supposed to reside in the eye.[38] Pliny, for instance, says expressly that "the soul dwells preeminently in the eyes,"[39] and the fabulist Babrius that "the souls of the dying are in their eyes."[40] The aforementioned Macusi assert that the disappearance of the mannikin at death marks the departure of the spirit (*emmawarri*), which thenceforth wanders abroad.[41] The Pygmies of Gabon likewise believe that the eye houses the soul.[42] It is for this reason, and not merely because they are the organs of sight, that the eyes are deemed especially precious. The idea is a commonplace of Classical literature.[43] People therefore swore oaths by their eyes.[44]

23–24

(e) The retribution which awaits faithless Israel is described in our poem in vivid terms:

> *I will sweep evils upon them,*
> *spend my arrows on them.*
> *They shall be drained by Famine,*
> *devoured by Pestilence* (Resheph)
> *and by Poisonous Plague* (Qeṭeb Mᵉriri).
> *The teeth of wild beasts also*
> *will I launch against them,*
> *together with the venom*
> *of creatures that crawl in the dust.*

Seven evils are here enumerated, and several of them, such as the "faery arrows," the monstrous Resheph, and the "poisonous plague" can be definitely identified as *demons* (see below, §§**242, 269, 275**). It is therefore probable that the poet is playing on the familiar concept of the Seven Evil Spirits, so frequently mentioned in Mesopotamian and later Semitic magical texts.[45] A similar attenuated reference to them is made in the great commination of Deuteronomy 28, where (v. 23) seven disasters are threatened against those who disobey Yahweh's commandments, and where it is said significantly that those disasters will *pursue* them.

The expression, "drained by Famine" reflects the widespread belief that demons and ogres suck the blood and marrow of their victims. The most familiar example of this is furnished by the Arabic Ghul, which derives its name from a word meaning "suck." The demonic Seven are likewise said, in Mesopotamian and Syriac charms, to eat flesh and suck blood,[46] and the belief that this is a peculiar feature of such fell beings comes subsequently to figure prominently in European witchcraft.[47] Thus, in Shakespeare's *Macbeth* one of the witches declares that she will drain her victim "like hay,"[48] and in *Richard the Third,* Gloucester exclaims:

> See how I am bewitch'd; behold, mine arm
> Is, like a blasted sapling, wither'd up.[49]

So too in the Jewish popular charm against the child-stealing Lilith, that beldam boasts that she is out to suck the blood of mother and babe.[50]

The belief finds expression also in folktales.[51] Siberian[52] and American Indian[53] stories alike know of an ogre who sucks blood, and cannibal giants appear also in Hindu[54] and Icelandic[55] lore. And who does not recall the familiar words of the ogre in *Jack the Giant-Killer: Fee, fo, fie, fum, I smell the blood of an Englishman?*

NOTES

▲ indicates material incorporated from Sir James G. Frazer's *Folklore in the Old Testament.*

IN THE BEGINNING

1 Creation as shaping

1. Thus the word *bara'* is related to the Arabic *b-r-y,* "pare, cut." On this term, see: F. Böhl, in Kittel Festschrift (1913), 42–60; J. van der Ploeg, in Mélanges Lefort (1946); R. J. Wilson, in ET 1953.94 f. Similarly, the name of the Australasian creator-god Baiame is derived by some scholars from a verb which means primarily, "to cut a sandal from a skin or a figure from bark": D. G. Brinton, Religions of Primitive Peoples (1899), 123.—The alternative word, *y-ṣ-r* means primarily "mould." On this term, see: P. Humbert, in Beihefte ZAW 77 (1958), 82–88. Similarly in Egyptian, the words *ḳ-d* and *n-ḥ-p,* used of creation, refer primarily to moulding: H. Grapow, Die bildlichen Ausdruecke des Aegyptischen (1924), 160 f.—It has now been recognized also that the word *q-n-ḥ,* usually rendered "own, acquire," sometimes possesses the meaning "fashion," deriving from quite a distinct root: P. Humbert, in Bertholet Festschrift (1950), 259–66; G. Rinaldi, in Aegyptus 34 (1954), 61 f.; W. F. Albright, in VTSuppl 3 (1955), 7, n.5; Vattioni, in RBib. It. 3 (1955), 218–20; M. Pope, El in the Ugaritic Texts (1955), 51–52. This is denied, however, by G. Levi della Vida, in JBL 63 (1944), 1, n.1; J. A. Montgomery, in JAOS 53 (1953), 107, n.6, and P. Katz, in JJS 5 (1954), 126–31.

The Akkadian word for "create," viz., *banū,* likewise means primarily "build."

2 Primordial water

1. On primordial water in general, see: Stith Thompson, MI i.121 ff.; O. Dähnhardt, Natursagen 1 (1909), 1–89; A. H. Krappe, La genèse des mythes (1938), 197 ff.; A. J. Wensinck, The Ocean in the Literature of the Western Semites (1919), 1–15, 40–46; M. Eliade, Patterns in Comparative Religion (1958), 188–215.

2. S. N. Kramer, Sumerian Mythology (1961), 39; id., From the Tablets of Sumer (1956), 71 ff.

3. Enuma Elish i.1–3.

4. CT XIII, Pl. 35–38.10 (= Heidel, Bab. Genesis, 50). This is the so-called "Eridu Creation Story," discovered by Rassam on the site of Sippar. The tablet dates to the 6th cent. B.C., but the contents are far older.

5. Thus, in the Heliopolitan and Hermopolitan cosmogonies, Nun, the primordial ocean, preceded all things: J. Vandier, La religion egypt. (1949), 33 f.—However, though primeval, Nun was *not* the substance out of which the world was made: S. Morenz, Aegypt. Religion (1960), 180.

6. BD, ch. 175, Pap. Ani (1550–1350 B.C.), ed. Budge, Sheet iii.29; trans. J. Wilson, in ANET 90.

7. Taittiriya Brahmana I.i.3, 5; Satapatha Br. xiv.1.2, 11; Ramayana, Ayodhya-Kanda 110.4; Mahabharata, Vana-Prana, 142.28–62; Bhagavata Purana 3:13 f.; cf. I. Scheftelowitz, Altpal. Bauernglaube (1935), 163.—Cf. also: Rig Veda x.129. Ib., vi.50, 7 the waters are described as "progenitresses" of all things. Similarly, in Bhaviçyottarapurana 31.14 water is addressed as "source of everything and of all existence."

8. Taittiriya Samhita V.6.4, 2.

9. Iliad 14.201, 246; cf. also: Plato, Cratylus 402B.—Thales (640–550 B.C.) claimed that water was the *genetic* origin of all things; cf. Eusebius, PE 1.8.1 Dindorf. Significantly, he was reputed to have been of Phoenician descent.—The Orphics likewise asserted that water was prior to all other things: Damascius, Quaest. de primis princip. 163 bis; cf. C. A. Lobeck, Aglaophamus (1826), i.484.

10. Kalevala, runo i.

11. J. de Angulo, in Anthropos 23 (1928), 583.

12. E. M. Loeb, in Amer. Anthropologist 28 (1926), 475; id., The Western Kaksu Cult (1934), 4.

13. A. L. Kroeber, The Valley Nisenan (1929), 275.

14. Id., Indian Myths of Central California (1907), 202.

15. T. T. Waterman, The Religious Practices of the Diegueno Indians (1910), 338.

16. G. A. Dorsey and A. L. Kroeber, Traditions of the Arapho (1903), 1 ff.

17. R. H. Lowie, Myths and Traditions of the Crow Indians (1918), 14 ff.

18. J. R. Swanton, Religious Beliefs of the Creek Indians (1928), 487 ff.

19. D. G. Brinton, Myths of the New World[3] (1905), 229.

20. L. Frobenius, Die altlantische Götterlehre. Atlantis 10 (1926), 109.

21. R. P. Trilles, Les pygmées de la forêt equatoriale (1933), 72.

22. See in general: K. Harte, Zum semitischen Wasserkultus (1921). Cf. also: M. Ninck, in Philologus, Suppl. vol. 14 (1921).—A representative instance of this concept is P. Haupt, Akkad.-Sum. Keilschrifttexte 75.1–2: "waters of incantation" (*mê išippûti*).

23. These primordial waters were known popularly as "the waters of Eridu," the oldest Babylonian city, on the Persian Gulf (mod. Abu Bahrein). Cf. Utukkê Limnûti iii.129–30: "I am the *ramku* of Eridu"; ib., iii.170 ff.: "I am an *ašipu* (magician) of Eridu"; ib., 185 ff.; R. C. Thompson, Devils xvi.205, 250: "incantation of Eridu." Cf. also: Ut. Limn. iii.83; iv.32: "the word of Ea"; ib., iii.207: "the spell of Ea"; ib., iii.239, 242: "I am the magician born of Eridu . . . may Ea, lord of the primal deep, protect me!" Ea was, indeed, the prime god of magic: G. Furlani, Rel, bab. e. ass. (1925), i.124 f.

24. Cf. KAT[3], 525; A. Jeremias, The Old Testament in the Light of the Ancient East (1911), i.211, 217. The *'a-p-š* mentioned in the Phoenician inscription of Zakir of Hamath, of the 8th cent. B.C. (M. Lidzbarski, Ephemeris, iii.1–11; tr. F. Rosenthal, in ANET[2], 502), is possibly such an artificial "ocean" (*apsu*).

25. E.g., Ut. Limn., iii.65 ff., 204; iii.105. 260–61; Thompson, Devils, "B" 47 ff., 59; Ut. Limn. iv.4, 1, etc.

26. In primitive belief, a man's reflection, like his shadow, was part of his essential self: Frazer-Gaster, NGB §158; J. Negelein, in ARW 5 (1902), 1–37.

27. Odyssey 4. 381 ff.

28. Hesiod, Theog. 233–36. The name Nereus is connected with modern Greek *nero*, "water."

29. Euripides, Helen 13 f.

30. F. Boas, in Bull. Amer. Mus. Nat. Hist., 15/i (1901), 129 ff.; cf. R. Pettazzoni, L'omniscienza di Dio (1955), 9, 208, 523.

31. They are called *apkallê*: H. Zimmern, in ZA, N.F. 1 (1924), 151 ff.; S. Smith, in JRAS 1926.605 ff.; O. R. Gurney, in AAA 22 (1935), 31 ff.—They hold a "purifier" (*mullilu*) in their right hands, a ewer (*banduddu*) in their left: E. D. Van Buren, Foundation Figurines and Offerings (1931), 58 ff.; M. E. Mallowan, in Iraq 16 (1954), 85 ff.; A. Goetze, in JCS 9 (1955), 15, n.53.—Berosus likewise tells a story of mythical beings who emerged from the sea: H. Zimmern, KAT[3], 530–39; S. Langdon, OECT ii.4; F. Hrozný, in MVAG 1903/v.94–106. For further evidence, cf. ZA 39.255, 5;

K 8444.8; ASKT 78.10. In Gilgamesh i.19 (p. 11, ed. Thompson), seven *muntalkê* ("Clever ones") help build a temple in Uruk.—Similarly, in the Egyptian Book of the Dead, ch. 71, "seven divine masters," offspring of Mehurit, are "the inventors and patrons of all the arts and sciences and assisted Thoth in the composition and measurement of the earth": H. Brugsch, in ZAS 1872.6; P. le Page Renouf, in PSBA 16 (1894), 67. They are sometimes depicted as hawk-headed, but on a sarcophagus in the Louvre (D 7) they have human heads. However, it does not appear that they rose from the waters.

32. Berosus, as quoted by Eusebius, Chron. 1. Helladius calls him Otos, and Hyginus (fab. 274, ed. Schmidt), Euvadores. The latter may be simply a textual corruption.

33. Sirach 24:2–6.—Note that in Babylonian glossaries, *ab-zu,* the primeval abyss, is popularly explained as derived from *ab* "abode" and *zu,* "wisdom": E. Dhorme, Rel. ass-bab. (1910), 73.

34. Job 28:12, 14. Note, however, that in Prov. 8:24, Wisdom exists prior to the creation of the deep.

3 Primordial wind

1. Eusebius, PE i.6; cf. S. Moscati, in JBL 66 (1947), 305–10. It is there called *kolpia,* of which there is so far no satisfactory explanation. W. F. Albright, in JBL 42 (1924), 363 ff., suggests that the Greek text is here corrupt and that ΚΟΛΙΙΑ ΑΝΕΜΟΥ should be read ΚΟΔΜ ΑΝΕΜΟΥ, "the east wind" (Heb. *qādîm*).

2. Cf. F. Rock, in Hommel Festschrift (1916), 270–83.

3. Job 41:10.

4. Exod. 15:8, 10.

5. K. Sethe, Amun (1909), 97.

6. E. C. T. Werner, Myths and Legends of China (1922), 77.

7. Rig Veda vii.87, 5.

8. On this problem see: W. B. Kristensen, in Theol. Tijdschr. 4 (1909), 398–400; E. Smoronski, in Biblica 6 (1935), 140–46, 275–93, 361–95; W. H. McClellan, ib., 15 (1944), 512–27; S. Moscati, in JBL 61 (1945), 305–10; J. P. Peters, in JBL 30 (1914), 44 f.; W. F. Albright, ib., 43 (1927), 363 ff.; K. Galling, in ZTK 47.145 ff.; B. S. Childs, Myth and Reality in the O.T. (1960), 33 ff.

9. Deut. 32:11 (*yᵉraḥef*).—The word *raḥefū* in Jer. 23:9 probably comes from a different root.

10. Cf. Epimenides (c. 600 B.C.), quoted by Damascius, 124; Aristophanes, Birds 639 ff.

11. Cf. S. G. Katawala, Cultural History from Matriyapurana (Baroda 1964), 212 f.; F. Lukas, in Zs. f. Vk. 4 (1894), 227–43; A. B. Heilborn, in Ethnos 28 (1963), 63–105.

12. III Aqhat i.20, 31. In a text (RS 24.252.8), discovered in 1960, the word is used to describe the gyrations of the goddess 'Anat in flight.

13. II Sam. 22:11; Ps. 18:11; Hos. 4:19; Ps. 104:3.

14. ANET 101.

15. Cf. T. H. Gaster, Thespis² (1961), 168.

16. F. Thureau-Dangin, in RA 24 (1927), 199–282.

17. Grimm-Stallybrass, TM 633–35.

18. P. Munsch, Norse Mythology (1926), 53 ff.

19. Samaveda 2.102.—The Indonesian national airline is today called Garuda.

20. G. Smith and A. H. Sayce, The Chaldean Genesis (1880), 123.

21. J. G. Scott, Indo-Chinese Mythology (1918), 323.

22. Grimm-Stallybrass, op. cit., 633.

23. Ib., 635.

24. L. Spence, Introduction to Mythology (1921), 123.

25. D. G. Brinton, Myths of the New World[3] (1905), 229.
26. Gracia, Or. de los Indias, V, ch. 4.
27. L. A. Magnus, ed., Tale of the Armament of Igor (1915), 18, line 633.

4 The firmament

1. The term derives from the Vulgate's *firmamentum,* which in turn goes back to the Septuagint's *stereōma.*
2. Heb.: *raqiᶜa;* cf. Exod. 39:3; Num. 17:3; Jer. 10:9; TB Sheqalim 95. So too Phoenician *m-r-q-ᶜ* in CIS i.90, but this reading has been disputed.
3. Job 26:13; 37:18.
4. Iliad 5.504; 18.425; Odyssey 3.2.
5. Pindar, Pyth. 10.27; Nem. 6.3.
6. Odyssey 15.329; 19.565.—Comparable is the German popular expression *eisene Himmel* (cf. H. Reichelt, in Indogerm. Forschungen 32.23 ff.; V. Pisani, in Archivio glottologico italiano 24:65 ff.).
7. Deveria, in Mel. d'archéol. égypt. et assyr. 1.9; [E. A. W. Budge,] BM Guide to the Egyptian Collections (1904), 145.
8. Kalevala, runo vii.332 ff.; tr. W. F. Kirby (Everyman's Library ed.), i.69.

5 Separation of heaven and earth

1. KUB XXXIII.106, iii.42' f., 52' f.; H. G. Güterbock, Kumarbi (1946), 27, *27–28; T. H. Gaster, The Oldest Stories in the World (1952), 133.
2. Enuma Elish iv.137–38.
3. On this motif, see: Stith Thompson, MI, A 625.2; A. H. Krappe, La genèse des mythes (1938), 78–80; K. Marot, in Act. Ant. Acad. Sc. Hung. i (1953), 35–63; K. Numazawa, in Scientia 88 (1953), 28–35; E. B. Tylor, Primitive Culture, i.322 ff.; A. Lang, Custom and Myth[2] (1885), 42–63; W. Radermacher, Die Trennung vom Himmel und Erde: ein vorgriechischer Schöpfungsmythus bei Hesiod und den Orphikern (1942); R. Dussaud, "Astarte, Pontos et Baal," in CRAIBL 1947.201–24; R. Pettazzoni, Dio (1922), i.130.
4. H. Kees, Götterglaube (1956), 226; Leyden Stele, V.12; S. Morenz, Aeg. Religion (1960), 182–83; P. Munro, in ZAS 85 (1960), 64. See also: S. Morenz, in RGG[3], iii (1959), 329.—Pyramid Text 1208ᶜ says that heaven was parted (*wpy*) from earth, and the gods ascended to the sky.
5. Aitareya Brahmana, in J. Muir, Original Sanskrit Texts (1858–72), V.23.
6. A. Lang, op. cit., 45 ff.; K. Ziegler and S. Oppenheim, Weltenstenhung in Sage und Wissenschaft (1925), 59.
7. J. G. Frazer, The Worship of Nature (1924), 627.
8. A. Bastian, Inselgruppen (1883), 1 f.
9. J. Doolittle, Social Life of the Chinese (1867), ii.396; R. Willhelm, Chinesische Volksmaerchen (1921), 29.
10. Koran 21:30, 32.
11. Ziegler and Oppenheim, op. cit., 53, 56; F. N. Numazama, Die Weltanfange in der japanischen Mythologie (1946), 317 ff.; R. Pettazzoni, La mitologia giapponese (1929), 39 f.

6 "God saw that it was good"

1. Gen. 1:12, 18, 21, 25, 31; cf. W. F. Albright, in Mélanges André Robert (1957).
2. L. Oppenheim, in Orientalia 16 (1947), 215. The technical term is *šuteṣbu.*
3. T. Bauer, Das Inschriftenwerk Assurbanipals (1933), ii.84.
4. Enuma Elish i.92.

7 The primal upsurge

1. Gen. 2:6. The Hebrew word is *'ed,* often rendered "mist," after the meaning which has been traditionally attached to it in Job 36:27.

2. E. A. Speiser, in BASOR 140 (1946), 9 ff.

3. Gen. 7:11.

4. Prov. 8:28.

5. CT XIII.35–38, 10–11 Heidel, Bab. Genesis[1] (1942), 49 ff. The Akkadian word is *ratu,* which is elsewhere written with the same logogram as also denotes *bitiqtu, pisannu,* "channel," etc.; cf. G. Howardy, Clavis Cuneorum, #348.18; #500.131.

6. A. J. Wensinck, The Ocean in the Literature of the Western Semites (1918), 17.

7. Ephraim Syrus, Opera i.11E, ed. Benedictus and Asserman.

8. Mas'udi, Les prairies d'or, ed. Barbier de Meynard et Pavet de Corteille (1861–77), i.203.

9. T. Canaan, Volksmedizin im Lande der Bibel (1914), 9.

10. See fully: T. H. Gaster, Thespis[2], 253, n.10.

11. KBo III.21, ii.8.

12. KBo VIII.3, i.20.

13. Gaster, op. cit., 261.

14. G. A. Smith, The Historical Geography of the Holy Land, 77.

ADAM AND EVE

▲ 8 Man formed from earth or clay

Literature: Stith Thompson, MI, A 1241; O. Dähnhardt, Natursagen, i.89–111; J. G. Frazer, Apollodorus, i.51, n.5; R. Briffault, The Mothers (1927), iii.57.

1. KAT[3], 506.

[1a. KARI 10.7.]

[1b. Epic of Gilgamesh ii.35 ff.]

[1c. CT vi.5; E. Ebeling, Tod und Leben (1931), 172–76; A. Heidel, The Babylonian Genesis[1] (1940), 54 f.; Speiser, in ANET 99[b].]

[1d. Atrahasis Epic (end); CT xv.49, iv; ANET 100[b].]

[1e. F. H. Weissbach, Bab. Misc. (1903), xv.26, pp. 32–34; Heidel, op. cit., 44 f. There would appear to be an allusion to this concept in Job 33:6, "I too was pinched out of clay."]

2. Eusebius, Chronicon, ed. Schoene, vol. i, col. 16. [See also: F. Lenormant, Essai de commentaire des fragments cosmogoniques de Bérose d'après les textes cuneiformes (1871); P. Schnabel, Berossus und die babylonisch-hellenistische Literatur (1923).]

3. H. Kees, Aegypten, in Bertholet's Religiongesch. Lesebuch 10 (1928), 19, No. 25; J. Černy, Ancient Egyptian Religion (1952), 49; A. M. Badawi, Der Gott Chnum (1937).

[3a. H. Frankfort, Kingship and the Gods (1948), fig. 23.]

[3b. ANET 441[b].]

[3c. Amen-em-opet, ch. 25; ANET 424[b].]

4. Pausanias, x.4, 4. Cf. Apollodorus, Bib. i.7, 1; Ovid, Met. i.82 ff.; Juvenal, xiv.35 [with Mayor's note, in loc. See also: Hesiod, Theog. 590; Aeschylus, fr. 373 Dindorf; Sophocles, Oedipus Tyr. 56; fr. 432 (Pandora), Dindorf; Euripides, Phoen. 1122; Ion 455; Aristophanes, Birds 686; Plato, Protagoras xi.320 f.; Callimachus, fr. 133 Schneider; Lucian, Prom. i.11–15; Oppian, Hal. v.9; Horace, Odes i.16, 13–15; Martial, x.39, 4; Hyginus, fab. 142; Claudian, In Eutrop. ii.450–501; Censorinus, 4. §6; Weiske, Prome-

theus und seine Mythenkreis (1842), 497; T. Konitzer, De fabula Prometheana in arte literisque usu (Diss. Königsberg, 1885); L. T. A. Bouché-Leclerq, Placita Graecorum de origine generis humani (1877); E. S. McCartney, "Unde humanum genus," in Classical Journal 20 (1925), 367–68.] The creation of man by Prometheus is figured on ancient works of art; cf. J. Toutain, Études de mythologie et d'histoire des religions antiques (1900), 190. According to Hesiod (Works and Days, 60 ff.), it was the smith-god Hephaestus who, at the bidding of Hera, moulded the first man out of clay. [C. Kerenyi, Miti e Misteri (1951), 376–406, maintains that according to the earlier Greek tradition, man was formed from earth, not clay.]

[4a. Herondas, ii.28; cf. Headlam-Knox in loc.]

5. R. Brough Smyth, The Aborigines of Australia (1878), i.424.

6. W. E. Gudgeon, "Maori Religion," in Journal of the Polynesian Society, 14 (1905), 125 ff.; R. Taylor, Te Ika a Maui, or New Zealand and Its Inhabitants[2] (1870), 117; E. Shortland, Maori Religion and Mythology (1882), 21 ff. (The name of the Creator varies in the three versions: Tu, Tiki and Tane respectively. The red color of the clay, and the kneading of it with the god's blood, are mentioned only by Taylor, but he is a good authority.) [Cf. also R. B. Dixon, Oceanic Mythology (1916), 107, 203.]

7. W. Ellis, Polynesian Researches[2] (1832–36), i.110 f. [Cf. also Dixon, op. cit., 24–26.]

8. G. Turner, Samoa (1884), 300 f.

9. J. Kubary, "Die Religion der Pelauer," in A. Bastian's Allerlei aus Volksund Menschenkunde (1888), i.3, 56.

10. R. H. Codrington, The Melanesians (1891), 158.

11. F. W. Leggat, "Maleluka, New Hebrides," in Report of the Fourth Meeting of the Australasian Association for the Advancement of Science (Hobart 1893), 707 f.

12. C. M. Pleyte, "Ethnographische Beschrijving der Kei-Eilanden," in TANAG, Second Series, 10 (1893), 564.

13. N. Adriani and A. C. Kruijt, De Bare'e-sprekende Toradjas's van Midden-Celebes (1912–14), i.3, 245 f.

14. Hosburgh, quoted by H. Ling Roth, The Natives of Sarawak and of British North Borneo (1896), i.299 ff.

15. E. H. Gomes, Seventeen Years among the Sea Dyaks of Borneo (1911), 197.

16. H. Sunderman, Die Insel Nias und die Mission dasselbst (Barmen 1905), 65 ff., 200 ff.

[16a. On the Indonesian myths, cf. also: Dixon, op. cit., 172 ff., nn.96–100, 104–6.]

17. Fay-Cooper Cole, The Wild Tribes of Davao District, Mindanao. Field Museum Publication, 170 (1913), 135 f.

18. Laura W. Benedict, "Bagobo Myths," in JAF 26 (1913), 15.

[18a. Sat. Brahm., vii.4, 2, 17. Cf. also: N. M. Penzer, The Ocean of Story, iii.59.]

19. T. H. Lewin, Wild Races of S. E. India (1870), 224–26.

20. P. R. T. Gordon, The Khasis[2] (1914), 106.

21. R. V. Russell, The Tribes and Castes of the Central Provinces of India (1916), iii.551 f.

22. S. Chandra Roy, "The Divine Myths of the Mundas," in Journal of the Bihar and Orissa Research Society, 2 (Bankipore 1916), 201 ff.

23. J. N. Smirnov, Les populations finnoises des bassins de la Volga et de la Kama, i (1898), 200. [Cf. also: W. Holmberg, Siberian Mythology (1927), 327.]

24. W. Hofmayr, in Anthropos 6 (1911), 128 f.

25. G. Tessmann, Die Pangwe (1913), ii.18.

26. J. Spieth, Die Ewe-Stämme (1906), 828, 840.

[26a. N. Griaull, in Journal de psychologie, 1947; S. Feldmann, African Myths and Tales (1963), 62 f.]

[26b. Priest Ofuntola Oserjeman, Orisha (Great Benin Books, African Library Series, New York 1960), 4.]

27. Report of the International Expedition to Point Barrow (Washington 1885), 47.

28. E. W. Nelson, "The Eskimo about Bering Strait," in 18th Annual Report of the Bureau of American Ethnology, Pt. i (1899), 854.

29. Father Geronimo Boscana, "Chingchinich," appended to [A. Robinson's] Life in California (1846), 247.

30. R. B. Dixon, "Maidu Myths," in Bulletin Amer. Museum of Natural History, 17/i (1902), 39, 41 f. [The name of the Creator is given by other authorities as Kodoyanpe (or Kodayampeh); see: ERE iii.66a, 560b; iv.12; vi.638b.]

31. T. T. Waterman, The Religious Practises of the Diegueño Indians (1910), 338 f.

[31a. P. G. Goddard, Kato Texts (UCP v/3, 1909), 184 ff.]

[31b. J. Adair, History of the American Indians (1775), 195.]

[31c. See in general: H. Baumann, Schöpfung und Urzeit des Menschens im Mythus der afrikanischen Völker (1936); W. Krickeberg, Indianermärchen (1924), 267, 307, 321 f.]

32. H. R. Voth, The Traditions of the Hopi (1905), 1 ff.

33. H. H. Bancroft, The Native Races of the Pacific States (1875–76), iii.78.

34. Le Page du Pratz, The History of Lousiana (1774), 330.

35. A. de Herrera, General History of the Vast Continent and Islands of America, tr. J. Stevens (1725–26), iii.254; Brasseur de Bourbourg, Histoire des nations civilisées du Mexique et de l'Amérique Centrale (1857–59), iii.80 f.

[35a. H. B. Alexander, Latin American Mythology (1920), 85.]

36. Cristoval de Molina, "The Fables and Rites of the Yncas," in Narratives, Rites and Laws of the Yncas, tr. C. R. Markham (1873), 4.

37. W. B. Grubb, An Unknown People in an Unknown Land (1911), 114 f.

38. Plato, Symposium 189D–191D.

[38a. Grubb, op. cit., 139–41.]

9 Man animated by divine breath

1. Maitrayani Upanishad ii.2, 6.

2. Steph. Byz., s.v. Ikonion. Cf. also: W. Kroll, in Rhein. Mus. 52 (1897), 340; C. A. Lobeck, Aglaophamus (1826), i.753–64.

3. Priest Ofuntola Oserjeman, Orisha (pamphlet issued by the Shango Temple in Harlem, New York 1960), 4.

4. L. Spence, in ERE iv.127.

5. E. W. Norton, in 18th Annual Report of the Bureau of American Ethnology (1899), 432 ff.

6. The word is actually used in certain passages of the O.T. (e.g., Jonah 2:6; Ps. 69:2; Job 7:15; 11:20; 31:39), as also in Akkadian (napištu) to mean "windpipe, throat."

7. A. Pott, Zigeuner (1844–45), ii.306; George Borrow, Lavengro, ii, ch. 26.

8. E. B. Tylor, Primitive Culture, ii.1617 (where references are given).

9. E. Rhode, Psyche[8] (1921), i.46 f.; T. H. Gaster, The Holy and the Profane (1955), 161 f.

10. Gen. 50:1.

11. Jubilees 23:10.

12. Vergil, Aeneid 4.686.

13. Cicero, In Verr. v.118.

14. Alexander Pope, Heloise and Abelard, 324; P. B. Shelley, Adonais.

15. E. B. Tylor, op. cit., i.391.

16. J. Hartland and T. T. Wilkinson, Lancashire Folklore (1882), 210.

17. Amarna Letters, ed. Winckler, 71.70; 122.36, 40; 128.7, 10; 130.1, 7, 9; 147.6, 8, etc. See on this: O. Weber, in J. A. Knudzton, Die Amarna Tafeln (1915), 1195 f.; J. de Köning, Studien over de El-Amarna brieven, etc. (1940), 503 ff.; CAH ii.342; I. Engnell, Studies in Divine Kingship in the Ancient Near East (1945), 93.

18. Lam. 4:20.

19. Job 32:8.

20. See below, §25.

21. Stith Thompson, MI, A 1211.1; Dahnhardt, loc. cit.

22. KARI i.4, 20 ff.; tr. E. Ebeling, in ZDMG 70 (1916), 532–38; A. Heidel, The Babylonian Genesis[1], 56 ff.

23. Enuma Elish vi.32–33.

24. Homeric Hymn to Apollo, 335; Dio Chrisost. 30; Acusilaus, cited by Scholiast on Nicander, Theriaca = F. G. Sturz, Phocylidis fragmenta . . . denique fragmenta Acusilai[2] (1824), 233, #35.—Ovid, Met. i.318 ff., says that Earth breathed new life into the gore of the ousted Titans, with which she had been drenched.

25. Ovid, Met. i.154 ff.; Servius, on Vergil, Ecl. vi.41 ff.

26. Julian, frag. epist. i.375, 21 ff., cf. A. B. Cook, Zeus ii (1925), 1032.

27. S. Eitrem, Opferritus und Voropfer der Griechen und Römer (1915), 426.

28. Koran 96:2.

10   Man made in the image of God

1. Teaching of Ani, LXVII = E. A. W. Budge, The Teaching of Amen-em-apt (1924), 249.

2. King Khety, xxvii.132 = ib., 22 = A. Erman, Die Literatur der Aegypter (1923), 119.

3. Quoted by Stobaeus, cxvii.8.

11   Woman

(a)   Woman formed from man's rib

1. V. Scheil, in CRAIBL 1915.334 f.; E. Villa, in SMSR 15 (1939), 126–29; H. Holma, in Orientalia 1 (1944), 225; S. N. Kramer, Enki and Ninhursag. BASOR Suppl. 1 (1954), 9. See also: T. Obbink, Het bijbelsch Paradijsverhael (1917), 123; J. Feldmann, Paradies und Sündenfall (1913), 242 f.; Against this view, see: J. Renié, in MScRel. 10 (1953), 9–12.

2. J. A. Mason, The Ethnology of the Salinan Indians, UCP X/4 (1912), 190 f.

3. A. L. Kroeber, in Anthropos 27 (1932), 907 ff.

4. E. W. Gifford, Clans and Moieties in Southern California, UCP XIV/2 (1918), 182 f.

5. C. E. Fox, The Threshold of the Pacific (1924), 238.

6. J. Grimm, TM[4], iii.162.

7. Op. cit. Mason's view is contested, however, by T. Waterman in UCP VIII/6 (1910), 339, n.149; while the Yuki myth which Kroeber attributes to missionary influence finds a striking parallel in a folktale from Bechuanaland: see R. Pettazzoni, Miti e Leggende, i, #28.

8. See: B. Landsberger, in ZA 25 (1911), 384 f.; A. Dillmann, Genesis[6] (1892), 53 f.

9. The possibility of missionary influence in fact bedevils most comparisons between primitive and Scriptural tales. The extent of such influence may be gauged from the development among several primitive peoples of newfangled "Biblical" cults fostered by missionaries or native converts. Thus, in 1825, Protestant missionaries in Hawaii introduced the Hapu cult, which stressed the worship of Jehovah on the grounds that the O.T. was more adaptable to native ideology than the N.T.: see V. Lanternari, The

Religions of the Oppressed (1965), 198.—By a similar process, a "Biblical" sect called "the Israelites" was established in the Tuamotu Islands of Polynesia: ib., 200; A. C. E. Caillot, Les polynesiens orientaux au contact de la civilisation (1909), 308.—Among the Hau-hau of New Zealand, a certain Te-Ua, who had become an Anglican convert, introduced a cult in which sacred songs were sung containing a mixture of Hebrew, Greek, English, German, and Italian words! He said that he was the new Moses, and was also known as Tiu, "Jew." New Zealand, he declared, was the new Canaan, and Jehovah would eventually speak to the Maoris from the top of a *niu*-pole, just as he had spoken of old to Moses from the top of Mt. Sinai. Native warrior bands called themselves "the Twelve," in reference to the twelve tribes of Israel: Lanternari, op. cit., 203 ff.; F. Vaggioli, Storia della Nuova Zelanda (1896), ii.360 ff. In light of such syncretistic developments, a certain degree of skepticism about primitive parallels to Bible stories may perhaps be permitted.

(b) The woman in Paradise

10. See: W. F. Albright, "The Goddess of Life and Wisdom," in AJSL 36 (1920), 258–94; C. A. Williams, Oriental Affinities of the Legend of the Hairy Anchorite, UILL X/2 (1925), 36 ff.

11. Gilgamesh ix.37 (Assyrian version: x.1 ff.) = ANET 90. A goddess named Shiduri, lady of wisdom and life, is mentioned in the Babylonian incantation series, Shurpu ii.172 f., and is identified by P. Jensen, Gilgames Epos (1926), 28, n.5 with Siduri.

12. Cf. E. A. Speiser, Introduction to Hurrian (1941), 55, 112.

13. Odyssey 5.282–493. See: H. Güntert, Kalypso (1919)—with exhaustive bibliography; L. Radermacher, "Die Erzaehlungen der Odysee," in Sitzb. Kais. Akad. Wien, 178 (1915), 27–31, 49–51; Cornelia G. Coulter, "The Happy Otherworld and Fairy Mistress Theme in the Odyssey," in TAPhil. Soc. 56 (1925), 37–53.

14. Tr. C. H. Tawney, Jaico paperback ed. (Bombay 1956), 82–93.

15. Cf. E. G. Cox, "Classical Traditions in Medieval Irish Literature," in PQ 3 (1924), 282–83.

16. Imram Malduin, §28; cf. W. Stokes, in Rev. Celt. 9. 447–95; 10. 50–95; A. C. L. Brown, Iwain (1903), 65.

17. A. Nutt, in Kuno Meyer's edition of The Voyage of Bran (1895), i.101–331; P. W. Joyce, Old Celtic Romances translated from the Gaelic (1907), 106–111, 152–56.

18. Cf. L. A. Paton, Studies in the Fairy Mythology of Arthurian Romance (1903).

19. Vita Merlini (1150).

20. W. H. Schofield, "The Lady of Guingamor," in [Harvard] Studies and Notes in Philology and Literature 5 (1896), 221–43, where a distinction is drawn between the fairy mistress and the swan-maiden.

21. T. P. Cross, "Celtic Elements in Lanval and Graelent," in Modern Philology 12 (1914–15), 585–644.

22. R. S. Loomis, in Speculum 20 (1945), 183 f.

23. Cf. E. S. Hartland, The Science of Fairy Tales (1891), 43, 204.

24. F. J. Child, English and Scottish Popular Ballads (1882), i.317–29.

25. M. W. Beckwith, The Hawaiian Romance of Laikawai (1918); id., "Polynesian Analogies to the Celtic Otherworld and Fairy Mistress Themes," in Vassar Medieval Studies (New Haven 1923), 27–55.

26. Cf. I. Zoller, "Lilith," in Filologische Schriften 2 (1929), 121–42; J. Montgomery, in The Museum Journal (Philadelphia) 41.62–65; A. S. Rappoport, Myth and Legend of Ancient Israel (reprint 1966), i.77–79; J. Trachtenberg, Jewish Magic and Superstition (1939), 277, n.33.

THE GARDEN OF EDEN

12 The Earthly Paradise

1. *Literature:* Stith Thompson, MI, A 151.2; H. Gressmann in ARW 10 (1907), 345–67; K. Budde, Die bibl. Paradiesgeschichte (1932); H. Schmidt, Die Erzählung von Paradies und Süundenfall (1931); P. Humbert, in RHPR 16 (1936), 445 ff.; A. Causse, in RHR 81 (1926), 289–315; A. Deimel, in Orientalia 16 (1925), 90–100; J. Morgenstern, "The Sources of the Paradise Story," in Journal of Jewish Lore and Philosophy 1 (Cincinnati 1919), 105–23, 225–40; A. Wuensche, "Schöpfung und Sündenfall des ersten Menschenpaares im Jüdischen und moslemischen Sagenkreise, etc.," in Ex Oriente Lux 11 (1906), 169–252; T. C. Vriezen, Onderzoek naar de Paradijsvoorstelling bij de onde semietische Voken (1937); W. Watson, "Paradise in the Apocrypha and Pseudepigrapha," in International Journal of Apocrypha, 1914.74 ff.—A. Brock-Utne, Der Gottesgarten (1936), propounds the curious view that the story is, *au fond,* a polemic against the cult of the serpent!

Modern critical analysis recognizes two hands in the composition of the Biblical tale. To J¹ are assigned: Gen. 2:4ᵇ–9, 13–25; 3:1–19, 21, 23. (This source knows of only *one* tree in the Garden.) To J² are assigned: 2:10–14 and 3:23–24, containing mention of the four rivers, the expulsion, the cherubim, and the revolving sword.

2. The name paradise is Iranian (*pairi-daeza*) and denotes properly a pleasure-park, such as embellished the palace of the Persian king. It came into general European usage through the ancient Greek (Septuagint) Version of the Bible, where it was used—in the naturalized form, *paradeisos*—to render the Hebrew, *Garden of Eden;* see fully: L. B. Paton, ICC on Esther 1:5. By analogy, temples of gods (*qua* divine kings) were likewise supplied with parks. Thus, at Mari we hear of the *kirum . . . ša ilim* (Dossin, ARM i.136.7) and in the Hittite myth of Illuyankas of the A. ŠAG. *siunas* attached to the temple. See fully: W. Andrae, "Der kultische Garten," WO 6 (1952), 485–94.—In the Canaanite texts from Ras Shamra-Ugarit the demesne of the supreme god (El) is styled not only *šd ilm* ("field of the gods") but also, more specifically, *qrš mlk* ("*qrš* of the king"), and Aistleitner would connect *qrš* with Arabic *q-r-s,* "cut off" in the sense of "park." I am not convinced by this.

3. S. N. Kramer, Enki and Ninhursag. BASOR Suppl. 1 (1945); id., ANET 37–41; M. Witzel, in Orientalia 15 (1946), 239–85; T. Jacobsen, in The Intellectual Adventure of Ancient Man, ed. H. Frankfort (1946), 157–60. See also: A. Dammron, La mythologie sumérienne et les premiers chapitres de la Genèse (1959); J. de Fraine, "Paradesus apud Sumeros?" in VD 25 (1947), 161–71; W. F. Albright, "The Vineyard Paradise," in AJSL 36.280–84.—The location of Paradise near the Persian Gulf (i.e., at Bahrein) seems to be reflected in Aristophanes, Birds 144 f., where mention is made of "a blessed city beside the Red Sea," i.e. (to the Greeks), the Persian Gulf. See further on that passage: E. Rohde, Griech. Roman (1914), 201 ff.

4. On this vexed problem, see: E. Burrows, "Tilmun, Bahrein and Paradise," in Orientalia, O.S. No. 30 (1928); S. N. Kramer, "Dilmun, the Land of the Living," in BASOR 96 (1944), 18–28 (somewhere in Iran); P. B. Cornwall, ib., 103 (1946), 3–11 (Bahrein); S. N. Kramer, "Dilmun, Quest for Paradise," in Antiquity 37 (1963), 111–15; J. Lazar, "Dilmun es Makan, problemaja az ujabb regeszeti kutatasok megvilagi tasaban," in An. Tan. 10 (1963), 112–15. (Ignorance of Georgian has prevented me from consulting this study.)

5. Sumerian Deluge Story from Nippur (= A. Poebel, Histor. and Grammatical

Texts (1914), P. 1 = A. Heidel, Gilgamesh, 105 = ANET 44), 21. In the Akkadian version (Gilgamesh xi.195) the name Dilmun is not mentioned.

6. Gilgamesh v.47. On the meaning of *ḫiṣṣu,* see: L. Oppenheim, in Orientalia 17 (1948), 47 f.

7. N. M. Penzer, Ocean of Story (1923 ff.), i.66, n.1; 68, 96; ii.34; iii.5, 24, 138; vi.82; vii.129, 148; viii.73, 165, 179; x.21, 87, n.4.

8. Ib., i.65; cf. Dunlop-F. Liebrecht, Gesch. d. Prosadichtungen (1851), 251, n.325.

9. Sukhavatiyuha 15–19, 21–22, 24, 26–27; tr. E. Conze, Buddhist Scriptures (1959), 232–36.

10. It is vividly described by Eumaeus in Odyssey 15.405 f., and the description accords remarkably with that of Dilmun in the Sumerian poem. See also: Sophocles, Ion, fr. 297 Nauck[2]; Eratosthenes, Catast. 3; Aristophanes, Birds 1758. See: A. B. Cook, Zeus ii (1925), 1017, 1021, 1027, 1119.—On Herakles' eleventh task, viz., fetching golden apples of the Hesperides, see: Hesiod, Theog. 215 f.; Euripides, Hercules Furens, 394 f.; Ap. Rhod. Argon. iv.1396 f.; Ovid, Met. iv.637 f.; Hyginus, fab. 30; Apollodorus, Bib. ii.5, 11.

11. Euripides, Hippolytus 749 (Gilbert Murray's translation).

12. T. H. Gaster, Thespis[2], 183.

13. J. A. MacCulloch, The Celtic and Scandinavian Religions (1948), 89.

14. E. Windisch, Irische Texte (1880–1909), i.197–227; A. C. L. Brown, Iwain (1903), 40, n.2. Cf. H. Zimmern, in Zeitschr. f. deutsch. Altertum 33.276. Cf. also: H. Patch, "Medieval Descriptions of the Otherworld," in PMLA 33 (1918), 619 f.

15. Cf. V. Rydberg, Teutonic Mythology, tr. R. Anderson (1889), 231.

16. L. C. Wimberly, Folklore in the English and Scottish Ballads (1928), 148. Cf. also the description of Paradise in the early English poem, *Pearl* (tr. Brian Stone), in Medieval English Verse (Penguin 1964), 145 ff.

17. D. G. Brinton, Myths of the New World[3] (1905), 104 f.; Peter Martyr, De Rebus Oceani (1574), Dec. iii, lib. x, p. 202.

18. Brinton, loc. cit.; id., Notes on the Floridian Peninsula (1859), 99 f.

19. Brinton, Myths, 108–9.

20. Ib., 105 f.

21. Ib., 107; Ximenes, Or. de Los Indios, 80.

13 The location of Paradise

(a) In the east

1. Gen. 2:8.

2. Pyramid Texts, 480, 487, 916, 928, 994, 1010, 1191, 1475, 1985. See: H. Kees, Totenglauben (1956), 119; R. Weil, Le champ des roseaux et le champ des offrandes (1936); A. Bayoumi, Autour du champ des souchets et du champs des offrandes (1941); J. H. Breasted, Development of Religion and Thought in Ancient Egypt (1912), 101–5. Book of the Dead, ch. 109 (ANET 32) likewise locates the blessed realm in the east.

3. J. Vandier, La religion égyptienne (1949), 85.

4. ERE, s.v. (Isles of the) Blest (Iranian).

5. S. D. F. Salmond, in Hastings' DB, s.v. Paradise.

6. H. H. Bancroft, Native Races of the Pacific States of N. America (1875–76), iii.529.

7. D. G. Brinton, Myths of the New World[3] (1905), 108–9.

8. J. A. McCulloch, ERE, s.v. Blest, Abode of the. The Mexicans say that the sun goes at evening to lighten the dead: Brasseur de Bourbourg, Histoire des nations civilisées du Mexique et de l'Amérique Centrale (1857–59), iii.496.

9. E. B. Tylor, Primitive Culture, ii.158.

10. F. Rinder, Old-World Japan (1895), 79.

(b) In the west

11. Hesiod, Works and Days, 165; Pindar, Ol. ii, antistr. 4; Strabo, iii.2, 13 Cf. also: Pliny, HN iv.36.

12. W. Stanbridge, in Trans. Ethnological Soc. of London, N.S. 1 (1861), 299; J. Bonwick, Daily Life and Origin of the Tasmanians (1870), 181.

13. W. Mariner, An Account of the Natives of the Tonga Islands[2] (1818), ii.107: Bolotu, the isle of gods and souls, lies in the northwest.

14. L. H. Morgan, League of the Iroquois (1851), 176.

15. J. J. Molina, Geographical, Natural and Civil History of Chili (1809), ii.89.

16. Peter the Martyr, Dec. i, lib. ix; W. Irving, Life of Columbus, ii.121.

(c) In the sky

17. H. Kees, Der Götterglaube im Alten Aegypten (1956), 247.

18. See: E. F. Weidner, "Das Paradies am Sternhimmel," in AfO 2 (1924–25), 124–30; J. Aistleitner, "Excurs ueber kosmologische Beziehungen der ugaritischen Mythologie," in Acta Orient. Hung. 5/i–ii (1955), 4–22.

19. Cf. Hyginus, fab. 152b, 154; Ps.-Eratosthenes, Catast. 37.—R. Anthes, in Mythologies of the Ancient World, ed. S. N. Kramer (1961), 20, doubts that the heavenly waters were identified as a counterpart of the Nile.

20. Cf. Hesiod, fr. 199 Rzach; Hyginus, loc. cit.; Ps.-Eratosthenes, loc. cit.; Aratus, Phaenom. 359 ff.; Claudian, De sixt. cons. hon. Aug. 175 ff.; Nonnus, Dionys. iii.326 ff. See: R. Brown, Eridanus, River and Constellation (1883); A. Jeremias, Handbuch d. altor. Geisterkultur[3] (1913), 60, 189.—Note too the remark of Strabo 215 that Eridanus is really "nowhere on earth, though alleged to be near the Po."

14   The Waters of the Garden

(a) The "Confluence of the Two Streams"

1. W. F. Albright, in AJSL 35 (1919), 161–95; ib., 39 (1922), 15–31; A. Causse, in RHR (1920), 289–315; A. Wuensche, Die Sagen vom Lebensbaum und Lebenswasser (1905). Cf. CT XVI.46, 18[3] ff.; XVII.26, 64 ff., 38.30 ff.

2. Egyptian Tale of the Shipwrecked Sailor, 85.

3. Odyssey 1.50. But in Hesiod, Theog. 215, the Garden of the Hesperides lies *beyond* the cosmic stream (Okeanos).

4. Koran 18:59 ff.; cf. W. F. Albright, in JPOS 12 (1932), 12, n.35. (On the broader implications of this passage, see: M. Lidzbarski, in ZA 7 [1892], 104 ff.; 8 [1893], 263 ff.; A. H. Krappe, in PQ 20 [1941], 125 f.; ib., 21 [1942], 334–46.)—There seems to be a further reference to the junction of all streams, this time located in the *north,* in the Syriac translation of Andronicus' On the Inhabitants of the Earth; cf. G. Furlani, in ZS 5.241, 245.

(b) The Paradisal River and the Four Streams

5. Gen. 2:10–14.

6. Stith Thompson, MI, F 162.2.1; H. Patch, in PMLA 33 (1918), 622 ff.; W. F. Albright, in AJSL 39 (1922), 40 ff.; F. Hommel, in Theol. Litbl. 47 (1901), 557 ff. (= Aufsaetze und Abhandlungen, 326–40), argues from references in II R 56.26–29 and V R 22.27 ff. that the Babylonians recognized *four* divine rivers; cf. also: H. Zimmern, KAT[3], 528.

7. D. G. Brinton, Myths of the New World[3] (1905), 102–3.

8. [T. W. Doane], Bible Myths (1883), 14.

9. Cf. ERE ii.706[b].

10. Brinton, loc. cit.

11. A. Fornander, The Polynesian Race (1878–85), i.79 ff.

12. Beowulf, 3337–84; Saemund, Voluspá, 9b.

13. Odyssey 5.59 ff.

14. Ch. Fries, in Neue Jahrb. für d. klass. Alt., 1902, i.689–707; H. Zimmern, KAT³, 642, n.4.

(c) The Paradisal Fountain

15. Heb.: ᶜadanim, plural of ᶜeden.

16. Prov. 10:11; 13:14; 14:27; 16:22.

17. Wuensche, op. cit., 77; J. A. McCulloch, The Childhood of Fiction (1905), 52–79; Bolte-Polivka, i.513; ii.400; W. Hertz, Ges. Abh. (1905), 49, 91; A. N. Vesselofsky, Iz istorii romana i povesti, i.229, 271.

18. Koran 76:12–22; 47:16–17.

19. Peter Martyr, De rebus Oceani (1574), Dec. iii, lib. x, p. 202; D. G. Brinton, op. cit., 104 f.

20. H. Draws-Tychsen, in Acta Tropica 1952.1–16.

21. Ancient poem in Villemarqué, Barz. Breiz. i.193.

22. Quoted in S. Baring-Gould, Curious Myths of the Middle Ages (1880), 408.

23. Cf. ERE vii.693ᵇ–694ᵃ; I. Friedlander, Die Chaḍirlegende und der Alexander-roman (1913).

24. See: E. W. Hopkins, in JAOS 26 (1905), 1–67; 27 (1906), 41 ff.; K. von Spiess, "Der Brunnen der ewigen Jugend," in Hommel Festschrift (1918), ii.328–41.

15   The land of gold and gems

1. On the jeweled trees of Paradise, see: Stith Thompson, MI, F 162.0.1; 163.3.1; 169.2; 771.1.8; 811.2.2; H. Patch, in PMLA 33 (1918), 625, n.83; N. M. Penzer, Ocean of Story (1923 ff.), iv.128.

2. Gilgamesh IX, v.45–51; cf. V. Christian, in WZKM 40 (1933), 148; L. Oppenheim, in Orientalia 17 (1948), 47.

3. Ezek. 28:13–14, 16. "Flashing gems" renders the Hebrew ’abnê ’eš, which is the Akkadian aban išāti, an equivalent of the precious stone called ḫipindû (CT XIX.5, obv. 5); see below, §213.

4. PRB xii. 270; F. Liebrecht, Des Gervasius von Tilbury Otia Imperialia (1856), 152n.

5. Ramayana iv. 43; cf. also: Mahabharata vi.7.

6. Tale of the Fairy Bride Mrigankavati and Yasahketu: tr. C. H. Tawney, Jaico paperback ed. (Bombay 1956), 82–93.

7. Sukhavatiyuha = E. Conze, Buddhist Scriptures (1959), 232 ff.; Ashvagosha Saundaranakavya X.3–4 (= ib., 223).

8. Ol. ii.67–74.

9. M. Anesaki, Japanese Mythology (1928), 242.

10. Voluspá 62.

11. H. R. Patch, Other World (1950), 375; Stokes-Windisch, Irische Texte 3 Ser., i.209.

12. F. J. Child, The English and Scottish Popular Ballads (1882–98), 41, A.7 f.; L. C. Wimberly, Folklore in the English and Scottish Ballads² (1959), 147.

13. Wimberly, ib. So too, in the ballad entitled Child Waters, the hero and Burd Ellen cross waters to the otherworld and come upon a hall with a tower and gates of red gold: Wimberly, op. cit., 145; W. M. Hart, Ballad and Epic (1907), 29.

14. E.g., Midrash Gedullath Mosheh, in A. Jellinek's Beth ha-Midrash (1853–78), ii; Revelation of R. Joshua ben Levi, Rec. B = Jellinek, ii.52; tr. M. Gaster, in JRAS 1893.596 f. Cf. L. Ginzberg, Legends of the Jews (1909 sqq.) v.32.

16   The Food of Paradise

1. Stith Thompson, MI, A 152; 153.2; 154; 154.1; Grimm-Stallybrass, TM 318 ff.
2. Iliad 5.340.
3. Iliad 19.38.
4. Iliad 16.670.
5. Iliad 23.186.
6. Homeric Hymn to Demeter, 236.
7. Ap. Rhod., Argon. 4.869; Apollodorus, Bib. iii.13, 6.
8. Theocritus, 15.106.
9. Ovid, Met. 14.606.
10. Odyssey 5.136 ff.
11. Pindar, Ol. i.98.
12. Met. ii.4.12.
13. Lucian, Dial. deorum 4; cf. W. H. Roscher, Nektar und Ambrosia (1883), 51–55.
14. H. D'Arbois de Jubainville, Cours de la littérature celtique (1883–1902), v.170 ff.
15. Ib., v.384. In the legend of Eithne, in the Book of Fermoy, Manaán settles the Tuatha de Danaan in beautiful lands, walled and impenetrable, and supplies them with the ale of Goibnenna the smith, which preserves them from old age and death: Todd, in R. J. A. Irish MS. series, I, i.46; A. C. L. Brown, Iwain (1903), 42, n.1.
16. Sn. 30a; on this motif, see: Grimm's Märchen, #37; Grimm-Stallybrass, TM 318 ff.
17. Revue Celtique 15.457.
18. H. Zimmern, in ARW 2.156–77; Ch. Virolleaud, in JA 239 (1951), 127–32.
19. Adapa, Amarna tablet, 60–63; tr. Speiser, ANET 102.
20. I Aqhat vi.25 ff.; cf. T. H. Gaster, Thespis[2], 347 f.
21. G. A. Cooke, A Text-book of North Semitic Inscriptions (1903), #61.21–22.
22. Enoch 25:4–5.
23. Test. Levi 18:11.
24. Vita Adae 40–42.
25. L. Ginzberg, Legends of the Jews, i.94.
26. Patrologia Orientalis i.1014.
27. F. Cumont, After Life in Roman Paganism (1923), 206 f.
28. Horace, Odes iii.3, 12.
29. Julian, Caes., p. 307C.
30. Exod. 16:15; see: H. Winckler, AOF ii.322 ff.
31. Ps. 78:25; cf. Wisdom of Solomon 16.20.
32. Exod. 16:31; Roscher, loc. cit.
33. See in general: Stith Thompson, MI, C 211, 241; E. S. Hartland, The Science of Fairy Tales (1891), 43 ff.; J. A. MacCulloch, The Childhood of Fiction (1905), 178; L. C. Wimberly, op. cit., 275 ff.; T. H. Gaster, Thespis[2], 208; F. J. Child, op. cit., i.322 and nn.; ii.505; G. Schambach and W. Mueller, Niedersaechsiche Sagen und Maerchen (1855), 373–424; Allen-Sikes-Halliday, The Homeric Hymns[2] (1936), on Demeter 372; J. G. Frazer, Apollodorus, Bib. xii.1.39, n4; A. Lang, A Collection of Ballads (1907), 232.
34. I* AB iii–iv; Gaster, op. cit., 203 f.
35. E. S. Drower, The Mandaeans of Iraq and Iran (1937), 351.
36. Homeric Hymn to Demeter, 372; see Allen-Sikes-Halliday, in loc.
37. W. G. Aston, Shinto (1921), 23.
38. O. Elton and F. Y. Powell, Saxo Grammaticus (1894), 344 ff.
39. Ib., 346.
40. R. C. A. Prior, Ancient Danish Ballads (1860), iii.320; Wimberly, op. cit., 278 f.

41. Andrew Lang, in EBrit.[9] x.134 (art. "Fairy").

42. Kalevala, runo xvi; frag. 293.

43. E. B. Tylor, Primitive Culture[3] (1891), ii.52n.

44. J. C. Poestion, Lappländische Märchen, etc. (1886), 111; Grimm-Stallybrass, TM 457n.; Hartland, op. cit., 38 f.

45. T. Keightley, The Fairy Mythology[2] (1882), 506.

46. Mélusine 1 (1878), 446; Hartland, op. cit., 42.

47. Hartland, loc. cit.

48. Wimberly, op. cit., 150.

49. Journal of the [Royal] Anthropological Institute, 10.282.

50. D. Leslie, Among the Zulus and Amatongas (1875), 121.

51. Gagnière, in Ann. de la Propag. de la Foi, 1860.439 ff.; R. H. Codrington, The Melanesians (1891), 277, 386; G. Landtmann, The Kiwai Papuans of British New Guinea (1927), 289.

52. Stith Thompson, MI, C 621; O. Dähnhardt, Natursagen, i.208 ff.; W. Holmberg, Siberian Mythology (1927), 381 ff.; H. Alexander, Latin American Mythology (1920), 171 (Quiché); 315 (Yuracare); J. G. Scott, Indo-Chinese Mythology (1918), 265, 289; A Carnoy, Iranian Mythology (1917), 296, 309.

53. H. Abrahamson, The Origin of Death: Studies in African Mythology (1957) = S. Feldmann, African Myths and Tales (1963), 118 f., #46.

54. Abrahamson, op. cit. = Feldmann, op. cit., 119 f.

55. J. A. Farrer, Primitive Manners and Customs (1879), 12, 141; G. Klemm, Allgemeine Culturgeschichte (1843–52), ii.155; Dorsey-Swanton, in Ann. Report of the Bureau of Amer. Ethnology, 47 (1922), 32 (Biloxi).—For an Andamanese legend of the same tenor, see: J. A. MacCulloch, in ERE v.707.

17   The Trees of Paradise

Literature: Skinner, in ICC ad loc.; P. Dhorme, in RB 4.271–74; A. Ungnad, in ZDMG 79 (1925), 111–18; W. Staerk, in RHPR 8 (1928), 66–69; G. Pidoux, in ZAW 66 (1954), 37–43.

(a) The Tree of Life

1. On the subject in general, see: R. Bauerkress, Arbor Vitae (1938); H. Bergema, De Boom des Levens (1938); W. Holmberg, Der Baum des Lebens (1922–23); H. Gunkel, Märchen in AT (1917), 45, 48, 152; Bolte-Polivka, i.513; O. Gruppe, Griechische Mythologie (1906), 872, n.l.; G. Widengren, The King and the Tree of Life in Ancient Near Eastern Religion (1951).—P. Humbert, Études sur le récit du paradis et la chute dans la Genèse (1940), 22 ff., holds that the Tree of Life was hidden, and revealed only when the fruit of the Tree of Knowledge was eaten.—P. A. H. de Boer, Genèse II en III (1941), argues that the Hebrew word rendered "tree" was originally a *collective* noun, referring to *all* the trees in the Garden.—H. Obbink, in ZAW 5 (1928), 105–12 contends that the fruit of the Tree of Life gave eternal life; but this is questioned (wrongly, I think) by K. Budde, ib., 6 (1929), 54–62.

2. K. Sethe, Pyr. Texts, i.484 = J. Breasted, Development of Religion and Thought in Ancient Egypt (1912), 134.

3. A good example comes from the "Astronomical Room" of the Ramesseum: see Paton-Moss, Topographical Bibliography, ii.155, #44; cf. E. Lefebvre, in Sphinx 5.1 ff., 65 ff.; C. J. Gadd, Ideas of Divine Rule in the Ancient East (1948), 91 f.

4. E. A. W. Budge, Osiris (1911), ii.327; id., BM Guide to the Egyptian Collections (1908), 43.—"Tree of life" is a not uncommon designation for a fruit tree in general: Pyr. Texts 1216; Ammon Hymn Cairo, i.7; Edfu, ed. Rochem., i.323; cf. H. Grapow, Die bildlichen Ausdruecken des Aegyptischen (1924), 137.

5. Gadd, loc. cit.; cf. also: R. Largement, "L'arbre de la vie dans la religion sumérienne," in AIDK 1959.188–91.

6. Gadd, loc. cit.

7. Cf. G. Howardy, Clavis Cuneorum, #272.290.

8. Ashvagosha, Saundarandakanvyga 10.4 = E. Conze, Buddhist Scriptures (Penguin ed.) 223.

9. Mrs. J. H. Philpot, The Sacred Tree (1897), 130.

10. R. F. Rattray, From Primitive to Modern Religion (1949), 16.

11. Enoch 24:4–25:6; Test. Levi 18:11; IV Ezra 8:52; Rev. 2:7; 22:2. For representations in art, see: Z. Ameisenowa, in Journal of the Warburg Institute, 1939.326–43.— The expression "tree of life" is used metaphorically in Prov. 3:18; 11:30; 13:12; and 15:4; but R. Marcus, in JBL 62 (1943), 119 f., argues that the reference is simply to a medicinal plant and has no mythological import. He recognizes an allusion to such a plant in the medieval Hebrew Book of Noah (in Jellinek, Beth ha-Midrash, i.156), which he attributes to Essene tradition.—A "balm of life," which the God-fearing may obtain, is mentioned in Sirach 6:15, though the Genizah Hebrew text there substitutes "bundle of life" (i.e., Heb.: ṣᵉrôr for ṣôrî), after II Sam. 25:29.

(b) The Tree of the Knowledge of Good and Evil

12. Stith Thompson, MI, J 165 (cf. also: C 621.1); Dähnhardt, Natursagen, i.212 ff.

13. On the subject in general, see: F. Asensio, in Gregorianum 30 (1949), 490–520; 31 (1950), 35–61; 136–91; 362–90; J. Coppens, in ETL 33 (1957), 506 f.; id., in Analecta Lovanensia Biblica et Orientalia, Ser. II, 35 (1952), 17 f.; J. Stoebe, in ZAW 65 (1953), 188–204; S. Munoz Inglesias, in Estudios biblicos 4 (1949), 441–63; J. Stegmeier, in Revista Biblica 13/60 (1951), 55 f.; T. Vriezen, Onderzoek naar de paradijsvoorstelling, etc. (1937), 142 ff.; P. Humbert, Études sur le récit du paradis (1940), 82 f.; A. Kolping, in Festschrift Nötscher (1950), 137 f.; H. S. Stern, in VT 8 (1958), 405–18.

14. Contrast II Sam. 19:36; I Kings 3:9; Isa. 7:15–16.

15. A. M. Honeyman, in JBL 71 (1952), 11 ff.; G. W. Buchanan, ib., 75 (1956), 114–20; C. H. Gordon, Introduction to O.T. Times (1953), 22–23.

18 The Serpent

(a) The Serpent as guardian

1. Stith Thompson, MI, B 11.6.2; D 950.0.1; N. W. Penzer, Ocean of Story (1923 sqq.), iii.133; G. Elliott Smith, The Evolution of the Dragon (1909), 157–65 [to be read with caution]; E. T. C. Werner, Myths and Legends of China (1922), 209; Grimm-Stallybrass, TM 689 f., 978 f.; M. Eliade, Patterns in Comparative Religion (1958), 291. —The theme is common in Classical literature: see J. E. B. Mayor, on Juvenal 14.114.

2. Hesiod, Theog. 333–35; Lucretius, 5.32–35; Propertius, iii (ii), 24, 26; Lucan, 9.356–66; Juvenal, 14.114; Pliny, HN v.3; Varro, Menipp. Meleagr. fr. 7 Buecheler; Hyginus, P.A. ii.6; Servius, on Vergil, Aeneid 4.184; Phaedrus, 4.21; E. Spannheim, on Callimachus, Del. 91.

3. Herodotus, 3.16.

4. A. H. Leahy, Heroic Romances of Ireland (1905), i.36.

5. Plutarch, Themistocles; so too at Lanuvium: Propertius, I.iv.8; Aelian, De animal. xi.16.

6. W. J. Hamilton, Researches in Asia Minor, Pontus and Armenia (1842), ii.275.

7. Nordenskiold, 288; G. N. Gould, Scandinavian Studies and Notes 9 (1917), 170, #4; T. Nordlind, Skattsägner (1918), 77 f.

8. W. Hinke, Boundary Stones (1907), 25, 28, 30, 97 ff.; S. Langdon, Tammuz and Ishtar (1914), 119.

9. Alföldi, in Gnomon 9 (1933), 517 f.

10. Aristeas, frags. 4, 7 Kinkel.

(b) The "subtil beast"

11. Prov. 12:16, 23; 13:16; 14:15, 18; 15:5; 22:3; 27:12.—On the wisdom of the serpent in general, see: Stith Thompson, MI, B 123; R. D. Scott, The Thumb of Knowledge (1930), 173; R. F. Burton, Arabian Nights (1894), iii.145; v.305, 328, 390; Marian R. Cox, Cinderella (1893), 496, n.32.—Cf. also: Matt. 10:6.

12. Ovid, Met. 4.563 f.

13. Plutarch, Cleomenes 39; cf. also: Porphyry, Vita Platonis 103.

14. H. A. Junod, The Life of a South African Tribe (1912–13), iii.351 f.

15. ERE vii.238[b].

16. E. Dunn, in Anthropos 1 (1906), 182.

17. A. Aymonier, in RHR 24 (1891), 267.

18. G. W. Stow, The Native Races of South Africa (1905), 148.

19. A. C. Hollis, The Nandi (1909), 90.

20. Cf. Aelian, De animal. ii.16; Artemidorus, Oneirocr. 4.69.

21. Cf. E. Spanheim, In Callimachi Hymnos Observationes (1697), on Del. 91.

22. G. Gamler, in R. Neuhaus, Deutsche Neu-Guinea (1911), iii.516.

23. Pliny, HN, 10.70; Apollodorus, Bib. i.9, §11 (legend of Melampus); Philostratus, Vita Apoll. i.20; iii.9. For the theme in modern folktales, cf. Bolte-Polivka, Anmerkungen zu . . . Grimm, i.131 ff.

24. J. Wellhausen, Reste d. arab. Heidentums[2] (1897), 137; T. Noeldeke, in ZDMG 64 (1910), 441; T. Canaan, Dämonenglaube im Lande der Bibel (1929), 13 f.

25. Koran 27:10; 28:31.

26. Relations des Jésuites 1678.75.

27. E. S. Parker, The Aborigines of Australia (1854), 25. The serpent is called Mindi.

28. Suffolk Folklore (Folklore Society), 32.

29. Artemidorus, Oneirocr. 2.13.

30. 'Abd-el-Gani of Nablus, quoted by T. Canaan, op. cit., 54, n.118.

31. James Furlong, Dictionary of Religions (reprint 1964), s.v. Mros.

32. T. Canaan, op. cit., 14; id., Mohammedan Saints (1927), 244 f.

▲ (c) The cast skin

33. Aristotle, Hist. anim. 8.17; Nicander, Ther. 137; Aristophanes, Pax 336; Ovid, Ars amat. 3.77; Met. 9.266; Vergil, Georgica 3.437; Aeneid 2.473; Statius, Theb. 4.97; Tibullus, i.4, 35.

34. Gilgamesh xi. 277–89 = ANET 96; cf. J. Morgenstern, in ZA 29 (1915), 284 ff.

35. A. Gardiner and N. E. Davis, Tombs of Menkheperransonb, etc. (EEF 1933), 26. See below, §277.

36. Plutarch, De Iside et Osiride 74.

37. Eusebius, PE i.10.

38. E.g., Pliny, HN 29.137 (senecta).

39. Mgr. Lechaptois, Aux rives du Tanganika (Algiers 1913), 195.

40. Ivor H. N. Evans, in JRAI 43 (1913), 478.

41. N. Adriani and A. C. Kruijt, De Bare'e-sprekende Toradja's van Midden-Celebes (1912–14), ii.83.

42. O. Meyer, in Anthropos, 5 (1910), 724.

43. H. Sundermann, Die Insel Nias (Barmen 1905), 68; E. Modigliani, Un viaggio a Nias (1890), 295.

44. A. Fehr, Der Niasser im Leben und Sterben (Barmen 1901), 8.

45. R. H. Codrington, The Melanesians (1891), 265.

46. C. Ribbe, Zwei Jahre unter den Kannibalen des Salomo-Inseln (1903), 148.

47. C. Keysser, "Aus dem Leben der Kaileute," in R. Neuhauss, Deutsch Neu-Guinea (1911), iii.161 ff. For a similar tale from the Admiralty Islands, see: J. Meier, in Anthropos, 3 (1908), 193.

48. Adriani-Kruijt, op. cit., ii.83.

49. Codrington, loc. cit.

▲ (d) The falsified message

50. J. E. Alexander, Expedition of Discovery into the Interior of Africa (1838), i.169; C. J. Anderson, Lake Ngami² (1856), 328 ff.; W. H. I. Bleek, Reynard the Fox in South Africa (1864), 71–73.

51. W. H. I. Bleek and L. C. Lloyd, Specimens of Bushman Folklore (1911), 57–65.

52. A. C. Hollis, The Nandi (1909), 98.

53. W. H. I. Bleek, Reynard, 69 ff.

54. S. S. Dornan, in JRAI 47 (1917), 80.

55. E. Jacottet, Études sur les langues du Haute Zambèze, iii. Textes Louyi (1901), 116 f.

56. P. A. Talbot, In the Shadow of the Bush (1912), 229.

57. J. G. Christaller, in Zs. für Afrikanische Sprachen, 1 (1887–88), 55.

58. Ib.

59. E. Perregaux, Chez les Achanti (1906), 198 ff.

60. Ib. 199.

61. C. W. Hobley, Ethnology of A-Kamba and other East African Tribes (1910), 107–9.

62. Fr. Müller, in Anthropos, 2 (1907), 203.

63. "Calabar Stories," in Journal of the African Society, No. 18 (Jan. 1906), 194.

64. H. Callaway, The Religious System of the Amazulu (1868), i.3 ff., ii.138; L. Grout, Zululand (Philadelphia, n.d.), 148 ff.; D. Kidd, The Essential Kafir (1904), 76 f.; Bleek, Reynard, 74; D. Leslie, Among the Zulus and Amatongas² (1875), 209.

65. J. Chapman, Travels in the Interior of S. Africa (1868), i.47.

66. E. Casalis, The Basutos (1861), 242; E. Jacottet, The Treasury of Ba-suto Lore, i (Morija, Basutoland 1908), 46 ff.

67. H. A. Junod, Les chantes et les contes des Ba-ronga (Lausanne, n.d.), 137; id., The Life of a S. African Tribe (1912–13), ii.328 f.

68. W. A. Elmslie, Among the Wild Ngami (1899), 70.

69. See: W. E. R. Barrett, in JRAI 41 (1911), 37.

70. J. G. Christaller, in Zs. für Afrikanische Sprachen, 1 (1887–88), 61.

71. Junod and Elmslie, locc. citt. (above, nn. 67–68).

72. Alice A. Werner, in Man, 13 (1913), 90 ff.

73. P. A. Kleintitschen, Die Küstenbewohner der Gazellehalbinsel (Hiltrup bei Münster, n.d.), 334.

74. A. Landes, in Cochinchine française, Excursions et Reconnaissances, No. 25 (Saigon 1886), 108 ff.

19 The Cherubim

1. See in general: W. F. Albright, in BA 1 (1937); R. H. Pfeiffer, in JBL 41 (1922), 249–50; P. Dhorme and L. Vincent, in RB 35 (1926), 328–58; 484–95; J. Pedersen, Cherubim (1897); A. S. Kapelrud, in JAOS 70 (1950), 151–56; R. de Vaux, in Mél. de la Faculté orientale de l'Université Saint Joseph, Beyrouth, 37 (1961), 93–124; R. L. Cleveland, in BASOR 172 (1963), 55–60 [South Arabian]; H. Schmidt, "Kerubenthron und Lade," in Gunkel Festschrift (1923), 120–44; F. N. Lindsay, Kerubim in Semitic Religion and Cult. PhD Diss. Columbia 1912.—On the motif in general, see: Stith Thompson, MI, B 11.6.2; D 950.0.1.

2. ANEP #654; cf. M. von Oppenheim, Der Tell Halaf (1931), Pl. 33.
3. ANEP #652.
4. ANEP #649; J. W. Crowfoot, Early Ivories from Samaria (1938), 18.
5. Gilgamesh ix/ii = ANET 88.
6. Rig Veda X.15; 7.55.
7. Notes and Queries 3/ix (1866), 23.

20 The Revolving Sword

1. Cf. Judg. 3:22; Nah. 3:3; cf. also: I Sam. 17:7; Job 29:23.—The Greek (Septuagint) Version renders *tēn phloginēn romphaian,* and it is interesting to observe that Tiglath Pileser I set up a "brazen lightning" over the site of a devastated city: I R vi.5; KB i.37; cf. Th. Dangin, in RHR 1, 146 ff.; H. Zimmern, KAT³, 530.—It should be noted too that the Hebrew word *ḥereb* does not necessarily mean a *sword.* It may be a *lance,* like the cognate term in Arabic (cf. J. Wellhausen, Reste, 142) or even a scimitar or scythelike weapon (cf. G. Chenet, in Mélanges Dussaud, i [1939], 49 ff.).
2. A. C. L. Brown, Iwain (1903), 80n.
3. Wigalis, ed. Pfeiffer (1847), cols. 173–81, vv. 6714–7053.
4. D. M. Méon, Nouveau Recueil de Fabliaux (1823), i.1 ff.
5. Iwain, 944.
6. Imram Malduin, §32; W. Stokes, in Revue Celtique 10.50–95; Brown, op. cit., 66.
—On the general theme of the revolving barrier to the otherworld, see: G. L. Kittredge, A Study of Sir Gawain and the Green Knight (1916), 244 f.

21 The role of man

1. A. Tiumenev, "O prednaznacenti ludei po miform deanego Dvurec'ia" (On the Destiny of Man according to the Myths of Ancient Mesopotamia), in Vestrik drevnei istorii 4 (1948), 14–23 [Georgian].—Similarly, among the Pygmies of Gabon it is held that man was created to tend and feed the gods: R. Pettazzoni, Miti e Leggende, i.384.
2. Enuma Elish vi.8, ff.
3. CT VI.5.6–10; A. Heidel, The Babylonian Genesis¹ (1942), 54 f.
4. E. Ebeling, in ZDMG 70 (1916), 532–38; Heidel, 56 f., lines 24 ff.
5. F. Weissbach, Miscellen (1903), Pl. 12, pp. 32–34; Heidel, 53 f., line 18.
6. A. Poebel, Historical and Grammatical Texts (1914), #1; Heidel, 59 f.

CAIN AND ABEL

Literature: A. Eberharter, "Der Brudermord Kains im Licht der ethnologischen und religionsgeschichtlichen Forschung" in Theol. Qu. 1916.355–65.

22 Behind the Biblical Story

(a) Smith and Herdsman

1. Cf. Arabic *qayin;* Aramaic *qena'â,* etc.; cf. P. Haupt, in Proc. Amer. Philos. Soc. 50.514.—The Biblical tribe of the Kenites (i.e., Cainites), who are associated with the Midianites (Num. 10:29) and the Amalekites (Num. 24:21), are thought to have been itinerant smiths. Indeed, a correct translation of Balaam's prophecy in Num. 24:22 seemingly alludes to this, for by word-play on their name it declares that someday the Kenite, i.e., the smith, will himself constitute the fuel of the forge: see W. F. Albright, in JBL 63 (1944), 222, n.102.
2. Cf. Syriac *ḥablâ,* "herdsman, swineherd," in Eliae Nisibeni interpres, ed. Lagarde (1879), 42, 48; Syrisch-Arabischen Glossen, ed. Hoffmann (1878), #3258; see: Haupt, op. cit., 513. The Syriac word *h-b-l-t-â,* which in the Peshitta version of Isa. 60:6 means

"a herd of camels," has often been compared, but this may be a mere variant spelling of *'a-b-l-t-â, for cf. Arabic *ibl,* S. Arab. *'a-b-l* (CIH 535.4) and Akkadian *ibilu,* "dromedary."

3. For bibliography on this point, see: J. G. Frazer, GB ii (Taboo and Perils of the Soul), 236n.

4. M. Eliade, Forgerons et Alchimistes (1956), 83 ff.; R. Andree, Ethnographische Parallelen i (1878), 153 ff.; B. Guttmann, in ZE 44 (1911), 81–93; R. Lasch, in Zs. fuer Sozialwissenschaft 4.78 f.; W. Wackernagel, Kleine Schriften (1872), i.49; P. Sartori, Sitte und Brauch ii (1912), 166; R. Eisler, The Messiah Jesus (1931), 327; F. J. Mone, Gesch. des Heidenthums in nördlichen Europa (1822–23), ii.430; Mélusine 4.368 f.; J. F. Campbell, Superstitions of the Scottish Highlands (1900), 246.

5. Eliade, op. cit., 92 f.

6. Von Harnier, in Petermann's Ergänzungshefte, No. 10, p. 133.

7. Pruyssenaere, ib., No. 50 (1877), 25.

8. G. Nachtigal, in Zs. d. Geselschaft fur Erdkunde zu Berlin 5 (1870), 312.

9. Haggenmacher, in Petermann's Ergänzungshefte, No. 47, p. 4.

10. A. von Maltzan, Reise nach Südarabien (1873), 309.

11. R. Hartmann, Die Nigritier (1876), i.374 ff.; M. Parkyns, Life in Abyssinia (1865), 300 f. So too among the Gallas: C. A. Doughty, Arabia Deserta (1888), ii.167. —F. A. Klein (the missionary who discovered the "Moabite Stone"), writing in 1881, says that skilled artisans in Palestine then operated mainly as journeymen; in some villages nary a one was to be found. The fellahin depended on German mechanics. In Transjordan, however, there were smiths in the smaller villages: PEFQS 1881.297; E. W. Rice, Orientalisms in Bible Lands (1910), 209.

12. W. Cline, Mining and Metallurgy in Negro Africa (1937), 114.

13. Cline, loc. cit.; H. Baumann and D. Westermann, Les peuples . . . de l'Afrique, tr. Hamberger (1948), 259.

14. Oral communication from Dr. W. Stockton Jr., who visited the Qashgai in 1961.

15. Raverty, in Globus 8.342.

16. Ausland, 1876:93.

17. Cline, op. cit., 115.

18. Ib., 119.

19. Ib., 122.

20. Ib., 125.

21. O. Lenz, Skizzen aus Westafrika (1878), 88; C. Seligman, Races of Africa (1930), 57.

22. R. J. Forbes, Metallurgy in Antiquity (1950), 68.

23. W. Jochelson, The Yakut (1931), 172 f.

24. Ib.

25. M. Eliade, Le chamanisme (1951), 408.

26. T. H. Gaster, Thespis², 162; R. Eisler, op. cit., 327.

27. D. Klementz, in ERE iii.4.

28. On the apotropaic properties of iron, see: Frazer-Gaster, NGB 100–102, 125, 240; I. Scheftelowitz, Altpal. Bauernglaube (1925), 66 f.; S. Seligmann, Magische Heil- und Schutzmittel (1927), 161–69; T. Höpfner, Griech.-aegypt. Offenbarungzauber (1921), §596; E. Clodd, Tom Tit-Tot (1898), 33–36; W. Abt, Apologie des Apuleius (1898), 86; S. Eitrem, Papyri Osloenses i (1925), 56 f.; O. Gruppe, Griech. Mythologie (1906), 895; F. T. Elworthy, The Evil Eye (1895), 220 f.; W. R. Halliday, Greek and Roman Folklore (1927), 31 f.; M. Eliade, Forgerons et alchimistes (1956), 26 ff., 70, 188; T. H. Gaster, The Holy and the Profane (1955), 9 f.; I. Goldziher, in ARW 10.41 ff. (Arabic); Tawney-Penzer, Ocean of Story, ii (1924), 166–168; W. Crooke, Natives of Northern India (1907), 203; G. Dumézil, in JA 1929.237–54 (Caucasus); E. Riess, in P–W i.59 ff.; Notes and Queries I/iii (1861), 56 (Lancashire, England).

29. F. C. Connybeare, in JQR 11.18.

30. J. Montgomery, Aramaic Incantation Texts from Nuppur (1913), #2; W. H. Rossell, A Handbook of Aramaic Magical Texts (1953), 104, #26.—E. Riess, in AJP 46 (1925), 228–29, so explains Odysseus' drawing a sword when he encounters the witch Circe: Odyssey 19.13. See also: T. G. Tucker, Aeschylus' Seven Against Thebes (1908), Introd., p. xxix, n.I; Gruppe, op. cit., 453.

31. M. Cox, Introduction to Folklore (1897), 8.

32. Ib., 16.

33. E. W. Lane, Arabian Society in the Middle Ages (1883), 36.

34. Clodd, op. cit., 35.

35. F. Nork, Die Sitten u. Gebräuche der Deutschen. Das Kloster XII (1849), 555.

36. O. Sprenger, Mohammad² (1861–69), i.142.

37. S. Seligmann, D. böse Blick (1910), ii.8.

38. G. Finamore, Tradizioni popolari abruzzesi (1890), 69.—The custom was known also to the Jews: Tosephta, Shabbat vi.4 (see: F. Perles, in MGWJ 19.428).

39. A. C. Kuijt, in BTLVNI 1901.157 ff.—Similarly, the Kols of India place iron in an earthen pot to protect mother and child: W. Crooke, Tribes and Castes of the North-West Provinces (1896), iii.307.

40. T. Keightley, Fairy Mythology (1850), 148, 488.

41. G. Pitré, Usi e costumi del popolo Siciliano (Universale Cappelli reprint, 1963), 85.

42. Ovid, Fasti 2.441.

43. P. Kretschmer, Neugr. Märchen (1917), #60.

44. A. Leskien, Balkanmärchen (1915), ##59, 63.

45. Grimm, Märchen #136.

46. J. Grimm, DM⁴, iii.453.

47. Oṣar Neḥmad 4 (1863), 189, 204; L. Löw, Die Lebensalter in der jüdischen Literatur (1875), 77; T. H. Gaster, The Holy and the Profane (1955), 9 f.

48. M. Abeghian, Der armenische Volksglaube (1899), 119.

49. T. Keightley, The Fairy Mythology (1850), 488.

50. F. Liebrecht, Zur Volkskunde (1879), 321.

51. Keightley, op. cit., 148.

(b) The rivalry of professions

52. S. N. Kramer, Sumerian Mythology (1944), 49–51.

53. Ib., 101 ff.

54. Th. Jacobsen, in Before Philosophy, ed. H. Frankfort (1949), 182.

55. Kramer, op. cit., 72–73.

56. See: E. K. Chambers, The Medieval Stage (1903), ii.78 ff.; F. M. Cornford, The Origins of Attic Comedy² (1961), 87 ff.; M. Steinschneider, "Rangstreitliteratur," in Szb. Akad. Wien 4 (1908), 155 f.

57. E. Chiera, Sumerian Religious Texts (1924), No. 4, obv., 17–22; Th. Jacobsen, in Before Philosophy, ed. H. Frankfort (1949), 179 f.

58. See: T. A. Sinclair, A History of Classical Greek Literature (1962), 270. So too in the play entitled Antiope (ed. Porter², 1929) the poet Amphion defends the role of the artist against that of the politician.

59. E. K. Chambers, The English Folk Play (1933), 13.

60. P. Haupt, Das babylonische Nimrod-Epos (1884–91), #28; B. Meissner, Bab. und Ass., ii (1925), 428 f.

61. Aesop, fab. 385, ed. Hahn.

62. CT xv. 31 ff. (fox); ib. (horse and ass); Meissner, op. cit., 427. Cf. also: C. Johnston, in AJSL 28 (1912), 81–100; E. Ebeling, in JCS 4 (1950), 215 ff.

63. Phaedrus iv.25.

64. Babrius, #180; Aesop, #40 Hahn; see: W. Wienert, Die Typen der griech.-röm. Fabeln, FFC 56 (1925), 42 ff.

65. T. H. Gaster, Purim and Hanukkah (1950), 60 ff.

66. Gen. 4:8. This supplement is adopted by most modern scholars, and indeed appears in RSV. KJV skirts the difficulty by rendering, *And Cain talked with his brother Abel;* but this violates Hebrew idiom.

23 "Sin crouches at the door"

1. Conventional translations take the words, *Sin crouches at the door,* to denote the consequence of *if thou doest not well.* But this ruins the point, which is that Sin is *always* lurking at the door and must be surmounted. Hence, the correct construction must be to assume an ominous aposiopesis after the former clause, as if to say, "Woe betide you!" The fate was too dreadful to utter.

2. Cf. C. F. Jean, Le péché chez les Babyloniens et les Assyriens (1925), 53–56; G. Furlani, La religione babilonese e assira (1929), i.339–40.

3. P. Haupt, ASKT II, iii.1 ff.

4. I Rawl. v.50, i.51.

5. Job 4:15.

6. Nergal and Ereshkigal, Amarna version, rev.68 = ANET 103.

7. C. H. Gordon, The Living Past (1944), 203, 213; J. A. Montgomery, Aramaic Incantation Texts from Nippur (1913), #6.6–7 ("Their doors and roofs are made fast," sc. against the demons). Cf. also: TB Pesaḥim 111b.

8. Pliny, HN xxviii. 33; cf. E. Riess, in Rhein. Mus. 2 (1894), 188 f.; Gruppe, op. cit., 859, n.l.

9. R. C. Thompson, Semitic Magic (1908), 40.

24 The mark of Cain

1. See in general: B. Stade, in ZAW 14 (1894), 250 ff.; R. Eisler, in Monde Orientale 21.48-112; H. Lilliebjörn, Ueber religiöse Signierung in der Antike. Diss. (1933); C. A. Lobeck, Aglaophamus (1829), i.658; Preller-Jordan, Röm. mythol. ii.389; F. Dölger, Sphragis (1911), 39 ff.; Wolters, in Hermes 38.265; R. Perdrizet, in ARW 14.54 f.; S. Eitrem, Papyri Osloenses i (1925), 40 f. (citing a Norwegian example from Sigrdrüf-mal 15 ff., Bugge).

2. III, iv.15–21; tr. Speiser, ANET 81.

3. R. P. Dougherty, The Shirkûtu of Babylonian Deities (1923), 81 ff.

4. L. Keimer, in Mem. de l'Inst. d'Égypte (1947), 53; S. Capart, Primitive Art in Egypt (1905), 22 f.; A. Erman, Aegypten² (1923), 257, n.l. See also: C. Schuster, "Modern Parallels for Ancient Egyptian Tatooing," in Sudan Notes and Queries 29 (1948), 71–77.

5. Herodotus, 2.113.

6. E. Norden, Die Geburt des Kindes (1924), 28, n.4.

7. W. Rapp, Die Beziehungen des Dionysuskultes zu Thrakien und Kleinasien (1882), 25; Wolters, in Hermes 38 (1903), 268 ff.

8. Herodotus, 5.6; cf. C.A. Böttiger, Kl. Schriften (1837), i.174.

9. Dittenberger, Sylloge #802.48 ff.

10. III Maccabees 2:29; see: J. Tordiau, in Aegyptus 30 (1950), 56–66.

11. Lucian, De dea Syria 59; cf. Joh. Lydus, De mens. 4.53.—Analogously, Syrian Christians who have been to Jerusalem are tattooed with a cross: C. H. Parry, Six Months in a Syrian Monastery (1895), 63.—Medieval pilgrims wore badges round their necks, or on their hats or scrips: R. Chambers, The Book of Days, i.338; E. L. Cutts, Scenes and Characters of the Middle Ages (1925), 167; W. W. Skeat, The Vision of Piers the Plowman, ii (1886), 101.

12. CIL III.686: *signatae mystides;* Tertullian, De praescr. haeret. 40; see: F. Cumont, Les mystères de Mithra² (1913), 131.

13. Prudentius, Peristeph. 10.1076 ff. (*sacrandus accipit sphragitidas*); G. Anrich, Das antike Mysterienwesen (1894), 124; W. Hepding, Attis (1903), 162 f.; R. Pettazzoni, I Misteri (1924), 106, 114, n.24.

14. Anrich, op. cit., 120 f.; G. Wobbermin, Religionsgesch. Studien (1896), 144 ff.

15. Right Ginza, 39; see: I. Scheftelowitz, in MGWJ 73 (1929), 216.

16. Rom. 4:11; Midrash Exodus Rabba 19; Yelammedenu, Ṣaw, §14; Grace After Meals, Circumcision Service (S. Singer, Authorized Daily Prayerbook, 305).

17. A. B. Ellis, The Ewe-speaking Peoples of the Slave Coast (1890), 146.

18. C. H. Huber, Journal d'une voyage en Arabie (1891), 196 f.; R. Eisler, op. cit., (though many of Eisler's deductions are untenable).

19. See fully: Headlam-Knox, on Hero[n]das, 5.79; J. E. B. Mayor, on Juvenal 14.24.

20. Bound captives were tattooed with the name of the god or king: Breasted, AR iii. §414; iv. §405.

21. Hammurapi, §226 f.; H. Holma, Koeperteile (1911), 55.120; a slave who denied his master was branded: S. Daiches, LSS I/ii, #26.9.

22. Holma, op. cit., 14, 55.

23. A temple officer called *gallabu* (ideogr. LU.ŠU.I) is mentioned in documents of the First Dynasty of Babylon (P. Kraus, Altbab. Briefe [1931], 64) and an analogous official appears in various Hittite texts (H. Ehelolf, in Kl. Forsch. i.147, and n.4), while a "*g-l-b* of the gods" figures in Phoenician temple tariffs of the 4th cent. B.C. from Citium, Cyprus (CIS I.86A, 257). This is commonly understood to be a barber, for that is the normal meaning of the word. However, *gullubu* was also the technical term, in Neo-Babylonian times, for a certain rite of initiation to priesthood (see: San Nicolo, in AOr 7 [1935], 25–28), and while this might possibly mean "tonsure," it has been pointed out that Akkadian *galābu* also means "cut, incise," so that *signing* by a form of cicatrization might be implied.

24. See: E. Spitz, De stigmatiis (1711), 21 f.; E. Tenzell, De stigmatibus in facie (1719), 6 ff.

25. E. Brewer, Dictionary of Phrase and Fable, s.v. "Mark with a B."

26. Ib., s.v. "F is written on his face."

27. Stephen, Criminal Law, iii.271 (quoted by Headlam-Knox, Herodas [1922], 264).

▲ 24a Excursus

1. Plato, Laws 865 D–866 A; Demosthenes, Orat., p. 643; Hesychius, s.v. *apentiautismos* [i.e., banishment for one year].

2. C. W. Hobley, in JRAI 40 (1910), 438 f. (It deserves to be noted that a Kikuyu homicide entails ceremonial pollution [*thaku*] only through the slaughter of a man of his own clan.)

3. J. Roscoe, The Northern Bantu (1915), 171.

4. Ib., 170.

5. Ib., 279 f.

6. J. H. Weeks, Among the Congo Cannibals (1913), 268.

7. J. Owen Dorsey, "Omaha Sociology," in Third Annual Report of the Bureau of [American] Ethnology (1884), 369.

8. J. H. Weeks, Among the Primitive Bakongo (1914), 62 f.

9. Father Baudin, "Féticheurs ou ministres religieux des Nègres de la Guinée," in Les missions catholiques, 16 (1884), 332.

10. G. Loyer, "Voyage to Issini on the Gold Coast," in T. Astley's New General Collection of Voyages and Travels, ii (1745), 444.

11. A. G. Leonard, The Lower Niger and Its Tribes (1906), 180 f.; Mrs. Leslie Milne, Shans at Home (1910), 192.

12. See further: J. G. Frazer, Psyche's Task² (1913), 117 ff.

13. A. Thevet, Les singularités de la France antarctique (Antwerp 1558), 74–76; id., Cosmographie universelle (1575), 994 [978] f.; J. Lerius [Lery], Historia navigationis in Brasiliam (1586), 183–94; The Captivity of Hans Stade of Hesse in A.D. 1547–55 among the Wild Tribes of Eastern Brazil, tr. A. Tootal (1874), 155–59; J. F. Lafitau, Moeurs des sauvages amériquains (1724), ii.292 ff.; R. Southey, History of Brazil, i² (1822), 232. G. Friederici, in Globus, 89 (1906), 56–63, interprets the incised marks on the executioner's body as intended to disguise him from the victim's ghost.

14. R. Hagen, Unter den Papuas (Wiesbaden 1899), 254. In the same tribe, at the conclusion of hostilities, the bravest of the victors puts a chalk mark on the brows of the vanquished "in order that they may not be exposed to the caprice of the ghosts"; see: H. Zahn, "Die Jabim," in R. Neuhauss, Deutsch Neu-Guinea (1911), iii.318.

15. See: Frazer-Gaster, NGB, §168.

16. E. Torday and T. A. Joyce, in JRAI 36 (1906), 50 f.

17. H. A. Junod, The Life of a S. African Tribe (1912–13), i.453 f.

18. Father Porte, in Les missions catholiques, 28 (1896), 371.

19. K. R. Dundas, in JRAI 43 (1913), 47.

20. H. Johnston, The Uganda Protectorate (1902), ii.743 f.; C. W. Hobley, Eastern Uganda (1902), 20.

21. Johnston, op. cit., ii.794; Hobley, loc. cit. For another account, see: J. Roscoe, The Northern Bantu (1915), 289.

22. D. Fraser, Winning a Primitive People (1914), 39 f.

23. P. Paulitschke, Ethnographie Nord-est-Afrikas (1893), 258.

24. A. C. Hollis, The Masai (1905), 353.

25. Id., The Nandi (1909), 74.

26. J. Teit, in Memoirs of the American Museum of Natural History, vol. ii; Anthropology i/4 (1900), 357.

27. S. Hearne, Journey from Prince of Wales's Fort in Hudson Bay to the Northern Ocean (1795), 204–6.

28. F. Boas, Chinook Texts (1894), 258.

29. V. Stefánsson, My Life among the Eskimos (1913), 367.

30. C. G. Seligman, The Melanesians of New Guinea (1910), 563 f.

31. B. Spencer and F. J. Gillen, Native Tribes of Central Australia (1899), 493–95; iid., Northern Tribes of Central Australia (1904), 563–68. The writers suggest that the practise of painting the slayers black is meant to render them invisible to the ghost.

32. T. Williams, Fiji and the Fijians² (1860), i.55 f.

33. John Jackson, quoted by J. E. Erskine, Journal of a Cruise among the Islands of the Western Pacific (1853), 477.

34. Charlevoix, Histoire de la Nouvelle France (1744), vi.77, 122 f.; J. F. Lafitau, Moeurs des sauvages amériquains (1724), ii.279.

35. R. E. Guise, in JAI, 28 (1899), 213 f.; J. L. D. van der Roest, in TITLV, 40 (1898), 157 f.; H. von Rosenberg, Der Malayische Archipel (1878), 461; R. Hagen, Unter den Papuas, 266; G. Brown, Melanesians and Polynesians (1910), 142, 145.

36. J. G. Frazer, in JRAI 15 (1886), 73.

37. J. G. F. Riedel, in Deutsche Geographische Blätter, 10.286.

38. G. Viehe, in [South African] Folk-lore Journal, 1 (1879), 51 f.

39. So Aeschylus tells us (Choephoroe 65 [59]) that "vengeful gore sets hard and will not run away."

40. A. Jaussen, Coutumes des Arabes au pays de Moab (1908), 227.

41. Cf. Frazer-Gaster, NGB §§407–16.

42. Mgr. Lechaptois, Aux rives de Tanganika (Algiers 1913), 194 f.

25 Abel's blood

1. Deut. 12:23.—For this notion, see: Frazer-Gaster, NGB §173 (and Additional Notes); W. Wundt, Elements of Folk Psychology, tr. Schaub (1916), 208 ff.; O. Gruppe, Griech. Mythologie (1906), 728, n.5; E. Rohde, Psyche[8] (1921), ii.176.—Among ancient writers, see: Sophocles, Electra 785; Aristophanes, Clouds 712; Theophrastus, De sens. 10.25 f.; Servius, on Vergil, Aen. 5.79.—For *Arabic* ideas on the subject, see: J. Wellhausen, Reste des arabischen Heidentums[2] (1897), 217; Mas'udi, Golden Meadows iii.309, says that the pagan Arabs believed that "the soul is really the blood"; cf. G. Jacob, Altarab. Parallelen zum AT (1897), 9 f.

2. Iliad 14.518; 17.86.

3. De sens. 10.23.

4. Hovorka-Kronfeld, Vergleichende Volksmedizin (1908–9), i.79.

5. Ib., 80.

6. P. Paulitschke, Ethnographie Nordost-Afrikas, i (1896), 186.

7. H. Spencer, Principles of Sociology (1876–82), i.116.

8. Hovorka-Kronfeld, op. cit., ii. 29.

9. Chateaubriand, Memoire d'outre tombe, iii.120.

10. F. Parkman, The Jesuits in North America in the Seventeenth Century[20] (1885), 389.

11. See: Brand-Ellis, Popular Antiquities of Great Britain (1882–83), iii.15–16; S. Seligman, D. Böse Blick (1927), ii. 218; Am Urquell 2 (1892), 1 (Sweden).

12. Job 16:18. The modern emendation to "*its* cry" is unperceptive; Job's self cries out *through* his blood. Cf. H. Duhm, Die bösen Geister im AT (1904), 22 f.; L. Bauer, Volksleben im Lande der Bibel (1903), 197.

13. II Maccabees 8:3.

14. T. Canaan, Dämonenglaube im Lande der Bibel (1929), 33.

15. Bolte-Polivka, ii.274, 526; M. Cox, Cinderella (1893), 518, n.69; C. L. Rochholz, Deutscher Glaube und Brauch (1867), i.54. (Rochholz says flatly that the blood is simply the soul.)

16. M. Cox, Introduction to Folklore (1895), 279.

17. Brand-Ellis, op. cit., iii.229–32.

18. L. Ginzberg, Legends of the Jews, iv.304; vi.354, n15.

19. Ib., vi.396, n.30.

20. Ib., v.140, n.21.

21. H. C. Trumbull, The Blood Covenant (1887), 143 f.; R. Scott, Discoverie of Witchcraft (1584); King James I, Demonologie (1597); Five Philosophical Questions Disputed (1650); H. C. Lea, Superstition and Force (1892), 315–23.

22. Matthew of Paris, ed. 1684, p. 126.

23. Shakespeare, Richard the Third, I.ii.

24. J. Stow, Annals (1631), 424.

25. R. Cobett, State Trials, xi.1371.

26. L. Benson, The Book of Remarkable Trials (1871), 94n.

27. Niebelungenlied, xix.

28. Aeschylus, Choephoroe 58–59, 63.

29. Shakespeare, Macbeth, V.i ("Out, damnèd spot!"); cf. also: Euripides, Heracles 1320 ff.; Ovid, Fasti 2.45.

30. R. Chambers, The Book of Days (1886), i.235.

31. Zimmern Chronicle, ii.262.

32. Chambers, loc. cit.

33. M. U. Green, in The Quest 21 (1929), 65.

34. Frazer-Gaster, NGB §173.

35. Ibn Hishām, 79 ult., p. 861.5, cited by W. R. Smith, The Religion of the Semites³ (1927), 417, n.5.

36. E. Westermarck, Pagan Survivals in Mohammedan Culture (1933), 71.

37. Mary Kingsley, Travels in West Africa (1897), 447.

38. G. F. Angus, Savage Life and Scenes in Australia and New Zealand (1847), i.110 f.

39. J. G. Frazer, GB i.554 f.

40. Col. Maclean, A Compendium of Kafir Laws and Customs (1866), 81.

41. J. G. Frazer, GB, i.684 ff.

42. Ib.

43. F. B. Jevons, Introduction to the History of Religion (1896), 73 f.; Frazer, GB iii.243 f.; J. L. Saalschutz, Das Mosäische Recht (1846), 457, n.243 ff.

44. Walter Scott, Peverel of the Peak, ch. 2, n.2.

26 The errant ghost

1. E. g., K 2175, i.6–8; cf. R. C. Thompson, in PSBA 1906.219 ff.; id., Semitic Magic (1908), 32.

2. C. A. Lobeck, Aglaophamus (1826), i.302*k;* A. Dieterich, in Phil. Jahrb. Suppl. 16 (1888), 792, n.2; B. Schmidt, Das Volksleben der Neugriechen (1871), 169, n.2.

3. A. Oldfield, in Trans. Ethn. Soc. London 3 (1865), 228, 236, 245.

4. L. H. Morgan, League of the Iroquois (1851), 174.

5. E. B. Cross, in JAOS 4 (1854), 309.

6. E. B. Tylor, Primitive Culture, ii.114.

7. O. Tobler, Die Epiphanie der Seele in deutschen Volksage (1911), 47.

8. Stith Thompson, MI, E 413.

9. This view was expressed already by Antiphon; see: G. Mouliner, Pur et impur (1950), 182.

▲   27 The contagion of bloodshed

(a) Banishment of homicides

1. Demosthenes, Orat. xxiii.77 f.; Aristotle, Constitution of Athens 57; Pausanias, i.28.11; Julius Pollux, Onomasticon 8.120; Helladius, quoted by Photius, Bibl. 535A, Bekker.

2. The rule forbidding the ship to cast anchor is mentioned only by Pollux, but he had access to excellent authorities, and we may therefore discard the contrary statement by Helladius that the ship did not cast anchor.

3. Plato, Laws 886 C–D.

[3a. See: R. J. Bonner-Smith, The Administration of Justice from Homer to Aristotle, i (1930), 1 ff., 111 ff.; G. Thomson, Aeschylus and Athens (1941), 34 f., 73 f., 435; G. Richard, in Rev. Et. Anciennes 37 (1935), 301 f.; O. Daube, Zu den Rechtsproblemen in Aeschylus' Agamemnon (1938), 50 f., 74 f., 85 f.; E. Balogh, Political Refugees in Ancient Greece (1943), 2, 88. Cf. especially: Aeschylus, Septem 274 f.; Supplices 6 f.; Pausanias, 5.1.6.—The Homeric evidence is inconclusive. All cases (e.g., Iliad 16.571–74; 23.85 ff.; Odyssey 13.259; 15.271–78) seem to refer to flight for fear of reprisals or vendetta, not to legal banishment. So too in the case of Drakontios the Spartiate mentioned in Xenophon, Anabasis 4.8.25.—C. H. Gordon, Before the Bible (1962), 15–16, aptly compares II Sam. 14:5–7, but I cannot accept the far-reaching conclusions which he draws from this concerning the relationship of Hellenic and Hebraic cultures.]

[3b. Lysias, Agoratos §§79, 82.]

[3c. Antiphon, Herod. §11; Choreut. §4.]

[3d. SEG #72, §20, line 137.]

[3e. Lycurgus, c. Leocrat. §133.]

[3f. Herodotus, 1.35 ff.]

[3g. SEG, loc. cit.; G. Moliner, Pur et impur (1950), 185.]

[3h. Demosthenes, Aristocrates 90; Plato, Laws 9.65E.]

[3i. T. H. Gaster, Thespis², 364 f.]

[3j. O. Proksch, Ueber die Blutrache der vorislamischen Arabern (1899), 31 ff.]

[3k. E. Westermarck, Pagan Survivals in Mohammedan Civilization (1933), 133.]

4. W. E. Bromilow, in Report of the 12th Meeting of the Australasian Association for the Advancement of Science (1910), 478.

5. C. W. Hobley, in JRAI 40 (1910), 431.

6. E. Westermarck, The Moorish Conception of Holiness (1916), 130 f.

(b) Bloodshed renders the soil barren

7. Aeschylus, Agamemnon 987 ff.

[7a. Cf. Isa. 26:21; Ezek. 24:7; 36:17–18, 30; Job 16:18. Cf. R. Patai, in JQR, N.S. 30 (1939), 59–69.]

[7b. Num. 35:33.]

[7c. Deut. 32:43.]

[7d. I Sam. 1:21.]

[7e. III Aqhat iii.28–37; cf. T. H. Gaster, Thespis², 357.]

8. Thucydides, ii.102; Apollodorus, Bib. iii.7, 5.

9. Apollodorus, loc. cit.; cf. Herodotus, 2.10.

10. Apollodorus, loc. cit.

[10a. Aeschylus, Eumenides 750 ff., 767 ff., ed. Paley.]

[10b. Sophocles, Oedipus Rex 22 ff., 96 ff.; cf. Hyginus, fab. 67.]

[10c. Isocrates, Evagoras, 14 f.; Diod. Sic., iv.61, 1 f.; Pausanias, ii.29, 7 f.; Apollodorus, Bib. ii.12, 6.]

[10d. Livy, 45.5: *pollui eam* (sc. *terram*) *homicida . . . sanguine velari.* Cf. R. Pettazzoni, La confessione dei peccati, iii (1936), 167.]

[10e. J. C. Lawson, Modern Greek Folklore (1910), 174 (quoting Kamporouglou, Historia tōn Anthenōn, i.224).]

[10f. Am Urquell 3 (1892), 5.]

28   The Curse of Wandering

1. Odyssey 15.343.

2. Breasted, AR iv.26, §46.

3. Statue Inscription, iii.1 f.; ANET², 500.

4. Judg. 5:6.

5. Tibullus, i.4, 69 (see: Kirby Smith, in loc.)

6. Ovid, Heroides 6.161.

29   The Land of Nod

1. The Ancient Versions caught the point. The Aramaic Targum, for instance, renders simply, "Land of Wandering (or, Exile)"; while the Vulgate (reading *nād* for *Nôd*) comes up with *Habitavit profugus in terra.*

2. See below, §117.

3. Fancifully derived from *naṣāru,* "preserve."

4. Cf. E. A. Speiser, Introduction to Hurrian (1911), 55, 112.

5. From ʿ-*t*-*q*, which is actually used in Akkadian (*etēqu mutanê*) of removing sicknesses; see: T. H. Gaster, in JQR 37 (1946), 287.

6. Odyssey 8.111 ff.

7. Iliad 18.39 ff.

8. Odyssey 1.154, 337; 17.263; 22.230 f.

9. Iliad 10.314 ff. On such names see: Gilbert Murray, The Rise of the Greek Epic (1907), 181 ff.

10. See: T. H. Gaster, in F. M. Cornford's The Origin of Attic Comedy, Anchor Books ed. (1961), xxi–xxiii.

11. E.g., A. E. Suffrin, in Hasting's DB, s.v. Nod.

THE SONG OF LAMECH

31   An ancient war cry

(a) Battle taunts

1. Enuma Elish iv.72–86.

2. Gilgamesh I, iv.47; cf. L. Oppenheim, in Orientalia 17 (1948), 28, n.l.

3. 137 Gordon; T. H. Gaster, Thespis[2] (1961), 153 f.

4. I Sam. 17:25–26, 43–46.

5. The technical Hebrew expression, hitherto unrecognized, is *hithgabber*.

6. Isa. 42:13.

7. Job 15:25–26. Cf. also Dan. 7:11; Rev. 13:5.

8. I. Goldziher, Abhandlungen (1895), i.1–121; G. Jacob, Leben der vorislam. Beduinen (1895), 144 ff.; R. A. Nicholson, A Literary History of the Arabs (1930), 72 ff.

9. G. B. Gray, ICC Numbers, 327 f.; D. S. Margoliouth, The Poetics of Aristotle, 192; G. A. Smith, Early Poetry of the Hebrews (1927), 44 f.; J. A. Montgomery, Arabia and the Bible (1934), 6, 15.

10. Mrs. E. A. Finn, Palestine Peasantry (1923), 26.

11. E. Welsford, The Fool (1935), 80, 89; Lord Raglan, The Hero (Thinker's Library ed., 1949), 217 ff.

12. M. Dillon, in Vishveshvaranand Indological Journal, 1 (1963), 203.

13. A. Goldenweiser, Early Civilization (1922), 39 f.

14. Ib., 97 ff.; cf. also ERE vi. 470.

15. E. K. Chambers, The English Folk-Play (1933), 13.

16. Tod, in Folk-Lore 46 (1935), 361 ff.

17. T. H. Gaster, Thespis[2], loc. cit.

18. M. W. Myers, in Folk-Lore 43 (1932), 97 ff.

(b) Adah and Zillah

19. Cf. Arabic ^c-d-d; an Akkadian equivalent (*edēdu*, "do early") is recognized by B. Landsberger, in AfO 3 (1926), 169, n.l; cf. also: T. Jacobsen, ib., 16 (1939), 365, line 25.

20. I am trying only to illustrate the general effect of the merism. In the Biblical context, the terms scarcely referred to color of hair, since the blonde was virtually unknown in ancient Palestine.

(c) "If Cain be avenged sevenfold"

21. This mode of invocation is a cliché of Ancient Near Eastern verse. It recurs in the Old Testament at Isa. 32:9. An earlier example is afforded by the Ugaritic "Nikkal-text" (77 Gordon), 11, 14–15 (*šm^c ilht Ktrt, šm^c lK̠trt*). Similarly, the Hittite Kumarpi myth (KUB XXXIII.120) begins with an invocation to all the gods to "hearken" (*istamaskandu*). This style evidently reflects the minstrel's invitation to the audience to gather around.

THE SONS OF GOD AND THE DAUGHTERS OF MAN

32 "Sons of God"

Literature: F. Schwally, in ZAW 18 (1898), 142 ff.; J. W. Rothstein, in BZAW 34 (1920), 150 ff.; H. Junker, in Biblica 16 (1935), 209 ff.; G. E. Closen, Die Sünde der "Söhne Gottes" (Rome 1939); E. Kraeling, in JNES 6 (1947), 193–208; J. Fischer, in Nötscher Festschrift (1950), 74 ff.; B. S. Childs, Myth and Reality in the Old Testament (1960), 49 ff.; G. Cooke, in ZAW 76 (1964), 22–47; O. Gruppe, in Philologus 47 (1889), 92 ff., 328 ff.; id., in ZAW 9 (1889), 307 ff.; A. Kolaska, Gottessohn und Engel in der vorexilischen Buchern des AT (Diss., Vienna 1953).

1. The Hebrew word *yadôn,* commonly rendered "judge" (as though from *d-y-n*), is here to be associated with the Arabic *dāna,* "persist," as rightly perceived by the Septuagint. E. A. Speiser suggests, however, that it is rather to be combined with the Akkadian *dinānu,* "substitute, surrogate": JBL 75 (1956), 126 ff. In that case, the most natural rendering would be, "My spirit is not to be duplicated (or, find a substitute) among men, "rather than" My spirit shall not shield man," as he himself translates in the Anchor Bible.

(a) "Sons of God"

2. It is regularly used in this sense in the Ugaritic texts and occurs also in a Canaanite magical plaque of the 8th cent. B.C. from Arslan Tash, as well as vestigially in the O.T. itself (e.g., Ps. 29:1); see: T. H. Gaster, in Orientalia 11 (1942), 59.

(b) Properties conveyed through sexual intercourse

3. E. Crawley, The Mystic Rose[2] (1927), i.223 ff.; Stith Thompson, MI, A 180; c 191.

4. KBo III.7; see: T. H. Gaster, Thespis[2] (1961), 257–59.

5. Hyginus, fab. 29.

6. Plutarch, Def. Or. 417 E.

7. Homeric Hymns, 5.188 f.; Vergil, Aeneid 2.647. H. J. Rose (in CQ 18 [1924], 1 ff.) suggests that Vergil's language implies an older myth in which Anchises was subsequently rendered impotent by a thunderbolt.

8. Odyssey 11.576–81; see: J. G. Frazer, Apollodorus, i.28, n.2.

9. F. York Powell, in O. Elton's translation of Saxo Grammaticus' Danish History (1894), lxiv.

10. L. C. Wimberly, Folklore in the English and Scottish Ballads[2] (1959), 282 ff.; F. Child, Ballads, 1.322; 5.500.

11. Andrew Lang, The Homeric Hymns (1899), 42 f.

12. Ib.

(c) The mortal span

13. Num. 7:86.

14. I Kings 9:14; 10:10.

15. II Chron. 5:12.

16. Judg. 8:10.

17. I Kings 8:63; II Chron. 7:5.

18. I Chron. 12:37.

19. II Chron. 28:6.

20. Cf. E. König, in ZDMG 61 (1907), 913 ff.; K. Bruns, "Die Zahl 40 im A.T.," in Paulus, Memorabilia, vii.55 f.; A. Jeremias, The Old Testament in the Light of the Ancient East (1911), i.43, n.4; id., Babylonisches im N.T. (1905), 111 f.—On forty as a round number in general folklore, cf. Stith Thompson, MI, Z 71.12; W. Roscher,

"Die Zahl 40 im Glauben, etc.," in ASAW, phil.-hist. Kl., xxvii/4 (1909); O. Rescher, in ZDMG 65 (1911), 512; K. Brunnhofer, Arische Urzeit (1910), 226 ff.; J. Grimm, Deutsche Rechtsaltertümer (1881), i.301; Diordorus, i.85, 90 (Egyptian). The number is so used frequently in Turkish folktales: T. Menzel, Türkische Märchen, Billur Köschk (1923), 17, 25, 35, 46, 70, 73, 130, etc. (cf. Rescher's review, in ZS 3.146).—In Arabic, *eighty* (i.e. 2×40) years denotes a long space of time.—According to P. le Page Renouf, in PSBA 14 (1892), 264, Egyptian *ḥn.t* denotes "an ideal span of 120 years," but A. H. Gardiner (Egyptian Grammar, Vocab., s.v.) and Erman-Grapow (Hand-wörterbuch, s.v.) define it more vaguely as "two eternities." Usually, the Egyptians reckoned the ideal life-span as 110 years (see below, §77,a).

21. Deut. 31:2; 34:7.

22. See below, §54.

23. So according to the reading of the Vatican and Sinaitic codices, but Codex Alexandrinus has 248.

THE DELUGE

Literature. Frazer was not the first, nor has he been the last, to point out that stories of a primeval flood exist in all parts of the world. Among his predecessors mention may be made especially of the following, upon whom, indeed, he drew lavishly: L. Diestel, Die Sintflut und die Flutsagen des Altertums[3] (1876); R. Andree, Die Flutsagen (1891); H. Usener, Die Sintflutsagen untersucht (1899); R. Gittée, "Les legendes du déluge devant l'ethnographie et l'histoire," in Rev. d. Belge, 1900.250–65, 350–62; M. Winternitz, Die Flutsagen des Altertums (1901); G. Gerland, Der Mythus von der Sintflut (1912).—Later studies include: I. Riem, Die Sintflut in Sage und Wissenschaft (1925); L. Rasnitzki, "Die Sintflut in Sage und Wissenschaft," in Der Morgen 3 (1927), 168–78; A. R. Hermann, "Die Sintflut in Völkerleben," in Benediktinische Monatsschrift 44 (1951), 153 ff.—Many of the primitive stories are conveniently reproduced in R. Pettazzoni's monumental Miti e Leggende (1948 ff.).—It was commonly assumed in Frazer's day that flood stories are rare in Northern Asia. Since he wrote, however, this view has been corrected by the publication of fresh material. The matter is fully dis-cussed in W. Anderson, Nordasiatische Flutsagen. Acta et Commentationes Univer-sitatis Dorpatensis, B. Humaniora iv/3 (1923).—Recent studies on the *Biblical* story are: E. G. Kraeling, in JBL 66 (1947), 279–93; J. Heuschen, in Revue Belge 1 (1951), 433–42; W. Dalton, in Australian Catholic Record 35 (1958), 29–39.—P. Romanoff, in JBL 50 (1931), 304 ff., recognized *three* sources in the Biblical narrative (J, E, and P), not *two,* as commonly assumed; this view has been endorsed in principle by W. F. Albright, in JBL 58 (1939), 98.

▲   **33 Mesopotamia**

1. The cuneiform tablets were unearthed in 1872 by George Smith. For reliable English translations, see: E. A. Speiser, in ANET 93–95; A. Heidel, The Gilgamesh Epic and Its Old Testament Parallels (1946). The standard edition of the original is R. C. Thompson, The Epic of Gilgamesh (1930). A suggestive commentary is: A. Ungnad and H. Gressmann, Das Gilgames Epos (1916). Useful also are L. Oppenheim's notes in Orientalia 17 (1948), 17 ff., and K. Saunders' popular The Epic of Gilgamesh in the Penguin Classics.—The far-reaching conclusions of P. Jensen, Gilgamesch-Epos, Judäische Nationalsagen, Ilias und Odysee (1924), are now generally regarded as fantastic.

2. For details of the various recensions, see: Speiser, op. cit., 72–73.

3. Speiser, op. cit., 104–6.

4. Translated by S. N. Kramer, in ANET 42–44, where bibliography is cited.

5. Eusebius, 5.8. The account is taken from the work (now lost) of Alexander Polyhistor, an Ionian or Phrygian scholar who was captured by the Romans in the war against Mithridates and brought to Rome by Cornelius Lentulus to serve as tutor to his sons (c. 85 B.C.). Alexander lost his life when Lentulus' house burned down. English translations in Cory's Ancient Fragments, ed. E. H. Hodges (1876), 60–63; G. A. Barton, Archaeology and the Bible² (1917).

34 Egypt

1. Book of the Dead, ch. 175-Papyrus of Ani, B.M. 10470. Cf. E. A. W. Budge, British Museum Guide to the Egyptian Collections (1908), 136 f.

▲ ## 35 Greece

1. C. Pascal, "La leggenda del diluvio nelle tradizioni Greche," in Atti d. Acad. Turin 30 (1895).

2. Apollodorus, Bib. i.7, 2. [Later sources are: Ovid, Met. i.125–415; Hyginus, fab. 153; Servius, on Vergil, Ecl. 6.41; Scriptores rerum mythicarum Latini, ed. Bode, i.57 ff., 99.]

3. Scholiast on Pindar, Ol. ix. 64; FHG i.48.

4. Pindar, Ol. ix.64.

5. Strabo, ix.4, 2.

6. Pausanias, x.6, 2.

7. Lucian, Timon 3.

8. EM 176, s.v. Aphesios.

9. I.e., from geranoi, "cranes"; Pausanias, i.40, 1.

10. Aristotle, Motenol. i.14.

11. Plutarch, Pyrrhus 1; Ovid, in his picaresque retelling of the story (Met. i.125–415), follows Greek tradition in having Deucalion and Pyrrha land on Parnassus. Later Roman writers, however, carried them further afield, e.g., to Mt. Athos (Servius, on Vergil, Ecl. vi.41), or even to Etna (Hyginus, fab. 153).

12. Marmor Parium, in FHG i.542.

13. Pausanias, i.18, 8; Strabo, ix.4, 2.

14. Pausanias, i.18,7.

15. De deâ Syriâ 5.

16. Ib., 12 ff.

17. Plutarch, De sollertiâ animalium 13.

18. Suidas, Lex., s.v. Nannakos; Zenobius, Cent. vi.10; Macarius, Cent. ii.23. [See also Headlam-Knox's commentary on Herodas, iii.10.]

19. Steph. Byz., s.v. Ikonion.

20. Nonnus, Dionysiaca iii.202–19; Scholiast on Plato, Timaeus 22A.

21. Pausanias, ix.5, 1; Servius, on Vergil, Ecl. vi.41.

22. Varro, De re rusticâ iii.i.

23. Africanus, quoted by Eusebius, Praep. ev. x.10, 9. Among the authorities cited by Africanus (ib., x.10, 5) are the Attic historians, Hellanicus and Philochorus.

24. Nonnus, Dionys. iii.206–8. [Cf. also: Mayor, on Juvenal, i.81–82. Another who is said to have escaped alive from the Flood was a certain Cerambus, who was wafted by nymphs over the Thessalian mountains; cf. Ovid, Met. 8.353 ff.; J. G. Frazer, Apollodorus (1926), i.55, n.1.]

25. E. Meyer, Gesch. d. Alterthums, ii.194.

26. See: Strabo, ix.2, 16–18; Pausanias, ix.24, 1 ff. (with Frazer's commentary); A. Philippson, in Zs. für der Ges. für Erdkunde zu Berlin, 29 (1894), 1–90.

27. Dio. Hal., Ant. Rom. i.61.

28. Servius, on Vergil, Aeneid iii.167.

29. Pliny, Nat. Hist. xxxi.54.

30. Plutarch, De serâ numinis vindictâ 12.

31. Pausanias, viii.14, 1–3.

32. J. F. Baker-Penoyre, in JHS 22 (1902), 228–40.

33. Pausanias, viii.14, 1.

34. Dio. Hal, Ant. Rom. i.61, 3.

35. Scholiast, on Plato, Timaeus 22A.

36. Lycophron, Cassandra 72 ff., with the scholia of Tzetzes; Scholiast on Iliad 20.215.

37. W. Smith, ed., Dictionary of Greek and Roman Geography, ii.901, s.v. Samothrace.

38. Diodorus Siculus, v. 47.

39. H. Carnoy and J. Nicolaides, Folklore de Constantinople (1894), 16–18.

[39a. Iliad 16.384–92.]

▲ **36 Europe**

1. K. Simrock, ed., Die Edda, übersetzt, etc.[8] (1882), 253; Grimm, DM[4], 463 ff. In this Norse legend, the word rendered "boat" (*lûdr*) is obscure; it might also mean "cradle."

2. J. Rhŷs, Celtic Folklore, Welsh and Manx (1901), ii.429 (referring to the Triads, iii.13, 97). But Rhŷs thinks (p. 440) that the story may have been developed on the basis of the Scriptural narrative.

3. T. Narbutta, Dzieje starožynte narodu liteswkiego (Wilno 1835), i.2, quoted by Grimm, DM[4], i.480 f. But Usener (Sintflutsagen, 3) doubts the authenticity of this legend.

4. J. Deniker, The Races of Man (1900), 351.

5. L. Adam, in Revue de Philologie et d'Ethnographie, 1.12 ff.

▲ **37 India**

1. Satapatha Brâhmaṇa, tr. Eggeling [SBE xii], i. (1882), 216–19; H. Usener, Die Sintflutsagen, 26 f. (A. Weber's translation).

2. Another version of the Flood legend occurs in the Mahabharata; see: J. Muir, Original Sanskrit Texts, i[3] (1890), 199–201; Usener, op. cit., 29–31 (Jacobi's translation). For a subsidiary version, in the Vayu Puraṇa (c. A.D. 320), see: Muir, op. cit., 211 ff. [See in general: A. Hohenberger, Der indische Flutsage und das Matsyapurana (1930).]

3. C. Luard, The Jungle Tribes of Malwa. Monograph II of the Ethnographical Survey of the Central India Agency (Lucknow 1909), 17.

4. R. V. Russell, Tribes and Castes of the Central Provinces of India (1916), iii.326 f.

5. Tickell, in JAS Bengal 9 (1840), ii.798.

6. J. Hooker, Himalayan Journals (1891), ch. v.

7. S. Turner, An Account of an Embassy to the Court of the Teshoo Lama in Tibet (1900), 224. (Durgeedin may be Darjeeling.)

8. A. Bastian, Die Völker des Oestlichen Asien, i (1866), 87.

9. J. Shakespear, The Lushei Kuki Clans (1912), 95.

10. Ib., 176 ff.

▲ **38 Eastern Asia**

1. J. G. Scott and P. Hardiman, Gazeteer of Upper Burma and the Shan States (Rangoon 1900–1901), Pt. I, i.417 ff.; C. Gilhodes, in Anthropos 3 (1908), 683–86.

2. Guerlach, in Les missions catholiques, xix (Lyons 1887), 479; cf. A. Bastian, in Zs. d. Gesell. für Erdkunde zu Berlin, 1 (1866), 42.

3. N. Mouhot, Travels in the Central Parts of Indo-China [Siam], Cambodia and Laos (1864), ii.28.

4. W. W. Skeat and C. O. Blagden, Pagan Races of the Malay Peninsula (1906), ii.355–57.

5. W. Skeat, Fables and Folklore from an Eastern Forest (1901), 62 ff.

6. A. Henry, in JRAI 33 (1903), 103, 105 f. To this day the ancestral tablets which the Lolos worship on set days of the year and on all the important occasions of life, are made out of the same sort of tree as that in which their great forefather found safety from the waters of the deluge; and nearly all the Lolo legends begin with some reference to him or to the great Flood. In considering the origin of this flood legend it should be mentioned that the Lolos generally keep a Sabbath of rest every sixth day, when ploughing is forbidden, and in some places women are not allowed to sew or wash clothes. Taken together with this custom, the Lolo traditions of the patriarchs and of the flood appear to betray Christian influence; and A. Henry may well be right in referring them all to the teaching of Nestorian missionaries; for Nestorian churches existed in Yunnan in the thirteenth century when Marco Polo travelled in the country, and the Nestorian Alopen is said to have arrived in China as early as A.D. 635.

7. G. W. Steller, Beschreibung von dem Lande Kamtschatka (1774), 273.

▲ 39 Indonesia

1. J. von Brenner, Besuch bei den Kannibelen Sumatras (1894), 218.

2. H. Sundermann, Die Insel Nias (Barmen 1905), 70 ff. [Chatelin, in TVITVL 26 (1881), 115 f.; R. Pettazzoni, Miti e Leggende ii (1963), 10.]

3. O. L. Helfrich, in BTLVNI 71 (1916), 543 ff.

4. H. Ling Roth, The Natives of Sarawak and British North Borneo (1896), i.301 ff.; C. Hose and W. McDougall, The Pagan Tribes of Borneo (1912), ii.144–47; J. Perham, in JRAS Bengal, Dec. 1880.289–91.

5. Ling Roth, op. cit., i.300.

6. C. A. Schwaner, Borneo (1853–54), ii.151.

7. N. Adriani and A. C. Kruijt, De Bare'e-sprekende Toradja's van Midden-Celebes (1912–14), i.20, 247; ii.258; iii.386. [See also: P. Arndt, in TVITVL 75 (1935), 347–51, for another deluge-myth from the Celebes.]

8. P. v. Crab, De Moluksche Einlanden (Batavia 1862), 212 ff.

9. J. Franggidaej, in BTLVNI 63 (1905), 427 ff.

10. G. Beker, in BTLVNI 67 (1913), 625.

11. Fay-Cooper Cole, The Wild Tribes of Davao District, Mindanao, Chicago Field Museum, Publication 170 (1913), 164.

12. Shinji Ishii, in Transactions of the Japan Society, 14 (1916).

[12a. H. O. Beyer, in Philippine Journal of Science, Sect. D.8 (1913), 85–118.]

13. E. H. Man, On the Aboriginal Inhabitants of the Andaman Islands (London, n.d.), 98 f.; cf. R. C. Temple, in Census of India 1901, iii (The Andaman and Nicobar Islands), 63.

▲ 40 New Guinea and Melanesia

1. J. Chalmers and W. W. Gill, Work and Adventure in New Guinea (1885), 164.

2. P. Schleiermacher, in Globus, 78 (1900), 6.

3. M. Moszkowski, in Zs. für Ethnologie, 43 (1911), 340 ff. [For a flood-story from the Mimika Papuans of New Guinea, see: P. Drabbe, in Oceania 20 (1949), 71–73.]

4. T. Williams, Fiji and the Fijians (1860), i.[157 f.], 252; H. Hale, U.S. Exploring

Expedition: Ethnography and Philology (1846), 55; C. Wilkes, Narrative of U.S. Exploring Expedition (1851), iii.82 ff.; B. Seeman, Viti (1862), 394 ff.

5. R. H. Codrington, The Melanesians (1891), 166 ff. The writer adds: "It is likely now that the story will be told of eight persons in the canoe, but it is certain that the story is older than any knowledge of Noah's ark among the people."

6. S. Macfarlane, The Story of the Lifu Mission (1873), 19–20.

▲ 41 Polynesia and Micronesia

1. W. Ellis, Polynesian Researches[2] (1832–36), i.386 f. See also: T. Henry, "Ancient Tahiti," in Bernice P. Bishop Museum Bulletin 48 (Honolulu 1928), 445.

2. Ib., i.387–89.

3. Ib., i.389–91.

4. Ib., i.391.

5. Ib., i.392 ff.

6. Ib., iv.441 ff. [See also: D. Malo, Hawaiian Antiquities, in Bernice P. Bishop Museum, Spec. Publications, 3 (1951), 234–37; R. Pettazzoni, Miti e Leggende, ii.461.]

7. J. White, The Ancient History of the Maori (1887–89), i.172–78.

8. G. Grey, Polynesian Mythology (1885), 60 ff.

9. J. White, op. cit., i.55; R. Taylor, Te Ika a Maui, or New Zealand and Its Inhabitants[2] (1870), 101, 115n.

10. White, op. cit., i.113 ff.

[10a. For a deluge-story from Hao, one of the Tuamotu Islands, see: A. C. E. Caillot, Mythes et traditions des polynésiens (1914), 7–11.]

11. K. Semper, Die Palau-Inseln (1873), 195 ff. [See also: J. Kubary, "Die Religion der Palauer," in A. Bastian's Allerlei aus Volks- und Menschenkunde (1888), 53–55; Pettazzoni, op. cit., 560 f.]

[11a. For a deluge-story from Yap, one of the Caroline Islands, see: F. W. Christian, The Caroline Islands (1899), 281 ff.]

[11b. We may safely leave out of account the deluge-story reported from the Marquesas Islands, since this is patently a "play-back" of the Biblical narrative; see: A. Fornander, An Account of the Polynesian Race (1880), i.90; H. Jouan, "Chants des naturels des îles Marquises sur la création et le déluge," in Ac. Cherb., 1894.—Similarly, we may discount the poetic legend published by T. Powell in The Journal of Transactions of the Victoria Institute, 20 (1887), 147–74, under the title, "A Samoan Tradition of Creation and the Deluge." It has in fact nothing to do with the Deluge, and is marred in presentation by an utterly preposterous theory of Israelite connections with the proto-Polynesians!]

▲ 42 Australia

1. A. W. Howitt, in R. Brough Smyth's Aborigines of Victoria (1878), i.477 ff.; id., Native Tribes of S. E. Australia (1904), 486.

2. Brough Smyth, op. cit., i.429; E. M. Carr, The Australian Race (1886–87), iii.547.

3. Brough Smyth, loc. cit.

▲ 43 North America

[1. For a useful survey, although now partly antiquated, see: D. G. Brinton, Myths of the New World[3] (1905), 245n.]

1a. H. H. Bancroft, The Native Races of the Pacific States (1875–76), ii.75 ff.

2. Ib., iii.78 ff.

3. Constance Goddard du Bois, The Religion of the Luiseno Indians of Southern California (1908).

[3a. J. R. Swanton, in Bulletin of the Bureau of American Ethnology, 103 (1931), 202.]

4. Le Page du Pratz, Histoire de la Lousiane (1758), iii.27 ff.

5. H. R. Schoolcraft, Notes on the Iroquois (1847), 358 ff.

6. Mgr. Faraud, in Annales de la Propagation de la Foi, 36 (1864), 388 ff.

7. E. Petitot, Traditions indiennes du Canada Nord-Ouest (1886), 146–49.

8. Id., Monographie des Dènè-Dindijé (1876), 74.

9. H. Holmberg, in Acta Societatis Scientiarum Fennicae, 4 (1856), 345 ff.; T. de Pauly, Description ethnographique des peuples de la Russie (1862): Peuples de l'Amérique Russe, 14. [See also: J. R. Swanton, in Bulletin of the Bureau of American Ethnology, 39 (1909), Nos. 1, 31; A. P. Niblack, The Coast Indians of Southern Alaska and Northern British Columbia (1890), 378 ff.]

[9a. F. Boas, in Bull. Bureau of Amer. Ethnology, 27 (1902), 86, 94.]

10. J. A. Teit, in JAF 30 (1917), 442 ff.

11. M. Eels, in The American Antiquarian, 1 (1878–79), 71.

12. Ib.

13. E. W. Nelson, in Eighteenth Annual Report of the Bureau of American Ethnology, Pt. i (1899), 452.

14. D. Crantz, History of Greenland (1767), i.204 ff.

15. C. F. Hall, Life with the Esquimaux (1864), ii.318.

16. A. Hamberger, in Anthropos, 4 (1909), 304.

▲ 44 Central America and Mexico

1. A. de Herrera, The General History of the Vast Continent and Islands of America, tr. J. Stevens, ii.414; Herrera's authority seems to have been Pascual de Andagoya; see the latter's Narrative of the Proceedings of Pedrarias Davila in the Provinces of Tierra Firme or Castilia del Oro (London, Hakluyt Society, 1865), 14.

2. G. F. de Oviedo y Valdés, Histoire de Nicaragua (1840), 21 ff. The ultimate source is an interview between Indians at the village of Teola, Nicaragua, and François de Bobadilla, Provincial of the Order of Mercy, on 28 September, 1528.

3. F. S. Clavigero, The History of Mexico, tr. C. Cullen (1807), i.244. Cf. H. H. Bancroft, The Native Races of the Pacific (1875–76), iii.66, who says: "In most of the painted manuscripts supposed to relate to this event, a kind of boat is represented floating over the waste of water, and containing a man and a woman. Even the Tlascaltecs, the Zapotecs, the Miztecs, and the people of Michoacan are said to have had such pictures."

4. Bancroft, op. cit., iii.69 ff.; v.192 ff.

5. A. de Herrera, op. cit., iii.254 ff.; Bancroft, op. cit., iii.66 ff.

6. C. Lumholtz, Unknown Mexico (1903), ii.22 ff.

7. Ib., i.191–93.

8. Ib., 193 ff.; K. T. Preuss, Die Nayarit-Expedition, i: Die Religion der Cora-Indianer (1912), 277 ff.

9. Preuss, op. cit., 201.

10. Lumholtz, op. cit., i.298 ff.

▲ 45 South America

1. J. Lerius [Lery], Historia Navigationis in Brasiliam (1586), 238 [220].

2. The Captivity of Hans Stade of Hesse, in A.D. 1547–55, among the Wild Tribes of Eastern Brazil, tr. A. Tootal and annotated by Richard F. Burton (London, Hakluyt Society, n.d.), 148.

3. C. Teschauer, in Anthropos, 9 (1914), 32 ff.

4. Id., in Anthropos, 1 (1906), 739.

5. Rivet, in L'Anthropologie, 19 (1908), 235 ff.

6. W. H. Brett, The Indian Tribes of Guiana (1868), 398 ff.

7. A. de Humboldt, Voyage aux régions equinoxiales du Nouveau Continent, i (1814), 238 ff.

8. R. Schomburgk, Reisen in Britisch Guiana (1847–48), ii.320.

9. Christoval de Molina, "The Fables and Rites of the Yncas," in The Rites and Laws of the Yncas, tr. and ed. C. R. Markham, 4 ff. Cf. also: Garcilasso de la Vega, First Part of the Royal Chronicles of the Yncas, tr. Markham (1869–71), i.71; J. de Acosta, Natural and Moral History of the Indies (1880), i.70 ff.

10. Bernadino de Nino, miscionero franciscano, Etnografia Chiriguana (La Paz, Bolivia, 1912), 131–33.

11. T. Bridges, in Bulletins de la Société d'Anthropologie de Paris, Troisième Série, 7 (1884), 181.

46 The mountain of deliverance

1. Stith Thompson, MI, A 1022.

2. Lucian, Tim. 3; Ovid, Met. 1.320–21.

3. Hyginus, fab. 153.

4. Servius, on Vergil, Aeneid 6.41.

5. Arrian, fr. 26 (quoted in Eym. Magn.).

6. Hellanicus, fr. 16 Mueller.

7. A. Humboldt, in R. Schomburgk, Reisen in Britisch-Guiana (1847–48), 35 f.

8. D. G. Brinton, Myths of the New World[3] (1905), 238.

9. Śatapatha Brahmaṇa, 1, 8, 1, 1–6.

10. E. A. Speiser, in JAOS 68 (1948), 8; L. Némethy, in Oriens Antiquus 5–12 (1944), 93–96; G. A. Melikichvili, in Mimomkhilweli 3 (1953), 169–91 [in Georgian, with Russian summary].—In the Hittite Story of Appu (KUB XXIV.8; J. Friedrich, in ZA 49 [1950], 215 ff.) that typical numskull (see: T. H. Gaster, The Oldest Stories in the World [1952], 159, 168) lives in the land of the Lullu "beside the sea (or, lake)." According to E. Forrer (in JA 1930.237), Lullu-land lay north of Zohab, its northern boundary being the Caspian Sea. However, A Ungnad (Subartu [1936], 146) thinks it extended only to Lake Urmia and was identical with modern Luristan and northwards (ib., 18). For a good discussion, see: M. Streck, in ZA 15.289 ff.

11. Cf. E. H. Berger, Mythische Kosmographie der Griechen (1904), 21 f.—On ancient ideas about the ends of the earth, see: W. Schwartz, Fünf Vorträge über den griechischen Roman (1896), 16–19, 100–105; J. Partsch, in BSGW, phil.-hist. Kl. 68 (1916), ii.4; G. Furlani, "Andronikos über die Bewohner der Grenzen der Erde in syrischen Sprache," in ZS 5.238–49; A. Zeki Validi, "Die Nordvölker bei Biruni," in ZDMG 90 (1936), 38–51.

12. Aeschylus, Prometheus Vinctus 1.

13. On this concept, see: Stith Thompson, MI, A 145; Gressmann-Ungnad, op. cit., 160 ff.—For a Teutonic parallel, cf. R. M. Meyer, Altgermanische Religionsgeschichte (1910), 468.

14. A. J. Wensinck, The Ideas of the Western Semites concerning the Navel of the Earth (1916), 6.

15. W. W. Skeat, in ERE, s.v. Malay.

16. CT XIII.35–38, 31 = A. Heidel, The Babylonian Genesis[1] (1942), 51. The mythical dam was probably identified at Eridu with the ridge at the Persian Gulf near Basra (Heidel).

17. Heb.: ḥôq ḥāg. (Perhaps we should here derive ḥôq from a root * ḥ-w-q, after Arabic ḥauq, "ring," rather than from ḥ-q-q, as it is usually taken.)

18. Gilgamesh xi.140. The name may have been chosen because of its resemblance to the Semitic naṣāru, "preserve." However, it can also be read Ninmush.

19. Annals ii.34.

20. A variant Jewish tradition calls it Lubar, not yet explained; see: L. Ginzberg, Legends of the Jews (1909 ff.), i.171; v.186. Can the mysterious Lubar be simply a distortion of Elburz?

47 The dispatch of the birds

1. Epic of Gilgamesh xi.145–54.

2. Callimachus 2.66.

3. Scholiast on Aristophanes, Clouds 133.

4. Strabo, xvii.i.43.

5. The dispatch of the birds appears also in the deluge myth of the Pomo of California (Pettazzoni, MeL iii.134); while in the Algonquin version, the god Michabo actually dispatches a *raven* in search of land: D. G. Brinton, Myths of the New World[3] (1905), 239. I am reluctant, however, to deduce anything from these parallels, since the form in which the myths were related to their rapporteurs may in fact owe something to missionary influence.

6. Cf. F. Liebrecht, Zur Volkskunde (1879), 405; L. Uhland, Schriften zur Dichtung und Saga (1865 sqq.), iii.111; W. Radloff, Proben der Volksliteratur der türkischen Stämme Süd-Siberiens (1866), i.69; v.266 f.

7. Pliny, HN vi.24.

8. F. Lee, in Raumer's Taschenbuch (1835), 388.

9. Cf. I. Scheftelowitz, Altpal. Bauernglaube (1925), §68; Bartholomeus, De proprietatibus (1536), fol. 168; O. Keller, "Rabe und Krähe im klassischen Altertum," in Kulturgeschichtliches aus der Tierwelt (Prag 1905), 8a; W. A. Clouston, "Folklore of the Raven," in Saxby's Birds of Omen (1893), 20. Cf. also: H. Heros, "The Crow of Noe," in CBQ 10 (1948), 131–39.

10. K. Macaulay, History of St. Kilda (1765), 165, 174, 176; Brand-Ellis, Popular Antiquities of Great Britain, iii.211–12.

11. E.g., L. Hopf, Thierorakel (1888), 110; J. Hunger, Babylonische Tieromina (1909), 36 ff.; M. Jastrow, Rel Bab. u. Assyr. (1905–12), iii.887 ff. Cf. also: Shakespeare, Macbeth, I,5.30.

12. R. F. Harper, Letters, #253; R. Pfeiffer, State Letters of Assyria (1935), #334; E. Klauber, Assyr. Beamtentum (1910), 71.

13. IV R 30*, obv. 36 = Jastrow, op. cit., ii.29, n.2; cf. F. Hommel, Geogr. u. Gesch. alten Orients (1904–26), 308.

14. See below, §**156**.

15. Plutarch, De sol. Anim. 13, §1, pp. 968 f.

48 The rainbow

1. On the rainbow in folklore and myth, see: A. Pott, in Zs. f. vergl. Sprachforschung 2.414; A. Wuensche, "Der Regenbogen in den Mythen und Sagen der Voelker," in Nord und Süd 82 (1898), 70–82; R. le Page Renouf, in TSBA 8 (1883), 220 ff.; Meusel, "Der Regenbogen nach heidnische Sage und im christlichen Gedanke," in Beweis des Glaubens, March 1882; Revue des traditions populaires, 23.221 f.

2. Stith Thompson, MI, A 791.1.

3. L. Moor, Hindu Pantheon (1810), 260; W. Crooke, The Popular Religion and Folk-lore of Northern India (1896), i.25.

4. P. Lagarde, Gesammelte Abhandlungen (1866), 58, n.2.

5. H. Massé, Persian Beliefs and Customs. Human Relations Area Files (1954), 178.

6. J. Wellhausen, Prolegomena[6] (1905), 311.

7. F. L. W. Schwartz, Der Ursprung der Mythologie (1860), 103.

8. Kalevala, runo iii.310 ff. (tr. W. F. Kirby).

9. U. Holmberg, Siberian Mythology (1927), 443 f.

10. Flags too are customarily hung in chapels.

11. Enuma Elish vi.84 ff.

12. Wellhausen, loc. cit.

13. CT XXVI.40; C. Virolleaud, L'astrologie chaldéenne (1909–12), Sin, iii.121; A. Jeremias, Handb. d. altorient. Gesisteskultur[2] (1929), 139 f. However, S. Langdon, Semitic Mythology (1931), 406, n.48, denies that this is the meaning of *marratu*, and other scholars take the term to denote the cosmic ocean.

14. Grimm-Stallybrass, TM (1880), 733.

15. Philo, Quaestiones et solutiones in Genesin et Exodum, ii.64 = 148 Archer (on Gen. 9:13–17); cf. R. Marcus, in JNES 7 (1948), 113.

16. Strictly speaking, the Bow (Sum. [mul]BAN; Semitic [kakkab]Qaštu) consists of the stars ϵ, σ, δ, τ of Canis Major, together with κ and λ of Puppis. It is identified in Astrolabe Pinches (JRAS 1900.573–55; E. F. Weidner, Handbuch i.65–66) as the regent of the first decan of the month of Tammuz during the Taurus period, corresponding to that of Ab in the Aries period, i.e., after c. 1100 B.C. Ab is defined as the month of the Bow: Streck, Ashurbanipal, 72.ix.9; KAVI, p. 125.5; CT XXXIII.2, 7. It is said to rise on Ab 5 (CT XXXIII.I.ii.44) or on Ab 15 (ib., 7.22–23). See further on this constellation: E. Dhorme, Rel. assyr.-bab. (1945), 71 (Mari); V R 46, A 23; Virolleaud, Ishtar, Suppl. ii, #67.15; S. Langdon, Babylonian Menologies (1935), 21, n.1.

17. See fully: Kirby Smith, on Tibullus i.4.43.

18. H. B. Alexander, Latin American Mythology (1920), 203.

19. J. Warneck, in ARW 18 (1915), 333 ff.; R. Pettazzoni, Dio (1922), 116.

THE TOWER OF BABEL

▲ 49 Scaling heaven

1. Stith Thompson, MI, F 722. 1.1 (Indo-Chinese, Mayan, Aztec, Kaffir, and Arabic parallels).

2. E. Jacotet, Études sur les langues du Haute Zambesi, iii (1901), 118.

3. E. Torday, Camp and Tramp in African Wilds (1913), 242 f.

4. A. Hamberger, in Anthropos 4 (1909), 304; R. Pettazzoni, MeL i.95, #53.

[4a. Fr. Spelling, in Zs. f. Ethnol. 59 (1927), 232.]

5. E. Perreaugaux, Chez les Ashanti (1906), 200.

6. J. Shakespear, The Lushei Kuki Clans (1912), 183 f.

[6a. R. de Nebesky-Wajkowitz, in Anthropos 48 (1953), 889–97; W. J. Mackean, in ERE xi.511[b], s.v. Sikkim.]

[6b. Satapatha Brahmana i.8.1.6; M. Blomfield, SBE xliii.500; cf. H. Heras, in Estudios Biblicos 7 (1948), 292–325.]

7. S. H. Ray, in The Story of the Lifu Mission (1873), 19.

8. Diego Duran, Historia de Nueva España y Islas de Terra Firme, 1 (1867), 1 ff.; Brasseur de Bourbourg, Histoire des nations civilisées du Mexique et de l'Amérique Centrale (1857–59), i.301 f.; W. H. Prescott, History of the Conquest of Mexico (London 1901), iii.365.

[8a. Stith Thompson, loc. cit.]

[8b. The so-called "Yuzgat Tablet": A. Goetze, Verstreute Boghazköi-Texte (1930), #58 (cuneiform text); T. H. Gaster, Thespis[2], 270–94 (translation and commentary).]

[8c. H. G. Güterbock, The Song of Ullikummi (1952); A. Goetze, in ANET 121 ff.; T. H. Gaster, The Oldest Stories in the World (1952), 110–33.]

[8d. The Hebrew words usually rendered, "I shall be like *the Most High*," may mean only, "I shall be like *a celestial being*"; see below, §180.]

[8e. Odyssey 11.312–20; Vergil, Georgica 1.281–83. Cf. J. G. Frazer, The Fasti of Ovid (1925), vol. ii, p. 136.]

▲ **50 The confusion of tongues**

[*Literature:* J. Chaine, "Une réponse du folklore biblique à la question de l'origine des langues," in Mélanges Podechard (Lyon 1945); L. Turado, in Cult. Bib. 5 (1948), 142–48; 6 (1949), 83–86. See also, on the motif in general: Stith Thompson, MI, A 1333.]

1. F. Mason, in JAS Bengal, N.S. 37 (1868), 163 f.

2. E. Stack, The Mikirs, ed. Chas. Lyall (1908), 72.

3. H. H. Bancroft, The Native Races, etc., v.19–21.

4. A. C. E. Caillot, Mythes et traditions des polynésiens (1914), 7–11.

5. Hyginus, fab. 143. The legend appears not to be mentioned by any extant Greek author.

6. W. E. H. Barrett, in JRAI 41 (1911), 37.

7. C. A. Soppitt, A Short Account of the Kachcha Nâga (Empêo) Tribe in the North Cachar Hills (Shillong 1885), 15 f.

8. W. McCulloch, Account of the Valley of Munnipore and of the Hill Tribes (Calcutta 1859), 56.

9. H. E. A. Meyer in The Native Tribes of South Australia (Adelaide 1879), 204.

10. R. B. Dixon, in Bulletin of the American Museum of Natural History, 17/ii (1902), 44 ff.

11. Brasseur de Bourbourg, Popul Vuh, le livre sacré et les mythes de l'antiquité américaine (1861), 211–17.

51 Babel

1. See: A. Parrot, The Tower of Babel, tr. W. E. Hudson (1955), 18 ff.; T. Dombart, Das Sakralturm (1930).

2. David Lord, in Layman's Magazine of the Living Church, Milwaukee, Wis., September 1941, p. 6.

3. For this concept, cf. Gen. 28:17.

THE PATRIARCHS

ABRAHAM

52 Abraham and Melchizedek

1. The Hebrew word *zebaḥ* here means "meal," not "sacrifice," as again in Zeph. 1:7 and in the Ugaritic Epic of K-r-t.

2. W. R. Smith, The Religion of the Semites[3] (1927), ch. viii, 267 ff.; E. Westermarck, The Origin and Development of the Moral Ideas (1906–8), i.593 ff.; A. van Gennep, Rites of Passage (English tr. 1960), 29 f.; E. S. Hartland, The Legend of Perseus (1894–96), iii, passim. Cf. also: W. T. McCree, "The Covenant Meal in the OT," in JBL 45 (1926), 120–28.

3. J. L. Burckhardt, Bedouins and Wahabys (1831), i.329; C. A. Doughty, Arabia Deserta (1888), i.228; J. Wellhausen, Reste des arabischen Heidentums[2] (1897), 124; E. Westermarck, Pagan Survivals in Mohammedan Civilization (1933), 85.

4. Herodotus, 4.172.

5. T. H. Gaster, Passover (1949), 17.

6. Ib.

7. E. S. Drower, in Folk-Lore 48 (1937), 226–44.

8. P. Pervanoglu, Das Familienmahl auf altgriechischen Grabsteinen (1872).

9. W. R. Smith, op. cit., ch. viii.

10. III Aqhat 203–4; cf. T. H. Gaster, Thespis[2], 375.

11. Vergil, Aeneid 1.728–40.

▲   53 "Cutting" a covenant

1. Jer. 34:18: "I will give [into the hands of their enemies] the men that have trans-gressed against My covenant, which have not performed the words of the covenant which they had made before Me, when they cut the calf in twain and passed between the parts thereof."

2. E.g., Gen. 21:27, 32; 26:28; Exod. 23:32; 34:10; Deut. 5.2; 7:2; Jos. 9:6; 24:25; Judg. 2:2; I Sam. 18:3; II Sam. 5:3; I Kings 5:12; Neh. 9:8; Ps. 105:9; Isa. 28:15; Ezek. 17:13; Hos. 12:1. [Cf. also: W. Gesenius, Thesaurus; s.w. *b-r-h, k-r-t.*]

[2a. J. Bottéro, in RA 44 (1950), 112 ff.; W. F. Albright, in BASOR 144 (1951), 22; E. Vogt, in Biblica 36 (1955), 566.]

3. *horkia temnein;* e.g., Iliad 2.124; Odyssey 24.483; Herodotus 7.132.

4. Euripides, Helen 1235: *spondas temnein.*

5. *Foedus ferire/ictum,* e.g., Livy, 1.24.

6. Dictys Cretensis, Bellum Troianum 1.15.

[6a. Chronicon Dubracense, 1351.]

7. H. Johnston, *The Uganda Protectorate[3]* (1904), ii.752 ff.

8. A. C. Hollis, The Nandi (1909), 84.

9. J. Roscoe, The Northern Bantu (1915), 170 ff.

10. J. Macdonald, in JRAI 29 (1899), 233.

11. J. Raum, in ARW 10 (1907), 285–88.

12. R. Moffat, Missionary Labours and Scenes in Southern Africa (1842), 278.

13. J. Mackenzie, Ten Years North of the Orange River (1871), 393; see also: W. C. Willoughby, in JAI 35 (1905), 306.

14. R. G. Woodthorpe, in JAI 11 (1882), 11. The *dâo* is a long knife or sword, nar-row at the haft, square, broad, and pointless at the tip, with only one edge sharpened.

15. J. Butler, Travels and Adventures in the Province of Assam (1853), i.154.

16. T. C. Hodson, The Nāga Tribes of Manipur (1911), 111.

[16a. W. R. Halliday, Greek and Roman Folklore (1927), 40 f.]

[16b. Cf. J. Henninger, in Biblica 34 (1953), 344–53.]

17. Letter from P. A. Talbot, District Commissioner in S. Nigeria, dated 12/7/1916.

18. Livy, 1.24.

19. Iliad 3.292 ff.

20. F. Peiser, in MVAG 1898.229 ff. Luckenbill, AR ii, §§750–54.

[20a. G. Furlani, Rel. bab. e. assir. (1925), ii.294; H. Zimmern, KAT[3], 49, n.1. 597.]

[20b. KBo II.3; tr. Goetze, ANET, 350 f.]

21. J. T. Nieuwenhuisen and H. C. B. Rosenberg, in Verhaendlingen van het Bataviaaasch Genootschap van Kunsten en Wetenschappen, 30 (1863), 105.

22. H. D. Wiggers, in TITLV 36 (1893), 279.

23. F. Junghuhn, Die Battaländer auf Sumatra (1847), ii.142.

24. W. Ellis, History of Madagascar (1838), i.368 ff.

25. P. Paulitschke, Ethnographie Nordost-Afrikas (1896), 52.

26. C. W. Hobley, Ethnology of A-Kamba and other East African Tribes (1910), 142 ff.

27. B. S. Carey and H. N. Tuck, The Chin Hills (1896), 195; W. G. Hughes, The Hill Tracts of Arakan (Rangoon 1881), 44.

28. F. Mason, in JRAS Bengal, N.S.37 (1868), 160 ff.

29. A. W. Nieuwenhuis, Quer durch Borneo (1904–7), i.62.

30. J. von Klaproth, Reise in den Kaukasus und nach Georgien (1812–14), ii.603.

31. For more examples of the symbolical or magical sacrifice of animals at taking oaths, see R. Lasch, Der Eid (1908), 51 f., 84–88, where many of the preceding instances are cited.

32. W. Robertson Smith, Religion of the Semites[3] (1927), 481.

33. Plutarch, Quaest. Rom. 111. [Cf. also: id., Vert. mul., 236[b]; Seneca, Deira 3.17.]

34. Livy, 40.6; Quintus Curtius, De gestis Alexandri Magni 10.9, 28.

35. Apollodorus, Bib. iii.13, 7. [Cf. Frazer, in loc.; M. Nilsson, in ARW 16 (1913), 314.]

36. Strabo, xi.4, 7.

37. E. Casalis, Les Bassoutos (1860), 270 ff.

38. A. Jaussen, Countumes des Arabes au pays de Moab (1908), 361–63.

39. B. S. Carey and H. N. Tuck, The Chin Hills (1896), i.200; H. W. Read, Handbook of Haka Chin Customs (Rangoon 1917), 40.

40. Carey-Tuck, op. cit., i.198.

41. S. Krascheninnikow, Beschreibung des Landes Kamtachatka (Lemgo 1766), 277 ff. This form of sacrifice would seem to have died out, since it is not mentioned by W. Jochelson in his later account in Jessup North Pacific Expedition, I.i (1905), 90 ff. He does refer, however, to the general sacrifice of dogs among the Koryats.

42. H. von Wislocki, Vom wandernden Zigeunervolke (1890), 92.

43. W. Robertson Smith, Religion of the Semites[3] (1927), 480. On the blood covenant in general, see: H. C. Trumbull, The Blood Covenant (1887).

44. H. H. Pritchard, Through the Heart of Patagonia (1902), 96.

45. W. R. Smith, op. cit., 402.

46. Lucian, De deâ Syriâ §55.

47. M. Merker, Rechtsverhältnisse und Sitten der Wadschagga (1902), 16.

48. Jaussen, op. cit., 361.

49. Ib., 362 f.

50. S. I. Curtiss, Primitive Semitic Religion Today (1902), 195 ff.

51. Ib., 196 f.

52. Ib., 197 f.

53. Ib., 196.

54. Ib., 202 f.

55. Ib., 205 f.

56. Ib., 191.

[56a. S. Eitrem, Beitraege zur griech. Religionsgeschichte, Vid. St. 1917, ii/2, 15–16.]

[56b. Landstad, Norse Folkeviser, 18.]

[56c. Axel Olrik, in Dania 1 (1890–92), 136 ff.]

[56d. C. Unger, Saga Didriks (1853), 22.]

[56e. Danmarks gamle folkeviser, No. 9. C, Str. 16.]

[56f. J. G. F. Riedel, De sluik- en kroeshaarige rassen tusschen Selebes en Papua (1886), 379, 389.]

[56g. E. Crawley, The Mystic Rose[2] (1927), i.295.]

[56h. Sometimes the piece was symbolically bent, rather than actually broken and divided; cf. Samuel Butler, Hudibras: "Like commendation ninepence crooked/With 'to and from my love' it looked."]

[56i. Isa. 15:5; Jer. 31:18; cf. S. Bochart, Hierozoicon[3] (1692), i.28.]

[56j. Theocritus, 29.17.]

[56k. Cf. E. A. Speiser, in BASOR 72 (1938), 15–17.]

[56l. Mishnah, Parah 1.1.]

[56m. KUB XXX.15, vs. 26: . . . III *ŠA.A.TI hi-wa-as-sal-wa-la-a-an* (raw).]

54 Seeing the fourth generation

1. Exod. 20:5; 34:7; Deut. 5:9. (RSV and most other versions miss the point by rendering "thousands" instead of "them of the thousandth generation.")
2. Job 41:16.
3. G. A. Cooke, A Textbook of North Semitic Inscriptions (1903), #65.2–4.
4. Herodotus, 2.142, 2; Livy, ix.15, 10.

SODOM AND GOMORRAH

55 Entertaining angels unawares

1. O. Dähnhardt, Natursagen (1907–12), ii.133 ff.; Aarne-Thompson, Types, ##750–51; Bolte-Polivka, ii.210; Pauly-Wissowa, s.v. Baukis.
2. Ovid, Fasti 5.447–83.

(a) The submerged city

3. Pausanias, 2.35.
4. The story is told by Hionen Thrang, a Chinese Buddhist pilgrim to India in the 7th cent. C.E.; cf. S. Julien, ed., Mémoires sur les contrées occidentales (1858), ii.243.
5. Tobler, Im neueren Reich (1873), 166 f.; Grimm, DM⁴, 546 f.; Hölty, Gedichte (1870), 6.
6. For other versions and parallels see: J. R. Wyss, Idyllen . . . aus der Schweiz (1815), i.62; J. F. Vonbun, Die Sagen Voralbergs (1858), No. 68; J. Jerglehner, Was die Sennen erzählen (1908), 80; G. Schambuch and W. Müller, Niedersächsische Sagen u. Märchen (1953), 51; G. Waibel and H. Flamm, Badische Sagenbuch (1859), ii.347; A. Heyl, Bräuche, u. Meinungen aus Tirol (1897), 680, No. 158.
7. Notes and Queries III/3 (1863), 362.—Not impossibly, the name Simmerwater is connected with French sous mer.
8. Ib., 479.
9. T. Rees, A Topographical and Historical Description of South Wales (1815), 46.
10. R. Busk, The Folklore of Rome (1874), No. 2.
11. J. F. Bladé, Contes de la Gascone (1883), iii.147. For parallels, see: P. Sébillot, a Folklore de France (1904–7), i.14, 184, 218, 254; ii.66, 334, 358; iv.458.
12. A. Merensky, Deutsche Arbeit am Nyassa (1884), 108.
13. See: "Les villes engloutées," in Revue des traditions locales, 1899–1900; P. Kraetzschmar, "Der Mythos von Sodoms Ende," in ZAW 17.81–92; Schmersel, "Die sage von der versunkenen Stadt," in Danske Studien 1925. 117 ff.; U. Jahn, Volksagen aus Pommern und Rügen (1889), Nos. 223, 249, 256, 293; F. G. Heins, Seespuk (1888), 168 ff.; F. v. d. Leyen, Deutsches Sagenbuch (1910–24), iv.234 ff.
14. P. Sébillot, in Revue de Bretagne, etc. 22 (1899), 414–25. It is perhaps to be identified with a city in the area named Christ (or Keris), mentioned by the Geographer of Ravenna.
15. C. Wetzstein, in Franz Delitzsch's Job² (1876), 197, where other Arabic parallels are cited.
16. The Hebrew word is "outcry." Conceivably, however, this here means "din, turmoil," for analogously, in the Babylonian story of the Deluge, destruction comes because of the "hubbub" created by the sinful.
17. The Lot version is clearly influenced by the same type of popular tale as also underlies the gruesome narrative in Judg. 19:22 ff.

(b) Itinerant strangers as gods in disguise

18. See in general: M. Landau, "Die Erdenwanderung der himmlischen und die Wünsche der Menschen," in Zeits. f. vgl. Literaturgeschichte, 14.1–41, with additions by Reuschel and Zuidema, ib., 472 f.

19. Odyssey 17.483 ff.

20. Acts 14:11.

21. Acts 28:1–6.

56 Blinding for impiety

1. T. H. Gaster, Thespis[2], 367; F. Kirby Smith, on Tibullus, i.6, 24; J. Vürtheim, Versl. en Meded. V.ii (1916), 409 f.; E. Spanheim, In Callimachi hymnos observationes (1697), 606; R. Pettazzoni, La Confessione dei Peccati, iii (1936), 99; J. E. B. Mayor, on Juvenal, 8.93; J. G. Frazer, on Pausanias, iii.19, 3.

2. III Aqhat 165–69.

3. III R, 41.ii.19–20.

4. M. Lidzbarski, Ephemeris für Semitische Epigraphik ii (1906), 33, 347.

5. KBo VI.34.

6. Apuleius, Met. 8.26.

7. Pausanias, viii.5.

8. Callimachus, Lavacrum Palladis 82; Apollodorus, Bib. iii.86.

9. W. Mannhardt, Germanische Mythen (1868), 668 ff.; J. Grimm, DM[4], ii.229; P. Sébillot, La folklore de France (1904–7), iii.117; W. Aly, Volksmärchen (1921), 217, f. 66; O. Weinreich, Heilungswunder (1909), 56 f., 189 ff.

10. F. Nork, Der Festkalender. Das Kloster, vii (1847), 41.

57 Taboo on looking back

1. J. G. Frazer, GB iii.104; A. S. Pease, Cicero's De Divinatione (1923), p. 334; Stith Thompson, MI, C 331; E. S. Hartland, The Science of Fairy Tales (1891), 236, 243; E. Samter, Geburt, Hochzeit und Tod (1911), 147 ff.; H. Usener, Kl. Schriften (1914), iv.455; E. Rohde, Psyche[7] (1921), ii.85, n.2; J. Lomeier, Epimenides[2] (1700), 455 ff.; L. Kohler, in ZAW 34 (1914), 149 ff.; Janiewitsch, in ARW 14 (1911), 317 ff.; G. F. Abbott, Macedonian Folklore (1903), 105; J. A. Dorsey, "Omaha Sociology," in Third Annual Report of the Amer. Bureau of Ethnology (1884), 369.

2. KUB XXVII.17.iv.3 ff.; trans. A. Goetze, ANET 348[b].

3. L. W. King, Babylonian Magic and Sorcery (1896), 58, 98 f.

4. W. Caland, Die altindischen Todten- und Bestattungsgebräuche (1888), 23, 73 ff.

5. Odyssey 10.528.

6. Odyssey 5.349.

7. Aeschylus, Choephoroe 90–91; Eumenides 430; Sophocles, Oedipus Col. 490.

8. Theocritus, Id. 24.94 ff.

9. Schol. in Theocr. l.c.; Plutarch, Quaestiones graecae 12; C. Picard, in RHR 93.75.

10. Lucian, Nek. 7.

11. Jamblichus, Protr. p. 114.29 Pist.

12. J. Grimm, DM[4], 435.14; 446.30.

13. Ovid, Fasti 5.436; see Frazer, in loc.

14. Vergil, Ecl. 8.102.

15. Pliny, HN xxi.176; Marcellus Empiricus, i.54; London Magical Papyrus, in F. G. Kenyon, Greek Papyri in the BM (1893–1917), i.98; Paris Magical Papyrus = Suppl. Gr. 2491.

16. Sophocles, fr. 491 (*Rhizotomoi*); Ap. Rhod., Argon. iv.1315.

17. R. C. Thompson in PSBA 1906.79 (Hebrew charm from Mossul); id., Semitic Magic (1908), 171, n.4.

18. B. Thorpe, Northern Mythology, ii (1852), 8.

19. Ovid, Met. 10.1–77; Vergil, Georgica iv.489 f.; E. Paratore, Introduzione alle Georgiche (1938), 60 ff.

20. The story is told in the Kojiki; see: R. Pettazzoni, La mitologia giapponese (1929), 48.

21. Cf. C. Pascal, Scritti vari di letteratura Latina (1920), 369 ff., where parallels are cited.

22. Goblet d'Alviella, Croyances, rites, institutions (1911), ii.287.

58   The pillar of salt

1. Cf. G. Cocchiara, Genesi dei leggende[3] (1940), 41–61; Stith Thompson, MI, C 961.1; H. F. Fielberg, Bidrag til en Ordbog over Jyske Almeuesmal (1886–1914), iii.173b; 553b; E. Sklarek, Ungarische Volksmärchen (1901), #2, p. 288n.—J. McCulloch, The Childhood of Fiction (1905), 156, and A. H. Krappe, La genèse des mythes (1938), 335 f., say that these stories were told to account for anthropomorphic megaliths; G. Cocchiara, op. cit., 61, disagrees. Cf. also: Bauer, in VD 38 (1960), 28–33.

2. G. Pitré, Spettacoli e feste popolari siciliane (1881), 274.

3. L. C. Wimberly, Folklore in the English and Scottish Ballads[2] (1959), 36.

4. L. Ranke, Die deutsche Volksagen[2] (1910), 235, ii.151; Zs. f. Vk. 16.393.

5. Bolte-Polivka, Index, s.v. versteinert.—E. Riess, in Latomus 2 (1938), 172, suggests that Propertius ii.9, 47 f. (Utinam . . . ille vir in medio fiat amore lapis), alludes to such a story, but this is surely far-fetched. A similar curse occurs in a modern Greek tale: J. C. Lawson, Modern Greek Folklore and Ancient Greek Religion (reprint, 1964), 393.

6. E. S. Hartland, The Legend of Perseus (1896), iii.132.

7. V. di Giacomo, Leggende del Diavolo (1963), 229.

8. Ib., 226.

9. G. Pitré, Usi e costumi . . . del popolo siciliano, iii (1889), 135 f.

10. Di Giacomo, op. cit., 225.

11. I find this story in a compilation the first page of which is headed "Relics for the Curious" (i.92), a torn copy of which I picked up in London some forty years ago. Unfortunately, I have not been able to trace the exact title.

12. Cf. Arabic gh-m-r; W. Gesenius, Thesaurus, s.v. ᶜ-m-r; E. Flasher, in ZAW 28.216; J. A. Montgomery, in JQR, N.S. 25 (1935), 262.

59   The proposed sacrifice of Isaac

1. Euripides, Iphigenia in Aulis 87 ff., 358 ff., 1541 ff.; Cypria, as summarized by Proclus, Epic. Frag. Graec., ed. Kinkel, 19; Apollodorus, Epitome iii.21–22.

2. Aristodemus, quoted by Plutarch, Hist. parall. Graec. et Rom. 35.

3. Aristides, Ital. hist. lib. xii, quoted by Plutarch, loc. cit.

JACOB

60   Twin culture-heroes

1. See in general: Rendell Harris, The Cult of the Heavenly Twins (1906); id., Boanerges (1913). Harris derives the idea from the cult of the Dioscuri, or Heavenly

Twins, but he has probably got things the wrong way around: Dioscurism is rather to be regarded as largely a projection into astral mythology of ideas and legends associated with earthly twins. See also: J. Lindsay, A Short History of Culture (1966), 80 f. Lindsay attributes the concept to the dual structure of many societies. ERE, s.v. Twins should also be consulted.

2. It has been suggested that the Romulus and Remus story was simply an adaptation of an earlier legend about Pelias and Neleus, as related by Apollodorus, Bib. i.9, 8. It would have been mediated by the Roman historian, Q. Fabius Pictor, who in turn got it from the Greek historian, Diocles of Peparethos: see C. Trieber, in Rhein. Mus. 43 (1888), 568 ff.

3. Lindsay, loc. cit.

4. Ib.

5. Ib.

6. Ib.

7. K. von den Steinen, Unter der Naturvölker Zentral-Brasiliens (1894), 37 ff.

8. Lindsay, loc. cit.

9. Relation des Jesuites 10, Hurons (1636) = reprint (1896), 125.

10. Harris, Boanerges, 155 ff.

11. Ib.

The hostile twins

12. Harris, op. cit., 381 f.; H. Usener, "Zwillingsbildung," in Kl. Schriften (1913), iv.351 f.

13. D. G. Brinton, Myths of the New World (1868), 169.

14. Ib.

15. Lindsay, loc. cit.

16. J. Batchelor, The Ainu and Their Folklore (1901), 536.

17. Lindsay, loc. cit.

Twins struggle in the womb

18. Cf. Stith Thompson, MI, T 575.1.3; Harris, Boanerges, 381 f.

19. Apollodorus, Bib. ii.2; Servius, on Vergil, Aen. 3.286; Schol. on Euripides, Orestes 965.

20. Stith Thompson, North American Tales (1919), 279, n.33; Standard Dict. of Folklore, s.v. Twins.—On the quarrelsome twins, see also: P. Ehrenreich, Die Mythen und Legenden der Sudaner, Urvölker, etc. in Suppl., Zs. f. Ethnol., 1905.51.—Eznik, an Armenian writer, in his Book of Heresies, says much the same thing about the twin Iranian gods, Ormazd and Ahriman: Harris, Boanerges, 381 f.—Two quarrelsome twins also appear in Assamese legend: ib., 179 f.

21. G. R. Driver, in Mélanges A. Robert (1957), 28 f.

61 The hairy man

1. See: F. L. W. Schwartz, Der Ursprung der Mythologie (1860), 138 ff.; A. B. Cook, Zeus, ii (1925), 447 ff.; Harris, The Cult of the Heavenly Twins (1906), 46, 91.

2. J. Lindsay, A Short History of Culture (1966), 80 f.

3. Stith Thompson, MI, F 521.1.

4. Gilgamesh, I.ii.35 ff. (tr. Speiser, ANET 74). The word is šu-'-u-ur; see: S. Schott, in ZA 42 (1934), 46.

5. K. Sklarek, Ungarische Volksmärchen (1901), 130 ff.

6. Grimm, #136. For further parallels see: R. Kohler, Kl. Schriften (1898–1910), i.133, n.1; H. Gressmann, in ZAW 30 (1910), 21, n.3.

7. See: A. Spamer, "Die wilden Leute im Sage und Bild," in Volkskunst und Volks-

kunde 9 (1911), 117–23. Cf. also (but with caution): C. A. Williams, Oriental Affinities of the Legend of the Hairy Anchorite, Pt. i (UILL 10/2 [1925]), 18 ff.

62 The sinister redhead

1. See: R. Andree, Ethnographische Parallelen, N.F. (189), 271 ff.; L. Radermacher, in Philologus 37.22 ff.; id., Jenseits im Myth. d. Hellen. (1903), 51 ff.; Notes and Queries, VI/6 (1882), 426; VI/7 (1883), 155, 616; VI/8 (1883), 172.

2. Oral information from the late Moses Gaster.

3. Montague Summers, The Vampire (1960), 183.

4. Ib., 182.

5. G. F. Abbott, Macedonian Folklore (1903), 105.

6. F. Redi, Bacco in Toscana (1804): "Guardati dal pelo rosso né valse a togliera la barba del Redentore."—Another Italian proverb runs: "Capelli rossi, o tutto foco, o tutto mosci": Summers, op. cit., 183.—An old Latin proverb (referring to Cain and Judas Iscariot) says: *Monet nos haec fabula rufos evitare, Quos color et fama notat (vetat?) illis sociare.* Cf. also Martial, 12.54: *Crine ruber, niger ore, brevis pede, lumine laesus, Rem magnam praestas, Zoile, si bonus es.*

7. E. Leigh, Certain Choyce French Proverbs (1657): "Homme roux et femme barbue, De trente pas les salue; Avec trois pierres au poing, Pour t'en aider à ton besoign." Cf. also: John Wodroephe, in The Spare Hours of a Soldier in His Travels (Dort 1623), 276: "Guarde toi bien des hommes rousseaux, des femmes barbues, et de ceux qui sont marqués au visage."

8. A. H. Krappe, The Science of Folklore (1930), 210.

9. T. F. Thiselton Dyer, Domestic Folklore[2] (1881), 75.

10. Quoted by Andree, op. cit., 272.

11. W. Wackernagel, Kl. Schriften (1872–74), i.172.

12. Shakespeare, As You Like It, III.iv. Cf. also: C. Middleton, A Chaste Maid in Cheapside (1630), iii.2.—Since 1300 Judas Iscariot was portrayed as a redhead—first, apparently, in the murals at Ranersdorf: Wackernagel, loc. cit.

13. Similarly, the Biblical writer uses the story of how Esau was robbed of the birthright for a "mess of *red* pottage" (*adom;* Gen. 25:30) to account for the name Edom. In point of fact, however, the Hebrew word which he interprets to mean *"red* pottage" has nothing to do with redness, but is connected with a quite distinct, though like-sounding Arabic word *idam* meaning something spread on bread.

▲   63   Jacob steals the blessing

(a) Sacrificial skins in ritual

1. P. Paulitschke, Ethnographie Nordost-Africas (1893), 193 f.

2. C. Dundas, in JAI 43 (1913), 528.

3. Ib., 546.

4. C. W. Hobley, in JAI 40 (1910), 431.

5. W. S. and K. Routledge, With a Prehistoric People, the Akikuyu of British East Africa (1910), 151–53.

6. Hobley, 440 f.

7. Ib., 441.

8. Ib.

9. Ib., 442.

10. A. Karašek, in Baessler-Archiv 1 (1911), 191.

11. M. Merker, Rechtsverhältnisse und Sitten der Wadschagga (1902), 14 ff.

12. E. G. Ravenstein, in Proc. Royal Geogr. Soc., N.S. 6 (1884), 271.

13. C. Dundas, in JAI 43 (1913), 39.

14. Ib., 541 f., 546.

15. W. E. H. Barrett, in JAI 41 (1911), 21.
16. A. C. Hollis, The Nandi (1909), 63.
17. C. New, Life, Wanderings and Labours in Eastern Africa (1873), 458.
18. J. M. Hildebrandt, in Zs. f. Ethnol. 10 (1878), 386.
19. Routledge, op. cit., 176 f.
20. Merker, op. cit., 20.
21. B. Guttmann, in Globus 89 (1906), 198.
22. K. Dundas, in JAI 43 (1913), 38.
23. Ib., 43.
24. J. Raum, in ARW 14 (1911), 189.
25. B. Gutmann, in Zs. f. Ethnol. 44 (1912), 82–84. On superstitions attaching to smiths and smithcraft, see above, §22.
26. B. Guttmann, in Zs. f. Ethnol. 45 (1913), 507 ff.
27. C. W. Hobley, in JAI 40 (1910), 432.
28. Ib.
29. Ib., 435.
30. Ib., 436.
31. Ib., 437.
32. Ib.
33. Id., in JAI 41 (1911), 425.
34. Dundas, op. cit., 46 ff.
35. Ib., 67 ff.
36. C. W. Hobley, Eastern Uganda (1902), 15; H. Johnston, The Uganda Protectorate² (1904), ii.732.
37. Hollis, op. cit., 12 ff.
38. C. W. Hobley, in JAI 41 (1911), 419 f., 421.
39. A. and G. Grandidier, Ethnographie de Madagascar, ii (1914), 278.
40. J. G. Frazer, GB³, Pt. vii (Balder the Beautiful), ii.168 ff.
41. See above, §53.

(b) The new birth

42. Diodorus Siculus, iv.39, 2.
43. C. Hose and W. McDougall, The Pagan Tribes of Borneo (1912), i.78 f.
44. J. Roscoe, The Northern Bantu (1915), 114.
45. Plutarch, Quaest. Rom. 5; Hesychius, s.v. Deuteropotmos.
46. W. Caland, Die altindischen Todten- und Bestattungsgebräuchen (1896), 89.
47. Reade, in Punjab Notes & Queries 2 (1885), 74, §452.
48. Satapatha Brahmaṇa, tr. Eggeling [SBE xxvi], ii.4, 20, 29, 38, 42, 44; H. Hubert and M. Mauss, in L'Année Sociologique 2 (1897–98), 48 ff.
49. Satapatha Brahmaṇa ii.18–20, 25–35, 73, v.23 f.; Sylvain Lévi, in La doctrine du sacrifice dans les Brâhmanas (1898), 102–7; Hubert Mauss, op. cit., 48 ff. [The ceremony is known as diksha and is mentioned in the Atharva Veda, xi.5–6; cf. also Aitareya Brahamaṇa, i.3; Maitrayani Samhita, iii.6, 1; cf. M. Eliade, Birth and Rebirth (1958), 54–56.]
50. R. V. Russell, The Tribes and Castes of the Central Provinces of India (1916), iii.568.
51. F. Wilford, "On Mount Caucasus," in Asiatick Researches 6 (1801), 537 ff. Raghu-Na'th-Ra'ya was an unsuccessful claimant for the Peshwaship of the Marathas, and his claims were supported by the British. His son succeeded to that office in 1796.
52. E. Thurston, Ethnographic Notes in Southern India (1906), 271 ff.
53. J. Forbes, Oriental Memoirs (1813, i.378; S. Mateer, The Land of Charity (1871), 169–71.

54. F. Liebrecht. Zur Volkskunde (1879), 379.

55. Northern Indian Notes & Queries 3 (1894), 215, §465.

56. E. T. Atkinson, The Himalayan Districts of the N. W. Provinces of India, ii (1884), 914.

57. J. A. Dubois, Moeurs, Institutions et Cérémonies des peuples de l'Inde (1825), i.42.

58. A. Mackintosh, Account of the Origin and Present Condition of the Tribe of Ramoosies (Bombay 1833), 124.

[58a. Cf. E. Crawley, Oath, Curse and Blessing (Thinker's Library ed., 1934), 17–19, whence our examples are drawn.]

[58b. Ecclus. 3:9.]

[58c. Grimm-Stallybrass, TM 1690.]

[58d. C. J. Anderson, Lake Ngami (1856), 228.]

[58e. J. Wellhausen, Reste des arabischen Heidentums[2] (1897), 139, 191.]

[58f. Iliad 15.204.]

[58g. Plato, Laws ix.881.]

[58h. H. H. Johnston, The Uganda Protectorate (1902), ii.879.]

[58i. J. L. Wilson, Western Africa (1856), 393.]

[58j. E. Westermarck, The Origin and Development of the Moral Ideas[2] (1912–17), i.627.]

▲   64   Jacob at Bethel

(a) Dreams of the gods

1. Pausanias, i.34, 5.

2. Pausanias, i.34, 2–5.

3. Strabo, viii.6, 15; Pausanias, ii.27, 3. [For a convenient selection of the tablets, see: G. Delling, ed., Antike Wundertexte (Kleine Texte für Vorlesungen und Übungen, No. 79), Berlin 1960, pp. 20–24.]

4. Pausanias, iii.26, 1; Plutarch, Agis 9; id., Clemenês 7; Cicero, De divinatione i.43, 96.

5. Strabo, vi.3, 9.

6. Vergil, Aeneid 8.81 ff.; Ovid, Fasti 4.649 ff.

(b) The heavenly ladder

7. Mary Kingsley, Travels in West Africa (1897), 507.

8. N. Adriani and A. C. Kruijt, De Bare'e-sprekende Toradja's van Midden-Celebes (1912–14), i.23 f., 273.

9. Ib., iii.396 ff.; 436 ff.; 440.

10. A. C. Kruijt, Het Animisme in den Indischen Archipelage (1906), 494 ff.

11. W. R. S. Ralston, The Songs of the Russian People[2] (1872), 111.

12. G. W. van Hoëvell, in Internationales Archiv für Ethnographie, 8 (1895), 134.

13. Adriani-Kruijt, op. cit., ii.163.

14. P. te Wechel, in Internationales Archiv für Ethnographie, 22 (1915), 45 ff.

15. J. H. Breasted, Development of Religion and Thought in Ancient Egypt (1912), 111 ff.; A. Erman, Die Aegyptische Religion[2] (1909), 112, 212 f. [H. P. Blok, in Acta Orientalia, 6 (1928), 257–69; see also: A. B. Cook, Zeus, ii (1925), 125 f.]

16. H. H. Risley, The Tribes and Castes of Bengal (1891), ii.75.

17. Ralston, op. cit., 110 f.

18. P. v. Stenin, in Globus 58 (1890), 202; J. N. Smirnov, Les populations finnoises des bassins de la Volga et de la Kama, i (1898), 141.

19. W. W. Skeat and C. O. Blagden, Pagan Races of the Malay Peninsula (1906), ii.108, 114.

(c) The sacred stone

20. Clement of Alexandria, Protrept. 4.1.
21. E. B. Tylor, Primitive Culture[2] (1873), ii.166.
22. Pausanias, vii.22, 4.
23. Pausanias, i.44, 2.
24. F. Imhoof-Blumer and P. Gardner, Numismatic Commentary on Pausanias, p. 6, with Pl. A, viii.
25. Pausanias, iii.22, 1.
26. Pausanias, ix.24, 3.
27. Pausanias, ix.27, 1–3.
28. Plutarch, Quaest, Graec. 13.
29. R. H. Codrington, The Melanesians (1891), 140 ff.
30. G. Turner, Samoa (1884), 327.
31. W. Gunn, The Gospel in Futuna (1914), 221 ff.
32. W. W. Gell, Life in the Southern Isles (London, n.d.), 217.
33. Turner, op. cit., 62.
34. Ib., 24 ff.
35. Ib., 268 ff.
36. Ib., 296.
37. W. H. Furness, in JAI 32 (1902), 457 ff.
38. W. Crooke, The Popular Religion and Folklore of Northern India (1896), ii.163 f.
39. P. N. Bose, in JRAS Bengal 59/i (1891), 275. Thakur Deo seems to be especially concerned with cultivation. The village priest of the Baigas and Bhainas sows a few seeds before him prior to the sowing of crops.
40. J. Biddulph, Tribes of the Hindoo Kush (1880), 114 ff.
41. La mission Lyonaise d'exploration commerciale en Chine (Lyons 1898), 361.
42. Potoki, Voyage dans les steps d'Astrakhan et du Caucase (1829), i.124, 126.
43. J. H. Speke, Journal of the Discovery of the Source of the Nile. Everyman's Library ed., 197.
44. J. Roscoe, The Northern Bantu (1915), 250.
45. L. Tauxier, Le Noir du Sudan (1912), 105.
46. Relations des Jesuites (Quebec 1858), i [1636], 108 ff.
47. M. Lewis and W. Clark, Travels to the Source of the Missouri River (1815), i.224.
48. Edwin James, Account of an Expedition from Pittsburgh to the Rocky Mountains (1823), i.252 ff.; cf. Maximilian zu Wied, Reise in das Innere Nord-Amerika (1839–41), ii.186 ff.
49. Sven Nilsson, The Primitive Inhabitants of Scandinavia (1868), 241 ff.
50. Pausanias, x.24, 6.
51. Theophrastus, Characters 16.5.
52. Lucian, Alexander 30.
53. Id., Deorum concilium, 12.
54. Arnobius, Adversus nationes i.39.
55. D. G. Hogarth, A Wandering Scholar in the Levant (1896), 179 ff.
56. JRAS 7 (1843), 20.
57. R. E. Enthoven, "Folklore of the Konkan," Supplement to the Indian Antiquary, 44 (1915), 81.
58. E. Moor, in Asiatick Researches, 7 (1803), 394 ff.
59. F. Buchanan, "Journey from Madras through the countries of Mysore, Canara, and Malabar," in John Pinkerton's Voyages and Travels (1804–14), vii.667; E. Thurston, Castes and Tribes of Southern India (1909), i.208 ff.
60. W. H. R. Rivers, The Todas (1906), 130 ff., 143.

61. J. G. F. Riedel, De sluik- en kroeshaarige rassen tusschen Selebes èn Papua (1886), 223.

62. J. Sibree, The Great African Island (1880), 305 f.; cf. A. and G. Grandidier, Ethnographie de Madagascar (1914), ii.246.

63. G. A. Shaw, "The Betsileo," in Antananarivo Annual and Madagascar Magazine, Reprint of the First Five Numbers (Antananarivo 1885), 404 ff.

64. J. Pearse, ib., 164.

65. J. M. Hildebrandt, in Zs. f. Ethnol., 10 (1878), 384.

▲   65   Jacob at the Well

[Literature: In addition to the sources cited by Frazer see: R. Lehmann-Nitsche, "Der Tränerguss im Alten Testament," in FF 12 (1936), 239 ff.; F. Hvidberg, "Vom Weinen und Lachen im Alten Testament," in ZAW 57 (1957), 150–52; id., Gradd og Latter i det Gamle Testament (1938); A. Van Selms, "Weenen als Aanvangsrite," in NTT 24 (1935), 119–27; L. Radermacher, Weinen und Lachen: Studien über antikes Liebesgefuhl (1947).]

1. W. Yate, An Account of New Zealand (1835), 100–2.

2. A. S. Thomson, The Story of New Zealand (1859), i.200; R. Taylor, Te Ika a Maui, or New Zealand and Its Inhabitants² (1870), 222.

3. E. H. Man, On the Aboriginal Inhabitants of the Andaman Islands² (London, n.d.), 79 ff.

4. E. M. Gordon, in JRAS Benegal, N.S. 1 (1905), 184.

5. R. V. Russell, The Tribes and Castes of the Central Provinces of India (1916), ii.428.

6. See fully: G. Friederici, "Der tränengruss der Indianer," in Globus 89 (1906), 30–34.

7. J. Lerius [Lery], Historia Navigationis in Brasiliam (1586), 251–53; A. Thevet, Les singularités de la France antarctique² (1878), 225 ff. (Thevet says that the host himself also wept in sign of welcome, sitting in his hammock.)

8. F. de Azara, Voyages dans l'Amérique méridionale (1809), ii.151.

9. A Nuñez Cabeza de Vaca, "Naufragos y Relacion," in E. de Vedia, Historiadores Primitivos de Indias (1852–53), i.529.

10. N. Perrot, Memoire sur les moeurs, coutumes et religion des sauvages de l'Amérique septentrionale (1864), 86.

11. De la Potherie, ii.182–84, quoted by J. Tailhan in his notes to Perrot, op. cit., 197 ff.

12. H. A. Rose, Glossary of the Tribes and Castes of the Punjab and N. W. Frontier Province, ii (Lahore 1911), 192.

13. P. Colle, in Bulletin des pères blancs, Antwerp, 15 August, 1908, pp. 229 ff.

14. J. Raum, in ARW 10 (1907), 290 f.

15. A. C. Hollis, The Nandi (1909), 78 ff.

16. Id., The Masai (1905), 316.

17. M. W. H. Beech, The Suk (1911), 25.

18. J. Johnston, The Uganda Protectorate² (1904), ii.833.

19. C. de Mensignac, Recherches ethnographiques sur la salive et le crachat (1892), 22.

66   Jacob's marriage

1. HWbDA ii.566.—For this custom as a motif in folktales, cf. Stith Thompson, MI, T 131.2; Arfert, Das Motiv von der unterschobenen Braut (1897); G. M. Gooden, "The False Bride," in Folklore 4 (1893), 142–48.

2. A. Rittershaus, Die neuisländischen Volksmärchen (1902), #2.

3. C. M. Pleyte, Bataksche Vertellingen (1894), 184 ff.

4. H. Calloway, Nursery Tales, Traditions, and Histories of the Zulus (1868), 323.

5. E. Westermarck, History of Human Marriage[5] (1921), ii.521 ff.

6. See also: I. von Duringsfeld, Hochzeitsbuch (1871), 53 (Roumania); 113 (Switzerland); 126 (Bavaria); 179, 190 ff. (Bohemia); 246 (Brittany); L. von Schroeder, Die Hochzeitsbräuche der Esten (1888), 68–72; E. Samter, Geburt, Hochzeit und Tod (1911), 98 ff.; P. Sartori, Sitte und Brauch (1910–14), i.75. Other references in Westermarck, loc. cit., and in J. G. Frazer, The Fasti of Ovid (1929), iii.127, n.l.—The Ben-Amir custom is reported by W. Munzinger, Ostafrikanische Studien (1864), 324.

7. A. John, Sitte, Brauch und Volksglaube in deutschen Westböhmen (1905), 127 ff.

8. W. B. d'Almeida, Life in Java (1864), ii.160 ff. There is, however, no mention of this usage in Clifford Geertz's exhaustive work, The Religion of Java (1964).

9. H. Usener, Kleine Schriften (1914), iv.94 ff.; see also: Frazer, loc. cit.

10. Stith Thompson, MI, K 1191.

11. Cf. E. Crawley, The Mystic Rose[2] (1927), ii.51 f.

67 Reuben and the Mandrakes

1. See: C. Brewster Randolph, "The Mandragora of the Ancients in Folklore and Medicine," in Proc. Amer. Assoc. Arts and Sciences, No. 12 (1905), 1 ff.; T. Starck, Der Alraun. Ottendorfer Memorial Series of Germanic Monographs, No. 14 (Baltimore 1917).

2. Dioscorides iv.76.

3. G. Dalman, in O. Procksch, Die Genesis (1913), 173; J. G. Wetzstein, in Keil-Delitzsch, Hohelied (Bibl. Comm. ueber das A.T., iv.1), 439 f.

4. Theophrastus, Hist. Plant. x.15, 7.

5. Josephus, Bellum Judaicum vii.6, 3.

6. Odyssey 10.302–6.

7. Andrew Lang, Custom and Myth (1885), 143 ff.

8. Alexis, Mandr., 141 ff., ed. Koch.

9. Hesychius, Lex., s.v. Mandragoritis.

10. The Hebrew word is *dūday*, seemingly connected with *dūd*, "to love."

11. R. Patai, in Talpioth 5 (1953), 248 [Hebrew].

12. G. Lammert, Volksmedizin und medizin. Aberglaube in Bayern (1869), 150; cf. also: HWbDA, s.v. Mandragora.

13. Brunetto Latini, Le Trésor, translated (in excerpts) in A. Flores, ed., The Medieval Age (Laurel paperback ed.), 319.

68 The theft of the teraphim

1. Representative studies are: F. Baumgartner, Teraphim (1900); G. Hoffmann, "Teraphim, Masken und Wind-Orakel in Aegyptian und Vorderasien," in ZAW 40 (1922), 75–137; B. Santos Olivera, in VD 8 (1928), 185–88; W. E. Barnes, in JTS 30 (1928–29), 177–79; I. Löw, "Zur Bedeutung der Teraphim," in MGWJ 73 (1929), 314 ff.; E. Sellin, "Ephod und Teraphim," in JPOS 14 (1934), 85–93; id., "Zu Ephod und Teraphim," in ZAW 14 (1937), 296–98.

2. C. J. Gadd, in RA 23 (1926), 49 ff.; S. Smith, in JTS 33 (1932), 33–36; C. H. Gordon, in BA 3 (1940), 6.

3. Vergil, Aeneid ii.293 f.: *Sacra suosque tibi commendat Troja Penates, / Hos cape fatorum comites*. Significantly enough, Aeneas declines to touch them with bloodstained hands and consigns them to his father, Anchises: ib., 717 ff.: "Take, father, in thy hand these holy things / And these ancestral gods, for I who come / Fresh from all this warfare and from blood / So lately spilled may touch them not until / In living waters I have purged the stain" (*Tu, genitor, cape sacra manu partrisque Penates; / Me, bello e tanto digressum et caede recenti / Attrectare nefas, donec me flumine vivo / Abluero*).

69   Stealing the heart

1. See: F. H. von Meyenfeldt, Het hart (Heb.-*lebab*) in het oude Testament (1950); C. Walker, " 'The Heart' in Scriptural Usage," in Homiletic Review, Nov. 1898; W. Spiegelberg, "Das Herz als zweites Wesen der Menschen," in ZÄS 66 (1930), 35–37; A. Piankoff, Le "coeur" dans les textes égyptiens (1930); J. Doresse, "Le coeur et les Égyptiens," in Études Carmelites 29 (1950), 82–97.—Among the Ba-huana of Africa there is only one word for both "heart" and "soul"; E. Jorday and T. A. Joyce, in JAI 36 (1906), 291. So too the Carib word *iouanni* means "heart," "soul," and "life"; while the Tongans say that the principal seat of the soul is the heart: E. B. Tylor, Primitive Culture, ii.15.

2. E.g., Gen. 17:17; Isa. 47:8; Pss. 10:6; 14:1. Cf. also Akkadian *qabû itti libbišu*.

3. Frazer-Gaster, NGB §152.—The Basutos say that a dead man's heart has "gone out"; Tylor, loc. cit.—Among the Bolivians, men and women called "midwives" (*thaliri*) set the heart in the right place after it has been supposedly dislocated by shock or accident: Standard Dict. of Folklore, s.v. *thaliri*.

4. Frazer-Gaster, NGB §§153–155.

5. Book of the Dead, chs. 26–30. Comparable is the primitive notion that the heart can be malevolently "eaten"; J. MacCulloch, ERE vi.55a.

6. D. S. Margoliouth, The Temple Bible: Proverbs (1902), 118.

▲   70   The covenant at the cairn

1. In Gen. 31:46, RSV translates, "And they ate there *by* the heap," whereas the King James Version renders "*upon* the heap." The Hebrew preposition (*ᶜal*) is ambiguous, and can be used in either sense, but the parallels which are here adduced would seem to lend probability to the latter version. [Cf. P. Suarez, in VD 42 (1964), 71–80.]

2. Oliver Elton, tr., The First Nine Books of the Danish History of Saxo Grammaticus (1894), 16.

3. T. S. Raffles, History of Java (1817), i.377.

4. The Grihya-Sûtras, tr. H. Oldenberg [SBE xxix–xxx], i (1886), 13, 168, 282 f.; ii (1892), 45, 188, 260 f.

5. E. Thurston, Ethnographic Notes in Southern India (1906), 1.

6. The Grihya-Sûtras, tr. Oldenberg, ii.146.

7. R. Stewart, in JAS Bengal, 24 (1855), 620 ff.

8. Census of India 1901, vol. xv. Madras, i. Report by W. Francis (1902), 138.

9. Father Abinale, in Les missions catholiques, 11 (1879), 482. [—The custom finds a striking parallel in an ancient Hittite ritual for the renovation of a house: KBo IV.i; tr. A. Goetze, in ANET 356ᵃ. At one point in the ceremony, the officiant declares: "Just as the four corner (stones) of the house are firm on the ground, and as they will not be overturned, so let the sacrificer's well-being not overturn in future before the gods!"]

10. For many examples of swearing on stones, see: R. Lasch, Der Eid (1908), 41 ff.

11. Aristotle, Constitution of Athens vii.55; Plutarch, Solon 25; Julius Pollux, Onomasticon viii.26. [—Similarly, European kings seem to have been placed on a stone when they were installed: A. Pictet, Les origines indoeuropéennes (1859-63), i.334; A. Kuhn, Studien² (1886 ff.), ii.394; Grant Allen, The Evolution of the Idea of God (Thinker's Library ed.), 162. See fully, below, §148.]

12. M. Martin, "Description of the Western Islands of Scotland," in Pinkerton's Voyages (1808–14), iii.657.

13. Ib., 627 ff.

14. Folk-Lore, 8 (1897), 399.

15. W. Munzinger, Sitten und Recht der Bogos (Winterthur 1859), 33 ff.

16. C. Dunda, in JRAI 45 (1915), 252.

17. T. C. Hodson, The Nāga Tribes of Manipur (1911), 110.

18. J. Eliot, in Asiatick Researches, 3 (1807), 30 ff. [—On the custom of concluding pacts over heaps of stones, cf. also: L. B. Farnell, in Anthropological Essays presented to E. B. Tylor (1907), 131 ff.; E. Westermarck, ib., 362.—The custom still obtains among the natives of New Caledonia: M. Leenhardt, Notes d'ethnologie néocalédonienne (1930), 30–31.—It is attested also among the Antimores of Madagascar: A. Van Gennep, Tabou et totémisme à Madagascar (1911), 18.]

19. A. Playfair, The Garos (1909), 75.

20. G. Turner, Samoa (1884), 184.

21. Gen. 31:47–52.

22. Josh. 24:26 ff.

23. S. I. Curtiss, Primitive Semitic Religion Today (1902), 79 ff.

71 Jacob at Mahanaim: The Furious Host

1. Heb.: *malaḵê elôhîm*. In a popular context like this, *elôhîm* means simply what the Scots call "unco beings," and it is a theological anachronism to render it "God."

2. See: H. Gunkel, Das Märchen im AT (1921), 21, 83 f.; P. Ch. Hilscher, Dissertationes de exercitu furioso (1688); H. Meisen, Die Sagen von wütenden Heer und vom wilden Jäger (1925); A. Endter, Die Sagen vom wilden Jäger (Diss., 1933); J. Grimm, DM², 760 ff.; P. Sartori, in Zs. f. Vk. 4 (1894), 289 ff.; A. Kuhn, in Zs. f. deutsch. Altertum 6 (1848), 13 ff.; K. Mannhardt, Antike Wald-und Feldkultur² (1904), i.149 ff.; F. Liebrecht, Gervasius (1856), 173–211; H. Usener, Göternamen (1896), 42; V. Schweda, Die Sagen vom wilden Jäger und vom Schlaffenden Heer in der Provinz Posen (1915); E. S. Hartland, The Science of Fairy Tales (1891), 234 ff.; Stith Thompson, MI, E 501.

3. In Germany it is commonly styled Wotan's host, but Grimm has shown that this is simply a corruption of *wütendes Heer,* i.e., Furious Host.—In England, it is represented as Gabriel's ratchets, i.e., hunting dogs: W. C. Hazlitt, Dictionary of Faiths and Folklore (1905), i.262.—Similarly, in Malaya it is known as "the huntsman and his dogs" (*hantu si buru*).

4. Guilelmus Avernus (d. 1248), p. 1056.

5. Standard Dictionary of Folklore, s.v.

6. Liebrecht, loc. cit.

7. Pliny, HN ii.57.

8. Dio. Halic. x.2.

9. G. Dalman, Arbeit und Sitte in Palästina i (1928), 119.

10. Hesychius Miles, in FHG iv.151, n.27.

11. Grimm-Stallybrass, TM 1591.

12. Pausanias, i.32, 4.

13. E. Rohde, Psyche, English tr. (Harper Torchbooks, 1966), ii.298.

14. O. Dilthey, in Rhein. Mus. 25 (1870), 321 ff.; O. Gruppe, Griechische Mythologie (1906), 406, n.l; 762; 840, n.3; 854, nn.5 ff.; 1203; 1290, n.2; 1293; F. Schönwerth, Aus der Opferpfalz (1857–59), ii.149 ff.

15. See below, §337.

▲ 72 Jacob at the ford of Jabbok

(a) The mysterious adversary

1. Plautus, Amphitryo 532 f.

2. Odyssey 4.354–570.

3. Apollodorus, Bib. iii.13, 5; Scholiast on Pindar, Nem. iii.60.

4. Ovid, Met. ix.62–86; cf. Sophocles, Trachiniae 9–21.

5. Works and Days, 737–41.

6. Herodotus, 6.76.

7. Herodotus, 7.113.

8. Plutarch, Lucullus 24.

9. E. B. Tylor, Primitive Culture[2] (1873), ii.210.

10. Marie Trevelyan, Folk-lore and Folk-stories of Wales (1909), 6.

11. Exod. 32:20.

12. H. Callaway, Nursery Tales, Traditions, and Histories of the Zulus (1868), 90.

13. D. Kidd, The Essential Kafir (1904), 9 ff.

14. S. L. and H. Hinde, The Last of the Masai (1901), 103 ff.

15. J. Roscoe, The Baganda (1911), 319.

16. Ib., 163.

17. J. H. Speke, Journal of the Discovery of the Sources of the Nile. Everyman's Library ed. (1912), 446 ff.

18. P. H. G. Powell-Cotton, in The Geographical Journal, 30 (1907), 374 ff.

19. N. W. Thomas, in JRAI 47 (1917), 165.

20. F. Metz, The Tribes Inhabiting the Neilgherry Hills[2] (1864), 68.

21. A. van Gennep, Tabou et totémisme à Madagascar (1904), 113.

22. J. B. L. Durand, Voyage au Sénégal (1802), 55.

23. R. S. Rattray, Some Folklore Stories and Songs in Chinyanja (1907), 190.

24. Ib., 194.

25. N. Adriani and A. C. Kruijt, De Bare'e-sprekende Toradja's van Midden-Celebes (1912–14), i.276.

26. Herodotus, vii.35.

27. Aelian, Varia Historia xii.23.

28. Whitley Stokes, in Folk-Lore, 4 (1893), 488. Concerning the theme in general, see: E. S. Hartland, Ritual and Belief (1914), 161 ff.

29. Adriani-Kruijt, op. cit., i.37.

30. P. E. Moodenburgh, in Tijdschrift van het Koninklijk Nederlandsch Aardrijkskundig Genootschap, Second series, 19 (1902), 169.

[30a. E. Sklarek, Ungarische Volksmärchen, N.F. (1901), 189.]

[30b. M. Preindlsberger-Mrazović, Bosnische Volksmärchen (1905), 42.]

(b) The shrinking sinew

31. See fully: J. G. Frazer, GB[3], Spirits of the Corn and Wild, 264 ff.

32. J. Mooney, in Seventh Annual Report of the Bureau of [American] Ethnology (1891), 323.

33. Id., in Nineteenth Annual Report (1900), i.263.

[33a. Cf. Gen. 24:2, 9; 46:28; 47:29; Exod. 1:5; see also: J. Wellhausen, Reste des arabischen Heidentums[2] (1897), 168; W. Robertson Smith, Rel. of the Semites[3] (1927), 380 f.; id., Kinship and Marriage in Early Arabia (1865), 38; R. B. Onians, Origins of European Thought about the Body, etc. (1951), 184 f.—For this notion among the Choctaws and Cherokees of North America, see: J. G. Frazer, GB vii.264 ff.]

[33b. Euripides, Bacchae 94 ff., 288 f.]

[33c. A. Erman, "Zaubersprüche für Mutter und Kind," in APAW, phil.-hist. Kl., 1901/i, 41 ff.]

[33d. D. Myhrman, Labartu [Lamashtu]-Texte (1901), ii, 1.51–52.]

[33e. G. Meier, Maqlû (1937), viii.1; R. C. Thompson, Devils (1904), ii.125, 84.]

[33f. T. H. Gaster, in Orientalia 11 (1942), 67 f.]

[33g. T. Pradel, Griech. und süditalienische Gebete (1907), 12.24.]

[33h. Papyrus Parthey, i.20, 60; Pap. Mag. Paris, 37.]

[33i. Lucian, Philopseud., 15; Philostratus, Vita Apollon., 4.16; Prudentius, Kathēmeron, hymn i.378.]

[33j. Stith Thompson, MI, F 420. 3. 4. 2; A. Schöppner, Sagenbuch der bayerischen Lände, (1852–53), i.221, 227; P. Sébillot, Le folklore de France (1904–7).]

[33k. Stith Thompson, op. cit., F 383.4; G 636.]

[33l. Ib., E 452.]

[33m. Ib., E 501.11.1.2.]

[33n. Cf. E. Westermarck, Morocco (1913), i.35–261; T. Plassmann, The Significance of Beraka (1913); E. Argues, in Africa 63 (1947), 125–29.]

[33o. Frazer-Gaster, NGB §126; E. Lefèbvre, in Mélusine 8 (1897), 229–31; G. Contenau, in RHR 41 (1920), 316–22; W. Kroll, in Mitt. d. Schles, Ges. für Volkskunde 16 (1914), 179 ff.; A. Abt, Apologie des Apuleius (1908), 44; 150 f.]

[33p. E. Clodd, Tom Tit-Tot (1898), 91.]

[33q. C. A. Doughty, Arabia Deserta (1888), i.329 f.]

[33r. T. H. Gaster, Customs and Folkways of Jewish Life (1965), 34n.]

[33s. J. von Klaproth, Reise in den Kaukasus (1812), i.253.]

[33t. R. Schmitz, Baholoho (1911), 327.]

[33u. W. H. Müller, Asien und Europa (1893), 163, n.1; B. Luther, in ZAW 21.57; E. Meyer, Israeliten (1906), 57; H. Gunkel, Comm. Genesis, 361.]

73 Guardian angels

1. Harper, Letters 453 (= R. Pfeiffer, State Letters of Assyria, #258), 9–10; L. W. King, Magic (1896), #12.105; KARI #58.64; ZDMG 69 (1915), 98.28; KAT³, 387.

2. TB, Ber. 60^b; Shabb. 119^b; Ta^{c}anith 119^b.

3. Matt. 13:10.

4. E.g., Hermae Vis. v.6, 2; Clem. Alex., Strom. vi.17.

5. Menander, fr. 18 Meineke. Cf. Censorinus, Die die natal. 3: *genius est deus cujus in tutela ut quisquis natus est vivit.* Cf. also: W. W. Hyde, Greek Religion and Its Survivals (1923), 198 ff.

6. Horace, Epistles ii.2, 188.

7. Plutarch, Caesar, ad fin.; cf. Shakespeare, Julius Caesar, V.v.

8. Appian, De bellis Parth, p. 156; cf. E. B. Tylor, Primitive Culture, ii.288.

9. Tibullus, iv.6.1; Pliny, HN ii.16; Petronius, 25, etc.

10. F. Kirby Smith, on Tibullus i.7, 49.

11. C. L. Rochholz, Deutscher Glaube und Brauch im Spiegel der heidnischen Vorzeit (1867), i.92 ff.; W. Schmidt, Geburtstag im Altertum (RVV vii/1, 1908), 10, 32; W. Mannhardt, Germanische Mythen (1858), 308.

12. Stith Thompson, MI, F 403.2.2.2.

13. Rev. des trad. populaires 10 (1895), 4.

14. Acta Sanct. Bolland., S. Francisca Romana, ix Mart., quoted by Tylor, op. cit., ii.289.

15. A. Calmet, Dissertation, ch. iv, §xxx; Tylor, loc. cit.

16. D. Monnier, Traditions populaires (1854), 7.

17. ERE xii.488 f.

18. Manual of Discipline, iii. 13– iv.26; tr. T. H. Gaster, The Dead Sea Scriptures in English Translation (1956), 43–46.

19. C. L. Rochholz, Deutscher Glaube und Brauch (1867), i.92 ff.; W. Mannhardt, Germanische Mythen (1858), 308; W. Schmidt, Geburtstag (1908), 10.2, 32.

74 Jacob's last words

1. On the historical background of the Blessing, see: J. Coppens, in VT Suppl. 4 (1946), 97–115; V. Amerding, in Bibliotheca Sacra 112 (1955), 320–28.

2. Deut. 33. It is plain that both "blessings" draw largely from a common source.

3. E. S. McCartney, "Folklore Heirlooms," in Papers of the Michigan Acad. of Science, Arts and Letters, 16 (1932), 171 f.; W. R. Halliday, Greek Divination (1913),

202 f.; E. Rohde, Psyche[7] (1921), i.44 f.; T. F. Thiselton Dyer, The Folklore of Shakespeare (1884), 340–41.

4. Cyrop. viii.7, 21; cf. Cicero, De Divinatione 1.23.

5. Quoted by E. R. Dodds, The Greeks and the Irrational (1957), 140.

6. Iliad 16.849 f.

7. Iliad 22.325.

8. Sophocles, Trachiniae 1148 ff.

9. Vergil, Aeneid 10.729–41.

10. Plato, Apol. 39c; cf. Xenophon, Anab. Apol. 30.

11. Cf. A. S. Pease, on Cicero, De Divinatione, 1.23.

12. Ib.

13. R. H. Charles, The Assumption of Moses (1897); id., The Ascension of Isaiah (1900).

14. D. S. Margoliouth, in ERE iv.818.

15. Shakespeare, King Richard the Second, II.ii, 31–32.

16. Id., The Merchant of Venice, I.i, 30–31.

17. Byron, Childe Harold, iii.23.

18. T. G. Thiselton Dyer, Domestic Folklore[2] (1881), 58.

19. Everyman's Library ed., 561, 567–70, 593, 628.

20. Schmidt, loc. cit.

21. Cf. A. H. Krappe, The Science of Folklore (1930), 217.

JOSEPH

75 The bloodstained coat

1. See: W. A. Clouston, The Childhood of Fiction (1887), ii.64; M. Cox, Cinderella (1893), 475.

2. Nights 169–249.

3. T. Menzel, Archiv für Märchenkunde des Morgenlandes, II: Türkische Märchen Billur Köschk (1923), 169 f.; 177 f.

4. J. Arnason, Icelandic Legends (1864), 413.

5. Folk-Lore Journal, 4.42. Further parallels occur in Madagascar, ib., 2.136; in Germany (Grimm, ##31, 33); and in the Gesta Romanorum (ch. 20, tr. Swan).

6. Aeschylus, Choephoroe 232 f.; Apollodorus, Epitome vi.24.

7. Euripides, fr. 105 Nauck; Aelian, Var. Hist. xii.42; Hyginus, fab. 38, 187, 252; R. Graves, Greek Myths (1955), #49.

8. The word occurs in this sense in post-Biblical Hebrew and in Syriac. Cognate are Arabic ƒ-sh-y, "extend" and Heb. p-ś-h. In Ps. 72:16 the expression pissat bar means simply "an expanse (RSV: abundance) of corn," and no emendation is needed.

9. LXX: poikilos chitōn; Vulg.: tunica polymita; similarly the Syriac Peshitta at II Sam. 13:18–19.

10. R. Eisler, in OLz 1908.368–71, ingeniously suggests that Heb. pasîm should be emended to <pas>pasîm, since a word paspas, denoting some kind of garment, occurs in Mishnah, Negaᶜim 9.

11. Stith Thompson, MI, M 370.

12. A. Leskien, Balkanmärchen (1915), 162.

13. Bolte-Polivka, i.324; A. Thimme, Das Märchen (1909), 51.

14. Stith Thompson, MI, K 1931.4.

15. Nights 482–535 ("The Queen of the Serpents").

16. Menzel, op. cit., 112; cf. O. Rescher, in Zs. f. Semitistik 3.147.

17. Cieza de Leon, The Chronicles of Peru, cf. R. Markham (1883), Pt. iii.5.

76 Potiphar's wife

1. Stith Thompson, MI, K 2111; see: N. Penzer, The Ocean of Story, ii.120; iv.104, 107; v.176; P. Wendland, De fabellis antiquis earumque ad Christianos propagatione (1911), 13 ff.; M. Braun, History and Romance in Graeco-Oriental Literature (1938), ch. ii; W. F. Albright, in JBL 37 (1918), 111–28; id., in AfO 5 (1930), 229 f.; id., in BASOR, No. 78 (1940), 26, n.1; E. Benveniste, in Mélanges Dussaud, i (1939), 249–58; J. G. Frazer, Apollodorus (1921), ii. p. 146n.

2. D'orbiney Papyrus, ANET 23 ff. Cf. R. J. Williams, "Ancient Egyptian Folktales," in Univ. Toronto Quarterly 37 (1958), 265 ff.; S. Donadoni, "La seduzione della moglie di Bata," in Riv. Stud. Or. 28 (1953), 143–48. C. W. von Sydow, in Yearbook of the New Society of Letters at Lund, 1930. 53–89, claims that the Egyptian story is a garbled version of an Indo-European myth!

3. Euripides, Hippolytus; Seneca, Phaedra; Diod. Sic., 4.62; Pausanias, i.22, 1 ff., ii.32, 1–4; Ovid, Met., 15.479 ff.; id., Heroides, iv; Apollodorus, Epitome, 1.19. Cf. J. G. Frazer, Apollodorus (1921), ii.146n.

4. Iliad, 6.160–65.

5. Apollodorus, Bib. 3.13, 3. Cf. Pindar, Nem., 4.54 (88) ff. (and Scholiast in loc.); Scholiast on Aristophanes, Clouds, 1063. (Pindar calls her Hippolytē, daughter of Cretheus, and the Scholiast on Aristophanes agrees, though he later changes the name to Astydameia.)

6. A. C. Pearson, in CR 33 (1909), 255, sees an allusion to this story in Pindar, Pyth., 4.162, but this is doubtful.

7. Jatāka, #472. Cf. M. Bloomfield, "Joseph and Potiphar in Hindu Fiction," in Trans. Amer. Philological Association, 54 (1923), 145–47.

8. A. Carnoy, Iranian Mythology (1927), 336 (from the Tutti Nameh).

9. E. T. C. Werner, Myths and Legends of China (1923), 192.

10. L. Soumelian, tr., The Daredevils of Sassoun (1965).

11. Boccaccio, Decameron, ii.8.

12. Stith Thompson, Tales of the North American Indians (1929), 326, n. 178.

13. The Thousand and One Nights, Nights 456–66.

14. For a translation of this text, cf. H. Otten, in MDOG, No. 85 (June 1953), 30 ff.

▲ 77 Joseph's Cup

1. Damascius, Vita Isidori, quoted in Photius, Bibliotheca 347 B, Bekker; cf. Jamblichus, De mysteriis iii.14.

2. C. B. Klunzinger, Upper Egypt (1878), 387 ff.

3. Sven Nilsson, The Primitive Inhabitants of Scandinavia[3] (1868), 241.

4. W. Ellis, Polynesian Researches[2] (1832–36), i.378 ff.

5. F. A. Swettenham, Malay Sketches (1895), 201–3; W. W. Skeat, Malay Magic (1900), 538 ff.

6. H. Newton, In Far New Guinea (1914), 89 ff.

7. L. Tauxier, Le Noir du Soudan (1912), 570, 572.

8. D. Crantz, History of Greenland (1767), i.214.

9. Hippolytus, Refutatio omnium haeresium iv.35.

10. J. Forbes, Oriental Memoirs (1813), ii.245 ff.

11. W. Hone, Year Book (London, n.d.), col. 1176.

12. C. S. Burne and G. F. Jackson, Shropshire Folk-Lore (1883), 179.

13. J. Roscoe, The Northern Bantu (1915), 135.

14. A. Playfair, The Garos (1909), 97.

15. W. Gregor, Notes on the Folk-lore of the N. E. of Scotland (1881), 31 ff.

16. J. G. Campbell, Superstitions of the Highlands and Islands of Scotland (1900), 266 ff.

17. J. Brand, Popular Antiquities of Great Britain (1882–83), iii.330.

18. G. F. Abbott, Macedonian Folklore (1903), 95.

19. J. Lascius, De diis Samagitarum caeterorumque Sarmatarum, reprinted in Magazin herausgegeben von der Lettisch Literärischen Gesellschaft, 14/i (Mitau 1868), 98; L. Lloyd, Peasant Life in Sweden (1870), 187; J. G. Dalyell, Darker Superstitions of Scotland (1834), 511 ff.; A. C. Haddon, "A Batch of Irish Folk-Lore," in Folk-Lore, 4 (1893), 361 ff.

20. William Camden, Britannia, tr. Philemon Holland (1610), 147. See also: N. W. Thomas, Crystal Gazing (1905), 42 ff.

77a   One hundred years and ten

1. Cf. J. M. Jaussen, in Oudheidkundige Mededelingen vit het Rijksmuseum van Oudeheiden te Leiden, N.S. 31 (1950), 33–43.—In the fourth story of the Westcar Papyrus, Djedi lives 110 years: cf. G. Lefebvre, in CRAIBL 1944.106.—At a much later date and in a different clime, Zosimus in his On the Decline of Rome, ii.6, remarks: *When now the longest time has run its course that man / May live, and years a century and ten have closed / Their circuit* (tr. F. C. Grant, Ancient Roman Religion [1957], 177).

MOSES

▲   **78   Moses in the Bulrushes**

[1. On the motif of the *exposed child*, cf. Stith Thompson, MI, S 144; Bolte-Polivka, i.489; ii.236 ff.; iii.2; E. Cosquin, Etudes folkloriques (1922), 199 ff.; E. S. Hartland, in Folk-Lore Journal 4 (1886), 308–49; A. Nutt, in Folk-Lore Record 4 (1881), 1 ff.; P. Sébillot, Incidents, s.v. enfant; G. Binder, Die Aussetzung des Königskindes Kyros und Romulus, Beitr. z. Klass. Philol. 10 (1964); A. Krappe, Balor and the Evil Eye (1927), 3 ff., 17 ff., nn.57–60; id., in RHR 107.126–33; J. de Vries, in FCC 24 (1928), 40 ff.; A. Hertel, in Zs. f. Vk. 19.83; A. Tille, ib., 29.22 ff.; H. Spaarnay, Verschmelzung legendarischer und weltliche Motive in der Poesie des Mittelalters (1922), 31 ff., 50; A. S. Pease, Cicero's De Divinatione, vol. ii (1923), 166; S. Luria, in ZAW 42 (1926), 101 ff.; H. Gunkel, Märchen im AT (1921), 113 ff.; K. Weinhold, Deutsche Frauen[2] (1882), i.79; H. Usener, Sintflutsagen (1899), 88, 110 ff.; P. Saintyves, Les vierges-mères et les naissances miraculeuses (1908), 87–109.—For INDIC parallels, cf. E. B. Cowell et al., Jataka (1895–1913), v.230; N. M. Penzer, The Ocean of Story, ii.4; vii.81, n.l.—An ITALIAN story containing the same motif may be found in Basile's Penta-merone, iii.2; and an INDONESIAN tale, from the Palaung tribe, in J. B. Scott, Indo-Chinese Mythology (1918), 276.—In an ancient HITTITE tale, a child begotten by the sun on a cow is exposed, washed by the river, and eventually reared by a fisherman: KUB XXIV.17; J. Friedrich, in ZA 49 (1950), 225 ff.; T. H. Gaster, The Oldest Stories in the World (1952), 159 ff., 170.]

[1a. Spaarnay, op. cit., 33; A. Dickson, Valentine and Orson (1920), 37, 170.]

[1b. Diodorus Siculus, ii.4.]

[1c. Aelian, VA xii.21.]

[1d. Hyginus, fab. 87, 88, 252; Lactantius Placidus, Theb., iv.306; First and Second Vatican Mythographers, in Scriptores reum mythicarum Latini, ed. Bode, i.7 ff., 126.]

[1e. Apollodorus, Bib. iii.5, 7; Sophocles, Oedipus Tyrannus, 711 ff., 944 ff., 1123 ff.]

[1f. Apollodorus, Bib. iii.12, 5 (v. Frazer, in loc.); Hyginus, fab. 91.]

[1g. Apollodorus, Bib. iii.5, 5.]

[1h. O. Gruppe, Gr. Mythol. (1906), 1171, n.l.]

[1i. B. H. Chamberlain, The Kojiki (1882), 21.]

[1j. Lord Raglan, The Hero (Thinker's Library ed., 1949), ch. xvi.]

2. Herodotus, i.107–22.—A different version is told by Justin (i.4). Cyrus, he says, was actually exposed by the herdsman, but later rescued by him upon the entreaty of his wife. When he went to retrieve the infant, he found a bitch suckling and protecting it, and when he carried the child home, the bitch trotted solicitously at his heels. Hence the herdsman's wife, who nursed the babe, received the name Spaco, which is said to mean "bitch" in Persian.—On this legend, see further: Ctesias, apud Nicol. Damasc., in FHG 90 F.66; Aelian, VA xii.42; Xenophon, Cyrop. i.4, 15; A. Bauer, "Der Kyros-Sage und Verwandtes," in Szb. Akad. Wien, phil.-hist. Kl. 100 (1862), 495 ff.; W. Aly, Volksmärchen, Sage u. Novellen bei Herodot und seinen Zeitgenossen (1921), 11 ff.; F. Lessmann, Die Kyrossage in Europa (1906), 160 ff.; Binder, op. cit., 175 ff.

3. CT XIII.42–43; L. W. King, Chronicles of Early Babylonian Kings, ii (1907), 87–96; H. G. Güterbock, in ZA 42 (1934), 62–64; tr. E. A. Speiser, in ANET 49.

4. Vana Parva, The Mahabharata of Krishna-Dvaipyara-Vysya, tr. R. C. Roy[2], ii.651 ff.; The Mahabharata, tr. Dutt (1846), 436–40; A. Wirth, Danae in Christlichen Legenden (1892).

5. Ghulam Muhammad, in Memoirs of the Asiatic Soc. of Bengal, i/7 (1905), 124 f. Binder, op. cit., 211.

[5a. Pausanias, iii.24, 3 ff.; Euripides, Bacchae 1 ff., 286 ff.]

[5b. Pherecydes, quoted by the Scholiast on Ap. Rhodius, Argon. iv.1091; cf. Apollodorus, Bib. ii.4.]

[5c. According to Aristotle, Poetics xvi, p. 1454, this was the version adopted by Sophocles in his lost play, Tyro. Others said that the infant was received by a keeper of horses.]

[5d. Strabo, xiii.1, 69.]

[5e. Livy, i.3–6; Ovid, Fasti ii.381 ff.; Plutarch, Romulus 3–9; Dio. Hal. i.76–85. Only Plutarch mentions the woodpecker. See also: E. Trieber, in Rhein. Mus. N.F. 43 (1888), 568 ff.; F. Soltau, Aufsätze d. röm. Geschichtschreibung (1909), 21 ff.]

[5f. S. Julien, Documents historiques sur les Tou-kioue Turcs, traduits du chinois (1887), 2 f., 25 f.; W. Radloff, Aus Sibirien[2] (1893), i.129 ff.; J. J. M. de Groot, Chinesische Urkunde zur Geschichte Asiens, i.–ii (1921–26); Binder, op. cit., 215 f.]

[5g. J. Hertel, Indische Erzählungen, iv (1922); Binder, op. cit., 196.]

[5h. Firdausi, Shah Nameh, xvii = v. 21–47 Mohl; Binder, op. cit., 184.]

[5i. P. Kretschmer, Neugr. Märchen (1917), 257 ff.; Binder, op. cit., 249 f.]

[5j. M. J. bin Gorion, Der born Judas[2] (1916–22), i.165 f.]

[5k. Golden Legend; L. Constans, La légende d'Oedipe (1881), 95–97; J. G. Frazer, Apollodorus (1921), ii.374–75.]

[5l. S. Przyluski, Etudes asiatiques, ii (1925), 276; M. Eliade, Patterns of Comparative Religion (1958), 208 ff.]

[5m. Eliade, op. cit., 210, n.2.]

[5n. Przyluski, loc. cit.]

[5o. Eliade, op. cit., 209.]

[5p. G. Furlani, La religione babilonese e assira (1928), i.126.]

[5q. ISA 38–39, 42–43, 67–68, 94–95.]

[5r. ISA 218–19.]

[5s. Code of Hammurapi, r.24, 26 ff.]

[5t. A. H. Gardiner, in JEA 36 (1950), 3–12; H. P. Block, in Acta Orientalia 8.208 ff.]

[5u. I Kings 9:33, 38; see below, §148.]

[5v. W. Webster, Basque Legends (1877), 22.]

[5w. J. T. Naake, Slavonic Fairy Tales (1874), 28; J. A. MacCulloch, The Childhood of Fiction (1905), 71.]

6. R. Cirilli, in Bulletins et Mémoires de la Societe d'Anthropologie de Paris, Vième sér., iii (1912), 80–88.

7. Exod. 6:20; cf. Num. 26:59.

8. Lev. 18:12.

9. Exod. 1:22.

10. Julian, Orat. ii; id., Epist. xvi, pp. 104, 495, ed. Hertlein; Libanius, Orat. xii.48; Nonnus, Dionysiaca xxiii.94–96; Claudian, In Rufinum ii.112; Eustathius, Comm. on Dionysius, in FHG ii.267 f.

11. J. H. Speke, Journal of the Discovery of the Source of the Nile, Everyman's Library ed. (1912), 444.

79 Moses at Horeb

(a) **The burning bush**

Literature: G. H. Skipwith, in JQR 10 (1898), 489 ff.

1. P. Haupt, in Proc. Amer. Philos. Soc., 48 (1909), 354–69.

2. For other explanations, see: A. S. Pease, Ciceronis De Divinatione (ILL viii/2 [1923]), ii.316; W. O. E. Oesterley, in ET 8 (1907), 510–12.

3. Guérin, Vie des Saints, vii (1880), as quoted by E. C. Brewer, Dictionary of Miracles, 55.

(b) **The removal of shoes**

4. Jos. 5:15.

5. ATOB, Pl. 323.

6. O. Weber, Altoriental. Siegelbilder (1912), #432.

7. Herodian, v.6, 11.

8. Silius Italicus, iii.28.

9. Dittenberger, Sylloge #357.25.

10. Eph. arch. 1898.249.

11. P. Kretschmer, in Jahresheft d. oester. arch. Inst., v (1902), 139 ff.; W. R. Paton, in CR 16 (1902), 290.—K. Esdaile, in JHS 29 (1909), 2 ff., assembles representations of one-sandaled offrants in Greek cults, and W. Amelung, in Diss. della pontif. acad. di archeol. ii/9 (1907), 113 ff., points out that it was usually the *left* foot that was unshod, suggesting a *chthonic* significance.

12. Illustrations in Bull. comm. arch, dom. di Roma 7 (1897), ii.4; iv.9. Cf. A. Dieterich, in Rhein. Mus. 48 (1893), 277.

13. Aristophanes, Clouds 719, 858.

14. Prudentius, Peristeph. x.154–60; H. Hepding, Attis (1906), 64.

15. Tertullian, Apol. 40.

16. T. Trede, Das Heidentum in der römischen Kirche (1889–91), i.151; ii.105, 165; iv.178; R. Wuensch, Das Fruehlingsfest der Insel Malta (1902), 59.

17. See: C. A. Lobeck, Aglaophamus (1829), i.249; K. Weinhold, in Abh. d. Berl. Akad., phil.-hist. Kl. 1896. 4 ff.; F. Dümmler, in Philologus 56 (1897), 6; H. Hepding, op. cit., 174; O. Gruppe, Gr. Mythol. (1906), 912; H. Usener, Das Weinachtsfest² (1911), 295; L. Dürr, in OLz 41 (1938), 410–12.

18. T. Wächter, Reinheitsvorschriften, RVV ix/9 (1919), 23 f.; J. Hackenbach, De nuditate sacra, RVV ix/3 (1919), 23 ff.

19. Penquitt, De Didonis vergilianae exitu (Königsberg 1910), 53.

20. Concerning this taboo, see: Frazer-Gaster, NGB §§482–87.

21. G. Contenau, Manuel (1927–47), i.441, 443, 474, 475.

22. E. Otto, Handb. d. Archäologie (1939), i. pl. 125.

23. OIC xiii, figs. 32–33. See also: E. Dhorme, Les religions de Bab. et d'Ass. (1945), 199; B. Meissner, Babylonien und Assyrien, ii (1925), 55, where it is explained as a survival from days when everyone went nude!

24. Hackenbach, op. cit.; S. Eitrem, Opferritus und Voropfer der Griechen und Römer (1915), 52.

25. J. Wellhausen, Reste arab. Heidentums[2] (1897), 110; W. Robertson Smith, The Religion of the Semites[3] (1907), 451 f., with S. A. Cook's note, ib., 687.

26. I. Goldziher, in Nöldeke Festschrift (1906), 328 f.

27. JPOS 6 (1926), 15.

28. JRAS 1897.47 f.

29. Cf. T. H. Gaster, Thespis[2], 330 f.

30. J. E. Padfield, The Hindu at Home (1896), 73.

31. E. J. Payne, History of the New World called America (1892–99), ii.495.

32. Ezek. 24:17, 20. There seems to be a further allusion to this custom in Mic. 1:8, where the correct rendering would appear to be: *For this will I lament and wail; I will go* barefoot *and naked,* rather than stripped *and naked,* as in RSV.

33. II Sam. 15:30.

34. See on this: A. Marmorstein, in SMSR 10 (1934), 90 f. Cf. also: Juvenal, vi.159.

35. A. J. Wensinck, Some Semitic Rites of Mourning and Religion (1917), 98 f., quoting Wetzstein, in Zs. f. Ethnologie 5.273 ff.

36. E. S. Drower, The Canonical Prayerbook of the Mandaeans (1959), 99, n.3.

37. Callimachus, Hymn to Demeter, 124.

38. Bion, i.20.

39. Nonnus, Dionys. v.374. Isis, too, is said thus to have mourned Osiris: Aelian, HA x.23.

40. Suetonius, Augustus 100.

41. See: Plutarch, De sera num. vindic. 12 (Locrian maidens at Troy); Ovid, Fasti i.629; vi.396–97; Statius, Theb. ix.572; Jamblichus, Vita Pythag. 85, 105; Marinus, Vita Procli 11; Varro, Pseudo-Ap., fr. 439; Servius, on Vergil, Aen. iv.518.—The custom was later interpreted as due to the fact that leather soles were made from dead animals: Varro, De lingua Latina, vii.84; Ovid, Fasti i.629. Other material was therefore substituted, instead of wearing no shoes at all: Appian, Bell. civ. v.11; Pausanias, ix.39, 8 (at Lebadeia); Dittenberger, Sylloge 388.15 (at Andania); see: O. Gruppe, op. cit., 912, n.5.

80 The three proofs of Moses' commission

1. This section is reprinted from T. H. Gaster, Passover (1949), 40 f.

2. Exod. 7:8–10.

3. Num. 12:1–15.

4. Exod. 7:19–25.

5. See fully: Stith Thompson, MI, H 900, 1000–1199.

81 The rod of Moses

1. See in general: I. Abrahams, in Papers read before the Jews' College Literary Society (London 1887).—On magical wands, see: Leclerq, in Cabirol's Dict. d'Archéol. chrétienne, ii/1 (1910), 60–70; R. Lankester, Diversions of a Naturalist (1915), 383–95; Gundel, in P–W. s.v. Rhabdomanteia.

2. E. O. James, in ERE., s.v. Staff.

3. Judges 6:21.

4. Hos. 4:12; cf. M. Gaster, in ERE iv.810[a].

5. Gordon, #127.7.

6. Odyssey 16.172.

7. Odyssey 5.47; cf. Vergil, Aen. 4.242 ff.

8. Homeric Hymn to Hermes 529 ff.

9. Odyssey 10.238.

10. Odyssey 11.91.

11. Aeschylus, Agamemnon 1265.

12. E.g., Parthey, in Abh. BAW 1865.128, 1.279; F. M. de Waele, The Magic Staff or Rod in Graeco-Roman Antiquity (1927); O. Gruppe, Gr. Mythologie (1906), 896, n.3.

13. N. M. Penzer, The Ocean of Story, i.22 ff.; ix.68 f.

14. Cf. Stith Thompson, MI, D 1551, 1567.

15. G. M. Theal, Kaffir Folk-Lore (1886), 129.

16. C. Plummer, Vitae Sactorum Hiberniae, i (1910), clxxiv, nn.2–3.

17. P. Saintyves, Essais de folklore biblique (1923), 139 ff.

18. Callimachus, Hymn to Zeus 31; Ap. Rhod., Argon., i.1146.

19. Hyginus, fab. 169, 169A.

20. Pausanias, iv.38.

21. Id., iii.28.

22. Les petits Bollandistes[7] (1880), v.232.

23. Ib., i.405.

24. E. C. Brewer, Dictionary of Miracles, 332 ff., where all of these instances are cited.

25. F. Giry, Bull and other Documents of the Canonization of St. Francis of Padua, quoted by Brewer, loc. cit.

26. Brewer, loc. cit.

27. Bollandus, Acta Sanctorum, i.170.

28. Gui of Burgundy, Life of St. James of Tarentaise.

29. D. Piolin, History of the Church of Mans, as quoted by Brewer, loc. cit.

30. Osbert of Canterbury, Life of St. Dunstan.

31. N. Adriani and A. C. Kruijt, De Bare'e-sprekende Toradja's van Midden-Celebes (1912–14), i.25.

32. J. Jegerlehner, Sagen und Märchen aus dem Oberwallis (1909), #21.

82   The incident at the inn

1. For suggested explanations, see: H. Junker, in Nötscher Festschrift (1950); S. Talmon, in Erez Israel 3 (1954), 93–96; J. Blau, in Tarbiz 26 (1957), 1–3; I. Ben-Shabbat, ib., 213; H. Kosmala, in VT 12 (1962), 14–28; J. Morgenstern, in HUCA 34 (1963), 35–70.—According to G. A. Barton (in ERE iii.697[b]), Zipporah placed the foreskin of Moses' son on Moses' genitals to simulate that the latter had been circumcised.

2. The Biblical writer fully understood this, for he took care to add the explicit gloss, *She was then using the expression "ḥatan of bloodshed" in reference to circumcision.* Unfortunately, however, this gloss has been misunderstood and therefore mistranslated (RSV: *Then it was that she said, "You are a bridegroom of blood," because of the circumcision*).

3. B. Spencer and F. J. Gillen, The Native Tribes of Central Australia (1899), 350, 368 ff.; id., The Northern Tribes of Central Australia (1904), 334, 361, 372. Cf. also: J. G. Frazer, GB i.92 ff.; H. P. Smith, in JBL 25 (1906), 14; S. A. Cook, in W. Robertson Smith, The Religion of The Semites[3] (1927), 609.—In the early nineteenth century, Charles Payne was adopted into a Gypsy tribe by mutual incisions in his own and the Gypsies' arms and mingling of the blood. The novice's oath was administered to him by touching with the point of a knife both his own chest and that of the representatives of the tribe: Jean-Paul Clébert, The Gypsies, tr. Ch. Duff (Penguin 1967), 160 (after J. Bloch, Les Tsiganes [1951]).

4. ERE iii.660[a]; J. G. Frazer, GB, Balder the Beautiful, ii.234.

83 The death of Moses

1. Num. 20:28.

2. J. G. Wetzstein, Reisebericht ueber Hauran und die Trachinen (1860), 26; J. L. Burckhardt, Bedouins and Wahabys (1830), 147; J. Wellhausen, Reste des arabischen Heidentums[2] (1897), 15 f.; W. W. von Baudissin, in PRE[3], viii.183.

3. B. Spence and F. J. Gillen, The Native Tribes of Central Australia (1899), 250, 268 ff.; id., The Northern Tribes of Central Australia (1904), 334, 361, 372.

4. J. A. MacCulloch, The Celtic and Scandinavian Religions (1948), 160.

5. H. R. Schoolcraft, Indian Tribes of the United States (1855–57), ii.133.

6. W. H. Brett, Indian Tribes of Guiana (1889), 125.

7. J. A. MacCulloch, in ERE viii.864; T. H. Gaster, in The Jewish Guardian (London), Dec. 23, 1930.

8. F. Thureau-Dangin, Une relation de la huitième campagne de Sargon (1912), r.150.

9. G. Brown, Melanesians and Polynesians (1910), 399 f.

10. W. Ellis, Polynesian Researches[2] (1832–36), i.331, 516.

11. W. Ellis, History of Madagascar (1838), i.429 f.

12. Folk-Lore 16 (1905), 115.

13. H. St. John, Life in the Forests of the Far East (1860), i.172, 278; C. Hose and W. McDougall, The Pagan Tribes of Borneo (1912), ii.10.

14. G. Dale, in JAI 25 (1896), 232 f.

15. J. J. de Groot, The Religious Systems of China (1892), 175.

16. Rigg, in Journal of the Indian Archipelago 4.119.

17. K. Schwenck, Die Mythologie der Slawen (1853), 263; W. R. S. Ralston, Songs of the Russian People[2] (1872), 109 f.

18. R. C. Maclagan, in Folk-Lore 8 (1897), 208.

19. Stith Thompson, MI, A 571; D 1960.2; Bolte-Polivka, iii.460 f.; R. Köhler, Kl. Schriften, ed. J. Bolte (1898), i.411; Grimm-Stallybrass, TM 953 ff.; A. H. Krappe, in Mitt. d. Schlesischen Ges. fuer Volkskunde 25 (1935), 76–102; E. S. Hartland, The Science of Fairy Tales (1891), 70 ff., 205, 258; K. Wehran, Die Sage (1908), 47 ff.; H. F. Feilberg, Danske Studien (1920), 97 ff.

20. Weltig, Der Sagenkreis des Kyffhäusers (1891).

21. M. H. Ananikian, Armenian Mythology (1925), 3 f.

22. A. Carnoy, Iranian Mythology (1917), 327.

23. A. B. Keith, Indian Mythology (1917), 173.

24. Folk-Lore 11 (1902), 327 f.

25. Moses Gaster, The Samaritans (1925), 91.

THE EXODUS

84 The "finger of God"

1. B. Couroyer, in RB 63 (1956), 481–95.

2. *dr.t ntr.*

3. *qât ilī.*

4. RS 54.11, Gordon (*yd ilm p kmt*).

5. ŠU. DINGIR. RA.

6. See W. F. Albright, in BASOR 94 (1944), 12 ff.; id., in ANET 490.

7. A. Deissmann, Light from the East (1911), 309, n.3.

8. ANEP, #473.10.

9. E. A. W. Budge, Amulets and Superstitions (reprint, 1961), 148.

85   The escorting angel

1. NABATEAN (Hauran, A.D. 96): R. Dussaud and F. Macler, Voyage archéologique au Safa et dans le Djebel-ed-Druz (1901), #62. PALMYRENE (132 A.D.): G. A. Cooke, A Text-Book of North Semitic Inscriptions (1903), #140, B.9 (p. 304). SAFAITIC: E. Littmann, Zur Entzifferung der Safa-Inschriften (1901), p. v.

2. KBo IV.iii, 35; KUB XIX.37.iii, 16; A. Goetze, Kleinasien[1] (1933), 136.

3. Iliad 3.381.

4. Iliad 18.205.

5. Iliad 21.549 (cf. 597).

6. Grimm-Stallybrass, TM 330.

▲   86   The passage through the Sea of Reeds

1. The narrative is held by modern scholars to be a compound of elements drawn from the Jehovistic (J), Elohistic (E), and Priestly (P) documents. The Jehovistic writer attempts to rationalize the miracle by the help of a "strong east wind" which drove the sea back and allowed the Israelites to cross the dry bed in safety (Exod. 14:21).

2. Josephus, Ant. ii.16, 5.

3. Plutarch, Alexander 17; cf. Appian, Civil Wars ii.149, where Alexander's passage through the sea is spoken of as if it were miraculous.

4. Arrian, Anabasis i.26.

5. Strabo, xiv.3, 9; Arrian, loc. cit.

6. Plutarch, Alexander 17.

7. Arrian, loc cit.

8. Polybius, x.9–15; Livy, xxvi.42–46; Appian, Hispan. 19–22.

[8a. See: E. Naville, in Journal of Transactions of the Victorian Institute, 26 (1893), 27–29; Tulloch, ib., 28 (1896), 267–68.]

9. Mgr. Lechaptois, Aux rives du Tanganika (Algiers 1913), 54.

10. A. Poupon, in L'Anthropologie, 26 (1915), 122.

87   The song at the Sea

1. J. A. McCulloch, The Childhood of Fiction (1905), 480 f.

2. E. Jacottet, Contes populaires des Basauttos (1895), p. ix.

3. A. R. Wallace, Narrative of Travels on the Amazon and the Rio Negro (1889), 64; R. E. Dennett, Notes on the Folklore of the Fjort.

4. J. Batchelor, The Ainu and Their Folklore (1901), 370; H. St. John, Life in the Forests of the Far East (1862), i.104.

5. Sixth Annual Report of the Bureau of Amer. Ethnology (1888), 409 f.

6. E. W. Lane, Manners and Customs of the Modern Egyptians, ch. xxi.

7. Joseph Jacobs, English Fairy Tales (1898), 247.

8. R. C. Temple, Legends of the Punjaub (n.d.), i.5.

9. On this myth, see: T. H. Gaster, Thespis[2], 85 ff.

10. Heb.: îš milḥāmah. So, in the Ugaritic poems, Baal is commonly styled aliyn, "Puissant," or aliy qrdm, "Puissant of warriors." The Babylonian Marduk is likewise called quradu, "warrior."

11. Marduk defeats Tiamat, and Baal defeats Yam (Sea), alias Nahar (Stream).

12. Enuma Elish ii.122 ff.; iii.59 ff., 115 ff.; iv.2 ff., 28.

13. Baal acquires "eternal kingship" (mlk 'lm), and Yam, after his defeat, seemingly declares "Let Baal be king!": III AB, A 8–10, 32.

14. Marduk builds Esagila in Babylon, or has it built for him by the gods: Enuma Elish vi.37–48. Baal builds a palace on Mt. Ṣapân (Casius): II AB, iv–v. Similarly, in Ps. 87:1, Zion is described as "the structure founded by Yahweh"; see below, §272.

15. Heb.: *har naḥ^alat^ekā;* Canaanite (Ugaritic): *ẓr nḥlty:* 'nt iv.64.

16. The same verb (*n-h-h*) is used of leading sheep in Pss. 23:3; 77:21; 78:53. Indeed, the metaphor is developed in the same context in Ps. 78:52–54 (where Heb. *g^ebūl* is the Arabic *jibl,* "mountain").

17. The same verb (*n-h-l*) is used in this sense in Isa. 40:11; 49:10; Ps. 23:2. So too is the cognate Arabic *nahāla.*

18. Heb.: *t^ebî'em.* The word carries this nuance in Arabic: see Lane, Lex. s.v. The same sense may be recognized also in Zeph. 3:20; Ps. 78:54, and possibly in Deut. 33:7 (cf. Gen. 49:22–24).

19. The Hebrew word is *naweh;* see: T. H. Gaster, in ET 47 (1936), 45.

87a Sweetening bitter waters

1. E. C. Brewer, Dictionary of Miracles, 239.

2. Pausanias, vii.38; cf. J. R. Smith, Springs and Wells in Greek and Roman Literature (1922), 3 f.

88 Manna—the "Bread of Angels"

1. Cf. F. S. Bodenheimer, in BA 10 (1947), 1–6; W. T. Pilter, in PSBA 39 (1917), 155–67, 187–206; M. J. Teesdale, in Science Gossip 3 (1897), 289–93.

2. Galen, On the Sustenance of Trees, vi.739 Kühn; Aelian, Hist. anim., cv.7; Pliny, HN xi.31.

3. Sn. 20.

4. J. Grimm, DM³, 659.

5. Theog. 581.

6. Historia anim. v.22, 4.

7. Columella, ix.14, ad fin.

8. Rig Veda i.112, 11.

9. Kalevala, runo xv.

10. W. H. Roscher, Nektar und Ambrosia (1883), 13–33.

11. Iliad 19.352; Odyssey 5.199; 9.359; Hesiod, Theog. 639, 796; Homeric Hymns, Hermes 248; Demeter 49; Aphrodite 231, etc.

12. Cf. Yalquṭ Shime'oni, §258.

13. Imram Curaig Maildiun, §16, ed. W. Stokes, in Rev. Celt. 9.447–95; 50–95.

▲ 89 The ox that gores

[1. Whatever be the date of its literary redaction, "it is now becoming a truism that the cultural background of the Book of the Covenant lies in the Bronze Age, not in the Iron; i.e., it must go back substantially to the Mosaic Age": W. F. Albright, in The Old Testament and Modern Study, ed. H. H. Rowley (1951), 39; see also: H. Cazelles, Études sur le Code de l'Alliance (1946).]

2. Gen. 9:5 ff.

3. J. Macrae, in Asiatic Records [Researches], 7 (1803), 189 ff.

4. T. J. Newbold, Political and Statistical Account of the British Settlement in the Straits of Malaca (1839), ii.257.

5. N. Adriani and A. C. Kuijt, De Bare'e-sprekende Toradja's van Midden-Celebes (1912–14), i.182.

6. Ib., ii.349 ff.

7. W. Munzinger, Sitten und Recht der Bogos (1859), 83.

8. E. Torday, Camp and Tramp in African Wilds (1913), 42.

9. A. Musil, Arabia Petraea, iii (1908), 368.

10. The Zend-Avesta, pt. i: The Vendidad, tr. J. Darmesteter, SBE iv.1880, 159 f.

11. Demosthenes, Contra Aristocratem, p. 654; Aeschines, Contra Ctesiph. 244; Aristotle, Constitution of Athens 57; Julius Pollux, Onomasticon viii.90, 120; Pausanias,

i.28, 10; vi.11, 6. Aristotle is the only author who mentions that *animals* were tried in the court of the Prytaneum.

12. Wasps, 835–1082.

13. Laws ix.12, 873D–874A.

14. Festus, De verborum significatione, p. 368 Müller.

15. Ib., 318, s.v. *sacrae leges;* Macrobius, Sat. iii.7; Dio. Hal. ii.74; G. Wissowa, Religion und Kultus der Römer² (1912), 388.

16. E. B. Tylor, Primitive Culture² (1873), i.372.—Another Irish saint, St. Yvorus, is said to have cursed and banished rats, and yet a third, St. Nannan, to have operated similarly on fleas: see Thos. Wright, ed., The Historical Works of Giraldus Cambrensis (1887), 95 ff.

17. H. H. Milman, History of Latin Christianity, iv (1905), 313, note p; "Procès contre les animaux," in La Tradition, 2, No. 12 (Dec. 15, 1888), 363, quoting St. Guillelm Abbas, Vita S. Bern., lib. x, cap. 12.

18. Mal. 3:7–12.

19. As to the trial of animals in ecclesiastical and civil courts in various parts of Europe, but particularly in France, cf. M. Delrio, Disquisitionum Magicarum libri sex (1624), lib. iii, pars ii, quaest. iv, sect. viii., pp. 460 ff.; Pierre le Brun, Histoire Critique des Pratiques Superstitieuses (1733–36), i.242 ff.; Berriat-Saint-Prix, in Mémoires et Dissertations publiées par la Société Royale des Antiquaires de France, 8 (1829), 303–50; Léon Ménabréa, in Mem. de la Soc. Royale Académique de Savoie, 12 (1846), 399–557; F. Nork, Die Sitten und Gebräuche der Deutschen und ihre Nachbarvölker (1849), 941 ff.; S. Baring-Gould, Curiosities of Olden Times (1869), 50–71; R. Chambers, The Book of Days (1886), i.126–29; E. Robert, in Bull. de l'Association Générale des Étudiants de Montpellier, i/6 (1888), 169–81; K. von Amira, in Mitt. d. Instituts für Oesterreichische Geschichtsforschung, 1891.545–601; E. Westermarck, Moral Ideas (1906–08), i.254 ff.; E. P. Evans, The Criminal Prosecution and Capital Punishment of Animals (1906), 1–192, 257–371. Canonists seem to differ as to the exact degree of damnation which the Church is empowered to hurl at these poor creatures. The celebrated case of the Archangel Michael *v.* the Devil is recorded in the Epistle of Jude, verse 9. That the best way of getting rid of caterpillars was to pay tithes was stated in so many words by the great French lawyer Barth. Cf. Chassenée (or Chasseneux) in his classical treatise on the subject, Consilium primum, quod Tractatus jure dici potest . . . ubi luculenter et accurate tractatur questio illa de excommunications animalium insectorum (1531).

20. Thos. Wright, Narratives of Sorcery and Magic (1851), ii.309.

21. R. Chambers, The Book of Days, i.129.

22. Benoit, Histoire de l'Edit de Nantes, v.754.

23. For varying interpretations of this law, see: Wm. Blackstone, Commentaries on the Laws of England¹⁸ (1829), i.299 ff.; E. B. Tylor, Primitive Culture² (1873), i.286 ff.

[23a. Cf. A. Van Selms, "The Goring Ox in Babylonian and Biblical Lore," in Archiv Orientální, 18 (1950), 321–30.]

[23b. Code of Eshnunna, §§53–57; tr. Goetze, ANET, 163ᵇ.]

[23c. Code of Hammurapi, §§250–52; tr. Meek, ANET, 176ᵇ.]

[23d. Cf. Exod. 19:13; Deut. 13:10; 17:5; 22:21, 24; Josh. 7:25; I Kings 21:10, 13; R. Hirzel, "Die Strafe der Steinigung," in ASG, phil.-hist. Kl. 27 (1909), 223–66.]

▲ 90 Not to seethe a kid in its mother's milk

1. Exod. 23:19 (E); 34:26 (J); Deut. 14:21.

2. Maimonides, Guide of the Perplexed, iii.48; W. R. Smith, The Religion of the Semites³ (1927), 221n. A good survey of traditional interpretations may be found in J. Spencer, De legibus Hebraeorum ritualibus (1686), i.270 ff., and in S. Bochart, Hierozoicon (1692), i.634 ff.

[2a. The Ugaritic Poem of the Gracious Gods, line 15; cf. T. H. Gaster, Thespis², 423. Meat stewed in milk is a favorite dish among the Arabs: Abraham ibn Ezra, Comm. on Exod. 23:19; J. Burckhardt, Bedouins and Wahabys (1831), 63; Mrs. E. A. Finn, Palestine Peasantry (1923), 71–72. It is to the preparation of such a dish for ritual purposes that the Canaanite text would seem to refer. The Biblical prohibition, however, is directed against the use of milk drawn from the animal's own dam, not against the practice in general.]

3. Quoted by Spencer, op. cit., i.271.

4. T. Winterbottom, An Account of the Native Africans in the Neighborhood of Sierra Leone (1803), 69 f.

5. E. Westermarck, The Moorish Conception of Holiness (1916), 144 f.

6. N. Adriani and A. C. Kruijt, De Bare'e-sprekende Toradja's van Midden-Celebes (1912–14), ii.209.

7. J. A. Grant, A Walk across Africa (1864), 89.

8. J. H. Speke, Journal of the Discovery of the Source of the Nile. Everyman's Library ed., 138.

9. J. Thomson, Through Masai Land (1885), 445; P. Reichard, Deutsch-Ostafrika (1892), 287 ff.—According to M. Merker, The Masai (1904), 32, unboiled milk is drunk by persons in health, boiled milk only by the sick.

10. J. Roscoe, The Baganda (1911), 418.

11. Id., The Northern Bantu (1915), 137.

12. H. A. Junod, The Life of a South African Tribe (1913), ii.51.

13. J. A. Meldon, in Journal of the African Society, No. 22 (Jan. 1907), 142.

14. C. G. Seligmann, "Some Aspects of the Hamitic Problem in the Anglo-Egyptian Sudan," in JRAI 43 (1913), 665.

15. A. C. Hollis, The Nandi (1909), 24.

16. Private information from J. Roscoe, who had personal contact with all three tribes.

17. Seligmann, loc. cit. However, the prohibition is not universal among pastoral tribes. Thus, among the Wa-taturu of E. Africa, who used to live mainly on fish and milk, the boiling of milk was quite common: O. Baumann, Durch Massailand zur Nilquelle (1894), 171. Similarly, it is quite usual among the bedouins of Arabia and Moab to boil meat in milk: C. M. Doughty, Arabia Deserta (1888), ii.671 A. Jaussen, Coutumes des Arabes au pays de Moab (1908), 68.

18. F. J. Wiedemann, Aus dem inneren and äusseren Leben der Ehsten (1876), 480.

19. W. H. Dall, in The American Naturalist, 12 (1878), 4.

20. Seligmann, op. cit., 655. Among the tribes which observe the prohibition are the Dinkas of the White Nile: ib., 656.

21. J. Roscoe, The Northern Bantu, 42.

22. Ib., 67.

23. Ib., 109, 122.

24. Ib., 126.

25. Id., The Baganda, 419.

26. J. Macdonald, Light in Africa² (1890), 221. See also: L. Alberti, De Kaffers aan de Zuidkust van Afrika (1810), 102 ff.; Col. Maclean, Compendium of Kafir Laws and Customs (1866), 91, 122.

27. Alberti, op. cit., 78 ff.; H. Lichtenstein, Reisen im südlichen Africa (1811–12), i.428; G. Thompson, Travels and Adventures in Southern Africa (1827), ii.354; Warner's notes in Maclean, op. cit., 98; G. McCall Theal, Kaffir Folk-lore (1886), 218; D. Kidd, The Essential Kafir (1904), 209.

28. H. A. Junod, in Rev. d'Ethnographie et de Sociologie, 1 (1910), 139; id., Life of a South African Tribe, ii.51.

29. Brownlee's note, in Maclean, op. cit., 122.

30. Kidd, op. cit., 238 ff.; Warner, op. cit., 93.

31. L. K. Anantha Krishna Iyer, The Cochin Tribes and Castes (1902–12), i.203.

32. Private communication from J. Roscoe.

33. N. Isaacs, Travels and Adventures in Eastern Africa (1836), i.203–5; Kidd, op. cit., 309 ff.

34. A. C. Hollis, *op. cit.*, 24, n.l.

35. R. Moffat, Missionary Labours and Scenes in Southern Africa (1842), 465.

36. Frazer-Gaster, NGB §167.

37. Junod, op. cit., i.51, 190; ii.51.

38. Roscoe, The Northern Bantu, 67.

39. Hollis, op. cit., 68.

40. C. W. Hobley, Eastern Uganda (1902), 39 ff.

41. M. W. H. Beech, The Suk, Their Language and Folklore (1911), 22.

42. J. G. Frazer, Totemism and Exogamy (1910), ii.521, n.3.

43. J. L. Burckhardt, op. cit., i.280 ff.

44. Seligmann, op. cit., 656.

45. Roscoe, The Northern Bantu, 59.

46. Hollis, op. cit., 70.

47. J. M. Hildebrandt, in Zs. für Ethnologie, 10 (1878), 404 ff.

48. A. F. Gardiner, Narrative of a Journey to the Zoolu Country in South Africa (1836), 81.

49. Kidd, op. cit., 249 (cf. 246).

50. Alberti, op. cit., 102 ff.

51. W. H. R. Rivers, The Todas (1906), 241.

52. R. E. Enthoven, in The Indian Antiquary, 44 (1915), Suppl. 69.

53. Hildebrandt, op. cit., 401.

54. "Folk-lore in the Old Testament," in Anthropological Essays presented to Edward Burnett Tylor (1907), 162.

55. C. W. Hobley, Ethnology of A-Kamba and Other East African Tribes (1910), 166; C. Dundas, in JRAI 43 (1913), 501; 45 (1915), 274.

56. C. W. Hobley, in JRAI 41 (1911), 412.

57. H. R. Tate, in JRAI 34 (1904), 261.

58. Rivers, op. cit., 236; F. Metz, The Tribes Inhabiting the Neilgherry Hills (Mangalore 1864), 20; W. E. Marshall, Travels amongst the Todas (1873), 137; J. W. Breeks, An Account of the Primitive Tribes and Monuments of the Nilagiris (1873), 14.

59. J. Shooter, The Kafirs of Natal and the Zulu Country (1857), 28.

60. E. Casalis, The Basutos (1861), 145.

61. H. Tönjes, Ovamboland (1911), 60 ff.

62. Roscoe, The Baganda, 418.

63. H. R. Tate, in JRAI 34 (1904), 259.

64. J. Campbell, Travels in South Africa: Second Journey (1822), ii.202.

65. E. Thurston, Castes and Tribes of Southern India (1909), i.88 ff.

66. F. Galton, Narrative of an Explorer in Tropical South Africa[2] (1890), 85; F. Fleming, Southern Africa (1856), 218 ff.; id., Kaffraria and Its Inhabitants (1853), 108 ff.; Alberti, op. cit., 36; Casalis, op. cit., 145; Kidd, op. cit., 59; F. Speckmann, Die Hermannsburger Mission in Afrika (Hermannsburg 1876), 107 ff.; E. Dannert, in South African Folklore Journal, 2 (1800), 63; H. H. Johnston, British Central Africa (1897), 431; H. R. Tate, in JRAI 34 (1904), 259.

67. J. A. Meldon, in Journal of the African Society, No. 22 (January 1907), 142.

68. Roscoe, The Northern Bantu, 108.

69. W. E. Marshall, op. cit., 145.—On the other hand, it is said that the village dairy-

man, who does not rank with the most holy dairyman (*palaul, palel*), is not allowed to taste milk during his period of office, but may help himself to as much clarified butter (ghee) as he likes: F. Metz, op. cit., 37.

70. When the Wa-Yamwesi are about to convert milk into butter, they mix it with the urine of cows or of human beings. The reason they gave to Stuhlmann was that it made the butter more saleable, but he believed, probably with justice, that the real motive was a fear that the cows would otherwise lose their milk: F. Stuhlmann, Mit Emin Pascha ins Herz von Afrika (1894), 78 ff.

71. M. Merker, Die Masai (1904), 33; M. Weiss, Die Völker-Stämme in Norden Deutsch-Ostafrikas (1910), 380; P. Reichard, Deutsch-Ostafrika (1892), 288.

72. Weiss, op. cit., 46; id., in Globus 91 (1907), 157.

73. "Dr. Fischer's Journey in the Masai Country," in Proc. Royal Geographical Society, New Monthly Series, 6 (1884), 80.

74. J. Thompson, op. cit., 429–31; H. H. Johnston, in JAI 15 (1886), 15; Reichard, op. cit., 287 ff.; O. Baumann, op. cit., 161 ff.; Merker, op. cit., 33; Weiss, op. cit., 380. Baumann and Merker give a rationalistic explanation of the rule not to eat boiled flesh and milk on the same day. They say that the Masai always cook flesh with the seasoning of a certain acacia bark called *mokota* (*Albizzia anthelmintica*), which, taken with milk, causes severe diarrhea or dysentery, and that the observation of this effect is the reason why the Masai do not partake of flesh and milk together. But that this is not the true explanation of the custom is strongly suggested by (1) Merker's own statements, on the same page, that the Masai "avoid more carefully bringing milk into contact with flesh, because according to the universal opinion the udder of the cow which yielded the milk would thereby be rendered permanently diseased," and that "if a man has eaten boiled flesh one day, he drinks some blood next morning before drinking milk, not on considerations of health, but because he believes that were this custom not observed the cattle would give less milk"; (2) the fact that the same rule is observed by other tribes who are not said to use the *mokota* bark, and with regard to some of whom (the Banyoro, Bahima, and Washamba) it is expressly affirmed that they believe the mixture of meat and milk in the stomach to be injurious to the cattle. Hence we may confidently conclude that the same belief is the motive of the same custom with the Masai and with all the other pastoral tribes of Africa who observe the rule.

75. A. Krasek, in Baesler Archiv, 3 (1913), 102.

76. Roscoe, The Northern Bantu, 108.

77. Ib., 64, 67, 71.

78. Hollis, op. cit., 24.

79. Beech, op. cit., 9.

80. J. Buxtorf, Synagoga Judaica (1661), 594–96.

81. Meldon, loc. cit.

82. Roscoe, The Northern Bantu, 70 ff.

83. Id., The Baganda, 418.

84. Beech, op. cit., 9.

▲   91   The golden bells

1. J. Wellhausen, Reste d. arab. Heidentums[2] (1887), 144; A. Jirku, Die Dämonen und ihre Abwehr im AT (1912), 85.

2. On the folklore of bells, see: P. Sartori, in Zs. f. Vlk. 7 (1897), 113–29, 270–86, 358–69; 8 (1898), 29–38; G. S. Tyack, A Book about Bells (1898), 170 ff. For beliefs in Classical antiquity, cf. A. B. Cook, in JHS 22 (1902), 5–28.

3. Lucian, Philopseud. 15.

4. Ovid, Fasti v.419–44.

5. Scholiast on Lycophron, 77.

6. Jean Baptiste Thiers, Traités des Cloches (1721), 145.

7. Ib., 44.

8. G. Durandus, Rationale Divinorum Officiorum, lib. i, cap. 4. 14 ff. (i.21, ed. Leyden, 1584).

9. According to the poet, Grose's valuable collection of antiquities included a cinder of Eve's first fire, Tubalcain's fire-shovel and fender, a part of the anatomy of Balaam's ass, and a brass-shod broomstick used by the witch of Endor! See the verses, On the late Captain Grose's Peregrinations thro' Scotland.

10. F. Grose, A Provincial Glossary, with a Collection of Local Proverbs and Popular Superstitions[2] (1811), 297 ff. Longfellow has introduced this picturesque superstition into his version of The Golden Legend.

11. Brand-Ellis, Popular Antiquities of Great Britain (1882–83), ii.202 ff.; Tyack, op. cit., 191 ff.

12. Ed. London 1836, p. 153.

13. Brand-Ellis, op. cit., 206.

14. R. Nelson, A Companion to the Festivals and Fasts of the Church of England (1732), 144.

15. J. H. Schmitz, Sitten und Bräuche, Lieder, Sprüchwörter und Räthsel des Eiflen Volkes (1856–58), i.65.

16. T. Vernaleken, Mythen und Bräuche des Volkes in Oesterreich (1859), 311.

17. C. L. Rochholz, Deutscher Glaube und Brauch (1867), i.179.

18. Thiers, op. cit., 269.

19. A. Birlinger, Volksthümliches aus Schwaben (1861–62), i.278, §437.

20. Frazer-Gaster, NGB, §451.

21. Il Penseroso 83 ff.

22. R. Chambers, The Book of Days (1886), i.496 ff.

23. Robert Herrick, Works (Edinburgh 1823), i.169.

24. T. Naogeorgus, The Popish Kingdom, Englished by Barnabe Googe, ed. R. C. Hope (1880), 41 ff.

25. H. Pfannenschmid, Germanische Erntefeste (1878), 90 f.; 394 f., 396 f.; W. Mannhardt, Die Götterwelt der deutschen und nordischen Völker, i (1860), 93; U. Jahn, Die deutschen Opfergebräuche bei Ackerbau und Viehzucht (1884), 56 ff.

26. A. Kuhn and W. Schwartz, Norddeutsche Sagen, Märchen und Gebräuche (1848), 454.

27. E. Meier, Deutsche Sagen, Sitten und Gebräuche aus Schwaben (1852), 260 ff.

28. Birlinger, op. cit., ii.443. Cf. also: F. Panzer, Beitrag zur Deutschen Mythologie (1848–55), ii.184, 417.

29. Pfannenschmid, op. cit., 609; Jahn, op. cit., 57.

30. C. Meyer, Der Aberglaube des Mittelalters und der nächtsfolgenden Jahrhunderte (1884), 186 ff.; H. B. Walters, Church Bells of England (1912), 256 ff.

31. Meyer, op. cit., 185 ff.; Pfannenschmid, op. cit., 395.

32. Quoted by Brand-Ellis, op. cit., ii.215.

33. M. Delrio, Disquisitionum Magicarum libri sex (1624), 1021–24.

34. Francis Bacon, "Natural History, " cent. ii.127.

35. J. Aubrey, Remaines of Gentilisme and Judaisme, ed. J. Britten (1881), 22, 96.

36. Walters, op. cit., 262. Cf. also: G. Juan and A. de Ullva, Voyage to South Africa[5] (1807), i.341–43.

37. A. L. Kitching, On the Backwaters of the Nile (1912), 264 ff.

38. J. Doolittle, Social Life of the Chinese (1868), 114.

39. J. Chalmers and W. W. Gill, Work and Adventure in New Guinea (1885), 259 ff.

40. J. G. Bourke, The Snake-dance of the Moquis of Arizona (1884), 258 ff.

41. J. J. M. de Groot, The Religious System of China, vi (1910), 945.

42. Ib., 981–86.

43. E. Diguet, Les Annamites (1906), 280.

44. Shway Yoe (G. George Scott), The Burman, His Life and Notions (1882), i.241 ff.; cf. A. Batian, Die Voelker des Oestlichen Asien (1866–71), ii.33, 105 ff.

45. Krick, in Annales de la Propagation de la Foi, 24 (1854), 86–88.

46. B. H. Hodgson, Miscellaneous Essays relating to Indian Subjects (1880), i.402.

47. Herodotus, vi.58.

48. C. W. Hobley, Eastern Uganda (1902), 17.

49. M. T. H. Perelaer, Ethnographische Beschrijving der Dajaks (Zalt-Bommel 1870), 220 ff.

50. F. Hatton, North Borneo (1885), 162 ff.

51. Ivor Evans, in JRAI 42 (1912), 382–84.

52. W. Crooke, Popular Religion and Folk-lore of Northern India (1896), i.168.

53. N. B. Dennys, The Folk-lore of China (1876), 55.

54. F. T. Elworthy, The Evil Eye (1895), 356–58, 368.

55. W. B. Heard, in JRAI 41 (1911), 214.

56. E. Thurston, Castes and Tribes of Southern India (1909), i.98 ff.

57. Father Baudin, in Les Missions Catholiques, 16 (1884), 249; P. Bouche, La cote des esclaves et le Dahomey (1885), 215 ff.; A. B. Ellis, The Yoruba-speaking Peoples of the Slave Coast of West Africa (1894), 112 ff.

58. J. Roscoe, The Baganda (1911), 444; id., The Northern Bantu (1915), 46.

59. Roscoe, The Baganda, 65.

60. W. Munzinger, Sitten und Recht der Bogos (1859), 37.

61. R. V. Russell, Tribes and Castes of the Central Provinces of India (1916), iii.88.

62. Callimachus, Hymns i.52–55; Apollodorus, Bib. I.i.7; Hyginus, fab. 139.—The legend was a favorite subject of ancient artists: J. Overbeck, Griechische Kunstmythologie, i (1871), 328, 331, 335–37.

63. F. Gardner, in JAF 19 (1906), 192 ff. This account is translated from Father Tomas Ortiz' La Practica del Minesterio (Manila 1713), of which only one copy is known.—The *bolo* is a broad-bladed knife or sword; and the spirit *patianak*, whom the priest calls a goblin or devil, is probably the ghost of a woman who has died in childbirth, for such ghosts are called by similar names in the East Indies: G. A. Wilken, De verspreide Geschriften (1912), iii.222–30; A. C. Kruijt, Het Animisme in den Indischen Archipel (1906), 245–51.

64. F. Blumentritt, in Mitt. der Wiener geograph. Gesellschaft, 1882.178; cf. J. Mallat, Les Philippines (1846), 65.

65. J. G. Scott and J. P. Hardiman, Gazetteer of Upper Burma and the Shan States (1900–1901), I, i.339.

66. P. S. Pallas, Reise durch verschiedene Provinzen des Russischen Reichs (1771–76), i.360; J. G. Georgi, Beschreibung alter Nationen des Russischen Reichs (1776), 412.

67. "Relation du Sieur Ferrand, Médecin du Kan des Tartares, touchant la Krime'e, les Tartares Nogäis, etc.," in Recueil de Voyages au Nord[2] (1731–78), iv.524.

68. "Het leenvorstendom Boni," in TITLV 15 (1865), 40, 117.—The instruments called *pabongka setangs* appear to be a sort of cymbals.

69. J. G. F. Riedel, De sluik- en kroesharige rassen tusschen Celebes en Papua (1886), 265.

70. Father Guillené, in Annales de la Propagation de la Foi, 60 (1880), 252.

71. A. A. Perera, in The Indian Antiquary, 31 (1902), 379.

72. Augustine, De civitate Dei, vi.9 (probably from Varro, who is named repeatedly throughout the chapter).

73. R. V. Russell, op. cit., iv.527.

74. A. C. Hollis, The Nandi (1909), 58 ff., 88; C. W. Hobley, in JRAI 33 (1903), 351 f.

75. Notes analytiques sur les collections ethnographiques du Musée du Congo, i. Les arts, religions (Brussels 1902–6), 164.

76. Ib., 161.

77. P. E. Hurtel, in Anthropos, 6 (1911), 74.

78. J. Macdonald, Religion and Myth (1893), 106.—On such periodic expulsions of demons in West Africa, see further: Frazer-Gaster, NGB §§444 ff.

79. J. Roscoe, The Northern Bantu, 90.—For further evidence of the use of bells by African priests or medicine men, see: J. H. Speke, Journal of the Discovery of the Source of the Nile, Everyman's Library ed., 419 ff.; Notes analytiques (as cited, n.75), 1888.300; A. Bastian, Die deutsche Expedition an der Loango-Küste (1874), i.46; P. B. du Chaillu, Explorations and Adventures in Equatorial Africa (1861), 253 ff.; P. A. Talbot, In the Shadow of the Bush (1912), 328; E. Perregaux, Chez les Achanti (1906), 269.

NUMBERS

▲   92   The poison ordeal

1. The text is composite; for the details, cf. G. B. Gray, ICC Numbers (1903), 49 f.

2. For examples, cf. E. B. Tylor's article, "Ordeal," in Encyc. Brit.[9]; C. J. Leendirtz, in Tijdschrift van het Kon. Nederlandsch Aarijkskundig Genootscchap, II Ser., V (1888), 1–29, 315–38.

[2a. G. R. Driver, in Syria 33 (1956), 73–77.]

3. See in general: A. H. Post, Afrikanische Jurisprudenz (1887), ii.110 ff.

4. L. J. B. Bérenger-Féraud, Les peuplades de la Sénégambie (1879), 299–306.

5. Ib., 239–99.

6. Ib., 273–78.

7. R. Caillié, Travels through Central Africa to Timbuctoo (1830), i.156 ff.

8. L. Tauxier, Le Noir du Soudan (1912), 580 ff.

9. Ib., 229 ff.

10. Ib., 292.

11. Ib., 375.

12. Ib., 376.

13. H. H. Johnston, Liberia (1906), ii.1064–70.

14. Gouvernment Général de l'Afrique Occidentale Française. Notices publiées par le Gouvernment Général à l'occasion de l'Exposition Coloniale de Marseille: la Cote d'Ivoire (Corbeil, S.-et-.0, 1906), 570–72.—The use of the poison ordeal at Great Bassam on the Ivory Coast is mentioned by H. Hecquard, Reise an die Küste und in das Innere von West-Afrika (1854), 48.

15. A. B. Ellis, The Tshi-speaking Peoples of the Gold Coast of West Africa (1887), 198 ff., 201; E. Perregaux, Chez les Ashanti (1906), 150; B. Cruickshank, Eighteen Years on the Gold Coast of Africa (1853), i.2871; ii.187.

16. Lt. Herold, in Mitt. von Forschungreisenden und Gelehrten aus den deutschen Schutzgebieten, v (1892).

17. A. B. Ellis, The Yoruba-speaking Peoples of the Slave Coast of West Africa (1894), 190 ff.; id., The Ewe-speaking Peoples (1890), 97; P. Bouche, La Cote des Esclaves et le Dahomey (1885), 174–76.

18. H. Ling Roth, Great Benin (1903), 88 ff.

19. H. Goldie, Calabar and Its Mission[2] (1901), 34 ff.

20. A. J. N. Tremearne, The Tailed Head-hunters of Nigeria (1912), 200 ff.

21. A. Mansfield, Urwald-Dokumente, Vier Jahre unter den Cross-flussnegern Kameruns (1908), 178 ff.; B. Schwarz, Kamerun (1866), 175.

22. A. Poupon, in L'Anthropologie, 26 (1915), 113, 130, 133.

23. The name of this people is variously spelled Fan, Fang, Pahouin, M'Pongos, Mpongwes and Pangwes.

24. J. L. Wilson, Western Africa (1856), 398 ff.

25. "The Strange Adventures of Andree Battel," in John Pinkerton's Collection of Voyages and Travels (1808–14), xvi.334.—The town of Longo is no doubt Loango, capital of the province of that name.

26. Notes analytiques sur les collections ethnographiques du Musée du Congo, I (1902–06), 188–93.

27. J. Halkin, Quelques peuplades du district de l'uelé, I. Introduction: les Ababua (1907), 95 ff.

28. G. Casati, Ten Years in Equatoria (1891), i.164.

29. E. Torday and T. A. Joyce, in JRAI 35 (1905), 416 ff.

30. Id., in JRAI 36 (1906), 48 ff., 291.

31. Id., Notes ethnographiques sur les peuples communément appelés Bakaba, etc. (1910), 78 ff.

32. "Mittheilungen aus Dr. Paul Pogge's Tagebücher," in Mitt. d. Afrik. Gesell. in Deutschland, 4 (1883–85), 258.

33. H. Wissmann, L. Wolf, C. von François and H. Mueller, Im Inneren Afrikas, Die Erforschung des Kassai (1888), 143 ff.

34. P. Pogge, Im Reiche des Muata Jamwo (1880), 36 ff.; L. Nagyar, Reisen in Südafrika, i (1859), 119, 123, 136; F. Travassos Valder, Six Years of a Traveller's Life in Western Africa (1861), ii.128 ff.

35. J. Irle, Die Herero (1906), 141.

36. "Mr. Farewell's Account of Chaka, the King of Natal," appended to W. F. W. Owen's Narrative of Voyages to explore the Shores of Africa, Arabia and Madagascar (1833), iii.398–400; D. Kidd, The Essential Kafir (1904), 185.

37. E. Gottschling, in JRAI 35 (1905), 375, 377 ff.

38. R. C. F. Maugham, Portuguese East Africa (1906), 276–78.

39. Kidd, op. cit., 185 ff.

40. Alice Werner, The Native Tribes of British Central Africa (1906), 90, 160 ff., 174.

41. Ib., 90, 170 ff., 263 ff.; D. Macdonald, Africana (1882), i.45, 159 ff., 200, 204 ff.; H. H. Johnston, British Central Africa (1897), 441, 468.

42. A. Hamburger, in Anthropos 4 (1909), 315.

43. F. Stuhlmann, Mit Emin Pascha ins Herz von Afrika (1894), 93.

44. H. Claus, Die Wagogo (1911), 55 ff.

45. E. Nigmann, Die Wahehe (1908), 71 ff. See also: O. Dempwolff, in Baessler-Archiv, 4 (1913), 109.

46. C. New, Life, Wanderings and Labours in Eastern Africa (1883), 111 ff.

47. K. R. Dundas, in JRAI 43 (1913), 42.

48. M. A. Condon, in Anthropos 6 (1911), 382.

49. J. Roscoe, The Baganda (1911), 341.

50. Id., The Northern Bantu (1915), 23 ff.

51. Stuhlmann, op. cit., 377, 394.

52. W. Ellis, History of Madagascar (1838), i.458–87; J. Sibree, The Great African

Island (1889), 281–83; E. Perrot and E. Vogt, Poisons des flèches et poisons d'épreuve (1913), 142 ff.

53. Ellis, op. cit., i.463–72, 477–79. (The long formula of adjuration has here been abridged.)

54. Ib., i.479 ff.

55. On the general suject of ordeals in India, see: A. I. Kuhn, in Asiatick Researches, i⁵ (1806), 389–404; J. A. Dubois, Moeurs, Institutions et Cérémonies des Peuples de l'Inde (1825), ii.546–54; A. F. Stenzler, in ZDMG 9 (1855), 661–82; E. Schlagintweit, Die Gottesurtheile der Inder (1866); G. Bühler, in Journal of the Asiatic Society of Bengal, 351 (1867), 14–49; J. Jolly, Recht und Sitte (1896), 144–46; E. Thurston, Ethnographic Studies in Southern India (1906), 421 ff.

56. A. A. Macdonell, in The Imperial Gazetteer of India: The Indian Empire (1909), ii.262.

57. The Institutes of Vishnu, tr. J. Jolly, SBE vii (1880), chs. ix–xiv, pp. 52–61.

58. Ib., ch. 13, p. 60.

59. Ib., ch. ix. 27–28, p. 55.

60. Ib., ch. xiv, pp. 60 ff.

61. Bühler, op. cit. (n.56), 42 ff.

62. Ib., 43.

63. Stenzler, op. cit., 675.

64. Ib., 674 f.; Schlagintweit, op. cit., 30.

65. Bühler, op. cit., 43.

66. Ib.; Schlagintweit, op. cit., 29.

67. Dubois, op. cit. (n.56), ii.554.—The Arab geographer and scholar Albiruni (c. A.D. 1030) gives an account of ordeals in India, but his description of the poison ordeal is slight and vague: E. Sachau, Alberuni's India (1880), ii.159 ff.

68. Stenzler, op. cit., 29.

69. Schlagintweit, op. cit., 29, n.43; L. A. Waddell, in JRAI 24 (1895), 57; Perror and Vogt, op. cit., 167 ff.

70. L. J. B. Bérenger-Ferand, Les peuplades de la Sénégambie (1879), 69; L. A. Waddell, The Buddhism of Tibet (1895), 401, n.2.

71. A. Leared, Morocco and the Moors (1876), 272.

72. E. Doutté, Magie et Religion dans l'Afrique du Nord (1908), 109.

73. E. W. Lane, Manners and Customs of the Modern Egyptians (1895), 263.

74. G. Grandidier, in L'Anthropologie 23 (1912), 321.

75. L. A. Waddell, The Buddhism of Tibet (1895), 401.

76. J. F. Davis, The Chinese (1845), ii.215.

77. E. Diguet, Les Annamites (1906), 282.

78. A. Bastian, Der Mensch in der Geschichte (1860), ii.211.

93   Leprosy as punishment

1. See: G. N. Münch, Die Zaraath der hebräischen Bibel (1893); R. G. Cochrane, in BT 12 (1961), 202 f.; K. P. Gramberg, ib., (1960), 10–23; J. L. Swellengrebel, ib., 69–80; D. H. Wallington, ib., 12 (1961), 75–79; J. Preuss, Bibl.-Talmudische Medizin (1911), 469 ff.

2. Aelian HA x.6; Plutarch, De Is. et Os. 8.

3. Herodotus, ii.47; Plutarch, Aelian, locc. cit.; Josephus, Contra Apionem ii.13. But see also W. R. Dawson, in JRAS 1928.597–608, who shows that the attitude of the Egyptians toward the pig was ambivalent.

4. J. C. Lawson, Modern Greek Folklore (1910), 87.

5. J. G. F. Riedel, De sluik- en kroesharige Rassen tusschen Selebes en Papua (1886), 432, 452.

6. H. Cole, in JRAI 32 (1902), 307.

7. R. S. Rattray, Some Folk-Stories and Songs in Chinyanja (1907), 174 ff.

8. A. C. Fletcher and F. la Flesche, in 28th Annual Report of the Bureau of American Ethnology (1911), 144.

9. J. Crevaux, Voyages dans l'Amérique du Sud (1883), 59.

10. Central Provinces of India Ethnographic Survey, II: Articles on Uriya Castes (Allahabad 1907), 16.

11. Aeschylus, Choephoroe 288 f.; cf. Lawson, op. cit., 453 f.

12. E. S. McCartney, in Papers of the Michigan Academy of Science, Arts and Letters 16 (1931), 144 f.

13. Theocritus, Id. ix.30 (cf. xii.24).

14. Horace, Odes ii.8, 1 ff.

15. Ovid, Amores iii.3, 1 f.

16. A. Lang, Theocritus, Bion and Moschus (1896), 53n.

17. M. Gaster, The Exempla of the Rabbis (1924), #313 (parallels, p. 237). The motif (C 941.1 in Stith Thompson's Index) appears also in Irish hagiography: C. Plummer, Vitae Sanctorum Hiberniae, i (1910), cliii.

18. Cf. Jer. 13:23: "Can the Ethiopian change his skin, or the leopard his spots?"

95 The Blossoming Rod

1. Cf. Barry, "The Blossoming Rod," in The Open Court, 31 (1917), 26–53; A. S. Pease, on Cicero, De Divinatione, i.30 (p. 229); G. C. Rawlinson, on Herodotus, iv.67–68; O. Dähnhart, Natursagen, ii.265 ff.; P. Saintyves, Essais de folklore biblique (1922), 61 ff.

2. Pausanias, ii.31.

3. Abbé Mazelin, Saints de la Haute Matne, quoted by E. C. Brewer, Dictionary of Miracles (1884), 53.

4. Morlezum, Histoire de Gascogne, quoted by Brewer, loc. cit.

5. Brewer, loc. cit.

6. Stith Thompson, MI, F 971.1; Bolte-Polivka, iii.471, n.1; Revue des traditions populaires, ix.65, 336, 532; xxi.123; xxii.289; xxviii.63 ("Le baton qui reverdit"); P. Toldo, Studien zur vergl. Literaturgeschichte viii.49–56; Zeitschrift für Volkskunde, x.196 f.; xiii.72; xv.393; A. Andrejev, in FFC 54.34; 62.126; 129 ff., 241 ff.

96 The Covenant of Salt

1. W. Robertson Smith, The Religion of the Semites[3] (1927), 270; R. Kraetschmar, Bundesvorstellung (1896), 206 f.; J. Wellhausen, Reste d. arabischen Heidentums[2] (1897), 124, 189; Trumbull, The Covenant of Salt (1899).

2. R. F. Burton, Pilgrimage to El-Medinah and Mecca (1857), iii.84.

3. I. Benzinger, in JE, s.v. Salt.

4. Sanchuniathon, quoted by Eusebius, Praep. Evangelica, i.10.

97 The Song at the Well

1. According to Karl Budde, the immediately following words, *And from the desert to Mattanah,* usually taken to continue the itinerary of the Israelites, are really part of the song and should be rendered, *Out of the desert—a gift* (Heb.: mattanah)!

2. See G. B. Gray, ICC Numbers, in loc.; G. A. Smith, The Early Poetry of Israel (1927), 63 f.; J. A. Montgomery, Arabia and the Bible (1934), 7.

3. On such *welis,* see: T. Canaan, in JPOS 1 (1921), 155 ff.; id., Dämonenglaube im Lande der Bibel (1929), 30 ff.

4. Migne, PG 79, col. 648. For examples of such songs, see: R. Nicholson, Literary History of the Arabs (1930), 73; A. Musil, Arabia Petraea (1908), iii.255 f.

5. Qazwini, i.189.

6. ZDPV 10.180.

7. Musil, op. cit., i.298.

8. J. Tod, Annals of Rajasthan[2] (1920), ii.1228; E. Thurston, Castes and Tribes of Southern India (1909), i.280; W. Crooke, in ERE xii.716[a].

9. For a convenient account of this role among African peoples, see: J. A. Hadfield, Traits of Divine Kingship in Africa (1949), 17 ff.

10. KBo III.7; cf. T. H. Gaster, Thespis[2], 261 f.

11. "The Kubban Stele," in Breasted, AR iii. §292; cf. S. A. Cook, in W. Robertson Smith, The Religion of the Semites[3] (1927), 559.

12. D. Crantz, History of Greenland (1767), 267; E. B. Tylor, Primitive Culture, ii.296.

98 Balaam

1. See fully: E. Crawley, Oath, Curse and Blessing (1934, reprinted from ERE, s.v.). —The Irish say that a curse can blister, and we still speak of "blistering" invective.

(a) Professional cursing

2. J. S. Polack, Manners and Customs of the New Zealanders (1840), i.248 f.

3. W. C. Harris, The Highlands of Aethiopia (1844), iii.50.

4. H. Zimmern, Beitraege zur Kenntniss der bab. Religion (1901), 172, #57; R. Labat, Le caractère religieux de la royauté assyro-babylonienne (1939), 258 f.; H. Frankfort, Kingship and the Gods (1948), 263.

5. Josephus, Ant. xiv.2, 1.

6. G. A. Smith, The Early Poetry of Israel (1927), 37.

(b) Augur consulted before battle

7. J. Wellhausen, Reste des arab. Heidentums[2] (1897), 130; I Goldziher, Abhandlungen (1896–99), i.26 ff.; G. Jacob, Das Leben der vorislamischen Beduinen (1895), 127.—Qazwini (ii.408) describes this officer as "one whose words bring blessing or curse": G. Jacob, Altarabsche Parallelen zum AT (1897), 12.

8. C. F. Jean, ARM i.22; tr. W. F. Albright, in ANET 482.

9. (By stars:) E. F. Weidner, in AfK 1 (1923), 1–12, 59–69; (by birds:) KBo III.16, ii.8e, 16–17; A. Goetze, Madduwatas (1928), 113; G. Furlani, Rel. d. Hittiti (1936), 160.

10. Cf. Iliad 2.299 ff.

11. I Kings 22:5.

12. II Kings 6:36 ff.

13. E. Hull, Folklore of the British Isles (1928), 176.

14. J. Burckardt, Bedouins and Wahabys (1831), 239.

15. The standard works on this subject, so far as Mesopotamia is concerned, are: J. A. Craig, Astrological-astronomical Texts . . . (1899); C. Virolleaud, L'astrologie chaldéenne (1909–12); R. C. Thompson, The Reports of the Magicians and Astrologers of Nineveh and Babylon (1900); C. Bezold, in Sitz. Heidelberg, Akad. Wiss., 1911/ii.

(c) Balaam as a typical soothsayer

16. See especially: S. Daiches, "Balaam—a Babylonian barū," in Hilprecht Anniversary Volume (1909), 60–70; R. de Largement, "Les oracles de Biléam et la mantique suméro-akkadienne," in Memorial du Cinquantennaire de l'École des langues orientales anciennes de l'Institute Catholique de Paris (1964), 35–51.

17. Cicero, De divinatione ii.35; Livy, i.18.

18. Cicero, De div. ii.35; Livy, viii.23 (media nocte); ix.38; xxxiv.14; Lucan, i.601; v.395; Aulus Gellius, iii.2 (post mediam noctem).

19. Quoted by Eusebius, Praep. evang. i.6.—The word ṣ-ph-', in the sense of "sooth-sayer, scryer," seems indeed to occur in a Phoenician inscription: M. Lidzbarski, Handbuch d. nordsem. Epigraphik (1898), 359.

20. E.g., R. F. Harper, Babylonian Letters (1902), ##423, obv. 13; 591, obv. 9; 671, rev. 1; 817, obv. 2; 829, rev. 2; 1157.7 (maṣṣarta nitaṣar).

21. The Masoretic text reads maṣôr, which would mean "entrenchment." Parallelism (mišmartî) and the Habakkuk Commentary from Qumran justify the reading, maṣṣôrî.

22. On seven in magic and ritual, see: J. H. Graf, Die Zahl Sieben (1917); F. von Andrian, "Die Siebenzahl im Geistesleben der Voelker," in Mitt. der anthropol. Gesell. in Wien 31 (1901), 225–74; H. Webster, Rest Days (1916), 208 ff.; O. Gruppe, in Bursians Jahresbericht 186.281 f.; S. Eitrem, Papyri Osloenses, i (1925), 61; B. Celada, "Numeros sagrados derivados del sietis," in Sefarad 10 (1950), 3–23; K. Sethe, Von Zahlen und Zahlworter bei den alten Aegyptern (1916), 33.

23. J. Bell, MS. on Witchcraft (1705), p. 48, quoted by Brand-Ellis, Popular Antiquities of Great Britain (1882–83), iii.266.

24. Pap. London, LXXI.1265.

25. F. Griffith and F. Thompson, Demotic Papyrus (1904), col. ii.15, 27; iii.5 ff.

26. TB Sabbath 66b.

27. L. Blau, Jüdische Zauberwesen2 (1914), 73 f. quotes a Jewish proverb, "All sevens are cherished."

28. J. A. Montgomery, Aramaic Incantation Texts from Nippur (1903), #5.2.

29. Daiches, loc. cit.

30. M. Höfner and N. Rhodokanakis, in WZKM 42 (1936), 218, n.l.

31. Gen. 24:12; 27:20; Exod. 3:18; Num. 11:23.

32. J. Pedersen, "The Islamic Preacher, waʿiz, mudhakkir, qaṣṣ," in Ignace Goldziher Memorial Volume, 1 (1946), 226–51; I. Goldziher, Ghazzali against al-batiniya, Introd. 97 ff.

33. E. S. Drower, The Canonical Prayerbook of the Mandaeans (1959), 87, ult.: galaia dᵒainh galian.

34. G. Furlani, Rel. bab. e assir. (1925), i.201, 238.

35. See on this: F. Nork, Das Kloster, xii (1849), 742.

36. W. W. Ellis, Polynesian Researches2 (1832–36), i.352, 373.

37. J. A. Morenhout, Voyages aux iles du Grand Ocean (1837), i.479; cf. E. B. Tylor, Primitive Culture, ii.220.

38. A. H. Sayce, Reminiscences (1923), 196.

39. Pliny, HN xi.147; cf. Plato, Ion 553E; E. Rohde, Psyche7 (1921), ix, n.18; E. R. Dodds, The Greeks and the Irrational (1957), 96, n.94.—G. Lanczkowski, Antike Prophetismus (1960), 13, thinks that this is what is meant in II Kings 8:11, where it is said that when Elisha apprised Hazael that King Ben-hadad of Aram would recover from his sickness, "he set his countenance" (Heb.: wayaᶜᵃmed eth pānāw). The prophet would have been in a trance. But this could just as well mean, as Moffatt has it, that "his face became rigid with horror." If Elisha were in a trance, he could scarcely have replied rationally, as he did, to Hazael's further question.

40. (a) Arslan Tash magical plaque (8th cent. B.C.), line 4 (aš tm py); cf. T. H. Gaster, in Orientalia 11 (1942), 62 f.; (b) Ugaritic text III AB, C 12, 18 = Syria 24 (1944–45), 6, 9 (dtm p(?)), but there applied to the god ᶜAthtar).

41. Akk. ša pušu ellu; cf. K. Tallquist, Maqlû (1895), 121.

(d) Balaam's oracles

42. Cf. Testaments of the XII Patriarchs; Levi, v.15; Judah, iv.20. Targum Onkelos likewise identifies the Star with the Messiah.

43. Zadokite Document iii.18; tr. T. H. Gaster, The Dead Sea Scriptures (1956), 70.

44. See E. Weidner, "Astrologische Geographie im Alten Orient," in AfO 20 (1963), 117–21.

45. E. Dhorme, Les religions de Babylonie et d'Assyrie (1945), 286.

46. M. Jastrow, Relig. Bab. und Ass. (1905–12), ii.629, 806.

47. Harper, Letters, #565, obv. 10.13; #744, rev. 10; #894, obv. 13, etc.—Note the common parallelism of n-d-d (= Akkad. nazāzu) and q-m in Ugaritic poetry.

48. Harper, Letters #113. 6 f.; 318, obv. 11–18.

49. ZÄS 69 (1933), 24–39.

50. J. Friedrich, in OLz 39 (1936), 135 f.

51. See: H. Usener, in Rhein Mus. 55 (1900), 286–87; Pfeiffer, Gestirne und Wetter (1914), 3; F. Boll, in ZNTW 18 (1918), 47, n.l.; A. S. Pease, Comm. on Cicero's De Divinatione, pp. 105–7; F. Stemplinger, in Neue Jahrb. 47 (1920), 37–38.—For references in Classical authors, see: Kirby Smith, on Tibullus ii.5, 71.—See also: Grimm-Stallybrass, TM 722.

52. H. A. Giles, Confucianism and Its Rivals (1915), 180.

53. Oracula Sibyllina, iii.334–40.

54. The same is said of shooting stars by Hephaistion of Thebes, i.21 p. 82.23, Engelbr.

55. Vergil, Ecl. ix.46; Aen. viii.691; Horace, Odes i.12, 47; Pliny, HN ii.93. Cf. H. Vagenvoort, "Virgil's Fourth Eclogue and the Sidus Julium," in his Studies in Roman Literature, Culture and Religion (1956).

56. Tacitus, Ann. xiv.22; Suetonius, Nero 36.

57. Pliny, HN ii.93; Lucan, i.526.

58. A. D. White, A History of the Warfare of Science with Technology and Christendom (1913), i.171 ff.; Grimm-Stallybrass, TM 722.

59. R. Chambers, The Book of Days (1886), ii.583 ff.

60. Ib.

61. Ib.

62. Ib.

63. Shakespeare, Julius Caesar, II.ii.

64. John Milton, Paradise Lost, ii.706 f.

65. Chambers, loc. cit.

66. On omens derived from animals, see: L. Hopf, Tierorakel und Orakelthiere in alter und neuer Zeit (1888). For Mesopotamian examples see: B. Meissner, Babylonien und Assyrien, ii (1925), 260 ff.; J. Hunger, Babylonische Tieromina, MVAG XIV (1909). See especially the text, KARI 394.ii, 5 ff.

67. This alternative rendering is based on connecting the Hebrew verb ś-y-m in this passage with the Akkadian šimtu, "fate."

68. The reconstruction is due in part to F. Hommel, but mainly to W. F. Albright, in JBL 63 (1944), 207–33. Although I accept all of Albright's readings, I have given to some of them a different interpretation.

69. For the traditional text's oy mî yihyeh mi-šûmô El, read 'iyyîm *yehawwū mi-Sama'l. The word 'iyyîm here does not mean "islanders" (from 'iy, "island, coastland"), as many scholars have supposed; the parallelism with the assonantal ṣiyyîm, "wild yowling beasts" (which is, indeed, something of a cliché since it recurs in Isa. 13:21–22; 34:14 and Jer. 50:39) determines the meaning, "howling beasts, jackals." The word occurs in Egyptian in the form 'iw, "jackal."

70. Reading yehawwū, with Hommel and Albright. The latter derives this from a root h-w-h, cognate with Arabic h-w-y, "congregate, foregather," but I would venture to suggest that, in view of the antithetical ᶜabārū, "they have passed by," which im-

mediately follows (see n.74), a better sense may be obtained by equating the word with Arabic *ḥ-w-y*, "hasten," or with *n-ḥ-y*, "make for a place." It may be recognized in this sense in the Ugaritic text 75.i.35, *yḥ pat mdbr*, "he hies to the outskirts of the desert" (|| *ytlk wyṣd*).

71. Reading *mi-Sama'l*.

72. The word *ṣiyyîm* here does not mean "ships" (*ṣy* I: Egyptian *ṣ⟩y*), as usually supposed and as the imitator in Dan. 11:30 evidently thought. The parallel with *'iyyîm*, "yowling beasts, jackals" (see n.69) establishes the true sense. The word *ṣy* occurs elsewhere in this sense in O.T. and is the equivalent of the Arabic *ḍayyūn*, "wild cat."

73. Following Albright's correction of the traditional *mi-yad Kittîm* to *mi-yarketê yam* —surely one of the most brilliant emendations ever made in the text of the O.T. The corruption, however, is as old as our present recension of Dan. 11:30, though even there what the author originally wrote has been altered by later editors to accommodate it to the current misreading of Balaam's oracle. The word rendered "West" literally means "sea," i.e., the Mediterranean.

74. Reading, with Albright, *wᵉ-ᶜad-mi 'ašūr ᶜabārū* for the traditional *wᵉᶜinnū' Aššur* (*wᵉᶜinnū*) *ᶜEber*. [But see now id., Yahweh and the Gods of Canaan (1968), 16, n. 40.]

75. On left and right in ancient superstition, see: A. S. Pease, on Cicero, De divinatione ii.82; S. Eitrem, Papyri Osloenses i (1925), 96 ff.; F. Boll, Sphaera (1903), 563 ff.; F. Dölger, Sonne der Gerechtigkeit (1918), 9 ff., 37 ff.; E. Pottier, in Mélanges Pedersen (1937), 405–13; G. Roeder, Urkunden zur Religion des alten Aegyptens (1923), 107, 109, 112.

76. Sm. 67 f. = Hunger, op. cit., 103 f. = Jastrow, op. cit., ii.821.—On omens from *jackals,* see: Rm. 155, obv. 11 = Jastrow, op. cit., ii.813.

77. Tosephta, Sabbath vii.13; Sanhedrin 65ᵇ; cf. I. Scheftelowitz, Altpal. Bauernglaube (1925), 141.

78. J. Wellhausen, Reste d. arab. Heidentums² (1897), 202. Not impossibly, this is the real meaning of the epithet *bāriᵃḥ*, usually rendered "evasive" (from *b-r-ḥ* "flee"), applied to Leviathan in the Ugaritic text 67.i.1, and in Isa. 27:1; Job 26:13; see T. H. Gaster, in JRAS 1944.47, n.49.

79. Admittedly, there is no corroboration from other Semitic languages, but Jewish tradition attests this meaning, and in later Hebrew the word *shebeṭ* (also *sharbîṭ*) is indeed so used.

80. On the Shutu, see: Albright, op. cit., n.89; A. Goetze, Kleinasien¹ (1933), 117.

81. In an imitation of this verse in Jer. 38:45, the word *šēt* is likewise taken as a common noun, but is equated with Heb. *šā'ôn*, "uproar, tumult."

82. The traditional text reads *w-q-r-q-r*, but this does not yield a satisfactory sense. The imitation in Jer. 48:45 has *w-q-d-q-d*, but vocalizes it *wᵉ-qadôd*, i.e., "and *the pate* of all the sons of Sheth." It seems to me that the poet intended a play on words between *q-d-q-d* "head" and **qidqed*, from the root *q-d-d*, "bow low." For an exact parallel to the sentiment, cf. Isa. 2:17; 10:33.

83. Albright, op. cit.

84. See n.73. This is the word actually used in 23:9.

85. That is, for the traditional *tiśbekā*, "shall carry thee away captive" (which has, in fact, been variously emended by modern scholars), I would propose to read *tᵉšubbekā*, from *š-b-b*, "burn." The prefix is the archaic *t-* of 3rd pl., as often in Ugaritic.

99 Balaam's ass

1. See: A. H. Krappe, "Spirit-Sighted Animals," in Folk-Lore 54 (1943), 391–401, from whom most of the following examples are taken. See also: H. Eising, "Balaams Eselin," in Bibel und Kirche 13 (1958), 45 ff.; F. Nork, Das Kloster, xii (1849), 744; Stith Thompson, MI, B 733, E 421.1.2; Grimm-Stallybrass, TM 667, 1107.

2. Od. 16.158 ff.
3. Pausanias, vi.20, 15–16.
4. Pliny, HN viii.40, 62.
5. *Grímnismal,* in L. M. Hollander, The Poetic Edda (1928), 352.
6. W. R. S. Ralston, Russian Folk-Tales (1873), 206.
7. A. Straus, Die Bulgaren (1898), 425.
8. K. Mauer, Isländische Volkssagen der Gegenwart (1860), 85.
9. Andrew Lang, in Anthropological Essays presented to Edward Tylor (1907), 11.
10. E. B. Tylor, Primitive Culture (1873), ii.196.
11. See Stith Thompson, MI[1], B 733; E 421.1.2; Grimm-Stallybrass, TM, 667, 1107.
12. E. Garlick, in PSBA 1910.64 f.
13. E. Westermarck, Ritual and Belief in Morocco (1926), i.270.
14. T. Gwynn Jones, Welsh Folklore and Folk-Custom (1930), 203. A similar belief obtains in Brittany: A. le Braz, La légende de la Mort chez les Bretains amorecains (1912), i.7.
15. I. Scheftelowitz, Altpalästinensicher Bauernglaube (1925), 142; J. A. Charap, in Am Urquell 4 (1893), 194.
16. V. di Giacome, Leggende del Diavolo (1963), 192.

DEUTERONOMY

100 Aborigines as giants

1. Num. 13:32–33; cf. Deut. 1:28; 9:2.
2. Deut. 3:11; cf. Jos. 12:4; 13:2.
3. Jos. 14:12–15; cf. Judg. 1:20.—The name, it would seem, was popularly derived from a root akin to Arabic *r-f-ᶜ,* "be tall, high."
4. Jos. 11:21–22.
5. II Sam. 21:20 ff. = I Chron. 20:6 ff.
6. See: O. Dähnhardt, Natursagen, i (1907), 242 ff.; E. B. Tylor, Anthropology (Thinker's Library ed.), ii.121 f.; id., Primitive Culture (1873), i.386 ff.; Grimm-Stallybrass, TM 518 ff.; J. G. Frazer, GB v.157 f.; A. H. Krappe, La genèse des mythes (1938), 329; J. E. B. Mayor, Thirteen Satires of Juvenal[2] (1878), ii.374–76; T. Ryk, Oratio de gigantibus, in the Leyden ed. of Stephanus Byzantinus (1685), ii.496 ff.; G. Siefert, in Neue Jahrb. f. klass. Phil. 10 (1902), 473 ff.
7. Krappe, loc. cit.
8. P. Sébillot, Le Folklore de France (1904–7), i.213, 309; ii.72.
9. J. Malalas, ed. Bonn, p. 282.
10. B. Schmidt, Das Volksleben der Neugriechen (1871), 204; R. Rodd, Customs and Lore of Modern Greece (1892), 172.
11. E.g., Yaqut i.130; Tabari, Chronique, tr. Zotenberg, i (1867), 51; G. Jacob, Altarab. Parallelen zum AT (1897), 12; C. H. Becker, Islamstudien (1924–32), i.150.
12. C. A. Doughty, Arabia Deserta (1888), i.22, 43, 134, 162, 388; ii.394.
13. J. Rhŷs, Celtic Folk-Lore (1901), i.286; T. Gwynn Jones, Welsh Folklore and Folk-Custom (1930), 80.
14. E.g., Philostratus, Hero ii.4–8; Pausanias, i.35, 6; Dio Cassius lxix.22, 2; cf. Lasaulx, in Abh. Münch. Akad. 6.517 ff.
15. See, for example: C. Squire, The Mythology of the British Isles (1905), 328; S. Reinach, Amalthée, i (1930), 151; A. Bastian, Die Voelker des oestlichen Asien (1866–71), i.121, 294; C. Lumholz, Unknown Mexico (1902), 299.
16. E. B. Tylor, History of Mankind[2] (1878), 322.

17. Cf. Gen. 6:4; IV (II) Esdras v.50–54; Philo, De opific. mundi xlix.1; Plutarch, Plac. phil. v.27; id., Sert. ix.5 (Sertorius found a tomb containing a skeleton sixty cubits long; it was held to be that of the giant Antaeus); Pliny, HN vii.73; Arnobius, Adversus nationes ii.75; Augustine, De civ. Dei xv.19.

18. TB Hagigah 12ᵃ; Sanhedrin 38ᵇ. Cf. M. Grünbaum, Neue Beitraege (1893), 55, 65; L. Ginzberg, Legends of the Jews (1909 ff.), i.59 f., 70, 86; v.79 f., 86, 99, 113, 126; A. S. Rappoport, Myth and Legend in Ancient Israel² (1966), i.142.

19. Thus in our passage; cf. also: Gen. 14:5; 15:20; Jos. 12:4; 13:12; 17:15.

20. So in our passage; cf. also Num. 13:22, 28; Jos. 11:21–22; 14:12, 15; 15:14; Judg. 1:20.

21. I Aqht 20, 36–37, 47, etc.

22. J. A. Wilson, in ANET 328 f.; R. Dussaud, in Syria 8 (1927), 219.

23. Grimm-Stallybrass, TM 518 ff.; O. Schrader, in Reallexicon d. indogerm. Alter-tumskunde, i.41.

24. The Emim have been identified with a people named A-y-m-m in South Arabian inscriptions: D. H. Müller, Sudar. Altertümer . . . Wien (1899), 15. This, however, is very doubtful.—The Zamzumim are evidently identical (by tendencious distortion of the name) with the Zuzim of Gen. 14:5.

25. W. Robertson Smith, apud S. R. Driver, ICC Deuteronomy, 40; F. Schwally, in ZAW 18.135; E. W. Lane, Lex. 1248–49.—The word z-m appears in this sense in an Aramaic magical incantation: J. A. Montgomery, Aramaic Incantation Texts from Nippur (1903), #6.11. Cf. also the Talmudic z-m-z-m-ê, the name of a musical instrument.—On the ᶜazif, cf. J. Wellhausen, Reste d. arab. Heidentums² (1897), 136, and see below, §177.

▲ 101 Boring a servant's ear

[1. See: O. Loretz, in Biblica 41 (1960), 167–75.]

2. Exod. 21:5–6.

[2a. There is no need to infer from the words "in the presence of the gods" (EV: "before God") that the ceremony took place at the entrance to the sanctuary. This is simply a time-honored cliché (cf. I Sam. 2:25) which has its counterpart (mahar ilim) in the Code of Ḥammurapi (§§20, 23, 103, 120, 126, 131, 240, 281) and bears reference to the household gods, represented by images in the home.]

3. It is little to the point to compare the enactment in the Code of Ḥammurapi, §282: "If a male slave has said to his master, 'You are not my master,' his master shall prove that the slave indeed belongs to him, and shall cut off his ear," for such mutilation need not necessarily have reference to the ear as an organ of hearing and obedience; it may be merely a form of punishment and a brand of infamy, as it con-tinued to be in English law down to the 17th cent.: see H. Hallam, Constitutional History of England (1876), ii.37 ff.

[3a. In Hebrew, the verb "to hear" (sh-m-ᶜ) also bears the correlative sense of "to obey," and in Phoenician, a noun formed from that root (m-sh-m-ᶜ-t) was a common term for "retinue, body of servants" (G. A. Cooke, A Text-book of North Semitic Inscriptions [1903], 14). Moreover, alike in Classical Arabic and in ancient South Arabian, words formed from the noun, "ear" (viz., '-dh-n) are similarly employed.]

4. Lt. Herold, in Mitt. von Forschungreisenden und Gelehreten aus den deutschen Schutzgebieten, 5/iv (1892), 147 ff.

5. Frazer-Gaster, NGB, §§34, 174–76.

6. A. C. Hollis, The Nandi (1909), 74 ff.

7. L. J. B. Bérenger-Ferand, Les peuplades de la Sénémgabie (1879), 59.

8. For many examples, cf. E. S. Hartland, The Legend of Perseus (1896), ii.86 ff.

9. N. Andriani and A. C. Kruijt, De Bare'e-sprekende Toradja's van Midden-Celebes (1912–14), i.198 f.

10. Ib., ii.173 f.

[10a. Tr. T. J. Meek, in ANET 183[b].]

102 Cultic transvestitism

1. Cf. Lev. 18:30; Deut. 7:25-26; 12:31; 32:16; II Kings 16:3; 21:2; Isa. 41:24; 44:19; Ezek. 7:20. The term is also used of foreign customs abhorred by the Egyptians: Gen. 43:32; Exod. 8.22.—In a Phoenician inscription (c. 300 B.C.), violation of the tomb of a priest of Astarte is termed an "abomination" to that goddess: G. A. Cooke, A Text-Book of North Semitic Inscriptions (1903), No. 4.6.

2. See in general: J. G. Frazer, GB vi.253–64; E. Crawley, The Mystic Rose[2] (1927), ii.110 ff., 318 ff.; R. Briffault, The Mothers (one-vol. ed., 1959), 276 f.; F. Liebrecht, Zur Volkskunde (1879), 410; H. Usener, in Rhein. Mus. N. F. 30 (1873), 195 ff.; A. Marmorstein, in Orient and Occident: (Moses) Gaster Anniversary Volume (1936), 409 ff.

3. Plutarch, Quaest. Graec. 58; cf. W. R. Halliday, The Greek Questions of Plutarch (1928), 217 f.

4. Joannes Lydus, De mensibus 4.46. (Women excluded from attendance at sacrifices to Hercules.)

5. Lucian, Calumniae non temere credendum, 16.

6. Plutarch, Theseus, 23.

7. O. Gruppe, Gr. Mythologie (1906), 904 f.

8. Ib., 159.

9. Lucian, De deâ Syriâ 27, 51.

10. G. Fawcett, in JASBombay 11 (1854), 343.

11. Tacitus, Germania 43.

12. Apollodorus, Bib. iii.5.1.

13. Ib., ii.6.2. (with Frazer's note); Ovid, Heroides, 9.55.

14. Varro, Men. 120; Arnobius, Adversus Nationes 5.17; cf. L. Gray, in ERE v.581.

15. S. St. John, Life in the Forests of the Far East[2] (1863), i.73.

16. B. F. Matthes, Over de Bissoes of heidensche Priesters en Priesteressen der Boeginezen (1872), 1 ff.

17. H. H. Bancroft, Native Races of the Pacific States (1875–76), i.82, 92, 415, 585, 774; J. F. Lafitau, Moeurs des sauvages amériquains (1724), i.52–54; G. Catlin, North American Indians[4] (1844), ii.214 f.; J. G. Müller, Gesch. d. amerikan. Urreligionen[2] (1867), 44 f.

18. J. Kubary, in A. Bastian's Allerlei aus Volks- und Menschenkunde (1888), i.35.

19. H. Callaway, The Religious System of the Amazulu (1868–70), 93; cf. also: A. C. Haddon, in JAI 19 (1890), 401.

20. J. B. Labat, Relation historique de l'Ethiopie occidentale (1732), ii.195–99.

21. Briffault, op. cit., 283.

22. H. G. Holmberg, in Acta Soc. Scient. Fennicae 4 (1856), 120.

23. W. Bogoras, The Chukchee (1904–09), 448–53.

24. W. Foley, in JASBengal 4 (1835), 199.

25. Monier Williams, Religious Life and Thought in India (1883), 136.

26. O. Dapper, Description de l'Afrique (1686), 467.

27. Briffault, op. cit., 276n.

28. J. Roscoe, as cited in Frazer, GB vi.257, n.3; id., The Baganda (1911), 297.

29. S. Meier, in Schweizerisches Archiv fuer Volkskunde 9 (1905), 128.

30. Cf. L. Farnell, in ARW 7 (1904), 93.

31. O. Gruppe, Gr. Mythologie (1906), 904 f.

32. J. G. Frazer, GB vi.264.

33. E. Fehrle, Kultische Keuschheit im Altertum (1910), 92.

34. R. Krafft-Ebbing, Psychopathia Sexualis (reprint, New York 1965), 382–89, 590 ff. Homosexuals have a regular vocabulary for the adoption of female costume; in general, it is termed "wearing drag."—On such effeminates (boté, berdashe) among N. American Indians, see: A. W. Holder, in The New York Medical Journal, Dec. 7, 1889.—Not impossibly, the "male-female" (zikru-sinništu) mentioned in ancient Mesopotamian Text (concerning which cf. G. R. Driver and J. C. Miles, in Iraq 6 [1939], 66–70) was of the same order.

103 Moses' farewell song

(a)

1. This is the reading of the Greek (Septuagint) and some other Ancient Versions, as well as of a Hebrew fragment discovered at Qumran (Biblica 36 [1958], 165). The traditional Hebrew text, in an evident attempt to palliate the pagan reference, reads, By the number of the Children of Israel!—On Heb. benê el as a generic term for pagan gods, see above, §6.

2. Trans. F. Rosenthal, in ANET², 503 f.

3. Eusebius, Praep. Ev. i.10.

4. Concerning this development, cf. R. Lack, in CBQ 24 (1962), 44–46.

5. See: J. Morgenstern, in HUCA 14 (1939), 29–126.

6. Originally, it would seem, ᶜelyôn meant simply a supernal, as distinct from an infernal or terrestrial, god. The Mesopotamians similarly distinguished between the upper Anunnaki and the lower Igigi, the Hittites between "those above" (sarrazês) and "those below" (katterês: cf. KUB XVII.14, i.17), and the Greeks and Romans between theoi hypatoi, di superi and theoi nerteroi, di inferi; see: T. H. Gaster, IDB, s.v. Angels, §2a.

7. Poem of the Gracious Gods, 3: ᶜl[nym]. The restoration is due to H. L. Ginsberg.

8. TB. Sanhedrin 20ᵇ; Ket. 104ᵃ.

9. Luke 6:35.

10. Enuma Elish vi.39–46.

11. Ecclus. 17:17 (cf. W. O. E. Oesterley, Cambridge Bible for Schools, in loc.).

(b)

12. Stith Thompson, MI, R 131; G. Binder, Die Aussetzung des Königskindes Kyros und Romulus (1964).

13. See in general: W. H. Roscher, Nektar und Ambrosia (1883), 62 ff.; K. F. Hermann, Lehrbuch der griechischen Privatalterthümer (1882), 33, n.9; ZEUS: Callimachus, Zeus 48; Diodorus, v.70; Aelian, xvii.35; O. Gruppe, Gr. Mythologie (1906), 249.

14. Ap. Rhod. Argon. iv.1134.

15. Pindar, Ol. vi.45 (v. Schneider-Böckh, p. 158, in loc.). See also: AP x.62.

16. Odyssey 10.69.

17. Bradaranyaka, vi.4; cf. A. Kuhn, Die Herabkunft des Feuers und des Göttertrankes² (1886), 137.

18. J. Grimm, DM³, 295; id., Deutsche Rechtsaltertümer³ (1881), 475 ff.

19. Tertullian, De coronâ militis 3; see fully: S. Bochart, Hierozoicon³ (1962), iii.388.—According to a letter from Johannes Diaconus to Senarius (6th cent.), honey, water, and milk were given to neophytes also in the Roman rite, but this is not attested in later documents: L. Duchesne, Christian Worship⁵ (1949), 315.—Honey was likewise given in Eastern churches which followed the Alexandrinian use: ib., 330.

20. E.g., Berlin Magical Papyrus, in AB. Berl. Akad. Wiss., 1865.120, 20; cf. Jane Harrison, Prolegomena to the Study of Greek Religion[2] (1922), 596; T. H. Gaster, Thespis[2], 222.

21. Aelian, HA xii.21; Binder, op. cit., 175 f., §60.

22. Firdausi, Shah Nameh vii; J. M. Mohl, Le livre des rois (1838–78), i.213–29; Binder, op. cit., 179 f., §62.

23. Pausanias, i.6, 2; Quintus Curtius, ix.8, 22; Binder, op. cit., 151 f., §37.

24. Aelian, loc. cit.

25. Pausanias, iv.18.

(c)

26. C. A. Doughty, Arabia Deserta (1888), i.307 f.; G. Jacob, Das Leben der vorislamischen Beduinen (1895), 122; P. Haupt, in JAOS 40.218, n.1; id., in JHUC 312.23; see above, §100.

27. Viz., *yabab;* cf. Kamūs 173.

28. Pal. Targum in loc: *atar dᵉ-mᵉyallᵉlîn shedîm wᵉ-yirurîn.*

(d)

29. Prov. 7:2.

30. See below, n.38.

31. Arabic: *insan.*

32. Persian: *merdek.*

33. Grimm-Stallybrass, TM 1546.

34. Plato, Alcibiades 1, p. 133A.

35. G. Claridge, Wild Bush Tribes of Tropical Africa (1922), 207.

36. H. Grapow, Die bildlichen Ausdrücke des Aegyptischen (1924), 131.

37. Pliny, HN xxviii.64; Servius, on Vergil, Aen. iv.244; E. Crawley, The Idea of the Soul (1909), 107.

38. V. S. Lean, Collectanea, ii (1904), 519; A. Waser, in ARW 16 (1913), 381 ff.; K. F. Smith, "Pupula Duplex," in Studies in honor of B. L. Gildersleeve (1902), 287–300; E. S. McCartney, in Papers of the Michigan Academy of Science, Arts and Letters 16 (1931), 187–89; E. Monseur, in RHR 51 (1905), 1–23; M. B. Ogle, in TAPA 73 (1942), 189–91; W. Wundt, Völkerpsychologie, ii/2 (1906), 27 f.; B. Schmidt, in Neue Jahrb. für Klass. Altertums 31 (1913), 574–613.

39. Pliny, HN xi.145.

40. Babrius, fab. xcv.35.

41. E. F. Im Thurn, in JRAI 2.365; J. H. Bernau, British Guiana (1847), 134.

42. A. Le Roy, Les Pygmées (1928), 187.

43. E.g., Aeschylus, Septem contra Thebas 516; Sophocles, Ajax 991; Moschus iv.9; Callimachus, Hymns iii.211; Terence, Adelphi 701, 903; Catullus, iii.5.

44. Headlam-Knox, on Hero[n]das vi.23 (p. 290).

(e)

45. R. C. Thompson, Semitic Magic (1908), 47 ff.

46. Id., The Devils and Evil Spirits of Babylonia (1904), i, Tab. V, iv.8 ff.; H. Gollancz, The Book of Protection (1912), 87.

47. Montague Summers, Witchcraft and Black Magic (Arrow Books, 1964), 253, 259.

48. Shakespeare, Macbeth, I.iii.18.

49. Id., King Richard the Third, III.iv.69–70.

50. T. H. Gaster, The Holy and the Profane: Folkways of Jewish Life (1955), 22.

51. Stith Thompson, MI, G 11.2; G 332.

52. H. J. Holmberg, Siberian Mythology (1927), 387.

53. S. Thompson, Tales of the North American Indians (1929), 321, n.158.

54. Id., MI, G 312 (Pišaka).

55. J. Arnason, Icelandic Legends, tr. G. Powell and E. Magnusson (1864), i.122, 125, 133.

FORMER
PROPHETS

Joshua

(a) "The walls came tumblin' down"

Despite extensive excavation of the site, archaeology can as yet say nothing definite about an Israelite invasion of Jericho. In the opinion of many scholars, the Biblical narrative really reflects the reminiscence of an earlier capture of the city by pre-Israelite Hebrews (Ḫabirû).[1] In any case, the account clearly incorporates several purely folkloristic traits.

(b) The circumambulation of the walls

Thus, Joshua's celebrated march around the walls of the beleagured city is based, in all probability, on the widespread custom of laying claim to territory by so tracing out its bounds.[2] Such circuitory marches often formed part of the ceremonies at the installation of kings.—In Egypt, for example, the new pharaoh circumambulated the fortified wall in a festal procession on the day of his enthronement. The ceremony, called "the circuit of the wall" (*phrr h inb*), was said to be as old as the time of Menes, the first monarch of United Egypt.[3]—Similarly, the Hittite king had to tour his realm at the annual winter festival of Nuntariyashas;[4] while in the Canaanite Poem of Baal, discovered at Ras Shamra-Ugarit, that god makes the rounds of "seventy-seven towns, eighty-eight cities" in order to assert his new kingship over gods and men.[5]—In India, the rajputs marched ceremoniously around a temple or stupa at the time of their installation;[6] and in Malaya, a new sultan was required to perambulate his territory seven times on the same occasion.[7]—In 1875, the new king of Thailand ritually circuited his palace and city at the time of his enthronement,[8] and the practice likewise figures in many African installation ceremonies.[9] A familiar survival of it is the ceremony of "beating the bounds" in British popular usage.[10] The local vicar marches around the confines of the parish in solemn procession; every so often a choirboy, or some other functionary, is lifted by his legs and his head "bumped" on the boundary line. The custom was observed as late as the twenties of the present century at such places as East Barnet, Datchet in Buckinghamshire, Bexhill, and St. Clement's parish in Hastings, Sussex.[11] It is recorded also from various rural areas of Germany.[12]

History records several instances in which territory was acquired by circumambulation.—Thus after Horatius Cocles had delivered Rome by his celebrated defense of the bridge against the Etruscans, the grateful city awarded him all the territory which he could encompass in a circuit traced out by his chariot.[13]—Similarly, in 496, Clovis awarded to the abbot John of Reomans all the land he could circuit while riding on an ass;[14] and some two centuries later, Dagobert, king of the Franks, gave to St. Florent as much of the land of Kircheim, in Alsace, as he could traverse riding on an ass while the king bathed and dressed.[15] It was in the same way, too, that King Waldemar of Denmark rewarded St. André in 1205; the holy man was granted all the territory he could encircle riding on a nine-day-old colt, while the king was bathing.[16] Of like tenor also is a legend current at Maccarese (ancient Castel St. Giorgio), near Rome, which tells of a knight who combatted a local dragon on condition that he might claim for himself as much land as he could cover at a gallop on a single day.[17]

(c) The seven circuits

Joshua's men, we are told, circuited the walls of Jericho for seven successive days. On each of the first six days, they made the rounds once, but on the seventh day, seven times. They were accompanied by seven priests blowing trumpets ahead of the ark of the Lord.

This emphasis on the sacred number seven shows clearly that the Biblical writer *is modeling his account upon a ritual ceremony,* and such ritual circum-ambulation is indeed attested in many parts of the world.—In ancient Rome, for instance, it was the custom in times of peril to circuit the city in a cere-mony called *amburbiam;*[18] and annually on the Feast of Lupercalia (Feb. 15) men were ritually scourged around its bounds.[19]—Ritual perambulations of this kind survived into Christian usage;[20] and it is recorded of both Dagobert (628–38) and Hugh Capet (967–96) that they used to march ceremoniously around cities, not only to assert possession of them but also to ensure public peace and well-being.[21]—The ancient kings of Sweden likewise made a prac-tice of marching around cities in a reverse direction to the sun's as a means of securing their safety.[22]

The purpose of this procedure was to form a closed circle which might ob-struct the entry of demons and noxious influences. As we shall see later (be-low, §257), altars were commonly circuited in this way during acts of worship; so was a bridal couple, and so too was the bier of the dead.—It has been sug-gested also that the rite was sometimes designed to keep the gods or beneficent spirits of a place accessible and to prevent their slipping away.[23] It is obvious, however, that when the Biblical writer patterned his account after the ancient ritual, he could not have had this meaning in mind, for the gods of Jericho would have been hostile to the invading Israelites and the latter would there-fore have had no reason to keep them where they were; and as for their own god, far from being within the beleagured city, he was in fact accompanying his people in their circuits in the form of his sacred ark!

(d) The trumpets[24]

On the seventh day, seven priests preceding the ark of the Lord blew seven times upon their trumpets. Thereupon the people uttered a loud shout and the wall collapsed.

Stories of magic horns the blasts of which raze walls are by no means uncommon in folktales the world over,[25] and it is therefore not at all impossible that the Biblical narrative is indebted to the influence of such popular lore. It should be observed, however, that noise is everywhere regarded as a method of expelling demons and hostile powers. Thus, New Year, regarded universally as a "critical" period, is very commonly inaugurated by the beating of drums, the rattling of kettles, the cracking of whips, the firing of guns, the ringing of bells, etc., in order to forefend noxious spirits which might otherwise infest it.[26] The Navaho, for example, employ a "groaning stick" on that occasion;[27] the Zuni of Mexico resort to the use of bull-roarers,[28] so do also the Kafirs of Africa.[29] In Estonia, hammers are beaten, and kettles rattled.[30] So too, it is common practice to sound drums, etc. at eclipses in order to frighten away the demon who is believed to be attacking the sun or moon;[31] while ancient Greek legend tells how King Salmoneus of Elis once tied kettles to his chariot in a bizarre attempt to intimidate Zeus![32] Not impossibly, then, the sounding of the trumpets before Jericho reflects a time-honored rite of frightening or expelling hostile demons in this fashion.

It is noteworthy that both the ancient Greek (Septuagint) Version of the Bible and the historian Josephus (*Ant.* VI.1.5) play down the miraculous character of the incident. The latter says that the trumpets were blown only *in order to encourage the troops.* Living in Roman times, he probably had in mind the *tuba concionis,* or "trumpet of assembly" which customarily rallied Roman soldiers to battle,[33] and in the shout uttered by Joshua's men he evidently saw the equivalent of the united war cry which the Romans used to emit before battle in order to strike terror into the heart of the foe.[34]

105 Foundation-sacrifice 6:26

After the destruction of Jericho, Joshua imposed an oath on the people never to rebuild it. The formula of the oath declared that anyone who might venture to do so would have to lay the foundations at the cost of his eldest son, and set up the gates at that of his youngest. This dire prediction, we are told, was fulfilled later during the reign of Ahab, when Hiel of Bethel had indeed to sacrifice in this way his eldest son, Abiram, and his youngest, Segub.[1]

The reference is to the worldwide institution of the *foundation-sacrifice:* at the construction of a new building a human being or animal is slain and buried under the threshold as an offering to spirits, demons, or deceased ancestors who might otherwise bring misfortune or ruin upon it.[2]

Popular tradition associated the sacrifice of a maiden in this way with the foundation of such famous Syrian cities as Antioch and Laodicea;[3] while the Arabic version of *The Travels of St. John of Zebedee* relates that a young girl was buried alive under the foundations of a bathhouse threatened by a satanic spirit.[4] Indeed, until recent times the belief persisted in various parts of the Orient that a Turkish bath had to be rendered immune from accidents and untoward influences by the inaugural sacrifice or inhumation of a Negro or Sudanese.[5]

Among the Arabs of Syria and Palestine,[6] and likewise among the peasantry in modern Greece,[7] it is common practice to slay a cock, ram, or lamb at the building of a house and to let the blood flow freely over the foundation stone; while the custom of human or animal sacrifice on such occasions is abundantly attested in European folklore.[8] In Papua, two old people, deemed expendable, are sacrificed whenever a "men's house"—that is, a communal meeting place for males—is completed.[9]

Nor is the custom confined to the actual building of a house: among Arab peasants, jinns or evil spirits are similarly placated when new land is broken up.[10]

Sometimes, as in ancient Mesopotamian and Palestinian buildings, images and figurines are substituted for real human beings.[11] On the other hand, however, the discovery of infant skeletons in the foundations of houses excavated at such sites as Gezer, Megiddo, and Ta'anek[12] is not necessarily to be interpreted as evidence of foundation-sacrifice, for it was in any case a not uncommon practice in the East to bury children in the corners of rooms.[13]

106   "Sun, stand thou still"   10:12–14

> *Joshua delivered the inhabitants of Gibeon from a threatened attack by the Amorites. In a popular song quoted by the Scriptural writer, that victory is said to have been attended by a singular miracle:*

> Said the LORD in the sight of Israel:
> "Sun, on Gibeon be still,
> and Moon in the Vale of Aijalon!"
> So sun stood still, and moon stayed
> until the nation took vengeance on its foes.[1]

Agamemnon prayed to Zeus for a similar miracle at Troy,[2] and such magical manipulation of the luminaries is a not uncommon motif in folktales.[3] Hera, says Homer, ordered the sun to set betimes so as to facilitate an attack of the Achaeans upon the Trojans.[4] Conversely, when Zeus was enjoying Alcmene, he commanded the sun to bank its fires and stay at home, so that the night might be prolonged, and at the same time Hermes bade the moon travel thrice more slowly than usual;[5] and this boon was granted by Athene when Odysseus was reunited with Penelope.[6]

The motif recurs both in German[7] and Australasian popular tales,[8] and even finds place in hagiography. Once, we are told, when St. Ludwin wished to perform ordination on the same day both at Rheims and Laon, the day was miraculously lengthened to enable him to accomplish this pious intent.[9]

Some scholars, to be sure, have attempted to dilute the miraculous element in our Biblical story.[10] It has been suggested, for instance, that what really happened was that, at Joshua's request, the hailstorm which had been harassing the Amorites, and which the Scriptural writer expressly mentions, lasted from noon on the day of battle until the following noon, blocking out the light of both sun and moon![11] An alternative explanation which has been proposed is that the Hebrew word conventionally rendered "be still" does not mean that the sun actually halted its course, but only that it desisted from aiding the Gibeonites, since Joshua wanted to confute their trust in heavenly bodies and demonstrate that the victory came from Yahweh![12]

The poem which the writer quotes is said to have formed part of the now lost *Book of Jashar*. This work is mentioned again in II Samuel 1:18 as the source of David's famous Lament over Saul and Jonathan; while in the Greek (Septuagint) Version the song chanted by Solomon at the dedication of the Temple is quoted as an excerpt from the Book of *Shîr,* i.e., Song, and many scholars regard this as a corruption of Jashar. Ostensibly, the name would mean *The Book of Upright,* but to explain this as a generic designation of the heroes there commemorated seems, to say the least, a trifle strained. Since ancient compositions were usually known by their opening words (e.g., the Babylonian poems *Enuma Elish* and *Ludlul bêl nimêqi*), and since we have elsewhere in the Bible (Exod. 15:1; Judg. 5:1) excerpts of songs actually introduced by the word *yashar* "he sang" (or *va-tashar,* "she sang"), it is not impossible that the book really derived its name from this standard prefatory phase.

Judges

The mutilation of captives   **Judg. 1:5–7**

> *During their invasion of Canaan, the men of Judah capture a prince of Bezek (modern Ḥirbet Bezḳa, near Gezer) and amputate his thumbs and big toes.*

The mutilation of the captured prince was not simply an act of savagery; it was designed to prevent his ever again taking up arms or marching to war.

The Greeks and Romans sometimes adopted the same practice.[1] Thus, when the Athenians captured the island of Aegina, in 458 B.C., they cut off the right hand of every enemy soldier, "lest he should again carry a spear or throw a lance";[2] and when the city of Uxellodunum (Puy d'Isolu?) surrendered to Julius Caesar in 52 B.C., he ordered the hands of any who had borne arms to be amputated.[3]

By an extension of the same idea, it has been a not uncommon practice among diverse peoples to mutilate the corpses of the slain in order to immobilize their vengeful spirits. The aborigines of Tasmania, for example, used to sever the right thumb of fallen foes lest their ghosts be able thereafter to wield a spear;[4] and similar mutilation was commonly practiced by Greek murderers upon their victims.[5] Clytaemnestra, we are told, so mangled Agamemnon;[6] and Lycurgus, king of the Edonians, cut off the extremities of his son Dryas whom he had struck dead with an ax in a fit of madness.[7] According to one account, murderers used even to attach the severed parts to their own clothing;[8] and an earlier instance of this is afforded by a Canaanite myth from Ras Shamra-Ugarit in which the goddess 'Anat hangs the shorn limbs of her slaughtered foes from her girdle.[9]

Sometimes, however, it was the criminal himself who was so treated. In an Ambrosian illustrated manuscript of the Iliad, Dolon, the Trojan spy slain by Diomedes (10.34), is shown with hands and feet bound;[10] and at Travancore they used to cut off the heels of a murderer when he was hanged to prevent his ghostly feet from "running to do evil."[11]

Sometimes, too, it is the perfectly innocent dead who are thus "disabled." The Romans, for instance, made a practice of cutting off a finger of the deceased before cremation;[12] and in early graves discovered at Gezer, in Palestine, the fingers of infants are buried separately.[13]

Often, for the same reason, the dead were *beheaded*. Thus, the kings of Assyria frequently refer in their annals to impaling the heads of their enemies,[14] and Herodotus informs us that this was also standard practice among the Scythians.[15] Greek legend furnishes instances of this custom in the cases of Eurystheus,[16] Antaeus,[17] Cyecnus,[18] and Oenomaeus;[19] while Evenus, the father of Marpessa, is said to have cut off the hands of his daughter's unsuccessful suitors and to have nailed them to the walls of his house.[20] Coming down to more recent times, Giraldus Cambrensis tells us that once, in the time of Fitzstephen, Irish foot soldiers placed some two hundred enemy heads at the feet of Dermitius, prince of Leicester.[21] In certain parts of Armenia[22] and Africa,[23] if a person falls sick after a funeral, the body of the deceased is disinterred and beheaded; and a case is on record in which a Chinese felon, condemned to death, begged not to be decapitated, so that he would not be immobilized in the next world.[24]

Other parts of the body were likewise mutilated. Constantine, for instance, is said to have cut off the noses of fallen foes,[25] and similar mutilations are attested among the Celts[26] and Berbers,[27] in Dahomey,[28] in Persia,[29] and in New Caledonia,[30] while in the ancient Mesopotamian Epic of Gilgamesh the hero chops off the testicles (or haunches?) of the divine *Alu*-bull after he has slain it.[31] William of Newbury relates that a Galway chieftain once captured a cousin of Henry II (1154–89), plucked out his eyes and his tongue, and severed his genitals[32]—an act of barbarism which may nevertheless have had its origins in superstition. It is recorded also that during the Greek War of Independence a fallen soldier from the island of Santorini (Thera) was mutilated by the enemy out of fear that he was a vampire.[33]

Lastly, it may be mentioned that among the Cheyenne Indians of North America the tribal sign, which consists in drawing the right index finger several times across the left forefinger, is commonly interpreted to indicate "cut finger" or "cut wrists" and "is said to be derived from their custom of cutting off the fingers and hands of slain enemies."[34]

108 Captives fed on scraps

The prince of Bezek reconciles himself to this fate by observing that God has requited him in kind for the fact that "seventy kings with their thumbs and big toes cut off used to gather scraps under my table."

There is an interesting parallel to this in a Canaanite mythological poem from Ras Shamra-Ugarit. The supreme god El invites the other gods to a banquet. Those who acknowledge him and are therefore regarded as his friends are offered viands, whereas those who do not, and are therefore regarded as "gate-crashers," are ordered to be "beaten with a stick (till they sink) under the table."[1]

In the Middle Ages, adulteresses were sometimes punished by being fed on scraps with the household dogs;[2] and the same ignominy was occasionally imposed as a penance.[3]

109   The Song of Deborah   5

(a) Long-haired warriors   1

The initial words of the Song of Deborah, rendered in RSV *That the leaders took the lead in Israel,* could also mean *When men let flow their locks in Israel* (KJV).[1] If this latter rendering be correct, we may see in them an allusion to the custom, attested alike in Greek,[2] Arabic,[3] Icelandic,[4] Swiss,[5] and Spanish[6] sources, whereby warriors kept their hair unshorn because it was regarded as an "index" or seat of their lives and strength.[7] In the Iliad the Achaeans are regularly described as "long-haired," and this has been thought to refer to the same usage;[8] while it is known that in Greek practice generally men who were bent on blood-vengeance kept their beards untrimmed until their mission had been accomplished.[9]

(b) Riding high and sitting low   10

The words, *Ye that ride on roan asses, yet that sit upon rugs* (lit. *cloaks*), constitute what is called a merism, that is, a figure of speech in which a whole is expressed in terms of two contrasting parts, e.g., *officers and men,* for *army,* or *dollars and cents* for *cash.* The expression thus embraces the entire population by specifying its two extremes.

He who rides on the ass is the grandee. In Amorite texts from the ancient city of Mari, "rider on the ass" (*rakib emerin*) is the title of a municipal officer.[10] On the other hand, he who sits, or squats, on his coat[11] is a lowly beggar by the wayside. The contrast is well illustrated by the Palestinian Arab proverb, "A prince remains a prince, even on a mat (*el 'amir ulauw innuh 'al ḥaṣīr*),"[12] while the words, "He is on the mat (*hū 'al ḥaṣireh*)" are, like the English, "He is on the floor," a common colloquial expression for utter abasement.[13]

Curiously enough, a Sumerian poet expresses this contrast between lord and commoner in precisely the opposite terms. In the Epic of Gilgamesh and Agga, the nobles are those "who are raised with the sons of the king," while the lowly poor are those "who press the donkey's thigh."[14]

Roan (RSV: tawny) asses are especially prized by the Arabs, and Arab stallions from the Nejd are usually of roan or chestnut color.[15] The Hebrew word so rendered, however, could also mean *white,*[16] and it is therefore worth observing that in other cultures riding on white steeds is indeed attested as a mark of distinction. In ancient Greece, for example, this was a sign of royalty or nobility,[17] and the Dioscuri, or Heavenly Twins, who were indeed known as "kings" or "lords" (*anakte*),[18] were said to ride on white horses.[19]

So too were their Indic counterparts, the Aśvins. In the Biblical Book of Revelation,[20] the King of Kings and his warriors ride on white horses; and the expression, "the man on a white horse," has become proverbial for an imperialistic ruler. In his final tenth avatar, say the Hindus, Vishnu (Kalki) will appear riding on a white horse.

(c) "Awake, awake,[21] Deborah, utter a song."   12

The reference is not to the present song but to that customarily chanted by the womenfolk when the warriors return with the loot. It is in this way that Saul and David were greeted after the slaying of Goliath,[22] and in Psalm 68:12 we are assured that once Yahweh takes command on the field of battle, one can rest assured that in due course a veritable army of women will come forth to cheer the visitors.[23] The custom still prevails among bedouin Arabs.[24]

(d) The cursing of Meroz   23

The "messenger (EV: angel) of Yahweh" who bade the Israelites curse Meroz for not coming to their help need not have been an angel, as is commonly supposed. He may have been simply the augur or "counsellor" who, as we have seen (above, §98) accompanied armies and advised their leaders as the spokesman of the god.

The site of Meroz has not yet been identified. Not impossibly, the introduction of this curse into the Song was motivated by a popular tradition which derived its name form a Semitic word meaning "calamity, doom," i.e., *Cry doom on Doomsville.*[25]

110   Gideon

(a) Gideon's fleece[1]   6:36–40

> *Gideon, leader of the Israelites, spreads a fleece on the ground at night. If it remains dry, while everything around it is covered with dew, this will be interpreted as a sign that Israel will overcome a coalition of Moabites, Amalekites, and others that has been mobilized against it. In the morning, however, the fleece is sopping wet. After imploring God's clemency, Gideon tries again the following night. This time the fleece remains dry.*

The idea that rain can fall miraculously in one place and leave the surrounding area dry, or vice versa, is a commonplace in legends of saints.[2] Rabbi Honi ben Dosa, says the Talmud, could stand in a drawn circle and by the effect of his prayer cause rain to fall all around him while none fell on him.[3] So too, when the body of Bishop Cerbonius of Populonium, on the isle of Elba, was being brought back to his see, heavy rain accompanied the voyage, but not a drop fell on the ship itself.[4] Again, when Fulgentius, Bishop of Otricoli, found himself surrounded by Goths who were praying to the sun,

he drew a circle, stood within it, and remained dry while a downpour miraculously drenched them.[5] In like manner, Albinus of Angers was once able to
stand immune in a rainstorm;[6] and St. Patrick, while observing the divine
office in the open air, found that he and his disciples remained dry while it
poured in torrents all around them.[7] Bishop Aridius of Limoges could ride
through rain without becoming wet;[8] and tales of the same general import
were told, in the twelfth, fourteenth, and fifteenth centuries, concerning
Gudwal, Petrocus, and Antoninus.[9]

The same motif appears also in connection with holy places. Rain never
fell, says the Talmud, on the altar of the Temple in Jerusalem;[10] and similar
legends were current in Classical antiquity concerning the statue of Diana at
Rhosus,[11] the temple of Venus at Paphos, and that of Minerva at Nea.[12] The
privilege was granted also to the home of John the Evangelist at Ephesus,[13]
and to the uncovered grave of the Lady Mary in the Valley of Jehosaphat;[14]
while William of Malmesbury relates the same thing of the churches built by
Aldhelm of Sherbourne in Dorsetshire, England.

Nor, indeed, is the notion excluded from secular tales, for it forms a leading
motif in a modern story from the Balkans.[15]

(b) Gideon's men[16]   7:1–8

▲ *Gideon rallies the Israelites against attack by the Midianites,
Amalekites, and neighboring bedouins. But Yahweh fears that if the
whole army of Israel triumphs over the whole army of their foes, the
people may be puffed up with pride and, forgetting Him to whom alone
they could owe the success of their arms, claim that "Our own hand
hath saved us." To prevent this deplorable illusion, he commands
Gideon to dismiss to their homes all the fearful and craven-hearted
and to retain only the valiant and brave. Twenty-five thousand recre-
ants readily avail themselves of this leave of absence, leaving only
ten thousand stalwarts to face the enemy. Even that number, however, appears too large to Yahweh. So the whole force is ordered to
march down the river, and the word is given to drink water. Immediately a marked distinction is observed in the manner in which the
command is carried out. The great majority of the men kneel down
and, applying their mouths to the water, imbibe it by suction. Three
hundred, however, scoop it up in their hands and, lifting it to their
mouths, lap it up with their tongues like dogs. These three hundred
are chosen for the campaign.*

The test is one of alertness: the men who drink standing up instead of
lying down show themselves more watchful and ready to meet any sudden
emergency, such as an attack from the rear. The point may be well illustrated
by noting corresponding differences in the modes of drinking adopted by various primitive peoples, for these suggest that the custom of throwing water

into the mouth with the hand, instead of kneeling or lying down and applying the lips to the stream, is characteristic of men like hunters or porters whose occupation renders it either unsafe or difficult to employ the other posture.

Speaking, for instance, of the Ogieg or Wandorobs of East Africa, Captain C. H. Stigand observes that "they drink from a stream on all fours, putting their mouths down to the water. Practically every other tribe drink, when no vessel is available, with the hand. They either take up water with one hand or both, or throw up water with the right hand and catch it in the mouth. The latter is the way most caravan porters drink."[17] Among the Bambalas of the Congo valley "water is the commonest drink, and in the village cups are used for drinking purposes; but on a march the water is thrown into the mouth with the hand; they lie down on their stomachs and, bending the fingers, scoop up the water without spilling a drop, though the hand never touches the mouth in the process."[18] When the Namaquas, a Hottentot tribe of South-West Africa, are out hunting, they always drink by throwing water into their mouths with their fingers, and they trace the custom to the Hottentot Adam or first man, who one day, hunting a lion, saw the animal lying in wait for him under a large mimosa tree beside a pool of water. The first man's dogs, on coming to the spot, lay down, lapped up the water, then shook themselves and frisked about. But the first man, more cautious, knelt down, holding his spear in his left hand, and drank the water by throwing it into his mouth with two fingers, while all the time he kept a sharp eye on the lion. When man and dogs had thus refreshed themselves, they attacked the lion and soon made an end of him. Since that time the Namaquas have always drunk water in the same way when they are out hunting.[19]

Again, a native of Cambodia, travelling through the forest, "ought not to drink by putting his mouth to the water, if he wishes not to be despised by tigers and other fierce animals. Let him drink by throwing water into his mouth with his hand, for then the denizens of the woods will respect him."[20] So, too, "a thirsty Samoan, in coming to a stream of water, stoops down, rests the palm of his left hand on his knee, and, with the right hand, throws the water up so quickly as to form a continued jet from the stream to his mouth, and there he laps until he is satisfied."[21] Similarly, the New Caledonians stoop till their head is a few inches above the water, and then throw the liquid into their mouth with one hand till their thirst is quenched.[22]

Commenting on the story of Gideon's men, a missionary to Melanesia observes that "this lapping of the water like a dog by Gideon's army was unintelligible to me until I came to the New Hebrides. Standing one day by a stream I heard a noise behind me like a dog lapping water. I turned and saw a woman bowing down and throwing the water rapidly into her mouth with her hand. This satisfactorily explained the action of Gideon's men. It showed care and watchfulness; for they could walk along the stream lapping the water as they went; and an enemy was less likely to take them unawares than if they bent on their knees to drink. Most of the natives, however, bend down and touch the water with their lips as the rejected men of Gideon's army did."[23]

[Similarly too, among the Arunta of Australia medicine men are instructed never to lie down or kneel when they wish to drink water, but always to use a small receptacle.[23a] ▼

111   The purple of kings   8:26

Purple,[1] or deep red, was the favored color of royalty or nobility in ancient times.

The Babylonian king wore a deep red garment, called *lamḫuššu,* which means just that.[2] Plutarch tells us that Artaxerxes of Persia was similarly clad.[3] The Cilician god Sandon is said to have worn a deep red robe, called *sandyx,*[4] and in the Homeric Hymn to Dionysus, he is depicted as being similarly attired.[5] In the Book of Daniel, to be clothed in purple is a sign of distinction;[6] and in the Book of Lamentations the nobility are described as "reared on purple."[7] Greek tyrants likewise wore purple,[8] and the *trabea* affected by the ancient kings of Rome was a toga striped with purple.[9] Romulus is said to have worn a deep red cloak.[10] The Jewish mystical classic, the *Zohar,* relates that in the fourth hall of Paradise those who mourn for Zion or who have been martyred for their faith stand clad in purple garments.[11]

All of this is simply a particularization of the more general use of red—the color of blood—as a means of fortifying oneself with extra life and thus counteracting hurtful elements or demons.[12] Babylonian magicians wore red garments, and this color was also affected in rites of expiation and in those concerning the dead.[13] Red pigment was applied to the eye to cure it from the asault of eye disease;[14] and the god Marduk himself smeared red ochre on his lips before he engaged the monster Tiamat in battle.[15] At the ancient Mexican festival of Titill, which was primarily a commemoration of the dead, the image of the god was clothed in red.[16] Red threads were wound by Jews around the throats of children to forefend sickness,[17] just as among the Tupis of Brazil the godfather of a child paints it red soon after its birth,[18] and in Japan a red cross is sometimes hung in a house to ward off demons.[19] Among the Greeks and Romans, red skeins had to be used for the symbolic "binding" of victims in homeopathic magic.[20] In England and elsewhere, red bands are tied around the thighs of a woman in labor, for apotropaic purposes;[21] and among the Tarascos of Mexico, babies are so bound for the same reason.[22] In Irish folklore, a man assailed by the "wee ones" sits up with a red handkerchief bound around his head. "Always red, if the fairies are about," says the rector's widow who records this superstition.[23] In the Canaanite *Poem of Aqhat,* discovered at Ras Shamra-Ugarit, one of the central characters is instructed to wash and rouge himself before performing a ritual ceremony.[24] Among the native tribes of Western Victoria (Australia), objects stolen in order to work magic on their owners have to be rubbed with red clay;[25] and among the Galellas and Tobelorese of Halmahera, the faces and bodies of boys are smeared with reddened water to ensure their wellbeing.[26] The Tlingits of Alaska paint children's noses red to the same end.[27]

Red animals are commonly used in cathartic rites.[28] The ancient Hindus offered red goats to the Aśvins;[29] and in Egypt oxen which were sacrificed had to be red.[30] In Israel, the ashes of a red heifer removed the effects of violating taboo—a custom preserved by the Samaritans until as late as 1348 and still current among the Falashas of Ethiopia.[31]

The altar in the Mosaic sanctuary was spread with a red cloth.[32] Red stones (e.g., coral, red agate, red jasper, carnelian) are used by Mediterranean peoples as a protection against the evil eye.[33]

Among the Greeks, red was the favorite funereal and chthonic color.[34] Hector's bones, for instance, were wrapped in red cloths.[35] Red is likewise the funereal color—to cite but two modern instances—in Ashanti[36] and among the Gypsies.[37] Similarly, among the Tartars of the Crimea and Southern China, as also among the Arabs of Egypt and in modern Greece and Albania,[38] the bridal veil is often red, as was the Roman *flammeum*.[39] "Scarlet stuff" was used in Israelite ritual to decontaminate persons who had recovered from leprosy or vitiligo;[40] and on Roman holidays, the faces of the divine images were painted red with *minium*.[41]

See also above, §62, concerning *red-haired persons*.

▲ 112 Jotham's parable[1]   9:7–15

In the mouth of Jotham the fable of the trees would seem to be a democratic, or perhaps rather theocratic, satire on kingship, for according to him all the noble and useful trees declined the office, so that in despair the trees were driven to offer the crown to the meanest and most useless of their number, who accepted it only on a condition which practically involved the destruction of the aristocracy of the woods, the cedars of Lebanon. The distrust of monarchy which the parable implies was natural enough in the honest son of an honest patriot, who had refused to rule over his people, and had declared that the rule of God was better than the rule of man; and the same distrust of kings and the same preference for a theocracy are expressed still more plainly by the Hebrew historian who records, with evident reluctance and regret, the institution of the monarchy under Saul. But apart from any political application the story of the rivalry between the trees for the primacy would seem to have been popular in antiquity. [Thus, a cuneiform text from the city of Ashur, the ancient capital of Assyria, tells the story of a quarrel between the tamarisk and the palm-tree, each claiming superiority over the other. The tamarisk boasts that it supplies the wood for axes which break open the dry clods, and also for plows and threshing wains. The palm retorts, however, that *its* wood furnishes the keels of ships, the roofs of houses, and many a domestic tool.[1a]] In Greek dress, the theme appears in one of the fables of Aesop. The fir-tree, we read, one day said boastfully to the bramble, "You are good for nothing, but I am useful in roofs and houses." To which the bramble replied, "O wretched creature, if you only remembered the axes and the saws that will chop and cut you, glad enough would you be to be a bramble instead of a fir."[2] Again, a pomegranate and an apple-tree disputed with each other as to which was the more fruitful, and when the dispute was at its height, a bramble called out from a neighbouring hedge, "O my friends, do let us stop fighting."[3] In these fables, it should be noted, as in Jotham's parable, the bramble is involved in a discussion with trees of higher pretensions.

The same theme was treated much more elaborately by the Alexandrian poet Callimachus in a poem, of which a copy, written on papyrus, was discovered in Egypt during the winter of 1905–1906. The verses unfortunately are mutilated and incomplete, but so far as they go they describe a contest for supremacy between a laurel and an olive-tree, in which, up to the point where the manuscript breaks off, the olive-tree appears to get much the better of the argument. So far as the lines can be read or probably restored, the fable runs as follows:[4]

"The ancient Lydians say that once on a time the laurel contended with the olive on Mount Tmolus. For the laurel was a tall tree and fair, and fluttering her branches thus she spoke: 'What house is there at whose doorposts I am not set up? What soothsayer or what sacrificer bears me not? The Pythian prophetess, too, she sits on laurel, eats of laurel,[5] lies on laurel. O foolish olive, did not Branchus heal Ionia's sons with but a stroke of laurel and a few muttered words, what time Phoebus was wroth with them? I go to feasts and to the Pythian choral dance, I am given as a prize in games, and the Dorians cut me at Tempe on the mountain tops and bear me thence to Delphi, whene'er Apollo's rites are solemnized. O foolish olive, no sorrow do I know, nor mine the path that the corpse-bearer treads. For I am pure, and men tread me not under foot, for I am holy. But with thee they crown themselves whene'er they are about to burn a corpse or lay it out for burial, and thee they duly spread under the dead man's ribs.'

"So spake she boasting; but the mother of the oil answered her calmly: 'O laurel, barren of all the things I bear, thou hast sung like a swan at the end. . . . I attend to the grave the men whom Ares slays, and [am spread under the heads] of heroes who [died gloriously]. And when children bear to the tomb their white-haired grandam or Tithonus old, I go with them and on the path am laid, (helping them) more than thou (doest help) the men who bring thee from Tempe's dale. But as for that thou spakest of, am not I a better prize than thou? for are not the games at Olympia greater than the games at Delphi?[6] But silence is best. Not a word more concerning thee shall I so much as mutter, neither good nor bad. Yet lo! the birds that perch among my leaves are twittering thus: "Who found the laurel? It was the earth who brought it forth as she brings forth the ilex, the oak, the galingale, or other woodland things. But who found the olive? Pallas it was, when she contended for the shore with him who dwells amid the sea-weed, and the ancient one gave judgment, he the man with snaky limbs below.[7] That is one fall for the laurel! But of the immortals, who honours the olive, and who the laurel? Apollo honours the laurel, and Pallas honours the olive, which she found. In that they are alike, for I distinguish not between the gods. But what is the laurel's fruit? How shall I use it? It is good neither to eat nor to drink nor to anoint one's self with. But pleasing is the olive's fruit in many ways, both as a food and as an unguent. . . . That is, I think, the laurel's second fall. And then what is the tree whose leaves the suppliants hold out? The olive's leaves. That is the laurel's third fall." But plague on these birds, will they never stop? They must still be chattering! Impudent crow, is thy beak not sore with croaking? "Whose trunk is it that the Delians preserve? It is the olive's, which gave a seat to Leto." ' . . . So spake the olive. But the laurel's rage swelled at the words, and the smart struck deeper than before. [And now an ancient spreading thorn-bush][8] spoke up, for she was not far from the trees. 'O my poor friends,' quoth she, 'do let us cease, lest we carry the quarrel too far. Come, let's give over bickering.' But the laurel glared daggers at the thorn, and thus she spake: 'O cursed wretch, don't preach patience to me, as if thou wert one of us. Thy very neighbourhood chokes me. By Phoebus, by Persephone, talk not of reconciliation! Slay me rather!' "

At this point the poem breaks off in the manuscript, and we cannot say how the quarrel between the trees ended, but from the poet's evident partiality for the olive, we may conjecture that the subsequent verses described the triumph of that pacific, fruitful, and useful tree over the bellicose, barren, and boastful laurel. What tree or shrub it was that attempted to intervene as peacemaker in the strife, and got small thanks for its pains from one at least of the disputants, we cannot say for certain, since the Greek text at this point is mutilated; but the analogy of Aesop's fable, in which a bramble attempts to end a dispute between a pomegranate and an apple-tree, suggests that the humble bush may have played the same benevolent but thankless part in the poem of Callimachus, and the suggestion is borne out by the sharp way in which the proud laurel turns on the would-be mediator, whose claim to meddle in a quarrel between trees she contemptuously rejects ("as if thou wert one of us").

[A similar fable concerning the rivalry of the pomegranate-tree and the bramble occurs in the Aramaic version of the celebrated Romance of Aḥikar, inscribed on a palimpsest papyrus of the late fifth century B.C. discovered, in 1906–7, at Elephantine in Upper Egypt. The bramble, we read, once taunted the pomegranate-tree by asking why anyone who tried to touch its fruit had always to encounter a mass of thorns. "True," rejoined the pomegranate tartly, "but you yourself offer nothing else."[8a]]

The rivalry between the trees appears to be a favourite theme of Armenian fables. For example, in one of them it is said that the plants held a council to decide which of them deserved to reign over the rest. Some proposed the date-palm, because he is tall and his fruits are sweet. But the vine resisted the proposal, saying, "It is I who diffuse joy; it is I who deserve to reign." The fig-tree said, "It is I, for I am sweet to the taste." The thorn said, "The honour should be mine, because I prick." Each of them thought himself better than the rest, and imagined that he could dispense with them. As for the date-palm, on reflection he perceived that the trees would not let him reign, because they were loth to share their honours with others. He said, "It belongs to me rather than to anybody else to be king." The other trees admitted his claim to a certain extent. They said, "Thou art tall and thy fruits are sweet, but thou lackest two things. Thou does not bear fruit at the same time that we do, and thou art not suitable for building. Besides, thou art so tall that it is impossible for many people to enjoy thy fruit." He answered, "I shall become king and make you princes, and after accomplishing my time I shall still reign over your sons." He set the kingdom in order, naming the rest to various offices. The vine he made chief cupbearer, the fig-tree consul, the thorn head executioner, the pomegranate head physician; other plants were to serve for medicines, the cedars for building, the forests for fuel, the bushes for prison; each was assigned its special task.[9]

A Malay story tells of a dispute between the plants as to their respective claims to precedence. Once upon a time, we are informed, the maize-plant boasted, saying, "If rice should cease to exist, I alone should suffice to sustain mankind." But the liane and the jungle yam each made a like boast, and as the parties could not agree, the case was brought before King Solomon. Said Solomon, "All three of you are perfectly right, albeit it were perhaps better that the maize-plant should sustain mankind because of his comradeship with the bean." Thereat the wrath of the liane and the yam waxed hot against the maize-plant, and they went off together to hunt for a fruit-spike of the jungle fig-tree whereon to impale him, but found none. And meanwhile the maize-plant, hearing news of their quest, set to work to find arrow-poison. And when he found it he poisoned the jungle yam therewith, wherefore to this day the jungle yam has narcotic properties. Then the jungle yam, being wroth thereat, speared the maize-plant in his turn, wherefore to this day the cobs of the maize are perforated. And the maize-plant, reaching out in turn, seized the pointed shoot of a *wilang* (?) stem and wounded the liane therewith. At this juncture the parties to the quarrel went before the prophet Elijah who said, "This matter is too great for me, take ye it before Solomon." And Solomon said, "Let them fight it out between them, that the rage of their hearts may be appeased." Wherefore there was battle between them for twice seven days. And when the twice seven days were needed, the battle being still undecided, the combatants were parted, and a space was set between them by Solomon. And the jungle yam he made to sit down, and the liane to lie down. But the maize-plant and the bean he made to stand together.[10]

Jotham's parable seems to have enjoyed a special popularity during the

Middle Ages, for we find it detached from its Biblical setting and inserted in various collections of fables which were derived, directly or indirectly, from Phaedrus. In some of these collections the story is taken with but slight verbal changes from the Vulgate,[11] but in a Latin version of the fables which pass under the name of the mediaeval French poetess Marie de France, the writer has handled the theme more freely. The trees, so runs the fable, once assembled and consulted about choosing a king. A tall and spreading tree proposed the vine for the kingly office, but the vine refused on the ground that he was weak and could do nothing without a support. So the trees offered to choose the whitethorn, saying that he deserved to reign because he was strong and handsome. But the whitethorn declined the offer, declaring that he was not worthy to reign because he bore no fruit. Several other trees were proposed, but they all excused themselves for various reasons. At last, when no tree could be found that would consent to be king, the broom got up and said, "The sceptre is mine by rights, because I desire to reign and I ought to be king, for my family is most opulent and noble." But the other trees answered the broom, "In the whole family of trees we know none meaner or poorer than thee." The broom replied, "If I am not made king, never will I honour him whom ye shall elect, neither will I love those who appoint another than me." The trees said to him, "What, then, will you be able to do to us if you do not love our king or us?" The broom answered, "Though I seem to you mean and needy, yet could I do that which I had thought to do if I were king." And they all asked him what that was. He said to them, "I had thought to prevent any tree from growing that stands under me or over me." "It is likely enough," replied the others, "that thou couldst do that to us if thou wert king and powerful; but what thinkest thou canst thou do when we are stronger than thou?" But the broom did not answer the question, he only said, "I cannot harm you without injuring myself. Yet I will carry out my intention. I can cause," said he, "that any herb or tree that is under me shall cease to grow, and that any that is above me shall wither. But to do that it is necessary that I myself should burn. Therefore I wish to be consumed with fire, with all my kindred that are about me, in order that those trees which deem themselves great and noble may perish with me in the flames."[12]

This fable is plainly nothing but a feeble expansion of the parable of Jotham.

[When the bramble says to the trees (v. 15), "If in good faith you are anointing me king over you, then come and take refuge in my shade (shadow)," the author of the fable is introducing a clever play on a popular expression associated with kingship. For in the royal letters of Assyria, persons under the special protection of the king, or officials traveling on missions of state are frequently said to be "in his shadow."[12a] Similarly, too, in an Egyptian inscription of Pharaoh Pi-ankhi (about 720 B.C.), courtiers entreat him to "set us in thy shadow."[12b] Not impossibly these expressions refer, if only metaphorically, to being sheltered under the royal parasol.[12c]] ▼

113   The navel of the earth   9:37

When Abimelech and his men come down from Mt. Gerizim to attack the city of Shechem, they are described by the enemy commander as "coming down from the navel of the earth (RSV: center of the land)."

Many ancient and primitive peoples identify their main city or principal shrine with the "navel" or center of the earth—the point where the world axis (often portrayed as a mountain), which reaches from the mid-point of heaven to the mid-point of the netherworld, penetrates its surface.[1] The idea is widely attested among the Sumerians and Semites of Mesopotamia.[2] Cities like Nippur, Larsa, and Sippar, for instance, were so regarded, while the great temple of Marduk in Babylon was held to be "the link between heaven and earth."[3] In Jewish tradition this is said likewise of Jerusalem;[4] and as late as the second and third century of the Common Era, the *omphalos* or navel of the earth was portrayed on coins from the whilom Phoenician city of Tyre.[5] Moreover, to this day, the Samaritans so characterize Gerizim, their sacred mountain, to which specific reference is made in our Biblical passage.[6]

In Greece this idea was entertained about Delos, Delphi, Pythoi, Paphos (in Cyprus), and other shrines;[7] and among the Arabs about the Ka'aba at Mecca.[8] The Hindus speak in the same vein of the mythical Mt. Meru in the Himalayas,[9] and the Buddhists of the spot where the Master received enlightenment under the banyan-tree.[10] That the Celts too shared the notion "is evidenced by such words as *medinemetum, mediolanum* which exist even today in French place names. . . . In the village of Armany (district of La Roche) can be found a 'Middle-of-the-Earth-Stone.' "[11] The notion obtains also among the Pygmies of Malacca,[12] and "seems, indeed, to be part of the symbolism of pre-historic monuments."[13]

114   Sowing a city with salt

After the defeat of the men of Shechem, Abimelech razed their city and strewed salt upon it.

The action is not unparalleled in the Ancient Near East. In a treaty concluded, around 750 B.C., between Barga'yah, king of a yet unidentified realm named K-t-k, and Matta'el, king of Arpad, in Syria, the curse is invoked on the latter that, if he break faith, his city "shall be sown with natron and salt."[1] Similarly, King Ashurbanipal of Assyria (688–33 B.C.) boasts that he "sowed with salt" the vanquished cities of Elam.[2] Moreover, in later times, Attila employed the same device after his conquest of Padua, and Frederick Barbarossa after the capitulation of Milan.[3]

In ancient and primitive thought salt has various connotations, and the practice has therefore been explained in several different ways.

(i) The older commentators saw in it *a symbol of devastation,* salt being indeed mentioned in this sense elsewhere in the Old Testament itself, viz., Jeremiah 17:6 ("saltland"||"wilderness"); Zephaniah 2:9 ("nettles and saltpits and a waste for ever"); Psalm 107:34 ("salty waste" × fruitful land"); and Job 39:6 (||"steppe").

(ii) Others, however, have suggested that it was *a symbol of sterility invoked as retribution for a breach of covenant*,[4] such as the men of Shechem are said explicitly (9:22) to have committed against Abimelech. This explanation is supported by the terms of the aforementioned ancient treaty, and salt is so used symbolically in the military oath of the Hittites: "[The officiant] places salt in their hands . . . and speaks as follows: '. . . Whoever breaks these oaths, shows disrespect to the king of the Hatti (Hittite) land, and turns his eyes in hostile fashion upon the Hatti land, . . . let him be scattered like salt! Just as salt has no seed, even so let that man's name, seed, house, cattle and sheep perish!' "[5]

(iii) A third view is that strewing a city with salt was *a means of putting it under a ban*.[6] The ban (Heb.: *ḥerem*) was a form of taboo, and since tabooed objects were regarded as numinous or "charged" they were treated in the same way as those deemed sacred.[7] Salt, we know, was often used to consecrate and purify the latter.[8]

(iv) The practice has been interpreted also as *a means of purifying the soil from the contamination of bloodshed*[9] This, of course, would likewise be based on the general use of salt as a purifying agent.

(v) Lastly, it has been suggested that the real purpose of the action was *to avert the vengeful spirits of the slain*—in this case more specifically, of Abimelech's seventy murdered brothers.[10] Salt, on account of its incorruptibility, is widely employed as a means of forefending demons or noxious spirits (see below, §211) and, as we have seen (above, §26), fear of the vengeful ghosts of the slain played an important role in ancient and primitive belief.

The first of these explanations is, on the whole, the most plausible. What argues especially in its favor is the fact that salt is often mentioned alongside of other substances which certainly symbolize devastation. Thus, in the aforementioned ancient Syrian treaty, as again in the inscription of Asnurbanipal and in a record of the early Hittite king, Anittas of Kussara, the vanquished city is sown also with *cress* or weeds,[11] and in the Hittite myth of the Snaring of the Dragon (Illuyankas), the same is done to a house consigned to destruction;[12] while in Deuteronomy 29:23 salt is conjoined with *brimstone*.[13] Furthermore, against the view that the practice was a form of curse for violation of a covenant it is to be observed that when Ashurbanipal strewed salt over the cities of Elam no such breach of faith was in fact involved; the Assyrian monarch was simply invading them on an imperialistic rampage. Significant too is the fact that in an Assyrian list of omens, salt "sprouting" from the soil is mentioned as a bad sign.[14]

It may be added, as a matter of curious interest, that the practice was based on the effect of salt on weeds and topsoil only; if it is sunk to the roots of vegetation, it in fact stimulates growth![15]

115   Jephthah's vow   11:30–40

> (a) *Jephthah, the Gileadite, champion of Israel, makes a vow that if Yahweh will grant him victory over the Ammonites who are waging war against his people, he will sacrifice to him the first person who meets him when he returns home. He is met by his daughter, who is his only child.*

Parallels to this story are to be found in the popular lore of several peoples.[1] The best known is probably the Greek legend of Idomeneus, king of Crete. Caught in a storm on his return from the Trojan War, he vowed to Poseidon, god of the sea, that he would sacrifice to him whomever he would first meet when he landed safely on his native shores. This turned out to be his own son.[2]

A similar tale was told by the Greeks about Maeander, the son of Cercaphos and Anaxibia. At war with the people of Perssinus, in Phrygia, he vowed to the Great Mother that if she granted him victory he would sacrifice to her the first person who came out to greet him when he returned home. The first to do so was his own son, Archelaos, together with his mother and sister.[3]

In modern European versions of the tale, it tends to be combined with the familiar theme of the prince bewitched into the form of an animal. From Hesse, Germany, for example, comes the story of a man who went on a journey and promised his youngest daughter to bring back to her a singing and soaring lark. When, however, he at last espied one, a lion stepped forth, ready to devour him. Thereupon the merchant promised the beast that if it would spare him and permit him to take the bird, he would give it the first thing that met him when he returned home. This turned out to be the daughter herself. However, the story has a happy ending, for the lion proves to be a handsome prince who has been bewitched but is eventually freed from the spell.[4]

A variant of this tale from Lorraine makes the promised gift a talking rose. This is found in the courtyard of a castle, but is guarded by a white wolf. A similar bargain is struck, with a similar result, but here too the wolf turns out to be an enchanted prince. In this case, however, the story does not end happily, for an equally familiar motif is tacked on to it: the wolf swears the girl to secrecy about his true identity, but she betrays it, and he instantly falls dead.[5]

Yet another variant, this time from Hanover, makes the prize a *Löwenblatt*, and the protector of it a black poodle. Once again, the same pact is concluded, with the same result, but here the additional element is introduced that the girl's father, a king, at first tries to palm the animal off with a goosegirl and then with a false princess. The fraud is detected each time, but when the real daughter is at last delivered up, it turns out that the poodle is really an enchanted prince.[6] (In versions of the same story from Schleswig-Holstein the enchanted prince takes the form of a bear or white wolf.[7])

As told in the Tyrol, it is a traveling merchant who promises his youngest daughter to bring her a leaf that dances, sings, and plays. The leaf, however, is guarded by a serpent who exacts the same bargains, again with the same result, but who is eventually revealed to be a bewitched youth.[8]

In a Lithuanian version it is a king who sets out for Wilna to find a woman who will clean and tend his palace. His youngest daughter, however, offers to do this herself, if he will bring her back a mat woven of living flowers. On the way home, he finds in a forest a wolf wearing a hood of just such blossoms. Same bargain; same result; and, once again, the wolf is really an enchanted prince.[9]

The story is known also in Sweden, but there it is a king who loses his way in a wood and is guided out of it by a man in a gray cloak, who demands as the price of his services the first person whom the king encounters on returning to his palace. It turns out, of course, to be his youngest and favorite daughter. He at first tries to palm off her two older sisters. The man sends them back, but when the youngest girl is indeed delivered to him, he once again proves to be an enchanted prince or nobleman.[10]

Somewhat similar in detail, but revolving around the same theme, is another Swedish story which tells how a mermaid once released a king's ship in exchange for a promise to give him the first thing which the king met on his return. It was his own son.[11]

In a Danish version, it is a dwarf who rescues a king from a swamp upon similar conditions. The eventual victim of the rash vow is the king's own son and heir, who has been born to him while he was on his travels.[12]

Nor is the story confined to Europe. An Arabic poem, dating before the time of Mohammed, relates how Al-Mundhir, king of Ḥira, once vowed that on a certain day each year he would sacrifice the first person he saw. On one occasion this turned out to be his favorite, 'Abid.[13]

> **(b)** *Jephthah's daughter, on hearing of the fate in store for her, begs her father to spare her for two months so that she may "go and wander[14] about on the mountains and bewail my virginity, along with my companions." This he grants. "It then became a custom in Israel," adds the writer, "that Israelite maidens went year by year to lament the daughter of Jephthah the Gileadite four days in the year."*

Modern scholars see in this a story based on the ancient and primitive custom of annually bewailing the dead or ousted spirit of fertility during the dry or winter season.[15] That spirit would here have been personified, like Persephone in Greek myth, as a female.

"Such lamentation for Osiris in Egypt, Altis in Asia Minor, and Adonis in

Syria are well known.[16] Similarly, in the Babylonian Epic of Gilgamesh (vi.46–47) and again in the poem of the Descent of Ishtar to the Netherworld (rev. 56–57)[17] mention is made specifically of the annual weeping of Tammuz. Moreover, an early Babylonian text published by Reisner[18] and another of Arsacid date[19] define the month of Tammuz (July) as a period of wailing (*tekiltu*), ritual mourning (*rikis sipitti*) and weeping (*bikîtum*);[20] while an old Assyrian almanac prescribes weeping for its second day.[21] This seasonal ululation, which obtained likewise in the Greek cult of Demeter and Kore,[22] survived, indeed, into the Christian era, for a medieval Arabic antiquary records the performance of it at Harren.[23] It is true that recent studies have thrown considerable doubt upon the time-honored identification of Tammuz with the spirit of fertility,[24] but for our present purpose this is not really important, for the analogy to the rite performed by Jephthah's daughter could still stand, even if Tammuz was in fact bewailed for other reasons.

The wailing for these seasonal spirits is, *au fond,* a mythological rationalization of an even more primitive custom of howling and shrieking at harvest ceremonies. "The Egyptians, says Diodorus, used to shed tears and cry upon Iris at the first cutting of the corn,[25] and their summer festival was marked, according to Herodotus, by the chanting of a doleful lay called Maneros[26]—a distortion of the Egyptian words, *maa n per.k,* "come to thy house,"[27] which constitute the initial phrase in seasonal dirges for Osiris which have actually come down to us.[28] The custom is attested also at a much later date by Firmicus Maternus, who reproaches the pagan Egyptians for "lamenting over the crops and wailing over the growing seed."[29]

In Mesopotamia, the harvest was accompanied by a ritual cry known as *alalu,* or "ululation";[30] and Plutarch informs us that the traditional cry at the Attic vintage festival of Oschophoria was *eleleu.*[31] Similarly, according to a writer quoted by Athenaeus, the ritual dirges uttered in the mysteries of Demeter and Kore went under the name of *iouloi* (or *houloi*), i.e., "howls."[32] . . . Lamentations were likewise a characteristic feature of the Eleusinian mysteries."[33]

The two-months which Jephthah's daughter spends in such rites correspond to the double-month of the early (10th cent. B.C.) Palestinian agricultural calendar discovered at Gezer,[34] and to the system of reckoning employed by the pre-Islamic Arabs.[35]

As for the four days of annual wailing in Israel, that is best illustrated by the Attis mysteries, where the god was ceremoniously interred on March 22, to be resurrected three days later.[36] As has often been observed, this survives in the third-day resurrection in Christianity, and there would appear to be a distinct allusion to it in Hosea 6:2.

Lastly, it should be noted that the ritual ululations are frequently satirized by the Hebrew prophets themselves (e.g., Hos. 7:14; Joel 1:5; Amos 5:16–17; Zeph. 1:10), showing the prevalence of this practice in popular Palestinian usage (see below, §221).

116 Shibboleth

The Ephraimites at first refuse aid to Jephthah and his men against the Ammonites. When they subsequently offer their services, Jephthah treats them as opportunistic "johnnies-come-lately," and when they retort that the Gileadites are simply secessionists from Ephraim, he sets his men against them and cuts off their retreat by occupying the fords of the Jordan. Any fugitive Ephraimite who tries to pass himself off as a Gileadite is made to repeat the word shibboleth *(ear of corn). But, invariably, he pronounces it* sibboleth, *thereby betraying himself. In this way no less than forty-two thousand Ephraimites meet their death.*

The device employed in this famous story has been repeated on several historical occasions.[1] Thus, when the English defeated the Danes on St. Bryce's day (November 13), 1002, fugitive enemies were detected by being made to utter the words "Chichester Church," which they pronounced, "Shishshester Shersh."[2] Similarly, during Wat Tyler's uprising in 1381, "many Flemings lost their heads" because "they could not say, 'Bread and cheese,' but said instead, 'Case and Brode.'"[3] Again, when the Frisians defeated the forces of William IV, Count of Holland, near Stavoren, in 1345, they recognized escaping Hollanders by making them recite verses, which they mispronounced.[4]

117 Samson

▲ Among the grave judges of Israel the burly hero Samson cuts a strange figure. That he judged Israel for twenty years we are indeed informed by the sacred writer, but of the judgments which he delivered in his judicial character not one has been recorded, and if the tenor of his pronouncements can be inferred from the nature of his acts, we may be allowed to doubt whether he particularly adorned the bench of justice. His talent would seem to have lain rather in the direction of brawling and fighting, burning down people's cornricks, and beating up the quarters of loose women; in short, he appears to have shone in the character of a libertine and a rakehell rather than in a strictly judicial capacity. Instead of a dull list of his legal decisions we are treated to an amusing, if not very edifying, narrative of his adventures in love and in war, or rather in filibustering; for if we accept, as we are bound to do, the scriptural account of this roystering swashbuckler, he never levied a regular war or headed a national insurrection against the Philistines, the oppressors of his people; he merely sallied forth from time to time as a solitary paladin or knight-errant, and mowed them down with the jawbone of an ass or any other equally serviceable weapon that came to his hand. And even on these predatory expeditions (for he had no scruple about relieving his victims of their clothes and probably of their purses) the idea of delivering his nation from servitude was to all appearance the last thing that would have occurred to him.

In the extravagance of its colouring the picture of Samson owes more to the brush of the story-teller than to the pen of the historian. The marvellous and diverting incidents of his career probably floated about loosely as popular tales on the current of oral tradition long before they crystallized around the memory of a real man, a doughty highlander and borderer, a sort of Hebrew Rob Roy, whose choleric temper, dauntless courage, and prodigious bodily strength marked him out as the champion of Israel in many a wild foray across the border into the rich lowlands of Philistia. For there is no sufficient reason to doubt that a firm basis of fact underlies the flimsy and transparent super-structure of fancy in the Samson saga. The particularity with which the scenes of his life, from birth to death, are laid in definite towns and places, speaks strongly in favour of a genuine local tradition, and as strongly against the theory of a solar myth, into which some writers would dissolve the story of the brawny hero. ▼

(a) Samson as a solar hero[1]

The basis of the solar-myth theory is as follows: (i) The name Samson derives from the Hebrew word *shemesh,* meaning "sun," and much of the action takes place near Beth-Shemesh (mod. Tell Rumeileh), presumably an ancient shrine of the sun-god, where solar myths would very probably have been current.[2] (ii) The story of how Samson burned up the standing grain and olive crop of the Philistines by sending into their fields foxes with fire-brands tied to their tails (15:4–6) might well represent the action of the scorching sun. (iii) The shearing of Samson's locks at the instigation of Delilah (16:16–19) might, in the same way, reflect the curtailment of the sun's rays by the shades of the night.[3]

In the light of Comparative Folklore, however, this interpretation can no longer be sustained. The incident of the foxes has, as we shall see, several parallels in other cultures, in all of which it possesses no symbolic significance, but can be readily explained as based either on a well-established ritual practice or an equally well-documented military stratagem. There are likewise plenty of analogues to the story of how a hero was enfeebled by the shearing of his locks, and in none of them does he bear a name which has anything whatsoever to do with the sun.[4] What is more, we now know both from Mesopotamian and from Canaanite sources that Samson (or its equivalent) was in fact a not uncommon name among ordinary mortals.[5]

(b) Samson and the foxes   15:4–5

Samson's first exploit was the firing of the Philistines' grainfields by sending into them foxes with lighted torches tied to their tails.

Modern scholars have advanced two alternative explanations of this in-cident, each based on popular practice. According to the one, it reflects, albeit in a distorting mirror, *a traditional ritual usage designed to remove mildew from crops*. The Roman poet Ovid tells us that at the annual Festival of Ceres (on April 19) it was customary to send into the fields foxes with firebrands tied to their tails.[6] Although he explains it on quasi-historical grounds, this custom (which is attested also by the fabulist Babrius)[7] was really a form of lustration by fire, mildew and other noxious elements being thereby consumed. Similarly, among the Arabs, foxes with torches attached to their tails were sometimes dispatched into the cornfields as a charm to promote rainfall and fertility;[8] while in European folklore the fox itself often personifies mildew because it is of the same color.[9] Moreover, in Paris and in parts of Savoy, foxes are (or once were) occasionally burned or singed in the midsummer bonfires,[10] though, admittedly, this may have been simply a ceremonious way of getting rid of the invaders.

The other explanation of Samson's exploit sees in it a *military stratagem*—part of the guerrilla tactics employed at the time by the Israelites against the Philistines.[11] For this an excellent parallel is offered by Livy's account of how Hannibal scared the Roman troops at Lake Trasimene, in 217 B.C., by launching into their fields oxen with firebrands tied to their horns.[12] In the same way, too, when in 1262 the Mongols were encamped against the Arabs in a field outside Aleppo, the latter frightened them off by dispatching into their midst foxes and hounds with torches attached to their tails;[13] and the redoubtable Timur (Tamurlane) is said to have routed an Indian army, in 1397, by striking panic in its elephants at the sight of a host of camels carrying flaming torches.[14] There is an interesting variation of this theme in the Icelandic *Heimskringla* of Snori Sturluson. Harald of Norway, we read, was laying siege to a large and populous town in Sicily, but came to realize that its walls were too stout to be broken down and that its townsmen had plenty of provisions with which to hold out. So "he thought up a scheme: he told his bird-catchers to catch the small birds that nested within the town and flew out to the woods each day in search of food. Harald had small shavings of fir tied to the backs of the birds, and then he smeared the shavings with wax and sulphur and set fire to them. As soon as the birds were released they all flew straight home to their young in their nests in the town; the nests were under the eaves of the roofs, which were thatched with reeds or straws. The thatched roofs caught fire from the birds, and although each bird could only carry a tiny flame, it quickly became a great fire; a host of birds set roofs alight all over the town. One house after another caught fire, and soon the whole town was ablaze. At that all the people came out of the town, begging for mercy."[15]

(c) Samson's riddle 14

The Biblical writer accounts for Samson's exploit as an act of revenge for a thwarted love affair. Samson, runs the story, had picked a wife from among the Philistines at Timnah (modern Tibneh, west of Beth Shemesh). At the wedding feast, as a typical Oriental form of entertainment, he had posed a riddle to the assembled company of thirty guests, but the bride had wheedled the solution out of him and had revealed it. In high dudgeon, Samson had betaken himself to Ashkelon and there slain thirty Philistines. Outraged at this savagery, his father-in-law had thereupon canceled the marriage, giving the girl to the best man and denying Samson any access to her. At this, Samson took three hundred foxes, turned them tail to tail, attached lighted torches to each pair of tails, and sent them into the Philistine's fields at the time of the wheat harvest.

The riddle which Samson's guests were invited to solve was to identify the object described in the following jingle:

> *It comes from "the eater"*
> *'tis something you eat,*
> *—from something fierce,*
> *but itself is sweet.*

The answer was, honey (14:18).

It has recently been shown that the point of the riddle lies—as usually—in a play on words.[16] The Hebrew word for *honey, viz., arî,* is identical in outward form with one meaning *lion.* The latter is the "something fierce." It is also "the eater," for this was a popular designation both among the Canaanite and (later) among the Arabs for a carnivorous beast.[17]

▲ (d) Samson and Delilah 16

The art and skill of the storyteller reveal themselves most clearly, however, in the account of the catastrophe which befell his hero through the wiles of his treacherous mistress, Delilah, who wormed from him the secret that his great strength lay in his hair, and then betrayed him to his enemies by having it shorn.

The story revolves around the widespread belief that the strength, or very life of men (especially of heroes), resides in their locks.[18] Thus, the natives of Amboyna, an island in the East Indies, used to think that their vigor would desert them if their locks were shorn. A criminal under torture in a Dutch court once persisted in denying his guilt until his hair was cut off, when he immediately confessed. One man, who was tried for murder, endured without flinching the utmost ingenuity of his torturers till he saw the surgeon standing by with a pair of shears. On asking what they were for, and being told that it was to shave his hair, he begged that they would not do it, and made a clean breast. In subsequent cases, when torture failed to wring a confession from a prisoner, the Dutch authorities made a practice of cutting off his hair.[19] The natives of Ceram, another East Indian Island, still believe that if young people have their hair cut they will be weakened and enervated.[20]

In Europe it used to be thought that the maleficent powers of witches and wizards resided in their hair, and that nothing could make any impression on these miscreants so long as they kept their hair on. Hence in France it was customary to shave the whole bodies of persons charged with sorcery before handing them over to the tormentor. Millaeus witnessed the torture of some persons at Toulouse, from whom no confession could be wrung until they were stripped and completely shaven, when they readily acknowledged the truth of the charge. A woman also, who apparently led a pious life, was put to the torture on suspicion of witchcraft, and bore her agonies with incredible constancy, until complete depilation drove her to admit her guilt. The noted inquisitor Sprenger contented himself with shaving the head of the suspected witch or warlock; but his more thoroughgoing colleague Cumanus shaved the whole bodies of forty-one women before committing them all to the flames. He had high authority for this rigorous scrutiny, since Satan himself, in a sermon preached from the pulpit of North Berwick church, comforted his many servants by assuring them that no harm could befall them "sa lang as their hair wes on, and sould newir latt ane teir fall fra thair ene."[21] Similarly in Bastar, a province of India, "if a man is adjudged guilty of witchcraft, he is beaten by the crowd, his hair is shaved, the hair being supposed to constitute his power of mischief, his front teeth are knocked out, in order, it is said, to prevent him from muttering incantations. . . . Women suspected of sorcery have to undergo the same ordeal; if found guilty, the same punishment is awarded, and after being shaved, their hair is attached to a tree in some public place."[22] So among the Bhils, a rude race of Central India, when a woman was convicted of witchcraft and had been subjected to various forms of persuasion, such as hanging head downwards from a tree and having pepper rubbed into her eyes, a lock of hair was cut from her head and buried in the ground, "that the last link between her and her former powers of mischief might be broken."[23] In like manner among the Aztecs of Mexico, when wizards and witches "had done their evil deeds, and the time came to put an end to their detestable life, some one laid hold of them and cropped the hair on the crown of their heads, which took from them all their power of sorcery and enchantment, and then it was that by death they put an end to their odious existence."[24]

[On the other hand, an ancient Mesopotamian magical text tells us that witches themselves contrived to pluck out hairs from their intended victims in order to work their evil upon them;[24a] and everyone knows of the use in spells of "a hair of the dog that bit you."

Nor are these the only illustrations of this widespread belief. In many cultures, as we have seen, warriors have to go unshorn lest they lose their power.[24b] A child's hair may not be cut during its first year, since this would prejudice its chances of survival.[24c] Among the Pennsylvania Dutch a woman may not cut her husband's hair lest he became enfeebled and impotent.[24d]

Elsewhere baldness is regarded as a sign of debility.[24e] Moreover, because the hair (like the fingernails) is symbolic of the total self, it is often surrendered in *rites de passage,* when a person "changes identity" by transition from one stage of life to another. In ancient Greece, for example, girls dedicated their tresses to Artemis when they reached puberty;[24f] and elsewhere brides are shorn at marriage,[24g] as are nuns when they become "brides of Christ." It is this belief too that underlies the Teutonic custom of shearing the locks of an adulteress[24h]—a custom known also to the Babylonians, Arabs, and Jews[24i] as also that of cutting the hair of prisoners[24j] or criminals.[24k] So also, the hair is sometimes surrendered in token of adoption, as among the Pawnee Indians of North America.[24l] It is related of Boson, king of Provence, that he had his hair cut off and dedicated to Pope John VIII when the latter adopted him; this signified surrender of personality.[24m]]

It is no wonder that a belief so widespread should find its way into fairy tales which, for all the seeming licence of fancy, reflect as in a mirror the real faith once held by the people among whom the stories circulated. The natives of Nias, an island off the west coast of Sumatra, relate that once upon a time a certain chief named Laubo Maros was driven by an earthquake from Macassar, in Celebes, and migrated with his followers to Nias. Among those who followed his fortunes to the new land were his uncle and his uncle's wife. But the rascally nephew fell in love with his uncle's wife and contrived by a stratagem to get possession of the lady. The injured husband fled to Malacca and besought the Sultan of Johore to assist him in avenging his wrongs. The Sultan consented and declared war on Laubo Maros. Meanwhile, however, that unscrupulous chief had fortified his settlement with an impenetrable hedge of prickly bamboo, which defied all the attempts of the Sultan and his troops to take it by storm. Defeated in open battle, the wily Sultan now had recourse to stratagem. He returned to Johore and there laded a ship with Spanish mats. Then he sailed back to Nias, and anchoring off his enemy's fort he loaded his guns with the Spanish mats instead of with shot and shell, and so opened fire on the place. The mats flew like hail through the air and soon were lying thick on the prickly hedge of the fort and on the shore in its neighbourhood. The trap was now set and the Sultan waited to see what would follow. He had not long to wait. An old woman, prowling along the beach, picked up one of the mats and saw the rest spread out temptingly around her. Overjoyed at the discovery she passed the good news among her neighbours, who hastened to the spot, and in a trice the prickly hedge was not only stripped bare of the mats but torn down and levelled with the ground. So the Sultan of Johore and his men had only to march into the fort and take possession. The defenders fled, but the wicked chief himself fell into the hands of the victors. He was condemned to death, but great difficulty was experienced in executing the sentence. They threw him into the sea, but the water would not drown him; they laid him on a blazing pyre, but the fire would not burn him;

they hacked at every part of his body with swords, but steel would not pierce him. Then they perceived that he was an enchanter, and they consulted his wife to learn how they might kill him. Like Delilah, she revealed the fatal secret. On the chief's head grew a hair as hard as a copper wire, and with this wire his life was bound up. So the hair was plucked out, and with it his spirit fled.[25] In this and some of the following tales it is not merely the strength but the life of the hero which is supposed to have its seat in his hair, so that the loss of the hair involves his death.

Tales like that of Samson and Delilah were current in the legendary lore of ancient Greece. It is said that Nisus, king of Megara, had a purple or golden hair on the middle of his head, and that he was doomed to die whenever that hair should be plucked out. When Megara was besieged by the Cretans, the king's daughter Scylla fell in love with Minos, their king, and pulled out the fatal hair from her father's head. So he died.[26] According to one account it was not the life but the strength of Nisus that was in his golden hair; when it was pulled out, he grew weak and was slain by Minos.[27] In this form the story of Nisus resembles still more closely the story of Samson. Again, Poseidon is said to have made Pterelaus immortal by giving him a golden hair on his head. But when Taphos, the home of Pterelaus was besieged by Amphitryo, the daughter of Pterelaus fell in love with Amphitryo and killed her father by plucking out the golden hair with which his life was bound up.[28] In a modern Greek folk-tale a man's strength lies in three golden hairs on his head. When his mother pulls them out, he grows weak and timid and is slain by his enemies.[29] Another Greek story, in which we may perhaps detect a reminiscence of Nisus and Scylla, relates how a certain king, who was the strongest man of his time, had three long hairs on his breast. But when he went to war with another king, and his own treacherous wife had cut off the three hairs, he became the weakest of men.[30]

[Celtic lore tells similarly how Blodenwedd disabled Llew Llaw by cutting off his hair and exposing him, at the vulnerable moment, to attack by her lover, Gromas; and in Irish legend, Blathnat is said likewise to have deprived Cu Roi of his strength and then invited her lover Cuchularin to slay him.[30a] The same motif appears also in Norse mythology: Loki shears the golden tresses of Sif, the wife of Thor.[30b] Stories of the same tenor are to be found also in The Arabian Nights[30c] and in Turkish popular tales.[30d]]

Sometimes the hero's strength is said to lie not in his hair but rather in some external object such as an egg or a bird.

A Russian story relates how a certain warlock called Kashtshei or Koshchei the Deathless carried off a princess and kept her prisoner in his golden castle. However, a prince made up to her one day as she was walking alone and disconsolate in the castle garden, and cheered by the prospect of escaping with him she went to the warlock and coaxed him with false and flattering words, saying, "My dearest friend, tell me, I pray you, will you never die?" "Certainly not," says he. "Well," says she, "and where is your death? Is it in your dwelling?" "To be sure it is," says he, "it is in the broom under the threshold." Thereupon the princess seized the broom and threw it on the fire, but although the broom burned, the deathless Koshchei remained alive; indeed not so much as a hair of him was singed. Balked in her first attempt, the artful hussy pouted and said, "You do not love me true, for you have not told me where your death is; yet I am not angry, but love you with all my heart." With these fawning words she besought the warlock to tell her truly where his death was. So he laughed and said, "Why do you wish to know? Well then, out of love I will tell you where it lies. In a certain field there stand three green oaks, and under the roots of the largest oak is a worm, and if ever this worm is found and crushed, I shall die." When the princess heard these words, she went straight to her lover and told him all; and he searched till he found the oaks and dug up the worm and crushed it. Then he hurried to the warlock's castle, but only to learn that the warlock was still alive. Then the princess fell to wheedling and coaxing Koshchei once more, and this time, overcome by her wiles, he opened his heart to her and told her the truth. "My death," said he, "is far from here and hard to find, on the wide ocean. In that sea is an island, and on the island grows a green oak, and beneath the oak is an iron chest, and in the chest is a small basket, and in the basket is a hare, and in the hare is a duck, and in the duck is an egg; and he who finds the egg and breaks it, kills me at the same time." The prince naturally procured the fateful egg and with it in his hands he confronted the deathless warlock. The monster would have killed him, but the prince began to squeeze the egg. At that the warlock shrieked with pain, and turning to the false princess, who stood smirking and smiling, "Was it not out of love for you," said he, "that I told you where my death was? And is this the return you make to me?" With that he grabbed at his sword, which hung from a peg on the wall; but before he could reach it, the prince had crushed the egg, and sure enough the deathless warlock found his death at the same moment."[31]

A Serbian story relates how a certain warlock called True Steel carried off a prince's wife and kept her shut up in his cave. But the prince contrived to get speech of her, and told her that she must persuade True Steel to reveal to her where his strength lay. So when True Steel came home, the prince's wife said to him, "Tell me, now, where is your great strength?" He answered, "My wife, my strength is in my sword." Then she began to pray and turned to his sword. When True Steel saw that, he laughed and said, "O foolish woman! my strength is not in my sword, but in my bow and arrows." Then she turned towards the bow and arrows and prayed. But True Steel said, "I see, my wife, you have a clever teacher who has taught you to find out where my strength lies. I could almost say that your husband is living, and it is he who teaches you." But she assured him that nobody had taught her. When she found he had deceived her again, she waited for some days and then asked him again about the secret of his strength. He answered, "Since you think so much of my strength, I will tell you truly where it is. Far away from here there is a very high mountain; in the mountain there is a fox; in the fox there is a heart; in the heart there is a bird, and in this bird is my strength. It is no easy task, however, to catch the fox, for she can transform herself into a multitude of creatures." Next day, when True Steel went forth from the cave, the prince came and learned from his wife the true secret of the warlock's strength. So away he hied to the mountain, and there, though the fox, or rather the vixen, turned herself into various shapes, he contrived, with the help of some friendly eagles, falcons, and dragons, to catch and kill her. Then he took out the fox's heart, and out of the heart he took the bird and burned it in a great fire. At that very moment True Steel fell down dead.[32]

In another Serbian story we read how a dragon resided in a water-mill and ate up two king's sons, one after the other. The third son went out to seek his brothers, and coming to the water-mill he found nobody in it but an old woman. She revealed to him the dreadful character of the being that kept the mill, and how he had devoured the prince's two elder brothers, and she implored him to go away home before a like fate should overtake him. But he was both brave and cunning, and he said to her, "Listen well to what I am going to say to you. Ask the dragon whither he goes and where his great strength is; then kiss all that place where he tells you his strength is, as if you loved it dearly, till you find it out, and afterwards tell me when I come." So when the dragon came home the old woman began to question him, "Where in God's name have you been? Whither do you go so far? You will never tell me whither you go." The dragon replied, "Well, my dear old woman, I do go far." Then the old woman coaxed him, saying, "And why do you go so far? Tell me where your strength is. If I knew where your strength is, I don't know what I should do for love; I would kiss all that place." Thereupon the dragon smiled and said to her, "Yonder is my strength in that fireplace." Then the old woman began to kiss and fondle the fireplace; and the dragon on seeing it burst into a laugh. "Silly old woman," he said, "my strength is not there. It is in the tree-fungus in front of the house." Then the old woman began to fondle and kiss the tree; but the dragon laughed again and said to her, "Away, old woman! my strength is not there." "Then where is it?" asked the old woman. "My strength," said he, "is a long way off, and you cannot go thither. Far in another kingdom under the king's city is a lake; in the lake is a dragon; in the dragon is a boar; in the boar is a pigeon, and in the pigeon is my strength." The secret was out; so next morning, when the dragon went away from the mill to attend to his usual business of gobbling people up, the prince came to the old woman and she let him into the mystery of the dragon's strength. Needless to say that the prince contrived to make his way to the lake in the far country, where after a terrible tussle he slew the water-dragon and extracted the pigeon, in which was the strength of the other unscrupulous dragon who kept the mill. Having questioned the pigeon, and ascertained from it how to restore his two murdered brothers to life, the prince wrung the bird's neck, and no doubt the wicked dragon perished miserably the very same moment, though the story-teller has omitted to mention the fact.[33]

Similar incidents occur in Celtic stories. Thus a tale, told by a blind fiddler in the island of Islay, relates how a giant carried off a king's wife and his two horses, and kept them in his den. But the horses attacked the giant and mauled him so that he could hardly crawl. He said to the queen, "If I myself had my soul to keep, those horses would have killed me long ago." "And where, my dear," said she, "is thy soul? By the books I will take care of it." "It is in the Bonnach stone," said he. So on the morrow when the giant went out, the queen set the Bonnach stone in order exceedingly. In the dusk of the evening the giant came back, and he said to the queen, "What made thee set the Bonnach stone in order like that?" "Because thy soul is in it," quoth she. "I perceive," said he, "that if thou didst know where my soul is, thou wouldst give it much respect." "That I would," said she. "It is not there," said he, "my soul is; it is in the threshold." On the morrow she set the threshold in order finely, and when the giant returned he asked her, "What brought thee to set the threshold in order like that?" "Because thy soul is in it," said she. "I perceive," said he, "that if thou knewest where my soul is, thou wouldst take care of it." "That I would," said she. "It is not there that my soul is," said he. "There is a great flagstone under the threshold. There is a wether under the flag; there is a duck in the wether's belly, and an egg in the belly of the duck, and it is in the egg that my soul is." On the morrow when the giant was gone, they raised the flagstone and out came the wether. They opened the wether and out came the duck. They split the duck, and out came the egg. And the queen took the egg and crushed it in her hands, and at that very moment the giant, who was coming home in the dusk, fell down dead.[34]

Once more, in an Argyleshire story we read how a big giant, King of Sorcha, stole away the wife of the herdsman of Cruachan, and hid her in the cave in which he dwelt. But by the help of some obliging animals the herdsman con-trived to discover the cave and his own lost wife in it. Fortunately the giant was not at home; so after giving her husband food to eat, she hid him under some clothes at the upper end of the cave. And when the giant came home he sniffed about and said, "The smell of a stranger is in the cave." But she said no, it was only a little bird she had roasted. "And I wish you would tell me," said she, "where you keep your life, that I might take good care of it." "It is in a grey stone over there," said he. So next day when he went away, she took the grey stone and dressed it well, and placed it in the upper end of the cave. When the giant came home in the evening he said to her, "What is it that you have dressed there?" "Your own life," said she, "and we must be careful of it." "I perceive that you are very fond of me, but it is not there," said he.

"Where is it?" said she. "It is in a grey sheep on yonder hillside," said he. On the morrow, when he went away, she got the grey sheep, dressed it well, and placed it in the upper end of the cave. When he came home in the evening, he said, "What is it that you have dressed there?" "Your own life, my love," said she. "It is not there as yet," said he. "Well!" said she, "you are putting me to great trouble taking care of it, and you have not told me the truth these two times." He then said, "I think that I may tell it to you now. My life is below the feet of the big horse in the stable. There is a place down there in which there is a small lake. Over the lake are seven grey hides, and over the hides are seven sods from the heath, and under all these are seven oak planks. There is a trout in the lake, and a duck in the belly of the trout, an egg in the belly of the duck, and a thorn of blackthorn inside of the egg, and till that thorn is chewed small I cannot be killed. Whenever the seven grey hides, the seven sods from the heath, and the seven oak planks are touched, I shall feel it wherever I shall be. I have an axe above the door, and unless all these are cut through with one blow of it, the lake will not be reached; and when it will be reached I shall feel it." Next day, when the giant had gone out hunting on the hill, the herdsman of Cruachan contrived, with the help of the same friendly animals, which had assisted him before, to get possession of the fateful thorn, and to chew it before the giant could reach him; and no sooner had he done so than the giant dropped stark and stiff, a corpse.[35] ▼

118 The woman divided into twelve parts   19

A levite, sojourning beside the highlands of Ephraim, has a concubine who hails from Bethlehem, in Judah. She deceives him by consorting with other men, and finally takes off for her hometown. He goes to fetch her back, and is hospitably received by her father. On the return journey, the party is accommodated overnight at Gibeah, a city in the territory of Benjamin, by an aged fellow-Ephraimite who has encountered the levite in the street after everyone else has refused him lodging. Hooligans, however, surround the house and demand that the old man's guest be surrendered to them for unnatural purposes. The old man offers his own virgin daughter and his guest's concubine instead. They choose the latter and abuse her all night. At dawn the levite finds her lying in a faint on the threshold. He takes her back to his hometown, but there slices her into twelve parts which he distributes "throughout all the territory of Israel." Thus the concubine pays in the end for her infidelity to him.

This gruesome story is, of course, simply a variant of the folktale related in the Book of Genesis (ch. 19) concerning Lot and the angels. Upon it, however, there has been engrafted the moralizing theme of "the postman always rings twice."

In the original version of the tale, the *twelve* parts into which the hapless woman is severed probably had nothing whatever to do with the twelve tribes of Israel, this being simply an Israelization of an older märchen-motif. They may have been the twelve parts in which the human body was anciently believed to consist. This notion is well attested, for instance, among the Hittites,[1] and in one Hittite ritual for curing sickness, the patient is magically healed by treatment of the twelve limbs of a sacrificial beast.[2]

Twelvefold offerings were likewise common. Thus, in a funeral ritual it is expressly prescribed that twelve loaves be placed beside the cremated corpse,[3] and at a subsequent stage of the proceedings the fleeces of twelve unblemished sheep are dedicated to the gods.[4] Similarly, in a ritual designed to expel pestilence, provision is made for the presentation of twelve vessels and twelve loaves of bread;[5] while in another, for the removal of evil spirits from a palace, twelve loaves of *ḫuri*-bread and twelve of some other kind are presented.[6]

Nor was this twelvefold offering confined to the Hittites. In the Homeric Hymn to Hermes, a sacrifice is likewise divided into twelve parts, but these are rationalized as having been presented to the twelve Olympian deities.[7]

By a similar development the twelve stones erected by the prophet Elijah on Mt. Carmel, in what was really an ancient rain-making ritual, are associated in the Scriptural account (I Kings 18:31) with the "twelve tribes of the sons of Jacob" and are said to have been built into an altar of Yahweh (see below §158).

119   The rape of the women of Shiloh   21:16–24

In vengeance for the outrage perpetrated by the men of Gibeah, the Israelites vowed never to give their daughters in marriage to any member of the tribe of Benjamin. Subsequently, however, after a reconciliation had been effected, it occurred to them that maintenance of this ban would result eventually in the extinction of a tribe of Israel. They therefore devised a way of circumventing the vow. The Benjaminites were informed that an annual festival was about to be celebrated at Shiloh, at which maidens would come out to dance. They were advised to lay in ambush in the vineyards and then pounce on the girls, taking whomever they desired. This they did.

On the face of it, the story here related is perfectly natural and intelligible. A country carnival is an obvious place for sex-starved males to go stalking mates. Indeed, throughout the centuries young men have been known to eye girls in church, and E. W. Lane, in his *Manners and Customs of the Modern Egyptians,* paints a vivid picture of the similar enterprise of Arabs in the mosque at Cairo.[1]

A close parallel to the incident here related is afforded, however, by the familiar Roman legend of the rape of the Sabine women at the agricultural festival of Consualia (in August).[2] "In the early days of Rome," runs the story, "the population consisted chiefly of broken men who had taken refuge in the asylum opened for them by Romulus. As the neighboring peoples refused to give their daughters in marriage to these ruffians, Romulus was obliged to resort to stratagem to procure wives for his subjects. So he issued a proclamation that he was about to celebrate the solemn games in honor of the equestrian Neptune. Many people flocked from the neighborhood of Rome to witness the spectacle; in particular the Sabines came in great force with their wives and children. When the games were about to begin, and the spectators were on the tiptoe of expectation, the young Roman men rushed upon them, singled out the likeliest young women, and carried them off. After some ado they succeeded in pacifying the damsels and so won brides for themselves."[3]

In the same way the Messenians are said, in Greek legend, to have carried off maidens from neighboring Laconia during the celebration of a festival of Artemis at Limnae.[4]

It has been suggested also that the famous Greek myth which tells how Persephone was abducted by Hades (Pluto) while gathering flowers may reflect a similar practice.[5] For, while it is true that the rape of maidens in such circumstances is something of a stock situation in Greek poetry,[6] "there is some evidence of a widespread custom of the ceremonial [i.e., ritual] gathering of flowers in spring, analogous to the modern Greek May Day Festival of Flower-gathering.[7] Herosantheia (or Heroantheia) was a Peloponnesian festival of this kind."[8]

It is possible, however, that our Biblical story is, *au fond,* an etiological legend told originally to account for an ancient practice of mass-mating at seasonal festivals.[9] Designed to regenerate and refecundate the human community at those regular intervals when its corporate life seemed to have completed a cycle, this practice is widely attested both in antiquity and among modern primitive peoples.[10] It obtained—to cite but a few examples—at the Roman festival of Anna Perenna on the Ides of March;[11] while among the Pipiles of Central America copulation takes place in the fields at the moment the first seeds are sown.[12] Similarly, in parts of the Ukraine, married couples copulate in the fields on St. George's Day (April 23) in order to promote the fertility of the crops and to achieve the renewal of the topocosm—that is, the corporate life of the area.[13] In certain districts of Portugal they likewise roll together in the meadows, in a ceremony called *rebolada,* before the reaping of flax, in May.[14] In Java, husbands and wives adopt the same practice as a means of stimulating the growth of rice;[15] while in Amboyna men indulge in mimetic sexual intercourse with trees whenever the harvest is threatened.[16] So too among the Hereros of South West Africa[17] and among various

Bantu tribes[18] mass-mating and sexual promiscuity are obligatory at specific seasons of the year; while the Garos of Assam encourage men and women to sleep together after certain major seasonal festivals.[19]

In a more ceremonial form of the custom, the king has at the same time to indulge in a ritual marriage with a chosen bride.[20]

An attenuated survival of this usage may be recognized in popular traditions that certain crucial days of the year are particularly auspicious for the choosing of husbands and wives.[21] The Talmud tells us, for example, that it was customary in Jerusalem to choose brides on the Day of Atonement— that is (originally), during the period of austerity and purification preceding the autumnal harvesting of fruits—and on the 15th day of the month of Ab (August), the occasion of an ancient festival.[22] Similarly, in some parts of England, St. Roch's day (August 16) and St. Luke's day (October 18) were deemed especially propitious for the choosing of mates.[23] In the same way too it is the custom in Spanish Galicia for girls to repair at harvest time to a duly selected barn, where their ardent swains make love to them;[24] and among the Thompson River Indians of British Columbia husbands and wives are chosen at a seasonal festival held in the "spring house."[25]

A further attenuation is the European popular custom of compulsory kissing or "lifting" on certain days of the year.[26] "Kissing fairs" and "hocking days" (cf. German hoch, "high") are well attested. Thus, in the Arad commune of Nagyhalmagy, in Hungary, a markt is (or was) held annually on March 15, at which women may be kissed without risk of rebuff.[27] Similarly, in certain parts of England, girls may be "lifted" with impunity on May 15; and at Hungerford, in Berkshire, the second Thursday after Easter is "hocking day," when the "tuttimen" go about the streets lifting or "hocking" the women and exacting a kiss from each.[28] Analogous, of course, is the religiously observed Yuletide custom of kissing under the mistletoe—a custom which derives, as every folklorist knows, from the cruder primitive usage of compulsory promiscuity at seasonal festivals.[29]

Ruth

120 Levirate marriage

The Book of Ruth turns largely around the ancient institution of Levirate marriage. A discussion of this belongs within the sphere of law rather than folklore. Since, however, certain elements of traditional custom are involved, the subject cannot be altogether excluded from this work. For the reader's convenience I therefore append a representative bibliography:

M. Burrows, in JBL 59 (1940), 23–33; id., in BASOR 77 (1940), 2–14; id., The Basis of Israelite Marriage (AASOR, No. 15); D. Jacobson, The Social Background of the OT (1942), 290 ff.; I. Mendelsohn, in The Biblical Archaeologist 11 (1948), 24 ff.; J. Mittelmann, Das althebräische Levirat (1939); H. Schaeffer, Social Legislation of the Primitive Semites (1915), 57–64; I. Mattuck, in Kaufmann Kohler Festschrift (1913), 210–22; S. A. Cook, The Laws of Moses and the Code of Hammurabi (1903), 144, n. 3; S. R. Driver, ICC on Deut. 25:6 f.; W. W. Davies, in The Christian Advocate 63 (1888), 820 f.; W. Redslob, Die Levirat-Ehe bei den Hebräern (1836); Rauschenbusch, De lege leviratus (1765).

For analogies in the Middle Assyrian Law Code (§43), cf. B. Cruvelier in RB 34 (1925), 524–46; G. R. Driver and J. C. Miles, The Assyrian Laws (1935), 240–50.

For a parallel in the Hittite Law-Code (§193), cf. A. Goetze, ANET 196; O. Gurney, The Hittites (1952), 101 f.

Among some bedouin tribes the brother of a man deceased must marry his widow: J. Burckhardt, Bedouins and Wahabys (1830), i.112; B. Jacob, Altarabische Parallelen zum AT (1897), 14; J. Wellhausen, Die Ehe bei den Arabern (1893), 435 f. Sometimes his nephew must do so, even if he himself has murdered the husband: C. A. Doughty, Travels in Arabia Deserta (1888), i.506; ii.20.

Cf. also the *niyoḡa*—marriage of a betrothed widow in the Laws of Manu, ix.59–64, and the so-called *čakar*—marriage among the Iranians and Parsis.

Among the Bushmen of South Africa a widow who does not remarry must be supported by her deceased husband's brother: C. G. Seligmann, Races of Africa (1930), 29.

On the institution in general, see: E. Westermarck, A History of Human Marriage (1921), iii.208 ff.; R. Briffault, The Mothers (1927), i.761; J. G. Frazer, Pausanias (1898), iii.198–200.

121   Covering with a garment in token of protection   Ruth 3:9

Ruth asks Boaz to cast his garment over her in token of his protection.

Covering with a garment is in several cultures a recognized method of taking
a person under one's protection; indeed, the very word "protect" carries this
meaning. In Ezekiel 16:8 Yahweh declares that he "adopted" the infant
Israel by spreading his garment over him, and in pre-Islamic times this was
the manner in which an Arab son took over his father's relicts.[1] It was by
this gesture too that Mohammed "married" the Jewess Safiya after the battle
near Khaibar;[2] and even in modern times it was customary in the Sinai peninsula for bridegrooms to cast their mantles over their brides.[3] So too, in the
marriage ceremony of the Russian Orthodox Church, the bridegroom casts
the lap of his gown over the bride;[4] and it is related of Maria Cantacuena that
she spread out her cloak and wrapped it around the children she adopted.[5]

In a figurative sense, reference is made to this custom in one of the
pseudepigraphic *Odes of Solomon,* dating (probably) from the first century
of the Common Era: *I have been prepared against the coming perdition,*
says the passage, *in that I have been placed under God's garment of non-
destruction, and in that he has enfolded me in life immortal and embraced
(kissed) me.*[6]

An interesting variation of this usage was the European practice whereby
children who had been born to a couple out of wedlock could be legitimized
by being covered with the nuptial veil or the pallium of the altar when their
parents married. Such children were known as *pueri mantellati* or—in German—*Mantelkinder.*[7] The custom was observed in Scotland as late as the
nineteenth century.[8] A fascinating survival of it may perhaps be detected in
the Jewish custom of spreading a prayer shawl (*ṭallîth*) over the heads of
minors when they are called to the rostrum for the reading of the Lesson at
the annual Festival of Rejoicing in the Law (*Simḥath Torah*). The synagogal
service on that occasion is cast in the form of a symbolic wedding between
Israel and the Law (Torah), and it is in extension of that symbolism that
children, who are not normally eligible to be called to the reading of the
Lesson from it until they attain the age of religious majority, are fancifully
"legitimized" *ad hoc!*[9]

122   Gestures of adoption   4:16

*Naomi takes the child born to Ruth and Boaz and lays him on her
bosom. Thereby she becomes his foster-mother.*

Placing a child upon the bosom was a gesture of adoption. It symbolizes
suckling, and it could be performed by men as well as by women. The Count
of Edessa, for instance, so adopted Baldwin.[1] The custom is well attested in

European usage,[2] but that it is indeed ancient and obtained also in the Orient is indicated not only by our present passage but also, it would seem, by Psalm 2:7, where, by the emendation of a single letter in the original Hebrew, the obscure and ungrammatical phrase usually rendered (as in RSV), *I will tell of the decree of the Lord: He said to me, You are my son, today I have begotten you,* may be made to yield the sense, *"I gather thee unto my bosom"*— *so saith the Lord unto me*—*"Thou art my son, this day have I acknowledged thee mine offspring."*[3]

A variant of the custom of placing a child on the bosom to symbolize adoption is mentioned in an ancient Mesopotamian document: if the real parents of a child wished to reclaim it from a foster-mother, they placed before it a vessel (*kabduqû*) filled with human milk. This likewise symbolized suckling.[4]

123 Removing the shoe 4:7–12

The symbolic meaning of removing the shoe as a gesture of divorce or repudiation[1] has been variously explained.

(i) Some scholars would illustrate it from the fact that in Arab ceremonies of divorce the man sometimes removes his shoe, saying, "she was my slipper; I cast (her) off."[2] Furthermore, a wife is sometimes called figuratively a "shoe" (*na'l*), and the expression "to tread" is used of sexual intercourse.[3]

(ii) In documents from the Mesopotamian city of Nuzu, dating from the thirteenth century B.C., a pair of shoes sometimes represents a "legal" payment of formal or fictional character.[4] That the same custom obtained later among the Israelites has been inferred from references in the Book of Amos (2:6; 8:6) to the transgression of selling the needy for a pair of shoes; while, according to the Greek (Septuagint) text of I Samuel 12:3, the aged Samuel declared to Israel: *Whose calf* (Heb.: *ox*) *have I ever taken? Or whose ass have I ever taken? Or whom of you have I ever overmastered and oppressed? Or from whose hand have I ever taken a bribe or* a pair of shoes (i.e., a purely fictitious payment, to deprive him of his property)?[5] In the present writer's opinion, however, the connection is doubtful, because in our passage the significance surely lies in the pulling off of the shoe, not in the shoe itself.

(iii) A third explanation derives from the fact that in those same documents from Nuzu "lifting the foot" is a technical term for releasing property.[6] This, however, really belongs to quite a different order of ideas. "Lifting the foot" is simply the opposite of "putting one's foot down" or setting someone or something "under one's heel" as a gesture of subjugation. The expression is used in this sense alike in the Old Testament itself (Ps. 8:7) and in Ugaritic[7] and Phoenician sources.[8] The Egyptians planted their feet on vanquished foes,[9] and in the Babylonian Epic of Creation the god Marduk does likewise to the vanquished Tiamat;[10] while the Romans spoke similarly of "laying all things underfoot."[11] The lifting of the foot would therefore very naturally imply release from such domination, but this is surely quite different from *the pulling off of a shoe.*

(iv) A curious interpretation advanced by some Jewish authorities (e.g., Jehiel of Paris) is that the drawing off of the shoe was simply the customary gesture of mourning.[12] When the potential levir refused to "raise up seed" for his deceased brother, the latter was indeed dead, and the widow signified this by drawing of the levir's shoe.

Not impossibly, the true explanation lies in the fact that the shoe was a symbol of authority; the ceremonial removal of it therefore indicated that such authority had been surrendered. True, we cannot yet authenticate such symbolism from any Ancient Near Eastern source, but in support of this interpretation it may be noted that, according to some later rabbinic authorities, a glove may be substituted for the shoe,[13] for this can be brought into relation with the custom, which persisted in English usage until recent times, of bestowing a pair of gloves "by way of delivery or investiture, in sales or conveyances of lands and goods."[14]

Samuel

124 Falling to the ground
I Sam. 3:19

Yahweh favors Samuel and "does not let any one of his words fall to the ground."

What falls to the ground loses its inherent power and is no longer "whole."[1]

Folklore expresses this idea in custom as well as in language. Pythagoras, for instance, forbade his followers to pick up anything that had fallen from the table,[2] and this became a law at Croton.[3] The same practice obtained also among the Romans[4] and the ancient Prussians.[5] In Greece it was held that what ever falls on the ground belongs to the "heroes,"[6] or ancestral spirits; while a modern German superstition assigns it to the Devil.[7]

When herbs are plucked, says Pliny, care must be taken that they are not subsequently dropped,[8] and the same caution is elsewhere prescribed concerning the gathering of stones.[9] Material used in magic or medicine was likewise believed to lose its efficacy if it fell.[10] Thus, a Greek spell for forcing locked doors instructs the operator to "take the navel of a firstborn ram, without letting it fall on the ground."[11]

124a Leaping over the threshold
5:5

See below, §243.

125 Of mice and men
5:6—6:5

The Philistines capture the ark of Yahweh. He retaliates by sending an epidemic of hemorrhoids.

Individuals who commit sacrilege or transgression are punished by blindness (§56), leprosy (§93), or paralysis (§154). Hence, when a whole people does so, this entails an epidemic.

Folklore knows several parallels to the incident here related. Callimachus tells us that when, in 652 B.C., Lygdamus led a host of Cimmerians against the temple of Artemis at Ephesus, the goddess turned her shafts upon them, and "no man of them was destined to return to Scythia";[1] and the lexicographer Hesychius adds that, on the score of this episode, "Scythian desolation" became a proverbial expression.[2] The shafts of Artemis, like those of her brother Apollo, and like those said in European folklore to be shot by elves, were the strokes of plague or disease.[3] Similarly, according to Herodotus, when some of the Scythians pillaged the shrine of Aphrodite (i.e., Astarte) at Ascalon, the outraged goddess visited upon them what he calls "the female sickness"—that is, an atrophy of the organs of generation.[4] Of the same tenor too, is a story related, in the fourth century C.E. by Ammianus Marcellinus, the last of the major Roman historians. He says that after the Romans had sacrilegiously deported the image of Apollo of Seleucia to the Palatine in Rome, certain soldiers peered into a crevice in the original Syrian temple in the hope of finding hidden treasure; whereupon a sudden and widespread contagion ensued.[5] Lastly, Dictys Cretensis, in his fabled narrative of the Trojan War, relates that after Agamemnon had impiously slain the sacred hind of Artemis, a plague broke out and grew in intensity from day to day, until everything fell prey to it.[6]

The Philistines decide to send the ark to the Israelites, but their priests and diviners advise that the restoration be accompanied by a tresspass-offering, or indemnity. The latter includes five golden images of mice, one for the lord of each of the five Philistine cities of Palestine.

The association of plague—especially bubonic plague—with mice was certainly observed in antiquity, even though the causal connection may still have been unknown; and it survives in European folklore.[7] Strabo tells us, for example, that the Iberians of Spain were regularly "tormented by vast swarms of mice, from which pestilential diseases have frequently ensued";[8] and it is a common superstition among the peasants in Germany that a procession of mice forebodes an epidemic;[9] while in Bohemia the mouse is (or was) popularly regarded as a symbol of plague and war.[10]

Some scholars have sought to discover an instance of this belief in the Old Testament itself. In the Second Book of Kings it is related that when Sennacherib laid siege to Jerusalem in 701 B.C., he was prevented from actually penetrating the city because "an angel of Yahweh went forth and smote in the camp of the Assyrians an hundred fourscore and five thousand men."[11] Now, according to Herodotus, when the same invader marched upon Egypt, he was stopped at the last moment by the fact that field mice gnawed the quivers and shield handles of his men overnight. Combining these two accounts, it has been suggested that Herodotus has garbled the details of an incident which really took place on the outskirts of Jerusalem and which consisted in the sudden onset of a plague brought by mice.[12] To be sure, this ingenious suggestion is not without its difficulties, first because the story of how rodents achieved an army's defeat by gnawing at its bowstrings is indeed paralleled elsewhere,[13] and second because, as Andrew Lang acutely pointed out,[14] the Father of History speaks specifically of *field* mice, and these do not in fact carry infection!

Be this as it may, mice are indeed associated in popular lore with gods who send or avert plague.[15] The prime example of this is Apollo. Apollo, as we know, was, among other things, a god of plague.[16] It is he who, in the

Iliad, shoots the shafts of pestilence at the Greeks before Troy;[17] who, in the Odyssey, kills Rhexenor through illness,[18] and whom Melanthios bids slay Telemachus,[19] and Penelope bids slay Antinous.[20] His arrows are called "arrows" of pestilence,"[21] and he is said once to have inflicted a plague on the Libyans.[22] In a Graeco-Phoenician bilingual inscription from Cition, in Cyprus, he is explicitly identified with the Phoenician plague-god, "Resheph of the arrow,"[23] and a place named Arsuf (i.e., Reshephville), near Jaffa, was known in Seleucid times as Apollonias.[24] Conversely, he was also the healer or averter of plague, bearing such titles as "Healer" (Akesios)[25] and "Physician" (Iatros).[26] Now, in several parts of the Greek world Apollo was known as Smintheus,[27] and this derives from an old Cretan word, sminthos, meaning "mouse."[28] At Hamaxitos the god was definitely associated with mice,[29] and at Chryse the sculptor Skopas embellished his statue with a mouse at its feet.[30] Here, then, we have the plague-god explicitly associated with mice, and what makes this the more interesting and the more pertinent to our Biblical narrative is that the Philistines are said to have come from Crete.[31] In sending the golden mice to Yahweh to avert plague they would therefore have been transferring to Israel's god a standard practice traditionally associated with his counterpart in their own religion. Such, at least, is the construction which many scholars have put upon this incident. A word of caution, however, is not inappropriate, for we must not lose sight of the possibility that Apollo Smintheus was not a plague-god at all, but simply one who kept mice away from the fields.[32]

It has been suggested also that Apollo's sister Artemis, who was likewise a sender and averter of pestilence, provides yet another example of a plague-deity associated with mice, for at Therapne, on the border of Arcadia, she was known by the curious epithet Mysia,[33] which may be explained, perhaps, from the word mus, "mouse."[34] Moreover, at Lysoi in Arcadia she was worshiped beside a spring in which mice were fabled to come to life and have their being.[35] A survival of this or an analogous mouse-goddess has been recognized in the figure of St. Gertrude who is said specifically to protect from mice and from diseases[36] and who is often portrayed accompanied by a mouse.[37]

126   Death for looking into the Ark of the Lord   6:19

When the Philistines were returning the captured Ark of the Lord to the Israelites, certain men of Beth Shemesh looked inside it. In retribution for this impiety the Lord slew them.

On the significance of this offense, see below, §138. The traditional text gives the number of those slain as "seventy men, five thousand men." The absence of the copula shows that the two numbers are variants. Folklore clarifies the variation, for the fact is that both seventy and five thousand are conventional round numbers in Hebrew.[1] The latter was evidently considered too implausible and was therefore duly "corrected." Both readings were then preserved side by side.[2]

127   Qualifications for kingship   9:21; 10:23; 16:7

Saul, chosen to be king of Israel, is "goodlier" and taller than any one of the people.

The king, in ancient and primitive thought, is the epitome of his people's corporate life and fortune. Therefore he must be without blemish and (at least in theory) physically superior to everyone else.

Examples of this belief are legion. Concerning the pretender Absalom it is said expressly, in the Old Testament itself, that he was the most beautiful man in Israel and "without blemish from top to toe";[1] while in the Babylonian Epic of Creation, Marduk, who becomes king of the gods, is described as the tallest among them and as endowed with a "surpassing stature."[2] According to Herodotus, Xerxes I was likewise the tallest and most handsome of the Persians;[3] and Athenaeus tells us that among the ancient Ethiopians the most handsome man was appointed king.[4]

In the Canaanite (Ugaritic) *Poem of Baal,* the god Ashtar though recommended by the queen goddess Asherat as "terrific" (*'arisu*), is disqualified from succeeding him after he has disappeared into the netherworld, because he is too small: "his head does not reach to the top of the throne, nor his feet to the footstool."[5] Similarly, the Konde of Lake Nyassa keep the king under surveillance before installing him, "lest, being a weakling, he should be a menace to the land";[6] while among the Varozwe, a Shona tribe of Africa, "absence of bodily blemishes was considered absolutely necessary in the occupant of the throne."[7]

A natural corollary is that the king is deposed or killed as soon as he shows signs of old age, debility, or physical defect. When Uzziah-Azariah of Judah became a leper, says the Book of Kings, the reins of government passed to his son Jotham.[8] In similar vein, in the Canaanite (Ugaritic) *Epic of K-r-t,* that monarch's upstart son, Yaṣṣib, claims the throne from him on the grounds that he has become sick and feeble, merely talks "blather" and is unable to dispense justice, redress oppression, or succor the widow and orphan.[9] In Western Africa, it is likewise the general rule that kings are dethroned or slain by reason of bodily defect. This is standard practice; for example, among the Fazoql, the Shilluk of the White Nile, the Bunyoro, the Kibanga of the Upper Congo, the Hausa of Northern Nigeria, and the Zulus.[10]

128   Eyes brightened by eating honey   14:24–30

When the Israelites engaged the Philistines at Beth-aven, Saul adjured his men to abstain from food until victory was won. Some of them found a honeycomb, but carefully refrained from tasting in obedience to the king's command. Saul's son, Jonathan, however, cavalierly broke the taboo, but instead of dire consequences found that as soon as the honey touched his lips, his eyes brightened.

Involved in this story is a widespread tradition of folk medicine. The physicians of ancient Egypt precribed honey for diseases of the eyes,[1] and the Greeks followed suit. Aristotle says that honey relieves dullness of vision,[2] and Dioscorides that it removes "whatever darkens the pupils."[3] Galen too recommended it for affections of the eyes,[4] and Pliny speaks in the same sense, adding that it is useful against cataract, and was employed for such purposes in India.[5] Celsus[6] and Marcellus of Bordeaux[7] likewise endorse it as a nostrum in diseases of the eyes; while even in modern times it has been held efficacious against trachoma.[8]

This is merely a particular application of the idea that honey is regenerative and expels or averts evil spirits.[9] Hindus and Moslems smear it on the lips and gums of newborn babes,[10] and in Greek myth this is said to have been done both to the infant Zeus[11] and to the infant Dionysus.[12] In the pseud-epigraphic story of Joseph and Asenath, the archangel Michael provides the Egyptian princess with a honeycomb by the use of which she achieves both purification and immortality;[13] while in the Finnish Kalevala, the slain hero Lemminkainen is revived by magic honey.[14] Initiants into the mysteries of Mithra were given honey as a means of regeneration.[15] Jews still eat honey at New Year, and in Babylon, honey was offered at the dedication of new images of the gods at the Akîtu (New Year) festival.[16] An ancient Egyptian charm prescribes honey as a means of keeping away the child-stealing witch.[17]

For the same reason rivers of honey are characteristic of the Golden age, and are said to flow in Paradise (see above, §14).

129 Agag

(a) Agag walks "delicately"   15:32

Agag, king of the Amalekites, defeated by Saul, is led into the presence of the prophet Samuel. He comes walking "delicately" and exclaiming, "Bitter indeed is death."[1]

The Hebrew word rendered "delicately" really means "with limping gait."[2] The reference is to a custom observed at Semitic funerals, whereby the mourners shuffle around the bier with a peculiar limping or hopping step.[3] An excellent description of the rite is given by Roger in his *La terre saincte,* published in 1664,[4] while Lane, in his famous *Manners and Customs of the Modern Egyptians,* informs us that

it is customary among the peasants of Upper Egypt for the female relations and friends of a person deceased to meet together by his house on the first three days after the funeral, and there to perform a lamentation and a strange kind of dance.

They daub their faces and bosoms and parts of their dress with mud; and tie a rope girdle . . . round the waist. Each flourishes in her hand a palm-stick or a nebroot (a long staff), or a drawn sword [so to forefend demons], and dances with a slow movement, and in an irregular manner; generally pacing about and raising and depressing the body.[5]

The custom was reported also by Wetzstein, the German consul at Damascus, as current among the peasants of Syria in the nineteenth century, and it was there known by the same term (*ma'id*) as in our Biblical text.[6] In Arabic and Syriac, the word "to skip, hop" (*r-q-d, r-q-ṣ*) also denotes the performance at a funeral of a special kind of limping dance,[7] and in an ancient Mesopotamian syllabary, the corresponding Akkadian word (*ruquddu*) is listed as the technical term for a professional manner.[8] The term seems also to occur, as early as the fourteenth century B.C., in the Canaanite (Ugaritic) *Poem of Aghat* in connection with the mourning for him by his father, Daniel.[9]

Not impossibly, it was because they had to accompany this limping dance that Hebrew dirges were usually composed in a peculiar limping (scazontic) meter, achieved by truncating the final beat of what would otherwise be a verse consisting of two balanced halves, each with three corresponding accents, e.g.,

> Outdóors they líe on the gróund
> yóung men and óld;
> My yóuths and máidens áll
> are sláin by the swórd;[10]

The point of our Scriptural narrative is, then, that Agag, like an arch-hypocrite, approaches the prophet in the manner of a mourner, intoning a typical dirge!

(b) Agag is hewn asunder   15:33

Samuel orders Agag to be hewn in pieces, as a condign punishment for his savagery.

Agag is not merely slain; he is slain "before Yahweh at Gilgal," and he is slain in a special way. This indicates that he became the victim of a ritual ceremony, and that ceremony is admirably illustrated from Arab sources. After a successful foray, the Arabs, we are told, used, before dividing the spoil, to select from it one choice beast which they sacrificed and upon the flesh of which they then feasted.[11] The technical name for the victim was *naqi,* which means properly "that which is split, rent, hewn." The Saracens, says Nilus, did not always use an animal for this purpose; by preference they would select a handsome boy.[12] It has therefore been suggested that the hewing asunder of Agag "before Yahweh" represents an earlier Israelite example of the same practice.[13] The *raison d'être* was probably the recementing by commensality (see above, §52) of kinship ties after the losses incurred in warfare or on forays.

130   Battle taunts   17:43–48

See above, §31.

131   Beheading fallen foes   17:46, 51

David cuts off the head of the defeated Goliath.

The decapitation of slain enemies is a widely attested custom. To confine ourselves to the ancient Semites: the Assyrian monarch Ashurbanipal boasts that he so treated his foes;[1] while a relief on a gate at Zenčirli, in North Syria (8th cent. B.C.), depicts a victorious warrior riding with the head of his victim in his hand.[2] Among the pre-Islamic Arabs it was likewise the custom to take the head of a vanquished enemy as trophy,[3] and in Persia, during Sassanian times, such heads were hung up in the fire-temple.[4]

This was not, however, simply an act of savagery. It was of a piece with the custom of cutting off the hands, lest the ghosts of the slain should move them again to take up arms.[5] The head was popularly regarded as one of the seats of the personal "genius," or individuality.[6] The Romans, for example, regarded the forehead as sacred to the genius natalis, and touched it in praying to him.[7] In Yoruba it is held that the principal of each man's three indwelling spirits, called Odori, dwells in the head.[8] In Cambodia[9] and in the Marquesas Islands,[10] the head is taboo, and in Thailand it is forbidden to touch the head of a fallen or sleeping man with the foot; those who thus come into contact with it must build chapels to the earth-demon to avert ill-omen; so too must the persons touched.[11]

An interesting survival of these ideas occurs in a recent Catholic work on baptism, where it is contended that "the water must touch the *head* . . . for the human soul functions principally in the head."[12]

Thus, the purpose of beheading a fallen foe is to accompany the destruction of his body with the annihilation of his "genius."

▲ 132   The bundle of the living   25:29

The traveller who, quitting the cultivated lands of central Judea, rides eastwards towards the Dead Sea, traverses at first a series of rolling hills and waterless valleys covered by broom and grass. But as he pursues his way onward the scenery changes; the grass and thistles disappear, and he gradually passes into a bare and arid region, where the wide expanse of brown or yellow sand, of crumbling limestone, and of scattered shingle is only relieved by thorny shrubs and succulent creepers. Not a tree is to be seen; not a human habitation, not a sign of life meets the eye for mile after mile. Ridge follows ridge in monotonous and seemingly endless succession, all equally white, steep, and narrow, their sides furrowed by the dry beds of innumerable torrents, and their crests looming sharp and ragged against the sky above him as the traveller ascends from the broad flats of soft white marl, interspersed with flints, which divide each isolated ridge from the one beyond it. The nearer slopes of these desolate hills look as if they were torn and rent by waterspouts; the more distant heights present the aspect of gigantic dustheaps. In some places the ground gives out a hollow sound under the horse's tread; in others the stones and sand slip from beneath the animal's hoofs; and in the frequent gullies the rocks glow with a furnace heat under the pitiless sun which beats down on them out of the cloudless firmament. Here and there, as we proceed eastward, the desolation of the landscape is momentarily lightened by a glimpse of the Dead Sea, its waters of a deep blue appearing in a hollow of the hills and contrasting refreshingly with the dull drab colouring of the desert foreground. When the last ridge is surmounted and he stands on the brink of the great cliffs, a wonderful panorama bursts upon the spectator. Some two thousand feet below him lies the Dead Sea, visible in its whole length from end to end, its banks a long succession of castellated crags, bastion beyond bastion, divided by deep gorges, with white capes running out into the calm blue water, while beyond the lake rise the mountains of Moab to melt in the far distance into the azure of the sky. If he has struck the lake above the springs of Engedi, he finds himself on the summit of an amphitheatre of nearly vertical cliffs, down which a rugged winding track, or rather staircase, cut in the face of the precipice, leads to a little horse-shoe shaped plain sloping to the water's edge. It is necessary to dismount and lead the horses carefully down this giddy descent, the last of the party picking their steps very warily, for a single slip might dislodge a stone, which, hurtling down the crag, and striking on the travellers below, would precipitate them to the bottom. At the foot of the cliffs the copious warm fountain of Engedi bursts in a foaming cascade from the rock amid a verdurous oasis of luxuriant semitropical vegetation, which strikes the wayfarer all the more by contrast with the dreary waterless wilderness through which he has been toiling for many hours. Hebrews called Jeshimmon, or desolation, the wilderness of Judea. From the bitter but brilliant water of the Dead Sea it stretches right up into the heart of the country, to the roots of the Mount of Olives, to within two hours of the gates of Hebron, Bethlehem, and Jerusalem.

To these dismal wilds the hunted David fled for refuge from the pursuit of his implacable enemy Saul. While he was in hiding there with the band of broken men he had gathered round him, he was visited by Abigail, the wise and beautiful wife of the rich sheep-farmer Nabal, whom the gallant outlaw had laid under a deep obligation by not stealing his sheep. Insensible of the services thus rendered to him by the caterans, the surly boor refused with contumely a request, couched in the most polite terms, which the captain of the band had sent in for the loan of provisions. The insult touched the captain's nice sense of honour to the quick, and he was marching over the hills at the head of four hundred pretty fellows, every man of them with his broadsword buckled at his side, and was making straight for the farm, when the farmer's wife met him on the moor. She had soft words to soothe the ruffled pride of the angry chieftain, and, better perhaps than words, a train of asses laden with meat and drink for the sharp-set brigands. David was melted. The beauty of the woman, her gentle words, the sight of the asses with their panniers, all had their effect. He received the wife, pleading for her husband, with the utmost courtesy, promised his protection, not without dark hints of the sight that the sun would have seen at the farm next morning if she had not met him, and so dismissed her with a blessing. The word was given. The outlaws faced to the right-about, and, followed no doubt by the asses with their panniers, marched off the way they had come. As she watched those stalwart, sunburnt figures stepping out briskly till the column disappeared over the nearest ridge, Abigail may have smiled and sighed. Then, turning homeward, she hastened with a lighter heart to the house where her boorish husband and his hinds, little wotting of what had passed on the hills, were drinking deep and late after the sheepshearing. That night over the wine she wisely said nothing. But next morning, when he was sober, she told him, and his heart died within him. The shock to his nervous system, or perhaps something stronger, was too much for him. Within ten days he was a dead man, and after a decent interval the widow was over the hills and far away with the captain of the brigands.

Among the compliments which the charming Abigail paid to the susceptible David at their first meeting, there is one, which deserves our attention. She said, "And though man be risen up to pursue thee, and to seek thy soul, yet the soul of my lord shall be bound in the bundle of life with the Lord thy God; and the souls of thine enemies, them shall he sling out, as from the hollow of a sling." No doubt the language is metaphorical, but to an English writer the metaphor is strange and obscure. It implies that the souls of living people could be tied up for safety in a bundle, and that, on the contrary, when the souls were those of enemies, the bundle might be undone and the souls scattered to the winds. Such an idea could hardly have occurred to a Hebrew even as a figure of speech, unless he were familiar with an actual belief that souls could thus be treated. To us, who conceive of a soul as immanent in its body so long as life lasts, the idea conveyed by the verse in question is naturally preposterous. But it would not be so to many peoples whose theory of life differs radically from ours. There is in fact a widespread belief among savages that the soul can be, and often is, extracted from the body during the lifetime of its owner without immediately causing his death. Commonly this is done by ghosts, demons, or evil-disposed persons, who have a grudge against a man and steal his soul; for if they succeed in their fell intent and detain long enough, the man will fall ill and die.[1] For that reason people who identify their souls with their shades or reflections are often in mortal terror of a camera, fearing lest the photographer who has taken their likeness has abstracted their souls or shades along with it.

Sometimes, however, souls are extracted from bodies with a kindly intention. The primitive seems to think that nobody can die properly so long as his soul remains intact, whether in or out of the body; hence he infers that if he can contrive to draw out his soul and stow it away in some place where nothing can injure it, he will be for all practical purposes immortal so long as it remains unharmed and undisturbed. Hence in time of danger the wary savage will sometimes carefully extract his own soul or the soul of a friend and leave it, so to say, at deposit account in some safe place till the danger is past and he can reclaim his spiritual property. For example, many people regard the removal to a new house as a crisis fraught with peril to their souls; hence in Minahassa, a district of Celebes, a priest then collects the souls of the whole family in a bag, and keeps them there till the danger is over.[2] Again, in Southern Celebes, when a woman's time is near, the messenger who goes to fetch the doctor or midwife takes with him a chopping-knife or something else made of iron. The thing, whatever it is, represents the woman's soul, which at this dangerous time is believed to be safer outside of her body than in it. Hence the doctor must take great care of it, for were it lost the woman's soul would with it be lost also. So he keeps it in his house till the confinement is over, when he gives back the precious object in return for a fee.[3] In the Kei Islands a hollowed-out coco-nut, split in two and carefully pieced together, may sometimes be seen hanging up. This is a receptacle in which the soul of a newly-born infant is kept lest it should fall a prey to demons. For in those parts the soul does not permanently lodge in its tabernacle of clay, until the clay has taken a firm consistency. The Eskimos of Alaska adopt a similar precaution for the soul of a sick child: the medicine-man conjures it into an amulet and then stows the amulet in his medicine-bag, where, if anywhere, the soul should be out of harm's way.[4] In some parts of South-Eastern New Guinea, when a woman walks abroad carrying her baby in a bag, she "must tie a long streamer of vine of some kind to her skirt, or better still to the baby's bag, so that it trails behind her on the ground. For should the child's spirit chance to wander from the body it must have some means of crawling back from the ground, and what so convenient as a vine trailing on the path?"[5]

But perhaps the closest analogy to the "bundle of life" is furnished by the bundles of *churinga,* that is, flattened and elongated stones and sticks, which the Arunta and other tribes of Central Australia keep with the greatest care and secrecy in caves and crevices of the rocks. Each of these mysterious stones or sticks is intimately associated with the spirit of a member of the clan, living or dead; for as soon as the spirit of a child enters into a woman to be born, one of these holy sticks or stones is dropped on the spot where the mother felt her womb quickened. Directed by her, the father searches for the stick or stone of his child, and having found it, or carved it out of the nearest hard-wood tree, he delivers it to the headman of the district, who deposits it with the rest in the sacred store-house among the rocks. These precious sticks and stones, closely bound up with the spirits of all the members of the clan, are often carefully tied up in bundles. They constitute the most sacred possession of the tribe, and the places where they are deposited are skilfully screened from observation, the entrance to the caves being blocked up with stones arranged so naturally as to disarm suspicion. Not only the spot itself but its surroundings are sacred. The plants and trees that grow there are never touched: the wild animals that find their way thither are never molested. And if a man fleeing from his enemies or from the avenger of blood succeeds in reaching the sanctuary, he is safe so long as he remains within its bounds. The loss of their *churinga,* as they call the sacred sticks and stones thus associated with the spirits of all the living and all the dead members of the community, is the most serious evil that can befall a tribe. Robbed of them by inconsiderate white men, the natives have been known to stay in camp for a fortnight, weeping and wailing over their loss and plastering their body with white pipeclay, the emblem of mourning for the dead.[6]

It would be rash to assert that the ancient Semites ever conserved their souls for safety in such sticks and stones, but it is not rash to affirm that some such practices would explain in a simple and natural way the words of Abigail to the hunted outlaw.

[There are, however, other possible explanations:

(a) The Hebrew word rendered *bundle* can also mean *wallet,*[6a] and in that case we may aptly compare the words of an Old Babylonian letter: "May thy god (lord) and thy goddess keep thee as (in) the wallet which they hold in their hands."[6b] A similar expression occurs also in the literature of the Mandeans of Iraq and Iran.[6c]

(b) L. Oppenheim has pointed out that at Nuzi, a city in Upper Mesopotamia which flourished in the sixteenth century B.C., it was apparently the custom to "keep tabs" on sheep and goats sold, sacrificed, moved for shearing and the like by means of pebbles. One pebble represented each animal, and could be transferred to a particular receptacle reserved for each category. An ovoid clay pouch so used has actually been discovered.[6d] O. Eissfeldt has suggested that the Biblical idiom refers to such a usage, the wish of Abigail being that the king's "soul," or life, may be included among the pebbles deposited in the pouch reserved for those who are to be kept alive.[6e] Marvin Pope records a similar method of checking guests and "no-shows" at social functions in Jerusalem,[6f] and it may be added that this device was also once used in the United States to register ballots at elections,[6g] and that it underlies the expression "to blackball," i.e., to exclude, or doom to rejection.] ▼

▲ 133   **The Witch of Endor**   28

Saul, frightened by the massing of the Philistines at Shunem, consults the oracle of the Lord, but this is denied him. He then goes in disguise to a witch who is clandestinely practicing her forbidden craft at Endor. He asks her to conjure the spirit of Samuel from the netherworld. The witch reports that she sees an elohim, *or otherworld being, coming up. He looks like an old man wrapped in a mantle. Saul recognizes him as Samuel.*

The practice of necromancy was shared by the Hebrews with other peoples of the Ancient Near East.[1] A clear reference to it appears to be contained in the twelfth canto of the Gilgamesh epic. There the hero Gilgamesh is represented mourning for his dead friend Eabani. In his sorrow he appeals to the gods to bring up for him the soul of his departed comrade from the nether world. But one after another the deities confess themselves powerless to grant his request. At last he prays to Nergal, the god of the dead, saying, "Break open the chamber of the grave *and open the ground,* that the spirit of Enkidu, like a wind, may rise out of the ground." The deity graciously listened to his prayer. "He broke open the chamber of the grave and opened the ground; and caused the spirit of Enkidu to rise out of the ground like a wind." With the ghost thus summoned from the vasty deep Gilgamesh converses, and learns from him the mournful state of the dead in the nether world, where is the devouring worm and all things are cloaked in dust. However, the gloominess of the picture is a little relieved by the information which the apparition vouchsafes as to the solace which the rites of burial afford to the souls of warriors fallen in battle, compared with the deplorable condition of those whose corpses have been suffered to welter unburied on the field.[2]

The ancient Greeks were familiar with the practice of evoking the souls of the dead in order either to obtain information from them or to appease their wrath. It would seem that the practice of calling up the shades from the nether regions was not carried on by necromancers at any place indiscriminately, but was restricted to certain definite spots which were supposed to communicate directly with the underworld by passages or apertures, through which the spirits could come up and go down as they were summoned or dismissed. Such spots were called oracles of the dead,[3] and at them alone, so far as appears, could legitimate business with the shades of the departed be transacted. There was one at Aornon in Thesprotis, where the legendary musician Orpheus is said to have called up, but in vain, the soul of his loved and lost Eurydice.[4] The whole vicinity of this oracular seat would seem to have been associated with, if not haunted by, the spirits of the dead; for the names of the infernal rivers were given to the neighbouring waters. Beside it ran the Acheron[5] and not far off flowed the Cocytus,[6] "named of lamentation loud heard on the rueful stream." The landscape combines the elements of grandeur, solitude, and desolation in a degree that is fitted to oppress the mind with a sense of awe and gloom, and thereby to predispose it for communion with supernatural beings. No wonder that in these rugged mountains, these dreary fens, these melancholy streams, the ancients fancied they beheld the haunts of the spirits of the dead.

Another oracle of the dead was established at Heraclea in Bithynia. The Spartan King Pausanias, who defeated the Persians in the battle of Plataea, resorted to this oracle, and there attempted to summon up and propitiate the ghost of a Byzantine maiden named Cleonice, whom he had accidentally killed. Her spirit appeared to him and announced in ambiguous language that all his troubles would cease when he should return to Sparta. The prophecy was fulfilled by the king's speedy death.[7]

We have no information as to the mode in which the ghosts were supposed to appear and reply to questions at these places; hence we cannot say whether the phantoms revealed themselves to the inquirer himself or only to the wizard who conjured them up; nor again do we know whether the person who was favoured with these manifestations beheld them awake or in dreams. However, at some Greek oracles of the dead the communication with the souls of the departed is known to have taken place in sleep. Such, for example, was the custom at the oracle of the soothsayer Mopsus in Cilicia. Plutarch tells us that on one occasion the governor of Cilicia, a sceptic in religion and a friend of Epicurean philosophers, who derided the supernatural, resolved to test the oracle. For that purpose he wrote a question on a tablet, and without revealing what he had written to anybody he sealed up the tablet and entrusted it to a freedman with orders to submit the question to the ghostly seer. Accordingly the man slept that night, according to custom, in the shrine of Mopsus, and next morning he reported to the governor that he had dreamed a dream. He thought he saw a handsome man standing by him, who opened his mouth, and, having uttered the single word "Black," immediately vanished. The friends of the governor, who had assembled to hear and to quiz the messenger from the other world, were at a loss what to make of this laconic message, but no sooner did the governor himself receive it than he fell on his knees in an attitude of devotion. The reason for this very unusual posture was revealed when the seal of the tablet was broken and its contents read aloud. For the question which the governor had written therein was this, "Shall I sacrifice a white bull or a black?" The appropriateness of the answer staggered even the incredulous Epicurean philosophers, and as for the governor himself, he sacrificed the black bull and continued to revere the dead soothsayer Mopsus to the end of his days.[8]

The pious Plutarch, who reports with obvious satisfaction this triumphant refutation of shallow infidelity, has related another incident of the same sort which was said to have occurred in Italy. A certain very rich man named Elysius, a native of the Greek city of Terina in Bruttium, lost his son and heir, Euthynus, by a sudden and mysterious death. Fearing that there might have been foul play in this loss of the heir to all his riches, the anxious father had recourse to an oracle of the dead. There he offered a sacrifice, and then, in accordance with the custom of the sanctuary, he fell asleep and dreamed a dream. It seemed to him that he saw his own father, and begged and prayed him to help in tracking down the author of his son's death. "For that very purpose am I come," answered the ghost, "and I beg you will accept my message from this young man," pointing, as he said so, to a youth who followed at his heels, and who resembled to the life the son whose loss Elysius mourned. Startled by the likeness, Elysius asked the young man, "And who are you?" to which the phantom answered, "I am your son's genius. Take that." So saying, he handed to Elysius a tablet inscribed with some verses, which declared that his son had died a natural death, because death was better for him than life.[9]

In antiquity the Nasamones, a tribe of northern Libya, used to seek for oracular dreams by sleeping on the tombs of their ancestors;[10] probably they imagined that the souls of the departed rose from their graves to advise and comfort their descendants. A similar custom is still practised by some of the Tuaregs of the Sahara. When the men are away on distant expeditions, their wives, dressed in their finest clothes, will go and lie on ancient tombs, where they call up the soul of one who will give them news of their husbands. At their call a spirit named Idebni appears in the form of a man. If the woman contrives to please this spirit, he tells her all that has happened on the expedition; but if she fails to win his favour, he strangles her.[11]

The most elaborate description of the evocation of a ghost in Greek literature is to be found in Aeschylus's tragedy, *The Persians*. The scene of the play is laid at the tomb of King Darius, where Queen Atossa, the wife of Xerxes, is anxiously waiting for news of her husband and the mighty host which he had led against Greece. A messenger arrives with tidings of the total defeat of the Persians at Salamis. In her grief and consternation the queen resolves to summon up the ghost of Darius from the grave, and to seek counsel of him in the great emergency. For that purpose she offers libations of milk, honey, water, wine, and olive oil at the tomb, while at the same time the chorus chants hymns calling on the gods of the nether world to send up the soul of the dead king to the light of day. The ghost accordingly emerges from the earth, and learning of the disaster that has befallen the Persian arms, he gives advice and warning to his afflicted people.[12] In this account it is clearly implied that the ghost appears in broad daylight, and not merely in a dream, to those who have evoked it; but whether the poet is describing a Greek or a Persian form of necromancy, or is simply drawing on his own imagination, we cannot say for certain. Probably the description is based on rites commonly performed by Greek necromancers, either at the regular oracles of the dead, or at the graves of the particular persons whose ghosts they desired to consult. The Pythagorean philosopher Apollonius of Tyana is reported by his biographer Philostratus to have conjured up the soul of Achilles from his grave in Thessaly. The hero appeared from the barrow in the likeness of a tall and handsome young man, and entered into conversation with the sage in the most affable manner, complaining that the Thessalians had long since ceased to bring offerings to his tomb, and begging him to remonstrate with them on their negligence.[13] In Pliny's youth a certain grammarian named Apion professed to have evoked the shade of Homer and questioned the poet as to his parents and his native land, but he refused to reveal the answers which he received from the ghost; hence later ages have not benefited by this bold attempt to solve the Homeric problem at the fountain head.[14]

The poet Lucan has given us, in his usual tawdry bombastic style, a tedious report of an interview which, according to the bard, Sextus Pompeius, son of Pompey the Great, had with a Thessalian witch before the battle of Pharsalia. Anxious to learn the issue of the war, the unworthy son of a great father, as Lucan calls him, has recourse, not to the legitimate oracles of the gods, but to the vile arts of witchcraft and necromancy. At his request a foul hag, whose dwelling is among the tombs, restores an unburied corpse to life, and the soul thus temporarily replaced in its earthly tabernacle tells of the commotion which it has witnessed among the shades at the prospect of the catastrophe so soon to befall the Roman world. Having delivered his message, the dead man requests as a particular favour to be allowed to die a second time for good and all. The witch grants his request, and considerately erects a pyre for his convenience, to which the corpse walks unassisted and is there comfortably burnt to ashes.[15] Thessalian witches were certainly notorious in antiquity, and it is likely enough that necromancy was one of the black arts which they professed; but no reliance can be placed on Lucan's highly coloured description of the rites which they observed in evoking the ghosts. More probable is the account which Horace gives of the proceedings of two witches, whom he represents as pouring the blood of a black lamb into a trench for the purpose of calling up ghosts to answer questions.[16] Tibullus speaks of a witch who conjured up the shades from their tombs by her chants;[17] and in the reign of Tiberius a highborn but feeble-minded youth, named Libo, who dabbled in the black arts, requested a certain Junius to evoke the spirits of the dead for him by incantations.[18]

More than one of the wicked Roman emperors are said to have had recourse to necromancy in the hope of allaying those terrors with which the memory of their crimes, like avenging spirits, visited their uneasy consciences. We are told that the monster Nero never knew peace of mind again after he had murdered his mother Agrippina: he often confessed that he was haunted by her spectre and by the Furies with whips and burning torches, and it was in vain that by magic rites he conjured up her ghost and attempted to appease her anger.[19] Similarly, the crazed and bloody tyrant Caracalla imagined that the phantoms of his father Severus and of his murdered brother Geta pursued him with drawn swords, and to obtain some alleviation of these horrors he called in the help of wizards. Among the ghosts which they evoked for him were those of the emperor's father and the Emperor Commodus. But of all the shades thus summoned to his aid none deigned to hold converse with the imperial assassin except the kindred spirit of Commodus, and even from him no words of consolation or hope could be elicited, nothing but dark hints of a fearful judgment to come, which only served to fill the guilty soul of Caracalla with a fresh access of terror.[20]

The art of necromancy has been practised by barbarous as well as civilized peoples. In some African tribes the practice has prevailed of consulting the ghosts of dead kings or chiefs as oracles through the medium of a priest or priestess, who professed to be inspired by the soul of a deceased ruler and to speak in his name. For example, among the Baganda of Central Africa a temple was built for the ghost of each dead king, and in it his lower jawbone was reverently preserved; for curiously enough the part of his body to which the ghost of a dead Baganda man clings most persistently is his jawbone. The temple, a large conical hut of the usual pattern, was divided into two chambers, an outer and an inner, and in the inner chamber or holy of holies the precious jawbone was kept for safety in a cell dug in the floor. The prophet or medium, whose business it was from time to time to be inspired by the ghost of the dead monarch, dedicated himself to his holy office by drinking a draught of beer and a draught of milk out of the royal skull. When the ghost held a reception, the jawbone, wrapt in a decorated packet, was brought forth from the inner shrine and set on a throne in the outer chamber, where the people assembled to hear the oracle. On such occasions the prophet stepped up to the throne, and addressing the spirit informed him of the business in hand. Then he smoked one or two pipes of homegrown tobacco, and the fumes bringing on the prophetic fit he began to rave and speak in the very voice and with the characteristic turns of speech of the departed monarch; for the king's soul was now supposed to be in him. However, his rapid utterances were hard to understand, and a priest was in attendance to interpret them to the inquirer. The living king thus consulted his dead predecessors periodically on affairs of state, visiting first one and then another of the temples in which their sacred relics were preserved with religious care.[21]

Again, among the Banyoro, another tribe of Central Africa, in the Uganda Protectorate, the ghosts of dead kings were consulted as oracles by their living successors. Over the king's grave a mound of earth was raised, with a flat top which was covered with a grass carpet and overlaid with cow-skins and leopard-skins. This served as the throne where the king's ghost was supposed to take its seat at any ceremony. Before this throne offerings were presented to the ghost, and there also requests were made, when the reigning king wished to consult his father on matters of state or when sickness appeared in the royal household. At the grave a large hut was built, and in it were lodged guards, whose duty it was to watch over the tomb and to present the offerings to the worshipful ghost.[22]

Among the Basoga of the Central District, in the Uganda Protectorate, the souls of dead chiefs are in like manner consulted as oracles through the medium of women, who act as their interpreters or prophets. When a chief has been dead and buried for some months, his ghost appears to one of his kinsmen and tells him, 'I' wish to move." On being informed of the ghost's desire, the new chief orders the grave of his predecessor to be opened and the skull removed. When the skull has been dried and enclosed in skins, the chief sends for a woman, who must be a member of the clan to which the nurse of the late chief belonged. To her he commits the duty of guarding the skull, interpreting the wishes of the ghost, and attending to its wants. She also receives a she-goat, a cow, and a hen, which are to provide food for the ghost. Having received her commission and the provender, the woman is escorted to a place called Nakazungu, on the Mpologoma river, where a large house is built for her. There the skull is deposited in a shrine or temple, which is deemed the house of the ghost, and there the woman becomes possessed by the ghost and reveals his wishes. Thither, too, the new chief sends offerings to the spirit of his father. However, the skull and the ghost remain in this place of honour only during the life of his successor. When the next chief dies, the old skull and the old ghost are compelled to vacate the premises and shift their quarters to a wooded island in the river, where the skulls and ghosts of all former chiefs are permanently lodged. No house there shelters them from the inclemency of the weather. Each skull is simply deposited in the open, with a spear stuck in the ground beside it. The prophetess who attended to its wants in the temple accompanies the skull to its long home in the island, and there she may continue to interpret the wishes and views of the ghost to any who care to consult it. But few people think it worth while to make a pilgrimage to the old ghosts in this oracular Golgotha or Place of Skulls in the forest; most persons prefer to ask the advice of the new ghost in the temple. Thus fashion runs after novelty in the world of the dead as in the world of the living.[23]

Among the Bantu tribes who inhabit the great tableland of Northern Rhodesia the spirits of dead chiefs sometimes take possession of the bodies of live men or women and prophesy through their mouths. When the spirit thus comes upon a man, he begins to roar like a lion, and the women gather together and beat the drums, shouting that the chief has come to visit the village. The possessed person will predict future wars, and warn the people of approaching visitations by lions. While the inspiration lasts, the medium may eat nothing cooked by fire, but only unfermented dough. However, this gift of prophecy usually descends on women rather than on men. Such prophetesses give out that they are possessed by the soul of some dead chief, and when they feel the divine afflatus they whiten their faces to attract attention, and they smear themselves with flour, which has a religious and sanctifying potency. One of their number beats a drum, and the others dance, singing at the same time a weird song, with curious intervals. Finally, when they have worked themselves up to the requisite pitch of religious exaltation, the possessed woman drops to the ground, and bursts out into a low and almost inarticulate chant, which amid the awestruck silence of the bystanders is interpreted by the medicine-men as the voice of the spirit.[24]

Again, among the Barotsé, a Bantu tribe of the Upper Zambesi, the souls of dead kings are consulted and give their responses through the mouth of a priest. Each royal tomb is indeed an oracle of the dead. It stands in a beautiful grove, and is enclosed by a palisade covered with fine mats, like the palisade which surrounds the residence of a living king. Such an enclosure is sacred; the people are forbidden to enter it, lest they should disturb the ghost of him who sleeps below. A priest acts as intermediary between the royal ghost and the people who come to pray to him at the shrine. He alone has the right to enter the sacred enclosure; the profane multitude must stand at a respectful distance. Even the king himself, when he comes to consult one of his ancestors, is forbidden to set foot on the holy ground. He kneels down at the entrance, claps his hands, and gives the royal salute, which is solemnly returned by the priest from within the enclosure. Then the suppliant, whether king or commoner, makes his petition to the worshipful spirit and deposits his offering; for no man may pray at the shrine with empty hands. Inside the enclosure, near the entrance, is a hole, which is supposed to serve as a channel of communication with the spirit of the deified king. In it the offerings are deposited. Often they consist of milk, which is poured into the hole; more solid offerings, such as flesh, clothes, and glass beads, become the property of the priest after they have lain for a decent time beside the sacred aperture. The spirits of dead kings are thus consulted on matters of public concern as well as by private persons on their own affairs. All over the country these temple-tombs may be seen, each in its shady grove; hence no man need have far to go to seek for ghostly counsel at an oracle of the dead.[25]

Among the Ewe-speaking Negroes of South Togoland, when the funeral celebration is over, it is customary to summon up the soul of the deceased. His relations take cooked food to the priest and tell him that they wish to bring water for the spirit of their departed brother. The priest accordingly receives food, palm-wine, and cowry-shells at their hands, and with them retires into his room and shuts the door behind him. Then he evokes the ghost, who on his arrival begins to weep and to converse with the priest, sometimes making some general observations on the difference between life in the upper and in the under world, sometimes entering into particulars as to the manner of his own death; often he mentions the name of the wicked sorcerer who has killed him by his enchantments. When the dead man's friends outside hear the lamentations and complaints of his ghost proceeding from the room, they are moved to tears and cry out, "We pity you!" Finally, the ghost bids them be comforted and takes his departure.[26] Among the Kissi, a tribe of Negroes on the border of Liberia, the souls of dead chiefs are consulted as oracles by means of the statuettes which are erected on their graves. For the purpose of the consultation the statuettes are placed on a board, which is carried by two men on their heads; if the bearers remain motionless, the answer of the spirit is assumed to be "No"; if they sway to and fro, the answer is "Yes."[27] In the island of Ambrym, one of the New Hebrides, wooden statues representing ancestors are similarly employed as a means of communicating with the souls of the dead. When a man is in trouble, he blows a whistle at nightfall near the statue of an ancestor, and if he hears a noise, he believes that the soul of the dead kinsman has entered into the image; thereupon he recounts his woes to the effigy and prays the spirit to help him.[28]

The Maoris of New Zealand feared and worshipped the spirits of their dead kinsfolk, especially dead chiefs and warriors, who were believed to be constantly watching over the living tribesmen, protecting them in war and marking any breach of the sacred law of taboo. These spirits dwelt normally below the earth, but they could return to the upper air at pleasure and enter into the bodies of men or even into the substance of inanimate objects. Some tribes kept in their houses small carved images of wood, each of which was dedicated to the spirit of an ancestor, who was supposed to enter into the image on particular occasions in order to hold converse with the living. Such an ancestral spirit (*atua*) might communicate with the living either in dreams or more directly by talking with them in their waking hours. Their voice, however, was not like that of mortals, but a mysterious kind of sound, half whistle, half whisper.[29]

An Irishman, who lived long among the Maoris and knew them intimately, witnessed many such exhibitions of necromancy, and has described one of them in detail. The priests, he tells us, undertook to call up the spirit of any dead person for a proper fee. On this particular occasion the ghost evoked was that of a very popular young chief (*rangatira*), whom the Irishman had known intimately, and who had been killed in battle. At the request of his nearest friends, a priest engaged to call up the dead man's spirit to speak to them and answer certain questions which they wished to put. The interview took place at night in a large house common to the whole population, where fires cast a flickering light through the gloom. The priest retired to the darkest corner. All was expectation, and the silence was broken only by the sobbing of the sister and other female relations of the dead man. About thirty persons were seated on the rush-strewn floor. At last, when the fire had died down, leaving only a heap of glowing charcoal, a voice issued from the darkness solemnly saluting the assembly. It was answered by a cry of affection and despair from the dead chief's sister, a fine handsome young woman, who rushed, with both arms distended, into the darkness from which the voice proceeded. She was instantly seized round the waist and restrained by main force by her brother, till, moaning and fainting, she lay still on the ground. At the same instant another female voice was heard from a young girl, who was held by the wrists by two young men, her brothers, "Is it you? is it you? truly is it you? *ane! ane!* they hold me, they restrain me; wonder not that I have not followed you; they restrain me, they watch me, but I go to you. The sun shall not rise, the sun shall not rise, *ane! ane!*" Here she fell insensible on the floor, and with the sister was carried out. Afterwards the ghost conversed with his brother in strange melancholy tones, like the sound of the wind blowing into a hollow vessel, and he answered a woman's inquiry about her dead sister. Having satisfied her affectionate anxiety, the ghost next requested that his tame pig and his double-barrelled gun might be given to the priest. The Irishman now struck in and questioned the ghost as to a book which the dead chief had left behind him. The ghost indicated correctly the place where the volume had been deposited, but on being pressed to mention some of its contents he took an abrupt leave of the assembly, his farewell sounding first from the room, next from deep beneath the ground, then from high in air, and finally dying away in the darkness of night. The company broke up after midnight, and the Irishman retired to rest. But he was soon wakened by the report of a musket, followed by the shouts of men and the screams of women. Hastening in the direction from which the sounds proceeded, he saw in the midst of a crowd, by the light of a burning house, the lifeless and bleeding body of the young girl who had said that she would follow the spirit to the spirit land. She had kept her word, having secretly procured a loaded musket and blown herself to pieces. The voice of the priest said, close to the Irishman, "She has followed her *rangatira.*"[30]

In Nukahiva, one of the Marquesas Islands, the priests and priestesses claimed to possess the power of evoking the spirits of the dead, who took up their abode for the time being in the bodies of the mediums and so conversed with their surviving relatives. The occasion for summoning up a ghost was usually the sickness of a member of the family, on whose behalf his friends desired to have the benefit of ghostly advice.[31]

At the initiation ceremonies, which they observe every year, the Marindineeze, a tribe on the southern coast of Dutch New Guinea, summon up the souls of their forefathers from the underworld by knocking hard on the ground with the lower ends of coco-nut leaves for an hour together. The evocation takes place by night.[32] Similarly at their festivals the Bare'e-speaking Toradjas of Central Celebes evoke the souls of dead chiefs and heroes, the guardian spirits of the village, by beating on the floor of the temple with a long stick.[33]

The Sea Dyaks of Borneo believe that the souls of their dead friends live and revisit them on earth. They are invoked in times of peril and distress; and on the hilltops or in the solitude of the jungle a man will often go by himself and spend the night, hoping that the spirit of a dead relative may visit him and reveal to him in a dream some charm by which he may extricate himself from his difficulties and grow rich and great.[34]

Among the Kayans of Borneo, when a dispute has arisen concerning the division of a dead man's property, recourse is sometimes had to a professional wizard or witch, who summons up the ghost of the deceased and questions him as to his intentions in the disposal of his estate. The evocation, however, cannot take place until after the harvest which follows upon the death. When the time comes for it, a small model of a house is made for the temporary accommodation of the ghost and is placed in the gallery of the common house, beside the door of the dead man's chamber. For the refreshment of the spirit, moreover, food, drink, and cigarettes are laid out in the little house. The wizard takes up his post beside the tiny dwelling and chants his invocation, calling upon the soul of the deceased to enter the soul-house, and mentioning the names of the members of his family. From time to time he looks in, and at last announces that all the food and drink have been consumed. The people believe that the ghost has now entered the soul-house; and the wizard pretends to listen to the whispering of the soul within the house, starting and clucking from time to time. Finally, he declares the will of the ghost in regard to the distribution of the property, speaking in the first person and mimicking the mode of speech and other peculiarities of the dead man. The directions so obtained are usually followed, and thus the dispute is settled.[35]

The Bataks of Central Sumatra believe that the souls of the dead, being incorporeal, can only communicate with the living through the person of a living man, and for the purpose of such communication they choose an appropriate medium, who, in serving as a vehicle for the ghostly message, imitates the voice, the manner, the walk, and even the dress of the deceased so closely, that his surviving relations are often moved to tears by the resemblance. By the mouth of the medium the spirit reveals his name, mentions his relations, and describes the pursuits he followed on earth. He discloses family secrets which he had kept during life, and the disclosure confirms his kinsfolk in the belief that it is really the ghost of their departed brother who is conversing with them. When a member of the family is sick, the ghost is consulted as to whether the patient will live or die. When an epidemic is raging, the ghost is evoked and sacrifices are offered to him, that he may guard the people against the infection. When a man is childless, he inquires of a ghost through a medium, how he can obtain offspring. When something has been lost or stolen, a ghost is conjured up to tell whether the missing property will be recovered. When any one has missed his way in the forest or elsewhere and has not returned home, it is still to a ghost, through the intervention of a medium, that the anxious friends apply in order to learn where the strayed wayfarer is to be sought. If a medium is questioned as to how the ghost takes possession of him, he says that he sees the ghost approaching and feels as if his body were being dragged away, his feet grow light and leap about, human beings seem small and reddish in colour, the houses appear to be turning round. But the possession is not continuous; from time to time during the fit the ghost leaves the medium and plays about. When the fit is over, the medium is often sick and sometimes dies.[36]

Necromancy has been practised by man amid Arctic snow and ice as well as in tropical forests and jungles. Among the Eskimo of Labrador we read of a shaman who used to oblige his friends by calling up the spirits of the dead, whenever the living desired to inquire concerning the welfare of the departed, or the whereabouts of absent relatives at sea. He would first blindfold the questioner, and then rap thrice on the ground with a stick. On the third rap the spirit appeared and answered the shaman's questions. Having supplied the information that was wanted, the ghost would be dismissed to his own place by three more raps on the ground. This sort of necromancy was called "conjuring with a stick" (*kilu'xin*). A similar method of evoking the souls of the dead is employed by the Eskimo of Alaska. They believe that the spirits ascend from the under world and pass through the body of the shaman, who converses audibly with them and, having learned all he desires, sends them back to their subterranean abode by a stamp of his foot. The answers of the ghosts to his questions are supposed by sceptics to be produced by ventriloquism.[37]

In China, the practice of necromancy was always common, and in recent times the practitioners were chiefly old women. Such necromancers, for example, abound in Canton and Amoy. During his residence at Canton, Archdeacon Gray witnessed many exhibitions of their skill, and he describes one of them as follows: "One day, in the month of January 1867, I was the guest of an old lady, a widow, who resided in the western suburb of the city. She desired to confer with her departed husband, who had been dead for several years. The witch who was called in, was of prepossessing appearance and well-dressed; and she commenced immediately to discharge the duties of her vocation. Her first act was to erect a temporary altar at the head of the hall in which we were assembled. Upon this she placed two burning tapers, and offerings of fruits and cakes. She then sat on the right side of the altar, and, burying her face in her hands, remained silent for several minutes. Having awakened from her supposed trance or dream, she began to utter in a singing tone some words of incantation, at the same time sprinkling handfuls of rice at intervals upon the floor. She then said that the spirit of the departed was once more in the midst of his family. They were greatly moved, and some of them burst into a flood of tears. Through the witch as a medium, the spirit of the old man then informed the family where he was, and of the state of happiness he was permitted to enjoy in the land of shades. He spoke on several family topics, and dwelt upon the condition of one of his sons who, since his death, had gone to the northern provinces of China—references which evidently astonished the members of the family who were present, and confirmed their belief in the supernatural powers of the female impostor before them. There can be no doubt that she had made suitable inquiries beforehand. After exhorting his widow to dry her tears, and on no account to summon him again from the world of shades, in which he was tolerably happy, the spirit of the old man retired."[38]

According to the account of a native Chinese author, it is customary in the province of Shantung to consult the ancestral spirits (*shen*), in the female apartments, when a member of the family is sick. The medium employed for the purpose is an old witch who dances, playing a tambourine and making grimaces, and is therefore called the dancing spirit. "But this practice," he proceeds, "flourishes specially in the capital of the empire, where even young married women in respectable families perform it from time to time. In the hall of the house they place on the table stands which are filled with meat, and goblets full of spirits, and they light large candles, so that it is clearer there than in the daytime; then the woman, tucking up her petticoat, draws up one leg and hops like a *shang-yang*,[a] while two grasp her arms, and support her on either side. She babbles in a monotonous tedious way, now in a sing song, now as if uttering conjurations, now with a flow of words, then with only a few, without any modulation or tune. Meanwhile drums are wildly banged in the apartment, so that their thunder stuns one, and in their noise the words which come from her opening and closing lips are far from distinct. In the end she droops her head, looks askance, and wants help to stand erect; but for her supporters she would tumble. But suddenly she stretches out her neck and jumps one or two feet into the air, and all the women in the apartment shiver and regard her with terror; thereupon she exclaims, 'The ancestor comes and eats!' Now they blow out the lights, so that it is pitch dark everywhere. Silent the bystanders stand in the dark, and speak not a word to each other; indeed, owing to the confused noise, nothing they might say would be understood. After a while they hear the woman mention with a shrill voice the (deceased) father or mother-in-law, or the husband or sister-in-law, by the name by which he or she was familiarly known, this being a sign to the whole company to re-light the candles. With outstretched necks they now ask the medium whether good or evil is to be expected, and in the mean time they inspect the goblets, baskets and cups, to find them altogether emptied; and they try to read on her face whether the spirit is contented or not; and, full of respect, they address a series of questions to her, which she answers as readily as an echo."[39]

The practice of calling up the spirits of the dead for consultation is said to be very common in Amoy, where the necromancers are professional

a A fabulous one-legged bird.

women. Among the male sex the reputation of these ladies for strict veracity seems not to stand very high, for to tell a man, in common parlance, that he is "bringing up the dead" is almost equivalent to saying that he is telling a lie. Hence these female necromancers often prefer to confine their ministrations to their own sex, lest they should expose their high mysteries to the derision of masculine sceptics. In that case the session is held with closed doors in the private apartments of the women; otherwise it takes place in the main hall, at the domestic altar, and all inmates of the house are free to attend. Many families, indeed, make a rule to question, by means of these witches, every deceased relation at least once not long after his or her death, in order to ascertain whether the souls are comfortable in the other world, and whether anything can be done by family affection to ameliorate their condition. An auspicious day having been chosen for the ceremony, the apartment is swept and watered, because spirits entertain an aversion to dirt and dust. To allure the ghost, food and dainties, together with burning incense, are placed on the domestic altar, or, should the conference take place in a secluded room, on an ordinary table. In the latter case, when the medium has come, it is necessary for one of the women to go to the altar, where the tablets are deposited in which the souls of the dead members of the family are believed to reside. Having lighted two candles and three incense-sticks at the altar, she invites the ghost to leave its tablet and follow her. Then, with the incense between her fingers, she slowly walks back into the room, and plants the sticks in a bowl or cup with some uncooked rice. The medium now goes to work, chanting conjurations, while she strums a lyre or beats a drum. In time her movements grow convulsive, she rocks to and fro, and sweat bursts from her body. These things are regarded as evidence that the ghost has arrived. Two women support the medium and place her in a chair, where she falls into a state of distraction or slumber, with her arms resting on the table. A black veil is next thrown over her head, and in her mesmeric state she can now answer questions, shivering, as she does so, rocking in her seat, and drumming the table nervously with her hands or with a stick. Through her mouth the ghost informs his relations of his state in the other world and what they can do to improve it or even to redeem him entirely from his sufferings. He mentions whether the sacrifices which are offered to him reach their destination intact or suffer loss and damage in process of transmission through the spiritual post; he states his preferences and he enumerates his wants. He also favours his kinsfolk with his advice on domestic affairs, though his language is often ambiguous and his remarks have sometimes little or no bearing on the questions submitted to him. Now and then the medium holds whispered monologues, or rather conversations with the ghost. At last she suddenly shivers, awakes, and raising herself up declares that the ghost has gone. Having pocketed the rice and the incense-sticks in the bowl, she receives her fee and takes her departure. "The various phases in the condition of the medium during the conference are, of course, taken by the onlookers for the several moments of her connection with the other world. Yet we remain entitled to consider them to be symptoms of psychical aberration and nervous affection. Her spasms and convulsions pass for possession, either by the ghost which is consulted, or by the spirit with which she usually has intercourse, and which thus imparts to her the faculty of second sight by which she sees that ghost. And her mesmeric fits confessedly are the moments when her soul leaves her, in order to visit the other world, there to see the ghost and speak with it. Her whispering lips indicate conversation with her spirit, or with the ghost which is consulted. It may be asked, why, since this ghost dwells in its tablet on the altar, her soul should travel to the other world to see it. We can give no answer."[40]

[The witch of Endor is described in the Hebrew text as "a woman who owns (or controls) an *'ob*" (KJV: "that hath a familiar spirit"; RSV: "a woman who is a medium"). This technical term (which recurs elsewhere in the Old Testament[40a]) has long proved a puzzle to interpreters. The older view was that it was the common Hebrew word for "bottle" and referred to a common belief —familiar especially from the story of Aladdin—that genii or familiar spirits can be kept in bottles.[40b] To this day, for example, the Galelas and Tobelorese think they reside in earthen pots.[40c] In a Canaanite (Ugaritic) poem from Ras Shamra, however, the "portmanteau" word *ilib* occurs with the sense of "ancestral spirit,"[40d] and W. F. Albright has ingeniously suggested that this is made up of *il* "god, otherworld being," and the Canaanite cognate of our puzzling *'ob*.[40e] The former would then relate to the fact that the beings whom the witch was ascending from the netherworld are indeed described in the Hebrew text by the comparable term *elohim*, likewise meaning "gods, otherworld beings"; while the latter might then be explained from the Arabic term *'abā*, "return" in the sense of our *revenant*, or the Danish *gienfard, gienganger*.[40f] ▼

134   Mutilation of fallen foes   **II Sam. 31:14**
See above, §**107.**

135   Signs of mourning   **1:2, 11**
See below, §§**202, 293.**

136   Bloodshed renders soil infertile   **1:21**
See above, §**27.**

137   The "holder of the spindle"   **3:29**

*Abner, a supporter of Saul, consorts with one of his master's con-
cubines. Upbraided for this, he decides to transfer his allegiance to
David. The latter receives him cordially, but David's general, Joab,
nurses a grudge against the new ally because he has been responsible*

*for the slaying of his (Joab's) brother, Asahel. Unbeknown to his
royal master, he summons Abner to the capital and there settles the
score by stabbing him. When David hears of this, he pronounces upon
Joab the curse that his household may never be without "a leper or
one that holds the spindle[1] or one that falls by the sword or one that
lacks bread."*

The sense of David's curse is that Joab's progeny may suffer disease,
effeminacy, ill-fortune in war, and starvation. The expression, "one that
holds the spindle," implies one who is fit only to do woman's work, and it
represents a common form of commination in the Ancient Near East. Thus,
in the treaty of Mat'ilu of Arpad, the curse is invoked that if either party
violate the provisions of the agreement, "he shall become like a whore, and
his people like women";[2] while in an inscription of Esarhaddon, now in Berlin,
Ishtar, "queen of combat and battle," is brought to turn the manhood of the
perfidious into womanhood.[3] Similarly, in a Hittite ritual text, the punishment
prescribed for disloyal citizens is that they be dressed in female clothing,
handed a spindle, and blinded.[4]

138   Taboo on touching the Ark of the Lord   6:6–7

*As David was bringing the sacred ark of Yahweh to Jerusalem, his
new capital, the oxen which were drawing it stumbled. A certain
Uzza caught hold of it, to steady it. This, however, was deemed sacrilege, and "God struck him down on the spot . . . and he died."*

That which is "holy" and otherworldly—what the Scots call "unco"—may
not be touched or approached by a mundane and mortal creature, except he
be in a state of absolute purity, lest it thereby become contaminated and lose
its "mana."[1]

The incident here recorded has two illuminating parallels in Classical lore.
When Troy was burning, we are told, Ilus took the Palladium—a counterpart
of the Biblical ark—from the shrine of Athene (or whatever the native goddess may have been called) in order to rescue it from the flames. He was
instantly blinded[2]—the standard punishment for sacrilege.[3] The same fate
also befell Metellus when he tried to snatch that sacred object from a fire in the
temple of Vesta.[4] (Both, it may be added, eventually had their sight restored.)

139   Shaving and shearing   10:1–6

*When the king of the Ammonites died, David sent a message of
condolence and goodwill to his son and successor, Hanun. The latter's
counselors, however, were suspicious of David's envoys and, on their
advice, Hanun had them arrested and "shaved off half of the beard of
each, and cut off their garments in the middle, at their hips, and sent*

*them away." David naturally resented this, and when the Ammonites
perceived that they had "become odious" to him,*[1] *they decided to
forestall his reprisals by hiring Syrian mercenaries to mount an attack
upon Israel.*

Comparative Folklore suggests a new interpretation of this bizarre incident. In Arab custom there are two different reasons for forcibly shaving a
man's beard. The one is as a gesture of reconciliation: the "blood-avenger"
of a slain man settles accounts with a repentant murderer by shearing his locks
instead of cutting his throat.[2] Thus the sheikh of Bweme in Adjlun told S. I.
Curtiss that one of the recognized ways in which a blood-avenger claims
satisfaction and makes peace with his kinsman's slayer, in lieu of accepting
payment or security or demanding surrender of property is to cut off some of
the latter's hair. Similarly, a bedouin wanderer informed the same scholar
that when a murderer brings to the avenger the customary sacrifice of peace
and reconciliation, "the avenger shaves off some of his (the murderer's)
beard." They then "kiss each other on the head and beard. If the avenger
refuses to claim damage from the murderer, he shaves off the lock of hair
on his forehead and lets him go."[3]

Similarly, among the Druzes, "if a murderer believes that he and his family
are too weak to defend themselves against the family of the murdered man,
he goes to the nearest relative of the latter with a cord or a cloth about his
neck. He excuses himself by pleading that since he is a man of honor, he
could not avoid committing the murder, since the other had applied a dis-
honorable epithet to him. He then gives the blood-avenger, amid compliments,
full freedom to take his life. Then the relative of the murdered man is obliged
to forgive him. Nevertheless, this does not proceed quite so inconsequentially.
The wronged man has a barber brought to shave off the beard of the murderer.[4]

"Among the Tiāhā a parallel practise is found. When a prisoner is taken
in war, and they do not wish to put him to death, he is led to the encampment,
where a corner of his head below the temples is shaved, and he is let go
free."[5]

It is also customary, however, to shear a prisoner's locks in token of
his subjection and surrender of personality (see above, §117).[6]

In the light of these usages the incident here recorded takes on quite a
different complexion. Hanun, it may be suggested, really intended no insult.
He was simply accepting a final reconciliation between the Israelites and the
Ammonites by a gesture customary in such circumstances among his own
people. David, however, interpreted it in the other sense, namely, as an indication that Hanun was treating Israel as a subjected people surrendering
to him. Such an explanation gives point to the Ammonites' subsequent amaze-

ment at David's reaction; they were surprised that what they had meant to signify reconciliation had been so misunderstood that they had now "become odious" to those with whom they had thought to be friends.

140   The Uriah letter   11

> David consorts with Bathsheba, the beautiful wife of Uriah, a paladin at his court. To further the intrigue, he sends Uriah with a letter to Joab, the commander of the army. The letter orders Joab to place Uriah in an exposed position in battle against the Ammonites. This is done, and Uriah is killed.

This is but a Hebrew version of a widespread folktale.[1] The most familiar parallel is the Greek story of Bellerophon.[2] Stheneboea,[3] the wife of Proetus, becomes infatuated with him and tries to seduce him. When he rejects her advances she plays the role of Potiphar's wife and falsely accuses him to her husband. Thereupon Proetus sends him with a letter to his (Proetus) father-in-law Iobates, requesting the latter to have him killed. Accordingly, Iobates dispatches him to fight the fearsome Chimaera. Bellerophon, however, mounts his winged horse Pegasus and shoots the monster from the air. He is then sent on other adventures designed to be fatal, but in each case emerges unscathed. Iobates then relents, marries Bellerophon to his daughter, and eventually bequeathes to him his kingdom.

An Indian version appears in one of the tales of Somadeva's Ocean of Story, where King Adityavaraman similarly disposes of his vizar Sivavaraman, whom he suspects of an intrigue with one of his concubines.[4]

Often the story takes the twist that the fatal letter is intercepted; the intended victim alters the name or someone else changes the contents to his advantage.[5] Thus, in Saxo's Historia Danica, Hamlet's wicked uncle Fengon sends him, with two companions, to England, bearing a letter to the English king requesting that monarch to put him to death. Hamlet, however, changes his own name to that of his companions, and they perish in his stead. This incident was taken over by Shakespeare who identified the two victims as Guildenstern and Rosencrantz.[6] Similarly, in Grimm's story of The Devil with Three Golden Hairs, a king tries to prevent a youth from marrying his daughter, as fated. Encountering him while on his travels, the king sends him to the palace with a letter to the queen, ordering her to have him killed. On the way, however, the youth rests in a robbers' hut. The robbers change the letter so that it orders the youth's marriage to the princess.[7] Again, in an Arabic version, the poet Mutalammis is given a letter ordering his death. He destroys it, but his companion Tarafah, who bears a similar missive, does not do so, and perishes. The motif recurs also in the Scandinavian Edda,[8] and stories of the same tenor are likewise reported from modern Greece[9] and Hungary.[10]

141 Regnal names   12:24–25

Bathsheba bears to David a son whom he calls Solomon. The child is subsequently renamed Jedidiah, "beloved of Yahweh," the change being made formally by the prophet Nathan.

In ancient times, as we have seen (above, §72), a person's name was not simply a verbal appellation, but a manifestation of his essential self. Kings, popes, and members of holy orders therefore assume new names when they enter upon their careers and thus assume, as it were, new characters. The custom goes back to ancient Egypt, and appears to have been fairly widespread in the Near East.[1]

The name Jedidiah, "beloved of Yahweh," is not chosen arbitrarily. It is the Hebrew equivalent of a title commonly affected in the Ancient Near East. Mesopotamian kings, for example, were often styled *naram ili*, "beloved of the god," or *migir ili*, "favored by the god";[2] while in the Canaanite myths discovered at Ras Shamra, "Prince (*zbl*) Sea" bears the common epithet *mdd Il,* "beloved (friend) of El (God),[3] and Môt, god of sterility and of the netherworld, is termed similarly *ydd Il.*[4]

142 The coal on the hearth   14:7

Joab, anxious to reconcile David to his upstart son, Absalom, sends to him a clever woman of Tekoa whom he instructs to win the king over by means of a parable. Clad in mourning, she tells David that she is the mother of two sons, one of whom killed the other during a quarrel. The clan is now demanding the manslayer's death, but this will mean that "they will extinguish the one coal that is left (on the hearth)."

> Put out the light, and then put out the light
> Shakespeare, *Othello,* V.ii.7.

The hearthfire is universally regarded as the symbol of family life. When it dies out, the family is extinct.

The idea is expressed several times in the Old Testament; compare, for instance, Job 18:5–6: "The light of the wicked is put out, and the spark of his fire doth not shine; the light in his tent is darkened, and his lamp above him is put out"; *ibid.* 21:17: "Dimmed is the light of the wicked"; Proverbs 13:9; 24:20: The lamp of the wicked is put out"; *ib.* 20:20: "Whoso curseth his father or his mother, his lamp shall be put out"; II Samuel 21:17: "Then David's men sware unto him, saying 'Thou shalt go no more out with us to battle, lest thou quench the lamps of Israel." Mesopotamian texts likewise mention the extinction of the hearthfire or the oven as a sign of family misfortune,[1] and it has been suggested that the Sumerian word for "heir" (IBILA) really means "one who keeps the oil (lamp) burning (I(A)+BIL)."[2] In Arabic idiom, the extinction of a light is likewise a synonym for disaster.[3]

The image is well known also to Classical writers.[4] Ovid, for instance, speaks of "extinguished hearths" as a symbol of exile,[5] and both Tibullus[6] and Martial[7] of the "ever-burning fire on the hearth" as betokening bliss and contentment.

A modern Greek belief on the island of Zacynthos (Zante) is that a light burns for every human life in the realm of Charos, god of death; when one of them goes out, a man dies.[8] Similarly, an English popular superstition holds that gathering candles betokens death,[9] and analogous notions appear in German folklore.[10]

Among the Tonga, Sothe, and Venda-Bantu tribes of Southeast Africa,[11] as also among the Zulus,[12] it is the practice to extinguish the main communal fire at the death of a chieftain; while among the Cwana, fires are put out at moments of public calamity, as when an epidemic occurs.[13] Along the same lines, a burning brazier was carried before Spartan[14] and Hellenistic kings.[15]

Conversely, the maintenance of the household fire implies the preservation of the home. Yahweh promises to "give a lamp to David and his sons for ever,"[16] and in the Canaanite Poem of Aqhat one of the reasons why a man wants a son is that he shall have someone "to make his smoke ascend from the ground."[17]

143   Absalom and his father's concubines   16:20–23

Absalom, in order to rally popular support for his ambitions, is anxious to demonstrate an open breach with David. On the advice of Ahitophel, he does so by publicly indulging in sexual relations with David's concubines.

There is more to this incident than an act of affront. Ahitophel's advice is based on the ancient custom whereby a son and heir inherited all of his father's wives and concubines except his own mother. This was, so to speak, part of the act of succession.

The custom is attested both in Semitic and in Classical sources. Molaika, wife of the Calif Ali, was thus "inherited"; so was Amina, the wife of Abu Mo'ayyit, and so too was the Fahmite widow of the Calif Omar.[1] Robertson Smith suggests[2] that desire to establish succession was what motivated Reuben to consort with Jacob's concubine, Bilhah,[3] and that when Ish-bosheth accused Saul's uncle and supporter, Abner, of consorting with the former's concubine, what he really meant was that Abner was not disinterested but conniving to secure the succession for himself.[4]

In the Odyssey, Telegonus, the son of Odysseus, "inherits" Penelope,[5] and Telemachus inherits Circe.[6] So too Herakles charged his son Hyllus to marry Iole when he came of age.[7] Several cases of this practice may be cited also from Syro-Roman times.[8]

144 King's misconduct affects soil 21:1–9

Because Saul had slain the Gibeonites, with whom Israel had concluded a treaty, the Lord sent a three-year famine during the reign of Saul's successor, David.

The king is the epitome of his people's life and destiny. Misconduct, like debility, on his part therefore impairs the fertility of the soil and the general welfare.[1]

In a Hittite text it is stated that a twenty-year blight has resulted from sins committed by the royal household,[2] and similar ideas appear in ancient Mesopotamian literature.[3] In the Canaanite (Ugaritic) *Epic of K-r-t*, drought follows that monarch's neglect of a vow he has made to the goddess Asherath;[4] while in an Aramaic treaty of the eighth century B.C., between the king of K-t-k and the king of Arpad, a seven-year scourge is invoked as sanction in case of breach by either party.[5]

In parts of Africa, drought is attributed to the king's unchastity,[6] and this is likewise a common theme of Irish legend[7] and of European folktales in general.[8] Ammianus Marcellinus, the last of the major Roman historians, has an interesting passage anent this concept. "Among the Burgundians," he tells us, "the king is removed from power and deposed by ancient rite, if during his reign the fortunes of war suffer reverse or the earth refuses to yield substantial crops." "The Egyptians," he adds, "used in the same way to attribute such disasters to their rulers."[9]

All of this, of course, is merely a particular application of the wider principle that misconduct in general—and especially, sexual misconduct—is reflected in the condition of the soil.[10] Thus the Kayans of Borneo hold that adultery is punished by the spirits, who withold crops;[11] while the Negroes of Lorango suppose that the intercourse of a man with an immature girl is punished by God with drought.[12] Job, protesting that he is no adulterer, declares that if he were, "fire would root out all my produce"; and in the Book of Leviticus we are told that misconduct pollutes the land and causes it to "vomit forth its inhabitants."[13] Indeed, in several passages of the Old Testament the same Hebrew word describes the infertility of the soil as normally denotes the defilement of a woman through unchastity.[14]

Conversely, a land prospers under a good king. For this reason, ancient Semitic monarchs, like Azitawad of Adana[15] and Zakir of Hamath,[16] both of the eighth century B.C., make a point, in their triumphal inscriptions, of boasting that during their reigns crops were abundant. So too, in Homer's Odyssey, Odysseus (still unrevealed to her) tells Penelope that her fame has risen to the broad heavens, "like that of a blameless king who is god-fearing and holds to justice . . . so that, through him, the black earth bears barley and wheat, and the trees burgeon with fruit, and the sheep breed in the plains, and the sea teems with fish."[17] The greatest bliss that could be invoked on a new king was, in fact, that he might serve as a symbol of his people's peace and prosperity. "May he be in the land," says the Psalmist, "like an expanse of corn which waves in the breeze on the hilltops; may he be like the fruit which in Lebanon grows, and may men blossom forth out of the city like grass of the earth."[18]

145   A Hebrew Niobe   21:10

> *In retribution for the massacre perpetrated by Saul, the Gibeonites request of David that seven of Saul's sons be handed over to them and be hung up before the Lord on a hill at Gibeon. David consents, but Rizpah, one of Saul's concubines, whose sons have been included among the seven, keeps continuous vigil over the bodies "from the early days of harvest until the rains, fell." David, told of her devotion, orders the bones collected, along with those of Saul and Jonathan, and gives them honorable burial. Thereupon, the Lord is propitiated, and the famine ends.*

(a) Rizpah is usually regarded as a kind of Hebrew Niobe,[1] but perhaps, in its original form, the story revolved around the widespread notion that the *essential vitality of a person lies in the bodily fluids,*[2] *so that a corpse must be "watered" before it can be assured of eventual resurrection.* It is for this reason that, for example, Arabs often make a practice of burying the dead near water,[3] and in an ancient Arabic poem the spirit of a deceased man prays that his burial mound as well as himself may "drink from the thunderclouds and raindrops."[4] The Babylonians made a practice of pouring water over the dead,[5] and a very common belief in Europe is that rain at a funeral is lucky;[6] as the English proverb puts it, "Blessed is the dead the rain rains on."[7] Not impossibly, there is an allusion to this idea in the words of Job 21:32–33:

> When he is borne to the grave,
> Watch is kept o'er his tomb;
> the clods of the valley are sweet unto him.

Associated with this notion is the belief that dew revives the dead. Mentioned already by Isaiah (*Thy dead shall live; those whom I have made corpses shall arise, for thy dew is a shimmering dew*),[8] the "dew of resurrection" features prominently in later Jewish folklore.[9]

(b) As we have seen in the story of Cain and Abel (above §14), the unavenged spirits of the slain can affect the fertility of the soil by causing drought or blight. Rizpah therefore keeps her vigil until the auspicious moment—the time when the rains would normally descend. At that time her action is reported to David, and he becomes anxious that the spirits be appeased.

What is here related is admirably illustrated by an incident recorded by

Plutarch. A plague broke out in Rome, and the Pythian oracle was consulted. It advised that the wrath of Saturn and the spirits (manes) of those unjustly slain should be appeased. Thereupon Lutatius Catulus created a temple to Saturn containing an altar with four faces.[10]

▲ 146 The sin of a census   24

The Lord is angry with the Israelites, so he inspires David to commit a crime which will bring dire consequences upon them. The crime is the taking of a census.

[To be able to identify a thing precisely is, in ancient and primitive thought, to have potential control over it. It is for this reason, as we have seen (above, §72), that knowledge of a person's name is all-important in working magic against him and, conversely, it is for this reason that otherworld beings refrain from disclosing it. To know the exact number of things can produce the same result. Accordingly, all over the world we find a popular resistance to taking a census, counting cattle, crops or fruits, and even to revealing one's age.]

This curious superstition is especially well attested among the Negroid races of Africa. For example, among the Bakongo of the Lower Congo "it is considered extremely unlucky for a woman to count her children one, two, three, and so on, for the evil spirits will hear and take some of them away by death. The people themselves do not like to be counted; for they fear that counting will draw to them the attention of the evil spirits, and as a result of the counting some of them will soon die. In 1908 the Congo State officials, desiring to number the people for the purpose of levying a tax, sent an officer with soldiers to count them. The natives would have resisted the officer, but he had too many soldiers with him; and it is not improbable that fights have taken place between whites and blacks in other parts of Africa, not that they resisted the taxation, but because they objected to be counted for fear the spirits would hear and kill them."[1] Similarly among the Boloki or Bangala of the Upper Congo, "the native has a very strong superstition and prejudice against counting his children, for he believes that if he does so, or if he states the proper number, the evil spirits will hear it and some of his children will die; hence when you ask him such a simple question as, 'How many children have you?' you stir up his superstitious fears, and he will answer: 'I don't know.' If you press him, he will tell you sixty, or one hundred children, or any other number that jumps to his tongue; and even then he is thinking of those who, from the native view of kinship, are regarded as his children, and desiring to deceive, not you, but those ubiquitous and prowling evil spirits, he states a large number that leaves a wide margin."[2]

Again, the Masai of East Africa count neither men nor beasts, believing that if they did so the men or beasts would die. Hence they reckon a great multitude of people or a large herd of cattle only in round numbers; of smaller groups of men or beasts they can reckon the totals with tolerable accuracy without numbering the individuals of the groups. Only dead men or dead beasts may be counted one by one, because naturally there is no risk of their dying again in consequence of their numeration.[3] [The Loango have a similar reluctance to numbering their cattle;[3a] while] the Wa-Sania of British East Africa "most strongly object to being counted, as they believe that one of those who were counted would die shortly afterwards."[4] To the Akamba, another tribe of the same region, the welfare of the cattle is a matter of great concern; hence the people observe certain superstitious rules, the breach of which is believed to entail misfortune on the herds. One of these rules is that the cattle may never be counted; so when the herd returns to the village, the owner will merely cast his eye over it to discover if a beast is missing. And in this tribe the unluckiness of counting is not limited to cattle, it extends to all living creatures, and particularly to girls.[5] On the other hand, another authority on the Akamba tells us that "there does not appear to be any superstition against counting stock; if a man has a large herd he does not know the number, but he or his wives when milking would quickly notice if a beast with certain markings was not present. A man however knows the number of his children but is averse to telling any one outside his family. There is a tradition that a man named Munda wa Ngola, who lived in the Ibeti Hills, had many sons and daughters, and boasted of the size of his family, saying that he and his sons could resist any attack from the Masai; one night however the Masai surprised him and killed him and his people, and the countryside considered that this was a judgement on him."[6] Again, among the Akikuyu, another tribe of British East Africa, "it is difficult to arrive at figures, even approximately correct, with regard to the size of the families. The natural method of conversing with the mothers as to the number of their children is soon found to be, to say the least, a tactless proceeding. It is considered most unlucky to give such figures. The inquiry is politely waived, with a resquest to 'come and see.' . . . The objection to giving family statistics was discovered not to be in force amongst other members than the parents; at any rate it did not seem to affect those Kikuyu boys who were continually in touch with us. These answered readily any questions as to the number of their father's wives, their grandfather's wives, and their respective children, and seemed to have a good acquaintance with their relations."[7] The Gallas of East Africa think that to count cattle is an evil omen, and that it impedes the increase of the herd.[8] To count the members of a community or company is reckoned by the Hottentots to be of very evil augury, for they believe that some member of the company will die. A missionary who once, in ignorance of this superstition, counted his workpeople, is said to have paid for his rashness with his life.[9]

The superstitious objection to numbering people seems to be general in North Africa; in Algeria the opposition offered by the natives to all French regulations which require an enumeration of the inhabitants is said to be based in great measure on this aversion to be counted. Nor is this repugnance limited to the counting of persons; it is exhibited also in the counting of measures of grain, an operation which has a sacred character. For example, at Oran the person who counts the measures of grain should be in a state of ceremonial purity, and instead of counting one, two, three, and so on, he says "In the name of God" for "one"; "two blessings" for "two"; "hospitality of the Prophet" for "three"; "we shall gain, please God" for "four"; "in the eye of the Devil" for "five"; "in the eye of his son" for "six"; "it is God who gives us our fill" for "seven"; and so on, up to "twelve," for which the expression is "the perfection for God."[10] So in Palestine, at counting the measures of grain, many Mohammedans say for the first one, "God is one," and for the next, "He has no second," then simply "Three," "Four," and so on. But "there are several unlucky numbers, the first being five, and therefore, instead of saying the number, they often say 'Your hand,' five being the number of the fingers; seven is another unlucky number, strange to say, and is passed over in silence, or the word 'A blessing' is used instead; at nine Moslems often say, 'Pray in the name of Mohammed'; eleven also is not unfrequently omitted, the measurer saying, 'There are ten,' and then passing on to twelve."[11] Perhaps such substitutes for the ordinary numbers are intended to deceive evil spirits, who may be lying in wait to steal or harm the corn, and who are presumably too dull-witted to comprehend these eccentric modes of numeration.

In the Shortlands group of islands, in the Western Pacific, the building of a chief's house is attended by a variety of ceremonies and observances. The roof is heavily thatched at each gable with thatch made of the leaves of the ivory-nut palm. In collecting these leaves the builders are not allowed to count the number, as the counting would be deemed unlucky; yet if the number of leaves collected should fall short of the number required, the house, though nearing completion, would be at once abandoned.[12] Thus the loss entailed by a miscalculation may be heavy, and from its possible extent we can judge how serious must, in the opinion of the natives, be the objection to counting the leaves, since rather than count them they are prepared to sacrifice the fruit of their labour. Among the Cherokee Indians of North America it is a rule that "melons and squashes must not be counted or examined too closely, while still growing upon the vine, or they will cease to thrive."[13] Once on a time the officer in charge of Fort Simpson, in British Columbia, took a census of the Indians in the neighbourhood, and very soon afterwards great numbers of them were swept away by measles. The Indians attributed the calamity to their having been numbered.[14] The Omaha Indians "preserve no account of their ages; they think that some evil will attend the numbering of their years."[15]

Similar superstitions are widespread in Europe. [The Roman poet Catullus tells Lesbia that they should "confound" the number of their kisses lest evil-minded persons cast the evil eye on them or bewitch them with spells;[15a] and

Muretus, the sixteenth-century scholar, notes that in his day Italian peasants avoided counting the fruit on a tree.[15b] The Lapps used to be, and perhaps are still unwilling, to count themselves and to declare the number, because they feared that such a reckoning would both forebode and cause a great mortality among their people;[16] [and Swedish fishermen still deem it unpropitious to count their catch[16a]]. In the Highlands of Scotland, "it is reckoned unlucky to number the people or cattle belonging to any family, but more particularly upon Friday. The cowherd knows every creature committed to his charge by the colour, size, and other particular marks, but is perhaps all along ignorant of the sum total of his flock. And fishermen do not care to confess the number of salmon or other fish which they have taken at a draught or in a day, imagining that this discovery would spoil their luck."[17] Though this account is derived from a writer of the eighteenth century, similar superstitions are known to have prevailed in Scotland far into the nineteenth century, and it is probable that they are not extinct at the present time. In Shetland, we are told, "counting the number of sheep, of cattle, of horses, of fish, or of any of a man's chattels, whether animate or inanimate, has always been considered as productive of bad luck. There is also said to have been an idea prevalent at one time, that an outbreak of small-pox always followed the census being taken."[18] Among the fisher folk on the north-east coast of Scotland on no account might the boats be counted when they were at sea, nor might any gathering of men, women, or children be numbered. Nothing aroused the indignation of a company of fisherwomen trudging along the road to sell their fish more than to point at them with the finger, and begin to number them aloud:

> Ane, twa, three,
> Faht a fishers I see
> Gyain our the brigg o' Dee,
> Deel pick their muckle greethy ee.[19]

So the fish-wives of Auchmithie, a village on the coast of Forfarshire, used to be irritated by mischievous children, who counted them with extended forefingers, repeating the verse:

> Ane, twa, three!
> Ane, twa, three!
> Sic a lot o' fisher-wifies
> I do see!

And the unluckiness extended to counting the fish caught or the boats in the herring-fleet.[20]

In Lincolnshire, England, "no farmer should count his lambs too closely during the lambing season. [As a French proverb puts it, *Brebis comptées, le loup les mange* (Number your sheep, and the wolf will eat them).[20a] I have seen a shepherd in obvious embarrassment because his employer knew so little of his own business that, though usually the most easy of masters, he would insist on learning every morning the exact number of lambs his flock had produced. For a cognate reason, it may be, some people when asked how old they are reply, 'As old as my tongue, and a little bit older than my teeth.' Gaidoz remarks in *Melusine* (ix. 35) that old people ought not to tell their age, and when importuned to reveal it they should answer that they are as old as their little finger. Inhabitants of Godarville, Hainault, reply, 'I am the age of a calf, every year twelve months' ";[21] [and Sardinian peasants have been known to resort to similar evasions[21a]]. In England, the superstitious objection to counting lambs is not confined to Lincolnshire. A friend, whose home is in a village of South Warwickshire, wrote to me some years ago, "Superstitions die hard. Yesterday I asked a woman how many lambs her husband had. She said she didn't know, then, perceiving the surprise in my face, added, 'You know, sir, it's unlucky to count them.' Then she went on, 'However we haven't lost any yet.' And her husband is postmaster and keeps the village shop, and, in his own esteem, stands high above a peasant."[22]

In Denmark they say that you should never count the eggs under a brooding hen, else the mother will tread on the eggs and kill the chickens. And when the chickens are hatched, you ought not to count them, or they will easily fall a prey to the glede or the hawk. So, too, blossoms and fruit should not be counted, or the blossoms will wither and the fruit will fall untimely from the bough.[23] In North Jutland people have a notion that if you count any mice which the cat has caught, or which you chance to discover, the mice will increase in number; and if you count lice, fleas, or any other vermin, they also will multiply in like manner.[24] It is said to be a Greek and Armenian superstition that if you count your warts they will increase in number.[25] On the other hand, it is a popular German belief that if you count your money often it will steadily decrease.[26] In the Upper Palatinate, a district of Bavaria, people think that loaves in the oven should not be counted, or they will not turn out well.[27] In Upper Franconia, another district of Bavaria, they say that, when dumplings are being cooked you should not count them, because if you do, the Little Wood Women, who like dumplings, could not fetch any away, and deprived of that form of nutriment they would perish, with the necessary consequence that the forest would dwindle and die. Therefore to prevent the country from being stripped bare of its woods, you are urged not to count dumplings in the pan.[28] [Elsewhere in Germany, it is considered unlucky to count fruit on a tree or fish which have been caught.[28a]]

On the whole we may assume, with a fair degree of probability, that the objection which the Israelites in King David's time felt to the taking of a census rested on no firmer foundation than sheer superstition, which may have been confirmed by an outbreak of plague immediately after the numbering of the people.[28b] [A striking parallel comes from Tiraspol, in Russia, where, in 1897, some twenty-eight persons buried themselves alive in order to escape a census, which they regarded as sinful.[28c] Similarly, it was reported from England, in the nineteenth century, that "some regard with feelings of strong antipathy our decennial census, and it is only the compulsion of the law which induces them to comply with this national means of ascertaining the state of the population."[28d] To this day the same repugnance to count or be counted appears to linger among the Arabs of Syria, for we are told that an Arab is averse to counting the tents, or horsemen, or cattle of his tribe, lest some misfortune befall them.[29]

At a later time, Hebrew Law so far relaxed the ban upon a census as to permit the nation to be numbered, on condition that every man paid half a shekel to the Lord as a ransom for his life, lest a plague should break out among the people.[30]

[On the popular level, however, the superstition continued among the Jews into relatively modern times, for the mystical Kabbalists laid it down that "Satan has power over things that have been counted."[30]] ▼

Kings

147 Abishag

I Kings 1:1-4

In David's old age, a beautiful maiden, Abishag of Shunem, is brought to him to lie in his bosom and keep him warm, though she does not serve as a concubine.

What is here involved is the principle known technically as *osphresiology*. This asserts that new vigor can be imparted to the aged and infirm by physical contact with, or proximity to, young persons.[1]

The physician Marcellus Empiricus of Bordeaux (4th cent.) recommends a poultice for chronic disorders of the stomach which had the same effect as though the patient were *adverso pectore cujuslibet tepefactus*.[2]

In eighteenth-century England "there was a belief that the breath of young women might be helpful in prolonging life. . . . One physician actually took lodgings in a girls' boarding-school for this purpose. 'I am myself,' wrote Philip Thicknesse in 1779, 'turned of sixty, and in general, though I have lived in various climates, and suffered severely both in body and mind, yet having always partaken of the breath of *young women, wherever they lay in my way*, I feel none of the infirmities which so often strike the eyes and ears in this great city of sickness [Bath] by men many years younger than myself."[3]

148 The ritual of enthronement

1:9, 33, 38

Adonijah, a pretender to the throne of David, stages a ceremony of installation and anointment at a certain stone beside the Fuller's Spring (En Rogel), near Jerusalem.[1] David retaliates by having his son Solomon formally anointed beside another spring, named Gihon.

(a) Water, as we have seen (above, §2), was the source of all primal virtues and wisdom. Accordingly, ancient kings often claimed descent from water-goddesses or asserted that they had been drawn out of the waters shortly after birth. In Southeast Asia, for example, the king is said to be the child of a mortal man and a *nagi,* or water-nymph.[2] In Indonesia, the kings of San-fo-ts'i were called for this reason "sperm of a naga" (*long tsin*);[3] while the Emperors of China, Palaung and Pagan were believed to have sprung from the union of Prince Thuriya, son of the sun, and the nagi of Thusandi, and the king of Palembang claimed that his parents were King Souran and the daughter of a submarine monarch.[4]

Alternatively, the special qualities of kingship were imparted by baptism at the time of installation. Thus, in the Hindu ceremony of *abhiṣeka*, or royal consecration, water taken from the sacred River Sarasvatī is sprinkled over the king's head and addressed: "O water, that art naturally a giver of kingship, give kingship to X."[5] The ceremony is called Sprinkling-with-Kingly-Dignity.[6] Similarly, in Egypt, the Pharaoh was baptized at his enthronement by the gods of the four quarters of the earth.[7]

Among the Sumerians of Mesopotamia, Ea, god of the primeval deep, was said to impart "intelligence" (IGI.GAL) to new kings.[8] This claim became, in fact, something of a standard cliché; it occurs in the inscriptions of Eanadu,[9] Entemena,[10] and Ur-Bau[11] of Lagash, as well as in those of Lugalzagissi of Uruk[12] and even in the Code of Hammurapi of Babylon.[13]

The power of special waters features also in European folktales.[14] In a Basque story, a hero who has subdued a dragon is unable to kill it until the princess whom he has rescued throws a bottle of water in his face; this gives him extra strength.[15] Similarly, in a Russian tale, a hero named Gol insists that a princess fortify him with "the water of heroes."[16]

(b) If water imparts strength and wisdom, stone imparts durability—especially since this is often regarded as emanating from a god who dwells within it.

Anglo-Saxon kings were customarily anointed standing on a stone at Kingston-on-Thames,[17] and to this day the throne of the king of England is mounted on the celebrated Stone of Scone when he is crowned in Westminster Abbey. Swedish monarchs likewise stood on a stone when they were installed at Uppsala, and the same practice is recorded also as current at the installation of kings at Antanarivo and Ambohimanga in Madagascar.[18] In Scotland, the chief of the Celtic O'Donnels was inaugurated on a special stone (called Flagstone), set on a mound; while the chief of the clan M'Donald was crowned "king of the isles" while standing on a sacred stone. A cylindrical obelisk said to have been used in connection with the enthronement of chieftains still stands in the Rath-na-Riegh. Similarly, German emperors and Lombard kings took their coronation oaths beside a stone pillar which now stands before the Church of St. Ambrosio at Milan.[19]

(Coronation beside a pillar, rather than directly on a stone, seems to be implied in two passages of the Old Testament itself. In Judges 9:6, Abimelech is installed as king "beside the oak of the pillar at Shechem";[20] while in II Kings 11:14, the priest Jehoiada crowns Joash while the latter "stands beside the pillar, according to custom."[21])

149   Asylum at the altar   1:50; 2:28

> *When Adonijah hears what has happened, he flees in terror of Solomon and rushes to lay hold on the "horns" (knobs) of the altar. Later, Joab, who has supported him, does likewise.*

Altars and sanctuaries were regarded throughout the Ancient Near East as places of asylum.[1] This is simply an extension of the common bedouin convention whereby a man who repairs to another's tent, touches the ropes, or eats three handfuls of food (be it only salt) can claim protection for a minimum of three days.[2] When men resort for refuge to an altar or sanctuary they are therefore styled "guests" of the god or goddess.

A Canaanite text of the fourteenth century B.C. from Ras Shamra-Ugarit mentions "guests of the sacred enclosure" (*gr ḥmt*),[3] and a mythological poem from the same site invokes upon an assassin who is still at large the curse that he may find himself perpetually seeking asylum as "a guest of the sanctuary" (*gr bt il*).[4] Right of asylum continued in Phoenician temples until relatively late times; we have evidence of it at the sanctuary of Melqarth at Tyre[5] and at the temple in Daphne, near Antioch,[6] even in the Hellenistic age, and "guests" (*grm*) are listed, in the fourth century B.C., among the personnel of a temple at Kition, in Cyprus.[7] Moreover, Tacitus tells us that the Emperor Tiberius instituted an inquiry into abuses of the system at Paphos and Amathus, on the same island.[8] In Arabic usage, a suppliant beside the Ka'aba at Mecca is known as a "guest of Allah" (*jār Allah*),[9] and Yakūt tells us that right of asylum prevailed in pre-Islamic times at the holy places of Jalṣ and Fals.[10]

A man pursued by a vendetta, or in danger of such pursuit, could seek refuge at an altar of sanctuary, where, under oath, he could protest his innocence in the form of a "negative confession" ("I have not lied, stolen, murdered," etc.). The god himself would then punish him if the oath were false.[11] It is, indeed, in this sense that we are to understand the Psalmist's statement that he who "walks blamelessly, does what is right, speaks truth in his heart, and . . . harms not his fellow" is fit to be a guest (RSV: sojourn) in the Lord's tent.[12]

The right of asylum at sanctuaries was, in fact, so standard an institution in Israel that the law of Exodus 21:14 finds it necessary expressly to withdraw it in cases of deliberate homicide.

Nor was this right by any means confined to the Semites. Classical writers tell us that after Ajax had violated Cassandra, the goddess Athene prevented the Greeks from sailing home from Troy. Thereupon they sought to kill the miscreant, but he fled to an altar and thus found safety.[13] Similarly, the Heraclids, fleeing from Eurystheus, found asylum beside the altar of Mercy at Athens.[14]

In Christian tradition, churches afford asylum. A decision of the American courts, however, has recently (1968) denied this right to draftees seeking thus to avoid military service.

▲ **150   The judgment of Solomon**   **3:16–28**

Two harlots come before Solomon to seek his judgment. Each, at about the same time, has borne a son in the same house. The one declares: We were alone in the place. During the night this woman ac-

cidentally smothered her child. While I was asleep, she took mine, laid it in her bosom, and put her dead child in mine. When daylight came, I saw what she had done. The other replies that the live child is indeed hers, and the dead child that of ther accuser. Solomon orders the child to be cut in half. The one woman immediately cries out, "No; no! Give her the child whole!" The other, however, says, "No, divide it." In this way the true mother is revealed.

Like much else that is told of King Solomon, this anecdote has the air rather of a popular tale than of an historical narrative. True or false, it has passed into folk-lore, having been incorporated into that vast legendary literature of the Jains, which as yet has been only partially explored by European scholars. Four of these Indian versions of the story have been discovered in recent times;[1] they all bear a family resemblance to each other and to their Hebrew; original. It will be enough to cite one of them, which runs as follows:

A certain merchant had two wives; one of them had a son and the other had not. But the childless wife also took good care of the other's child, and the child was not able to distinguish, "This is my mother, that is not." Once on a time the merchant, with his wives and his son, went to another country, and just after his arrival there he died. Then the two wives fell to quarrelling. One of them said, "Mine is this child," and the other said just the same. One said, "It is I who am the mistress of the house"; and the other said, "It is I." At last they carried the dispute before a royal court of justice. The presiding minister of justice gave an order to his men, "First divide the whole property, then saw the child in two with a saw, and give one part to the one woman and the other part to the other." But when the mother heard the minister's sentence, it was as if a thunderbolt, enveloped in a thousand flames, had fallen on her head, and with her heart all trembling as if it had been pierced by a crooked dart, she contrived with difficulty to speak. "Ah, sire! Great minister!" she said, "it is not mine, this child! The money is of no use to me! Let the child be the son of that woman, and let her be the mistress of the house. As for me, it is no matter if I drag out an indigent life in strange houses; though it be from a distance, yet shall I see that child living, and so shall I attain the object of my life. Whereas, without my son, even now the whole living world is dead to me." But the other woman uttered never a word. Then the minister, beholding the distress of the former woman, said, "To her belongs the child, but not to that one." And he made the mother the mistress of the house, but the other woman he rebuked.[2]

[This celebrated story has far more parallels in world folklore than Frazer has cited.[2a]

An Indian (Prakrit) tale, for instance, tells of two women who set out for a feast, each with an infant child. While they are sleeping in a forest, a wolf kills one of the children. Its mother substitutes it for that of her companion before the latter wakes. At the court of Gopicandra a wise parrot advises that the child be cut in half. The true mother reveals herself by demurring.[2b]

A Buddhist Jataka tale, preserved in a Singalese version of the fifth or sixth century C.E., relates that a female cannibal demon (*yakinni*) once stole the child of a woman who was bathing. The demon and the mother appealed to Buddha for judgment. He drew a line on the ground and ordered them to draw the child across it in a tug of war. The true mother refused.[2c]

Again, in a Tibetan tale, a man has both a wife and a concubine. The former is barren, but the latter bears a son. When the man dies, the wife claims the son as hers in order to inherit the estate. The sage Vičakha orders a tug of war. The true mother refuses.[2d]

A Chinese story of the same type by Ying Shao (178–97 C.E.) is quoted in Mo Tsing's *Yilin,* dating from the time of the Tang Dynasty (7th–9th centuries C.E.). This is based in turn on an earlier work by Chung-Yung of the Liang Dynasty (546–56 C.E.). A charming translation of it will be found in Lin Yutang's *The Wisdom of China.*[2e] From China also comes the celebrated Story of the Chalk Circle (*Huei-lan-ki*), based on a corpus of plays (*Yuen-jin-pe-chang*) compiled under the Yuen rulers (1259–1368). In this version, Pao-Čing, chief of the city, orders the child to be pulled out of a circle drawn in chalk on the ground. The true mother objects.[2f]

Nor is it only in the classic literature of the country that the story is known. A modern Chinese folktale tells of two women who contend for possession of a child. The wife of the mandarin suggests that a live fish be put into its clothing and that it then be thrown into the water. When the true mother sees the fish struggling to get free and thereby harming the infant, she plunges in to rescue him, thus proving the truth of her claim.[2g] In another version, the child is ordered, as in the Biblical tale, to be cut in two.[2h]

There is also an Iranian version of the tale;[2i] while in a Bosnian variant, which otherwise follows the Scriptural narrative, the wise decision is attributed to the celebrated sage and wit, Nasreddin Hodja.[2j]

Different in detail, but identical in basic theme, is a tale from Cairo recorded by a Paduan traveler in the eighteenth century. Two men claim the paternity of a child. The judge orders it starved for three days and then fed a bowl of milk. The child gulps and slops. The "false" father chides it for its bad manners; the true father pitifully excuses it.[2k]

The story is also portrayed—of all places—on a wall painting at Pompeii. Since the characters are there depicted as pygmies, and since there are in the same room frescoes of hippopotami and crocodiles, it has been suggested that the tale may have been of Egyptian origin;[2l] but, as the famous folklorist Gaidoz pointed out, this need indicate only that the artist was an Egyptian or worked under Egyptian influence, not that the story itself came from Egypt.[2m]

Other representations of the tale are to be found in the grave chamber of the Villa Pamphili[2n] and in a house near the Farnesina in Rome.[2o]

Theodor Benfey claimed that the story was of Tibetan provenience,[2p] but this view is not accepted by more recent scholars. Hermann Gunkel suggested, on the other hand, that it came ultimately from India and dealt, in its original form, with the claims of two women to the same man's estate, for in India a childless widow has no rights to inheritance.[2q] ▼

151   The dedication of the Temple   8

Solomon builds a temple to the LORD in Jerusalem, and dedicates it in the seventh month of the year, at the onset of the rainy season. The Scriptural writer gives the text of a hymn which the king is said to have recited.

The date of the dedication of the Temple is not fortuitous; it follows an ancient precedent of installing the god of rainfall and fertility in a new fane after he has vanquished the marplot of Chaos and the contumacious dragon who tries either to impound the waters or else to send them in floods at the onset of the wet season. This triumph and enthronement, which inaugurated the world order in the past, was thought to be repeated each year and therefore formed the central theme of myths recited at the New Year Festival. Examples are the Canaanite *Poem of Baal,* the Mesopotamian Epic of Creation (*Enuma Elish*) and the Hittite myth of the Slaying of the Dragon (Illuyankas).[1]

The date chosen is also important in the solar year, for it is the time of the autumnal equinox.[2] In the Canaanite myth, a major role is assigned for this reason to the sun-goddess ($\check{S}$-p-$\check{s}$).[3]

Against this background, the song intoned by Solomon at the dedication ceremony takes on a new significance. In the traditional Hebrew text it runs as follows:

> *YAHWEH said that he would dwell in thick cloud.*
> *A lofty house have I indeed built for thee,*
> *a place for thee to dwell in for ever.*

This, however, obscures the point, for the crucial opening line has dropped out! It can be restored, however, from the ancient Greek (Septuagint) Version, and it contains, significantly, an allusion to the sun at its zenith.[4] Now, a Hebrew word for zenith was *zebul,*[5] and the "lofty house" which Solomon declares that he has indeed built for Yahweh is, in the original, "a *zebul*-house." The whole point now becomes clear as the sunlight itself: the little poem is a sublime satire on the pagan rites, the implication being that the new temple of Yahweh is to enshrine him perpetually in a blaze of glory, whereas the sun can always be obscured by cloudmists! The point can be baldly reproduced as follows:

> *Yahweh set the sun on high*
> *In the topmost of the sky,*
> *But then in turn he bade it dwell*
> *Where the cloudmists round it swell.*
> *Yet, for Thee Thyself right here*
> *I a lofty house uprear,*
> *Where, as at Thy zenith-tide,*
> *Thou for evermore may'st bide!*[6]

152 Settlement of disputes beside the altar   8:31-32

See §§149, 271.

▲ 153 Solomon and the Queen of Sheba   10

According to Israelite tradition King Solomon was a sage whose reputation for wisdom spread to the ends of the earth, and from all quarters kings sent envoys to Jerusalem to profit by the sagacity and learning of the Hebrew monarch.[1] Amongst the rest the Queen of Sheba, not content to receive at second hand the treasures of knowledge which he dispensed to his hearers, came in person from her home in southern Arabia to question Solomon with her own lips and to listen to his wise answers. We are told that she put riddles to him, and that he read them all; not one of them did he fail to answer.[2]

In Central Celebes similar stories are told of contests of wit between the rival Rajahs of Loowoo and Mori. It is said, for example, that the Rajah of Mori, hearing reports of the other's greatness, resolved to test his power and glory. For this purpose he sent him an iron staff bent into a loop, with a request that he would straighten it out. The Rajah of Loowoo put the staff in a furnace, and when it was red-hot, he straightened it out, as he had been requested to do. Having performed the task set him, he now in his turn tested his rival by sending the Rajah of Mori a tube of sago, baked in a bamboo and bent into a loop while it was still warm. This tube he begged the Rajah of Mori to straighten out The Rajah of Mori accordingly set to work on the tube of sago, but do what he would, he could not straighten it out. If he tried to do it when the sago was dry, the tube threatened to break in his hands; if he tried to do it when the sago was damp, by being dipped in water, the tube dissolved; and if he warmed it up to dry it again, the sago melted into a solid mass. So in this trial of skill the Rajah of Loowoo got the better of the Rajah of Mori.

However, in another story the Rajah of Mori contrives to defeat his rival. The Rajah of Loowoo had sent him a piece of cotton with a request that he would draw out all the threads. This the Rajah of Mori contrived to do, and having executed the task, he sent the Rajah of Loowoo in return a piece of bark-cloth with a request that the Rajah would be so good as to draw out all the threads from *that*. In vain the Rajah of Loowoo struggled to disentangle all the fibres of the bark; at last he had to give it up and acknowledge that the Rajah of Mori was at least his peer.

Yet another story, however, reverses the parts played by the two potentates and assigns the superiority to the Rajah of Loowoo. It is said that the Rajah of Loowoo came to visit the Rajah of Mori, and that the two sat up late at night talking by the light of a resin-torch, after all the other folk in the palace had gone to sleep. As the torch guttered and threatened to go out, the Rajah of Mori took a stick and directed the flow of resin so that the flame burst out again as bright as ever. Now this is a task which is usually performed by a slave, and the good-natured Rajah only did it with his own hands because all his slaves were abed. However, his astute rival at once took advantage of his politeness to place him in a position of inferiority. "Because you have snuffed the torch," said he to the Rajah of Mori, "you are less than I, and you must pay me homage." The crestfallen but candid Rajah of Mori acknowledged the justness of the observation, and confessed the superiority of the Rajah of Loowoo.[1]

If we had the Queen of Sheba's version of her interview with King Solomon, we might perhaps discover that in the war of wit she was at least able to hold her own against the Hebrew monarch.

In the dreary wilderness of the Koran, which by comparison with the glorious literature of the Old Testament remains an eternal monument of the inferiority of the Arab to the Hebrew genius, we read how Solomon tested the discernment of the Queen of Sheba by overlaying his court of audience with glass, and how the Queen of Sheba, falling into the trap, mistook the glass for water and drew up her skirts to wade through it.[2] Later Arab tradition has not unnaturally dwelt by predilection on the visit of a native Arab princess to the wise king at Jerusalem, and has adorned or disfigured the simple theme by many fanciful details. Among the rest it enlarges on the trivial incident of the glassy pavement. Envious or malignant demons had whispered, so it is alleged, in Solomon's ear that the Queen had hairy legs or the feet of an ass, and in order to prove or disprove the truth of the accusation the sage king resorted to the expedient of the crystal floor. When the Queen raised her skirts to wade through the imaginary water, Solomon saw that the story of her deformity was a vile calumny, and, his too susceptible heart receiving a strong impression of her charms, he added her to the numerous ladies of his harem.[3] At Jerusalem the legend is told to this day, and the very spot where the incident happened is pointed out. It is a few yards within the gate called Bâb el Asbât, or the Gate of the Tribes, the only gateway now left open in the eastern wall of the city. Here down to the summer of 1906 there stood an old bath house, which dated from the days of the Saracens, but which, according to tradition, had been built by King Solomon for the use of the Queen of Sheba.⁴

The deception of the crystal pavement occurs also as an incident in the great Indian epic, the *Mahabharata*. We there read how on one occasion the dull-witted king Duryodhana mistook a sheet of crystal for a sheet of water, and tucked up his skirts to wade through it; how another time he on the contrary mistook a lake of crystal water for dry land, and fell splash into it with all his clothes on, to the amusement of the spectators and even of his own servants; how he tried to pass through a crystal door, which he supposed to be open, but knocked his brow against its hard surface till his head ached and his brains reeled; and how after this painful experience, he came to an open door, but turned away from it, because he feared to encounter the obstruction of crystal again.⁵

Despite the resemblance between the two stories in the Koran and the *Mahabharata*, neither the prophet nor the poet can well have copied directly the one from the other, the prophet because he did not read Sanskrit, and the poet because he died before the prophet was born. If they did not both draw independently from the well-spring of fancy an incident, for the creation of which an imagination less than Miltonic might conceivably have sufficed, they may have borrowed it from a popular tale which circulated alike in the bazaars of India and the tents of Arabia. ▼

154 Hand withers for impiety 13:4

An ecstatic ("man of God") appears at Bethel and denounces the pagan practices of Jeroboam. The king stretches out his hand to lay hold of him, but it withers.

This is a common motif in later Christian legend. In the apocryphal Infancy gospel, Salome doubts the virgin birth of Jesus, whereupon her hand withers. She is cured only when an angel descends from heaven and when she touches the child's swaddling bands.¹ Similarly, when Aurelius (270 C.E.) ordered St. Vitus, then only twelve years old, to be scourged for worshiping Christ, both the lictor's and his own hand withered, though the latter was subsequently healed by the saint.² So too it is related of the Empress Eudoxia (c. 400 C.E.) that she once tried to force her way into the cathedral at Constantinople after Chrysostom had expressly barred her from it and ordered it shut and bolted in her face. The soldier who, at her command, raised his ax to burst open the doors found his arm paralyzed. Only when the empress withdrew did Chrysostom heal him.³

Elijah

155 The "man of God"

Elijah is described as a *man of God*.[1] So are Moses,[2] Samuel,[3] and Elisha,[4] as well as the anonymous messengers of Yahweh who come to Eli at Shiloh,[5] to Jeroboam at Bethel,[6] and to the parents of Samson.[7] The term does not refer, as in modern speech, to piety or devotion, but characterizes men subject to suprasensuous experiences;[8] it is virtually the equivalent of *shaman,* and it is significant that in the cases of Elijah and Elisha it is applied to them in connection with quasi-magical performances on their part.

In precisely the same way, the Hittites used the expression "man of the gods" to denote one who was crazed or who possessed the mantic powers of a soothsayer,[9] and a verb formed from the word "god" signified this type of "possession."[10] The Arabs likewise called a mantic "he of Allah";[11] while the Greeks spoke of him as "one with a god inside him"[12] or as "one seized by a god."[13] So too among the Japanese, the victim of a hypnotic trance is known as "one to whom a god has attached himself";[14] and in the language of the Quiché of Peru, "the word *huaca* is the most general term for the divine, but *huaca runa,* "divine man," means "one who is crazy."[15]

(It should be observed that the Hebrew expression does not really mean "man of God"—with a capital G—but simply one possessed by the supernormal. In the same way, the Suffering Servant of Isaiah who is said, in the usual rendering, to be "smitten of God" [53:4] is simply one who has been plagued by demonic influences—what the Arabs would call "jinn-struck" [*majnun*].)

▲ 156 Elijah and the Ravens   17:2–6

According to the Hebrew historian, the first mission entrusted by God to the prophet Elijah was to go to Ahab, king of Israel, and announce to him that neither dew nor rain should fall on the land for several years. But having discharged his divine commission, the ambassador of the deity was not left to perish in the long drought. For the word of the Lord came to him, saying, "Get thee hence, and turn thee eastward, and hide thyself by the brook Cherith, that is before Jordan. And it shall be, that thou shalt drink of the brook; and I have commanded the ravens to feed thee there." So Elijah went and dwelt by the brook Cherith, that is before Jordan. And the ravens brought him bread and flesh in the morning, and bread and flesh in the evening; and he drank of the brook. But it came to pass after a while that the brook dried up, because there was no rain in the land.

The brook Cherith has been identified with the Wady Kelt, which descends eastward from the highlands of Judea and opens out on the plain of the Jordan not far from Jericho. The glen is one of the wildest and most romantic in Palestine. It is a tremendous gorge cleft through the mountains, shut in by sheer precipices, and so narrow that the bottom scarcely measures twenty yards across. There the stream forces its way through brakes of cane, rushes, and oleanders, the strip of verdure contrasting with the nakedness of the rocky walls on all sides. In its depth and narrowness the ravine reminds the traveller of the famous defile which leads through the red cliffs to Petra. A magnificent view into the glen is obtained from some points on the road which leads down from Jerusalem into the valley of the Jordan. After traversing for hours the almost total desolation which marks that long descent through the bare, torrent-furrowed limestone hills, the wayfarer is refreshed by the sight of the green thread far below, and by the murmurous sound of water which comes up, even on autumn days after the parching drought of summer, from the depths of the profound ravine. Peering over the giddy brink he may see ravens, eagles, and huge griffon-vultures wheeling beneath him.[1]

To this wild solitude, where water seldom fails throughout the year, the prophet Elijah may well have retired to live out the years of drought which he foresaw and foretold, and there he may have tarried with no neighbours but the wild beasts and the wild birds.

[The story of the helpful (or grateful) birds who bring food to a man (especially a hero) in distress is a favorite of popular literature in many lands.[1a] Achaemenes, the ancestor of the Persian king, is said to have been nurtured by an eagle;[1b] and of Semiramis, the wife of Ninus, mythical founder of Nineveh, it is related that she was fed in childhood by doves until found by the shepherd Simmas.[1c] Ptolemy I and his mother Arsinoe are two others who are reputed to have been succored by an eagle after they had been exposed to die;[1d] and according to Ovid, Romulus and Remus were fed by a woodpecker when the wolf failed them.[1e] In Indic myth, the beauteous Sakuntala, abandoned in a forest after birth, is tended by birds.[1f]

The theme appears frequently in legends of Christian saints.[1g] St. Catherine, imprisoned by Maxentius, is fed for twelve days by a dove.[1h] St. Vitus, fleeing the persecution of the Christians in Sicily (303), is fed on the way to Naples by an eagle.[1i] St. Peter, the hermit of the Lower Thebaid (341), is fed daily for sixty years by a crow.[1j] St. Auxentius is fed daily at Sinope by a pigeon.[1k] St. Cuthbert (7th cent.) is fed by rooks on the isle of Farne.[1l]]

There was, however, a special propriety in the employment of ravens to minister to the prophet in the wilderness; for the raven has often been regarded as a bird of omen and even as itself endowed with prophetic power. [Indeed, the expression, "to have the foresight of a raven," was proverbial in the British Isles.[1m] Examples of this belief are legion. A Babylonian magician, for example, advises King Esarhaddon (680–69 B.C.) that it presages ill if a raven flies into a house carrying something in its bill;[1n] while an ancient Mesopotamian manual of divination says that if a raven croaks when an army is setting out, this betokens coming defeat.[1o]] The Greeks, for their part, deemed the bird sacred to Apollo, the god of prophecy, and Greek augurs drew omens from its croaking;[2] [while one of Aesop's fables relates that the goddess Athene came to hate it because she grew jealous of its prophetic powers.[2a]] Persons who sought the gift of divination, says Porphyry, used to eat the hearts of ravens, believing that they thus acquired the bird's prophetic soul.[3] The Romans credited the raven with the ability to foretell rain and storm. [Vergil, for instance, records the belief that a raven, stalking up and down on the sands and croaking, was calling for rain.[3a] Similarly, Horace called it a "water-augur,"[3b] and Aelian, writing in the second century C.E., says that it foretells tempests.[3c]]

In European folklore the raven is preeminently an omen of death and misfortune. [There are several allusions to this in English literature.[3d] Lady Macbeth exclaims in a famous passage,

> The raven himself is hoarse
> That croaks the fatal entrance of Duncan
> Under my battlements;[3e]

and in Butler's *Hudibras* the question is put:

> Is it not om'nous in all countries
> When crows and ravens croak on trees?[3f]

The bird was particularly ill-omened if it croaked directly over a housetop. Says John Gay in his pastoral, *The Dirge:*

> And with hoarse croakings warn'd us of our fate;[3g]
> The boding raven on her cottage sat,

and in Shakespeare's *Othello* occur the lines:

> it comes in my memory
> As doth the raven, o'er the infected house,
> Boding to all.[3h]

Nor is this notion confined to Europe. It is attested equally in Australia[31] and in America,[3j] while] the Lillooet Indians of British Columbia imagine that he who has a raven for his guardian spirit possesses the gift of prophecy.[4]

The sagacity and solemn deportment of this sable bird may have had much to do with throwing a glamour of mystery and sanctity about it. According to an eminent authority the raven is "probably the most highly developed of all birds. Quick-sighted, sagacious, and bold, it must have followed the pre-historic fisher and hunter, and generally without molestation from them, to prey on the refuse of their spoils, just as it now waits, with the same intent, on the movements of their successors; while it must have likewise attended the earliest herdsmen, who could not have regarded it with equal indifference, since its now notorious character for attacking and putting to death a weakly animal was doubtless in those days manifested. Yet the raven is no mere dependent upon man, being always able to get a living for itself; and, moreover, a sentiment of veneration or superstition has from very remote ages and among many races of men attached to it—a sentiment so strong as often to overcome the feeling of distrust not to say of hatred which its deeds inspired, and, though rapidly decreasing, even to survive in some places until the present time."[5]

Pliny tells a story which strikingly illustrates the veneration in which the raven was popularly held at Rome, when Rome was at the height of her glory. Under the reign of Tiberius it happened that a pair of ravens had built their nest on the roof of the temple of Castor and Pollux. One of the young birds in time flew down, stalked into a shoemaker's shop, and took up its quarters there, the shoemaker not venturing to molest a creature which he looked upon with religious awe, partly perhaps for its own sake and partly for the sake of the holy place where it had been hatched. Every morning the sagacious bird flew out of the shop, perched on the rostra in the forum, and there in a distinct voice saluted the emperor and his two sons, Drusus and Germanicus, by name, after which he greeted in an affable manner the people passing to their business. Having discharged these offices of civility he returned to the shop. This he continued to do regularly for many years, till at last another shoemaker in the neighbourhood killed the bird, either out of spite, as was suspected, at the custom which the raven brought to his rival, or, as the shoemaker himself alleged, in a fit of passion because the bird had befouled the shoes in his shop. Whatever his motive, it was a bad day's work for him; for the people, thunder-struck at the death of their old favourite, rose in their wrath, drove the corbi-cidal shoemaker from his shop, and never rested till they had the miscreant's blood. As for the dead raven, it received a public funeral, which was attended by thousands. The bier was supported on the shoulders of two Ethiopians as black as the corpse they carried; a flute-player marched in front discoursing solemn music, while wreaths of flowers of all sorts, carried in the procession, testified to the general respect and sorrow for the deceased. In this impressive manner the funeral cortege made its way to the pyre, which had been erected two miles out on the Appian Way. The historian concludes by remarking that the bird received a grander funeral than many a prince before him, and that the death of the fowl was more signally avenged than the murder of Scipio Africanus.[6]

Among the qualities which have procured for the raven a certain degree of popular veneration may be its power of imitating the human voice. That power is attested not only by Pliny's anecdote but by modern writers. Thus Oliver Goldsmith affirms that "a raven may be reclaimed to almost every purpose to which birds can be converted. He may be trained up for fowling like an hawk; he may be taught to fetch and carry like a spaniel; he may be taught to speak like a parrot; but the most extraordinary of all is, that he can be taught to sing like a man. I have heard a raven sing the Black Joke with great distinctness, truth, and humour."[7] And Yarrell, in his *History of British Birds,* writes, "Among British birds, the power of imitating the sounds of the human voice is possessed in the greatest perfection by the raven, the magpie, the jay, and the starling. In proof of this power in the raven, many anecdotes might be repeated; the two following, derived from unquestionable authorities, are perhaps less known than many others: 'Ravens have been taught to articulate short sentences as distinctly as any parrot. One, belonging to Mr. Henslow, of St. Alban's, speaks so distinctly that, when we first heard it, we were actually deceived in thinking it was a human voice: and there is another at Chatham which has made equal proficiency; for, living within the vicinity of a guardhouse, it has more than once turned out the guard, who thought they were called by the sentinel on duty.' "[8]

It is possible, too, that the raven's habit of preying on the human dead may have helped to invest it with an atmosphere of mystery and awe; for as savages commonly suppose that they themselves can acquire the desirable properties of the dead by eating some part of their corpses, so they may have imagined that birds of prey, which batten on the slain, absorb thereby the wisdom and other qualities which the dead men possessed in their lifetime. This suggestion is supported by the analogy of the superstitious veneration in which the hyena is held by many tribes of East Africa appears to arise in large measure from the custom, which these tribes observe, of exposing their dead to be devoured by hyenas. For example, the Nandi, who follow that practice, hold hyenas in great respect, and believe that the animals talk like human beings and converse with the spirits of the dead. When several children in one family have died, the parents will place a newly-born babe for a few minutes in a path along which hyenas are known to walk, hoping that the brutes will intercede for the child with the spirits of the dead and induce them to spare its life. If such a child lives, it receives the name of Hyena.[9] Similarly the Bagesu and the Wanyamwesi, two other tribes of East Africa who throw out their dead to be devoured by hyenas, regard these animals as sacred and often take the cry of a hyena in the evening to be the voice of the last person who died in the neighbourhood. The Wanyamwesi say that they could not kill a hyena, because they do not know whether the creature might not be a relation of theirs, an aunt, a grandmother, or what not.[10] These beliefs appear to imply that the souls of the dead are reborn in the hyenas which devour their bodies. Thus the practice of exposing the dead, combined with the belief in the transmigration of human souls into animal bodies, may suffice to establish an imaginary kinship between men and beasts and birds of prey, such as hyenas, eagles, vultures, and ravens. How far its predatory habits have contributed to surround the raven in particular with that degree of respect which it enjoys among the vulgar, is a question which might be worth considering.

[Otto Gruppe has suggested,[10a] however, that the specification of ravens as the succorers of Elijah has in fact quite a different explanation. The raven, he says, is simply a substitute for the *eagle* who, at least in Greek legend, was believed to be the purveyor of celestial ambrosia. It was on such food that, in the original form of the story, the prophet was nourished. If it be asked why specifically the raven was substituted, the answer may lie in the fact that this bird appears to obtrude itself on the attention of the traveler all over the desolate region, from Jerusalem to the Dead Sea, in which the Biblical story plays.

Yet a third possibility is that the raven was specified because of a belief that it was especially adept at bringing succor in thirsty climes, seeing that, according to Classical writers, it reared its own young in the hottest and driest period of the year.[10b]

At all events, whichever explanation be adopted, the prevalence of the story in so many different parts of the world sufficiently disposes of the prosaic suggestion advanced by some Biblical scholars that the Hebrew word *'orebim,* "ravens," should really be read *'Arabim,* "Arabs"![10c]] ▼

157 "Measuring" the sick 17:7–24

Elijah revives the dead son of the woman of Zarephath by placing him on his own bed and then stretching himself out upon him thrice.

The same story is told, with significant variations, about Elisha (II Kings 4:32–37). There the prophet not only stretches himself upon the child, but also "places his mouth upon its mouth, his eyes upon its eyes, and his hands upon its hands" until "the flesh of the child becomes warm."

The Hebrew word rendered "stretched himself out" means literally "measured himself." Two ideas appear to be combined. The first is that a sick or dead person can be cured or revived by having the "essence" of a numinous or holy being superimposed upon him. This is, *au fond,* an extreme expression of the notion which underlies the touching of or by a holy man, or of the king's curing scrofula by touch.[1] Analogous too is the old German usage whereby pregnant women used to measure a wick around a saint's image and then tie it round their own bodies.[2]

The other idea is that the measuring of a sick person effects a cure. This also may be illustrated from old German lore. In the medieval Bîhtebuoch, the confessant is asked whether he has ever allowed himself to be measured by witches; while in the Liegnitz district old women called "measurers" (Messer-innen) used to measure people from head to foot to see whether they had consumption.[3] The basic notion underlies our own popular expression, "to take a man's measure, size him up."

Note also the threefold repetition of the action—a characteristic feature of magical procedures,[4] as also of folktales.[5]

(It should be observed that in the Elisha version of the story the point of the prophet's action has been forgotten, and the writer substitutes for the term "stretched himself out" the more neutral "bent over." The ancient Greek (Septuagint) translators were likewise unaware of the true import, for they substituted for the crucial word the simpler, "he *breathed into* (ἐνεφύσησεν) the child.")

158   The confrontation on Carmel   18

For several months the soil had suffered a severe drought. Elijah, the prophet of the LORD (Yahweh), seized the opportunity to discredit the growing faith in Baal, the Canaanite god of rain. He therefore staged a dramatic "competition" on Mt. Carmel between the latter's priests and himself. Each party was to erect altars, offer sacrifices, and call on its god with appropriate rites. The god who answered by consuming the sacrifice by fire from heaven would be the winner.

The pagan priests went through their accustomed ritual, gashing themselves with knives until their blood flowed and performing a limping dance about the altar, while they cried loudly, "Baal, answer us!" Nothing happened. It was then Elijah's turn. The prophet erected an altar made out of twelve stones. Then he dug a trench around it and filled it with water poured from twelve vessels. This done, he taunted his antagonists by bidding them call "in a loud voice" because their god might perchance be asleep or away or otherwise preoccupied. Finally, he offered the sacrifice. Fire descended miraculously from heaven, and the multitude shouted, "Yahweh—He is the god!"

Few stories in the Old Testament can be more amply illustrated by Comparative Folklore and Religion than that of the contest between Elijah and the prophets of Baal on Mt. Carmel. What is involved in this incident is, essentially, a competition in rain-making during a period of drought. Each side employs standard, established rain-making techniques, but by the time the traditional story came to be written down, the true significance of these techniques had long been forgotten. It is only by their recurrence elsewhere that we are now able to recover it and thus to reconstruct the incident as it may really have occurred.

(a) Baal

The first thing to observe, then, is that Baal, the rival of Yahweh, to whom the pagan prophets address themselves, is not just a vague and general god of the heathen. To the Canaanites he was specifically the *god of rainfall*. In the *Poem of Baal,* discovered at Ras Shamra-Ugarit (14th cent. B.C.), it is said expressly that when the furrows of the fields are parched, it is because Baal has been neglecting his duty or is absent from the earth;[1] while in the same poem, when the supreme god El grants permission to Baal to have a palace of his own, he expresses the hope that thenceforth Baal will send his rains at appropriate seasons, and not merely by caprice.[2] Again, in the Ugaritic *Poem of Aqhat,* when King Daniel learns of the murder of his son, he prays that Baal may withhold his rains from the polluted soil.[3] The Arabic writer Bukhari defines "land of Baal" as "soil watered by fountains or clouds";[4] while in the Jewish Mishnah "field of Baal" is cited as a popular designation of land watered by rain rather than by artificial irrigation.[5]

That there was indeed an ancient sanctuary on Carmel is suggested by the fact that even in later Roman times it was still regarded as a traditional holy place.[6] Tacitus tells us that Carmel was the name of a god as well as of a mountain,[7] and his statement is confirmed by the discovery there, in recent years, of a stone foot dedicated to Zeus Heliopoleites Carmelos—clearly a Hellenized form of the more ancient local deity.[8] Similarly, Suetonius says that in the days of Vespasian, the mountain was the seat of an oracle;[9] and the neo-Platonic philosopher Jamblichus, writing in the reign of Constantine, characterizes it as "sacred above all mountains and out-of-bounds to the vulgar."[10]

(b) The fire upon the altar

The proof of whether Yahweh or Baal is the true god lies in which of them answers his suppliants by sudden, unlit fire upon the altar.

Gods are, to a large extent, personifications of what *we* would call natural forces. Lambent fire of unknown origin was therefore regarded as a manifestation of their presence. It was in this form, for instance, that the deity revealed himself both to Gudea, governor (*ensi*) of the Sumerian city of Lagash,[11] and to Moses.[12] The mysterious appearance of so-called "automatic fire" on an altar was therefore considered in antiquity a token of divine favor.[13] Pausanias tells us that when Seleucus, together with Alexander, offered sacrifice to Zeus at Pella, the wood on the altar blazed automatically,[14] and he reports also that at Hierocaesarea, in Lydia, he himself saw upon an altar ashes which burst into flame when priests prayed over them.[15] Valerius Maximus mentions a similar "miracle" at Egnatia,[16] and in one of Vergil's Eclogues, a sudden blaze upon an altar is deemed an auspicious omen.[17] Conversely, the extinction of altar-fire was taken to indicate the withdrawal of the god or goddess.[18]

The production of such fire by hocus-pocus was, we are told, part of the stock-in-trade of ancient magicians. Pausanias says that it was a common feature of Iranian magic,[19] and other Classical writers declare that it was a common trick on the part of profane conjurers.[20] Maximus, for example, is said to have made a statue of Hecate laugh and to have caused the torches in her hands to light up automatically.[21] On a more exalted level, Caesarius von Heisterbach attributes similar feats to several Christian saints.[22] It has therefore been suggested by some scholars that Elijah practiced a similar feint, surreptitiously substituting naphtha (kindled by the sun or by a concealed mirror) for the water which he is said to have poured over the altar![23] Sober readers, however, will scarcely be fired by this suggestion; one might as well try to identify botanically the species of beanstalk which Jack climbed! Moreover, it has been shrewdly pointed out that, since Elijah performed *in the late afternoon,* the sun would in any case scarcely have been strong enough to work such a trick.[24]

(c) The limping dance and the gashing with knives

> *After dressing the altar, the priests of Baal commence their performance by limping beside* (KJV, wrongly: *leaping upon*) *it. Then they gash themselves with knives, "as was their wont," until the blood flows.*

The prophets of Baal were performing a type of ritual dance which is attested also from other sources. Heliodorus (3rd cent. B.C.), in his romance *Aethiopica,* describes how Tyrian seafarers performed a dance of "hops and skips" in honor of the local god, "Heracles," i.e., Melqarth. "They now jumped with light leaps," he says, "and now limped along on the ground."[25] His account is doubly pertinent to our theme, because the cult of Baal, against which Elijah was contending, appears to have been promoted in Israel especially by Jezebel, the Tyrian princess whom King Ahab had married. Again, from Deir al Qa'la, near Beirut, comes an inscription of the third century B.C. which mentions specifically a "Baal of the Skipping Dance" (*Ba'al marqôd*);[26] while Herodian, the historian of the Roman Empire, paints a graphic picture of the Emperor Heliogabalus (218–22 C.E.) executing a dance around the altar of his god at Emesa (Homs), in Syria.[27]

The custom is also known elsewhere. In modern Palestine, for instance, Arabs sometimes dance and leap with bent knees as a means of magically producing rain;[28] while on a curious bas-relief found at Aricia (La Riccia), near Rome, men and women are depicted "tripping the light fantastic" in the

Romanized cult of Isis.[29] Analogous procedures are reported also from India[30] and Iceland.[31]

The limping dance was, as we have seen (above, §**129**), associated especially with *funeral ceremonies,* and it is thus that it is to be interpreted also in the present instance. We now know, from the mythological poems discovered at Ras Shamra-Ugarit, that when drought beset the land, it was popularly believed that Baal had sunk into the netherworld, and the cry went up, *"Baal is dead!"*[32]

It is likewise as a *funeral rite* for Baal that we should understand the concomitant action of his prophets, when they "gashed themselves with knives and lancets, as was their wont, until the blood gushed out upon them." Such laceration was and still is a common rite of mourning in many parts of the world, its primary purpose being to revivify the deceased.

The practice was common in cults revolving around the figure of a dying and reviving god of fertility.[33] Herodotus tells us, for example, that as a part of the worship of Osiris in the Egyptian city of Busiris, "at the conclusion of the sacrifice, the whole crowd, men and women alike, proceed to beat themselves in honor of the god . . . while the Carian element of the population go even further, gashing their faces with knives."[34] Similarly, when Lucian of Samosata (2nd cent. C.E.) describes the rites performed at the temple of "the Syrian Goddess" at Hierapolis (Membij), he makes a point of telling us that "on certain days a crowd flocks into the temple, and the sacred eunuch (*galli*) in great number perform "the ceremony of men" (i.e., castrate themselves) and gash their arms."[35]

As is well known, orgiastic cults of this type, imported largely from Asia Minor, attained something of a vogue in Rome from the dawn of the Imperial Age onward, and Roman authors frequently allude to this characteristic practice of laceration.[36] Particularly lurid is the description given by the poet Tibullus, who says of the exotic priestess of such a cult:

> Frenzied, with battle-ax she rends her arms,
> And o'er the image of the goddess sheds
> Her streaming blood, unheeding. There she stands,
> The blade plung'd in her side, her bosom torn.[37]

Similarly, his contemporary, Propertius, poses the agonizing question:

> Why should any man with sacred spear
> Gash his own arms and tear his flesh to shreds,
> The while those mad, wild Phrygian cries ring out?[38]

while Statius (c. 61–96 C.E.) compares the melee of battle, with its clashing spears and freely flowing blood, to an orgy in the cult of the Asianic Mother-goddess, when her devotees pour pell-mell out of her temple, gashing their arms in frenzy.[39]

In such ceremonies, however, it is also possible that the shedding of blood served quite a different purpose. As we have seen (above, §144), drought and blight were popularly regarded as the consequence of misconduct. Hence, as Pettazzoni has suggested, the underlying idea may have been to eliminate "sin" from the inner man along with the discharge of his blood, i.e., his contaminated vital essence. Blood-letting for this purpose actually obtains in the Malaccas among the Bechuanas of South Africa, the Yuchi Indians of California, the Aztecs and Totonacs of Mexico, in Nicaragua, Guatemala, Peru, and China, and it is attested also in ancient Greece.[40]

Again, it should not be overlooked that in some parts of the world, bloodletting is an act of imitative magic, to produce rain.[41] In Java, for instance, people thrash themselves in times of drought until the blood flows,[42] and in Eggibiu, a region of Ethiopia, they stage sanguinary conflicts to the same end.[43]

(d) Elijah's taunts

> *The prophets of Baal receive no response from him. Thereupon Elijah taunts them, bidding them, "Cry aloud, for he is a god. Maybe he is engaged or busy,[44] or on a journey; maybe he is asleep, and will wake."*

There is a subtle point in these taunts, and Comparative Folklore brings it out. *Elijah is deliberately satirizing certain standard pagan procedures.* Thus, when he urges his opponents to "cry loudly," he is mocking the practice of magically promoting thunderstorms (and hence rainfall) by imitating its loud noise. In many parts of the world, for instance, bull-roarers are used for this purpose;[45] the Zuñi of Mexico also crack whips,[46] and at Tartu, in Estonia, men rattle kettles and bang with hammers.[47] Similarly, when Elijah bids the prophets of Baal to arouse the god because he may be asleep, he is taking a sly dig at the custom in pagan temples of awakening the god each morning or in times of distress.[48] "Awake, O Judge!" says an Egyptian pyramid text of the third millennium B.C., "Rouse thyself. O Thoth! Awake, ye sleepers! Awake, ye that dwell in Kenset!"[49] and Porphyry tells us that the ceremony of waking the god was part of the Egyptian daily ritual even in Roman times.[50] At Delphi, the Greek Dionysus was similarly roused by the Thyades,[51] as was Bacchus at Rome.[52] Nor indeed was the usage unknown to the Hebrews themselves; Yahweh was roused daily in the Second Temple by an order of priests called "awakeners" ($m^e\hat{o}r^er\hat{i}m$), who chanted the words, "Awake, Lord! Why sleepest thou?" (Ps. 44:23),[53] and thrice in the Psalms, Yahweh is bidden "Awake!"[54] At Tyre there was an annual ceremony of awakening the god "Herakles" (i.e., Melqarth) in the month of Peritios;[55] and it has been suggested that an official called "he who makes the god stand up" (*m-q-m i-l-m*), who is mentioned in connection with various Phoenician temples, was really the priest who roused him every morning.[56]

The general tenor of Elijah's taunts, it may be added, finds a striking parallel in a passage of the *Deipnosophistae* (Banquet of the Learned) by the Greek grammarian, Athenaeus (c. 230 C.E.). "When," we read, "Demetrius Poliorketes returned to Athens from Leucas and Corcyra, the Athenians welcomed him with an extraordinary ovation . . . dancing and singing praises to the effect that he was the only true god, whereas the others were asleep or away from home or had no ears."[57]

(e) Rain-stones

> *It is now Elijah's turn. He first takes twelve stones and with them builds an altar to Yahweh. Then, after dressing that altar, and digging a trench around it, he orders twelve barrel-fulls of water to be poured over it. The water also fills the trench.*

The Biblical writer explains the prophet's action as the renovation of an altar of Yahweh which had been overthrown, and interprets the twelve stones as symbolic of the twelve tribes of Israel. Comparative Folklore suggests, however, that this is simply an *interpretatio israelitica* of a more ancient practice.

"Stones," says Frazer in *The Golden Bough*,[58] "are often supposed to possess the property of bringing on rain, provided they be dipped in water or sprinkled with it. . . . In a Samoan village a certain stone was carefully housed as the representative of the rain-making god, and in time of drought his priests carried the stone in procession and dipped it in a stream. . . ."[59] At Sagami in Japan there is a stone which draws down rain whenever water is poured on it.[60] In Behar people think to put an end to drought by keeping a holy stone named Narayan-chakra in a vessel of water. . . ."[61] At Barenton, Breton peasants used, when they needed rain, to draw water from a special fountain and pour it over a slab.[62] "On Snowdon, . . . a row of stepping-stones runs out into the Black Lake (Dulyn), and if anyone steps on the stones and throws water so as to wet the farthest stone, which is called the Red Altar, 'it is but a chance that you do not get rain before night, even when it is hot weather.' "[63] At Uskub, in Turkey, in a time of drought, both Christians and Moslems set up a fallen altar of Jupiter Optimus Maximus and poured wine over it.[64] Analogous procedures are reported also from Africa, India, and Mexico.[65] Often, too, the ceremony has been transmogrified into the Christian rite of dipping the statue of a saint in water.

It has been suggested that the celebrated *lapis manalis* at Rome was originally such a "rain-stone" and came later to be integrated with the cult of Jupiter in order to give sanction to traditional prayers and sacrifices associated with it.[66] According to Pliny, the theory underlying the use of "rain-stones" was that they housed the rain-spirit, and that the latter could be "manipulated" by inciting or influencing other spirits who were resident there.

The selection of *twelve* stones need originally have had no reference to the twelve tribes of Israel, for twelve is often used as a round number in ancient rituals.

The ritualistic twelve appears again in the twelve barrels of water poured over the stones, and here the major religious character of the procedure comes out even more clearly in the fact that the aspersion is made in *three* installments, such threefold iteration ("holy, holy, holy") being commonplace in such cases.

(f) The filling of the trench with water

This may likewise be interpreted as a procedure designed to procure water for the parched soil, for it possesses an arresting parallel in an ancient custom performed both in Syria and in Greece to the same end. When the ground was dry, it was believed that the waters of the subterranean ocean, which normally welled up in the form of springs, had disappeared down a crevice; by pouring more water into a ditch, they could be made to rise and overflow.[67] The custom is mentioned by Lucian as having been performed twice yearly in the temple of the Syrian Goddess at Hierapolis (Membij). The water, he says, was brought from the sea and poured out within the sacred precincts. It passed down into a chasm, identified in local myth with that which had received the waters of the Deluge.[68] A similar procedure has been witnessed in recent times at Tyre,[69] and it has been suggested that this was also the real purport of a strange rite performed by the Greeks on the last day of the Mysteries at Eleusis. "They fill two vessels (*plēmochoai*)," says the grammarian Athenaeus, "and, turning with one towards the east, and with the other towards the west, recite over them a ritual formula." The rite, he adds, was mentioned in the now lost Cretans of Euripides, where it was said expressly that the contents of the vessels were poured into a "chasm of the earth."[70]

(g) Elijah on the summit of Carmel

After the fire had duly fallen upon the altar of Yahweh, and the assembled multitudes have therefore acknowledged him as the true god, Elijah repairs, accompanied only by his servant, to the top of the mountain. There he "bows himself to the ground and puts his face between his knees." Six times he bids his servant look out to sea, but each time the lad brings back word, "There is nothing." The seventh time, however, he reports: "Behold, a little cloud is rising from the sea, like a man's hand." Presently the heavens lower, and rain falls.

To put one's head between one's knees would normally suggest a gesture of despondency, and the expression indeed occurs in this sense both in Egyptian[71] and in Ugaritic.[72] Elijah, however, has just scored an impressive triumph, and it is therefore difficult to see why he should be in despair. Accordingly, it may be suggested—albeit with reserve—that what he really did was to adopt a posture of divinatory trance, for this may be illustrated by the fact that to this day just such a posture is characteristic of fetish-women in Guinea during the act of divination.[73]

(h) The raincloud

The comparison of the raincloud to a man's hand finds an interesting parallel in Finnish and Estonian folklore, where a thundercloud is envisaged as "a little man with a copper hand who, rising from the water, becomes a giant."[74]

159   The ascension of Elijah

Elijah and his disciple Elisha are walking beside the Jordan. Suddenly they are parted from each other by a fiery chariot driven by fiery horses. Elijah is caught up in a stormwind and raised to heaven. He vanishes from Elisha's sight.

This is simply a Hebrew version of the well-known folktale of the *Wild Hunt* (E 501), the gist of which is that a deity or famous historical character rides across the sky on stormy nights, or appears in moments of crisis, accompanied by a ghostly troop of followers. In Teutonic folklore, the host is usually known as the *wütendes Heer,* or Wild Host, but this is simply a popular corruption of *Wotan's Heer,* i.e., the army of Wotan, or Odin. An earlier form of it has been seen by some scholars in the bacchic routs of Artemis and Dionysus in Greek belief, for these are sometimes said to be celestial.[1]—Tales of the Wild Hunt are ubiquitous, and it would be tedious to cite them in detail. It is, however, especially pertinent that the Hunt often appears as an army of old soldiers who "never die, but simply fade away."[2] Dio Halicarnassus, for example, speaks of it specifically as a "celestial *army,"*[3] and it is so designated also in Spanish tradition. Indeed, it is in this form that it is said to have been seen near Worms in 1098,[4] at the siege of Byzantium by Philip II of France in 1204,[5] and at the battle of Mons in World War I (Aug. 23, 1914).—Arthur of Britain is reported so to have appeared at various times in the forests of Brittany, in Savoy, in parts of Scotland, and—as late as the nineteenth century—at Cadbury Castle, in Somerset.[6]—In Germany, similar tales are told about Rupprecht and other national heroes.[7]

All the characteristic details of the Wild Hunt occur in our Biblical narrative. Thus (a) it is often said to appear beside a body of water[8] as here it appears beside the River Jordan—a notion evidently derived from the rising of mists from rivers, lakes, and marshes. (b) It is usually accompanied by a chariot or wagon.[9] (c) It exhales fire, is wreathed in fire, and leaves a trail of sparks.[10] (d) It appears on stormy nights, is heralded by a storm, and disappears in a storm, or in a sudden blast of wind.[11]

When Elijah disappears, Elisha exclaims: *My father, my father! the chariots of Israel and the horsemen thereof!* In these words the Biblical writer merely works in a standard cliché, for exactly the same expression is employed also by King Joash when Elisha himself falls sick (II Kings 13:14). In both of their present contexts, the words clearly mean no more than that the hero in question is tantamount in power and prowess to an entire protective army;[12] but it may be suggested that originally they possessed quite a different meaning and were intended to identify the ghostly chariot and horses as those of Jacob—the ancestral hero of the Israelites.[13] The expression, *My father, my father,* would then be simply an exclamation of surprise or alarm, exactly like the Arabic *ya abu, ya abu,* commonly employed in this way.[14]

Combined with that of the Wild Hunt is the equally familiar motif of the *translation of a hero to heaven.*[15]—The god Mithra, for instance, was said to have been borne aloft in the chariot of the sun after his earthly mission had been fulfilled.[16]—Hercules, too, was believed to have ascended in a cloud from his funeral pyre;[17] and Roman emperors were held to ride with the Sun-god after death. A papyrus from Egypt has Phoebus announce the death of Trajan by saying, "I have just ridden with Trajan in a chariot drawn by white horses";[18] and even on the tombs of very humble persons a chariot is often figured to suggest their lot in the afterlife.[19]

160   The mantle of Elijah   19:19

In primitive thought, "clothes makyth man" in a very real sense, since a person's garments are considered not merely as vestments but as part of his essential self. Conferment of them upon another therefore signifies transference of personality. It is, indeed, for this reason that a king is clothed in traditional robes; he inherits a traditional "self."[1]

In Morocco, chieftains exchange cloaks or turbans as earnests in concluding covenants; they thereby pledge themselves.[2] Similarly, one can work magic against a person if one secures even the smallest portion of his clothing as does Simaetha in Theocritus' famous idyll.[3]

The belief has curious offshoots. The clothes of the Mikado, for example, are so sacred—that is, so intimately bound up with his divine "self"—that it is fatal for anyone to wear them;[4] while a man who dons the robes of a Maori chieftain, will face certain death,[5] just as in Fiji, a similar act of presumption entails a special disease.[6]

Conversely, removal of clothes implies loss of identity or extreme self-abasement. It was for this reason that worshipers often appeared before their gods in *puris naturalibus,* though here the additional factor of possibly contaminating the divine also operates.[7] It is for this reason too that mourners and penitents doffed their garments, and that divorcees were stripped when dismissed from their husbands.[8] A particularly interesting example of this symbolism occurs in a Jewish anecdote concerning one Rabbi David ben Daniel of Mosul who pronounced a ban (*ḥerem*) on detractors of the philosopher Maimonides. They could clear themselves only if they asked forgiveness at the sage's tomb and deposited their turbans upon it, i.e., symbolically divested themselves of their offending "selves."[9]

The haircloth worn by Elijah[10] was, of course, a characteristic sign of humility. Manu prescribed similarly that the devout should wear garments of cow hair.[11] Buddhist monks are sometimes encouraged to wear rags, and rags[12] were likewise worn in penance in medieval Christendom.[13] Strabo tells us that at Palmetum, in the Suez area, men and women who guarded the sacred grove of palms wore skins.[14]

161   Harlots bathe in Ahab's blood   22:38

The harlots were not merely having fun; they were giving themselves a tonic and probably also, in their estimation, a beauty treatment. "The blood is the life,"[1] and throughout the ages it has been believed that bathing in it can reinvigorate the body and cure afflictions of the skin.[2] Pliny tells us, for instance, that the ancient Egyptians used to bathe in blood as a cure for leprosy or elephantiasis;[3] while from modern India comes the story of a woman who had lost her child and was told by a fakir to bathe daily in a boy's blood in order to ensure that her next would be healthy.[4] In Bechuanaland, the blood of a goat is sprinkled over a sick man to cure him;[5] while among the Caribs a newborn boy is "anointed" with drops of his father's blood so that the latter's vitality and courage may be transmitted to him.[6] Constantine, we are told, desisted from this practice only as the result of a vision; while, on the other hand, in one version of the notorious "blood-libel,"[7] Richard I of England is alleged to have been advised by a Jew to bathe in the blood of a newly slain child in order to gain strength and relieve bodily infirmities.[8] Bathing in the blood of a bull (*taurobolium*) or of a ram (*criobolium*) was also one of the principal rites of regeneration in the so-called Mystery Religions of the Hellenistic age.[9]

The notion is introduced frequently into popular legend and fiction.[10] Thus, in one of the "vampire tales" included in Somadeva's *Ocean of Story* (*Kathasaritsagara*), the Indian princess Mrigenkavati, wife of Sahasranika, asks for a bloodbath to cure her malady;[11] and in the medieval English romance of *Amys and Amylion,* one of those knightly brothers has his two children slain so that their blood may relieve the other of leprosy.[12] In the Arthurian cycle of legends, Galahad is told by the maiden daughter of King Pellinore that in a certain castle lies a lady sick to death who can recover only if she is anointed with the blood of a pure princess;[13] and very much the same thing is related in Longfellow's *Golden Legend* concerning Prince Henry who lies sick of a strange disease in the castle of Vautberg, on the Rhine.[14] A Jewish legend associates the medieval bloodbath with the pharaoh who oppressed the Israelites in Egypt;[15] and the basic motif occurs also in Syrian,[16] Tibetan,[17] German,[18] Italian,[19] and Czech[20] folktales.

Sometimes the regenerative blood is absorbed by *drinking* rather than bathing.[21] The ancient Scythians, for example, mutilated the bodies of fallen foes and drank their blood in order to imbibe their strength;[22] and a medieval chronicler says the same of the Hungarians,[23] while in the *Nibelungenlied* the brave Burgundians so use the blood of the Huns whom they have slain in battle.[24] Similarly, it is recorded that when the Count of Montmorency was put to death at Toulouse in 1632, the troops drank his blood in order to fill their veins with his intrepid valor;[25] and the Iroquois are said to have done likewise when the Jesuit missionary Jean de Brébeuf was martyred by them in 1648.[26] Moreover, even at the present day, the wounded Somali sucks his blood in order to regain his strength,[27] and it is customary among huntsmen in Upper Austria to quaff the blood of a newborn beast so as to acquire what they call "a sturdy breast."[28]

When, in 1483, Louis XI of France lay near to death, he attempted to revive himself by daily draughts of the blood of young children.[29] On the same principle the blood of slain dragons or monsters is credited in legend with medicinal and regenerative properties. Sifrit, it will be remembered, became invulnerable by drinking the blood of Fafnir,[30] and in the German romance of Kudrun, Hagen drinks the blood of a monster whom he has killed; while in a Danish legend an ailing king can be cured only by drinking dragon's blood.[31] In allusion to such legends a well-known Rhenish wine is still called *Drachenblut*.

162   Baal Zebub, "Lord of the Flies"   II Kings 1:2, 3, 6, 16

Ahab, king of Israel, falls from an upper window of his palace at Samaria. He sends to the heathen god Baal Zebub of Ekron to inquire whether he will live.

The Hebrew word *zebūb* means "fly," but why should Ahaziah send to a Lord of Flies to inquire whether he would recover from sickness?

Scholars have cited in explanation the apparent analogies of the Greek god Zeus *apomyios* (Averter of Flies)[1] and in the demon Myagros (Driver of Flies), worshiped at Aliphora in Arcadia,[2] both of whom were, it is asserted, regarded as averters of pestilence. The apparent analogy, however, is really no analogy at all, for the deities in question were not in fact averters of pestilence in general; they were simply propitiated before sacrifice in order to keep flies away from the altar.[3] Besides, Ahaziah fell from a window; so why, in any case, should he resort to a god who averted plague?

An alternative explanation is, therefore, that Baal Zebub, "Lord of the Flies," was a god who gave oracles through the buzzing of flies. Such an oracle indeed existed—to cite but one arresting example—at the holy well of Kirkmichael in Bannfshire, Scotland.[4] There seems, however, to be no evidence of such a practice on Semitic soil.

Yet, even if the fly was not an averter of plague or a giver of oracles by means of buzzing, he may well have been a symbol of death and disease, for this idea is widespread both in the ancient world and in modern folklore.[5] Thus, in the Iranian Avesta, the demon of death (*Naças*) is said to take the form of a fly.[6] In Greece, Eurynomos, the demon of decay and putrefaction, is similarly portrayed;[7] and so too is death in several parts of Africa.[8] In medieval Europe, plague and sickness were commonly represented as flies.[9] In the French areas of Switzerland, witches are said to send blue flies against men in order to bring death or sickness upon them;[10] while a legend current at St. Gall tells of a beldam who brought death by stinging in the form of a fly.[11] In German folklore the Devil its often depicted as a fly;[12] and among the Lapps, Finns, and Norwegians flies are popularly regarded as demons in disguise.[13]

If, however, Ahaziah resorted to Baal Zebub as a god of death, he probably did so only on the bases of a popular etymology of that deity's name. For the god of Ekron was, in all probability, a *Philistine,* not a *Semitic,* deity, so that the word which the Hebrews interpreted as *zebūb,* "fly," would really have been a like-sounding *Philistine* term, of quite different meaning.[14]

Elisha

163   Waters purified by salt   2:19 ff.

The men of Jericho complain to Elisha that, despite the pleasing location of the city, there is no water and the ground is barren. The prophet fills a new cruse with salt and casts it into a spring. Instantly the waters are "healed."

Contamination is attributed in ancient and primitive thought to the machinations of demons. Salt, being an incorruptible substance, is universally regarded as potent against them.[1] It was for this reason, for instance, that newborn children were commonly "salted" among the Hebrews[2] and Greeks,[3] as they are still by Balkan peasants[4] and by the Todas of Southern India.[5] The Arabs protect children from the evil eye by placing salt in their hands on the eve of the seventh day after birth; the following morning, the midwife or some other woman strews it about, crying, "Salt in the eye of all who look with malice!"[6] The Germans used to put salt under a child's tongue as soon as it was born,[7] and in the Catholic rite of baptism this is still done as a means of exorcizing the Devil. Laotian and Thai women "wash" with salt after childbirth as a protection against demons;[8] and in the northern counties of England a sachet of salt is tucked into a baby's clothing on its first outing.[9] As late as 1946, a couple was arraigned at Trowbridge, Wiltshire, for burning salt over a child in order to stop it from crying. The father attributed the cries to witchcraft, and pleaded in defense that "he felt he had to counteract the evil influences that were around."[10] The basis of such practices lies—in the words of an old writer—in the belief that witches and warlocks, "like their master, the Devil, abhor salt as the emblem of immortality." Indeed, because of its potency against them witches allowed no salt in their kitchens, and no salt was used in their "Devil's feasts."[11]

By similar reasoning, the Romans made use of salt in purificatory rites, e.g., to avert the fulfillment of a bad dream.[12]

The properties attaching to salt extended, of course, to saline waters. Thus the well of Zeus Asbamaios, which was of that character, was held to afford special protection against evil influences,[13] while Clement of Alexandria records a superstition that water drawn from three wells and mixed with salt provided immunity against the "princes of darkness."[14]

Elisha places the salt in a *new* bowl. The efficacy of a magical procedure can be impaired if the material used has been contaminated. Accordingly, it is commonly specified in charms and recipes that only *new* vessels and implements may be employed.[15] Thus, in the great Greek magical papyri there is frequent reference to *new* pots and bowls,[16] and Pliny likewise endorses this requirement.[17] Similarly, the medieval Jewish book of magic entitled *The Sword of Moses* lays it down that a *new* potsherd is to be used for inscribing charms designed to "make a man follow thee,"[18] to fructify a barren tree,[19] to cure a sick dog,[20] and to send plague;[21] while in modern Egyptian folklore it is held that a murdered person's ghost can be pinned down by driving a *new* nail into the ground at the scene of the crime.[22]

The same provision applied in more formal ritual. Thus—to cite but a few examples—at the games celebrated in honor of Poseidon at Onchestos, the race had to be run by a *new-broken* colt;[23] and a *new* cart was required to transport the ark of Yahweh to Jerusalem.[24] So too the Roman poet Tibullus, in entreating the acceptance of an offering, stresses that it has been presented in pure, i.e., hitherto unused vessels.[25]

164   Elisha called "baldpate"   2:23

Urchins in the city of Bethel mock Elisha as he passes by, crying after him "Baldpate."

The urchins who cried "Baldpate" after Elisha were simply behaving like all ill-bred children everywhere, and the modern reader cannot but be a trifle shocked at the prophet's humorless and savage reaction. Behind the insult, however, lies an interesting piece of folklore. As we have seen (above, §117), hair is popularly regarded as the seat of vitality. Accordingly, a bald man was, in antiquity, an object not only of fun but also of opprobrium, because he was believed to have lost his vital essence and consequently to be impotent. Aristotle says, for example, that baldness is due to loss of semen,[1] and that boys maimed in the sexual organs do not grow beards.[2] Hairy men, he says also[3]—and in this Pliny agrees with him[4]—have the strongest sexual bent, and the sexual appetite even of mares can be extinguished by cutting off their manes.[5] The belief survives in our own concept of the "hairy-chested he-man" and in the superstition current among British schoolboys that, if they masturbate, they will lose their strength and their hair will fall out.

In Balkan folkore a bald man is regarded as outside the human race and cannot marry;[6] while a popular German expression for the Devil is "Baldpate" (*Kahlkopf, Snoyen*).[7]

The bald man was a constant butt of jokes in Classical antiquity.[8] Indeed, Juvenal is said to have been banished to Egypt for ridiculing the baldness of

Nero—which, in fact, other writers did too.[9] Jesters at banquets were commonly bald, to raise a laugh from the guests, and this custom continued into medieval times.[10]

165   The inexhaustible cruse   4:1–7

At Zarephath, Elijah is given hospitality by a poor widow. She has only a handful of meal in a barrel and a little oil in a cruse, but, at the prophet's request, she makes a cake for him before serving herself and her son. The prophet promises her that neither the barrel nor her cruse will ever be empty throughout the time of drought. So it turns out.

This is simply a Hebrew version of the familiar folktale, known technically as *Tischlein deck' dich,* the theme of which is that scant food is miraculously increased as a reward for hospitality to itinerant gods or saints.[1]

The theme is best known to Western readers from the tale, *Vom süssen Brei* in the Grimm collection,[2] but it has plenty of parallels elsewhere. An Indian variant tells, for instance, how in similar circumstances a single grain of rice was made to yield inexhaustible sustenance;[3] while in a modern Turkish version it is a coffee mill that becomes endowed with this magical property.[4] From the Pelew Islands comes the tale of a magic bird, called Peaged arsai, which alights beside a poor boy and sets before him a single morsel of meat and some *toro.* "What good is that?" cries the lad. "I am hungry!" "Then eat, only eat," replies the bird, and lo and behold, every time the boy takes a bite, what he eats is immediately replaced. When he is so full that he cannot manage a single further bite, and is therefore constrained to break the Pelew custom of eating either everything served at a meal or taking the leftovers with one, and when in this dilemma, he looks anxiously at the bird, the latter cries, "Enough! Finished!" and the miraculous increase stops.[5]

Finnish and Hungarian versions relate how a poor girl is enabled to feed a guest to satiety from three grains of corn which continuously multiply, and how a samovar miraculously develops twelve spouts, each yielding a different drink.[6]

In Classical literature we have, of course, the famous story of Philemon and Baucis who entertain Jupiter and Mercury out of their scant store, only to discover at their amazement that every time the wine bowl is emptied, it fills up again of its own accord.[7] The story served as the subject of well-known paintings by Bramantino (1455–1536) and the Zuccari, and was especially popular with Flemish, Dutch, and German artists of the seventeenth century. It was likewise adopted frequently (under the influence of the New Testament story of the Loaves and Fishes) in Christian hagiologies.[8]

The Western versions of the tale have been traced to a lost comedy (*Thēria*) by the Greek playwright Kratês (c. 470 B.C.),[9] but the theme

itself may perhaps be recognized, at a far earlier date, in a Canaanite mythological text from Ras Shamra-Ugarit, our extant copy of which goes back to
the fourteenth century B.C. This text relates how two sons of the supreme god
El, distinguished from birth by a voracious appetite, are left by him to forage
for themselves on the edges of the steppeland. There they encounter a man
(possibly an official) storing grain. They beg him for bread and wine, but
he replies—the text is incomplete—that he has only a meager quantity of
either. Nevertheles, they break into his store and eat lavishly. The text then
continues with lines which have been imperfectly preserved but which seem
to say that what had at first been small quantities of grain and drink now
become larger quantities and that the jar of wine becomes full. Now, this
text was composed for a celebration in honor of those two gods, and it is
difficult to see why they should have been thus honored unless they had com-
pensated their greedy consumption of the victuals with some promise for future
increase. The celebration, so the text says clearly, took place at the time
when the sun was ripening the grapes and the vines were blooming. It would
seem possible, therefore, that this explanatory myth turned on the theme of
Tischlein deck' dich: the generous host was rewarded by a promise of increase and prosperity—a promise that the steppeland, seemingly barren,
would yet yield produce year by year—as in fact it does. The annual fulfillment
of the promise would thus have been the occasion of the festival for which
the text was designed![10]

165a Elisha revives a dead boy   4:34

This is a duplicate of the incident related concerning Elijah (see above,
§157).

166 Bathing cures leprosy   5:10

*Naaman, commander-in-chief of the king of Syria, is a leper. At the
suggestion of a handmaid, appeal is made to Elisha. The prophet bids
him to bathe seven times in the Jordan.*

(a) What is involved in this procedure is not ablution, or the washing off
of impurity, but what we may call *illution*—the washing *in* of the properties
of primordial waters (see above, §2), here identified as the River Jordan.
This, indeed, is the real meaning of *baptism* in general; and it is worthy of
note that among the Mandeans of Iraq and Iran the baptismal river is still
called Jordan.

The Biblical incident served as a precedent in later Jewish magic, for the
medieval collection of charms entitled *The Sword of Moses* says that a leper
can be cured if he dips seven times in a river.[1]

The vital essence can, however, be renewed also by an infusion of *blood,*
for "the blood is the life" (see above, §26).[2] Such immersion in blood, says
Pliny, was common in Egypt;[3] while the Emperor Constantine is said to have

desisted from this practice only when so warned by a vision.[4] In Somadeva's *Ocean of Story,* the Indian princess Mṛigavāti asks to bathe in blood to cure herself of an ailment;[5] and in the medieval romance of Amys and Amylion two children are slain to provide blood through which one of the heroes may be cured of leprosy.[6] Tales of the same purport are to be found in Basile's *Pentamerone,*[7] and in Sicilian,[8] German,[9] Syrian,[10] and Tibetan lore.[11] A rabbinic legend (*midrash*) has it that the Pharaoh of the Exodus suffered from leprosy and therefore bathed daily in the blood of the Hebrew children whom he ordered slain;[12] while, *en revanche,* a variant of the infamous "blood libel" asserted that Richard I of England had been advised by a Jew to achieve the same end by bathing in the blood of a slain newborn child.[13] Similarly, in 1870 a Moslem butcher in Northern India, who had lost a son, was told by a Hindu fakir that if he washed his wife daily in blood, his next child would be healthy.[14] In Bechuanaland, the blood of a goat is poured over a sick person.[15]

(b) Waving in magic

> *Naaman is at first indignant since he expects an instant cure by a mere* waving *of the prophet's hands over his body and deems the prosaic instructions given him something of an insult to his dignity. Urged by his servants, however, he eventually complies and is healed.*

Waving motions are a common feature of magical procedures; their purpose is to *diffuse* the otherworldly quality by which the magic is worked.[16]

In the Hittite myth of Telepinu, the divine sorceress Kamrusepas makes waving motions to remove from him all the anger and umbrage which have caused him to withdraw his ministrations from the earth;[17] and the same technique is mentioned in other Hittite texts.[18] Moslem midwives sometimes wave vessels full of water over the heads and feet of newborn babes in order to forefend demons;[19] and at Moslem weddings the bride's mother sometimes sprinkles red-dyed water in a waving motion over the bridegroom.[20] At Hoshangabād, in Northern India, it is customary to wave a handful of corn over a sick person, thereby conveying to him the essence of healthy development;[21] and in parts of Afghanistan three shots of pepper are waved in the face of a person believed to be possessed by a demon.[22]

Waving motions were likewise made over offerings in Israelitic ritual— evidently as a survival of an earlier device for keeping off evil influences.[23] This was the practice at the ordination of the high priest,[24] at the presentation of *shelamim* (EV: "peace-offerings"),[25] guilt-offerings,[26] and first fruits,[27] in the ceremony of trial by ordeal,[28] and at the consecration of nazirites.[29]

167   Iron floats   6:5–7

> *The guild of professional prophets ("the sons of the prophets") complain to Elisha that their quarters are too constricted. He bids them repair to the banks of the Jordan and there construct a more com-*

modious abode. One of the guild asks him to accompany them and bring along his servants to help in the work. While they are felling timber, one of the laborers drops his ax into the water—a disaster heightened by the fact that he had it only on loan from someone else! The prophet thereupon cuts down a stick and throws it toward the spot where the ax fell. Instantly the ax floats on the surface.

The miracle of floating iron occurs in Christian hagiology.[1] A novice clearing the bank of a lake near the monastery of St. Clement at Monte Cassino accidentally dropped the head of his ax into the water. St. Benedict (480–543) laid his hands on the haft; instantly the iron head rose and fitted itself to the handle.[2] It was thus too that St. Leufredus retrieved an ax dropped into the water by one of the monks at La Croix (738 C.E.).[3] Similarly, while St. Wolfram was sailing from Candebec to Frisia, St. Vando, during the celebration of the Mass on board, accidentally dropped the paten and it fell into the water. Wolfram took a stick and dipped it into the waters. The paten then floated on the surface.[4]

168 The use of corpses in magic 13:21

The life essence or any special qualities which once inhabited the dead can, according to widespread popular belief, be transferred to the living and afford them extra strength when their own is failing. By an extension of this idea, a dead person may himself be reanimated, if brought into contact with the bodily remains of a saint, since the latter are endorsed with numinous properties.[1]

An Arabic superstition holds that if one lies between the graves of holy men, one can be relieved of fever;[2] and in parts of Germany it is believed that one can acquire health by disturbing the dead.[3] In Armenia, a piece of a dead man's hand is given to a sick person;[4] and similarly in Ireland a dead man's hand can cure ailments.[5] This latter belief obtained also among the Jews, and is mentioned in the Talmud.[6] Analogously the Romans thought that one could induce health by stroking a patient with a dead man's hand,[7] and that a tooth drawn from a cadaver could cure toothache.[8] In Thomas Hardy's story, *The Withered Arm* (included in his *Wessex Tales*), touching the neck of a man who had been hanged is said to affect a cure;[9] and certain primitive tribes of South Africa maintain that magic can be worked from a decoction of the left hand and foot of a person slain for ritual purposes.[10] A trial for murder committed to this end was reported in 1957.[11] In much the same vein Pliny declares that the hair of a man who has been crucified protects from quartan fever;[12] while Jewish sources record a popular notion that a barren woman can induce conception by applying to her person the water or soap in which a corpse has been washed.[13]

The bodies of the dead can also be used magically to inflict harm. The Belep of New Caledonia, for example, believe that they can disable an enemy from flight through magic worked with the leg bone of a dead foe;[14] and the ancient Greeks seem to have thought that to set a young male child on a tomb would be to rob him of his manhood by infecting him with the impotence of the dead.[15] A South Slavonian housebreaker often begins operations by throwing a dead man's bone into the house. "May you have as much chance of waking," he says cynically of the sleeping inmates, "as has this bone!"[16]

▲ 169   Yahweh's Lions   17:24–28

[*In 722* B.C. *the king of Assyria invaded the territory of Israel, deported its inhabitants, and replaced them by people drawn from his own dominions. The latter, of course, did not worship Yahweh, and when the God of Israel saw how they ignored him, he "sent lions among them, which killed some of them." On hearing of this, the Assyrian monarch ordered one of the deported priests of Yahweh to be repatriated in order to teach the newly settled population "the law of the god of the land."*]

The incident illustrates a not uncommon belief that every land has its own local deity, who can be propitiated only by the natives of the country, since they alone are acquainted with the particular form of religious ritual which he expects.[1] For example, the Toradjas of Central Celebes hold that "every district has its own earth-spirit, or rather earth-spirits, which can only be invoked by members of the tribe which inhabits the district." Hence, when a man has obtained leave to lay out a rice-field in the territory of another tribe, and the time comes for him to make an offering to the earth-spirit Toompoo ntana, "Owner of the Ground," "the stranger always invites for that purpose the help of one of the garden-priests of the tribe in whose land he has come to dwell, because they say that such a stranger does not know how he ought to invoke the spirit of that land; he is not yet accustomed to that earth-spirit."[2]

Again, among the aboriginal tribes of the Upper Niger valley, the Earth is a very important deity, whose worship is cared for by a priest called the Chief of the Earth. Each village, as a rule, has its Chief of the Earth, who is the religious, but not the political, head of the community, being charged with the duty of offering sacrifices to Earth and the other local deities, and of acting generally as the indispensable intermediary between the gods and the people. For example, it is his business to sacrifice for good crops at sowing, to offer thank-offerings after harvest, to perform the rites necessary for procuring rain in seasons of drought, and to make atonement whenever Earth has been offended by the spilling of human blood on the ground, whether in murder or in simple assault and battery.[3] Moreover, as representative of the Earth-deity, and therefore himself master of the earth, it is the prerogative of the priest to grant permission to dig graves and to prescribe their dimensions.[4]

This important priesthood continues to be filled by members of the old aboriginal race under the rule of an alien people, the Mossi, who have invaded and conquered a large part of the country. "The existence of these Chiefs of the Earth among the Mossi is explained very probably by the superposition of the conquering on the conquered race. When the Mossi invaded and conquered the country, in proportion as they spread their dominion they put men of their own race at the head of all the villages and cantons to ensure the submission of the vanquished population. But they never thought—and this is a notion to be found in the whole of West Africa—that they were qualified to offer sacrifices to the Earth-god of the place and the local divinities. It was only the vanquished, the ancient owners of the soil, with which they continued in good relations, who were qualified for that. Hence the old political head of the aborigines was bound to become naturally a religious chief under the rule of the Mossi. Thus we have seen that the king (*Moro-Naba*) never himself offers the sacrifices to Earth at Wagadugu, nor does he allow such sacrifices to be offered by his minister of religion, the Gandé-Naba. He lays the duty on the king of Wagadugu (*Wagadugu-Naba*), the grandson of the aborigines, who as such is viewed favourably by the local divinities. Similarly, when he sacrifices to the little rising-grounds in the neighbourhood of Wagadugu, he commits the charge of the offerings and sacrifices to the local chief. But what the king (*Moro-Naba*) actually does now at Wagadugu, the Mossi kings (*naba*) doubtless did formerly, more or less everywhere after the conquest, as soon as the submission of the aborigines was assured. Hence the institution of the Chiefs of the Earth (*Tensoba*)."[5]

The historian has not described the rites and ceremonies by which the Israelitish priest at Bethel succeeded in staying the ravages of the man-eating lions; we can, therefore, only compare the intention, but not the form, of the rites and ceremonies which a priest of one of the aboriginal tribes in India at the present day performs for the purpose of staying the ravages of man-eating tigers and laying the ghosts of such persons as have fallen victims to the ravening maw of these dangerous brutes. The Baigas (or Bygas) are one of the wildest of the primitive Dravidian tribes that roam the dense *sal* forests which clothe the hills of Mandla in the Central Provinces of India. They lead a very secluded life in the wilderness, and down to the middle of the nineteenth century, when they first came under the exact observation of English officers, they were even more solitary and retired than they are now.[6]

In the country where they dwell they are regarded as the most ancient inhabitants and accordingly they usually act as priests of the indigenous gods.[7] Certainly there is reason to believe that in this part of the hills they are predecessors of the Gonds, towards whom they occupy a position of acknowledged superiority, refusing to eat with them and lending them their priests or enchanters for the performance of those rites which the Gonds, as newcomers, could not properly celebrate. Among these rites the most dangerous is that of laying the ghost of a man who has been killed by a tiger. When such an event has taken place, the Baiga priest or enchanter proceeds to the scene of the catastrophe, provided with articles, such as fowls and rice, which are to be offered to the ghost of the deceased. Arrived at the spot, he makes a small cone out of the blood-stained earth to represent either the dead man or one of his living relatives. His companions having retired a few paces, the priest drops on his hands and knees, and in that posture performs a series of antics which are supposed to represent the tiger in the act of destroying the man, while at the same time he seizes the lump of blood-stained earth in his teeth. One of the party then runs up and taps him on the back with a small stick. This perhaps means that the tiger is killed or otherwise rendered harmless, for the priest at once lets the mud cone fall into the hands of one of the party. It is then placed in an ant-hill and a pig is sacrificed over it. Next day a small chicken is taken to the place, and after a mark, supposed to be the dead man's name, has been made on the fowl's head with red ochre, it is thrown back into the forest, while the priest cries out "Take this and go home." The ceremony is thought to lay the dead man's ghost, and at the same time to keep the tiger from doing any more harm. For the Baigas believe that if the ghost were not charmed to rest, it would ride on the tiger's head and incite to fresh deeds of blood, guarding at the same time from the attacks of human foes by his preternatural watchfulness.[8]

If we cannot suppose that the Israelitish priest at Bethel performed a similar pantomime for the repression of man-eating lions among the woods of Samaria, we shall perhaps be justified in assuming that the rites which he did celebrate were neither less nor more effectual than those which the jungle-priests of Mandla still observe for a like purpose over the blood-stained earth in their native forests. At all events, with these parallels before us we can better appreciate the gross religious impropriety of which the foreign settlers in Palestine were deemed to be guilty, when they began by completely ignoring the old god of the land; it is no wonder that he is represented as being nettled at such treatment and as taking strong measures to impress his claims on the attention of the newcomers. ▼

170   The horses and chariots of the sun   23:11

He also removes the model horses and burns the model chariots set up by previous kings at the entrance to the Temple in honor of the sun.

The idea that the sun drives a chariot was commonplace in the Ancient Near East. Shamash, the sun-god of the Mesopotamians, is described in their literature as "the Charioteer" (*rakib narkabti*),[1] and in a Phoenician inscription of the eighth century B.C., from Zenčirli, in Syria, he is associated with another called Rkb-el, which would seem to denote a divine charioteer.[2] Pottery models of horses and chariots, found at pre-Israelite levels in several Palestinian cities, have been related by some scholars to such a solar cult, but this is doubtful.[3]

The concept is likewise well attested outside the Semitic world.[4] In the Indic Rig Veda, Surya, the sun-god, rides a chariot,[5] and a similar notion attached to the sun among the Iranians.[6] The chariot of the sun is not mentioned, however, in the Iliad and Odyssey, but first occurs among the Greeks in the Homeric Hymns[7] and in Hesiod.[8] Thereafter it becomes a commonplace.[9]

A cognate concept is that of the *horses* of the sun.[10] The Iranian Avesta speaks of "the sun's swift steeds,"[11] and horses were dedicated and sacrificed to the solar deity.[12] The Rhodians offered a chariot and four horses annually to the sun;[13] and the Spartans sacrificed horses to the sun on Mount Taygetus.[14] A similar practice was observed, says Herodotus, by the Massagetae of Turkestan;[15] while the Romans annually threw a chariot and horses into the sea in honor of the sun.[16] The Icelandic saga of Hrafnkell revolves around a horse consecrated to Frey, a solar deity;[17] and in medieval Sweden, the day of St. Etienne, the Christian successor of Frey, was dedicated to horses.[18]

NOTES

JOSHUA

104 Joshua at Jericho

(a) "The walls came tumblin' down"

1. See: G. E. Wright, Biblical Archaeology (1960), 47 f.

(b) The circumambulation of the walls

2. P. Saintyves, Essais de folklore biblique (1902), 177–204; W. Pax, in WS 8 (1937), 1–88.

3. K. Sethe, Untersuchungen, iii (1905), 133–35; J. Vandier, La religion égyptienne (1949), 181 f.; S. S. B. Mercer, The Religion of Ancient Egypt (1949), 351.

4. A. Goetze, Kleinasien[1] (1933), 154.

5. T. H. Gaster, Thespis[2], 193 f.

6. The ceremony was called *pradaksina;* see: M. Eliade, Patterns in Comparative Religion (1958), 373 f.; C. H. Tawney, Ocean of Story (1880), i.190–93.

7. R. O. Winstedt, in JRAS 1945.139 f.

8. W. Simpson, The Buddhist Praying Wheel (1896), 275.

9. Tor Irstam, King of Ganda (1944), 176 ff.

10. Brand-Ellis, Popular Antiquities of Great Britain (1882–83), i.197 f.; T. F. Thiselton Dyer, British Popular Customs (1876), 204 ff., 208–11; 213 f.; E. M. Hull, The Folklore of the British Isles (1928), 77–80; E. M. Leather, The Folklore of Herefordshire (1912), 149–51.

11. A. R. Wright, English Folklore (1928), 44–45.

12. P. Sartori, Sitte und Brauch (1910–14), iii.168, 216, 268.

13. Livy, ii.10; Valerius Maximus, iii.2, 1.

14. Bouquet, Recueil des historiens de la Gaule (1840 ff.), iv.

15. M. Diemer, Légende dorée de l'alsace (1905), 115–18.

16. J. Michelet, Origin du droit français (1837), 63–64.

17. Il Messagero (Rome), Sept. 8, 1967, p. 3.

(c) The seven circuits

18. Lucan, Phars. i.592 ff.; Apuleius, Met. iii, init.; Servius, on Virgil, Ecl. iii.77.

19. Plutarch, Romulus xxi.4; Ward Fowler, Roman Festivals at the Period of the Republic (1899), 319; J. G. Frazer, The Fasti of Ovid (1929), vol. ii, p. 335 f.; E. Samter, in ARW 16 (1913), 137 ff.

20. Saintyves, loc. cit.

21. Gesta Ambrosiensium, apud Scriptores Rer. Franc., x.228.

22. Michelet, op. cit., 128.

23. M. Haberlandt, in Corr. Bl. d. Ges. f. Anthropol., Ethnol., und Urgeschichte, 21.9.

(d) The trumpets

24. P. Haupt, in WZKM 23 (1909), 355–65.

25. Stith Thompson, MI, D 1562.3; Bolte-Polivka, i.464 ff.; Aarne-Thompson, Types, #569.

26. T. H. Gaster, New Year (1955), 45–49; Frazer-Gaster, NGB §41.

27. W. Matthews, in RBEW 5 (1887), 435 f.
28. E. O. James, in ERE x.562[b].
29. D. Kidd, The Essential Kafir (1904), 333.
30. W. Mannhardt, Antike Wald- und Feldkulte (1877), 342n.
31. Cf. A. H. Krappe, La genèse des mythes (1938), 135, R. Lasch, in ARW 3 (1900), 97 ff.
32. Apollodorus, Bib. i.9, 7.
33. Livy, vii.36; viii.7, 32.
34. Caesar, Bell. Civ. iii.92; Livy, vii.36; Sallust, Catiline 60.

105   Foundation-sacrifice

1. I Kings 16:34.
2. See: P. Sartori, in Zs. f. Ethnologie 30 (1898), 1–54; S. Baring-Gould, in Murray's Magazine, 1 (1887), 363–77; H. Trumbull, The Threshold Covenant (1896), 45 ff.; H. Naumann, Primitive Gemeinschaft-kultur (1921), 70 ff.—For the Semitic Field, see: S. A. Cook, in W. Robertson Smith, The Religion of the Semites[3] (1927), 632 f.; F. W. S. O'Neill, in ET 21 (1909), 43 f.
3. Joh. Malalas, 37; 200; 203.
4. Ed. Mrs. A. S. Lewis, p. 43.
5. T. Canaan, in JPOS 6 (1927), 63; cf. Mishnah, Ohol. 18.7; Niddah 7.4.
6. S. I. Curtiss, Ursemitische Religion im Volksleben des heutigen Orients, tr. H. Stocks (1913), xvi f., 73, 209, 219, 229.
7. J. G. Frazer, GB iii.89.
8. See, for example: S. Gaidoz, in Mélusine 4 (1888), No. 2; P. Sébillot, Le folklore de France (1904–7), 165 ff.; A. H. Krappe, Balor with the Evil Eye (1927), 165 ff.; Revue Celtique 41 (1924), 187.
9. K. Landtmann, in Acta Acad. Aboensis, 1920, i.5.
10. C. A. Doughty, Arabia Deserta (1888), i.136; ii.100, 198.
11. Cf. R. A. S. Macalister, Gezer (1902–9), ii.426 ff.; ATAOB[2], ii, fig. 231 (Gezer); A. Lods, Israel (1930), 114.—J. Gray, Archaeology and the Old Testament World (Torchbook ed., 1965), 45, identifies images buried in Palestinian houses with the *teraphim,* or household gods (see above, §68), but I see no authority for this.
12. H. Vincent, Canaan d'après l'exploration récente (1907), 282 ff.; A. Lods, Israel (1930), 113 ff.; S. A. Cook, The Religion of Ancient Palestine in the Light of Archaeology (1925), 84 ff.
13. Vincent, loc. cit.; T. Canaan, in JPOS 4 (1925), 8n.; 6 (1927), 118, n.3; A. B. Cook, Zeus ii (1925), 1059.

106   "Sun, stand thou still"

1. There are further allusions to this miracle in Hab. 3:11; Ecclus. 46:4–7.
2. Iliad 2.413 ff.
3. Stith Thompson, MI, D 2146.1; cf. Plautus, Amphitryo 113 f.; A. Dillmann, Comm. on Jos. 10:12.
4. Iliad 18.439 f.
5. Hesiod, Shield 1–56; Pindar, Isthm. vii.5; Lucian, Dial. deorum 10; Apollodorus, Bib. ii.4, 7–8; Hyginus, fab. 28; Seneca, Phaedra 315.
6. Odyssey 23.241 ff.
7. P. Zaunert, Deutsche Märchen seit Grimm (1912–23), 143.
8. C. Schirren, Die Wandersagen der Neuseeländer (1856), 37 ff.
9. Acta Boll., Sept. viii.171; H. Delahaye, The Legends of the Saints (1961), 51.
10. See in general: Badger, in PEFQS, July 1900; S. Birch, ib., April 1900; Matthes, in ThT 1908.461–94; Kelly, in ET 1909.566; B. Alfrink, in StC 24 (1949), 238–69;

J. de Fraine, in Verbum Domini 28 (1950), 227–36; Van der Busche, in Collationes Gandavenses, ii/1 (1951), 48–53.—Standard Bible commentaries are full of tiresome homiletical nonsense about this incident.

11. R. C. Fuller, in Scripture iv/10 (1951).

12. E. C. Brewer, Dictionary of Miracles, 295 f.—It may be pertinent, alternatively, to compare the Hebrew word with the Arabic *d-w-m,* used specifically of *the sun's turning in its course.*

JUDGES

107   The mutilation of captives

1. Xenophon, Hist. gr. ii.1, 31; Plutarch, Lysander 9; Cicero, De officiis iii.11; Valerius Maximus ix.2, ext. 8.

2. Aelian, VH ii.29.

3. Caesar, Bell. Gall. viii.44.

4. A. Oldfield, in Trans. Ethnol. Soc. of London 3 (1865), 287.

5. Cf. Hesychius, Photius, s.v. *maschalismata;* Schol. on Ap. Rhod., Argon. iv.477; E. Riess, in Rhein. Mus. 49 (1894), 182 f.; F. Dümmler, in Philologus 56 (1897), 13 ff.; E. Rohde, Psyche[1], 322–26; O. Gruppe, Gr. Mythol. (1906), 903, n.1; Metzger, in Mélanges Chas. Andler (Strasbourg 1924), 251–68; J. G. Frazer, Apollodorus, vol. i, p. 328, n.1.

6. Aeschylus, Choephoroe 349 (v. T. G. Tucker, Comm. in loc.); Sophocles, Electra 439 (v. Schol. in loc.).

7. Apollodorus, Bib. iii.5, 1.

8. Rohde, loc. cit.; R. C. Jebb, Electra of Sophocles (1892–1900), 211 ff.

9. V AB, B 5–13; tr. H. L. Ginsberg, ANET 136. Cf. Strabo, 5.302; Diod. Sic., 5.29. Cf. also G. L. Gomme, Ethnology in Folklore (1892), 148.

10. A. Baumeister, Denkmäler des klass. Altertums (1855–88), i.460 f., fig. 506.

11. S. Mateer, The Land of Charity (1871), 203 ff.

12. Festus, 135 Lindsay, s.v. *os resectum.*

13. PEFQS 1903.32 ff.

14. E.g., Shalmaneser, in ANET 277; Esarhaddon, ib., 290.

15. Herodotus, iv.103.—Certain tribes in Borneo do the same thing: J. G. Frazer, GB vii.294 ff.

16. Strabo, viii.6, 19, p. 337; Apollodorus, Bib. ii.8, 1.

17. Apollodorus, Bib. ii.5, 11.

18. Ib., ii.7, 7.

19. Ib., Epitome ii.5.

20. Scholiast on Iliad 9.557; Eustathius, in loc., p. 776.

21. Giraldus Cambrensis, Conquest of Ireland, i.4; cf. G. L. Gomme, Ethnology in Folklore (1892), 149.

22. M. Abeghian, Das Armenische Volksglaube (1899), 11.

23. J. B. Labat, Relation historique de l'Ethiopie occidentale (1732), i.208.

24. J. Jones, in Trans. Ethnol. Soc. of London, 3 (1865), 138; E. B. Tylor, Primitive Culture, ii.35.

25. E. Gibbon, The Decline and Fall of the Roman Empire, ed. J. B. Bury, v.186.

26. Silus Italicus, 4.213; Diod. Siculus, 14.115; Livy, 10.26; Strabo, 198. Cf. M. W. Dunbar, History of Antiquity (1877–87), i.176.

27. Ibn Batuta 17, ed. S. Lee.

28. A. Dalzel, History of Dahomey (1793), 76.

29. J. Morier, A Second Journey through Persia (1818), 186.

30. ERE, s.v. Mutilation.

31. Epic of Gilgamesh vi.161. (E. Speiser, in ANET 85, renders "right thigh.").

32. William of Newbury, G. Nub. 281.

33. J. C. Lawson, Modern Greek Folklore and Ancient Greek Religion (reprint, 1964), 435 ff.

34. J. Mooney, The Ghost-Dance Religion (reprint, 1965), 264.

108 Captives fed on scraps

1. Ugaritica V (1967), i.6–8: dyd^cnn y^cdb lḥm lh, wdl yd^cnn ylmn tḥt ṭlḥn.

2. G. Kittredge, "Arthur and Gorlagon," in Harvard Studies and Notes in Philology and Literature, 8 (1903), 252n.; Stith Thompson, MI, Q 478.2–3.—This practice lends itself readily to incorporation as a motif in the widespread story of the adulteress who mistreats a dog which eventually betrays her to her husband: see E. J. Gibb, The History of the Forty Vizirs (1886), 331 f., and versions of the legend of Robert of Sicily cited by Kittredge, loc. cit.

3. Stith Thompson, MI, Q 523.3.

109 The Song of Deborah

(a) Long-haired warriors

1. The Hebrew expression is, bi-ph^ero^{ca} ph^era^côth b^e-Yisraël. The verb p-r-^c means primarily, "to break loose, be unrestrained," and is then used metaphorically of behaving lawlessly (Prov. 29:18), or of keeping the hair untrimmed (Lev. 10:16; 13:45). Hence, the only legitimate translations are, When men cast off restraint (i.e., inhibitions), or When locks flowed freely in Israel. For my own part, I confess that the former seems to me more likely, since it provides a stricter parallel to the following, When men offered themselves freely (i.e., volunteered).—RSV's rendering is based on the fact that in Deut. 32:42, where the crucial word recurs in the expression, the head of p^era^côth of the enemy, it has been traditionally taken to mean "leaders." This, however, is tenuous, for that verse can equally well be rendered, I will make my arrows drunk with blood . . . with the blood of the slain and the captives—(blood) from the long-haired heads of the enemy, as RSV itself indeed translates it.

2. W. H. Roscher, ed., Lex. Myth, s.v. Achilles.

3. J. Wellhausen, Reste d. arab. Heidentums² (1897), 123.

4. Edda vii.116; cf. S. Bugge, Heldensage (1889), 222 f. (Haralds haarfagres Løfte).

5. O. Jegerlehner, Oberwallis (1906), 308, #39.

6. S. Boggs, in FCC 90.53, #400* B.

7. See in general: Frazer-Gaster, NGB, §§167, 502; Bolte-Polivka, ii.413 ff.; Eitrem, Opferritus und Voropfer der Griechen und Römer (1915), 400; E. Bi., s.v. Nazirite. See also below, §117, d.

8. Gilbert Murray, The Rise of the Greek Epic (1907), 123.—It has been objected that the Myceneans are known to have worn their hair long in any case; see fully: D. L. Page, The Homeric Iliad (1963), 243, 282, nn.67–68.

9. Nicetas, Lacon, Chronogr. v.260; G. L. von Maurer, Das griechische Volk (1835), 10.

(b) Riding high and sitting low

10. G. Dossin, ARM i.45; 5–6; 72.6, etc.; cf. A. Salonen, in AOr. 17/ii.320; S. Feigin, in Studies in Memory of Moses Schorr (1944), 227–40.

11. RSV's rich carpets misses the point. The Hebrew word middîn, admittedly difficult, is best taken as an "Aramaic" plural of mad, madū, "cloak." LXX and Vulgate's in judgment arises from fanciful combination of the word with dîn, "judgment," but

this involves impossible syntax.—An alternative suggestion is that *m-d-n* should be interpreted after the Ugaritic *m-d-l*, "caparison," and that (by adding *'ayr*, "male donkey," at
the end) the clause should be rendered, "Ye who sit on caparisoned [male donkeys]"; cf.
D. Hillers, *apud* W. F. Albright, Yahweh and the Gods of Canaan (1968), 49, n. 102.
But this destroys the pointed contrast between *riding* (rkb), *walking* (hlk) and *sitting*
(yšb). Furthermore, I know of no other place where *y-š-b* ("sit") is used of *being
mounted*.

12. T. Canaan, in JPOS 19 (1939), 225, No. 38.

13. Ib.

14. Tr. S. N. Kramer, ANET 44.

15. G. Jacob, Studien in arabischen Dichtern, ii (1894), 115; G. A. Doughty, Arabia
Deserta (1888), ii.231.

16. The word is *ṣeḥôrôth;* see GB[16], s.v. *ṣāḥôr*. Vulg. renders "gleaming" (*nitentes*).

17. Pindar, Pyth. i.66; Sophocles, Electra 706.

18. Pausanias, ii.32, 7; Sophocles, frag. 871.2, Nauck; CIA iii.1015.

19. Pindar, Pyth. i.127.

20. Rev. 19:11, 14.

(c) "Awake, awake, Deborah, utter a song"

21. This conventional rendering is not quite accurate. Deborah was wide awake. What
the Hebrew word really means here is "vent your passion."

22. I Sam. 18:7 ff.

23. RSV: *The Lord gives the command; great is the host of those who bore the tidings.*
But this misses the force of the Hebrew original. The first clause is *conditional,* and in
the second, the word rendered *those that bore the tidings* is feminine. Moreover, the
description of them as *a great host* is the whole point of the verse: the victorious army
of men will be greeted by what amounts to another vast army of their joyous womenfolk!

24. Doughty, op. cit., i.452; G. Jacob, Das Leben der vorislamischen Beduinen
(1895), 125.

(d) The cursing of Meroz

25. Cf. Heb. *rôzî-li,* "woe is me!" (Isa. 24:16), and Arabic cognate. The name of
the city may really have been Hurrian, with the characteristic ending *-zzi;* on the latter,
see: E. Speiser, Mesopotamian Origins (1930), 141; A. L. Oppenheim, in WZKM
44 (1937), 206; T. H. Gaster, in JRAS 1935.38, n.117.

110 Gideon

(a) Gideon's fleece

1. E. Nestle, in ARW 12 (1909), 154–58; W. Schultz, in OLz 1910.241–45.

2. H. Günthert, Die Christliche Legende des Abendlandes (1910), 78 f., whence our
examples are taken.

3. TB Yoma 53[b].

4. Günthert, loc. cit.

5. Ib.

6. Venantius Fortunatus, Vita S. Albini, c.7; Monumenta Germaniae historica, auct.
antiqu. iv[2], 29.

7. Jocelin, Vita 17.

8. Gregory of Tours, Hist. x.29.

9. See: A. Franz, Die kirchliche Benediktionen im Mittelalter, ii (1909), 16 f., as
cited by Günthert.

10. TB Yoma 21[a].

11. Günthert, loc. cit.
12. Ib.
13. Bernardi Itinerarium, in Tobler, Descriptiones terrae sanctae (1874), 94.
14. Günthert, op. cit., 173.
15. J. v. Hahn, Griech. u. albanes. Märchen (1864), i.227.

(b) Gideon's men

16. See: S. Tolkowsky, in JPOS 5 (1925), 69–74; D. Daube, in JJS 7 (1956), 155–61; Y. Yadin, The Art of Warfare in Biblical Lands (1963), ii.257.
17. C. H. Stigand, The Land of Zini (1913), 274 ff.
18. E. Torday, Camp and Tramp in African Wilds (1913), 85.
19. T. Hahn, in Globus, 12/ix.277; id., Tsuni- || Goam, The Supreme Being of the Khoi-Khoi (1881), 71.
20. E. Aymonier, in Cochinchine Française, Excursions et Reconnaissances, No. 16 (Saigon 1883), 165.
21. G. Turner, Nineteen Years in Polynesia (1861), 332.
22. Labillardière, Relation du voyage à la recherche de la Pérouse (1800), ii.196.
23. W. Gunn, The Gospel in Futuna (1914), 276.
23a. Paul Radin, Primitive Religion (reprint, 1957), 114.

111 The purple of kings

1. On purple dye in antiquity, cf. E. Bask, Dissertatio de purpura (Uppsala 1686); G. Wilckius, De purpura varia speciatim regia (Wittenberg 1706); A. Steger, Diss. de purpura sacra dignitatis insigni (Leipzig 1744); B. Roswall, Diss. de purpura (Lund 1750); A. Dedekind, Ein Beitrag zur Purpurkunde. Appendix to Neue Ausgabe seltenen Schriften über Purpur (1898); H. Blümner, Purpureus (1892); J. B. Mayor, Thirteen Satires of Juvenal (1872), ad i.27; Faymonville, Die Purpurfarberei d. versch. Kulturvölker d. Klass Altertums (Diss., Heidelberg 1900). Cf. also: Rachel Carson, The Sea Around Us (Mentor Books ed.), 148.
2. W. Muss-Arnolt, Assyrian Dictionary, s.v.
3. Plutarch, Artaxerxes 5.
4. Joh. Lydus, De magistratibus iii.64.
5. Homeric Hymn to Dionysus, 5–6.
6. Dan. 5:7, 16, 29.
7. Lam. 4:5.
8. Horace, Odes i.35, 2; see fully: J. B. Mayor, on Juvenal i.27.
9. Pliny, HN viii.195; ix.136; Livy, i.41, 6; Cicero, Brutus 56; Servius, on Vergil, Aen. vii.612; J. G. Frazer, The Fasti of Ovid (1929), ii.33 (on i.37).
10. Plutarch, Romulus 14.
11. Zohar, i.38^b–39^b.
12. F. von Duhn, "Rot und Tot," in ARW 7 (1906), 1–24; Eva Wunderlich, Die Bedeutung der roten Farbe im Kultus der Griechen und Römer, RVV 20/i (1927); I. Scheftelowitz, in ZAW 39 (1921), 117 f.; E. Samter, Geburt, Hochziet und Tod (1911), 190 f.; P. Henisch, Die Trauergebräuche bei den Israeliten (1931), 59 ff.; G. B. Luquet, L'art et la religion des hommes fossiles (1926), 185; L. Deubner, De incubatione (1909), 25; H. Kees, "Farbensymbolik in aegyptischen religiösen Texten," in Nachr. Akad. Wiss. Göttingen, Phil.-hist. Kl. 11 (1943).
13. W. Schrank, Babyl. Sühnriten (1908), 28 ff.; K. Frank, Babyl. Beschwörungsreliefs (1908), 44; H. Zimmern, Ritualtafeln (1901), #26.i.14–15; G. Furlani, La relig. bab. e assira (1929), ii.167, 351.
14. E. Ebeling, Tod und Leben (1923), No. 30, A. 25.
15. Enuma Elish iv.61.

16. ERE viii.616.

17. TB Shabbath vii.11; see on this: I. Scheftelowitz, Schlingen- und Netzmotif (1912), 32 ff.

18. Globus, 89.60.

19. G. H. Simon, in JAF 65 (1952), 291.

20. Theocritus, Ib., ii.2; Petronius, Satyricon 131; Pap. London 46.402, Wünche. (The reference in Pap. Paris, Suppl. Gr. 574.2704 to wrapping an amulet in a *red* skin is here inapposite. It is to be explained by the fact that codices were commonly bound in red leather: see Catullus, xxxvii.6–7; T. Birt, Antikes Buchwesen [1882], 64 f.).

21. Folklore 9 (1898), 79; T. H. Gaster, The Holy and the Profane (1955), 13; A. E. Crawley, The Mystic Rose² (1927), i.333.

22. C. Lumholtz, Unknown Mexico (1902), ii.423.

23. Mrs. Wm. Hunt, in Folk-Lore 44 (1938), 194.

24. I Aqhat 204.

25. Crawley, op. cit., i.158.

26. Ib., ii.19.

27. R. Briffault, The Mothers (one-vol. ed., 1963), 248.

28. K. Latte, in ARW 26 (1928), 41 ff.

29. Satapatha Brahmana V.5.4, 1; cf. A. B. Keith, in JRAS 1938.603.

30. J. G. Frazer, GB, ed. min., 380.

31. Num. 19:2; cf. R. Patai, in JQR, N.S. 20 (1939), 59–70.

32. Num. 4.13.

33. E. A. W. Budge, Amulets and Superstitions (1930), 314.

34. Plutarch, Lyc. 27; Artemidorus, i.77; Aeschylus, Eumenides 1028. See fully: E. Rohde, Psyche⁷, ch. v, n.61.

35. Iliad xxiv.796.

36. G. Parrinder, La religion en Afrique centrale (1950), 134.

37. T. W. Thompson, in Journal of the Gipsy Lore Society, 3.1.

38. D. Seligmann, D. böse Blick (1910), 252–57.

39. Festus, s.v. *flammeum* = p. 89, ed. Mommsen.

40. Lev. 14:2 ff.

41. Pliny, HN xxxiii.11; Plutarch, Quaest. Rom. 98; Arnobius, Adversus nationes vi.10; Vergil, Ecl. vi.20; x.27; Tibullus, i.1, 17 (v. Kirby Smith in loc.). Cf. also: E. Nestle, in Philologus 50.501 ff.

▲   112   Jotham's parable

[1. Cf. M. Adinolfi, in Rivista Biblica Italiana 7 (1959), 322-42; H. Gunkel, Das Märchen im AT (1917), 16 ff.; W. Wienert, Die Typen der griechisch-röm. Fabel, FCC 56 (1925), 73–74; E. Ebeling, Die babylonische Fabel . . . , MVOG 2/iii (1927); id., in JCS 4 (1950), 215–22; R. J. Williams, "The Fable in the Ancient Near East," in A Stubborn Faith: W. A. Irwin Volume (1956), 3–26.]

[1a. KARI ##145, 324; cf. B. Meissner, Babylonien und Assyrien, ii (1925), 428 f.]

2. Fabulae Aesopicae #125, Hahn; Babrius, fab. 64.

3. Fab. Aesop. #385, Hahn.

4. A. S. Hunt, Oxyrinchus Papyri, vii (1910), 39 ff. [R. Pfeiffer, ed., Callimachi Fragmenta (1925), 51 ff.; H. Diels, "Orientalische Fabeln in griechischen Gewand," in Internat. Wochenschrift f. Wiss., 4 (1910), 995 ff.]

5. The Greek says, *"sings* of laurel," but the text is probably to be emended, as suggested by Diels. The prophetess chewed laurel as a mode of inspiration: Lucian, Bis accusatus 1; Tzetzes, Scholia on Lycophron 6; [Plutarch, E apud Delphos 2; id., De Pythiae oraculis 6; cf. A. Abt, Apologie des Apuleius (1908), 77 ff.].

6. An olive wreath was the prize at Olympia; a laurel wreath at Delphi.

7. An allusion to the contest of Athene and Poseidon for possession of Attica: [Herodotus, viii.55; Ovid, Met. vi.70 ff.; cf. J. G. Frazer, Apollodorus (1921), vol. ii, p. 78a].

8. The text is here fragmentary. The words in brackets are supplied by Diels. [8a. Aḥiqar xi.168 f.; tr. H. L. Ginsberg, ANET², 429.]

9. F. Macler, in JA, N.S. 19 (1902), 467 ff.

10. W. Skeat, Fables and Folktales from an Eastern Front (1901), 13–15.

11. L. Hervieux, Les fabulistes latines: Phèdre et ses anciens imitateurs (1884), ii.589 ff., 761.

12. Ib., 581 ff.

[12a. See fully: A. L. Oppenheim, in BASOR 107 (1947), 7–11.]

[12b. Pi-ankhi 53.]

[12c. This suggestion is made by Oppenheim, loc. cit.]

113 The navel of the earth

1. M. Eliade, Patterns in Comparative Religion (1958), 231 f., 374 ff.; id., The Eternal Return (1955), 12 ff.; W. M. Roscher, Omphalos (1913); id., Neue Omphalosstudien (1915); id., in Sitzb. Kön. Ges. d. Wiss. 80 (1918), 2 ff.; R. Meninger, in Wörter und Sachen 5 (1913), 43–91; 6 (1914) [critique of Roscher]; W. Gaerte, in Anthropos 5 (1916), 956–79; A. S. Pease, in UCILL 8 (1923), 535 (on Cicero, De Divinatione lxvi.15).

2. A. J. Wensinck, The Ideas of the Western Semites concerning the Navel of the Earth (1916); A. Jeremias, Handbuch d. altorientalischen Geisteskultur² (1936), 33 f.; T. H. Gaster, Thespis², 183.

3. E. Burrows, in The Labyrinth, ed. S. H. Hooke (1935), 45–70.

4. Ezek. 38:12; Enoch 26:1; Jubilees 8:2; Tertullian, Contra Marcionem ii.196; A. Jellinek, Beth ha-Midrash (1853–78), v.63; Ethiopic Synaxaria, in Dillman's Chrestomathia 16 [Calvary]. Cf. M. Grünbaum, in ZDMG 31 (1887), 199; J. Jeremias, in Ἄγγελος II (1926), ii.92 ff.

5. S. A. Cook, The Religion of Ancient Palestine in the Light of Archaeology (1925), 164.

6. M. Gaster, in ZAW 17 (1911), 448.

7. Pausanias, x.13, 7; Pindar, Pyth., iv.4; vi.3; Plutarch, Moralia 409E; Lucian, De saltatione 39, 147; Strabo, x.65. See: Robert-Preller, Griech. Mythologie⁴ (1894), 226; Jane Harrison, Themis² (1927), 396; A. B. Cook, Zeus ii (1925), 166–68; O. Gruppe, Gr. Mythol. (1906), 723, n.2.

8. Ibn Haukal, Oriental Geography, ed. Ouseley (1800), 2.

9. W. Kirfel, Die Kosmographie der Inder (1920), 18.

10. Kalingabodhi Jataka, #479; H. T. Francis and E. J. Thomas, Jataka Tales (Jaico paperback, 1957), 317.

11. P. Saintyves, Corpus de folklore préhistorique en France, ii (1936), 327.

12. P. Schebesta, Les Pygmées (1940), 156.

13. Gaerte, op. cit.; Eliade, Patterns, loc. cit.

114 Sowing a city with salt

1. Sujin (Sefiré) Inscription, 17; tr. F. Rosenthal, ANET², 504.

2. Annals vi.79 = Luckenbill, ARAB ii. §811.

3. Encyclopaedia Biblica, s.v. Salt.

4. F. C. Fensham, in The Biblical Archaeologist 25 (1962), 48–50.

5. KBo VI.34, ii.15 ff.; tr. A. Goetze, ANET 353.

6. W. R. Smith, The Religion of the Semites² (1894), 454, n.1.

7. Cf. EBib., s.v. Ban; F. Schwally, Semitische Kriegsaltertümer, i (1901), 37.

8. Cf. Lev. 2:13 (see: Dillmann, in loc.); Ezek. 43:24. So too among the Greeks and Romans: Theocritus, Id. xxiv.97; Tibullus iii.4, 10; J. G. Frazer, The Fasti of Ovid (1925), ii.142 f., 283; Arnobius, Adv. nationes ii.67. See also: Grimm-Stallybrass, TM 1047.

9. S. Gevirtz, in VT 13 (1963), 56–62.

10. A. M. Honeyman, in VT 3 (1953), 192–95; A. Jirku, Materialen zum Volksreligion Israels (1914), 13 ff.

11. Trans. A. Goetze, ANET 126; cf. T. H. Gaster, Thespis[2], 261.

12. B. Hrozný, in AOr 1 (1929), 273 ff.; tr. J. Friedrich, AO 24/ii.6.—The operative word is Akkadian *siḫlu;* Aramaic *šeḥalîn;* Hittite *zaḫliya(s)*; see on this: J. Friedrich and B. Landsberger, in ZA, N.F.7 (1931), 313 f.

13. Cf. Gen. 19:24; Ezek.: 38:22; Ps. 11:8. Note, however, that in Theocritus, Id. xxiv.97 brimstone is mentioned along with salt as a purifying agent.—Tiglath-Pileser (Pr. vi.14) says that he strewed "*ṣipu-*stones" over a conquered city, but what this means is uncertain.

14. M. Jastrow, Religion Babyloniens und Assyriens (1905–12), ii.716.

15. E. P. Deatrick, in The Biblical Archaeologist 25 (1962), 41–47.

115　Jephthah's vow

(a)

1. See: Stith Thompson, MI, S 241; W. Baumgartner, in ARW 18.240 ff.; E. Oca, in RBCalz. 26 (1965), 167–71; Th. Barbes, in ThT. 1909.137–43; Feilberg, Bidrag til en Ordbeg over Jyske Almusmal (1886–1914), i.404; ii.647a; Andrejev, in FCC 69.58, 62, 225n.; M. Cox, Cinderella (1893), 511.

2. Servius, on Vergil, Aen. iii.121 f.; xi.264; First and Second Vatican Mythographers, in Scriptores rerum mythicarum Latini, ed. G. H. Bode (1834), i.195, 210.—The story is here combined, as in the Swedish version (see n.11), with the familiar motif that an embroiled sea must be appeased by a human sacrifice; on this, see below, §236 (Jonah).

3. Plutarch, De fluviis ix.1.

4. Grimm's Tales, #88.

5. E. Cosquin, Contes populaires de Lorraine (n.d.), ii.215–17.

6. C. and Th. Colshorn, Märchen und Sagen (1854), #20. Cf. also: P. Zaunert, Deutsche Märchen seit Grimm (1919), 303 ff.

7. K. Müllenhoff, Sagen Märchen und Lieder der Herzogthümer Schleswig-Hollstein und Lauenberg (1843), 285–88.

8. Ch. Schneller, Märchen und Sagen aus Wälschtirol (1867), #25.

9. A. Leskien and K. Brugmann, Litauische Volkslieder und Märchen (1882), #23.

10. Bolte-Polivika, i (1913), 16 ff.

11. B. Thorpe, Yule-Tide Stories (1853), 44 f.

12. Svend-Grundtvig (tr. Mulley), Fairy Tales from Afar (1900), 166.

13. C. J. Lyall, Ancient Arabian Poetry (reprint, 1930), p. xxviii.

(b)

14. The traditional Hebrew text reads, "and go down" (*we-yaradtî*); the correction (*we-radtî*) is due to Robertson Smith. It may be added that the emended reading corresponds to the term employed in mythological accounts of the search for the vanished deity, viz., Bion, Epitaphion Adônidos 18: *alalêtai;* Homeric Hymn to Demeter, 43: *strôphat'*. Note also the use of the same word in this connection in a Babylonian commentary on the rites of the Akitu festival, VAT 9555. 29 *ši-i ta-ta-rad* (cuneiform text: *ta-da-ra;* correxit Langdon).

15. T. H. Gaster, Thespis[2], 30 ff.

16. J. G. Frazer, GB vii (Spirits of the Corn and Wild), ch. vii; A. Moret, in An-

nuaire de l'hist., de phil., et d'hist. orientales 3 (1935), 311 ff.; H. Hepding, Attis (1903), 128, 186. For the weeping in the Babylonian Akitu rites, cf. VAT 9555.29.

17. CT XV, Pl. 48.

18. G. Reisner, Sumerisch-babyl. Hymnen aus Tontafeln Griechischer Zeit (1896), 145, iii. 12–15.

19. ZA 6 (1891), 243. 34.

20. S. Langdon, Babylonian Menologies and the Semitic Calendars (1935), 120 f.

21. R. Labat, in RA 38 (1941), 28.

22. Cf. Proclus, on Plato, Rep. i.215 Kroll; Marius, Vita Procli, c.33 Boissonade.

23. D. Chwolson, Die Sabier (1856), ii.27.

24. O. R. Gurney, in JSS 7 (1962), 147–60; E. M. Yamauchi, in JBL 84 (1965), 283–90.

25. Diodorus Siculus, i.14.

26. Herodotus, ii.79; cf. Julius Pollux, iv.54; Pausanias, ix.29, 7; Athenaeus, 620A.

27. H. Brugsch, Die Adonisklage und das Linoslied (1852), 24; A. Wiedemann, Herodots zweites Buch (1890), 24–26.

28. J. de Hoorack, Les lamentations d'Isis et de Nephthys (1866); E. A. W. Budge, Osiris and the Egyptian Resurrection (1911), ii.59–66; A. Moret, Mystères égyptiennes (1913), 24–26.

29. De errore prof. relig., ii.7 (addressed to the Egyptians); cf. also: Diod. Sic. i.14, 2; A. Moret, La mise à mort du dieu en Égypte (1927), 19 ff.

30. A. L. Oppenheim, in BASOR 103 (1946), 11–14.—For a similar custom in modern Palestine, see: G. Dalman, Arbeit und Sitte in Palästina, i (1928), 566.

31. Plutarch, Theseus 22 (reading *spendontes*, with Cornford, for the *speudontes* of the MSS.).

32. Semus, quoted by Athenaeus, iv.618 f.; cf. E. Spanheim, In Callimachi hymnos Observationes (1697), 649.

33. E. Rohde, Psyche² (1897), 289.

34. D. Diringer, Le iscrizioni anticho-ebraiche palestinesi (1934), 1–20; tr. W. F. Albright, ANET 320.

35. A. Jeremias, The Old Testament in the Light of the Ancient East, tr. Beaumont (1911), ii.168.

36. H. Hepding, Attis (1903), 151 ff.

116 Shibboleth

1. See: Notes and Queries 10/x (1908), 408; 10/xi (1909), 36, 233.

2. E. C. Brewer, Dictionary of Miracles, 228.

3. C. L. Kingsford, ed., Chronicles of London (1827), 15.

4. A. M. Kramer, in Notes and Queries, 10/xi (1909), 36.

117 Samson

(a) Samson as a solar hero

1. Cf. I. Goldziher, Hebrew Mythology, tr. R. Martineau (1877), 392–446; E. Stucken, Astralmythen (1907), i.70–75; H. Steinthal, in Zs. für Völkerpsychologie und Sprachwissenschaft 2 (1862); H. Stahn, Die Simsonsage (1908); A. Smythe Palmer, The Samson-saga and Its Place in Comparative Religion (1913); P. Carus, The Story of Samson (1907); S. Reinach, Samson. Bibl. de vulgaris. du Musée Guimet (1912); H. Gunkel, in Internat. Monatsschrift für Wiss., Kunst und Technik, 1913.875–94. Even W. F. Albright once leaned to this view (JBL 37 [1919], 130), but he subsequently modified it (JPOS 1 [1922], 51, n.2).—A. Lods, in Actes du congrès internat. d'histoire des religions, 1923.504–16, and again in Israel (1930), 406, while conceding that Samson was originally a solar hero, thinks that the story was of pre-Israelitic

Horite provenience. Manoah, the father of Samson (a name which does not recur in the O.T.) is, he claims, simply the eponymous hero of the Horite clan of Manaḥat (possibly modern el-Menaḥ, near 'Ain Šams) mentioned in Gen. 36:23, and Samson himself a doublet of Sheshai, the pre-Israelitic giant of Hebron (Num. 13:22; Jos. 15:14). The connection of Manoah with Manaḥat was previously adumbrated by Robertson Smith in EBib., s.v. Samson.

2. Zorah (modern Sara'a), the hometown of Samson's father, Eshtaol (modern Eshwa), Timnah (mod. Tibneh), where Samson took a Philistine bride, and the Valley of Sorek (mod. Wadi Sarar), where Delilah lived, all lie within a five-mile range of Beth Shemesh (mod. Tell Rumeileh).

3. Cf. Greek komē; Latin coma, both "tress" and "ray."

4. Stith Thompson, MI, K 976.

5. Babylonian Shamshanu, BEUP ix.7, 20; Ugaritic Špšyn, RS 80.i.20; 321.ii.25; Špš (a man's name), RS 80.i.11; 321.iv.6. Cf. also Babylonian Shimshai (S. Daiches, in OLz 11.277) and Biblical Shimshai (Ezra 4:8).

(b) Samson and the foxes

6. Ovid, Fasti iv.680 ff.

7. Babrius, fab.i.11.

8. I. Goldziher, Muhammedanische Studien (1889–90), i.35; J. Wellhausen, Reste d. arabischen Heidentums[2] (1897), 167.

9. O. Preller, Röm. Mythologie[3] (1875), ii.43 f.; F. Baethgen, Beiträge zur sem. Religionsgeschichte (1888), 170 f.

10. J. W. Wolf, Beiträge zur deutschen Mythologie (1852–57), ii.388; Subsidia i (1873), 269.

11. R. Hartmann, in ZAW 31 (1911), 69–72.

12. Livy, xxii.16 f. This, however, may have been simply part of a "scorched earth" policy, such as the forces of Julian later (A.D. 323) employed against the Persians: Ammianus Marcellinus, xviii.7.

13. Maqrizi, tr. Quatremière (1837–45), I.i.179; Sihab ad-Din ibn Faḍallah al'-'Omari, Al-ta'rif bil-muṣtlaḥ aš-Šarif (Cairo 1894), 201 f.

14. John Schiltberger, ed. Neumann, 78, as quoted by Hartmann, loc. cit.

15. M. Magnusson and H. Palsson, King Harald's Saga (1966), 52 f.

(c) Samson's riddle

16. H. Bauer, in ZDMG.1912.473 f.; see also: J. R. Porter, in JTS 13 (1962), 106–9.

17. Cf. the mythological beasts called "eaters" (aklm) in the Ugaritic Hunting of Baal (75 Gordon, i.26, 36), and the Arabic 'akīl, "eater," as an epithet of the lion: Freytag, Lex. Arab., s.v.

▲ **(d) Samson and Delilah**

18. Frazer-Gaster, NGB §§26, 500–02; Schredelseker, De superstitionibus Graecorum quare ad crines pertinent (Diss. Heidelberg 1913); L. Sommer, Das Haar im Religion und Aberglauben der Griechen (Diss. Munich 1912); O. Waser, in ARW 16 (1913), 381 ff.; H. Günthert, in Sitzb. Heidelb. Akad. Wiss., 1915.11 f.; O. Gruppe, Griech. Mythologie (1906), 187, n.2; 882, nn.2 ff.; S. Reinach, Samson (1912), 23 f.; G. A. Wilken, Verspreide Geschriften (1912), iii.551 ff.; W. R. Smith, The Religion of the Semites[3] (1927), 342, n.2; HWbDA, iii.1258; Stith Thompson, MI, D 1831; J. Morgenstern, Rites of Birth, Marriage, Death and Kindred Occasions among the Semites (1966), 84 ff.; W. Abt, Apologie des Apuleius (1908), 179 ff.—Sommer, op. cit., thinks that this belief underlies the Homeric references to swearing by the beard (Iliad 2.501 ff.; 8.371; 10.454).—In Jewish legend, the strength of Judah is said to have resided in his hair: L. Ginzberg, Legends of the Jews, v.277, 354.

19. F. Valentyn, Oud en Nieuw Oost-Indien (1724–26), ii.143 ff.—Several of the folklore parallels here cited were first adduced by G. A. Wilken in his essay, "De Simsonsage," reprinted in his De Verspreide Geschriften (1912), iii.551–79.

20. J. G. F. Riedel, De sluik- en kreishaarige rassen tusschen Selebes en Papua (1886), 137.

21. J. G. Dalzyell, The Darker Superstitions of Scotland (1834), 637–39.

22. W. Crooke, Popular Religion and Folk-Lore of Northern India (1896), ii.281.

23. Ib.

24. B. de Sahagun, Histoire des choses de la Nouvelle Espagne, tr. D. Jourdanet and R. Simeon (1880), 374.

[24a. KAR II.80.32 (= Ebeling, Quellen, i [1918], 29, 32): *šarta imlušu.*]

[24b. See above, §109.]

[24c. Zs. für Mythologie 2.336; 4.299; Notes and Queries 1/vi (1852), 312; II.xii (1861), 500; VI/vi (1882), 249, 416.]

[24d. E. M. Fogel, Beliefs and Superstitions of the Pennsylvania Germans (1915), #1831.]

[24e. See below, §164.]

[24f. Sozomen, v. 10, 7; E. Samter, Familienfeste der Griecher und Römer (1901), 64 ff.; A. B. Cook, Zeus i (1923), 68.]

[24g. E.g., in the steppes of Russia: R. Chambers, The Book of Days (1880), i.721; in Prussia: F. Nork, Die Sitte und Gebräuche d. Deutscher, etc. Das Kloster, xii (1849), 163; at Trapani, Sicily: H. N. Hutchinson, Marriage Customs (1879), 275; in Japan: Notes and Queries III/ii (1862), 67; among the Kaffirs of Natal: J. Shooter, The Kaffirs of Natal (1857), 75; among Jews: T. H. Gaster, The Holy and the Profane, 106 f.]

[24h. J. Grimm, Deutsche Rechtsaltertümer[3] (1881), ii.287; H. Vordemfelds, Die germ. Religion in der deutschen Volksrechten, RVV 18/i (1923), i.113 ff.; K. Müllenhoff, Deutsche Altertumskunde, iv (1920), 309 f.—During the Hitler regime in Germany, the Nazis cut off the hair of "Aryan" women who engaged in liaisons with Jews. —The custom was known also to the Slavs: F. S. Krauss, Sitte und Brauch der Südslaven (1885), 192 f.]

[24i. A. Poebel, Legal and Business Documents from the Time of the First Dynasty of Babylon (1909), No. 48.14–16; I. Goldziher, Muhamm. Studien (189–90), i.85; J. L. Burckhardt, Travels in Nubia (1819), 146: A. Büchler, in WZKM 18.91–138.]

[24j. See below, §139.]

[24k. Morgenstern, op. cit., 238 f.; cf. Isa. 7:20.]

[24l. J. O. Dorsey, in MAFLS 8.113, No. 31.]

[24m. E. C. Brewer, Dictionary of Phrase and Fable, s.v. Adoption by hair.]

25. J T. Nieuwenhuisen and H. C. B. Rosenberg, in Verhandl. van het Batav. Genootschap van Kunsten en Wetenschappen, 30 (1863), 110 ff.; cf. H. Sundermann, Die Insel Nias (1905), 71.

26. Apollodorus, Bib. iii.15, 8; Aeschylus, Choephoroe 612 ff.; Pausanias, i.19, 4; Ciris 116 ff.; Ovid, Met. viii.8 ff.

27. Tzetzes, Scholia on Lycophron, 650.

28. Apollodorus, Bib. ii.4, 5 and 7.

29. J. G. von Hahn, Griechische und Albanesische Märchen (1864), i.217; a similar story, ib., ii.282.

30. B. Schmidt, Griechische Märchen (1877), 91 f. The same writer found in the island of Zacynthus [Zante] a belief that the whole strength of the ancient Greeks resided in three hairs on their chests, and that it vanished whenever those hairs were cut, but returned if they were allowed to grow again: see: B. Schmidt, Das Volksleben der Neugriechen (1871), 206. [A variant in a Greek folksong relates that once, during

the Turkish domination, an agha managed to overcome a Greek hero in combat but could not kill him until an obliging stork fortuitously plucked out some of his hair: Lucy Garnett, Greek Folk Poesy (1896), ii.175.]

[30a. Robert Graves, The Greek Myths (1955), i.310.]

[30b. H. van d. Leyen, Deutsches Sagenbuch (1920), i.26 f. Like the story of Samson and Delilah, this too is often interpreted as a solar myth.]

[30c. W. Henning, The Thousand and One Nights, xii.67.]

[30d. R. Menzel, Bilur Köschk (1923), 16.]

31. A. Dietrich, Russian Popular Tales (1857), 21–24.

32. C. Mijatovich, Serbian Folk-Lore, ed. W. Denton (1874), 167–72; F. S. Krauss, Sagen und Märchen der Südslaven (1883–84), i.164–69.

33. A. H. Wratislaw, Sixty Folk-tales from Exclusively Slavonic Sources (1889), 224–31.

34. J. F. Campbell, Popular Tales of the West Highlands[2] (1890), i.7–11.

35. D. MacInnes, Folk and Hero Tales (1890), 103–21.

118 The woman divided into twelve parts

1. KUB IX.4, i.3 ff., 22 ff.; iii.33 ff.; IX.34, ii.23 ff., 38 ff.; cf. T. H. Gaster, Thespis[2], 307 f.

2. KUB IX.4 and 34 (duplicates); cf. A. Goetze, The Hittite Ritual of Tunnawi (1933), 42 ff.—For analogous magical practices based on the assumed number of the bodily parts, see: F. Boll, Sphaera (1903), 471 ff.; S. Eitrem, Papyri Osloenes, i (1925), 41 ff.

3. KUB XXX.15, i.11.—Curiously enough, a Christian epitaph of the early 5th cent., discovered at Tanagra, in Boeotia, calls for the regular offering to the dead of *"twelve round loaves and goodly wines"*; cf. H. Musarillo, in Theological Studies 11 (1950), 567–69; id., The Fathers of the Primitive Church (1966), 264.—In SMSR 23 (1952), 19, I have suggested that the sacrifice of the *twelve* Trojans at the funeral of Patroclus (Iliad 23.175 f.) was simply a cruel variation on such twelvefold funeral offerings. It is noteworthy that Homer shows the same distaste for this gruesome story (ib., 176) as does our Biblical writer for the ancient Hebrew tale (cf. Judg. 19:30)!

4. Ib., i. 23–24.

5. KUB IX.32; tr. J. Friedrich, AO 24/iv.12.

6. KUB IV.12; tr. Friedrich, ib., 14.

7. Homeric Hymn to Hermes, 128. Twelvefold sacrifices among the Greeks are mentioned also by Eustathius on Iliad 6.93; cf. also: Sophocles, Trachiniae 760 f.

119 The rape of the women of Shiloh

1. E. W. Lane, Manners and Customs of the Modern Egyptians (Minerva Library ed., 1890), 396.

2. Livy, i.9; Plutarch, Romulus 14; Ovid, Fasti ii.139 ff.

3. This account is taken from J. G. Frazer, The Fasti of Ovid (1929), ii.311.

4. Pausanias, iv.4, 2; iv.16, 9; iv.31, 3; Strabo, viii.4, 9.

5. L. R. Farnell, Cults of the Greek States (1896–1909), ii.124; cf. also: Roscher's Lexicon d. Griech. Mythologie, ii.1313.

6. E.g., Euripides, Ion 857; Helen 242–48; Hypsipyle, fr. 734; Plutarch, Ait. phys. 217F.

7. Allen-Sikes-Halliday, The Homeric Hymns[2] (1936), 128 f.

8. Hesychius, Photius, Lexx., s.v. μασχαλισμος.

9. Cf. T. H. Gaster, Thespis[2] (1961), 41.

10. Frazer-Gaster, NGB §§118–21, and Additional Notes thereto.

11. Ovid, Fasti iii.523 f. (v. Frazer, in loc.); W. Ward Fowler, The Roman Festivals of the Period of the Republic (1899), 50–54.

12. H. H. Bancroft, Native Races of the Pacific States (1856–76), ii.719 f., iii.507.

13. W. W. Mannhardt, Mythologische Forschungen (1884), 341.

14. R. Gallop, Portugal (1936), 11. For analogous customs in England, see: Brand-Ellis, Popular Antiquities of Great Britain (1882–83), i.181. So too in Germany: Mannhardt, op. cit., 340; T. Siebs, in Zs. für Volkskunde 3 (1893), 277.

15. G. A. Wilken, in De Indische Gido, June 1884, p. 958.

16. J. G. Frazer, GB ii.100.

17. P. Brincker, in Mitt. f. orient. Sprachen zu Berlin, 3 (1900), 2.

18. H. Fehlinger, Sexual Life of Primitive Peoples (1921), 23.

19. A. Playfair, The Garos (1909), 68.

20. T. H. Gaster, Thespis², 78 f., 413 ff.; see below, §176.

21. E. Westermarck, A Short History of Human Marriage (1926), 28.

22. Mishnah, Taᶜanith iv.8.

23. W. C. Hazlitt, Dictionary of Faith and Folklore (1905), 193.

24. Howes, in Folk-Lore 40 (1929), 56 f.

25. L. Spence, in ERE iii.67ᵃ.

26. Gaster, op. cit., 41 f.

27. Lorenz, in ARW 17 (1915), 342.

28. A. R. Wright, English Folklore (1928), 43.

29. For a different explanation, see: L. Spence, Myth and Ritual in Dance, Games and Rhyme (1947), 42 f.

RUTH

121 Covering with a garment in token of protection

1. G. W. Freytag, Einleitung in d. Stud. d. arab. Sprache (1861), 223; G. A. Wilken, Das Matriarchat bei den alten Araben (1864), 69; G. Jacob, Das Leben der vorislamischen Beduinen (1895), 58 f.; id., Altarabische Parallelen zum AT (1897), 27 f.—A paper on this usage (ḥillat) was read by F. W. Buckler before the Twentieth International Congress of Orientalists at Brussels in 1928, but I have been unable to trace publication of it.

2. Ibn Hisham, ed. Wüstenfeld, 763.

3. J. L. Burckhardt, Bedouins and Wahabys (1830), 213.

4. H. N. Hutchinson, Marriage Customs of Many Lands (1897), 199.

5. Zs.f. Vk. 20 (1910), 146.

6. Odes of Solomon 28:5. J. Rendell Harris renders the crucial phrase, "I have been set on his immortal pinions," but I think the Syriac word k-n-ph-â here has the meaning "skirt" rather than "pinion." Cf. also Gesenius, Thesaurus, s.v. k-n-f.

7. Ducange, iii.114c, s.v. pallio cooperire. Hommel, Jurisprudentia numismatibus illustrata (1763), 214–18; J. Grimm, Deutsche Rechtsaltertümer³ (1881), i.220; F. Nork, Die Sitten und Gebräuche der Deutschen. Das Kloster xii (1849), 161.—There is an interesting reference to this custom in a letter (Ep. 13) of Robert Grosseteste, the great bishop of Lincoln, to William de Raleigh, bishop of Winchester.* Raleigh replies that he has verified this usage in English law on the authority of Richard de Luce, a jurist of the time of Henry III. John Selden, in his Table Talk, also alludes to it.

8. Notes and Queries, I/vii (1853), 17, 243 f.; A. L. Gilchrist, in Folk-Lore 49 (1938), 192 f.

9. T. H. Gaster, Customs and Folkways of Jewish Life (1965), 132 f.

---

* Du Cange says strangely, Walter Raleigh, who lived some three centuries later and whose connection with cloaks was, as we know, something else again!

122　Gestures of adoption

1. F. Liebrecht, Zur Volkskunde (1879), 439.

2. L. Kohler, in ZAW 29 (1909), 312–14; Zs. f. Vk. 20 (1910), 140 ff.; J. Grimm, Deutsche Rechtsaltertümer³ (1881), i.219, 638.

3. I.e., for *'aSaPPeRaH 'eL HôQ*, read *'ôSîPHeKaH 'eL HeQî*. The emendation is due to H. Torczyner (Tur Sinai); see also: H. Ringgren, in ZAW 64 (1952), 123. Note that the Hebrew word *'-s-ph*, which is thus restored to the text, is indeed the technical term for adoption: cf. Ps. 27:10 and post-Biblical usage.

4. B. Landsberger, *Ana ittišu* (1937), 51–57.

123　Removing the shoe

1. Cf. Deut. 25:9; see: L. Dürr, in OLz 41 (1938), 410–12.

2. R. Burton, Land of Midian (1857), ii.197; I. Goldziher, Abh. arab. Philologie (1896–99), i.47; W. R. Smith, Kinship and Marriage in Early Arabia (1885), 269.

3. J. L. Burckhardt, Bedouins and Wahabys (1830), i.113.

4. HSS V.17, 76; tr. E. Speiser, AASOR 10 (1930), 63–64, 66. See also: E. A. Speiser, in BASOR 77 (1940), 15 ff.

5. I.e., for the traditional text, which reads *We'aeLîM eêNi Bô*, "(From whose hand have I ever taken a bribe) to blind my eyes therewith?" the Greek Version presupposes, by a change of but a single letter, *WeNa'Laim 'āNū Bî*, "Or a pair of shoes? Testify against me!"

6. E. R. Lacheman, in JBL 56 (1937), 53–56.

7. II Aqhat vi.44–45.

8. Aztwd Inscription from Karatepe; tr. F. Rosenthal, ANET², 499 f.

9. J. G. Wilkinson, The Ancient Egyptians (1878), ii.337.

10. Enuma Elish iv.104, 118; tr. E. A. Speiser, ANET 67.

11. Vergil, Aen. vii.99 f.; Livy, xxxiv.22. Cf. also *pedem opponere;* Ovid, Pont. iv.6–7.

12. Cf. J. D. Eisenstein, JE, s.v. Halizah.

13. L. Lewy, in MGWJ 62 (1918), 178–85.—For other Jewish interpretations of the custom, see: M. Guttmann, in Wissensch. Zeitschr. für jüd. Theologie 4 (1839), 61–87; A. Büchler, in ZAW 21 (1901), 81–92; J. Nact, in JQR 6 (1915), 1–22.

14. F. Thiselton Dyer, Domestic Folklore (n.d.), 92.—For a similar usage in Germany, see HwBDA, i.1405.

S A M U E L

124　Falling to the ground

1. H. Spencer, Principles of Sociology (1897), i.318; E. Rohde, Psyche⁷ (1921), 245, n.1.

2. Diogenes Laertius, viii.34.

3. Jamblichus, Vita Pythag. 126.

4. Pliny, HN xxviii.27.

5. C. Hatknoch, Alt und neues Preussen (1684), 188.

6. Aristophanes, frag. 291, Dindorf (= Athenaeus, 427E).

7. A. Wuttke, Der deutsche Aberglaube der Gegenwart³ (1900), §458.

8. Pliny, HN xxviii.6.

9. Orphica, Lithica 383.

10. S. Eitrem, Papyri Osloenses i (1925), 114 f.

11. Eitrem, op. cit., Text 1.313.

125 Of mice and men

1. Callimachus, Hymns iii.251–58.
2. Lex., s.v. *Skythôn erêmia*. The expression is echoed in Aeschylus, Prometheus Vinctus 1–2.
3. O. Gruppe, Griech. Mythologie (1906), 1269 ff.
4. Herodotus, i.105 f.
5. Ammianus Marcellinus xxiii.6, 24; cf. B. Gildersleeve, in AJP 29 (1908), 97 f.; P. Svoronos, in Journ. internat. d'archéologie num. 13 (1911), 115 f.
6. De bello Troiano i.19.
7. For examples, see: J. V. Grohmann, Apollo Smintheus und die Bedeutung der Mäuse in der Mythologie der Indogermanen (1862), 28 f.; HWbDA vi.43.
8. Strabo, iii.4, 18.
9. A. Wuttke, Der deutsche Volksaberglaube der Gegenwart[2] (1925), 201.
10. Grohmann, loc. cit.
11. II Kings 19:35.
12. Herodotus, ii.141; see: A. Godley, in CR 15 (1901), 194 ff.; J. H. Moulton, ib., 281 f.; J. Oestrup, in Noeldeke Festschrift (1906), ii.86 ff.; D. M. Robinson, in AJP 29 (1908), 97, n.1.
13. Cf. Strabo, xiii. §604.—For a Chinese parallel, cf. F. Liebrecht, Zur Volkskunde (1879), 13.
14. CR 15 (1901), 319 f.
15. J. U. Powell, "Rodent Gods in Ancient and Modern Times," in Folk-Lore 40 (1929), 173 ff.
16. F. G. Welcker, Kleinere Schriften (1844–67), iii.33–45.
17. Iliad 1.39 ff.
18. Odyssey 7.64.
19. Odyssey 17.251.
20. Ib., 494.
21. Iliad 1.10; Lycophron, 1205; Apollodorus, Bib. ii.103; Macrobius, Sat. i.17, 9; Gruppe, op. cit., 1238 f.
22. Macrobius, Sat. i.17, 24.
23. CIS I.110 (341 BC); G. A. Cooke, A Text-Book of North Semitic Inscriptions (1903), 55 f.
24. F. Clermont-Ganneau, Récueil d'archéologie orientale (1888–1907), i.176 ff.
25. At Elis: Pausanias, vi.24, 6; cf. Euripides, Andromache 880.
26. Aristophanes, Birds 584; Gruppe, op. cit., 1238, n.4.
27. Grohmann, op. cit.; Gruppe, op. cit., 1229, n.2; A. Lang, Custom and Myth[2] (1885), 103–20 [superficial]; J. G. Frazer, GB viii.282 f.; A. H. Krappe, in ARW 33 (1936), 40–46; id., in Class. Phil. 36 (1941), 133–41.
28. Scholiast, on Lycophron 1303; Schol., on Iliad 1.39 (ed min., Heyne [1834] i.12).
29. Aelian, Hist. animal. xii.5.
30. Strabo, xiii.1, 45. Menandros, *Peri epideiktiôn*, in Rhetores Graeci, ed. Spengel (1856), iii.445 f., identifies Apollo with Horus. It is therefore not without interest that porcelain images of mice dedicated to Horus have been found in Egypt: Lang, op. cit., 113.
31. In Amos 9:7 they are said to have come from Caphtor, usually identified with Crete. On this identification, see: T. H. Gaster, Thespis[2], 163. Cf. also Deut. 2:3.
32. Polemo, quoted by Scholiast on Iliad 1.39; cf. Gruppe, op. cit., 1229.—The Chams of Indo-China have a rude idol called Good Rat whom they propitiate when rats infest fields excessively: E. Aumonier, in BPHR 24 (1891), 236; J. G. Frazer, GB viii.283.

33. Pausanias, iii.20, 9.
34. So S. Wide, Lakonishe Kulte (1893), 118; A. H. Krappe, in Class. Phil. 39 (1944), 178–93.
35. Pseudo-Aristotle, Mirab. auscult. 125 (137); cf. Wide, op. cit., 119.
36. F. Panzer, Bayerische Sagen und Gebräuche (1848–56), ii.157.
37. C. L. Rochholz, Deutsche Glaube (1897), i.158.—In a painting at Strasbourg Cathedral, for instance, she is portrayed surrounded by mice; while on a metal collar preserved in the Collegiate Church at Nivelles, Belgium, she has a mouse on the hem of her garment: Powell, op. cit., 177; Krappe, in Class. Phil. 36 (1944), 138. It should be observed, however, that "in medieval tradition the souls of the departed were believed to spend the first night in the Great Beyond with St. Gertrude" (Krappe, loc. cit.; Grohmann, op. cit., 34, 38), and souls were commonly assumed to take the form of mice: H. Pfannenschmid, Germ. Erntefeste (1878), 163, 433; J. Wellhausen, Reste d. arab. Heidentums[2] (1897), 152; Matthew of Paris, quoted by M. Cox, Introduction to Folklore[2] (1897), 43. This, therefore, may be what is intended. But even so, this may be simply a Christian interpretation of the mouse's association with the older plague-goddess who had been transmogrified into St. Gertrude. We know, in fact, that in pre-Christian times the cult of a Teutonic goddess of death, variously named Nehalennia or Hludana, flourished in Belgium, and it has long been suspected that St. Gertrude is but her Christian successor: Krappe, loc. cit.; H. Güntert, Kalypso (1919), 62.

126 Death for looking into the Ark of the Lord

1. For 5000 as a round number, cf. Judg. 8:10; 20:45; I Sam. 17:5.
2. RSV omits the "five thousand."

127 Qualifications for Kingship

1. II Sam. 14:25; see: R. Patai, in HUCA 20 (1947), 155 ff.
2. Enuma Elish i.99.
3. Herodotus, vii.187.
4. Athenaeus, xiii.20.
5. II AB, i.59–60; cf. T. H. Gaster, Thespis[2], 218 f.
6. D. R. Mackenzie, The Spirit-ridden Konde (1925), 72 f.
7. S. S. Doran, in South African Journal of Science 15 (1918), 397.
8. II Kings 15:5.
9. Krt C, vi.44 f.; tr. H. L. Ginsberg, ANET 148[a].
10. Frazer-Gaster, NGB §190.

128 Eyes brightened by eating honey

1. B. F. Beck, Honey and Health (1938), 86.
2. Aristotle, De animal. hist. ix.40, 21; Probl. ined. i.2.
3. Dioscorides, ii.
4. Galen, xi.34, xii.70; xiii.731, etc.—A recipe inscribed on a marble tablet (after A.D. 138) probably from the temple of Asclepius on an isle in the Tiber, prescribes honey for sick eyes: Dittenberger, Sylloge[2], 807.15 ff.; A. Deissmann, Light from the Ancient East[2] (1911), 132.
5. Pliny, HN xi.37, 38; xxix.128.
6. Celsus, vi. 34.
7. Beck, op. cit., 88.
8. Ib., 118.
9. E. N. Fallaize, in ERE vi.770; Stith Thompson, MI, D 1338.9.
10. Beck, op. cit., 223 f.; W. R. Smith, in Journal of Philology 14.125; J. Wellhausen,

Reste d. arab. Heidentums[2] (1897), 173; J. Morgenstern, Rites of Birth, Marriage, Death and Kindred Occasions among the Semites (1966), 34–35. Photographs of the ceremony appeared in Life magazine, July 12, 1954, p. 52.

11. Vergil, Georgica iv.451.
12. Ap. Rhodius, Argon. iv.1136.
13. Cf. J. A. Fabricius, Codex pseudepigraphus Veteris Testamenti (1722), 780–81.
14. Kalevala, runo xv.385 ff.; tr. Kirby (Everyman's Library ed.), i.159 f.
15. Headlam-Knox, Herodas (1922), 271.
16. KB vi/2, 48.21.
17. Translated in ANET 328. The charm dates from the 13th cent. B.C.

129 Agag

(a) Agag walks "delicately"

1. The traditional Hebrew text reads, *Surely the bitterness of death is past,* but the Hebrew word *sar,* rendered *is past,* is probably a mere variant of the following *mar,* which means *is bitter,* rather than *bitterness of.* The Greek (Septuagint) Version so reads the phrase.

2. The word is $m^c dn\hat{\imath}t$, which KJV and RV (after Symmachus and the Aramaic Targum) vocalize $ma^{ca}dan\hat{\imath}t$ and derive from ^{c}-d-n, "be delicate." But it should really be read $m^{ec}\hat{o}dan\hat{\imath}t$, from m-^{c}-d, "totter, stagger," as both the Greek Septuagint and the Latin Vulgate recognized.

3. See: A. J. Wensinck, Some Semitic Rites of Mourning and Religion (1917), 43; H. Jahnow, Das hebräische Leichenlied (1923), 75, n.6.

4. E. Roger, La terre saincte (1664), 265.

5. Minerva Library ed. (London 1890), 488.

6. J. Wetzstein, in Zs. für Ethnologie 5 (1873), 296 ff.

7. Jahnow, loc. cit.; Wensinck, loc. cit.; S. A. Cook, in Essays and Studies presented to Wm. Ridgeway, ed. E. C. Quiggin (1913), 397 ff.

8. BM 83–1–18, 1846, rev. i.6–7 T. G. Pinches, in PSBA 18 (1896), 253. The Sumerian equivalent is LÚ. TU. IGI. GUGU(?), which Pinches interprets as "one who weeps with troubled eye."

9. III Aqhat 189 (reading: *ltm mrqdm*); see: T. H. Gaster, Thespis[2], 370 f.

10. Lam. 2:21.

(b) Agag is hewn asunder

11. Abu ᶜObaida, Ham, 458; Reiske, An. Musl. i.26 ff., of the notes; Lisan al-ᶜarab x.240; cf. W. Robertson Smith, The Religion of the Semites[3] (1927), 491 f.; J. Wellhausen, Reste d. arab. Heidentums[2] (1887), 112.

12. Nilus, in Migne, PG lxxix.66.

13. Smith, loc. cit.

131 Beheading fallen foes

1. KB ii.197.

2. Cf. A. Jeremias, The Old Testament in the Light of the Ancient East (1911), ii.183, fig. 165.

3. G. Jacob, Das Leben der vorislamischen Beduinen (1895), 28, n.2 (where full references are given).

4. Th. Noeldeke, Aufsätze zur pers. Geschichte (1887), 90; cf. also: Firdausi, i.129, 8; i.324, 141, ed. Vullers.

5. See above, §107.

6. R. B. Onians, The Origins of European Thought, etc. (1951), 95 ff.; J. A. Mac-Culloch, ERE, s.v. Head; Frazer-Gaster, NGB §174.

7. Servius, on Vergil, Ecl. vi.3; Aen. iii.607.—K. Bethe, in Rhein. Mus. 62 (1907), 465, so explains the Homeric expression, *amenêna karêna* (Odyssey 10.521, 536; 11.29, 49), but L. Radermacher, in ARW 11 (1908), 414, objects that this refers simply to the fact that the people were counted *per capita!*

8. A. B. Ellis, The Yoruba-speaking Peoples of the Slave Coast (1894), 125 ff.

9. R. Verneau and Pennatier, in L'Anthropologie 36 (1921), 317.

10. J. Langsdorff, Reise um die Welt (1812), i.115 f.

11. A. Bastian, Die Völker des östlichen Asiens (1866–71), ii.256.

12. Rev. Francis Connell, Baptism (1938), 13 f.

132 The bundle of the living

1. On the concept of the external (or separable) soul, see: Frazer-Gaster, NGB, §§148–49, and additional note, p. 123.

2. P. N. Wilken, in Mededeelingen van wege het Nederlandsche Zendeling-genootschap, 7 (1863), 146 ff.

3. B. F. Matthes, Bijdragen tot de Ethnologie van Zuid-Celebes (1873), 74.

4. J. A. Jacobsen, Reisen in die Inselwelt des Banda-Meeres (1896), 199.

5. H. Newton, In Far New Guinea (1914), 186.

6. B. Spencer and F. J. Gillen, The Native Tribes of Central Australia (1899), 128–36; cf. iid., The Northern Tribes of Central Australia (1904), 257–82.

[6a. E.g., Prov. 7:20.]

[6b. VS XVI.1 (= P. Kraus, Altbabylonische Briefe 1931, 49, 51), 11–12: *be-el-ki u be-li-it-ki ki-ma ki-[si] sá qa-ti-šu-nu li-iṣ-ṣu-ru-ki.*]

[6c. M. Lizbarski, Ginza, r., p. vii; E. S. Drower, The Canonical Prayerbook of the Mandaeans (1949), 80, n.4 (in reference to *laufa*).]

[6d. L. Oppenheim, in JNES 18 (1959), 121–28.]

[6e. O. Eissfeldt, in BASW 105 (1960), 60 f.]

[6f. M. Pope, Job (Anchor Bible, 1965), 104.]

[6g. The present writer acquired at a country fair in Vermont an antique ballot box designed for such a purpose.]

▲ 133 The Witch of Endor

1. Cf. CT, XXIII; A. Jeremias, The Old Testament in the Light of the Ancient East (1911), ii.184 f.

2. Epic of Gilgamesh xii.78 ff.; tr. Speiser, ANET 98 f.

3. *Nekyomanteia,* less commonly *nekromanteia* or *psychomanteia.*

4. Pausanias, ix.30, 6.

5. Herodotus, v.92, 7.

6. Pausanias, i.17, 5.

7. Plutarch, Cimon 8; id., De serâ numinis vindictâ, 10. Cf. Pausanias, iii.17, 8 f.

8. Id., De defectu oraculorum 45.

9. Id., Consolatio ad Apollonium, 14.

10. Herodotus, iv.172.

11. H. Duveyrier, Exploration du Sahara: les Touareg du Nord (1864), 415.

12. Aeschylus, Persae 600–838.

13. Philostratus, Vita Apollonii iv.16.

14. Pliny, Nat. Hist. xxx.18.

15. Lucan, Pharsalia xi.413–830.

16. Horace, Sat. i.26–29.

17. Tibullus, i.2, 47 ff. [with Kirby Smith's commentary, in loc.].

18. Tacitus, Annals ii.271 ff.

19. Suetonius, Nero xxxiv.4.

20. Dio Cassius, lxxvii.15.

21. J. Roscoe, in JRAI 31 (1901), 129 ff.; 32 (1902), 44 ff.; id., The Baganda (1911), 283–85; id., "Worship of the Dead as Practised by some African Tribes," in Harvard African Studies, 1 (1917), 39 ff.

22. Id., The Northern Bantu (1915), 53.

23. Ib., 226 ff.

24. C. Goldsbury and H. Sheane, The Great Plateau of Northern Rhodesia (1911), 83.

25. E. Beguin, Les Ma-rotsé (1903), 120–23.

26. J. Spieth, Die Religion der Eweer in Süd-Togo (1911), 238.

27. H. Néel, in L'Anthropologie, 24 (1913), 461.

28. F. Speiser, Two Years with the Natives in the Western Pacific (1913), 206.

29. E. Shorthand, Traditions and Superstitions of the New Zealanders[2] (1856), 81–96.

30. Old New Zealand, by a Pakeha Maori (London 1884), 122–28.

31. M. Radiguet, Les derniers sauvages: la vie et les moeurs aux Îles Marquises[2] (1882), 226–32. (The author first went to the Marquesas Islands in 1842.)

32. J. Viegen, in Tijdschrift van het Koninklijk Nederlaandsch Aardrijkskundig Genootschap, Second ser. 29 (1912), 149; A. J. Gooszen, in BTLVNI, 69 (1914), 377.

33. N. Adriani and A. C. Kruijt, De Bare'e-sprejende Toradja's van Midden-Celebes (1912–14), i.330.

34. E. H. Gomes, Seventeen Years among the Sea-Dyaks of Borneo (1911), 142.

35. C. Hose and W. McDougall, The Pagan Tribes of Borneo (1912), ii.38 ff.

36. J. Warneck, Die Religion der Batak (1909), 89 ff.

37. E. W. Hawes, The Labrador Eskimo. Canada, Department of Mines, Geological Survey, Memoir 91 (1916), 132.

38. J. H. Gray, China (1878), ii.22 ff.

39. J. J. M. de Groot, The Religious System of China, vi (1910), 1330 ff.

40. Ib., 1332–35.

[40a. E.g., Lev. 19:31; Deut. 18:11; Isa. 8:19; 19:3; 29:4; I Chron. 10:13. Cf. Th. Noeldeke, in ZDMG 28.667.]

[40b. See fully: J. Negelein, "Die Luft- und Wasserblase im Volksglauben," in ARW 5 (1902), 145–49.]

[40c. Zs. für Ethnologie 17 (1875), 86.]

[40d. II Aqhat i.27, 45; cf. T. H. Gaster, Thespis[2], 334.]

[40e. Archaeology and the Religion of Israel (1942), 203, n.31.]

[40f. For these terms, see: Grimm-Stallybrass, TM, 915.]

137 The "holder of the spindle"

1. KJV (following the Greek Septuagint and many of the older commentators) misses the point by rendering, *one that leaneth on a staff*, i.e., is crippled or feeble. But the Hebrew word (*pelek*) definitely means "spindle," not "staff."

2. MVAG 1898.234 f. Cf. Nah. 3:13: "Thy people in the midst of thee are women."

3. Berlin Esarhaddon Stele (= KB VI/i.62 ff.), rev. 56 f.

4. KBo VI.34; cf. T. H. Gaster, Thespis[2], 367.

138 Taboo on touching the Ark of the Lord

1. See Frazer-Gaster, NGB §§170–80 (and Additional Notes).

2. Plutarch, Greek and Roman Parallel Hist., c.17.

3. On blinding as a standard punishment for sacrilege, see above, §56.

4. Plutarch, loc. cit.

139 Shaving and shearing

1. The Hebrew original says more directly, "had become a stench."

2. See: J. Morgenstern, Rites of Birth, Marriage, Death and Kindred Occasions among

the Semites (1966), 84 ff.; P. Jaussen, Coutumes des arabes au pays de Moab (1908), 94 ff.

3. S. I. Curtiss, Ursemitische Religion im Volksleben des heutigen Orients, tr. H. Stocks (1913), 246–51.—A similar usage has been reported from the Sinai Peninsula: W. E. Jennings-Bramley, in PEFQS 1907.34 f.

4. F. Niebuhr, Reisebeschreibung nach Arabien (1774–1857), ii.431, as quoted by Morgenstern, loc. cit.

5. Morgenstern, op. cit., 86.

6. ᶜAntar, tr. Hamilton, i.149; ii.30; iii.92 f.; I. Goldziher, Muhamm. Studien (1889–90), i.250; Kitab al-Aghani, ed. Bulac (A.H. 1285), xii.128, 1; G. A. Wilken, Ueber das Haaropfer, etc. (1886–97), iii; W. Robertson Smith, The Religion of the Semites[3] (1927), 325n.

140 The Uriah letter

1. Stith Thompson, MI, K 978; H. Gunkel, Das Märchen im AT (1921), 132; Bolte-Polivka, i.286 ff.; A. Aarne, Finnische Märchenvarianten (FCC 33), 64 ff., 91.

2. Iliad 6.155 ff.; Apollodorus, Bib. ii.3; Hyginus, fab. 57; Tzetzes, Schol. on Lycophron 171 id., Chiliades vii.816 ff.; Euripides wrote a tragedy (now lost) on this subject.

3. Homer calls her Anteia.

4. Somadeva, Ocean of Story, i.52; cf. Penzer, ch. xiii.

5. Stith Thompson, MI, K 511.

6. Shakespeare, Hamlet, V.ii; cf. J. Schick, "Hamlet in China," in Jahrbuch der deutschen Shakespeare-Gesellschaft, 50 (1914), 31 ff.

7. Jacob and Wilhelm Grimm, Kinder- und Hausmärchen, #29. The story comes from Zwehrn, the Main district, and Hesse.

8. F. v. d. Leyen, Märchen in der Göttersagen der Edda (1898), 19.

9. B. P. Kretschmer, Neugriechische Märchen (1917), 205; J. G. von Hahn, Griechische und Albanesische Märchen (1864), 162.

10. E. Sklarek, Ungarische Märchen (1901), 26.

141 Regnal names

1. On such "regnal names," see: A. M. Honeyman, in JBL 67 (1948), 13 ff.; A. Alt, in Bertholet Festschrift (1950), 219; S. Hermann, in Wiss. Zs. des Karl Marx Universität Leipzig. Gesellsch. u. sprachwiss. Reihe, iii (1953–54), i.55; R. de Vaux, Les institutions de l'Ancien Testament, i (1958), 165 f.

2. Examples are cited in R. Labat, Le caractère réligieux de la royauté assyro-babylonienne (1939), 113 f.

3. II AB, ii.34; v.12; vii.3–4; V AB, D 35–36.

4. II AB, vii.46–47; I*AB, ii.8, 13; vi.31.

142 The coal on the hearth

1. KB VI/2.132, ii.86–87; cf. P. Haupt, in JBL 33 (1914), 166; 35 (1916), 319; B. Landsberger, in OLz 19 (1916), 33–39; A. Ungnad, Babylonische Briefe (1914), #229; P. Koschaker and A. Ungnad, Hammurabis Gesetze (1923), §1741; S. Smith, Isaiah XL–LV (1944), 164.

2. F. Thureau Dangin, in RA 10.93–97.

3. A. Schultens, Liber Iobi (1737), 440 f.

4. Fustel de Coulanges, The Ancient City (Anchor Books ed.), 25, n.2; F. Kirby Smith, on Tibullus i.1, 5. Cf. also: Aeschylus, Choeph. 629; Theocritus, Id., ii.51; Propertius, iv.8, 43; Ovid, Heroides xix.151–54.

5. Ovid, Tristia i.3, 44.

6. Tibullus, i.1, 6.

7. Martial, x.47, 4; xi. 56, 4.

8. B. Schmidt, Das Volksleben der Neugriechen (1871), 24c; D. C. Hesseling, Charos (1897), 53.

9. E. Thomas, in Notes and Queries, 6/iv (1881), 74.

10. J. Grimm, DM⁴, 812 f.

11. O. Petersson, Chiefs and Gods (1953), 214 f.; E. J. and J. D. Kriege, The Realm of a Rain Queen (1947), 168.

12. A. C. Bryant, The Zulu People (1949), 469.

13. Petersson, op. cit., 339.

14. J. G. Frazer, GB ii.363 f.

15. Quintus Curtius, iii.3, 9; Clem. Rom., hom. ix.6 (ii.245 Migne). Cf. A. B. Cook, Zeus ii (1925), 34, n.1, citing A. C. Eschenbach, Diss. Acad., 519 ff. (which I have not seen); W. Otto, "Zum Hofzeremoniell der Hellenismus," in Epitymbion Swoboda (Reichenberg 1927), 194 ff.

16. II Kings 8:19; Ps. 132:17.

17. II Aqhat i.28, but the interpretation is uncertain, and some scholars think that the reference is to the evocation of the father's ghost in the form of a wisp of smoke.

143 Absalom and his father's concubines

1. W. Robertson Smith, Kinship and Marriage in Early Arabia² (1903), 107 ff.

2. Ib.

3. Gen. 35:22; 49:4.

4. II Sam. 3:7.

5. Apollodorus, Epitome vii.37; Hyginus, fab. 127.

6. Eugammon of Cyrene, Telegony, abstracted by Proclus; see: EGF, ed. Kaibel, 57 f.

7. Sophocles, Trachiniae 1216 f.; Ovid, Met. ix.278 ff.; Apollodorus, Bib. ii.7, 7.

8. Bruns-Sachau, §§109 f.

144 King's misconduct affects soil

1. See above, §127.

2. Prayer of Mursilis, II; A. Goetze, in Kleinas. Forschungen 1 (1930), 175; O. Gurney, in Annals of Art and Archaeology 27 (1940), 27, 37.

3. C. Virolleaud, L'astrologie chaldéenne, IIème suppl., ix.42; Ier suppl. (Adad), lix.26; R. Labat, Le caractere réligieux de la royauté assyrobabylonienne (1939), 121 f.

4. Krt = ANET 148 (iii); cf. T. H. Gaster, The Oldest Stories in the World (1952), 199, 206 f.; id., in JQR 37 (1946), 285 ff.

5. Tr. F. Rosenthal, ANET², 504.

6. J. G. Frazer, The Fasti of Ovid (1929), vol. ii, p. 297.

7. J. MacCulloch, Celtic Mythology (1918), 72.

8. Cf. Stith Thompson, MI, Q 552.3.

9. Ammianus Marcellinus, xxviii.5, 14.

10. See: E. Spanheim, on Callimachus, Artemis 125 f.; Plato, Legg. 906; M. Delcourt, Stérilités mysterieuses et naissances maléfiques dans l'antiquité classique (1938), 17; R. Patai, in JQR, N.S. 30 (1939), 59–69; id., Man and Temple (1947), 151–52.

11. A. W. Nieuwenhuis, Quer durch Borneo (1904–07), i.367.

12. R. E. Dennett, At the Back of the Black Man's Mind (1906), 53, 67–71.

13. Job 31:11 f.

14. The word is ḥ-n-p; cf. Isa. 24:5; Jer. 3:1, 2, 9; Ps. 106:38.

15. Tr. F. Rosenthal, in ANET², 499 f.

16. Ib.

17. Odyssey 19.109 f.

18. Ps. 72:16. (There is no need to emend the traditional text, as do several modern scholars.)

145   A Hebrew Niobe

(a)

1. The expression is due to Hugo Winckler, Geschichte Israels, ii.241.

2. R. B. Onians, The Origins of European Thought about the Body, etc. (1951), 213 (aiōn as liquid), 285 f.; Hippocrates, A 11 Diels; M. A. Canney, Givers of Life (1923), 55; M. Eliade, Patterns in Comparative Religion (1958), 193–99.

3. C. A. Doughty, Arabia Deserta (1888), i.349; W. E. Jennings-Bramley, in PEFQS 1907.26 f.; I. Goldziher, in ARW 13 (1910), 20 ff.; J. Morgenstern, Rites of Birth, Marriage, Death . . . among the Semites (1966), 122 f.

4. Goldziher, op. cit., 45, cited in connection with our Biblical passage by A. Jirku, Die Dämonen und ihre Abwehr im AT (1912), 65 f.

5. CT XVI, PL. 10. v.10–14. It must be conceded, however, that this may have been connected with the belief that *the dead are thirsty;* see: T. H. Gaster, Thespis[2], 334.

6. J. V. Grohmann, Aberglauben und Gebräuche aus Böhmen und Mähren (1864), 189; G. Lammert, Volksmediziniches und medizinisches Aberglaube in Bayern (1869), 105; C. L. Rochholz, Deutsche Glaube und Brauch im Spiegel der heidnischen Vorzeit (1870), i.198; A. le Braz, La légende de la Mort chez les Brétons américains (1923), i.365; E. M. Fogel, Beliefs and Superstitions of the Pennsylvania Germans (1915), 91, #361; Geiger, in HWbDA i.996; A. H. Krappe, The Science of Folklore (1930), 222.

7. W. C. Hazlitt, Dictionary of Faiths and Folklore (1905), i.249; A. R. Wright, English Folklore (1928), 21; H. M. Hyatt, Folk-Lore from Adams County, Illinois (1935), ##10039–44.

8. Isa. 22:16.

9. Syr. Apoc. Baruch 29:7; 73:2; Slavonic Enoch 22:9; TJ Berakoth v.9ᵇ; Taᶜanith i.63ᵈ; TB Hagigah 12ᵇ; Pirqê de R. Eleazar 34 (end); cf. L. Ginzberg, The Legends of the Jews (1909 sqq.), v.11, n.22.

(b)

10. Plutarch, Par. Graec. et Rom. 9, quoting Critolaus.—Saturn is here obviously the god of sowing.

▲   146   The sin of a census

1. J. H. Weekes, Among the Primitive Bakongo (1914), 292.

2. Id., Among the Congo Cannibals (1913), 136.

3. M. Merker, Die Masai (1904), 152.

[3a. Pechuel-Loesche, in Zs. f. Ethnologie 10 (1878), 234.]

4. W. E. H. Barrett, in JRAI 41 (1911), 36.

5. C. Dundas, in JRAI 43 (1913), 501 ff., 526.

6. C. W. Hobley, Ethnology of A-Kamba and Other E. African Tribes (1910), 165.

7. W. S. and K. Routledge, With a Prehistoric People (1910), 135 f.

8. P. Paulitschke, Ethnographie Nordest-Afrikas (1896), 31.

9. T. Hahn, in Globus, 12.227.

10. E. Doutté, Magie et Religion dans l'Afrique du Nord (1908), 179 ff. For special expressions used in counting measures of corn in Morocco, see: E. Westermarck, Ceremonies and Beliefs Connected with Agriculture, etc. (1913), 31 ff.

11. C. T. Wilson, Peasant Life in the Holy Land (1906), 212 ff.

12. G. Brown, Melanesians and Polynesians (1910), 204.

13. J. Mooney, "Myths of the Cherokee," in 19th Annual Report of the Bureau of American Ethnology (1900), i.424.

14. R. C. Mayne, Four Years in British Columbia and Vancouver Island (1862), 313.

15. E. James, Account of an Expedition from Pittsburgh to the Rocky Mountains (1823), i.235.

[15a. Catullus, 5.11–13; 7.11–12.]

[15b. Cited by Robinson Ellis, Comm. on Catullus, 5.11.]

16. C. Leemius, De Lapponibus Finmarchiae eorumque linguâ, vitâ, et religione pristinâ Commentatio (1767), 499.

[16a. Lilian Eichler, The Customs of Mankind (1924), 667.]

17. J. Ramsay, Scotland and Scotsmen in the Eighteenth Century, ed. A. Allardyce (1888), ii.449.

18. J. R. Tudor, The Orkneys and Shetland (1883), 173; C. Rogers, Social Life in Scotland (1884–86), iii.224 ff.

19. W. Gregor, Notes on the Folk-Lore of the North-East of Scotland (1881), 200.

20. County Folk-lore, vii. Fife, collected by J. E. Simkins (1914), 418.

[20a. Quoted by Robinson Ellis, Comm. on Catullus, 5.12.]

21. Mabel Peacock, in Folk-Lore, 12 (1901), 179.

[21a. F. Nork, Das Kloster, xii (1849), 761.]

22. Letter from William Wyse, 2/25/1908.

23. H. Feilberg, "Die Zahlen im dänischen Brauch und Volksglauben," in Zs. für Ver. f. Volkskunde, 4 (1894), 383.

24. Ib., 384.

25. W. Henderson, Notes on the Folk-Lore of the Northern Countries of England and the Borders (1879), 140.

26. A. Wuttke, Der deutsche Volksaberglaube2 (1869), 384, §633.

27. Ib., 378, §620.

28. A. Witzschel, Sagen, Sitten, und Gebräuche aus Thüringen (1878), 285, §100.

[28a. Am Urquell, 6 (1895), 10.]

[28b. See now: E. A. Speiser, "Census and Ritual Expiation in Mari and Israel," in BASOR 149 (1958), 17–25.]

[28c. I. Stchoukine, Le suicide collectif dans le Raskol russe (Paris 1903), cited by H. J. Rose, in ERE xii. 22b.]

[28d. T. F. Thiselton-Dyer, Domestic Folklore2 (n.d.), 133.]

29. J. Burckhardt, Travels in Nubia (1819), 741.

30. Exod. 30:11–16. The passage is assigned by most modern scholars to a late section of the Priestly Code (P), of exilic or post-exilic date.

[30a. F. Nork, Das Kloster, xii (1849), 761.]

KINGS

147 Abishag

1. See: A. Hagen, Die sexuelle Osphresiologie (Berlin 1901), 191–219 ("Shunamitism").

2. Marcellus Empiricus, De medicamentis empiricis, ed. Helmreich (1889); cf. E. Riess, in The New York Latin Leaflet, May 2, 1904.

3. T. H. White, The Age of Scandal (Penguin ed., 1962), 32 ff.

148 The ritual of enthronement

1. The spring lay on the boundary line between Judah and Benjamin: Jos. 15:1, 7; 18:11, 16; II Sam. 17:17. Josephus (Ant. viii.14, 4) locates it in the King's Garden.— The stone is called "the stone of Zoheleth," and since the Hebrew word z-ḥ-l means

"to creep," this is commonly rendered "Serpent's Stone." For a fascinating, though highly speculative, explanation of the name, see: R. Eisler, in OLz 16.397 f. Cf. also: G. von Rad, in TLZ., 72 (1947), 211–16.

2. J. Przyluski, "La princesse à l'odeur de poisson et la nagi dans les traditions de l'Asie orientale," in Études asiatiques, 2 (1925), 276. Cf. also: M. Eliade, Patterns in Comparative Religion (1958), 208 f., who suggests that the descent of Greek heroes from water-goddesses (e.g., Achilles) may reflect the same idea.

3. Przyluski, loc. cit.

4. Eliade, op. cit., 209.

5. Rajendralala Mitra, Indo-Aryans (London-Calcutta 1881), ii.3, 37 ff., 46 ff.; cf. E. Crawley, Oath, Curse and Blessing (Thinker's Library, No. 40), 87.

6. Satapatha Brahmana, V.iii.3; cf. A. Weber, Ueber die Königsweihe den Rajasâya (1893), 4, 33 f., 42–45, 110–17.

7. A. H. Gardiner, in JEA 36 (1950), 3–12.

8. E. Dhorme, Les religions de Babylonie et d'Assyrie (1945), 34; G. Furlani, La religione babilonese e assira (1928), i.129.

9. ISA, 38–39.

10. Ib., 67–68.

11. Ib., 94–95.

12. Ib., 218–19.

13. Code, rev. xxiv, 26 ff. (Meek, in ANET, renders "insight").

14. J. McCulloch, The Childhood of Fiction (1905), 71.

15. W. Webster, Basque Legends (1879), 22.

16. J. T. Naake, Slavonic Fairy Tales (1874), 28.

17. Grant Allen, The Evolution of the Idea of God (Thinker's Library ed., 1931), 78 f.; cf. A. Kuhn, Indogermanische Studien, i.334.

18. Antanarivo Annual, 1892.485, 492 f.; A. van Gennep, Tabou et totémisme à Madagascar (1904), 82.

19. Grant Allen, loc. cit.

20. But the meaning of the Hebrew text is not entirely certain.

21. Here too the translation is not entirely certain. The Hebrew word, 'ammud, rendered "pillar," in accordance with its usual sense, could here mean "dais" (cf. Akkadian kussu nimêdi).

149 Asylum at the altar

1. See: M. Lohr, Das Asylwesen im Alten Testament (1930); W. Robertson Smith, Religion of the Semites[3] (1927), 75–77, 149, 543; L. Wenger, "Asylrecht," in RAC i.836–44; J. G. Frazer, Totemism and Exogamy (1910), i.96 ff.; E. Westermarck, The Origin and Development of the Moral Ideas (1906), ii.628 ff.

2. Smith, op. cit., 76; id., Kinship and Marriage in Early Arabia[2] (1894), 48–52; Hariri, ed. de Sacy, 177.

3. RS 2.27–28.

4. III Aqhat, 151 ff.; cf. T. H. Gaster, Thespis[2], 364 f.

5. Diodorus, xvii.41.8.

6. Strabo, xvi.2.6; II Macc. 4:33. Cf. also: B. W. Head, Historia Nummorum (1887), Index, iv, s.v.

7. CIS i.86 A 15, B 10; G. A. Cooke, North Semitic Inscriptions (1903), 67 f.

8. Tacitus, Ann., iii. 60 f.

9. Smith, op. cit., 77.

10. Yacut, ed. Wüstenfeld, s.vv. Jalsad, Fals; cf. J. Wellhausen, Reste des arabischen Heidentums[2] (1897), 52–54. See further: Quatremére, "Les asyles chez les Arabes," in Mém. Acad. Inscr., 15 (1845), 307 ff.; I. Goldziher, Muhammedanische Studien, i

(1889), 236 ff.; G. Jacob, Altarabische Parallelen zum Alten Testament (1897), 12, points out that to the bedouin graves sc. of saints are the main asyla.

11. See below, §313.

12. Ps. 15:1 ff.

13. Apollodorus, Epitome 5.23; Aretinus, Ilii Persis, summarized by Proclus = EPG, ed. Kinkel, 49 ff.

14. Apollodorus, Bib., ii.8.1; Schol. on Aristophanes, Knights, 1151.

▲ 150 The judgment of Solomon

1. L. P. Tessitori, "Two Jaina Versions of the Story of Solomon's Judgment," in The Indian Antiquity, 43 (1913), 148–52. The writer gives all four versions; two of them had been published previously by his fellow-countryman, F. L. Pulle.

2. This version of the story is from the Antarakathâsamgraha of Râjasekhara, a work apparently of the 14th cent.

[2a. The most exhaustive treatment will be found in F. M. Goebel, Juedische Motive in maerchenhaften Erzaehlungsgut (Gleiwitz 1932). Cf. also: Gaidoz, in Mélusine iv, Nos. 14, 15, 19; V. Chauvin, Bibliographie des oeuvres arabes (1892–1922), vi.63, No. 231; R. Köhler, Kleinere Schriften, ed. J. Bolte (1898–1900), 531; T. Zachariae, in Zs. f. Volkskunde 16.136 f.; A. Hertel, Geist des Ostens (1913), 6 f.]

[2b. Vikramodaya, No. 14 in Hertel's Pančatantra (1914), 154; Id., Panchakyana-Wartikka (1923), 157 f. A Tamil version is preserved in the Kathmanjari.]

[2c. Jataka, No. 546; T. Steele, An Eastern Love Story, Kusa Jatakaya (1871), 247–57; T. Rhys Davids, Buddhist Birth Stories (1880), i, pp. xiv–xvi.]

[2d. Tibetan Dsanglun; cf. J. J. Schmidt, in Mélusine, iv.367; F. A. von Schiefner, in Mélanges asiatiques, 8.527; F. A. von Schiefner and W. Ralston, Tibetan Tales (1882), 120; F. Köhler, in Zs. f. Missionsk. 42 (1927), 65–68 dates this version to the 7th cent.]

[2e. Lin Yutang, The Wisdom of China (1955), Sect. "Chinese Tales."]

[2f. Klein, Geschichte des Dramas (1865–86), iii.460 ff.]

[2g. The Academy, April 16, 1887, p. 275.]

[2h. N. B. Dennys, The Folklore of China (1876), 139.]

[2i. J. Gladwyn, Persian Moonshee² (1840), i.132.]

[2j. F. S. Krauss, cited by Gaidoz, in Mélusine, iv.414.]

[2k. Lumbroso, in L'archivio per lo studio delle tradizione popolari, 2 (1883), 574.]

[2l. Lumbroso, in M. R. Ac. d. Lincei, iii/9 (June 3, 1883); R. Engelmann, in Hermes 39 (1904), 146–54.]

[2m. Gaidoz, in Mélusine, iv.414 f.]

[2n. Abh. Bayer, Akad., Phil. Kl. 8 (1856–58), i.3, 9.]

[2o. E. Samter, in Archäologischer Anzeiger, 1898. 50.]

[2p. Th. Benfey, Pantshatantra (1859), ii.544.]

[2q. H. Gunkel, Märchen im Alten Testament (1921), 144 f.]

151 The dedication of the Temple

1. See fully T. H. Gaster, Thespis² (1961), where the subject is worked out in detail.

2. The coincidence did not escape the ancient rabbis: see TJ Sanhedrin 18ᵇ.

3. Gaster, op. cit., 47 f.

4. H. St. John Thackeray, The Septuagint in Jewish Worship (1921), 76 ff.

5. Hab. 3:5.

6. Some technicalities need to be discussed in order to reinforce the argument. (a) The missing opening line may be restored, after the Greek Version, to read, Šemeš hêḳîn ba-šamayim (or Šemeš bašamayim hêḳîn), which would mean ostensibly, "He (i.e., Yahweh) fixed the sun in heaven," but it is worthy of note that in Akkadian, the

equivalent of the verb *hêkîn* is used specifically in speaking of a heavenly body which reaches its zenith (see: G. Meier, in AfO 12 [1938], 240, n.24; R. C. Thompson, Reports, #206; M. Jastrow, Rel. Bab. u. Assyr. [1905–12], ii.614, n.6). To this in turn corresponds the word *mākôn*, the fixed place now built for Yahweh (cf. Exod. 15:17); (*b*) the emphatic, "I have indeed built" (Heb.: *banôh banîthî*) now receives its proper emphasis.

▲ **153 Solomon and the Queen of Sheba**

1. N. Adriani and A. C. Kruijt, De Bare' e-sprekende Toradja's van Midden-Celebes (1912–14), i.133.
2. Koran, Sura 27 (tr. E. H. Palmer).
3. W. Hertz, "Die Rätsel der Königin von Saba," reprinted in his Gesammelte Abhandlungen (1905), 419 ff. In Arab tradition, the queen's name is Balqis.
4. J. E. Hanauer, Folk-Lore of the Holy Land (1910), 97 ff.
5. The Mahabharata, tr. M. N. Dutt (1895), ch. xlvii. Cf. C. Lassen, Indische Alterthumskunde, i² (1867), 825; G. A. Grierson, "Dwryodhana and the Queen of Sheba," in JRAS 1913.684 ff.; W. Crooke, ib., 685 f.; C. H. Tawney, ib., 1048. Tawney cites another parallel in an Indian tale: "In the Jyotishkavadana, 108, artificial fishes which can be set in motion by machinery, appear under a crystal floor. The entering guest takes this for water, and is therefore about to remove his shoes"; see: F. A. von Schiefner, Tibetan Tales, tr. W. R. S. Ralston (1882), 361, n.2. In the Jerusalemitan version of the story, a stream of water, with fish swimming in it, flowed under the crystal pavement: Hanauer, loc. cit.

154 Hand withers from impiety

1. Protevangelium xiv.18 ff.; M. R. James, The Apocryphal New Testament (1924), 47; Cotton MS, Pageant xv, "The Miraculous Birth and the Midwives," in W. Hone, Ancient Mysteries (1823), 71. Cf. also: Gospel of Pseudo-Matthew 13 = James, op. cit., 74.
2. E. Kinesman, Lives of the Saints (1623), 381.
3. Socrates, Hist. Eccles. vi.16.

ELIJAH

155 The "man of God"

1. Heb.: *'îš ha-'elôhîm*.
2. Deut. 33:1; Jos. 14:6; Ezra 3:2; Ps. 90:1.
3. I Sam. 9:6–8, 10.
4. II Kings 4:7.
5. I Sam. 2:27.
6. I Kings 13:1.
7. Judg. 3:5, 8 (cf. also v.2). In a somewhat attenuated sense, Nehemiah (12:24, 36) so characterizes David.
8. Cf. H. Duhm, Der Verkehr Gottes mit den Menschen im AT (1926), §11. Duhm compares the "man of God" with a dervish; ib., 61.
9. *Siunan antuhsas*: BoTU 23A, ii.32; cf. A. Goetze, in Kleinasiatische Forschungen 1 (1929), 219, n.3; O. Gurney, in AAA 27 (1940), 27, n.20.
10. LÚDINGIR*LIM*-*niyant*- (= *siuniyant*-): Ehelolf, in ZA, N.F. 9 (1936), 180. *siyaniahh-:* BoTU 23B, iv.15.
11. *Dhu Allah:* I. Goldziher, Abh. z. ar. Phil. (1896–99), 18.—It is often asserted

that there is an Arabic verb *aliha,* derived from Allah, which has a similar meaning, but this is simply a variant of *waliha;* see: A. Fischer, in Islamica 1.390–97.

12. *Entheos:* e.g., Aeschylus, Eumenides 17; Agamennon 1209; Plato, Phaedrus 244*b*.

13. *Theoleptos:* Aristotle, Ethics E 1.1.4; *theolêpsia:* Plutarch, ii.763A.

14. *Kangakari:* W. Aston, in ERE xi.470*b*.

15. D. G. Brinton, Religions of Primitive Peoples (1889), 59 (citing Middendorf's Keshua Wörterbuch, s.v.).

▲ 156 Elijah and the Ravens

1. E. Robinson, Biblical Researches in Palestine[2] (1856), i.557 f.

[1a. See: R. Basset, Mille et un contes (1925–27), iii.295; A. Wesselski, Märchen des Mittelalters (1925), 249, #57; H. Gunkel, Das Märchen in A.T. (1921), 34.]

[1b. Aelian, HA xii.21.]

[1c. Diodorus, ii.4; cf. G. Binder, Aussetzung (1964), 163 f.]

[1d. Suidas, Lex., s.v. *lagôs;* cf. F. Cumont, Études syriennes (1917), 82 ff.]

[1e. Ovid, Fasti iii.37, 54.]

[1f. Kalidasa; Shakuntala and Other Writings, tr. A. W. Ryder (1939).]

[1g. Cf. P. Toldo, in Studien zur vergleichende Literaturgeschichte, II (1902), 87 ff.]

[1h. Metaphrastes, Lives.]

[1i. Guérin, Vie des saints[12] (1892), viii.29 f.]

[1j. Jerome, Life of Paul, First Hermit of Egypt.]

[1k. Brewer, loc. cit.]

[1l. Les petits Bollandistes, iii.550.]

[1m. K. Macaulay, History of St. Kilda (1765), 174.]

[1n. Letter of Balasi: R. F. Harper, Assyrian and Babylonian Letters belonging to the K Collection in the British Museum (1892–1914), #353 = R. H. Pfeiffer, State Letters of Assyria (1935), 3334; cf. J. Hunger, Babylonische Tieromina nebst griechisch-römischen Parallelen (1909), 33.]

[1o. Rm. ii.138; Bezold, Catalogue 1650; M. Jastrow, Rel. Bab. u. Assyr. ii (1912), 808.]

2. Aelian, HA i.48.

[2a. Cf. A. S. Pease, Comm. on Cicero, De Divinatione, vol. ii, p. 76.]

3. Porphyry, De abstinentia ii.48.

[3a. Vergil, Georgica i.388 ff.]

[3b. Horace, Odes iii.17, 3.]

[3c. Aelian, HA viii.7; Geoponica i.37. Cf. O. Keller, "Rabe und Krähe im Altertum," in Jahresber. d. wiss. Vereins f. Volkskunde und Linguistik (Prague 1873), 8 ff.]

[3d. Cf. Brand-Ellis, Popular Antiquities of Great Britain, iii (1849), 210–12.]

[3e. Shakespeare, Macbeth, I.v; C. Swainson, The Folklore and Provincial Names of British Birds (1886), 9 f.; T. F. Thiselton Dyer, The Folk-Lore of Shakespeare (1883), 149 f.

[3f. Samuel Butler, Hudibras, II, iii.707.]

[3g. Quoted by Brand-Ellis, loc. cit.]

[3h. Shakespeare, Othello, IV.i.]

[3i. JRAI 20.90.]

[3j. H. R. Schoolcraft, Indian Tribes of the United States (1853–56), iv.491. Cf. also: W. A. Clouston, "Folklore of the Raven," in Saxby's Birds of Omen (1893), 20.]

4. J. Tait, The Lillooet Indians (1906), 283.

5. A. Newton, Dictionary of Birds (1893–96), 766.

6. Pliny, HN x.121–23.

7. Oliver Goldsmith, History of the Earth and of Animated Nature (1776), v.226.

8. W. Yarrell, History of British Birds (1843), ii.68 ff.

9. A. C. Hollis, The Nandi (1909), 7, 70 ff.

10. J. G. Frazer, Totemism and Exogamy (1910), iv.305.

[10a. O. Gruppe, Griechische Mythologie (1906), 820, n.1.]

[10b. Petronius, frag. 26 Buecheler; Fulgentius, i.13.]

[10c. E.g., J. Gray, in The Interpreter's Bible, in loc.]

157 "Measuring" the sick

1. Gaster-Frazer, NGB §76; E. Law Hussey, in The Archaeological Journal, No. 39.

2. Grimm-Stallybrass, TM 1163.

3. Ib., 1165.

4. Cf. S. Eitrem, Opferritus und Voropfer der Griechen und Römer (1915), 485; O. Gruppe, in Bursians Jahresberichte 186 (1921), 281; O. Weinreich, in ARW 20.474.

5. Cf. G. Huet, Les contes populaires (1923), 72.

158 The confrontation on Carmel

Literature: H. H. Rowley, "Elijah on Carmel," in BJRL 43 (1960), 190–219 (with exhaustive bibliography of recent studies); R. de Vaux, "Les prophètes de Baal sur le Mont Carmel," in Bulletin du Musée de Beyrouth 5 (1941), 8–20; E. Würthwein, in Zs. für Theologie und Kirche, 59 (1962), 131–44.

(a) Baal

1. I AB iv.26–27, 37–38.

2. II AB v.68–69 = T. H. Gaster, Thespis², 185.

3. I Aqhat 25–45 = Gaster, op. cit., 358.

4. Bokhari, 95 Bulac; cf. Gaster, op. cit., 130, n.13.

5. TB, Sheb. ii.19; Sukkah iii.9; Ter. x.11; cf. Epstein, in ZAW 33 (1913), 82–83.

6. Cf. K. Galling, in Alt Festschrift (1953), 105 ff.; O. Eissfeldt, "Der Gott Karmel," in Sitzb. d. deutsch. Akad. d. Wiss. zu Berlin, Kl. für Sprachen, Literatur u. Kunst, 1953/i; A. Alt, Kleine Schriften (1953), 135 ff.

7. Tacitus, Hist. ii.78; cf. K. Scott, in JRS 24 (1934), 138 ff.

8. Avi-Yonah, in IEJ 2 (1952); summarized in SOTS Book List, 1954, p. 60.

9. Suetonius, Vespasian 5.

10. Jamblichus, Vita Pythag. iii (15).

(b) The fire upon the altar

11. Gudea Cylinder 1 = F. Thureau Dangin, Die sumer. Königsinschriften (1907), 102 f.

12. Exod. 3:3 ff.

13. Cf. E. Dodds, The Greeks and the Irrational (1957), 294, 307, n.95.

14. Pausanias, i.16.

15. Id., v.27.

16. Valerius Maximus, viii.2, 111.

17. Vergil, Ecl. viii.106; cf. also: Servius, on Vergil, Aen. xii.20; Solinus, v. 23.

18. F. Bötticher, in Philologus 25 (1867), 34.

19. Pausanias, v.27, 5 f.

20. Athenaeus, 19E; Julius Africanus, Kestoi, ed. Vielleford; cf. also: Hippolytus, Ref. haeres. iv.33; Dodds, loc. cit.

21. Enapius, Vita soph. 475; Migne, PG xii.12.

22. Caesarius von Heisterbach, Dial. Mirac. vii.46.

23. F. Hitzig, Gesch. d. Volk Israels (1869), 176; R. H. Kennett, in Old Testament Essays (1928), 91 ff.; A. Lucas, in PEQ 1945.5 f. Reference is made to a similar manner of kindling altar-fire, mentioned in II Maccabees 1:29 ff.

24. Cf. Rowley, op. cit., 211 f.

(c) The limping dance and the gashing with knives

25. Heliodorus, Aethiopica iv.17, 1.

26. C. Clermont-Ganneau, in Réc. d'archéol. orientale, i (1888), 101 f.; R. Pietsch-mann, Gesch. d. Phönizier (1889), 220; F. Cumont, in P-W ii (1896), 2834 f.; S. Ronze-valle, in Rev. archéol. Sér. IV/ii (1903), 29 f.

27. Herodian, v.5, 9; cf. Heliodorus, Aethiopica iv.5, 9.

28. R. Patai, in HUCA 14 (1939), 255. This, however, may be a leaping, rather than a limping, dance, and that is something quite different, concerning which see: Frazer-Gaster, NGB §23 (with Additional Note).

29. R. Paribeni, Notizie degli scavi (1919), 106 f.; F. Cumont, Les religions orien-tales dans le paganisme romain[4] (1929), Pl. viii.2 (facing p. 90). See on this: de Vaux, op. cit., 111; H. Gressmann, AO 23/viii (1923), 27.

30. Encyc. Brit.[10], vii.795.

31. S. Eitrem, Opferritus und Voropfer d. Griechen und Römer (1915), 479.

32. I*AB, i.6 = Gaster, op. cit., 213.

33. Cf. T. H. Gaster, Thespis[2], 213.

34. Herodotus, ii.61.

35. Lucian, De dea Syria 50.

36. E.g., Seneca, Agamemnon 686 ff.; Minucius Felix, Octav. xxiv.4; Apuleius, Met. viii.28; Horace, Sat. ii.3, 223; Lucan, Pharsalia i.365; Lucian, Asin. 37; Jamblichus, De mysteriis iii.4; cf. H. Hepding, Attis (1903), 159 f.; H. Graillot, Le culte de Cybéle (1912), 305 f.; F. Cumont, op. cit., 50–51 and nn.; T. Noeldeke, in ARW 10 (1907), 149 ff.

37. Tibullus, i.6, 44 f.

38. Propertius, ii.22, 15.

39. Statius, Theb. x.170.

40. R. Petazzoni, Confession des pechés (1931), i.151n.; 149, n.4; id., in SMSR 1930.285; id., La Confessione dei Peccati, iii (1936), 24, 38.

41. Frazer-Gaster, NGB §41 (with Additional Note).

42. J. Kreemer, in Mendel. Zendel. 30 (1886), 113.

43. Fr. Coulbeaux, in Missions catholiques 30 (1898), 455.

(d) Elijah's taunts

44. The meaning of the assonantal phrase, *kî sî‹a›h we-kî sîg lô* is uncertain. LXX paraphrases, "And maybe he is busy." So too Vet. Lat. Vulgate has *aut in diversorio est*. RSV renders, "Either he is musing or he is gone aside" (i.e., to the privy); KJV, "Either he is talking, or he is pursuing." I take the phrase as simply an example of the figure of speech known to Arab grammarians as *itba‹*, whereby effect is heightened by juxtaposing like-sounding words, one of which may be invented *ad hoc;* e.g., in English, "helter-skelter, pell-mell," etc. In that case, an approximate rendering would be, "He is all a-hustle and a-bustle," "he is in a stir and a stew"; "he is huffing and puffing around"; "he is in a dizzy tizzy."

45. Frazer-Gaster, NGB §41; D. Kidd, The Essential Kaffir (1904), 333.

46. E. O. James, in ERE x.562[b].

47. W. Mannhardt, Antike Wald-und Feldkulte (1877), 342n.

48. De Vaux, loc. cit.

49. A. Erman, Die Literatur d. Aegypter (1923), 37.

50. De abstinentia iv.9. See: A. Moret, Le rituel du culte divin journalier en Égypte (1902), 121 ff.; W. Spiegelberg, in ARW 23 (1925), 348; Cumont, op. cit., 89, 241, n.84.

51. Plutarch, De Iside et Osiride 35.

52. Inscription published in Jahreshefte d. oester. Archeol. Instituts 7 (1904), 93.

53. The order was abolished by John Hyrcanus: MIshnah, Ma^{c}aser Sheni v.15; Soṭah ix.10.

54. Pss. 7:7; 59:5; 88:65.

55. Menander, quoted by Josephus, Antiqu. Jud. viii.5.3; cf. Athenaeus, ix. 47; Stark, in SSGW 8 (1856), 132.

56. The title occurs on: (a) Larnax Lapethou iii = A. M. Honeyman, in Le Muséon 51 (1938), 288 (4th cent. b.c.); (b) a Rhodian inscription: A. Maiuri, Annuario della regia scuola di Atene, 2 (1916), 267–69; (c) Carthaginian inscriptions: CIS i.227, 260–62, 351, 377; Rép. i. ##13, 360, 537, 553, 554, 1569; (d) Jol (Shershel) 2 = G. A. Cooke, A Text-book of North Semitic Inscriptions (1903), #57.4. Cf. de Vaux, op. cit., 17 f.

57. Athenaeus, vi.253, b-f.

(e) Rain-stones

58. Frazer-Gaster, NGB §52. On the subject in general, see: R. Eisler, in Philologus 68 (1909), 42, n.222; M. Eliade, Patterns of Comparative Religion (1958), 226 f.; G. A. Wainwright, The Sky-Religion in Egypt (1938), 76; G. F. Kunz, The Magic of Jewels and Charms (1915), 5 f., 34; W. J. Perry, The Children of the Sun^2 (1926), 392; J. Rendell Harris, in Folk-Lore 15 (1905), 427 ff., 434 ff.; Notes and Queries III/iv (1864), 338.

59. G. Turner, Samoa, a hundred years ago and long before (1884), 145.

60. W. G. Aston, Shinto (1905), 330.

61. W. Crooke, Popular Religion and Folklore of Northern India (1896), i.75 f.

62. J. Rhys, Celtic Heathendom (1888), 184.

63. Ib., 185 f.

64. F. A. Hasluck, in Annual of the British School at Athens 21 (1914–16), 78.

65. Margaret Murray, in ZÄS 51 (1913), 131; S. G. Mitra, in Folk-Lore 9 (1898), 277.

66. Frazer-Gaster, loc. cit.; L. Deubner, in Neue Jahrb. 27 (1911), 334, n.3.

(f) The filling of the trench with water

67. O. Gruppe, Griech. Mythologie (1906), 446.—That Elijah's act was a magical rite is argued also by: P. Volz, Das Neujahrfest Yahwehs (1912), 31; R. Dussaud, Les origines canaanéennes du sacrifice israélite (1921), 205 f.; R. Patai, in HUCA 14 (1939), 256 f.; S. Mowinckel, Religion und Kultus (1953), 99; N. H. Snaith, in Interpreter's Bible, iii.157. It is denied, however, by R. de Vaux, Élie, 63; S. Garofalo, La Sacra Biblia (1951), 141.

68. Lucian, De dea Syria 13; Melito, in Cureton's Spec. Syr. (1885), 45.

69. Volney, Voyages en Syrie et en Égypte (= Études pol. de la Syrie [1787], ii.197).

70. Athenaeus, 496A; cf. Euripides, frag. 592, Nauck; Proclus, Tim. v.293^b (v. Bötticher, in Philologus 24 [1886], 235).

(g) Elijah on the summit of Carmel

71. Sinuhe R (= Pap. Berlin 3022), 10; W. C. Hayes, in JNES 7 (1948) 9, n.44 (tp ḥr m ⟩ st).

72. RS 137.23, Gordon (tǵly rišthm lẓr brkhm); cf. J. B. Bauer, in Hermes 87 (1959), 383 f.; A. Jirku, in ZDMG 103 (1953), 372.

73. Römer, Guinea, 57; Schlegel, Ewe-sprache, p. xvi, as quoted by E. B. Tylor, Primitive Culture, ii.221.

(h) The raincloud

74. S. Baring-Gould, Curious Myths of the Middle Ages (New York 1884), 201 f.

159 The ascension of Elijah

1. Dilthey, in Rhein. Mus. 25 (1870), 321 ff. See further: F. Schönwerth, Aus der Oberpfalz (1857–59), ii.149 ff.; O. Gruppe, Griech, Mythologie (1906), 406, n.l; 762; 840, n.5; 854, nn.5 ff.; 1203; 1209, n.2; 1293.

2. J. Grimm, DM⁴, 768 ff.; Sartori, in Zs. f. Vk. 4 (1894), 289 ff.; A. Kuhn, in Zs. f. deutsch. Altertum 6 (1848), 13 ff.; W. Mannhardt, Antike Wald- und Feldkulte² (1904–5), i.149 ff.; H. Meisen, Die Sagen vom wütenden Heer und vom Wilden Jäger (1925); A. Endter, Die Sage vom wilden Jäger (Diss. 1933); V. Schweda, Die Sagen vom Wilden Jäger, etc. (1915); H. Plischke, Die Sage vom Wilden Heer im deutschen Volke (1914); E. S. Hartland, The Science of Fairy Tales (1891), 234 ff.; Ch. Hilscher, Diss. de exercitu furioso (1688, 1702).—In France, the Host is known as *mesnie furieuse.*

3. Dio. Hal. x.2.

4. Grimm-Stallybrass, TM 1591.

5. FHG iv.151.27.

6. F. Liebrecht, Des Gervasius von Tilbury Otia Imperialia (1856), 173–211.

7. J. Grimm, DM⁴, loc. cit.

8. Schweda, op. cit., 13; Stith Thompson, MI, E 501.12.4.

9. Plischke, op. cit., 36; Stith Thompson, MI, E 501.10.3.

10. Schweda, op. cit., 28–29; Stith Thompson, MI, E 501.7.6, 1–4.

11. Plischke, op. cit., 55; Stith Thompson, MI, E 501.11.4; Plischke, op. cit., 37; Stith Thompson, MI, E 501.16.5.—Storms likewise occur at the death of witches: G. Kittredge, Witchcraft in Old and New England (1929), 158 f., 477, n.64.

12. In much the same way, in the old song chanted when the Ark of the Lord was brought back after a campaign, it was described as the equivalent of the "myriads (and) thousands of Israel": Num. 10:36.

13. Israel would then mean simply, Jacob. For a similar learned misunderstanding of a popular expression, we may refer to the famous words, *Is Saul also among the prophets?* (I Sam. 10:11, 12; 19:24), for—as Robert Eisler ingeniously suggested—the Hebrew word *shaūl* (Saul) may there have meant originally, "one loaned to the temple."

14. The expression, *y ad ad,* "Oh, daddy, daddy" (paralleled by *y um um,* "Oh, mummy, mummy") occurs in the same sense in the Ugaritic text, The Gracious Gods, 32.

15. E. Rhode, Psyche ⁷ (1921), ii.375, n.1.

16. J. Vermaseren, Mithras (Urban Bücher, 1965), 84 f.

17. Sophocles, Trach. 1193 ff.; Euripides, Heraclidae 910 ff.; Ovid, Met. x.134–275; Apollodorus, Bib. ii.158 ff.—Late Greek sources, however, discard the element of the fiery chariot. In Lucian, Hermot. vii, Heracles simply *flies* to heaven, and in Lysias, iii.11, he simply *disappears.*

18. Kornemann, in Klio 8.278; F. Cumont, The Mysteries of Mithra (1903), 157.

19. F. Cumont, After Life in Roman Paganism (1923), 157.

160 The mantle of Elijah

1. A. E. Crawley, ERE, s.v. Dress; cf. also: A. Jirku, in ZAW 37 (1917–18), 109–25.

2. E. Westermarck, The Origin and Development of the Moral Ideas (106–8), ii.623.

3. Theocritus, Id., ii.53–54.

4. E. Kaempfer, "History of Japan," in J. Pinkerton's Voyages and Travels (1808–14), vii.717; cf. E. Crawley, Oath, Curse and Blessing (1934), 99.

5. R. Taylor, Te ika Maui² (1870), 164.

6. J. G. Frazer, GB³ (1911–15), iii.131.

7. See above, §79.

8. See below, §218.

9. S. Dahn, in Me'oroth: Quarterly for Oriental Jews. Special Issue for the 750th Anniversary of Maimonides (Tel Aviv 1954), 25.

10. Cf. P. Joüon, in Biblica 16 (1935), 74–81.—Haircloth is mentioned also in Zech. 13:4 as the characteristic garb of prophets.

11. SBE xxv.449.

12. H. Kern, Manual of Indian Buddhism (1896), 75.

13. Westermarck, op. cit., ii.356; Crawley, ERE v.569.

14. Strabo, xvi.4, 8; cf. W. Robertson Smith, The Religion of the Semites[3] (1927), 437 f.

161 Harlots bathe in Ahab's blood

1. See above, §25.

2. Cf. H. C. Trumbull, The Blood Covenant (1887), 116 ff., 224; H. L. Strack, Der Blutaberglaube (1892), 14 ff., 44 f.; L. Kohler, in ZAW 34 (1914), 147; E. W. Lane, Manners and Customs of the Modern Egyptians[1] (1836), i.33; H. Gunkel, Das Märchen im AT (1921), 142.

3. Pliny, HN xxvi.5.

4. W. Crooke, The Popular Religion and Folklore of Northern India (1896), ii.172 f.

5. R. Moffatt, Missionary Labours and Scenes in Southern Africa (1842), 277.

6. H. Spencer, Principles of Sociology (1876–82), i.116.

7. Notes and Queries, Feb. 28, 1857.

8. Strack, op. cit., 36 ff.

9. *Taurobolium:* H. Hepding, Attis (1903), 196 ff.; S. Angus, The Mystery-Religions and Christianity (reprint, 1966), 94 ff. *Criobolium:* C. A. Lobeck, Aglaophamus (1829), 797; A. Dieterich, Eine Mithrasliturgie[2] (1922), 157 ff.; E. Rohde, Psyche[7] (1921), ii.421 ff.

10. J. Dunlop, Geschichte der Prosadichtung, ed. and tr. F. Liebrecht (1851), 135.

11. N. M. Penzer, The Ocean of Story (1923 sqq.), i.97.

12. Trumbull, op. cit., 117.

13. Ib., 120 f.

14. E. W. Cox and E. H. Jones, Popular Romances of the Middle Ages (1871), 292, as cited by Trumbull, op. cit., 121 f.

15. Midrash Rabbah, on Exod. 2:23.

16. E. Prym and A. Socin, Syrische Sagen und Märchen (1881), 73.

17. F. A. Schiefner, Tibetan Tales (1882), 160.

18. E.g., Grimm's story "Faithful John"; Bolte-Polivka, i.56 ff.; G. Huet, in Le Moyen Age, 21 (1919), 162–84.

19. G. Basile, Pentamerone, ix.3; L. Gonzenbach, Sicilianische Märchen (1870), 354 (with R. Köhler's notes).

20. J. Grohmann, Sagen aus Böhmen (1863), 268.

21. Frazer-Gaster, NGB §393.

22. Herodotus, iv.26.

23. O. Hovorka and A. Kronfeld, Vergleichendes Volksmedizin (1908–9), i.180.

24. Cox and Jones, op. cit., 310.

25. Chateaubriand, Mémoire d'autre tombe, iii.120.

26. P. Parkman, The Jesuits in Northern America in the Seventeenth Century[20] (1885), 389.

27. P. Paulitschke, Ethnographie Nordost Afrikas i (1886), 186.

28. Hvorka-Kronfeld, op. cit., ii.29.

29. Chronique de France, 1516, feuillet 202, as cited by Soane, in Notes and Queries, Feb. 28, 1857.

30. Norma L. Goodrich, The Medieval Myths (1961), 142.

31. A. Aarne and S. Thompson, Types of the Folk-Tale (1928), #305; Stith Thompson, MI, D 1500.1.9.3.

162 Baal Zebub, "Lord of the Flies"

1. Pausanias, v.14, 1.

2. Ib., viii.26, 7.

3. Cf. FHG iii.197; Aelian, NA ii.18; v.17; Antiphanes, in Fragmenta Comicorum Graecorum, ed. Meineke, iii.134; A. B. Cook, Zeus ii (1925), 781–83; L. R. Farnell, Cults of the Greek States (1896–1909), i.45.

4. R. A. S. Macalister, The Philistines (1914), 91–93.

5. O. Keller, Antike Tierwelt (1909–13), ii.448 ff.

6. Vendidad vii.2; viii.71.

7. Pausanias, x.28, 7.

8. K. Knortz, Die Insekten in Sage (Annaberg 1910), 88.

9. A. Wuttke, Der deutsche Volksaberglaube der Gegenwart[5] (1900), 207; ARW 2.132.

10. Schweiz. Archiv für Volkskunde 25.190.

11. J. Kuoni, Sagen des Kantons S. Gallen (St. Gallen 1903), 5.

12. Grimm-Stallybrass, TM iii.998 f.; HWbDA ii.1626 f.; G. Simrock, Deutsche Mythologie (1874), 95, 479.

13. G. Kittredge, Witchcraft in Old and New England (1929), 180 f.—The Lithuanians had a fly-god called *mussubinbiks*.

14. A monster called *žbb* is mentioned in a Ugaritic text: 'nt iii.43.—W. C. Graham and H. G. May, Culture and Conscience (1936), 154, accepting the connection with *zebub* "fly" as authentic, observe that "the Philistines readily and easily adopted that type of nature-worship, which had probably been brought to that region [i.e., Ekron] by the Hyksos." This view (anticipated by F. C. Movers in JA 1878.220–25) goes beyond the evidence.

ELISHA

163 Waters purified by salt

1. T. H. Gaster, The Holy and the Profane (1955), 13–14; O. Gruppe, Griech. Mythologie (1906), 889, n.3.

2. Ezek. 16:4.

3. Jalen, De sanitate tenenda, i.7.

4. E. Samter, Geburt, Hochzeit und Tod (1911), 152, n.6.

5. W. H. Rivers, The Todas (1906), 265 ff.

6. E. W. Lane, Arabian Society in the Middle Ages (1883), 188.

7. A. Wuttke, Deutscher Volksaberglaube der Gegenwart[2] (1900), 91; E. Mogk, ERE ii.633[a]; J. Grimm, DM[2] (1844), ii.999.

8. C. Bock, Temples and Elephants (1884), 260.

9. Notes and Queries 6/iii (1881), 73 f.

10. Manchester Guardian Weekly. March 22, 1947.

11. Grimm-Stallybrass, TM 1049.

12. Tibullus, iii.4, 9–10.

13. Strabo, xii.2, 6.

14. Clem. Alex., Strom. vii.4, 37.

15. J. G. Frazer, GB[2], ii.230; S. Eitrem, Opferritus und Voropfer der Griechen und Römer (1915), 38 f.

16. K. Preisendanz, Die griech. Zauberpapyri (1928–31), iv.2952, 3191; S. Eitrem, Papyri Osloenses i (1925), 100; Pap. Holn., col. ix.42; xii.5; Kyranides, p. 58.18; 77.32; Index of Wessely's Zauberpapyrus in Wiener Denkschriften xxiv, xlii, s.v. *kainos.*

17. Pliny, HN xxii.76, 85; cf. also: Marcell. Empir., xxvi.107.

18. M. Gaster, The Sword of Moses (1896), #46.

19. Ib., #57.

20. Ib., #58.

21. Ib., #69.

22. A. H. Sayce, in Folk-Lore 2.389.

23. Homeric Hymn to Apollo, 231.

24. II Sam. 6:3.

25. Tibullus, i.1, 38.

164   Elisha called "baldpate"

1. Aristotle, Problemata 878ᵇ, 21 ff.; 879ᵇ, 23 ff.; cf. R. B. Onians, The Origins of European Thought about the Body, etc. (1951), 232–33.

2. Id., De gener. animalium 746ᵇ.21 ff.

3. Id., Fr. vii.285.8; Probl. 880ᵃ.35 ff.

4. Pliny, HN xi.39.

5. Aristotle, Hist. anim. vi.57ᵇ, 9; Pliny, HN viii.42, 164.

6. Zs. f. Vk. 9 (1899), 68; Flügel, Volksmedizin und Aberglaube in Frankenwald (1863), 62 f.

7. Grimm-Stallybrass, TM 1606 (*snoyen, kahlkopf*).

8. Mayor, on Juvenal, v.171; cf. also: Aristophanes, Clouds 540 f.; Brunck, Analecta ii.311 (= Lucian, Epigr. gr. 18).

9. Mayor, loc. cit.

10. Dunlop-Liebrecht, Gesch. der Prosadichtungen (1851), 72a.

165   The inexhaustible cruse

1. Bolte-Polivka, i.361; ii.438. G. Jacob, Märchen und Traum (1923), 47, regards it as a dream-motif!

2. Grimm's Märchen, ed. 1819, #103.

3. A. L. H. von Polier, Mythol. des Indous (1809), ii.45.

4. J. Kunos, Ozman-török népköltesi-gijütemeny (Budapest 1887–89), #17.

5. P. Hambruch, Südseemärchen (1916), #37.

6. A. Löwis of Menar, Finnische und estnische Volksmärchen der Weltliteratur (1922), 36, #10; E. Sklarek, Ungarische Märchen, N.F. (1909), 54, 66; cf. H. Gunkel, Das Märchen im A.T. (1925), 58 f.

7. Ovid, Met. viii.679–80.

8. P. Toldo, Studien zur vergl. Literaturgeschichte, 6 (1906), 289–97; H. Gunther, Die christliche Legende des Abendlandes (1910), 97.

9. Bolte-Polivka, i.361.

10. Cf. T. H. Gaster, Thespis², 434 f.

166   Bathing cures leprosy

(a)

1. M. Gaster, The Sword of Moses (1896), #46.

2. H. C. Trumbull, The Blood Covenant (1887), 116 ff.; H. Strack, Das Blut im Glauben und Aberglaube (1900); Dunlop-Liebrecht, Ges. d. Prosaliteratur (1851), 135.

3. Pliny, HN xxvi.5.

4. Notes and Queries, Feb. 28, 1857.

5. Tawney-Penzer, Ocean of Story (1924–28), i.97.

6. Ellis, Early English Romances, 597 f.
7. G. Basile, Pentamerone, ix.3.
8. L. Gonzenbach, Sicilianische Märchen (1870), 354 (with R. Köhler's notes).
9. J. Grohmann, Sagen aus Böhmen (1863), 268.
10. E. Prym and A. Socin, Syrische Sagenund Märchen (1881), 73.
11. A. Schiefner and W. R. S. Ralston, Tibetan Tales (1882), 60.
12. L. Ginzberg, Legends of the Jews (1909 ff.), v.413, n.10; cf. Midrash Rabbah on Exod. 2:23.
13. Strack, op. cit., 36 ff.
14. W. W. Crooke, Popular Religion and Folklore of Northern India (1896), ii.172 f.
15. R. Moffatt, Missionary Labours and Scenes in Southern Africa (1842), 277; Trumbull, op. cit., 324.

(b) Waving in Magic

16. I. Scheftelowitz, Das stellvertretende Huhnopfer (1914), 28 f.
17. T. H. Gaster, Thespis[2], 310. (The Hittite term is *waḫnu-*.)
18. KUB IX 13 + XXIV.5, obv. 26 ff. = M. Vieyra, in RHR 118 (1939), 121 f.; tr. A. Goetze, ANET 355.
19. S. Seligmann, D. böse Blick (1910), ii.236.
20. Ib., ii.256.
21. W. Crooke, Popular Religion and Folklore of Northern India[2] (1896), i.153.
22. Seligmann, op. cit., i.383.
23. Heb.: *tᵉnûphah*. Cf. the expression *tšnpn* in a Canaanite ritual tariff from Ras Shamra-Ugarit: RS 23.6, Gordon.
24. Exod. 29:26; Lev. 8:29.
25. Lev. 7:30; 9:21; 10:15.
26. Lev. 14:12, 24.
27. Lev. 23:11, 20.
28. Num. 5:26.
29. Num. 6:20.

167 Iron floats

1. E. C. Brewer, Dictionary of Miracles, 133.
2. Gregory the Great, Dialogues, book ii.
3. Guérin, Vies des saints[12] (1892), vii.188.
4. L'abbé Corblet, Hagiography of the Diocese of Amiens, quoted in Brewer, loc. cit.

168 The use of corpses in magic

1. O. Weinreich, Antike Heilungswunder (1910), 64; I. Scheftelowitz, Altpales. Bauernglaube (1925), 122 f.; T. J. Pettigrew, On Superstitions Connected with the History and Practice of Medicine and Surgery (1844), 100; E. S. McCartney, in Papers of the Michigan Academy of Science, Arts and Letters 16 (1931), 189–90; Frazer-Gaster, NGB §§26–27, and Additional Notes.
2. P. Kahle, in Palest. Jahrbuch, vii.112.
3. Am Urquell, 4.70.
4. M. Abeghian, Der armenische Volksglaube (1899), 11.
5. W. Wood-Martin, Traces of the Elder Faiths in Ireland (1911), i.295.
6. TB Giṭṭin 69ᵇ.
7. Pliny, HN 28.45.
8. Ib.
9. Cited by McCartney, loc. cit.
10. Frazer-Gaster, loc. cit.

11. New York Herald Tribune, June 6, 1957.
12. Pliny, HN xxviii.41.
13. TB Sanhedrin 47[b].
14. Fr. Lambert, Moeurs et supersitions des Néo-Calédoniens (Nouméa 1900), 30 f.
15. Hesiod, Works and Days, 750 ff.
16. F. S. Krauss, Volksglaube und religiöser Brauch der Südslaven (1890), 146.

▲ **169 Yahweh's Lions**

1. W. Robertson Smith, The Religion of the Semites[2] (1894), 92 ff.
2. N. Adriani and A. C. Kruijt, De Bare'e-sprekende Toradja's van Midden-Celebes (1912–14), ii.233, 345 f.
3. L. Tauxier, Le Noir du Sudan pays Mossi et Gourounsi (1912), passim.
4. Id., 267 f., 310, 320.
5. Id., 461, 567 f.
6. J. Forsyth, The Highlands of India (1871), 357 f., 359 ff.; R. V. Russell, Tribes and Castes of the Central Provinces of India (1916), ii.77, 80.
7. Russell, op. cit., ii.78.
8. Forsyth, op. cit., 362 f.; Russell, op. cit., ii.84.

170 Horses and chariots of the sun

1. M. Jastrow, Rel. Bab. u. Assyriens (1905–12), 461.
2. G. A. Cooke, A Text-Book of North Semitic Inscriptions (1903), 165.
3. W. C. Graham and H. G. May, Culture and Conscience (1936), 242 f.
4. See: Stith Thompson, MI, A 724; Frazer-Gaster, NGB §56 and Additional Notes; A. B. Cook, Zeus i (1923), 205 f.; J. A. MacCulloch, Celtic Mythology (1918), 198; K. Helm, Altgerm. Religionsgeschichte (1913), i.178, 256; A. H. Krappe, La genese des mythes (1938), 85 f.; M. O. Howey, The Horse in Magic and Myth (1923), 114 f.
5. Rig Veda i.115, 3–4; viii.60, 3; ix.63, 8. Cf. N. M. Penzer, The Ocean of Story (1924–28), i.143, n.2; ii.150 f.
6. Xenophon, Cyrop. viii.3, 4, 12.
7. Hom. Hymns ii.63; iii.69; iv.69; v.88; xxviii.44; xxxi.15.—However, in Odyssey 23.244 Eos (Dawn) rides a chariot.
8. Hesiod, fr. 67, Rzach.
9. E.g., Pindar, Ol. vii.71; Sophocles, Ajax 845, 857; Euripides, Phoen. 1–3; cf. O. Robert, Theogonie und Götter[4] (1894), 431; O. Gruppe, Griech. Mythologie (1906), 381, n.14.
10. Cf. R. Eisler, in ARW 9 (1908), 150 f.; L. V. Schröder, Mysterium und Mimus (1908), 429 ff.; Krappe, loc. cit.
11. Vendiad xxi.5 (20); cf. Herodotus, vii.55.
12. Qunitus Curtius, iii.3, 8, 11.
13. Festus, s.v. October equus.
14. Pausanias, iii.20, 4.
15. Herodotus, i.216.
16. J. G. Frazer, The Fasti of Ovid (1929), ii.165–66.
17. Krappe, loc. cit.
18. J. W. Boecler, in Scriptores rerum Livonicarum, ii.674; J. Negelein, Germ. Mythologie (1912), 84; Krappe, loc. cit.

LATTER
PROPHETS

Isaiah

The LORD threatens to remove from Judah and Jerusalem every soldier and warrior, every governor and prophet, every wizard and senator, every petty official and nabob, every counsellor, every man expert in magic and charms.

The Hebrew word rendered *charm* means properly *whisper,* and is so used regularly in Semitic magic.[1] Charms are whispered, murmured, or hissed,[2] not only among the Semites, but also everywhere else for two reasons. First, this keeps the secret formula from the ears of "outsiders." Second, in the case of black magic, this prevents the spell's working on persons for whom it was not intended.

The whispering of spells is mentioned in other passages of the Old Testament itself. In Psalm 41:8 the writer complains that "all that hate me whisper against me," and that this refers specifically to magical incantations is evident from the fact that immediately afterward comes an allusion to the well-attested practice of pouring a magical substance over a man in order to bewitch him (see below, §**260**). Similarly, in Psalm 58:5 reference is made to a deaf adder "which will not hearken to the voice of *charmers,*" and the same Hebrew word is employed. In Mesopotamian magical texts the spell is said to be "chirped" like a sparrow's song;[3] and in Arabic, the recitation of runes is expressed by the imitative word *waswas,* suggesting a hiss.[4] Lucian, in his entertaining *Dialogues of the Demi-monde,* speaks of a witch who "murmurs her spell" over and over again;[5] while German warlocks are said habitually to have resorted to a low-pitched croon.[6]

Instructions to punctuate the words of a charm with hisses are a feature of several ancient magical texts that have come down to us. Such rubrics appear, for instance, in the famous Second Leyden Papyrus and in the equally well-known incantation which its editor Dieterich took mistakenly for a liturgy in the cult of Mithra.[7] An Aramaic magical document from Nippur includes the notation *sh, sh,* indicative of hissing;[8] and so too does a celebrated Ethiopic charm known as the *Net of Solomon.*[9] Tibullus, the Roman poet, speaks of conjuring ghosts by emitting a strident sound;[10] and Petronius says of certain witches that "they began to screech, so that you might have thought a hound was chasing a hare."

565

In the latter half of the nineteenth century there arose in the Tuamotu islands in the Pacific a cult of "Hissers" who hissed loudly to evoke the dead. Soft hissing sounds, interpreted by priests in a trance, were returned from the roof of the house of worship.[11]

▲ 172　Soul-boxes 3:20

After describing, in a strain of Puritan invective and scorn, the haughty daughters of Zion who tripped about with languishing eyes, mincing steps, and tinkling feet, Isaiah proceeds to give a long catalogue of the jewels and trinkets, robes and shawls, the veils and turbans, all the finery and frippery of these fashionable and luxurious dames.[1] In his list of feminine gauds he mentions "houses of the soul."[2] The expression thus literally translated is unique in the Old Testament. Modern translators and commentators, following Jerome, render it "perfume boxes," "scent-bottles," or the like.[3] Not impossibly, however, these "houses of the soul" were *amulets in which the soul of the wearer was supposed to lodge.*[4] Nor, indeed, are the two interpretations mutually exclusive; for in the eyes of a people who, like the Hebrews, identified the principle of life with the breath,[5] the mere act of smelling a perfume might easily assume a spiritual aspect; the scented breath inhaled might seem an accession of life, an addition made to the essence of the soul. Hence it would be natural to regard the fragrant object itself, whether a scent-bottle, incense, or a flower, as a centre of radiant spiritual energy, and therefore as a fitting place into which to breathe out the soul whenever it was deemed desirable to do so for a time. Far-fetched as this idea may appear to us, it may seem natural enough to the folk and to their best interpreters the poets:

> I sent thee late a rosy wreath,
> 　Not so much honouring thee
> As giving it a hope that there
> 　It could not wither'd be;
> But thou thereon didst only breathe
> 　And sent'st it back to me;
> Since when it grows, and smells, I swear,
> 　Not of itself but thee![6]

But if beauty can thus be thought to give of her life, her soul, to the soul of the rose to keep it fadeless, it is not extravagant to suppose that she can breathe her soul into her scent-bottle. At all events these old-world fancies, if such indeed they are, would explain very naturally why a scent-bottle should be called a "house of the soul." Poets perceive by intuition what most of us have to learn by a laborious collection of facts. Indeed, without some touch of poetic fancy, it is hardly possible to enter into the heart of the people. A frigid rationalist will knock in vain at the magic rose-wreathed portal of fairyland. The porter will not upon to Mr. Gradgrind. ▼

173 Waistcloths and shoestrings 5:27

Not a waistcloth is loose,
Not a sandal-thong broken.

This has more than a literal meaning. In ancient thought, "clothes makyth man" in a very real sense, being regarded not merely as vestments, but as an integral part of the person or "self." Accordingly, the loosening of the waistcloth or shoestrings means that their wearer has himself "become undone." The former idiom occurs in the Old Testament; in Job 12:21 it is said of Yahweh that "he pours contempt on princes and looses the waistband of the strong," while, according to Isaiah 45:1, Cyrus was called by Yahweh to "subdue nations and ungird the loins of kings." Similarly, in a Canaanite mythological text from Ras Shamra-Ugarit, the god Baal is warned by his adversary Mot that if he tussles with him, the girdle of his robe—which is heaven itself (see below, §278)—will become loosed.[1]

The loosening or snapping of shoestrings was also interpreted, however, as signifying the removal of impediments, and was therefore considered a *good* omen. A character in one of Menander's comedies calls on the gods to send him good fortune, seeing that his shoestring has indeed snapped,[2] and John of Salisbury relates that when Mark the evangelist accidently broke his sandal thong when leaving ship on a proselytizing mission to Alexandria, he gave thanks for this good omen.[3] Both Cicero[4] and Pliny[5] mention the practice of deriving omens from the loosing of latchets; and this superstition obtained in the Hebrides as late as the nineteenth century.[6]

174 Seraphim 6:2

Isaiah sees a vision of the LORD seated on a high and lofty throne,
with six-winged seraphs hovering around him.

The six-winged seraphim have been traditionally identified as flaming angels, but this rests solely on a fanciful association of the word with the Hebrew *ś-r-ph,* "burn." In Isaiah 14:29, the winged seraph is described as the offspring of an adder; and in Numbers 21:6, 8 and Deuteronomy 8:15 "seraph-serpents" are said to inhabit the wilderness, just as Herodotus speaks of fiery serpents which dwell there.[1] It is therefore more likely that we are to see in the seraph a mythological demon, and it may then be identified with the grim six-winged creature holding a serpent in either hand, who is portrayed on a relief of the eighth century B.C. from Tell Halaf, in Syria.[2] An Egyptian word *srrf,* which may be related, appears to mean "griffin" or "dragon."[3]

175 Invaders characterized as "tails of smoking firebrands" 7:4

We often miss the full point and irony of a prophetic utterance by failing to recognize a piece of folklore on which it is based. So, in the present instance, the real meaning is lost unless it is realized that Isaiah is alluding to what must have been a popular military stratagem of striking terror in an enemy by dispatching foxes through the battlefield with blazing torches tied to their tails. This, for instance, was the tactic adopted by Samson against the Philistines (see above §117).

Thus interpreted, added point is lent to the fact that the prophet is ordered to deliver his message of encouragement against the invaders in the vicinity of "the conduit of the Upper *Pool*," i.e., destined to quench the brands, and "on the highway to the Fuller's *Field*."

(This interpretation also avoids the necessity of twisting the Hebrew word [*zanab*], which normally denotes "tail" into the meaning "stump," as is usually done [LXX: *faggots;* RSV: *smoldering stumps;* MOFFATT: *faggots*]).

176   A virgin shall conceive:[1] Immanuel   7:14–16

> *When Rezin, king of Syria, and Pekah, king of Israel, unite to attack Judah, the latter's king Ahaz receives assurances from Isaiah that the LORD will yet protect his people. A sign of things to come will be that a young woman will conceive and bear a son, and name him Immanuel, i.e., "God is with us." From earliest infancy, the child will feed on curds and honey.*

This famous prophecy is susceptible of two alternative interpretations:

1. The reference is purely general, i.e., an era of such prosperity will ensue that any young woman now pregnant will be justified in naming her child Immanuel, "God is with us." This interpretation is supported by the fact that the words "Behold, the young woman (*ǵlmt* = Heb.: *'almah* of our text) shall bear a son" occur as part of a hymeneal in a Canaanite text from Ras Shamra-Ugarit,[2] suggesting that they were a traditional marriage formula, somewhat like the Italian *fighli maschi!*

2. The reference is to an ancient myth which told of the birth of a Wondrous Child as a presage of the coming of Age of Bliss.[3] This myth—familiar especially from Vergil's *Fourth Eclogue*—was a "projection" of a Seasonal Rite at which the Spirit of the New Year, and hence of returning fertility and increase, was represented as the newborn offspring of a "sacred marriage" between the king (impersonating the god) and a hierodule (impersonating the goddess). This "marriage" is well-attested in the Ancient Near East.[4] It was a recognized element of the New Year festivities at Babylon, and other Mesopotamian cities.[5] Toward the end of the third millennium B.C., the inscription on a statue of Gudea, governor of Lagash, refers to "bringing wedding-gifts on New Year's Day, the festival of the goddess Baú";[6] while a cylinder of the same ruler speaks of the marriage of that divine bride and the god Ningirsu.[7] Similarly, a long Sumerian hymn describes the spreading of the nuptial couch for the "sacred marriage" of Idin-Dagan, third king of the Isin dynasty (ca.

1918–1897 B.C.) and the goddess Innini.[8] Further, a late commentary on the New Year (*Akîtu*) festivities in Babylon relates how, on the eleventh day of the month of Nisan, the god Marduk "speeds to the marriage";[9] while the same and other documents also describe the nuptials, at Borsippa and Calah, of the god Nabu and the goddess Tahsmetu in the following month of Adar.[10] Lastly, brick couches used in this ceremony have actually been found in the ancient temple at Mari,[11] while the ceremony itself is starkly reproduced on a seal from Tell Asmar.[12]

Egyptian texts give evidence of a similar "sacred marriage" between the god Horus and the goddess Hathor celebrated annually at Edfu on the first day of the month of Epiphi (May-June), and followed three days later by the conception of the younger Horus.[13] So too, a feature of the Theban festival of Opet, held annually in the autumn month of Paophi (December-January), was the "sacred marriage" of the god Amon and the goddess Mut;[14] while an inscription in the temple at Deir-el-Bahri, accompanying reliefs which depict the event, describes the mating of god and goddess, impersonated (on the "punctual" and ritual level) by the pharaoh and his consort.[15]

The rite also obtained in ancient Greece. Aristotle informs us, for instance, that the Boukolikon at Athens was primitively the scene of Dionysus' "sacred marriage" with the king's consort;[16] while Lucian describes a three-day festival, blasphemously travestied by the false prophet Alexander, at which the nuptials of Leto and the birth of Apollo, and those of Koronis and the birth of Asklepios, were celebrated.[17] Moreover, the anonymous author of the Philoso-phoumena relates that at one stage of the Eleusinian Mysteries the hierophant "shouted and exclaimed in a loud voice, 'Holy Brimo hath given birth to a holy child, Brimos' ";[18] while we are told by Strabo that the birth of Zeus was enacted ritually in Crete.[19] Both marriage and nativity survive, albeit in attenuated and garbled form in the modern mumming plays performed in Thessaly, Macedonia, Epirus, and in the Northern Islands of Greece on such crucial seasonal dates as New Year, May Day, and the like; for the leading characters of those plays are often a bride and a groom, and the upshot of the dramatic action is the birth of a prodigious child.[20]

The offspring of the "sacred marriage" was, as we have seen, regarded as divine; and a standard term for a temple-woman in Phoenician was *glmt,* the exact equivalent of the Hebrew word rendered "young woman (KJV: *virgin*)" in the scriptural text.[21] Hence, the prophet speaks of such a woman's bearing a son, who should be named Immanuel, i.e. (on this interpretation), "*a god is with us.*"

The seasonal festival at which the "sacred marriage" was celebrated often coincided with the winter solstice, wherefore the child was identified as the re-emergent sun[22]—an idea eventually adopted (through Hellenistic channels) by Christianity, which came to observe that date as the birthday of him who was regarded as Lux Mundi.[23]

If this second interpretation be adopted, the prophecy may be linked to that in 9:1 ff. ("Unto us a child is given," etc.), and the solstitial background of the underlying rite will lend added point to the words: *The people that walked in darkness have seen a great light; they that dwelt in a land of gloom—over them has daylight shone!*[24]

177   Gibbering ghosts and mediums   8:19

Consult the mediums and the wizards who chirp and mutter.

On chirping and muttering in magic, see above, §171. It was especially appropriate in necromancy, because in the folklore of most peoples, the ghosts of the dead are believed to gibber or to speak in a thin, piping voice. This is known technically as the *sursurrus necromanticus.*[1]

Homer says, for example, that the spirit of the deceased ascended from the netherworld like smoke, emitting twittering sounds;[2] and Vergil has the shades of the departed "lift their feeble voices."[3] Horace,[4] Lucan,[5] Statius,[6] Ovid,[7] Petronius,[8] and Claudian[9] describe them in the same way. Nor is this notion confined to the ancient world. The Zulus of Africa call ancestral spirits "whisperers" (*imilozi*);[10] the aborigines of New Zealand say that they whistle,[11] the Solomon Islanders that they speak in a "low whisper,"[12] and the Polynesians that they squeak;[13] while the Algonquins declare that shadow-souls chirp like crickets.[14] Among the Arabs, it is deemed appropriate to whistle when talking to devils.[15]

178   Cursing by king and god   8:21

Apostates, says the prophet, will be visited with hardship and hunger. They will then become embittered and start pronouncing curses by their king and their gods.[1]

A curse, like an oath, can be effective only if it is pronounced in the name—that is, on the authority—of that which has power.[2] To cite but two representative examples from contemporary primitive cultures: among the Melanesians, curses are usually invoked in the name of a *li'oa,* or powerful spirit,[3] while on Banks Island, *vagona,* the direst execrations, consists in procuring the intervention of a supernatural force.[4]

In accordance with this principle, it was customary in the Ancient Near East to pronounce curses or swear oaths in the name either of the god, as the source of continuous and indesinent power, or of the king, as his punctual embodiment, or of both. The oath by the god (*niš ili,* or *niš zikir ili*) is frequently mentioned in Mesopotamian texts,[5] while in the time of the Amorite dynasty of Hammurapi (seventeenth century B.C.),[6] and later at Nuzi, oaths by the king became particularly common.[7] In Egypt, oaths were often sworn by the god Thoth and the pharaoh combined;[8] and it is to be noted that in Genesis 42:15 Joseph swears by the life of the latter.

179   The dawn of salvation   **9:1**

> *The people who walked in darkness*
> *have seen a great light;*
> *they who dwelt in a land of gloom,*
> *on them has daylight shone.*

These famous words are perhaps a quotation from an ancient poem, for a perfect parallel to them may be found in a Mesopotamian oracular text, which reads: *He that dwelt in darkness unlit now exults, he sees the light of the sun!*[1]

180   "Lucifer, son of the morning"   **14:12–15**

> *In 705 B.C., Sargon of Assyria, who had been threatening Judah, was defeated in battle in a distant land. Isaiah scornfully compares the fallen monarch to a certain Hêlal, son of Dawn (EV: "Lucifer, son of the Morning"), who aspired to enthrone himself on the mountain of the gods, but was thrust down into the netherworld.*

Sargon, it would seem, was not only defeated, but also abandoned on the battlefield and left to perish. The fallen monarch is fancifully identified with the central character of an ancient myth relating how an overweening upstart who threatened the supremacy of the Most High God was eventually thrust from heaven to the nethermost Pit.

Stories of such celestial upstarts indeed occur in the literature of the Ancient Near East. A Cappadocian cuneiform tablet, dating about 2000 B.C., tells of a female deity who was cast from heaven by the supreme god Anu because of some evil, jealous, or rebellious purpose on her part.[1] Sanchuniathon, the Phoenician mythographer, tells how "Kronos," after removing his father "Ouranos" from sovereignty in heaven and seizing power for himself, became apprehensive of his brother "Atlas" and cast him from heaven into a deep cavern in the earth. Unfortunately, however, we are not yet able to recognize the Phoenician (or Canaanite) gods who lie beneath the Greek names which Sanchuniathon's translator, Philo of Byblus, has fastened upon them.[2] Hittite myth tells likewise of a struggle between the gods for the hegemony in heaven. Originally, we are told, Alalu ruled. After nine years, Anu deposed him. Nine years later, Anu was in turn dethroned by Kumarbi.[3] In another Hittite tale, a monster called Hahhimas—evidently a form of Jack Frost—after paralyzing the earth and seizing a number of gods who have been dispatched to bring relief, eventually threatens to scale heaven and attack the supreme weather-god. The upshot of this threat is unknown to us, since only a portion of the text has been preserved, but from the fact that the tale is told in connection with the worship of the sun and of one of the gods whom Hahhimas is said to have seized, it is apparent that he was defeated—that is, thrust down from heaven—and order restored.[4]

The Greek myth of the *Theomachia,* or battle of the gods, in which Ouranos is dethroned by Kronos, and the latter in turn by Zeus, is, of course, well known from Hesiod's *Theogony,*[5] and has been frequently compared in recent years with the Hittite story of Kumarbi.[6]

Stories of the removal of rebellious angels or celestial beings from heaven may be detected even in the Old Testament itself. Ezekiel (28:11 f.) likens the king of Tyre to an upstart thrust from the paradisal "mountain of the gods," and his picture is evidently derived from a traditional Phoenician myth familiar to the object of his scorn (see below, §213). Again, in Psalm 82:6 f., wicked rulers who arrogate to themselves divine status and honors are warned that they are really men after all and are destined "to fall like one of the princes," where there is possibly an allusion to a story about "fallen angels."[7]

The tale was a favorite of pseudepigraphic literature,[8] where the upstarts are usually identified with the mysterious angelic "watchers" of the Book of Daniel, or with the impious "sons of God" who, in the story related in Genesis 6:1–3, consorted with the daughters of men and are seemingly associated with beings called *nephilîm*—a name popularly derived from the Hebrew *n-ph-l,* "fall" (see above, §32).

181   The fate of Sargon   14:18–20

> *While all the kings of the nations,*
>   *yea, all of them, rest in glory.*
>   *each in his separate tomb,*
> *thou art cast forth without a grave,*[1]
>   *like a (fallen) twig bemired,*[2]
> *swathed in the (spattered) robes*
>   *of murdered men,*
> *of those whom the sword has transpierced*
>   *—a trampled corpse!*
> *With those that (duly) go down*
>   *to the bedrock of the Pit*
>   *thou art not joined in burial. . . .*

There is a subtle point of folklore in this excoriation of the Assyrian king: *he is condemned to wander like an errant and restless ghost,* for it was a common belief of the Mesopotamians—as it is of many other peoples—that those who had died by the sword enjoyed no repose in the netherworld.[3]

The point is caught up in the succeeding verses, where it is said that Babylon will be reduced to "a possession of the hedgehog, and pools of water," for these are the typical haunts of ghosts (see below, §188).

We do not know where exactly Sargon met his defeat, but an Assyrian text has his son Sennacherib order the soothsayers to inquire what sin his father had committed that he was not buried in his own "house."

182 Flying serpents   14:29

Flying serpents are said in Numbers 21:6–8 and in Deuteronomy 8:15 to haunt the wilderness, and in Isaiah 30:6 to dwell in the inhospitable tracts of the Negev. They belong to the large class of mythical animals familiar from travelers' and sailors' yarns, and are mentioned again by Herodotus.[1] Lucan too speaks of the "flying serpents of the Arabs" (*Arabum volucer serpens*),[2] and references to them (*ḥaiyê ṭaiyara*) are to be found also in native Arab sources.[3] Among the Indians of Canada, lightning is portrayed as a flying serpent.[4]

183 Shaving the beard in mourning   15:2
See §§135, 293.

184 The gardens of Adonis   17:10
RSV: *Though you plant pleasant plants,*
         and set out slips of an alien god,
       though you make them grow on the day that you
                                       plant them,
       and make them blossom in the morning that you sow,
         yet the harvest will flee away
       in a day of grief and incurable pain.

These lines allude to the widespread custom of planting little seedboxes at crucial times in the seasonal calendar, watering them for a few days, and then regarding their germination as symbolic of revitalized fertility or even of the resurrection of the dead god (or spirit) of vegetation. "It is the custom," says a scholiast on Theocritus, "to plant wheat and barley in seedboxes during the festival of Adonis, and to call what is thus planted 'gardens of Adonis' ";[1] and references to such "gardens" are indeed made by Euripides,[2] Plato,[3] Theophrastus,[4] and other Greek writers.[5] "Just before New Year," reports the Jewish scholar Rashi in the eleventh century, "Jews plant seedboxes, water them, and watch them grow. They are kept until the Day of Atonement [ten days later]";[6] and the custom still survives among their modern co-religionists in parts of Italy.[7] In both Sicily[8] and Sardinia,[9] women sow wheat in plates shortly before Easter. These are then kept in a dark place and watered daily. Plants soon shoot up, and are tied with red ribbons. The plates are deposited on tombs along with effigies of the dead Christ, which are made up in Catholic and Greek Orthodox churches on Good Friday. The rite symbolizes the Resurrection.

In ancient Egypt, a similar custom was observed annually, to represent the resurrection of Osiris;[10] while in parts of India analogous ceremonies celebrated the seasonal revival of vegetation. Thus, at Udeipur, barley is sown in a small trench, then watered and heated artificially until the grain sprouts, whereupon the young women distribute the sprigs to the men, who wear them in their turbans.[11] Similarly, too, among the Oraons and Mundas of Bengal, it is customary for the daughters of the village headsman to sow blades of barley, mixed with turmeric, in moist, sandy soil. When presently they sprout, the girls carry them in baskets to the karma tree, in the central dancing place. They are set down beside it to stimulate its growth.[12]

The prophet's allusion to such "gardens of Adonis" is more apparent in the original Hebrew than in the usual English versions; for what is rendered *pleasant plants* is really *plants of Na'amans,* and Na'aman ("comely, pleasant") seems to have been an ancient Semitic byname of Adonis.[13] Indeed, this name is believed to underlie the name *anemone,* which the Arabs call "the wounds of Na'aman" and which is held to have been stained red by the god's blood.[14]

185 The rebel constellations   24:21-23

> *It shall come to pass on that day*
>> *that the LORD will punish the host of heaven in heaven,*
>> *and the kings of the earth on the earth.*
> *They will be gathered together as prisoners in a pit;*
>> *they will be imprisoned in a prison*
>
> . . . .
>
> *The moon will be confounded*
>> *and the sun ashamed,*
> *for He who is indeed the LORD of HOSTS*
>> *will reign in Mount Zion and in Jerusalem,*
>> *and his glory be fully displayed*
>> *before the elders of his court!*

The prophet is alluding to an ancient myth which told how, in primeval times, the supreme god imprisoned certain rebellious powers in subterranean vaults, himself asserting his sovereignty and establishing the world order. Thus, in the Mesopotamian Epic of Creation, the victorious Marduk imprisons them in "cells,"[1] and elsewhere in Akkadian literature they are commonly styled "the bound (or, chained) gods."[2] Similarly, in the Biblical Book of Revelation, the angelic allies of Satan are "cast down to the earth."[3] The analogy, in Greek myth, of the contumacious Cyclopes and Titans, similarly dispatched to Tartaros by Ouranos, will spring readily to mind.[4]

In later ages, these ousted rebels came to be identified with *stars* or *planets.*[5] Enoch, for example, sees in hell "seven stars like great burning mountains." Inquiring about them, he is told that what he is beholding is "the prison for the stars and host of heaven," who primevally "transgressed God's command by not coming forth at the right time."[6] So too Jude speaks of "wandering stars (Greek: *asteres planētai*) for whom nether darkness has been reserved for ever";[7] while in an Aramaic magical incantation from Nippur reference is made to "the seven stars (i.e., planets) and the twelve signs of the Zodiac which have been sealed until the great Day of Judgment,"[8] and allusion to the same myth is found in the liturgy of the Mandaeans of Iraq and Iran.[9]

It will be observed that in our quotation of the Biblical text one line has been omitted owing to uncertainty about the translation. It can mean either "And they shall be deprived of a large number of their days,"[10] or "And after many days they shall be visited." If the former rendering be adopted, the reference will be simply to the "blank days" of incarceration. If, however, we prefer the latter, the prophet's words may be understood to hark back to the ancient myth, for the Mesopotamian epic indeed speaks of Marduk's eventually having mercy on the vanquished gods and removing their yoke,[11] while a text published by T. G. Pinches describes how the god went down to their prison and freed them.[12] Enoch too says that they will be bound only for ten thousand years,[13] and the Aramaic charm that they will ultimately witness "a great hour of release."[14]

(It is possible also that the prophet is indulging in studied irony, for the Hebrew words (viz., *p-q-d* and *'a-s-f*) here rendered "punished" and "gathered together" are also military terms meaning "muster" and "assemble troops."[15] The idea would then be that Yahweh, the Lord of Hosts, will indeed muster the celestial hosts and assemble the earthly kings—not, however, for a victorious campaign but simply to mass them for judgment and to round them up like captives led to prison!)

186 Leviathan 27:1

Eschatology is cosmogony in the future tense: the age to come will be inaugurated in the same way as was the present age—by the Lord's subjugation of the rebellious Dragon of chaos and disorder. This myth is itself the counterpart of a ritual, surviving sporadically in folk usage, whereby the dragon of the nether waters is subdued at the beginning of the year, lest he prevent them from rising and moistening the earth or lest he send them in devastating flood.[1]

Ancient Near Eastern literature knows several forms of this myth. In Sumeria, it was related that the god Ninurta (or, in another version, the goddess Inanna) had primevally vanquished a draconic marplot and channeled the subterranean waters between the banks of the Tigris and Euphrates.[2] In Babylon, a myth recited at New Year (Akitu) related how, at the gray beginning of time, Marduk had conquered the draconic Tiamat and thus established the order of the world.[3] The Hittites likewise recited at New Year (Puruli) the tale of how the Weather God (or, in another version, a mortal named Hupasiyas) had overcome the primordial Dragon (Illuyankas) and how, in consequence of his triumph, rainfall had been assured.[4]

In a long mythological poem discovered at Ras Shamra-Ugarit, Baal, the Canaanite god of rainfall and fertility, does battle against Yam, *alias* Nahar, the genius of sea and streams, and, by subduing him, acquires dominion over gods and men and is able to regulate the seasons of the rains.[5] It is this feat which the prophet here appropriates to Yahweh and projects into the future. His very words, and especially the unusual epithets ("fleeing" and "tortuous") which he applies to the Dragon, reproduce exactly the lines of the older text, in which Baal is said to smite "Leviathan, the fleeing serpent" and the "Dragon Tortuous."[6]

The myth evidently enjoyed considerable popularity in Israelite folklore, for there are several allusions to it in the poetic books of the Old Testament, the Dragon being variously named Leviathan (Wriggly), Rahab (Blusterer), or Tannin (Sea-monster).

Thus (a) Isaiah himself elsewhere (51:9–10) describes Yahweh as he who hewed the Blusterer (Rahab) in pieces, transfixed the Dragon (Tannin), and dried up the sea (Yam).

(b) Habakkuk, envisioning the imminent approach of Yahweh to deliver his people from their oppressors, asks rhetorically (3:8) whether he is again about to launch an attack, as of old, upon Sea (Yam) and River (Nahar).

(c) In Psalm 74:13–14, Yahweh is addressed as the ancient King who by his strength broke up the sea (Yam), shattered the heads of the Dragon (Tannin), and crushed those of Leviathan.

(d) Similarly, in Psalm 89:9–10, Yahweh is pictured as establishing dominion over the proud and towering sea (Yam) and crushing the Blusterer (Rahab) like a slain man.

(e) In Psalm 93, Yahweh is hailed as a god who has acquired kingship and stabilized the world by subduing the contumacious rivers and sea.

(f) Lastly, the afflicted Job likens himself in one passage (7:12) to the sea (Yam) and Dragon (Tannin) whom Yahweh of old put under guard; and in another (26:12–13) he describes his God as having of old quelled the sea (Yam) by his strength and smitten the Blusterer (Rahab) by his skill.

In a manner characteristic of ancient myths, this tale was later embodied in a spell against evil spirits, for in an Aramaic incantation from Nippur demons are exorcized by "the charm which operated against the sea (Yam) and against Leviathan the Dragon (Tannin)," and it is said of the latter that he was smitten by "a fate laid upon him by God."[7]

Parallels to the story abound outside the Semitic area. In Indian mythology, one of the principal feats of Indra was the defeat of the monster Vrtra and the release of the waters which the latter had "impounded."[8] In Greek myth, we have the familiar victory of Zeus over Typhon (though the marine aspects of the monster have been obscured),[9] and among the Teutons that of Thor over Midhgardsormr, the serpent who encircles the earth.[10]

The name Leviathan is a fanciful invention of popular lore. It means properly "Coiling" or "Wriggly," and the monster is also called, both here and in the Canaanite text from Ugarit, 'Aqaltan, "the Tortuous." Similarly, in a Ugaritic charm against snakebite, a mythological serpent is called '-q-š-r, which means, in the same way, "Twist-and-Twine,"[11] while in Egyptian incantations of analogous type, a cobra is designated "Head-rearer."[12]

187   The "Name of the LORD" as his agent   30:27–28

> Behold, the Name of the LORD comes from afar,
> burning with his anger and with thick rising smoke;
> his lips are full of fury.
>   and his tongue is like a devouring fire;
> his breath is like an overflowing torrent
> that reaches up to the neck.

In Semitic thought, a person's *name* is, as we have seen (above, §72), his *manifested identity,* not merely a *verbal appellation.* When, for instance, God does something "for His name's sake," he is simply being true to his known and revealed character, and the more correct translation is, *true to his nature.* Since, however, a god may reveal himself through envoys or appointed agents, any such may also be described as his "name." In the mythological poems from Ras Shamra-Ugarit, the goddess Ashtareth is styled "the name of Baal,"[1] and she is so characterized also in an inscription of Eshmun'azar of Sidon, of the fifth century B.C.[2]

The personified "Name of the LORD" is here portrayed in terms of the typical ogre of folktales.[3] The prophet's words reproduce to a nicety the description of Ḥumbaba, the Rübezahl of the sacred wood, in the Mesopotamian Epic of Gilgamesh. *His roar is like the flood-storm, his mouth is fire, his breath is death* (or, *pestilence*).[4] The monstrous Typhon is similarly depicted in Greek myth.[5]

188   The haunts of demons   34:13–14

Deserts and solitary places, including ruins, on account of their eeriness, are universally regarded as inhabited by demons. Mesopotamian magical incantations, for example, speak of them constantly as haunting the wilderness, and it is thither that they are exorcized.[1] The same notion obtains also in Arabic folklore,[2] and is likewise mentioned in the Talmud and other Jewish sources.[3] In Syriac, Thomas of Marga's *History* says expressly that devils come from ruins in the form of black ravens;[4] and an Ethiopic prayer specifies the wasteland as their normal abode.[5] In a Canaanite mythological text from Ras Shamra-Ugarit, Baal is assailed in the desert by certain demonic creatures, called "renders" and "devourers" especially fashioned by El to lure him to his doom;[6] and it is in the desert that Jesus is tempted by Satan.[7] In Iranian belief, Ahriman and his evil spirits inhabit the desert;[8] and a similar European superstition is alluded to both by Milton in his *Comus*[9] and by Burton in his *Anatomy of Melancholy*.[10] Marco Polo records that he found the same idea current in the Far East,[11] and in more recent times it has been reported from Mongolia.[12] Somewhat analogous is the belief of the Finns that demons frequent the sequestered tracts of Lapland.[13]

In ancient Mesopotamia, the netherworld—the other natural habitat of demons—was sometimes described as a plain.[14]

189   Hairy devils   34:14

The satyr shall cry to his fellow

The Hebrew word rendered *satyr* means simply *hairy one* (Vulgate: *pilosus*), and thus reflects a common belief in hirsute demons who frequent desolate places. The belief is attested alike in Aramaic magical texts from Nippur[1] and in pre-Islamic Arabic sources;[2] while a familiar Moslem story relates that Bilkis, queen of Sheba, was revealed as of demonic descent by the fact that she had hair on her ankles.[3] The Mandaeans of Iraq and Iran speak of a shaggy female demon named Kaftâr who appears at full moon;[4] and Teutonic folklore knows of scrawny and scraggy demons called *scrats*.[5] Both Ephialtes, the proverbial *incubus,* and Pan are sometimes portrayed in ancient Greek folklore as goat-shaped satyrs.[6] (The Hebrew word which we have been discussing can also mean simply "goat.")

190   Lilith   34:14

In the future, the ruins of Edom will be haunted by demons; the night-hag will make herself at home there.

The word rendered "night-hag" is *lilith*. The rendering is based on a traditional, but quite erroneous, association of it with the Hebrew *lāyil,* "night." In reality, it derives from the Sumerian *lil,* "wind." In the form *lîlu* it was then adopted by the Semites of Mesopotamia as the name of a demon; and the corresponding feminine is *lilîtu,* whence *Lilith.*[1] Lilu, Lilitu, and "the handmaid of Lilu" (*Ardat Lîli*) constituted a triad of what were originally perhaps no more than wind-spirits.[2] Later, however—possibly through false etymology of their names—they came to be regarded as night wraiths or nocturnal demons, Lilith herself becoming the *succuba,* or faery sylph who consorted with men in sexual dreams.

As early, however, as the eighth century B.C., Lilith was in turn confused— at least in Syria—with what had originally been the quite distinct demonic figure of the child-stealing witch, known to the Mesopotamians as Lamashtu.[3] This we know from a curious amuletic plaque of that date discovered at Arslan Tash (ancient Ḥadatu) in the Upper Euphrates Valley. This plaque was designed to protect an expectant mother from Lilith's asaults, and the beldam is there portrayed, in two different representations, as a vixen swallowing a diminutive human figure and as a winged monster. The accompanying inscription names her explicitly "Lilith," "Winged One" (*'aftâ*), and "Strangleress" (*Ḥaniqatu*).[4]

In this aspect Lilith has worldwide analogues.[5] The Hittite knew of a demonic beldam called "the Strangleress" (*Wesuriyanza*) who was exorcized by taking her image down to a river and then giving her a sop of bread conveyed to her in the mouth of a fish.[6] Among the Semites of Mesopotamia she was portrayed as a hideous hybrid monster with a lion's head, ass's teeth, and bird's claws, holding a snake in either hand and suckling a dog and a pig at her breasts.[7] A Babylonian text now in the Yale collection describes her explicitly as "strangling children,"[8] and she was exorcized by being sent downstream in a boat[9]—a magical practice still observed in Indonesia.[10] The Egyptians saw her as a female who slipped into the house under cover of darkness and with face averted.[11] The Greeks were acquainted with her in several guises.[12] As Empousa, she had one foot made of brass and the other of cow dung. Alternatively, she was known as Dame Donkey-legs (*Onoskelis*),[13] or as *Mormō*, "Bogey,"[14] or as *Mormolukeion*, "Vixen-bogey."[15] She was also named Gello—a name which is probably connected with the word *ghoul* (properly "blood-sucker") but which was popularly interpreted as that of a lady-love of Zeus whose children had been slain by the jealous Hera and who took her revenge on human mothers![16] Again, she was recognized in the form of an owllike vampire, or as a plain owl (Bubo),[17] and, above all, a screeching nightjar, or strix. The later became one of her standard names in later European folklore; in the Balkans she is still called Strygoi; in Switzerland, Streggele; and in Italian, *strega* is, of course, the normal word for "witch."[18]

The parallels are, in fact, virtually endless; and the method of forefending her has now become virtually standard. Alike in the Balkans, in Ethiopia, and among more superstitious Jews it is customary for expectant mothers to carry an amulet the text of which describes how a saintly character (variously identified as St. Sisinnius or as the prophet Elijah) once encountered the beldam and her companions and exorcized her, in the name of God, by forcing her to disclose her various aliases. These were then recorded, and whenever a pregnant woman carries them on her person or has them written up in her chamber, the demons are rendered powerless.[19]

The varied migrations of this charm against Lilith may be seen in the fact that even in its modern Jewish form mention is made—incongruously and as a meaningless magical formula—of the names of S.S. Sisinnius and Sinoe, while the aliases of the beldam include *Aello*, "Stormwind," and *Okypodē*,

"Swift-footed," the two analogous harpies mentioned by the Greek poet, Hesiod![20] Even Shakespeare alludes to the charm, for in *King Lear* occurs the familiar doggerel:

> Saint Withold was walking over the [w]old,
> He met the witch and her ninefold;
> Said, "Aroint thee, witch! aroint thee!"[21]

In light of her common identification with owls, nightjars, and the like, it will now be clear why the prophet associates her, in our passage, with jackals, ostriches, and kites. In Malaya she is likewise identified with a screech owl and known as *langsuyar*;[22] while a popular Jewish name for her is Bruxa or Bruesche, which is simply the Portuguese *broxa*, "nightjar."[23]

191   The loom of life   38:12

> *Like a weaver I have rolled up my life,*
> *He cuts me off from the loom.*

On the concept of *life as a thread,* see below, §218.—A striking parallel to the prophet's phrase is afforded by the modern Greek euphemism, "His spindle is wound full (*mazōthēke to koubar' tou*) for "he died."[1] Cf. also Job 27:8.

192   Heaven as a muslin curtain   48:22

This is an alternative to the conception of the firmament as a sheet of metal (see above, §4). Similarly, in the Egyptian *Book of the Dead* (ch. 85), mention is made of "the firmament which constitutes a skin (*šet*),"[1] and in the Greek (Septuagint) and Vulgate's rendering of Psalm 104:2, "who stretchest out the heavens like a curtain," the latter word is translated "skin." The Indic Rig Veda says likewise that the sky is stretched out like a hide;[2] in parts of Africa it is called a cloth;[3] as again in the Finnish Kalevala.[4] The Assyrians called it "the piece of embroidery";[5] and in German riddles it is a curtain.[6]

193   Battle vaunts   42:13

> *The LORD sallies forth like a champion*
> *like a warrior vents (his) passion,*
> *shouts and raises his war cry,*
> *vaunts himself over his foes.*

See above, §31.

193a   The combat against the Dragon   51:9–10
See above, §186.

194   The Suffering Servant   53
> *The prophet comforts his oppressed compatriots by reminding them*
> *of a certain character who, though traduced, smitten, tortured, and*

*vilified, bears all this in equanimity, as a kind of human scapegoat
serving to make expiation for public sin and wrongdoing. A feature
of this martyr is that he is of unsightly appearance, like "one from
whom men turn their face."*

(a) We need not enter here into the vexed question of who the Suffering
Servant was intended to be—a problem as chronic and as seemingly insoluble
as the identity of the Dark Lady of the Sonnets.[1] Our concern is solely with
the folkloristic background of this image.

The picture is drawn, we suggest, from the widespread institution of the
human scapegoat, usually a misshapen person or one already under sentence
of death, upon whom is saddled the taint of all sins and offenses which might
otherwise be visited on the community, but precise responsibility for which
cannot be placed, for one reason or another, on any particular individual.[2]

In Babylon, a condemned felon (*bêl ḫiṭṭi*) was paraded through the streets,
scourged and expelled at the New Year (*Akîtu*) festival.[3] At Athens in times
of drought or calamity, a misshapen man and woman were driven out of town
as a public expiation; they were called *pharmakoi.*[4] At Chaeronea, during a
famine, a slave was ceremoniously beaten with twigs of *agnus castus* (a kind
of willow);[5] and at Marseilles, this was done in time of plague.[6] At Ephesus,
Apollonius of Tyana, the shamanistic "prophet" and charlatan, had a beggar
stoned to relieve pestilence;[7] and a similar use of human scapegoats is recorded from Abdera.[8] In Athens, a misshapen man and woman were scourged
with squills;[9] while similarly in Rome, an old man known as Mamurius
Veturus was clad in skins and beaten with white rods annually on the Ides of
March, evidently an ancient method of forefending evil at the beginning of the
year.[10] At Oritsha, on the Niger, two sickly persons act as human scapegoats
in moments of public crisis;[11] while in Thailand, purification is effected by
parading on a litter a woman broken down by debauchery, pelting her with
offal, and subsequently throwing her on a dunghill.[12] Among the aboriginal
tribes of China, a man of great muscular strength is expelled in times of
crisis, his face having first been disfigured by paints.[13] In Switzerland, a lad
disguised as a witch, goat or ass is driven out of town on the second Thursday
before Christmas;[14] and at Munich, Germany, the same custom used to
prevail on Ascension Eve.[15]

Now observe how perfectly all this chimes with the prophet's description of
the Suffering Servant. He is disfigured and sickly (Isa. 52:14; 53:2–3). He
bears physical sickness and pain on behalf of the community (53:4, 10). He
is expelled, "cut off" (53:8).[16] He is treated as a felon (53:9). He is subjected to stripes, i.e., trounced (53:5).

53:3

(b) The Suffering Servant is described also as *one from whom men hide
their face.* On this expression too Comparative Folklore sheds interesting light.

The Servant is a sick man, and, in ancient and primitive thought, sickness implies possession by a demon; indeed, he is said expressly (53:4) to be "smitten of God (i.e., demon-struck) and afflicted (i.e., plagued)."[17] Now, such demonic influences can be relayed to others by a mere glance. Hence, those who wish to avoid being so "infected"—especially persons possessed of some special or divine power—customarily veil their faces.[18] Moses, we are told (Exod. 34:33), veiled his face when addressing the people after his descent from Mt. Sinai. However, it may later have been re-interpreted, the real purpose of this action was to protect from untoward and demonic glances that divine glory with which he had become suffused. In the same way, the kings and sultans of several African peoples often keep their faces veiled;[19] and in ancient Persia only the seven highest courtiers were normally permitted to look upon the countenance of their sovereign at all times.[20]

Alternatively, the person who is demonically possessed had to keep *his* face covered, lest he pass the evil to others. In ancient Greece, for example, a man guilty of unwitting homicide had to keep his head covered;[21] and among West African primitives, human sacrifices are often veiled.[22] Not improbably, this is also the true basis of the law which anciently required lepers to wear hoods. Sometimes too, as in the case of the human scapegoats described above, the necessary disguise is effected by *whitewash*.[23]

195   The faery city   54:11–12

> *O thou forlorn, storm-racked, disconsolate,*
>   *Lo, I—even I myself—*
> *will yet lay thy stones with carbuncles.*[1]
>   *and thy foundations with sapphires;*
> *and I will make thy pinnacles of agate,*
>   *gleaming like little suns,*[2]
> *and thy gates of crystal,*
>   *and thine every boundary-mark of precious stones.*

This picture of the future Jerusalem is modeled after the *faery or heavenly city of folktales.*

Alike in the Old Testament itself (Exod. 24:10) and in Mesopotamian sources the floor or lowest register of heaven is said to be made of sapphires or lapis lazuli.[3] In Canaanite myth, the palace of Baal, built on the holy mountain of the gods, is made of silver and gold and ornamented with gems and lapis,[4] and in Ezekiel's description of the paradisial abode (Eden) on the sacred hill, those who inhabit it "walk about amid flashing gems" (Ezek. 28:14, 16; see below §213).

The theme enjoyed great popularity in later Jewish and Christian literature. The Greek version of Enoch speaks of the crystal palace and bdellium walls of heaven,[5] and the pseudepigraphic Testament of Abraham of God's crystal throne and table.[6] Tobit's "prayer of rejoicing" celebrates the future Jerusalem as a city built of sapphires, emeralds, and precious stones, with towers and battlements of pure gold, and streets paved with beryl, ruby, and "stones of Ophir."[7] The Book of Revelation elaborates the description by speaking of twelve foundations made of twelve different precious stones like those in the breastplate of Aaron, and adds the touch of the pearly gates and of the street "of pure gold, as it were transparent glass."[8]

The hymnographers virtually run riot with the picture. To quote but a few examples, one recalls first the famous lines of Hildebert of Lavardin, in the eleventh century:

> What joy the blessèd find in thee!
> Oh, how deep their revelry!
> Oh, what thrill unites them all!
> Oh, what gems adorn thy wall!
> What agates there and jacinths glow,
> None but they who dwell there know.[9]

Similar are the words of his great contemporary, Peter Damiani:

> Pearly mansions rise and, lo.
> Golden rooftops gleam and glow;
> Banquet-halls all crystal bright
> Twinkle in the morning light.
> Fashioned not of common stone,
> But of precious gems alone.
> The streets whereon the blessèd pass
> Are purest gold, transparent glass.[10]

To the same century belongs also the description of Paradise in a celebrated Jewish hymn entitled *Aqdamûth*. Composed in Aramaic by a certain Meir ben Isaac Nehorai (probably of Orleans), this is customarily recited in the synagogue on Pentecost:

> Lo, when the exiles He hath led
> To Jerusalem, there shall be shed
> Upon that city, day and night,
> The splendor of his radiant light;
> And silver-linèd clouds shall be
> Spread o'er it for a canopy.
> When He doth like a bridegroom ride
> At last, at last, to claim His bride.
> Then round about, on golden chairs
> (Each one approach'd by seven stairs)
> The righteous as His guests shall dine,
> And perfect bliss shall be their wine;
> And o'er their heads, for chandeliers,
> Shall hang the radiance of the spheres;

A beauty which no lips can tell,
Whereon no earthly eye can dwell,
A starry glory which of old
No prophet's vision could unfold.[11]

The picture appears, indeed, almost everywhere in world folklore. Thus, for example, in the Celtic legend of Sir Owayne, Paradise is enclosed by shining walls of glass; and in the fairy land of Ogygia, whither Meriddin Emorys sails, there is a glass palace of souls.[12] A Bosnian tale tells similarly of a faery castle made of diamonds,[13] in modern Greek tales it is wrought of gold and silver,[14] and in a Russian tale it is fashioned with columns of silver and steps of mother-of-pearl, and is ornamented with precious stones.[15] The Caribs and Arawaks of America spoke in the same vein of the fabulous realm of El Dorado with its imperial capital Manoa, "abounding in precious metals and all manner of gems."[16]

On the theme in general, see also above, §15.

196   Gad and Meni   65:11

In castigating his countrymen for forsaking Yahweh and forgetting his holy mountain, Isaiah describes them as men who spread a table for Gad [RSV: Fortune] *and* fill cups of mixed wine for Meni [RSV: Destiny].

Gad was the Canaanite god of luck.[1] When her handmaid Zilpah bore a son to Jacob, Leah exclaimed, (*This comes*) *through Gad,* and the child was named after that god.[2] The deity figures in several Biblical personal names, e.g., Gadi-el, a Zebulunite (Num. 13:10), Gaddi (Num. 13:11), and Gadi (II Kings 15:14, 17), as well as in the toponyms, Baal-Gad (Josh. 11:17) and Migdal-Gad, "tower of Gad" (Josh. 15:37).[3] A man named Gad-yô is mentioned several times in the celebrated Samarian ostraca (778–770 B.C.),[4] and such names as Gad-melek, "Gad is king,"[5] Gad-ram, "Gad is exalted,"[6] and Gad-na'im, "Gad is kindly,"[7] are found on Palestinian seals. The latter, however, are of uncertain date.

In Hellenistic and Roman times, when national religons broke down and men turned increasingly to the more personal mystery cults, the adoration of the Emperor, and the worship of such cosmic forces as the heavenly bodies or of such universal abstractions as Fate, special prominence was given to Tyche, or Chance.[8] In the Semitic area the ancient deity Gad came to serve as her masculine equivalent. He is accordingly mentioned with some frequency in Nabatean[9] and Palmyrene[10] inscriptions of this later period, and in the Greek (Septuagint) Version of our Biblical passage the name Gad is indeed rendered Tyche.

Eventually, the name of the god developed, by metonymy, into a common noun meaning "fortune, luck."[11]

Among the Jews a particularly interesting development took place. The expression, *couch of Gad,* came to be applied to a table decked with delicacies, or to an ornamented sofa, especially set aside, on the occasion of a circumcision. This was simply an imitation of the *lectus* which the Romans used to spread for Hercules or Juno at the birth of a boy or girl.[12] A parallel to this exists in modern Greece, where, on the third or fifth night after a child's birth, a table laden with honey, almonds, bread, and water, as well as with jewelry and coins, is set out for the three Fates, who are believed then to visit the house.[13]

The Talmud mentions also a popular custom of consigning the leavings of a meal to Gad, or Fortune[14]—a usage which survived among superstitious persons in Jerusalem as late as the nineteenth century.[15]

Moreover, as in ancient times, Gad continued to be invoked for prosperity, the popular expression, *Gad, spread luck and be not laggard about it,* being quoted in rabbinic sources.[16] In the same way, too, the Arabs sometimes called upon him when swearing oaths.[17]

Meni was a god who allotted fates.[18] His name derives from the Semitic word, *m-n-y,* "apportion," on the exact analogy of the Greek Moira, "Fate," which is connected with *meros,* "portion," and this inspires the prophet's declaration that Yahweh will *apportion* the worshipers of that deity to the sword.

Apart from our present passage, Meni is not mentioned in earlier Semitic sources. Like Gad, however, the deity became popular (evidently as an equivalent of Moira) in the Graeco-Roman age, appearing, in the form M-n-w-t-w, in Nabatean inscriptions.[19] It is mentioned also, in the feminine form Manat, in a passage of the Koran.[20] Tradition asserts that Mohammed at first countenanced the recognition of this goddess, describing her (along with the pre-Islamic Allat and Al-'Uzza),[21] as one of the three "exalted ladies" who might be expected to make intercession for the faithful. Later, however, his attitude toward such relics of heathendon stiffened, and he excised the conciliatory reference.

Jeremiah

197 Man from stones
Jeremiah 2:27

Saying to a stock, Thou art my father:
and to a stone, Thou hast brought me forth.

That mankind sprang from stones or rocks is a commonplace of popular belief in many parts of the world.[1] The Khasis of Assam, for instance, assert (with obvious sexual symbolism) that the Great Mother of the race is represented by cromlechs (called "female stone"), and the Great Father by menhirs (called "male stone").[2] In New Caledonia, Malekula, Achin, and other parts of Polynesia, stones were regarded as ancestral deities;[3] and among both the Zulus of Africa[4] and the Indians of Colombia[5] it is held that the first men either were or emerged from stones. The Paressi Indians of Matto Grosso say that the first man, a certain Darakavaitere, was made of stone, being born of a stone mother named Maiso.[6] Stories of particular men born from stone are common in the folklore of North Caucasian peoples;[7] while the Arab tribe of the Beni Sahr, in Moab, fancifully derive their name from the belief that their prime ancestor was a *ṣahr*,[8] or rock. Readers of the classics will at once recall the myth of Deucalion and Pyrrha, which relates how the world was repeopled after the Flood from stones which those two survivors cast behind their backs;[9] and that this story did not originate simply from the similarity of the Greek words, *laas* "stone," and *laos,* "people" (as the ancient mythographers supposed) is evidenced by the primitive parallels which we have cited.[10] In Tahiti, the wife of the first man is called *Papa,* or "Rock."[11]

There is an interesting survival of the belief in a famous passage of the Odyssey, where, before he has revealed his identity, Penelope says to the re-returning Odysseus:

> Say whence thou art, for not of fabulous birth
> Art thou, not from the oak nor from the rock.[12]

198 Land made barren through unchastity
3:2–3

See above, §144.

199 Passing children through fire
7:31; 19:5

Usually explained as a form of human sacrifice and sometimes so described by the Biblical writers themselves,[1] the heathen practice of passing children through fire is really something quite different. Fire purifies as well as consumes, and what is here involved is the widespread custom of passing children (and adults) through fire in order to "sain" them—that is, to purge them of human imperfections and (in myth and story) render them immortal.[2]

In ancient Greece, newborn males were carried around the hearth for this purpose,[3] and a similar rite was performed in the cult of Artemis Perasia at Kastabala, in Asia Minor.[4] Plutarch tells us that a certain Malkandros, king of Byblus (in Syria), was passed through fire to make him immortal;[5] and the Roman custom of leaping through fire at the festival of Palilia—a rite paralleled in many European harvest celebrations—is similarly interpreted by several modern scholars.[6] In reference to such usages, the neo-Platonic philosophers speak figuratively of "the ascent through fire" as a means by which devotees of theurgy sought to escape fate and ensure the immortality of the soul.[7]

The custom is well attested in many parts of the world.[8] Jakun tribes of the Malay Peninsula, for example, pass newborn children over fire.[9] Moreover, although the custom is proscribed in the classic lawbook of India,[10] it still persists in various parts of that country;[11] while a nocturnal ceremony of the same order has been witnessed among the Ali-Ilahis of Persia.[12] So too the practice is (or was) by no means uncommon in the Scottish Highlands,[13] and Jamieson, in his famous Scottish Dictionary, thence derives the English popular expression, "to haul over the coals."[14] In Siberian shamanism, boiling or roasting in a pot signifies rejuvenation or regeneration. "A Teleut woman," we are told, "became a shamaness after a vision in which unknown men cut her body to pieces and boiled it."[15] Similarly, an Avam-Samoyed shaman, while stricken with smallpox, dreamed that a naked man on a mountain chopped up his body and boiled it in a kettle for three years.[16] In various Australian tribes, initiation includes being roasted in or at a fire in order to achieve new birth.[17] This is also a frequent motif in folktales.[18] Indeed, Christ himself is said in one such tale to have rejuvenated an old woman by putting her on the fire.[19]

In ancient mythology, the idea underlies the story of how Demeter tried to make the infant Demophoon immortal by passing him through fire at night;[20] while of the same tenor is the tale of Thetis burning six of her and Peleus' sons in order to ensure their deathlessness.[21]

More often, the process is represented as that of being boiled in a Cauldron of Immortality.[22] Classical instances of this are the stories of Medea and Aison,[23] and of Thetis and Achilles;[24] while in the Welsh *Mabinogion Branwen,* Bendigeldfraen offers Matholoch a magic cauldron of this type.[25] The motif recurs also in more modern folktales from Sicily and Wallachia.[26]

An inscription of the Roman emperor Elagabalus (reigned A.D. 218–22) found at the foot of Mt. Hermon describes him as having been "deified in the cauldron," and this has been interpreted in reference to the same notion.[27] In early Christian thought, regeneration was likewise believed to be accomplished by baptism in fire.[28]

The children are said to have been passed through fire to Molech—a statement repeated elsewhere in the Old Testament. The usual view is that Molech is a tendentious misvocalization of the word *Melech,* "King," the original vowels being replaced by those of the word *bosheth,* "shame," just as Baal himself was called Bosheth by Israelite writers, and just as Ashtareth was vocalized Ashtoreth in the same way.[29] An Ammonite god named M-l-ch (or Milcom) is indeed mentioned in the Old Testament,[30] and a deity of the same name appears in an Amorite text of the eighteenth century B.C. from Mari,[31] in texts from Ras Shamra-Ugarit,[32] in documents from the Third Dynasty of Ur[33] and from Drehem.[34]

O. Eissfeldt has contended, however, that the Biblical *molech* is not the name of a god at all, but a common noun to be connected with a Phoenician (Punic) word, *molk* meaning "votive offering."[35] This view is today accepted by a large number of scholars, though dissident voices have indeed been raised.[36] As I see it, the difficulty with Eissfeldt's view lies not so much in the evidence elsewhere of a god M-l-ch as in the fact that the rite mentioned in the Old Testament need not have been sacrificial at all.

200   Creation of heaven and earth   10:12

> *It was He who formed the earth by His might,*
> *Who by His wisdom formed the firm ground,*
> *Who by His discernment stretched out heaven.*

These lines, together with those which immediately follow, recur at Jeremiah 15:15, and this particular sentence is quoted also in Psalm 135:7. It may therefore be assumed that it derives from a familiar hymn or other form of popular literature.

Now, it is significant that earth and sky (i.e., the firmament) are here said to have been created by a combination of Yahweh's physical prowess and mental shrewdness—of his brawn and brain—for exactly the same combination recurs in Job 26:12, where his primordial victory over the monster Sea (alias *Rahab,* the Blusterer) is described in the words:

> *By His strength He stilled Sea,*
> *by His perspicacity smote Rahab.*

We are therefore able to recognize in the prophet's words (i.e., in those of the popular poem he is quoting) an allusion to a cosmogonic myth parallel to that related in the Mesopotamian Epic of Creation (iv. 136–38), where, after subduing the analogous Tiamat, the victorious Marduk is said to have created heaven and earth by slitting her body lengthwise, suspending the upper half to form the firmament and submerging the lower half to constitute the bedrock of the earth. This is described expressly not only as an act of heroic prowess but also as the product of a "cunning plan," i.e., as a manifestation of his perspicacity!

201 "The wind and the rain"   **10:13; 51:16**

(a) Fissures for the rain

> *When He gives forth His voice,*
> *there is surging of water in heaven;*
> *out on the far horizon*
> *He causes vapors to rise;*
> *Lightning, He makes for the rain,*
> *and brings forth the wind from His stores.*

The phrase, *Lightnings he makes for the rain,* is readily explicable from the fact that in Palestine and Syria the advent of the "early rains" in October is heralded by electric storms.[1] Indeed, the native Arabs have a saying, "The lightning is a presage of rain."[2] Similarly, in the Canaanite *Poem of Baal* the imminent return of that god of rainfall, after he has been lured beneath the earth, is indicated by a display of lightning from his holy hill; and it is said of him also that "he will send his rain in due season . . . and give forth his voice from the clouds (and) his gleam earthwards as lightning-flashes."[3]

On the other hand, it has been ingeniously suggested[4] that in place of the word, *lightnings,* we should read, by a very slight change in the Hebrew text, (viz., *beDāqîm* for *beRāqîm*), *chinks, fissures.* The reference will then be to a popular belief that the rain was precipitated through chinks in the firmament, conceived as a solid dam holding back the upper waters of the cosmic ocean.[5] In the aforementioned Canaanite *Poem of Baal,* that god is indeed said to send rain through "chinks" in the sky, a form of the same word (viz., *bdqt*) being employed.[6] The concept of the celestial "chinks," it may be added, is an alternative to that of the celestial "grilles" or sluices (EV: "the windows of heaven"), often mentioned in the Old Testament (Gen. 7:113; 8:2; II Kings 7:2, 19; Isa. 24:18; Mal. 3:10). These are the supernal counterparts of the clefts in the surface of the earth through which springs gush forth. The former release the upper; the latter, the nether waters. The Deluge was caused by the opening of both simultaneously (Gen. 7:11; 8:2).

Similarly, according to Herodotus, it was believed in Libya that rain was precipitated by piercing the sky;[7] while some of the aborigines of New Zealand entertain the fancy that heaven is a solid septum provided with cracks through which the rain descends.[8]

(b) Promptuaries for the wind

The notion that meteorological phenomena are stored in promptuaries recurs elsewhere in the Old Testament: in Job 38:22, hail is so stored, and in Isaiah 45:3, reference is made to "storehouses of darkness." An elaborate description of the treasuries of the winds is given in the pseudepigraphic Book of Enoch.[9]

There is an interesting twist to this idea in the Dead Sea *Hymns of Thanksgiving.* Because the Hebrew word for winds also means spirits, it is there stated that sensate spirits (subsequently transformed into angels) were appointed by God to regulate natural phenomena and were stored in promptuaries. In the same way, man is guided by such a spirit, placed in his flesh![10]

The celestial promptuaries of the winds are a Hebrew counterpart to the widespread belief that the winds are imprisoned in *caves* or special houses. This idea is most familiar, of course, from the Greek story of Aeolus, who so guards them on an island,[11] but it occurs also among primitive peoples of the present day. The New Zealanders assert, for instance, that the god Maiu keeps the winds in check by rolling boulders over the mouths of caves in which they are confined.[12] Similarly, the Iroquois say that the god Gaoh imprisons them in a "home of the winds";[13] and the Eskimos identify the abode of the dead with a "house of the winds" and offer prayers to a spirit known as "Owner of the Winds (*Sillam Innua*)."[14]

202 Rites of mourning   16:6; 48:37

▲ (a) Cuttings for the dead

The customs of cropping or shaving the hair and cutting or mutilating the body in mourning have been very widespread among mankind.

Among Semitic peoples the ancient Arabs, like the ancient Jews, practised both customs. Arab women in mourning rent their upper garments, scratched their faces and breasts with their nails, beat and bruised themselves with their shoes, and cut off their hair. When the great warrior Chalid ibn al Valid died, there was not a single woman of his tribe, the Banu Mugira, who did not shear her locks and lay them on his grave.[1] To this day similar practices are in vogue among the Arabs of Moab. As soon as a death has taken place, the women of the family scratch their faces to the effusion of blood and rend their robes to the waist.[2] And if the deceased was a husband, a father, or other near relation, they cut off their long tresses and spread them out on the grave or wind them about the headstone. Or they insert two stakes in the earth, one at the head and the other at the foot of the grave, and join them by a string, to which they attach their shorn locks.[3]

Similarly in ancient Greece women in mourning for near and dear relatives cut off their hair and scratched their cheeks, and sometimes their necks, with their nails till they bled.[4] Greek men also shore their hair as a token of sorrow and respect for the dead. Homer tells how the Greek warriors before Troy covered the corpse of Patroclus with their shorn tresses, and how Achilles laid in the hand of his dead friend the lock of hair which his father Peleus had vowed that his son should dedicate to the river Sperchius whenever he returned home from the war.[5] So Orestes is said to have laid a lock of his hair on the tomb of his murdered father Agamemnon.[6] But the humane legislation of Solon at Athens, like the humane legislation of Deuteronomy at Jerusalem, forbade the barbarous custom of scratching and scarifying the person in mourning,[7] and though the practice of shearing the hair in honour of the dead appears not to have been expressly prohibited by law, it perhaps also fell into abeyance in Greece under the influence of advancing civilization; at last it is significant that both these forms of mourning are known to us chiefly from the writings of poets who depicted the life and manners of the heroic age, which lay far behind them in the past.

Assyrian and Armenian women in antiquity were also wont to scratch their cheeks in token of sorrow, as we learn from Xenophon,[8] who may have witnessed these demonstrations of grief on that retreat of the Ten Thousand which he shared as a soldier and immortalized as a writer.

Nor was the custom unknown in ancient Rome; for one of the laws of the Ten Tables, based on the legislation of Solon, forbade women to lacerate their cheeks with their nails in mourning.[9] (The learned Roman antiquary Varro held that the essence of the custom consisted in an offering of blood to the dead, the blood drawn from the cheeks of the women being an imperfect substitute for the blood of captives or gladiators sacrificed at the grave.[10] The usages of modern savages, as we shall see presently, confirm to some extent this interpretation of the rite.) Vergil represents Anna disfiguring her face with her nails and beating her breasts with her fist at the tidings of the death of her sister Dido on the pyre,[11] but whether in this description the poet had in mind the Carthaginian or the old Roman practice of mourners is open to question.

When they mourned the death of a king, the ancient Scythians cropped their hair all round their heads, made incisions in their arms, lacerated their foreheads and noses, cut off pieces of their ears, and thrust arrows through their left hands.[12]

Among the Huns it was customary for mourners to gash their faces and crop their hair; it was thus that Attila was mourned, "not with womanish lamentations and tears, but with the blood of men."[13]

"In all Slavonic countries great stress has from time immemorial been laid on loud expressions of grief for the dead. These were formerly attended by laceration of the faces of the mourners, a custom still preserved among some of the inhabitants of Dalmatia and Montenegro."[14] Among the Mingrelians of the Caucasus, when a death has taken place in a house, the mourners scratch their faces and tear out their hair,[15] according to one account they shave their faces entirely, including their eyebrows.[16] However, from another report it would seem that only the women indulge in these demonstrations of grief. Assembled in the chamber of death, the widow and the nearest female relations of the deceased abandon themselves to the vehemence, or at all events to the display, of their sorrow, wrenching out their hair, rending their faces and breasts, and remonstrating with the dead man on his undutiful conduct in dying. The hair which the widow tears from her head on this occasion is afterwards deposited by her in the coffin.[17] Among the Ossetes of the Caucasus on similar occasions the relatives assemble: the men bare their heads and hips, and lash themselves with whips till the blood streams forth; the women scratch their faces, bite their arms, wrench out their hair, and beat their breasts with lamentable howls.[18]

The Turks of old used to cut their faces with knives in mourning for the dead, so that their blood and tears ran down their cheeks together.[19]

In Africa the custom of cutting the body in mourning, apart from the reported practice of lopping off finger-joints, appears to be comparatively rare. Among the Abyssinians, in deep mourning for a blood relation, it is customary to shear the hair, strew ashes on the head, and scratch the skin of the temples till the blood flows.[20] When a death has taken place among the Wanika of East Africa, the relations and friends assemble, lament loudly, poll their heads, and scratch their faces.[21] Among the Kissi, a tribe on the border of Liberia, women in mourning cover their bodies, and especially their hair, with a thick coating of mud, and scratch their faces and their breasts with their nails.[22] In some Kafir tribes of South Africa a widow used to be secluded in a solitary place for a month after her husband's death, and before she returned home at the expiration of that period she had to throw her clothes away, wash her whole body, and lacerate her breast, arms, and legs with sharp stones.[23]

On the other hand, the laceration of the body in mourning, if rarely practised in Africa, was common among the Indian tribes of North America. Thus on the death of a relative, the Tinneh or Déné Indians of North-Western America used to make incisions in their flesh, cut off their hair, rend their garments, and roll in the dust.[24] Again, on the occasion of a death among the Crees, who ranged over a vast extent of territory in Western Canada, "great lamentations are made, and if the departed person is very much regretted the near relations cut off their hair, pierce the fleshy part of their thighs and arms with arrows, knives, etc., and blacken their faces with charcoal."[25] Among the Kyganis, a branch of the Tlingit Indians of Alaska, while a body was burning on the funeral pyre, the assembled kinsfolk used to torture themselves mercilessly, slashing and lacerating their arms, thumping their faces with stones, and so forth.[26] With the Chinooks and other Indian tribes of the Oregon or Columbia River it was customary for the relations of a deceased person to destroy his property, to cut their hair, and to disfigure and wound their bodies.[27]

Among the Indians of the Californian peninsula, "when a death has taken place, those who want to show the relations of the deceased their respect for the latter lie in wait for these people, and if they pass they come out from their hiding-place, almost creeping, and intonate a mournful, plaintive *hu, hu, hu!* wounding their heads with pointed, sharp stones, until the blood flows down to their shoulders.[28] In some tribes of Californian Indians the nearest relations cut off their hair and throw it on the burning pyre, while they beat their bodies with stones till they bleed.[29]

To testify their grief for the death of a relative or friend the Snake Indians of the Rocky Mountains used to make incisions in all the fleshy parts of their bodies, and the greater their affection for the deceased, the deeper they cut into their own persons. They assured a French missionary that the pain which they felt in their minds escaped by these wounds.[30] The same missionary tells us how he met groups of Crow women in mourning, their bodies so covered and disfigured by clotted blood that they presented a spectacle as pitiable as it was horrible. For several years after a death the poor creatures were bound to renew the rites of mourning every time they passed near the graves of their relations; and so long as a single clot of blood remained on their persons, they were forbidden to wash themselves.[31]

Among the Arapaho Indians women in mourning gash themselves lightly across the lower and upper arms and below the knees. Mourners in that tribe unbraid their hair and sometimes cut it off; the greater their love for their departed friend, the more hair they cut off. The severed locks are buried with the corpse.[32] After a bereavement the Sauks and Foxes, another tribe of Indians, "make incisions in their arms, legs, and other parts of the body; these are not made for the purposes of mortification, or to create a pain, which shall, by diverting their attention, efface the recollection of their loss, but entirely from a belief that their grief is internal, and that the only way of dispelling it is to give it a vent through which to escape."[33] The Dakotas or Sioux in like manner lacerated their arms, thighs, legs, breast, and so on, after the death of a friend; and the writer who reports the custom thinks it probable that they did so for the purpose of relieving their mental pain, for these same Indians, in order to cure a physical pain, used frequently to make incisions in their skin and suck up the blood, accompanying the operation with songs,[34] or rather incantations, which were no doubt supposed to assist the cure.

Among the Kansas, a branch of the Siouan stock who have given their name to a State of the American Union, a widow after the death of her husband used to scarify herself and rub her body with clay; she also became negligent of her dress, and in this melancholy state she continued for a year, after which the eldest surviving brother of her deceased husband took her to wife without ceremony.[35] The custom was similar among the Omahas of Nebraska, another branch of the Siouan family. "On the death of the husband, the squaws exhibit the sincerity of their grief by giving away to their neighbours every thing they possess, excepting only a bare sufficiency of clothing to cover their persons with decency. They go out from the village, and build for themselves a small shelter of grass or bark; they mortify themselves by cutting off their hair, scarifying their skin, and, in their insulated hut, they lament incessantly. If the deceased has left a brother, he takes the widow to his lodge after a proper interval, and considers her as his wife, without any preparatory formality."[36] But among the Omahas it was not widows only who subjected themselves to these austerities in mourning. "The relatives bedaub their persons with white clay, scarify themselves with a flint, cut out pieces of their skin and flesh, pass arrows through their skin; and, if on a march, they walk barefoot at a distance from their people, in testimony of the sincerity of their mourning."[37] Among these Indians, "when a man or woman greatly respected died, the following ceremony sometimes took place. The young men in the prime of life met at a lodge near that of the deceased, and divested themselves of all clothing except the breechcloth; each person made two incisions in the upper left arm, and under the loop of flesh thus made thrust a small willow twig having on its end a spray of leaves. With the blood dripping on the leaves of the sprays that hung from their arms, the men moved in single file to the lodge where the dead lay. There, ranging themselves in a line shoulder to shoulder facing the tent, and marking the rhythm of the music with the willow sprigs they sang in unison the funeral song—the only one of its kind in the tribe. . . . At the close of the song a near relative of the dead advanced toward the singers and, raising a hand in the attitude of thanks, withdrew the willow twigs from their arms and threw them on the ground."[38] Further, as a token of grief at the death of a relative or friend, the Omahas used to cut off locks of their hair and throw them on the corpse.[39] Similarly among the Indians of Virginia the women in mourning would sometimes sever their tresses and throw them on the grave.[40]

Among the Indians of Patagonia, when a death took place, mourners used to pay visits of condolence to the widow or other relations of the deceased, crying, howling, and singing in the most dismal manner, squeezing out tears, and pricking their arms and thighs with sharps thorns to make them bleed. For these demonstrations of woe they were paid with glass beads and other baubles.[41] As soon as the Fuegians learn of the death of a relative or friend, they break into vehement demonstrations of sorrow, weeping and groaning; they lacerate their faces with the sharp edges of shells and cut the hair short on the crowns of their heads.[42] Among the Onas, a Fuegian tribe, the custom of lacerating the face in mourning is confined to the widows or other female relations of the deceased.[43]

Among the Orang Sakai, a primitive pagan tribe, who subsist by agriculture and hunting in the almost impenetrable forests of Eastern Sumatra, it is customary before a burial for the relations to cut their heads with knives and let the flowing blood drip on the face of the corpse.[44] Again, among the Roro-speaking tribes, who occupy a territory at the mouth of St. Joseph River in New Guinea, when a death has taken place, the female relations of the deceased cut their skulls, faces, breast, bellies, arms, and legs with sharp shells, till they stream with blood and fall down exhausted.[45] In the Koiari and Toaripi tribes of New Guinea mourners cut themselves with shells or flints till the blood flows freely.[46] So in Vate (or Efate), an island of the New Hebrides, a death was the occasion of great wailing, and the mourners scratched their faces till they streamed with blood.[47] Similarly in Malekula, another island of the New Hebrides, gashes are or were cut in the bodies of mourners.[48]

The Galelarese of Halmahera, an island to the west of New Guinea, make an offering of their hair to the soul of a deceased relative on the third day after his or her death, which is the day after burial. Should the survivors fail to offer their hair to the deceased and to cleanse themselves afterwards, it is believed that they do not get rid of the soul of their departed brother or sister. For instance, if some one has died away from home, and his family has had no news of his death, so that they have not shorn their hair nor bathed on the third day, the ghost (*soso*) of the dead man will haunt them and hinder them in all their work. When they crush coco-nuts, they will get no oil: when they pound sago, they will obtain no meal: when they are hunting, they will see no game. Not until they have learned of the death, and shorn their hair, and bathed, will the ghost cease thus to thwart and baffle them in their under-takings.[49] Customs of the same sort appear to have been observed by all the widely spread branches of the Polynesian race in the Pacific. Thus in Otaheite, when a death occurred, the corpse used to be conveyed to a house or hut, called *tupapow,* built specially for the purpose, where it was left to putrefy till the flesh had wholly wasted from the bones. "As soon as the body is deposited in the *tupapow,* the mourning is renewed. The women assemble, and are led to the door by the nearest relation, who strikes a shark's tooth several times into the crown of her head: the blood copiously follows, and is carefully re-ceived upon pieces of linen, which are thrown into the bier. The rest of the women follow this example, and the ceremony is repeated at the interval of two or three days, as long as the zeal and sorrow of the parties hold out. The tears also which are shed upon these occasions, are received upon pieces of cloth, and offered as oblations to the dead; some of the younger people cut off their hair, and that is thrown under the bier with the other offerings. This custom is founded upon a notion that the soul of the deceased, which they be-lieve to exist in a separate state, is hovering about the place where the body is deposited: that it observes the actions of the survivors, and is gratified by such testimonies of their affection and grief."[50]

Among the women of Otaheite the use of shark's teeth as a lancet to draw blood from their heads was not limited to occasions of death. If any accident befell a woman's husband, his relations or friends, or her own child, she went to work on herself with the shark's teeth; even if the child had only fallen down and hurt itself, the mother mingled her blood with its tears. But when a child died, the whole house was filled with kinsfolk, cutting their heads and making loud lamentations. "On this occasion, in addition to other tokens of grief, the parents cut their hair short on one part of their heads, leaving the rest long. Sometimes this is confined to a square patch on the forehead; at others they leave that, and cut off all the rest: sometimes a bunch is left over both ears, sometimes over one only; and sometimes one half is clipped quite close, and the other left to grow long: and these tokens of mourning are sometimes prolonged for two or three years."[51] This description may illustrate the Israelitish practice of making bald places on the head in sign of mourning.

Similarly the Tongans in mourning beat their teeth with stones, burned circles and scars on their flesh, struck shark's teeth into their heads until the blood flowed in streams, and thrust spears into the inner parts of their thighs, into their sides below the arm-pits, and through their cheeks into their mouths.[52]

In the Samoan Islands it was in like manner customary for mourners to manifest their grief by frantic lamentation and wailing, by rending the garments, tearing out the hair, burning their flesh with firebrands, bruising their bodies with stones, and gashing themselves with sharp stones, shells, and shark's teeth, till they were covered with blood. This was called an "offering of blood" (taulanga toto).[53] Similarly in Mangaia, one of the Hervey Islands, no sooner did a sick person expire than the near relatives blackened their faces, cut off their hair, and slashed their bodies with shark's teeth so that the blood streamed down.[54] So, too, in the Marquesas Islands, "on the death of a great chief, his widow and the women of the tribe uttered piercing shrieks, whilst they slashed their foreheads, cheeks, and breasts with splinters of bamboo."[55]

Among the Maoris of New Zealand the mourning customs were similar. "All the immediate relatives and friends of the deceased, with the slaves, or other servants or dependants, if he possessd any, cut themselves most grievously, and present a frightful picture to a European eye. A piece of flint (made sacred on account of the blood which it has shed, and the purpose for which it has been used) is held between the third finger and the thumb; the depth to which it is to enter the skin appearing beyond the nails. The operation commences in the middle of the forehead; and the cut extends, in a curve, all down the face, on either side: the legs, arms, and chest are then most miserably scratched; and the breasts of the women, who cut themselves more extensively and deeper than the men, are sometimes woefully gashed."[56]

Nowhere, perhaps, has this custom of cutting the bodies of the living in honour of the dead been practised more systematically or with greater severity than among the rude aborigines of Australia, who stand at the foot of the social ladder. Thus among the tribes of Western Victoria a widower mourned his wife for three moons. Every second night he wailed and recounted her good qualities, and lacerated his forehead with his nails till the blood flowed down his cheeks; also he covered his head and face with white clay. If he loved her very dearly and wished to express his grief at her loss, he would burn himself across the waist in three lines with a red-hot piece of bark. A widow mourned for her husband for twelve moons. She cut her hair quite close, and burned her thighs with hot ashes pressed down on them with a piece of bark till she screamed with agony. Every second night she wailed and recounted his good qualities, and lacerated her forehead till the blood flowed down her cheeks. At the same time she covered her head and face with white clay. This she must do for three moons on pain of death. Children in mourning for their parents lacerated their brows.[57] Among the natives of Central Victoria the parents of the deceased were wont to lacerate themselves fearfully, the father beating and cutting his head with a tomahawk, and the mother burning her breasts and belly with a firestick. This they did daily for hours until the period of mourning was over.[58] Widows in these tribes not only burned their breasts, arms, legs, and thighs with firesticks, but rubbed ashes into their wounds and scratched their faces till the blood mingled with the ashes.[59] Among the Kurnai of South-Eastern Victoria mourners cut and gashed themselves with sharp stones and tomahawks until their heads and bodies streamed with blood.[60] In the Mukjarawaint tribe of Western Victoria, when a man died, his relatives cried over him and cut themselves with tomahawks and other sharp instruments for a week.[61]

Among the tribes of the Lower Murray and Lower Darling rivers mourners scored their backs and arms, sometimes even their faces, with red-hot brands, which raised hideous ulcers; afterwards they flung themselves prone on the grave, tore out their hair by handfuls, rubbed earth over their heads and bodies in great profusion, and ripped up their green ulcers till the mingled blood and grime presented a ghastly spectacle.[62] Among the Kamilaroi, a large tribe of Eastern New South Wales, the mourners, especially the women, used to plaster their heads and faces with white clay, and then cut gashes in their heads with axes, so that the blood flowed down over the clay to their shoulders, where it was allowed to dry.[63]

In the Kabi and Wakka tribes of South-Eastern Queensland, about the Mary River, mourning lasted approximately six weeks. "Every night a general, loud wailing was sustained for hours, and was accompanied by personal laceration with sharp flints or other cutting instruments. The men would be content with a few incisions on the back of the head, but the women would gash themselves from head to foot and allow the blood to dry upon the skin."[64] In the Boulia district of Central Queensland women in mourning score their thighs, both inside and outside, with sharp stones or bits of glass, so as to make a series of parallel cuts; in neighbouring districts of Queensland the men make a single large and much deeper cruciform cut in the corresponding part of the thigh.[65] Members of the Kakadu tribe, in the Northern Territory of Australia, cut their heads in mourning till the blood flows down their faces on to their bodies This is done by men and women alike. Some of the blood is afterwards collected in a piece of bark and apparently deposited in a tree close to the spot where the person died.[66]

In the Kariera tribe of Western Australia, when a death has occurred, the relations, both male and female, wail and cut their scalps until the blood trickles from their heads.[67]

In the Arunta tribe of Central Australia a man is bound to cut himself on the shoulder in mourning for his father-in-law; if he does not do so, his wife may be given away to another man in order to appease the wrath of the ghost at his undutiful son-in-law. Arunta men regularly bear on their shoulders the raised scars which show that they have done their duty by their dead fathers-in-law.[68] The female relations of a dead man in the Arunta tribe also cut and hack themselves in token of sorrow, working themselves up into a sort of frenzy as they do so, yet in all their apparent excitement they take care never to wound a vital part, but vent their fury on their scalps, their shoulders, and their legs.[69] In the Warramunga tribe of Central Australia widows crop their hair short, and, after cutting upen the middle line of the scalp, run firesticks along the wounds, often with serious consequences.[70] Other female relations of the deceased among the Warramunga content themselves with cutting their scalps open by repeated blows of yam-sticks till the blood streams down over their faces; while men gash their thighs more or less deeply with knives. In addition, some Warramunga men in mourning cut off their hair closely, burn it, and smear their scalps with pipeclay, while other men cut off their whiskers.[71]

It deserves to be noticed that in these cuttings for the dead among the Australians the blood drawn from the bodies of the mourners is sometimes applied directly to the corpse, or at least allowed to drop into the grave. Thus among some tribes on the Darling River several men used to stand by the open grave and cut each other's heads with a boomerang; then they held their bleeding heads over the grave, so that the blood dripped on the corpse lying in it. If the deceased was held in high esteem, the bleeding was repeated after some earth had been thrown on the corpse.[72] Similarly in the Milya-uppa tribe, which occupied the country about the Torrowotta Lake in the north-west of New South Wales, when the dead man had been a warrior, the mourners cut each other's heads and let the blood fall on the corpse as it lay in the grave.[73] Again, among the Arunta of Central Australia the female relations of the dead used to throw themselves on the grave and there cut their own and each other's heads with fighting-clubs or digging-sticks till the blood, streaming down over the pipe-clay with which their bodies were whitened, dripped upon the grave.[74] Again, at a burial on the Vasse River, in Western Australia, a writer describes how, when the grave was dug, the natives placed the corpse beside it, then "gashed their thighs, and at the flowing of the blood they all said, 'I have brought blood,' and they stamped the foot forcibly on the ground, sprinkling the blood around them; then wiping the wounds with a wisp of leaves, they threw it, bloody as it was, on the dead man."[75]

Further, it is deserving of notice that the Australian aborigines sometimes apply their severed hair, as well as their spilt blood, to the bodies of their dead friends. Thus, Sir George Grey tells us that "the natives of many parts of Australia, when at a funeral, cut off portions of their beards, and singeing these, throw them upon the dead body; in some instances they cut off the beard of the corpse, and burning it, rub themselves and the body with the singed portions of it."[76] Comparing the modern Australian with the ancient Hebrew usages in mourning, this writer adds, "The native females invariably cut themselves and scratch their faces in mourning for the dead; they also literally make a baldness between their eyes, this being always one of the places where they tear the skin with the finger nails."[77]

Among the rude aborigines of Tasmania the mourning customs appear to have been similar. "Plastering their shaven heads with pipe-clay, and covering their faces with a mixture of charcoal and emu fat, or mutton-bird grease, the women not only wept, but lacerated their bodies with sharp shells and stones, even burning their thighs with a firestick. Flowers would be thrown on the grave, and trees entwined to cover their beloved ones. The hair cut off in grief was thrown upon the mound."[78]

The customs of cutting the body and shearing the hair in token of mourning for the dead have now been traced throughout a considerable portion of mankind, from the most highly civilized nations of antiquity down to the lowest savages of modern times. It remains to ask, What is the meaning of these practices? A clue is perhaps afforded by the Nicobarese custom (to which we have elsewhere referred) of shaving the hair and eyebrows in mourning for the alleged purpose of disguising oneself from the ghost, whose unwelcome attentions they desire to avoid, and whom they apparently imagine to be incapable of recognizing them with their hair cut. Can it be, then, that both customs originated as devices for deceiving or repelling the ghost of the deceased?

How does this hypothesis square with the facts which we have passed in review? The fear of the ghost certainly counts for something in the Australian ceremonies of mourning; for we have seen that among the Arunta, if a man does not cut himself properly in mourning for his father-in-law, the old man's ghost is supposed to be so angry that the only way of appeasing his wrath is to take away his daughter from the arms of his undutiful son-in-law. Further, in the Unmatjera and Kaitish tribes of Central Australia a widow covers her body with ashes and renews this token of grief during the whole period of mourning, because, if she failed to do so, "the *atnirinja,* or spirit of the dead man, who constantly follows her about, will kill her and strip all the flesh off her bones."[79] In these customs the fear of the ghost is manifest, but there is apparently no intention either to deceive or to disgust him by rendering the person of the mourner unrecognizable or repulsive. On the contrary, the Australian practices in mourning seem to aim rather at obtruding the mourners on the attention of the ghost, in order that he may be satisfied with their demonstrations of sorrow at the irreparable loss they have sustained through his death. The Arunta and other tribes of Central Australia fear that if they do not display a sufficient amount of grief, the spirit of the dead man will be offended and do them a mischief. And with regard to their practice of whitening the mourner's body with pipe-clay, we are told that "there is no idea of concealing from the spirit of the dead person the identity of the mourner; on the other hand, the idea is to render him or her more conspicuous, and so to

allow the spirit to see that it is being properly mourned for."[80] In short, the
Central Australian customs in mourning appear designed to please or propitiate
the ghost rather than to elude his observation or excite his disgust. That this is
the real intention of the Australian usages in general is strongly suggested by
the practices of allowing the mourner's blood to drop on the corpse or into the
grave, and depositing his severed locks on the lifeless body; for these acts
can hardly be interpreted otherwise than as tribute paid or offerings presented
to the spirit of the dead in order either to gratify his wishes or to avert his
wrath. Similarly we saw that among the Orang Sakai of Sumatra mourners
allow the blood dripping from their wounded heads to fall on the face of the
corpse, and that in Otaheite the blood flowing from the self-inflicted wounds
of mourners used to be caught in pieces of cloth, which were then laid beside
the dead body on the bier. Further, the custom of depositing the shorn hair
of mourners on the corpse or in the grave has been observed in ancient or
modern times by Arabs, Greeks, Mingrelians, North American Indians,
Tahitians, and Tasmanians, as well as by the aborigines of Australia. Hence
we seem to be justified in concluding that the desire to benefit or please the
ghost has been at least one motive which has led many peoples to practice
those mutilations with which we are here concerned.

To say this, however, is not to affirm that the propitiation of the ghost has
been the *sole* intention with which these austerities have been practised. Different peoples may well have inflicted these sufferings or disfigurements on themselves from different motives, and amongst these various motives the wish to
elude or deceive the dangerous spirit of the dead may sometimes indeed have
played a part. We have still to inquire how the offering of blood and hair is
supposed to benefit or please the ghost? Is he thought to delight in them
merely as expressions of the unfeigned sorrow which his friends feel at his
death? That certainly would seem to have been the interpretation which the
Tahitians put upon the custom; for along with their blood and hair they offered
to the soul of the deceased their tears, and they believed that the ghost "observes the actions of the survivors, and is gratified by such testimonies of their
affection and grief." Yet even when we have made every allowance for the
selfishness of the savage, we should probably do injustice to the primitive
ghost if we supposed that he exacted a tribute of blood and tears and hair from
no other motive than a ghoulish delight in the sufferings and privations of his
surviving kinsfolk. It seems likely that originally he was believed to reap some
more tangible and material benefit from these demonstrations of affection and
devotion. Robertson Smith suggested that the intention of offering the blood of
the mourners to the spirit of the departed was to create a blood covenant between the living and the dead, and thus to confirm or establish friendly relations with the spiritual powers.[81] In support of this view he referred to the
practice of some Australian tribes on the Darling River, who, besides wounding
their heads and allowing the blood from the wounds to drop on the corpse,

were wont to cut a piece of flesh from the dead body, dry it in the sun, cut it in small pieces, and distribute the pieces among the relatives and friends, some of whom sucked it to get strength and courage, while others threw it into the river to bring a flood and fish, when both were wanted.[82] Here the giving of blood to the dead and the sucking of his flesh appear undoubtedly to imply a relation of mutual benefit between the survivors and the deceased, whether or not that relation be properly described as a covenant. Similarly among the Kariera of Western Australia, who bleed themselves in mourning, the hair of the deceased is cut off and worn by the relatives in the form of string. Here, again, there seems to be an exchange of benefits between the living and the dead, the survivors giving their blood to their departed kinsman and receiving his hair in return. The fact is, however, that these indications of an interchange of good offices between the mourners and the mourned are too few and slight to warrant the conclusion that bodily mutilations and wounds inflicted on themselves by bereaved relatives are always or even generally intended to establish a covenant of mutual help and protection with the dead. The great majority of the practices which we have surveyed in this chapter can reasonably be interpreted as benefits supposed to be conferred by the living on the dead, but few or none of them, apart from the Australian practices just cited, appear to imply any corresponding return of kindness made by the ghost to his surviving kinsfolk.

There is a simpler and more obvious explanation. We have seen that the practice of wounding the heads of mourners and letting the blood drip on the corpse was prevalent among the Australian tribes of the Darling River. Now among these same tribes it is, or rather used to be, the custom that on undergoing the ceremony of initiation into manhoood "during the first two days the youth drinks only blood from the veins in the arms of his friends, who willingly supply the required food. Having bound a ligature round the upper part of the arm they cut a vein on the under side of the forearm, and run the blood into a wooden vessel, or a dish-shaped piece of bark. The youth, kneeling on his bed, made of the small branches of a fuchsia shrub, leans forward, while holding his hands behind him, and licks up the blood from the vessel placed in front of him with his tongue, like a dog. Later he is allowed to eat the flesh of ducks as well as the blood."[83] Again, among these same tribes of the Darling River, we are informed, "a very sick or weak person is fed upon blood which the male friends provide, taken from their bodies in the way already described. It is generally taken in a raw state by the invalid, who lifts it to his mouth like jelly between his fingers and thumb." I have seen it cooked in a wooden vessel by putting a few red-hot ashes among it."[84] Again, speaking of the same tribes, the same informant tells us that "it sometimes happens that a change of camp has to be made, and a long journey over a dry country undertaken, with a helpless invalid, who is carried by the strong men, who willingly bleed themselves until they are weak and faint, to provide the food they consider is the

best for a sick person."[85] Now, if these savages gave their own blood to feed
the weak and sickly among their living friends, why should they not have
given it for the same purpose to their dead kinsfolk? Like almost all savages,
the Australian aborigines believed that the human soul survives the death of
the body; what more natural, then, than that in its disembodied state the soul
should be supplied by its loving relatives with the same sustaining nourishment
with which they may have often strengthened it in life? On the same principle,
when Ulysses was come to deadland in the far country of Cimmerian darkness,
he sacrificed sheep and caused their blood to flow into a trench, and the weak
ghosts, gathering eagerly about it, drank the blood and so acquired the strength
to speak with him.[86]

But if the blood offered by mourners was designed for the refreshment of
the ghost, what are we to say of the parallel offering of their hair? The ghost
may have been thought to drink the blood, but we can hardly suppose that
he was reduced to such extremities of hunger as to eat the hair. Nevertheless
it is to be remembered that in the opinion of some peoples the hair is the
special seat of its owner's strength,[87] and that accordingly in cutting their hair
and presenting it to the dead they may have imagined that they were supplying him with a source of energy not less ample and certain than when they
provided him with their blood to drink. If that were so, the parallelism which
runs through the mourning customs of cutting the body and polling the hair
would be intelligible. That this is the true explanation of both practices, however,
the evidence at our command is hardly sufficient to enable us to pronounce
with confidence.

So far as it goes, however, the preceding inquiry tends to confirm the view
that the widespread practices of cutting the bodies and shearing the hair of
the living after a death were originally designed to gratify or benefit in some
way the spirit of the departed; and accordingly, wherever such customs have
prevailed, they may be taken as evidence that the people who observed them
believed in the survival of the human soul after death and desired to maintain friendly relations with it. ▼

16:7

(b) Funeral meats

> *No one shall break bread for the mourner, to comfort him for
> the dead; nor shall any one give him the cup of consolation
> to drink for his father or his mother.*

The custom of serving and partaking of funeral meats is virtually universal.
However much they may later have been interpreted as mere "pick-me-ups" in
a time of grief and dejection, their original purpose was, on the one hand, to
recement by commensality the ruptured ties of kinship, and on the other to
forge a link with the dead by sharing a meal with his spirit.[88]

The custom is mentioned elsewhere in the Old Testament. When the wife of the prophet Ezekiel dies, in token of the grief and mourning which God has in store for Israel, he is admonished to dispense with the usual rites of mourning and not to eat "the bread of mourners";[89] while Hosea warns his recalcitrant compatriots that their offerings of food are unwelcome to Yahweh and are "like the bread of mourners, all who eat of which are defiled," i.e., with the contagion of death.[90]

Amorite texts of the eighteenth century B.C. mention the funeral meal (*ukkulum*) beside the wake (*maṣṣartum*) and the lament (*naḫādum*) as standard rites of mourning;[91] and in Mesopotamia, the proffering of food (*kasap kispi*), pouring of water (*niq mê*), and invocation of the name (*zikir šumi*) of the dead—together amounting to an invitation to a commensal meal with the survivors—likewise constituted the prescribed duties of mourners.[92] The same offices are likewise enjoined in a Phoenician inscription from Zen-čirli, where we are told also that a son was expected to "eat in the presence" of his departed father.[93] Similarly in the Ugaritic *Poem of Aqhat*, filial duties are said to include that of eating funeral meals in the sanctuary in connection with the cult of ancestors.[94]

Lucian of Samosata, in the second century C.E., cannot eschew his usual touch of satire in describing such meals. "The funeral meal," he writes, "is a universal custom. Neighbors come around and comfort the relatives of the deceased and induce them to take a bite. To be sure, the latter are not pressed unduly, but they are none the less somewhat worn down by three days of continuous hunger (between the demise and the obsequies). 'How long,' they ask, 'are we going to keep up this moping? Let the spirits of the departed have a rest! Even if you want to go weeping your heart out, that's no reason for going without food, and you shouldn't lose weight through grief.' What's more, they start reciting the verses in Homer about Niobe's at last realizing that she was hungry and about the Achaeans' not 'mourning the dead with their bellies.' Thereupon the bereaved indeed touch the food, though at first they are a bit bashful about it, wary lest they may seem to be lacking in human feeling after the demise of their loved ones."[95]

Clement of Alexandria[96] and Chrysostom[97] both attest the custom as current among the early Christians, and it has been suggested that the bench-lined "anterooms" sometimes found in the Christian catacombs at Rome originally served this purpose. So too, at the present day, Arabs conclude funeral ceremonies by slaughtering a lamb of which all the bereaved then partake.[98]

In traditional Jewish usage, a meal (*habra'ah*) of hard-boiled eggs, bread, and lentils (or beans) is served to mourners on their return from the cemetery.[99] This is especially interesting because eggs and beans appear elsewhere as characteristic funeral fare. In Rome, for example, eggs were a common offering to the dead[100]—a usage which still survived in the nineteenth century at Beihingen, in Germany.[101] In the Ukraine, eggs are given to the dead on St. Thomas' day;[102] and the Maori place an egg in the hands of the deceased.[103] Beans, says Pliny,[104] were commonly eaten at Roman funerals, and they were offered to the dead at the Lemuria, the annual Feast of Ghosts.[105] During the Middle Ages, it was customary in the Tyrol to eat bean soup on All Souls' Day.[106] The funeral fare of the Jews is thus identical with that believed to be consumed by the dead themselves; and this once again strengthens the view that the original purpose of the rite was to sustain relationship with them by an act of commensality.

A secondary motive, however, should not be overlooked: in many cultures mourners are indeed required to fast until burial has taken place.[107] To cite but a few representative examples, this custom is attested in the Andaman[108] and Fiji islands,[109] in Samoa,[110] China[111], Korea,[112] and among several African peoples.[113] Orthodox Jews likewise abstain from food on the day of interment, until they come home from the graveyard. Such fasting seems originally to have been a method of expressing the fact that, though death happens to a particular person, it happens in a group, and everyone else is therefore sympathetically affected by it and temporarily in a state of suspended animation. This explanation is supported by the fact that fasting is likewise a common custom at all times when an individual is thought to "put off" his personality and assume a new one, e.g., at initiation and marriage.[114]

Sometimes, to be sure, the custom of "eating with the dead" was regarded in Israel as a heathen rite, evidently smacking of ancestor worship. Thus, in Psalm 106:28, eating the meals of (not, as RSV: sacrifices offered to) the dead is classed with attaching oneself to the Baal of Peor.[115]

203   The ritual lament   22:18

> They shall not lament for him:
> "Ah, my brother!" or "Ah, sister!"[1]
> They shall not lament for him:
> "Ah, Lord [Heb.: adôn]!". . .

The prophet is quoting a standard form of lamentation, for it recurs at 34:5. This identical form is found again in a Mesopotamian text describing and explaining the rites of the New Year (Akitu) Festival. At a certain point of the proceedings, we are told, a wailing woman paraded around crying *ma-a aḫu-u-a, ma-a aḫu-u-a,* "Ah, brother! Ah, brother!"[2]

Moreover, a fragment of Sappho[3] preserves the analogous lamentation, *Oh, for Adonis!* where Adonis is, of course, simply the Semitic *adon,* "lord." This form of lament was likewise standard, for it is cited also by Aristophanes[4] and Bion,[5] and later also by Ammianus Marcellinus.[6]

204   Invoking the Earth   22:29

> O Land, land, land,
>   hear the word of the LORD!

The threefold repetition of the word, *Land* (or, *earth*), suggests that this reproduces an incantatory or liturgical formula. We may therefore pertinently compare the words of a Mesopotamian incantation: *Earth, earth, earth, Gilgamesh casts a spell upon you![1]*

205 Rachel weeping for her children 31:15

RSV: *Thus says the LORD:*
        "A voice is heard in Ramah,
            Lamentation and bitter weeping.
        Rachel is weeping for her children;
        she refuses to be comforted for her children,
            because they are not."

Since Rachel in fact died in childbirth (Gen. 35:16–20), it has been suggested that these famous lines reflect the common belief that women who suffer this fate haunt the earth in search of their babes, or return to suckle and tend them.[1]

A Mesopotamian magical text classes among errant spirits that of the woman who has died in childbirth,[2] and among Arabs of the present day the notion prevails that she returns in the form of an owl.[3] In Malaya, the nightjar, called Langsuyar, is thought to embody such a hapless mother;[4] while among the Banks Islanders it is held that the spirit of such a woman cannot go to Panoi, a ghostland, but must roam the earth.[5] Similarly, in the Pelew Islands, she is thought to wander eternally, crying: "Give me my child!"[6]

This is, of course, merely one particular form of the belief, widely attested in ancient Greek sources, that those who have died an untimely or violent death (*aōroi* or *biaiothanatoi*) are not admitted to Hades, but must wander.[7] In German folklore, the ghosts of little children are said to flit around as jack-o'-lanterns.[8]

It is possible, however, to interpret the lines in quite a different manner. Seeing that the prophet has just used the image of the ingathering of scattered sheep (31:10), the word *Rachel* may be no proper name at all, but simply the regular Hebrew word for *ewe-lamb,* while Ramah could be a common noun meaning *height, upland.* The passage would then read:

    Thus says the LORD:
    "Hark! in the upland is heard
    Lamentation and bitter weeping—
    a ewe-lamb weeping for her young,
    refusing to be solaced for her young,
        because they are not."

As a matter of fact, the affection of the ewe for her lamb was proverbial in Ancient Near Eastern literature. A Mesopotamian magical text says expressly: "As a ewe loves its lamb, a gazelle its young, a she-ass its foal . . . so do I love thee, mine own body";[9] while a Hittite text declares likewise: "as the ewe loves the lamb, the cow its calf, parents the child, so, O Sun-god, do thou also . . . etc.[10] The simile recurs also in Egyptian[11] and Sumerian[12] literature.

Even more to the point is the picture drawn in the Canaanite *Poem of Baal* of the goddess 'Anat's distress at his disappearance from the earth: "Like the heart of a cow for her calf, like the heart of a ewe for her lamb, so is the heart of 'Anat on account of Baal."[13] Moreover, precisely the same image is used by Ovid in describing Demeter's search for Persephone. *Ut vitulo mugit sua mater at ubere rapto Et querit fetus per nemus omne suos, Sie dea nec retinet gemitus et concita cursu Fertur.* (Even as the ewe lamb lows when the calf is snatched from her udder, and goes seeking her offspring through every grove, so the goddess restrains not her sighs and is borne along on her headlong course.)[14]

205a David redivivus   34:23–24

> *And I will set up over them one shepherd, my servant*
> *David . . . and my servant David shall be prince among them.*

Here, as again in Ezekiel 37:24 and in Hosea 3:5, the name David is used to denote the future king of a restored Israel.[1] The notion of the heroic king who will reappear in the hour of his people's need is widespread.[2] In Rome it was applied even to Nero.[3] The Welsh held the same belief about Arthur,[4] and the motif appears also in the Finnish Kalevala[5] and in Danish and Norse lore.[6] It is likewise attested among North American Indians and among the Aztecs,[7] while during World War I, the British attached this superstition to Lord Kitchener after he had drowned in the sinking of H.M.S. *Hampshire.*

Ezekiel

I

In the fifth or sixth[1] month of the Hebrew year, at the season when vines were pruned and summer fruit was reaped,[2] the prophet Ezekiel was transported in a vision to the precincts of the temple of Yahweh in Jerusalem. This is what he saw:

(i) At the northern gate of the inner courtyard, a seat had been set up for an idol whom he calls ironically "the idol of jealousy (or, of passion)."[3]

(ii) In a frescoed cavern,[4] a small congregation of men—described in round figures as seventy in number—was engaged in performing certain rites.

(iii) At the northern gate, women were sitting weeping for "the Tammuz," i.e., the god of vegetation and fertility, who was believed to withdraw from the earth during the summer months, and whom the prophet, living in Babylon, designates by his characteristic Babylonian name.

(iv) In the inner courtyard, between the porch and the altar, a group of men were turning toward the east and prostrating themselves before the rising sun.

The prophet denounced these rites as heathen abominations. Comparative Religion and Folklore now help us to understand what they were.

(a) The "seat of the idol of jealousy"

Among the Canaanite documents unearthed at Ras Shamra, in North Syria, is one which sets forth the ritual and accompanying myth of an agricultural and viticultural festival.[5] A rubric in this text[6] prescribes that at a certain stage of the proceedings, "seats" are to be set up for various deities—precisely the same term being used as is employed by the prophet. Moreover, in another document from the same site, the erection of such seats for gods is again mentioned as part of a ritual ceremony,[7] while elsewhere we read of "a throne for Elath" and a "tribune for 'Ashtareth."[8] A much later inscription from Teima likewise makes reference to such a "seat," again using the same word.[8a]

What is here implied is a *lectisternium,* or spreading of couches (seats) for the divine guests at a *theoxenia,* or seasonal banquet. This was a common feature of calendar festivals.[9] Thus, the so-called Egyptian Ramesseum Drama ends with the installation of the revived Horus and the celebration of a banquet attended, on the durative and mythic level, by the gods, and on the punctual and ritual level, by the princes of the several nomes of Upper and Lower Egypt.[10] in the Hittite myth designed for the annual "Festival of the Earth (Puruli)," the weather-god is installed at Nerik, with the gods around him;[11] while in the Telepinu myth, that god's return is celebrated at a banquet.[12] In the Babylonian New Year (Akîtu) myth, Marduk, duly installed as king, presides at a banquet of the gods;[13] and at Asshur, the ancient capital of Assyria, the festival itself is described as a "banquet (*kirêtu*)."[14] Further, we know from Assyrian sources that once a year the king invited the gods to a banquet and invoked them to bless himself, the city, the land, and the people. This ceremony was termed "the collation (*tâkultu*)."[15] Couches which were probably used in such a ceremony have actually been found at Palmyra and in the Hauran;[16] and inscriptional evidence attests the same usage in the Asianic cult of Attis, wherein it was the duty of the priest to "spread the couch" for the gods at annual panegyries.[17] Lastly, as F. M. Cornford has pointed out, Greek comedies, which evolved out of the primitive seasonal drama, often end in a scene of banqueting and in this we may perhaps recognize, albeit through a glass darkly, a lingering trace of the original *lectisternium*.[18]

In the mouth of Ezekiel, the expression "idol of jealousy" probably stigmatizes the divine occupant of the "seat" as a mere image destined to evoke the passionate jealousy of Yahweh. Not impossibly, however, the prophet uses this strange designation with particular satirical intent, for in the aforementioned Canaanite text the rubric prescribing the setting up to the "seats" is followed immediately by the opening words of a hymn then to be recited; and these words are: *I am jealous for the names of the gods*.[19] The implication would be, therefore, that the gods which excite the jealous devotion of their worshipers are but idols which excite the jealous wrath of Yahweh!

(b) The frescoed cavern

The prophet speaks of a "hole in the wall," through which he is told to dig. On doing so, he sees walls frescoed with pictures of "creeping things and loathsome beasts, and all the idols of the house of Israel." Before them stands a crowd of men holding smoking censers, but a discreet veil is drawn over what they were doing. Perhaps Comparative Religion can illuminate what "the elders of the house of Israel were doing in the dark, each in his frescoed chamber."

The first thing to observe is that the Greek (Septuagint) Version omits all reference to a *wall,* and that the Hebrew word (*hôr*) translated "hole" can also mean "cave." Not impossibly, therefore, the prophet misunderstood what was really taking place, and interpreted a rite in a subterranean vault as something which he knew in other connections, namely, the adoration of animals depicted, as in prehistoric caves, on the walls of such chambers.[20] But what was really going on? Could it perhaps have been something in connection with the cult of the "dying and resurrected god," symbolically placed in an underground cavern, or a symbolic union of worshipers with the earth?

What lends plausibility to this suggestion is the importance of such subterranean caverns in the later mystery cults. Thus, a scholiast on the *Alexipharmakon* of the Alexandrian poet Nicander explains the curious expression, "marriage-bowers of Rhea Lobrinē," as denoting subterranean chambers used in the rites of that mother-goddess and of her paramour, Attis;[21] while an epitaph on a priest of Cybele, preserved in the Greek Anthology, speaks of his having "descended into the evening darkness, gone down into the cavern."[22] Similarly, the lexicographer Hesychius defines the word *Cybela* as meaning "both caverns and marriage-chambers";[23] and the church father Arnobius, fulminating against the heathen mysteries, scornfully describes how the Mother of the gods "carries off the pine-log [representing Attis] into her cavern."[24]

Descent into a subterranean vault was also regarded, in several mystery cults, as symbolizing an *unio mystica* with the regenerative powers of Mother Earth.[25]

(c) Women weeping for Tammuz

Further researches on Sumerian texts have cast doubt on the old view (espoused especially by Frazer) that Tammuz was a "dying and reviving" god of fertility, of the order of Osiris, Attis, and Adonis. It now seems probable—if not altogether certain—that the Tammuz myth really ran on somewhat different lines.[26] Nevertheless, there is definite evidence that the god was indeed bewailed in annual rites. In the Mesopotamian Epic of Gilgamesh, that hero, rejecting the advances of the goddess Ishtar, brusquely points out to her that her lover Tammuz came to a bad end, and is now the subject of "wailing" year after year.[27] Similarly, in the *Poem of Ishtar's Descent to the Netherworld* there is a reference, albeit obscure, to male and female wailers who annually greet the goddess on the day when Tammuz "jubilates" over her arrival to rescue him.[28] Furthermore, an Old Babylonian text[29] and another of Arsacid date[30] describe the midsummer month of Tammuz as a period of wailing, ritual lamentation, and weeping; while an Old Assyrian almanac prescribes weeping for the second day in it.[31]

These rites have their counterpart, of course, in the well-known ritual laments for the Egyptian Osiris, the Phrygian Attis, and the Syrian Adonis (see above, §203). It survived in the Middle Ages at Harran, where women annually bewailed a log called Ta'uz, i.e., Tammuz.[32]

A modern parallel may also be cited. In Roumania, on the Monday before the Feast of Assumption (in August), groups of girls go out from the villages, carrying under a pall a miniature coffin in which is deposited a clay image called Kalojan. The coffin is subsequently interred, and for two days the girls ceremonially bewail it. Kalojan—i.e., *kalos Ioannēs* (beautiful John)—is here but a Christian substitution for the more ancient *kalos Adonis* (beautiful Adonis).[33]

The women who weep for Tammuz play the role of professional mourners at a funeral ceremony. Such female mourners are, of course, familiar enough, especially from modern Arab usage,[34] but it is noteworthy that they occur already not only in ancient Egypt[35] but also among the Hittites,[36] while in the Canaanite *Poem of Aqhat,* they are said to enter the house of King Daniel in order to perform a keening for his slain son.[36a] Homer likewise mentions them in his account of the obsequies of Hector.[37] They are the later Roman *praeficae*,[38] who lead the dirge; and in modern Armenia they are known as "dirge-mothers."[39]

In illustration of the fact that the lamentation is performed *at the entrance* of the temple, it may be noted that in modern Anatolia rites of mourning take place in the courtyard of the deceased's house and are attended by professional wailing women and relatives; the public exercises, which take place at the actual interment, are quite distinct.[40]

On the significance of the fact that the rite is performed at the *northern* gate, see below, §233.

(d) The adoration of the rising sun

Festivals which evolve around the concept of the dying and reviving god of fertility *are often made to coincide with the solstice or equinox*.[41] The mysteries of Attis, for example, culminated in the triumphant re-emergence of that god on the day of the vernal solstice (March 25); while an Old Assyrian calendar for the month of Tammuz prescribes signficantly that the "weeping" for him, which is to take place on the first day in it, is to be followed immediately, on the second by "the presentation of gifts to the sun-god."[42] A Babylonian hymn belonging to the Tammuz cycle represents the sun-god as assuring his sisters that he himself would restore to her "the verdure which hath been removed" and "the crushed grain which hath been carried away."[43] Similarly, in a Hittite text celebrating the discomfiture of "Jack Frost (*Hahhimas*)," joint honors are paid to Telipinu, the genius of vegetation, and the sun-god;[44] while in the Canaanite *Poem of Baal,* it is the sun-goddess that retrieves Baal from the netherworld and urges his rival Môt, genius of drought and sterility, to give up the fight against him.[45] Similarly, the *Poem of the Gracious Gods,* which was designed for a spring festival, includes a liturgical invocation in which in addition to those deities, the sun-goddess too is adored.[46]

Significant also is the fact that among the Israelites both the vernal festival of Pentecost and the autumnal festival of Ingathering fell in the months of the equinoxes, the latter being explicitly associated with that event in the ritual calendar of Exodus 34:22.[47]

Again, it should be observed that in Syria and in the eastern portions of the Roman Empire the Festival of the "new Age" was likewise combined with an important solar date, viz., the alleged birthday of the sun on November 18.[48] The same date, it may be added, was claimed by Clement of Alexandria as the birthday of the Christian Savior.[49] Indeed, so firmly established was the connection between festivals of the new life and the worship of the sun that the Church was obliged to fix Christmas on what had originally been the birthday of the solarized savior Mithra and to associate the date of Christ's resurrection (Easter) with the vernal equinox.[50] Similarly, the Irish celebration of Lammastide, in August, was associated with the worship of Lug, the sun-god.[51] As the Pervigilium Veneris puts it, *vere natus orbis est.*[52]

II

(e) Ezekiel's satire

If, then, we assume that Ezekiel's sermon was directed against pagan practices at a harvest festival, it becomes possible to recognize throughout his discourse sly allusions to features of that occasion. We may suppose, in fact, that the prophet used the same technique as is today a standard tactic of "hot gospellers" and evangelical revivalists: he drew metaphors from the familiar symbols of the heathen cult, giving to each a peculiar homiletical twist.

Thus he opens his discourse (7:2) with the words, *The end is coming.* The Hebrew word for "end" is *qêṣ,* and he would have been preaching at the very season of the year anciently called *qêṣ,* "the reaping of summer fruit." Is it not possible, therefore, that in these striking words he is giving a forceful meaning to a traditional cry of the season, viz., "Late Summer (*qêṣ*) is icumen in?" If anyone think this suggestion bizarre, let him turn to Amos 8:3, where exactly the same pun is employed: *The LORD God showed me, and behold, there was a basket of summer fruit* (qaiṣ, *i.e.,* qêṣ). *And he said, What seest thou, Amos? And I said, A basket of summer fruit. Then said the LORD unto me: The end* (qêṣ) *is coming for my people Israel. . . .* We may represent the point by rendering "fall," i.e., *The fall is coming!*

The prophet continues (7:7): *Doom is coming.* Here the Hebrew word rendered "doom" is *ṣᵉfîrah,* which does not occur in this sense elsewhere in the Old Testament. In several of the cognate Semitic languages, however, the basic root *ṣ-f-r* means "make a circuit." The sense will thus be, *"The cyclic point has come,"* i.e., things have come round full cycle, and the term will be an exact synonym of *tᵉqûfah,* which means literally "cyclic point" (from root *q-w-f*) and then comes to denote "equinox." We may represent the effect by rendering "turning-point," i.e., *the turning-point is coming* (or, *has come*)!

The fateful day is described (*ibid.*) as one in which *tumult, and not joyful sound, will re-echo on the hills.* It has been recognized by all commentators that the rare Hebrew word *hēd*, rendered "joyful sound," is simply an alternative form of *hēdād*, elsewhere (Isa. 16:10; Jer. 25:30; 48:29) stated to be the cry used by vintners when treading the grape. Thus it is apparent again that the prophet is alluding to features of the season, for an ancient agricultural calendar from Gezer (ninth century B.C.) tell us expressly that the period of *qêṣ* was preceded immediately by that of *zmr*, "trimming vines," when the dominant thought in everyone's mind would have been that of the coming vintage; while in Ezekiel 3:17 there is (apparently) reference to a ceremony in which a vine branch (*zᵉmōrah*) was used. We may convey the point by rendering freely, *Horror and not hurrah will re-echo on the hills.*

In verses 10–11, despite the uncertainty of the text, it is at least clear that the prophet is likening the wickedness and violence of his coreligionists to a shoot which grows up apace and, apparently, is destined eventually to wither.[53] Here again it seems not impossible that he is alluding slyly to a feature of the pagan ceremonies—namely, the custom of carrying or erecting garlanded poles or branches at harvest festivals. Such a pole, called *eyan,* is frequently mentioned in Hittite ritual texts;[54] and its most familiar analogues are, of course, the *eiresione* of the Greeks,[55] the palm branch (*lulab*) of the Jewish Feast of Ingathering, and the European maypole. According to both Johannes Lydus[56] and Julian,[57] a prominent feature of the later "mysteries" of Attis was the introduction of a pine log into the sacred precincts. One of the days of the festival was called, in fact, "Day when the Log comes in (*canna intrat*), and the priests who bore it were known as "carriers of the tree" (*dendrofori*).[58] Analogous rites were performed also, according to Firmicus Maternus, in the "mysteries" of Isis, Adonis, and Persephone.[59] In modern times, we may recognize a survival of the rite in the custom reported, at the end of the nineteenth century, from Banga, in Asianic Georgia, where a felled oak was brought into church during the last days of April.[60] Significant also is the fact that on the famous "Minoan" signet-ring discovered by Sir Arthur Evans at Thisbe, in Crete, the Mother and Child are depicted receiving adoration from armed priests (cf. Ezek. 9:1!) who hold flowering reeds in their hands.[61] These Evans rightly identifies with the priestly "reed-bearers" (*cannoforoi*) mentioned in divers sources concerned with the cult of Rhea and Attis.

The prophet's diatribe gains momentum. *They sound the trumpets,* he cries, *and there is general preparation, but no one goes out to battle!* The outward purport of the words is clear enough: we know that the trumpet was sounded at the beginning of a military campaign. What, however, inspired the image? Perhaps, once again, the answer may come from the analogy of the Attis "mysteries," for the priests were there called "spear-bearers" (*aichmoforoi;* Latin, *hastiferi*),[62] and Lucretius, in describing analogous rites, says distinctly that the priests carried weapons (*telaque praeportant*).[63] Moreover, as stated above, on the signet ring from Thisbe, in Crete, the votaries of the Great Mother are shown armed.

As for the sounding of the trumpet, it is sufficient to note that such blasts are a common method of scaring demons, especially at New Year and seasonal festivals.[64] The Hebrews, for example, sounded the ram's horn on such occasions,[65] as also at every new moon[66]—a time when the "princes of darkness" are believed to be particularly rampant. Similarly, it is customary in the Isle of Man to blow trumpets on the mountains at the Feast of Laa Boaldyn, on May 1, first to summon the demons, and then to drive them home;[67] and a similar practice obtains at religious gatherings in Bali.[68] On the same basis too, the Cheremiss use long trumpets of lime-tree bark to scare Satan[69]—a usage recorded in rabbinic literature as current also among the Jews.[70] The Aymara Indians employ the same device to forefend hail.[71]

Trumpets are also blown, in order to arouse dormant or "dead" gods of fertility. Julian tells us that they were so sounded at the annual festival of Attis;[72] while both Pausanias and Plutarch attest that the Argives used year by year to summon Dionysus from the Alyconian lake through which he descended to Hades by blowing trumpets on its shores.[73]

In the light of such comparative material it does not seem far-fetched to assume that Ezekiel may have been satirizing a specific heathen rite.

The prophet now passes on (v. 20) to a pointed jibe at the gaudy raiment and the parade of statuettes (Heb.: *ṣᵉlāmîm*) which characterized the pagan ceremonies.

> *Their silver shall they cast into the streets,*
> *and their gods shall become an unclean thing;*
> *neither their silver nor their gold shall be able to save them,*
> *in the day of the LORD'S wrath.*
> *Their hunger shall they not satisfy,*
> *their bellies not fill,*
> *for this iniquity of theirs shall prove a stumbling block.*
> *The finery which went with it*
> *they assumed for proud show,*
> *and images of their loathsome idols*
> *did they make in connection with it.*
> *Therefore I will make it an unclean thing unto them!*

It is not difficult to recognize in these words an allusion to the *masquerade* typical of a pagan festival,[74] and to the custom of carrying images of the gods in a ceremonial procession. Herodian tells us expressly that at the celebration of the mysteries of Attis, "unlimited permission was given to all for all manner of frivolity, and everyone donned whatever raiment he liked";[75] and a similar practice marked the festival of Anthesteria in Greece.[76] Indeed, even at the present day, "Sunday best" is considered *de rigueur* in religious occasions.

The parading of special statuettes of the gods, called by the same term (viz., *ṣalmê*) as in our Biblical text, is mentioned in a Babylonian document as a feature of the great New Year (Akîtu) Festival; and we are informed also that on the same occasion images of the god Marduk and of his bride Zarpanitum were made by craftsmen.[77]

Again, verse 22 emerges in a new light, if read as a satire on specific pagan practices. Says the prophet, in the name of Yahweh:

> *I shall turn my face from them,*
> *and men shall profane my hidden place;*
> *intruders shall enter it and profane it.*

In the first part of this statement we may now detect a pointed reference to the so-called *epopteia,* or "beholding of the (divine) face," which was a central element of pagan festivals. In several Babylonian texts, votaries are said then to have preceded to the temple in order to "see the face" of the god;[78] while in the Israelitic laws concerning the pilgrim feasts (Exod. 23:17; 34:23) the beholding of the face of Yahweh is likewise expressly mentioned. On Greek soil, the *epopteia* is best known to us from the Eleusinian Mysteries,[79] but it is attested also in Samothrace[80] and in other parts. It is with reference to this feature of the pagan ceremonies that Yahweh here pointedly declares, *I shall turn my face from them.*

In the reference to the profanation of "my hidden place" (for so the Hebrew word may fairly be rendered), we may see an allusion to the adyton, where the holiest part of the pagan ceremony took place. Similarly, in Babylonian texts, this adyton goes by the strictly comparable name of "place of the mystery, secret (*ashar puzri*)."[81] The unusual Hebrew word may be, in fact, a translation of this technical term.

The word rendered "intruders" likewise has special point. Usually rendered "robbers," it means literally "men who break through," and it is therefore by no means implausible that in this context it denotes the uninitiated who break in unlawfully upon the sanctity of the innermost shrine.

The prophet's final taunt may be recognized in the words of verse 25:

> *Spasm*[82] *shall ensue; and they shall seek peace,*
> *but it shall not be.*

Here, it may be suggested, he is alluding slyly to the pagan seasonal ceremony of seeking the lost or ousted god of fertility. The expression, "to seek" the god, was, in fact, a cardinal *terminus technicus* alike in the Egyptian cult of

Isis and Osiris and in the Greek worship of Demeter and Persephone.[83] It occurs also in the Canaanite *Poem of Baal,* when the goddess 'Anat declares her intention of setting forth to "seek" that vanquished deity.[84]

The reference to "spasm" which will overtake the participants in the heathen rites will then fall readily into place in the light of Themstius' description of the scene attending the "resurrection" of the god in the mysteries of Attis; the event was received, he tell us, with "tremor and trembling and perspiration and amazement." The prophet of Yahweh is scornfully satirizing such a scene.[85]

▲ 208   **Trapping the soul**   13:18

> *Woe to the women who sew fillets upon all wrists and make scarves for the heads of all upstanding people, thereby to entrap souls! The souls which belong to my people you entrap, but your own you keep alive! You also profane Me to My people by (using) handfuls of barley and pieces of bread in order to bring about the death of souls [persons] which ought not to die and to keep alive those which ought not to live. . . .*

> *Wherefore thus says the LORD God: Behold, I am against your fillets with which you go trapping souls, and I will tear them from your arms and release the souls which you would entrap, that they may fly away like birds.*[1]

The nefarious practices which the prophet here denounces apparently consisted in attempts to catch stray souls in fillets and cloths, and so to kill some people by keeping their souls in durance vile, and to save the lives of others, probably of sick people, by capturing their vagabond souls and restoring them to their bodies. Similar devices have been and still are adopted for the same purpose by sorcerers and witches in many parts of the world. For example, Fijian chiefs used to whisk away the souls of criminals in scarves, whereupon the poor wretches, deprived of this indispensable part of their persons, used to pine and die.[2] The sorcerers of Danger Island, in the Pacific, caught the souls of sick people in snares, which they set up near the houses of the sufferers, and watched till a soul came fluttering into the trap and was entangled in its meshes, after which the death of the patient was, sooner or later, inevitable. The snares were made of stout cinet with loops of various sizes adapted to catch souls of all sizes, whether large or small, fat or thin.[3] Among the Negroes of West Africa "witches are continually setting traps to catch the soul that wanders from the body when a man is sleeping; and when they have caught this soul, they tie it up over the canoe fire and its owner sickens as the soul shrivels. This is merely a regular line of business, and not an affair of individual hate or revenge. The witch does not care whose dream-soul gets into the trap, and will restore it on payment. Also witch-doctors, men of unblemished professional reputation, will keep asylums for lost souls, *i.e.* souls who have been out wandering and found on their return to their body that their place had been filled up by a Sisa, a low-class soul. . . . These doctors keep souls, and administer them to patients who are short of the article."[4] Among the Baoules of the Ivory Coast it happened once that a chief's soul was extracted by the magic of an enemy, who succeeded in shutting it up in a box. To recover it, two men held a garment of the sufferer, while a witch performed certain enchantments. After a time she declared that the soul was now in the garment, which was accordingly rolled up and hastily wrapped about the invalid for the purpose of restoring his spirit to him.[5] Malay wizards catch the souls of women whom they love in the folds of their turbans, and then go about with the dear souls in their girdles by day and sleep with them under their pillows by night.[6] Among the Toradjas of Central Celebes the priest who accompanied an armed force on an expedition used to wear a string of seashells hanging down over his breast and back for the purpose of catching the souls of the enemy; the shells were branched and hooked, and it was supposed that, once the souls were conjured into the shells, the branches and hooks would prevent them from escaping. When the warriors had entered the hostile territory, the priest went by night to the village which they intended to attack, and there, close by the entrance, he laid down his string of shells on the path so as to form a circle, and inside of the circle he buried an egg and the guts of a fowl, from which omens had been drawn before the troop set out from their own land. Then the priest took up the string of shells and waved it seven times over the spot, calling quietly on the souls of the enemy and saying, "Oh, soul of So-and-So, come, tread on my fowl; thou art guilty, thou hast done wrong, come!" Then he waited, and if the string of shells gave out a tinkling sound, it was a sign that the soul of an enemy had really come and was held fast by the shells. Next day the man, whose soul had thus been ensnared, would be drawn, in spite of himself, to the spot where the foes who had captured his soul were lying in wait, and thus he would fall an easy prey to their weapons.[7]

[In the South Celebes[7a] and among the Minangkabau of Sumatra,[7b] the body of a woman in childbirth is bound tightly lest her soul escape—a practice which has parallels in European folklore[7c]—and when a man falls sick, the latter people fasten fishhooks to his nose, navel, and feet for the same purpose. Similar practices obtain among the Taradjas[7d] and the Olu Dusun Dayaks of southern Borneo.[7e] In the same way, the Minahassa of the Celebes tie the soul of an ailing man to his head;[7f] while the Belong Mongondo of the same area lure it into a doll which is then wrapped in a cloth bound around his temples.[7g] The Papuans of Geelrink Bay, in New Guinea, bind cords around the wrists of sick persons, and retrieve their souls in a bag which is then emptied over their heads.[7h] In Thailand, when a child has intermittent fever, or when its mother is obliged to leave it overnight, she or somebody else binds both its wrists with a piece of unspun thread, tying the knot tightly. Such an operation is termed "binding the soul" (*phuk khwan*). "The sign of life," it is explained, "is visible on either wrist, for the pulse throbs. If a binding is made, the fickle soul (*khwan*) will not play truant.[71] In Fiji, corpses are trussed up, lest the departed soul walk by night and harm the living.[7j] Siberian shamans and spiritualistic mediums are likewise adept at "binding souls" with cords;[7k] and it is not without significance that in ancient Mesopotamian magical texts a sorceress is sometimes called "a woman who goes catching by night."[71]

Of special interest also is the prophet's reference to the practice of encompassing the death or preservation of souls by *handfuls of barley and pieces of bread*. On the face of it, this looks like a denunciation of those who try to starve their enemies by scant rations and to preserve their friends by handouts of food, and this is how it is commonly interpreted. Since, however, these words are closely conjoined with an excoriation of magical practices, and since the divine subversion of this device is said to consist in releasing the trapped souls like flying birds, it may be suggested that here too the prophet is alluding to a piece of magic. In that case, it may perhaps be explained in the light of the widespread belief that the soul has the form of a bird (see below, §**274**), so that it can be entrapped or enticed by the symbolic act of strewing grain or breadcrumbs. Such a magical practice is in fact common in Indonesia and the Malay Peninsula, where it is customary to strew rice on a man's hand in order to prevent his soul from "flying away like a bird."[7m] There, to be sure, the idea is to *hold in* the soul of a sick person, but it is not difficult to see that by the same line of thought the practice could have been employed in "black" as well as "white" magic, and have served, like the fillets and scarves, to bind an enemy's soul in captivity.] ▼

209 Yahweh's scourges   **14:12–20**

In predicting imminent disaster upon Judah, the prophet warns, in the name of Yahweh, that while the righteous might be delivered, they will not be able to achieve expiation for the people in general. To illustrate this message, he observes that even if such paragons of piety as Noah, Daniel, and Job were to be living in a sinful land doomed to destruction, and if Yahweh were to inflict that punishment in the form of famine, noisome beasts, the sword, or plague, they would not be able to deliver anyone but themselves.

The prophet living in Babylon appears to have in mind a passage in the Babylonian Epic of Gilgamesh. After the Deluge, we read,[1] the god Ea objected to Enlil, the supreme deity, that such wholesale destruction of mankind was unnecesary and involved the innocent as well as the guilty. Enlil, he says, should have taken counsel and adopted a more selective form of punishment, such as the dispatch of a *lion* or a *wolf*, or of *famine* or *plague*.

The specific reference to Noah, the hero of the Hebrew story of the Deluge, suggests that Ezekiel was indeed alluding to this passage.[2] Moreover, in the so-called *Little Genesis* (*Biblical Antiquities*), a paraphrase of early Biblical history composed (probably) in the first century C.E., it is stated expressly[3] that, after the Flood, God assured Noah that in the future He would punish mankind only by *famine, sword, fire,* or *pestilence.*[4]

210   The righteous Daniel   14:14

> *Even if these three men, Noah, Daniel and Job, were in it (i.e., the land), they would deliver but their own lives by their own righteousness, says the Lord GOD.*

We now know that the Daniel who is here classed among the paragons of righteousness is not the prophet of that name nor the "Daniel come to judgment" of the legend of Susanna, but a figure drawn from an ancient Canaanite folktale, the *Poem of Aqhat,* discovered in 1930 at Ras Shamra-Ugarit. King of H-r-n-m, in southern Syria, he is given a male heir (Aqht) as a reward for his piety in serving as a humble scullion in the temple of Baal for seven days. For this reason, the supreme god El issues the order that "the soul of Daniel is indeed to be kept in life" (I Aqhat, i.35–38). He is described also (*ib.,* v. 8) as dispensing justice to the widow and the fatherless.

211   Salting newborn children   16:4

> *On the day you were born your navel string was not cut nor were you washed with water to cleanse you, nor rubbed with salt nor swathed with bands.*

Salt, being incorruptible, averts demons and protects against black magic.[1] As an old writer puts it, witches and warlocks "like their master, the Devil, abhor salt as the emblem of immortality."[2]

Both the Talmud[3] and St. Jerome[4] attest the salting of newborn babies as standard procedure among the Jews in the early centuries of the Common Era; while, according to the physician Galen (130–c. 200 C.E.), this practice obtained also among the ancient Greeks.[5] The Arabs protect their children from the evil eye by placing salt in their hands on the eve of the seventh day after birth; the following morning the midwife or some other woman strews it about the house, crying, "Salt in every envious eye!"[6] "To salt" is a regular expression for "to rear a child";[7] and a Palestinian proverb declares that "the skin which is not salted will suppurate."[8] In standard Catholic ritual, salt is applied to the lips in baptism to exorcize the Devil,[9] and in medieval Sweden it was then put under the infant's tongue.[10] The Germans did the same thing immediately after the child had been delivered,[11] and salt was also placed near the child to forefend demons.[12] In the Balkans[13] and among the Todas of Southern India,[14] newborn children are immediately salted; while Laotian and Thai women "wash" with salt after childbirth to immunize themselves from demonic assault.[15] In the northern counties of England, it is customary to tuck a small bag of salt into a baby's clothing on its first outing.[16] As late as 1946, a couple was arraigned at Trowbridge, Wiltshire, for burning salt over a child in order to stop its hysterical crying. The father attributed the cries to witchcraft and pleaded in defense that "he felt he had to counteract the evil influences that were around."[17] In Italy, salt is often placed under the pillow of a woman in labor;[18] and at Marsala, in Sicily, it is put behind the door, on the day after delivery, to prevent the entry of the evil spirit, 'Nserra. Says a local proverb:

> Water and salt: no matter what they say,
> Thereby can the witches never thee affray
> (Acqua e sali: e zoccu dicinu li magari
>   non possa guivari)![19]

The apotropaic quality of salt underlies also the modern Egyptian custom of rubbing a bride with it to protect her against the evil eye;[20] while in Morocco, Jewish women used to dip their hands in it before embarking on a journey.[21] In the Isle of Man, an application of salt in the churning of butter is thought to keep away the "bad people" (*queeltah*).[22]

212   Rites of divination   21:26

(a) Crossroads

> *The king of Babylon stands at the parting of the two ways, to practice divination.*

A man who stands at the crossroads has several alternative courses before him, each beset with its own hazards. In the idiom of ancient thought, therefore, the crossroads are a meeting place of demons and spooks and also of witches and warlocks who would enlist their powers.[1] Thus, among the Greeks, Hecate, divine queen of the witches, appeared where three roads met,[2] as did her Roman counterpart, Trevia;[3] and there too—as in ancient Iran[4] and today in the Abruzzi[5]—superstitious persons propitiated the dead. In India, *bhuts;*[6] among Arabs, jinns;[7] and in Africa,[8] evil spirits in general frequent crossroads; while in German grimoires they are mentioned often as the haunt of demons.[9] It is there that witches dance with the Devil,[10] that he appears at midnight as a black cat,[11] that he concludes his bargain with Faust,[12] and that the Wild Hunt foregathers.[13] Similarly, in Slavonic folklore, it is at the crossroads that sorceresses brew their hell-broth and spin their magic threads;[14] while according to the pseudepigraphic *Testament of Solomon,* it is there that the beldam Envy lurks.[15]

If, however, roads part at the crossways, they also converge there; which means, in primitive idiom, that divers potencies there coalesce. Accordingly, anything associated with crossways is endowed, in popular belief, with especial "virtue" and efficacy. In medico-magical recipes, herbs gathered there are especially potent.[16] In Bombay, a charm against the evil eye is to carry seven pebbles picked up at a spot where three roads meet;[17] and in a Judaeo-German work of the fifteenth century, the burial there of a jet-black hen is recommended as a means of bringing one's true love to one's side.[18]

By the same reasoning, however, devils can themselves be bedeviled at crossroads. A widespread notion in this respect is that ghosts and witches are rendered powerless at places where roads meet, and that furies cannot pass such a spot.[19] A story from Mecklenburg relates, for instance, that a man once eluded a one-legged elf who was pursuing him by reaching the crossroads first; beyond that point he could not be followed.[20] In parts of India, demons are exorcized at crossroads by drawing a circle, protecting it with iron and water, and sitting inside it mumbling spells.[21]

Because they are intrinsically numinous, or haunted by otherworld beings, crossroads are a favorite spot for divination. An excellent illustration of this is the Japanese practice known as *tsujiura*. At dusk, when the spirits convene, a stick is planted in the ground at a crossroads. It represents Funado, the staff which the mythical hero Izanagi similarly emplanted to check the pursuit of infernal demons when he was escaping from the netherworld after his attempt to rescue his sister Izanami. Questions are then asked, and the casual remarks of passers-by counted as the oracular responses. Alternatively, a number of women foregather at the crossroads and draw a line of demarcation. Then, after sprinkling rice against evil spirits, each turns to a different road and summons the otherworld beings by blowing on a boxwood comb held between her teeth. The questions are then posed, and anything said by chance by the first person to pass within the line is taken as the answer.[22] A similar practice is recorded from Iran,[23] while again in India it is not uncommon usage to resort to divination at a crossroads when lost objects are sought. The location is believed to be indicated by the maniuplation of some twenty-one pebbles which are there placed on the ground after a benedictory formula from the Atharva Veda has been pronounced over them.[24]

(b) Belomancy

Divination by shaking arrows from a quiver and then drawing omens from the way they fall is well attested in antiquity.[25] Quintus Fabius Maximus, we read, used this method when moving his camp from Tarentum to Metapontum;[26] while Macrobius recalls the same practice among the Etruscans.[27] A Jewish legend says that Nero did likewise before attacking Jerusalem,[28] while Arab tradition relates that the device was adopted by Imr-al-Qais before his expedition against Asad, but was prohibited by Mohammed.[29] "The custom was," says Pockocke, "that when anyone was about to undertake a journey or to marry or to embark on any important project, he would seek an oracle from three arrows which he put in a container. The first of these was inscribed, *God has commanded me;* the second, *God has forbidden me;* the third was blank. If he drew out the first, he would proceed with alacrity, as though ordered by God; if the second, he would desist; if the third, he would replace it and try again."[30]

Arrowheads of the Middle Bronze Age found in Palestine sometimes bear a legend beginning with the Hebrew word, *ḥ-ṣ*. At first blush, this would appear to be simply the normal term for *arrow*. It has been suggested, however, that it is rather to be connected with a similar Semitic word meaning "fortune," and that the arrows were used in belomancy, or the type of divination described above.[31]

The present writer has himself seen a similar practice, performed with little sticks from a "quiver," at the Wat Po in Bangkok; and it is current also among the Dakotas of North America.[32]

(c) Hepatoscopy

On *hepatoscopy,* or inspection of the liver, as a technique in Mesopotamian divination, see: Von Oefele, in ZAW (1900), 311–14; J. Hunger, Babylonische Tieromina nebst griech.-rom. Parallelen (1909); A. Ungnad, in Babyloniaca 2 (1908), 257–74; G. Furlani, in SMSR 4 (1929), 243–85.—For Greek parallels, see A. G. Bäckström, De hierascopia Graecorum (1910). The custom was common also among the Etruscans: CIL vi. 32328.78; Servius, on Vergil, Aen. 4.56; Macrobius, Sat. iii.5.1.—It survived among the Arabs until the fourth century: A. Marmorstein, in ARW 15 (1912), 320.

213   The fallen paragon   28:11–19

When Nebuchadnezzar laid siege to the proud emporium of Tyre— a siege which lasted thirteen years (585–73 B.C.)—the prophet Ezekiel, in anticipation of the city's downfall, addressed to its king the following scornful and satirical "dirge":

Thou wast the crowning achievement of art,
the sum of wisdom,
the total of beauty.
In Eden, the garden divine, thou wast,
sheathed in all precious stones,
carnelian, topaz and jasper,
chrysolite, beryl and onyx,
sapphire, carbuncle and emerald;
thy bosses and sockets were made of gold,
set upon thee on the day thou wast created.
I placed thee upon the holy mount,
a guardian cherub with wings outspanned;
thou wast a being divine;
amid flashing gems didst thou walk.

Blameless, indeed, thou wast in thy ways,
from the day thou wast created
until vice was discovered within thee.
Through thine abundant trading

thou hadst filled thyself inwardly with crime,
and didst fall afoul.
So, I cast thee out as a thing profane
from the mountain divine;
guardian cherub though thou wast,
I banished thee from amid those flashing gems.
By reason of thy beauty,
thy heart had grown proud;
not only thy radiance didst thou tarnish,
but also the wisdom that thou hadst!
So I flung thee upon the earth,
exposed thee before kings
to feast their eyes upon thee.
Because of thy manifold wrongdoing,
thy vicious trafficking,
thou hadst profaned the holiness thou hadst.
So I brought forth fire from within thee
—this it is that hath consumed thee!—
and I turned thee to ashes on the ground
before the eyes of all who beheld thee.
All they among the nations
who once acknowledged thee
became appalled at thee;
thou hadst become a portent horrendous
—gone for evermore!

It has been commonly supposed in recent years that this passage, in which affluent Tyre is likened to some denizen of Paradise eventually cast out for his sins, reflects a variant (probably Phoenician) version of the expulsion of Adam from the Garden of Eden.[1] Anyone who reads it attentively, however, will see at once that the differences are so cardinal as to preclude such a comparison. In the Adam story, Adam is expelled for aspiring to divine prerogatives and in order to prevent his acquiring divine knowledge, whereas the mythological subject of our dirge possesses both from the start and is punished for profaning them. In the Adam story, Adam is condemned to spend the rest of his days on earth, working for his daily bread in the sweat of his brow, and the story is told precisely in order to account for that condition. The subject of our dirge, on the other hand, is doomed to immediate and summary extinction. Furthermore, there is here no mention of such crucial elements of the Adam story as the forbidden fruit and the temptation.

It may be suggested, therefore, that what we have here is a parallel not to the Adam story but to the myth of Prometheus. The culprit is not a man at all, but a divine being, who somehow defiles his divine status and privilege. Just how is not quite clear, for in order to make the parable more applicable, the prophet substitutes for any reference to the mythic offense a direct condemnation of Tyre's commercialism and huckster frame of mind. It is significant, however, that just as the subject of our dirge is characterized as originally "blameless," so Prometheus is specifically described by Hesiod as originally "without evil,"[2] and just as the subject of our dirge is distinguished for his wisdom (which he eventually pollutes), so Prometheus was the teacher of arts and sciences to mankind.[3] (Indeed, his powers of sapience and insight are implicit in his very name, which means properly, Forethought.) Suggestive also of a connection of our hero with some prototype of Prometheus is the prophet's emphasis on his fiery character—the flame which destroys him is extracted, apparently, from his own body—for Prometheus is, of course, associated preeminently with fire and was even worshiped at Athens as a god of that element.[4] Nor need it be objected that Prometheus, after all, did not die in flames or that he was subsequently released. In the first place, there actually existed a tradition that he *was* blasted by lightning and thrust into Tartaros[5]—a tradition elsewhere associated with his brother Menoetius, who is said to have suffered this fate on account of his "savage insolence and overbearing boldness,"[6] comparable with the "proud heart" of our "hero" in Ezekiel's dirge. Second, the tradition that Prometheus was eventually released seems to have been a later innovation—some scholars even credit it to Aeschylus[7]—for Hesiod says clearly that his punishment was to last forever.[8]

Several subsidiary features of Ezekiel's "myth" lend themselves to illustration from Comparative Folklore.

1. The paradisal abode is here located not, as in Genesis, at the source of four rivers, nor in the east, but on the top of a mountain. On this concept, see above, §13.

2. The inhabitants of that realm are compact of precious stones and of gold.[9] The latter is strongly reminiscent of the ancient notion that divine beings have golden limbs. Thus, in the famous Egyptian Hymn of Ani, Osiris is said to possess "limbs of gold, head of lapis, and crown of turquoise";[10] while in the inscription of Redseyeh "the god's flesh is of gold" (*nbw ḥʿw nṯrw*),[11] and in the Middle Kingdom *Legend of the Contendings of Horus and Set,* the former is similarly described.[12] A story preserved in the Westcar Papyrus asserts that royal children of the Fifth Dynasty had golden limbs,[13] and in inscriptions at Thebes, Ramses II and III are credited with the same distinction.[14] So too a statue of Baal discovered at Ras Shamra is covered with gold leaf,[15] and it still is the custom of the faithful to attach little patches of golden trefoil to the image of the reclining Buddha at the Wat Po in Bangkok.

3. The statement that the denizen of Paradise walks about "amid flashing gems"[16] reflects the notion that the divine abode or garden is a place of jewels. On this notion, see above, §15.

4. The fiery character of our "hero," if not directly derived from some prototype of the Prometheus myth, perhaps reflects the belief that divine beings are enveloped in a perpetual sheen—a belief which obtains alike in Ancient Near Eastern and Classical lore, and which survives in the Christian idea that angels are made of fire.[17]

5. Finally, the idea that the wicked can be punished by being suddenly reduced to ashes finds several parallels in myth and story. The rebellious Titans, for example, are said in Greek legend to have been cast into Tartaros, where their bodies were burned to cinders.[18] Man, adds one version, arose out of those ashes.[19] Similarly, a modern Greek folktale, current alike on the islands of Zacynthos (Zante)[20] and Chios,[21] tells how, after the War against the Giants, one of their number tried to ascend to heaven, but was promptly smitten with a thunderbolt and reduced to ashes, as were several others who subsequently followed his example.

Sometimes, to be sure, it is not an offender that is threatened with this fate. Thus, in the ancient Egyptian Tale of the Shipwrecked Sailor, the serpent whom he encounters on a lonely island at first terrifies him with such a threat;[22] and the same motif occurs in Indian folklore.

214 Pharaoh and the Nile   29:3

(a)   *Thus saith the Lord GOD: Behold, I am against thee, Pharaoh*
        king of Egypt, the great dragon that croucheth in the midst of
        his Nile, which saith, My Nile is my own, and it is I that made it!

Comparative Folklore enables us to bring out the subtle point of the prophet's words. The Egyptian pharaoh, as the embodiment of the divine norm, or order of nature (*ma'at*), was considered to be responsible for the annual rising of the Nile and consequently for the fertility of his country.[1] Thus, an encomium addressed to Ramses II says explicitly, albeit in fulsome tones: "If thou say to the water, rise to the crest of the mountain, the flood straightway ensues in obedience to thy word";[2] while a similar statement is made also in the same monarch's so-called "Marriage Stele" at Abu Simbel.[3] Moreover, the power extended even to the dead pharaoh.[4] When Thothmes III passed away at a season of year when the Nile was at its lowest, scarabs were put into circulation, bearing the reassuring legend that the river was nonetheless at his command since he had now become one with Osiris.[5]

Basically, of course, this is simply a facet of the widespread idea that the king is the responsible agent of nature—especially of the weather, rainfall, and fertility—in his area.[6]

                                                                          32:2–9

(b)   *Raise a lament over Pharaoh, king of Egypt, and say unto him:*
        Thou wast like the Dragon in the seas,
        puffing amid thy streams,

> *muddying the waters with thy feet,*
> *turning their streams to mud.*

> *Thus saith the Lord GOD:*
> *I will spread My net over thee,*
> *and haul thee up in my drag,*
> *and cast thee upon the land,*
> *fling thee out on the fields,*
> *and make all the fowl of the air settle on thee,*
> *and sate all the beasts of the earth on thee.*
> *I will lay thy flesh on the hills,*
> *and fill the dales with thy rot,*
> *and drench the earth with what oozes from thee,*
> *and fill the watercourses with thy blood.*
> *When thou thyself art extinguished,*
> *I will cover the heavens too,*
> *and clothe their stars in mourning black;*
> *I will cover the sun with a cloud,*
> *and the moon shall not give forth its light.*
> *All the bright lights of heaven*
> *will I shroud in mourning for thee,*
> *and set darkness upon thy land. . . .*
> *Peoples far and wide will I make aghast over thee,*
> *and their kings will bristle with fright*
> *on account of thee,*
> *when I wave My sword in their face.*

Reading these verses, the student of folkore can scarcely resist the suspicion that what the prophet has at the back of his mind is not only the aforementioned concept of Pharaoh as master and controller of the Nile, but also the Egyptian Myth of 'Apep, the dragon wo lives in the cosmic ocean and who tries daily to swallow up the sun (Re') as he crosses the sky in his bark, but is daily subdued and pierced with his adversary's sword.[7] Basically, this myth links up with the common belief that eclipses and obscurations of the sun and moon are caused by a dragon or similar monster who temporarily gobbles them up.[8] "Thus, in Indic belief, it is the dragon Rahu (who in this capacity bears the name Svarbhanu) who periodically swallows the sun or moon;[9] and this piece of mythology was adopted in turn by the Buddhists.[10] In China, eclipses were likewise attributed to the devouring of sun or moon by a monstrous beast; and in the Confucian classic, *Tsun Tsiu* ("Springs and Autumns"), the word "eat" is employed to describe the eclipse of April 20, 610 B.C.[11] Similarly, in Scandinavian lore, the sun is believed to be pursued constantly by a wolf called Skoll.[12] The Tartar tribe of Chuwashes use the phrase "a demon has eaten it" to denote an eclipse.[13] The Estonians have a similar expression; while the Lithuanians assert that quasi-serpentine creatures lie in wait for sun and moon; and in the region south of Lake Baikal it is held that the king of hell tries to swallow the moon.[14] In Jewish folklore, the sun was said to be swallowed by a great fish;[15] and the same notion was entertained by spectators of a lunar eclipse at Hastaya, west of Hermon, in 1891.[16] Lastly, the Negritos of Borneo say that eclipses are caused by a python who attempts to swallow the sun or moon;[17] and the idea is attested also in ancient Greek mythology.[18] In the Canaanite *Poem of Baal,* after the sun-goddess (Shapash) has succeeded in retrieving that god from the netherworld, she is promised that ever after she will enjoy the escort of Kôthar-wa-Ḥasis, the god who once "tossed the Dragon into the sea."[19]

In the light of this fairly universal belief, the prophet's words take on an added subtlety: the Lord God will not only subdue the Dragon but also punish the land of Egypt by Himself, obscuring *all* the lights of heaven!

215   The parable of the cedar   31

The most obvious analogue to this parable is the story related both by Herodotus[1] and by Valerius Maximus[2] that when Cyrus was about to be born, his grandfather Astyages had a dream in which he saw his own daughter Mandane in the form of a vine which grew so tall that it overshadowed all the provinces. A similar story is related also concerning Xerxes.[3] Moreover, the comparison of a king to a cypress or palm appears in sundry Babylonian inscriptions.[4]

In a more general setting we are reminded of a passage in the Finnish Kalevala which tells of a gigantic oak which obscured both sun and moon and obstructed the course of the clouds until a dwarf rose from the sea, was transformed into a giant, and felled it.[5] Stories of similar import are told in Syriac,[6] Hungarian,[7] and German[8] sources;[9] and the image is used again, within the Old Testament itself in the Book of Daniel.[10]

Hermann Gunkel (to whom the citation of these parallels is due) has made the interesting suggestion that Ezekiel's parable reflects a folktale concerning a wondrous tree, "child of the deep (*tehôm*)," which shot up to heaven and grew so proud that it had to be felled; whereupon its mother wore mourning, as did also the whole of Lebanon, which had seen it in its glory. Moreover, all the trees that had previously been felled took comfort when they realized that they were not alone in their fate. Gunkel further identifies the tree with the world-tree (e.g., Yggdrasill) of familiar legend.[11]

There is, however, another possibility. Since the prohpet lived in Babylon, this passage may contain a reminiscence of the Mesopotamian story concerning the felling of the sacred cedar(s) by the hero Gilgamesh and his companion(s). This story is known not only from the famous Humbaba-Huwawa episode of the Akkadian Epic of Gilgamesh (III-IV),[12] but also from a far older Sumerian version, the so-called myth of *Gilgamesh and the Land of the Living*.[13] There are some arresting points of similarity:

1. Although this prophecy is addressed to the Pharaoh of Egypt, the scene is set in Lebanon, and it is now generally agreed that the Humbaba episode is to be located in that area.

2. The region is described specifically as a "shady thicket" (v. 3), and this accords perfectly with the description of the grove of Humbaba in the Epic of Gilgamesh (vv. 2–3).

3. The proud cedar is destroyed by the "hero (paladin) of the nations" (Hebrew, *êl goyîm*) and by the "violent men of the nations" (vv. 11–12), and this accords with the description of Gilgamesh in the Sumerian tale (88: *ur-sag*[dGIŠ] *gibil-ga-meš*) and with the fact that *he is accompanied by fifty braves* (99–100).

4. The fellers of the cedar are said to "leave it upon (LXX) the mountains" (v. 12).[14] In the Sumerian tale (139–42), the stalwarts "hew down its crown, bundle it, and lay it at the foot of the mountain."

5. It is said of the felled cedar that it will henceforth lie in the netherworld "among the uncircumcised" (v. 18). The Hebrew word for "uncircumcised" is *'arēlîm,* and it is therefore not impossible that the prophet was playing (as again in 32:19, 24–29, 30, 32) on the Mesopotamian name of the netherworld, viz., *Arallû.*

The background of the story lies in the taboo on felling trees beside a shrine. This still obtains in respect of Moslem holy places in Palestine.[15]

(Not impossibly, this was originally a parable directed against *Assyria,* and then boldly transferred to the Pharaoh of Egypt. This would account for its curious opening phrase, *Behold,* Assyria *is a cedar in Lebanon*—a phrase which has otherwise to be emended, as for instance in RSV.[16] The allusion to the Mesopotamian Gilgamesh legend would then have been more telling.)

216 The dimming of the sun 32:7–8

In predicting the downfall of the Egyptian monarch, Ezekiel declares that the heavens will be covered and the stars obscured; the sun will be veiled with clouds, and the moon will not give light.

The sentiment recurs elsewhere in Biblical prophecy. Joel declares, for example, that on the coming Day of the Lord, sun and moon will be darkened, and the stars withdraw their shining.[1] In the present passage, however, two different ideas are combined. The first is that the heavenly lights will go into mourning for the fallen pharaoh and be clothed, as it were, in funereal raiment.[2] The second is that the sun grows dim in times of disaster. This latter notion has an interesting Classical parallel, for several Roman writers tell us that after the assassination of Julius Caesar, the sun was dim for about a year,[3] and Pliny adds the same thing happened during the subsequent war between Octavian and Mark Antony. Vergil elaborates on this theme in a famous passage of his *Georgics:*

> Is there a man would venture to declare
> The sun plays false? Nay, for oftimes it warns
> When tumult stirs in darkness or when crime
> And wars are surging to the bursting point
> To break into the open. Thus it was,
> When Caesar's light was dimmed, the sun itself
> Grew sad for Rome, and with a veil opaque
> Covered its shining head, so that men feared
> Lest times so lost to ancient loyalties
> Would be enveloped in eternal night.[4]

In the same vein Ovid asserts that

> Sad Phoebus' face showed clouded eyes,[5]

and Tibullus that

> The year beclouded saw the sun
> Shorn of its light.[6]

217   Kôshar, the god of minstrelsy   33:32

The people listen to the words of the prophet, but pay no heed. Yahweh therefore characterizes him as *one that sings* (Heb.: *kᵉshîr*) *with a beautiful voice and plays well on an instrument* (RSV), i.e., as being treated like a performing artist rather than as a messenger of God.

Since the Hebrew word *shîr,* which is here employed, usually means *song* rather than *singer,* the reading and rendering have alike been questioned. The clever suggestion has been made, however,[1] that the word should be vocalized *kôshar* rather than *kᵉshir,* and that we should therefore recognize an allusion to the Canaanite god Kôshar (*K-t̠-r*) of the Ugaritic texts,[2] who is said by the Phoenician mythographer Sanchuniathon[3] to have been expert in "tricking out words in song."[4] A common noun *kôsharôth* (*k-t̠-r-t*) indeed means "professional singing women."[5]

(This ingenious suggestion, however, is not really necessary, for the word *shîr* could indeed mean "singer" as well as "song," the formation being like that of *ṣîr,* "messenger."[6] Indeed, the feminine plural shîrôth seems to occur in this sense in Amos 8:3.)

218   The thread of life   37:11

> Our bones are dried up, and our hope is lost;
> we are clean cut off.

An interesting folkloristic suggestion has been made about this verse.[1] The Hebrew words (*NiGZaRNW LaNU*) rendered *We are clean cut off* can be so rendered only by torturing the normal rules of syntax. If, however, the letters of which they are compounded be differently divided (viz., *NiGZaR NaWLeNU*), we may obtain the sense *Our thread is cut off*,[2] and this would connect at once with the familar conception of *life or fate as a thread* (see above, §191).

The imagery may be detected again in the Old Testament in Isaiah 38:12: *Like a weaver have I rolled up my life; God cuts me off from the loom.* Moreover, in further support of the proposed interpretation, it may be observed that the word here rendered *our hope* actually lends itself to a double-entendre, for it can also mean, *our skein.*[3]

See also, below, §311.

219   The navel of the earth   **38:12**
   See above, §113.

The Minor Prophets

220   Introduction

A Hebrew prophet was more than a mere predictor. His role was to interpret passing events in terms of God's ongoing plan and purpose. To do this, he had to look backward as well as forward, to see what had led up to them as well as how they were likely to turn out. Moreover, in order to trace God's hand in the present, he had to recognize comparable operations in the past. That past, however, was not always historical. Traditional myth likewise told many a story of how God (or, in pagan versions, this or that particular god) had acted in primeval or primordial times, and it was sometimes possible to recognize in such mythical exploits precedents for what he was actually doing on the stage of history. These more ancient myths have become known to us only in recent times with the recovery, through archaeological excavations, of so much of Ancient Near Eastern literature; and one of the major contributions which Comparative Folklore has now to make to the interpretation and understanding of the Old Testament is to detect allusions to them in the sacred text. In the following pages, therefore, special attention is paid to these parallels.

The Hebrew prophet was essentially a *speaker,* not a writer. This means that he had always to be on the lookout for an audience, and one of the best ways of ensuring one was to wait for occasions when crowds would gather for the celebration of seasonal festivals or the performance of public rites of religion. Against this background it is possible, I suggest, to discern in many a prophetic utterance (particularly in the twelve Minor Prophets) pointed jibes at standard pagan rites and ceremonies and to recognize *satire* as a cardinal element of the prophetic technique. *Mutatis mutandis,* and on a far more exalted level, this technique was the same as that which is employed in our own day by revivalist preachers and "hot gospelers" who frequent ball games and boxing matches, holding aloft among the spectators or pacing the sidewalks bearing such messages as "Kick off with Jesus" or "the Lord will K.O. the Devil." If, for instance, the people were performing the traditional rite of pouring water as a rain charm, the Hebrew prophet, standing as it were on the sidelines, might hurl at them the taunt that Yahweh would shortly pour upon them the vials of his wrath (Hos. 5:10), or if they paraded around the town in a torchlight procession—a familiar feature of popular festivals—he might warn them that Yahweh too was carrying his torch—to search out sin in every nook and cranny (Zeph. 1:12). Other standard elements of the pagan festivals which lent themselves likewise to satirical castigation are the nocturnal vigil (Joel 1.13), the ululation for the vanished god of fertility (Joel 2:17; Zeph. 1:11; Zech. 12:11–14), the search for him (Hos. 5:6, 15; 6:3; Zeph. 2:3), and the divine banquet (Zeph. 1:7). Sometimes too the assurance of Yahweh's eventual triumph and favor is couched in terms of what was conventionally attributed to the pagan gods in the myths associated with seasonal festivals: he will free his people from the grasp of Death—the Canaanite Môt, genius of sterility (Hos. 13:14), assert his kingship (Zeph. 3:15; Zech. 14:9, 16), and restore rainfall and fertility (Hos. 14:6–8; Joel 2:21–24; 4:18; Zech. 14:8). Thus, by aligning the successive metaphors employed by a Scriptural prophet with the successive elements of a standard seasonal festival, it becomes possible in several instances to recover a sustained satire and in this way to add a new dimension to Hebrew prophecy. Such an approach tends also to offset the tendency of modern Biblical scholars to fragmentize the prophetic discourses by attributing to different authors passages which exhibit a rapid transition and diversity of themes. This too is one of the major contributions which Comparative Folklore has to offer to the interpretation of the Old Testament, and this too receives particular attention in the following pages.

The prophets did not write in a study; they spoke in a passion. Images, metaphors, and tropes came tumbling out of them, and almost every sentence they uttered was charged also with subconscious associations and with suggestions drawn from traditional lore. If, for example, a prophet spoke of the sun's being dimmed in the Last Days (Joel 2:10), he was not simply inventing this picture out of his head; he was drawing, albeit subconsciously, on the storehouse of inherited popular fancies, and he was relying on his listeners' doing the same. The full impact of his words—as, indeed, of those of any creative author—depended therefore at least as much on what was suggested as on what was stated; on what was, so to speak, subliminal as on what was patent. Consequently, it is the business of a modern exegete to try to bring out the implicit as well as the explicit meaning. Accordingly, I have made a special point, in the following pages, of trying to illustrate images and metaphors from folklore. Admittedly, this involves a process of reading into the text (*eisegesis*) as well as out of them (*exegesis*), and the danger of subjectivism is ever-present; but this is, in the last analysis, a danger implicit in attributing meaning to anything, and the notion that there is such a thing as the objective interpretation of literature or art is—at least to me—itself meaningless, the tired cliché of tired scholars. Moreover, even if some of the material here assembled may eventually turn out to be irrelevant to the correct explication of a particular passage, the collection may perhaps prove of service in other contexts.

Hosea

221 Hosea and the pagan festivals

Much of the Book of Hosea may be read as a sustained satire on pagan seasonal festivals.[1] Not only are there significant references to sowing, plowing, and reaping,[2] threats of drought and sterility and promises of dewfall and increase,[3] but there seem also to be a number of sly allusions to standard seasonal rites and myths. The following are the more arresting instances.

Hos. 5:6

(a) *Israel will go seeking Yahweh, but will not find him, since he will have "slipped away" from them.*

The reference here is to the ritual search for the vanished god of fertility. In the Egyptian "mysteries" of Osiris, "seek" was a technical term.[4] In the Canaanite *Poem of Baal,* which is basically a seasonal myth, the goodess 'Anat says expressly that she will "go in search" (*b-q-š*) of the ousted lord of the rains.[5] In the Hittite myth of Telipinu, that god is said to have "taken himself off . . . flown into a rage, and carried away everything good";[6] while the search of Demeter for Persephone is familiar to every reader of Classical literature.[7]

The prophet chooses his words exquisitely. In the original Hebrew, the god is said not merely to depart or withdraw, but to slip away (Heb.: *ḥalaṣ*), suggesting graphically the gradual disappearance of the green summer.[8]

5:8

(b)
> Blow the horn in Gibeah,
> the trumpet in Ramah.
> Sound the alarm at Beth-aven;
> they are after you,[9] Benjamin!

The prophet is obviously thinking in terms of warfare, the trumpet being the signal for battle. It should be observed, however, that the trumpet was also sounded at festivals, to scare away the demons, and it is to this pagan rite that he may here be giving an ironic twist (see above, §207).

5:10

(c) *The princes of Judah have become like men who remove landmarks;*
I will pour out my wrath upon them like water.

The effect of this image is enhanced if it is read as a satire on the common practice of pouring water as a rain-charm at seasonal festivals (see above, §158). This took place, for instance, in the Jewish ritual for the Feast of Ingathering at Jerusalem,[10] and twice yearly at the Syrian temple of the Great Goddess at Hierapolis-Membij.[11]

6:1-2

(d)   *Come, let us return to the Lord;*
              though he has torn, he will heal us;
              though he has stricken, he will bind us up.
              After two days he will revive us;
              on the third day he will raise us up,[12]
              and we shall be revived in his presence.

A not uncommon feature of seasonal festivals is the staging of a mock funeral and subsequent resurrection of the spirit of fertility.[13] In Egypt, it was Osiris who was thus buried and revived;[14] in Syria, it was Adonis,[15] and in Asia Minor it was Attis.[16] In Russia, the interment and resurrection of Kostrubonko, deity of the spring, was solemnly celebrated in popular custom at Eastertide;[17] and in Roumania, on the Monday before Assumption (in August), a clay image of the analogous Kalojan is deposited in the earth, to be dug up after a few days.[18] The prophet's words may well have been inspired by such a spectacle.

6:3

(e)   *Let us know, let us press on to know, the Lord;*
              his emergence is as sure as the dawn;
              he will come to us as the showers,
              as the spring rains that water the earth.

These lines receive added significance when it is borne in mind that seasonal festivals are often made to coincide with the solstice or equinox.[19] The Asianic mysteries of Attis, for example, culminated in the triumphant reemergence of that god of fertility on the day of the vernal equinox (March 25).[20] Similarly, in Mesopotamia, the rites of Tammuz were held in the month of the spring solstice;[21] and the prophet Ezekiel expressly associates the weeping for that god with a ceremony of adoring the rising sun.[22] Moreover, an Old Assyrian calendar for the month of Tammuz prescribes significantly that the weeping for that god, which is to take place on the first day, is to be followed immediately, on the second, by "the presentation of gifts to the sun-god";[23] while a Babylonian hymn belonging to the Tammuz cycle represents the sun-god as assuring the sister of the dead genius of fertility that he himself would restore to her "the verdure which has been removed" and "the crushed grain which has been carried away."[24] In a Hittite ritual myth, the restoration of Telipinu, the god of fertility, is associated with the worship of the sun,[25] and in the Canaanite *Poem of Baal* a particularly important role is assigned to the sun-goddess. It is she that retrieves Baal from the netherworld,[26] and it is she that urges his rival Môt, genius of drought and sterility, to give up the fight against him.[27] Indeed, so cardinal a part does she play in the action that she is formally commended in words which sound uncommonly as though they had been incorporated by the poet from some traditional hymn.[28] Again, it should be observed that in Syria and the eastern portions of the Roman Empire, the Festival of the "New Age" was likewise combined with an important solar date, viz., the alleged birthday of the sun on November 18.[29] The same date was claimed by Clement of Alexandria as the birthday of the Christian Savior.[30] Indeed, so firmly established was the connection between the festivals of the new life and the worship of the sun that the Church was obliged to fix Christmas on what had originally been the birthday of the solarized savior Mithra and to associate the date of Christ's resurrection (Easter) with the vernal equinox.[31] Significant also is the fact that among the Israelites themselves, both the spring festival (Pentecost) and the autumn Festival of Ingathering fell in the months of the equinoxes, the latter being expressly associated with that event in the ritual calendar of Exodus 34:22.[32]

7:14

(f)   *For grain and new wine they gash themselves;*[33]
              against me they rebel.

Gashing the flesh was, as we have seen (above, §**158**), a standard procedure in rites of mourning, and the vanished god of fertility was everywhere lamented in this manner.[34] Once again, therefore, the prophet is alluding to pagan seasonal practices.

9:1

(g)   *You have made love for a harlot's hire*
              on all the threshing floors.

Ritual promiscuity, designed to promote increase of men, cattle, and crops, is everywhere a standard feature of seasonal festivals.[35] According to Herodotus, it took place both at Babylon[36] and in Cyprus,[37] and it is attested also in the cult of the Great Goddess (Ma) at Comana, in Pontus.[38] In Java, as also among the Fan of West Africa, the Hereros, the Garos, and the natives of Amboyna, men and women are expected to copulate openly in the fields at major agricultural festivals; while the Indians of Peru do so as soon as the alligator pears ripen.[39]

(h)
> I am the Lord your God
> from the land of Egypt;
> I will again make you dwell in tents
> as on the days of the seasonal festival.

Dwelling in tents is, of course, a natural concomitant of pilgrim festivals. The Samaritans, for instance, still do so when they repair to Mt. Gerizim for the celebration of the Passover. An inscription from the island of Cos, dated in the second century B.C., mentions an annual religious festival at which worshipers were required to erect booths (*skênopagisthôn*),[40] and the rare Greek word which denotes this practice is actually employed by the Septuagint to render the Hebrew "Feast of Booths" (*ḥag ha-sukkôth*), the Feast of Ingathering.[41] The custom is well attested elsewhere in Classical antiquity.[42] Tibullus tells us, for example, that at the Roman festival of Sementivae Feriae (in January) "the crowd makes merry and erects wattled cabins."[43] Somewhat similarly, the celebrated *Pervigilium Veneris*, which really has reference to the festival of Venus Verticordia and Fortuna Virilis, in April, says specifically: *Cras amorum copulatrix inter umbras arborum / Implicat casas virentes de flagello myrteo,* and this, as Clementi has pointed out, bears allusion to the same custom.[44] Yet again, therefore, the prophet's words may have been suggested by the sight of such temporary structures at a pagan festival.

Nor is it only to the *ritual* of these occasions that Hosea appears to allude. Some of his images seem likewise to be drawn from the *myths* associated with such ceremonies. It has been suggested,[45] for instance, that his celebrated picture of Yahweh's marriage to Israel (chs. 1–3) may have been inspired by the fact that a cardinal element of seasonal festivals was often a mimetic "sacred marriage" between god and goddess, customarily impersonated by the king and a hierodule (see above, §176). The prophet lifts this primitive rite to a sublime spiritual plane. Similarly, when he declares in the name of Yahweh (5:14)

> I will be like a lion to Ephraim
> and like a young lion to the house of Judah;
> I, even I, will ravin and depart,
> carry off, with no one to rescue,

he may be drawing his image from a myth which related that the missing god of fertility had been savaged by a boar or some similar wild beast.[46] This, for example, is said to have been the fate of Adonis,[47] Attis,[48] Hyas,[49] Linos,[50] Bormos,[51] and Idmon,[52] all of whom are regarded by Gruppe as variants of the fertility-spirit.[53] To be sure, the evidence here is late and, in some cases, dubious,[54] yet it is significant that, at a far earlier date, the Canaanite Baal himself is said, in a poem from Ras Shamra-Ugarit, to have been attacked by wild beasts called "renders" (*'qqm*) and "devourers" (*aklm*).[55] Thus, what the prophet would be saying is that the horrible doom which attended the hero of the pagan seasonal myth would yet be visited upon recalcitrant Israel, and that he himself ("I, even I") would be the attacker.

That Hosea has in mind specifically the traditional usages and myths *of Canaan* is suggested further by the statement in 13:14 that Yahweh has been provoked beyond compassion, so that he will not redeem his people from Death (Heb.: *Maweth*). For here we may detect a reference to the Canaanite god of that name (Môt), from whom Baal was eventually redeemed, after he had been trapped in the netherworld. The implication thus is that the "happy ending" of the pagan ritual pantomime will not be repeated in the case of rebellious Israel, because "compassion is hidden from my eyes."

A final example of how Hosea may have been alluding to pagan myth is afforded in 14:8. The Hebrew text of this verse is notoriously obscure and has been variously translated and emended. RSV's *It is I who answer and look after you* can scarcely be extracted from it.[56] Some scholars, by different vocalization of the consonants, obtain the sense, *It is I that have bound and will now set loose*. In view, however, of the preceding, *What has Ephraim to do more with idols?* (LXX text), a better sequence results by adopting a clever emendation by Julius Wellhausen, who for the Hebrew *'ᵃNî 'ANîTHî Wᵉ-'AŠūReNNū* suggests the very similar *'ᵃNî 'ANāTHô Wᵉ-AŠRāTHô,* "I am his 'Anat and his Asherah." These were the two primary goddesses of the Canaanites.[57] The implication is, therefore, that Yahweh will do for Israel all that these deities were popularly credited with doing in the pagan myth and cult.

That the prophet was indeed indulging in a series of sly allusions is seemingly indicated by his own concluding words (14:9): *Whoever is wise will understand these things; whoever is discerning, will know them.*[58] A similar formula occurs in Psalm 107:43, and it resembles one subjoined to the Mesopotamian Epic of Creation. As Oppenheim has shown,[59] this is representative of standard practice. It is the equivalent of the classic tag, *Verbum sapienti sat,* and harks back to the notion that cultic texts contain a symbolic as well as a literal meaning.

222   Gomer, daughter of Diblaim   1:3

Diblaim is either the lady's father or else her hometown.[1] Since, however, the whole story is told as a parable, it is not improbable that the writer chose this name on account of some latent signficance.[2] Now, Diblaim (a dual form) at once suggests the Hebrew word, *dᵉbelah,* "a cake of pressed figs," and what may have been implied by calling a woman a "two-fig-cake wench" is perhaps suggested by a statement made, several centuries later, by the Arabic writer, Jabir ibn Abdullah, concerning popular usages during the early days of Islam. Until Abu Bekr forbade it, he tells us, it was possible to contract a temporary alliance (*"mota'*-marriage") with a woman for "a handful of dates or a small quantity of grain"[3]—just as in World War II soldiers overseas could "pick up" accommodating girls for a pack of cigarettes. Nor need we depend only on such late evidence. The Assyrian king Ashurbanipal (699–633 B.C.) informs us, in somewhat similar vein, that after he had suppressed the insubordinate Arabs, there ensued among them such an economic slump that a farmer was able to acquire a camel for the paltry price of "a basket of fresh dates."[4] To call a woman a "two-fig-cake wench" might therefore very well have been the ancient equivalent of calling her a "two-bit whore."

It should be observed, however, that this has nothing whatsoever to do with the common English expression "not worth a fig," for there the word "fig" is connected rather with the Spanish *fico,* and refers to the obscene gesture of contempt made by thrusting the thumb between the first and second fingers in imitation of coitus.[5] Nor has it any relation to the ancient Greek use of the term "fig-like" (*sykinos*) to denote "worthless,"[6] for that derives from the fact that the wood of the fig-tree is too soft to be used in carpentry.[7] Indeed, in Greek popular lore, it was deemed unlucky.[8]

223 Gomer's children 1:6–9

Two of the children of Hosea's union with Gomer are to be called respectively Lo-Ruḥamah and Lo-'Ammi. Within the context of the parable, these names mean simply, "Unpitied" and "Not-My-people." But they too may also conceal a more subtle point, for *ruḥamah* could also mean "a woman united to one by kinship" (cf. Arabic *raḥîm,* and Heb. *reḥem,* "womb");[1] while *'ammî* may be compared with the Arabic *ibn 'amm,* "a man of the same stock-group."[2] Hence, besides their symbolic connotation, Lo Ruḥamah and Lo 'Ammi could both mean simply, *bastard.*

224 Stripping a divorcee 2:2–3

It was an Ancient Near Eastern custom to strip a woman of her clothing when she was divorced or if she was discovered to be unfaithful.[1] An Old Babylonian letter has a man declare that if, after his death, his wife take another man, his own sons are to strip her and expell her from the house.[2] Legal documents from Nuzi, of the sixteenth century B.C., attest the stripping of a wife who is put away;[3] while in a late Aramaic charm against the demon Lilith, a writ of divorce is symbolically served upon her and she is ordered to go forth stripped.[4] Tacitus tells us that among the ancient Germans faithless wives were similarly treated.[5]

The practice was based on the ancient and primitive notion that *clothes symbolize their wearer's person.*[6] In Mesopotamia, for example, an illiterate could "sign" a legal document by pressing the fringe of his (or her) garment against the wet clay of the tablet on which it was inscribed;[7] while the Greek poet Theocritus (third cent. B.C.) tells how a lovesick woman tried to bewitch the object of her passion by shedding and burning the fringe (or tassel) of his garment, which had come by chance into her possession.[8] Analogous, too, is a modern tale from Prussia, which relates how a man who had been caught looting shed his coat while trying to escape, but fell dead the moment he heard that it was being cut to pieces by the man he had robbed.[9] To strip the clothing from a divorcee was therefore to *cancel her out.* By precisely the same symbolism the Babylonian king was annually stripped of his robes at the Akîtu (New Year) festival, in order to show that he was temporarily deposed;[10] and in the same way too—as in the notorious case of Captain Dreyfus—an army officer is stripped of his epaulets and buttons when he is "drummed out" in disgrace. The idea leaves its trace in popular parlance, for we still speak of *divesting* (or *stripping*) a person of authority or dignity.

Other ideas, however, also come into play, and these are even more clearly articulated in a variant form of the custom, wherein the faithless wife's garment is not stripped from her, but merely *cut.* Thus, a Babylonian who divorced his wife might sometimes content himself with snipping off the fringed hem of her robe;[11] while among the Chuwash, Chremiss, Mordvinians, Votyaks, and Voguls of Russia, a husband who desires to part from his wife does so by tearing her veil;[12] and in Wales, a woman who could not clear herself of a charge of adultery had her shift torn.[13] In such cases, what is thereby symbolized is not merely the diminution or annulment of her person, but also the severance of it from any further association with her husband: he *cuts her off.*

Then, too, it should be borne in mind that in several cultures, husband and wife are portrayed figuratively as each other's *raiment.*[14] Mohammed, for instance, in permitting sexual intercourse on the night of the Fast—a concession directly opposed to Jewish law—tells his followers that, after all, "your wives are your garments, and you are theirs";[15] while, in more cynical vein, a Chinese proverb remarks that "a wife is like one's clothes—replaceable when worn out!"[16] To remove the clothing of a divorcee was thus a symbolic gesture of *shedding* her—a figure of speech still affected by gossip columnists in our own day. This aspect of the custom is brought out arrestingly in a marriage contract from the Ḫabur Valley, dating around 1700 B.C. There it is stipulated that if *either party* unilaterally repudiate the other, *he or she* is to leave the house "naked."[17] Similarly, it is not without significance that an early Arabic term for "divorce" was *ḥol'*, which means properly, *divestiture.*[18]

Lastly, it should be observed that the stripping of the divorced wife is, in fact, the converse of the widespread custom whereby the husband casts his mantle over her during the marriage ceremony (see above, §121). This is at once a gesture of protection and of covenant. Among the Moslems of Morocco, for example, it symbolizes not only a voluntary but also a compulsory bond; for when a man casts an *'ar,* or "conditional curse," upon another, he sometimes moves toward him a fold of his garment, or throws his cloak over him.[19] The withdrawal of the wife's raiment would thus represent the withdrawal of that protection and the termination of the bond.

225 Marriage formulas 2:19–20

> *I will betroth thee unto me for ever;*
> *I will betroth thee unto me in righteousness, and*
> *in judgment, and in loving-kindness, and in mercies.*
> *I will betroth thee unto me in faithfulness:*
> *and thou shalt know the LORD.*

Note the threefold repetition of *I will betroth thee,* suggestive of a legal (or ritual) formula. The conventional rendering does not bring out the full meaning, for the word translated "in righteousness" really means "by due protocol," that rendered "in judgment" means "by legal process," that rendered "in loving-kindness" means "by mutual bond," and that rendered "in mercies" means "by ties of kinship." Lastly, "in faithfulness" is an inaccurate translation of a word which really means "by pledge." Hence, all are juridical terms.

> *And I said unto her, Thou shalt abide for*
> *me many days; thou shalt not play the harlot,*
> *and thou shalt not consort with another man;*
> *so will I consort with thee.*

This too was probably a standard marriage formula, possibly only for a temporary alliance. The expression "thout shalt abide for me" corresponds to the technical term for marriage in the legal documents from Nuzi.

226 Ephôd and teraphîm 3:5

> *The children of Israel shall dwell many days without king*
> *or prince, without sacrifice or pillar, without* ephôd *or*
> teraphîm.

It has been commonly supposed that *ephôd* and *teraphîm* denote objects used in divination. This, however, is scarcely correct. The *teraphîm,* as we have seen (above, §**68**), are images of the household gods. While they were certainly objects of cult, there is nothing to show that they were used in divination. The *ephôd* is simply a wrap worn in ritual ceremonies. Not only was it part of the official garb of the priests of Israel,[1] but it is said also to have been worn by the young Samuel when he served as an acolyte in the sanctuary at Shiloh,[2] and by David when he performed religious exercises.[3] In the form, *epadâtum* the word has now turned up in the sense of "mantle, wrap" in Old Assyrian texts. It has also been recognized in a poetic text from Ras Shamra-Ugarit.[4]

The combination, *ephôd and teraphîm,* therefore constitutes a merism meaning simply, "regular worship"—the equivalent, so to speak, of "vestments and ikons." Older views about them can now be safely discarded.[5]

227 David redivivus   3:5

> *Afterward the children of Israel shall return and
> seek the Lord their God and David their king.*

See above, §205, a.

228 El the Bull   8:6

> KJV: *For from Israel was it:*
> *the workman made it;*
> *therefore it is not God:*
> *but the calf of Samaria shall be broken in pieces.*

It is generally recognized that the traditional text of this verse is corrupt and barely translatable. Modern scholars join the opening clause to the last words of the preceding verse and, by slight emendation, obtain the sense, *How long will they be unable to obtain cleanliness (or, acquittal) in Israel?* Comparative Religion, however, comes to the rescue. As H. Tur-Sinai has acutely discerned, by mere redivision of the Hebrew consonants, the verse may be made to read:

> *For who is El the Bull?*
> *Something a workman made.*
> *No god is he!*
> *That Samarian calf will eventually be dashed to splinters.*[1]

"El the Bull" is a stock title of the supreme god in the Canaanite texts from Ras Shamra-Ugarit[2] and finds a counterpart also in the "Bull-Baal" (*Tr-B'l*) of early South Arabian inscriptions.[3] The "calf of Samaria," which was supposed to represent him, was thus an idolatrous image (cf. Hos. 10:5; 13:2; I Kings 12:28; II Kings 10:29),[4] here held up to scorn.

229 The bread of mourners   9:4

> *Theirs shall be bread like that of mourners;*
> *all that eat of it shall be deemed unclean.*

See above, §202.

230 Oil in the making of covenants   12:1

> (Of Ephraim:) *They make a covenant with Assyria,*
> *and oil is carried to Egypt.*

Interesting light is cast on these words by the observation that in neo-Assyrian business contracts the sincerity of the parties is sometimes said to be put to the test by means of a rite performed by a professional diviner (*barû*) "with water and oil."

(If the prophet is indeed alluding to this practice, it is probable that, by deriving the relevant Hebrew word from a different root, the second line should rather be rendered, *And oil* is poured *for Egypt.*)[1]

Joel

231 Joel and the pagan festivals

Comparative Folklore illustrates the Book of Joel in the same way as it does that of Hosea (see above, §221), suggesting that it may be read as a sustained satire on a pagan seasonal festival. Each of the characteristic features of that occasion serves, by a homiletic twist, to convey a message from Yahweh to his enemies and to apostates in Israel, while at the same time certain elements are exploited to bring tidings of hope to the oppressed.[1] The following are the more arresting instances.

Joel 1:5

> (a) *Drunkards and winebibbers are bidden "wail over the juice which has been cut off from their mouths."*

The reference here is to the ritual wailing for the discomfited god of the vine. The most familiar example of this comes from ancient Greece, where the "passion" of Dionysus was a common theme of vintage ritual. Thus, Diodorus mentions a *"linos-*song," or threnody, in ancient "Pelasgian" script, which recorded it;[2] while Clement of Alexandria speaks of a "rustic song dealing with the dismemberment of Dionysus,"[3] and Plutarch refers to the practice of intoning a direg (*eleleu*) at the Attic vintage festival of Oschophoria, in June–July.[4] The pruned vine was personified as Dionysus, and the idea was, indeed, taken over into Christianity. Thus Clement speaks of Christ as "that great grape-cluster . . . which was crushed for one benefit"; while a Middle German paternoster by Johann von Krolewitz refers to him as *gemen und gebunden als man ein Garten tut.*[5] In the same way, too, it is recorded in an Arabic source that when plague raged in Iraq in 1204, the warning was issued that all who failed to participate in the time-honored rite of bewailing the lost son of the mythical Um Unkud, "Mother of the Grape," would inevitably fall victim to it.[6] Of the same tenor also is a modern French song chanted at the pruning of vines:

> *Vignon, vignette,*
> *Vignon, vignette,*

Qui te planta il fut preudon,
Tu fus taillée à la serpette![7]

The practice was certainly known among the ancient Canaanites, for a vintage song of similar purport is embedded in a mythological text of the fourteenth century B.C. from Ras Shamra-Ugarit:[8]

> Death-and Rot has sat enthroned,
>   firm ensconced in regal sway,
> In his either hand a rood—
>   Loss of Children, Widowhood;
> Yet, when men now prune the vine,
>   *he* it is that they entwine;
> When they grub the soil all round,
>   'tis from *him* they pluck the ground!

1:8

(b) *Israel is bidden wail for "the husband* (Heb.: baal) *of her youth."*

Here the prophet is again satirizing the ritual ululation for the vanished god of fertility, actually named Baal among the Canaanites. "Such howling and wailing is well attested throughout ancient civilizations." The Egyptians, says Diodorus,[9] used to shed tears and cry upon Isis at the first cutting of the corn; and their summer festival was marked, according to Herodotus,[10] by the chanting of a doleful lay called Maneros. This latter, it is believed, is a distortion of the Egyptian words, *maa n per.k,* "come to thy house," which constitute the opening phrase of a seasonal dirge, that has actually come down to us.[11] The custom is attested also, at a much later date, by Firmicus Maternus, who reproaches the pagan Egyptians for "lamenting over the crops and wailing over the growing seed."[12] In Mesopotamia, the harvest was likewise accompanied by the utterance of a ritual cry known as *alalu* or "ululation"—corresponding exactly to the *eleleu* of Plutarch.[13] Similarly, according to a writer quoted by Athenaeus, ritual dirges called *iouloi* (or *houloi*), i.e., howls, characterized the mysteries of Demeter and Kore (Persephone).[14]

1:9–12

(c) *The land is portrayed as suffering from drought and blight. This has denied Yahweh his wonted offerings.*

Seasonal festivals are everywhere introduced by a period of "mortification," in which life and fertility are represented as suffering a temporary standstill.[15] The language on which this is described in the seasonal myth is more or less stereotyped, and it looks uncommonly as though the prophet is playing on the traditional phraseology. Thus, in the Hittite myth of Telipinu, god of vegetation and fertility, it is said that when he withdraws from the earth in a temper, not only do "the hillsides, trees and pasturelands become bare, and the springs dry up, but the gods themselves are threatened with starvation."[16] So too in the Homeric *Hymn to Demeter,* that goddess is said to have kept the seed buried in the ground while she mourned for Persephone, with the result that not only would the entire human race have perished of starvation but also that "they who dwell on Olympus would have been deprived of their offerings," had not Zeus intervened.[17]

For the rest, the terms in which Joel describes the sterility on earth accord closely with the ancient myths. Thus, in the Hittite "Yuzgat Tablet," which describes the ravages of Hahhimas (Torpor, or perhaps Jack Frost), he is said to have "paralyzed plants, oxen, sheep, hounds and pigs" and to be about to do the same to human beings and vegetation;[18] while in the Canaanite *Poem of Baal,* the disappearance of that god into the netherworld evokes the cry, "The furrows of the fields have gone dry. . . . Baal is neglecting the furrows of the plowlands!"[19]

1:13

(d) *In consequence of this disaster, the priests of Yahweh are bidden to don mourning garb and "pass the night in sackcloth."*[20]

Here it is possible to detect a satirical allusion to the seasonal custom of keeping an all-night vigil for the lost god of fertility, somewhat like the Catholic *tenebrae*-service in Holy Week. The mystery cults both of Dionysus[21] and Attis[22] celebrated some of their main rites at night, while at Eleusis a nocturnal vigil on Boedromion (roughly, September) 19 was taken to represent the wandering of Demeter through darkness in search of Persephone.[23] In Roman Egypt the faithful gathered in an underground chamber at the winter solstice and emerged at dawn carrying the image of a man-child (like the Bambino in the Christmas ceremonies at the church of Aracoeli in Rome) and proclaiming, "The Virgin has given birth! Light has increased!"[24] That ceremonies of this kind indeed go back to far earlier times is indicated by the fact the prophet Ezekiel expressly mentions rites in a cavern in connection with the annual bewailing of Tammuz, and there too they are associated with an adoration of the rising sun![25]

2:15

(e) *A sacred fast and period of abstinence* (Heb.: *ʿᵃṣārāh*) *are ordained.*

This, to be sure, does not come out clearly in the English Version, because the Hebrew word for "period of abstinence" has been confused by the translators with another meaning "solemn assembly."[26] Periods of abstinence are, however, the usual thing before a harvest festival. They indicate that one lease of life has come to an end, before the beginning of another.[27] Thus the Babylonians recognized the first week or even the first sixteen days of the New Year month of Teshrit as a lenten period;[28] while among the Israelites the autumnal Feast of Ingathering was preceded by a solemn Day of Catharsis (*Yôm ha-kippurîm*, "Day of Atonement"), when all activity stopped.[29] In Greece, the festival of Thesmophória, in October, was characterized by fasting; indeed, the third day was called specifically "the Fast,"[30] and in Cyprus, abstention from food obtained throughout the preceding nine days.[31] So too, the Feast of the Yellow Grain-Mother (Demeter Chloē), held in Athens in mid-May, was marked by rites of mortification.[32] In the Attis-cult, the annual resurrection of that spirit of fertility was introduced by a few days of fasting and ceremonial austerity (*hagisteiai, castus*);[33] and at Rome, the Festival of Ceres, in April, was prefaced by a fast.[34]

Modern parallels abound.[35] In Cambodia, for instance, the first three days of the year (which begins in mid-March) are a period of solemn abstinence.[36] Among the Cherokees and Choctaws of America, the New Year festival in August is called *Busk,* "the Fast," and no food is consumed for two nights and one day before the eating of the new crops.[37] The Mao of Manipur observe a *genna,* or period of taboo, for four days at the beginning of the harvest.[38] In South Massam, fasting takes places before the Walaga festival;[39] among the Natchez of Mississippi, for three days before harvest;[40] in New Guinea, before the yam festival;[41] and in Peru before the summer festival of Raymi.[42]

2:20

(f) *The "northerner" will be expelled and driven into parched and desolated land, "his front into the eastern sea, and his rear into the western sea."*

In the immediate context of the prophet's message, this evidently denoted an historical foe. Nevertheless, there is also a subliminal mythological allusion. The prophet is likening that invader to the figure of Death, Blight, or the like ceremonially expelled in seasonal ceremonies.[43] The Incas of Peru, for example, used ceremonially to expel disease at the festival of Situa, celebrated just before the onset of the rainy season in September.[44] Similarly in Thailand,[45] and likewise among the Woyaks of East Russia,[46] the forces of evil are solemnly banished on the last day of the year, and among the Hos of Togoland (W. Africa)[47] and the Kiriwina of southeastern New Guinea,[48] they are exorcized before the eating of new yams. At Cape Coast Castle the demon Abonsam is driven forth annually after a four-week period of mortification;[49] and in Tonquin, there is a similar expulsion once a year.[50]

The custom survives, as we shall see later (§**238**), in many parts of Europe, and it is significant, in connection with the prophet's words, that the dread spirits are often driven *into the sea.*

3:9–12

(g) *There will be a final warfare of Yahweh against his enemies.*

This is simply a projection into eschatology of the seasonal defeat of Death, Blight, Old Year, Winter, Chaos, and similar beings. The Ritual Combat, as has long been observed, is a standard element of seasonal festivals and is considered a necessary prelude to the restoration of rainfall and fertility. For this reason it is likewise retrojected into cosmogony, for what happens at the beginning of each year had obviously to have happened also at the beginning of time. Marduk defeats the rebel forces of Ti'amat and her allies before being installed as king and as lord of fertility (*bêl ḥegalli*); Baal similarly defeats Yam and Môt (Death) in the corresponding Canaanite myth; and the Hittite storm-god discomfits the dragon Illuyankas. Ritual equivalents of this myth are legion; the reader may find any number of examples in Frazer's *Golden Bough*[51] or in the present writer's *Thespis*,[52] and it is scarcely necessary to cite them. Representative of them all is the custom observed by women in the Brahmi Confederacy of Baluchistan of staging a ritual combat whenever rain is needed.[53] Similarly, in parts of Malaya, such a combat takes place every three or four years in order to expel demons.[54]

3:12

(h) The consequence of victory in the Combat is the holding of an assize at which the triumphant god is installed as king (e.g., Marduk at Esagila) and the order of "nature" reestablished for the ensuing year.[55] This involves the determination of the individual destinies of men. At the Babylonian New Year Festival, for example, the gods so assembled in the Chamber of Destinies (*parak shimātē*),[56] and to this day Jewish belief asserts that the fates of men are reviewed in heaven on New Year's Day. The ritual equivalent of the myth is the installation of a new king or the formal reinduction of the old one.

Out of this myth and ritual Joel develops the warning that the Last Days will be marked by Yahweh's pronouncing judgment[57] upon the enemies of his people. This, he adds, will take place appropriately in the Valley of Jehosaphat, since that name means properly "Yahweh (Jehovah) judges."

3:18

(i) But harvest and fertility *do* follow. Baal, or the vanished god, returns and brings rainfall and increase, and it is this that marks the concluding stage of the seasonal festival. In the Canaanite *Poem of Baal* the imminent return of the deity is harbingered by a dream in which "the skies rain fatness, and the wadies run with honey."[58] So here, harking back to these ancient words, the prophet declares that in the end

> *The mountains shall drip sweet wine,*
> *and the hills be awash with milk,*
> *and all the wadies of Judah shall flow with water.*

232   The dimming of the sun   2:10
See above, §**216.**

233   The foe from the north   2:20
The prophecy that Israel's enemy will be driven into the sea harkens back
to a popular custom of so expelling demons and noxious powers (see below,
§**238**). The designation of that enemy as "the northerner" likewise combines
a mythological with an historical allusion,[1] for it is a widespread belief that
the north is the natural habitat of such spirits.[2]

This belief is attested, for instance, among such ancient peoples as the Indians of the Vedic period[3] and the Iranians.[4] It survived later among the
Mandeans[5] and the Jews;[6] ineed, a Jewish tradition asserted specifically that
certain sacrifices were slaughtered in the north of the temple area at Jerusalem
in order to protect Israel from demons who lived there.[7] The Manichaeans too
regarded the north as especially sinister.[8]

Nor is the idea confined to Oriental cultures. In late Greek magical literature, demons are conjured from the north,[9] and it is there that Plutarch locates
the monster Typhon.[10] Similarly, in Mexican mythology, Mictlan, "the Country of the North," is the home of demonic spirits called *tzitzimitles.*[11]

The concept prevails especially in European folklore. Thus, in Chaucer's
Frere's Tale, the fiend who comes in disguise declares that he lives "in the
north countree": while in the English ballad entitled *Riddles Wisely Explained,* the riddle-mongering wooer—a fiend in disguise—lies in the north,
and in some versions of *Lady Isabel and the Elf-Knight* the supernatural suitor
hails from "the north lands."[12] Michael Behaim of Sulzbach, a German poet
of the fifteenth century, expressly ridicules the superstition that devils live in
Norway[13]—a popular notion mentioned also in a contemporary Jewish
source.[14]

The north side of a church is often held to be unlucky, and the northern
door is left open at baptism to give egress to the Evil One.[15] By the same
token, burial on the north side of a cemetery is commonly disdained, this
situation being reserved for unbaptized infants, persons excommunicated, executed criminals, and suicides.[16]

Amos

234   Amos and the pagan festivals

Like those of Hosea (§221) and Zephaniah (§243), the prophecies of Amos appear to be studded with jibes at pagan seasonal practices, suggesting that they may have been delivered at festive assemblies.

Amos 4:4, 6–9

(a) Thus, when the prophet ironically summons Israel to present its daily sacrifices and its "three-day tithes" at the pagan shrines of Bethel and Gilgal, he may perhaps be alluding to the fact that the seasonal festivals seem sometimes to have lasted for three days, beginning with a mock funeral, and ending with the "resurrection" of the god of fertility (see above, §221, d).[1]

(b) Similarly, when he threatens famine, blight, and drought as the punishment for such apostasy, it is not difficult to recognize a sly reference to the fact that the pagan festivals were resigned primarily to ensure regular rainfall and fertility.[2]

4:12

(c) Again, when he urges his brethren to "prepare to meet your God," he may well be playing on the fact that a main reason for repairing to pagan sanctuaries was to "see the face of the god" (see below, §251). Moreover, in the later mystery religions, the proceedings often culminated in the "vision" (*epopteia*) of the risen lord of fertility.[3]

4:13

(d) The pointed declaration that the Lord of Hosts is the real creator of the mountains[4] and of the wind, and the real fructifier of the soil, may have been designed more specifically as a counterblow against the pretensions of the Canaanite Baal, whose command of the rains and fertilization of the earth were the particular theme of seasonal myths and ceremonies.[5]

5:6

(e) So too, when the people are bidden "seek" the Lord so that they may "live," we are reminded once again of the ritual "search" for the vanished spirit of vegetation in the pagan seasonal ceremonies (see above, §221, e).

(f) The assertion that there will be public wailing in the streets, and that the farmer especially will participate in it, likewise recalls a characteristic feature of the pagan ceremonies—the ululation over the dead or vanished deity (see above, §§**158, 203**).

(g) The famous statement,

> *Let justice roll down like the waters,*
> *and righteousness like a perpetual stream* (êthan),

assumes added force if it is read as a satire on the rite of pouring water as a rain-charm (see above, §**221, c**). This took place at Jerusalem during the month of "perpetual streams" (*Ethanîm*), i.e., September–October.

(h) Again, when the future restoration of Israel's fortunes is described as the raising of the fallen booth (*sukkah*) of David, the prophet may well be drawing his imagery from the temporary booths or tents which studded the landscape at the pilgrim festivals (see above, §**221, h**). Frail structures, they would often have been blown down by the wind.

A further allusion to the ritual of pagan festivals may perhaps be recognized in the prophet's call to his countrymen (5:15) to "set up justice in the gate." The Hebrew word rendered "set up" is usually employed of erecting statues, and nowhere else does it occur in a metaphorical sense. The phrase is therefore somewhat strained and bizarre. But perhaps it is a deliberate "dig" at the pagan practice of putting up statues of the gods beside the gate of a city or temple in seasonal processions.[6] Such gates were statutory places of judgment,[7] and this would, of course, lend added force to the prophet's words.

That the prophet was indeed alluding to pagan festivals seems also to be indicated by the express declaration which he puts into the mouth of the Lord (5:21):

> *I hate, I reject your festivals,*
> *and take no delight in your days of restraint.*[8]

235 Judgment by fire 7:4

> RSV: *Thus the Lord GOD showed me: behold, the Lord GOD was calling for a judgment by fire, and it devoured the great deep and was eating up the land.*[1]

The notion of a final judgment of the world by fire recurs elsewhere in the Old Testament. Thus, the so-called farewell song of Moses (Deut. 32:22)—

which is dated by Eissfeldt to the eleventh century B.C.[2]—includes a prophecy that the fire which has been kindled in Yahweh's wrath and which "burns down to deepest hell" will yet "devour the earth and its produce and set the foundations of the mountains ablaze." Similarly, Isaiah speaks of Yahweh's "day of vengeance, the year of settling accounts in his suit against Zion," when "rivers will be turned into pitch, and dust to brimstone, and when the soil of Zion will become burning pitch."[3] Malachi[4] and Daniel[5] likewise paint a grim picture of a final conflagration, but it is possible that they were influenced more directly by Iranian ideas (see below, §247).

The conflagration became a prominent element of the eschatological nightmare portrayed in intertestamental literature. The Book of Enoch, for instance, threatens the heathen with the prospect of being "cast into the judgment of fire,"[6] and one of the Psalms of Solomon refers in a vivid passage to "the flame of fire and wrath" destined for the unrighteous.[7] In the same vein, too, the Manual of Discipline found among the Dead Sea Scrolls prescribes that at the ceremony of initiation into the brotherhood the levites are to pronounce the curse that all who have cast their lot with Belial "shall be damned in the gloom of the fire eternal,"[8] and in one of the Qumran hymns there is a lurid description (indebted partly to our passage) of the final conflagration.[9]

The New Testament likewise speaks in several places of the final "Gehenna (RSV: hell) of fire."[10]

Nor is the idea confined to the Bible. It features prominently in Zoroastrian doctrine,[11] although there the fire is regarded as purificatory as well as punitive. One of the Yashts, in predicting it, portrays it as the medium whereby the imperfections or dross of the world will be purged away;[12] and the later Bundahishn depicts in horrendous terms this coming disaster.[13]

According to Berosus (as quoted by Seneca),[14] the Neo-Stoics likewise espoused the belief in a final conflagration (*ekpyrōsis*), and it seems to have enjoyed considerable popularity in Imperial Rome.[15] Some scholars believe that this was borrowed, albeit indirectly, from the Iranians, while others see in it a moralizing development of Heraclitus' view that, since all things spring from fire, they will ultimately return to the same element.[16]

According to Eliade, ideas of a similar character are entertained by the Mayas of Yucatan and the Aztecs of Mexico.[17]

It may be suggested that in articulating this age-old belief our present passage also works in an allusion to traditional myth. Eschatology is, after all, simply cosmogony in the future tense: the new world will be born in much the same way as was the present one.[18] *Magnus ab integro saeclorum nascitur ordo.*[19] Hence, the concept of an eschatological world-fire ought to correspond to some cosmogonic event or incident of the same order, and traces of such a mythical event can indeed be detected in Ancient Near Eastern literature. A commentary on the ritual of the Babylonian Akîtu (New Year) festival interprets the ceremonial act of firing an oven as symbolizing the burning of Kingu, husband of the marplot Tiamat and commander of the rebel hosts in the primordial battle of the gods.[20] This lends added point to Amos' specific reference to the burning of "the great deep," seeing that the Hebrew word for "deep" is in fact *tehôm*, the equivalent of Tiamat.[21] Similarly, too, the act of burning the heads of two statues at the same festival is taken to represent the burning of the dragon Mušḫuššu and of the "scorpion man"—two monsters subdued by the god Ninurta in an earlier version of the cosmogonic myth.[22] True, these incidents do not appear in the more or less standardized form of the myth (*Enuma Elish*) which was actually recited at the festival, but we may be reasonably sure that Mesopotamian popular lore knew also of variant tales concerning these primordial events.

In view of the frequent appearance in rabbinic literature of the concept of a final "deluge of fire" (*mabbūl shel 'esh*)[23] it has recently been suggested that it is more specifically to this that Amos here refers, and the suggestion has been bolstered by the further proposal that the traditional text's *QôRē' La-RîB Ba-'ESH*, "calling *for a judgment by* fire," should rather be read (by mere redivision of the consonants) *QôRē' Li-RᵉBîB 'ESH*, "calling for a *rain of* fire."[24] This, however, misses the point of the prophet's phrase. The word, *QôRē'*, "calling," is here used, as in Isaiah 59:4, in the technical sense of *summoning to a court of law;* hence, the traditional *La-RîB*, which properly means "to litigation" (rather than "for a judgment"), is both apposite and necessary. Moreover, the sentiment finds a perfect parallel in Isaiah 34:8–9, where, as mentioned above, the final conflagration is explicitly associated with the year in which Yahweh will settle accounts in his long-standing litigation, or lawsuit (*RîB*) against Zion.[25]

Jonah

236 The story of Jonah

▲ We have all been familiar from childhood with the story of the prophet Jonah, who, fleeing from the presence of the Lord, took passage in a ship for Tarshish, where he evidently expected to be beyond the reach of the deity. However, he miscalculated the power of the Lord; for while he was still at sea, the Lord sent a great wind in pursuit of him, and the storm was such that the ship, in which the renegade prophet had taken his passage, was like to be broken in pieces. But, amid all the tumult of the tempest, Jonah slept soundly in his bunk down below, till the skipper came and, waking him from his slumber, bade him betake himself to prayer as the only way to save the ship. However, when he came on deck, the prophet found that the question with the crew was not so much one of prayer as of pitching somebody overboard as a propitiatory offering to the raging waters, or to the god who had lashed them into fury. So they drew lots to see who should perish to save the rest, and the lot fell upon Jonah. Accordingly with his consent, indeed at his own urgent request, and not until they had very humanely exhausted every effort by hard rowing to make the land, they took up the now conscience-stricken prophet and heaved him over the gunwale into the foaming billows. No sooner did he fall with a splash into the water than the sea went down. But the Lord had mercy on the repentant prophet, and prepared a great fish which swallowed up Jonah; and Jonah was in the belly of the fish three days and three nights. And Jonah prayed to the Lord out of the fish's belly, and the Lord spoke to the fish, and it vomited up Jonah, safe and sound, on the dry land. ▲

The story lends itself to considerable illustration from Comparative Folklore.

(a) Sailing with an "unholy" person

Jonah 1:4–7

It is a common superstition that *it is dangerous to sail with an impious or wicked person,* since his presence aboard will inevitably provoke an outraged god to embroil the sea and possibly wreck the ship. Aeschylus, for example, declares explicitly that

The pious man who on a ship embarks
With hothead crew or other villainy
Goes to his doom with that god-hated brood;[1]

while the orator Antiphon asserts in similar vein that persons suffering from physical or moral contagion can imperil the lives of other passengers on a voyage.[2] So too Theophrastus characterizes the timid and cowardly man as one who, when a great wave breaks against a ship, immediately inquires whether any of his companions is "tainted";[3] while Plautus, in his comedy *Rudens,* has one of the characters twit another with the taunt that any ship in which he sailed would be likely to founder,[4] and Horace asserts that he would not risk letting anyone who had divulged the secret rites of Ceres set foot on his boat.[5]

Nor is the belief confined to ancient times. A well-known anecdote relates that when the late Olive Schreiner was about to be lowered into a lifeboat at the wreck of the *Titanic,* some of its occupants objected, "Don't put her in here; she's an atheist and will wreck us."[6]

1:11–12

(b) *The guilty passenger, once identified, is usually thrown overboard.*[7]

Thus, in a Buddhist story, a certain Mittavindaka, son of a merchant of Benares, who has been disobedient to his mother, is put out on a raft because he might spoil the luck of a ship on which he has embarked.[8] Similarly, in the Scottish ballad of *Bonnie Annie,* a ship will not move because "fey folk" are aboard. Lots are cast to determine who should be sacrificed, and the lot falls, quite unreasonably, on Annie instead of on the captain who has in fact betrayed her. At first he refuses to throw her to the waves, but eventually

He has tane her in his arms twa, lo, lifted her cannie;
He has thrown her out owre board, his ain dear Annie.[9]

In the same vein, in the English ballad, *Brown Robyn's Confession,* that "hero" guilty of incest is tied to a plank and cast adrift because his presence prevents the ship from sailing. His "fair confession," however, brings him the aid of the Blessed Virgin and her Son, and he is ultimately translated to heaven.[10] Analogues to such tales are to be found also in Scandinavian folklore (especially in Lappland);[11] while in a French version, it is not one of the passengers but the ship's cat that is thrown as a sop to the angry billows.[12]

1:17; 2–10

(c) *The person cast overboard is sometimes said to be swallowed by a sea monster and subsequently disgorged intact.*[13]

An ancient Indian tale relates, for example, that once upon a time there lived a princess who refused to marry anyone except the man who had set

eyes on the Golden City of Legend. The hero Saktidêva accepted the challenge, and proceeded to roam the world in search of that fabulous place. In
the course of his travels he set sail for the island of Usthala, to seek directions
from the king of the fishermen who dwelt there. On the way, a storm arose,
and the ship capsized. Saktidêva, however, was swallowed by a great fish
which carried him to the isle. When the king of the fishermen slit it open, the
hero emerged unharmed.[14] The same story is told in Ceylon about the hero
Bahudama;[15] while an ancient Greek legend relates that Heracles was once
swallowed by a whale near the port of Jaffa—Jonah's own point of embarka-
tion!—and remained within the animal's belly for three days.[16] Similar stories
are current to this day in the popular lore of Melanesia and Indonesia[17] and
among the French Canadians,[18] and there is a parallel even in Basile's famous
Pentamerone.[19]

A less artistic, but equally veracious, variant of the Biblical story is told by
the natives of Windesi, on the northern coast of New Guinea. The inhabitants
of the island of Jop, they say, formerly dwelt at Batewaar. One day five of
them rowed in a canoe across to Waropen to fetch sago. But out on the high
sea a whale swallowed them, canoe and all, and they sank with the fish to the
bottom. As they sat in the fish's belly, they cut slices of its liver and guts,
hacked the canoe in pieces, and, lighting a fire, roasted the liver and guts and
ate them. But the fish, thus mangled in its vitals, died, and its carcass drifted
to shore. Thereupon, the men, sitting in the fish's belly, heard the cry of a
hornbill. They said, "Is that land?" They opened the fish's snout, they saw
that it was land, and they went forth. Then the bird came to them and said,
"I did it; it is my doing that you people are still alive. Go now home; fetch
your people and dwell on this island." So to sea they went, fetched their people,
and took up their abode on the island. That is why the inhabitants of the
island of Jop do not eat any hornbills.[20]

What is alleged to be an authentic counterpart to Jonah's adventures is
related on the authority of no less redoubtable a man of science than Linné.
In 1758, we are informed, a shipwrecked sailor in the Mediterranean had the
ill fortune to be swallowed by a shark. When, however, the latter was subsequently harpooned and opened, the sailor emerged intact![21]

Bible scholars often cite as parallels to the story of Jonah the classical
legend of Phalanthus, the mythic hero of Brundisium and Tarentum, who was
saved from shipwreck by a dolphin,[22] as well as the similar tales of Eikadios,[23]
Korianos,[24] and Arion.[25] These stories, however, are really quite irrelevant,
since in none of them is the hero swallowed, much less disgorged, by a sea
monster. On the other hand, it is indeed permissible to see in our tale a mari-
time variant of the same motif as is represented, for instance, in the story of
Red Riding Hood and the Wolf and of Tom Thumb extricated whole from a
crow.[26]

In ages[27] less enlightened than our own, when it was considered blasphemous to see in the stories of the Bible anything but the record of historical fact, commentators and ecclesiastics were often put to considerable pains to "authenticate" our bizarre narrative, and wondrous and ingenious were some of the explanations they propounded. What troubled them especially was that the more common type of whale or shark does not in fact possess a gullet wide enough to swallow a human being whole. The creature in question, it was pointed out, was a special kind of whale—the so-called right whale, described in *Moby Dick* as having a mouth which "would accommodate a couple of whist-tables and comfortably seat all the players." But even if the prophet was swallowed by such a monster, how, it was asked, could he have managed to survive in its belly for three days and three nights, seeing that its gastric juices would surely have poisoned him? Not so, replied the learned Bishop Jebb; the "great fish" which the Lord prepared was a *dead* fish, in which all such noxious elements had already ceased to function. That, too, was why the prophet eventually emerged unchewed and undigested!

Others found even more fantastic explanations. "Great Fish," they said, was the name of a ship which God provided to rescue his servant, and its "belly" was simply the hold or steerage. Maybe, it was added, the vessel was so named because it carried the figure of a fish on its prow! Alternatively, could not *Great Fish* have been the name of an inn at which Jonah put up when he reached land?

2:1–9

(**d**) *While he is in the belly of the "great fish," the prophet passes the time by intoning a prayer.*

Any attentive reader of the Bible will recognize at once that this consists largely of standard clichés many of which are actually to be found in the Psalter. What we have, then, is simply another example of the *cante-fable,* concerning which see above, §**31**. Until Jonah is disgorged, the action of the story comes to a standstill. When that story is recited, the intermission is filled by "audience participation" in the form of chanting a well-known hymn, artfully put into the mouth of the prophet.[28]

3:6–8

(**e**) *Animals dressed in mourning.*

When Jonah proclaims the impending doom of Nineveh, the king decrees a public fast and orders that *beasts as well as men be clad in the sackcloth of mourning.*

Animals are part of the "topocosm"—that is, of the aggregate of living beings and inanimate objects which together constitute the corporate entity and "atmosphere" of a place.[29] Hence, in popular belief, they participate in its fate and fortune. It is in this spirit, for instance, that cattle as well as men are victims of the plagues inflicted upon Egypt at the time of the exodus,[30] and that the prophet Joel can declare, when disaster befalls his country, that "the flocks of sheep too are held guilty."[31] Accordingly, animals can be made to share in any national mourning. The Persians, we are told, shaved the manes of their horses and mules when Masistius fell at Plataea,[32] and Alexander ordered a similar token of mourning after the death of Hephaistion.[33] Plutarch relates that the priests of Egypt shrouded the gilded ox with a linen veil, when they performed rites expressing their participation in the mourning of Isis for Osiris;[34] and somewhat similarly in a modern Greek folktale the king's chargers are said to have been dyed black in a time of national grief.[35]

In our Biblical narrative, the animals not only wear mourning but also *fast;* and this finds a parallel in the medieval Irish romance of Lebar Brec,[36] and even in ancient Mesopotamian sources.[37]

Micah

Nomina omina sunt. In ancient and primitive thought, a name is more than an appellation; it is an integral element of being. Accordingly, the very name of a person or object can betoken his or its fate and fortune.[1] One can curse a man by reading a derogatory or sinister meaning into his name, and the same can be done to hostile or impious cities and peoples. The first chapter of Micah is based largely on this practice, though the point is inevitably obscured in translation.

Tell it not in Gath (1:10), for example, is a proverbial expression—it recurs in II Samuel 1:20—depending on the similarity in sound between the name of that city and the Hebrew word, *ta-gidh-ū,* "tell." Similarly, when the city of Beth-le-'aphrah is told (*ib.*) to *"roll" in dust,* the point lies in a pun between its name and the Hebrew word *'aphar,* meaning "dust." Again, when it is said (1:11) of Za'anan (Heb.: Ṣa'anan) that its inhabitants, being beleaguered, *will not be able to come forth,* there is a play of sound between that name and the word *yasa,* "come forth"; and when the inhabitants of Lachish are warned (1:13) to *harness the steed to the chariot* and make their escape, the point lies in the similarity of the name Lachish to the word *rechesh,* "pack-horse," as who should say, *Latch on the horses in Lachish.* So too when the houses of Achzib are likened (1:14) to a "deceptive brook (RSV: wrongly, a deceitful thing)," i.e., one that dries up in summer, the English reader must be told that the Hebrew word for such a brook is the like-sounding *achzab.* Finally, when the prophet declares (1:15) that *God will bring a dispossessor* (RSV: *conqueror*) *to Mareshah,* his audience saw at once that he was reading into the name of that city a play on the word *yarash,* "(dis)possess."

Puns, however, are often tortured, and the punster is driven to the use of rare and recondite words. In course of time the true meaning of these tends to be forgotten. Therefore, if the prophecy is to retain its message, a contemporary synonym must be substituted, even at the sacrifice of the original play on words. This, it appears, has sometimes happened in the present case.

657

Thus, when we are told (1:11) that *the wailing of Beth-ezel* (Heb.: *eṣel*) *shall take from you its standing-place*—words which are in any case difficult to interpret—it may well be that in place of the Hebrew word rendered "standing-place" the prophet employed an archaic term *eṣel* (recoverable from the cognate Semitic languages)[2] which meant "grounding, origin." And when he said (*ibd.*), *Pass on your way, inhabitant of Shaphir*—words which in the Hebrew original contain no pun and have, indeed, been variously emended by modern scholars in order to introduce one—it may well be that in place of the more usual and intelligible word *'ibrî*, he used for "pass on your way" an archaic word *sh-p-r*, "travel along," recoverable from Arabic, as who should say, *shift yourselves, inhabitants of Shaphir*.[3]

Sometimes, too, the play on words is implicit rather than overt. Thus in the statement (1:12) that *the inhabitants of Maroth wait anxiously for good (bliss)*, the point may well lie in the fact that Maroth is the Hebrew word for "sorrow(s)," i.e., *Sorely she waits for bliss, who dwells in Sorrowtown*. Similarly, when the prophet's listeners are bidden (1:14) to *give parting gifts to Moresheth-gath*, the point depends on the resemblance of the name Moresheth to the Hebrew word *me'oreseth* meaning "betrothed" and on the fact that what is conventionally rendered "parting gifts" properly denotes "instruments of divorce." Finally, when he declares (1:12) that *Evil has come down from the Lord* to the gate of Jerusalem, it is not difficult to see that he is ironically interpreting the name of that city to mean "city of peace (Heb.: *shalôm*)."

The same device as is here employed by Micah was used also by other Old Testament prophets. Isaiah, for example, in castigating the Moabite city of Dibon (15:9), deliberately distorts its name to *Dimon,* in order to permit the declaration that it will be filled with *dam,* or blood. Jeremiah (48:2) fulminates against Ḥeshbon by warning that men are *ḥashab*-ing—that is, plotting—evil against it, and against Madmen that *it will be reduced to silence,* for which the Hebrew word is the like-sounding *tid-dom-mî.* Ezekiel (25:16) tells the Cherethim (Cretans?) that *God will curtail them* (Heb.: *k-r-t*); Amos (5:5) warns Gilgal that *it will be driven into exile,* for which the Hebrew word is *galah;* and Zephaniah (2:4–5) has a string of puns on the names of excoriated Philistine cities.

Examples of the same technique may be found also outside of the Bible. Thus, one of the so-called Sibylline Oracles (written during the Hellenistic age) condemns the island of Samos to the state of a sandy beach, the Greek for "sand" being *psammos.* Delos, says the same prophecy, will become *a-dêlos,* that is, "undistinguished," and Rome will be but a *rumê*—an alley.[4]

Illustrative of the same principle and technique is the Arabic story of how Omar, hearing a certain Jamrah ibn Shihâb (Coal, son of Flame) declare that his tribal and local names were both connected with fire, foretold that his house and family would be burned; and this actually happened.[5] One recalls also Catullus' scurrilous puns on the names of his personal enemies.[6]

238   Casting sins into the sea   **7:19**

RSV: *He will again have compassion upon us;*
        he will tread our iniquities under foot.
        Thou wilt cast all our[1] *sins*
        into the depths of the sea.

In the original Hebrew these verses are a jingle, the general effect of which may be reproduced as follows:

He will show us his mercy once more,
        stamp our misdeeds to the floor,
and all their sins shall be
        tossed in the depths of the sea.

The words may perhaps be those of a traditional chant which accompanied a symbolic ceremony, for the casting of death, blight, noxiousness, contagion, and the like into the waters is a widespread seasonal rite in several parts of the world.[2] At Nuremberg, in Germany, for example, an image of Death used annually to be carried out of the city and plunged into a neighboring stream, the bearers chanting the words, "We are carrying Death to the waters."[3] Similarly at Tabor, in Czechoslovakia, the effigy of Death was transported out of town and then floated downstream;[4] while at Chrudim it was flung into the waters on "Black Sunday."[5] At Bielsk, in Podlachia,[6] and among the Serbs of Upper Lausitz, it was drowned in a nearby pool or marsh.[7] In Silesia, children used to throw a puppet into the river;[8] and a similar practice obtained in various parts of Thüringen.[9] At Leipzig this was done by the local prostitutes and bastards;[10] at Dobschwitz, near Gera, the rite was performed on March 1,[11] and in a number of villages near Erlangen on the fourth Sunday in Lent.[12]

The custom can be traced to far earlier times. On March 15 the Roman vestal virgins flung puppets into the Tiber,[13] just as Indians cast them into the Ganges during the festival in honor of the goddess Kali.[14]

But we can go even further back. In the Canaanite *Poem of Baal,* that god's rival Yam, genius of sea and river, is apparently cast "into the sea with the streams." In terms of the story, he is, of course, merely shown back where he belongs, but since the entire myth seems to reflect the pattern of seasonal ceremonies, this incident may well have been suggested by a ritual practice.[15]

Alike among the Semites and the Greeks, moral as well as physical impurity was often cast into the sea or into running water.[16] Thus the carcass of the ram used in the purification (*kuppuru*) rite of the Babylonian New Year was subsequently tossed into the river;[17] while in the Iliad, Agamemnon orders his men to perform rites of purgation and to cast their impurities into the sea.[18] So too, in the *Supplices* of Aeschylus, the chorus beseeches Zeus to cast into "the darkling deep" the black fate which hangs over the daughters of Danaus.[19]

In Sophocles' *Oedipus Rex* there is a prayer that the spirit of war (Ares) may be plunged "into the great chamber of Amphitrite (i.e., the sea) . . . and into the Thracian billows."[20] In Euripides' *Iphigenia in Tauris* that hapless maiden expresses a wish to bathe in the sea because "the sea whirls away all mortal ills,"[21] and in the same writer's *Hercules Furens* the chorus voice the prayer that "grievous old age may vanish 'neath the waves."[22] Both Plutarch and the comic dramatist Diphylos expressly describe the sea as purificatory.[23] Indeed, even objects used in rites of purification were often cast subsequently into the sea;[24] so among the Romans, were *prodigia* and monstrous births,[25] while in Car Nicobar it is the custom, when a man is sick, to rub him with pigs' blood and beat him with leaves, and then to throw the leaves into the sea.[26]

The spirit of all these ceremonies is summed up by the Roman poet Tibullus in the well-known lines:

> Whatsoe'er of evil there may be,
> and whatsoe'er of sorrow that we dread,
> May sea and rapid rivers bear away.[27]

Nahum

239 The burden of Nineveh

The historical background of Nahum's prophecy is the capture of Nineveh, the proud capital of Assyria, by a coalition of Medes, Babylonians, and Scythians in the summer of 612 B.C. The details can be pieced together from a Babylonian chronicle now in the British Museum[1] and from later accounts by the Classical writers, Xenophon and Diodorus.

The siege lasted from June (Sivan) until August (Ab).[2] Three assaults were mounted by the Medes; the second of these began under cover of night, and though highly successful, was not conclusive.[3] The eventual sack of the city was facilitated by a vehement storm, which caused the River Tigris to rise in flood and sweep away some twelve hundred feet (twenty stadia) of the embankment.[4] A force of Bactrians sent to lift the siege were won over to the enemy's cause by the Median commander. The Assyrian king, ignorant of this defection, was lulled into a sense of security and passed the time regaling his troops at lavish entertainments. During one of their carousals, Median partisans attacked by night, destroyed the camp, put large numbers of its inmates to the sword, and drove others back into the city.[5] The Assyrian king then set his palace afire, and died in the flames.[6]

In a graphic portrayal of the disaster (2:3–8) the Hebrew prophet describes the final agony of the city—the fruitless defense and the desperate but frustrated hopes of its king, recalling the past glories of his "stalwarts" only to see them routed and the palace flooded:

> *Reddened are the shields of his warriors,*
> *his troops incarnadined,[7]*
> *on the day he makes his preparations.*
> *Aflame are the wheel-spokes of his chariots;*
> *the fir-trees are rustled (as they pass).*
> *Through the streets the chariots dash,*
> *jostle one another in the squares.*
> *Like firebrands—so they seem;*
> *like lightning-flashes they dart.*

He recalls (the past glories of) his braves,
  they come scurrying to the wall,
pitching and lurching as they go;
  and the mantelet is set up.
But the sluice-gates have been opened,
  and the palace now rocks and is awash.[8]

Like a lady she is
  stripped and carried off,
while her maids lead the way before her.
  <moaning>[9] *like doves,*
taboring—but on their own breasts!
  Yea Nineveh is like a pool
whose waters are ebbing away;
  "Halt, halt!" (men cry),
but none can turn them back!

In these events the prophet saw the hand of Israel's champion, Yahweh, performing in the manner of the familiar storm-god of the Mesopotamians themselves and translating into history the feats traditionally ascribed to him in myth. The prophet brought home his message by prefixing to his denunciation of Nineveh a poem of more general tenor (ch. 1) in which these feats were recited, with sidelong glances, as it were, toward the main features of the city's fall. (The poem appears to have been adapted from an older hymn, composed in the form of an alphabetical acrostic, in which the prowess of the storm-god was related; but this was freely adapted, so that the original alphabetic form and order of the verses has sometimes been disturbed.)[10]

1:2–3

A passionate, vengeful god,
  vengeful and wrathful is he,
taking revenge on opponents,
  nursing rage against foes.
Patient though he be,
  yet he is great in strength,
and lets not the guilty go free.

In gust and gale in his way,
  and clouds are the dust at his feet.

Yahweh plays the role of an Adad, Marduk, or Ninurta; he rides the storm. So Baal-Hadad is described in the Canaanite texts from Ras Shamra as "Rider on the Clouds,"[11] and in Mesopotamian hymns the storm-god is likewise the "rider on the great cloud"[12] or the "lord of the avalanche."[13] In the Babylonian Epic of Creation, Marduk is said specifically to ride the storm against Tiamat.[14]

1:4ᵃ

> *'Tis he that rebuked the sea*
> *and dried it up,*
> *and made all the rivers parched.*

The reference is, in the first place, to the general action of the stormwind on ocean and stream. It is to be noted, however, that the succeeding verbs are all in the past tense. The allusion is, therefore, to specific occasions when the prowess of the storm-god was evinced, i.e., to specific exploits attributed to him in the traditional myth.

In the Canaanite *Poem of Baal* (Hadad) that god conquers Yam, "Sea," *alias* T̤-p-t̤ N-h-r, "Prince Stream." Allusion to this is made also in a Hittite version of the Canaanite myth, where the storm-god is described as "he who vanquished the Sea."[15] Old Testament poetry also contains several allusions to this exploit, there attributed to Yahweh: see Isa. 50:2; 51:10; Pss. 74:13; 89:10; 93; Job 7:12; 26:12; 38:10.

There is no clear parallel in Ancient Near Eastern texts to the drying up of sea and streams, but allusions to this as a cosmic event is indeed made in Psalm 74:15. Elsewhere in the Old Testament, this exploit is seen *historically* rather than *mythically,* and is referred to the parting of the Sea of Reeds at the Exodus: Isa. 50:2; 51:10; Ps. 106:9. But the Hebrew poets may well have viewed this as the "actualization" in history of an archetypal mythical event.

1:4ᵇ–5

> *Awilt*[16] *were Bashán and Carmél,*
> *and the flowers of Lebanon drooped.*
> *Mountains were shaken before him,*
> *and hills were aquake.*
> *The earth was laid waste*[17] *before him,*
> *the world and all that dwell in it.*

So, in the aforementioned Canaanite poem, it is said of Baal-Hadad:

> When Baal's holy voice rings out,
> when Baal's thunders peal,
> the earth doth shake   the mountains quake,
> the highlands rock and reel.[18]

Similarly, one of the celebrated Tell Amarna Letters declares that "when Pharaoh gives forth his voice like Haddu (Hadad), all the mountains quake.[19] This is echoed in turn by a Mesopotamian hymn:

> When Baal rages, heaven is commov'd,
> When Hadad storms, the mightly mounts are rent;[20]

or again:

> Hadad doth his thunder send,
> and [sha]ken are the mounts.[21]

1:6

> *His fury who can withstand?*
> *who abide the blaze of his wrath?*
> *His anger was poured out like fire;*
> *the rocks were riven by him.*

In the Sumerian poem *Lugal-u₂-me-lám-bi-nir-gal,* Ninurta, the warrior-god, is described as assailing the mountains with his special weapon(s).[22] He declares explicitly—in agreement with the opening verse of our poem!—that he wreaks vengeance on them; and he is described as "unrivalled destroyer of mountains."[23]

1:7–8

> *Good is he as a refuge*
> *in the day of distress,*
> *and duly takes note of them*
> *that seek their shelter in him.*
> *Yet, with a flood overflowing*
> *he makes a full end of them*
> *that rise up against him*
> *and chases his foes into darkness.*

The storm-god is, of course, the god of inundations, Adad it was who brought the Deluge,[24] and one of his stock epithets is "lord of the avalanche" (*bêl abûbi*).[25] So too Marduk's word is described as "an advancing flood" (*mīlum tebū*).[26] The prophet, however, cleverly employs these standard clichés in order to show that the unusual rising of the Tigris, which has facilitated the fall of Nineveh (*see above*) is indeed the characteristic work of a deity—but this time, of Yahweh!

The reference to the god's chasing his foes into darkness likewise has special meaning when it is remembered that the final destruction of the Assyrian army took place at night (*see above*). Furthermore, according to Herodotus, the fall of the city coincided with a solar eclipse![27] The prophet sees in these events a translation into history of what was related in myth concerning the Deluge:

> From the horizon rose a darkling cloud . . .
> All that had been bright was turned to dark . . .

No man could see his neighbor, and the view
Of humankind from heaven was black'd out.[28]

1:9–10

What (more) would ye plot against him?. .
a full end it is that he makes;
rebellion ne'er rises twice!
See, it is come to the point
that, tangled like thorns though they were,
and sodden with drink,
yet have they been consumed
as though they were straw!

The prophet is perhaps harking back to the mythical defeat of the sea-god
and his confederates.

In the Babylonian Epic of Creation, Tiamat and her allies are said to
"plot" (*kapdū*) against the authority of heaven,[29] and the victorious Marduk
is described expressly as "the crusher of rebellion" (*ḥalaš tuqmati*).[30] Moreover, the Hebrew word (viz., *ṣārāh*) here rendered "rebellion" is identical
with that which is there employed (iii.15; iv.80, 116–18) to describe the
activity of Tiamat's horde, just as in the Canaanite *Poem of Baal* (V AB. D.
36) it describes that of the contumacious Yam ("Sir Sea").

1:11, 14, 12–13

The subsequent words of this verse are so terse and compact that their
meaning and point have escaped most commentators, and various emendations of the text have been proposed. But when we recall that the final attack
of the Medes was made while the Assyrian generals and troops were in fact
carousing and "sodden with drink," and that, according to Diodorus and
Abydenus, the Assyrian king finally committed both himself and his palace
to the flames, the brilliant irony of the prophet's words becomes apparent:
in these events he sees a parallel to the action of lightning upon thick thorn
bushes! Even though damp and sodden, and densely knit, they still burn!

Was it not out of thee,[31]
(O Nineveh), that he came
who plotted mischief against him
—that devilish counsellor?
So[32] *the LORD has commanded about thee:*
"No seed of thy name shall be sown.
Out of the house of thy gods
will I cut off image and idol;

thy very grave will I turn
into a desolate place,[33]
for thou art disgraced!"

(Yet, to Israel) thus saith the LORD:
"What though whole oceans gushed,
yet have they ebbed and passed o'er;
though I afflicted thee,
I shall afflict thee no more.[34]
Now burst I his bonds from thee,
and rend asunder his cords!"

Here again the prophet is playing on the fact that Nineveh met its doom, to
no small extent, through an exceptional flooding of the Tigris.

The siege of Nineveh lasted, as we have seen, from June (Sivan) until
August (Ab). It therefore covered the month of July (Tammuz, Dûzu), and
this month was regarded by the Mesopotamians as sacred to the storm-god
and divine warrior, Ninurta.[35] What happened during this period might therefore be attributed, with peculiar appropriateness, to the action of a god oper-
ating as a zealous warrior and as the lord of storm and tempest!

240 "The mills of God grind slowly"   1:3

Assyria had been supreme for a long time, and the retribution had been
slow to come. In his opening hymn, therefore, Nahum is careful to assure
his listeners that

Patient, yet great in strength is the Lord;
he lets not the guilty go free.

This notion of God's slow but inexorable justice ("The mills of God grind
slowly, yet they grind exceeding small")[1] is a commonplace of Greek literature,[2] and it is not impossible that our Scriptural writer was echoing a corresponding Oriental proverb. Says Sophocles, for instance:

Whene'er a man casts off the things of God
And turns to mad unreason, then the gods,
Albeit slowly, yet do see it clear.[3]

And Euripides observes to the same effect:

The gods may bide their time, but are not weak
In moving to their ends.[4]

The sentiment was likewise common among Roman writers. Tibullus, for
example, declares roundly that

> At first, indeed, a man may hide his crimes,
> Yet with soft steps doth Retribution come,
> Albeit late;[5]

and Horace that

> Though she be lame, yet Vengeance seldom fails
> To follow crime;[6]

while, more directly in consonance with our Biblical poet, Seneca affirms that "the immortal gods may take their time but they can nevertheless be relied upon to exact retributions on the human race,"[7] and Juvenal, more succinctly, that

> Great, though tardy, is the wrath of gods.[8]

Valerius Maximus likewise speaks of the slow-footed anger of the gods,[9] and his statement is echoed in Voltaire's famous dictum that *La peine suite le crime; elle arrive à pas lents.*[10]

Habakkuk

241 "Hush before the Lord" Hab. 1:20

Before the presence of the Lord in his temple, or when he stirs therefrom (Zech. 2:17), or when he prepares his banquet and invites his guests (Zeph. 1:7), all men are to keep silent. Why? Not merely because silence is the natural concomitant of awe—"the positive expression of the inexpressible, the language of the unutterable"[1]—but also because words have power, and untoward or inappropriate words can therefore impair holy things or defile sacred occasions. To utter unseemly words, or even to make unseemly noises, in the presence of sacred beings is tantamount to sacrilege or blasphemy, or to appearing before them in dirty clothes or in a state of physical impurity.

The Egyptian *Maxims of Ani* declares explicitly that noise in the house of God is an abomination;[2] while both Greeks and Romans (the former already in Homeric times) prefaced the performance of public rites with an order for silence (εὐφημεῖτε; *favete linguis*).[3] In the Ion of Euripides, when a slave hurls unseemly invective at the hero while the latter is serving in the temple, that slave is at once replaced, lest the sacred rites be thereby impaired.[4] Somewhat similarly after the slaying of their mother Clytaemnestra, both Orestes and Electra may neither speak to, nor be addressed by, anyone lest in conversation they transmit their own "contagion."[5] For the same reason, too, tombs of ancient worthies had to be passed in silence—a custom attested alike in Classical antiquity,[6] in German popular usage,[7] and among savages in West Africa.[8] Jews who follow orthodox tradition prepare corpses for burial and attend funerals in absolute silence—today interpreted as a mark of respect.[9] Magical rites, and the gathering of magical herbs, must likewise often be performed in silence.[10]

242 The prayer of Habakkuk 3

(a) To the main prophecy of Habakkuk there is appended a "prayer" (ch. 3) in which the prophet envisages the imminent discomfiture of Israel's foes as a repetition in history of the deeds attributed to Yahweh in time-honored myth and legend.[1] Many of these are in turn adaptations of still older legends associated with the pagan gods:

3:2

> *I have heard tell of thee, LORD;*
>   *LORD, I am filled with awe*
>   *at what thou hast done.*
> *Now, in this present time,[2]*
>   *make it a living thing;[3]*
> *show, in this present time,*
>   *that even when thou art raging*
> *thou rememberest ties of love!*

3:3–4

(b) *In the dark night of Israel's despair, Yahweh is about to appear as a rising sun:*

> *Here comes he, a very godhead,*
>   *out of the Southern Land,*
> *yea, a being divine,*
>   *from the hillsides of Parán.[4]*
> *His splendor has mantled the heavens,*
>   *and the earth is filled with his sheen.[5]*
> *It is as the glow of the dayspring;*
>   *rays shoot forth from his side,*
> *though still in the darkness yonder*
>   *lies hid the full force of his strength![6]*

The description of the theophany is based on the conventional portrayal of the sun-god (Shamash) in Mesopotamian art, e.g., on cylinder seals. He rises between twin mountains, with rays issuing from his shoulders or sides.[7] The glow betokens the approach of a god or otherworldly being.[8] In Mesopotamian belief, gods were enveloped in a sheen, called "luster" (*melammu*) or "terror" (*puluḫtu*),[9] or were said to be "clothed in light."[10] In the Epic of Creation, Marduk is described, indeed, as invested with the luster of ten gods.[11] The Hittites too envisaged their gods as wreathed in a nimbus called "terror" (*hatugatar*);[12] and a characteristic of Iranian deities was their *khvareno* (Old Persian, *farnah*), or brilliant radiance.[13] In the Old Testament itself this is evidently what is meant by "the glory of Yahweh";[14] and it is significant that the divine being whom Ezekiel describes as having been cast out of the divine assembly is said to have been distinguished not only by wisdom and beauty but also by "the sheen of a rising sun" (Heb.: *yif'ah*).[15] Greek gods too were signalized by a dazzling brightness,[16] though in sculpture this is portrayed only after the fifth century B.C.[17] Jamblichus (c. A.D. 250–325) preserves the ancient tradition in the statement that "when archangels appear, certain portions of the world are thrown into convulsion, and at their approach a light precedes them, but divided (i.e., forked)."[18] The divine light, it should be added, is not merely a sign of inner radiance; it symbolizes also the be-dazzlement of men at the sight of that which is otherworldly. It is therefore also a divine weapon, appropriately known as "the terror."

3:5

(c) *When Yahweh takes to the warpath he is attended by two escorts:*

> *Catastrophe is his vanguard;*
> *Pestilence brings up the rear.*

What is here reflected is an ancient notion that major gods are attended, when they stir abroad, by two servitors. Thus, in the Mesopotamian Epic of Gilgamesh, when Adad brings the deluge, he is accompanied by the two gods Šullat and Ḥanis.[19] In the Iliad, Phoebus and Ares are accompanied by Deimos, "Dread," and Phobos, "Fear";[20] and in Roman mythology Mars is similarly escorted by Pallor and Pavor. Somewhat analogously, in Czech folklore, the two demons Trâs, "Tremor," and Strakh, "Terror," leap on foes in battle.[21]—A poetic twist is given to this ancient concept in Psalm 89:14, where it is said that Steadfast Love (*Ḥesed*) and Faithfulness (or Truth: *Emeth*) attend upon Yahweh like courtiers.[22]

The concept is based on the ancient practice of dispatching messengers in pairs, lest one alone meet with mishap en route. Thus, in the Canaanite myths from Ras Shamra-Ugarit, Baal has two messengers, Gpn ("Sir Vine") and Ugr ("Sir Field"), just as the goddess 'Anat has at her command the pair Q-d-š and A-m-r-r.[23] In the Egyptian *Poem of Pentaur,* describing the battle of Kadesh in 1286 B.C., *two* bedouins (Šaśu) come from the Shabtuna district to speak with Ramses II, and *two* scouts are dispatched by the Hittite king.[24] In the Iliad, Talthybios and Eurybates are the two regular heralds of Agamemnon.[25] Indeed, the tradition that such envoys went in pairs was so ingrained that even when Homer is in fact speaking of *three* messengers, he automatically employs the dual form of the relevant verbs![26] In the Iranian national epic, Ayatar-i-Zareran, two messengers come from Arzasp to Vishtasp to urge him to give up Mazdaeism.[27]

There is a trace of the same notion elsewhere in the Old Testament itself in Gen. 19:1 ff., where *two* angels (messengers) visit Lot in Sodom (in con-trast to the *three* mentioned in the preceding chapter).

In the original Hebrew, the escort here rendered "Pestilence" is named *Resheph.* This is a clear mythological allusion, for Resheph is is now well at-tested as the Canaanite god of plague.[28] He is portrayed in numerous figurines standing erect and brandishing a lance, but he also assailed his victims with arrows.[29] Indeed, in a text from Ugarit he is styled explicitly "Resheph the archer" (*b'l ḥẓ Ršp*),[30] and in a far later Phoenician-Greek bilingual inscription from Cyprus (363 B.C.) he is called "Resheph of the arrow" (*Ršp ḥṣ*) and is equated with "far-darting Apollo."[31] The arrows are, of course, the faery darts of disease and disaster such as Apollo indeed hurled upon the Achaeans at Troy (Iliad, 1.40) and are familiar to all students of folklore (see below, §275). In the ritual texts from Ugarit, Resheph is associated with the goddess 'Anat,[32] just as is Apollo with her Greek counterpart, Artemis.

In Phoenician texts from Zenčirli (9th cent. B.C.) Resheph is conjoined with El, the supreme deity, Hadad, god of the storm, and a certain Rkb-el, evidently a divine charioteer.[33] In the inscription of King Azitawadda from Karatepe (approximately the same date, or a little earlier), the god is associated with Baal and is styled "Resheph of the *ṣ-p-r-m*."[34] Some scholars explain this epithet from the Hebrew *ṣippôr*, "bird," and refer to the fact that at Ischiali, terra-cotta figurines supposedly representing Resheph's Mesopotamian counterpart Nergal, show a heavily armed god encased in feathers and with talons for feet.[35] Similarly in Greek lore, Eurynomos, a god of the netherworld, is sometimes portrayed with a vulture's head,[36] and at Lipsos in Ephesus, Apollo—Resheph's equivalent—was indeed called "Vulturine Apollo" (Apollōn Gypaieas).[37] In further support of this explanation it is pointed out that in Job 5:7 the "sons of Resheph" (KJV: wrongly, "sparks"!) are said to fly, and the Septuagint Version actually renders the expression "fledglings," while in Deuteronomy 32:24 it translates Resheph by "birds." It should be observed, however, that the Hebrew word *ṣippôr* properly refers to a twittering songbird (cf. Akkadian *ṣapāru*, "twitter") and can thus scarcely be applied to a vulture or bird of prey. It would seem preferable, therefore, to connect the epithet with the Hebrew *ṣaphîr*, "buck," seeing that Resheph is indeed sometimes associated with gazelles.[38]

Resheph was known in Egypt as early as the time of Amenhotep II.[39] That monarch is described in one inscription as "striding across the River Orontes with all the fury of Resheph"[40] and in another, dealing with his association with the Great Sphinx at Gizeh, the god is again mentioned.[41] A hymn to Resheph in Egyptian is also extant.[42]

The name is sometimes used, by metonymy, in the plural to denote various forms of affliction. In Psalm 76:3 arrows are described as "Reshephs of the bow" (RSV, wrongly: "flashing arrows"), i.e., satanic shafts; and in Song of Songs 8:6 the pangs of love are "fiery Reshephs" (RSV: "flashes of fire"). In Job 5:7, the "sons of Resheph" is a generic term for demons who hover in the air, in contrast to the "trouble" which seems to sprout out of the very earth. A similar usage appears in Egyptian.[43]

The derivation of the name is obscure.[44] Certainly, it has no connection, as was once supposed, with the Semitic *š-r-p*, "burn"—an idea which was evidently inspired by false exegesis of Song of Songs 8:6. Most probably it is connected with an Akkadian word *rašāpu* which seems to mean "assail."[45]

In the original Hebrew, the other escort of Yahweh, here rendered "Catastrophe," is Deber, who is likewise a demonic figure of ancient folklore (see below, §275).

3:6–7

(d)   *He has halted, and shaken[46] the earth,*
                                       looked and convulsed[47] the nations.
                                       Age-old mountains are riven,
                                          time-hallow'd hills sink low,
                                       as again he takes to those highways
                                          he trod so long ago.[48]
                                       When Cushan's tents were rustled,
                                          when Midian's tent-cloths shook.[49]

This description of Yahweh on the warpath echoes standard clichés which would have been familiar to the prophet's audience. In an Egyptian hymn to Amon, dating from the time of the New Kingdom, it is said of him that

> Earth trembles when his word resounds;
>   all peoples shudder at his might;[50]

while elsewhere we read of the same god that

> When he rages, mountains tremble;
>   when he roars, the earth doth shake.[51]

Similarly, in Mesopotamian hymns:

> When Adad rages, earth doth shake
>   and peoples are a-tremble;[52]

and

> When he walks abroad,
>   heaven and earth do quiver.[53]

Of the god Ninurta it is related specifically that he attacks mountains.[54]

3:15

Yahweh rides the waves, which are likened to his chargers:

> *Thou hast trodden the sea; thy chargers*
>   *the foam of the ocean waves.[55]*

Waves are often so described in popular lore. In Old Irish poetry, for instance, "sea horse" is a common expression for "billow,"[56] and in Celtic verse, raging breakers are "the son of Ler's horses."[57] In the French district of Tréguier, an embroiled sea is called "the white mare,"[58] and the Italians speak of the waves as "charging like horses" (*acavallarsi delle onde*).[59] In English idiom, foaming waves are known popularly as "wild horses"; one recalls Matthew Arnold's lines:

> The wild horses play,
> Champ and chafe and toss in the spray.[60]

Connected with this is the representation of sea-gods and of the spirits of lakes and rivers in equine form. Poseidon, for example, is often styled "equine" (*hippios*), and the famous fountain on Mount Helicon was named "Fountain of the Horse" (Hippocrene).[61] In Scotland, the kwelpis, or spirits, who inhabit lochs are thought to be horses.[62] In Ireland, the same is said of the corresponding pookas;[63] and in Iceland, lakes are believed to be infested with sea horses called *vatnahesturs*.[64] A white horse, it is said, appears at dusk at the source of the River Seine.[65]

3:8

(e) Yahweh's onslaught is seen by the prophet as a repetition in history of the storm-god's primordial defeat of the contumacious god of the sea—the theme of the celebrated Canaanite *Poem of Baal* discovered at Ras Shamra-Ugarit.

> *Is it again the rivers,*[66]
>   *against the rivers, O LORD,*
> *that thine anger (again) has been kindled,*
>   *or thy wrath against the Sea,*
> *that thou comest riding thy chargers,*
>   *(riding) thy chariots in triumph?*

The myth appears to have been widespread throughout the Ancient Near East. An Egyptian text, the Hearst Papyrus, alludes to the combat between Seth (i.e., Baal) and the Sea;[67] and a Hittite myth, probably redacted from a Canaanite original, has the personified Mt. Pisaisa, in Syria, exclaim: "See with what [vehemence] the storm-god attacked the sea!"[68]

The picture of Yahweh riding a chariot into battle is taken directly from more ancient pagan mythology. The Canaanite Baal is described as "he that chariots upon the clouds" (*Rkb 'rpt*)[69]—a concept likewise applied to Yahweh in divers passages of the Psalms and by the prophet Zechariah.[70] Similarly, in the Mesopotamian Epic of Creation, Marduk launches his chariot against his adversary Tiamat,[71] and such an attack is indeed portrayed on a cylinder seal of the Akkadian period (c. 2360–2150 B.C.) now in the Morgan Library in New York.[72] Chariots are likewise associated in Hittite myth with the attack of the gods upon the stone monster Ullikummi;[73] and reliefs at Imankulu and Malatya portray the weather-god riding an ox-drawn chariot.[74] In Teutonic mythology, Thor is sometimes styled Rheidhertyr, "god of the chariot";[75] and the Greek lexicographer Hesychius (4th cent. A.D.) says that "lightning is regarded as the chariot of Zeus."[76]

3:9-11

(f)

> *No sooner thy bow is filled*
> *with the shafts at thy command,*
> *than lo, it is empty again![77]*

> *Thou hast carved out streams in the earth;*
> *Mountains have seen thee and quailed;*
> *the torrent has overflowed;*
> *loudly the deep has roared.*
> *The sun has forgotten to shine;*
> *the moon has stood still in the height,*
> *at the flash of thy darts as they speed,*
> *at the lightning glint of thy spear.*

In the Canaanite (Ugaritic) myth of the fight against the Sea, Baal is armed with *clubs*,[78] but in the Mesopotamian counterpart, Marduk does indeed carry bow and arrows against Tiamat.[79]

The arrows are simply shafts of lightning. Indeed, in several poetic passages of the Old Testament (Pss. 18:15; 77:18; 144:6; Zech. 9:14), "arrows" is a synonym for "flashes of lightning." Parallels to this notion are legion. In Finnish folklore, lightning is called "the shaft of the storm-god Juoma" (*Jumolan nuoli*); in Lithuanian, it is "the arrows of Perkunos" (*Perkuno strelos*); and in Estonian, *pikse nool*. The Russians call it analogously *gromovaya strela*, and the Hungarians say that it is the dart of the god Isten (*istenyala*).[80] The Ewe of Togoland assert that the thunder-god Sogba forges arrows;[81] and a similar belief is held by the Peruvians.[82] Among both the Cheyenne and Arapaho Indians of North America, "the thunder (*bá á*) is a large bird, with a brood of smaller ones, and carries in its talons a number of arrows with which it strikes the victims of lightning."[83]

The reference to cleaving out the rivers continues the reminiscence of the ancient cosmogonic myth: after the defeat of the dragon (Sea), the waters which would otherwise have flooded the earth are confined in rivers. There is a similar allusion to this in Psalm 74:13-15:

> *Thou it was shattered Sir Sea by thy strength,*
> *brake the heads of the dragons on the waters.*
> *Thou it was crushed Leviathan's heads,*
> *gave him as public food to hyenas.[84]*
> *Thou it was cleaved out fountain and river. . . .*

Similarly, in a Sumerian myth, after the god (or, in another version, the goddess) has subdued the demon of the subterranean floods, the waters are channeled between the banks of the Tigris and Euphrates.[85]

There is an interesting reference to this myth in the Egyptian Leyden Magical Papyrus.[86] Hadad and his consort Shala are there said to have made *ḥʿpy* burst forth by striking a mountain. Now, the word *ḥʿpy* normally means "Nile," but to give it that sense in the passage in question would be plainly absurd because there are in fact no mountains in Egypt! It has therefore been suggested—particularly in view of the mention of the Semitic god Hadad —that this is simply a Syrian myth mechanically translated. In the original version, the word which was rendered *ḥʿpy,* i.e., Nile, would probably have been the common noun for "river," for in Syria and Canaan rivers are indeed opened up by lightning's striking mountains![87]

By a change of but a single letter in the consonantal Hebrew text, a parallel passage in Psalm 77:18 substitutes for the words, *The torrent has overflowed,* the clause, *(The) clouds poured water in torrents,* and this is adopted by many modern scholars. But it misses the mythological allusion, which is to the up-surging of the nether waters, eventually subdued by the storm-god when he defeats the dragon (see below, **§258**, on Ps. 29:10). Moreover, this meaning is developed in the parallel clause: *Loudly the deep has roared.*

3:11

(g)   *Sun and moon stood still*

Notice the poet's artistry: he has just described the effect of Yahweh's actions upon mountains, rivers, and deep (vv. 6–10ᶜ), and later he portrays his furious march through the earth and his "threshing" of the nations (v. 12). Between these two passages he deftly introduces a picture of what happens meanwhile in heaven (vv. 10ᵈ–11). Unfortunately, the traditional Hebrew text is here corrupt, but a very simple emendation[88] restores yet another cliché drawn from the traditional vocabulary of pagan theophanies. In very similar terms, a Mesopotamian hymn declares that when the storm-god Adad raged,

> The sun sank to the foundation of heaven;
> the moon rose to its height.[89]

The prophet, however, also has in mind the historic realization of this scene in the incident connected with Joshua's defeat of the Amorites, when "the sun stood still in Gibeon, and the moon in the Valley of Ajalon" (Josh. 10:12–14) —an incident which must have been especially familiar through its incorporation into the popular repertoire of ballads known as the Book of Jashar (*loc. cit.*).

3:12–14

(h) *The prophet now passes to Yahweh's triumphant march through the earth:*

> *In fury the earth thou bestridest,*
> *in anger art threshing the nations,*
> *as forth to the fray thou hast sallied,*

> for the victory of thy people,
>   the victory of thine anointed,
> unroofing the home of the wicked,
>   as though striking him on the head,
> razing it down to bedrock,
>   as though stripping him top to toe.[90]
> Thou hast split the heads of his braves (?),[91]
>   as down like a whirlwind they sweep,
>   ready to blow us away,
> raising their gleeful cry
>   like < a lion poised > to[92] devour
> some hapless wretch in the dark.

The threshing of enemies is mentioned also in early Arabic poetry. Says 'Adi ibn Riqâ:

> When the battle raged at Rial,
>   like chaff our chariots threshed the foe.[93]

Yahweh, says the prophet, has sallied forth into the battle for the victory of his people and his anointed. The latter expression would refer most naturally to the *king*. However, it is not impossible that it here refers to warriors anointed before battle. In the Canaanite *Poem of Baal,* the goddess 'Anat is anointed by that deity before embarking on a warlike mission;[94] and in the Hittite myth of Kumarbi, the chariot and equipment of an attacking god are anointed before he goes into combat.[95] Such anointment would be but a stylized conventionalization of the widespread custom of smearing warriors with animal fat in order to give them added vigor.[96]

3:16

(i) *Through all the turmoil the prophet waits with confidence:*

> Though, when I heard the sound,
>   mine inwards were all aquiver,
> my lips did twitch,
> my bones began to crumble,
> my foothold gave way,[97]
>   yet will I wait with calm
>   till the day of disaster break
>   on the horde now sweeping upon us!

Note again the poet's consummate artistry: the reference to the day which is about to break balances the initial description of Yahweh as a god who appears like sunrise in darkened skies. But there may also be a touch of satire in his words, for it was the practice of bedouin raiders to creep up on their victims under cover of night and then sweep down on them at daybreak;[98]

and that this tactic was employed also in ancient times is shown by the fact that in the Canaanite *Epic of K-r-t,* the attack on the cities of Udum is mounted at daybreak (*špšm*).[99] Hence, the prophet's meaning would be that in the present case daybreak will bring defeat, not victory, to the marauding hosts.[100]

3:17–19

(j)

> Though fig-trees blossom not,
> nor fruit be on the vines,
> though olive-crop has failed,
> and fields produce no food;
> though sheep from pen have dwindled,[101]
> nor cattle remain in the byres,
> I even now will go singing
> paeans unto the LORD,
> cry in joy to the God
> who wins my battles for me:
> "LORD, LORD, my riches thou!"[102]
> For he will yet send me pacing
> light-footed like a hind
> upon my native heights!

Once again, Comparative Folklore throws unexpected light on the prophet's words: he is drawing on traditional popular poetry associated with the cult and myth of the god of fertility, whose annual disappearance caused the earth to languish, but who eventually returned to usher in a new lease of prosperity and increase. The words read, in fact, like a string of standard clichés from the liturgy of such cults. Here, for instance, are typical laments for the Mesopotamian Tammuz:

> The wailing is for the plants . . . they grow not.
> The wailing is for the barley; the ears grow not.
> The wailing is for homes and flocks; they produce not.
> . . . .
> The wailing is for the fields of men; the *gunu* grows no more.
> . . . .
> The wailing is for the garden storehouse: honey and wine fail.[103]

And when Tammuz is restored, it is said (in another poem):

> The figs grew large; in the plains the trees thrived(?).[104]

In the same vein, the Canaanite Baal is thus bewailed:

> The furrows of the field have gone dry. . . .
> the furrows of (all) the vast fields have gone dry!
> Baal is neglecting the furrow of the plowlands.

> Where now is Baal Puissant?
> Where is his Highness, the lord (baal) of the earth?[105]

Of the Hittite Telipinu, it is said analogously:

> Off stalked Telipinu.
> Grain and . . . increase and abundance he took away from field and meadow.
> . . . .
> Forthwith the seed ceased to yield produce;
> forthwith oxen, sheep and men ceased to breed,
> while even those that had conceived did not give birth.
> Hillsides were bare;
> trees were bare and put forth no new boughs;
> pastures were bare; springs ran dry.[106]

And this in turn recalls the description, in the Homeric *Hymn to Demeter,* of the languor which befell the earth through the rape of Persephone:

> No shoots did the earth put forth, for the fair-crowned Demeter kept the seed hidden in the ground. And many a crooked plow did the oxen drag in vain across the fields and many a stalk of barley fell fruitless and unripened to the ground. The goddess would, indeed, have destroyed the entire race of mortal men with grievous famine and have deprived of their offerings them that dwell in the Olympian mansions, had not Zeus taken thought and reflected.[107]

Zephaniah

243 Zephaniah and the pagan festivals

Comparative Folklore does for the Book of Zephaniah what it does for those of Hosea and Joel: it presents a good case for assuming that the prophet spoke against the background of a pagan seasonal festival, the principal features of which served as pegs on which to hang his message.

1:2–3

(a) The prophet opens with the words:

> Yes, I will make an ingathering ('-s-f),
> quoth the LORD,
> of all things off the face of the earth—
> an ingathering of man and beast,
> of fowl of the air and fish of the sea,
>
> . . . .
> and I will cut off all earthlings
> from the face of the earth!

These opening words would have sounded with special effect if the prophet were addressing the crowds at the Feast of Ingathering ('Asîf)—the autumnal harvest home. They parody the standard descriptions of the languishing earth in myths connected with the "vanished and returning" (or "dying and reviving") deities of fertility, e.g., the Canaanite myth of Baal, the Hittite myth of Telipinu, the Babylonian Tammuz dirges, and the Homeric *Hymn to Demeter* (see above, §242).

Moreover, that they were indeed uttered against the background of ritual practices is shown clearly by the reference, in the very next verse, to the eunuch priests of Baal and to the custom, attested also in a Canaanite text from Ras Shamra-Ugarit,[1] of worshiping the host of heaven on rooftops.

1:7

(b) 　　　　　　　　　　　　　　　Yahweh has arranged a banquet[2]
　　　　　　　　　　　　　　　　　has invited his guests.

679

A common feature of seasonal festivals is a banquet of the gods, designed originally to recement by commensality their ties of "kinship" with their worshipers.[3]

The Mesopotamian New Year (Akîtu) Festival is sometimes characterized as a "banquet" (kirêtu)[4] or "collation (tâkaltu).[5] This is mythologized in the Epic of Creation, then recited, as the banquet of the gods after Marduk has defeated Tiamat and been installed in his newly built palace (temple), Esagila.[6] Similarly, in the Canaanite Poem of Baal, that god, after vanquishing his rival Yam, regales the gods in a newly built palace.[7]

In the Hittite myth of Telipinu, the return of that lord of fertility to the earth is celebrated by a banquet attended by the gods, notably by the Ladies of Fate (Gulses), the goddess of increase (Miyantazipas) and the god of grain (Halkis).[8] So too, in the cult-text of the Puruli-festival, after the Weather-god has subdued the Dragon the gods convene, and food (galaktar) is served to them.[9]

In Greece, an annual regalement of the gods (theoxenia) was held at Delphi in the month of Boedromion (Sept.-Oct.);[10] and such a banquet was likewise a feature of the later mysteries of Attis.[11]

A vivid description of such feasts, as seen through Canaanite eyes in the second millennium B.C., is afforded by three mutually complementary (or parallel) texts discovered at Ras Shamra-Ugarit.[12]

The occasion is the return to the earth and the installation of Baal, lord of rainfall and fructifier of the soil. It takes place at the season when summer fruits are gathered, i.e., in September-October.[13] Various gods are invited to a banquet lasting several days. The affair is designated a "council" or "moot" (sd).[14] They come riding to their host's "place" (atr) in chariots, or mounted on asses, and foregather appropriately at the threshing floors or plantations, where they are regaled by the mortal king Daniel, known to us also from the Poem of Aqhat.[15] They are accompanied by their sons (bn) and grandsons (bn bn), and each of the youngsters (sgr) is assured that the beautiful goddess 'Anat herself will clasp his hand and kiss his lips.[16] At the scene of assembly they find a mighty host of their divine brethren engaged, "shoulder to shoulder," oldsters and youngsters alike, in various kinds of diversion, and forming a bodyguard for (or: paying honor to) the newly appointed lord and king.[17] 'Anat herself—the Canaanite Diana—fares forth to catch game for the repast, and herself flushes fowl from the bushes.[18] The fare consists of oxen, fatted sheep, lambs, and tender yearling kids. Olive branches shimmer like silver,[19] and dates gleam like gold before the eyes of all who frequent the scene, and the table is fragrant with vine blossoms fit for kings. The wine is of the finest, not just such as comes from spare gleanings.[20] Crescent-shaped loaves of fine Lebanese flour are served,[21] and the drink is so profuse that one might fancy all the wells of Lebanon had poured forth their contents.[22] The guest of honor

has been appointed by divine decree to reign over the land of Amurru,[23] i.e.,
Syria, and, as the divine cultivator of the soil,[24] he is regaled with new wine
fresh as dew.[25] Oil is poured over his head, and on the seventh day of the
feast—the Israelite Feast of Ingathering lasted seven days—he apparently
addresses his colleagues (the text is here defective) and formally announces
to them that "My father [has appointed me your king]."[26]

Jewish popular lore projected this annual banquet into eschatology: just
as at the beginning of each year, so at the beginning of the New Age, Yahweh
would tender a banquet to the faithful, the viands being the flesh of the
monsters Leviathan and Behemoth.[27] Says a liturgical poet of the eleventh
century:

> Then round about, on golden chairs
> (Each one approach'd by seven stairs)
> The righteous as His guests shall dine,
> And perfect bliss shall be their wine;
> And overhead, for chandeliers,
> Shall hang the radiance of the spheres,
> A beauty which no lips can tell,
> Whereon no earthly eye can dwell,
> A starry glory which of old
> No prophet's vision e'er foretold.[28]

1:5

(c) *Punishment will be meted out upon those who have sworn
allegiance to Yahweh, yet now take oaths by their king.*

In the seasonal myths, the banquet provides an opportunity for acknowledging the new divine king—evidently a projection of the rite in which the
sovereign was annually reinstated or reconfirmed.[29] Once this is realized, the
standard modern emendation of the Hebrew word, *malkam,* "their king," to
Milkôm, the god of the Ammonites, is seen to be unnecessary and, indeed, to
spoil the point of the prophet's words![30]

(d) *Likewise destined for punishment are those "who have not
gone seeking the LORD or inquiring after him."*

The words are suggested by the ritual *search* for the departed god of fertility
—a common feature of pagan seasonal rituals (see above, §221).

1:8ª

(e) *When Yahweh tenders his banquet, he will* lay charges against
(RSV: *punish*) *the attendant officials and the royal entourage.*

Banquets were the regular concomitants, in antiquity, of parliamentary
assemblies. This was the case, for instance, in Mesopotamia[31] and it finds
mythological expression in the aforementioned episode of the Epic of Creation.

Similarly, in the Egyptian *Ramesseum Drama,* which celebrates the installation of Horus as king (i.e., on the punctual level, the reconfirmation of the pharaoh), the proceedings end with a regalement of the lords of the realm.[32]

The "parliamentary banquet" was likewise a regular institution among the Persians,[33] the Homeric Greeks,[34] and the Teutons.[35]

At such assemblies the king would give his orders to his ministers (mythologically, the norms of the world would be determined) for the ensuing year.

The prophet plays satirically on this usage, for the Hebrew word for "laying charges *against*" (RSV: "punish") also means "laying charges *upon.*"[36] What he is saying, therefore, is that, in accordance with established custom, Yahweh will indeed charge his guests—but with their sins!

The members of the royal entourage are designated "sons of the king,"[37] and this at once recalls the fact that in the Canaanite "banquet" text discussed above, the guests are expressly invited to bring their sons and grandsons. The lesser members of the court are likened satirically to these youngsters at the divine banquet.

1:8ᵇ

(f) *Punishment will be visited also on "all who dress in foreign raiment."*

In the context of the prophet's message this means, of course, all who affect alien modes. The particular image may have been suggested, however, by the spectacle of the pagan worshipers wearing "fancy dress" at the seasonal festival. Designed originally to deceive the demons who were thought to be rampant on such critical occasions, this widespread custom survives in European Carnival masquerades.[38]

The general tone of the prophet's words, it may be added, find their counterpart in the contemptuous jibes leveled by Roman and Christian writers at the foppish and exotic garb affected by the devotees of Attis and Adonis.[39] In a religious medium, it is the superpatriot's cry against "foreign isms."

1:9

(g) *Likewise destined for punishment is "everyone who leaps over the threshold—men who fill their master's house with crime and fraud."*

The expression, "everyone who leaps over the threshold" is simply the Hebrew equivalent of our own colloquial "gatecrasher," and refers to those who are so eager to gain entrée into court circles that they virtually rush into the palace without decency or decorum. Once again, however, there is exquisite satire in the prophet's choice of words, for they are evidently suggested by the widespread practice of stepping over the threshold in order not to tread on the household spirits or the sainted dead, who lie beneath it. In I Samuel 5:5 it is said expressly that this custom was observed by the Philistine priests when they entered the temple of Dagon at Ashdod (I Samuel, 5:5). It is clearly to some such ritual practice that the prophet alludes. Not impossibly, however, this was also standard etiquette at court. If so, we may aptly compare Marco Polo's account of the same custom at the court of the Great Chan.⁴⁰

1:10-11

(h)   *It shall come to pass in that day*
that a loud cry will resound from the Fish-gate,
and a howl from the Second Quarter

. . . .
Howl, ye that dwell in Maktesh. . . .

A satirical allusion to the ceremonial *howling* for the vanished god of fertility (see above, §221).

1:12

(i)   *Yahweh "will search out*
Jerusalem with lamps."

The transition of thought, otherwise somewhat abrupt and inconsequential, becomes immediately intelligible when it is remembered that a very common feature of seasonal festivals was a *torchlight procession*.⁴¹ This was an element, for instance, of the Babylonian New Year (Akîtu) ceremonies,⁴² and an ancient Mesopotamian oracle mentions it as standard festal procedure.⁴³ In Greek usage, when the god Iacchos arrived in procession at Eleusis on Boedromian 20, he was welcomed by a nocturnal torchlight dance at the Callichoron,⁴⁴ and such dances were, indeed, a prominent feature of the cult of Dionysus.⁴⁵ At the festival of Thesmophoria, women paraded across the fields carrying torches,⁴⁶ and it has been suggested that it is this rite that is mythologized in the Homeric *Hymn to Demeter,* where that goddess and Hecate are portrayed as searching by torchlight for the lost Persephone.⁴⁷ Torchlight processions were likewise a feature of the mysteries of Attis.⁴⁸ The original motivation of this practice was, in the opinion of several modern scholars, to fructify the fields by warmth.⁴⁹

As the procession wends its way through the streets, the prophet, standing as it were on the sidewalk, comments sardonically that Yahweh too has his torches—wherewith to search out sin from every nook and cranny!

1:14

(j)   *Bitter is the sound of the day of the LORD;*
('tis that of) a warrior raising his war-cry!

A further reference to pagan seasonal ceremonies may perhaps be dug out from under the traditional Hebrew text of this verse. To be sure, as it stands it yields eminently intelligible sense, and may well be correct. It has been suggested, however, that by a change of but a single letter and the regrouping of others to form different words, these lines may be made to yield the sense:

> *Swifter than a racer comes the day of the LORD,*
> *and quicker than a champion!*[50]

If this is right, it is not impossible that the words were suggested by the
spectacle of a ritual *race*—a not uncommon feature of seasonal festivals. Such
a race was run—to cite but a few examples—at the Babylonian New Year,[51]
at the Greek Eleusinian mysteries,[52] and at the Roman festival of Robigalia,[53]
and the practice is still widespread in European and Oriental calendar customs.[54] Moreover, in the Canaanite "banquet text" from Ras Shamra, which
we have discussed above, there is an obscure passage which seems to say that
the gods engaged in races.[55] I confess, however, that I drop this suggestion
and run for my life.

3:15–19

(k) In spite of all his dire warnings, Zephaniah concludes his prophecy on
a note of hope. But this too is conveyed through a skillful use of the traditional
pagan pattern. Just as Baal and the other "vanished" gods of the pagan myths
and rituals eventually subdue their enemies and return as conquering heroes
and kings, to restore the fortunes of the languishing earth and bring "salvation"
to their worshipers, so will Yahweh:

> *The LORD hath removed those things*
> *that were as judgments upon thee;*[56]
> *He hath swept away thy foes.*
> *The LORD shall yet be in thy midst*
> *as king of Israel:*
> *thou shalt fear evil no more.*
> *In that day shall it be said unto Jerusalem:*
> *"The LORD thy God is in thy midst,*
> *a hero triumphant."*
> *He will rejoice over thee with gladness.*
> *Though now he keep silent about his love,*
> *he then will exult over thee in a burst of song,*[57]
> *(saying) "Them that I thrust forth from the assembly*
> *I now have gathered in;*
> *Albeit they were the cause*
> *of insults levelled at me,*
> *yet, withal, they came from thee.*[58]
> *See, I will press hard*[59] *at that time*
> *on all who have oppressed thee;*
> *The lame will I rescue, the lorn retrieve,*
> *and make them praised and renowned*
> *who were shamed throughout the earth!*

The reference in these lines to "them that I thrust forth from the assembly" may perhaps echo the Canaanite myth of the divine banquet, for it is significant that when the gods are invited to that repast, their host declares: "Eat, ye gods, and drink: drink wine to satiety, new wine unto drunkenness. . . . He that acknowledges (lit. knows) me—let food be set for him, but he that does not acknowledge me—let them batter him under the table with a stick!"[60]

244 Ravens in ruins   2:14

> The raven and the hedgehog shall lodge in her capitals;
> the owl shall hoot in the window,
> the raven croak[1] on the threshold.

An ancient Arabic name for the *owl* is "mother of ruins" (*imm el-ḥarâb*).[2]

The *raven* is everywhere regarded as a prophet of woe (see above, §47). In the Semitic world, the idea appears already in Babylonian literature[3] and it has counterparts in modern Arabic proverbial lore. Says one popular saying: "He is like a raven, bespeaking nothing but ruin." Says another: "Follow the raven, and he will show you nothing but ruin."[4] Such birds, haunting ruins, were thought to be demons. The Syriac writer Thomas of Marga tells us, for instance, that "while a certain man was passing at night along the road by the side of a fire temple of the Magians which had been a ruin for some time, devils sprung out upon him in the form of black ravens."[5]

Zechariah

Zechariah is yet another of the minor prophets who evidently spoke against the background of pagan seasonal festivals—in this case, the Feast of Ingathering which inaugurated the rainy season. Thus, when he describes the final Day of Doom as *a singular kind of day . . . neither day nor night, seeing that at eventide it shall be light* (14:7), the image may well have been suggested by the fact that ancient seasonal festivals were commonly celebrated at solstice or equinox.[1] In Mesopotamia, for example, the rites of Tammuz were held in the month of the vernal solstice,[2] and the prophet Ezekiel—though he seems to have muddled his dates—expressly associates the weeping for that god with a ceremony of adoring the rising sun (Ezek. 8:14–16). Similarly, the Ugaritic *Poem of the Gracious Gods,* which can be shown to have been the "book of words" for a spring festival, includes a liturgical invocation addressed not only to the gods responsible for grain and wine, but also to the Sun-goddess;[3] while in the *Poem of Baal,* which is really the cult-myth of the autumn festival, a particularly important role is assigned to that same deity. She is, in fact, formally commended for the part she plays in retrieving Baal from the netherworld.[4] Significant also is the fact that among the Israelites themselves both the spring festival (Pentecost) and the autumnal Feast of Ingathering fell in the months of the equinoxes.[5]

The Asianic "mysteries" of Attis likewise culminated on the day of the vernal equinox (March 25);[6] while it should be observed also that in Syria and the Eastern portions of the Roman Empire, the Festival of the New Age (Aiōn) was combined with the alleged birthday of the sun on November 18.[7] Indeed, so firmly established was the connection between festivals of the New Life and these crucial solar dates that the Church was eventually obliged to fix Christmas on what originally had been the birthday of the solarized hero Mithra, and to associate the date of Christ's resurrection with the vernal equinox.[8]

Again, when the prophet holds out to his people the hope that eventually *Living waters shall go out from Jerusalem, in summer and winter alike* (14:8), his words are probably motivated by the thought that at the season of

686

the autumn festival the riverbeds have not yet been replenished and the soil still depends for its moisture on those "perpetual streams" (Heb.: *'ethanim*) after which the relevant month was indeed named. Moreover, when he adds to this assurance the dire warning (*ib.*) that the punishment of the impious will consist of a dearth of winter rains (Heb.: *geshem*), what he clearly has in mind is that the autumnal festival marks the official beginning of the rainy season.[9] So too, when he describes how pilgrims will *come annually to pay homage to the King, the Lord of Hosts at the Feast of Booths* (14:16, 18), he is quite obviously thinking of the fact that an essential feature of Ancient Near Eastern seasonal festivals was the ceremonial installation of the god as king, or of the mortal king as his human embodiment or viceroy.[10]

Nor is it only by inference and innuendo that the prophet alludes to these pagan rites, for when he admonishes his listeners that in the last days *the mourning in Jerusalem will be as great as that for Hadad-Rimmon in the plain of Megiddo* (12:11), he is making direct reference to the standard ritual wailing for Baal-Hadad, the god of rainfall and fertility, who is ousted from the earth during the dry summer.[11] In the Canaanite (Ugaritic) *Poem of Baal,* the goddess 'Anat is said to roam the uplands (like Demeter in search of Persephone), gashing her flesh and crying, "Baal is dead!"[12]

246 Teraphîm   10:2

> *The teraphîm utter nonsense,*
> *and the diviners claim visions falsely.*

The teraphîm are the household gods, from whom oracles were sought (see above, §68).

Malachi

247 Malachi's picture of the Last Days

The prophecies which go under the name of "Malachi" were composed in the fifth century B.C., when, after the conquest of Babylon by Cyrus (539), the Jews had come under Persian rule. This brought them into direct contact with Zoroastrian and earlier Mazdean lore and—at least on the popular level, profoundly influenced the traditional patterns of religious thought. From the Persians the Jews adopted and adapted an extensive folklore of angels, archangels, spirits, and demons. Ahriman, captain of the evil ones, became Satan, "the Obstructer," or Belial, "the Good-for-Nothing"; Druj, the spirit of falsehood, who constantly opposed Asha, "the Right," became Mastemah, the female demon of Hostility. The elaborate and lurid eschatology of the Iranians also found its way into popular Jewish thought: there would be a final ordeal by fire, in which wickedness would be purged, to be followed by the appearance of a savior or champion who would bring about the regeneration of the world and usher in a golden age of prodigious increase and prosperity. These apocalyptic ideas, which are extensively developed in the intertestamental literature and in the Dead Sea Scriptures,[1] have long been recognized in the Biblical Book of Daniel, written during the Hellenistic period, but they may also be detected, if one look closely, in the graphic description of the Last Days which forms the concluding portion of the prophecies of "Malachi."[2] The following are the more arresting parallels:

3:1

    (a) *Yahweh will send his messenger, to prepare the way before him.*

The Renewal of the World (*frashokereti*) will be inaugurated by the appearance of a "savior" (*saoshyant*).[3]

    (b) *The Lord* (Heb.: 'ādôn), *for whom people are looking, will then return suddenly to his palace,*
The 'messenger (angel) of the covenant'[4] is already on his way.

688

Ahura Mazdāh, "the Wise Lord," will reassert his sovereignty over men.

A leading aide of Ahura Mazdāh, often regarded as virtually his equal, is *Mithra,* who is the genius of covenants or contracts.[5] (In Avestan literature *mithra* indeed occurs as a common noun meaning "covenant").[6]

3:2

(c) *The Final Day (era) will be "like a refiner's fire, and like fuller's soap."*

The Iranians held that the Renewal of the World would be preceded by an "ordeal of molten metal" (*aya khshusta*) in which the wicked would be refined, while to the righteous it would be like warm milk.[7] The Book of Daniel (12:10) speaks similarly of a final "refinement" of "many men"; and in the Dead Sea Scrolls, the "era of refinement" is a specific eschatological period.[8]

The doctrine easily gets confused, alike in the intertestamental literature and in the New Testament, with the alternative notion that the present world will end in a conflagration (*ekpyrōsis*)[9]—a notion common also in the Neo-Stoic speculation.[10]

3:5

(d) *This will be followed by a Judgment in which Yahweh will appear as a "swift (or, expert?) witness" against sorcerers and other evildoers.*

In Iranian doctrine, the Ordeal of Molten Metal is followed in short order by a Last Judgment.[11]

Moreover, the specification of sorcerers is especially interesting in view of the fact that Zoroastrianism made a particular point of denouncing sorcery as an evil creation of Angra Mainyu (Ahriman). Not only is it condemned in native works of all periods,[12] but testimony to the same effect is also borne unanimously by Greek writers. Dino, for example, states in his *Persica* that the Magi abhorred divination;[13] and Sotion, on the authority of the same writer and Aristotle, says that sorcery was unknown among them.[14]

3:6

(e) *The pious and God-fearing have been registered in God's special record.*

In later Pahlevi works of Zoroastrianism it is said that thrice daily, the spirit Vohuman ("Good Mind") notes down the good and evil deeds of everyone in the Book of Life.[15] True, the idea does not seem to be attested in earlier Iranian sources. Nevertheless, it appears not infrequently in intertestamental literature and is therefore certainly of higher antiquity.[16]

248 The sun of righteousness   **4:2**

After the annihilation of the wicked by fire, the "sun of righteousness" will rise for the God-fearing "with healing in its wings."

The "sun of righteousness" is a Hebrew counterpart of Mithra, who is also the lord of light and the champion of righteousness and truth.[1]

The notion is influenced also by the pagan notion that the savior-god or savior-king will appear at the dawn of the New Age in the form of an effulgent sun.[2] The idea originated in the fact that the Festival of the New Age—itself a projection of the seasonal regeneration—often coincided with the winter solstice, when the sun began its ascent from the nether regions.[3] The major festival of Mithra was celebrated on that date,[4] as was also the birthday of Aron (the New Age) in Hellenistic times.[5] In Imperial Rome, this was likewise the birthday of Sol Invictus,[6] and at Durostorum in Silestria, the Roman troops held the festival of Kronos-Helios on that day.[7] The Egyptians said that Osiris had been born at the winter solstice,[8] and the Nabateans said the same of their god Dusares.[9] It was, indeed, on account of such time-honored associations that Pope Julius, in the fourth century, chose December 25 as the birthday of him who was to the Christians *lux mundi*.[10]

The solar disc is often portrayed with wings in Ancient Near Eastern art,[11] and this form of representation is increasingly common in Achaemenian times.—An interesting parallel to the notion occurs among the Ibo-Itsi of Africa, where one of the tribal scarification marks is a winged sun.[12]

Mithra is indeed a god of healing,[13] but the notion of the sun with healing in its wings is probably indebted also to ideas associated with the Semitic Shamash, who is frequently invoked in Mesopotamian texts to provide cures for ailments.[14] Similarly, too, in a Canaanite text from Ras Shamra-Ugarit, the sun-goddess is besought, while on her daily round, to bring a charm against snakebite to various cities whose own gods have remained powerless against it.[15]

A more familiar parallel is afforded by the healing powers of the Greek Phoebus-Apollo.[16]

Not impossibly, the prophet's words are also inspired by a popular belief, attested elsewhere, that the sun is refreshed nightly by a healing draught or by some other substance hidden in the nether waters.[17]

249   The Second Coming of Elijah   4:5

> *The "savior" and regenerator in the Last Days is identified as the prophet Elijah.*

The immediate reason for this identification is that Elijah was translated to heaven in a fiery chariot (see above, §159). He therefore never died, but will eventually return—a notion which is commonplace in later Jewish folklore.[1] It is significant, however, that in this manner of disappearance Elijah duplicates Mithra, who was likewise carried aloft in the chariot of the sun, but who will likewise return in the Last Days to do battle against the forces of evil and help bring about the Renewal of the World.[2]

In Christian art, the ascent of the soul after death is sometimes symbolized on sarcophagi by the portrayal of Elijah ascending in the fiery chariot. Not impossibly, this mode of representation was influenced, or even suggested, by similar portrayals on the tombstones of the followers of Mithra.[3] This would then be an excellent parallel to what Malachi is here doing.

NOTES

ISAIAH

171 Whispering in charms

1. T. H. Gaster, in Orientalia 11 (1942), 64.
2. Andrew Lang, Custom and Myth (1885), 43; A. Dieterich, Mithrasliturgie[3] (1910), 42; W. Gesenius, Thesaurus, s.v. *ṣ-f-f*; P. Lagarde, Ges. Abh. (1866), 45, n.4.
3. Maqlû, ed. Tallquist, ii.17, 68, 91 (*šaptu muṣṣapratu*); IV R 16, rev. 60 f.; P. Jensen, in ZK 2 (1885), 310.
4. I. Goldziher, in Noeldeke Festschrift (1906), i.306; cf. also: Bar Bahlul 337.
5. Lucian, Dial. meretr. iv.5; cf. Ovid, Met. xiv.57; Apuleius, Met. 23.
6. Grimm-Stallybrass, TM 1224.
7. A. Dieterich, Abraxas (1891), 177.6–7; id., Mithrasliturgie[3], 5.23; S. Eitrem, Papyri Osloenses i (1925), i.356; K. Preisendanz, Papyri magici Graeci (1928–31), #12.40, 49; E. Riess, in Latomus 2 (1938), 173.
8. J. Montgomery, Aramaic Incantation Texts from Nippur (1913), 60.
9. S. Euringer, in ZS 6 (1925), 178.25 (and 185n.).
10. Tibullus, i.2, 47.
11. V. Lanternari, The Religions of the Oppressed (1965), 199; Robert Louis Stevenson, In the South Seas, 274 f.

▲ 172 Soul-boxes

1. Isa. 3:16–24.
2. Isa. 3:20.
3. "Johnson's learned sock" was on when he wrote these beautiful verses, for the idea was borrowed from Philostratus, Epist. ii: "I have sent thee a wreath of roses, not to honor thee but to grace them, that they wither not." Similarly, the thought of the first stanza derives from Philostratus, Epist. xxxiii.

173 Waistcloths and shoestrings

1. I*AB i.4; T. H. Gaster, Thespis[2], 201 f.
2. Superstit. 109, Kock.
3. Policrat. ii.8.
4. Cf. A. S. Pease, on Cicero, De Divinatione ii.84 (*abruptio corrigiae*).
5. HN viii.221.
6. Folk-Lore 13 (1902), 50.

174 Seraphim

1. Herodotus, ii.75; iii.109.
2. Max von Oppenheim, Der Tell Halaf (1943–50), Pl. xxxi*b*.
3. Gesenius-Buhl, HWb 794[b].

176 "A virgin shall conceive": Immanuel

1. *Literature:* Aziz, in Al Mashriq 24 (1900); C. F. Burney, in JTS 10 (1909), 580 f.; K. Fullerton, in JBL 35 (1916), 134 ff.; id., in AJSL 34 (1918), 256–83; F. C. Ackerman, in AJSL 35 (1919), 205–14; E. G. Kraeling, in JBL 50 (1931), 277–97; K. Budde,

in JBL 52 (1933), 22–24; A. von Bulmerincq, in Acta et Commentationes Univ. Tartuensis, B 37/i (1935), 1–17; E. Hamershaib, in Studia Theologica 3 (1949), 124 ff.; J. Coppens, in Analecta Lovanensiana bibl. et or. ii/35 (1952); J. J. Stamm, in VT 4 (1954), 20 ff.; id., in ZAW 68 (1956), 46 ff.; id., in TZ (Basle) 16 (1960), 439–55; L. Koehler, in ZAW 67 (1955), 48 ff.; J. Lindblom, A Study in the Immanuel Section in Isaiah (1957–58); F. L. Moriarty, in CBQ 19 (1957), 226 ff.; H. L. Ginsberg, in J. N. Epstein Denkschrift (1950), 29–32. See also: G. Gutknecht, Das Motiv der Jungfraugeburt in religionsgesch. Beleuchtung (Diss. Greifswald 1953).

2. Nikkal 7 (*hl ǵlmt tld b*[*n*]).

3. E. Norden, Die Geburt des Kindes (1924).

4. For the evidence, see: T. H. Gaster, Thespis[2], 414 f.

5. Mrs. E. D. von Buren, in Orientalia 13 (1944), 1–72.

6. Statue E, 51–53.

7. Cyliner B, iv.23–v.19.

8. S. Langdon, PBS X.1 (JRAS 1926.36 ff.)

9. VAT 633, obv. 1–10.

10. Ib., 14–21; G. Reisner, Sum.-bab. Hymnen (1896), ii.12–32; R. Pfeiffer, State Letters of Assyria (1935), #217 (reign of Esarhaddon, 681–668 B.C.).

11. Syria 19 (1938), 23.

12. H. Frankfort, OIC 17, p. 48, fig. 42.

13. H. Junker, Die Onurislegende (1917), 116 ff.

14. W. Wolf, Das schöne Fest von Opet (1931), 72 ff.; A. Blavkman, Luxor and Its Temples (1923), 70.

15. K. Sethe, Untersuchungen, iv (1905), 219 f.

16. De rep. ath. iii.5.

17. Alexander, 38.

18. Philosophoumena, p. 170, ed. Cruice.

19. Strabo, x.3, 11.

20. R. M. Dawkins, in JHS 26 (1906), 191; M. Beza, Paganism in Roumanian Folklore (1928), 51.

21. E.g., CIS I.86, B 9 (from Citium, Cyprus). Note, however, that L. Koehler (loc. cit.) would interpret the word in Isaiah as a collective, i.e., "Young women, when they bear sons, will give them such significant names as Immanuel (God-is-with-us)."

22. See: O. S. Rankin, The Origin of the Feast of Hanukkah (1930), and cf. Macrobius, Sat. i.18; Claudian De iv. Caes. honor. 570 ff.; Norden, op. cit., 25; Schol. Greg. Naz.: *hê parthenos tetoken, auxei phôs* ("the virgin has given birth; light will increase"); cf. K. Holl, in Sitzb. Berlin. Akad. 1917.427, n.4.

23. L. Duchesne, Christian Worship[2], tr. McClure (1904), 261 f.—In an earlier period, the solstice fell on January 6–7; hence, the birth of the Savior or New Aion was celebrated on that date: Epiphanius, haeres. li.22, 8 f.; cf. H. Engberding, in ALW 2 (1952); L. Fend, in TLZ 78 (1953), i.1–10; R. J. Z. Werblowsky, in RHR 145 (1954), 35 ff.

24. Isa. 9:1.

177 Gibbering ghosts and mediums

1. E. B. Tylor, Primitive Culture, ii.540; Nicolaus Remigius, Daemonolatria (1596), i. ch. 8 (on the authority of Psellus).

2. Iliad 23.100; Odyssey 23.101; 24.5.

3. Vergil, Aeneid vi.492.

4. Sat. i.8, 40.

5. Phars. vi.23.

6. Theb. vii.770.

7. Fasti v.458.
8. Satyricon 122, 137.
9. In Ruf. i.126.
10. H. Callaway, Religious Systems of the Amazulu (1868–70), 265, 348, 370.
11. E. Shortland, Traditions and Superstitions of the New Zealanders[2] (1856), 92.
12. E. Crawley, The Idea of the Soul (1909), 102.
13. W. Ellis, Polynesian Researches[2] (1832–36), i.406.
14. Fr. Lejeune, in Relations des Jesuites 1634.13; 1639.43.
15. R. F. Burton, First Footsteps in East Africa (1910), 42 (sifr).

178 Cursing by king and god

1. This is commonly rendered, after Septuagint and Vulgate, They . . . will curse their king and their god, though RSV, in a footnote, concedes the alternative translation. The common rendering, however, involves a grammatical anomaly in the Hebrew text, for nowhere else is the word for "curse," viz., q-l-l, construed, as here, with the preposition b- of the direct object. Indeed, the true meaning comes out very clearly from the next verse, where that preposition is omitted in speaking of the cursing of the territories of Zebulun and Naphtali (direct object). A distinction in sense must therefore be implied by the variant constructions, and this can be elucidated from the fact that the preposition b- is similarly employed after the same verb in I Samuel 17:43, to indicate that by which one curses.—Interestingly enough, the Greek (Septuagint) Version, according to the best reading, renders "his gods" by the word patakhra, "idols"—a loanword from Iranian which is widely employed in Aramaic and Mandaean magical incantations: see J. A. Montgomery, Aramaic Incantation Texts from Nippur (1913), 72.
2. See: E. Westermarck, The Origin and Development of the Moral Ideas[2] (1912–17), i.564; E. Crawley, Oath, Curse and Blessing [reprint of art. Oath in ERE] (1934), 36 f.
3. R. H. Codrington, The Melanesians (1891), 51.
4. Ib., 217.
5. G. Furlani, La religione babilonese e assira (1929), ii.292 ff.; J. Pedersen, Der Eid bei den Semiten (1914).
6. S. A. B. Mercer, The Oath in Babylonian and Assyrian Literature (1912), 7 ff.
7. Cf. H. Liebesny, in JAOS 61 (1941), 62–63.
8. See: J. A. Wilson, in JNES 7 (1948), 129–56; J. G. Frazer, GB[2], i.419.

179 The dawn of salvation

1. VAT 8896.1.

180 "Lucifer, son of the morning"

Literature: N. König, in ET 1907.479; K. Schmidt, in ThZ 3 (1951); T. H. Gaster, Thespis[2], 412; B. Bamberger, Fallen Angels (1952); R. de Vaux, in RB 46 (1937), 546 f.
1. J. Lewy, in RHR 110 (1934), 43 f.
2. E. R. Hodges, ed., Cory's Ancient Fragments (1876), 12. The comparison was made by O. Eissfeldt at the Twentieth International Congress of Orientalists, Brussels, 1938.
3. H. G. Güterbock, Kumarbi (1946); A. Goetze, ANET 120 ff.; T. H. Gaster, The Oldest Stories in the World (1952), 110.
4. A. Goetze, Verstreute Boghazköi-Texte (1930), #58; T. H. Gaster, Thespis[2], 270 ff.
5. Hesiod, Theogony 154–210, 453 ff.
6. H. G. Güterbock, in AJA 52 (1948), 123–34; N. O. Brown, Hesiod's Theogony (1953), 36 ff.; F. M. Cornford, Principium Sapientiae (1952), 209 ff.; F. Vian, La

guerre des géants (1952); A. Lesky, "Hethitische Texte und griechischen Mythos"; "Osterreichische Anzeiger 51 (1952), 137–59.

7. Cf. J. Morgenstern, in HUCA 14 (1939), 70, n.4; 112, n.153; Gaster, op. cit., 412.

8. Enoch 1:5; 10:9; 12:2; 13:10, etc., and esp. 15:8; II Enoch 18:1–6; 24:4–5; Vita Adae et Evae, chs. 13–16; Qumran Genesis Aprocryphon, tr. T. H. Gaster, The Scriptures of the Dead Sea Sect in English Translation (1957), 330.

181 The fate of Sargon

1. For the traditional text's *mi-qibreka* read simply *mi-qeber* (with prefix in privative sense). The final letter of the traditional reading is simply dittography from the next word.

2. Heb. *ke-neṣer niteab*. There is no need to emend the text, as is usually done. Heb. *neṣer* means "twig," as in Isa. 60:21; Dan. 11:7 (cf. also Aramaic *niẓrâ;* Arabic *n-ẓ-r,* "be green"). The proud king is likened to foliage once blossoming gloriously but eventually fallen, sodden and mired. Moreover, if, as some scholars think, the prophecy really refers to Nebuchadnezzar, rather than to Sargon, the word *neṣer* would contain a pun on the second element of his name, as written in Hebrew. The Septuagint Version, however, has *nekros* ("corpse"); Aquila has *ichôr,* and the Vulgate *sanies,* while the Syriac and Aramaic versions render "untimely birth." This may point to a variant reading *neṣel* (as in post-Biblical Hebrew) or even to *nephel* (cf. Ps. 58:9; Eccles. 6:3).

3. R. C. Thompson, Semitic Magic (1908), 17; W. A. I. 17; P. Haupt, Akkad. und Sumer. Keilschrifttexte (1881), 11.ii, 6; K. 2175.i, 6–8 = Thompson, in PSBA 1906.219 ff.

4. Josephus, Contra Apionem 1.20.

182 Flying serpents

1. Herodotus, ii.75; iii.109.

2. Lucan, Phars. vi.677.

3. C. Clermont-Ganneau, in Réc. d'archéol. orientale 4 (1880), 319; C. Landberg, Hadramout (1901), 137. Cf. A. Lods, Israël (1930), 275.

4. S. Baring-Gould, Curious Myths of the Middle Ages (New York 1884), 201.

184 The gardens of Adonis

1. Scholiast, on Theocritus, Id., xv.112. See further: Greve, De Adonide (1877), 37–41; Rochette, in Rev. archéol. 8 (1881), 97–123; W. von Baudissin, Adonis und Esmun (1911), 87 ff., 139 ff.; W. H. Engel, Kypros (1841), ii.548 ff.; Ohnefalsch-Richter, Kypros, die Bibel und Homer (1893), i.139 f.

2. Frag. 514 (Melanippe).

3. Phaedrus, 276B.

4. Hist. plant. vi.7, 3.

5. E.g., Zenobius i.29; Philostratus, Vita Apoll. vii.32; Julian, Conviv. 423 Hertlein; Suidas, Lex. s.v.

6. Rashi, on TB Shabbath 81ᵇ. (The boxes are called *p-r-p-s-y-a,* which is the Greek *paropsis.*)

7. A. Neppi Modena, in Bylinchis: fascicolo in ommagio al Congresso internat. di storia delle religioni a Parigi, 1923.

8. G. Pitré, Spettacoli e feste populari siciliani (1881), 211; E. Caetani-Lavatelli, Antichi Monumenti (1889), 61 ff.; Frazer-Gaster, NGB §216.

9. A. Bresciani, Dei costumi dell' isola di Sardegna (1886), 427 f.; W. Baumgartner, in Archives suisses des traditions populaires 43 (1946), 122–48; V. Dorsa, La tradizione greco-latina negli usi populari della Calabria Citeriore (Cosenza 1884), 50.

10. A. Mariette, Denderah (1873–80), iv.35; A. Moret, Rois et dieux d'Égypte

(1922), 102; id., La mise à mort du dieu en Égypte (1927), 39; N. G. Davies and A. H. Gardiner, The Tomb of Amenemhet (1915), 115; H. Carter, The Tomb of Tutankhamen (1923–27), iii.161, pl. 64.

11. E. Thurston, Ethnographic Notes in Southern India (1906), 2.

12. E. T. Dalton, Descriptive Ethnography of Bengal (1872), 259; S. C. Roy, The Oraons (1915), 243.

13. F. C. Movers, Die Phönizier (1841–56), i.217; A. Jirku, in VT 7 (1956), 201 f.

14. J. Wellhausen, Reste d. arab. Heidentums² (1897), 110. Cf. Ovid, Met. x.735; Servius, on Vergil, Aen. v.72. This etymology, however, is disputed by Wellhausen, op. cit., 70, and by I. Löw, Aramäische Pflanzennamen (1881), 201n.; 411, n.90.

185 The rebel constellations

1. Enuma Elish vii.27.

2. S. Langdon, The Epic of Creation (1923), 34 ff. See also the text published by T. G. Pinches in PSBA 1908.53 ff.

3. Rev. 12:7–9.

4. Hesiod, Theog. 617 ff.; Apollodorus, Bib. i.2, 4.

5. Enoch 86:1; 88; 90:20–21; J. Morgenstern, in HUCA 14 (1939), 100; T. H. Gaster, Thespis², 412; B. Bamberger, Fallen Angels (1952).

6. Enoch 21:3 ff.; cf. also ib., 18:13 ff.

7. Jude 13.

8. J. Montgomery, Aramaic Incantation Texts from Nippur (1913), #4.4–5.

9. Qolasta, 75; M. Lidzbarski, Liturgien, 127; E. S. Drower, The Canonical Prayer-book of the Mandaeans (1959), 75.

10. For this sense of the verb p-q-d, cf. Isa. 38:10.

11. Enuma Elish, loc. cit.

12. PSBA 1908.53, col. i.

13. Enoch 21:3 ff.

14. Montgomery, loc. cit.: w'd š'tâ rbty dprqnâ.

15. For the verb 'a-s-f in this sense, cf. I Sam. 14:52; 17:1; Zech. 14:2.

186 Leviathan

1. Cf. T. H. Gaster, Thespis², 249 f.

2. S. N. Kramer, Sumerian Mythology (1944), 80 ff.; T. Jacobsen, in JNES 5 (1946), 146–47.

3. Enuma Elish, tab. iv.

4. KBo III.7; KUB XII.66; XVII.5–6; tr. A. Goetze, ANET 125–26; T. H. Gaster, op. cit., 245–67.

5. The so-called Poem of Baal; cf. Gaster, op. cit., 134–244.

6. I*AB, 1–2; Gaster, op. cit., 201 f.

7. J. Montgomery, Aramaic Incantation Texts from Nippur (1903), #2.4, 6. The word here rendered "fate" is the Aramaic š-m-t-â = Akkadian šimtu.

8. Rig Veda i.32; cf. A. A. Macdonell, Vedic Mythology (1897), 56–60, 158 f.

9. Hesiod, Theogony 820 ff.; Aeschylus, Prometheus Vinctus 351 ff.; Apollodorus, Bib. i.6, 3; Ovid, Met. v.319 ff.; Hyginus, fab. 152. Cf. Porzig, in KlF 1 (1930), 376–86.

10. L. Bechstein, Thüringer Sagenbuch (1885), #190.

11. Ugaritica V (1967), #7. The explanation of the name is my own.

12. Egyptian djeser tep (Chicago Oriental Institute, #16881.14); cf. K. C. Steele, in JNES 6 (1947), 47, n.56.

187 The "Name of the LORD" as his agent

1. II AB, B 8; Krt c, vi.55.

2. G. A. Cooke, A Text-book of North Semitic Inscriptions (1903), 37.

3. Cf. Stith Thompson, MI, F. 531.3.8; B 14.1.
4. Gilgamesh iii.109–111.
5. Hesiod, Theogony 820 ff.; cf. Aeschylus, Prometheus Vinctus 351 ff.

188 The haunts of demons

1. R. C. Thompson, Semitic Magic (1908), 92; K 4347, obv. ii.50–51 = S. Langdon, in AJSL 28 (1911), 222. See also: A. Smythe Palmer, Babylonian Influences in the Bible, etc. (1897), 72 ff.; A. Lods, Israël (1930), 276.
2. J. Wellhausen, Reste d. arab. Heidentums[2] (1897), 135–40.
3. Zohar i.188a–b; Sepher ha-Yashar, Wa-tišlaḥ, 70a; L. Ginzberg, Legends of the Jews (1909 sqq.), v.322.
4. ii.599, ed. Budge.
5. E. W. Budge, Lady Meux MSS, Nos. 2–5.216.
6. T. H. Gaster, Thespis[2], 218, n.9.
7. Matt. 12:43; Luke 4:1–2.
8. R. Trench, Studies in the Gospels (1867), 7.
9. John Milton, Comus 207–9.
10. R. Burton, Anatomie of Melancholy, i.2, 2.
11. I, p. xxix, and ch. 57 *sub init.*, ed. Yule.
12. N. Prejevalsky, Mongolia (1876), i.194.
13. F. Lenormant, Chaldaean Magic (1877), 245 f.
14. K. Tallquist, Namen der Totenwelt (1934), 17 ff. See also (but with caution): A. Haldar, The Notion of the Desert in Sumero-accadian and West Semitic Religions (1950).

189 Hairy devils

1. J. Montgomery, Aramaic Incantation Texts from Nippur (1913), #5.4.
2. Maimonides, Guide for the Perplexed, iii.46, says that the Sabaeans regarded certain demons as goats and so called them.
3. Jewish Encyclopaedia, i.605.
4. E. S. Drower, The Mandaeans of Iraq and Iran (1937), 349–50.
5. Grimm-Stallybrass, TM ii.478 ff.; J. Schmidt, "Der Schkrat," in Edda 4 (1892), 218–21, 251–54.
6. Cf. W. Roscher, Ephialtes (1900), 29 f., 62, 285; O. Gruppe, Griech. Mythologie (1906), 1386, n.2.

190 Lilith

1. R. C. Thompson, The Devils and Evil Spirits of Babylonia (1904), i. p. xxxvii; KAT[3] 460; J. Montgomery, Aramaic Incantation Texts from Nippur (1913), 75 ff.; T. H. Gaster, in Orientalia 11 (1941), 40 ff.; C. Frank, Bab. Beschwörungsreliefs (1900); id., Lamashtu, Pazuzu, und andere Dämonen (1940); D. Myhrman, Labartu-Texte (1901); F. Thureau-Dangin, in RA 18 (1921), 161–98; H. Klengel, "Neue Lamaštu-Amulette," in MIOr 7 (1960), 334–55.
2. R. C. Thompson, Semitic Magic (1908), 65 ff.
3. T. H. Gaster, The Holy and the Profane (1955), 18–27.
4. Id., in Orientalia 11 (1942), 41–76.
5. See: M. Gaster, in Folklore 1900.126–62; I. Zolli, in Filologische Schriften 2 (1929), 121–42; G. Kittredge, Witchcraft in Old and New England (1929), 224 ff., 522, nn.104–8; A. H. Krappe, Balor with the Evil Eye (1927), 87 ff.; H. A. Winkler, Salomo und die Karina (1911).
6. T. H. Gaster, in SMSR 25 (1951–52), 154–57.
7. C. Frank, Bab. Beschwörungsreliefs (1900), 78.

8. VAB XI.17, 4 f. (not yet published, but quoted, in another connection, by A. Goetze, in JCS 11 [1957], 81).

9. Frank, Beschwörungsreliefs, 77 f.; Myhrman, op. cit. 11.44–48a.—The Babylonians observed a similar practice in exorcizing demons from a new or renovated house or temple: text and translation in P. Jensen, KB vi/2.

10. Frazer-Gaster, NGB §454.

11. ANET 328.

12. S. G. Oliphant, in TAPA 44 (1913), 127 ff.; L. Oppenheim, in WZKM 30 (1908), 158 ff.; W. Klinger, in Philologus 66 (1907), 344, cites modern parallels.

13. Aristophanes, Frogs 294–95; Suidas, Lex., s.v. Empousa.

14. Aristophanes, Acharn. 574; Theocritus, Id., 15.40.—The name survived in English folklore as a "bogey-word" used to scare unruly children: Notes and Queries, 5/xi (1879), 427; 5/xii (1879), 18.

15. Aristophanes, Thesm. 417; Plato, Phaedo 77E.

16. Diodorus, xx.41; Photius, s.v. LAMIA; Oliphant, loc. cit., Sappho, 94 Wharton. Cf. Gaster, The Holy and the Profane, 229, n.13.

17. On the ominous character of the owl, of Kirby Smith, on Tibullus, i.5, 52.

18. Ib.

19. Gaster, The Holy and the Profane, 21 ff.

20. Hesiod, Theogony 267; cf. Apollodorus, Bib. i.9.21.

21. III.iv.

22. W. W. Skeat, Malay Magic (1900), 325.

23. J. Trachtenberg, Jewish Magic and Superstition (1939), 278, n.34.

191   The loom of life

1. B. Schmidt, Das Volksleben der Neugriechen (1871), 220.

192   Heaven as a muslin curtain

1. BD 85. The Egyptian word is *šet;* cf. P. le Page Renouf, in PSBA 16 (1894), 182.

2. A. C. Blank, Il sacro presso i primitivi (1945), 71.

3. H. Güntert, Von der Sprache der Götter und Geister (1921), 142.

4. Cf. KB i.174–75; P. Jensen, Die Kosmologie der Babylonier (1890), 6 ff.

5. L. Strackerjan, Sagen aus dem Herzogtum Oldenburg² (1907), ii.108.

6. Daniel Defoe, History of the Devil (1739), 50.

194   The Suffering Servant

1. The Suffering Servant has been identified by some scholars with the mythological "dying and reviving god": H. Gressmann, Der Ursprung d. israel.-jüdische Eschatologie (1905), 312–33; id., Der Messias (1929), 287–323; H. Gunkel, RGG, col. 1543; W. Staerk, in ZAW, N.F. 3 (1926), 259 f.; A. Jeremias, The Old Testament in the Light of the Ancient East (1911), ii.278; G. H. Dix, in JTS (1925), 241 ff.; S. Mowinckel, in ZAW, N.F. 8 (1931), 259 f. These views are rejected—in my opinion, on inadequate grounds—by H. Orlinsky, The so-called Suffering Servant in Isaiah and alleged Near Eastern Parallels. Gittelson Lecture, 1965.—An interpretation approximating my own is offered by L. Dürr, Ursprung und Ausbau d. israel.-jüd. Heilandserwartung (1925), 125 ff.

(a)

2. See fully: Frazer-Gaster, NGB §§456–67, and Additional Notes thereto.

3. VAT 9555, rev. 10–11; S. Langdon, The Babylonian Epic of Creation (1923), 34 ff.

4. Texts are assembled and discussed in Gilbert Murray, The Rise of the Greek Epic

(1907), Appendix A, pp. 253–58. See also: Jane Harrison, Prolegomena to the Study of Greek Religion[3] (1922), 95 ff., 105 f.

5. Plutarch, Quaest. symp. vi.8.

6. Servius on Vergil, Aen. iii.57; Lactantius Placidus, Comm. on Statius, Theb. x.793 p. 452, ed. Jahnke; Petronius, fr. 1, Buecheler.

7. Philostratus, Vita Apoll. vi.10.

8. Harpocration, s.v. *pharmakos;* cf. J. Töpfer, Beitraege zur griech. Altertumswissenschaft (1897), 130 ff.; M. P. Nilsson, Griechische Feste (1906), 105 ff.

9. Helladius, cited by Photius, Bib. 534; Lysias, Orat. vii.53; Hesychius, s.v. *pharmakos.*

10. Joannes Lydus, De mensibus iii.29; iv.36; Varro, De lingua Latina vi.45; Festus 131 Müller; Plutarch, Numa 13. See: L. Preller, Röm. Mythologie[3] (1881–82), i.360; W. H. Roscher, Apollon und Mars (1873), 49; H. Usener, Kl. Schriften (1913), iv.125 f.

11. S. Crowther and J. C. Taylor, The Gospel on the Banks of the Niger (1859), 344–45; Frazer-Gaster, NGB §459.

12. Turpin, "History of Siam," in J. Pinkerton's Voyages and Travels (1808–14), ix.579.

13. J. H. Gray, China (1875), ii.306; Frazer-Gaster, NGB §456.

14. H. Herzog, Schweizerische Voksfeste (1884), 293 f.

15. L. Curtius, in ARW 14 (1911), 307.—To be sure, the rite was sometimes interpreted as a means of flogging *in* fertility and increase, just as parents today speak alternatively of beating the nonsense *out* of their unruly children or of beating sense *into* them. For this alternative view, see: W. Mannhardt, Mythologische Forschungen (1884), 113–40; S. Reinach, Cultes, Mythes et Religions (1905–12), i.180–83; L. R. Farnell, The Cults of the Greek States (1896–1909), v.163.—Women were struck for fertility in the Arcadian rites of Dionysus and of Demeter: Pausanias, viii.23, 1; Hesychius, s.v. Morotton.—Beating with thongs likewise figured prominently in the Roman rite of the Lupercalia: A. M. Franklin, The Lupercalia (1921), 59 f.—The custom is well attested in European folklore. In Croatia, people beat one another for "freshness and health" after church on Good Friday and the two previous days: F. S. Krauss, Kroatien und Slavonien (1889), 108; while in some parts of Russia people returning from church on Palm Sunday beat with their branches the children and servants who have stayed at home, saying "Sickness into the forest, health into the bones"; W. Mannhardt, Baumkultus (1875), 257. A similar custom, known as "Easter smacks," prevailed around Eastertide in several parts of Germany: Frazer-Gaster, NGB §470. Jews perform a similar rite on the seventh day of the autumnal festival of Ingathering (Booths): H. Graetz, in MGWJ 36 (1887), 509–21.

16. Heb.: *nigzar.* The expression echoes the wording of the scapegoat ritual in Lev. 16:22, where the beast is ordered to be dispatched to "a land of cutting off" (Heb.: *gᵉzerah*), i.e., a desert.

(b)

17. For similar conceptions in Classical antiquity, see: T. Wächter, Reinheitsvorschriften (1910), 39 ff. Cf. especially: Iliad 1.413; 5.394 ff.; Herodotus, i.138 (lepers among the Persians). So too among African primitives: J. Spieth, Die Ewe-stämme (1906), 255.

18. See: J. Heller, "Hiding the Face" (Isa. 53:3), in Communio Viatorum 1 (1958), 263–66.—In Arabia, the face is veiled against the evil eye: J. Wellhausen, Skizzen (1889), iii.146. Alternatively, a disguise is adopted: W. Mannhardt, Antike Wald- und Feldkulte (1904), i.543; E. Nestle, in Philologus, N.F. 4 (1891), 502; M. Grünbaum, in ZDMG 21 (1877), 263.

19. E.g., the Darfur: Mohammed ibn Omar el-Tunisi, Voyage en Daufar (1845),

203; BORNU: Ibn Batutah, ed. Deffrémery-Sanguinetti (1855–58), iv.441; CHONGA: Mattei, Bas-Niger, etc. (1895), 90 f.; JEBU: A. B. Ellis, The Yoruba-speaking Peoples of the Slave Coast (1894), 190. See Frazer-Gaster, NGB §162.

20. Cf. L. B. Paton, ICC on Esther 1:14.

21. Scholiast on Iliad 24.480; Ap. Rhod., Argon. iv.697 f.; Euripides, Iphigenia in Tauris 1206 f. Cf. Wächter, op. cit., 70.

22. G. Parrinder, La religion en Afrique centrale (1950), 95.

23. O. Gruppe, Griech. Mythologie (1906), 903, n.2, would so explain the Graeco-Roman custom of besmearing with gypsum initiants to the mysteries. See on this: Demosthenes, xiii.239; Plutarch, Superstit. 3; Apuleius, Met. vii.27; Augustine, De civ. Dei viii.26. Cf. also: A. Dieterich, in Rhein. Mus. 48 (1893), 279.

195 The faery city

1. Reading, with LXX, ba-<no>phek for the traditional ba-pūk ("with stibium"). It occurs to me, however, that this widely accepted emendation may be, in fact, a little too facile and obscure the true sense. The prophet likens Zion to a "forlorn, storm-tossed, disconsolate" woman who will yet be restored to her former glory and beauty. This verse, therefore, may really contain an extension of that metaphor, involving a subtle double-entendre: the very stones of the city will be, in their new brilliance, like a woman whose features are enhanced by cosmetic "eye-shade," for which stibium is regularly employed in the Near East. Similarly, when he describes the gleaming pinnacles as "suns," he may be intending an allusion to the familiar brooches in the form of sun discs. Bizarre as this may sound to Western ears, it is in keeping with the common extravagance of Oriental poetry.

2. Literally, "And I will make thy suns of agate." Cf. Akkadian šamsātê, "ornaments in the form of solar discs."

3. KARI #307.30 ff.; B. Meissner, Babylonien und Assyrien (1925), ii.108.

4. II AB, iv-v.77–81.

5. Enoch 14:9 ff.

6. Test. Abraham, ch. xii; tr. Box (1927), 19.

7. Tobit 13:16 f.

8. Rev. 21:18 f., 21 f.

9. Cf. F. Brittain, ed., The Penguin Book of Latin Verse (1962), 191.

10. Ib., 176.

11. Tr. T. H. Gaster, Festivals of the Jewish Year (1953), 72; id., in Commentary, June 1953.

12. Ib., 405 f.; E. Davies, Myths and Rites of the British Druids (1809), 522; R. Southey, Madoc, ix.

13. M. Preindlsberger-Mrazović, Bosnische Volksmärchen (1905), 110 f.; cf. H. Gunkel, Das Märchen im AT (1925), 63 f.

14. J. G. von Hahn, Griechisch und albanesische Märchen (1864), i.147, 194.

15. A. N. Afansjev. Narodnyja russkija skazki[3] (1897), 73.

16. D. G. Brinton, The Myths of the New World[3] (1905), 105.

196 Gad and Meni

1. See: F. Baethgen, Beitraege zur sem. Religionsgeschichte (1888), 76 ff.; W. C. Wood, in JBL 35 (1916), 266 ff.—The name is strangely absent from the Canaanite texts from Ras Shamra-Ugarit.

2. Gen. 30:11. The Masoretes, however, took the Hebrew word be-Gad to stand for bā' Gad, "Gad (Fortune) has come!"

3. On the other hand, the name 'Azgad (Ezra 2:12; 8:12; Neh. 7:17; 10:16), which

might appear at first blush to be the Semitic *'az-Gad,* "Gad is strong," could equally well be the Iranian *izgad,* "messenger."

4. Nos. 2, 4, 7, 18, etc.

5. M. Lizbarski, Ephemeris fuer Semitische Epigraphik, i (1902), 15.

6. A. Reifenberg, in PEQ 70 (1938), 114.

7. M. Lidzbarski, Handbuch der nordsemitischen Epigraphik (1898), 249.

8. Cf. Pliny, NH ii.5.22; G. A. Cooke, A Text-book of North Semitic Inscriptions (1903), 269; S. A. Cook, The Religion of Ancient Palestine in the Light of Archaeology (1930), 226 ff.—Significantly enough, Jacob of Serug states explicitly (ZDMG 29.138) that the Christians turned many of the sanctuaries of Tyche (in Syriac: *beth gadde!*) into churches.

9. E.g., Cooke, op. cit., 245n. (from El-Qanawat, in the Ḥauran).

10. Ib., 79; 112.4 (A.D. 140).

11. So, for instance, in Nabatean (Cooke, op. cit., 145.4–5: "He shall have neither seed nor *gad* for ever!"); Syriac, Ethiopic, South Arabian, and Mandaean (*gada taba,* "good luck").

12. TB Mo'ed Qatan 27a; Nᵉdarim 56a; Sanhedrin 20a. See: Joseph Karo, Shulhan 'Aruk, Yoreh De'ah §170.7 (with H. J. D. Azulai, Birkê Joseph [1774–76] in loc.); M. Schul, Superstitions et coutumes populaires du judaïsme contemporaine (1886), 6; T. H. Gaster, Folkways of Jewish Life (1965), 64 f.—On the Roman custom, cf. Varrus, cited by Servius, on Vergil, Aeneid 10.76; G. Wissowa, Religion und Kultus der Römer (1932), 357, n.1.

13. G. F. Abbott, Macedonian Folklore (1903), 125 f.; J. C. Lawson, Modern Greek Folklore (1910), 125 f.; Kamporouglou, Historia tôn Athênôn, iii.67 f.

14. TB Shabbath 92b; cf. also Yalquṭ Shime'oni §509 (on our passage from Isaiah).

15. A. Berliner, Aus dem leben der deutschen Juden im Mittelalter (1900), 105.

16. TB Shabbath 67b; Yalquṭ Shime'oni, §587.

17. Th. Noeldeke, Beitraege zur sem. Sprachwissenschaft (1904), 94.—On Gad among the Arabs in general, see: J. Wellhausen, Reste des arabischen Heidentums³ (1897), 146; R. Dussaud, Les Arabes en Syrie (1907), 147 ff.; Th. Noeldeke, in ERE i.662a.

18. See: H. Zimmern, in Islamica 2.574–84; S. H. Langdon, in JRAS 1930.21–29.

19. Cooke, op. cit., 79 (from El-Hejra, 1st cent. B.C.); 80.4 (A.D. 1); 86.8 (A.D. 26). —The form *M-n-w-t-w* appears to be feminine. I. Goldziher (in Archäol. epigr. Mitteilungen aus Oesterreich 6 [1882], 109) reads it as a plural (*maniyat*).

20. Koran 53:20.

21. *M-n-w-t-w* is indeed associated with the ancient goddess Allat in the Nabatean inscription, Cooke, op. cit., 80.4.

JEREMIAH

197 Man from stones

1. Stith Thompson, MI, T 544.1; M. Eliade, Patterns in Comparative Religion (1958), 237; M. Semper, Rassen und Religionen im alten Vorderasien (1930), 179–86; J. Layard, Stone Men of Malekula (1942); G. Dumézil, Légendes sur les Nartes (1930), 75–77; W. J. Perry, Children of the Sun² (1926), 255 ff.; W. Jackson Knight, Cumaean Gates (1936), 9 ff.

2. R. Pettazzoni, Dio i (1922), 10.

3. R. W. Williamson, The Social and Political System of Polynesia (1924), ii.242–43; M. Leenhardt, Notes d'éthnologie néocaledonienne (1930), 183.

4. H. Callaway, The Religious System of the Amazulu (1868–70), 34.
5. D. G. Brinton, Religions of Primitive Peoples (1899), 147.
6. T. H. Gaster, The Oldest Stories in the World (1955), 125.
7. A. v. Löwis of Menar, in ARW 13 (1910), 509–24.
8. J. A. Jaussen, Coutumes des arabes au pays de Moab (1908), 107.
9. Ovid, Met. i.125–415; Lucian, De dea Syria, 12 ff.; Apollodorus, Bib. i.7.2.
10. Cf. Stith Thompson, MI, T 544.1.
11. Fornander, The Polynesian Race, as quoted by Brinton, loc. cit.
12. Odyssey 19.163; cf. also: Juvenal, vi.12.

199 Passing children through fire

1. Note that in II Chron. 28:3, which parallels our passage, the Hebrew word for "pass through fire" is replaced by "burned." Cf. also Jer. 7:31 and 19:5, which speak of *burning* children.
2. J. G. Frazer, The Fasti of Ovid (1925), iii.293 ff.; G. Glotz, L'ordalie dans la Grèce primitive (1904), 105 f.; O. Gruppe, Griech. Mythologie (1906), 898, n.4.
3. Preuner, Hestia-Vesta (1864), 60; A. Mommsen, Feste d. Stadt Athen (1898), 274; W. R. Halliday, in CR 25 (1901), 8 f. Cf. also: E. H. Meyer, Indogermanische Mythen, ii (1877), 512 f.
4. Strabo, xii.2, 7.
5. Plutarch, De Iside et Osiride 16.
6. Ovid, Fasti iv.423 ff.; Tibullus, ii.5, 89 f.; Propertius, v (iv).4, 77 f.; Dio Hal., Ant. i.88; Pliny, HN vi.19.
7. Jamblichus, De mysteriis clxxix.8; Proclus, In Rem. i.152, 10. Cf. E. R. Dodds, The Greeks and the Irrational (reprint, 1957), 305, n.66.
8. J. G. Frazer, Apollodorus (1921), ii.311–17; A. Lang, "The Fire Walk," in his Modern Mythology (1897); J. Grimm, DM² i.592; W. Mannhardt, Antike Wald- und Feldkulte (1877), i.497 ff.; ii.302 ff.
9. Journal of the Indian Archipelago 2.264.
10. E.g., Yajnavalk i.137.
11. Meyer, loc. cit.
12. H. Massé, Persian Beliefs and Customs (1954), 499 (citing Layard).
13. T. Pennant, in J. Pinkerton's General Collection of Voyages and Travels (1808–14), iii.383.
14. *s.v.* coals.
15. M. Eliade, Birth and Rebirth (1950), 91.
16. A. Popov, Tavagijcy: Trudy Instituta Antropologii i Etnografi (Moscow-Leningrad), i/5 (1936), 84 ff., as quoted by Eliade, *op. cit.*, 90.
17. B. Spencer and F. Gillen, The Northern Tribes of Australia (1904), 389 ff.; id., The Arunta (1927), i.295 ff.; W. L. Warner, A Black Civilization (1937), 325; F. Speiser, in Verhandlungen der Naturforschenden Gesell. in Basel, 1929, 216–18; A. P. Elkin, Aboriginal Men of High Degree (1946), 91, 193.
18. See below, n22.
19. A. Aarne and S. Thompson, Types of the Folk Tale. FCC #74 (1928), #753.
20. Homeric Hymn to Demeter, 237 ff. (v. Allen-Sikes-Halliday, in loc.).
21. Apollodorus, Bib. iii.13.6.
22. Stith Thompson, MI, D 1885–86; Grimm, ##81, 147; Bolte-Polivka, i.412; iii.198; O. Dähnhardt, Natursagen (1907–12), iii.154; 162 ff., 288; R. Kohler, Kl. Schriften (1894), i.298; J. G. Frazer, Apollodorus (1921), i.121, n.4; A. Ritterhaus, Die neuisländischen Volksmärchen (1902), 338 (Iceland); Hartung, in Zs. f. Volkskunde 8.89; Piger, ib., 10.84 (Germany); P. Sébillot, Incidents, s.v. "four" (Breton); W. Mannhardt, Germanische Mythen (1858), 64–75; A. B. Cook, Zeus ii (1925), 210 ff.;

O. Gruppe, Griech. Mythologie (1906), 546; M. Eliade, Birth and Rebirth (1958), 90 f.; A. H. Krappe, La genèse des mythes (1938), 209; J. G. Frazer, GB iii.872; iv.96; R. B. Onians, The Origins of European Thought about the Body, etc. (1952), 289, n.5.

23. Pausanias ii.3, 2; Ovid, Met. vii.297–349.

24. Apollodorus, loc. cit.; Ap. Rhodius, Argon. iv.869.

25. G. and T. L. Jones, The Mabinogion (Everyman's Library ed.), 29 ff.

26. A. B. Cook, Zeus i (1923), 786.

27. R. Dussaud, in RHR 58 (1909), 309 (apotheôsis en tô lebêti).

28. Matt. 3:10; Luke 3:16. See fully: C. Edsman, Le baptême du feu (1949).

29. Concerning Moloch, cf. Daumer, Le culte de Moloch (1842); G. E. Moore, in JBL 16 (1897) 161 ff.; E. Dhorme, in Anatolian Studies 6 (1956), 57–61; H. Cazelles, in Suppl. Dict. de la Bible, cols. 1337–46; cf. also: H. Donkert, Het Mensenoffer in de OTsche Wereld (Baarn 1955).

30. II Kings 23:15; Jer. 49:1; Amos 5:26.—For mlk in Phoenician names, cf. G. A. Cooke, A Text-book of North Semitic Inscriptions (1903), 49; S. R. Driver, ICC Deuteronomy, 223.

31. A. Bea, in Biblica 20 (1939), 415; E. Vogt, ib., 38 (1957), 471 f.; H. Cazelles, ib., 485 f.; R. Dussaud, in Syria 35 (1957), 349 f.

32. Ugaritica V (1967), #7.

33. N. Schneider, in Biblica 18 (1937), 337–43.

34. Id., in Biblica 19 (138), 204.

35. O. Eissfeldt, Molk als Opferbegriff im Punischen und Hebräisch, und das Ende des Gottes Moloch (1935), W. Kornfeld, in WZKM 1952.287–313 (against Eissfeldt); cf. also: J. G. Février, in JA 248 (1960), 167–87; C. Virolleaud et al., in CRAIBL 1956.61, 67.—J. Hoftzijzer, in VT 8 (1958), 92 interprets a Punic inscription reading mlk adm bšrm b(n) btm to mean "A human sacrifice—his own child in perfect health," but this is very dubious.

36. See: W. Kornfeld, in WZKM 1952.267–313; A. Jirku, in ARW 53 (1938), 178; N. Schlögl, in WZKM 45.203–11.

201 "The wind and the rain"

(a) Fissures for the rain

1. G. Dalman, Arbeit und Sitte in Palästina (1928–37), iii/i.114.

2. Ib.

3. II AB, iv–v.68–71.

4. J. Kissane, in JTS 1952.214 f.

5. See above, §4.

6. II AB, vii. 19; cf. T. H. Gaster, Thespis², 195.

7. Herodotus, iv.158, 185.

8. E. B. Tylor, Primitive Culture, ii.157.

(b) Promptuaries for the wind

9. Enoch 17:3; 18:1; 41:4; 60:12–24; 71:4, 9.—Note also the reference in Aeschylus, Eumenides 813 ff., to a mansion of the lightning.

10. Hymn i; tr. T. H. Gaster, The Dead Sea Scriptures in English Translation² (1964), 135.

11. Iliad 23.192; Odyssey 20.66, 77; Apollodorus, Bib. i.9.21; cf. F. G. Welcker, Griechische Götterlehre (1857–62), i.707; iii.67. Cf. also: Vergil, Aen. i.56.

12. W. Ellis, Polynesian Researches² (1832–36), i.329; E. B. Tylor, Primitive Culture, ii.360.

13. H. R. Schoolcraft, Algic Researches (1839), i.139; ii.214.

14. D. G. Brinton, Myths of the New World³ (1905), 93.

202 Rites of mourning

▲ (a) Cuttings for the dead

1. J. Wellhausen, Reste d. arab. Heidentums[2] (1897), 181 f.; I. Goldziher, Muhammedanische Studien (1888–90), i.248; G. Jacob, Das Leben der vorislamischen Beduinen (1897), 139 ff.

2. A. Jaussen, Coutumes des arabes au pays de Moab (1908), 96; S. Merill, East of the Jordan (1881), 51.

3. Jaussen, op. cit., 94.

4. Euripides, Electra 145 ff.; Hecuba 650 ff.; Hesiod, Shield of Heracles 242 ff.; Lucian, De luctu xii; cf. Ovid, Met. xiii.427 ff.; Heroides ix.91 f., 115 ff.

5. Iliad 23.135–53.

6. Aeschylus, Choephoroe 4 ff.; Sophocles, Electra 51–63, 900 ff.; Euripides, Electra 90 ff., 513 ff.

7. Plutarch, Solon 21.

8. Xenophon, Cyropaedia iii.1, 13, iii.3, 67.

9. Cicero, De legibus ii.23, 59; Festus, De verborum significatione 273 Müller; Pliny, HN ii.157; Fontes Juris Romani Antiqui[7], ed. Bruns-Gradenwitz (1909), 36.

10. Servius, on Vergil, Aen. iii.67; xii.606.

11. Vergil, Aen. iv.672 ff.

12. Herodotus, iv.71.

13. Jornandes, Romana et Getica, ed. Mommsen (1882), 124.

14. W. R. S. Ralston, The Songs of the Russian People[2] (1872), 316.

15. A. Lamberti, in Recueil de Voyages au Nord, vii (1725), 153.

16. G. M. Zampi, ib., 221.

17. G. Mourier, in RHR 16 (1887), 90, 93.

18. J. von Klaproth, Reise in den Kaukasus und nach Georgien (1814), ii.604 ff.

19. Stanislas Julien, Documents historiques sur les Tou-Kioue [Turcs] traduits du Chinoise (1877), 10, 28; L. Cahun, Introduction à l'histoire de l'Asie, Turcs et Mongols (1896), 59.

20. E. Rüppell, Reise in Abyssinien (1838–40), ii.57.

21. J. L. Krapf, Reisen in Ost-Afrika (1858), i.325.

22. H. Néel, in L'anthropologie 24 (1913), 458.

23. L. Alberti, De Kaffers aan de Zuidkust van Afrika (1910), 201; H. Lichtenstein, Reisen im südlichen Africa (1811–12), i.421 ff.; S. Kay, Travels and Researches in Caffraria (1833), 199 ff.

24. E. Petitot, Monographie des Déne-Dindijé (1876), 61.

25. A. Mackenzie, Voyages from Montreal through . . . North America (1801), p. xcviii.

26. H. J. Holmberg, in Acta Societatis Scientiarum Fennicae 4 (1856), 324; cf. also: W. H. Dall, Alaska and Its Resources (1870), 417; H. H. Bancroft, The Native Races of the Pacific States (1875–76), i.173.

27. A. Ross, Adventures of the First Settlers on the Oregon or Columbia River (1849), 97.

28. J. Baegert, in Annual Report of the Board of Regents of the Smithsonian Institution for the year 1864, p. 387.

29. Bancroft, op. cit., i.397, n.142.

30. Father de Smet, Voyages aux Montagnes Rocheuses (1873), 28.

31. Ib. 66.

32. A. L. Kroeber, in Bull. Amer. Museum of Natural History 18/i (1902), 16 ff.

33. W. H. Keating, Narrative of an Expedition to the Source of St. Peter's River (1825), i.232.

34. Ib., i.433.

35. Edwin James, Account of an Expedition from Pittsburgh to the Rocky Mountains (1823), i.116.

36. Ib., i.222 ff.

37. Ib., ii.2.

38. Alice C. Fletcher and F. la Flesche, in XXVIIth Annual Report of the Bureau of American Ethnology (1911), 592–94.

39. Ib., 591.

40. J. F. Lafitau, Moeurs des sauvages amériquains (1724), ii.441.

41. T. Falkner, A Description of Patagonia (1774), 118.

42. P. Hyades and J. Deniker, Mission scientifique du Cap Horn, vii (1891), 379.

43. J. M. Cooper, Analytical and Critical Bibliography of the Tribes of Tierra del Fuego and Adjacent Territory. Bull. Amer. Bureau of Amer. Ethnology, #63 (1917), 160.

44. J. A. van Rijn van Alkemarde, in Tijdschrift van het Nederlandsch Aardrijkskundig Genootschap, II Ser. ii (1884), 238 ff.; H. A. Hijmans van Androoij, in TITLV 30 (1885), 347–49.

45. V. Jouet, La Société des Missionaires du Sacré-Coeur dans les Vicariats Apostoliques de la Mélanésie et de la Micronésie (Issoudin 1887), 292; Father Guis, "Les Canaques. Mort-deuil," in Les Missions Catholiques 34 (1902), 186.

46. J. Chalmers, "New Guinea, Toaripi and Koiari Tribes," in Report of the Second Meeting of the Australasian Association for the Advancement of Science (1890), 316, 322.

47. G. Turner, Samoa, a Hundred Years Ago (1884), 335.

48. T. W. Leggart, "Maleluka, New Hebrides," in Report of the Fourth Meeting of the Australasian Society for the Advancement of Science (1892), 700.

49. M. J. van Baarda, in BTLVNI 69 (1913), 64 ff.

50. The Voyages of Captain Cook Round the World (1809), i.218 ff.

51. J. Wilson, Missionary Voyage to the South Pacific (1799), 352 ff.

52. Voyages of Captain James Cook, v.420.

53. Ch. Wilkes, Narrative of the U.S. Exploring Expedition[2] (1851), ii.139; Turner, op. cit., 144; J. B. Stair, Old Samoa (1897), 182; G. Brown, Melanesians and Polynesians (1910), 401 ff.

54. W. W. Gill, "Mangaria Hervey Islands," in Report of the Second Meeting of the Australasian Society for the Advancement of Science (1890), 344.

55. C. Clavel, Les Marquisiens (1885), 39, 44. Cf. also: M. Radiguet, Les derniers sauvages (1882), 284.

56. W. Yate, An Account of New Zealand (1835), 136 ff.; E. Dieffenbach, Travels in New Zealand (1843), ii.62; W. Brown, New Zealand and Its Aborigines (1845), 19; A. S. Thomson, The Story of New Zealand (1859), i.186; E. Tregear, in JAI 19 (1890), 104 ff.

57. J. Dawson, Australian Aborigines (1881), 66.

58. W. Stanbridge, in Trans. Ethnological Soc. of London, N.S. 1 (1861), 298.

59. R. Brough Smyth, The Aborigines of Victoria (1878), i.105.

60. A. W. Howitt, The Native Tribes of S. E. Australia (1904), 459.

61. Ib. 453.

62. P. Beveridge, in Journal and Proc. of the Royal Society of New South Wales for 1883 (1884), 28 f.

63. W. Ridley, Kamilaroi and Other Australian Languages (1875), 160; Howitt, op. cit., 467.

64. J. Mathew, Two Representative Tribes of Queensland (1910), 115; E. M. Curr, The Australian Race (1886–87), iii.165; A. McDonald, in JAI 1 (1872), 216, 219.

65. W. E. Roth, Studies among the North-West-Central Queensland Aborigines (1897), 164.

66. B. Spencer, Native Tribes of the Northern Territory of Australia (1914) 241 ff. (The writer's account of the use made of the blood is not quite clear.)

67. A. R. Brown, in JRAI 43 (1913), 169; E. Clement, in Internat. Archiv für Ethnographie 16 (1904), 8 ff.

68. B. Spencer and F. Gillen, The Native Tribes of Central Australia (1899), 500.

69. Ib., 510.

70. Ib., 500, n.1.

71. Ib., 516–23; id., Across Australia (1912), ii.426–30.

72. F. Bonney, in JAI 13 (1884), 134 ff.

73. J. A. Reid, in E. M. Curr, op. cit., ii.179.

74. Spencer-Gillen, Native Tribes, 507, 509 ff.

75. G. Grey, Journals of Two Expeditions of Discovery in North-West and Western Australia (1841), ii.332 (quoting a letter from a certain Mr. Bussel).

76. Ib., ii.335.

77. Ib.—For other evidence of cuttings for the dead among the Australian aborigines, see: T. L. Mitchell, Three Expeditions into the Interior of Eastern Australia[2] (1839), ii.346; J. Fraser, in Journal and Proc. of the Royal Soc. of New South Wales 16 (1882), 229, 231; E. Palmer, in JAI 13 (1884), 298; J. F. Mann, in Proc. Geogr. Soc. of Australia 1 (1885), 47; E. M. Curr, op. cit., i.330; ii.249, 346, 443, 465; iii.21, 29.

78. J. Bonwick, Daily Life and Origin of the Tasmanians (1870), 97 ff.

79. Spencer-Gillen, Native Tribes, 507.

80. Ib., 510 f.

81. W. R. Smith, The Religion of the Semites[3] (1927), 322 ff.

82. Bonney, loc. cit.

83. Ib., 128.

84. Ib., 132.

85. Ib., 133.

86. Odyssey 11.13 ff. The drinking of the blood by the ghosts is mentioned explicitly in verses 98, 153, 232, 390.

87. See above, §117.

(b) Funeral meats

88. Cf. E. Bendann, Death Customs (1930), ch. ix, pp. 147–61, where examples are quoted from Melanesia, Barthe Bay, Koita, Massim, Santa Cruz, etc. The feasts take place variously two, ten, forty, or a hundred days after death, and are often repeated at spaced intervals.—In the New Hebrides, the dead are believed to join the feast: R. H. Codrington, The Melanesians (1891), 259.—The Greeks held such feasts on the third, ninth, and thirtieth day after a death: Pollux, xiii.146.—The Roman funeral feast took place on the ninth day after a death, and on the birthday of the deceased: E. Aust, Die Religion der Römer[2] (1899), 288 ff.; G. Wissowa, Religion und Kultus der Römer[2] (1912), 235. Cf. also: T. Klaufer, Die Cathedra im Totenkult der heidnischen und christlichen Antike. Liturgesch. Forschungen 9 (1927), 54, 82.—The Patagonians hold funeral feasts every three years: Koch, in Internat. Archiv 13 (1900), suppl. 103.

89. Ezek. 24:17; Heb.: leḥem ᵃnāšim, lit. "bread of men." This is usually "corrected," after Vulgate, Targum, and Hos. 9:4, to leḥem ônîm, "bread of mourners." But the emendation is unnecessary, for the received text can stand in the sense of "bread of fellowship, communion" (cf. Arabic '-n-s in precisely this sense): T. H. Gaster, Communication to the New York Oriental Club, October 1964 (unpublished).

90. Hos. 9:4.

91. G. Dossin, Archives Royales de Mari, i (1946), 8.14. The terms are absent from Akkadian texts: L. Oppenheim, in JNES 11 (1942), 131.

92. CT XVI, p. 10, v.10–14.

93. G. A. Cooke, A Text-book of North Semitic Inscriptions (1903), #61.14–18.

94. T. H. Gaster, Thespis², 334.

95. Lucian, De luctu 24.

96. Clem. Alex., Const. viii, c.24.

97. Chrysostom, Homil. in Matth. 37.

98. E. W. Lane, Manners and Customs of the Modern Egyptians (Minerva Library ed.), 488.

99. T. H. Gaster, The Holy and the Profane (1955), 176 f.

100. Varro, Nonn. i.235; Servius, on Vergil, Aen. v.92; cf. ARW 11 (1909), 330–46.

101. H. Höhn, Sitte und Gebräuche bei Tod, etc. (1913), 333.

102. Am Urquell 6.26.

103. P. Sartori, Die Speisung der Toten (1913), 11.

104. Pliny, HN xviii.12, 30.

105. Ovid, Fasti vi.438 (v. Frazer, in loc.).

106. P. Sartoti, Sitte und Brauch iii (1914), 262, n.16.

107. T. H. Gaster, Thespis², 29 f.

108. JAI 12 (1882), 142.

109. T. Williams and J. Calvert, Fiji and the Fijians (1858), i.169.

110. G. Turner, Samoa a hundred years ago and long before (1884), 142.

111. Ki Li, in SBE xxvii.87.—Ting Ho-Nien (1335–1424) abstained from salt and lao (a milk product) for five years after the death of his mother: L. C. G(oodrich), in Draft Ming Biographies (MBHD), 1964, a.2.

112. J. Ross, A History of Corea (1897), 222.

113. ERE v.760ᵇ; JAI 19 (1890), 28.

114. Gaster, Thespis², loc. cit.

115. In this passage, the word *zebaḥ* means "meal" not "sacrifice," as in Zeph. 1:7 and as sometimes in Ugaritic.

203 The ritual lament

1. LXX omits, "Ah, sister!" M. Dahood has suggested that *adôn* here means simply "daddy," after Ugaritic *ad,* etc. But the parallel from Sappho shows that he is mistaken.

2. VAT 9555.29.

3. Sappho, fr. 63, 108 Wharton.

4. Aristophanes, Lys. 365–66.

5. Bion, Epitaphion Adônidos 1, 40.

6. Ammianus Marcellinus, xix.1, 11; xxii.9, 15.

204 Invoking the earth

1. K 43, obv. 37 (cited by P. Jensen, KB VI/i.270): *EN irṣitum, irṣitum, irṣitum,* ᵈ*Gilgameš bêl ma-mi-ti-ku-nu.*

205 Rachel weeping for her children

1. R. C. Thompson, Semitic Magic (1908), 19 ff.; J. G. Frazer, GB v (Spirits of the Corn and Wild), ii.97 ff.

2. Utukkê Limnûti IV.v.25; V.i.53 (*bakîtu mušeniqtu*); R. C. Thompson, The Devils and Evil Spirits of Babylonia (1903), i.40, 54.

3. C. M. Doughty, Travels in Arabia Deserta (1888), i.305.

4. W. W. Skeat, Malay Magic (1900), 325; id., and C. O. Blagden, Pagan Races of the Malay Peninsula (1906), i.153 (the Sakai of Perak).

5. R. H. Codrington, The Melanesians (1891), 275.

6. J. Kubary, in A. Bastian's Allerlei aus Volks- und Menschenkunde (1888), i.9.

7. S. Wide, in ARW 12 (1909), 224–33; cf. BCH 12 (1888), 297; Pap. Paris Mag. 322 ff., 342 f., 1410, 2215, etc.; O. Dilthey, in Rhein. Mus. 27 (1872), 387 ff.; O. Gruppe, Griech. Mythologie (1906), 761.

8. A. Wuttke, Deutsche Aberglaube d. Gegenwart (1900), 447 ff.

9. Maqlu vii.25.

10. KUB XXX.70, iii(?).14 ff.

11. W. Spiegelberg, Sonnenauge (1917), 7.31.

12. SRT #5.34–36.

13. T. H. Gaster, Thespis[2], 220.

14. Ovid, Fasti iv.495 ff.; cf.; Lucretius, ii.355–63.

205a David redivivus

1. Cf. H. Schmidt, Der Mythos vom wiederkehrenden König im AT (1925); A. W. Hands, in International Journal of Apocrypha, 1916.39.

2. Cf. Stith Thompson, MI, A 580; T. Norlind, Skattsänger (1916).

3. Suetonius, Nero 57; cf. J. Geffcken, in Gött. Gelehrt. Nachrichten, 1899.441–62.

4. J. A. McCulloch, Celtic Mythology (1918), 194.

5. Kalevala, runo 50.

6. Cf. J. Bolte, in ZfVK 29.74; H. Feilberg, Bidrag til en Ordbog over Jyske Almusmal (1886–94); A. Olrick, Ragnarök, tr. Ranisch (1922), 103 ff., 478 [Balder].

7. Stith Thompson, Tales of the North American Indians (1929), 274, n.11a; N. Alexander, Latin American Mythology (1920), 66.

EZEKIEL

207   Ezekiel's vision of heathen worship

1. LXX says "fifth"; Massoretic text, "sixth."

2. The Gezer Agricultural Calendar (10th cent. B.C.?) assigns these months to zmr, "late trimming of the vines," and to qṣ, "reaping of summer fruits." A Canaanite gloss in a letter from Tell el Amarna (97.11, Winckler) gives qêṣ (gi-e-zi) as a statutory season, and the Ugaritic text, I Aqhat i.41 describes it as the time of the early rain (yr).

3. The Masoretic text adds the gloss, "which provokes (Yahweh's) jealousy." LXX and Syriac (Peshitta) omit.

4. The Masoretic text, taking the Hebrew word ḥôr to mean "hole," explains that this was a hole in the wall. LXX omits this gloss.

(a) The "seat of the idol of jealousy"

5. The Gracious Gods (SS); cf. T. H. Gaster, Thespis[2], 406–35; id., in JBL 60 (1941), 290, n.9.

6. The Gracious Gods, 19.

7. RS 1929, #33.

8. RS. 1929. #48, r.2.

8a. CIS ii.114.

9. H. Hepding, Attis (1903), 136–37; E. Rohde, Psyche[7] (1921), i.129, n.3; Gaster, op. cit., 64, 311 f.

10. The Ramesseum Drama = K. Sethe, Dramatische Texte zu altägyptischen Mysterienspiele, ii (1928), lines 132–133a; Gaster, op. cit. 398.

11. KBo III.7; KUB XII.66; Gaster, op. cit. 265 f.

12. KUB XVII.10, iii.20–34; Gaster, op. cit., 311.

13. Enuma Elish vi.53–54.

14. MDOG 38 (1908), 19; S. A. Pallis, The Babylonian Akitu Festival (1926), 173.

15. Cf. T. Frankema, Tâkultu (1954). Two recensions of the ritual are extant, viz. (a) II R 66 (duplicate, KAVI 57), of the reign of Sennacherib; and (b) KARI 214 (duplicates, KAVI 83; KARI 325). The ceremony is mentioned in inscriptions of Adad-nirari and of Shalmaneser I; cf. R. Labat, Le caractère réligieux de la royauté assyro-babylonienne (1939), 286–87.

16. H. Seyrig, in Syria 14 (1933), 262 f.; R. Dussaud, Mission dans les regions désertiques de la Syrie moyenne (1903), #19; M. Lidzbarski, Ephemeris für Semitische Epigraphik (1902–15), ii.356.

17. CIA II.i.624, 662; IV.ii.624b; cf. Livy, xxix.14, 13.

18. F. M. Cornford, The Origins of Attic Comedy (1934), 99.

19. Gracious Gods, 21–22.

(b) The frescoed cavern

20. Such pictures have been found in caves at Gezer.

21. Schol. on Nikander, Alexipharmakon 7–8.

22. Dioscorides, in AP vi.220, 3.

23. Hesychius, s.v. KYBELA: *kai antra kai thalamai.*

24. Arnobius, Adv. nationes, v.7.

25. H. Hepding, Attis (1903), 195–96; A. Dieterich, Mithrasliturgie[2] (1910), 157 ff.

(c) Women weeping for Tammuz

26. See: O. Gurney, in JSS 7 (1962), 147–60; S. N. Kramer, in Studia Biblica et Orientalia 3 (1939), 198n.; id., in Trans. XXVth Internat. Congress of Orientalists, i (1962), 169–73; W. W. Hallo, in JBL 82 (1963), 339.

27. Epic of Gilgamesh vi.46–47.

28. CT, P. 48. rev. 56–57.

29. G. Reisner, Sumerisch-babylonische Hymnen aus Tontafeln Griechischer Zeit (1896), 145, iii.12–15.

30. ZA 6 (1891), 243.24.

31. KARI 178.vi, 10.

32. D. Chwolson, Die Ssabier (1856), ii.27.

33. M. Beza, Paganism in Roumanian Folklore (1928), 27 ff. It should be observed, however, that the name of the puppet is given by other authorities as Scalojan, which is the Roumanian word for "drought, dearth": cf. E. Fischer, in Globus 93 (1908), 13–16.

34. E. W. Lane, Manners and Customs of the Modern Egyptians (Minerva Library ed.), 478.

35. M. Werbrouck, Les pleureuses dans l'Égypte ancienne (1939).

36. KUB XXX.15, 27.

36a. III D 170 ff.; Gaster, op. cit., 368 f.

37. Iliad 24.746.

38. Festus, 223 Mommsen; Ovid, Met. ii.340–43; J. E. B. Mayor, on Juvenal, x.261.

39. M. Ananikian, Armenian Mythology (1920), 95.

40. W. M. Ramsay, Asianic Elements in Greek Civilisation[2] (1928), 93 ff.

(d) The adoration of the rising sun

41. Gaster, op. cit. 47 f.

42. R. Labat, in RA 38 (1941), 28.

43. S. Langdon, Tammuz and Ishtar (1914), 32.

44. Yuzgat Tablet (= A. Goetze, Verstreute Boghazköi-Texte [1930], #58), rev.; Gaster, op. cit. 272 f., 291 f.

45. I AB, i.8–16; vi.22–29.
46. Gracious Gods, 23–27.
47. Cf. also: TJ Sanhedrin 18ᵈ.
48. O. S. Rankin, The Origin of the Festival of Hanukkah (1930), 205 f.
49. Cf. O. Weber, in ARW 19 (1916–19), 325 f.
50. O. S. Rankin, op. cit., 201 f.
51. E. Hull, Folklore of the British Isles (1928), 280.
52. Pervigilium Veneris, 3.

(e) Ezekiel's satire

53. For suggestions concerning the text, see: T. H. Gaster, in JBL 60 (1941), 299 f. In verse 11, for the traditional text's *qām lᵉmaṭṭeh resha'* I read, with Cornill, *qāmal maṭṭeh resha'*.
54. Cf. KUB XXV.31, 7; cf. also: H. Ehelolf, KUB XXIX, Vorwort, iii; C. G. von Brandenstein, in Orientalia 8 (1939), 75 f.
55. Cf. M. Nilsson, Greek Folk Religion (1940), 36 f.; Frazer-Gaster, NGB §§108–10 (with Additional Notes).
56. Joh. Lydus, De mensibus iv.59.
57. Julian, Orat. V, p. 188C.
58. Hepding, op. cit., 152 ff.
59. Firmicus Maternus, c.27.1–2; Hepding, op. cit. 51.
60. C. F. Lehmann, in Die Zeit 2 (1902), 468.
61. Arthur Evans, The Early Religion of Greece in the Light of Cretan Discoveries (1931), 35.
62. Hepding, op. cit., 169 ff.
63. Lucretius, ii.598.
64. See: I. Scheftelowitz, in ARW 15 (1912), 485 ff.; A. Eberharter, in Zs. für katholische Theologie 52 (1928), 492–518; H. Feilberg, in ARW 4 (1901), 170–77; 274–89; J. G. Frazer, GB ix.116 f., 156.
65. Lev. 22:24; Num. 29:1.
66. Num. 10:10; Ps. 81:4.
67. Hull, op. cit. 251.
68. Standard Dict. of Folklore, etc., 1127ᵃ.
69. P. von Stenin, in Globus 58 (1890), 204.
70. TB Rosh ha-Shanah 28ᵃ, Rashi, in loc.; Yalqut Zech. §578.
71. Standard Dictionary of Folklore, etc., 1127ᵈ.
72. Julian, *Eis tēn Mētera tôn theôn*, 169C; cf. Catullus, 63.9.
73. Cf. Plutarch, Is. 35; id., Quaest. conviv., 4.6, 2; Pollux 4.86; O. Gruppe, Griech. Mythologie (1906), 180.
74. See below §243.
75. Herodian, i.10, 5–7.
76. C. A. Lobeck, Aglaophamus (1829), i.173 ff. Cf. also: T. Trede, Das Heidentum in der römischen Kirche (1889–91), iii.70.
77. Pallis, op. cit. 123, 201.
78. Cf. F. Nötscher, 'Das Angesicht Gottes schauen' nach babylonischer und alttestamentlicher Auffassung (1924).
79. Plato, Phaedrus 250C; Plutarch, Demeter 26; Dittenberger, Sylloge², 646.40.
80. Dittenberger, op. cit., 657–59.
81. CT IV.5, 18; cf. B. Landsberger, Das kultische Kalender der Babylonier und Assyrer (1915), 124.
82. Heb.: *qᵉfādah*. The root of the word means primarily "constrict."
83. See: A. Moret, La mise à mort du dieu en Égypte (1927), 18. Cf. also: Hos. 5:15.

84. V AB iii.41; cf. T. H. Gaster, in Iraq 6 (1939), 138, n.183.

85. Themistius, quoted by Stobaeus, Anthol. iv.52, 49 (*phrikē kai tromos kai hidrôs kai thambos*).

▲ **208 Trapping the soul**

Literature: H. Torczyner, in JPES 1934.257–60; W. H. Brownless, in JBL 69 (1950), 367–73.

1. The traditional text of the passage appears to be corrupt. In v.20, the first *l^ephor^ehôth* ("like birds," KJV) is here omitted [with RSV] as a mere doublet of the second, and the obscure words, *eth n^ephāshîm* ("the souls," KJV) are emended, [again with RSV and many modern scholars,] to the very similar *ôtham hôpshîm* ("them free"). [LXX, it may be observed, missed the point entirely by confusing the Hebrew word *ṣ-w-d*, "hunt, entrap," with the like-sounding *ṣ-d-d* and *ṣ-d-h*, "turn aside"—a confusion influenced, perhaps, by the association of the latter word with the *soul* in I Sam. 24:12.]

2. T. Williams, Fiji and the Fijians² (1860), i.250.

3. W. W. Gill, Myths and Songs from the South Pacific (1876), 171; id., Life in the Southern Isles (London, n.d.), 181 ff. (Cimet is cordage made from the dried fibre of coconut husk.)

4. Mary Kingsley, Travels in West Africa (1897), 461 ff.

5. M. Delafosse, in l'Anthropologie 11 (1900), 558.

6. W. W. Skeat, Malay Magic (1900), 576 ff.

7. N. Andriani and A. C. Kruijt, De Bare'e-sprekende Toradja's van Midden-Celebes (1912–14), i.233 f., 236 f.

[7a. B. F. Matthes, Bijdragen tot de Ethnologie vun Zuid-Celebes (1875), 35, 56, 59; id., Ouer de Bissie's of heidensche priesters en priesteressen da Boeginezen (1872), 24; A. E. Crawley, The Idea of the Soul (1909), 118.]

[7b. J. L. van der Toorn, in BTLVNI 39 (1890), 48–49, 56, 58; Crawley, op. cit., 114 f.]

[7c. T. H. Gaster, The Holy and the Profane (1955), 12 f.; Folk-Lore 9 (1898), 79.]

[7d. Crawley, op. cit. 117.]

[7e. A. C. Kruijt, Het Animismus in der Indischen Archipel (1906), 120.]

[7f. N. Graffland, De Minahassa (1867), i.248, 321 f., 331; J. G. F. Riedel, in TITLV 18 (1872), 523.]

[7g. N. P. Wilken and J. A. Schwarz, in Med. van wege het Nederlandsche Zendeling-genootschap 7 (1863), 263 f.]

[7h. A. B. Meyer, in Jahresber. des Vereins für Erdkunde 12 (1875), 26; Crawley, op. cit. 104.]

[7i. Phya Anuman Rajadhon, Chao Thi, or Some Traditions of Thai. Thailand Culture Series, #6 (Bangkok 1952), 15.]

[7j L. Fison, in JAI 10 (1881), 145 f.]

[7k. Fr. Dummeruth, in VT 13 (1963), 228–29.]

[7l. Maqlu iii.46, 59–61 (*ba'artum ša muši*).—A further allusion to this may perhaps be detected in Nah. 3:4 if, with several modern scholars, we emend the traditional text's "mistress of magic arts, who *sells* (Heb.: *ha-môkereth*) whole nations with her harlotries, and families with her charms," to "who *entraps* (Heb.: *ha-kômereth*) whole nations," etc.]

[7m. G. A. Wilken, Verspreide Geschriften (1912), i.20; B. F. Matthes, op. cit., 33; G. K. Nieman, in BTLVNI 38 (1889), 281; W. W. Skeat, Malay Magic (1900), 47.]

209 Yahweh's scourges

1. Epic of Gilgamesh xi.180–94; tr. Speiser, ANET 95.

2. Cf. S. Daiches, in JQR 17 (1905), 441 f.

3. The Biblical Antiquities of Philo 3.19; cf. L. W. King, Legends of Babylon and Egypt in Relation to Hebrew Tradition (1918), 132 ff.

4. Literally, "death," but since the work seems to have been composed in Hebrew or Aramaic, this evidently reflects *môtânâ* or the like in the original text—a word which means both "death" and "plague."

211　Salting newborn children

1. See: I. Scheftelowitz, Altpal. Bauernglaube (1925), 78–79; E. Samter, Geburt, Hochzeit und Tod (1911), 151–61; T. Ploss, Das Kind³ (1911–12), i.227 ff.; I. Löw, "Das Salz," in G. A. Kohut Memorial Volume (1935), 429–62; Notes and Queries V/xi (1879), 206.

2. Cf. T. H. Gaster, The Holy and the Profane (1955), 14.

3. TB Shabbath 129ᵇ. So too among modern Arabs: ZDPV 4.63.

4. Wieser, Scholien, ii.248.

5. Galen, De sanitate tenenda, i.7.

6. E. W. Lane, Arabian Society in the Middle Ages (1883), 188.

7. J. Wellhausen, tr., Al-Wākidî al-Madani, Muhammad in Medina (1882), 378.

8. T. Canaan, in JPOS 19 (1944), 239.

9. Cf. W. Kroll, "Alte Taufgebräuche," in Beiheft ARW 8.32 f.—In Britain, salt is sometimes carried around a child at baptism: ERE viii.592ᵃ.

10. Globus 89.587.

11. J. Grimm, DM² (1844), ii.999; A. Wuttke, D. deutscher Volksaberglaube der Gegenwart³ (1900), 91; E. Mogk, in ERE ii.633ᵇ.

12. Grimm-Stallybrass, TM 1049.

13. E. Samter, Geburt, Hochzeit und Tod (1911), 52, A.6.

14. W. H. Rivers, The Todas (1906), 263 ff.

15. C. Bock, Temples and Elephants (1884), 260.

16. Notes and Queries VI/iii (1881), 73 f.

17. Times (London) Weekly Edition, Oct. 16, 1946; Manchester Guardian Weekly, May 22, 1947.

18. G. Finamore, Credenze, usi e costumi Abruzzesi (1890), 69.

19. G. Pitré, Usi e costumi . . . del popolo Siciliano (abridged reprint, 1963), 31.

20. A. Kremer, Aegypten (1863), i.59, 151.

21. J. Richardson, Travels in Morocco (1860), ii.21.

22. Notes and Queries 1/viii (1853), 617.

212　Rites of divination

(a) Crossroads

1. See: Stith Thompson, MI, D 1786; ERE iv.330–36; E. Westermarck, The Origin and Development of the Moral Ideas (1912–17), ii.256 ff.; J. G. Frazer, GB ii.340; iii.59; ix.61, 68 ff.; x.229; N. M. Penzer, The Ocean of Story (1923 ff.), iii.37 f.; S. Eitrem, Papyri Osloenses, i (1930), 95; E. Riess, P–W, s.v. Aberglaube; Theophrastus, Characters, 28; Pap. Bib. Nat. 2943; Pap. Mag. London cxxv.3.

2. Orphic Hymns i.1; Athenaeus, vii.126; Cornutus, c.34; Scholiast on Aristophanes, Plut. 594; Lucian, Dial. mort. i.1; Eupolis, Dem. 120, Koch; O. Gruppe, Griech. Mythologie (1906), 760, n.1.

3. A. Wunsch, ERE, s.v. Crossroads; cf. Vergil, Aen. iv.609.

4. SBE xxxi (1887), 291.

5. G. Finamore, Credenze, usi e costumi Abruzzesi (1890), 180–82.

6. W. Crooke, The Popular Religion and Folklore of Northern India (1896), 65, 126–7, 140, 157, 201; cf. H. Oldenberg, Die Religion des Veda (1894), 267 ff.

7. E. W. Lane, Arabian Society in the Middle Ages (1883), 37.

8. J. G. Frazer, The Fasti of Ovid (1925), vol. ii, p. 459 ff.

9. Düntzer, in Scheible's Das Kloster V (1847), 120, n. 42.

10. Grimm-Stallybrass, TM 1074, 1115, 1799, 1803.

11. P. Drechsler, Sitte, Brauch und Kolksglaube in Schlesien (1903–6), 234.

12. Goethe, Faust III.i.40.

13. F. Panzer, Beitrag zur deutschen Mythologie (1845–55), i.16, 93, 98, 198 ff., 260.

14. F. S. Krauss, Volksglaube und religiöser Brauch der Südslaven (1890), 116.

15. F. C. Connybeare, in JQR 11.26.

16. E. Samter, op. cit., 145; S. Seligmann, D. böse Blick (1927), 151 ff.; A. Wuttke, D. deutsche Volksaberglaube der Gegenwart[3] (1900), 89; J. Trachtenberg, Jewish Magic and Superstition (1939), 207.

17. J. Campbell, Spirit Basis of Belief and Custom (1855), 208.

18. F. Perles, in Heinrich Graetz Jubelschrift (1887), 24–25.

19. H. Feilberg, Bijdrag til en Ordbog over Jyske Almuesmal (1886–1914), ii.277a.

20. E. S. Hartland, The Science of Fairy Tales (1891), 142.

21. Folk-Lore 34.281 f.

22. ERE iv.802a.

23. J. Atkinson, Women of Persia (1832), 11.

24. ERE iv.828b.

(b) Belomancy

25. See: F. Schwally, in ZAW 11.170 ff.; W. R. Smith, in JOP 13.276–87. For Sumerian evidence, cf. W. W. Struve, in Trans. XXIVth Internat. Congress of Orientalists, i (1962), 178–86. Cf. also: F. Lenormant, La divination et la science des présages chez les Chaldéens (1875), 17–32; A. Ungnad, in AO X/ii (1909), 15.—For the practice in China, cf. J. B. du Halde, The General History of China[2] (1741), iii.§100.

26. Livy, xxvii.16, 15.

27. Macrobius, Sat. iii.5, 1; cf. Servius, on Vergil, Aen. iv.56.

28. TB Gittin 56a; M. Gaster, The Exampla of the Rabbis (1924), #70.

29. Koran 5:92; cf. J. Wellhausen, Reste d. arab. Heidentums[2] (1897), 132.

30. E. Pocock, Specimen historiae Arabum (1806), 323 ff.

31. S. Iwry, in JAOS 81 (1961), 27–34.

32. A. Lang, Cultes, Mythes et Religions (French tr., 1896), 94.

213 The fallen paragon

THE TRANSLATION: In the opening verse, I take the Hebrew words *attah ḥôtem taknîth* to mean literally, "Thou wast the one that set the seal on (all) design," i.e., wast the crowning masterpiece of art. No emendation is required. In v. 14, I derive *mimšaḥ* from *m-š-ḥ* II, "extend, spread," rather than from *m-š-ḥ* I, "anoint." I suspect also that we should read *kᵉrūb-ma/i mošeᵃḥ* (with archaic enclitic *-ma/i*) in place of the traditional *kᵉrūb mimšaḥ*. In the same verse, I construe *ᵉlôhîm hayyîthā* as a separate clause, viz., "Thou wast a being divine," for metrical and syntactical reasons. In v. 16 I read, with most modern scholars, *mille'tā* for *māl'ū*, though it has occurred to me that the correct reading may be *mill'ūkā tôk wᵉ-ḥamas*, "trickery and crime had filled thee." In v. 18, I read *ḥillalta-ma(i) qôdšᵉkā*, though *ḥullaltā mi-qôdšᵉkā* would also be possible.—It should be observed that, according to LXX and the Syriac (Peshitta) Version, the expelled denizen of Paradise was not himself a guardian cherub; he was placed on the divine mountain *along with* (or, *beside*) such a creature, and it was that creature that eventually banished him therefrom (v. 16).

1. See in particular: H. Gunkel, Genesis[5] (1922), 34; T. H. Robinson, in Myth and Ritual, ed. S. H. Hooke (1933), 180 ff.; G. W. Widengren, Psalm 110 (1941), 15 ff.; id., Myth, Ritual and Kingship, ed. S. H. Hooke (1958), 164 ff. But see also on this passage: K. Yaron, in ASTI 3 (1964), 28–57; F. L. Moriarty, in Gregorianum 46 (1965), 83–88; H. G. May, in Essays for J. Muilenburg (1962), 166–76.

2. Hesiod, Theogony 614.

3. Hesiod, Theog. 565–616; Aeschylus, Prometheus Vinctus 218, 282, 445 ff., 478 ff.; Theophrastus, apud Ap. Rh. ii.1248 (philosophy); Servius, on Vergil, Ecl. vi.42 (astronomy); I. Bekker, Anecdot. ii.781, 28 (letters); O. Gruppe, Griech. Mythologie (1906), 1025, n.4.

4. An early name for him was Ithas, which may be connected with Greek *aithô*, Sanskrit *idh-*, "burn."

5. The tradition seems to be mentioned in Horace, Odes ii.18, 34 ff.; cf. S. Reinach, in Rev. archéol. 1903.176.

6. Hesiod, Theog. 507 ff.; Apollodorus, Bib. i.11.3. Apollodorus uses the word *katatartaroô*, with which may be compared *tartaroô*, used of the expulsion of the rebel angels, in I Pet. 2:4.

7. Cf. H. Weil, in RÉG 6 (1893), 304; Gruppe, op. cit. 1026, n.1.

8. Hesiod, Theog. 613–16.

9. I take the "bosses" and "sockets" mentioned in v. 13 to denote the protuberances and orifices of the body.—E. Lipinski, in Syria 42 (1965), 49–52, suggests that the "socket" (read as sg.) is the vagina, and the "boss" the *membrum virile,* the king of Tyre being thus portrayed as a hermaphrodite! This interpretation seems to me to emasculate the point.

10. E. A. W. Budge, The Egyptian Book of the Dead (1895), 14.6–7.

11. Bibl. Aegyptiaca, iv.27, 16.

12. The Contendings of Horus and Seth, 14 = G. Lefebvre, Romans égyptiens (1949), 197.

13. Westcar Papyrus, App. iv.10, 11 = Lefebvre, op. cit. 87, n.78.

14. Ch. Maystre, in BIFAO 40 (1941), 53–73; A. Erman, Literatur der Aegypter (1923), 47–49; J. A. Wilson, in ANET 10–11.

15. F. A. Schaeffer, The Cuneiform Texts from Ras Shamra-Ugarit (1939), Pl. xxxv.1, p. 93.

16. The Hebrew is usually rendered "stones of fire," about which wondrous theories have been spun. My translation rests on the fact that in an Akkadian lexical text (CT XIX.5, obv.5) the expression "stone of fire" identifies a particular gem called *ḫipindû.* What this was, however, is as yet unknown. The name has been connected with the Semitic *pindu = pêmtu,* "coal," but this leaves the first syllable unexplained. I suspect that *ḫipindû* is an Anatolian word with the same ending as in jac*inth,* hyac*inth,* etc. (The long final *-û* suggests, in any case, that the word is a loan.)

17. Cf., for example, Pseudo-Epiphanius, Hexaemeron 226, ed. Trumpp (Abh. Bay. Akad. Wiss. 16, 1882): "God took fire and made garments of light for the angels."

18. Nonnus, Dionys. vi.260 ff.; Proclus, on Plato, Timaeus i.188.26 ff.; id., in Rep. i.93, 22 f.; Eusthathius in Iliadem, pp. 231 f., 332.

19. Olympiodorus, on Plato, Phaedo 61E (p. 227 f., ed. Norwin).

20. B. Schmidt, Griechische Märchen, etc. (1887), 131.

21. J. C. Lawson, Modern Greek Folklore and Ancient Greek Religion (reprint, 1966) 73.

22. Tale of the Shipwrecked Sailor, 73–74 Lefebvre, op. cit., 35.

214　Pharaoh and the Nile

1. See: H. Frankfort, Kingship and the Gods (1948), 58 f.

2. Kubban Stele, 17–18 = Breasted, AR iii.§288.

3. Breasted, op. cit. §423.

4. E. Drioton, in Egyptian Religion 1 (1933), 39 ff.

5. Frankfort, op. cit. 94–95.

6. See: Frazer-Gaster, NGB §§65–75; P. Hadfield, Traits of Divine Kingship in

Africa (1949), 17 ff.; C. Seligman, Pagan Tribes of Nilotic Sudan (1932), 329 ff.; S. S. Doran, "Rain-making in South Africa," in Bantu Studies 3 (1927–29), 185–95; W. E. R. Cole, "African Rain-making Chiefs," in Man (1910); O. Petersson, Chiefs and Gods (1953).

7. Book of the Dead, ch. 29; Papyrus of Nesi-Amsu, ed. Budge, in Archaeologia 52 (1890), 502 ff.; id., The Gods of the Egyptians (1904), 324–28; G. Roeder, Urkunden zur Religion des alten Aegyptens (1923), 98–115. Useful also, even though partially antiquated, is P. le Page Renouf's article in TSBA 8 (1883), 217 ff.

8. See: E. Tylor, Primitive Culture³ (1891), 325 f.; H. Gunkel, Schöpfung und Chaos in Urzeit und Endzeit (1895), 41–69.

9. Rig Veda v.40.

10. Buddhagosa i.9; Samyutta i.50, tr. C. A. F. Rhys Davids, Kindred Sayings (1918), i.71.

11. T. Fu, in ERE xii.77.

12. E. Welsford, ib., 102ª.

13. W. Schott, De lingua Tschuwaschorum (1841), 5.

14. Grimm-Stallybrass, TM (1880), 707.

15. Saᶜadyah, Introd. to Emunôth wᵉ-Deᶜôth; L. Ginzberg, Legends of the Jews (1909 sqq.), v. 108, 116. Cf. also: Maximus of Turin, in Migne PL vii.337; Hrabanus Maurus, Op. v. 606, Colyr.; Tacitus, Ann. i.28.

16. G. A. Smith, The Book of the Twelve Prophets² (1904), ii.524.

17. C. O. Blagden, Pagan Races of the Malay Peninsula (1906), ii.203–4.

18. R. Lasch, in ARW 3 (1900), 136.

19. T. H. Gaster, Thespis², 228 f.

215 The parable of the cedar

1. Herodotus, i.108.

2. Valerius Maximus, i.7, extr. v.7.

3. Herodotus, vii.19.

4. E.g., R. F. Harper, Assyrian and Babylonian Letters (1902), #656, rev. 6 ff.; KARI #324.9.

5. Kalevala, runo ii.111–224; tr. Kirby (Everyman's Library ed.), i.13–16.

6. Vita Ephraem, cited in Brockelmann, Syr. Gr. 29** 16 ff.

7. E. Sklarek, Ungarische Volksmärchen, N.F. (1901), 13 ff., 26 ff.

8. P. Zaunert, Deutsche Märchen seit Grimm (1919), 1 ff.; cf. W. Wundt, Völker-psychologie² (1915), ii/3, 192.

9. Concerning this motif in general, see: Deonna, in RHR 84 (1921), 36 ff.; E. Meyer, Ursprung und Anfänge des Christenthums, iii (1921), 36 ff.; E. L. Ehrlich, Der Traum im AT (1953), 117 f.

10. Dan. 4:10–12.

11. H. Gunkel, Das Märchen im AT (1921), 24 ff.—On the world-tree, see: Stith Thompson, MI, A 652.

12. Trans. Speiser, ANET 78–82.

13. S. N. Kramer, in JCS 1 (1947), 3–56; id., ANET 47–50.

14. The traditional Hebrew text reads: Unto (sic!) the mountains and in all the valleys, after its branches have fallen, will its boughs lie broken. Reading, with LXX, upon (Heb.: ᶜal) for unto (Heb.: 'el), I construe the first clause with the preceding will leave it.

15. Cf. T. Canaan, in JPOS 4 (1929), 35 ff.

16. The Hebrew for "Assyria" is 'aššûr. By a very slight emendation this can be made to yield tᵉ'aššûr, "pine"—a reading which many modern scholars adopt. Another suggestion is to read 'ašwᵉkā, "I will liken thee (to a cedar)" which is followed by RSV.

216 The dimming of the sun

1. Joel 2:10; 4:15.
2. On dark raiment in Semitic mourning, see: A. J. Wensinck, Some Semitic Rites of Mourning and Religion (1917), 60 ff.; E. W. Lane, Arabic Lexicon, i.86. Cf. also: T. H. Gaster, Thespis², 214.
3. Pliny, HN ii.98; Plutarch, Caesar 68; Dio Cassius, xlv.17, 5; Appian, Bellum civile iv.4, 14; Servius, on Vergil, Georgica i.472.
4. Vergil, Georgica i.462 ff.
5. Ovid, Met. xv.785 f.
6. Tibullus, ii.5, 75 f. (F. Kirby Smith, in his commentary ad loc., attributes the darkness to an eruption of Mt. Etna, and compares the effects of the volcanic disturbances in the Pacific in 1883. The Italian sun, he adds, was unusually dim in the summer of 1906, after a great eruption of Vesuvius.)

217 Kôshar, the god of minstrelsy

1. M. Dahood, in Biblica 44 (1963), 531–32.
2. See fully: T. H. Gaster, Thespis², 162 f., 339.
3. Quoted, from the Greek rendering by Philo of Byblus, in Eusebius, Praep. evangelica i.10, 1 f.
4. It should be observed, however, that—strictly speaking—Sanchuniathon speaks of *incantations* (*epōdai*), not of songs in general. This connects with the fact that Kôshar was primarily the god of smithcraft, and the smith is commonly regarded as a master of magic; see above, §22. In exactly the same way, the Greeks regarded the mythical Daktyloi as both the discoverers and first workers in iron and as the founders of the magical arts.—The point, however, need not be pressed, for the analogous *kôsharôth* certainly meant "songstresses" in general, and there are good parallels (e.g., Greek *poiêtês*, Sanskrit *takś-*, German *Reimschmied*) for the transference of meaning from *artisan* to *artist;* see: Gaster, loc. cit.
5. Cf. H. L. Ginsberg, in BASOR 72 (1938), 13–15.
6. Cf. J. Barth, Die Nominalbildung in der semitischen (1889–91), §127c.

218 The thread of life

1. F. Perles, in OLz 12 (1909), 251 f.
2. The word rendered *thread,* vix., *nawel,* does not recur in the Old Testament, and this would readily account for the misreading of it. It is, however, not uncommon in post-Biblical Hebrew, and possesses an Akkadian cognate in *nam/wālu.*
3. Cf. Jos. 2:18,21 (RSV: cord).—Such double-entendre, called *tawriyya* by Arab rhetoricians, is a common device in Biblical and Semitic poetry: see J. Finkel, in Joshua Starr Memorial Volume (1952), 29 ff.

HOSEA

221 Hosea and the pagan festivals

1. Cf. E. Jacob, "L'héritage canaanéen dans le livre du prophète Osée," in RHPR 43 (1963), 250–59; H. G. May, "The Fertility Cult in Hosea," in AJSL 48 (1932), 93–98.
2. Israel sows the wind and reaps the whirlwind (8:7). She is likened to grapes and new figs (9:10); Ephraim, to blighted fruit (9:16). She was originally like a spreading vine (10:1). Judgment will spring up like noxious weeds (10:4). Judah must plow,

and Israel harrow for herself (10:10). Israel has planted iniquity, reaped injustice, and fed on the fruit of lies (10:13).—If the text be read against the background of a harvest festival, added point is given also to the words of 6:11: *Also, O Judah, he (Yahweh) hath set a harvest for thee"*—words usually "emended" by modern scholars.

3. Hos. 13:15. Cf., conversely, the promise of eventual dewfall and fertility in 14:5–8.

4. A. Moret, La mise à mort du dieu en Égypte (1927), 18n.

5. I AB, v.23; cf. V AB, iii.41.

6. T. H. Gaster, Thespis², 303 f.

7. Cf. the Homeric Hymn to Demeter.

8. There is also, of course, the notion of "giving us the slip"; cf. Akkadian *ḫalāṣu*.

9. Heb., simply, "Behind you!" which means properly, "Look to your rear!" There is a good Arabic parallel to this idiom, and the text need not be emended (as in RSV).

10. Mishnah, Sukkah iv.9; cf. D. Feuchtwang, in MGWJ 54 (1910), 535 ff.; I. Scheftelowitz, Altpal. Bauernglaube (1925), 93–95.

11. Lucian, De dea Syria 3, 48.

12. The Hebrew word does not refer to resurrection, but simply to bringing a sick man to his feet.

13. Frazer-Gaster, NGB §§207, 231–32.

14. Plutarch, De Is. et Os. 39; Frazer-Gaster, NGB §259.

15. Plutarch, Alcibiades 18; Lucian, De dea Syria 6.

16. Diodorus, iii.59, 7; cf. H. Hepding, Attis (1903), 131 f.

17. Frazer-Gaster, NGB §207.

18. M. Beza, Paganism in Roumanian Folklore (1928), 30. Analogous is the Pietro Puco of the Abruzzi: E. Canziani, in Folk-Lore 39 (1928), 218.

19. This paragraph is taken substantially from the writer's Thespis², 47 f.

20. Arnobius, Adversus nationes v.42; Macrobius, Sat. i.21, 7–11; cf. H. Hepding, Attis (1903), 44, 63.

21. S. Langdon, Babylonian Menologies and the Semitic Calendars (1935), 119 f.

22. Ezek. 8:14–16.

23. R. Labat, in RA 38 (1941), 28.

24. S. Langdon, Tammuz and Ishtar (1914), 32.

25. The so-called "Yuzgat Tablet" = A. Goetze, Verstreute Texte (1935), #58; cf. T. H. Gaster, Thespis², 273.

26. I AB, i.8–16.

27. I AB, vi.22–29.

28. I AB, vi.40–52.

29. Cf. O. Rankin, The Origin of the Feast of Hanukkah (1930), 205 f. Cf. also: F. Boll, in ARW 19 (1916–19), 240, 342; O. Weber, ib., 315 f.

30. Weber, op. cit., 325 f.

31. Rankin, op. cit., 201 f.

32. Cf. also: TJ Sanhedrin, 18d.

33. Reading *yithgôDᵉDŪ* for the traditional text's *yithgôRāRū*.

34. Cf. Hepding, op. cit., 159.

35. Gaster, Thespis², 41.

36. Herodotus, i.199; cf. Strabo, xvi.1, 20.

37. Herodotus, ib.; cf. Athenaeus, xi.11; Justin, xviii.5, 4.

38. Strabo, xii.3, 32–36.

39. Gaster, Thespis², loc. cit.

40. J. Toepfer, in Athenische Mitteilungen, 1898.415.

41. A. Deissmann, Light from the East² (1911), 116.

42. Toepfer, loc. cit.

43. Tibullus, ii.i., 24.

44. Pervigilium Veneris, 5.

45. Cf. May, op. cit.

46. A similar metaphor occurs in 13:7–8.

47. Apollodorus, Bib. iii.14, 4; Bion, i; Athenaeus, ii.80; Plutarch, Quaest. conviv. iv.5, 3 §8; Ovid, Met. 10.710 ff.; Hyginus, #248. Cf. O. Gruppe, Griechische Mythologie (1906), 1277.

48. Hermesianax, cited by Pausanias, vii.17, 9; Scholiast on Nikander, Alex. 8.

49. Hyginus, #192; Gruppe, op. cit., 950, n.1.

50. Schol. in Iliad 18.570; Propertius, iii (ii.13), 4; Gruppe, op. cit., 968, n.3.

51. Pollux 4.55; Eustathius, on Iliad 4.791.

52. Apoll. Rhod., Argon. 2.815–50; cf. Kraack, in GGA 1896.873.

53. Gruppe, op. cit., 968.

54. W. von Baudissin, Adonis und Esmun (1911), 142, gives reasons for believing that in the myth of Adonis this element is a later intrusion.

55. Gaster, Thespis[1], 217 ff. (omitted in the second ed.).

56. The usual Hebrew word for "look after" is *p-q-d,* not *šûr.*

57. Concerning these goddesses, cf. T. H. Gaster, "The Religion of the Canaanites," in V. Ferm's Ancient (Forgotten) Religions, 125–29; E. Pilz, in ZDPV 47 (1924), 129–68; J. Pritchard, Palestinian Figurines in relation to Certain Goddesses known through Literature (1943).

58. Or, *Whoever is wise,* let him understand, etc.

59. L. Oppenheim, in Orientalia 16 (1947), 237.

222   Gomer, daughter of Diblaim

1. So far, no Semitic personal name is known containing the element *d-b-l,* whereas, as a place-name, Diblaim may be compared with (Beth) Diblathaim, in Moab, and with Dibl, in Galilee.

2. We may compare how Joel (3:12) locates the final judgment on the nations at the Valley of Jehoshapat, i.e., "Yahweh judges," and how Hosea himself declares (2:15) that the Valley of Achor, i.e., "tribulation," will yet become a "gateway of hope."

3. E. Nestle, in ZAW 29 (1909), 233 f.

4. Rassam Cylinder, §ix.; tr. L. Oppenheim, in ANET 299[b]. The American equivalent would be "a row of beans."

5. On this gesture, see HWbDA, s.v. *Feige.*

6. Theocritus, x.45; Antiphon, Cleoph. ii.4; Lucian, Indoct. vi.

7. Scholiast on Theocritus, loc. cit. T. Gaisford, Poetae Minores Graeci (1830), iv.152 f.; Hemsterhuis, on Aristophanes, Ploutos, p. 328.

8. Comicorum Atticorum Fragmenta, ed. Kock, Anon. 7.

223   Gomer's children

1. W. R. Smith, Kinship and Marriage in Early Arabia[2] (1903), 32, 37, 72, 177. The expressions *'akka 'l-raḥim* and *kata'a 'l-raḥim* mean "to rupture the ties of kinship." The Hebrew equivalent is *š-ḥ-ṭ raḥ^{a}mîm* (RSV: "cast off all pity"), in Amos 1:11. It seems to me that meter and sense alike demand the restoration of this idiom in Ps. 78:38, where for the traditional text's *w^{e}hû' RaḤūM y^{e}kapper 'āwôn w^{e}lô' yaŠḤîTH* we should read, by transposition, *w^{e}hû' y^{e}kapper 'awôn w^{e}lô' y^{e}ŠaḤeTH RaḤ^{a}Māw,* thus obtaining the sense, "But He—He shrives wrongdoing, and breaks not the ties of love," in place of the usual, "But He, being compassionate, forgave their iniquity, and did not destroy them."

2. Smith, loc. cit.; J. Wellhausen, Ehe bei den Arabern (1893), 480, n.4; G. Jacob, Studien in arabischen Dichtern, I: Noten zum Verständniss der Mu'allaqat (1894), 92.

224 Stripping a divorcee

1. Cf. L. Kohler, in ZAW 34 (1914), 146, who sees further allusions to this custom in Isa. 47:4 and Ezek. 16:35. See also: S. Smith, Isaiah xl–xlv (1944), 98, n.90.

2. A 3534.26 (unpublished; cited in CAD, s.v. ḥamāṣu).

3. JEN 444.22. The late Isaac Mendelsohn referred me also to HSS XIX.10.13–15; 19.22–24.

4. J. A. Montgomery, Aramaic Incantation Texts from Nippur (1913), 158.

5. Tacitus, Germania xix; cf. C. H. Gordon, The Living Past (1941), 171, 215 f.

6. Cf. A. E. Crawley, in ERE v.51[b].

7. A. T. Clay, in BEUP XV.55, 10–11; A. Ungnad, in OLz 9.163 f.; 12.479; G. R. Driver, Semitic Writing (1948), 63.

8. Theocritus, ii.53–55. The Greek word is kraspedôn, which in LXX Num. 15:36 renders Heb. ṣiṣîth, the tassel on the fringe of a robe. It is therefore of interest to observe that in a modern Hebrew charm from Mossul the ṣiṣith is likewise used for purposes of envoûtement. Theocritus says explicitly (line 162) that the lovelorn woman learned her magic from "an Assyrian (i.e., Semitic) stranger."

9. Tetian-Temme, Volksagen Ostpreussens (1837), 883 f.

10. F. Thureau-Dangin, Rituels accadiens (1921), 127–54, lines 415 ff.; tr. A. Sachs, ANET 334.

11. B. Landsberger, Die Serie ana ittišu (1937), 99, ii.50; cf. also: L. Boyer, in Studies and Documents, ii.208–18; Driver, loc. cit., n.5.

12. J. Georgi, Russia (1780–83), i.42.

13. F. Nork, in Das Kloster 12 (1849), 1136; J. Grimm, Deutsche Rechtsalterthümer[3] (1881), 712.

14. W. Gesenius, Thesaurus, 742[b], s.v. l[e]būš. Gesenius would recognize this sense in Mal. 2:16, which he would render: But the Lord God of Israel has declared that he has always hated divorce and always been prepared to hide (lit. has always hidden) the (signs of) crime on a man's garment (i.e., his wife). This has been followed by many more recent interpreters, but I think the whole passage (14–16) has been commonly misunderstood or "emended" out of its plain sense. I would suggest the following rendering: Yahweh himself was the witness (to the troth) between you and the wife of your youth, whom you have betrayed, even though she was your comrade and the woman to whom you had pledged your faith. There is no one man (on earth), who has a vestige of spirit within him, who has ever acted like that. What would such a man be seeking? Some sort of divine offspring? . . . Nay, let no man betray the wife of his youth! For Yahweh, God of Israel, has declared that he has (always) hated divorce and been ready to cover up (lit. has always covered up) the (marks of) crime which are (all too patently visible) on such a man's garment, i.e., the man is all too often himself culpable, but God prefers to help him conceal his faults rather than be exposed to the scandal and recriminations of divorce. The expression, signs of crime on his garment, thus refers to his, rather than his wife's, guilt. Consequently, his garment cannot here stand for his wife, for that would yield just the wrong sense.

15. Koran 2:183.

16. Indo-Chinese Gleaner (Malacca 1818), i.164.

17. C. H. W. Johns, in PSBA 29 (1907), 180.

18. W. R. Smith, Kinship and Marriage in Early Arabia[2] (1903), 112 f.

19. E. Westermarck, Pagan Survivals in Mohammedan Civilization (1933), 68 f.

225 Marriage formulas

1. Exod. 25:7; I Sam. 14:3; 22:18, etc.

2. I Sam. 2:18.

3. II. Sam. 6:14.

4. RŠ 67.i, 4–5; Gordon: *ttrp šmm krs ipdk,* where *ttrp* is a verb and has nothing to do with *teraphîm.* The passage probably means "the heavens will sag like the girdle [read *kr<k>s;* cf. the verb *r-k-s* used of the fastening of the ephôd in Exod. 28:28; 39:21] of thy wrap"; cf. W. F. Albright, in BASOR 83 (1941), 40 f.—In Isa. 30:22, the golden *'aphūdah* of a molten image is probably a sheath of gold plating, or a covering of gold leaf such as has actually been found on a statue of Baal at Ras Shamra.

5. E.G., W. R. Arnold, The Ephôd and the Ark (1917); E. Sellin, in Nöldeke Festschrift (1906), 699 ff.; J. Morgenstern, in HUCA 18 (1944), 1–17.

227 David redivivus

1. EBB I, col. 31a. What is involved is the change of *Kî M-YŚRaEL* to *Kî My Šôr EL.*

2. E.g., I AB, iii–iv.34; vi.37; II AB, ii.10; iii.31; iv–v.47; V AB, E 18, 43; I Krt, 41, 59, 76, 169. Cf. M. Pope, El in the Ugaritic Texts (1955), 35 f.; F. L. Løkegaard, "A Plea for El the Bull," in Studia Orientalia J. Perdersen (1953), 219–53.

3. Cf. T. H. Gaster, Thespis², 172. E. Burrows, in PEFQS 1935.87 ff., finds the divine name *Šw[r]*, "Bull," on the celebrated Tell ed-Duweir Ewer.

4. Note, significantly, the personal name *'glyw,* composed of *'gl,* "calf," and the shorter form of Yahweh, on a Samarian ostracon of the 8th cent. B.C.

230 Oil in the making of covenants

1. Cf. K. Deller, in Biblica 46 (1965), 349–52. Cf. also: D. J. McCarthy, in VT 14 (1964), 215–21.

JOEL

231 Joel and the pagan festivals

1. Cf. T. H. Gaster, Thespis², 71–76. The same idea underlies A. S. Kapelrud's Joel Studies (1948).

(a)

2. Diodorus Siculus, iii.67 (from Dionysus Skythobracchion).

3. Scholiast on Clem. Alex., Protrept., p. 297.4, Stählin.

4. Plutarch, Theseus 22.

5. Clem. Alex., Paidag. II.1.ii, 2; Johann von Krolewitz, ed. Lisch, in Kirchner's Bib. d. deutsch. Nationalliteratur 19 (1839), 26; cf. R. Eisler, Orphisch-Dionysische Mysteriengedanken (1925), 226 ff.

6. Ibn al-Athir, 10.28, ed. Toraberg.

7. K. Bücher, Arbeit und Rhythmus⁶ (1924), 124.

8. The Poem of the Gracious Gods (52, Gordon), 8–11; cf. Gaster, op. cit., 420 f.; J. Finkel, in Joshua Starr Memorial Volume (1952), 29 ff.

(b)

9. Diodorus Siculus, i.14.

10. Herodotus, ii.79; cf. Julius Pollux, iv.54; Pausanias, ix.29, 7; Athenaeus, xiv.11, p. 620A.

11. See J. de Hoorack, Les lamentations d'Isis et Nephthys (1866); E. A. W. Budge,

Osiris and the Egyptian Resurrection (1911), ii.59–66; A. Moret, Mystères égyptiens (1913), 24–26.

12. Firmicus Maternus, De errore profanarum religionum ii.7; cf. also: A. Moret, La mise à mort du dieu en Égypte (1927), 19 ff.

13. A. L. Oppenheim, in BASOR 103 (1946), 11–14.

14. Semus, quoted by Athenaeus 618E; cf. E. Spanheim, In Callimachi hymnos observationes (1967), 649.

(c)

15. T. H. Gaster, op. cit., 26–28.

16. KUB XVII.10, i.16–18; Gaster, op. cit., 303; A. Goetze, in ANET 126[b].

17. Hymn to Demeter, 302–13.

18. Gaster, op. cit., 286.

19. I AB, iii–iv.25–27, 36–38; Gaster, op. cit., 223; H. L. Ginsberg, in ANET 141[a].

(d)

20. The Hebrew word ba-śaqqîm, "in sackcloth," goes with the preceding verb ḥigrū, "begird yourselves," as well as with lînū, "pass the night."

21. Sophocles, Antigone 1146 f.; Euripides, Bacchae 485–86, 862 ff.; Aristophanes, Frogs 340. Cf. also: Herodotus, iv.76; Pindar, fr. 79.

22. Firmicus Maternus, De errore prof. relig. xxii.1–3.

23. Vassits, Die Fackel in Kult und Kunst der Griechen (1900), 18 ff.; Allen-Sikes-Halliday, The Homeric Hymns[2] (1936), 120 f.

24. Macrobius, Sat. i.18, 10; Epiphanius, Panarion 51; cf. E. Norden, Die Geburt des Kindes (1924), 25; Gaster, op. cit. 276.

25. Ezek. 8:7–16.

(e)

26. Gaster, op. cit. 30 f., 52, n.60.

27. Ib., 27 f.

28. KAV p. 20, ii.22–28; KAR 177, rev. 3; cf. R. Labat, Le caractère religieux de la royauté assyro-babylonienne (1939), 315.

29. Leviticus, ch. 16.

30. Aristophanes, Birds 1519; Plutarch, De Iside et Osiride 69.—In corresponding myth, Demeter was said to have abstained from food while searching for Persephone: Homeric Hymn to Demeter, 49–50; Callimachus, Demeter 17 (cf. Spanheim, op. cit., 671 f.)

31. Diodorus Siculus, v.4; Plato, Epist. 349D; Allen-Sikes-Halliday, op. cit., 135.

32. L. R. Farnell, Cults of the Greek States (1896–1909), iii.34.

33. Julian, Or. v.173D, 177A; Arnobius, Adversus nationes v.16; Tertullian, Adversus physicos de jejunio, c.16; cf. H. Hepding, Attis (1903), 182 ff.; G. A. Lobeck, Aglaophamus (1829), 247 ff.

34. For the fast in October, cf. Livy, xxxvi.37; cf. also: Ovid, Met. x.432; id., Fasti iv.535; G. Wissowa, in P-W, iii.1780.

35. Gaster, op. cit., 27 f.

36. Cabaton, in ERE iii.161[a].

37. L. Spence, in ERE iii.507[a], 568[b].

38. T. C. Hodson, The Naga Tribes of Manipur (1911), 167; id., in JAI 36 (1906), 94 f.

39. C. Seligman, The Melanesians of British New Guinea (1910), 590.

40. Chateaubriand, Voyage en Amérique (1870), 130 f.

41. W. Brown, New Zealand and Its Aborigines (1845), 113.

42. W. H. Prescott, History of the Conquest of Peru (1890), 50.

(f)

43. Frazer-Gaster, NGB §§444–52.

44. G. Gay, in Bull. soc. géogr. de Paris, III/19 (1843), 29 f.

45. J. G. Frazer, GB, one-vol. ed., 554.

46. M. Buch, Die Wotjäken (1882), 153 f.

47. J. G. Frazer, GB, one-vol. ed., 555.

48. G. Brown, Melanesians and Polynesians (1910), 413 f.

49. Frazer, op. cit., 555.

50. Ib., 558.

(g)

51. Frazer-Gaster, NGB §206.

52. T. H. Gaster, Thespis², 37–40, 63, 77, 89, 268.

53. Census of India 1911, IV/i.65 ff. (as quoted by J. G. Frazer, Aftermath [1936], 75–77).

54. R. O. Winstedt, Shama, Saiwa and Sufi (1925), 92.

(h)

55. H. Frankfort, Kingship and the Gods (1948), 168–69, 183–84, 320.

56. S. A. Pallis, The Babylonian Akîtu Festival (1926), 183–97; mythologized in Enuma Elish vi.69 ff.

57. Note that the Hebrew word here employed is *šaphaṭ,* which refers to the rendering of legal decisions, rather than *dîn* (elsewhere used of God's rule: Gen. 49:16; Deut. 32:36; Pss. 9:9; 72:7, etc.), which refers to general administration and government.

(i)

58. I AB, iii.7; Gaster, op. cit., 222.

233 The foe from the north

1. For the historical implications, see: Stocks, in NKZ 1908.725–50; K. Budde, in OLz 22 (1919), 1–5.

2. Stith Thompson, MI, G 633; T. H. Gaster, Thespis², 182.

3. Satapatha Brahmana I.2, 4, 10; XII. 5, i, 11, etc.

4. I. Scheftelowitz, Die altpersische Religion und das Judenthum (1920), 59.

5. W. M. Brandt, Die mandäische Religion (1889), 67 ff.

6. J. L. Lauterbach, in HUCA 2 (1925), 364; n.31; Sepher Raziel (1701), 15ᵃ; Chronicles of Jerahmeel, i.17 (p. 6, ed. M. Gaster).

7. Moses Isserles, *Torath ha-ʿolah* (1858), ii.25.

8. G. Flügel, Mani, seine Lehre und seine Schriften (1862), 101.

9. Pap. Bibl. Nat. 269; Pap. Leyden W, col. xviii.27.

10. Plutarch, De Iside et Osiride 21; cf. S. Eitrem, Papyri Osloenses, i (1925), 34.

11. L. Spence, The Mythologies of Mexico and Peru (1907), 24.

12. L. C. Wimberly, Folklore in the English and Scottish Ballads (reprint, 1959), 137 ff.; F. B. Gummere, Germanic Origins (1892), 418n.

13. J. Hansen, Quellen und Untersuchungen zur Gesch. des Hexenwahns . . . im Mittelalter (1901), 208.

14. Menahem Ziyyuni of Speyer, Sepher Ziyyuni 48ᵈ; cf. J. Trachtenberg, Jewish Magic and Superstition (1939), 34.

15. T. H. Gaster, Customs and Folkways of Jewish Life (1964), 61.

16. Brand-Ellis, Popular Antiquities of Great Britain (1900), ii.292.

AMOS

234 Amos and the pagan festivals

1. Cf. T. H. Gaster, Thespis[2], 68; H. Hepding, Attis (1903), 44, 49, 54.
2. Gaster, op. cit., 66, 124, 195 ff.
3. Cf. Hepding, op. cit., 165 f.
4. LXX reads "thunder" (Heb.: *hara'am*) for "mountains" (*hārîm*). If this is correct, it is worth noting that the Canaanite Baal was recognized as the lord of thunder, his alternative name being Hadad (or Hadd), "the Crasher." The LXX reading, however, involves an odd use of the Hebrew word (*y-ṣ-r*) rendered "creator." This means primarily "moulder, shaper," and although it is sometimes employed in an extended sense (as in Isa. 47:5; Ps. 74:17), one can scarcely *mould* a noise.
5. Gaster, op. cit., 124 f.
6. Cf. G. Furlani, Rel. bab. e assira (1929), ii.216 f.
7. Gaster, op. cit., 342; S. Smith, in PEQ 78 (1946), 5–14.
8. Heb. *'aṣārah*, often rendered "solemn assembly," is here derived from *'-ṣ-r*, "restrain." The reference is to the characteristic austerities (Greek: *hagisteiai;* Latin: *castus*) of seasonal ceremonies; cf. Gaster, op. cit., 26 ff., 62.

235 Judgment by fire

1. The rendering "earth" is approximate, but not exact. The Hebrew word (*ḥeleq*) means properly "field, groundplot" (cf. Akkadian *eqlu*, etc.), but by a clever play it also suggests that the field or territory in question is the peculiar "portion" (Heb. *ḥeleq*), or estate, of Yahweh; cf. Deut. 32.9. For a parallel picture, cf. Isa. 27:4.
2. O. Eissfeldt, The Old Testament: an Introduction (1965), 227. I. Seligmann, in VT 14 (1964), 75–92, dates it to "pre-regnal times."
3. Isa. 34:8–9.
4. Mal. 3:19.
5. Dan. 7:10 f.
6. Enoch 91:9.
7. Psalms of Solomon, 15:14 f.
8. Manual of Discipline, ii.8 = T. H. Gaster, The Dead Sea Scriptures[2] (1964), 48.
9. Hymns, iii.19 f. = Gaster, op. cit., 146.
10. Matt. 18:9; Mark 9:43; Luke 17:28; II Pet. 3:7 ff.
11. It is called "the ordeal of molten metal" (*aya khshusta*); cf. Yasna 31:3; 43:4; 47:6; 51:9; Yasht 22:33. See especially: R. Mayer, Ist die biblische Vorstellung vom Weltenbrand eine Entlehnung aus dem Parsismus? (1947); C. Clemen, Primitive Christianity and Its non-Jewish Sources (1912), 161 f.
12. Yasht 19:14, 89.
13. Bundahisn 30:18.
14. Seneca, Nat. Qu., ii.29.1.
15. Cf. F. Cumont, The Oriental Religions in Roman Paganism (1911), 210.
16. H. Diels, Die Fragmente der Vorsokratiker[1] (1903), 62 f. (quotations from Theophrastus and Aetius).
17. M. Eliade, The Myth of the Eternal Return (1954), 88.
18. Cf. T. H. Gaster, "Cosmogony," in IDB.
19. Vergil, Ecl., 4.5.
20. S. Langdon, Semitic Mythology (1931), 320.
21. This quasi-mythological designation recurs in Ps. 36:7 (also, in the Masoretic text, in Gen. 7:11, but the Greek Version there omits the adjective).

22. Langdon, op. cit., 315.
23. Cf. L. Ginzberg, Legends of the Jews, v.149–50.
24. D. R. Hillers, in CBQ 26 (1964), 221–25.
25. Others have emended *La-RîB* to *Li-ŠᵉBîB,* i.e., "to a spark," or to *LaHaB,* "a flame." These emendations too miss the point.

JONAH

236 The story of Jonah

(a) Sailing with an "unholy" person

1. Aeschylus, Septem contra Thebas 602 ff.
2. Antiphon, De caed. Herod. 82.
3. Theophrastus, Characters xxv.l.
4. Plautus, Rudens 505.
5. Horace, Odes iii.2, 26.
6. The Times Literary Supplement, Dec. 13, 1957, as quoted in R. G. Ussher, The Characters of Theophrastus (1960), 211.

(b) Man cast overboard to allay storm

7. Stith Thompson, MI, S 264.1.
8. Jataka #439; cf. E. G. Hardy, in ZDMG 50 (1896), 153.
9. F. J. Child, The English and Scottish Popular Ballards (1882–98), #24; F. B. Gummere, The Popular Ballad (reprint, 1959), 214; L. C. Wimberly, Folklore in the English and Scottish Ballards (reprint 1959), 98.
10. Child, op. cit., #57; ib., v.496; Gummere, loc. cit.
11. A. Aarne and S. Thompson, The Types of the Folktale (1928), #973*. Cf. also: V. Chauvin, Bibliographie des oeuvres arabes (1892–1909), vii.30, #212, n.2.
12. Notes and Queries I/x (1854), 26.

(c) Swallowed and disgorged intact

13. Stith Thompson, op. cit., F 911.4; J. MacCulloch, The Childhood of Fiction (1905), 50; W. A. Clouston, Popular Tales and Fictions (1887), i.403 ff.
14. Somadeva, Katha Sarit Sagara, ch. 25, 139 f. ed. Brockhaus (1839); N. M. Penzer, The Ocean of Story (1923–29), ii.193; iv.154, n.3.
15. H. Schmidt, Jona (1907), 127 f.
16. Tzetzes, Scholiast on Lycophron, 34; Scholiast on Iliad 20.146. This is a variant of the story of how Heracles rescued Hesione, daughter of Laomedon (cf. Apollodorus, Bib., II.5.9, and Frazer, in loc.)
17. R. B. Dixon, Oceanic Mythology (1916), 69.
18. E. Petitot, Trad. ind. du Canada Nord-ouest (1886), 319; M. Barbeau, in JAFL 39.11.
19. G. Basile, Pentamerone v.8.—There are also variants from Samoa (G. Turner, Samoa a hundred years ago and long before [1884], 331, 337) and Guiana (F. Im Thurm, Among the Indians of Guiana [1883], 385).
20. J. A. van Balen, in BTLVNI 70 (1915), 465.
21. Quoted by J. G. Einhorn, Einleitung in das AT (1780–86), 249, from Müller's translation of Linné. Cf. also: E. Perowne, Jonah, in the Cambridge Bible for Schools, App. ii.
22. Probus, on Vergil, Georgica ii.197; cf. Pausanias, x.13, 10.
23. Servius, on Vergil, Aen. iii.332.
24. Koiranos was on his way between Naxos and Paros. A brigand crew threw him

overboard, but a dolphin rescued him and carried him to Sikunthos (? Sikenos): Plutarch, De sollert. animalium xxxvi.12; Aelian, De natura animalium viii.3.

25. Herodotus, i.24; Pausanias, iii.25, 5; Hyginus, fab. 194.

26. Aarne-Thompson, op. cit., ##333, 700; Penzer, op. cit. vi.154, n.3; P. Saintyves, Les contes de Perrault (1923), 227 ff.; Bolte-Polivka i.37, 40, 389.

27. The following two paragraphs are adapted from my Festivals of the Jewish Year (1953), 174 f. Cf. also: Notes and Queries 1/iv (1851), 45, 178 f.

(d) Jonah's prayer

28. In 2:7 I read: *ha-areṣ bᵉrîḥêhā ba'adî Nᵉ'ūLîM* for the traditional text's *ha-areṣ bᵉrîḥêhā ba'adî Lᵉ'ôLaM*, i.e., "Earth's bars *were bolted* against me." The roots of the mountains are likewise mentioned in Babylonian literature as the bars of the earth: cf. M. Jastrow, Rel. Bab. und Ass. (1905–12), i.30.4.

(e) Animals dressed in mourning

29. On this concept, see: T. H. Gaster, Thespis[2], 24; W. R. Smith, The Religion of the Semites[3] (1927), 271 ff.

30. Exod. 8:8; 9:3, 6, 9–10, 19, 25; 11:4; 12:12, 29.

31. Joel 1:18. This is the correct rendering. RSV's "are dismayed" depends on an emendation (supported by LXX), which in fact destroys the point.

32. Herodotus, xi.24. For further examples, see: C. G. Rawlinson, History of Herodotus (1880), iv.389, n.7.

33. Plutarch, Aristides 14.

34. Plutarch, De Iside et Osiride 29.

35. P. Kretschmer, Neugriechische Märchen (1917), 2.

36. Lebar Brec, 259, cited by Whitley Stokes in The Academy, Aug. 15, 1896, p. 155.

37. Schaumberger, in Misc. Bib. 2 (1934), 123–34.

MICAH

237 Prophecy by puns

1. See above, §98; cf. also: A. S. Pease, on Cicero, De Divinatione i.102; E. S. McCartney, in Classical Journal 14 (1919), 343–58; id., in Papers of the Michigan Academy 16 (1932), 120 f.

2. Cf. Arabic '-ṣ-l, "be firmly rooted"; Nabataean *'aṣlâ,* "foundation, bedrock"; Heb. *'aṣîlîm,* "chief men," in Exod. 24:11 is probably related, in the sense of "the Establishment."

3. There is a further pun in this verse, for the subsequent words, usually rendered, (*in*) *nakedness and shame,* should probably be translated, *Exposed is (thy) shame,* playing on the fact that the name Shaphir suggests a Hebrew word for "beautiful," as who should say contemptuously, *Shift along, Miss Shapely, your ugly spot is bared.*

4. Oracula Sibyllina iii.363–64; iv.165–66; cf. Tertullian, De Pall. 2; Lactantius, vii.25. Note also Shakespeare's pun in *Julius Caesar,* I.ii: *Is it* Rome *indeed, and* room *enough,* etc.

5. Muwatta (Cairo, A. H. 1280), iv.205, as quoted by D. S. Margoliouth, in ERE ix. 140[a].

6. E.g., 55 (*Camerius: camerium;* see F. O. Copley, in AJP 73 [1952], 295–97); 94; 105 (*mentula*).

238 Casting sins into the sea

1. The traditional (Masoretic) Hebrew text reads, their *sins.* RSV follows the ancient Greek, Syriac and Aramaic versions. The mistake is, to be sure, very simple in archaic

Hebrew script. Nevertheless, *praestat arduor lectio*. If we assume that the prophet was quoting a traditional formula, the anomalous *their* could have been a part of that formula, referring originally to the attendant crowds. It should be observed also that by reading *their,* the jingle in the Hebrew is preserved.

2. Frazer-Gaster, NGB §203.

3. Grimm-Stallybrass, TM, 767.

4. Ib., 771.

5. Th. Vernaleken, Mythen und Bräuche des Volkes in Oesterreich (1859), 29 ff.

6. Grimm-Stallybrass, op. cit., 771.

7. Ib.

8. P. Drechsler, Sitte, Brauch und Volksglaube in Silesien (1903–6), i.70.

9. A. Witzschel, Sagen, Sitten und Gebräuche aus Thüringen (1878), 193.

10. P. Sartori, Sitte und Brauch (1910–14), iii.131, n.2.

11. J. G. Frazer, GB, one-vol. ed. 308.

12. Bavaria: Landes- und Volkskunde des Königsreiches Bayern (1860–67), iii.958.

13. Ovid, Fasti v.62 ff.; Varro, De lingua Latina v.45; Plutarch, Quaest. Rom. 32, 86. For varying modern interpretations, see: L. Preller, Römische Mythologie³ (1881–83), iii.134 ff.; W. W. Fowler, The Roman Festivals of the Period of the Republic (1899), 111 ff.; J. G. Frazer, GB viii.107 f.

14. J. G. Frazer, The Fasti of Ovid (1925), iv.53, 74 ff.

15. T. H. Gaster, Thespis², 175 f. (But H. L. Ginsberg, in ANET 132, translates the passage somewhat differently.)

16. See: I. Goldziher, in ARW 13 (1910), 20 ff.; R. Wuensch, in Festschrift d. Schles, Gesell. für Volkskunde (1911), 25; O. Gruppe, Griechische Mythologie (1906), 895, n.5; L. Radermacher, in Anzeiger d. oesterr. Akad. Wiss., Phil.-hist. Kl. 1949/xvi, 307–15.

17. F. Thureau-Dangin, Rituels accadiens (1921), 127 ff., lines 350–60; trans. A. Sachs, in ANET 333.

18. Iliad 1.312–13.

19. Aeschylus, Supplices 529 f.

20. Sophocles, Oedipus Rex 193.

21. Euripides, Iphigenia in Tauris 1191–93.

22. Id., Hercules Furens 649 ff.

23. Plutarch, Superst. 3; Diphylos, Incert 126, Koch.

24. Pausanias, viii.41, 2; cf. P. Stengel, Die griechische Kultusaltertümer² (1920), 163.

25. Cicero, Rosc. Am. 70; Livy, xxxi.12, 8; Tibullus, ii.5, 80 (with Kirby Smith's note); Valerius Maximus, i.1, 13.

26. V. Solomon, in JAI 32 (1902), 227.

27. Tibullus, iv.4, 7.

NAHUM

239 The burden of Nineveh

1. BM 21, 901, obv. 24–30; C. J. Gadd, The Fall of Nineveh (1923); ANET 304.

2. Gadd, op. cit., 17.

3. Diodorus, ii.25, 6.

4. Diodorus, ii.26, 9–27, 1; Xenophon, Anabasis iii.4, 7–12; Gadd, loc. cit.; P. Haupt, in JAOS 28 (1907), 99–107.

5. Diodorus, ii.26, 1–4.

6. Id., ii.27,2; Abydenus, cited by Eusebius, Chron. i.35, 28–37, 13.

7. What the prophet means, of course, is that the shields and uniforms of the soldiers were bloodstained. But, by a clever choice of words, he likens these braves to princes stoled in scarlet.

8. I follow Gesenius in deriving Heb. *huṣṣab* (RSV, arbitrarily: "its mistress") from a root *ṣ-b-b*, "flow," and joining it to the end of the preceding verse.

9. Inserting *hôgôth*, which has dropped out through haplography.

10. Note especially that in vv. 2, 3, 7, and 11 the divine name YHWH overloads the meter. This suggests that it has been interpolated into an older hymn in which the name of the god was not mentioned or in which he was specified, once for all, in an opening verse which has been suppressed. (In v. 12, *Thus saith YHWH* is, of course, a prose insertion; while in v. 9 the present text's *'el YHWH* may have been originally *'elāw.*)

11. T. H. Gaster, Thespis[2], 194, n.4.

12. K. Tallquist, Akkadische Götterepitheta (1938), 175.

13. CT XXIV.40, 43; cf. KAT[2], 448.

14. Enuma Elish iv.50.

15. KUB XXXIII, 18.17; cf. J. Friedrich, in Jahrb. für kleinas. Forschung 2 (1952), 148–49.

16. For the sake of the acrostic, read *dālū* (or some other word beginning with *d*) in place of the traditional text's erroneously repeated *'umlallū*.

17. For the traditional text's *wa-tiśśa'* read *wa-tiśśa'*.

18. II AB, vii.29 ff.

19. EA 147.14–15.

20. IV R[2], 28.2 = S. A. Strong, in PSBA 20 (1891), 61.

21. L. W. King, Babylonian Magic and Sorcery (1896), 21.83.

22. S. N. Kramer, Sumerian Mythology (1944), 117 ff.; S. Langdon, Semitic Mythology (1931), 119 f., 125, 128; M. Jastrow, Rel. Bab. u. Ass. (1905–12), i.461.

23. F. Hrozný, Sumerisch-babylonische Mythen von dem Gott Ninrag, i.e., Ninurta (1903), #4.14–21; K 4829; Jastrow, op. cit., i.458.

24. Epic of Gilgamesh ix.17, 102; cf. E. Dhorme, in RB 39 (1930), 489, 495.

25. See above, n.13.

26. M. Witzel, Tammuz-Liturgien und Verwandtes (1935), 208.31; 269.71; cf. also: A. Haldar, Studies in the Book of Nahum (1946), 106.

27. E. Mahler, in Sitzb. Akad. Wien, Abt. ii, 93 (1886). Mahler's conclusions, however, are disputed.

28. Epic of Gilgamesh xi.96, 106, 111–12.

29. Enuma Elish iii.20, 74.

30. Ib., ii.95.

31. For the traditional text's *mālē'* read, with many modern scholars, *hᵃlô'*, and join to the next verse.

32. Verses 12–13 must be placed after v. 14, since the latter is the logical sequel to v. 11, addressed to Nineveh, whereas the former are clearly words of comfort directed toward Israel.

33. For the traditional text's *'āśîm* read *'aśśîm*.

34. For the traditional text's notoriously obscure *'im šᵉlēmîm wᵉ-kēn rabbîm wᵉ-kēn nāgōzū wᵉ-ᶜabār wᵉ-ᶜinnitik* read, by mere re-division of the consonants and omission (with LXX) of the first *wᵉ-kēn: 'im šālū mayyim rabbîm wᵉ-kēn gāzū wᵉ-ᶜabārū ᶜinnitik,* etc. The word *šālū* means "overwhelm with flood"; cf. in Akkadian, Shalmaneser I, Asshur Inscription (KAVI, p. 24), iv.22: *ina šamni tâbi e-ri-ni dišpi ù ḫimêti še-la-ar-šu a-še-el* (cf. M. Kmosko, in ZA 31 [1917–18], 83); Arabic *sayyil*, "flood"; see: T. H. Gaster, in JBL 63 (1944), 51 f.

35. IV R 33, iv.13.

240 "The mills of God grind slowly"

1. Plutarch, ii.549 f.; Paroemiographi Graeci, ed. E. Leutsch and F. G. Schneidewin (1839–51), i.444.
2. Cf. Kirby Flower Smith, The Elegies of Albius Tibullus (1913), 360 f.; J. E. B. Mayor, on Juvenal, xiii.100.
3. Sophocles, Oedipus Coloneus 1536 f.
4. Euripides, Ion 1615.
5. Tibullus, i.9, 4.
6. Horace, Odes iii.2, 31.
7. Seneca, Rhet. controv. x, praef. 6.
8. Juvenal, xiii.100.
9. Valerius Maximus, 1.1, ext. 3.
10. Other Classical references are: Plato, Legg. 899A; Livy, iii.56, 7; Persius, ii.24–30.

HABAKKUK

241 "Hush before the Lord"

1. G. van der Leeuw, Religion in Essence and Manifestation (1963), §63.3; "Silences in worship," says Amiel, "are not the empty moments of devotion, but the full moments." See also: G. Mensching, Das heilige Schweigen (1926).
2. Maxims of Ani, §xi.
3. Iliad 9.171; Aristophanes, Thesm. 39 f.; see: E. Spanheim, In Callimachi hymnos observationes (1697), on Apollo 17–18; F. Stengel, Die griechische Kultusaltertümer[2] (1920), 111. Cf. also: Cicero, De Div. i.45, 102; Horace, Odes iii.1, 2; Ovid, Fasti ii.654; Tibullus, ii.1, 1; ii.2, 2; Pliny, HN xxviii.11.
4. Cf. W. Kroll, Antiker Aberglaube (1897), 32.
5. Kroll, loc. cit.
6. Scholiast on Aristophanes, Birds 1490; cf. E. Rohde, Psyche[7] (1921), 244, n.1.
7. J. Grimm, Deutsche Mythologie[4] (1875–78), iii.463, #830.
8. J. Reville, Les religion des peuples non-civilisées (1883), i.73.
9. T. H. Gaster, Customs and Folkways of Jewish Life (1965), 138.
10. W. Kroll, Antiker Aberglaube (1897), 32.

242 The prayer of Habakkuk

1. See: F. J. Stephens, in JBL 43 (1924), 290–93; U. Cassuto, in Ann. Stud. ebrei 1936–37 (1938), 7–22; W. A. Irwin, in JNES 1 (1942), 10–40; 15 (1956), 47–50; W. F. Albright, in Theodore H. Robinson Volume (1950), 1–18; S. Mowinckel, in ThZ 9 (1953), 1–23; J. H. Eaton, in ZAW 76 (1964), 144–71.
2. Literally, *amid years*, i.e., in actual time.
3. The traditional text's *ḥayyêhū* has point: the mythic exploits are to be actualized in history. The commonly accepted emendation, *ḥawwêhū*, "reveal it," is both unnecessary and banal.
4. Not, as commonly rendered, *God came from Teman, and the Holy One from Mount Paran*. The point is that the sheen indicates that he who is approaching is a god or otherworldly being; *god* and *holy one* are therefore common nouns. For the latter in this sense, cf. the Canaanite inscription from Arslan Tash and the Yeḥimilk inscription from Byblus. So too sometimes in O.T. (e.g., Hos. 16:3; Zech. 14:5; Pss. 16:3; 89:8; Job 5:1; 15:15); see: J. Wellhausen, SBOT Psalms, on Pss. 29 and 58; S. R. Driver, ICC Deut. 4:19; P. Haupt, in Hebraica 20 (1904), 161, 172; T. H. Gaster, in Orientalia 11 (1942), 17; C. Shedl, in VT 14 (1964), 310–18.

5. Heb. *tᵉhillātô* here derives from *h-l-l* I, "shine" (Isa. 13:10; Job 41:10), not from *h-l-l* II, "praise," as usually rendered.

6. I.e., the first glow of the sun has already appeared over the horizon, but its full strength still lies *yonder* (Heb.: *šām*—deictic) beneath it. No emendation is needed!

7. O. Weber, Altorientalische Siegelbilder (1920), i.101–103; ii. ##373–76; G. Furlani, Rel. bab. e ass. (1925), i.167 f.

8. L. Stephani, "Nimbus und Strahlenkranz," in Mém. de l'Acad. des Sciences de St. Petersbourg, Vi sér., Sc. pol.-hist. et phil. ix (1859); R. B. Onians, The Origins of European Thought about the Body, etc. (1951), 165 ff.; A. Smythe-Palmer, Jacob at Bethel (1899), 47 ff.

9. L. Oppenheim, in JAOS 63 (1943), 31–33; G. Furlani, "L'aureola delle divinità assire," in Rendiconti Acad. Lincei 6–7 (1931), 223–37.

10. JVAI 39.24: *illabiš nûri*.

11. Enuma Elish i.103; iv.57–58. Tiamat so arrays her monsters: ib., ii.22–23, 117–18.

12. KBo III.2i̇, ii.14; J. Friedrich, in AO 25/ii, 190; G. Furlani, Rel. degli Hittiti (1936), 24.

13. Iranian *khvarenah;* Yasht 19; cf. A. Christensen, Die Iranier (1933), 229.

14. Isa. 4:5; 10:16 f.; 24:23; Ezek. 10:19; 11:1; 43:2; Zech. 2:9. Cf. J. Morgenstern, in ZA 25 (1910), 139–93; 28 (1913), 15 ff.; id., in HUCA 6 (1929), 34 ff.; T. Paffrath, Das Gotteslicht im AT (1936); W. F. Albright, From the Stone Age to Christianity[2] (1957), 262.—The O.T. passages in which light is associated with God need, however, to be carefully sifted, for they reflect various conceptions: (*a*) in Micah 7.8; Pss. 27:1; 80:20, all that is meant is that God will dissipate spiritual darkness, as sunrise dissipates the shades of night; (*b*) in Isa. 2:5 the idea is simply that God will be like a torch lighting a path; (*c*) in Num. 6:25; Pss. 4:7; 31:17; 44:4; 67:2; 89:16 the light of God's countenance is simply a Semitic idiom for "favor, benevolent mien" (cf. Prov. 16:15; Eccles. 8:1); (*d*) in Deut. 33:2; Ps. 76:5, the poet is expressly comparing the theophany to sunrise; (*e*) in Ps. 104:2 the light is simply the bright sky, as in Rig Veda I.25, 13 and in the Iranian Avesta, Yasht xiii.3; cf. T. H. Gaster, Thespis[2], 201 f.

15. Ezek. 28:7, 17.

16. Hom. Hymns, Apollo 444; Demeter 189, 278; Aphrodite 173 f.; Euripides, Bacchae 1083 (Dionysus); Aristophanes, Birds 1709–13; Bacchylides xvii.102 (Nereids). Cf. also: Ovid, Fasti i.94; vi.251–52; Vergil, Aeneid ii.615; x.634; Horace, Odes i.2, 31.

17. O. Gruppe, Griechische Mythologie (1906), 382.

18. Jamblichus, De mysteriis ii.4.

19. Epic of Gilgamesh ix.98–100; cf. I. Gelb, in AOr 18/iii (1950), 189–98.

20. Iliad 4.440; 15.119.

21. Grimm-Stallybrass, TM 208.

22. Heb. *yᵉqadᵉmū pānāw*, "stand before him," is a technical expression for the office of a courtier; cf. Akkadian *nazāzu ina pani*.

23. Cf. H. L. Ginsberg, in BASOR 72 (1938), 13–15.

24. Breasted, AR iii.144–45, §§319, 321–22.

25. Iliad 1.320–21.

26. Iliad 9.181 ff.; cf. C. H. Whitman, Homer and the Homeric Tradition (1958), 344, n.25.

27. E. Pagliaro, Epica e romanzo nel medievo persano (1927), 4.

28. Concerning RESHEPH, see: W. D. van Wijngaarden, in Internat. Archiv fuer Ethnographie, Oudheidkundige Medeeling 31 (1931), 28–42; A. Caquot, in Semitica 6 (1956), 53–68; W. K. Simpson, in JAOS 72 (1953), 86–89; id., in Bulletin of the Metropolitan Museum of Art 10 (1952), 182–87; P. Matthiae, in Oriens Antiquus 2 (1963), 27–43; A. Eisenlohr, in PSBA 14 (1892), 368 f.; W. Spiegelberg, in OLz 11 (1908), 529–31; S. A. Cook, The Religion of Ancient Palestine in the Light of Archaeology (1925), 112 f.; W. F. Albright, in Paul Haupt Festschrift (1926), 143–58.—

Resheph occurs in proper names from Mari in the forms Rashap and Rushpan: J. Lewy in Mélanges Dussaud i (1939), 275; also at Ḫana: ib., 274; M. Schorr, in Babyloniaca 3 (1910), 266 f. A n. pr. 'Ebed-Resheph occurs in a text from Elephantine: P. 11438 = Sachau, Pl. 70, No. 13.

29. L. Vincent, in RB, 1938.512 ff.

30. RS 15.134; C. Virolleaud, in CRAIBL 1952.30.

31. G. A. Cook, A Text-book of North Semitic Inscriptions (1905), #30. A Resheph of Amyclae (Mkl) is mentioned in CIL I.89; 91.2. Arsippos, father of Aesculapius, mentioned in Cicero, De natura deorum iii.22, 57, is identified by Clermont-Ganneau (Réc. vii.173) with Resheph. Arsuf, near Jaffa, was the Seleucid Apollonias.

32. RS i.7; iii.16; Krt B ii.6. So in the Hurrian Text, RS.4.42, 44–45, *Iršpn* precedes *'nt Amrn*, "Amorite 'Anat."—Drexler, in Roscher's Lex. Myth. ii.1117, identifies the Cypriotic Keraunios and Keraunia with *Ršp ḥṣ* and *'Anat*.

33. Panamuwa inscription, 2–3, 11.

34. Aztwd Inscription, iii.89–9.

35. H. Frankfort, in OIC, figs. 69–70; id., in Afo 12 (1938), 134.

36. Pausanias, x.28, 7.

37. O. Gruppe, op. cit., 1231.

38. T. H. Gaster, *apud* C. H. Gordon, in JQR, N.S. 39 (1948), 50; see: E. Meyer, Gesch. des Altertums[3] (1910), ii.134; W. K. Simpson, in JAOS 72 (1953), 86–89.

39. Concerning Resheph in Egypt, see: B. Grdsellof, Les débuts du culte de Resef en Égypte (1942); W. C. Hayes, in JNES 10 (1951), 234, and fig. 34, No. R. 43; M. Leibovitch, in ASAE 39 (1939), 145 ff.; PSBA 1901.83, #339 (name on 18th Dyn. scarab); J. M. A. Jaussen, in Chronique d'Égypte 50 (1950), 209–12.

40. Stele of Amenhotep II at Mit-Rahineh: A. Badawi, in ASAE 42 (1943), 1 ff; E. Drioton, ib., 45 (1947), 61–64.

41. S. Hassan, in ASAE 37 (1937), 129–34.

42. H. R. Hall, Hieroglyphic Texts from Egyptian Stelae in the British Museum (1925), Pl. vii.

43. W. Edgerton and J. A. Wilson, Historical Records (Medinet Habu), 27. 25*d*; also in n.pr. 'pr-Ršpw in a papyrus dated 1743 B.C., now in the Brooklyn Museum No. 35, 1446. (For these references I am indebted to Professor W. K. Simpson.)

44. W. F. Albright, in Archaeology and the Religion of Israel (1942), 79, derives the name from a root *r-š-p*, "burn," but this meaning of the word is not entirely certain.

45. A. H. Sayce, in PSBA 39 (1917), 207, citing a syllabary (CT XVIII.27, 27): *rašāpu‖rašu*. But Sayce's interpretation is uncertain.

46. Heb.: *wa-yᵉmôded*. There is no need to emend this word, as do most modern scholars. It connects with Arabic *mâda*, "shake, convulse," rather than with Heb. *m-d-d*, "measure," as usually understood.

47. Heb. *wa-yatter*, to be derived from *n-t-r*, "leap," or vocalized *wa-yater*, from *t-r-r*, Akkadian *tarāru*, Arabic *t-r-t-r*, "quiver."

48. I eschew all emendations of these lines, because they all rest on the assumption that the Hebrew word *hᵃlîkah* means "path," whereas it really denotes *the process of going*. What is implied, therefore, is simply that Yahweh has marched against his foes in his ancient manner; and this makes perfect sense.

49. Cushan is simply Cush, the ending being added for the sake of euphonious harmony with Midian. In the traditional text the verse is corrupt and ungrammatical. I read simply: *ratᵉtū 'oholê Cushan, tᵉḥaṭ'enā yᵉrîᶜôth Midian*. (The ungrammatical *yirgᵉzū* is a gloss.)

50. New Leyden Papyrus, ed. A. Gardiner, in ÄZ 42.14 ff.; A. Erman, Die Literatur der Aegypter (1923), 367, Abschnitt 50.

51. Erman, op. cit., 371, Abschnitt 500.

52. IV R², ii.*a*, 11–12.

53. II R 19a, 3–4.

54. F. Hrozný, Sumerisch-babylonische Mythen von dem Gott Ninrag (1903), 8 ff.; P. Jensen, Kosmologie (1890), 455, 460.

55. Heb. *mayyîm rabbîm,* "many waters," is a common expression for "ocean," like Akkadian *mê rabbûti.*

56. K. Meyer, Selections from Ancient Irish Poetry (1911), 3, 7.

57. J. A. MacCulloch, Celtic Mythology (1918), 128.

58. P. Sébillot, Le folklore de France (1904–07), ii.12.

59. R. Battaglia, in Rivista di Antropologia 27 (1925), 25; cf. I. Zolli, in Actes du XXeme Congrès des Orientalistes (1940), 284.

60. Matthew Arnold, The Forsaken Mermaid, 6.

61. O. Gruppe, op. cit., 1147; U. von Wilamowitz-Moellendorf, Griechische Tragödien ii (1907), 230; H. J. Rose, in Folk-Lore 45 (1933), 21.

62. J. F. Campbell, Popular Tales of the West Highlands (1860–62), iv.331, 337, 342; J. MacDougall, Folk Tales and Fairy Lore (1910), 309; J. F. Black, Orkney and Shetland Folklore (1905), 189 ff.; Teutonia 2 (1902), 72.

63. W. B. Yeats, Irish Faery and Folk Tales (n.d.), 100.

64. Powell-Magnusson, Icelandic Legends (1866), i.106 ff.

65. Sébillot, op. cit., ii.207; A. H. Krappe, La genèse des mythes (1938), 203 (whence many of the foregoing examples are taken).

66. Heb.: *ha-binehārîm.* Since the plural of the word *nahar,* "river," occurs in the very next verse in the form *nehārôth,* it has been suggested that we should read here *ha-ba-Nahar-ma/mi* (with archaic enclitic *-ma/mi*), and see a direct reference to the proper name Nahar, the alternative designation of Yam (Sea) in the Canaanite myth.

67. Hearst Papyrus, ed. G. Reisner (1905 ff.), ii.13.

68. KUB XXXIII.108, 16–17; cf. H. Güterbock, Kumarbi (1946), 112; J. Friedrich, in Jahrb. fuer kleinas. Forschung 2 (1952), 147–50.

69. II AB iii, ii, 18; I*AB ii.7; III AB, A 29, 33; IV AB i.7; iii.22, 37; cf. T. H. Gaster, Thespis², 124, 211.

70. Ps. 18:15; 77:18; 144:6; Zech. 9:14.

71. Enuma Elish iv.40 f.

72. ANEP, #689.

73. H. Otten, Mythen vom Gott Kumarbi (1950), #12, 1 ff. (pp. 23 ff.); KUB XXXIII.106, 1, 3 ff.; Güterbock, op. cit., 24, 76.

74. H. Bossert, Altanatolien (1942), Nos. 563, 778.

75. Grimm-Stallybrass, TM 166 f.

76. Hesychius, Lex., s.v. *elasibronta.*

77. This verse has been variously emended, but it makes perfect sense if only MT's obscure *šebu'ôth* be vocalized *śibb'athā* or *šebē'ath.* The word is exquisitely chosen, for it plays by hyperbole on the common expression *malle' qešeth* (also in Akkadian), lit. *"fill* a bow," in the sense of charging it with an arrow. Translate literally, *Utterly empty is thy bow, replete though it was* (or, *which thou hadst constantly filled) with the arrows of (thy) command.*—For *'omer* in the sense of "command," cf. Pss. 68:12; 106:34; I Sam. 24:11; Job 9:7, and the Arabic equivalent in Koran 10:25; 11:42; 16:1.

78. T. H. Gaster, Thespis², 164 f.

79. Enuma Elish iv.35 ff.

80. For these examples, cf. M. Haavio, in Journal of the Folklore Institute 1 (1965), 45 f.

81. E. Dammann, Die Religionen Afrikas (1963), 24.

82. W. Krickberg, Märchen der Azteken und Inkaperuvianer Maya und Muesca (1928), 285.

83. J. Mooney, The Ghost-Dance Religion (reprint, 1965), 218.

84. Heb.: *tittenennū ma'akal le'am le-ṣiyyîm.* There is no need to emend the text;

ma'ªkal lᵉ'am go together, with the meaning of "food for (the) people, for public consumption," while *ṣî* is the Arabic word for "wild cat, hyena."

85. S. N. Kramer, Sumerian Mythology (1944), 80, 82 f.

86. Leyden Magical Papyrus, ed. Mossart, 84–85.

87. E. Drioton, in BOr. 12 (1955), 165.

88. For *rôm yadêhū nāśā'*: *šemeš* I read *hôdêhū* (cf. v. 2) *našah šemeš*. The initial *rôm* is either a gloss on *zᵉbul*, "height, zenith," at the end of the verse, or else vertical dittography from (*ze*)*rem* in the preceding line. One wonders, however, whether *yadêhū našah*, lit. "forgot its hands," may not be an idiomatic expression for "lost its power."

89. IV R² 28.ii, 22–26.

90. The sense of this verse depends on a double-entendre. The point is that Heb. *rô'š* means both "head" and "top of a building," so that the unroofing of buildings—called "slighting" in medieval England—is likened to beheading. Similarly, the word *yᵉsôd* means both "heel" (Ugaritic *ysd*) and "foundation," so that the act of razing down to bedrock (cf. Ps. 137:7) is compared to stripping a person from head to toe.

91. The meaning of Heb. *pᵉrāzāw* is uncertain.

92. The defective meter shows that a word has dropped out. I restore *'ªrî*, "lion," on the basis of the similar expression in Ps. 10:9; Lam. 3:10.

93. G. Jacob, Altarabische Parallelen zum AT (1897), 17.

94. IV AB, ii.22–23.

95. Otten, op. cit., No. 12, iii.3–4.

96. J. Wellhausen, in ARW 7.33; 9.140; Weinel, in ZAW 18.1 ff.; E. Crawley, in ERE i.550.

97. I retain the traditional text, rendering literally, "and where I stand, I tremble, I who . . ." The conventional emendation of *'ašer* to *ašūr(a)i*, overlooks the fact that *'ašūr* means "foot*step*, foot*print*," not simply "foot."

98. G. Jacob, Studien in arabischen Dichtern, ii (1894), 119; id., Das Leben der vorislamischen Beduinen (1895), 124.

99. Krt A, 108 ff.

100. The point is reinforced by the use of the verb *yᵉgudennū*, which refers properly to marauding raids.

101. Heb. *gazar*, here to be explained from Arabic *j-z-r*, "dwindle."

102. That these are the actual words of the paean is shown by the iterated "LORD, LORD," since this corresponds to the Semitic form of address: cf. Gen. 22:11; Exod. 3:4; 34:6, and cf. in the Canaanite Poem of the Gracious Gods (#52 Gordon), 32–33, *ad ad*, "Daddy, daddy," and *um um*, "Mummy, mummy!"—The context demands that the Heb. word *ḥeylî* here mean "my substance, wealth," rather than "my strength," as usually rendered.

103. S. Langdon, Sumerian and Babylonian Psalms (1909), 332. 1–21; id., Tammuz and Ishtar (1914), 11.

104. S. Langdon, Tammuz and Ishtar (1914), 23.

105. I AB, iii–iv.25–27, 36–38; T. H. Gaster, Thespis², 223.

106. KUB XVII.10, i.16–18; Gaster, op. cit., 303.

107. Homeric Hymn to Demeter, 302–13.

ZEPHANIAH

243 Zephaniah and the pagan festivals

1. RS. 3.50 ff.

2. Heb. *zebaḥ* here means "meal, banquet," (not "sacrifice"). For this meaning, cf. Prov. 7:14 and the Ugaritic Epic of Keret = 128 Gordon vi.5.

3. T. H. Gaster, Thespis[2], 93 f.

4. B. Landsberger, Der kultische Kalendar der Babylonier und Assyrer, i (1915), 14; S. A. Pallis, The Babylonian Akitu Festival (1926), 173; D. Luckenbill, ARAB ii.§456.

5. R. Labat, Le caractère religieux de la royauté assyro-babylonienne (1939), 286 f.; T. Frankema, Tâkultu (1954).

6. Enuma Elish vi.72–81. A similar situation obtains earlier when Kingu claims sovereignty: iii.61–62.

7. II AB, vi–vii; tr. H. L. Ginsberg, in ANET 134 f.; Gaster, op. cit., 190 f.

8. KUB XVII.10, iii.30 ff.; Gaster, op. cit., 311.

9. KBo III.7; Gaster, op. cit., 265 ff.

10. Pindar, Paeans vi; cf. R. Pfister, in P-W V/ii, 2256–58.

11. H. Hepding, Attis (1903), 136 f.

12. Rephaim (Rp), i–iii; C. Virolleaud, in Syria 22 (1946), 1–30; Gordon, UH ##121–24; G. R. Driver, Canaanite Myths and Legends (1946), 66–70.

13. II Rp A.4: bym qz. Cf. yrḥw qs, Sept.-Oct. in the Gezer Agricultural Calendar (10th cent. B.C.). In the Amarna letter 131.15 gi-e-zi (= qêz) is the Canaanite equivalent of eburu, "harvest," and in the Ugaritic Poem of Aqhat 1.41, q-z is the season of the early rain (yr).

14. I Rp a.4: t'rb sd (cf. Gen. 49:6). For the basic meaning of s-d (Heb.: sôd) cf. L. Kohler, Hebrew Man (1956), 87 ff.

15. I Rp B 7–11. The reason why Daniel is introduced may be that the divine guests are characterized as rpum, and he himself usually bears the title mt Rpi, "rpu-man." He would therefore be regarded as an appropriate mortal host.

16. III Rp, B 2–4. For 'Anat as a paragon of beauty, cf. the Ugaritic of K-r-t, i.145 (ANET 144[b]).

17. The passage is still obscure in details.

18. In the Poem of Aqhat II r. 25–30, 'Anat offers to teach him the art of archery; see: Gaster, Thespis[2], 351.—The word here rendered "flushes" is tštr, which I interpret as a causative form of t-r-r = Akkadian tarāru, or of n-t-r = Heb. id., "startle"; cf. Vergil, Georgica i.56: sonitu terrebis aves.

19. III Rp, B 14–17. The lower leaves of the Syrian olive are silvery, and from a distance create the effect of a shimmer: G. E. Poste, in Hastings' Dictionary of the Bible, s.v. Olive.

20. III Rp, B 17–18: yn bl d-ǵll. The interpretation is due to Gordon.

21. Ib., 19–20: ᶜnq smd Lbnn. Cf. Arabic 'anāq, "croissant." This is the zalabiyeh, still eaten in the Hejaz: see: W. R. Smith, Lectures and Esays (1912), 511. Crescent-shaped loaves, called armanni-bread (cf. armas, "crescent moon") are mentioned in Hittite texts. Smd is the Arabic and Neo-Hebrew samîd, Turkish and Georgian simidi, and Greek semidalis, whence our semolina.

22. III Rp. B 25: bṣq birt Lbnn.

23. Ib., A 13–15: prst . . . [ym]lk . . . 'l Amr, "My decree (cf. Akkadian purussu) it is that he shall rei[gn] over Amurru."

24. Ib., B 20: Baal is hailed as y ḫrt Il; cf. I AB iv.27 f.

25. Ib.: ṭl mrṭ cf. Syriac-Aramaic meritâ; Heb. ṯirôš, "new wine." For the idiom, cf. Pindar, Ol. vii.2: drosos ampelou. A modern Irish liquor is called "dew-mist."

26. Ib., 26–27.

27. Syr. Apocal. Baruch 29:3–8; IV Ezra 6:32; TB Baba Bathra 74[a]–75[b]; Targum Ps.-Jon. to Num. 9:26 ff.

28. Moses ben Isaac of Orleans(?), Aqdamuth, recited in the Ashkenazic liturgy on the first day of Pentecost: trans. T. H. Gaster, in Commentary, June 1953; id., Festivals of the Jewish Year (1953), 72.

29. So the gods acknowledge Marduk at the banquet described in Enuma Elish, loc. cit.

30. This also chimes with the subsequent description of the guests (i.8) as "sons of the king"; see below, n.37.

31. T. Jacobsen, in JNES 2 (1943), 167, n.49.

32. K. Sethe, Dramatische Texte, ii (1928), Ramesseum Drama, lines 89–90, 132–33; Gaster, Thespis², 392 (Scene xxx), 398 (Scene xliii).

33. Herodotus, i.133.

34. G. Glotz, The Greek City and Its Institutions (1930), 37.

35. Tacitus, Germania 22; O. Schrader, in RIA², ii.30.

36. Cf. II Chron. 36:23; Ezra 1:21; Job 36:23, and nouns pᵉqūdîm (Num. 31:14, 48; (II Kings 11:15) and piqqūdîm (Pss. 19:9; 103:18; 117:7; 119 passim).

37. Note that the Hebrew says "sons of the king," not "sons of kings." The expression need not be taken literally; it may be a title, i.e., "members of the royal entourage": cf. Jer. 36:26; 38:6.

38. On festal garb, see: ERE, s.v. Dress (reprinted in E. Crawley, Oath, Curse and Blessing, Thinker's Library, #40, 113–15); C. A. Lobeck, Aglaophamus (1829), 173 ff.; P. Stengel, Die griechischen Kultusalterthümer² (1898), 209; T. H. Gaster, in JBL 60 (1941), 302.—The Hebrew word rendered "foreign" is nôkrî. In a text from Mari the same word (nukru) is used to denote exotic hand-made articles produced in Anatolia: see W. F. Albright, in BASOR 77 (1940), 31.

39. E.g., Dionysius of Halicarnassus, Antiqu. Rom., ii.19, 5; Ovid, Met. iv.339; Herodian, Post Marcum i.10, 5; Sallustius, De diis et mundo, iv.—In the mysteries of the Syrian Goddess the castrated votaries (galli) wore female raiment: Lucian, De de Syria xv. Cf. H. Hepding, Attis (1903), 169.

40. Marco Polo, Travels, tr. R.E. Latham (Penguin 1958), 107 f.

41. Vassits, Fackel (1900), 18 f.; Gaster, Thespis², 465, n.22. Zephaniah's specific mention of lamps indicates that he is referring to the torches rather than to seasonal bonfires.

42. K. 3476.5, 29 H. Zimmern, in BSGW 58 (1903), 130, 133. Cf. also F. Thureau-Dangin, Rituels accadiens (1921), 118 ff., obv. 28, rev. 2, 13, 15, 19, 20; K 3050 (VAB vii/2. 252 ff.), iii.5–20 (Ashurbanipal).

43. IV R 61.54a ff. (oracle of the Arbelite priest Ladagilili to Esarhaddon).

44. Euripides, Ion 1074; Aristophanes, Frogs 340.

45. Pindar, fr. 79; AP; vi.173 (Rhianus); Cornutus 6.

46. Aristophanes, Thesm. 101, 1151.

47. Homeric Hymn to Demeter, 48 f. (see: Allen-Sikes-Halliday, in loc.)

48. Julian, Crat. v.179B; Hepding, op. cit., 129, 165.

49. H. Diels, Sibyllinische Blätter (1890), 47 f.; L. R. Farnell, Cults of the Greek States (1896–1909), iii.103; J. G. Frazer, GB x.329.

50. I.e., instead of QôL YôM YHWH MaR ṢōReᵃH ŠaM GiBBôR read QaL YôM YHWH Me-RāṢ Wᵉ-ḤaŠ Mi-GiBBôR. For the speed of the "champion," cf. Ps. 19:6.

51. VAT 9555, rev. 7–9 (lismu); H. Zimmern, in BSGW 70 (1918), fasc. 5, p. 6.

52. J. G. Frazer, GB viii.72 f.

53. C. Fries, in MVAG 15 (1910), ii.4.

54. Gaster, Thespis², 40 f.

55. III Rp, B 5–6.

56. Literally, "thy judgments." Some scholars prefer to read, "The Lord hath removed them that wrought judgment upon thee."

57. For this interpretation, cf. T. H. Gaster, in ET 78 (1967), 27.

58. RSV, by emendation of the text, renders: He will exult over you with gladness; /

he will renew (i.e., *yḥdš*, with LXX, for *yḥrš*) *in his love; / he will exult over you with loud singing / as on the day of the festival* (i.e., *kym m'd*, with LXX and Peshitta, for *nūgê mi-mô'ed*). */ I will remove disaster* (i.e., *hôwah* for *hāyū*) *from you, / so that you will not bear* (i.e., *mi-š'eth* for *maśś'eth*) *reproach for it.* In my judgment, this is wrong for several reasons: (*a*) the change of *yḥrš*, "keep silent," to *yḥdš*, "renew," overlooks the pointed contrast between now being silent and eventually breaking into song; (*b*) the emendation of *nūgê mi-mô'ed*, "them that were thrust forth from the assembly," overlooks a mythological allusion; (*c*) the word *hôwah*, "disaster," which is read in place of *hāyū*, "they were," means properly "a fall," so that the concrete verb "remove" cannot be applied to it; (*d*) the emendation of *maśś'eth* to *mi-š'eth* overlooks the fact that *maśś'eth ḥerpah* is the nominal equivalent of the verbal *naś'a ḥerpah*, "to heap insults." All that is really necessary to make sense of the passage is simply to vocalize *nūgai* for *nūgê*, deriving from *y-g-h* I, "thrust away," and to read *maśś'eth 'alai ha-ḥerpah* for *maśś'eth aleihā ḥerpah*, with pointed contrast between *mi-mᵉkā hāyū*, i.e., from *you* they came forth who brought insult to *me*. (Note that *mi-mᵉkā* goes with *hāyū*, not with *'asaftî*.)

59. Heb. *'ōśeh*, here to be derived from *'-š-h* II, "press" (cf. Ezek. 23:3, 21).

60. Ugaritica V (1967), #1.5–6.

244 Ravens in ruins

1. The traditional (Masoretic) text reads *ḥôreb*, "ruin, devastation," but this is simply a scribal error for *'oreb*, "raven"—the reading actually presupposed by the Greek (LXX) and Latin (Vulgate) Versions.

2. Ad-Damiri, i.135.

3. Zs. für Volkskunde 1913.386 ff. So too in Jewish lore: Tosefta, Shabbath vi.6; vii.17; cf. I. Scheftelowitz, Altpalestinensicher Bauernglaube (1925), 140.

4. T. Canaan, Dämonenglaube im Lande der Bibel (1929), 15.

5. Thomas of Marga, The Book of Governors, ed. E. A. W. Budge (1893), ii.599.

ZECHARIAH

245 Zechariah and the pagan festivals

1. Cf. T. H. Gaster, Thespis², 47 f., 66.

2. S. Langdon, Babylonian Menologies and the Semitic Calendars (1935), 119 ff.

3. Gordon #52.23–27; Gaster, op. cit., 426.

4. I AB vi.40–52; Gaster, op. cit., 227 f.

5. Cf. Exod. 34:22; TJ Sanhedrin 18d.

6. Arnobius, Adversus Nationes v.2; Macrobius, Sat. i.21, 7–11; cf. H. Hepding, Attis (1903), 44, 63.

7. Cf. O. S. Rankin, The Origin of the Festival of Hanukkah (1930), 205 f.; O. Weber, in ARW 19 (1916–19), 315 f., F. Boll, ib., 342.

8. Rankin, op. cit., 201 f.

9. Rain-making ceremonies took place in the temple at Jerusalem on the first night of the festival: Mishnah, Sukkah iv.9; D. Feuchtwang, in MGWJ 54 (1910), 535 ff.; cf. also: Tos. Sukkah iii.18, p. 197 f.; Pᵉsiqtâ dᵉ-Rab Kahana 193ᵇ, Buber. Prayers for rain are still offered in the synagogue on the first day.

10. Gaster, op. cit., 49, 63, 78, 300.

11. On ritual ululations at seasonal festivals, cf. Gaster, op. cit., 30 f.

12. I*AB i.6.

MALACHI

247 Malachi's picture of the Last Days

1. Cf. T. H. Gaster, The Dead Sea Scriptures in English Translation[2] (1964), 24–27; id., IDB, s.v. Angels, Demons, Resurrection.

2. On Malachi's eschatology, cf. E. Margolioth, in Studies in the Bible: M. H. Segal Festschrift (1964). Our presentation is independent of this study.

3. Yasna 48.9; 53.2; 49.9; Yasht 13.129, 142; 19.32; Vendidad 19.5. Cf. M. Dhalla, Zoroastrian Theology (1914), 60, 181 f.; J. H. Moulton, The Treasure of the Magi (1917), 43 f., 105.

4. The Iranian parallel disposes of the facile emendation of Heb. *mala'k,* "messenger, angel," to *melek,* "king"—yet another of those tiresome "corrections" which, by missing an allusion, destroy an author's point.

5. Yasht 10.2.

6. Yasht 10.116–17; Vendiad 4.2–16.

7. Yasna 30.7; 31.3, 19; 32.7; 34.4; 43.4; 47.6; 51.9; Dhalla, op. cit. 291 (Pehlevi).

8. Dead Sea Scrolls, Comm. on Ps. 37, *b* 4; Florilegium 2.1.

9. Dead Sea Scriptures, Hymns 3.29; War 14.17; Manual of Discipline 2.8; Dan. 7:10; Enoch 77:6; Psalms of Solomon 15:14; Or. Sib. 2.253 f.; 3.542, 689; 4.176; Luke 17:28; II Pet. 3:6 f.; II Thess. 1:7 f.; Rev. 19:20; 21:10, 14 f.; 21:8. See: R. Mayer, Ist die biblische Vorstellung vom Weltenbrand eine Entlehnung aus dem Parsismus? (1947).

10. Berosus, quoted by Seneca, Nat. Quaest. ii.29, 1; cf. C. Clemen, Primitive Christianity and Its Non-Jewish Sources (1912), 161 f.; M. Eliade, The Myth of the Eternal Return (1954), 87–88.

11. Dhalla, op. cit., 60f.

12. E.g., Videvdat i.14, 5; cf. Dhalla, op. cit., 173.

13. Dino, Persica 5 (FHG ii.90).

14. Diogenes Laertius, Proaem. 8.

15. Dadistan-i-Denak (West, SBH xviii), 14.2; Dhalla, op. cit., 162.

16. Dan. 12:1; DSS Hymns 1.23–24; 16.10; Slavonic Enoch 50.1; Odes of Solomon 9.12. For rabbinic parallels, cf. L. Ginzberg, Legends of the Jews (1909 ff.), v.128, n.141.

248 The sun of righteousness

1. Dhalla, Zoroastrian Theology (1914), 106; M. J. Vermasseren, Mithras (Urban Bücher 1965), 75 ff.

2. O. S. Rankin, The Origin of the Festival of Hanukkah (1930), 200 f.

3. T. H. Gaster, Thespis[2], 47 f.

4. CIL I, p. 410.

5. Joh. Lydus, De mensibus 4.1; Macrobius, Sat. 1.18,9.

6. G. Wissowa, Religion und Kultus d. Römer[2] (1912), 367.

7. F. Boll, in ARW 19 (1916)–19), 342; O. Weber, ib., 315 f. On the identification of Kronos with Helios (the sun), see: Rankin, op. cit., 206 f.

8. Plutarch, De Iside et Osiride 12.

9. K. Holl, in Sitzb. Berl. Akad. 1917.428; O. Weber, in ARW 18 (1919), 300 ff.; E. Norden, Die Geburt des Kindes (1924), 27, n.2.

10. L. Duchesne, Christian Worship, tr. McClure (1920), 261 f. Cf. Philip le Grève's hymn, *In nativitate Christi,* quoted in Gaster, Thespis[2], 280, n.18.

11. See: S. A. Cook, The Religion of Ancient Palestine in the Light of Archaeology (1925), 47–48; F. v. Bissing, in ZÄS 64 (1929), 112; B. Perring, in AfO 8 (1933), 281–96; V. Christian, ib., 9 (1934), 30; O. Eissfeldt, in Forsch. und Fortschritte 18 (1942), 145–47; J. Pritchard, ed., ANEP ##442, 443, 493.

12. M. O. W. Jeffreys, in Africa 31 (1951), 94–111.

13. Yasht 10.5.

14. E. Dhorme, Les religions de Babylonie et d'Assyrie (1945), 61; B. Meissner, Babylonien und Assyrien, ii (1925), 20.

15. Ugaritica V (1967), #7.

16. See fully: O Gruppe, Griechische Mythologie (1906), 1237 ff.

249 The Second Coming of Elijah

1. E.g., TB Menaḥoth 45a; Baba Meṣi'a 3a; Aboth de-Rabbi Nathan 24.4; cf. also: Matt. 11:14; 17:10 ff.; Mark 9:11 f.

2. M. J. Vermasseren, Mithras (Urban Bücher, 1965), 84 f.

3. Ib., 85.

THE HOLY WRITINGS

Psalms

---

250   The divine adoption of kings   **Ps. 2:6-7**

This psalm was designed for the installation of a king. In ancient times, the primary function of a king (as it still is among primitive peoples) was to mediate what *we* call "nature" to the community. The king was responsible for the weather, the rhythm of the seasons, and, in general, the life and increase of his people. He was therefore a representation in present time of the god, who exercised the same office on a continuous plane, extending over all generations.[1] To articulate this relationship in intelligible terms, various images and symbols were employed: the king could be envisaged as the god in the flesh, or as an offspring of the god's body, or as the recipient of insignia and tokens of authority handed to him from "on high." These images and symbols condition the forms of installation ceremonies.

In the present case, the pattern used is that of genealogy. The king is formally acknowledged by the god as his son: *Yahweh hath said unto me, Thou art my son; this day have I begotten thee.* Parallels to this are to be found throughout the Ancient Near East. An Egyptian text has the god Re' declare to Sesostris III (c. 1880–40 B.C.): "Thou art the son of my body, whom I have begotten";[2] while elsewhere the Pharaoh is described explicitly as "the son of his (Re''s) body."[3] The Babylonians conveyed the same idea by having the king placed on the knees of a divine image during a solemn ceremony in the temple[4]—an act which in secular life, signified acknowledgment of paternity.[5] In a Canaanite myth from Ras Shamra-Ugarit, the imminent death of the king excites surprise on the grounds that he is "a son of God (El)," and therefore presumably immortal;[6] while among the Iranians all kings were deemed descendants of the god Mithra,[7] and in ancient South Arabia as the sons of gods.[8]

(The idea could be expressed also by saying that the king had been suckled at the breasts of the major goddess. Two Egyptian texts have Hathor make such a statement to the Pharaoh;[9] and a relief at Abydos portrays Seti I (c. 1318–01 B.C.) imbibing from the udders of that cow-deity.[10] Similarly, the early Babylonian king Entemena is "nourished by the life-giving milk of the goddess Ninḫursag";[11] while Ashurbanipal (668–63 B.C.) is informed by the divine messenger Nabu that he is indeed a suckling of divine teats.[12])

Alternatively, a god is said to have contrived the human birth of the sovereign and thus to be, in a sense, his real father. Thus Hatchepsut, Ramses II and Amenhotep III of Egypt are alike represented as "adopted" by Amun.[13]

We have seen above (§**122**) that a standard method of adopting a child was to clasp it to the bosom, in imitation of suckling by the mother. This too appears as part of our present ceremony of installation. Unfortunately, however, the point is obscured in the traditional text because the ancient editors, unaware of it, put the wrong vowel points to the Hebrew consonants and also ventured a slight emendation, thereby obtaining a false meaning. In place of the words (v. 7), *I will publish the decree* (a translation which is, in any case, grammatically untenable), we must read, by a very slight restoration, *I will gather thee unto My bosom.*[14]

King installed on holy mountain

The king is said (v. 6) to be installed on the holy mountain, here identified as Mt. Zion. This, again, reflects a piece of ancient symbolism. As the punctual representation of the god, the king had to imitate him on the present scene. Gods—especially supreme gods—characteristically dwell on the top of a mountain regarded as the axis of the world.[15] We think immediately of the Olympus of the Greeks, but there are also the Uttarakuru of the Hindus,[16] the Haraberezaiti (Elburz) of the Iranians,[17] the Meru of the Aryans, the Himavata of the Tibetans, the Kwan-lun of the Chinese, the Mtemnoh Toung of the Burmese,[18] the Northern Mountain of the Caucasian Khevsurs[19] and of the North American Dakotas,[20] and countless others. In religious cult, these mythical mountains were usually localized at the most prominent peak in the area, e.g., Casius in Syria, Tabor, Zion, Gerizim; and where no such peak existed, fiction supplied it by identifying the local cult center, albeit low-lying, with this eminence. The Egyptian queen Hatchepsut, for example, extols Karnak as representing "the light-mountain, the favorite place of Re',"[21] and similar praise is lavished also on the cities of Thebes and Hermonthis.[22] The Mesopotamians appear to have identified their stepped temples (ziggurats) with the mythical cosmic mountain,[23] as the Javanese do their famous temple at Barabudur.[24] Nor, indeed, is the idea unattested in the Old Testament itself; for in Psalm 48:2, Mt. Zion is hailed as something called "the far extremes of the North," and we now know from the Canaanite texts discovered at Ras Shamra that this was a standard designation of the mythical mountain of the gods. So too in Psalm 87:1, the temple on Zion was apostrophized as "the structure founded by God on the holy hills," and here again the point is that it is fancifully identified with the mythical mansion which the god (e.g., Baal in the Ras Shamra texts) upreared on the mythical mountain where the divine hosts convened.[25]

Accordingly, when the king is here said to be installed on "Zion, My holy hill," the meaning is not merely that Zion, by virtue of the Temple's being upon it, happens to be a cultically sacred spot, but rather that it stands for the mythical mountain of the god, the king thus reproducing on the real plane the status of the god on the ideal one.[26]

A further significance may also be involved. Since, as we have seen, the king was but a punctual embodiment of the sempiternal, continuous god, the beginning of his reign could be envisaged as the repetition of the primordial beginning of all things. The ceremony of installation would therefore have had to reproduce the primordial archetype. Now, the belief was entertained by many ancient peoples (as it is also by many modern primitives) that the earth had risen out of the primeval waters in the form of a hill or mound.[27] Accordingly, at his coming into power, the new king would have had symbolically to stand on such a hill or mound—a practice which we have already discussed (above, §148) in connection with the installation of Solomon.

251 Seeing the face of God 17:15

I shall behold Thy face in righteousness
when I awake, have full enjoyment of thy visage.

This psalm is written for the occasion when a man seeks refuge at a sanctuary from men who are bringing charges against him or actually pursuing him in order to wreak vengeance.[1] Such suppliants were regarded as the temporary "guests" (Heb.: *gērim*) of the god, claiming from him the customary rights of hospitality and protection (see above, §149). They slept in the sacred precincts and trusted to wake up safe and sound in the morning. It is to this rather than to the resurrection or judgment after death—as has been commonly supposed—that our concluding verse alludes.[2] The immediate reference is to what came later to be termed the *epopteia*—that is, the vision of the god in a dream or ecstatic experience,[3] though here it is conceived rather as the act of beholding the divine host's friendly countenance on awaking. The *epopteia* later became a prominent element of the Graeco-Roman mystery cults,[4] though it is mentioned already in connection with the Eleusinian mysteries.[5]

A further reference to this usage may be detected in the concluding words of Psalm 11—likewise a "psalm of asylum," viz., *The upright shall see thy face*.[6]

252 The breakers of Death 18:4–5

"Death" is here used by metonomy, as elsewhere in the Old Testament,[1] for the netherworld. The river (or rivers) of the netherworld figure ubiquitously in world folklore.[2] Usually, it is regarded as a barrier at the edge of the world of the living.[3] There is evidence of such a concept among the Egyptians, though admittedly of doubtful interpretation.[4] The Mesopotamians, however, spoke clearly of an infernal stream named Ḥubur, which all mortals were destined to cross.[5] In one Mesopotamian text, a man's deliverance from misfortunes is described as being plucked from the waters of Ḥubur.[6] Gilgamesh, in his quest for immortality, is eventually directed to a distant island beyond "the waters of death," where dwells the ancient worthy Utnapishtim, survivor of the Flood.[7] The Odyssey speaks likewise of a river (Acheron) which compasses the realm of the dead;[8] and the figure of the ferryman (Charon) who rows souls across it is, of course, a commonplace of Classical mythology and survives in modern Greek folklore.[9] King Arthur of England was transported on a barge to the Land of the Dead, and the hapless Lady of Shallot requested that, after her death, "her body be placed in a skiff and left to drift to the underworld, led only by the winds"[10]—a faded reminiscence of the same concept. The gravedigger in *Hamlet* also alludes to it when he declares that old age "hath *shipped* me into the Land";[11] while the old English Ballad of Johnnie Cock speaks significantly of "the *ford* of Hell."[12]

Attempts were sometimes made to determine the earthly location of this River of Death. German popular belief, for instance, identified it with the Rhine;[13] Procopius, the Byzantine historian, writing in the early sixth century, says that the English Channel was once so regarded;[14] while according to Pliny, the Cimbri—the ancient inhabitants of Jutland—called an arm of the North Sea "the sea of the dead."[15] Similarly, in France, an arm of the River Tréguier was known popularly as *le passage de l'enfer.*[16]

Nor is this fancy confined to ancient peoples. In a funeral dirge current among the Badaga of the Nilgrit Hills, the departing soul is said to encounter the "sea rising in waves" before it reaches the bridge dividing this world from the next.[17] The infernal or otherworld stream figures also in the popular fancy of many North American Indian tribes, such as the Ojibway, the Araucanians, the Algonqins, and the Sioux of Dakota.[18] The Aztecs speak of "Nine Rivers (Chicuroapa)";[19] the Greenlanders sail after death to an unfathomable abyss;[20] and analogous beliefs obtain among the Tupis of Brazil[21] and the Caribs.[22]

(If the Biblical writer is indeed referring to this Barrier Stream, the plural *rivers* [KJV: floods] must be understood as mere poetic idiom, like ῥοαί so used by Homer [e.g., Il. 19.229; Od. 6.216] or *rivi* by Latin authors [e.g., Horace, Odes 3.13.7; Tibullus 1.1, 28; Juvenal 6.490].)

To be sure, the concept is fluid in more than one sense, and the River (or Rivers) of Death are sometimes envisaged not as barriers but as actually flowing in the netherworld; and it is equally possible that this is what the Psalmist has in mind. Especially familiar in this respect are the four rivers of Hades in Greek myth—possibly an infernal counterpart of the four rivers of the Earthly Paradise (see above, §14).[23] But these are by no means the only example. In the Hindu Rig Veda we hear similarly of the "hellish" Vaitârâṇi river;[24] and in the Finnish Kalevala, the gruesome realm of Tuonela contains a "murky lake" and a "raging whirlpool."[25] The funeral liturgy of the Mandaeans of Iraq and Iran includes mention of a river which the dead must cross;[26] while Dante, gilding the Classical lily (if one can use such a metaphor of such darkling things), speaks of "infernal rivers fed by human tears."[27]

253 The bonds of Death

If Death can be portrayed mercifully as a shepherd (Ps. 49:14), he can also be pictured more harshly as a huntsman armed with snares and toils. This concept is by no means the peculiar invention of the Hebrew Psalmist. A Mesopotamian magical text likewise speaks of a man's being "bound in death."[1] In Hindu belief, Yama, the god of death, comes equipped with nets,[2] and among the Iranians the demon Astoridhotush stalks abroad in this fashion.[3] A Mandaean text speaks in the same way of "the bonds and toils of Death."[4]

The picture is common also in European lore. It is said, for instance, in the poem *Beowulf* that if any man gazed upon Thryth "he might reckon death-bonds prepared for him,"[5] and in the Anglo-Saxon *Exodus,* when Moses slays the Egyptian (Exod. 2:12), the latter falls "in dede's bond."[6] Shakespeare too speaks of the "bonds of death,"[7] and in medieval German poetry, Death is armed, like the Devil himself, with traps and bonds.[8]

The same is said too of Death's brother, Sleep. Sophocles speaks of "almighty Sleep who binds men,"[9] and Plato of being "fettered by Sleep."[10] In one of the Orphic Hymns, Hypnos (Sleep) is said to "tie men in indissoluble bonds";[11] and the Roman poet Ennius expresses a similar sentiment.[12] A Jewish prayer, still recited on retiring at night, alludes to "the bonds of sleep,"[13] and everyone familiar with English literature will at once recall Thomas Moore's "Oft in the stilly night, Ere slumber's chain hath bound me."

The idea is, of course, simply a variation on the common motif of *demoniacal binding,*[14] concerning which see above, §**208.**

(Most versions obscure the point by confusing the Hebrew word for "bonds" or "snares" with that which means "sorrows" (KJV) or "pangs." The word is *ḥebel,* and it is here to be associated rather with the Akkadian *naḥbalu,* "snare.")

254 Riding a cherub   18:10

We have already seen (above, §**18**) that a cherub is not a nightgowned angel, but a griffonlike monster; and since the words, *He mounted a cherub and flew,* here stand parallel to *He darted on the wings of the wind,* it is apparent that the reference is to the mythological storm-bird—the Im. Dugud of the Sumerians,[1] the Anzu (formerly read Zu) of the Akkadians,[2] the Hraesveglr of the Eddas,[3] the Garuda-bird, mount of Vishnu, of the Hindus,[4] and their congenors in other mythologies (*loc. cit.*).[5]

That gods ride the winds is a commonplace of Mesopotamian religious literature.[6] Ninlil, for instance, is described expressly as "rider on the great storms."[7] A variant of the idea is that gods are shod with the winds. They are said in the Hittite myth of Kumarbi to be so accoutred;[8] and a dim echo of the same notion may perhaps be heard in Homer's statement that Hermes and

Athene flew with the aid of winged sandals,[9] for this may represent a conflation of the originally distinct ideas that (a) gods were shod with the winds
and (b) the winds were winged. In Sassanian and Byzantine iconography, gods
are often portrayed riding in chariots drawn by griffins or similar mythical
beasts.[10]

255   The heavenly sieve   18:11

> *His pavilion round about*
> *were dark waters and thick clouds of the skies* (KJV)

Comparison with the parallel passage in II Samuel 22:12 shows that the
Hebrew word rendered *dark* (viz., *ḤeŠKaT*) is simply a substitution for a very
similar archaic word (viz., *ḤaŠRaT*) which does not occur elsewhere in the
Old Testament and which the ancient editors therefore could not understand.
Now, this rarer word is identical in outward form with one which occurs
in post-Biblical Hebrew and in other Semitic languages with the meaning,
sieve. It has therefore been suggested[1] that the Psalmist is here alluding to a
widespread popular notion that rain is precipitated through a celestial sieve.
Among the Kandhs of India, for example, it is believed that rain is sent in
this manner by the god Pidzin Pennu;[2] while the Greek comedian Aristophanes
has one of his characters declare ribaldly that it is Zeus urinating through a
sieve;[3] and even at the present day, in certain districts of Boeotia, "God is
plying his sieve" is a common popular expression for "it is hailing."[4]

The belief also underlies a very common practice of weather magic. In
times of drought, the Ainus of Japan scatter water through a sieve in order
"homeopathically" to influence the precipitation of rain.[5] German witches used
to do likewise;[6] and it is recorded that in the middle of the nineteenth century
the inhabitants of the Tarashchansk area of Russia poured water through a
sieve over an exhumed corpse to the same end.[7]

This interpretation of the Biblical verse has, however, itself to be passed
through a sieve, for it turns out to be a parade example of how Comparative
Folklore can be *wrongly* invoked in the exegesis of Scripture. The stark and
prosaic fact is that the obscure word *ḥašᵉrah*, which has been taken to mean
sieve, and which stands parallel in the text to *thick clouds of the skies*, is
really to be connected with a quite distinct Arabic *ḥathara*, "condense," and
therefore means no more than *condensation*, i.e., thick mass, *of waters!*[8]

256   Lightning as an arrow   18:14

See above, §242.

257   Walking round the altar   26:6

> *I will wash my hands in innocency,*
> *and compass Thine altar*

Circumambulation is a common device in folk custom for keeping noxious spirits from a place or person. The object is to make a closed circle which they cannot penetrate.[1]

The custom is well attested in Semitic antiquity.[2] The Akkadian word *saḥāru,* which comes to mean, "to resort to a shrine, perform cultic practices, worship," means literally, "to circuit," and probably referred in the first place to ritual circumambulation.[3] Similarly, in ancient South Arabian inscriptions, a not uncommon term for "altar" or "cultic standing stone" is *q-y-f* or *m-q-f,* the literal meaning of which is "object of circuit";[4] while a prominent feature of pre-Islamic worship was the rite known as *tawwaf,* in which the altar was solemnly circuited, in a peculiar limping gait, amid wild ejaculations of praise (*tahlil*).[5]

As with so much of primitive usage, the idiom may be rude and antiquated, but the content is profound and meaningful: the holy must be protected by a spiritual *cordon sanitaire,* and that cordon must be provided by human beings who are on their feet and moving.

258 A Canaanite psalm? 29

It is now commonly recognized that the Babylonian poem *Enuma Elish*— the so-called "Epic of Creation"—is really the cult-myth of the New Year (Akîtu) Festival, as part of the ceremonies of which it was indeed recited.[1] The sixth tablet of that poem relates how, following his victory over the monster Tiamat, the god Marduk (or, in the earlier Sumerian version, Ninurta)[2] was acclaimed king of the divine hosts and how, after being installed in an especially constructed palace, he received the adoration of his subjects. This episode of the myth evidently corresponded to that stage of the ritual in which the image of the god was conducted ceremoniously to his temple and there enthroned.

Precisely the same thing is represented also in Hittite myth and ritual. A text discovered at Boghazköi[3] which preserves the cultic legend and ritual of the annual Puruli festival held in spring deals with the triumph of the god of storm and weather over a dragon (*illuyankas*) and describes how, as the climax of that festival a parade was organized to the city of Nerik and how, on arrival at that cultic center, the victorious god was enthroned as king.[4]

The same pattern obtained likewise in the Canaanite world. In the *Poem of Baal,* the story is told how that god, after defeating the monster Yam (Sea) was acclaimed king of the gods and how, duly installed in an especially constructed palace, he received the adoration of his divine subjects.[5] The *Poem of Baal,* like its Mesopotamian and Hittite counterparts, was in all probability the cult-myth of a seasonal festival, its main episodes corresponding to the main stages of the ritual.[6]

In both cases the pattern is the same: the god of the weather defeats a rebellious dragon or monster, thereby acquires dominion and is installed in a new palace; and in both cases the occasion is marked by the recitation of a paean rehearsing his glory and prowess.

This mythological situation certainly finds expression in the Old Testament, for, as we shall see later, it provides the true interpretation of Psalm 93.[7] That psalm begins with a reference to Yahweh's having acquired kingship and to his being arrayed in the robes of majesty. It then alludes to the firm establishment of his throne and of the world order, and to his prowess over the raging force of Sea (*Yam*) and Streams (*Nᵉharōth*), the very antagonists specifically mentioned in the Canaanite *Poem of Baal*.[8] Next it makes reference to the reliability of his decrees—a phrase readily explicable from the fact that, in the analogous Babylonian myth, Marduk inaugurates his new regime by issuing orders and decrees designed to regulate the world.[9] Lastly, there is an allusion to a "house" which Yahweh is destined to occupy for all eternity.

Psalm 29 may be regarded as of the same order and as being really the typical "hymn of laudation" detached from its mythic context, Yahwized and preserved as an independent liturgical composition.[10] There is a complete correspondence in details between the Hebrew psalm and the texts to which we have referred, and several passages of the former which are at present difficult of interpretation are at once clarified and illuminated by comparison with the latter.

The psalm begins (v. 1) with an invocation to the *bᵉnê elim* or members of the pantheon, to pay homage to Yahweh.[11] Now, in *Enuma Elish* it is the company of the gods who render homage to Marduk after his victory,[12] while in the Canaanite *Poem of Baal* it is the "threescore and ten sons of Asherat,"[13] identical with what are elsewhere called specifically the *bn ilm*,[14] who are summoned to the new-built palace to perform the same function.

These lesser gods are invited (v. 2) to ascribe unto Yahweh "the glory of His name." This last expression recurs elsewhere,[15] and the whole phrase is usually taken to mean that the divine hosts are summoned to acknowledge the innate majesty of Yahweh. But it is significant that in *Enuma Elish* the adoration takes the particular form of reciting the god's honorific name and titles,[16] and that there is repeated reference in that poem to the celebration of Marduk's *name;* cf. vi, 117: "verily, we will acclaim his name in our assembly"; *ib.* 143–44: "in their convocation they acclaim his essence; in the fane they all of them celebrate His name." Hence, it would appear plausible that the expression "glory/honor of His name" possesses a more specific meaning and denotes the recitation, with appropriate laudatory embellishments, of his honorific names.[17] In other words, the ensuing description of Yahweh's prowess as a "god of glory" who convulses nature by his storms would be the actual "glory of his name" which the divine hosts are bidden recite.

The gods are invited (v. 2b) to "prostrate themselves" in "holy awe." Now, for the latter phrase (Heb.: *bᵉhadrath qōdeš*) the Septuagint and Peshitta Versions read, significantly, "in the court of the/His sanctuary (*beḥad/ṣrath qōdeš*),[18] and this links up at once with the fact that in *Enuma Elish* the gods are said explicitly to render homage to Marduk "in the great court (*paramaḫḫu*) of his temple Esagila in Babylon (vi, 51) and "in the fane" (*ib.* 144). while in the *Poem of Baal* they are invited into the "mansion" (II AB vi, 44: "he invited his brethren into his mansion, his kinsmen into the midst of his palace, he invited the seventy sons of Asherath").

There follows (vv. 3–9b) a vivid description of Yahweh's prowess in storm and tempest. This, as suggested above, must be regarded as the actual honorification which the lesser gods are invited to recite; it is not merely a series of laudatory observations by the poet. Yahweh's thunder (lit. "voice") is said to convulse forest and ocean; it comes with strength and awe-inspiring vehemence. Particularly, it is stated that by means of it Yahweh shatters the cedars of Lebanon. Now, the language of this laudation runs parallel, to a remarkable degree, with that of the paean recited to Baal in the Canaanite poem. The latter is put into the mouth of Kôshar, the divine architect,[19] who, after some argument, has at last received Baal's consent to install windows and skylights in the new palace. The plan is that whenever the latter are opened it will be a sign to Baal correspondingly to open "a rift in the clouds" and send rain. Kôshar is so delighted at Baal's final acquiescence in this plan that he breaks out into a hymn of glory celebrating the powers of the god as genius of the storm. The hymn reads as follows:[20]

> When Baal opens a rift in the clouds,
> When Baal gives forth his holy voice,[21]
> When Baal keeps discharging the utterances of his lips
> His ho[ly] voice [convul]ses the earth,
> . . . . the mountains quake,
> A-tremble are the . . . .
> East and west the high places of the e[arth] reel;
> The enemies of Baal take to the woods,
> The foes of Hadad to the sides of the mountains!

Baal replies:

> The eyes of Baal mark down, then his hand strikes,[a]
> Yea, cedars quiver at the touch of his right hand![22]

That this paean is based upon standard hymns to the storm-god is shown by the fact that parallel phrases are indeed quoted by Abimilki of Tyre in the Tell Amarna letter 149:14–15 Winckler:

> Who giveth forth his voice in heaven like Hadad,
> And all the mountains quake at his voice.

Similarly, a hymn to Hadad printed in King's *Magic and Sorcery,* 21:22 contains the directly comparable expression:

> Hadad giveth forth thunders,
> The mountains are shaken.

In the light of these parallels the conclusion seems inescapable that the "glory of his name" of our Hebrew psalm reproduces the mythic laudation uttered by the lesser gods, itself projected from a standard hymn recited at the festival in the ceremonies of which the myth was recited or enacted.

At the end of the laudation (v. 9c) occur the obscure words "and in His palace all of it saith, Glory." The abruptness of this clause has been duly observed by most modern commentators, and the usual way of surmounting the difficulty is to assume an immediately antecedent lacuna, which must have also contained the subject to which the expression "all *of it*" referred.[23] With this solution we may readily agree, but exactly how the lacuna should be filled is indicated clearly by a comparison with *Enuma Elish* vi, 144. There we are told that the gods, duly assembled in the new-built palace of Esagila, *sat in the fane and recited the "name" of Marduk*. The words are a virtually exact translation of our Hebrew phrase, "all of them" answering precisely to "all of it" (*kullô*) and thus showing that the missing subject is the assembly of the gods. Indeed, the preceding verse in *Enuma Elish* (vi, 143) reads explicitly: "in their convocation they celebrated his essence." Hence it is apparent that we must restore something like:

> The congregation of the holy ones[24] praise him
> And in his palace all of it recites the Glory.

The Glory is, of course, the foregoing laudation.

"Yahweh," continues the Psalmist (v. 10), "sat (enthroned) at the storm-flood, and Yahweh will sit (enthroned) for ever." The abruptness of this statement is likewise perplexing, while scholars have also been exercised to determine whether the reference to the stormflood is to the specific Noachic Deluge or to *any* inundation caused by the display of Yahweh's powers. The difficulty is removed, however, when the mythological background of the psalm is kept in mind. In *Enuma Elish* it is stated *specifically* (vi, 47, 51) that Esagila, the newly-built palace of Marduk, *was upreared upon the nether sea;*[25] while the temple of E-ninu at Lagash was said likewise to have been founded on the nether ocean,[26] and that in Eridu was termed "House of the nether sea."[27] In the sanctuary at Hierapolis (Membij), Lucian was shown a chasm into which the waters of the Deluge were supposed to have gathered,[28] and Jewish tradition asserted that the foundation stone of the temple at Jerusalem held down the flood.[29] An analogous myth was current in the sanctuary of Olympian Zeus at Athens.[30] Even more pertinent is the fact that in the Hittite cult-myth of the Puruli festival, the god who vanquishes the dragon (*illuyankas*) is said subsequently to be enthroned in the temple "over the well."[31] As for the phrase "and Yahweh will sit (enthroned) for ever," this must be regarded as

something like a "God save the king!" In precisely the same way, the divine ancestors of Marduk are said, in *Enuma Elish* iv 28, to hail him with the cry
"Marduk is king", while in the Canaanite *Poem of Baal* (III AB, A 32) the
defeated monster Yam explains: "Let Baal be king."[32]

The concluding verse (11) of the Psalm ("Yahweh giveth strength to
His people; Yahweh blesseth His people with peace") is usually regarded as
an addition made when the poem was incorporated into or adapted for the
public liturgy, and analogies to it may certainly be found in Psalm 28:8; 68:36,
etc. It should be observed, however, that an exactly comparable expression
occurs in *Enuma Eelish* vi 113, where the minor gods hail their new king
Marduk in the words "Verily, Marduk is the strength of his land and of his
people." This suggests that it was part of the original mythological hymn. In
itself, of course, it was a liturgical formula, probably used at ceremonies of
enthronization and therefore adopted into the liturgy whenever a god was
hymned in the role of king; this would account for its substantial recurrence in
Psalms 28:8; 68:36, etc. The point is, however, that its presence in our psalm
is not due to such adoption at a later date; on the contrary, it was adopted
already in the original composition.

Thus it would appear that Psalm 29 is a form of the ritual laudation of the
victorious god which formed part of the seasonal pantomime of the New
Year Festival. It must be emphasized, however, that this in no way implies
that the seasonal pantomime actually obtained in official Israelitic cultus, as
has been so frequently supposed. All that we are here suggesting is that certain
hymnodic patterns, derived from these earlier usages, survived in literary
convention.[33] This is, of course, a very different thing, and the difference is
salient. At the same time, we would not deny that the survival often involved
more than a mere persistence of forms. Evidence is increasing daily that many
of the psalms were conscious and deliberate Yahwizations of current "pagan"
compositions; and we believe that this was the case in the present instance.[34] It
can scarcely be doubted that beside the official cult of Yahweh in Jerusalem
there existed a more primitive folk-religion throughout the length and breadth
of Palestine. This may have taken the form of mere folkloristic and unmean-
ing customs rather than of formal religion, but it must certainly have had its
influence upon the cult of Yahweh, and it is not unreasonable to suppose that
the zealous propagandists of the latter may frequently have tried to "fetch the
public" by adopting and adapting the songs and airs current in the former, on
the same principle as induced Rowland Hill to suggest that hymns be set to
popular melodies on the grounds that "the Devil shouldn't have the best
tunes." Has not Professor Soothill told us[35] that he once heard children in India
singing enthusiastically in imitation of a well-known Christian hymn:

> Buddha loves me; this I know
> For the Sutras tell me so?

259 Paradisal bliss   36:7–9

> *O LORD, how precious is Thy loving-kindness!*
> *Gods and men take refuge under the shadow of Thy wings.*
> *They are sated on the richness of Thy house,*
> *and Thou givest them to drink of the River of Thy delights.*
> *For with Thee is the Fountain of Life;*
> *in Thy light do we see light.*

The Psalmist is painting a picture of paradisal bliss, and draws on characteristic mythical traits. The "river of delights" is the celebrated Paradisal Stream, source of the world's rivers (see above, §14). The word rendered *delights* is the plural of *'eden,* "luxuriance," and pointedly suggests the Garden of Eden. The "fountain of life" is the paradisal Fountain of Immortality or Eternal Youth, so ubiquitous in world folklore (see above, §14). The "light" is the special glow of the paradisal realm, derived in large measure from the fact that it lies near the rising sun (see above, §13).

(The traditional rendering misses the mythological allusion by construing the word "gods" in the second line as a vocative, i.e., "O God"; it really provides the complement to "and men," and is simply a poetic vestige of ancient pagan myth.

The words, "with Thee is the Fountain of Life, in Thy light do we see light," are often emended by modern scholars who have simply failed to drink from it. Once the underlying mythology is appreciated, there is no need to "correct" the text.)

260 Magical waters   41:7–9

> RSV: *All who hate me whisper together about me;*
> *they imagine the worst for me.*
> *(They say,) "A deadly thing has fastened upon him;*
> *he will nor rise up again from where he lies."*

This rendering again misses the underlying folklore. The word "whisper" refers specificially to the murmuring of spells (see above, §171), and the phrase translated, *(They say,) "A deadly thing has fastened upon him,"* is really a direct statement meaning, *A noxious thing is poured upon him.*[1] The allusion is then clarified by a famous passage in the Babylonian Epic of Creation (*Enuma Elish* 1.61 ff.), where the rebellious god Apsu is finally dispatched (perhaps "liquidated" would be the better word) by Ea, genius of all arts, knowledge, and magic, by having a magical concoction poured over him in his sleep, so that he never wakes! The passage runs:

> Ea, the all-wise, divined their plan.
> A master design he contrived and wrought.

Cunningly wrought he his spell, high and pure.
He . . . ed it, set it in water.
Then, while he (Apsu) was lying in a cavern,
he poured sleep over him.
He made Apsu lie supine, drenched with sleep.

(In the light of this parallel it is apparent that the Hebrew words usually rendered, *They imagine the worst for me,* really mean more specifically, *They devise an evil plot against me.*)

261 An ancient Hebrew wedding song 45

Psalm 45 is expressly entitled "a song of loves," and if one reads it attentively in the light of Comparative Folklore it becomes immediately apparent that it is in fact an ancient Hebrew hymeneal.[1]

Unfortunately, the true sense of the poem has been but imperfectly perceived and is therefore not brought out clearly in the standard English translations. Because it is said to have been indited for a "king" (v. 1), and because it refers to his anointment (v. 2) and enthronement (v. 6), and makes specific mention of a "princess" (v. 12), it has been commonly assumed that it was composed for the marriage of a particular monarch, and scholars have broken their heads to determine who he may have been.[2] Once we bear in mind, however, that in the Near East, as elsewhere, it is a common convention to treat a bridal couple as royalty,[3] it becomes apparent that "His Majesty" is simply an ordinary bridegroom and the princess an ordinary bride, and that the reference to their regal status and dignity are no more than *jeux d'esprit.*

Oriental weddings invariably involve the presence of a professional poet or minstrel (Arabic: *sha'ir*) who improvises songs in honor of the bridal couple and leads the guests in chanting them. Accordingly, our poem begins with the songster's reaction to the summons for his services. He playfully expresses his excitement at being called to a "command performance":

> *My heart is a-flutter—oh joy!*
> *'Tis for a king himself*
> *I am now to indite my works!*
> *My tongue shall be like the pen of a fluent scribe!*

The scene then turns to the bridegroom's house. He is being robed and perfumed for the ceremony, and each stage of the procedure is accompanied by appropriate verses. As the unguents are poured over him, the poet exclaims:

> *Fairer thou wast than human kind,*
> *with a magic[4] shed o'er thy lips!*
> *Some godhead must have endowed thee*
> *with an immortal grace!*

In these words the poet plays on the custom of sprinkling date juice, clarified butter, or honey on the lips of a child shortly after birth.[5] No ordinary juice or honey was it that was shed on *your* lips, he says in a graceful compliment to the bridegroom, but rather divine magic or charm. You were born super-humanly handsome; some god must have conferred upon you the quality of immortal grace (Heb.: *b*ᵉ*rakah,* "blessing").[6]

The idea that privileged beings were fed at birth on heavenly food or that they were especially annealed by gods is commonplace in the folklore of many peoples. It may be illustrated especially from ancient Greek poetry. In the Homeric *Hymn to Demeter* we read how that goddess anointed the newborn Demophon so that he resembled a god.[7] Appolonius Rhodius relates how Thetis tried by similar means to render Achilles immortal;[8] and Theocritus asserts that Aphrodite likewise "immortalized" Berenice.[9] So too Athene poured ambrosial grace on the infant Telemachus,[10] and so too was Penelope endowed;[11] while Ovid declares of Aeneas that his divine mother (Venus) touched his baby lips with nectar and ambrosia and "thus made a god of him."[12] True, none of these references comes from an Oriental source, but that the basic idea was not foreign to Ancient Near Eastern thought is attested by the frequent insistence in both Mesopotamian and Egyptian documents that the king "imbibed" divinity at birth by being suckled at the breasts of a goddess (see below, §284).

Once attired, the bridegroom buckles on his sword. Such a sword is a standard article of equipment at Arab weddings.[13] Thus, when a Palestinian Arab bridegroom goes out to usher his bride into his house, he usually carries a sword, which he presses against her face and with the tip of which he eventually raises her veil.[14] Alternatively, he stands on the flat roof and waves a sword over the bride as she crosses the threshold.[15] The purpose in either case is to forefend demons.[16] Sometimes, to be sure, the sword is carried by a grooms-man.[17] Indeed, the Song of Songs expressly alludes to this custom when it speaks of the threescore "mighty men" who escort the bridegroom's palanquin, "each with his sword on his thigh against the Terror at Night" (i.e., demon; cf. Ps. 91:15);[18] and the usage survives in modern times in the crossed swords held over the bridal couple when they leave the church at a military wedding. Sometimes, too, it is the bride rather than the groom who carries a sword. This is not uncommon among the Arabs,[19] and readers of Norse literature will recall that in pagan Norway, Erik's daughter carried a sword at her marriage to Rolf.[20] In medieval Egypt, Jewish brides not only carried a sword but also wore a helmet;[21] and it is reported that in the Usambara territory of East Africa, the chief bridesmaid, dressed as a man, carries a sword before the bride.[22]

Likening the bridegroom to a king, the poet identifies the sword with that carried by a warrior monarch or handed to him—as in the British coronation ceremony—at the time of his investiture. He therefore bids him gird it on by way of insignia and regalia:

> *Champion that thou art,*
> *gird the sword on thy thigh*
> *as thy regal array and adornment!*[23]

The "conquering hero" is now ready to go forth to meet the bridal procession in order to lead it into the house. The bridegroom usually goes mounted on a horse or a camel.[24] As he mounts, the minstrel, playing on that action and continuing the comparison with a valiant monarch, bids him:

> *Ride forth, fare on, in the cause of Truth!*

As he leaves the precincts of his house, the bridegroom customarily distributes largesse to the poor, who crowd around the gate.[25] Now, in Hebrew popular speech such largesse was called "righteousness" (*ṣᵉdāqāh*).[26] Accordingly, by a neat double-entendre, the minstrel likens this act of charity to the typical duty of a king (cf. Pss. 72:2–4; 82:3), bidding him

> *do the right thing by the poor.*[27]

Finally, as the party is about to move off, minstrel and friends exclaim:

> *May thy right hand guide thee on thy way*
> *by awe-inspiring feats!*
> *May thine arrows (well-sharpened, to boot)*
> *sink into the heart of thy Majesty's foes!*
> *May (whole) peoples fall at thy feet!*

In these words there is, it would seem, yet another artful allusion to a wedding custom, for among the Arabs and among several other peoples it is a common practice for the bridegroom and/or his escorts to shoot arrows in order to ward off malevolent spirits.[28] At ancient Indian weddings, for example, he used to shoot them while he cried out, "I pierce the eyes of the demons who are surrounding the bride!"[29] The modern equivalent is the firing of rifles.[30] Moreover, it is worth noting that, according to some authorities, discharge of arrows was likewise an element of Egyptian coronation ceremonies,[31] and it still obtains at the installation rites of the Bar-Kitara of Africa.[32] If, therefore, such a rite could be attested in ancient Palestine or Syria, we might find in the minstrel's words a further parallelism between the features of wedding ceremonies and those of enthronement.

As the bridegroom rides through the courtyard, looking to all the world like a king, the bystanders—again led by the chief minstrel—chant appropriate verses extolling his regal state:

> *Thy throne hath some god <set firm>*[33]
> *to endure for all time!*
> *A sceptre of equity is the sceptre of thy kingship!*
> *Because thou hast loved the right,*
> *and hated the wrong,*

some god with (this) festive oil[34]
hath now anointed thee (king)!

These verses deliberately imitate the kind of salutation which loyal subjects were wont to address to their sovereign. We need quote only such common expressions in the state letters of Assyria as: *May the royal throne of my lord stand firm for ever,*[35] or *May the gods Nabu and Marduk . . . grant unto my lord, the king of countries, a sceptre of equity and an enduring throne!*[36]

The bride's procession is now in view, or at least within earshot. The bridegroom's party therefore feels called upon to give him a special "build-up" as an enviable "catch." Accordingly, with typical Oriental exuberance, it pays tribute to his former triumphs in the lists of love:

Among thy lady loves,
who have brought delight unto thee
have been very princesses themselves
hailing from ivory halls!
At thy right hand hath stood
(full many) a harem-queen
Decked in the gold of Ophir![37]

Meanwhile, corresponding ceremonies have been taking place in the home of the bride, and the next verses of our poem represent the snatches of song sung by *her* relatives and friends as she is being prepared for the ceremony. As they dress and undress her, they seek to allay her apprehensions and to overcome that bashfulness which convention demands of her:[38]

Hearken, maiden, and see,
and incline thine ear;
forget thy kith and kin;
His Majesty craves thy beauty;
He is thy lord—make obeissance to him!

Then, as a counterpart to what the bridegroom's friends have been chanting about *him* while they have been preparing him for the ceremony, they make a point of complimenting the girl on her powers of captivation:

Thyself a Tyrian heiress,[39]
the richest men of the people
have come courting thee with gifts![40]

This is followed, in turn, by what the Arabs call the *jelwe*—that is, the formal display of the bride in all her finery.[41] As they turn her this way and that and take in the various details of her costume, they break out into enthusiastic cries:

Very princess that she is,
her finery is of pearls[42]
set amid braids of gold!
She is clothed in broidered robes![43]

The general sentiment of these verses is well illustrated by the modern Arab practice of referring to the bride's trousseau as "royal garments,"[44] while the mention of the pearls and the braids of gold alludes to the fact that the bridal crown often consists of strings of pearls set amid golden braids or chains of golden coins.[45]

When all is in readiness, the procession moves off to conduct the bride into the presence of the groom. The procession is accompanied by gay music, and the guests shout in chorus:

Let her be led to the king!
Let virgins, walking behind her,
escort her with gladness and glee,
bring her into his Majesty's halls!

After the ceremony, the company turns once more to shower congratulations upon the bridegroom:

In place of thy fathers be thy sons!
Mayest thou make them to be lords throughout the earth!
May they keep thy name in remembrance[46]
for age upon age!
May peoples heap upon thee
everlasting praise!

Such outspoken wishes for offspring—reminiscent of the Italian greeting, *figli maschi*—were and still are quite common at Syrian weddings. In the Canaanite (Ugaritic) *Poem of K-r-t,* The supreme god El himself, on behalf of the divine guests, proposes such a toast to the hero at his marriage to the princess Ḥurraya.[47] The point to be observed, however, is that the formula here employed reproduces at the same time the type of salutation customarily addressed by courtiers to their sovereign. In one of the state letters of Assyria, for example, we find the expression, *May the gods grant kingship to thine offspring, to thy seed, for all time![48]* Comparable also is the Homeric formula addressed by Odysseus to the queen of the Phaeacians: *May the gods grant these thy friends that they may be prosperous while they live and that each may rear up children to inherit the wealth which lies in his halls and the honorable place which the people have given him![49]*

262 Mountains in midsea   46:2

We shall not fear though God rock[1] the earth,
though mountains totter into midsea.

This hyperbole finds an excellent parallel in an Icelandic poem by the skald Kormak (10th cent.): *Flagstones will float like corn on water,* and great mountains move out into the deep sea *ere there be born again a lady so illustrious and fair as Steingard.*[2]

263 The far reaches of the North 48:2

His holy hill, towering superb,
joy of the whole earth,
Mt. Zion, thou "far reaches of the North,"
an emperor's citadel!

Mt. Zion is here likened to the mythical northern mountain of ancient lore, on which the gods held session and where their overlord sat ensconced in his palace.[1] Thus, in the Canaanite texts from Ras Shamra-Ugarit, the abode of El and the seat of the divine parliament lies in the "far reaches of the North," popularly identified with neighboring Jebel el Akra (ancient Mt. Ḥazzi, Casius), the tallest peak in Syria;[2] and this belief is echoed in Isaiah 14:13, where the rebellious "Lucifer" declares, "I will sit throned on the Mount of Assembly, in the far reaches of the North." The Babylonian supreme god Anu dwelt atop a great mountain—the "axle of the world"—near the North Star.[3] The celestial Uttarakuru of the Hindus,[4] the Himavata of the Tibetans, the Meru of the Aryans, the Kwan-lun of the Chinese, the Myemnoh Toung of the Burmese, and the Asaheim of the Norsemen likewise lay in the north.[5] In the north too, on the summit of a mountain, sat Heyoka, the weather-god of the North American Dakotas,[6] and there also the Khevsurs of the Caucasus locate the lord of storms.[7] The Masai believe in a northern paradise,[8] as do also the Finns.[9] In the Syriac Alexander-legend, that hero sees Paradise from a place in the north;[10] and in the Scandinavian Flatey-book (14th cent.), the hero Holge Thoresen goes to the north in order to join the blessed.[11]

The numinous quality of the north also inspires the belief that it is the seat of demons. This idea obtained among the Iranians,[12] the Mandaeans of Iraq and Iran,[13] the Hindus of the Vedic age,[14] the Greeks,[15] Jews,[16] and Mexicans,[17] and was a tenet also of Manichaean belief.[18] In late Greek magical spells, demons are conjured from the north,[19] and Plutarch there locates the monster Typhon.[20] Milton, in his *Paradise Lost,* makes the rebel angels muster in the north; and in Shakespeare's *I Henry the Sixth* (v. 3), La Pucelle invokes the aid of spirits "under the lordly monarch of the north." In English popular superstition, the north door of a church is sometimes regarded as that through which the Devil enters.[21]

264 Death as a shepherd 49:14

The conception of Death as a shepherd is not so common in folklore as one might suspect.[1] Nevertheless, this Biblical image has interesting parallels. In Greek mythology, Menoetēs, the son of Keuthonymos, is said to herd sheep at the far western entrance to Hades;[2] and a statement by Plato that the soul is shepherded has been so interpreted.[3]

265 Bottled tears 56:8

Put Thou my tears in Thy bottle!

This curious image may well have been suggested by the widespread practice of conserving tears in a bottle at funerals and other occasions of lamentation. Thus, when the Shi'ite Moslems of Iran celebrate the annual Commemoration of Hosein, their tears are often wiped with a cloth or a piece of cotton-wool and then squeezed into a bottle. They are held to possess amuletic virtue, and popular superstition asserts that an angel keeps them until the Day of Judgment.[1] Originally, such tear-bottles were buried with the dead, the idea being that the moisture would preserve their desiccated bodies and compensate for the vital fluids that had ebbed out of them. This custom obtained, for instance, in many parts of Germany until recent times;[2] while in Russia tear-stained handkerchiefs were often thrown into graves.[3] In ancient Egypt, the tears shed by Isis and Nephthys were believed to revive Osiris,[4] and similar notions appear in several Indonesian folktales.[5] A frequent theme of Greek and Latin poetry is the craving of the dead for tears;[6] what was really besought was not a token of grief but a means of "survival." Analogous is the common idea that "Blessed are the dead whom the rain rains on."[7]

On the other hand, such tears are sometimes regarded as an encumbrance to the deceased. There are, for example, many European folktales which tell how the ghosts of children return and complain of being troubled by the presence of tear-bottles in their graves;[8] while the Iranians say that the tears of mourners form a river which impedes the passage of the dead to the other world.

266 Yahweh's processional 68

(a) It was the custom both among the Mesopotamians and the Hittites solemnly to induct the major national or local god as king during the New Year ceremonies. He was led to his palace in a festal parade, accompanied by the lesser gods who had come to pay him homage. The procession assumed the form of a triumph, for the god was thought to have secured his dominion by vanquishing the contumacious dragon of the waters, who might otherwise have flooded the earth.[1] Whether such a ceremony actually occurred also among the Canaanites is at present unknown, but it was certainly represented by them in myth, for the conquest of the draconic Sir Sea (Yam), and the consequent induction as king of his victor, Baal, form the central theme of a mythological poem discovered at Ras Shamra-Ugarit.[2]

It is not necessary to suppose that the actual ceremony persisted in Israel. The type of liturgical composition which originally accompanied it may well have survived simply as a conventional genre of hymns, and it is on this assumption that the long and otherwise disjointed Psalm 68 becomes at once coherent and intelligible. The psalm moves, as it were, through the successive moments of the celebration and may be read as a kind of "processional." Indeed, this is explicitly indicated by the words of v. 25: *How awe-inspiring*[3] *are thy processions, O God, the processions of my God, my King, into the sanctuary.*

> 1. *When God but takes the field,*[4]
>   *his enemies are scattered,*
>   *and his foremen flee from his face.*

These proud opening words echo the traditional cry uttered when the ark (palladium) of Yahweh moved forward: cf. Numbers 10:35. The ark, we know, represented the presence of Yahweh on the field of battle: cf. I Samuel 4:5–7. Accordingly, this verse places us in imagination at the scene of the combat wherein the god vanquished his adversary and thereby acquired kingship.

> 4. *Cast up a way*[5] *for him*
>   *who chariots through the deserts*

The Hebrew for "chariots through the deserts" is *Rokeb ⁽ᵃ⁾rābōth.* This is simply a popular distortion of *Rokeb 'araphôth* "He that chariots upon the clouds"—the constant epithet of Baal in the mythological texts from Ras Shamra-Ugarit.[6] It is clear, therefore, that the Hebrew poet has this ancient myth in mind.

> 6. *God . . . leads out prisoners to*
>   *prosperity.*

It was the custom among the Babylonians to release a prisoner at the New Year festival;[7] and this usage prevailed also at several Greek festivals.[8] Moreover, Livy tells us that at the celebration of a *lectisternium,* or "banquet offered to the gods," the bonds of prisoners were untied.[9]

A more familiar example of this custom is afforded by the incident of Barabbas in the New Testament.[10] The Psalmist plays on this standard element of the ceremonies, using it to point up the clemency and mercy of God in general.

> 9. *A liberal rain dost thou shed, O God,*
>   *over thine estate;*
>   *and when it waxes faint,*
>   *thou dost hold it firm.*

The victory of the newly inducted god is everywhere associated with the securing of adequate rainfall for the ensuing year. Thus, in the Canaanite myth, Baal's triumph over Yam and over Mot (Death, Sterility) culminates in his "furnishing his rains in their due seasons";[11] and when, in the corresponding Babylonian version, Marduk has subdued Tiamat, he is hailed as "Lord of luxuriance" (*bêl ḫêgalli*).[12] Similarly, too, the victory of the Hittite storm-god over the dragon Illuyankas—the theme of the annual Puruli festival—is associated with the supply of rain.[13]

> 16. *Why look ye askance, ye many-peaked hills,*
> *at the mount which (this) God has favored*
> *as his dwelling?*
> *Surely, Yahweh too can take up an eternal*
> *dwelling!*

In the Canaanite *Poem of Baal,* that victorious god is installed on his holy mountain;[14] just as is Marduk in the lofty ziggurat of Esagila, especially built for him.

> 17. *The chariotry of God is twice ten thousand;*
> *bowmen there are by the thousands;*
> *Yahweh comes from Sinai into the sanctuary!*[15]

The allusion is to the triumphal march (Babylonian *tebû*)[16] of the divine victor into his palace, or temple. This is conceived of in terms of a military parade.

The word rendered "bowmen" (viz., Heb.: *šin'an*) has long proved a puzzle to commentators and, by false etymology, is usually rendered "thousands *twice-told.*" But the word has now turned up as a military term in documents from Alalaḫ[17] and it has been recognized as the equivalent of the Egyptian *snni,* which means bowmen who fought from chariots.[18]

> 18. *Thou hast ascended the height.*

The expression occurs in reference to a conquering hero, in Psalm 7:8.[19] It echoes the technical language of the ancient myth, for Baal too is said after his victory to ascend the "height" (*mrym*) of Zaphon, i.e., Mt. Casius.[20]

> 20. *To God, the Lord, belongs escape*
> *from death* (RSV).

The Hebrew word rendered "escape" also means "ruin, discomfiture."[21] The poet is giving a universal meaning to the fact that in the ancient myth Baal secured his sovereignty by discomfiting Môt, the god of death.

> 21. *God smites the head of his foes.*

Again the poet is giving a general meaning to a specific feature of the celebrations. A commentary on the Babylonian New Year ceremonies mentions that at one stage of the proceedings a felon (*bêl ḫiṭṭi*) was marched through the streets and beaten about the head.[22] He probably served as a human scapegoat (see above, §**194**).

> 22.   *Said Yahweh; I will muzzle Bashan,*
>   *capture Yam in the depths!*
> (RSV: *I will bring them back from Bashan,*
>   *I will bring them back from the depth of the sea.*)

At first blush one would assume that Bashan meant the volcanic plateau east of the Jordan (as in v. 15), and that what the poet intended to convey was that Yahweh delivers from loftiest height to lowest depth. We now know, however, from the Canaanite texts discovered at Ras Shamra that another word B-sh-n (vocalization uncertain) was one of the names of the mythological dragon muzzled and subdued by Baal.[23] We know also that another of his names was simply "Sea" (Yammu) and that the archaic Canaanite word for "muzzle" was very similar in form to that usually rendered "I will bring (them) back."[24] Accordingly, what the first line of our verse really meant was: *Said Yahweh, I will muzzle the Dragon!* To this the second line now provides an appropriate parallel, for here the Hebrew word usually rendered, *I will bring back,* is identical in form (in the original spelling) with one meaning, *I will capture,*[25] and this is in fact the very term used in the Canaanite myth to describe the discomfiture of Sea (Yammu) at the hands of Baal![26] Hence, the second part of the verse really means, *Yea, I will capture Sir Sea in the depth!*

In the Canaanite poem, Baal shatters the multiple heads of his adversary with a bludgeon;[27] while in the corresponding Babylonian myth, the victorious Marduk does likewise to the monster Tiamat.[28] That the myth was familiar to the Hebrews is clear from the explicit allusion to it in Psalm 74:14: *Thou it was that didst crush the heads of Leviathan.*

By a natural association, therefore, the poet connects the belaboring of the condemned felon (see above §**194**) with the similar punishment inflicted, in the traditional myth, upon the god's adversary.

> 35.   *Awe-inspiring is God amid the holy beings.*[29]

The poet is here alluding to the fact that when the victorious god is finally enthroned, he is surrounded by the lesser gods, who come to pay him homage and to participate in the divine "parliament" at which the fates of the ensuing year are determined.

This is the culminating scene of the Babylonian myth;[30] while in the corresponding Hittite version there is even a description of the protocol which is to govern the order of seating![31] Baal too, when he is finally enthroned in his new-built palace, tenders a banquet to the gods.[32]

(In the traditional Hebrew text the point of this verse is obscured by the false reading: *Awe-inspiring art thou, O God, from thy sanctuary.* The correct reading can, however, be elicited from a variant in the Greek Septuagint Version.)

(b) Yellow garments **68:13**

> *Shall ye still go lying 'mid the slagheaps,*
> *ye wings of a dove silver-spangled,*
> *whose pinnions are yellow gold?*[33]

The poet is addressing the womenfolk of Israel who are thus exhorted to emerge from their gloom and dejection and preen themselves in celebration of Yahweh's triumph over His and their enemies.

The imagery becomes even more effective when it is observed that yellow was highly favored in the costume of women alike in Oriental and Classical antiquity. "Like all Oriental women," we are told of the Arabian 'Aisha, "they love yellow. Often they dress entirely in that color. . . . Their garments are dipped in saffron whenever they are laundered."[34] In Malaya, yellow is the regal hue;[35] and in the famous Syriac *Hymn of the Soul*, it wears a yellow robe.[36] Cassandra, says Aeschylus, was clothed in yellow at the sack of Troy;[37] and in the same poet's *Persians,* the ghost of Darius is bidden rise from the netherworld clothed in yellow.[38] Greek courtesans and temple women affected yellow garb[39] as did also the eunuch priests of the Syrian Goddess whom Lucian saw at Hierapolis (Membij)[40] and as do Buddhist monks (*bhikkus*) and Indian ascetics at the present day.[41] The wife of the priest of Jupiter (*flamen Dialis*) at Rome likewise wore yellow,[42] and, on a less exalted plane, such Roman poets as Catullus, Tibullus, and Ovid frequently make mention of the yellow raiment of brides, ladyloves, and mythological heroines.[43]

Yellow is considered also to have special virtue in forefending demons,[44] and this too is a reason for its popularity. Modern brides in India, for example, wear tattered yellow raiment for six days before marriage, to avert evil spirits;[45] and a wife who greets her husband after his return from a long absence wears yellow.[46] Similarly, the Mundas and Santals of Bengal smear yellow dye on bridal couples;[47] and the Hindus of western India rub their bodies with yellow turmeric against assault by the "princes of darkness."[48] In Sicily, yellow threads (*nastro gallo intrecciato*) are worn against the evil eye.[49]

Since, in popular usage, anything that excites observation usually does so ambivalently—that is, for evil as well as for good—yellow comes to be regarded also as an ominous and evil color. In medieval Germany, a yellow badge was placed around the neck of a condemned heretic; and this, of course, is the origin of the infamous "Yellow Badge" imposed on Jews.[50] Furthermore, in medieval art, Cain and Judas were often portrayed with yellow beards.[51] Says Simple in Shakespeare's *Merry Wives of Windsor: He hath but a little wee face, with a little yellow beard—a Cain-colour'd beard.*[52]

267   The Book of Fate   69:29

The concept of a Book of Fate was not uncommon in the Ancient Near East.

The Babylonians believed that Nabu, the divine scribe, kept such a record. Ashurbanipal, for instance, addresses to him the words, "My life is inscribed before thee,"[1] and similar expressions occur in other texts.[2]

Among the Hittites, the goddesses who presided over individual destinies were called Gulses, a name which is probably to be derived from the verb GUL-, "write, inscribe."[3] Similarly, both the Roman Parcae and the Teutonic Norns are said to have kept a written record of men's fates,[4] the latter being sometimes designated Die Schreiberinnen.[5] In the same vein, too, Tertullian tells us that at the conclusion of a child's first week of life, prayers were offered to Fata *Scribunda.*[6]

In the Old Testament itself, the notion reappears in Psalm 139:15:

> *My frame was not hidden from thee,*
> *when I was being fashioned in secret,*
> *knit together (as though) in the depths of the earth.*
> *Thine eyes beheld mine unformed substance,*
> *and in Thy book were all of them written*
> *—the days when men were to be created,*
> *and among them was one (assigned) thereto.*[7]

A further allusion to it has been recognized in a Punic inscription of the second or third century B.C., which has been interpreted to read: "Moreover, the gods have . . . my name; my mark . . . along with their names have they inscribed, and the glory and splendor of my name have they recorded for all time right from the beginning."[8]

268   The combat against the Dragon   74:13–14

See §§186, 299, 310.

269   Demon shafts   76:3

RSV: *There He broke the flashing arrows*

The Hebrew says nothing about *flashing arrows;* it speaks of *Reshephs of the bow.* Resheph was the Canaanite god of pestilence. He was popularly regarded as being armed (like Cupid) with arrows—a concept which survived in the medieval notion of *elf-shot* (see below, §275). In a cuneiform text from Ras Shamra-Ugarit he is designated "Resheph the archer,"[1] and in a far later Phoenician-Greek bilingual inscription from Cyprus, where he is equated with the arrow-shooting Apollo, as "Resheph of the arrow."[2] In the plural, the word came to be used as a general term for "demons."[3] Accordingly, there is here an allusion to popular lore, the reference being to "the slings and arrows of outrageous fortune," particularized as the hazards of war.

(A similar mistake has converted the fiery *reshephs* of love mentioned in Song of Songs 8:6 into *flashes* [or *coals*] of love [see below, §338].)

270   Food of angels   78:25

Man did eat angels' food

The word traditionally rendered *angels* means simply, *divine beings*. The reference is, of course, to the manna supplied in the wilderness; and on manna as the Hebrew equivalent of the Classical nectar and ambrosia and of the Indic soma and amrita, see above, §§**16, 88**.

▲ 271   The bird sanctuary   84:1–3

How dear is thy dwelling place,
O LORD of hosts!
My soul longeth, yea, even fainteth
for the courts of the LORD;
my heart and flesh sing for joy
unto the living God.
Even the sparrow hath found a house,
and the swallow a nest for herself,
where she may lay her young
—thine altars, O LORD of hosts,
my King and my God.

These words seem to imply that birds might build their nests and roost unmolested within the precincts and even upon the very altars of the temple at Jerusalem. There is no improbability in the supposition, for the Greeks in like manner respected the birds which had built their nests on holy ground. Herodotus tells us that when the rebel Pactyas, the Lydian, fled from the wrath of Cyrus and took refuge with the Greeks of Cyme, the oracle of Apollo commanded his hosts to surrender the fugitive to the vengeance of the angry king. Thinking it impossible that the god could be so merciless, we may almost say so inhuman, as to bid them betray to his ruthless enemies the man who had put his trust in them, one of the citizens of Cyme, by name Aristodicus, repaired to the sanctuary of Apollo, and there going round the temple he tore down the nests of the sparrows and all the other birds which had built their little houses within the sacred place. Thereupon, we are told, a voice was heard from the Holy of Holies saying, "Most impious of men, how dare you do so? how dare you wrench my suppliants from my temple?" To which Aristodicus promptly retorted, "So you defend your own suppliants, O Lord, but you order the people of Cyme to betray theirs?"[1]

Again, we read in Aelian that the Athenians put a man to death for killing a sacred sparrow of Aesculapius.[2] In the great sanctuary of the Syrian goddess at Hierapolis on the Euphrates, the doves were held to be most sacred, and no man might touch, far less molest or kill them. If any person accidentally harmed a dove he was deemed to be in a state of ceremonial pollution or taboo for the rest of that day. Hence the birds became perfectly tame, entering into people's houses and picking up their food on the ground.[3] We must remember that in antiquity the windows of temples as well as of houses were unglazed, so that birds could fly freely out and in, and build their nests, not only in the eaves, but in the interior of the sacred edifices. In his mockery of the heathen, the Christian Father, Clement of Alexandria, twits them with the disrespect shown to the greatest of their gods by swallows and other birds, which flew into the temples and defiled the images by their droppings.[4]

The reason for not molesting wild birds and their nests within the precincts of a temple was no doubt a belief that everything there was too sacred to be meddled with or removed. It is the same feeling which prompts the aborigines of Central Australia to spare any bird or beast that has taken refuge in one of the spots which these savages deem holy, because the most precious relics of their forefathers are there deposited in the holes and crannies of the rocks.[5]

The divine protection thus extended to birds in the ancient world and particularly, as it would seem, in the temple at Jerusalem lends fresh tenderness to the beautiful saying of Jesus, "Are not two sparrows sold for a penny, yet not one of them will fall to the ground without your Father's will?" (Matt. 10:29). We may perhaps indulge the fancy that these words were spoken within the sacred precinct at Jerusalem, while the temple sparrows fluttered and twittered in the sunshine about the speaker.

[Every living being that lodges in a sanctuary is automatically a guest of the god and therefore sacrosanct under his protection (see above, §149). In many parts of the world, this status extends to animals and birds. Thus, among the protestations of innocence (the so-called "negative confession") which the Egyptian dead were required to make before the judges in the afterworld was the statement, "I have never driven cattle from the gods' pastures . . . never netted birds in the gods' manors."[5a] Artemidorus, author of a famous Greek dream book, says similarly that fowl nesting beside an altar are inviolable;[5b] while in German,[5c] Russian,[5d] and English[5e] folklore, birds found in a church enjoy the same immunity.] ▼

272 The heavenly and earthly Zion   87

Zion, says the Psalmist, is a structure reared by God (Yahweh) "on holy hills." These hills, however, are not (as usually supposed) merely the hills of Jerusalem. The phrase contains a subtle mythological allusion and is charged with far deeper import. What the Psalmist is really saying is that the habitation of Yahweh on Zion is the earthly counterpart of the glorious mansion which, in traditional popular lore (e.g., the Canaanite *Poem of Baal*), the divine overlord is said to have built for himself on the supernal hill of the gods.[1] The statement is, in fact, exactly parallel to the identification of Zion, in Psalm 48:2, with the mythical "far reaches of the north"—a standard synonym for that mountain (see above, §**263**).

The comparison reflects a basic tenet of all ancient and of much primitive thought: things on earth correspond to things in heaven or in the otherworld; the real has its counterpart in the ideal; the immediate and punctual is but an aspect of the continuous and durative.[2]

In accordance with this idea, for instance, the Babylonians worked out a comprehensive celestial geography, in which the counterparts of such prominent earthly cities as Babylon, Ashur, and Susa were recognized in the constellations;[3] while Judeo-Christian literature is full of the "Jerusalem on high," counterpart of the "Jerusalem below," which will eventually come down to earth, "prepared like a bride adorned for her husband" (Rev. 21:2).[4] So too, during the Han period in China (206 B.C.–221 C.E.), popular fancy traced an equivalent of the capital city in the stars.[5]

What held good for cities held good also for *temples*. Gudea of Lagash claimed that the blueprint of the major sanctuary in that city had been conveyed to him by the goddess Nisaba and followed a celestial archetype.[6] Hammurapi says that the temple at Sippar corresponded to one in heaven;[7] and the same is affirmed concerning Esagila, the great fane of Marduk in Babylon.[8] Moses, we are told, saw the model of the Tabernacle while he was standing before God on Mt. Sinai.[9]

Just as the relation between durative god and punctual king was often articulated by the fiction that the former had handed down the insignia to the latter (see below, §**284**), so that between the celestial and terrestial temple was often conveyed by the notion that the latter had actually been built by the god who inhabited it. Egyptian temples, for example, were commonly held to have been designed by the gods;[10] while a Babylonian hymn to Enlil of Nippur hails him as the builder of his local shrine,[11] and Ishtar herself is said to have upreared one of her major shrines at Nineveh.[12] Similarly too, the ancient song preserved in Exodus 15 speaks (v. 17) of "the place, O Yahweh, which Thou hast made for Thine abode, the sanctuary which Thine own hands have established"; while Moslem tradition asserts that the Haram (sacred enclosure) at Mecca was planned by the angels.[13]

Against this background, other phrases in our psalm acquire new point and significance. Thus it now becomes apparent that in v. 3, which is usually rendered, *Glorious things are spoken of thee, O city of God,* the last phrase is really not a vocative at all, but means rather, *City of the gods,* and itself constitutes the "glorious things" spoken of, i.e., the glorious epithet applied to, Zion. Thereby it is likened to the celestial city.

Similarly, in v. 6, the words usually rendered, *For the Most High himself will establish her,* really carry an even richer meaning. For while it is true that *'elyôn,* the Hebrew original of *Most High,* is indeed attested as the name of a specific deity,[14] the word itself means simply "supernal being" and was applied also to any celestial god, in contrast to those who were believed to dwell on or under the earth.[15] Hence, what the Psalmist is really saying is that an added distinction of Zion is that *He* (virtually pointing upward)—a celestial being, and no mere mortal—is its founder! Note, in confirmation of this, that in Isaiah 14:14 the typical inhabitant of the celestial "Mount of Assembly" is similarly designated an *'elyôn (I will mount the back of a cloud, be like an* 'elyôn).

Excursus. Because the psalm has, in my opinion, been persistently misunderstood, I append a new translation (bald and literal, to be sure) showing what I believe to be its true meaning:

1   *It is, it is the structure*
      which He Himself upreared
      upon the holy mountains!

2   *Yahweh loves the gates of Zion*
      more than Jacob's dwellings all!

3   *Glorious words applied to thee:*
      "City of the gods!"

                                        Selah

4   *Unto my friends I tell the fame*
      of Egypt proud and Babylon;
      say, "Here is Philistia, Tyre and Cush:[a]
      Such-and-such was born there!"

5   *But when it comes to Zion,*
      each man born therein is mentioned,
      for He, yes He, a heavenly being,
      it is that founded it!

6   *'Tis Yahweh who Himself records,*
      in writing up peoples and princes:[b]
      "Such-and-such was born there."

                                        Selah

7   *Within thee all of them together*
      like minstrels raise their song.[c]

[a] I.e., Ethiopia.

[b] With the Greek (LXX) Version, I transfer the obscure *wešārîm* of v.7 to this place, reading *wešārîm.* For the contrast of "peoples" with "princes," cf. Jer. 25:19; 26:11, 12, 16; II Chron. 24:10.

[c] For *kôl ma'yanai bak* I read, by redivision of the consonants, *kullam 'ānū bak.*

273 The throne founded on righteousness **89:14**

Right and Justice are the foundation of Thy throne

This metaphor is admirably illustrated by the fact that the Egyptian hieroglyphic sign for "right, normalcy" (*mu'at*), viz., ▭, originally meant *the base of a throne.*[1]

274 The winged soul **90:10**

The days of our years are threescore years and ten,
or even by reason of strength fourscore years;
yet is their pride but toil and trouble,
for swiftly it passes, and we fly away.

Among peoples which believe that the soul of the departed goes to heaven, it is often depicted as winged.[1] Thus, among the Egyptians, both the *ba* and the *akh,* two aspects of the essential self, were alike portrayed as birds,[2] and in the *Tale of the Two Brothers,* preserved in the famous D'Orbiney Papyrus, the dead pharaoh is said to have "flown aloft."[3] Similarly, in India, the *pitaras,* or spirits of the ancestral dead, were believed to hover around the offerings presented to them in the form of birds.[4] Homer too pictures the souls of the deceased as birds;[5] and the psyche is often so represented in paintings on Greek vases.[6] The pre-Islamic Arabs entertained the same fancy,[7] and it survives in the folklore of the Moslems of Abyssinia[8] and likewise among the Mandaeans of Iraq and Iran.[9] The idea is further attested in China[10] and in several parts of Indonesia (notably, on the island of Bali);[11] while the Semangs of Malacca assert that the soul of the dying often soars aloft in the form of a small bird.[12] German popular lore is full of stories about birds (usually doves) which ascend into the air beside a deathbed;[13] and in the Czech traditional poem of *Czestmir and Wslaslaw,* they are turned after death into nesting doves.[14] In England, white pigeons are sometimes regarded, on the same basis, as omens of death,[15] as are also white moths;[16] and in the Breton ballad of *Le Seigneur Nann et la Fée,* souls appear as white doves perched in the branches of a tree.[17] Readers of Thornton Wilder's *The Bridge of San Luis Rey* will recall the discussion between two Peruvians whether "the soul can be seen like a dove fluttering away at the moment of death."

The notion finds place also in Christian hagiology. To quote but a few instances: the friends of Polycarp maintained that as the martyr died, a white dove flew from his mouth;[18] and the same phenomenon was said to have characterized the deaths of St. Eulalia,[19] of the abbot of Nuria,[20] and of St. Benedict's sister, Scholastica.[21] In Catholic ritual, white doves are released from cages at the canonization of a saint.

275 A coven of demons[1] **91:5–6**

Thou shalt not be afraid of the terror by night,
of the arrow that flieth by day,

> *of the pestilence that stalketh in darkness,*
> *of the destruction that ravageth at noon.*

Although the Psalmist is speaking only in a vague and general way, like the famous Cornish prayer with its comprehensive reference to "ghoulies and ghosties and long-leggity beasties and things that go bump in the night," the disasters which he lists are in fact specific demons believed to operate at specific hours. He commences with the "terror by night" because the Hebrew day began at the preceding nightfall.

The TERROR BY NIGHT, who is mentioned again in Song of Songs 3:8 (see below, §335), is simply the *nightmare.* This is a universal figure in folklore.[2] A Mesopotamian magical text speaks expressly of "the terror of the nights,"[3] and in many primitive cultures bad dreams are personified as demons. Among the aborigines of Australia, for example, a demon named Koin is said to throttle people when they are asleep;[4] while the Caribs say the same of a spirit called Mboya,[5] and the Karens of Burma tell of the noxious *na* who crouches on the stomach.[6]

The ARROW THAT FLIETH BY DAY is the "faery arrow" of pestilence and disaster. This concept too is ubiquitous.[7] The anguished Job cries out that "the arrows of Shaddai (EV: the Almighty) are with me";[8] while in the Iliad, Apollo shoots arrows of plague at the Achaeans.[9] The Canaanite god Resheph, genius of plague and adversity, was known popularly as a demonic archer;[10] and in Hindu myth the hero Krishna is finally killed by the arrows of the demon Jara, who personifies old age.[11] In medieval European folklore, diseases were attributed to the shafts of elves,[12] and sudden pain in the side is still called "stitch," i.e., prick of an arrow (cf. German *stechen*). The Scandinavian Eddas speak analogously of an elf-*ray*.[13]

Wielders of these demonic shafts can be thwarted by receiving what they give. Arrows were discharged against them, for instance, as part of the Babylonian New Year (Akitu) ceremonies;[14] and in certain parts of Germany they are still so discharged on January 1,[15] as well as at such crucial seasonal festivals as those of Easter and May Day.[16] An Aramaic magical spell from Nippur inveighs against demons with the threat that "a bow has been drawn against you, and its string pulled taut";[17] while in a Manichaean text from Chinese Turkestan, a conjuror (shaman) is said to fell demons by aiming darts at them.[18]

The DESTRUCTION THAT RAVAGETH AT NOON is *sunstroke,* the demon of the torrid noonday heat in which only "mad dogs and Englishmen" venture abroad.[19] Theocritus, the Alexandrian poet, has one goatherd counsel another not to sit piping at noon for fear of this demon, whom he identifies with Pan.[20] Pliny the Elder likewise discourses about the noonday demon;[21] and belief in him is still very much alive among the peasantry of Greece[22] and Italy.[23] German popular lore also knows of formidable *Mittagsgespenster,*[24] and Slavonic peoples tell of an ominous being (variously named Ozwita, Poludnitza, Preypoludnitza, and Szépassony) who wanders in the woods at noon to strike terror in men.[25]

The noonday demon also figures in legend. The faery mistress of Gilbert, later Pope Sylvester II, is called Meridiana, and he first makes her acquaintance at noon;[26] while Joan of Arc hears her "voices" at midday.[27]

The PESTILENCE THAT STALKETH IN DARKNESS is the demon *Debher,* whose name means simply, "Reverse, Catastrophe"[28] (see above, §242).

276 From Canaanite hymn to Israelite psalm   93

The Chinese scholar Soothill has recorded that he sometimes heard children in India paraphrase a well-known Christian hymn in the words, "Buddha loves me, this I know / For the Sutras tell me so";[1] while of Rowland Hill it is related that he used to set his hymns to catchy music-hall airs on the grounds that "the Devil shouldn't have the best tunes." The ancient Israelites did likewise, and this psalm provides an excellent illustration of their methods.

Yahweh is acclaimed as king of the earth. Why? Because he has subdued the raging and contumacious floods. Where is he enthroned? In his special house which "holiness beseemeth for evermore." What does he do there? He issues decrees which are "very sure." At first blush, this sequence is somewhat bewildering, but to anyone who has read the Canaanite poems from Ras Shamra the implication is obvious: the psalm is an adaptation to the cult of Yahweh of the Canaanite myth of Baal.[2] Baal succeeds to kingship by vanquishing the contumacious Yammu-Nahru, the genius of sea and rivers. Once he has subdued his adversary, he is enthroned "for evermore."[3] He builds himself a special palace on the heights of Ṣaphon, the mountain of the gods.[4] From that eminence he regulates the order of nature, causing the rains thenceforth to fall in due season, rather than by caprice.[5]

The story has several parallels in Ancient Near Eastern literature.[6] In the Mesopotamian Epic of Creation (*Enuma Elish*), for example, the god Marduk (or, in the earlier version, Enlil) attains sovereignty by conquering the marine monster Tiamat and her cohorts, and then builds himself a sumptuous palace whence he issues ordinances for the regulation of the world.[7] Similarly, in the cult-myth of the Hittite Puruli-festival, the god subjugates the marine Dragon (*Illuyankas*) and is therefore installed as king.[8]

Basically, this is a seasonal myth designed to explain how, at the beginning of the agricultural year, increase and the "benefits of nature" can be assured only if the surging streams and upwelling springs can be kept in check (see above, §258). There is no reason to suppose, however, that the battle of Yahweh against Sea and River was necessarily enacted in Israelitic ritual; the theme survives only as a literary relic or fossil.

277   Renewing youth like the eagle   103:5

Thy youth is renewed like the eagle's.

Says the medieval *Bestiary:*

It is a true fact that when the eagle grows old, and his wings become weary, and his eyes become darkened with a mist, then he goes in search of a fountain. . . . At length, taking a header down into the fountain, he dips himself three times in it, and instantly he is renewed with a great vigor of plumage and splendor of vision.[1]

There is an amusing allusion to this traditional belief in the *Heauton Timoroumenos* of the Roman comedian, Terence: in reply to his protest that he has not been drinking too much, the old codger Chremes is told that, in any case, he seems so spry early in the morning that "the old saying seems to hold true; you've got yourself the old age of an eagle!"[2] The Greeks too used the expression "eagle's eld" to denote longevity.

278   Heaven as a garment   104:2

To Thee, to Thee, all royal pomps belong,
*   Clothed art Thou in state and glory bright:*
For what is else this eye-delighting light
*   But unto Thee a garment wide and long?*
The vaulted heaven but a curtain right,
*   A canopy Thou over Thee hast hung?*

(trans. Mary, Countess of Pembroke)

The portrayal of heaven as a garment or curtain is one of the most widespread images of the world's folklore.[1] It recurs again in the Old Testament itself in the familiar words of Isaiah (40:22) who describes Yahweh as "stretching out the heavens like a muslin curtain, spreading them like a tent wherein to dwell." In Mesopotamia, the cloud-hung sky was called poetically "the heavenly garment,"[2] and the star-spangled firmament "the embroidered robe";[3] while in a Greek magical text, the moon is hailed as "wearing a jerkin of stars."[4] The Sumerians spoke similarly of the goddess Innini's "donning the garment of heaven,"[5] just as in a hymn of the Indic Rig Veda, Indra is said to "wear heaven as a crown";[6] and the Iranians said likewise of the supreme god Mazda that "he takes heaven to himself as a garment star-embroidered, god-woven."[7] In Teutonic mythology, Odin wears a blue or azure mantle representing the sky;[8] while among the Ewe-speaking peoples of Africa the azure sky is the veil with which Maiu, the supreme god, covers his face, and the clouds are his garments and ornaments.[9] Herakles (i.e., Baal) of Tyre is depicted by the Byzantine poet Nonnus as "wearing a jacket of stars" and as being wrapped in a garment which lights up the sky at night;[10] while Daniel Defoe, in his *History of the Devil,* calls the sky "the blue blanket."[11]

The idea is implicit also in the Greek (Septuagint) Version of Job 14:12, where, by vocalizing the Hebrew consonants differently from the received text, an allusion is introduced to "heaven's becoming unstitched."[12] Similarly, in Isaiah 64:1 (Heb. 63:19), where Yahweh is besought to "rend the heavens and come down," and word "rend" is that employed of rending garments.[13] Not impossibly, a further reference to this concept is to be recognized in an obscure passage of the Canaanite *Poem of Baal* which seems to speak of heaven as the *ephod,* or wrap, of Baal.[14]

Because kings were considered to be the punctual incarnations of gods (see above, §250), they were sometimes invested, especially in Sassanian and Byzantine usage, with star-spangled robes;[15] and it has been suggested that even in a more ancient Mesopotamian text, the expression "robe of heaven" really denotes such a royal garment.[16]

279   The wings of the wind   **104:3**
See above, §254.

280   The clouds as chariots   **104:3**
See above, **ibidem.**

281   The kindly stork   **104:17**
The stork has its home in the fir trees.

The Hebrew word for "stork" (viz., *ḥᵃsîdah*) means literally, one imbued with loyalty or affection (*ḥesed*)." This reflects a popular belief that the bird in question is especially solicitous towards its parents.[1] "I am a most pious creature," says the stork in one of Aesop's fables, "in that I honor and serve my father";[2] and similar testimony is given by other ancient writers.[3]

282   The bread of angels   **105:40**
See above, §270.

283   The right hand   **109:31**
He stands at the right hand of the needy,
to save him from those who condemn him to death.

See below, §284.

284   The ritual of enthronement   **110**
The LORD said unto my lord,
Sit thou at my right hand,
until I make thine enemies thy footstool.

The LORD shall send the rod of thy strength out of Zion:
rule thou in the midst of thine enemies.
Thy people shall be willing in the day of thy power,
in the beauties of holiness from the womb of the morning:
thou hast the dew of thy youth.
The LORD hath sworn, and will not repent,
Thou art a priest for ever after the order of Melchizedek.
The LORD at thy right hand
shall strike through kings in the day of his wrath.
He shall judge among the heathen,
he shall fill the places with the dead bodies;
he shall wound the heads over many countries.
He shall drink of the brook in the way:
therefore shall he lift up the head.

So, in the stately cadences of the King James Version, runs the famous 110th Psalm. But to whom it is addressed, and what is its wider background been, throughout the centuries, anybody's guess. Older generations of scholars thought that the man who was to be at once king and priest "for ever" and to sit at the right hand of God, could be only the future Messiah, or Davidic prince (in a Christian interpretation, Jesus); while in recent times it has been suggested that the psalm was composed at a relatively late date and refers to Simon the Maccabee who, in reward for his military prowess and religious zeal, was in fact appointed ethnarch and "perpetual" high priest of the Jews in 141 B.C.[1] Indeed, some scholars have sought ingeniously to detect an acrostic on his name in the first four verses of the Hebrew text![2]

Comparative Religion and Folklore, however, put things in a very different perspective. For if we align the several statements made in the psalm with ancient beliefs and practices relating to the installation of kings, it becomes immediately apparent that what we have before us is really *the "book of words" for a coronation ceremony, each verse being uttered by the officiant as he performed an act of the traditional ritual.*[3] Especially illuminating in this respect is a long inscription describing in detail the coronation of Queen Hatshepsut of Egypt (c. 1500 B.C), for this runs parallel to a remarkable degree with the ideas which inform our Hebrew composition.[4]

The king is the punctual counterpart of the durative god,[5] and the main function of all coronation ceremonies everywhere is to demonstrate in a series of symbolic acts his absorption of divine power and authority.[6]

(a) The proceedings here begin with the actual *installation*. In token of his divine appointment, the new king is conducted to a throne placed to the right of the god's statue. Thereupon the officiant says:

The pronouncement of Yahweh to my lord:
"Sit thou at my right hand. . . ."

This divine summons is couched in terms of a formal *edict,* being introduced in the original Hebrew by the term *ne'ūm* (attenuated in the King James Version to the colorless "said"), which is the standard technical word for an oracular utterance. In precisely the same way, in the account of Queen Hatshepsut's enthronement, it is Thoth, the spokesman of the supreme god— counterpart of the Greek Hermes—who pronounces the appropriate formula when the royal tiaras are placed on her head.[7] Similarly too, the Assyrian king Ashurbanipal says that his divine appointment was ordained by Ninlil.[8]

Ancient Oriental monarchs frequently articulated their divine character by declaring that thy had been especially selected or commissioned by the gods.[9] Both Hammurapi[10] and Mardukbaladan II,[11] for instance, assert explicitly that they had been nominated by Marduk, god of Babylon; and Esarhaddon that he had been appointed by Ashur, Bel, Nabu, and Shamash jointly.[12] Elsewhere in the Old Testament itself, the new king is formally "adopted" by Yahweh (Ps. 2:6), receives "authorization"[13] from him (Ps. 72:1–2), or "grasps his hand" (Isa. 45:1; cf. 42:6).[14]

(b) To sit at the *right hand* was to sit in the seat of honor. In the Canaanite *Poem of Baal,* the divine architect Koshar sits at the right hand of that god when plans for the latter's temple are drawn up.[15] In Psalm 45:9 the king's favorite odalisque (*not* "queen" as in EV) stands at his right hand; and in I Esdras 4:29 the concubine Apamē sits at the right hand of Darius. According to Josephus,[16] this was likewise the position occupied by Jonathan at the court of Saul; and Jesus, of course, is said to sit at the right hand of God the Father in heaven.

The underlying idea is that the right side is auspicious; the left, ominous.[17] In Psalm 16:11, favors are bestowed by God's right hand, and in Psalm 80:17, one who enjoys them is styled "a man of Thy right hand." Conversely, in Psalm 77:10, misfortune is described as "a change (in position) of the celestial right hand." Rachel, dying in childbirth, calls her last son Ben-oni, "son of my sorrow," but Jacob changes the name to the more auspicious Benjamin, "son of the right hand."[18] In Arabic, "at the right hand (*yamin*)" means "fortunate";[19] and it has been suggested that the Babylonian word for "evil," viz., *limnu,* really stands for *la imnu,* "not (at) the right hand," i.e., sinister.[20] In Chinese script, the notion of "protection, providence" is expressed by a sign composed of the right hand plus the mark of divinity.[21] The right hand was likewise deemed auspicious by the Egyptians,[22] and the notion is also abundantly attested in Greek and Roman literature.[23] The helping hand of a god was the right hand, and it was the ham of the right leg that became the god's share of a sacrifice and was therefore allotted to the priest.[24] In Plato's famous myth of Er, the souls of the righteous pass by a right-hand path to heaven, while the wicked go left to hell.[25] The right foot, said the Romans, was the lucky one, and one should step forth with it foremost or enter a house on it[26]—a superstition which even the rugged Sam Johnson punctiliously observed[27] and which survives also in the widespread notion that "a bride must step over the church sill with her right foot."[28] Finally, among the Yoruba of West Africa, the highest court functionary is called "the right-hand minister."[29]

(c) Next, the *footstool* is placed in position. A symbolic meaning is read into this act, and the officiant, continuing the divine pronouncement, utters the words:

> . . . *while that I set thy foemen*
> *a footstool at thy feet!*

From the ritual standpoint, there is a special significance in these words. As the mediator of what *we* would call "the order of nature" to his people, the king is responsible not only for the positive benefits of weather, fertility, and increase but also for the expulsion or aversion of all noxious influences, whether demonic or human.[30] Accordingly, an essential element of the installation ceremony is that he receive the power to do so, and the purpose of this statement is to serve formal notice that he indeed possesses it. Exactly comparable is the assurance given at the coronation of the Egyptian Pharaoh Thothmes III that "all lands are under thy sandals."[31]

(d) Once enthroned, the king is handed the royal scepter, while the officiant declares:

> *Yahweh extends the rod of thy might;*
> *from Zion exact subjection 'mid thy foes!*[32]

This again is a way of articulating the subtle relationship of punctual king to durative god: the latter bestows the insignia upon him. So, in the Egyptian account, Amon-Re' confers the "magical powers" of the diadem on Hatshepsut, while Thoth recites the accompanying formula.[33] So too, the Sumerian King List asserts that the regalia came down primevally from on high,[34] and the Sumerian Story of the Deluge corroborates the statement;[35] while in the Akkadian Legend of Etana, those marks of kingship are said to be reserved in heaven during a period of divine displeasure.[36] Hammurapi states that he was invested by the mother-goddess;[37] Esarhaddon, by Shamash, Bel, and Nabu;[38] and Nabuna'id (Nabonidus) by Sin and Nabu together;[39] while elsewhere we are told that the insignia are held by the supreme god Anu, who delegates them to mortal kings.[40]

Nor is this idea confined to the Ancient Near East. Homer says in the same vein that the scepter of Agamemnon came ultimately from Zeus;[41] while in Japanese tradition, the Imperial Sword (Kusangi no Tsurugi) is believed to have come, in the first instance, from heaven and to have been acquired, through a feat of gallantry and daring, by the ancestor of the Mikados.[42] Analogously too, in Tahiti, the native king is invested in the presence of the god Oro, and the royal cincture is solemnly addressed as the "parent" or "progenitor" of the king's power.[43]

(e) In contrast to the subdued enemies of the king are his loyal subjects. Speaking, as it were, in their name, the officiant declares that they are willing at all times to take up arms in their royal master's cause:

> *Thy people freely volunteer*
> *whensoever thou musterest thy forces!*

(This is the correct translation.[44]) Not impossibly, these words constitute a formal expression of fealty, as in the British coronation ceremony, where the investiture is followed by pledges of allegiance from the peers.[45]

(f) What follows is, as all scholars admit, somewhat obscure. The King James Version's *In the beauties of holiness from the womb of the morning: thou hast the dew of thy youth,* is, perhaps, the best that can be made out of the traditional Hebrew text. This is usually taken to mean that whenever the king sallies forth to war, his youthful warriors, attired in stately and sacred garments, will press forward in his service, countless as dewdrops at dawn.[46] Such an interpretation, however, is open to at least three objections. First, the word rendered *thy youth,* and taken to mean the collective youth of the country, could mean at best *thy childhood,* or the collective children of the country; and children do not go to war.[47] More probably, however, it means simply *thy birth* and connects somehow with the expression, *womb of the morning.*[48] Second, warriors do not normally go into battle dressed in sacred or ecclesiastical vestments. Third, in the Old Testament, as in other literatures, dew is usually a symbol of freshness, or even of fragrance, rather than of innumerability.[49]

Perhaps here again Comparative Religion and Folklore can throw a ray of light. Whatever the verse may mean in detail, it seems to be saying something about the new king's birth or childhood. May it not be, then, that it is really alluding to that cardinal doctrine of ancient and primitive peoples that the king is of divine, "supernatural" birth and predestined for his role? In the ceremony of Queen Hatshepsut's corronation, for example, the supreme god Amon-Re' declares explicitly that he is her true supernal begetter, and the fact is formally acknowledged by the other gods.[50] In line with such ideas, coronation elsewhere involves a symbolic demonstration that the new king, though indeed born of mortal parents, is, from the moment of his investiture, really the incarnation of a divine being. Thus, in ancient India, he was thought, when crowned, to discard his natural parentage and to be born anew, his royal robe being sometimes described as "the caul (or womb) of sovereignty."[51]

Similarly, among several West African peoples, he has on that occasion to renounce his human parents, and is given an official divine pedigree;[52] while in Fiji, the symbolism is carried to such lengths that the new king is nursed as a baby for four days after his installation![53] If this is, indeed, the general purport of our verse, what it seems specifically to be saying is that the new king comes "trailing clouds of glory," like the sun emerging from the womb of dawn, and with all the freshness and fragrance of the morning dew still clinging to him.

This picture too is suffused with ancient and primitive imagery. In Egypt, the king was indeed portrayed as a sun, offspring of the solar deity Re',[54] and in the Tell Amarna Letters, "sun" is one of his regular titles. Similarly, in Hittite hieroglyphic script, the sign for "sun" enters into the names of several kings of the Neo-Hittites.[55] Mesopotamian kings also often affect the same style;[56] while in the New World, the Natchez of Mississippi say that their original culture-hero was a "sun-child," and call his progeny, "suns."[57] Pertinent also is the fact that in a number of modern Greek folktales, maidens who consort with kings or princes are said to give birth to Sun, Moon, or Morning Star, or to offspring with starlight in their faces.[58] Directly comparable with this last is the statement in our psalm that the new king comes bathed with the morning dew of his birth or childhood, especially when it is borne in mind that dew was often regarded in antiquity as an effluvium from the stars.[59] In sundry Egyptian texts, the pharaoh is likewise described as bathed in fragrant and invigorating dew.[60]

Not impossibly, the recital of this verse accompanied the act of anointment, the dew being symbolized by the oil. What makes this suggestion the more plausible is that otherwise there would be a strange omission of any reference to this essential element of the installation ceremony.[61]

(g) As the mediator of the divine order, the king functioned, both in Egypt and in Mesopotamia, as a *priest;*[62] and this, it will be recalled, was likewise the role of Melchizedek, king of Salem, in Genesis 14:18. His formal authorization in this office therefore forms the next element of the coronation ritual:

> *Yahweh has sworn, and will not relent:*
> *"Thou art a priest for ever,*
> *on the pattern of Melchizedek!"*

The royal priesthood is perpetual because the king is the punctual embodiment of a continuous, indesinent being: *Le roi est mort, vive le roi!*[63] In the same way, at the coronation of Queen Hatshepsut, her royal names and titles are bestowed on her by Amon-Re' "for ever."[64]

To be sure, the institution of royal priesthood did not obtain in Israel; the reference to it here is therefore an example of what may be termed "literary atavism"—a mere survival of an element common in the traditional form of composition on which this one is based.

(h) We have already observed that, as steward of the divine order, the king is responsible for "security" in the wider sense of the word—that is, for eliminating all noxious influences from his people, and this includes the subjugation of his enemies. The assumption is, however, that he does the latter not merely through the fortunes of war but necessarily and automatically by virtue of his divine character. If ever he is defeated (or if prosperity fail), it is simply because the vessel is not functioning properly; the king's human shortcomings ("sins") have impaired it. In the long run, therefore, victory comes from the durative god whom the king embodies. It is that god who has stood.

> (*ever*) *at thy right hand,*
> *has smitten kings whenso he was angry.*

Moreover, with the defeat of their sovereigns, it is that same god who now himself

> *wields government*[65] *among the nations,*
> *having filled the valleys with corpses,*[66]
> *smashed heads far and wide.*[67]

Again there is an exact parallel in the Egyptian texts describing the coronations of Thothmes III and of Hatshepsut: the gods, we read, "give victory" to the king and fight on behalf of the queen.[68]

(i) In its final verse, the psalm swells to a dramatic crescendo. In contrast to the heads of his enemies which will be smashed, the king, it is said, will always lift his own proudly and triumphantly; and, while *their* corpses fill the valleys and are strewn "far and wide" over the fields, *he* will go drinking nonchalantly from the wayside brook!

The sense (despite the insensitive skepticism of some modern scholars) seems plain enough;[69] but what, we may ask, prompted the introduction of this somewhat bizarre image? The answer, it may be suggested, is that *the recital of this verse accompanied the act of proffering to the new king a ceremonial chalice.*

Such royal chalices are well attested in the Ancient Near East. In the Canaanite *Poem of Baal,* that god is described as "our king, our governor . . . to whom we bring goblet of tribute, to whom we bring cup of tribute";[70] while in the Hittite *Yuzgat Tablet,* Jack Frost (*Hahhimas*) challenges the sovereignty of the supreme god by telling him that his hands no longer "retain firm hold on the chalice," only to receive the retort that they are in fact virtually glued to it![71] Moreover, the literary evidence is supported in turn by artistic representations. Thus, on the sarcophagus of King Ahiram of Byblus,[72] and again on the Megiddo ivories[73] and on two Phoenician bowls, the king is depicted holding a cup in his right hand and a lotus in his left;[74] while on cylinder seals gods are often portrayed holding goblets, while their votaries stand before them.[75] The Holy Grail (in its original form) probably also comes into the picture.[76] The goblet or chalice evidently represents that primordial water which, as we have seen (above, §**148**), the new king had to absorb in order to acquire divine wisdom and power.

* * *

For the reader's convenience, I append a new translation of the psalm embodying the above interpretation:

The king is enthroned

> 1. *The pronouncement of Yahweh to my lord:*
> *"Sit thou at my right hand,*

The footstool is placed in position

> *while that I make thy foemen*
> *a footstool at thy feet!"*

The scepter is handed to the king

> 2. *Yahweh extends the rod of thy might;*
> *from Zion subdue thy foes!*

The attendant crowd signify their allegiance

> 3. *Thy people shall offer ready service*
> *whensoever thou musterest thy host!*

The king is invested and anointed

> *(Clad) in (all) the tokens*
> *of awesome, sacred state,*
> *thou comest besprent from birth*
> *with dew from the womb of dawn!*

The king is consecrated as priest

> 4. *Yahweh has sworn, and will not relent:*
> *thou art perpetual priest,*
> *on the pattern of Melchizedek!*

The king is assured of military success

> 5. *Yahweh, at thy right hand,*
> *crushing kings whenso he grows angry,*
> 6. *will himself bear rule 'mid the nations,*

filling <the valleys> with corpses,
crushing heads far and wide;

A chalice is proffered

7.   *(yet) he*[a] *will go (calmly) drinking*
   (meanwhile) from the wayside brook,
(and) by reason of this,
   (proudly) lift his head!

285   Jordan turned back   **114:3**

The sea looked and fled,
Jordan turned back

The picture is drawn from popular lore: the reversal of rivers betokens world upheaval and a change in the prevailing order of things. In a famous chorus of Euripides' *Medea,* the universal breakdown of things as they were is conveyed by the words:

Back flow the streams on the ever-running river;
Life, life is changed, and the laws of it o'ertrod.[1]
   —trans. Gilbert Murray

while the diversion or entire arrest of the rivers was regarded in Classical antiquity as a typical accomplishment of witches.[2]

286   Snares of death   **116:3**
See above, §**253.**

287   Tears fertilize   **126:5–6**

They that sow in tears
   shall reap with shouts of joy.
Though one go forth weeping,
   bearing the trail of seed,
he shall come home with shouts of joy,
   bearing his bounden sheaves!

Though employed in a wide and general sense, this image may well have been suggested by the common practice of bewailing the dead or vanished god of fertility at agricultural ceremonies. The Egyptians, says Diodorus, used to shed tears and cry upon Isis when they began cutting their corn,[1] and their summer festival was marked, according to Herodotus, by the chanting of a doleful lay called Maneros.[2] The latter, it is now known, is simply a distortion of the Egyptian words, *maa n per.k,* "come to thy house," which constitute

---

[a] I.e., the king.

the initial phrase in seasonal lamentations for Osiris which have actually come down to us.[3] The custom is attested also, at a much later date, by Firmicus Maternus, who reproaches the pagan Egyptians for "lamenting over the crops and wailing over the growing seed."[4] The lamentations, say Herodotus and various other Classical writers, were accompanied on the flute,[5] and one of the scenes sculptured on the walls of the Fifth Dynasty tomb of Ti indeed portrays a man piping beside reapers![6]

In Mesopotamia, the harvest was accompanied by the chanting of an ululation (*alalu*),[7] and this is paralleled in other parts of the ancient world. Thus, in the Biblical Book of Judges (9:27) it is stated expressly that the inhabitants of Shechem performed the analogous rite of *hillulim* (RSV: lamely, "held festival") on the occasion of the vintage,[8] and the custom still obtains in parts of the Holy Land;[9] while Plutarch informs us that the traditional cry at the Attic vintage festival of Oschophoria was *eleleu*.[10] Similarly, according to a writer quoted by Athenaeus, the ritual dirges uttered in the mysteries of Demeter and Kore—basically an agricultural rite—went under the name of *iouloi* (or *houloi*), i.e., "howls";[11] and it is possibly to such a cry that the prophet Micah consciously alludes when he exclaims (7:1): *"Al*e*lai li* (Woe is me!), for I am become as when the summer fruit has been gathered, the vintage gleaned!"

These traditional howlings and wailings were popularly interpreted as dirges over gods or spirits of fertility who were believed to have died or temporarily withdrawn themselves from the earth. The lamentations for Osiris in Egypt, Adonis in Syria, and Attis in Asia Minor are well known. Similarly, in the Babylonian Epic of Gilgamesh,[12] and again in the *Poem of the Descent of Ishtar to the Netherworld*,[13] mention is made explicitly of the annual weeping for Tammuz, and other texts prescribe wailing in midsummer.[14] This seasonal ululation survived, indeed, into the Christian era, for a medieval Arab antiquary records the performance of it at Harran.[15]

Yet, despite these later mythological interpretations, there is reason to suspect that the howlings and wailings in question were not originally signs of mourning at all. First, it is significant that in several cases the gods or spirits who are supposedly lamented bear names which are really nothing but artificial personifications of the wailings themselves! The Greeks, for example, promptly invented a corn-goddess Ioulo whom the *iouloi* or "howls" of the Demeter-cult were supposed to invoke.[16] Similarly, the Phoenician refrain, *ai lanu*, "woe unto us," was transformed into the Greek *ai Linou*, "woe for Linos," and gave birth to the Adonis-like figure of that name;[17] just as among the Basques the traditional *lelo*, or lamentation, has begotten a legendary hero Lelo, for whom they are held to be chanted.[18]

Second, it should be observed that weeping is, in any case, not necessarily evidence of mourning, for it can be produced also by any violent excitement.[19] Accordingly, seasonal weeping may have been but the natural accompaniment of frenzy and hysteria, and the loud cries mere shrieks and yells of agitation. Moreover, it is to be borne in mind that in several cultures—as, for instance, among the Toradjas, Galelarese, and Javanese of Indonesia[20]—tears are regarded (like blood, sweat, semen, and urine elsewhere)[21] as effusions of the "soul-substance," so that the shedding of them serves as a means of reinvigorating the earth and even of reviving the dead. Thus, at Great Bassam, in Guinea, oxen are slaughtered annually as part of a procedure designed to ensure a good harvest, and it is an essential part of the ceremony that they must weep. To this end, manioc meal and palm wine are thrown into their eyes.[22] Again, among the Khonds of Bengal,[23] and likewise in Mexico,[24] the shedding of tears is believed to be a homoeopathic method of producing rain. It is therefore something of this kind that may have underlain the practice reflected in the Psalmist's language.

288 The winds of fortune   143:10

RSV: *Let Thy good spirit lead me*
on a level path!

Once again, the conventional rendering obscures an interesting piece of folklore. The Hebrew words translated *good spirit* really mean *goodly wind,* and hark back to the ancient conception of good and bad fortune as favorable and unfavorable winds.[1] Such an image would readily have suggested itself to Phoenicians sailing the Mediterranean or to Mesopotamians plying their crafts along the Tigris and Euphrates.

To cite but a few examples. Ashurbanipal "waits upon a goodly wind."[2] A Mesopotamian magical text includes the invocation that the god "may cause his goodly wind to blow," and prolong a man's life;[3] while in a prayer a suppliant entreats, "May I live through thy wind!"[4] The wind is, of course, the divine breath, so that when Isaiah says of Israel (63:14) that it is guided by the same gentle "breath of Yahweh" as guides cattle which roam the valley for pasture,[5] or when the "Babylonian Ecclesiastes" advises men to "seek ever the good breath of the gods,"[6] the same image is involved. Aeschylus too describes good fortune as the wind, or breeze, of the gods.[7]

Conversely, evil spirits are frequently portrayed as fierce stormwinds,[8] and in an incantation from the time of Hammurapi, winds are bringers of illness[9]—a notion which survives sporadically in European folklore.[10] Euripides speaks analogously of "the blast of Fate."[11]

Job

The Biblical Book of Job is a poetic and quasi-philosophic treatment of an ancient pagan legend, the outlines of which are sketched in the prose prologue and epilogue. From the fact that all of the principle characters are said to come from Arabian lands,[1] that Job's estate is raided by Arabian Sabaeans,[2] and that many words are used in a sense common in Arabic but unparalleled in classical Hebrew,[3] it has been conjectured that the book emanates from Edom,[4] whose "sages" are indeed mentioned as proverbial in sundry passages of Scripture.[5]

The description of Job's physical sufferings, and his protest of seeming innocence, find a striking parallel in a Mesopotamian poem often styled *The Babylonian Job*.[6] It should be observed, however, that while the Biblical writer has indeed been influenced by that composition, his work is far from a mere slavish imitation of it, for the plight of Job is merely the background, but not the essence, of the book. The latter lies rather in the argument that by virtue of man's finite nature and intellect, there can be no rational discourse between him and God, so that all attempted justifications of God's dealings with him are necessarily futile. In other words, the book is not a philosophical theodicy but rather a protest against any such thing. Viewed in this light, it is quite mistaken to object, as many critics have done, that God answers Job with thunder rather than with reason; the whole point is that this is the only plane on which He can communicate with man, for "justification" implies a satisfaction of purely human standards by that which *ex hypothesi* transcends them. We have in this book the direct antithesis of Greek moral philosophy.[7]

Scholars have assumed that the speeches of Elihu were added later, the reason being that he speaks in a style different linguistically from the rest of the book and says nothing which God himself does not say.[8] I believe this argument to be false and unperceptive. The introduction of Elihu is essential to the real point and irony of the book. He is, so to speak, the brash young theological student who "knows all the answers" and fancies himself superior to the homespun philosophies of Job's middle-class friends.[9] He speaks in a somewhat different dialect precisely in order to point up the difference between his background and theirs; he knows the "seminary jargon." But he gets his eloquent come-uppance from God himself, who exposes the limitations and impudence of "theology," and he is hoisted with his own petard by having his ratiocinations condemned as mere plebeian mortal arguments! Inured as we are to Greek patterns of thought and criteria of discourse, this primitive Oriental line of approach may indeed fail to satisfy our more sophisticated minds, but that is no reason for distorting the author's own attitude, which is precisely that our minds are inadequate vehicles for the comprehension of the problem which Job's experience raises.

290   The Devil's wager

The folktale around which the Book of Job revolves finds an interesting parallel in the Indian legend of King Harischandra. Once upon a time, we are told, at a combined assembly of the gods, saints, and patriarchs, the question was propounded whether any entirely faultless prince could be found on earth. The majority, headed by the god Rudra, said, No, but the sage Vasesta nominated his disciple Harischandra. Rudra accepted this challenge and obtained permission to put the matter to the test. He therefore subjected Harischandra to the most abject poverty, compassed the execution of his only son, and took away his wife. Harischandra, however, withstood all these afflictions without relinquishing his piety. In reward for such virtue, the gods restored his property, revived his son, and brought back his wife, while Rudra retired discomfited. It should be observed, however, that this story—which is told in connection with a passage in the Markandcya Puraṇa—appears to be no older than the third century A.D., and may itself reflect the story of Job, picked up from Christian missionaries.[1]

291   The Sons of God   1:6–12

The opening scene of the book is set in the court of God, which is portrayed in terms of ancient pagan belief, since the story itself is of pagan origin. The "sons of God," therefore, are not angels—which belong to a much later theology; they are simply the junior members of the pantheon, this being their common designation in the Canaanite texts from Ras Shamra-Ugarit,[1] and again in a magical inscription of the Eighth century B.C., from Arslan Tash in the Upper Euphrates Valley.[2] The same style recurs, as a mythological relic, in such ancient passages of the Old Testament as Genesis 6:2,4 (see above, §32), Deuteronomy 32:8, and Psalms 29:1 and 89:7.

292   Satan

The *satan* in this narrative is not the archfiend, perpetually opposed to God. Such a conception, again, belongs to later thought, when Iranian dualism had made inroads into traditional Hebrew thinking.[1] Here the name denotes simply a member of the pantheon who happens on this particular occasion to "throw a monkey wrench" into the proceedings, but who is subject to God. The word means simply "obstructor."

293　Signs of mourning　　　　　　　　　　　　　　　　　　1:20

See above, §§135, 202.

294　Mother Earth　　　　　　　　　　　　　　　　　　　　1:21

> *Naked I came from my mother's womb,*
> *and naked I return thither.*

(a) No one returns to his mother's womb. Hence, *thither* must be understood deictally: the speaker points to the earth with the added implication that it is the mother of all men.

(On the concept of *Mother Earth* among the Semites, cf. E. Dhorme, in ARW 7 (1905), 550 ff.; Noeldeke, *ib.,* 8 (1906), 161 ff.; Briem, *ib.,* 24 (1926), 179–85; Stein, in *Tarbiz* 9 (1938), 257–77; Volmer, in ZNTW 10 (1910), 324 f.; W. von Baudissin, *Adonis und Esmun* (1911), 20, n. 1, 443 f., 505 f.
On the concept in general, cf.: A. Dieterich, *Mutter Erde*[2] (1913); Dittmar, in ZNTW 9 (1908), 341–44; E. H. Jones, *The Earth Goddess* (1936).)

In token of return to Mother Earth, it is customary in many parts of the world to lay the deceased on the ground shortly after death.[1] The custom can be traced back to ancient India,[2] and Servius, the famous fourth-century commentator on Vergil, tells us that it was likewise the practice of the Romans, when men lay dangerously ill, to place them on the ground outside their houses, "so that they might return their last breath to the earth" whence they sprang.[3] Similarly, Aelfric, the celebrated medieval English churchman, says that in his day it was the custom to spread a sheet of sackcloth on the floor and on this to sprinkle ashes in the shape of a cross. Just as the dying person was in the last agony, he was taken out of bed and stretched on the sackcloth and ashes; it being deemed more becoming "that sinful man should yield up his soul thus than on a soft bed, when his divine Redeemer died on the hard wood of the cross."[4] Moreover, it is related both of Bishop Benno of Osnabruck, in the eleventh century,[5] and of St. Francis of Assisi, in the thirteenth,[6] that they ordered their disciples to deposit them on the ground during their last moments. Nor, indeed, was the custom altogether extinct in more recent times; it was common as late as the nineteenth century in several parts of England and Ireland,[7] and it still obtains sporadically in such regions of Germany as Vogtland, Silesia, and East Prussia.[8] It is also standard usage among Orthodox Jews to lay a corpse on the ground for one hour.

Earth appears as a deity in sundry passages of Ancient Near Eastern literature. She is included, beside various celestial phenomena, in a list of gods from Asshur, the older capital of Assyria;[9] while in the Canaanite myths from Ras Shamra-Ugarit, "Miss Earth" (*Arṣaya*) is one of the brides of Baal.[10] The female Omorka mentioned in Sanchuniathon's account of ancient Phoenician cosmogony is identified by many scholars as *em arqâ*, "Mother Earth," though his Greek translator, Philo of Byblus, says that she is the same as Tiamat, the primordial ocean.[11] In the Book of Enoch mention is made of an angel Arqiel, who is probably a transmogrification of an older god of the earth (cf. Aramaic, *arqâ*, "earth").[12]

(b) Job's pious exclamation finds an arresting parallel, albeit in a somewhat different vein, in an epigram by Palladas of Alexandria (4th cent. C.E.) in the Greek Anthology:

> Naked I came unto earth;
> naked to earth I descend.
> Why should I labor for naught,
> seeing how naked the end?[13]

Similarly too, an old Norse expression for "die" was "fall back into mother's womb" (*i mooturaett falla*).[14]

> *The LORD gave, and the LORD has taken;*
> *blessed be the name of the LORD!*

We now know that Job was adapting a traditional proverb, for another version of it has turned up in a Mesopotamian cuneiform text: *The king gave, and the king has taken; long live the king!*[15]

295 Rousing Leviathan 3:8

> *May they curse it who pronounce days accursed,*
> *who will in the future rouse up Leviathan!*

Since Job has just expressed the wish that the day of his birth may be shrouded in darkness, it is usually supposed that Leviathan here denotes the celestial dragon who, in many mythologies, causes eclipses by swallowing up the sun or moon.[1]

Thus, in Indic belief, it is the dragon Rahu (Svarbhanu) who periodically swallows the sun or moon,[2] and this notion was adopted also by the Buddhists.[3] In China, eclipses were likewise attributed to the devouring of sun or moon by a monster, and in the Confucian classic, *Tsun Tsiu* ("Springs and Autumns") the word "eaten" is employed to describe the eclipse of April 20, 610 B.C.[4] Among the Burmese, it is a white dog (*shittakwā*) that swallows the moon;[5] and in Scandinavian lore the sun is continually pursued by a wolf named Skoll.[6] The Tartar tribe of the Chuwashes use the phrase, "a demon has eaten it" (*vabur siat*) to denote a lunar eclipse;[7] while the Lithuanians assert that the demon Tiknis (Tiklis) attacks the chariot of the sun.[8] A Mongolian myth says that dragons lie in wait for sun and moon[9]—a belief which possesses a well-known analogue in ancient Egypt.[10] In Iraq, the popular cry at an eclipse is, "O serpent who art swallowing it up, disgorge the moon!"[11] In Jewish folklore, the sun was said to be swallowed by a great fish,[12] and the same notion is mentioned, but refuted, by Maximus of Turin[13] and Hrabanus Maurus.[14] Spectators of a lunar eclipse near Mt. Hermon, in 1891, held that a large fish had devoured the moon,[15] and Tacitus attests a similar belief among the Romans.[16] The Greeks maintained that eclipses were caused in like fashion by a python;[17] and this fancy obtains also among the Negritos of Borneo.[18] In the Canaanite *Poem of Baal,* the sun-goddess is assured of the protection of the god Kothar "who hurls both Monster and Dragon into the sea."[19]

It may be suggested, however, that Job is really alluding to quite a different myth. Leviathan, as we have seen (above, §186), is the monster whom the regnant god (Baal, Yahweh) subdues at the beginning of the present era. But, though imprisoned, it is destined to break lose when that era reaches its close, and then the combat will be repeated. A famous passage in Isaiah (27:1) alludes to this coming event; while in the Book of Revelation (20:1–3) we read similarly of "the ancient serpent" (*not* the snake in Eden!) who will break his bonds after a thousand years and "be loosed for a little while." The same picture is painted also in later pseudepigraphic[20] and rabbinic literature.[21] In Iranian myth, the rebellious serpent Azhi Dahak, imprisoned beneath Mt. Demawend, will eventually burst forth, only to be subdued by the hero Keresaspa,[22] while in Classical lore, the volcanic fires of Etna are attributed to the snortings of the dragon Typhon incarcerated beneath it.[23] The curse which Job invokes, therefore, would be that the day of his birth may be deemed so ill-starred that it will be the one on the anniversary of which the Dragon will emerge and "all hell break loose."

296   Father's knees   3:12

Why did knees receive me?
or breasts, that I should suck?

The knees were those of Job's father, for a father acknowledged paternity by setting his child on his knees. In the Hittite myth of Ullikummi, for example, after the god Kumarbi has created the stone monster, he dandles it on his knee and gives it a name;[1] while in reliefs at Der-el-Bahri, Queen Hathepsut of Egypt is shown perched on the knee of the god Amon in token of her divine parentage.[2] The custom was standard also in pagan Germany[3] and, indeed, throughout Europe:[4] Harald the Dane adopted the son of Erik by placing him on his knees,[5] and Harald Haarfagre wrested the succession from the true offspring of the English king Aethelstan by setting the son of a handmaid on the latter's knee.[6] Even grandfathers sometimes authenticated

their descendants in this way; those of Joseph, for example, are said to have
been born "on his knees."[7]

The basis of this custom was a widespread belief that the knee was a seat
of the seminal fluid—an idea attested by the very etymology of the word
(knee-*genu*-generate).[8] Indeed, the word *genuine* meant originally "one whose
paternity had been authenticated by his having been placed on his father's knee
(*genu*)";[9] and in ancient Mesopotamian speech the word for "knee" (*birku*)
was sometimes used in the sense of the male organ.[10]

297   The weary dead   3:17

> *There the wicked cease from raging,*
> *and there the weary are at rest.*

A common euphemism for "the dead" in Egyptian is "the weary" (*nn.y*)
or "the languid at heart" (*wrd 'ib*);[1] while the Greeks likewise called them
"the weary" or "toilworn" (*hoi kamontes*).[2] The name Rephaim by which
they are designated both in the Old Testament and in Canaanite and Phoenician texts has been derived by some scholars from a verbal root (*r-ph-h/y*)
of the same meaning, but this is uncertain.[3]

298   The sons of Resheph   5:7

> *For affliction does not come from the dust,*
> *nor does trouble sprout from the ground;*
> *but man is born to trouble,*
> *as the sparks fly upward.*

This familiar rendering must now be given up, for the Hebrew words translated *sparks* really mean *sons of Resheph,* and we now know that Resheph was
the Canaanite god of plague and pestilence.[1] The reference is, therefore, to
the band of demons who are ever on the wing, hovering over men. Moreover,
the words rendered *for not . . . nor* really mean (by an idiom found in the
Amarna Letters and sporadically also in the Old Testament itself)[2] *how not?,
surely.* Hence, the correct translation is:

> *Verily, affliction springs from the very dust,*
> *and trouble sprouts from the very ground;*
> *yea, man is born to trouble,*
> *and Resheph's band wings ever on high.*

In other words, this is again a mythological allusion, the sense of which is
that man is beset on all sides, above and below; he "gets it coming and going."

(On Resheph as winged, see F. Matthiae in *Oriens Antiquus*[2] [1963], 39.
Note also that the Greek (Septuagint) Version renders here, "vulture's fledglings," and that the Egyptian *r-sh-f*—perhaps a loanword from Canaanite—
denotes a winged being.[3])

299   Guard over Sea and Dragon   7:12

> *Am I, then, sea or dragon,*
> *that Thou shouldst set guard over me?*

Again a mythological allusion. Sea is here personified, the reference being
to the contumacious Sir Sea (Yammu) of the Canaanite *Poem of Baal,* where
the Dragon (Tannin) is also mentioned (see above, §186). The monster represented the raging floods, and had therefore to be clamped down and guarded
(see above, §258). In the Babylonian Epic of Creation (*Enuma Elish* 4.139)
it is said explicitly that after the defeat of Tiamat, Marduk posted guards over
her confederates "and ordered them not to let the waters escape."

300   Orion   9:9

> *Who made the Bear and Orion.*

The Hebrew word for Orion (viz., *Ke sil*) means properly "a lumbering
gawk, clod" (not simply, fool, as commonly rendered).[1] In Classical tradition,
Orion was a giant. Homer speaks of him as "prodigious in size,"[2] and he is
so portrayed in Greek art.[3] Latin writers call him *Gigas,*[4] and in Arabic
literature he is termed analogously, "the Giant" (*al jabar*).[5] The Hebrew
name therefore reflects a common ancient belief that giants are gawkish
dunderheads. Thus in German folklore they are frequently styled *dumme
Lutten,* or "lubbers,"[6] and in Old Norse, *dumbr,* or "numskulls."[7] Some two
hundred stories about stupid giants and ogres are listed in Aarne-Thompson's
standard *Types of the Folk-Tale.*[8]

301   The whip of God   9:23

> *When a scourge brings sudden death,*
> *He (God) but mocks at the anguish(?) of the innocent.*

It was a common belief in antiquity that disaster and disease were caused
by the stroke of a divine or demonic whip. In the Iliad, the Achaeans and
Argives are defeated by "the whip of Zeus";[1] while Aeschylus ascribes military reverse to lashes of the whip of Ares, god of war.[2] The Furies too are
said to brandish whips;[3] and the hapless Io complains that she is being
driven from pillar to post by the "scourge of Zeus."[4] Similarly, the Egyptian
demon Seth is often figured wielding a whip, and so too is the cock-headed
demon Iao on Gnostic gems.[5] A late Greek magical spell offers protection
in the divine name against "any whip's coming near you,"[6] and in a prayer
for a sick person composed by Bishop Serapion of Thmuis, in the fourth
century, immunity is besought against "every whip (scourge), every pain,
every trouble."[7] In medieval folklore, the Devil often carries a whip.[8]

Lightning too was regarded as a lash.[9] Capaneus, who, in Greek legend, was struck by lightning for attempting to scale the walls of Thebes, is said by the Alexandrian poetaster Lycophron—surely the greatest bore in all Greek literature—to have been flailed by the whip of Zeus;[10] and Oppian (c. A.D. 180)—who runs him a close second—describes Zeus as lashing the waves in a sea storm[11]—an idiom which survives, of course, in modern speech. Lightning is similarly conceived in India, China, and Wallachia;[12] while in medieval German folklore it is portrayed as a blue flail.[13]

302 The disappearing shadow   **15:29**

> *He shall not grow rich, neither shall the substance which he has continue, nor will he strike root in the earth.*

The Hebrew of the second line is obscure, and the text is probably corrupt, but RSV's rendering, given above, is pure conjecture. The Greek (Septuagint) and Old Latin versions have the interesting variant: *Nor will his shadow extend upon the ground.* If this is correct, we are once more in the realm of folklore, for the verse will then reflect a widespread popular belief that the disappearance of one's shadow—regarded as one's alter ego—betokens death. Pausanias, Polybius, and Plutarch all attest the ancient Greek superstition that anyone who trespassed on the sacred precinct of Lycaean Zeus would lose his shadow and die within the year.[1] Similarly, it is believed in various parts of Germany that if one's shadow be invisible on Christmas Eve, one will not live through the ensuing twelve months;[2] and in Jewish popular lore, the same consequence is said to be entailed if one's shadow cannot be seen on the wall of the synagogue during the public devotions on Hoshanna Rabbah, the seventh day of the Feast of Booths.[3] A Japanese proverb says that "When death approaches, a man's shadow fades, although he seems healthy,"[4] and people are warned not to tread on a man's shadow, "for shadow is life."[5] On the general notion of the shadow as a life index, see above, §94.

303 The hawsers of the heart   **17:11**

> RSV: *My days are past; my plans are broken off, the desires of my heart.*

This conventional rendering obscures an effective metaphor drawn from popular lore and fancy. The Hebrew word rendered *broken off* is usually employed of snapping a rope or thread,[1] and in Isaiah 33:20, specifically of a ship's cable. That rendered *plans,* if derived from a different verbal root, can mean *things that tie, restrain, curb;*[2] while that rendered *desires* can be connected with a Syriac term for *hawser.*[3] The verse would then read:

> *Spent are my days; snapped are my hawsers, the moorings of my heart.*

The picture now finds a perfect parallel in Shakespeare's *King John,* where that monarch exclaims:

> The tackle of my heart is crackt and burned,
> And all the shrouds wherewith my life should sail
> Are turned to a thread, one little hair:
> My heart hath one poor string to stay it by.[4]

This is a natural counterpart to the familiar figure of "the desired haven."[5] If the fulfillment of life's dreams and ambitions can be described as reaching port, the frustration of them can obviously be represented as a sudden snapping of the hawsers, so that the ship drifts from its moorings.

304   The King of Terrors   18:14

Bildad warns Job that the affluence and security of the impious are short-lived:

> His strength is hunger-bitten,
> and disaster stands poised at his side.
> Death's firstborn feeds on his limbs,
> feeds on the thews of his flesh.[a]
> He is torn from the tent where he felt secure,[b]
> to be led in triumphal progress[c]
> unto the King of Terrors!

The last line has greatly perplexed commentators, and various emendations have been proposed.[1] Once again, however, Comparative Folklore clarifies what is otherwise obscure, for the fact is that the expression "King of Terrors" finds its exact counterpart in Sumerian texts where Nergal, lord of the netherworld, is characterized as "king of the land of terror" (*lugal ḫuš-ki-a*),[2] and that realm itself as "the terrible house" (*eš ḫuluḫ*).[3] Similarly too, Vergil describes Pluto as *rex tremendus.*[4] The words are thus a perfect parallel to the personification of wasting disease as "the firstborn of Death."

The picture is completed by the word here rendered "led in triumphal progress," for this refers primarily to *marching in a procession* (cf. II Sam. 6:13). The irony should not be missed: the affluent, but impious, "tycoon," whose greatest ambition is to be "presented at court," finds himself eventually escorted to the court of Hades!

Thus interpreted, the sentiment finds a striking echo in a passage of Aeschylus' *Seven against Thebes,* where the seer Amphiaraus, who has encouraged Polyneikes to attack his paternal city, is castigated by Eteocles as

---

[a] There is no need to emend the text, as is usually done; the subject of *both* clauses is "the firstborn of death."

[b] Or, His security is plucked out of his tent.

[c] For this nuance of the verb *ṣ-ᶜ-d,* cf. Ps. 68:8.

one who is bound in the end to be conducted, along with the impious invaders, to the "far city," i.e., Hades.[5]

305 God's net   19:6

See above, §**253**.

306 Razed foundations and faery gold   22:15–30

Are you taking note
of the fate that once attended
certain impious men?[1]

Though God himself had filled
their houses with all good things,
they said to him, "Begone!
What can Shaddaí[2] *do for us?"*
   (Oh, wicked, wicked counsel!
   Be it ever far from me!)
So they became (like plants)
shrivelled betimes,[3]
their foundation turned to a quagmire.
The righteous looked on and made merry;
the guiltless laughed them to scorn:
"Though our *mainstay proves not delusive,*[4]
their tent-ropes[5] *are set ablaze!"*

Pay heed, then, to God, and submit;
thereby shall you get rich yield.
Take guidance from his mouth,
and store his words in your heart.
If you return to Shaddaí[6]
(and) keep frowardness far from your tent,
you will (again) be built up.
You will find a treasure-trove
lying there in the dust,
and amid the stones of the brook
there will be gold of Ophir!
Shaddaí himself will be
that treasure-trove of yours,
and he will be to you
like silver massed in heaps![7]
You will find in Shaddaí
a mooring taut and secure,[8]
and be able to face him with calm.

When you pray, he will hear you;
you will (live to) fulfill your vows.
When you decide on a matter,
you will find that it comes to fruition,
and sunlight shall shine on your ways.
Though others lower their eyes,
you will say to yours, "Be raised!"[9]
For God is wont to save
a man downcast in meekness.
Even to him whose hands
are soiled with the taint of guilt
God grants a means of escape.
How much more, then, will you escape,
if yours, in fact, are clean![10]

It is evident that in these lines (somewhat obscured in the standard translations) the author is alluding to familiar popular lore. The reference in the
first part, it may be suggested, is to the widespread tale of the city that was
suddenly flooded or burned on account of the impiety of its inhabitants[11]—a
tale represented in the Old Testament by the legend of Sodom and Gomorrah
(see above, §55). Of the same tenor too is an early Arabic story which tells
of a certain Ḥimar who had been practising exemplary piety for forty years
when, one day, all of his ten sons were killed by a thunderbolt while they
were out hunting. Thereupon their father vowed that he would no longer
serve a god who acted so cruelly. In punishment, however, for this impious
resolve, his property was destroyed and his valley turned into a desert.[12]

In the second part, the poet seems to be alluding to the popular belief—
well attested in European folktales—that "faery gold" can be found in rivers
and mountains ("There's gold in them thar hills"),[13] or that the dust of the
earth can be turned miraculously into gold as a reward for piety or good
deeds.[14]

307   The shades beneath the waters   26:5

The Shades (Rephaim) tremble beneath the waters;
so too do they who dwell therein.

It is a not uncommon belief among primitive peoples that the abode of the
dead lies beneath the sea. The Polynesians there locate the underworld,
Puloto;[1] while the Eskimos contrast a submarine hell named Adlivum with
a celestial paradise, Quidlivum.[2] The Massims of New Guinea know of a
realm of bliss under the waters, called Hyoyoa;[3] and similar ideas are entertained also by the Papuans;[4] while in New Caledonia, the domain of the
blessed (Tsiabiloum) is likewise thought to lie beneath the ocean.[5]

A curious variation on this theme appears among certain Bantu tribes of West Africa: the submarine paradise, it is held, is White Man's Land, and Negroes who go there become white and happy![6]

Nor are such notions confined to primitive peoples. In the Irish tale of Laegaire mac Crimthainn, related in the fifteenth-century Book of Lisinore, the abode of the blessed is Tir fa Tonn, "the Land under the Waters";[7] and Radermacher has tried to make out a case for such a belief among the Greeks.[8]

To be sure, this was not the usual view of the netherworld among the ancient Semites, but it should be observed that in some of the Mesopotamian hymns relating the fate of Tammuz, he is said to have been dragged down *beneath the waters*.[9]

308   Binding waters in the clouds   26:8
See below, §319.

309   The pillars of heaven   26:11

The notion that heaven rests on pillars is virtually universal.[1] The Egyptians spoke of four columns of iron or alabaster which held up the sky and which were controlled by the four sons of Horus—Mesthi, Hapi, Tuatmutef, and Qebhsenuf—who sat on them. They were regarded as the four cardinal points. This concept was so ancient that even by the time the Pyramid Texts came to be written, the true nature of the pillars was no longer clearly discerned.[2]

The pillars of heaven were likewise a common feature of Indo-European mythology. Not only are they mentioned in a hymn of the Rig Veda[3] and in sundry passages of ancient Iranian literature,[4] but they were also, from very early times, so standard an element of Greek popular lore that they were variously associated with different gods and heroes, being connected now with Atlas, now with Heracles, and now with Briareus.[5] Among modern primitives, the concept is attested in such divers parts of the world as Africa,[6] Indonesia,[7] North and South America,[8] Australasia,[9] and Finland.[10]

If it is true, as has often been asserted, that the temples of the Ancient Near East were built to represent the world in miniature,[11] then the twin pillars which are frequently associated with them (e.g., Jachin and Boaz at Jerusalem) may be taken as further evidence that the sky was believed to rest on such supports.[12]

Two curious survivals of the concept perhaps deserve special mention. Among the Skidi in the southwest region of North America, a "Pole Ceremony" is held periodically in which the posts are supposed to support the sky, represented by a domed roof;[13] while in the medieval right of High Mass, three ministers stood under a domelike canopy, or ciborium, painted blue and ornamented with stars in imitation of the sky, and this rested on four posts.[14]

310   The Dragon in the net   26:12–13

> By his strength he stilled the sea,
>   and by his intelligence smote the Proud Dragon.[a]
> By his breath the heavens were made fair,
>   his hand pierced the Evasive Serpent.

These lines clearly refer to the well-known myth of God's defeat of the primeval Dragon (see above, §186). The third line, however, seems out of place in such a context; yet Comparative Folklore enables us at once to recognize a lost allusion and thus to restore the true sense. For the traditional text's *ShāMaYiM,* "heavens," we must read, by mere redivision of the consonants, *ŚāM YāM,*[1] and we must interpret the Hebrew word *shifrah,* commonly rendered "made fair," from the Akkadian *saparu,* "net."[2] Thus the line will mean *By his wind he put Sir Sea in a net.* The allusion will then be to the incident related in the Mesopotamian Epic of Creation,[3] where the god Marduk subdues the monster Tiamat by driving the "evil wind" into her mouth and the stormwinds into her belly, and by spreading a net to catch her in it.[4]

311   The thread of life   27:8

See above, §191.

312   The legend of the phoenix   29:18

> RSV: *Then I thought, "I shall die in my nest,*
>   *and I shall multiply my days as the sand."*

The Hebrew says literally, "I shall die *with* my nest," and this has inspired some ancient translators and commentators with the notion that the word *ḥôl,* rendered "sand," is here to be taken as a homonym allegedly meaning "phoenix."[1] The reference would then be to the legend, recorded by Pliny, that at the close of its long life, the miraculous bird called phoenix (of which there is only one at a time) builds itself a nest out of cassia and frankincense, and dies in it. From its corpse is generated a worm which grows into the young phoenix.[2] (Variations on this legend, in which the long-lived bird is said finally to burn itself alive but subsequently to rise from its own ashes, are related by other Classical authors.[3])

Analogous stories are told in Arabic literature. Kazwini relates, for instance, that a mysterious bird called the *'anka* lives for seventeen hundred years, and that, when it is hatched, the parent of the opposite sex burns itself alive;[4] while Damiri speaks of a long-lived and periodically rejuvenated creature named *samand* or *samandal,* i.e., salamander, variously represented as a quadruped and as a bird.[5] The story also finds place in medieval bestiaries.[6]

[a] Heb.: *Rahab,* i.e., Braggart.

It has been suggested that the phoenix is really a transmogrification of the Egyptian mythical *bennu*-bird, regarded as symbolizing the rising sun and often described as "self-generating."[7]

(On the history of the legend, see fully: J. Hubaux and M. Leroy, *La mythe du phénix dans les litteratures grecque et latine* (Liège, Faculté des Lettres, 1939); R. T. Rundle Clark, "The Origin of the Phoenix," in *University of Birmingham Historical Journal*, 2 (1949), 1–29, 105–40.)

Against the proposed interpretation of our verse stand the following facts: (1) There is no evidence of a word *ḥôl* meaning "phoenix" in any Semitic or Ancient Near Eastern language;[8] (2) sand as a symbol of multiplicity is a commonplace of Biblical literature (see above, §**59**).

On the other hand, the reference in the first line of the verse to "dying with my nest" ought indeed, by normal laws of parallelism, to comport with what is said in the second line and to repeat the same sentiment. Moreover, there are indeed traces in Ancient Near Eastern literature of a belief in the rejuvenation of certain birds. Thus in Psalm 103:5, the Psalmist bids his soul bless the Lord who causes his youth to "renew itself like the eagle," and it is significant that Herodotus (ii.73) actually likens the phoenix to an eagle. Similarly, an inscription in an Egyptian tomb says of the deceased: "Mayest thou have the life of a *ḳḳ*-bird, and mayest thou wax old like the *nʿy*-serpent!"[9]

313 The negative confession 31

Job protests his innocence by reciting a list of offenses for which condign punishment would indeed be merited but each of which he claims never to have committed. These include: practice of fraud and deceit, rape of virgins, liaisons with other men's wives, denial of legal rights to servants, oppression of widows, refusal of hospitality to wanderers, and adoration of the sun or moon.

This catalogue is patterned after a type of composition known in the Ancient Near East as the *Negative Confession*.[1] Egyptian texts dating as far back as the sixteenth century B.C. contain a form of protestation believed to have been uttered by the deceased before the tribunal of the netherworld, and among the offenses of which he claims to be innocent specific mention is made of: blasphemy, sacrilege, assault, theft, perversion of justice, falsehood, trespass, usury, slander, and lust.[2] Such protestations are likewise incorporated into the autobiographical inscriptions found in tombs. Thus, in a Twelfth Dynasty tomb at Beni Hasan the occupant declares that he has never violated the daughter of a fellow-Egyptian, nor forced anyone to labor, nor denied food to the hungry;[3] while in the far older Pyramid Texts, the defunct proclaim in similar fashion that they have never done physical violence to anyone, nor refused succor to the starving or raiment to the naked.[4]

From Babylon too come examples of similar "negative confessions" recited by the deceased before the court of the netherworld;[5] and the analogous "oath of purgation," whereby a person might clear himself of a proffered charge by swearing innocence at an altar or sanctuary, is mentioned expressly in the Book of Kings (I Kings 8:31 f.) and seems to have been a standard judicial procedure among the Semites.[6]

Negative confessions (especially on the part of women in respect of sexual delinquency) are also part of the sun-dance ritual of the Crow Indians, the Cheyennes, the Sarsi, and the Dakota Oglala of America,[7] and obtain likewise among the Negroes of Calabar.[8]

In the Old Testament itself a similar literary imitation of the Negative Confession may be recognized in Isaiah 59:12 ff.:

> Our transgressions have abounded[9] before thee,
>   and our sins have borne witness against us.
> Verily, our transgressions are ever with us,
>   and as for our iniquities—they are our familiars:
> transgression and denial of the Lord,
> backsliding from our God,
> giving utterance to oppression[10] and revolt,
> conceiving and emitting from our hearts
>   words of falsehood.

That the author of Job is indeed imitating the "negative confessions" of the deceased is shown clearly by his telltale reference to the *scales of justice* (vv. 5–6):

> *Have I consorted with fraud,*
>   *or has my foot sped to deceit?*
> *Let God weigh me in the scales of justice,*
>   *and he will know how blameless I am!*

For, although the concept of the scales of justice indeed appears also in Indic,[11] Zoroastrian,[12] and Greek[13] lore, as well as in Japanese Buddhism,[14] the fact is that in ancient Egypt and similarly in Babylon the negative confession was thought to be accompanied in the court of the netherworld by a weighing of the heart or soul;[15] and a similar fancy is entertained to this day among the Negroes of Calabar.[16]

314 Blowing kisses to the sun and moon 31:27

> *If I have looked at the sun when it shone,*
>   *or at the moon passing in beauty,*
> *and my heart has been secretly enticed,*
>   *so that my mouth has kissed my hand,*
> *this too would be an iniquity. . . .*

This passage is admirably illustrated by the fact that the word *adore* means primarily "to put the hand to the mouth" (Latin: *ad + os, oris*) in a gesture of blowing kisses. This form of worship was known already to the ancient Sumerians, for it is portrayed on a statuette of Awil-Nannar of Larsa.[1] In later times, Pliny attests it as a common usage among the Romans.[2]

The origin of the gesture, as of kissing in general, probably lay in the notion that a portion of one's own *élan vitale* could thereby be conveyed to another—even to a god as an act of submission.[3]

315   Man pinched out of clay   33:6

> *Behold, I am toward God as you are;*
> *I too was pinched out of clay.*

On this concept, see above, §8.

316   Cattle presage storms   36:33

> *The peal of his thunder announces him,*
> *(as do) cattle a storm when it is but rising.*

This is perhaps the only possible translation of the Hebrew original.[1] The Ancient Versions could make little of it, and modern commentators have resorted to various emendations.[2] Folklore, however, may perhaps clarify the meaning, or (if the text be indeed corrupt) at least what the ancient editors intended, for it is a widespread popular belief that sheep and cattle sense a rising storm and indicate its approach by their behavior. In England, for example, it is said among farmers that when sheep put their feet into the hedges for shelter, this is a sign of impending rain;[3] while the Kashmir goats that were formerly kept in Windsor Park were reputed to remain instinctively in the barn when a downpour was imminent.[4]

317   Gold from the north   37:22

> *Out of the north cometh gold;*
> *round about God is a wondrous sheen.*

It was thought by some older commentators that the reference here was to the provenience of gold from northerly countries—a fact attested by Herodotus (iii.116)! The parallelism shows clearly, however, that the "gold" is the luster of divinity. Accordingly, this is a further instance of the popular belief that God (or the gods) dwelt in the far reaches of the north, on the summit of a mountain (cf. Ps. 48:2, and see above, §263).

318   Stars divine   38:7

> *When the morning stars sang together,*
> *and all the sons of God shouted for joy.*

The parallelism demands that "stars" be regarded as equivalent to "sons of God," i.e., members of the heavenly court (see above, §32). Precisely the same parallelism occurs in a Canaanite mythological text from Ras Shamra-Ugarit;[1] while in Mesopotamian belief, each of the main deities had his or her distinctive star.[2]

The picture recurs in Lucian of Samosata's burlesque hymn celebrating the birth of Gout (*Podagra*):

> All the bright heaven into laughter broke,
> And o'er the radiant sky loud thunder pealed.[3]

319 Rain from bottles   38:37

> RSV: *Who can number the clouds by wisdom?*
>   *or who can tilt the waterskins of heaven?*

On an enamel of the time of the Assyrian king Tukulti-Ninurta II (c. 890 B.C.) raindrops are depicted stored in skins.[1] In the Indic Rig Veda, the rain-god Parjanya is invoked: "Thine opened waterskin draw with thee downward. . . . Lift up the mighty vessel, pour down water."[2] A Turkish popular expression for rainfall is "the bottles are emptied."[3] The Peruvians believed in a rain-goddess who sat in the clouds and sent rain by emptying a pitcher;[4] while in Teutonic mythology,[5] rain was said to be poured by the gods out of celestial bowls. The same idea occurs also in Edna St. Vincent Millay's poem, "Renascence":

> O God. . . .
> Upset each cloud's gigantic gourd
> And let the heavy rain, downpoured
> In one big torrent, set me free,
> Washing my grave away from me![a]

[a] *Collected Poems* (New York: Harper & Row). Copyright 1917, 1944, by Edna St. Vincent Millay. By permission of Norma Millay Ellis.

Proverbs

320 Introductory

Surprisingly enough, the Book of Proverbs contains but few overt allusions to popular lore, though D. S. Margoliouth (in *The Temple Bible* [1902]) has made the attractive suggestion that some of its maxims which are now obscure to us might have been clarified for their original readers by accompanying tales to which they served as introductory or concluding "morals." That such moral apophthegms were indeed attached to folktales in the Ancient Near East we now know from the case of the Hittite story of Master Good and Master Bad (retold in the present writer's *Oldest Stories in the World*), where the narrative is introduced by a version of the familiar proverb, *One rotten apple in the basket spoils all the others* (*Pomum compunctum corrupuit sibi junctum*).

In several cases, allusions to popular lore may be pretty confidently suspected, even though they cannot yet be precisely identified. Thus, there seem's little doubt that Wisdom's seven-pillared mansion (9:1 ff.) reflects the faery castle of some familiar folktale; while the leech and her two (LXX: three) greedy daughters (30:15) may be safely recognized as a prototype of the child-stealing hag and her nine (or seven) beldams of later folklore. Similarly, the comparison, in 23:34, of the intemperate drunkard to "one who lies on the top of a mast"—a comparison which already nonplused the ancient Greek (Septuagint) translators—looks uncommonly like an allusion to some traditional numskull. An attentive reader will doubtless find many more such possible reflections of popular lore. Here we must perforce confine ourselves to those cases which permit of more adequate illustration.

321 The house that leads down to Death   Prov. 2:18–19
7:27

The house of the wanton woman, who lurks in the street to seduce wayward young men, is said to sink down to Death, i.e., the netherworld.[1]

The late D. S. Margoliouth has made the attractive suggestion[2] that there is here an allusion to the widespread folktale of the castle or mansion which sinks miraculously into the earth.[3] More probably, however, the writer is referring to a somewhat different tale, best exemplified by the legend of Tannhaüser and by the ballad of *Thomas the Rhymer,* which tells of a Fairy Mistress who lures her mortal lovers into a subterranean (or submarine) palace or realm, whence they cannot escape.[4] This story is familiar also from the Celtic *imramas* of Malduin, Bran, Connla, Cuchulainn, Teigue, Guingamor, Lanval, and Desiré, as well as from the legend of Moran la Fay in the Arthurian cycle. An Indian counterpart is the story of the princess Mrangakavati and Yasahketu in Somadeva's *Ocean of Story.*[5]

322   Ants store food in summer   6:6,8

> *Go to the ant, thou sluggard;*
> *consider her ways, and be wise*
>
> . . . .
>
> *She prepares her food in summer,*
> *gathers her sustenance in harvest.*
> *The ants are a people not strong,*   30:25
> *yet they prepare their food in summer.*

That ants store food in summer against the lack of it in winter is stated also by Ovid:

> Be sparing of the grain on which ye prey,
> Ye ants; thereby, when harvest-time is o'er,
> Ye will enjoy a larger wealth of loot;[1]

while Vergil likewise alludes to the prudence with which the ant provides for its needy old age.[2]

The truth of this popular notion, it may be added, was denied, in the nineteenth century, by the entomologist Grimes,[3] but it is said to have been amply confirmed by observations made in Southern Europe, India, and America.[4]

323   Pointing the finger   6:13

> *A vicious person, a mischievous man,*
> *goes about with a twisted mouth,*
> *winking with his eyes, scraping with his feet,*
> *pointing with his finger.*
> *Perversion is in his heart;*
> *he fabricates evil;*
> *sows discord every moment.*

The prophet Isaiah (58:9) likewise denounces pointing with the finger as a wicked act, associated with "uttering mischief." In many cultures, this gesture is one not merely of insult but also of black magic, the idea being that a potential victim is thus indicated to the demons.[1] In Mesopotamian magical texts "stretching out the finger" is listed among noxious acts,[2] and in modern Algeria the gesture strikes positive terror in the person at whom it is directed.[3]

Nor is it only persons who can be thus affected. Among the Ilocoans of Luzon, in the Philippines, it is forbidden to point at the seeds of cucumbers, on the grounds that this will prevent their growth;[4] and in several parts of Europe, fishermen grow angry when anyone points at them or at their catch, since this is deemed the equivalent of casting the evil eye.[5]

(That the Biblical writer indeed had a magical practice in mind is suggested also by the fact that the Hebrew words here rendered "mischievous man" are, literally, "man of *'awen*," and it has been pointed out that the analogous expression, "workers of *'awen*," when it occurs in the Psalms [e.g., Ps. 5:6], often means "magicians": see N. M. Nicolsky, Spuren magischen Formeln in den Psalmen [1927]; S. Mowinckel, Segen und Fluch in Israels Kult und Psalmendichtung [1924.])

324 Wisdom as God's master craftsman   8:30–31

> *Then was I* [Wisdom] *beside him like a master craftsman;*
> *I was his daily playmate,*
> *making merry before him every moment.*

In the conventional rendering, Wisdom is described as God's *nursling,* but it is now commonly agreed among Biblical scholars that the Hebrew word (*'amôn*) so translated really means, *expert, master craftsman,*[1] like the corresponding Babylonian *ummanu;*[2] and this interpretation is supported by a passage in the apocryphal Wisdom of Solomon, where it is styled "the *artificer* of all things."[3]

There is, however, more to the picture than this. The Babylonian *ummanu* was also a court official, and one of the functions of such officials was to cheer up their royal masters when the latter were depressed or overburdened by the cares of state.[4] Thus the vizier of Sennacherib (704–681 B.C.) is described as "the one who puts him in good humor,"[5] and elsewhere we read of a court secretary who served as the "cheerer" of his lord—a kind of court jester.[6] In the so-called Epic of Creation (*Enuma Elish*), Mummu plays this role before the god Apsu.[7] Accordingly, the words, *I was his daily gossip,*[8] *making merry in his presence at all times,* may refer to Wisdom's duty as God's *ummanu.*[9]

325 The seven pillars of Wisdom   9:1

> *Wisdom is said to have embellished her house with a portico of*
> *seven pillars.*[1]

It has been suggested that this picture reflects a traditional type of Ancient Near Eastern temple, for on the site of the very ancient "holy place" at

Bab ed-Dra', in Moab (third millennium B.C.), seven such menhirs have indeed been found lying on the ground.[2] Moreover, a later Greek inscription from Amathus, in Cyprus, records the dedication of a seven-pillared shrine to the local Aphrodite (i.e., Astarte?).[3]

An alternative view[4] is that the Biblical writer is portraying Dame Wisdom's mansion in terms of the "stately homes" of ancient Palestine, for a later rabbinic source states expressly that these were sometimes adorned with seven pillars,[5] as were indeed their counterparts in India.[6]

Perhaps, however, the whole picture is simply a folkloristic cliché—what the Greeks called a *topos*—for the number seven often figures in descriptions of ancient buildings and furnishings merely as a symbol of grandiose multiplicity.[7] Thus, according to Herodotus, the famous stepped temple (*ziggurat*) at Babylon had seven tiers.[8] In the Old Testament itself, Solomon's throne is said to be mounted upon seven steps,[9] and in medieval Jewish lore the seats of the righteous at the celestial banquet tendered them by God are each reached by seven stairs.[10] The Mandaeans of Iraq and Iran say that Jerusalem rests on seven pillars;[11] and the pseudepigraphic Book of Enoch goes so far as to assert that the Sovereign of the universe is enthroned upon seven jewelled hills.[12] Similarly, the *śakra* of the ancient Indic Ruler of the World rises to the height of seven palmtrees,[13] and the goddess Śrī inhabits a palace adorned with seven kinds of jewels.[14]

The folkloristic seven likewise enters into architectural convention. The walls of ancient Persian palaces were colored in seven hues,[15] and the first Armenian church was raised on seven pillars.[16] At Rostock, in Germany, the Church of the Lady Mary has seven doors; there are seven bridges across the river; and the Rathaus has seven towers. A similar predilection for seven can be observed in the architectural layout of Jena, Lübeck, Altmark, and several other cities.[17]

326   The Fountain of Life   10:11

The mouth of the righteous is a fountain of life

13:14

The teaching of the wise is a fountain of life

Concerning the mythological Fountain of Life, see above, §**14**.

327   The lamp of the soul   20:27

RSV: *The spirit of man is the lamp of the Lord,*
searching all his inner parts.[a]

[a] Several modern commentators, who have found difficulty in this expression, have suggested that the Hebrew word *nēr*, "lamp," is a scribal error for *n<ôṣ>er*, "preserves," i.e., *The Lord preserves the spirit of man, searching all his inner parts.* But the juxtaposition of the words "lamp" and "search" in Zephaniah 1:12 seemingly confirms the traditional text.

The author of this proverb is probably giving a special twist to the wide-spread notion that the soul, or *élan vitale,* is a light or candle. This notion is virtually ubiquitous in European folklore,[1] and there are many stories which revolve around the idea that life ends when a light goes out.[2] Related too is the motif, exemplified especially by the well-known stories of Meleager[3] and of Olger the Dane,[4] that the life of a hero is bound up with a blazing torch.

Because of its symbolic significance, says Plutarch, the Romans had an aversion to snuffing a lamp; they preferred to let it go out by itself.[5]

In Greek mysticism of the sixth century B.C. it was commonly held that the soul itself was made of the fire stolen from heaven by Prometheus.[6]

328   Coals of fire on the head   25:21–22

> *If thine enemy be hungry, give him bread to eat,*
> *and if he be thirsty, water to drink,*
> *for (so) wilt thou be heaping coals of fire on his head,*
> *and the Lord will reward thee.*

A late Egyptian text speaks of a custom of pouring coals of fire on the head of an offender as part of the ritual ceremony of penitence.[1] This was evidently a kind of ordeal, comparable with that which underlies our own popular expression, "to rake over the coals,"[2] and which may be paralleled also from the practice of throwing fire over the heads of novices in certain Australian initiatory rites.[3] Since Egyptian influence can be traced elsewhere in the Book of Proverbs,[4] it has been suggested that the proverb alludes to this usage, the general meaning then being that charity shown to an enemy in need will be just as effective in moving him to expressions of regret and contrition.

To this ingenious interpretation it may be objected, however, that the Hebrew word rendered "heaping" means properly "shoveling," and is usually used of shoveling coals *off* a fire rather than *on* to it.[5] This suggests quite a different picture. In the Oriental,[6] as in the Classical,[7] languages and in English, anger, jealousy, love, and similar passions are commonly portrayed as fires burning in the heart or soul. In Egyptian, an intemperate man is a "hot man," or, as we would say, "incensed";[8] and in Arabic, "coals of the heart" is a popular expression for strong emotion.[9] Sometimes, however, the fire is said to rage *in the head*—a concept which survives, indeed, in our own colloquial "hothead"—because the head was regarded as the seat of personality or of the *élan vitale.*[10] Thus, in one of the comedies of Plautus, when a pander complains to the slaves who have tricked him that his heart is incensed, they at once suggest that he should be given a drink lest "his head too catch fire!"[11] Similarly, a man in love declares that if the tears in his eyes did not prevent it, his head would already be blazing.[12] In the Iliad and Odyssey, flames of valor are seen over the heads of heroes,[13] and in Vergil's *Aeneid,* when Turnus rages for combat, it is said that sparks leaped from his face.[14]

Nor is the idea confined to Classical authors. Of the Irish Cuchulain it is said that when he was enraged "you might have thought that a spark burned on his every hair."[15]

Thus, all that our proverb might really mean is that an act of charity toward an enemy in need will not only douse the flames of his passion or enmity but also earn reward from God.[16]

329   Mythological riddles   30:4

> Who went up to heaven and came down?
> Who gathered the wind in his fists?
> Who tied up the waters in a garment?
> Who upheld all the ends of the earth?
> What is his name, and what is his son's name?
> Surely you know!

It is commonly supposed that these are merely rhetorical questions and that the answer to each of them is, God. In that case, however, the words, *What is his name, and what is his son's name?* sound strangely odd from Hebrew lips. It may therefore be suggested that, however the Scriptural compiler may later have understood them, they were originally riddles employed, on a well-known pedagogical principle, to teach that special knowledge of which the writer professes himself ignorant (vv. 2–3). Each would then refer to a standard myth.

(a) *Who went up to heaven and came down?* would refer to Etana, the central figure of a famous Mesopotamian story which related how he was persuaded to attempt ascent to heaven on the back of an eagle, but eventually slipped off and plunged into the sea[1]—an Ancient Near Eastern variant of the Classical tale of Icarus and his waxen wings and, indeed, of the widespread motif of "Borrowed Plumes."[2]

(b) The second question should probably be read, after the Greek (Septuagint) Version and with a change of but a single letter in the consonantal Hebrew text,[3] *Who gathered the wind in his bosom* (or rather, *in the sinus of his robe*)?[4] The allusion will then be to a mythological figure like the Classical Aeolus, who kept the winds tied in a bag.[5] This in turn is simply a translation into myth of a practice attributed to witches and warlocks in several parts of the world.[6] In the Isle of Man, for instance, witches are said to tie up the winds with three knots of thread; when these are loosened, fresh breezes ensue.[7] In Lapland and Finland they sell bags of wind to sailors.[8] Similarly, a priest of the Bagaba in Togoland was credited with the power of shutting up the wind in a pot.[9] A Norwegian tale relates that a witch once sunk a ship by opening a bag in which she had imprisoned the wind;[10] and in Mecklenburg, whenever a storm blew up, local sailors were wont to exclaim, *Nu hebben de Jungens den Sack wedder open makt* (The youngsters have gone and opened the sack again)![11]

(c) *Who tied up the waters in a garment?* This might refer to a folktale which accounted for a drought on the supposition that someone had maliciously kept the rainwaters tied up. That rain was indeed believed to be bound in skins is stated expressly in Job 38:37 (see above, §319), and God himself is said to tie it up in the cloudbanks (*ib.*, 26:8). Australian folklore likewise knows of waters tied in a bag.[12] The story would be a variant of the well-known motif of Impounded Waters (see above, §258). I must confess, however, that I have thus far been unable to identify a particular story of this nature.

(d) *Who upheld all the ends of the earth?* The word "upheld" (Heb.: *heqim*) is nowhere else applied to the "ends of the earth," and the seeming strangeness of the expression has led several modern scholars to suspect that the traditional text is corrupt and should be emended (after the Greek Version) to read, *Who has* laid hold *of all the ends of the earth?* It was, however, common Hebrew belief that the earth rested on pillars (see above, §309), so that the allusion may be to some mythological figure like Atlas, who was sometimes believed to support not only the heavens but also the earth.[13] Such a figure appears indeed in Ancient Near Eastern mythology in the Hittite *Myth of Ullikummi*, where the giant Upelluri carries the world on his shoulder.[14] Similarly, too, the Chibchas (Muyscas) of Colombia say that the earth is upheld by a giant named Chibchachum,[15] and the Tlingits and Athapascans of North America by Hayicanako, "the Old Lady beneath us."[16]

330 'Aluqah the vampire 30:15

RSV: *The leech has two daughters;*
"Give, give," they cry.[1]

This conventional rendering misses an interesting piece of folklore. The Hebrew word rendered "leech" is 'Aluqah, and in Arabic the corresponding word, 'Alauq, is the name of a vampyric demon.[2] Accordingly, this may be a reference to a Lilith-like creature with her attendant gang. Note that in Jewish charms Lilith is usually accompanied by a band of nine beldams,[3] just as in Shakespeare's *King Lear*,

> Saint Withold footed thrice the [w]old,
> He met the night-mare and her nine-fold.[4]

The Song of Songs

The Song of Songs has been interpreted traditionally as an allegory of the union between God and Israel, Christ and the Church, or even of the intellect and the soul.[1] Such homiletic exegesis, however, is now, by and large, a thing of the past. Among modern scholars three principal views prevail.

(1) The song is a pastoral drama. A girl from the village of Shunem (i.e., the Shulamite; cf. 7:1) has been abducted by the king to his harem in Jerusalem (1:4). Her lover, a peasant lad, visits her, "peers through the lattice" (2:9), and sings his love for her. She reciprocates, and they are eventually reunited.[2]

This view, however, rests on a flimsy foundation. For one thing, such secular drama does not appear elsewhere in the whole range of ancient Semitic literature, and was therefore probably unknown to the Hebrews. For another, to interpret the Song in this manner entails making some of the scenes consist only of a single verse or even less! And in the third place, the crucial verse *The king hath brought me into his chambers; we will exult and rejoice in thee* (1:4) can equally well be rendered, *Were even the king to have brought me to his chambers, 'tis in thee we would exult and rejoice.*

(2) It has been suggested that the Song represents, *au fond*, a repertoire of love-poems originally chanted in the pagan worship of such divine lovers as Ishtar and Tammuz or Astarte and Adonis.[3] The fact is, however, that the parallels which have been adduced between the wording of the Song and the ritual chants of such cults are scarcely convincing,[4] and it must be borne in mind in any case that the language used in such cultic songs would be bound to imitate that current among ordinary human lovers.

(3) Comparative Folklore has furnished a third interpretation. This derives from observations made nearly a century ago by the German consul, Johann Gottfried Wetzstein, among the Syrian peasantry. Wetzstein noticed that Syrian wedding festivities lasted for seven days, and that during this period bride and groom were enthroned as king and queen. Each danced before the other, while

the assembled company joined them in outspoken eulogies of their bodily charms. The Song of Songs, it is held, is a collection of such chants, known as *waṣfs*.[5] The long descriptions of bodily charms (e.g., 4:1–7; 5:10–16; 6:4–7; 7:2–10) would then fall into place, while the references to the king and to Solomon would be complimentary allusions to the bridegroom. Similarly, "Shulamite," the name given to the bride (7:1), would be a dialectical pronunciation of Shunemite, and the point of the compliment would be to liken her to Abishag, the Shunemite beauty who comforted David in his old age (cf. I Kings 1:1–4; see above, §147). Again, the obscure lines, *What see ye in the Shulamite? As it were, the dance of Mahanaim* (6:13) would be an allusion to the customary sword dance performed by the bride, seeing that Mahanaim could mean "the two camps."

It must be admitted that this theory is, at first blush, not unattractive. However, a closer comparison of the Syrian usages with the Hebrew text of the Song does not fully bear it out. We need cite but two glaring discrepancies. The sword dance is performed *barefoot,* whereas the Song declares expressly, *How fair are thy feet in sandals* (7:1). The Syrian bridegroom is not crowned, whereas the Song speaks specifically of *the crown with which his mother crowned him on the day of his espousals* (3:11).[6]

Nor is it necesary to assume that the descriptions of bodily beauties necessarily indicate an origin of the Song in some earlier analogy of the Syrian *waṣfs*. Such descriptions are the stock-in-trade of love lyrics all over the world and in all ages. Many of the phrases and images used in the Song find parallels, for instance, in ancient Egyptian love songs. The following are representative examples drawn from S. Schott's *Altägyptische Liebeslieder* (1950):

1:2:	*Thy caresses are better than wine*	Schott, 66.5
2:6:	*Oh that his right hand would embrace me!*	ib., 52.5
2:9:17:	*the lover is likened to a gazelle*	ib., 44.3
4:9:	*Thou hast ravished my heart with one glance of thine eyes*	ib., 44[b]
4:11:	*Thy lips drop honey*	ib., 57.2
4:12–16:	*A garden locked is my sister, my bride*	
	. . . .	
	Let my lover come to his garden,	ib., 56.2
	and eat his choice fruits!	Pap. Harris, 500
7:5:	*The king is held captive in thy tresses*	Schott, 63.3
8:6:	*Set me as a seal upon thy heart*	ib., 67.6

Other arresting parallels can be culled from both ancient and modern Arabic poems.[7] The Arabs too, for example, take the gazelle as the paragon of grace and beauty,[8] liken the tresses of the beloved to waving palms (Song 5:11),[9] and compare the legs of the beloved to marble pillars (5:15).[10]

Equally striking, though less familiar, are the parallels afforded by the love songs of modern primitive peoples.[11] Thus, the comparison of the beloved to "a mare of Pharaoh's chariots" (1:9) is echoed both in a song of the Kirghiz of Siberia, where she is likened to "the steed of nobles,"[12] and in a chant of the Fulbé of the Sudan, where she is addressed as "the steed of the king of all kings."[13] Somewhat analogously too, a popular chant of the Hausa speaks of her as "a camel with slender neck."[14] Again, in a popular ditty from Malaysia, the maiden's locks are likened to palms;[15] and the Jaggas of East Africa speak of the lips of cherished friends as having "the savor of honey, the sweet savor of honey from the Sahara."[16]

The aforementioned Malayan chant may serve as a representative example of these primitive parallels:

> Mabrûka is a camel with slender neck.
> Her teeth are like gold,
> her hands are of gold,
> her ring is of gold.
> Her arm is pliant like a rush;
> her nose is like a rose,
> her face like a mirror.
> Her shoulders are of gold,
> her shawl is of gold,
> her locks are like gold.
> Her apron is broidered with silver,
> her blouse is broidered all over with silver,
> her drawers are of silk.
> Her locks are tightly bound;
> her breasts are like silver cups;
> look on those breasts, and it dazzles your eyes!
> look too on her body, how it sways
> like a reed!

Is this derived from a Syrian *waṣf?*[17]

It would be safer, then, to say only that certain portions of the Song may have been taken from wedding chants, but to regard the book as a whole as simply a collection of Palestinian love songs. These need not have been written in any one single place nor at any one single time. Moreover, the fact that certain verses recur does not prove unity of authorship, for the incorporation of popular lines from one song to another is a commonplace of all folk poetry.[18]

Naturally, in the course of transmission through the ages the original wording would often have been "modernized"—as happens in all popular songs—so that we cannot cite the relatively late language of the present Hebrew text as evidence for the original date of composition.[19]

332 The banner of Love

> *He brought me to the banqueting house*
> *and his banner over me was love.*

It has been suggested that these words contain an allusion to the custom of marking taverns with distinctive banners. Inns were certainly so marked by the pre-Islamic Arabs,[1] but there appears to be no evidence of the usage in the Ancient Near East. If the interpretation is correct, the banner would be comparable to the old English ale-stake, a pole set up before an alehouse by way of sign, often surmounted by a bush or garland (cf. the proverbial saying, "Good wine needs no bush"). In the Prologue to *The Canterbury Tales*, Chaucer refers to this custom in the words:

> A garland hath he set upon his head
> As great as it were for an ale-stake. . . .[2]

An alternative suggestion is that this is a military metaphor: when the girl is "taken places" by her escort, she sallies forth under the banner of his love, like an army under that of its commander. The difficulty with this interpretation is, however, that the Hebrew word (*degel*) traditionally rendered "banner" probably means simply "regiment," or division of the army.[3]

This brings us to the third view, which is that the word in question is rather to be connected with an Akkadian word meaning "look at." The sense will then be that the escort casts loving looks on his inamorata.[4]

333 Apples and love   2:5

> *Comfort* (RSV: *refresh*) *me with apples,*
> *for I am sick with love.*

In the folklore of many peoples the apple has erotic associations. In Classical antiquity, to throw apples at a person was an invitation to dalliance.[1] Thus, in the *Clouds* of Aristophanes, young men are warned not to frequent the houses of dancing girls, where "while they are gaping at some cute strumpet, she might get them involved by tossing an apple at them." Similarly, in Vergil's *Third Eclogue,* the goatherd Damoetas boasts that Galatea, "that wanton minx," keeps egging him on by throwing apples at him;[3] and in one of Lucian's *Conversations of Harlots,* a jealous courtesan complains that her fickle lover keeps pelting her rival with apples.[4] In the story of Acontius and Cydippe, the former sends a love note to the latter by inscribing it on an apple which he arranges to have cast at her feet.[5] A similar erotic quality is attached to the apple even at the present day in the popular lore of Kentucky, in the United States;[6] and it has been suggested that it was this association that inspired the medieval identification of the forbidden fruit of Paradise with an apple.

Among the Mesopotamians, apples and pomegranates were thought to give sexual potency;[7] and a Jewish superstition asserts that the sap of an apple tree can induce conception in a barren woman.[8]

Our passage is commonly interpreted in the light of these ideas. But it is difficult to see why a girl who is already lovesick should demand an aphrodisiac. Besides, the text says distinctly that she asks for apples in order to *restore*, not *lose*, her equilibrium; for the Hebrew word rendered *comfort* (or *refresh*) means properly *stabilize, support*. Hence it would seem more apposite to regard the apples as a kind of restorative "smelling salt," and this is supported by the fact that the Hebrew word so rendered (viz., *tappuᵃh*) actually derives from a verbal root (*n-p-ḥ*) meaning "blow," i.e., diffuses aroma. Moreover, we may aptly compare what the ancient botanist Simeo Sethus says of apples: "They are a useful aid against failure of spirit and irregular heartbeat."[9]

(This interpretation also surmounts the difficulty that Heb. *tappūᵉh* may in fact be a more generic term than our *apple,* including quince and apricot, since it is still an open question whether apples grew in the Holy Land in ancient times. [Note, incidentally, that in English itself, *apple* originally possessed a wider meaning.])

Further support for this interpretation comes from the parallel phrase, *Sustain me with raisins,* for this would reflect a popular belief that raisins and other dried fruits are effective against fatigue and nervous debility. In 1881, Sir William Gull, M.D. testified before the Committee of the House of Lords on Intemperance that he had always found raisins useful to this end![10]

334 Solomon's groomsmen   3:7–8

> *Behold, here is Solomon's litter;*
> *threescore warriors stand around it,*
>   *of the warriors of Israel,*
> *all of them girt with swords,*
> *trained for battle;*
> *each with his sword at his thigh,*
> *against terror by night.*

This little song was probably designed to accompany the procession of a The bridegroom, as also the bride's procession, is customarily escorted by an such occasions. In Oriental weddings, as elsewhere, the bridal couple is likened to a king and queen;[1] in Malaya, for example, they are called "sovereigns for a day" (*raja sari*).[2] Hence the bridegroom is here fancifully identified with King Solomon—the Harun al Rashid of ancient Israelitic folklore.

The bridegroom, as also the bride's procession, is customarily escorted by an armed bodyguard, designed originally to ward off those hovering demons who, in the fancy of ancient and primitive peoples, personify the hazards of marriage.[3] Often the bride herself carries a sword;[4] and in medieval Jewish usage, she sometimes wore a helmet.[5] In the Usambara region of West Africa, an armed bridesmaid procedes her with drawn sword.[6]

Analogously, because demons also hover at death, Baltic funeral corteges used anciently to be escorted by an armed bodyguard.[7]

335 The "Terror by Night" 3:8

In the Hebrew, this is an extended use of a term which, in a stricter sense, denoted the nightmare; cf. Ps. 91:5 (see above, §275). It finds an exact parallel in the description of Zaqar, god of dreams, as "the terror of the nights" (*puluḥtu ša lilâti*) in an ancient Mesopotamian magical incantation.[1]

Two ideas are here combined. On the one hand, the "terror by night" denotes simply the dangers which may beset the wedding procession, since weddings are usually celebrated in the East at nightfall. On the other, however, it alludes slyly to untoward happenings during the bridal night,[2] and to nightmare in general.[3]

336 The separable soul 5:6

My soul failed *when he spoke*

The Hebrew word rendered *failed* means literally *went out*. The idiom thus reflects the widespread notion that the "soul," or inner self, leaves the body in sleep, trance, ecstasy, or unusual excitement.[1]

337 The dance of Mahanaim 6:13 [Heb. 7:1]

What see ye in the Shulamite?
As it were, the dance of Mahanaim.

W. F. Albright has suggested that "Shulamite" is here the Hebrew equivalent of the Mesopotamian Shulmanitu, a title of the goddess Ishtar at Ashur.[1] Now, since Ishtar was also a goddess of battle, and since the word Mahanaim could conceivably mean "camps," the meaning would be that the gyrations of the girl in her dance resemble those of the goddess in her war dance.

An alternative interpretation might start from the legend that Mahanaim was the place where Jacob saw "the camp of otherworldly beings" (Gen. 32:1–2). As we have seen (above, §71), this was simply a Hebrew variant of the Wild Hunt, or Furious Host. Now, alike in Greek and European folklore, the latter is often associated with such goddesses as Artemis or Berchta and her troupe of ghostly dancers.[2] Thus the meaning would be that the wild gyrations of the girl in her dance are such as to suggest to the onlookers that they are witnessing the "furious rout." (It might then be significant that the word rendered "see" often denotes *prophetic or imaginative vision.*)

338 The Reshephs of love 8:6

> *The flashes* (KJV: *coals*) *thereof are flashes of fire,*
> *a most vehement flame.*

It seems a pity to eliminate this familar and graphic description of love. The stark fact is, however, that the Hebrew word does not mean flash (or coal). It is the name *Resheph,* which designates the Canaanite god of plague and pestilence (see above, §242) and which came to be used in the plural to denote demons in general.[1]

The point of the picture is brought out more clearly when it is borne in mind that in Arab folklore, *demons are often believed to be made of fire.*[2]

Lamentations

339 Dirges over cities; the weeping "daughter of Zion"

A common feature of Oriental funerals was (and is) the employment of professional wailing women.[1] Not only is this usage well attested among the Egyptians,[2] but likewise in a description of Hittite funeral rites the leading role is said to be played by women.[3] In the Canaanite *Poem of Aqhat* "weeping women" (*bkyt*) and "female mourners" (*mšspdt*) repair to the palace and perform a keening for the slain prince;[4] and the custom is mentioned also in several passages of the Old Testament itself.[5] So too, in Homer's account of the burial of Hector, the laments are uttered by women, led by the hero's mother, wife, and daughter;[6] and such wailing women appear later in the Roman *praeficae,* who lead dirges.[7] E. W. Lane describes graphically the "crying and shrieking" of women at Moslem funerals, despite the Prophet's express prohibition of such excesses.[8] In Armenia, professional wailing women are known popularly as "dirge-mothers."[9]

Out of this custom there developed a literary convention of composing lamentations over fallen cities in the form of dirges sung by some imaginary female citizen. A song of this type, written partly in the so-called Eme-sal dialect, usually reserved for speeches by females, is preserved on Sumerian cuneiform tablets of the early second millennium B.C., discovered at Nippur. It bewails the destruction of the city of Ur.[10] Later specimens of the same genre, written in the Akkadian language, are also known, one of them being put into the mouth of "the daughter of Sin (the moon-god."[11] The Biblical Book of Lamentations, which may indeed have been composed in the exile in Babylon, belongs to the same class of composition, and employs the analogous figure of the weeping "daughter of Zion" (cf. 1:16, 21; 2:19, etc.).

Our Biblical poems follow the older Mesopotamian models, working in more or less standard clichés of this genre. The following parallels will best illustrate this point.

A. Sumerian Lamentation over the Destruction of the city of Ur by the Elamites and Subarians: trans. S. N. Kramer, in *ANET* 455–63.

B. Rm. iv. 97 (3334): trans. T. G. Pinches, in *PSBA* 23 (1901), 197 ff.

C. "The Lament of the Daughter of Sin": T. G. Pinches, in *PSBA* 17 (1895), 64–74.

1.

1. (*The city*) *is become like a widow*

B 5: *The woman of Hursag-kalama moans for the husband of her youth*

2. *Bitterly weeps she at night*

A 100: *Because of its [affliction], in my sleeping-place . . . verily there is no peace for me*

3. *She finds no resting place*

B 2, 3: *The maiden of Arka weeps . . . the daughter of Uruk weeps*

6. *From the daughter of Zion has departed all her beauty*

B 2: *The maiden of Arka weeps, whose youthful grace is departed*

9. *Her uncleanness is in her skirts*

B 7: *The maiden of Masha weeps, whose garment is sullied*

10. *The foeman has put forth his hand against all her precious things*

A 279: *My treasure verily has been dissipated*

They have entered her holy place

C i.6: *He has entered my shrine*

13. *From on high has God sent fire*

A 180: *Enlil brings Gibil, the fire-god, to his aid in destroying Ur*

15. *He has summoned a battle-line against me to crush my young men*

B 14–15: *The maiden of Durilu weeps for all of Qutu, for the son of her city crushed, for her family brought to ruin*

16. *I weep*

B 1, 18: *I lament, I wail*

17. *Zion stretches out her hands*

A 371: *The house stretches out the hands to thee*

19. *My priests and my elders are dying in the city*

B 8: *The maiden of Agade weeps, whose elders are killed*

2. 1. *The Lord in his anger beclouds the daughter of Zion*

A 190: *The day was deprived of the rising of the bright sun, the goodly light*

    He has taken no thought of his footstool

B 22: *His platformed throne is overturned* . . .

2. *The Lord has destroyed . . . all the pastures of Jacob*

A 1: *He has abandoned his stable, his sheepfold (has been delivered) to the wind*

6. *He has broken down his booth like that of a garden*

A 128: *My house . . . like a garden hut, verily on its side has caved in*

17. *The Lord has done what he purposed, has consummated his word which he ordained of old*

A 168–69: *Anu changes not his command; Enlil alters not the command which he had issued*

19. *Pour out thy heart like water*

A 331: *O queen, make thy heart like water!*

4. 1. *The holy stones (gems?) lie scattered at the top of every street*

A 278: *My (precious) metal, stone and lapis lazuli have been scattered about*

5. *those who feasted on dainties perish in the streets*

A 271 f.: *In its boulevards, where the feasts were celebrated, scattered they lay, etc.*

8. *Blacker than soot is their visage; they are not recognized in the streets*

A 358: *Dirt has been decreed for them; verily, their appearance has changed*

11. *He has kindled a fire in Zion and it has consumed her foundations*

A 180: *Enlil calls Gibil, the fire-god, to his aid*

5. 15. *Our dance is turned to a dirge*   A 359–60: *Thy song has been turned into weeping; thy . . . -music has been turned into lamentation*

18. *. . . Mount Zion which lies desolate; foxes walk upon it.*   A 269: *In the rivers of my city dust has gathered; into fox-dens verily have they been made*

340 The limping meter

The first three chapters of the Book of Lamentations are composed in the "limping meter" characteristic of Hebrew dirges. Whereas normal Hebrew verse—there are, of course, variations—consists of two stichs each containing three accentual beats, in the dirge the final beat of the second stich is cut off, e.g.,

> *Outdoórs they líe on the groúnd,*
> *yoúng men and óld;*
> *My yóuths and máidens áll*
> *fáll by the swórd.*

> (2:21)

This produces a distinctly limping (scazonic) effect, and it may therefore be suggested that the dirges were originally designed to accompany a limping dance of mourning. An excellent description of such a dance is given by Lane in his famous *Manners and Customs of the Modern Egyptians:*

> It is customary among the peasants of Egypt for the female relatives and friends of a person deceased to meet together at his house on the first three days after the funeral, and there to perform a lamentation and a strange kind of dance. They daub their faces and bosoms and part of their dress with mud and tie a rope girdle . . . round the waist. Each flourishes in her hand a palm-stick or a *nebroot* (a long staff) or a drawn sword [i.e., to forefend demons], and dances with a slow movement and in an irregular manner, generally pacing about and raising and depressing the body.[1]

The custom was current also, we are informed, among the Syrian peasantry, who gave it the name of *ma'îd,* or "limping."[2] (This last, as we have seen above, §**129**, is the real explanation of Agag's "walking delicately" in the famous incident related in I Samuel 15:32.)

Furthermore, it is significant that both in Syriac and Arabic, a word which normally means "skipping" (*r-q-d, r-q-z*) is a technical term for "funeral exercises"; while an Akkadian lexical text lists a cognate word (*ru-qu-ud-du*) among names of professional mourners.[3]

See further, above, §158.

341 Sitting apart 1:1

RSV: *How lonely sits the city*
that was full of people!

This rendering misses a subtle point: the reference is not to the contrast between a crowded and a deserted city, for the Hebrew word translated *lonely* really means *apart,* and the allusion is to the ritual seclusion of menstruous women and diseased persons.[1] Exactly the same expression occurs in Leviticus 13:46 in reference to the segregation of lepers; while in verse 8 of this very lamentation Jerusalem is described explicitly as having "become like a menstrual woman" (RSV, wrongly: *therefore she became filthy*).

▲ 342 The silent widow 1:1

[The vanquished city of Jerusalem is likened not only to a leper segregated from the community[1] but also to a *widow*. Comparative Folklore throws interesting light on this comparison.]

Among many, if not all, peoples of the world the occurrence of a death in a family has entailed on the survivors the obligation of observing certain rules, the general effect of which is to limit in various directions the liberty enjoyed in ordinary life; and the nearer the relationship of the survivor to the deceased, the more stringent and burdensome these restrictions become. Though the reasons for imposing them are often unknown to the people who submit to them, a large body of evidence points to the conclusion that many, perhaps most, of them originated in a fear of the ghost and a desire to escape his unwelcome attentions by eluding his observation, repelling his advances, or otherwise inducing or compelling him to acquiesce in his fate, so far at least as to abstain from molesting his kinsfolk and friends.[1a]

The ancient Hebrews observed many restrictions on the occurrence of a death, which are either expressly enjoined or incidentally referred to in the Old Testament.[2] To the list of rules for the conduct of mourners, which can thus be collected from Scripture, may perhaps be added one which, though it is neither inculcated nor alluded to by the sacred writers, is suggested by etymology and confirmed by the analogous usages of other peoples.

The Hebrew word for a widow (*'almanah*) is perhaps etymologically connected with an adjective meaning "dumb" (*'illem*). If this etymology is correct, it would seem that the Hebrew name for a widow is "a silent woman." Why should a widow be called a silent woman? I conjecture, with all due diffidence, that the epithet may be explained by a widespread custom which imposes the duty of absolute silence on a widow for some time after the death of her husband.

Thus among the Kutus, a tribe on the Congo, widows observe mourning for three lunar months. They shave their heads, strip themselves almost naked, daub their bodies all over with white clay, and pass the whole of the three months in the house without speaking.[3] Among the Sihanaka in Madagascar the observances are similar, but the period of silence is still longer, lasting for at least eight months, and sometimes for a year. During the whole of that time the widow is stripped of all her ornaments and covered up with a coarse mat, and she is given only a broken spoon and a broken dish to eat out of. She may not wash her face or her hands, but only the tips of her fingers. In this state she remains all day long in the house and may not speak to any one who enters it.[4] Among the Nandi, of British East Africa, as long as a widow is in mourning she is considered unclean and may not speak above a whisper, though she is not absolutely forbidden to speak at all.[5] In describing the Nishinam tribe of Californian Indians, a writer who knew these Indians well, as they were in the third quarter of the nineteenth century, mentions that "around Auburn, a devoted widow never speaks, on any occasion or upon any pretext, for several months, sometimes a year or more, after the death of her husband. Of this singular fact I had ocular demonstration. Elsewhere, as on the American River, she speaks only in a whisper for several months. As you go down towards the Cosumnes this custom disappears."[6] Among the Kwakiutl Indians of British Columbia, for four days after the death of her husband a widow must sit motionless, with her knees drawn up to her chin. For sixteen days after that she is bound to remain on the same spot, but she enjoys the privilege of stretching her legs, though not of moving her hands. During all that time nobody may speak to her. It is thought that if any one dared to break the rule of silence and speak to the widow, he would be punished by the death of one of his relatives. A widower has to observe precisely the same restrictions on the death of his wife.[7] Similarly among the Bella Coola Indians of the same region a widow must fast for four days, and during that time she may not speak a word; otherwise they think that her husband's ghost would come and lay a hand on her mouth, and she would die. The same rule of silence has to be observed by a widower on the death of his wife, and for a similar reason.[8]

But by no people is this curious custom of silence more strictly observed than by some of the savage tribes of Central and Northern Australia. Thus, among the Waduman and Mudburra, two tribes on the Victoria River in the Northern Territory, not only a man's widows but also the wives of his brothers are under a ban of silence until the final disposal of his bones three or four weeks after death. After that ceremony, animals of the deceased's totem are placed on a fire. While they are cooking, the women who have been under a ban of silence go up to the fire and, after calling out *"Yakai! Yakai!"* put their heads in the smoke. An old man then hits them lightly on the head and afterwards holds out his hand for them to bite a finger. This ceremony removes the ban of silence under which the women had hitherto laboured.[9]

Again, in the Arunta tribe of Central Australia a man's widows smear their hair, faces, and breasts with white pipeclay and remain silent for a certain time, until a ceremony has been performed which restores to them the use of their tongues. The ceremony is as follows. When a widow wishes the ban of silence to be removed, she gathers a large wooden vessel full of some edible seed or small tuber, and smears herself with white pipeclay at the women's camp, where she has been living ever since her husband's death. Carrying the vessel, and accompanied by the women whom she has collected for the purpose, she walks to the centre of the general camp, midway between the two sections occupied by the two halves of the tribe. There they all sit down and cry loudly, whereupon the men, who stand to them either in the actual or in the classificatory relationship of sons and younger brothers of the dead man, come up and join the party. Next, these men take the vessel of seeds or tubers from the hands of the widow, and as many as possible laying hold of it, they shout loudly, *"Wah! wah! wah!"* All the women, except the widow, stop crying and join in the shout. After a short time the men hold the vessel of seeds or tubers close to, but not touching, the widow's face, and make passes to right and left of her cheeks, while all again shout *"Wah! wah! wah!"* The widow now stops her crying and utters the same shout, only in subdued tones. After a few minutes the vessel of seeds or tubers is passed to the rear of the men, who now, squatting on the ground and holding their shields in both hands, strike them heavily on the ground in front of the women, who are standing. When that has been done the men disperse to their camps and eat the food brought in the vessel by the widow, who is now free to speak to them, though she still continues to smear herself with pipeclay.[10]

The significance of this curious rite, by which an Arunta widow recovers her freedom of speech, is explained as follows by Messrs. Spencer and Gillen: "The meaning of this ceremony, as symbolised by the gathering of the tubers or grass seed, is that the widow is about to resume the ordinary occupations of a woman's life, which have been to a large extent suspended while she remained in camp in what we may call deep mourning. It is in fact closely akin in feeling to the transition from deep to narrow black-edged paper amongst certain more highly civilised peoples. The offering to the sons and younger brothers is intended both to show them that she has properly carried out the first period of mourning, and to gain their goodwill, as they, especially the younger brothers, are supposed to be for some time displeased with a woman when her husband is dead and she is alive. In fact a younger brother meeting the wife of a dead elder brother, out in the bush performing the ordinary duties of a woman, such as hunting for 'yams,' within a short time of her husband's death, would be quite justified in spearing her. The only reason that the natives give for this hostile feeling is that it grieves them too much when they see the widow, because it reminds them of the dead man. This, however, can scarcely be the whole reason, as the same rule does not apply to the elder brothers, and very probably the real explanation of the feeling is associated, in some way, with the custom according to which the widow will, when the final stage of mourning is over, become the wife of one of these younger brothers whom at first she has carefully to avoid."[11]

Again, among the Unmatjera and Kaitish, two other tribes of Central Australia, a widow observes the ban of silence until, usually many months after her husband's death, she is released from it by her husband's younger brother. When this takes place she makes an offering to him of a very considerable quantity of food, and with a fragment of it he touches her mouth, thus indicating to her that she is once more free to talk and to take part in the ordinary duties of a woman.[12]

Among the Warramunga, another tribe of Central Australia, the command of silence imposed on women after a death is much more comprehensive and extraordinary. With them it is not only the dead man's widow who must be silent during the whole time of mourning, which may last for one or even two years; his mother, his sisters, his daughters, his mother-in-law or mothers-in-law, must all equally be dumb and for the same protracted period. More than that, not only his real wife, real mother, real sisters, and real mothers-in-law are subjected to this rule of silence, but a great many more women whom the natives, on the classificatory principle, reckon in these relationships, though we should not do so, are similarly bound over to hold their tongues, it may be for a year, or it may be for two years. As a consequence it is no uncommon thing in a Warramunga camp to find the majority of women prohibited from speaking. Even when the period of mourning is over, some women prefer to remain silent and to use only the gesture language, in the practice of which they become remarkably proficient. Not seldom, when a party of women are in camp, there will be almost perfect silence, and yet a brisk conversation is all the while being conducted among them on their fingers, or rather with their hands and arms, for many of the signs are made by putting the hands or elbows in varying positions. At Tennant's Creek some years ago there was an old woman who had not opened her mouth, except to eat or drink, for more than twenty-five years, and who has probably since then gone down to her grave without uttering another syllable. When, however, after a longer or a shorter interval of absolute silence, a Warramunga widow desires to recover her liberty to speak, she applies to the men who stand to her in the classificatory or tribal relationship of sons, to whom, as is customary in such cases, she has to make a present of food. The ceremony itself is a very simple one; the woman brings the food, usually a large cake of grass seed, and in turn bites the finger of each of the men who are releasing her from the ban of silence. After that she is free to talk as much as she likes.[13]

Again, in the Dieri tribe of Central Australia a widow was not allowed to speak until the whole of the white clay, which she had smeared on her body in token of mourning, had crumbled and fallen away of itself. During this intermediate period, which might last for months, she might communicate with others only by means of the gesture language.[14]

But why should a widow be bound over to silence for a longer or a shorter time after the death of her spouse? The motive for observing the custom is probably a dread of attracting the dangerous attentions of her late husband's ghost. This fear is indeed plainly alleged as the reason by the Bella Coola Indians, and it is assigned by the Unmatjera and Kaitish as the motive for covering the widow's body with ashes. The whole intention of these customs is apparently either to elude or to disgust and repel the ghost. The widow eludes him by remaining silent; she disgusts and repels him by discarding her finery, shaving or burning her hair, and daubing herself with clay or ashes. This interpretation is confirmed by certain particularities of the Australian usages.

In the first place, among the Waduman and Mudburra the custom of silence is observed by the widow only so long as the flesh adheres to her late husband's bones; as soon as it has quite decayed and the bones are bare, she is made free of the use of her tongue once more. But it appears to be a common notion that the ghost lingers about his mouldering remains while any of the flesh is left, and that only after the flesh has wholly vanished does he take his departure for the more or less distant spirit-land.[15] Where such a belief prevails it is perfectly natural that the widow should hold her tongue so long as the decomposition of her husband's body is still incomplete, for so long may his spirit be supposed to haunt the neighbourhood and to be liable at any moment to be attracted by the sound of her familiar voice.

In the second place, the relation in which among the Arunta, the Unmatjera, and the Kaitish the widow stands to her late husband's younger brother favours the supposition that the motive of the restrictions laid on her is the fear of the ghost. In these tribes the younger brother of her late husband appears to exercise a special superintendence over the widow during the period of mourning; he sees to it that she strictly observes the rules enjoined by custom at such times, and he has the right severely to punish or even to kill her for breaches of them. Further, among the Unmatjera and Kaitish it is the younger brother of the deceased who finally releases the widow from the ban of silence, and thereby restores her to the freedom of ordinary life. Now this special relationship in which the widow stands to her late husband's younger brother is quite intelligible on the supposition that at the end of mourning she is to become his wife, as regularly happens under the common form of the levirate which assigns

a man's widow to one of his younger brothers. This custom actually obtains
in all the three tribes—the Arunta, the Unmatjera, and the Kaitish—in which
the widow observes the rule of silence and stands in this special relation to the
younger brothers of her late husband. In the Arunta it is the custom that on
the conclusion of mourning the widow becomes the wife of one of her deceased
husband's younger brothers;[16] and with regard to the Unmatjera and Kaitish
we are told that "this passing on of the widow to a younger, but never to an
elder, brother is a very characteristic feature of these tribes."[17] Similarly in the
Dieri tribe, which enforced the rule of silence on widows during the period of
mourning, a man's widow passed at his death to his brother, who became her
husband, and her children called him father.[18] But among rude races, who believe that a man's ghost haunts his widow and pesters her with his unwelcome
attentions, marriage with a widow is naturally thought to involve the bridegroom in certain risks arising from the jealousy of his deceased rival, who is
loth to resign his spouse to the arms of another. This may help us to understand why, among the Australian tribes in question, a man keeps such a vigi-
lant watch over the conduct of his deceased elder brother's widow. The motive
is probably not so much a disinterested respect for the honour of his dead
brother as a selfish regard for his own personal safety, which would be put
in jeopardy if he were to marry the widow before she had completely got rid
of her late husband's ghost by strictly observing all the precautions usually
taken for that purpose, including the rule of silence.

    Thus the analogy of customs observed among widely separated peoples sup-
ports the conjecture that among the ancient Hebrews also, at some early time
of their history, a widow may have been expected to keep silence for a certain
time after the death of her husband for the sake of giving the slip to his ghost;
and further, perhaps, that the observance of this precaution may have been
particularly enforced by her late husband's younger brother, who, in accordance with the custom of the levirate, proposed to marry her when the days of
her mourning were over. But it should be observed that, apart from analogy,
the direct evidence for such an enforced silence of widows among the Hebrews
is no more than a doubtful etymology; and as all inferences from etymology
to custom are exceedingly precarious, I cannot claim any high degree of probability for the present conjecture.

                        *   *   *

[Proceed with caution. It is true that among many primitive peoples a
woman is condemned to a period of silence and to other austerities on the
death of her husband;[18a] but Frazer's theory that such a practice obtained also
in ancient Israel rests solely on a supposed connection of the Hebrew word
'almanah, "widow," with a like-sounding 'illem, "dumb," and this, though

superficially alluring, is not accepted by the best Semitic philologists, who relate it rather to the Arabic *'a-l-m,* "be in pain, forlorn."[18b] Besides, the word *'illem,* wherever it occurs in the Hebrew Bible, means "to be voiceless by nature or by physical defect," not simply "to be muted, hushed, silenced";[18c] for the doleful silence observed by persons in distress the quite distinct verb *d-m-m* is employed.[18d] It is to be observed also that the cognate of Hebrew *'almanah* has now turned up in Akkadian and in Ugaritic, yet no Akkadian or Ugaritic text speaks of a ritual silence of widows, even though they indeed describe procedures of mourning. Moreover, among primitive peoples such silences are by no means confined to widows, but are usually imposed on *all* mourners and kinsfolk.[18e] Accordingly, philological objections apart, it would be difficult to explain why "the female silent one" should have to mean the widow exclusively.] ▼

343 Cannibalism in a time of famine   **2:20; 3:10**

> *Should women eat their offsprings*
> *the babes whom they have dandled?*

> *The hands of compassionate women have boiled their own children:*
> *they (the children) have become as food for them.*

Allegations of cannibalism are something of a cliché in ancient literary accounts of famines and sieges. Thus, Ashurbanipal relates that during his campaign against the Arabs "famine broke out among them, and they ate the flesh of their children against their hunger."[1] Similarly, the inhabitants of Tauromenium, in Sicily, are said to have eaten their slaves when they were beleaguered by the Romans during the Servile War of 104 B.C.;[2] and it is reported of the Vascones (Basques) of the city of Calahorra that they ate their children to stave off hunger when they were resisting the Romans after the death of Sertorius in 72 B.C.[3] Procopius, in his Gotica, tells of two women who slew and devoured their offspring during a famine;[4] and Strabo relates that the practice was not unknown, in similar circumstances, among the ancient Irish.[5]

What happened in the time of the Biblical writer seems to have been repeated later when Jerusalem fell to the Romans in 70 C.E., for Josephus reports the unnatural behavior of a woman who then ate her own suckling.[6]

The word rendered above as *food* is *leḇārôt.* This has inspired the suggestion that it really conceals the name of Labartu, the cannibalistic child-stealing hag of Mesopotamian folklore, the correct translation being, *They became unto them like child-eating hags.*[7] Since this suggestion has found its way into several modern commentaries, it may be well to point out that the reading of the demon's name as Labartu is in fact erroneous. The cuneiform sign for the syllable *bar* can also be read as *mash,* and that the correct reading in the present case is LaMAShtu is now proved by the discovery of a text in which it is actually spelled out: La-ma-ash-tu.[8]

344   Drinking gall   3:15

> *He hath filled me with gall,*
> *sated me with wormwood.*

This expression recurs twice in the Book of Jeremiah.[1] Drinking gall is frequently invoked as a curse in Classical literature.[2] It was not only a symbol of bitterness, but was believed also to cause madness.

We may aptly compare the famous lines in Shakespeare's *Macbeth*:[3]

> Come to my woman's breasts
> And take my milk for gall, you murdering monsters,
> Whenever in your sightless substances
> You wait on nature's mischief.[4]

345   Gravel and dust in the mouth   3:16

> *He has ground my teeth on gravel,*
> *and made me cower in ashes.*

The Greek (Septuagint) and Latin (Vulgate) Versions render the second clause, *And has fed me on ashes.* There does not appear to be any philological authority for this rendering, but it rests on an interesting piece of folklore. The ancient translators were evidently nonplused by the Hebrew word which, though it can be satisfactorily explained from the cognate Semitic languages, does not in fact recur in the Old Testament.[1] They therefore saw in the phrase an allusion to the custom of stuffing a man's mouth with dust or with a pebble against adverse spells or utterances.[2] This custom is attested by the popular expression, "Dust (or, stone) in thy mouth!" which is found alike in the Talmud[3] and in Arabic[4] and Mandaean[5] sources. The same custom likewise underlies the words of Proverbs 20:17:

> Though the bread of deceit may be pleasant to a man,
> his mouth will thereafter be filled with gravel.

According to Herodotus,[6] Ctesias,[7] and other ancient writers,[8] it was the custom of the Iranians to throw condemned felons into a room filled with ashes, with meat and drink in sight, but out of reach. Similarly, in the *History of Tamurlane,* it is recorded that men sentenced to death were given a cake of dust and ashes.[9]

346   The king as the life-breath of his people   4:20

> *The breath of our nostrils, the Lord's anointed*
> *is taken in their net.*[1]

The portrayal of the king as the *élan vitale* of his people occurs also in Egyptian literature.[2] Sesostris III, for instance, is described as "he that gives breath to his subjects' throats,"[3] and as "the herdsman that gives breath."[4] Elsewhere, the pharaoh is styled analogously, "the breath of our nostrils,"[5] "our life-breath,"[6] and "the *élan vitale* of mankind";[7] while in the Tell el Amarna Letters he is sometimes addressed as the breath of his servant's life.[8]

Similar expressions are also found in Mesopotamian literature.[9]

The idea is applied also to divine beings. In Genesis 2:7 and in Job 27:3; 32:8; and 33:4, it is the breath of God that not only animates man but also gives him intelligence and moral sense. The concept is familiar especially from the great verses of Psalm 104:29–30: *When Thou withdrawest Thy breath,*[10] *they die, and return to their dust. When Thou sendest forth Thy breath, they are created; (thereby) also Thou renewest* (i.e., by Thy wind) *the face of the earth.*

Two ideas are in fact combined. The first is that the king, as the embodiment of the god,[11] furnishes the breath of life to his people. The second is that, as the embodiment of the community, he is at the same time the epitome, rather than the endower, of its corporate vitality.[12] He is that in which "they live and move and have their being."

347 The king's shadow
4:20

. . . in his shadow we live.

Two ideas are here combined.

(i) The king, as the embodiment of the god, is a *protective shade* to his people. In Mesopotamian belief "to stay (or serve) in the sweet and fine shadow of the king" meant to belong to his immediate entourage. "Persons so described enjoyed special privileges. . . . Officials on missions were considered to be 'travelling in the shadow of the king.'" The notion seems to have originated in Egypt and to have been introduced into Mesopotamia toward the beginning of the first millennium B.C.[1] In a hymn from Kahun, the Northerners are said to exclaim, "Set us in thy shadow, O king!"[2] Elsewhere Pharaoh is described as being "like a shadow in spring, a cooling shade in summer."[3]

In the celebrated Travels of Wen-Amun, when that official is brought before the king of Byblus, he accidentally steps into the latter's shadow. A courtier at once interposes himself, and it has been suggested that the motive for his action was to prevent the stranger's thus coming within the ambit of the royal favor and privilege.[4]

The notion is applied also to the protection afforded by gods. Many Akkadian names begin with the element Ṣilli, "in the shadow of," followed by mention of a specific deity.[5] A Hebrew name of this type is Bezalel, meaning properly, "In the shadow of God."[6] Similarly, in an Aramaic papyrus from Elephantine, the expression, "in the shadow of Ahuramazda," means "under the protection of that god.[7]

(ii) Associated with this notion is the more basic concept that, since the shadow is a part of the self, to be in the king's (or in anyone's) shadow is to absorb his royal (divine) essence.[8]

Esther

The Book of Esther relates a story designed to account for a festival named Purim. Scholars are virtually agreed, however, that the story is fiction rather than history, and that the festival must consequently have had quite a different origin.[2] In the first place, none of the Persian kings who bore the name Xerxes (Ahasuerus) had a wife called Esther. Second, there is no mention anywhere but in the Book of Esther of a queen named Vashti, a vizier named Haman, or of a courtier named Mordecai who eventually replaced Haman.[3] Third, there is no Hebrew, Aramaic, or Persian word *pur* denoting "lot"; this explanation of the name Purim could be, at best, a piece of folk etymology by which the exiled Jews attempted to account for the name of an already existent festival through fanciful association of it with a *Babylonian* word of that meaning![4]

Thus the book presents two problems: (*a*) What is the real origin of the story, independent of its connection with Purim? (*b*) What is the real origin of Purim?

(a) It is to be noted, first, that the Book of Esther really consists of *two* stories now artificially linked together. The one is the story of Vashti; the other, that of Esther. Now, in each of them the central figure is a woman, and both revolve around the same central theme of how a beautiful woman outwits the designs of kings and princes. Vashti frustrates her lord's plan to make a vulgar display of her; Esther foils the plot of Haman against Mordecai and the Jews. Both stories belong, therefore, to that well-known class of folktales which deal with the wiles of women. Such tales, of course, would have been especially popular with the fair sex, and doubtless have been told and retold with relish in the harems of Persia or wherever else women came together in purely feminine converse. They are, essentially, "Kaffee-klatsch" talk at the expense of the menfolk. It is, accordingly, from a repertoire of such novellae that the Book of Esther may be supposed to have stemmed. Originally, the two stories would have been purely Persian compositions, dealing with intrigues at the Persian court. In course of time, however, it would have been picked up and adapted by the Jews living under Persian rule, and eventually used to explain a popular festival called something like Purim.

The stories have been linked together in the manner of most Oriental romances. They are enclosed in a general cadre of adventures at the court of the Great King. This is the kind of thing which one finds again in such well-known collections as the Pančatantra, the Twenty-five Vampire Tales (Vetalapanchavimsati) of Somadeva, and the Thousand and One Nights.

That the story of Esther was originally independent of that of Vashti is plain on the surface. In the story of Vashti, the succession falls to the next harem favorite (1:19). Esther, however, is chosen only after a nation-wide beauty contest. Moreover, whereas the deposition of Vashti is said to have taken place in the *third* year of the king's reign (1:3), the appointment of Esther occurs in the *seventh* (2:16)—surely, too long an interval, if the events were really connected.[5]

Furthermore, although the story of Esther purports to be of essentially *Jewish* interest, dealing with a situation affecting Jews and explaining the origin of a Jewish festival, the fact is that every detail of its Jewish coloration is either anomalous or incredible. Mordecai and Esther bear non-Jewish names. This is like calling a French heroine, Gretchen. The king authorizes the massacre of the Jews on the grounds that they are a refractory people (3:11); yet, he heaps honors on Mordecai, who openly admits to being a Jew (6:10)!

Lastly, as it now stands, the story bears clear evidence of having been manipulated from some earlier original. The king, for instance, himself approves the plan of Haman (3:10–11); yet, when Esther discloses it to him, he expresses surprise and demands to know the villain's name (7:2–5). So too, although Esther makes a great fuss about the danger of interceding with the king (4:10–11), when she finally musters the courage to do so and is assured explicitly that any request she might make will be granted, she fails to use the opportunity and resorts, instead, to the elaborate and quite unnecessary procedure of inviting the king and Haman to a couple of dinners! Not only is the point of this procedure obscured, but it also remains unexplained why Haman could not just as well have been denounced *in absentia*.

Now, once the Jewish veneer is removed, the earlier pattern begins to emerge, even though some of its features remain but faintly limned. The original story was simply a Persian tale of court life, with a Persian setting and Persian characters; and it was later adapted to account, in terms acceptable to the Jews, for the origin of a Persian festival which they had come to adopt. Moreover, the dénouement is now seen to have involved a motif which is in fact extremely common in folktales throughout the world, namely, that of maneuvering a culprit into an unwitting confession. The most familiar example of this occurs in the play scene of Shakespeare's *Hamlet*.[6]

It is, of course, impossible to be certain about all the details, but the main outlines of the earlier story may be reconstructed somewhat as follows:

Once upon a time, at the court of the Persian king Ahasuerus (Xerxes), a feud broke out between two courtiers, one named Haman, and the other Mardaka (a good Persian name).[7] In consequence of this feud and the intense hatred which he entertained against Mardaka, Haman represented to the king that his rival and his rival's kinsfolk were disobedient and disloyal citizens, and thereby obtained the royal assent to have them put to death.

What Haman did not know, however, was that one of those kinsfolk was the current royal favorite, the beautiful Esther (Persian, Sitireh, "star"; cf. our *Stella*). He did not realize either that she was a girl of great courage, shrewdness, and resource. Esther found a way of foiling his evil designs. She invited him to dine privately with the king and herself and, when the two men were in their cups, she entertained them by telling a seemingly fictitious tale of how a wicked courtier had once plotted the destruction of the reigning favorite and her entire kinsfolk merely to pay off a score against one of his rivals. The king, intrigued by the tale and thoroughly befuddled with drink, thereupon broke in with the rhetorical question, "What kind of man could he have been to fill his heart with such designs?" Haman, however, equally befuddled, interpreted this as a direct and specific inquiry and, his lips loosed by wine, clumsily blurted out, "Why, that's me, of course," thereby betraying himself. Esther's purpose was thus achieved, and the villain was exposed and put to death with all his family—an admirably satisfying illustration of the principle, "measure for measure."

In the Jewish retelling of this tale, the Persian Mardaka was transmogrified into Mordecai, a name (derived from that of the Babylonian god Marduk) actually affected by Jews in the Babylonian Exile,[8] and he was said to descend from one of his coreligionists who had actually been deported to Babylon after the capture of Jerusalem by Nebuchadnezzar.[9] Conversely, Haman was made to trace his pedigree to Agag, king of the Amalekites (cf. I Sam. 15:32) and hence to be a member of that accursed race against whom the God of the Jews had sworn warfare "from generation to generation" (Exod. 17:16).[10]

(b) As for the origin of Purim, here we are confronted with a wide variety of theories. There is no need to waste space mentioning them all.[11] Two, however, invite special comment.

The first[12] asserts that the festival originated not in Persia, but in Babylon, and that it was adopted by the Jews in the Babylonian Exile. Its prototype was the Babylonian New Year festival, held at the beginning of spring. At that festival, it is supposed, a ritual pantomime was enacted portraying the victory of Babylon's leading deities, the male Marduk and the female Ishtar, over those of the neighboring state of Elam, the male Humman and the female

Kiririsha. This pantomime was later transmogrified by the Jews, when Babylon fell under Persian rule, into the story of Mordecai and Esther's triumph over Haman and his wife Zeresh, the setting being changed appropriately to the Persian court. On this hypothesis, the name of the festival would be connected with the Babylonian word *puru*, "lot," but it would originally have referred to the fact that on New Year's the gods were believed to meet in conclave and determine the fates of men by the casting of lots.

Attractive as all this sounds, it is nevertheless riddled with fatal objections. The Babylonian New Year took place in the month of Nisan; hence it could not have been the origin of a festival which is said explicitly to have fallen on the fourteenth and fifteenth days of the preceding month of Adar! Second, there is no evidence that the Babylonian New Year was ever known as "the day of lots," nor that the destinies of men were thought to be determined by this method. Third, although an Elamite Khumban is indeed attested, there is no Humman or Haman, and there is nothing to show that Khumban's consort was Kiririsha (i.e., Zeresh).

The second theory[13] contends that the Book of Esther is really a political squib, and that what it actually celebrates is the victory of Judah the Maccabee over the Syrian general Nicanor on the thirteenth day of Adar, 161 B.C. On this assumption, Xerxes stands for Antiochus IV; Haman for Nicanor; and Mordecai for Judah the Maccabee. But here again there are fatal objections. The Second Book of Maccabees, in the Apocrypha of the Bible, states clearly (15:36) that the victory of Nicanor was celebrated "on the day preceding the day of Mordecai." Furthermore, the name of the festival (viz., Purim) remains unexplained, and there is no historical character to correspond to Esther.

Comparative Religion and Folklore may perhaps lead us out of the labyrinth. A story designed to explain a festival has obviously to account for its leading features. Working backward, therefore, we may attempt to recognize in various features of the story of Esther allusions to characteristic seasonal customs, and thence to reconstruct the nature and pattern of the underlying festival. The factors of the story which then come into consideration are the following:

(1) The selection of a queen and the celebration of her accession by a public holiday (2:17–18).

(2) The parading of an ordinary citizen in the garb of the king (6:1–11).

(3) The observance of a fast (4:15–16).

(4) The execution of a malefactor (7:10; 9:14, 25).

(5) An armed combat between two parties (9:1–17).

(6) The distribution of gifts (9:22).

(7) The celebration of the festival around the time of the vernal equinox (9:18–21).

Now, it so happens that all of these features are characteristic of seasonal festivals in many parts of the world.

(1) The selection of the queen connects at once with the common practice

of appointing kings and queens at the beginning of the year, and of celebrating their nuptials at the seasonal festival.[14] The most familiar example is the election of European kings and queens of the May, but Aristotle informs us that the marriage of a king and queen formed part of Dionysia at Athens.[15] In Egypt, the wedding of god and goddess was likewise celebrated both at the summer festival in Edfu[16] and at the winter festival in Luxor,[17] and Mesopotamian parallels can also be adduced.[18]

(2) The parade of Mordecai in the royal robes would reflect the equally common custom of appointing temporary kings to reign during the few days which often intervene, in ancient and primitive calendars, between the end of one year and the beginning of the next.[19] Such temporary kings, usually ordinary citizens, are attested, for instance, at Lhasa in Tibet,[20] among the Kwottos of Northern Nigeria,[21] among the Bakitara of Uganda,[22] among the Bastars of the Central Provinces of India,[23] and in Cambodia.[24] We are told also that at the Persian festival of Sacaea, held in July, one of the royal domestics was installed as temporary king and paraded in the royal attire.[25] Even more significantly, the Arab writer al-Biruni (973–1048) relates that it was customary in Persia to lead a thin-bearded man around on horseback, attended by the king's servants, just before the spring festival.[26]

(3) The observance of a fast accords with the fact that New Year is usually preceded by a period of abstinence.[27] The Babylonians, for example, recognized the first six or even sixteen days of the year as a lenten period.[28] The Hebrews prefaced the autumnal feast of Ingathering by the solemn Day of Atonement, observed as a fast. In Rome, the festival of Ceres, goddess of crops, in April, was introduced by a fast.[29] Similarly, in modern Cambodia, the first three days of the year (in March) are a period of abstinence;[30] while among the Cherokees and Choctaws of North America, the New Year feast (in August) is called the Fast.[31] The purpose of such fasts and lents is to express the state of suspended animation in which a community finds itself at the end of its annual or seasonal lease of life.

(4) The execution of Haman would go back to the annual dispatch of a human scapegoat at the beginning of the year, in order to drive out all blight and noxiousness.[32] At the Athenian festival of Thargelia, in May, a male and a female were thus expelled and scourged; and the same thing took place at Abdera.[33] In European usage, the unfortunate wretch is often identified with Death, Disease, Old Year, or the like.[34] Sometimes too the rite is performed in symbolic form, the part of the victim being taken by an effigy which is drowned or burned.[35] In Cambodia for example, such a rite is performed in March;[36] and among the Eskimos of Point Barrow, Alaska, the evil spirit Tuña is driven out with contumely as soon as the sun reappears.[37] (On such usages, see above, §194.)

(5) The combat between the Jews and their antagonists is similarly explicable as reflecting the characteristic seasonal combat between Summer and Winter, Old and New Year, Life and Death, Fertility and Drought, or the like, which is a feature of seasonal festivals in many parts of the world,[38] and which are attested even among the ancient Egyptians[39] and Hittites.[40]

(6) The distribution of gifts as a New Year custom still obtains at the present day, so that little need be said about it. It is worth noting, however, that the Romans used likewise to distribute presents, called *strenae,* on the first of January, and that the French term, *jour d'étrennes,* meaning New Year's Day, is thence derived. Indeed, it has been suggested that Purim itself may have a similar meaning, being connected with an assumed Old Persian word, *purti,* and with our own *portion.*

(7) Purim usually falls within the week of the vernal equinox; it has done so, for example, no less than twenty times during the past fifty years. Now, in ancient and primitive calendars, equinox and solstice, or (in lunar systems) the new moons nearest to them, are often regarded as the beginning of the year. Thus, the Babylonians and the Jews reckoned their year from the month of Nisan (roughly, mid-March until mid-April) or Tishri (roughly, mid-September until mid-October). The Roman year, before the Julian reform, likewise began on March 1, and it is significant that the vernal equinox was the beginning of the year in Euroepan countries until comparatively modern times. Under Charlemagne, it began on March 25, and it was only in the eighteenth century that January 1 became the official date in Holland, Protestant Germany, Russia, and Sweden.[41] Moreover—and this is especially important—the Old Persian year began at the vernal equinox.

Purim, then, would have been the ancient New Year festival, and in explanation of the name it is noteworthy that in modern Arabic, New Year is indeed sometimes called *phur.* The word has, apparently, no satisfactory etymology in the Arabic language. It must therefore have been borrowed, and a not unreasonable conjecture would associate it with the Persian word for "first," when it would bear the same general connotation as the French *printemps* or as the Spanish and Italian *primavera.*

349   The Iranian background
The Book of Esther is full of little touches which can be illustrated from Persian lore and custom.

(a) The court at Susa   1:2
The incident concerning Vashti is said to have taken place "when King Ahasuerus was occupying his royal throne in Susa the capital." This has a special meaning, for Xenophon tells us that the Persian king used to make the

rounds of his three capitals, spending the spring in Susa, the summer in Ecbatana, and the winter in Babylon.[1] What is indicated, therefore, is that the
incident took place in the spring, while the court was in residence at the first-
named city.

(b) The royal banquet   1:3

The banquet tendered by the king lasted one hundred and eighty days.
Scholars have long wondered how officers of state could have absented themselves from their duties so long. The answer is simple: the author modeled
his account on the practice which obtained at the annual feasts of Nauroz
(New Year) and Mihrajan, when the sovereign entertained his ministers and
friends *in relays,* according to order of rank.[2]

(c) The one hundred and eighty days   1:4

The mention of 180 days is a clever touch. To be sure, in the mouth of one
who had lived in the Babylonian Exile, this could be nothing more than a
round number, consisting of the basic Babylonian sixty multiplied thrice for
exaggeration. There may, however, be more to the matter than this, for the
fact is that the ancient Persian year was divided into six parts, called *gahan-
bars,* and it so happens that 180 days comprise exactly the first three of them,
beginning in spring. The scheme is as follows:

maidyoizaremaya (mid-spring) — *maidyoišema* (mid-summer)	45 days
maidyoišema — *paitshaya* (grain-bringing)	60 days
paitshaya — *ayathrima* (home-coming)	75 days
	180 days

The total period lasted from May 1 until October 16.[3] The Jewish author,
however, was not quite *au fait* with the details, for, as we have seen, Xenophon
says that the court moved to Ecbatana over the summer months, whereas it
is here represented as spending both spring and summer at Susa.

(d) "Men who knew the law"   1:13

After Vashti has refused to appear at the banquet, the king consults men
"who know law and protocol." Cambyses, says Herodotus, married his own
sister after consulting the judges, described as "certain picked men, appointed
for life or until found guilty of misconduct. It is by them that justice is administered in Persia, and they are the interpreters of the old laws."[4]

The Hebrew word (*dath*) here rendered "law," it should be added, is a
Persian term.

(e) The seven who saw the king's face   1:14

The king's special counselors are seven men privileged to see his face.
Heracleides Commanus, quoted by the antiquarian Athenaeus, informs us that
the Persian king used to dine alone behind a curtain, and only seven men had
the right to see him.[5]

Similar taboos obtain among the Loango[6] and Coango[7] of West Africa and in Susa, a region to the south of Abyssinia.[8] They are explained by Frazer from the belief that a man's "spirit," or *élan vitale,* can be elicited by ill-wishers when he opens his mouth.[9] Possibly, however, this is simply a particularization of the rule that the king, as the embodiment of deity, must be kept inviolate.[10] The king of Jebu, in West Africa, for example, has always to remain veiled or screened,[11] and among the Ewe-speaking peoples of the same area only three chosen men may have direct converse with him.[12]

(f) The crazy edict 1:22

After Vashti has rebuffed him, the king, fearful lest the other ladies of the realm might be encouraged by her example to defy their husbands, issues a decree that every man is to be "ruler in his own house and (entitled to) speak the language of his people." Scholars have long wondered why Ahasuerus should have had to give special permission to husbands to use their native tongues in their own homes.[13] The answer is really very simple. This is a deliberately humorous touch. The only way in which the proud and ostentatious monarch can guarantee his male subjects authority in their own households is formally to appoint them "governors" therein, and this appointment is made, under full protocol, in the same terms as were used in letters patent accrediting governors to their several provinces! Such letters evidently contained a clause sanctioning the use of native tongues. The diplomatic phraseology is here reproduced with delightful humor, and one can readily imagine that when our story was told and retold in the harems of Persia, this little detail must have roused a particularly uproarious laugh.[14]

(g) The royal crown 2:17

As a mark of favor to Esther, the king places a crown on her head. The crown is called *kether.* Although common in later Hebrew, this word does not occur in the Old Testament except here. The reason is that it is a Persian technical term, for Greek writers mention the *kidaris* (or *kitaris*) as the royal headgear of Persian monarchs.[15]

(h) Haman's boast 5:11

Elated at the impending ruin of Mordecai and the Jews, Haman summons his wife and friends and recounts to them "the splendor of his riches, the number of his sons, and all the promotions with which the king had honored him" (RSV). At first blush, the reference to *the number of his sons* sounds somewhat odd and, as a matter of fact, the historian Josephus was so nonplused by it that he simply left it out in his retelling of the tale! But it is, once again, a genuine Persian touch. "Next to prominence in arms," says Herodotus, the Persians "regarded it as the greatest proof of manly prowess to be the father of many sons. Every year the king sends rich gifts to the man who can show the largest number, since they hold that number is strength."[16]

(i) "Whom the king delights to honor" 6:8–11

As a reward for having saved the king's life from conspirators, Mordecai is paraded around the city wearing a royal robe and mounted on a royal steed. It has been suggested above that this incident was intended to account for the parade of the "temporary king" at the festival which underlies Purim. Within the framework of the story itself, however, it can be illustrated from the assertion of Plutarch[17] that when the Persian king wished to show special favor to a subject, he gave him one of his own robes.

(j) Covering the head 6:12

Thoroughly put out by the honor which he has had to pay to Mordecai, Haman rushes home "in mourning and with head covered." Again a Persian touch. Quintus Curtius informs us that when a Persian wept in mourning, he kept his head covered.[18] The Hebrews, on the other hand, strewed ashes over it.

Ecclesiastes

350　The telltale bird　　　　　　　　　　**Eccles. 10:20**

A bird of the air shall carry the voice,
and that which hath wings shall tell the matter.

The allusion in this proverbial phrase is to the widespread tale of *The Bird of Truth,* who discloses treachery, murder, marital infidelity, and the like.[1] Tales of this type are to be found in Grimm,[2] in *The Arabian Nights,*[3] in the famous *Legend of the Seven Sages,*[4] and in the English and Scottish ballads.[5] A classic Greek example is the familiar story of the cranes of Ibycus.[6]

The motif is very ancient. In the recently discovered Hittite *Tale of Elkunirša* (which evidently goes back to a Canaanite original), "Ishtar," disguised as a bird, overhears the love-making of Baal and Asherath and reports it to the latter's husband, Elkunirša (i.e., *El qôneh 'eres,* "the god who owns the earth"; cf. Gen. 14:19).[7]

Related to this theme is the popular expression, "A little bird told me,"[8] the prototype of which occurs already in Aristophanes.[9] A popular belief in Norway is that if a bird flies to a window, this signifies news.[10]

NOTES

PSALMS

250 The divine adoption of kings

1. On this concept, see: A. M. Hocart, Kingship (1927); Frazer-Gaster, NGB §§125–27; T. H. Gaster, in Numen 1 (1954), 193–94.—On sacred kingship in the Ancient Near East, see: M. Canney, in JMEOS 10 (1923), 53–58; A. Moret, Du caractére religieux de la royauté pharaonique (1902); R. Labat, Le caractére religieux de la royauté assyro-babylonienne (1939); C. Jeremias, Die Vergöttlichung der bab.-ass. Könige, AO 19/iii-iv (1919); I. Engnell, Studies in Divine Kingship in the Ancient Near East (1943); T. H. Gaster, in Review of Religion 9 (1945), 267–81; C. J. Gadd, Ideas of Divine Rule in the Ancient Near East (1948); H. Frankfort, Kingship and the Gods (1948); A. Bentzen, Det sakrale Kongedomme (1945); S. Smith, "The Practice of Kingship in Early Semitic Kingdoms," in S. H. Hooke, ed., Myth, Ritual and Kingship (1958).—On kingship in Canaan and Israel, see: M. Noth, in Zeitschr. für Theol. und Kirche 47 (1950), 157–91; G. Widengren, Sakrales Königtum im AT und in Judentum (1955); J. de Fraine, L'aspect religieux de la royauté israélite (1954); A. Johnson, Sacral Kingship in Ancient Israel (1959); J. Gray, in VT 2 (1952), 199–220; A. Bentzen, Det sakrale Kongedomme (1945).—For modern African parallels, see: C. G. Seligman, Egypt and Negro Africa (1934); P. Hadfield, Traits of Divine Kingship in Africa (1949); C. Petersson, Chiefs and Gods: Social and Religious Elements in the S. E. Bantu Kingship (1953).

2. Cf. S. A. B. Mercer, The Religion of Ancient Egypt (1949), 248 ff.; H. Nelson, in JNES 1 (1942), 127–55.

3. Inscription of Khenzer, in Breasted, AR i.§786. In the Stela of Kubban (ib., iii.285), 18, he is regarded as "Re'incarnate," and in Pyramid Texts, Ut. 362, 1146, 1156, as "a vast cosmic figure."

4. T. Paffrath, in Hommel Festschrift (1917), i.157–59; G. Furlani, La religione babilonese e assira (1928), i.353.

5. See below, §296.

6. Krt C = 125 Gordon, 20–22.

7. E. Casartelli, in ERE vii.722–23.

8. M. Lidzbarski, Ephemeris ii (1908), 383 f.

9. E. Naville, Deir-el-Bahri iv (1913), pl. 96.4; id., Osorkon (1892), ii.25.

10. H. Gressmann, ATOB, #88; cf. G. Maspero, in PSBA 14 (1892), 308 ff.; A. Jacoby, in ARW 13 (1906), 547 ff.; K. Sethe, Altaeg. Pyramidentexte ii (1910), §§910–13.

11. ISA 58, g.7–8.

12. P. Jensen, KB vi/2. 140–41; M. Streck, Assurbanipal (1916), ii.348–49, 8; Labat, op. cit., 64–66; A. Boissier, in OLz 1908.234 f.; H. Zimmern, in ZA 36 (1925), 85, n.1; T. H. Gaster, Thespis², 179, 254.

13. See below, §284.

14. For the traditional text's 'aSaPPᵉRaH 'el HôQ read 'ôSîPhᵉKaH 'el ḤêQî.

King installed on holy mountain

15. See: M. Canney, in JMEOS 20 (1936), 25–40; M. Eliade, The Myth of the Eternal Return (1954), 12 ff.; W. Gaerte, in Anthropos 9 (1914), 956–79; T. H. Gaster, Thespis², 183 f.

16. Lassen, in ZKM 2 (1839), 62 ff.

17. C. Meinhold, in Baudissin Festschrift (1918), 382.

18. A. Smythe-Palmer, Jacob at Bethel (1899), 17 ff.

19. ERE xii.485ᵇ, n.3.

20. D. G. Brinton, Myths of the New World³ (1905), 95.

21. K. Sethe, Urkunden (1927–30), iv.364.

22. K. Sethe, Amun (1929), §250 f.

23. Sethe, ib., 117–18; A. de Buck, Oersheuvel (1937), 72–84; H. Frankfort, Kingship and the Gods (1948), 151–54. Cf. also: S. Morenz, Aeg. Religion (1960), 45.

24. T. Dombart, Der Sakralturm, I: Zikkurat (1920), 34.

25. P. Mus, Barabudur (1935), i.68 ff., 94 ff.

26. See below, §272; Gaster, op. cit., 156 f.

27. W. Dunbar, in Antiquity 3 (1929), 408–13.—The Egyptians held that earth had been formed from the gathering of primordial sand at Thebes: NK Leyden Papyrus, ed. A. H. Gardiner, in ÄZ 42.14 f. A. Erman, Literatur d. Aegypter (1923), 365, #10.— On Jerusalem as the cosmic hill, see: E. Burrows, in The Labyrinth, ed. S. H. Hooke (1935), 53 ff.—In Ezekiel's blueprint of the future temple (43:15), part of the altar is termed *hril*, which W. F. Albright (Archaeology and the Religion of Israel [1942], 151) identifies as a symbol of the divine mountain (*har el*), in accordance with the notion that the temple was a microcosm.

251   Seeing the face of God

1. The psalm bears all the hallmarks of such compositions. The god is besought to hear the suppliant's defense (Heb.: *ṣedeq:* v. 1); to let the verdict issue in his favor (v. 2); to investigate his state of heart (v. 3). He is addressed as "savior of those that *seek refuge*" (v. 7), and specific reference is made to guilty men (RSV: "the wicked," v. 9), who "despoil" him (ib.) or "track him down" (v.10). Many of these expressions possess a juridical nuance.

2. Cf. T. H. Gaster, IDB, s.v. Resurrection.

3. Cf. F. Nötscher, "Die Angesicht Gottes schauen" nach biblischer und babylonischer Auffassung (1924).

4. Cf. Apuleius, Met. ii.24: *inexplicabili voluptate divini simulacri perfruebar;* cf. F. Cumont, After Life in Roman Paganism (1922), 121 f.; A. D. Nock, Early Gentile Christianity and Its Hellenic Background (1964), 6, 111–13, 139.

5. L. R. Farnell, Cults of the Greek States (1896–1909), iii.126 ff.

6. For the traditional text's *yašar yeḥᵉzū panêmô* we should probably read *yᵉšārîm yeḥᵉzū pānāw.*

252   The breakers of Death

1. Isa. 28:15; 38:18; Hos. 13:14; Ps. 6:6; Job 28:22; 30:23, etc.

2. Stith Thompson, MI, A 672; F 93.1.

3. M. Cox, Introduction to Folklore (1897), 184 ff.; T. Waitz, Anthropologie der Naturvölker (1860–77), iii.197; W. Mannhardt, Germ. Mythen (1858), 364 ff. Cf. also the familiar Negro spiritual: "One more river, / And that's the River of Jordan, / One more river, / There's one more river to cross."

4. G. Maspero, in JA, IVème sér. 15 (1880), 161; W. Müller, Egyptian Mythology (1918), 176.

5. *Ludlul bêl nimêqi* iii.16 = ANET 438 f.

6. Ib., iv.6 = ANET, 437.

7. Epic of Gilgamesh x.21–27, 50.

8. Hesiod, Theog. 774 ff; cf. also: Ps.-Plato, Axioch 12, p. 371B; Plutarch, De orac. defec. ii.

9. E.g., Euripides, Herakles 431 ff.; id., Alcestis 253 ff., 440; Aristophanes, Lys. 606 ff.; id., Frogs 185 ff.; Vergil, Aen. vi.290 ff.; Juvenal, iii.260 f.; B. Schmidt, Das Volksleben der Neugriechen (1871), 222, 237; D. Hesseling, Charos (1897).—Neither in Homer nor in Aeschylus, Septem 857 is the ferryman named Charon.

10. Lancelot du lac, ed. 1591, p. 147; cf. F. Nork, Das Kloster xii (1849), 249 ff., 260 ff.

11. Shakespeare, Hamlet, V.i (song).

12. F. J. Child, English and Scottish Ballads (1882–98), #114; L. C. Wimberly, Folklore in the English and Scottish Ballads² (1959), 108 ff. Cf. also the ballads of Edward, Lizzie Wan, and The Two Brothers (ib.). For a Slavonic parallel, cf. K. Schwenk, Die Mythologie der Slawen (1853), 334; and for a Finnish parallel, ib., 389.

13. A. Kuhn, Westfalische Märchen, i (1859), 129.

14. Procopius, Goth. iv.20.

15. Pliny, HN iv.27.

16. Cox, op. cit., 188 f.; cf. Villemarqué, Barz. breiz. i.169: "En passant le lac de l'angoisse, elle vit une bande des morts, des morts, vetus de blanc, dans les petites barques."

17. E. Martinengo Cesaresco, Essays in the Study of Folk Songs (Everyman's Library ed.), 295.

18. A. B. Alexander, Latin American Mythology (1920), 198; D. G. Brinton, Myths of the New World³ (1905), 288 f.

19. D. G. Brinton, Essays of an Americanist (1890), 135–47.

20. Id., Myths, loc. cit.

21. Ib.

22. Ib., 290.

23. Odyssey 10.514; Plato, Phaedo 112–13C; O. Gruppe, Griechische Mythologie (1906), 402 f.; C. G. Heyne, Excursus ix. to Comm. on Vergil, Aen. vi.

24. Rig Veda x.63.

25. Kalevala, runo xvi.

26. E. S. Drower, The Canonical Prayerbook of the Mandaeans (1959), 63.4, 5, 9.

27. M. Pope, Job (Anchor Bible, 1965), 218, would recognize a reference to the river of the underworld in the expression "pass over the *shelaḥ*" in Job 33:18; 36:12— both times in allusion to death. The word is commonly rendered "weapon" (i.e., pass away by means of a weapon), but Pope here combines it with the Akkadian *šilḫu, šiliḫtu,* Heb. *šelaḥ* (Neh. 3:15), "channel." Cf. also the Coptic loanword *šoleḥ,* "canal."

253 The bonds of Death

1. Ti꜀i Series, IX.i, 25 = R. C. Thompson, Devils (1904), ii.66 (*itti mûti rakis*).

2. Atharva Veda vi.92, 2; viii.7, 28 (*Yamasya padbića*); id., vii.112, 2; viii.7, 28 (*mtryupâçah*). Cf. I. Scheftelowitz, Schlingen- und Netzmotiv (1912), 6; M. Eliade Images et Symboles (1952), 132 ff.

3. Yasna 53.8; Vendidad 5.8 (*mərəithyaosh*).

4. Alma Rišaia Zuṭa (Drower Coll. 48), 317 (*giṭria usqupata d-muta*).

5. Beowulf, 1936 ff.

6. Genesis-Exodus, 2716.

7. Shakespeare, Cymbeline, I.ii.

8. Grimm-Stallybrass, TM 845 ff., 1557.

9. Sophocles, Ajax 675 f.

10. Plato, Timaeus 71E.

11. Orphic Hymns, 35.85; cf. R. B. Onians, Origin of European Ideas about the Body, etc. (1951), 422, n.5.

12. Ennius, Ann. 5, Vaal. (*somno levi placidoque revinctus*).

13. TB, Ber. 60[b] (heblê šênah).

14. Cf. S. Eitrem, Papyri Osloenses, i (1925), 71; A. Deissmann, Light from the Ancient East (1911), 306 f.; M. Lidzbarski, Ephemeris, i (1902), 31.

254 Riding a cherub

1. F. Thureau Dangin, in RA 24 (1927), 199–202.

2. T. Fish, in BJRL 31 (1948), 162–71; S. Langdon, Semitic Mythology (1931), 115 f.

3. Grimm-Stallybrass, TM 633.

4. Samadeva 2.102.

5. T. H. Gaster, Thespis[2], 168 f.; Stith Thompson, MI, A 284.2.

6. Examples are collected in MAOG xi/1–2.69.

7. R. C. Thompson, in AAA 20.8, 8 (Ninlil).

8. H. Güterbock, in JCS 6 (1952), 34.

9. Iliad 24.341–45; Odyssey 1.97; 5.45–49.

10. H. P. L'Orage, Symbols of Cosmic Kingship in the Ancient World (1953), 49–51.

255 The heavenly sieve

1. S. Feigin, in JNES 9 (1953), 40 ff.—This interpretation is anticipated in TB Ta`anith 9[b] (cf. Rashi in loc.).

2. S. C. Macpherson, Memorials of Service in India (1865), 89, 355.

3. Aristophanes, Clouds 367. Cf. also: Plautus, Pseudol. 1.1.100; Pliny, HN xxviii.2 (imbrem in cribro).

4. W. W. Hyde, Greek Religion and Its Survivals (1923), 225, n.16.

5. J. Batchelor, The Ainu and Their Folklore (1901), 333.

6. A. Kuhn, Westfälische Sagen, Gebräuche und Märchen (1859), i.18, 203; J. Grimm, DM[4], 231.—In Grimms' Märchen, #178, Master Pfriem sees people in heaven pouring water in a tub full of holes; cf. Stith Thompson, MI, F 171.6.2; H 1023.2; Q 512.1.—O. Gruppe, Griech. Mythologie (1906), 831, suggests that a rain-making rite underlies the myth relating that the daughters of Danaos were compelled to pour water into a perforated jar in the underworld as a punishment for killing their husbands, the sons of Aegyptos. On this myth, see further: Campbell Bonner, in Harvard Studies xxiii.1291 ff.

7. J. G. Frazer, GB i.285.

8. E. Kutscher, in Leshonenu 21 (1956), 252 [Hebrew].

257 Walking round the altar

1. On the subject in general, see: M. Haberlandt, in Correspondenzblatt der. Gesell. für Anthropologie, Ethnologie und Urgeschichte, 21.9; A. Hillebrand, in Festschrift d. schles. Gesell. für Volkskunde (1911), 1 ff.; S. Eitrem, Opferritus und Voropfer der Griechen und Römer (1915), 6–75; F. Nötscher, "Die Angesicht Gottes schauen" nach biblischer und babylonischer Auffassung (1924), 66–67, n.l.; W. Upright, in ET 22 (1911), 563 ff.; F. Heiler, Das Gebet (1918), 176.

2. Cf. Jubilees 16:31; cf. A. J. Wensinck, in Theol. Tidjsk. 1919.103 f.

3. G. Furlani, Rel. bab. e ass. (1928), ii.286. So too in Sabaean: G. Ryckmans, in Le Muséon 71 (1958), 127 f.

4. CIS iv.19, 392, 395; Glaser 425, 1402; Jaussen, Himyar. 120; Mittwoch-Mordtmann, 24.1. Cf. M. Höffner and N. Rhodokanakis, in WZKM 1936.216 ff.

5. J. Wellhausen, Reste d. arab. Heidentums[2] (1897), 110 ff.; W. Robertson Smith, The Religion of the Semites[3] (1927), 340. Full description in H. St. John Philby, A Pilgrim in Arabia (1946).—For a Classical parallel, cf. Ovid, Met. vii.257 f.: Sparsis Medea capillis / Bacchantum ritu flagrantes circuit aras.

258 A Canaanite psalm?

1. Cf. S. A. Pallis, The Babylonian Akitu Festival (1926), 221 f., 249–306.

2. Cf. S. Langdon, The Epic of Creation (1923), 16 ff. For the earlier Sumerian myths, cf, T. Jacobsen, in JNES 5 (1946), 146–47; S. N. Kramer, Sumerian Mythology (1944), 82 ff.

3. See: T. H. Gaster, Thespis² (1961), 245–67; A. Goetze, in ANET 125 f. The original texts are: KBo III.7, i.9–27; KUB VII.v.6–24; KBo III.7, iii.4–33. The god is aided by the mortal hero, Hupasiyas.

4. KBo III.7, col. iv.

5. III AB, A; III AB; cf. especially II AB vi.44 ff.

6. Gaster, op. cit. 114–244.

7. Ib. 443.

8. III AB, A. The antagonist is there called Prince Sea (*Zbl Ym*) and Lord Stream (*Ṭpṭ Nhr*); cf. Hab. 3:8.

9. Enuma Elish vi.32, 56.

10. T. H. Gaster, in Folk-Lore 1933, 382, n.13; id., Thespis², 443–46; H. L. Ginsberg, The Ugaritic Texts (1936), 129–31 [Hebrew].

11. Note the *threefold* invocation—a common liturgical device.

12. Cf. vi.47, 51, etc.

13. II AB vi.44. "Threescore and ten" is, of course, merely a round number, signifying multitude.

14. See above, §32.

15. Pss. 66:2; 79:9; I Chron. 16:29.

16. Cf. vi.98–99, 142, 144; vii.118, 120, 124–25.

17. Note that in the Ugaritic texts the verb *k-b-d*, "pay homage," is a regular complement of *q-l*, "fall," and (*h*)*šthwy*, "prostrate oneself"; cf. I AB i.37–38; II AB iv.25–26, etc. The rendering to Yahweh of "the glory (*kabôd*) of his name," accomplished as it is by prostration, might therefore be a formal act of homage consisting in a ceremonial recitation of his honorific names and titles; cf. Enuma Elish vii.120: "he (Marduk) whose name his fathers glorified."

18. So also in Ps. 96:9, where the expression recurs. (Note that the traditional text's *hadrath qôdeš* means "holy *awe*," after Akkadian *adāru*, not "beauty of holiness," as commonly rendered.)

19. Concerning this god, see: T. H. Gaster, Thespis², 162 f.

20. II AB vii.27a–41.

21. The "voice of Baal" is mentioned again in II AB iv-v.70 and in III Aqhat 45–46.

22. The translation is, however, uncertain. Ginsberg, in ANET 135, suggests that the meaning of the clause is rather, "A yew-club swings in his right hand." This might be supported by a passage in an Egyptian magical text (Leyden Papyrus 235, recto iv.12 —v.2 = ANET 249), where it is said of Baal that he smites his enemies "with the cedar which is in his right hand."

23. See Kittel, BH³ in loc.

24. For this expression, cf. Ps. 89:6. It corresponds to the "Assembly of the Holy Ones (*mpḫrt qdšm*)" in the inscription of Yeḥimilk of Byblos (tr. Rosenthal, ANET², 499). The term "holy ones" denotes the pantheon in the 8th cent. B.C. Canaanite magical plaque from Arslan Tash, and the same usage may be recognized in Ps. 16:3; Job 5:1; 15:15; Hos. 12:1 and Zech. 14:5; cf. T. H. Gaster, in Orientalia 11 (1942), 59.

25. Similarly, in CT VIII.35, i.17 Marduk is said to have established his dwelling on the waters; cf. also: Ps. 104.3.

26. Gudea Cylinder A, xii.11–13; cf. JNES 2 (1943), 118.

27. Cf. T. Jacobsen, in JNES 5 (1946), 145, n.28.

28. Lucian, De Dea Syria, 13.
29. Targum Ps.-Jonathan, Exod. 28:30; Midrash Tanḥuma, Qedošim, §10.
30. Pausanias, i.18, 7.
31. KBo III.7 (duplicates, KUB XII.66; XVII.5–6); cf. Gaster, Thespis², 251 f., 256.
32. Cf. also: Enuma Elish vi.114–15.
33. Cf. T. H. Gaster, in Folk-Lore 1933. 382, n.13.
34. Cf. particularly Ginsberg's brilliant recognition of a Canaanite grammatical form in v.6, where for the traditional text's *wa-yarqidem* we should read *wa-yarqed-ma* (or, *wa-yirqod-ma?*), with the archaic coordinative enclitic *-ma*. Other instances of this may be detected in Num. 24:17; Deut. 33:3; Isa. 35:1; Joel 1:17; Pss. 42:5; 110:3.
35. The Modern Churchman 12 (1922), 390.

260   Magic waters

1. G. R. Driver has suggested that the Heb. word *dabar*, "thing," should be vocalized *deber*, "plague," the verb being derived, not from *y-ṣ-q* "pour," but from *ṣ-w-q*, "be attached closely." The sense will then be: "A noxious plague has fastened upon him." This, however, is thinking in English, not in Hebrew, for the word *deber* really means "reverse, catastrophe" (cf. Akkadian *dab/pāru*, "thrust back"), so that a very mixed metaphor results!

261   An ancient Hebrew wedding song

1. See: T. H. Gaster, in JBL 74 (1955), 239–51; J. H. Darly, in Ir. E. Rec. 91 (1959), 249–55.—The best accounts of modern Arab wedding customs are: H. Granquist, Marriage Customs in a Palestinian Village (1931–33); W. Rothstein, "Moslemische Hochzeitsgebräuche bei Jerusalem," in Palästinajahrbuch 6 (1910); E. W. Lane, Manners and Customs of the Modern Egyptians, ch. vi.
2. The bridal couple has been identified, for instance, with David and Maacah (Abraham ibn Ezra); Solomon and Pharaoh's daughter (Kirkpatrick); Ahab and Jezebel (Hitzig); Joram and Athaliah (Delitzsch); Alexander Balas and Cleopatra, daughter of Ptolemy Philometer (Olshausen, Haupt); Aristobulus I and Salome (Duhm). These are just wild stabs.
3. See: E. Westermarck, History of Human Marriage (1925), ii.261, n.5; id., Marriage Customs in Morocco (1914), 118, 274; J. G. Wetzstein, in Zeitschr. für Ethnologie 5 (1873), 288. At Malayan weddings, bride and groom are called "sovereigns for a day" (*raja sari*): W. W. Skeat, Malay Magic (1900), 388. In Java too they are treated as royalty: G. Geertz, The Religion of Java (1960), 57. In a wedding song of the Mandaeans of Iraq and Iran the groom is hailed as "king": M. Lidzbarski, Mandäische Liturgien (1920), p. x, n.3.
4. Literally, "grace" (Heb.: *ḥēn*).
5. W. Robertson Smith, in JP 14.125; J. Wellhausen, Reste des arabischen Heidentums² (1897), 173; J. Morgenstern, Rites of Birth, Marriage, etc. among the Semites (1966), 34–35. Photographs of the ceremony appeared in Life magazine, July 12, 1954, p. 52.
6. Literally, "some god hath endowed thee with *berākah*" (RSV: "God has blessed you"). *Berākah* is a kind of magical aura: E. Westermarck, Pagan Survivals in Mohammedan Civilisation (1933), 87 ff.; J. Chalhod, in RHR 148 (1955), 68–88. For this sense of the word in O.T., see: M. Canney, in ET 39 (1928), 381–85. A good example is Isa. 65:8: "When wine is found in a cluster of grapes, men say, 'Destroy it not, for there is *berākah* in it.'" See also: J. Pedersen, Israel i–ii (1926), 198 ff.
7. Homeric Hymn to Demeter, 236 ff.
8. Apollonius Rhodius, Argonautica iv.571 f.
9. Theocritus, Id., xv.106 f.

10. Odyssey 2.12.

11. Ib., 18.193 f.

12. Ovid, Met. xv.606 f.

13. Granquist, op. cit., ii.113, 117.

14. Ib.

15. C. R. Conder, Heth and Moab (1885), 295.

16. E. Crawley, The Mystic Rose² (1927), ii.33 ff.; P. Sartori, Sitte und Brauch (1910–14), i.114; E. Westermarck, History, ii.449 ff.

17. Granquist, op. cit., ii.60.

18. Song of Songs 3:7–8.

19. Granquist, op. cit., ii.85 ff.; Rothstein, op. cit., 121, 135; J. A. Jaussen, Coutumes des arabes au pays de Moab (1908), 55.

20. R. Chambers, The Book of Days (1886), i.721.

21. I Abrahams, Jewish Life in the Middle Ages² (1927), 267.

22. Notes and Queries VI/ii (1880), 245.

23. The expression recurs in Ps. 21:6 in the specific sense of *insignia and regalia.*

24. Granquist, op. cit., ii.95 ff.

25. Ib., i.124; ii.78; Lane, op. cit. (Minerva Library ed., 1891), 156; H. N. Hutchinson, Marriage Customs of Many Lands (1897), 66.

26. Cf. F. Rosenthal, in HUCA 33 (1950–51), 411 ff. The adjective *ṣadîq* bears this sense in Arabic, and it may be recognized in O.T. in such passages as Pss. 112:4; 116:5.

27. For the traditional text's *wᵉ-ᶜanwah ṣedeq,* which is barely translatable, read, by mere redivision of the consonants, *wᵉ-ᶜanî haṣdeq* (Melville Scott). The expression recurs in Ps. 82:3; cf. also: Ps. 72:2–4.

28. Crawley, op. cit., ii.37 f.

29. H. Oldenberg, Die Religion des Veda (1894), 271.

30. Granquist, op. cit., ii.90, n.1; Sartori, op. cit., i.92.

31. C. Seligman, Egypt and Negro Africa (1934), 15–18, 59.

32. J. Roscoe, The Bakitara (1912), 134.

33. The traditional text reads literally, *Thy throne God for ever.* This is a famous puzzle. The usual solution is to render, *Thy throne is as God is—everlasting,* or to assume that the word *God* has been substituted for an original YHWH (Yahweh), which was itself a corruption of the similar *yhyh,* "shall be." This, however, overlooks the parallelism of such phrases as "some god (*elohim*) has endowed thee with *bᵉrākah*" in v. 3, and "some god (*elohim*) has anointed thee," in v. 8, whence it is apparent that *God* (*elohim*) is here likewise the subject of the clause and that a verb describing his action has dropped out. Such passages as I Sam. 13:3; II Sam. 7:12, Isa. 9:6, and I Chron. 17:11, as well as a parallel Akkadian formula of salutation (cited above in the text) show that the missing word was *hêkîn,* "has set firm," as suggested long ago by Street (1790) and Olshausen (1853).

34. The *festive oil* is mentioned also in Isa. 61:3.

35. R. H. Pfeiffer, State Letters of Assyria (1935), #267.3–6.

36. R. F. Harper, Assyrian and Babylonian Letters belonging to the Kouyunjik Collections of the British Museum (1902), #330.3–6.

37. RSV: *From ivory palaces stringed instruments make thee glad; daughters of kings are among your ladies of honor; at your right hand stands the queen in gold of Ophir.* In my opinion, this rendering is impossible. First, the word translated "stringed instruments" (in any case an unusual form) could mean only "strings," and the assumed synechdoche is, at least to my ears, too harsh to be probable. Second, the word rendered "queen" means properly "concubine," and so to describe the bride herself would be, to put it mildly, indelicate! I would therefore make sense by simply deleting the word

rendered "stringed instruments" (viz., *mînî*), as vertical dittography from *li-yᵉMINekā* in the line below.—The reference to the ivory halls is admirably illustrated by Euripides, Iphigenia in Aulis 581 f., where Helen is said to have been abducted by Paris "from ivory halls."

38. Granquist has pointed out that such last-minute exhortations and admonitions are a standard element of Arab wedding ceremonies at the present day.

39. Literally, "daughter of Tyre." Tyre was the proverbial "affluent society" of the Ancient Near East; cf. Ezek. 26–27. The implication—allowing for the anachronism— is, so to speak, "Yourself a daughter of Croesus, you have been courted by millionaires!"

40. For the tradtional text's *panāyik yehallū*, "now come courting thee," I read, in the past tense, *panāyki hillū*.

41. Granquist, op. cit., ii.118, n.11; Rothstein, op. cit., 122, n.2; G. Dalman, Palästinischer Diwan (1908), 254. This is believed to be the background of Song of Songs 7:1 f., *How fair are thy feet in sandals, O prince's daughter,* etc.

42. For the traditional text's *kôl kᵉbūdah bath-melek pᵉnîmah* (KJV: The king's daughter is all glorious within) read *kᵉlê kᵉbôdah bath-melek pᵉnînîm*. The expression *kᵉlê kabôd* is matched by *kᵉlê tiphēreth* (glorious ornaments)—likewise associated with broidery—in Ezek. 16:17; cf. also Isa. 61:10. The emendation *pᵉnînîm* is due to Krochmal.

43. The word *li-rᵉqāmôth* at the beginning of v. 14 really belongs at the end of v. 13.

44. Granquist, op. cit., ii.42.

45. P. Haupt, The Book of Canticles (1912), 31 (on Song of Songs 1:9).

46. So with the Greek Version; the traditional text reads, I *will keep your name in remembrance.*

47. II Krt ii.16 ff. Birth of daughters is also invoked: ib., iii.5 ff.

48. Pfeiffer, op. cit., #125.14–18.

49. Odyssey 7.148–50.

262 Mountains in midsea

1. The Heb. word *bᵉ-hāmîr* requires no emendation. It is here to be connected with Arabic *m-r-m-r,* "be agitated," used especially of an embroiled sea.

2. Finmor Jónsson, Der norsk-islandike Skaldedighting, BI 79.—On such stylized exaggerations in general, see: S. Eitrem, Papyri Osloenses i (1925), 69.

263 The far reaches of the North

1. T. H. Gaster, Thespis², 181 f., 452. Cf. also: B. Alfrink, in Biblica 14 (1933), 60 f.; C. Virolleaud, in CRAIBL 1937.67–68; J. Morgenstern, in HUCA 16 (1941), 65; H. Dunbar, in Antiquity 3 (1924), 408–13.

2. I AB i.57, vi.12, vii.5; IV AB iii.31; V AB i.21, etc. (*ṣrrt Ṣpn*).

3. P. Jensen, Die Kosmologie der Babylonier (1890), 23; A. Jeremias, The Old Testament in the Light of the Ancient East (1911), i.20; F. Delitzsch, Wo lag das Paradies? (1881), 117; Krappe, in JA 1897.86 ff.

4. Lassen, in ZKM 2 (1839), 62 ff.

5. A. Smythe Palmer, Jacob at Bethel (1899), 17 ff.

6. D. G. Brinton, Myths of the New World³ (1905), 95.

7. ERE xii.485ᵇ, n.3.

8. R. Merker, Die Masai (1904), 197, 199.

9. K. Schwenk, Die Mythologie der Slawen (1853), 386.

10. Pseudo-Callisthenes, ii.32.

11. Gaster, loc. cit.

12. I. Scheftelowitz, Die altpersische Religion und das Judentum (1920), 59.

13. W. M. Brandt, Die mandäische Religion (1889), 67 ff.

14. Satapatha Brahmana i.2, 4, 10; xii.5, 1, 11, etc.
15. O. Gruppe, Griechische Mythologie (1906), 815 ff.
16. Ziyyuni 48d; Jerahmeel i.17 (p. 6, ed. M. Gaster).
17. L. Spence, The Mythologies of Mexico and Peru (1907), 24.
18. G. Flügel, Mani (1862), 101.
19. Pap. Bib. Nat. 269; Pap. Leyden, Wesselski, col. xviii.27.
20. Plutarch, De Iside et Osiride 21.
21. T. H. Gaster, Customs and Folkways of Jewish Life (1965), 61.

264 Death as a shepherd

1. On the theme in general, see: S. J. Lessing, De Mortis apud veteres figura (Diss., Bonn 1866); S. G. F. Brandon, in BJRL 43 (1961), 317–35.—On specifically *Greek* conceptions of Death, see: C. Robert, "Thanatos," in XXXIX Berl Winckelmanns Progr. Arch. März., 170, 175 ff.; E. Gaetani-Lovatelli, Thanatos (1888); Preller-Robert, Griech. Mythologie⁴ (1894), i.842 f.; J. H. Croon, The Herdsman of the Dead (Diss.) Utrecht 1952).
2. Apollodorus, Bib. ii.5, 10; vi.12, 7; see: J. H. Croon, The Herdsman of the Dead (Diss., Utrecht 1952).
3. Plato, Phaedo 62B (*en phrourâ*); cf. Espinas, in Archiv für Ges. der Philosophie 8.452. However, Cicero (Cat. Maj. 73) interpreted Plato's expression to mean simply that souls are "in the keeping of God," and this interpretation is followed by E. Rohde, Psyche⁷ (1921), iii.161, n.2.—See also: Euxitheos (a Pythagorean), in Athenaeus, iv.137.

265 Bottled tears

1. S. G. Wilson, Persian Life and Customs² (1896), 190 ff.; J. Perkins, A Residence of Eight Years in Persia among the Nestorian Christians (1843), 209; J. Morier, quoted by E. W. Rice, Orientalisms in Bible Lands (1910), 124.
2. J. A. E. Köhler, Volksbrauch . . . im Voigtlande (1867), 492; W. von Schulenburg, Wendisches Volksthum (1882), 280.—The custom was known also in Switzerland: F. Stählin, Die Schweiz in römisch. Zeit (1927), 361.
3. Niederdeutsch. Zs. für Volkskunde 7 (1932), 47.
4. W. Ebers, in Abh. Bay. Akad. Wiss. 1 Kl. 20/i.140 ff.; cf. R. B. Onians, Origins of European Thought about the Body, etc. (1951), 201 f., 283.
5. A. C. Kruijt, in ERE vii.234ª.
6. On tears as generative, cf. Onians, op. cit., 205; Proclus, fr. 354, in Orphicorum Fragmenta, ed. Kern; Pap. Leyden iv.1.395.
7. E. Rohde, Psyche⁷ (1921), i.223, n.2; Levi, in Philologus 63.55; A. Wright, English Folklore (1928), 21.
8. Grimm, Märchen #109; Bolte-Polivka, iii.483 ff.; W. Wackernagel, Kl. Schriften (1872–74), ii.400 ff.; A. Wirth, Beiträge zur Volkskunde von Anhalt (Dessau, s.a.), ii/3.67.

266 Yahweh's processional

Literature: T. H. Gaster, Thespis¹ (1950), 87–97; W. F. Albright, in HUCA 23 (1951), 1–39; S. Mowinckel, Der 68te Psalm (1953); P. Haupt, in AJSL 23 (1901), 220–40; R. Podechard, in RB 54 (1947), 502–20; R. Tournay, ib., 51 (1942), 227–45; F. C. Fensham, in JNES 19 (1960), 292–93.

(a)

1. Cf. S. A. Pallis, The Babylonian Akitu Festival (1926). Good popular accounts are: H. Zimmern, AO 25/iii; C. J. Gadd in S. H. Hooke's Myth and Ritual (1933),

47–58.—The procession of the gods is described in the text published by T. G. Pinches in PSBA 30 (1908), 62.—The Hittite material will be found in KBo III.7; cf. T. H. Gaster, Thespis², 245–67.

2. Gaster, op. cit., 114–244.

3. Reading with Torczyner (Tur-Sinai), *mah norā'ū* for the obscure *minnēhū rā'ū* of the traditional text.

4. Literally, "arises," but this is also a military term; cf. Num. 10:35; Amos 7:9; Ob 1, etc.

5. Others render, "Raise a song," but this meaning of the word is not well attested, and the context surely supports the normal translation.

6. III AB iii.11, 18; I*AB ii.7; III AB, A 8, 29, 33; IV AB i.7; iii.22.

7. IV R 33*, 21*d*, 22*b*; cf. B. Landsberger, Kultische Kalendar (1915), 116 f.; L. Dürr, Ursprung und Ausbau der israelit.-jüdischen Heilandserwarterung (1925), 141.

8. Athenaeus, 639–640A (Crete, Troezen, Thessaly); Schol. on Demosthenes 22.68; 614.23 (Athens); Ephorus, cited by Athenaeus, 263F (Cydonia). See fully: Headlam-Knox, Herodas (1922), 266 f.

9. Livy, v. 13; cf. also: Heliodorus, Aeth. viii.7.

10. Matt. 27:15.

11. II AB vi.68 (*Bᶜl yᶜdn ᶜdn mṭrh*).

12. Enuma Elish vii. 21 (*mukin hêgalli*).

13. Gaster, op. cit., 261–62.

14. II AB iv.19, v.85; I*AB i.11; ᶜnt iv.82, etc.

15. Reading, with most modern scholars, *bā' mi-Sinai* for the *bam Sinai* of the traditional text.

16. Cf. E. Behrens, Assyrisch-bab. Briefe kultischen Inhalts aus der Sargonidenzeit (1906), 31–32; Pallis, op. cit., 202 ff.

17. Nos. 145, 183, 352, ed. Wiseman; cf. also *šnnm* as a military term in the Ugaritic text, Krt A ii.91.

18. Cf. A. R. Schulman, Military Rank, Title and Organization of the Egyptian New Kingdom (1962), 96 ff.

19. For the traditional text's *ᶜalêhā la-mārôm šūbah*, which is barely translatable, I read *ᶜaleh la-mārôm šᵃbeh*, in accordance with the passage in our psalm.

20. See above, n.14.

21. Heb.: *tôṣā'ôth;* cf. Akkadian *ušêṣi* and Aramaic cognate, meaning "bring to ruin."

22. VAT 9555.10–11.

23. I*AB i.1. This is the Akkadian *bašmu*, "serpent." The identification is due to S. Feigin, *Mi-sitrê he-ᶜavar* (1943), 407.

24. Viz. *'ašbm*, confused with *'ašîb;* cf. S. E. Lowenstamm, in IEJ 9 (1959), 260 f.; J. L. McKenzie, in Theological Studies 2 (1950), 275–82; M. Dahood, in RB 43 (1962), 365.

25. I.e., *'ašb* for *'ašîb*.

26. III AB, B 29–30.

27. III AB, A 11 ff.; Gaster, op. cit., 163 ff.

28. Enuma Elish iv.130.

29. "Holy beings" (*qdšm*) is a common name for the gods in general both in Canaanite-Phoenician texts and vestigially also in O.T.: see T. H. Gaster, in Orientalia 11 (1942), 59 f.

30. Enuma Elish vi.70 ff.

31. Gaster, op. cit., 266.

32. II AB vi.39 ff.; Gaster, op. cit., 109 f.

(b) Yellow garments

33. Heb. *y^eraqraq ḥārūṣ*, sometimes rendered *"greenish* gold"; but the word *w-r-q* is used of gold in S. Arabian, and Ugaritic has the comparable expression *yrq ḥrṣ* (Krt A 138). Strictly speaking, *yrq*, like Greek *chlôros*, oscillates between yellow and green.

34. A. Sprenger, Muhammad (1851), iii.63; cf. Mu^callaqat, Tarafa 49; G. Jacob, Studien in arabischen Dichtern ii (1894), 90.

35. W. W. Skeat, Malay Magic (1900), 51.

36. Acts of Thomas 5.11; cf. M. R. James, The Apocryphal NT (1924), 411.

37. Aeschylus, Agamemnon 224 f.

38. Id., Persae 662.

39. Kirby Smith, on Tibullus i.7.46.

40. Cf. Apuleius, Met. viii.27.

41. W. Crooke, The Popular Religion and Folklore of Northern India (1896), ii.20, 26; E. Crawley, in ERE v.47.

42. Lucan, Phars. iii.361.

43. Catullus, lxi.9–10; Tibullus, i.7.46; Ovid, Met x.1. Cf. also: Vergil, Aen. ix.614 (Trojan); Seneca, Oed. 421; Pliny, HN xxi.46; Clem. Alex., Paidag. ii.10.

44. Zs. für Volkskunde 23 (1913), 262 f.

45. Crawley, loc. cit.

46. Ib.

47. Zs. für Volkskunde 23 (1913), 262 f.

48. Crawley, loc. cit.

49. G. Pitré, quoted by T. Ellworthy, in ERE v.614^a.

50. J. Grimm, Wörterbuch (1854), iv/i.2883; Goethe, Farbenlehre, §771.—In France, the doors of traitors used to be daubed with yellow paint: St. Swithin, in Notes and Queries VI/8 (1883), 172.

51. T. F. Thiselton Dyer, Domestic Folklore[2] (s.a.), 75.

52. Shakespeare, The Merry Wives of Windsor, I.iv.

267 The Book of Fate

1. P. Jensen, KB VI/i (1900), 136 f.; J. A. Craig, Assyrian and Babylonian Religious Texts (1895–97), i.5 ff.; ii.ix.

2. H. Zimmern and H. Winckler, KAT[3] (1903), 401; A. Jeremias, Babylonisches im Neuen Testament (1905), 69–73.

3. J. Friedrich, in JCS 1 (1947), 283 f.; cf. also: T. H. Gaster, Thespis[2], 288.

4. A. Klausen, in Zs. für deutsch. Alt. 1840.226.

5. Grimm-Stallybrass, TM 406.

6. Tertullian, De anima c.39.

7. Some details of this passage are still not quite clear, and various emendations of the text have been proposed. The general sense, however, is sufficiently apparent, and that is all that here concerns us.

8. M. Lidzbarski, Ephemeris für semitische Epigraphik (1902–15), i.164 ff.

268 The combat against the Dragon

1. Cf. J. L. McKenzie, in Theological Studies 2 (1950), 275–82.

269 Demon shafts

1. RS 15.134; C. Virolleaud, in CRAIBL 1952.30 (*b^cl ḥẓ Ršp*).

2. G. A. Cooke, A Text-book of North Semitic Inscriptions (1903), 56 f.

3. Song of Songs 8:6. So too in Ugaritic: Virolleaud, in CRAIBL 1952.62 (*kt^crbn ršpm bt mlk*). Also in Egyptian: Edgerton-Wilson, Historical Records of Ramses III,

Medinet Habu i–ii.24 (*snnw shmty.w mi' Ršp*). A "land of Reshephs" (*'rṣ ršpm*) is mentioned in an inscription of the 4th cent. B.C. found near Sidon: Cooke, op. cit., 401.

271 The bird sanctuary

1. Herodotus, i.157–59.
2. Aelian, Var. Hist. v.17.
3. Lucian, De dea Syria, 54.
4. Clement of Alexandria, Protrept. iv.52.
5. B. Spencer and F. J. Gillen, The Native Tribes of Central Australia (1899), 134 ff.
[5a. Book of the Dead 125; tr. J. A. Wilson, in ANET 34. Cf. C. Maystre, Les declarations d'innocence (1937), A.29.]
[5b. Artemidorus, Oneirocrit. 16.]
[5c. P. Sartori, Sitte und Brauch (1910–14), ii.13, n.4.]
[5d. Archiv für Russland 1 (1848), 628.]
[5e. J. Harland and T. Wilkinson, Lancashire Legends, etc. (1873), 143.]

272 The earthly and heavenly Zion

1. II AB iv–v.
2. M. Eliade, Traité d'histoire des religions (1949), 324 f.; T. H. Gaster, Thespis², ch. 1; id., in Numen 1 (1954), 195.—Egypt was called "the replica of heaven": Ps.-Apuleius, in Höpfner, Fontes rel. aegypt. 620. The Egyptians spoke of "two heavens" corresponding to the two lands of Egypt: Pyr. Texts 406b, 541c; S. Morenz, Aeg. Religion (1960), 47. The shrine of a god was called "heaven": J. Cerný, in JEA 34 (1948), 120.
3. Cf. B. Meissner, Babylonien and Assyrien ii (1925), 107, 110, 409 f.; H. Winckler, Babyl. Geisteskultur (1919), 93 f.
4. Test. XII Patr., Dan 5; II Baruch 59:4; Syr. Apoc. Baruch 4:3 ff.; IV Ezra 40:49; cf. G. H. Box, Liber Esdrae (1912), 198 f.; TB Taʿanith 5a, Hagigah 121; L. Ginzberg, Legends of the Jews, v.292. Cf. also: Matt. 5:35; Heb. 8:5; 11:10, 16; 12:22; 13.14.
5. J. Duyvendak, in Proc. Congress Hist. of Religions 7 (1951), 137.
6. F. Thureau Dangin, Die sumerischen und akkadischen Königsinschriften (1907), #140. 19 f.
7. Ḥammurapi, Code iii.29 ff.
8. KARI #164.38 ff.
9. Exod. 25:9, 40.
10. A. Moret, Du caractère réligieux de la royauté pharaonique (1902), 13.
11. M. Jastrow, Religion Babyloniens und Assyriens (1905–12), i.542; V. Scheil, in ZA 10.291, 3–4.
12. J. A. Craig, Assyrian and Babylonian Religious Texts (1895–97), i. Pl. 7–8.4.
13. I. A. Matthews, in JPOS 15 (1935), 351; J. Pedersen, Israel, iii–iv (1940), 263, 639.
14. Gen. 14:18; Sujin Inscription (c. 750 B.C.) = ANET², 504; Sanchuniathon, apud Eusebius, PE i.6.
15. See above, §180.

273 The throne founded on righteousness

1. Brunner, in VT 8 (1958), 426 ff.; S. Morenz, Aegyptische Religion (1960), 120.

274 The winged soul

1. Cf. G. Weicker, Der Seelenvogel in der alten Literatur und Kunst (1902); O. Waser, in ARW 16 (1913), 337 ff.; V. Aptowitzer, Die Seele als Vogel (1925); O. Dähnhardt, Natursagen (1907–12), iii.476 f.; A. B. Cook, Zeus, ii (1925), 524,

697n., 1132; O. Gruppe, Griechische Mythologie (1906), 1502, n.1; 1618, n.1; A. de Gubernatis, Die Thiere in indogerm. Mythen (1874), 469 ff.; I. Scheftelowitz, Altpal. Bauernglaube (1925), 12 ff.; E. S. McCartney, in Papers of the Michigan Acad. of Science, Arts and Letters 16 (1932), 162 ff.; A. H. Krappe, Balor with the Evil Eye (1927), 95 ff.; Frazer-Gaster, NGB §151 (and Additional Note).

2. H. Kees, Totenglauben und Jenseitsvorstellungen der alten Aegypter (1926), 57–66; L. Klebs, in ZÄS 61 (1926), 104–8; W. Spiegelberg, in OLz 29 (1926), 393–95.

3. Tale of the Two Brothers, xix.3; cf. H. Grapow, Die bildlichen Ausdrücke des Aegyptischen (1924), 93 f.

4. Atharva Veda iv.34, 4; cf. H. Oldenberg, Religion des Veda (1894), 563.

5. Cf. O. Falsirol, in SMSR 1951–52.102–16; McCartney, op. cit., 162 ff.

6. E. Rohde, Psyche[7] (1921), i.244; O. Jahn, Archaeologische Beitraege (1847), 128 ff.—When Alexander died, an eagle suddenly appeared, representing his soul ascending to heaven: Ps.-Callisthenes, iii.33. Similarly, when Peregrinus was cast on the pyre, an eagle rose from it, crying, "I have left the earth, and am going to Olympus": Lucian, Peregr. 39.

7. G. Jacob, Das Leben der vorislamischen Beduinen (1895), 122, n.2, 143, citing Masᶜudi, Muruj edh-dhahab iii.311 ff.; Diwan der Hudhaliten, #141.5; ᶜOrwa b. al-Ward iii.3–4; cf. also: ZDMG 12 (1858), 63.

8. I. Goldziher, in Globus 83.301.

9. E. S. Drower, The Canonical Prayerbook of the Mandaeans (1959), #73 (p. 62), lines 12, 27; (p. 63), lines 3, 10.

10. Inst. Arch. f. Ethnologie, 11.86 f.

11. H. Tonkes, Volkskunde von Bali (1888), 29; H. Ling Roth, Natives of Sarawak (1896), i.224.

12. W. Wundt, Elements of Folk Psychology, tr. Schaub[2] (1916), 82.

13. Grimm-Stallybrass, TM 828 f.; F. Nork, in Das Kloster xii (1845), 271; R. Kühnau, in Mitt. d. sachs. Ges. f. Volkskunde, Heft 16 (1906), 96 f.

14. K. Schwenk, Die Mythologie der Slawen (1853), 274 f.

15. The Gentleman's Magazine 92 (1822), pt. i.311; Byron, Don Juan, stanza 94; Notes and Queries VI/vi (1882), 269, 452 f.; Thos. Hardy, "The Superstitious Man's Story," in Life's Little Ironies.—In Cornwall, cloughs are protected because the soul of King Arthur is said to have migrated into one. Similarly, stormy petrels ("Mother Carey's chickens") are protected by sailors because they are believed to be the souls of dead mariners: E. Brewer, Dictionary of Phrase and Fable, s.v. Bird.—Other examples—not all of them convincing—are assembled by L. C. Wimberly, Folklore of the English and Scottish Ballads[2] (1959), 44 ff.

16. T. G. Thiselton Dyer, English Folklore (1880), 134 (Yorkshire).

17. T. Keightley, Fairy Mythology (1854), 436.—So too in Armenia, souls are thought to fly near graves in the form of doves: M. Abeghian, Der armen. Volksaberglaube (1899), 10.

18. Letter to the Smyrneans, 16.

19. Prudentius, Perist., #3.

20. Gregory of Tours, Dial. iv.10 (Migne, PL 77, col. 386).

21. Migne, PL 66, col. 196.

275 A coven of demons

1. See on this psalm: W. O. E. Oesterley, in The Expositor, 1907.132–51; Charbel, in REB 17 (1957), 281–300; A. Caquot, in Semitica 6 (1956), 281–300.—In Jewish tradition this psalm is recited at the expiration of the sabbath, when the demons who have been confined during the day of rest are again let loose. It is likewise recited at a funeral—originally to exorcize the princes of darkness both from the deceased and

from the mourners: T. H. Gaster, Festivals of the Jewish Year (1953), 279 f.—Conversely, in a sixteenth century German grimoire, it forms part of a magical ritual for *invoking* spirits: Wahrafter Jesuiten Höllenzwang, reprinted in J. Scheible's Das Kloster v (1847), 110.

2. E. B. Tylor, Primitive Culture, i.275 f.; J. Grimm, DM⁴, 1193; A. Wuttke, Der deutsche Volksaberglaube (1869), 122; J. Brand, Popular Antiquities of Great Britain (1882–83), iii.279.

3. KARL ii.58, r.2 (*mušitu puluḫtu ša li-la-a-ti*).

4. J. Backhouse, A Narrative of a Visit to the Australian Colonies (1843), 555.

5. De Rochefort, Histoire naturelle et morale des Iles Antilles² (1665), 419.

6. F. Mason, The Karens (1842), 211.

7. M. Höfler, in ARW 2 (1899), 127 f.; S. Eitrem, Papyri Osloenses (1925), 53 f.; Grimm-Stallybrass, TM 23, 443, 846, 1182, 1244 f.

8. Job 6:4.

9. Iliad 1.44. Sudden death was represented by the Greeks as a visitation by painless arrows, shot at men by Apollo, and at women by Artemis: Odyssey 3.280; 5.124; 11.173, 199; 15.140.

10. See above, §269.

11. A. B. Keith, Indian Mythology (1917), 125, 225.

12. Notes and Queries I/iv (1851), 500.—The idea appears in the famous Song in Time of Plague by Thomas Nashe (1567–1601): *Fond are life's lustful joys./Death proves them all but toys./None from his darts can fly.*

13. J. A. MacCulloch, Eddic Mythology (1930), 192, 222.

14. K. 3476, obv. 14; S. A. Pallis, The Babylonian Akitu Festival (1926), 215.

15. P. Sartori, Sitte und Brauch (1910–14), iii.67, 68, n.2.

16. Ib., iii.157, 171.

17. J. A. Montgomery, Aramaic Incantation Texts from Nippur (1913), #2.4–5.

18. Sitzb. Berl. Akad. 1908.401 (cited by Montgomery).

19. See: K. Haberlandt, in Zs. für Völkerpsychologie 13 (1882), 310–24; L. Laistner, Das Rätsel der Sphinx (1882), i.1 ff., 310 ff.; W. Mannhardt, Antike Wald- und Feldkulte (1875–77), ii.8, 37, 114, 135; A. H. Krappe, La genèse des mythes (1938), 163 f.; M. Grünbaum, Gesammelte Aufsätze (1901), 96 ff.; O. Crusius, in Philologus 50.70 ff.; B. Caillois, in RHR 115 (1937), 142–73, 116 (1938), 54–63; S. Landersdorfer, in BZ 18 (1929), 294 ff.; J. de Fraine, in Biblica 40 (1959), 372–83; W. H. Worrel, in JAOS 38 (1918), 160–66; W. H. Roscher, in ARW 1 (1898), 76 ff.; O. Gruppe, Griechische Mythologie (1906), 759; K. Schwenck, Die Mythologie der Slawen (1853), 319; T. H. Gaster, in Folk-Lore 1938. 361–63.

20. Theocritus, Id., i.15 ff. Cf. also Lucian, Philos. 22, where the midday spirit is identified with Artemis or Hecate, just as Christian authors sometimes call it Diana: C. A. Lobeck, Aglaophamus (1829), 1092. In Schol. ad Aristoph., Frogas 239 it is equated with Empusa, the child-stealing witch.

21. Pliny, HN xviii.330.

22. J. C. Lawson, Modern Greek Folklore (1910), 79, 139, 143, 148, 150, 160, 164, 168, 170, 172; B. Schmidt, Das Volksleben der Neugriechen (1871), 94 ff.

23. T. Trede, Das Heidentum in der römischen Kirche (1889–91), iv.362.

24. L. Korth, Mittagsgespenster (Cologne 1915); Grimm, DM⁴, 342.

25. J. V. Grohmann, Aberglauben und Gebräuche aus Böhmen und Mähren (1864), 108, 111, 125; Grimm, op. cit., ii.778, n.2; B. Caillois, in Revue des études slaves 16 (1936), 18–37; A. Strausz, Die Bulgaren (1898), 152; W. R. S. Ralston, Songs of the Russian People² (1872), 147; A.H. Wratislaw, Sixty Folk-tales from exclusively Slavonic Sources (1889), 45; Mitt. d. schles. Ges. für Volkskunde 1 (1894), 6; Am Urquell 3 (1892), 202.

26. K. Liebrecht, Zur Volkskunde (1879), 46 f.

27. Anatole France, Vie de Jeanne d'Arc, in Oeuvres complètes xvi.250 (as cited by Krappe, loc. cit.).

28. Cf. Akkadian *dab/pāru,* "thrust back"; cf. also: Caquot, loc. cit.

276   From Canaanite hymn to Israelite psalm

1. The Modern Churchman 12 (1922), 390.

2. Cf. T. H. Gaster, Thespis², 443.

3. III AB, B 10 (*tqḥ mlk ᶜlmk*); Thespis², 162.

4. II AB iv–v; Thespis², 185 ff.

5. II AB iv.68 (Thespis², 185); ib., v–vi (Thespis², 195 f.).

6. Thespis², 137–49.

7. Enuma Elish vii.78–79.

8. KBo III.7; KUB xii.66; xvii.5–6; Thespis², 256 ff.

277   Renewing youth like the eagle

1. T. H. White, The Bestiary (1960), s.v. Aquila; cf. S. Bochart, Hierozoicon (1962), II.ii, 1.

2. Terence, Heauton Timoroumenos iii.2, 10 f.

278   Heaven as a garment

1. R. Eisler, Weltmantel und Himmelszelt (1910).

2. B. Meissner, in AJSL 47 (1931), 202 (*nalbaš šamê/urpiti*); but see: E. Weidner, in Afo 7 (1931), 115 f.

3. Akkadian *burrumu* (cf. Heb. *bᵉrômîm,* Ezek. 27:24): P. Jensen, Kosmologie der Babylonier (1890), 6 ff.; cf. II R 48 c–d 54: *šupuk bu-ru-me;* K 3528.38 *šiṭir bu-ru-um-mi;* KB i.174–75.

4. Pap. Paris, Suppl. Gr. 574. 2259 = R. Wuensch, Aus einem griech. Zauberpapyrus (Kleine Texte 84), 15.

5. E. Chiera, Sumerian Religious Texts (1924), iii.17, 37; cf. S. Langdon, in JRAS 1925.717 f.

6. Rig Veda i.173, 6.

7. Yasht 13.3; Yasna 30.5.

8. P. Hermann, Nordische Mythologie (1903), 259; E. H. Meyer, Mythologie der Germanen (1903), 370.

9. A. Blanc, Il sacro presso i primitivi (1945), 71.

10. Nonnus, Dionys. xi.367–577.

11. Daniel Defoe, History of the Devil (1939), 50.

12. I.e., for the traditional text's *ᶜad BiLTî šamāyim* they read *ᶜad BᵉLôT šamāyim,* lit. "until the heavens wear out."—Not impossibly, this image also underlies Isa. 51:6, which rsv renders, "The heavens will vanish like smoke, and the earth will wear out like a garment." The Heb. word rendered "vanish" is *nimlāḥū,* but this meaning is conjectural. If, however, we combine it with Arabic *malāḥa* and with the noun *mᵉlāḥîm,* "tatters," in Jer. 38:11–12, and if we emend the inapposite *kᵉ-ᶜašan,* "like smoke," to *kᵉ-ᶜaš* (error through dittography), we may obtain the sense, "The heavens will become tattered (fretted) as by a moth, and the earth wear out like a garment."

13. Heb.: *q-r-ᶜ.*

14. I*AB i.1–5; cf. T. H. Gaster, Thespis², 201 f.

15. H. P. L'Orage, Studies in the Iconography of Cosmic Kingship in the Ancient World (1953).

16. Weidner, loc. cit.

281 The kindly stork

1. Cf. S. Bochart, Hierozoicon[3] (1692), ii.327 ff.
2. Aesop, Fables, #110.
3. E.g., St. Basil, Hexaëm., hom. viii; St. Ambrose, Hexaëm., c. xvi.

284 The ritual of enthronement

1. Cf. I Maccabees 14:41.
2. R. Pfeiffer, Introduction to the O.T. (1944), 630.
3. T. H. Gaster, in JMEOS 21 (1937), 47–44. Cf. also: J. Coppens, "Les rapports du psaulme cx à l'idéologie royale israélite," in Proc. VIIIth Internat. Congress of the History of Religions (1959); G. R. Driver, "Psalm cx: its meaning and purpose," in Studies in the Bible presented to Prof. M. H. Segal (1964).
4. J. Breasted, AR iii.§§216 ff.
5. On the subject in general, cf. T. H. Gaster, in Numen 1 (1954), 188 f.; id., in RR 9 (1945), 267 ff.; Lord Raglan, The Origins of Religion (1949), 81; Frazer-Gaster, NGB §§70, 73–75.—On divine kingship *in Israel*, see: M. Noth, in Zeitschr. für Theologie und Kirche 47 (1950), 157–91; A. R. Johnson, in ET 62 (1950), 36–42; J. Kroeker, Das Koenigtum und die Theokratie in Israel (1931); C. R. North, in ZAW 50 (1932), 8–38; G. Widengren, in Horae Soederblomianae (1947); F. Gypkens, Koenig und Kult im At (Diss., Emsdetten 1940).
6. Cf. Lord Raglan, "Patterns in the Ritual of Coronation and Royal Funerals," in Folk-Lore 64 (1953), 257 ff.; H. Thurston, The Coronation Ceremony[2] (1911).
7. Breasted, op. cit. §220.
8. S. A. Strong, in BA 2 (1884), 645; tr. Pfeiffer, in ANET 451[a].
9. Cf. K. Tallquist, Der Assyrische Gott (1932), 86 ff.
10. Ḫammurapi, Code v. 11–12; rev. xxiv. *a* 14.
11. F. Delitzsch, in BA 2 (1894), 267.
12. Prism B = ANET 288[a].
13. Heb. *ṣedāqah* means here the quality of preserving the norm (*ṣedeq*).
14. In the celebrated Cylinder Inscription of Cyrus, it is said similarly that Marduk, god of Babylon, selected him as "the upright man whose hand he would grasp": ANET 315.
15. II AB iv–v.109; T. H. Gaster, Thespis[2], 187. Cf. Callimachus, Apollo 29.
16. Josephus, Ant. vi.11, 9.
17. See: C. Meloni, "Sedet ad dexteram patris," in Saggi di Filologia semitica, iii (1913); E. Pottier, in Mélanges Boissier (1903), 405–13; S. Eitrem, Papyri Osloenses i (1925), 96 f.; O. Weinreich, in Göttingen Gelehr. Anzeiger 1912, No. 7–9. 135 ff.; F. Boll, Sphaera (1903), 563 f.; F. Dölger, Die Sonne der Gerechtigkeit (1918), 9 ff., 37 ff.
18. Gen. 35:18.
19. J. Wellhausen, Reste d. arab. Heidentums[2] (1897), 202.
20. P. Haupt, in BA 1 (1889), 170.
21. Tchang, L'écriture chinoise et le geste humaine (1939), 145.
22. G. Roeder, Urkunden z. Rel. d. alten Aegypter (1915), 107, 109, 112.
23. Cf. Iliad 2.353; Odyssey 24.312; A. S. Pease, on Cicero, De Divinatione ii.82; A. P. Wagener, Popular Associations of Right and Left in Roman Literature (Baltimore 1912); E. S. McCartney, in Papers of the Michigan Academy 16 (1932), 140 ff.; S. Eitrem, Opferritus und Voropfer der Griechen und Römer (1915), 29 ff.
24. Exod. 29:22; Lev. 8:25, 26; 9:21; Lev. 7:32–34; Num. 6:20; I Sam. 9:24.
25. This tradition is preserved also in the Koran, Sura 56.
26. See: J. E. B. Mayor, on Juvenal, x.5; M. B. Ogle, in AJP 32 (1911), 254, n.2;

so too in Madagascar: M. Cox, Introduction to Folklore (1897), 9; likewise in parts of the United States: D. L. and L. B. Thomas, Kentucky Superstitions (1920), #1001; C. J. Johnson, What They Say in New England (1897), 93.

27. Jas. Boswell, Life of Dr. Samuel Johnson, end of entries for 1764.

28. F. D. Bergen, Current Superstitions (1896), #355; A. Wuttke, Der deutsche Volksaberglaube der Gegenwart³ (1900), 371.

29. G. Parrinder, La religion en Afrique occidentale (1950), 216.

30. Frazer-Gaster, NGB §§69–76, 86.

31. Breasted, op. cit. §148. Enemies are portrayed as the footstool of Amenhotep III on a wall of tomb #226 at Thebes: N. M. Davies and A. H. Gardiner, Ancient Egyptian Paintings (1936), ii.Pl. 38; ANEP #4.

32. The usual translation is, *Yahweh sends the rod of thy strength out of Zion;* but the scepter is sent from heaven, not from Zion. Hence the words "out of Zion" must go with the verb "exact subjection," making a neat balance of four words in each half of the verse.

33. Breasted, op. cit. §§227, 235, 237.

34. T. Jacobsen, Sumerian King-List, #11.1–2; tr. Oppenheim, in ANET 365ᵇ.

35. Deluge Tablet 88–89; ANET 43ᵇ.

36. Etana Myth, Old Bab. Version A.I. i.11 ff.; tr. Speiser, in ANET 114. Cf. also: KARI i.19, obv. 14 f. = E. Ebeling, in Orientalia 23 (1954), 210 f. So also in the Neo-Assyrian Version, C.I. 13–16.

37. L. W. King, Letters and Inscriptions of Ḥammurabi (1898–1900), #61 f. In Code xxiv, *a*14, the sovereignty is conferred by Marduk.

38. Prism B; ANET 288ᵃ.

39. ANET 310.

40. AO 6461 = F. Thureau Dangin, Rituels accadiens (1921), 70.108.—In Egypt, the scepter (*šḥm*) was thought to possess divinity: W. Spiegelberg, in Rec. des Trav. 25 (1903), 184; 28 (1906), 136 f.—On the divinity of scepters in general, cf. G. van der Leeuw, Religion in Essence and Manifestation (1963), i.41.

41. Iliad 2.100–108; 204–6; 9.99. Agamemnon's scepter was worshiped at Chaeronea: Pausanias ix.40, 1.

42. N. Muccioli, Lo Shintoismo (1948), 21n. The myth relating to this sword is narrated in the *Kojiki;* cf. R. Peltazzoni, La Mitologia Giapponese (1929), 73.

43. W. Ellis, Polynesian Researches (1832–36), iii.103.

44. The correctness of the traditional text's *ᶜammᵉkā nᵉdābôth* (against LXX's *ᶜimmᵉkā nᵉdābôth,* "with thee is nobility") is avouched by similar phrasing in Judg. 5:2, and by the effective contrast it provides between the king and his people.

45. On *acclamatio* in ritual, cf. van de Leeuw, op. cit. 431; cf. also: E. Spanheim, In Callimachi hymnos observationes (1697), 647.

46. See Briggs, ICC, in loc.

47. According to Num. 1:3, the minimum age for military service was twenty.

48. For *me-reḥem mišḥar* I read *me-reḥem-ma šaḥar,* with the archaic enclitic *-ma;* a similar error in Joel 1:17 and possibly also in Ezek. 28:14.

49. Deut. 32:1; Hos. 14:6; Prov. 19:12; Isa. 26:19; Mic. 5:6.

50. Breasted, op. cit., §§216–17.

51. Lord Raglan, The Hero (Thinker's Library ed.), 169.

52. G. Parrinder, Les religions de l'Afrique occidentale (1950), 227.

53. Raglan, loc. cit.

54. See above, §251.

55. E. F. Weidner, AOF 1 (1927), 135–37; P. Jensen, in ZA, N.F.i (1924), 267–74; A. Goetze, Kleinasien¹ (1933), 82 f.

56. E.g., Ashurnasirpal (ARAB i, §437); Shalmaneser (ib., §§556, 596).

57. Le Page du Praz, Histoire de la Lousiane (1758), tr. K. T. Preuss, in Bertholet's Religionsgesch. Lesebuch (1926), pt. ii.35 ff.

58. A. B. Cook, Zeus ii (1925), 1003 ff.; cf. T. H. Gaster, Thespis[2], 431.

59. Cf. Pervigilium Veneris 20; O. Gruppe, Griechische Mythologie (1906), 823–24; J. Wellhausen, op. cit., 210. So also in Ugaritic: Gaster, op. cit., 237.

60. Cf. H. Grapow, Die bildlichen Ausdrücke des Aegyptischen (1924), 39 f.

61. The anointing of kings is mentioned in the Tel el Amarna Letter 34.50 ff. For the custom in Assyria, cf. K. Müller, in MVAG xii/3.9, line 33. See also: F. Steinmetzer, in BZ 1909.17–29.

62. Cf. S. Morenz, Aegyptische Religion (1960), 42 f.; A. Moret, Le rituel du culte journalier en Égypte (1902), 56 ff.; C. Aldred, The Egyptians (1963), 158 f.; G. Furlani, Rel. bab. e ass. (1928), i.355.

63. Cf. J. Jelito, "Tu es sacerdos," in Ruch Biblijny i Liturgiczny (Cracow), 3/i, 1–6 (1951), 251–64; B. Holwerda, De Priesterkoning in het OT (1946).

64. Breasted, op. cit., §§187–212.

65. Heb. yādîn, which implies more than merely "judging" (yišpôṭ).

66. Reading, millē' gē'āyôth gᵉwîyôth—error through haplography. Exactly the same expression occurs in the Victory Hymn of Thothmes III at Thebes: Breasted, op. cit. §660. ad fin.

67. Literally, "Over a great land (area)."

68. Breasted, op. cit. §237.

69. Heb. mᵉnahal ba-derek yišteh. As an example of insensitive cacoethes emendandi I record simply (with disgust) the conventional modern "correction," nᵉhalîm bᵉdāmām Yašqeh, "valleys will he make to drink of their blood," which is, to boot, bad Hebrew, since š-q-h takes the direct accusative (without b-) of the substance which is proffered. —Cf. also: P. Nober, in Verbum Domini 26 (1948), 351–53; C. Schedl, in ZAW 73 (1961), 290–97.

70. II AB iv.45.

71. Yuzgat Tablet, obv. 38–41; Gaster, op. cit. 291.—In the Kumarpi myth (KUB XXXIII 120, 1, 11, 17) the divine chamberlain proffers goblets to the divine king. Cf. also: Gen. 40:11 ff. (Egypt).

72. P. Montet, Byblus et l'Égypte (1929), pl. 130; cf. G. Widengren, King and Savior IV (1951), 28 f.; R. Giveon, "King or God in the Sarcophagus of Ahiram?" in IEJ 9/i (1959).

73. G. Loud, The Megiddo Ivories (1939), Pl. 4, 2 a–b; Widengren, op. cit. fig. 8.

74. Widengren, op. cit., figs. 10–11.

75. E.g., W. H. Ward, Seal Cylinders of Western Asia (1910), #917; E. Porada, Mesopotamian Art in Cylinder Seals (1947), #44 (III Ur); O. Weber, Altorientalische Siegelbilder (1920), 111.

76. Cf. (but with caution) Jessie Weston, From Ritual to Romance (Anchor reprint, 1957), ch. vi.

285 Jordan turned back

1. Euripides, Medea 410 f.

2. Apollonius Rhodius, Argonautica iii.532; Vergil, Aeneid iv.489; Horace, Odes i.29, 10; Tibullus i.2, 44 (see: Kirby Smith, in loc.); Propertius, i.1, 23; ii.15, 30 f.; cf. also: A. S. Pease, Comm. on Cicero, De Divinatione, pt. ii, p. 288.

287 Tears fertilize

1. Diodorus Siculus, i.14.

2. Herodotus, ii.79. Cf. also: Pausanias, ix.29, 7; Athenaeus, 620A; Julius Pollux, iv.54.

3. Cf. J. de Horrack, Les lamentations d'Isis et Nephthys (1866); E. A. W. Budge, Osiris and the Egyptian Resurrection (1911), ii.59–66; A. Moret, Mystères égyptiens (1913), 24–26.

4. Firmicus Maternus, De errore profanarum religionum, ii.7.

5. Herodotus, ii.48. So too at the festival of Adonis: G. Glotz, in RGG 33 (1920), 206.

6. A. Moret, La mise à mort du dieu en Égypte (1927), 21; P. Montet, Les scènes de la vie privée de l'ancien empire (1925), 201–2, Pl. cvi.

7. A. L. Oppenheim, in BASOR 103 (1946), 11–14.

8. RSV renders neutrally, "held festival."

9. G. Dalman, Arbeit und Sitte in Palästina (1928–37), i.566.

10. Plutarch, Theseus 22.

11. Semus, quoted by Athenaeus, 618E; cf. E. Spanheim, In Callimachi hymnos observationes (1697), 649.

12. Epic of Gilgamesh vi.46–47.

13. Descent of Ishtar, rev. 56–57.

14. G. Reisner, Sumerisch-babylonische Hymnen (1896), #145.iii.12–15; ZA 6 (1891), 243.34; KARI #178.vi.10.

15. D. Chwolson, Die Ssabier (1856), ii.27.

16. See above, n.11.

17. H. Brugsch, Die Adonisklage und das Linoslied (1852); F. C. Movers, Die Phönizier (1841–56), i.246; W. Mannhardt, Antike Wald- und Feldkulte (1904–5), ii.281; O. Eissfeldt, "Linos and Aliyan," in Mélanges Dussaud i (1939), 161 ff.

18. F. G. Welcker, Schriften (1844–47), i.27 ff.; cf. also K. Schwenck, Die Mythologie der Slawen (1853), 227–29.

19. M. Canney, "The Magic of Tears," in JMEOS 12 (1926), 47–54.

20. A. Kruijt, in ERE vii.234ª.

21. ERE vii.234; xii.127ª.

22. H. Hecquard, Reise an die Küste und in das Innere von West-Afrika (1854), 41–43.

23. S. C. Macpherson, Memorials of Service in India (1865), 113–31.

24. B. de Sahagun, Histoire générale des choses de la Nouvelle-Espagne, tr. D. Jourdanet et R. Siméon (1880), ii.86.

288 The winds of fortune

1. Cf. S. Langdon, The Babylonian Epic of Creation (1923), ad vii.15; T. H. Gaster, in JRAS 1932.892.—In the Sumerian Deluge Tablet (ANET 446) the breath of Enlil brings fertility.—It is worth observing also in this connection that the colloquial term *bonanza* is really a Spanish and Portuguese word for *fair weather at sea.*

2. E. Klauber, Politisch-religiöse Texte aus der Sargonidenzeit (1913), #112, rev.4.

3. L. W. King, Babylonian Magic and Sorcery (1896), #18, rev.3.—A similar petition is made in an Egyptian penitential hymn dating toward the end of the empire: Turin Museum #102; B. Gunn, in JEA 3 (1916), 86–87; tr. Wilson, in ANET 381.

4. BA 5.312.21.

5. For the traditional text's *tered,* "goes down," I read *tarîd,* from the root **r-w-d* = Arabic *râda,* "roam for pasture." Also, for *TeNiḤeNū,* "gives it rest," I read *TaNḤeNū,* "guides it."

6. "Babylonian Ecclesiastes," 241 = ANET 440.

7. Aeschylus, Septem contra Thebas 688; Persae 604 f.

8. R. C. Thompson, Semitic Magic (1908), 7, 54.

9. T. Fish, in Iraq 6 (1939), 184.

10. R. Corso, in Rivista di Anthropologia 22 (1918), 80; I. Zolli, ib., 27 (1926), 9–10.

11. Euripides, Iphigenia in Tauris 1317.

JOB

289 Introductory

1. Job himself hails from Uz, described in Gen. 10:23 as an Aramean tribe, but said in Lam. 4:21 to have been occupied by Edomites at the time of the fall of Jerusalem in 586 B.C. Two of Job's "comforters," viz., Eliphaz and Bildad, come respectively from Teman, specifically located in Jer. 49:20 and Amos 1:12 in Edom, and from Shuªḥ, which is probably the Šuḫu of Akkadian records, lying on the west of the Euphrates, near the mouths of the rivers Baliḫ and Ḫabur.

2. Job. 1:13. Note that the Sabaean raid is succeeded (v. 17) by one on the part of the Chaldeans of Mesopotamia!

3. See: F. H. Foster, in AJSL 49 (1933), 21–45; A. Guillaume, in S. H. Hooke Volume (1963), 106–27; E. Dhorme, Job (1926), pp. cxl–cxliii.

4. See: R. H. Pfeiffer, Introduction to the O.T. (1941), 669 f. Pfeiffer holds, however, that the prologue was added later by an Israelite writer, since no Edomite would have regarded Yahweh as the supreme god. But Yahweh seems indeed to have had early connections with Edom; cf. Judg. 5:4, and note that the name Yahweh-in-Edom occurs in an inscription of Ramses II at Amarah West: H. W. Fairman, in ILN, April 17, 1948. In Deut. 33:2 Yahweh comes from Seir, which is Edom, and in Hab. 3:3 from Teman.—See, however, J. Pedersen, in RPHR 10 (1930), 317–70, for arguments against the Edomite provenience of the book.

5. Jer. 49:7; Obad. 8.

6. Ludlul bêl nimêqi, tr. Pfeiffer, in ANET 434–37; cf. also: R. J. Williams, in Canadian Journal of Theology 2 (1956), 14–26. Analogous Mesopotamian texts are: (a) "The Babylonian Ecclesiastes," tr. Pfeiffer, op. cit. 438 ff.; cf. also: B. Landsberger, in ZA 43 (1936), 32–76; (b) "The Righteous Sufferer," ed. O. Lambert and O. Gurney, in Anatolian Studies 4 (1954), 65–99; (c) the Sumerian poem, "Man and his God," ed. S. N. Kramer, in VT Suppl. 3 (1955), 170–82.

7. The same argument informs T. E. Brown's famous poem, Sunset at Chingford; cf. The Week-End Book (1928), 102 ff.

8. E.g., G. B. Gray and S. R. Driver, Job (ICC), i, pp. xli–xlvii; W. A. Irwin, in JR 17 (1937), 37–47; E. Fohrer, in AFO 19 (1960), 83–94; R. H. Pfeiffer, Introduction, 673 f.; O. Eissfeldt, The O.T.: an Introduction (1965), 458.—On the other hand, the authenticity of the Elihu speeches is upheld, among others, by: C. H. Cornill, Einletung in das AT⁴ (1913), 249; N. H. Ridderbos, in GThT 38 (1937), 353–82; L. Dennefeld, in RB 48 (1939), 163–80; R. Gordis, in Biblical Studies, ed. A. Altmann (1963), 60–78.

9. So too Pfeiffer, Introduction, 673 f.

290 The Devil's wager

1. J. Muir, Original Sanskrit Texts i (1872), 179 ff.; cf. K. Schlottmann, in Deutsche Zeitschrift für christl. Wiss. und christl. Leben, 1850, No. 23; A. Jeremias, The Old Testament in the Light of the Ancient East (1911), ii.252 f.; O. Eissfeldt, op. cit., 468, n.44.—Cf. also: M. B. Cook and S. A. Eliot, "Tracing Job's Story," in The Hibbert Journal 60 (1962), 323–29.

291 The Sons of God

1. RS 1929.ii.16 f.; II AB iii.15; III AB, B 20–21; III AB, C 19–20; Krt C i–ii.9–11, etc.
2. T. H. Gaster, in Orientalia 11 (1942), 44.

292 Satan

1. Cf. T. H. Gaster, IDB, s.v. Satan; Faivre, Personnalité de Satan d'après la bible (Diss. Montauban-Granié, 1900); S. Kluger, Satan in the OT (1967).

294 Mother Earth

1. This paragraph is excerpted from T. H. Gaster, The Holy and the Profane (1955), 161 f.
2. W. Caland, Altindische Toten- und Bestattungsgebräuche (1896), 8.
3. Servius, on Vergil, Aeneid xii.395.
4. Aelfric, Anglo-Saxon Homilies, ed. B. Thorpe (1841), i.623.
5. A. Dieterich, Mutter Erde (1913), 25 ff.
6. Ib.
7. Notes and Queries VI/ii (1860), 87, 214.
8. Dieterich, loc. cit.; P. Sartori, Sitte und Brauch (1910–14), i.134; Rider, in Zs. für Kulturgeschichte 1.59 ff., 97 ff.; Stolz, in Zs. für oesterreiche Volkskunde 12, fasc. iv–v; E. Rohde, Psyche[7] (1921), 204.
9. VAT 10173, ii.14; O. Schröder, in ZA 33 (1921), 130.
10. II AB i.18; I*AB v.11; V AB, A 24, C 4, E 4, 50; cf. T. H. Gaster, Thespis[2], 128.
11. E. H. Hodge, ed., Cory's Ancient Fragments (1876), 59.
12. J. Lewy, in HUCA 19 (1945–46), 429, n.134, sees a relic of such an earth-god in the name Arqiel (i.e., Earth-god) given to one of the fallen angels in Enoch 6.
13. AP x.58.
14. Grimm-Stallybrass, TM 642.
15. Orientalia 19 (1950), 382.

295 Rousing Leviathan

1. Stith Thompson, MI, A 737.1; E. B. Tylor, Primitive Culture[2], i.325 ff.; H. Gunkel, Schöpfung und Chaos (1895), 41–69.
2. Rig Veda v.40.
3. Buddhagosa i.9; Samyutta i.50; tr. C.A.F. Rhys Davids, Kindred Sayings (1918), i.71.
4. Ti Fu, in ERE xii.77.
5. R. C. Temple, in ERE iii.36[a].
6. E. Welsford, in ERE xii.102[a].
7. W. Scott, De lingua Tschwaschorum (1841), 5.
8. Grimm-Stallybrass, TM 707.
9. Ib.
10. P. le Page Renouf, in PSBA 7 (1885), 163–70.
11. A. M. Layard, Discoveries in the Ruins of Nineveh and Babylon (1853), 442; B. Meissner, in ARW 5 (1902), 225.
12. Sa[c]adya, Introd. to Emunoth w[e]-De[c]oth; L. Zunz, Gesammelt Schriften (1875), ix.245, n.2; L. Ginzberg, Legends of the Jews, v.108, 116.
13. Migne, PL vii.337.
14. Hrabanus Maurus, Opera v.606, Colyr.
15. G. A. Smith, The Book of the Twelve Prophets (New York 1944), ii.524.
16. Tacitus, Ann. i.28.
17. R. Lasch, in ARW 3 (1900), 136.

18. C. O. Blagden, Pagan Races of the Malay Peninsula (1906), ii.203 f.

19. I AB vi.35–52; cf. T. H. Gaster, Thespis[2], 228 f.

20. E.g., II Esdras 6:49–52; Apoc. Baruch 29: 3–8.

21. TB Baba Bathra 74ᵃ–75ᵃ; Shabbath 30ᵇ; Kethub. 11ᵇ; Pal. Targum, Num. 9:26 ff.

22. Yasht xiii.62; cf. also: W. Bousset, Rel. des Judentums in NTlicher Zeitalter (1903), 271, where Behemoth is compared with the ox Hadhayos.

23. Hesiod, Theog. 820 ff.; Aeschylus, Prometheus Vinctus 351 ff.; Ovid, Met. v.319 ff.; Apollodorus, Bib. i.6, 3.

296   Father's knees

1. KUB XXIV 7 iv.38; XXIV 8 iii.4 ff.; cf. H. Ehelolf, in OLz 1926.767; A. Goetze, in JAOS 69 (1949), 180.

2. Breasted, AR ii, §§187–212.

3. J. Grimm, Deutsche Rechtsaltertümer[4] (1899), 598; M. Cahen, in Bull. de la Société de Linguistique, Paris 27.56–57; K. Beth, in HWbDA i.195.

4. For its prevalence among the Celts, cf. J. Loth, in Revue celtique 40.143–52.— The custom was known also to the Greeks: B. Haussolier, ib., 43.168–73; P. Suys, ib., 45.322–24.—So too among the Iranians: E. Beneviste, in Bull. de la Soc. de Linguistique 27.51–53.

5. HWbDA, loc. cit.

6. Ib.

7. Gen. 50:23.

8. See: M. W. Déonna, in Rev. arch. 1 (1939), 224–35; R. Meringer, in Wörter und Sachen 11 (1928), 114 ff.; K. Simyoni, "Knie und Geburt," in Kuhns Zeitschrift für vergl. Sprachwiss. i (1923), 152 ff.; R. B. Onians, The Origins of European Thought about the Body, etc. (1951), 174–86. Cf. also: E. Schwyzer, in Antidoron, Wackernagel Festschrift (1923), 283 ff.

9. A. Meillet, in Bull. de la Soc. de Linguistique 27 (1926), 54 f.; id., in CRAIBL 1926.45 ff.

10. Cf. H. Holma, Namen der Körperteile im Assyrisch-Babylonischen (1911), 96.

297   The weary dead

1. A. Erman and H. Grapow, Handwörterbuch d. aeg. Sprache, 38.

2. Odyssey 11.474 f.—In later Roman times, the dead were sometimes termed *securi* (free from care) and were said to enjoy *securitas aeterna*: Dessau, Inscr. sel. #8025, 8149; F. Cumont, After Life in Roman Paganism (1922), 191. Cf. also: Cicero, In Catil. iv.7: *mors laborum et miseriarum quies*.

3. Not impossibly, in view of the antithetical *rogez*, the Heb. word *rᵉšaᶜîm*, commonly rendered "the wicked" (its usual sense), should here be emended to *roᶜašîm*, "stormtossed, restless."

298   The sons of Resheph

1. See above, §242.

2. E.g., I Sam. 23:5. The words were anciently written *k l*, and in Hos. 14:3 this has been misvocalized as *kôl*, "all," the correct rendering being, *Say unto him, Surely thou wilt remit the penalty of wrongdoing.* Cf. also Neo-Hebrew *hᵃ-kî lō'*.—For the Amarna usage, cf. H. Holma, in ZA 28.102.

3. W. Müller, apud Gesenius-Buhl, s.v. *r-š-f*.

300   Orion

1. T. H. Gaster, Thespis[2], 323. It derives from a root meaning properly "to have collops of fat on the loins." Cf. also: G. R. Driver, in JTS 7 (1956), 2.

2. Odyssey 11.572.

3. Cf. E. Babelon, in Rev. belge de numismatique 1898.20 ff.; A. B. Cook, Zeus ii (1925), 430.

4. Cf. R. Allen, Star-names and Their Meanings (1899), 306.

5. The word is rendered similarly (*gabrâ*) in the Syriac (Peshitta) Version of our passage.

6. Grimm-Stallybrass, TM 66.

7. Ib., 525–29.

8. A. Aarne and S. Thompson, Types of the Folktale (1928), #1000–1099.

301 The whip of God

1. Iliad 12.37; 13.812; cf. Hesychius, s.v. *Dios mastigi*. Cf. also: J. E. B. Mayor, on Juvenal, xiii.195; H. J. Munro, on Lucretius, iii.1203; v.1154.

2. Aeschylus, Choephoroe 290.

3. Aeschylus, Eumenides 155–60; Heliodorus, Aethiopica ii.11.

4. Aeschylus, Prometheus Vinctus 681–82.

5. S. Eitrem, Papyri Osloenses: (1930), 53.

6. T. Pradel, Griech, Gebete (1907), 259.

7. Eitrem, op. cit., 52.

8. Grimm-Stallybrass, TM, 1003.

9. R. Harris, Picus who is also Zeus (1916), 57 ff.; A. B. Cook, Zeus ii (1925), 824 f.; T. H. Gaster, Thespis², 165 f.

10. Aeschylus, Septem contra Thebas, 423 ff.; Euripides, Phoenissae 1172 f.; id., Supplices 496 ff.; Lycophron, Alex. 433 ff.

11. Oppian, De pisc. 5.282 ff.

12. Harris, loc. cit.

13. Grimm-Stallybrass, TM 178.

302 The disappearing shadow

1. Pausanias, viii.38, 6; Polybius, xvi.12, 7; Plutarch, Quaest. Graec. 39; cf. J. Negelein, in ARW 5 (1902), 1–37.

2. P. Drechsler, Sitte, Brauch und Volksglauben in Schlesien (1905–6), i.31.

3. Cf. A. Löwinger, in Grunwald's Mitteilungen zur jüd. Volkskunde (Vienna 1910).

4. G. H. Simon, in JAFL 65 (1952), 1920.

5. Ib.

303 The hawsers of the heart

1. Cf. Judg. 16:9; Isa. 5:27.

2. Root *z-m-m*, akin to **ṣ-m-m*.

3. Syriac *maršô*.

4. Shakespeare, King John, V.vii.52 ff.

5. On the universal prevalence of this concept, see H. Campbell Bonner in HTR 34 (1941), 49–68.

304 The King of Terrors

1. The Heb. runs: *wᵉ-taṣᶜîdēhū lᵉ-melek balāhôt*. LXX's σχοίη δὲ αὐτὸν ἀνάγκη αἰτίᾳ βασιλικῇ is scarcely translatable, but perhaps presupposes the reading *wᵉ-taṣᶜîRēhū Kᵉ-melek bal-heyôt*. Vulgate renders: *Et calcet super eum, quasi rex, interitus* = *wᵉ-taṣᶜîdēhū Kᵉ-melek bᵉlôt*. The verb *wᵉtaṣᶜîdēhū* means literally "thou wilt cause him to march," and may be understood, without facile emendation, in the sense, "you will eventually see him escorted, conducted."

2. CT XXIV 36.52; 47.10.

3. E. Ebeling, Tod und Leben (1931), 166.14.

4. Vergil, Georgica iv.464.

5. Aeschylus, Septem contra Thebas 608 ff.

306   Razed foundations and faery gold

1. Literally, *Of the ancient way, which impious men (once) trod.* If the allusion is indeed to a time-honored story, the word "ancient" is pertinent and need not be emended, as some modern scholars have suggested.

2. EV: the Almighty.

3. RSV: *They were snatched away before their time,* but the precise meaning of the Hebrew verb is *shrink, contract.* The picture is drawn from plant life, and I have therefore inserted the words, *like plants,* to bring out explicitly what is implicit in the original.

4. Another reading is, *Why, their mainstay* (or, *substance*) *has proved delusive.*

5. The context requires that the Hebrew word *yeter* be taken in the sense of *tent-rope* (cf. Job 4:21), rather than *remainder, surplus,* as usually rendered.

6. EV: *the Almighty.*

7. KLV: *You shall have plenty of silver;* RSV: *Your precious silver.* For the true sense of the Hebrew word *to‘aphôth,* see Ps. 95:4; cf., by metathesis, Arabic *y-f-‘,* "be high, tower."

8. For this expression, cf. Job 27:10. The Hebrew word (*tith‘annag*) is usually rendered, "thou shalt delight thyself," but it is here better explained from an homophonous root akin to Arabic *‘-n-j,* "moor, tie, attach," and (by metathesis) Neo-Hebrew *‘-g-n,* since the point is that the tents of the pious stand firm, in contrast to what has just been said about the foundation of the wicked.

9. There is no need to emend this verse, as is usually done by modern commentators. The subject of the Hebrew verb *hišpîlū* is *‘eynaim* ("eyes") at the end of the sentence, and the point lies in a contrast between men who cannot "look God in the face" and those who lower their eyes through genuine humility.

10. Here again, no radical emendation is required. The renderings in the Ancient Versions merely indicate perplexity over a difficult phrase. The expression *î-nāqî* means simply "not guiltless," but it also includes the notion of not having clean hands; cf. Ps. 24:4. The traditional text's *nimlaṭ* must be vocalized *nimlaṭâ = nimlaṭethā.*

11. Stith Thompson, MI, F 944.

12. Commentary on First Mu‘allaqah, v.49, ed. Arnold, quoted by D. D. Margoliouth, The Relations between Arabs and Israelites Prior to the Rise of Islam (1924), 32.

13. Stith Thompson, op. cit., F 475.

14. Ib., D 1201; HWbDA, s.v. Gold.

307   The shades beneath the waters

1. J. A. MacCulloch, in ERE xii.518.

2. S. Reinach, Cultes, mythes et religions, i (1922), 184–94; A. H. Krappe, La genèse des mythes (1938), 216 f.

3. C. Seligmann, The Melanesians of British New Guinea (1910), 610, 655; cf. also: C. Clemen, Religionsgesch. Europas (1926–31), i.47; MacCulloch, loc. cit.

4. O. Finsch, Neu-Guinea und seine Bewohner (1865), 104 f.

5. R. Lambert, Moeurs et superstitions des néo-Caledoniens (1900), 13 f.; J. G. Frazer, The Belief in Immortality (1913), i.326.

6. R. Nassau, Fetichism in West Africa (1904), 56 ff., 237.

7. O'Grady, Sylva Gadelica (1842), 290; A. McBain, Celtic Mythology (1917), 91; J. A. MacCulloch, in ERE ii.689.

8. L. Radermacher, in Anz. d.Oesterreich. Akad. d. Wiss., phil.-hist. Kl. 1949, #16.307–15.

9. Cf. CT XVI.10*b*; IV R, 30.2.

309 The pillars of heaven

1. Stith Thompson, MI, A 665.2.1; A 841.

2. R. Anthes, in Mythologies of the Ancient World, ed. S. N. Kramer (1961), 31 f.; G. Maspero, in Rev. archéol., N.S. 34 (1877), 322; Guide to the Egyptian Collections in the British Museum (1908), 145.

3. Rig Veda vi.67, 6.

4. J. Scheftelowitz, Das altpers. Religion und das Judentum (1920), 106.

5. Odyssey 1.53–54; cf. O. Gruppe, Griechische Mythologie (1906), 382; A. B. Cook, Zeus ii (1925), 140 ff.

6. L. Frobenius, Erlebte Erdteile (1925), 163.

7. R. B. Dixon, Oceanic Mythology (1916), 163.

8. Stith Thompson, Tales of the North American Indians (1929), 286, n.56; A. B. Alexander, Latin American Mythology (1920), 154 (Mayan).

9. A. Bastian, Inselgruppen (1883), 218 (Maori); C. Strehlow, Die Aranda und Loutja-Stämme in Zentral-Australien (1907–20), i.2.

10. Kalevala, runo xvii.551, tr. W. F. Kirby (Everyman's Library ed.), i.191.

11. Cf. G. B. Gray, Sacrifice in the O.T. (1925), 152 (on Ps. 78:69); H. P. L'Orage, Iconography of Cosmic Kingship in the Ancient World (1953), 9–17; G. Martiny, in OLz 41 (1938), 665–72; F. Jeremias, in Bertholet-Lehmann, Handbuch i.523 ff.; I. Benzinger, Hebräische Archäologie² (1927), 329; R. Patai, Man and Temple (1947), 105 ff.; A. Piankoff, Les chapelles de Toutankhamen (1901), pl. ix; T. H. Gaster, in Numen 1 (1954), 195 f.—Among ancient writers, cf. Josephus, Ant. iii.7, 7; Clem. Alex., Strom. 562 ff.; Justin, Cohortatio ad gentes 29; Heb. 9:8 ff.—Against this view, however, cf. A. Parrot, Ziggurat et Tour de Babel (1949); J. Nougayrol, in Symbolisme cosmique et monuments réligieux, Musée Guimet, July 1953, pp. 13 f.; H. Nelson, in BA 7 (1944), 77.

12. Cf. A. Audin, in AOr 21 (1953), 430–39.

13. J. R. Murie, Anthropological Papers of the American Museum of Natural History 11 (1916), 551.

14. E. O. James, in The Labyrinth, ed. S. H. Hooke (1935), 245.

310 The Dragon in the net

1. This brilliant emendation is due to Tur Sinai.

2. The corresponding verb may be recognized, I suggest, in the Heb. text of Ps. 59:12, where in place of the usual *Let them be trapped in their pride, for the cursing and lies which they utter* (yᵉsapperū), we should render, *Let them be trapped in their pride, and enmeshed in their intrigue and deceit.*

3. Enuma Elish iv. 97 ff.

4. The Greek (Septuagint) Version, by a change of but one letter, obtains the sense, *The bolts of heaven were terrified at him; his hand pierced the Evasive Serpent.* But this destroys the pointed contrast between the actions of God's *hand* and of his *breath,* balancing that between his *strength* and his *understanding* (as if to say, his *brawn* and *brain*) in the immediately preceding line.

312 The legend of the phoenix

1. The tradition that our verse refers to the phoenix is due also to a misunderstanding of the Septuagint's Greek rendering, "I will live a long while like a branch of the *phoinix,*" where *phoinix* really means "palm-tree" (cf. Vulgate's *et sicut palma multiplicabo dies*). However, there is no solid basis for this rendering of the Heb. word, *ḥôl;* cf. E. Dhorme, Job (1926), in loc.

2. Pliny, HN x.2.

3. Cf. Herodotus, ii.73; Ovid. Met. xv.391; Tacitus, Ann. vi.34; Aelian, NA vi.58; Statius, Silv. ii.4, 37; Martial v.7, 1. Cf. also: II Enoch 12, 15; III Baruch 6:4 ff.

4. Kazwini, i.420.

5. Damiri, ii.36 f.

6. T. H. White, The Bestiary (1960), s.v.

7. A. Wiedemann, in ZÄS 16.89 f.

8. The word was recognized by Virolleaud in a passage of the Ugaritic Epic of K-r-t (c,109), but this is now otherwise explained; cf. H. L. Ginsberg, The Epic of Keret (1946), 44.

9. A. H. Gardiner and N. G. Davies, Tombs of Menkheperrasonb (1933), 26.

313 The negative confession

1. Cf. R. Pettazzoni, La confessione dei peccati, iii (1935), 1–24.

2. Book of the Dead, ch. 125; tr. J. A. Wilson, in ANET 34. Cf. C. Maystre, Les déclarations d'innocence (1937); E. A. W. Budge, Osiris and the Egyptian Resurrection (1911), i.315 ff.

3. Breasted, AR i (1906), 523.

4. Ib., 252, 281.

5. E. Ebeling, Tod und Leben nach den Vorstellungen der Babylonier, i (1931), 20–21.

6. Cf. S. A. Cook, The Laws of Moses and the Code of Hammurabi (1903), 62 f.

7. Pettazzoni, op. cit., 21.

8. Budge, op. cit., i. 339; Mary Kingsley, Travels in West Africa (1897), 465.

9. Heb.: *rabbū*. But I suspect that we should read *rābū*," have entered suit."

10. Heb.: *ᶜošeq*. It has been suggested that we should read **ᶜoqeš*, "distortion." An alternative might be *ᶜathaq*, "arrogance," as in I Sam. 2:3; Pss. 31:19; 75:6; 94:4.

11. Satapatha Brahmana xi.2, 7.33.

12. Cf. A. W. Jackson, in Actes du Xᵉ Congrès des Orientalistes (1897), II.i.67 ff.— The concept passed thence into Islam (cf. Tor Andrae, Der Ursprung des Islams und des Christentums [1926], 69) and into the lore of the Mandaeans of Iraq and Iran (Left Ginza iii.19, Lidzbarski).

13. Cf. M. Nilsson, in Bull. de la Soc. Royale des Lettres de Lund, 1921–23. 29 ff.

14. Pettazzoni, op. cit., i.186.

15. In the Egyptian conception, the forty-two judges were ranged in equal number on the left and the right, with the scale in the middle: H. Kees, Totenglauben und Jenseitsvorstellungen des alten Aegypten (1926), 450; G. Roeder, Urkunden zur Religion des alten Aegypten (1923), 244.—For the Babylonian view, cf. Ebeling, loc. cit.

16. Budge, op. cit., i.339.

314 Blowing kisses to the moon

1. S. Langdon, in JRAS 1919.531 f.; A. Malraux and G. Salles, Arts of Mankind: Sumer, tr. Giebert-Emmons (1960), fig. 350. Cf. also: A. Goetze, in JNES 4 (1945), 248, n.2.

2. Pliny, HN xviii.2, 5: *inter adorandum dexteram ad osculum referimus.*

3. Cf. E. Crawley, The Mystic Rose² (1927), i.343–49.

316 Cattle presage storms

1. Heb.: *yaggîd ᶜalāw rēᶜô miqneh 'af ᶜal ᶜôleh.*

2. By one such emendation (viz., *mᵉqanne' 'af ᶜal ᶜawlah*) RSV obtains the sense, *Its crashing declares concerning Him, Who is jealous with anger against iniquity.* Other suggestions are: (a) *yaggîd ᶜalāw rēᶜô wi-yᵉhawweh' apô ᶜaloleh,* i.e., *God's thunder bespeaks him, and the stormwind discloses his anger.* This is simply an arbitrary

rewriting of the text; (*b*) *yaggîd* ^c*alāw* *rô*^c*ô* *miqneh* <š*ō*>'*ef* ^c*aloleh* (Dhorme), *Its shepherd tells of him, (and) the cattle itself snuffs the stormwind*(!); (*c*) *yaggîd* ^c*Aliy rē*^c*ô* *maqnî' 'af* ^c*al* ^c*awlah* (Pope), ^c*Aliy* (i.e., *the High One*) *speaks with his thunder, venting his anger against evil*. This is barely Hebrew.

The preceding verse, to which this is the logical complement, has also given headaches to commentators. The traditional text reads: ^c*al kappaim kissah 'ôr wa-y*^e*ṣaw* ^c*alêhā* *b*^e*-mafgî*^{ca}. KJV renders arbitrarily, *With clouds he covereth the light, and commandeth it (not to shine) by (the cloud) that cometh betwixt*. Heb. *kappaim*, however, can only mean "palms, hands," not "clouds." RSV, reading *ba-mifga*^c, improves this to, *He covers his hands with lightning, and commands it to strike the mark*. It seems to me that perfect sense can be obtained simply by revocalizing the word *kappaim* to read *kēfîm*, "rocks," and by assuming a haplography in the second hemistich, to read, *wa-y*^e*ṣaw* ^c*alê lahab mifga*^c, i.e., *O'er rocks he casts the lightning as a mantle, and commands the flash to strike the mark*.

3. W. C. Hazlitt, Dictionary of Faiths and Folklore (1905), ii.624^b.
4. Ib.

318 Stars divine

1. IV AB i.4 (*bn il* || [*p*]*ḫr kkbm*); cf. T. H. Gaster, in Iraq 6 (1939), 125, n.5.
2. G. Furlani, Rel. Bab. e assir., i (1928), 95 f.; A. Deimel, Pantheon babylonicum¹ (1914), passim.
3. Lucian, Tragopodagra 108 f.

319 Rain from bottles

1. H. Gressmann, Texte und Bilder² (1926–27), #303; S. A. Cook, The Religion of Ancient Palestine in the Light of Archaeology (1925), 49.
2. Rig Veda v.83, 7–8, tr. R. H. Griffith.
3. G. Jacob, Altarabische Parallelen zum AT (1897), 20.
4. Garcilasso de la Vega, Royal Commentaries of the Yncas, tr. C. R. Markham (1869–71), ii.27.
5. Grimm-Stallybrass, TM 593.

PROVERBS

321 The house that leads down to death

1. For this sense of the word "death" in the Old Testament, see: Isa. 38:18; Pss. 6:6; 9:14; 22:16; Job 28:22; 30:23.
2. Temple Bible: Proverbs, in loc.
3. Stith Thompson, MI, F 941.1; A. Wesselski, Märchen des Mittelalters (1925), 200.
4. Stith Thompson, op. cit., F 302; W. A. Clouston, Tales and Popular Fictions (1887), i.212 ff.; S. Baring-Gould, Curious Myths of the Middle Ages² (1869), ch. 10, "The Mountain of Venus"; E. Hoffmann-Krayer, in Zeitschrift für Volkskunde 25.120, n.4; C. A. Williams, Oriental Affinities of the Legend of the Hairy Anchorite (1925), i.13–25; Myra Olstead, "Lancelot at the Grail Gate," in Folk-Lore 76 (1963), 48–55.
5. See above, §11.

322 Ants store food in summer

1. Ovid, Fasti i.685 ff.—A similar observation is made by the Hellenistic poet, Pseudo-Phocylides, 164 ff. (= T. Gaisford, Poeti Minores Graeci [1814], ii.458), but this writer appears to have been a Jew, and his statement seems to be derived directly from

Prov. 30:25, for his description of the ants as *phylon oligon* reproduces to a nicety the Heb. expression, *ᶜam lô' ᶜaz* (EV: a people not strong); cf. J. Bernays, in Jahresber. des jüdisch-theologischen Seminars Fraenckelscher Stiftung (Breslau 1856), xxx, n.2.

2. Vergil, Georgica i.186: *inopi metuens formica senectae.*

3. Notes and Queries II/xi (1861), 475 f.

4. J. Lubbock, Ants, Bees and Wasps[3] (1882), 59–61, cited by Frazer, Comm. on Ovid, Fasti, loc. cit.; Chambers' Encyclopaedia (1925), i.302, s.v. Ant. Cf. also: S. Bochart, Hierozoicon (1663), ii.591.

323 Pointing the finger

1. See in general: S. Seligmann, D. böse Blick (1910), ii.183; F. G. Groschuff, Abhandlung von der Finger, deren Verichtungen und symbolische Bedeutung (1756), 312 f.; Echtermeyer, Ueber Namen und symbolische Bedeutung der Finger bei den Griechen und Römer (1835); I. Löw, "Die Finger in Literatur und Folklore der Juden," in Gedenkbuch D. Kaufmann (1900), 61–85; Am Urquell 6. 49 ff.—Diogenes affronted Demosthenes by pointing his finger at him: C. Sittl, Die Gebärden der Griecher und Römer (1890), 51, 110 f.

2. Šurpu ii.88; cf. also: Maqlu iii.8, 11, with Tallquist's note, in loc.; KARI #118.4 f.; MDOG 1918/i.78 ff.; A. Jirku, Altor. Kommentar zum AT (1923), 234 f.

3. Seligmann, op. cit., ii.262; cf. I. Goldziher, Abhandlungen zur arab. Philologie (1896–99), i.57.

4. Globus 46.202.

5. Am Urquell 6.10 ff.; F. G. Heins, Seespuk (1888), 142.

324 Wisdom as God's master craftsman

1. Cf. Heb. *'ammān,* Song of Songs 7:2.

2. See fully: F. L. Moriarty, in Verbum Domini 27 (1947), 291–93.

3. Wisdom of Solomon 7:22 (*technitis*).

4. Cf. L. Oppenheim, in Orientalia 16 (1947), 212, n.4.

5. S. Smith, First Campaign of Sennacherib, line 33.

6. D. Luckenbill, ARAB i.§63.

7. Enuma Elish i.30–31.

8. The Heb. word (*šaᶜᵃšūᶜîm*), usually rendered "delight," is connected with a verbal root (*š-ᶜ-ᶜ* II) meaning "converse, chat." Cf. Prov. 19:24.

9. Cf. T. H. Gaster, in Vetus Testamentum 4 (1954), 77 f.

325 The seven pillars of Wisdom

1. For the traditional text's *ḥaṣbah,* "has hewn out," we must read, with LXX, *hiṣ-ṣîbah,* "has set up." (RSV adopts this reading.)

2. W. F. Albright, in Wisdom in Israel and the East: Rowley Volume (1958), 9; cf. id., in BASOR 14 (1924), 10; 53 (1933), 13 ff.; Nelson Glueck, in AASOR 14 (1934), 45 ff.

3. The inscription was discovered by T. B. Mitford in 1948; cf. JHS 66.40; Albright, in Wisdom in Israel, etc., loc. cit.

4. S. Krauss, Talmudische Archäologie (1910–12), i.53.

5. Bᵉrešîth Rabbah 78.

6. I. Scheftelowitz, Die Entstehung der manichäischen Religion (1922), 5.

7. The examples here cited are drawn mainly from I. Scheftelowitz, Altpalest. Bauernglaube (1925), 29 f.

8. Herodotus, i.181.

9. I Kings 10:19.

10. E.g., in Meir of Orleans' poem Aqdamûth; tr. T. H. Gaster, in Commentary, June 1953.

11. Right Ginza xiv.11, Lidzbarski.

12. Enoch, chs. 24–25.

13. Lal. Vist. xiv.11, ed. Lefmann.

14. Scheftelowitz, Altpal. Bauernglaube, loc. cit., n.1.

15. Id., Entstehung, loc. cit.

16. O. Wardrop and F. C. Connybeare, eds., Studia Biblica v (1908), 38 f., 83 f.

17. F. Nork, in Scheible's Das Kloster xii (1849), 765 f.

327   The lamp of the soul

1. J. Grimm, DM⁴, 1559; Bötticher, in Philologus 25 (1867), 27 ff.; R. S. Boggs, Index of Spanish Folktales: FCC #90 (1930), No. 708A; J. Jegerlehner, Sagen und Märchen aus dem Oberwallis (1909), 313; C. Plummer, Vitae Sanctorum Hiberniae (1910), #138; Bolte-Polivka i.377 ff., 388.

2. Stith Thompson, MI, E 761.7.4; 765.1.1; J. Bolte, in Zeitschrift für Volkskunde 20.70, n.11; A. H. Krappe, apud N. S. Penzer, The Ocean of Story (1913 ff.), viii.107.

3. Aeschylus, Choephoroe 604 ff.; Bacchylides, v.136 ff.; Apollodorus, Bib. I.7, 2 (see: Frazer, in loc.); Ovid, Met viii.445–525; Hyginus, fab. 171, 174.

4. Cf. E. S. Hartland, The Science of Fairy Tales (1891), 205.

5. Plutarch, Quaest. Rom.

6. Cf. O. Gruppe, Griechische Mythologie (1906), 848, n.10.—For the general notion that the soul was made of fire, cf. Cornutus ii.8; Orphica lxvi.2, 13.

328   Coals of fire on the head

1. S. Morenz, in Theologische Literaturzeitung 78 (1953), 187–92.

2. J. Jamieson, Etymological Dictionary of the Scottish Language² (1879–82), s.v. coal.

3. M. Gusinde, Die Yamana (Mödling 1937), 942 ff.

4. Thus, it is now recognized that Prov. 22:17—24:22 stand in very close relation to the Egyptian Maxims of Amenemope (ANET 421 ff.); while in Prov. 17:10 the hundred blows may be explained from an Egyptian form of punishment, seeing that the Deuteronomic law (Deut. 28:3) restricted the maximum to forty: cf. B. Couroyer, in RB.1950.331–35.

5. On this point, see fully: F. Vattioni, in Studiorum Paulinorum Congressus Internationalis Catholicus (1963), 341–45.

6. Cf. such verbs as ḥ-r-ḥ (blaze, kindle) and ᶜ-š-n (fume) applied to the passions.

7. Cf. Latin ignesco, etc.

8. Cf. H. Grapow, Die bildlichen Ausdrücke des Aegyptischen (1924), 48.

9. W. Gesenius, Thesaurus, s.v. g-ḥ-l.

10. R. B. Onians, Origins of European Thought about the Body, etc. (1951), 147 f. (where, however, sound observations are mixed with untenable conjectures).

11. Plautus, Poen. 770.

12. Id., Merc. 590.

13. Iliad 18.207 f.; Odyssey 18.353 ff.

14. Vergil, Aeneid xii.101 f.

15. Táin Bó Cúalnge, quoted by Onians, op. cit., 157.

16. Admittedly, the preposition ᶜal, "upon," creates a difficulty, for we should normally expect min, "from." However, it might be justified as brachylogical, the meaning being, "You will be shoveling away coals of fire which are on his head."

329 Mythological riddles

1. ANET 114 ff.

2. Stith Thompson, MI, K 1041. Variants are to be found in Spain, Indonesia, among the North American Indians, and even in one of the Uncle Remus stories.

3. I.e., *be-ḥiSnô* for *be-ḥôFnô*.

4. For this sense of the word, cf. Neh. 5:13.

5. Cf. Odyssey 10.1–76; Ovid, Met. xiv.223–32; Apollodorus, Epitome vii.10; Hyginus, fab. 125.—On this myth, see: Schwartz, in Zeitschrift d. Vereins f. Volkskunde 1 (1893), 448–51; id., Nachklänge. prähist. Volksglaube (1894), 20; R. Stroemberg, "The Aeolus Episode and Greek Wind Magic," in Symbolae Phil. Goteb. 1950.71–84.

6. Cf. Grimm-Stallybrass, TM 640, 1087; G. Kittredge, Witchcraft in Old and New England (1929), 159, 477, nn.65–66; Gaster-Frazer, NGB §60; Miss Macdonald, in PSBA 13 (1891), 162; L. Gomme, Ethnology in Folklore (1892), 48–49.

7. Higden (14th cent.), Polychronicon, ed. Babington, ii.43.

8. J. Scheffer, Lapponia (1674), 144 f.; Kalevala x.159–84; K. Krohn, Finnisch-Ungrische Forschungen, vi (1906), 173–75.—Elizabethan playwrights allude to this custom. Says Webster: *Henceforward I will rather trust / The winds which Lapland witches sell to men;* and Nashe: *For, as in Ireland and in Denmark both, / Witches for gold will sell a man a wind, / Which, in the corner of a napkin wrapped, / Shall blow him safe unto what coast he will.*

9. H. Klose, Togo unter deutscher Flagge (1899), 189.

10. C. Leemius, De Lapponibus Finnmarchiae, etc. (1767), 454.

11. K. Wehran, Die Sage (1908), 63.—I have a lurking suspicion that the practice here discussed really underlies the difficult Hebrew text of Hos. 4:19.

12. R. B. Dixon, Oceanic Mythology (1916), 296 f.

13. Stith Thompson, op. cit., A 842.

14. A. Goetze, in ANET 125; H. G. Güterbock, The Song of Ullikummi (1952); T. H. Gaster, The Oldest Stories in the World (1952), 122 f., 129.

15. H. B. Alexander, Latin American Mythology (1920), 203.

16. S. Thompson, Tales of the North American Indians (1929), 286, n.56b.

330 'Aluqah the vampire

1. The insertion of the words "they cry," which are not in the Hebrew, spoils the point. The expression "two give-give daughters" is a colloquialism, like the American "a gimme girl," i.e., a "gold-digger."

2. W. Gesenius, Comm. on Isa. 34:14; J. Wellhausen, Reste d. arabischen Heidentums (1897), 149; H. Schneider, in Junker Festschrift (1961), 257–64.

3. Cf. T. H. Gaster, The Holy and the Profane (1955), 25 ff.

4. Shakespeare, King Lear, III.iv (Withold is a popular form of St. Vitalis.)

THE SONG OF SONGS

331 Introductory

1. For a convenient summary of the various interpretations, cf. H. Rowley, in JRAS 1938.251–76. For a popular treatment, cf. T. H. Gaster, in Commentary 13 (1952), 316–22.

2. Cf. W. W. Cannon, The Song of Songs edited as a Dramatic Poem (1913). For recent renderings along these lines, cf. L. Waterman, The Song of Songs translated and

interpreted as a Dramatic Poem (1948); D. de Sola Pool, in The Menorah Journal, Spring 1945.

3. For this view, cf. especially, T. J. Meek, in AJSL 39 (1923), 1–14; id., in The Song of Songs: a Symposium (1924), 48–79; W. Wittekindt, Das Hohe Lied und seine Beziehungen zum Istarkult (1927); H. Schmökel, Heilige Hochzeit und Hohelied (1956). But cf. also: F. Horst's critique, in ThLz 83 (1958), 184–86.

4. Thus, there is no proof that *Dôd*, the Hebrew word for "lover," used throughout the Song, was ever a title of Tammuz or Adonis. Nor does the catalogue of Mesopotamian love-songs (?) cited and translated by Meek (Song of Songs: a Symposium, 70–79) necessarily emanate, as supposed, from the Ishtar-Tammuz cult, so that its phraseological similarities with the Song of Songs prove nothing more than that all lovers speak the same language everywhere.

5. J. G. Wetzstein, "Die Syrische Dreschtafel," in ZE 5 (1875), 270–302. These observations were first applied to the interpretation of the Song of Songs by Karl Budde, in his commentary (1898). For an excellent critique of the theory, cf. Cannon, op. cit., 28–40.

6. Cannon, op. cit., 32, 35.

7. Cf. G. Jacob, Das Hohelied auf arabische und andere Parallelen untersucht (1902); H. Stephan, "Modern Palestinian Parallels to the Song of Songs," in JPOS 2 (1922), 199–278.

8. Cf. G. Jacob, Altarabische Parallelen zum AT (1897), 20 f.

9. Id., Das Leben der vorislamischen Beduinen (1895), 46 f.

10. Cf. Amr's Muᶜallaqa, 18 (= Jacob, Altarab. Parallelen, 22).

11. A representative selection of these may be found in E. von Sydow's Dichtungen der Naturvölker. (I have used the Italian translation, Poesia dei Popoli Primitivi [1951]).

12. W. Radloff, Proben der Volkliteratur der türkischen Stämme Süd-Siberiens (1870), iii.155 = von Sydow, op. cit., .

13. Von Sydow, op. cit., #83.

14. R. Prietze, Haussa Sprichwörter und Lieder (1904), 26 = von Sydow, op. cit., #85.

15. H. Overbeck, Malaische Erzählungen (1925), 91 = von Sydow, op. cit., #68.

16. B. Gutmann, "Lider der Dschagga," in Zeitschrift . . . Eingeborenen Sprachen, 17 (1928), 179 ff. = von Sydow, op. cit., #96.

17. Comparisons have also been made with Greek poetry, especially with the Idylls of Theocritus; cf. H. Graetz, Schir ha-Schirim (1871); W. W. Hyde, in The Song of Songs: a Symposium (1924), 31–42. Once again, however, these scarcely show direct indebtedness. Thus, the statement that there is honey under the beloved's tongue (4:11) certainly finds its analogue in Theocritus' description of her voice as sweeter than honey (Id., xx.27), but "mellifluous" is a term applied everywhere to speech or voice and, as we have seen, this expression occurs already in an ancient Egyptian lyric!—Much has been made also of the similarity between the words, *I have likened thee, my beloved, to my mare in Pharaoh's chariot* (1:9) and Theocritus' statement (Id., xviii.30–31) that Helen was to Sparta what a Thessalian mare was to a chariot. But the two statements are not really parallel. In Theocritus, the comparison is between the glory which a cypress lends to a garden or a Thessalian horse to a chariot and that which Helen's beauty lent to Sparta. In the Song of Songs, on the other hand, the lover is likening his peasant inamorata (cf. 1:5–6) to the richly caparisoned mare in some pharaoh's equipage! (The words, *my mare* are therefore pointed, and should not be emended.)

18. Anyone can check this readily by leafing through Child's English and Scottish Popular Ballads or Percy's Reliques.

19. Failure to recognize this essential feature of popular literature bedevils much of modern Biblical criticism. All that the language of the extant Hebrew text can ever indicate is the date of that particular redaction, not of the original composition. It is strange that so blatant an error of method should still persist.

332   The banner of Love

1. Cf. ᶜAntara, Moᶜall, 52 (v. Noeldeke, in loc.); Landberg, Dat., 1432; BGA 8,xxii.
2. Chaucer, Canterbury Tales, Prologue, 666 f.
3. Cf. G. B. Gray, in JQR 11 (1899), 92–101; R. de Vaux, Ancient Israel (1965), 226 f.
4. Some scholars would vocalize the Hebrew word as an imperative of the corresponding verb (Akkadian *dagālu*), thus obtaining the sense, "Look lovingly upon me." The words would then be addressed to "the daughters of Jerusalem."

333   Apples and love

1. See: H. Gaidoz, "La réquisition d'amour et la symbolisme de la pomme," in Annuaire de l'École Pratique des Hautes Études 1902.5–23; B. O. Foster, "Notes on the Symbolism of the Apple in Classical Antiquity," in Harvard Studies in Classical Philology 10 (1899), 39–55; E. S. McCartney, "How the Apple became the Token of Love," in Trans. and Proc. Amer. Philos. Assoc. 56 (1925), 76–81; R. Aigremont, Volkserotik und Pflanzenwelt (n.d.), 59 ff.; A. de Gubernatis, Mythologie des Plantes (1878–82), iii.301 ff.; L. Bianchi, in Hessische Blätter für Volkskunde 13 (1914), 107; Bolte-Polivka iii.11; Zs. für Volkskunde 13.318; M. J. Gurion, Der Born Judas² (1916–22), i.192; T. Menzel, Türkische Märchen ii (1924), 69.
2. Clouds 996–97.
3. Ecl. iii.64; cf. Theocritus, Id. v.88; Propertius, ii.34, 69.
4. Dial. meretr. 12.
5. R. Flacalière, Love in Ancient Greece (paperback ed. 1964), 106, 136.
6. D. B. Thomas, Kentucky Superstitions (1920), 25–26, 41.
7. KARI ii.61, vs. 2–3 = E. Ebeling, Liebeszauber (1925), 12–13 (ᴳᴵˢMA = ḫašḫuru-ᴳᴵˢnu-ur-mu, which is also taken to mean *fig;* see: KARI ii.69).
8. R. Patai, in Talpioth 5 (1953), 248.—On apples in magic, see also: K. Helbig, in ZNTW 44 (1953), 111–17.
9. 64, ed. Langkavel.
10. Report, ii.243 (cited by W. Platt, in Notes and Queries, VI/5 (1882), 174).

334   Solomon's groomsmen

1. E. Westermarck, A History of Human Marriage (1925), ii.261, n.5; id., Marriage Customs in Morocco (1914), 118, 274; J. G. Wetzstein, in Zs. für Ethnologie 5 (1873), 288 (Syria); T. H. Gaster, in JBL 74 (1955), 239 ff.
2. W. W. Skeat, Malay Magic (1900), 388.
3. A. E. Crawley, The Mystic Rose² (1927), ii.33 ff.; P. Sartori, Sitte und Brauch, i (1910), 114.
4. H. Granqvist, Marriage Conditions in a Palestinian Village, ii (1933), 85 ff.; W. Rothstein, in Palätinajahrbuch 6 (1910), 121, 135; J. A. Jaussen, Coutumes des Arabes au pays de Moab (1908), 295; T. H. Gaster, in JBL 74 (1955), 241 f.
5. I. Abrahams, Jewish Life in the Middle Ages² (1927), 267.
6. Notes and Queries, IX/ii (1880), 245.
7. Jan Malecki, De religione et sacrificiis veterum Borussorum (1551), quoted by V. Pisani, La religione dei Celti e dei Balto-Slavi nell'Europa precristiana (1950), 88.

335 The "Terror by Night"

1. KARI ii.58 (= E. Ebeling, in MVAG 28 [1918], i/3), rev. 10–12.

2. See: S. Krauss, in Orient and Occident: Moses Gaster Anniversary Volume (1936), 323–30.

3. The verse is included in the Jewish prayer recited on retiring at night: S. Singer, Authorised Daily Prayer Book (1890), 296.

336 The separable soul

1. Frazer-Gaster, NGB §§149, 152; Stith Thompson, MI, E 721; A. E. Crawley, The Idea of the Soul (1909), 278, 280; J. J. de Groot, The Religious System of China (1892) sqq.), iv.105.—A. B. Cook (Zeus ii [1925], 1039 f.) would thence derive the Orphic notion of creation from *erôs* (i.e., inner ergative passion) emanating from Zeus.

337 The dance of Maḥanaim

1. Cf. W. F. Albright, in Hebrew and Semitic Studies . . . G. R. Driver (1963), 5–6; cf. also: L. Rost, Tiglathpileser (1893), iii.73.10; K. Tallquist, Akkadische Götterepitheta (1938), 34 (where for Di-ni-tu read Šulmanitu).

2. Cf. O. Gruppe, Griechische Mythologie (1906), 840, n.5; Grimm-Stallybrass, Teutonic Mythology (1880–88), 935, 1589.

338 The Reshephs of love

1. The name is likewise used in the plural in Ugaritic (C. Virolleaud, in CRAIBL 1956.60–67, #19.5 J. Nougayrol, ib., 126–35) and, as a loanword, in Egyptian (e.g., Edgerton-Wilson, Historical Records: Medinet Habu 27.25*d*).

2. Koran, Sura 55.; T. Canaan, Dämonenglaube im Lande der Bibel (1929), 5.

LAMENTATIONS

339 Dirges over cities; the weeping "daughter of Zion"

1. Cf. I. Scheftelowitz, in ARW 19 (1916–19), 221, n.1.

2. Cf. M. Werbrouck, Les pleureuses dans l'Egypte ancienne (1939).

3. KUB XXX.15, 27; cf. H. Otten, in ZA 46 (1942), 206–24; O. Gurney, The Hittites (1952), 164 f.

4. III Aqhat 170 ff.; cf. T. H. Gaster, Thespis², 369 f. Note that the women are called *mšspdt*, which is a causative form of the verb, indicating that they *lead* the dirge, which is then, apparently, taken up by others.

5. Cf. Jer. 9:16, 19; Ezek. 8:14 ("women weeping for Tammuz"); 32:16. Cf. also: H. Jahnow, Das hebräische Leichenlied (1923); P. Heinisch, Die Trauergebräuche bei den Israeliten (1931), 91 f.; id., Die Totenklage in AT (1931).

6. Iliad 24.746.

7. Cf. J. E. B. Mayor, on Juvenal, x.261; cf. also Ovid, Met. ii.340–43. Festus, 223.

8. E. W. Lane, Manners and Customs of the Modern Egyptians (Minerva Library ed., 1890), 478; G. Jacob, Das Leben der vorislâmischen Beduinen (1895), 140 f.; P. Kahle, "Die Totenklage in heutigen Aegypten," in Forschungen zu Religion und Lit. d. AT und NT, 19 (1923), 346 ff.

9. M. Ananikian, Armenian Mythology (1920), 95.

10. Tr. S. N. Kramer, in ANET, 455–63.

11. Rm. iv.97 (3334), translated by T. G. Pinches, in PSBA 23 (1901), 197 ff.; id., "The Lament of the Daughter of Sin," in PSBA 17 (1895), 64–74.

340 The limping meter

1. E. W. Lane, Manners and Customs of the Modern Egyptians (Minerva Library ed., 1890), 488.

2. C. Wetzstein, in Zeitschrift für Ethnologie 5 (1873), 296 ff. For other descriptions of the rite, see: E. Roger, La terre saincte (1664), 265; H. Jahnow, Das hebräische Leichenlied im Rahmen der Völkerdichtung (1923), 75, n.6; A. J. Wensinck, Some Semitic Rites of Mourning and Religion (1917), 43; E. C. Quiggin, ed., Essays and Studies presented to William Ridgeway (1913), 379 ff.; T. H. Gaster, Thespis², 370 f.

3. T. G. Pinches, in PSBA 18 (1896), 253.

341 Sitting apart

1. Concerning menstrual segregation and taboos, see: Frazer-Gaster, NGB §166; W. Robertson Smith, Religion of the Semites³ (1927), 446 ff.; R. C. Thompson, Semitic Magic (1908), 116 ff.; J. Wellhausen, Reste d. arab. Heidentums² (1897), 170 ff.; T. Canaan, Dämonenglaube im Lande der Bibel (1929), 43 f. Cf. also: Koran 2:222; Fihrist 319, line 18 (Syria).

▲ 342 The silent widow

[1. For this nuance of the expression, "sit apart," cf. Lev. 13:46.]

[1a. Frazer-Gaster, NGB §172; J. G. Frazer, Psyche's Task² (1913), 111 ff.]

2. Cf. especially Numbers, ch. 19, with G. B. Gray's Commentary (ICC, 1903), 241 ff.

3. Notes analytiques sur les collections ethnographiques du Musée du Congo I/ii, Religion (Brussels 1906), 186.

4. Rabesihanaka [a native Malagese], "The Sihanaka and their Country," in The Antananarivo Annual and Madagascar Magazine, Reprint of the First Four Numbers (1885), 326.

5. A. C. Hollis, The Nandi (1909), 72.

6. S. Powers, Tribes of California (1877), 327.

7. F. Boas, "Fifth Report of the Committee on the North-Western Tribes of Canada," in Report of the British Association . . . Meeting, 1889, p. 43.

8. Id., Seventh Report . . ." in Report of the British Association . . . Meeting, 1891, p. 13.

9. B. Spencer, Native Tribes of the Northern Territory of Australia (1914), 249 ff.

10. B. Spencer and F. Gillen, The Native Tribes of Central Australia (1899), 500–502.

11. Id., The Northern Tribes of Central Australia (1904), 507 ff.

12. Ib., 502.

13. Ib., 525 ff.; id., Native Tribes, 500 ff.

14. A. W. Howitt, Native Tribes of S. E. Australia (1904), 724 ff.; S. Gason, in JAI 24 (1895), 171.

15. Cf. Frazer-Gaster, NGB, loc. cit.

16. Spencer-Gillen, Native Tribes, 502.

17. Spencer-Gillen, Northern Tribes, 510.

18. Gason, op. cit., 170.

[18a. See fully: E. Bendann, Death Customs (1930), 125, 138, 229 f.]

[18b. T. Noeldeke, Mandäische Grammatik (1875), 128; F. Růžička, in BA 6.44, 104. —For another view, see: H. Bauer, in ZDMG 67.342 f.]

[18c. Cf. Exod. 4:11; Isa. 35:6; 53:7; 56:10; Ezek. 3:26; 24:27; 33:22; Hab. 2:18; Pss. 38:13; 32:2, 9 (I became "like a mute, reduced to silence"); Prov. 3:1, 8.]

[18d. Cf. Lam. 2:10; 3:28.]
[18e. Bendann, op. cit.]

343 Cannibalism in time of famine

1. Ashurbanipal, Rassam Cylinder ix; tr. L. Oppenheim, in ANET 300.
2. Diodorus Siculus, xxxiv.2, 20.
3. Juvenal, xv.92 ff.; Valerius Maximus vii. E §3; Orosius v.23; Prudentius, Perist. i.94.
4. Procopius, Got. ii.20.
5. Strabo, 201.
6. Josephus, Bell. Jud. vi.3, 3–4.
7. F. Peries, in OLz 6.244 f.
8. Cf. A. Ungnad, in ZA 36.108; S. Langdon, Semitic Mythology (1931), 416, n.34.

344 Drinking gall

1. Jer. 9:14; 23:15.
2. Cf. Kirby Smith, on Tibullus I.v, 50 (*Tristia cum multo pocula felle bibit*).
3. Cf. E. Oppenheim, in Wiener Studien, 30 (1908), 146.
4. Shakespeare, Macbeth, I.v.48–51.

345 Gravel and dust in the mouth

1. The word is *k-p-sh*, readily explicable as a bye-form of *k-b-sh*, "tread," on the analogy of Neo-Heb. *c-p-sh*, "shrivel," = *c-b-sh* (Joel 1:17); Heb. *n-p-sh* = Zenčirli *n-b-sh;* Ugaritic *l-p-sh* = Heb. *l-b-sh*.
2. Cf. I. Goldziher, in ZDMG 47.588 f.; id., in Vienna Oriental Journal 16 (1902), 144, n.4.
3. TB Baba Bathra 16 (Resh Lakish to Abbayê).
4. Goldziher, loc. cit.
5. The Canonical Prayerbook of the Mandaeans, ed. E. S. Drower (1949), 137.13; Johannisbuch, 131.8, Lidzbarski (*giṭma ᶜl pumaihun d-kalhun kahnia*).
6. Herodotus, ii.100, 7.
7. Ctesias, Pers. xviii.48.
8. Cf. Ovid, Ibis 317: *Utque necatorum Darei fraude secundi / Sic tua subsidens devoret ora cinis;* Valerius Maximus, ix.27.—In II Maccabees 13:5 ff. this is said to have been the fate of the priest Menelaus.
9. Hist. Timuri ii.124, 142, 926 (cited by Schleussner, Novus Thesaurus [1821], v.569).

346 The king as the life-breath of his people

1. Heb.: *bi-šeḥîthôthām;* cf. Akkadian *šêtu,* "net."
2. Cf. H. Grapow, Die bildliche Ausdrücke des Aegyptischen (1924), 122.
3. F. L. Griffith, Hieratic Papyri from Kahun and Gurob (1898), Hymn #4 = Erman-Blackman, The Ancient Egyptians (Harper Torchbook ed., 1966), 186.
4. Ib., Hymn #5 = Erman-Blackman, op. cit., 187.
5. Inscrip. inédit., cited by Grapow, loc. cit.
6. N. de G. Davies, The Rock Tombs of El Amarna (1903), ii.21.
7. Grapow, loc. cit. (Medinet Habu).
8. EA 128.7, 10; 130.7, 9, Winckler.
9. Cf. KAT³, 526.
10. Reading *rūḥᵃkā* for the *rūḥām* ("their wind") of the traditional text.
11. Cf. Frazer-Gaster, NGB §§77–93.

12. On this concept, cf. T. H. Gaster, in Review of Religion, 9 (1945), 270 f.; id., NGB, Add. Note to §1.

347 The king's shadow

1. Cf. A. L. Oppenheim, in BASOR 107 (1947), 7–11, citing R. F. Harper, Assyrian and Babylonian Letters belonging to the Kouyunjik Collection of the British Museum (1892–1914), #264.6–11; #595.4-r.1; #652.12-r.1–3; #886.r.1–4. Cf. also ib., #152.8-r.2; #456.4-r.16; #852.r.2–18; #925.5–7.

2. Kahun Hymn, ii.17 = A. Erman, Literatur, 181.

3. H. Grapow, Die bildliche Ausdrücke des Aegyptischens (1924), 45 f.

4. Text in A. Erman, The Ancient Egyptians, tr. A. M. Blackman (Torchbook ed., 1966), 182. For the interpretation, cf. Oppenheim, loc. cit.

5. Cf. J. Stamm, Die akkadische Namengebung (1939), 276.

6. Cf. G. B. Gray, Hebrew Proper Names (1896), 207.

7. A. Ungnad, Aramäische Papyrus aus Elephantine (1911), #65.5.

8. Cf. Frazer-Gaster, NGB §157, and Additional Note.

ESTHER

348 Introductory

1. Much of this section is condensed from the present writer's Purim and Hanukkah in Custom and Tradition (1950), 6–38.

2. For a resumé of modern critical views, cf. L. B. Paton, Esther (ICC, 1908), 77–94. On the other hand, some scholars have affirmed the historicity of the book: cf. S. Jampel, Das Buch Esther auf seine Geschichtlichkeit kritisch untersucht (1907); J. Hoschander, The Book of Esther in the Light of History (1923).

3. A minor official named Mardukâ, serving at the court of Darius I or of Xerxes at Susa, is mentioned in a cuneiform text cited by A. Ungnad in ZAW 58 (1941), 243; 59 (1943), 219.

4. The Babylonian word *pûru* means properly, "urn," i.e. into which lots are cast. Then, by metonymy, it comes to mean "lot"; cf. A. Bea, in Biblica 21 (1940), 198.

5. The Syriac (Peshitta) Version indeed saw the difficulty and substituted *fourth* for *seventh*.

6. Cf. Stith Thompson, MI, N.275; Bolte-Polivka, ii. 412.

7. Cf. Mardonius, etc. The final *-ka* is a regular Persian ending.

8. Cf. Ezra 2:2; Neh. 7:7.

9. It is not, as modern scholars commonly assert, Mordecai himself, but his ancestor, who is thus described.

10. To enhance the contrast with Agag, Mordecai himself is said to trace his descent from Kish, the father of Saul!

11. Cf. V. Christian, "Zur Herkunft des Purim-Festes," in F. Nötscher Festschrift (1950), 33–37; W. Erbt, Die Purimsage in der Bibel (1900); K. Ringgren, "Esther und Purim," in Svensk Exegetisk Arsbok, 20 (1956), 5–24; N. S. Doniach, Purim or the Feast of Esther (1933); J. Lewy, in HUCA 14 (1939), 127–51.—J. von Hammer (in Wiener Jahrbuch für Literatur, 38 [1872], 49) and P. de Lagarde (Purim [1887]) would derive the feast from the Persian festival of Farvadigan, celebrated in honor of the dead. This theory has been supported by the fact that the Greek (Septuagint) Version calls the feast Furdia, rather than Purim; but this may be merely a scribal error of ΦΟΥΡΔΙΑ for ΦΟΥΡΙΜ.

12. Cf. P. Jensen, in WZKM 6 (1892), 47–70, 209–26; H. Zimmern, KAT³, 514–20.

13. On such theories, cf. R. H. Pfeiffer, Introduction to the Old Testament (1941), 737 ff.; O. Eissfeldt, The Old Testament (1965), 509.

14. Frazer-Gaster, NGB §118; T. H. Gaster, Thespis², 49.

15. Aristotle, Const. Athen. iii.5; cf. Gaster, Thespis², 60, n.260, for further references.

16. Cf. H. Junker, Die Onurislegende (1917), 116 ff.

17. Cf. W. Wolf, Das schöne Fest von Opet (1931), 72 ff.; K. Sethe, Untersuchungen zur Geschichte und Altertumskunde Aegyptens (1902 ff.), iv.219 f.

18. E.g., Gudea Statue E, 51–53; Gudea Cylinder B, iv.23–v.19; S. Langdon, in JRAS 1926.36 ff. (Iddin-Dagan); VAT 633, obv. 1–40; R. H. Pfeiffer, State Letters of Assyria (1935), #217 (Esarhaddon).

19. Cf. Frazer-Gaster, NGB §196.

20. L. A. Waddell, The Buddhism of Tibet (1895), 504 ff.; Frazer-Gaster, op. cit., 462.

21. J. R. Wilson-Hoffenden, in Journal of the African Society 27 (1928), 385 f.

22. J. G. Frazer, The Golden Bough, one-vol. ed., 382 ff.

23. Ib.

24. J. Moura, Le royaume de Cambodge (1883), i.327 f.

25. Ctesias, quoted by Athenaeus, xi.44; cf. Ctesias, ed. F. Baehr (1824), 449 f.; S. Langdon, in JRAS 1924.65–72 (to be read with caution).

26. Cf. P. de Lagarde, "Purim," Abh. d. Kön. Ges. d. Wiss. zu Göttingen, 1887.

27. T. H. Gaster, Thespis², 26 ff.

28. KAV 120, ii.22–28; KAR #177, rev.iii; cf. R. Labat, Le caractère réligieux de la royauté assyro-babylonienne (1939), 315.

29. Livy, xxxvi.37; Ovid, Met. x.432; Fasti, iv.353; cf. G. Wissowa, Rel. und Kultur der Römer² (1912), 246.

30. E. Cabaton, in ERE iii.161a.

31. L. Spence, in ERE iii.507a, 568b.

32. Frazer-Gaster, NGB §§456–67; T. H. Gaster, Thespis², 34 ff.

33. Cf. Gilbert Murray, The Rise of the Greek Epic (1907), Appendix A; Jane Harrison, Prolegomena to the Study of Greek Religion (1922), 95 ff.

34. Grimm-Stallybrass, TM 767 ff.

35. Cf. Gaster, Thespis², 175 f.

36. J. G. Frazer, The Golden Bough, one-vol. ed., 559.

37. Ib., 551.

38. Cf. Gaster, Thespis², 37 ff.

39. Cf. Herodotus, ii.63; K. Sethe, op. cit., iii.134; A. Erman, Handbook of Egyptian Religion, tr. F. Griffith (1907), 215.

40. KUB XVII.35, iii.9–17; cf. A. Lesky, in ARW 24 (1927), 73–82; Gaster, Thespis, 267 ff.

41. Cf. T. H. Gaster, Purim and Hanukkah (1950), 17.

349 The Iranian background

(a) The court at Susa

1. Xenophon, Cyrop. viii. 6, 22; Anabasis iii.5, 15.

(b) The royal banquet

2. Al-Biruni, 203 f.; cf. L. H. Gray, in ERE v.872b.

(c) The one hundred and eighty days

3. L. H. Gray, in ERE iii.129a.

(d) "Men who knew the law"

4. Herodotus, iii.31.

(e) The seven who saw the king's face

5. Athenaeus, xii.514*b*. Concerning the *seven* counsellors, cf. Xenophon, *Anabasis* i.6, 4; A. Christensen, Die Iranier (1933), 256.

6. A. Bastian, Die deutsche Expedition an der Loango-Küste (1874–75), i.262 ff.

7. Proyart's "History of Loango, etc." in Pinkerton's Voyages and Travels, xvi.584.

8. W. C. Harris, The Highlands of Aethiopia (1844), iii.78.

9. Frazer-Gaster, NGB §162.

10. Ib., §146.

11. A. B. Ellis, The Yoruba-speaking Peoples of the Slave Coast (1894), 170.

12. G. Zündel, in Zeitschr. der Ges. für Erdkunde zu Berlin, 12 (1877), 402.

(f) The crazy edict

13. It has been proposed to read *U-MᵉDaBbeR KôL SHôVeH ᶜiMmô*, "and to speak all that beseems him," in place of *U-MᵉDaBbeR Ki-LᵉSHôN ᶜaMmô*, but this is not Hebrew, for the verb *sh-v-h* is construed with the preposition *l-*, not with *ᶜim;* cf. Esther 3:8; 5:13.

14. Cf. T. H. Gaster, in JBL 69 (1950), 381.

(g) The royal crown

15. Cf. P. de Lagarde, Gesammelte Abhandlungen (1866), 207; F. Baehr, Ctesiae Cnidii Operum Reliquiae (1824), 191 f.

(h) Haman's boast

16. Herodotus, i.134.

17. Plutarch, Artaxerxes 5.

(i) Covering the head

18. Quintus Curtius, iv, x.

ECCLESIASTES

350   The telltale bird

1. Cf. Stith Thompson, MI, B 131; Bolte-Polivka, ii.380 ff.; A. Aarne and S. Thompson, Types of the Folktale (1928), #781; V. Chauvin, Bibliographie des ouvrages arabes (1892–1922), ii.107.

2. Grimm's Märchen, #76; cf. Bolte-Polivka, i.275.

3. Ed. Burton, SV 245.

4. Cf. K. Campbell, The Seven Sages of Rome (1907), xcvii.

5. F. J. Child, The English and Scottish Popular Ballads (1882–98), ii.146–55, 260.

6. Cf. Stith Thompson, MI, N 271.3.

7. H. Otten, in MDOG, No. 85 (1953), 33. In the original Canaanite version, the telltale goddess would probably have been Ashtareth (Astarte).

8. Concerning this expression, cf. Notes and Queries, 1/iv (1851), 232, 284, 394; 4/iv (1869), 292; 6/iv (1891), 366; A. de Cock, in Volkskunde 22 (1911), 96–100; W. Wackernagel, Ἔπεα πτερόεντα (1864), 14.

9. Aristophanes, Birds, 600.

10. F. Liebrecht, Zur Volkskunde (1879), 329, No. 140.

ADDENDA

11b Eve

The Hebrew word for Eve is *h a w w a h*. Since this can be connected with a Semitic word meaning "serpent," it has been suggested that the mother of mankind was originally regarded as a serpent—an idea which recurs in many cultures; cf. Th. Noeldeke, in ZDMG 42. 487; J. Wellhausen, Reste[2] (1897), 154; H. Gressmann, in Harnack Festschrift, 24 ff.; W. F. Albright, in AJSL 36 (1928), 284, n.l.—Concerning the ophidian life-goddess of the Mesopotamians, cf. S. Langdon, Tammuz and Ishtar (1914), 114 ff., and note that in a cuneiform text published in BA iii.348, the deity KADI is described as "divine serpent, lady of life." Cf. also: ERE xi.410.—On this hypothesis, the Serpent in Eden would arise from a later differentiation.

13 Localization of Paradise

There are several interesting parallels to the Bible's attempt to localize the mythical Garden. In Classical tradition, the mythical Eridanus (which A. B. Cook [Zeus, ii.1025] would interpret to mean "river of life") was variously identified with the Rhodanne, a stream near Danzig (Rawlinson, Herodotus, iii, pp. 416–17), the Transalpine Rhone, the Italian R. Po (cf. Strabo, 215) and even with the Rhine! Similarly, the Greek Aigle, the mythical "bright land," was located at various places (Preller-Robert, Gr. Mythol.[4] [1894], i.569), as was also Mt. Olympus. Corbenic, the mythical castle of the Grail romances, was likewise localized, in the later *Morte Artu,* at Winchester, Edinburgh, on the R. Humber, on Salisbury Plain, and even at the Tower of London (cf. R. S. Loomis, The Development of Arthurian Romance [1964], 107 f.).

17a The Tree of Life

The tree has also been identified as a fig-tree; cf. L. Ozer, in Acta Antiqua 10 (1962), 1–16.

22 Iron as apotropaic

For this belief in Egypt and Africa, cf. J. Leclant, in Annales de l'Est, Mém. 16. (Nancy 1956), 83–91.

24 Signing of votaries

At Mecca, every male child receives three slashes on the cheek to signify that he is a servant of Allah's house: R. F. Burton, Pilgrimage to Mecca and Medinah[3] (1898), 456.—In India, menials used to be branded on the shoulder: J. A. Dubois, Moeurs, institutions, et cérémonies des peuples de l'Inde (1825), Pt. iii, ch. 3.—Cf. also: Gal. 6:17, "Henceforth let no man trouble me, for I bear branded in my body the marks of Jesus," which does not mean "I share figuratively in the Crucifixion," but "I am God's bondsman."—Witches were often signed at initiation into the coven by being pricked painfully on the shoulder or other part of the body: Margaret A. Murray, The God of the Witches (1952), 99 f.—On the branding of slaves in Babylon, cf. Marx, in BA 4.11.—Cf. also Pseudo-Phocylides 212 (= Gaisford, Poetae Minores Graeci [1824], ii.460): "Do not make brand-marks, thus putting a servant to shame."

25 Corpses of murdered men bleed posthumously

For an American instance of this belief, cf. The Farmer's Almanac, 1968.—For Jewish legends to the same effect, cf. TB Giṭṭin 54; Pesiqta Rabbathi, 25; Deut. Rabbah §1; M. Grunwald, Yalquṭ Sippurîm u-Midrashîm (1923), i.44.

31 The Song of Lamech

The initial words represent a cliché which recurs in Isa. 32:9.

70 Swearing on stones

Both the Danes and the islanders of Iona swore on stones: J. G. Frazer, GB³, i.160.— The Samoans swear by the sacred stone of the village: G. Turner, Samoa (1884), 30, 184.

81 The Rod of Moses

Cf. M. Grünbaum, Neue Beiträge (1893), 161–64; P. Saintyves, Essais de folklore biblique (1923), 90 f.; B. Heller, in MGWJ 80 (1936), 47.—For Jewish traditions on the subject, cf. Aaron Rosmarin, Moses im Licht der Agada (1932), 75 f.; I. Löw, Flora der Juden (reprint, 1966), iv.408–10; L. Ginzberg, Legends of the Jews, ii.291; v.411–12.

86 The passage through the Sea of Reeds

Cf. V. Lauha, in VT Suppl. 9 (1963), 32–46.

93 Leprosy as punishment

In Jewish belief, leprosy is the punishment meted out by God for murder, adultery, false suspicion, perjury, impiety, and eight other offenses: cf. Midrash Tanḥuma, Meṣora §4; Tosefta, Negaʻim, vii.7; Pirqê dᵉ-R. Kahana, 37a. David and Reuben were so chastised for adultery: Ginzberg, Legends, ii.190; iii.266, n.96; vi.305; cf. also: Josephus, Ant. vii.9, 4.

128 Eyes brightened by eating honey

A recipe inscribed on a marble tablet (after A.D. 138), probably from the temple of Asclepius on the Isola Tiburina, prescribes honey for sick eyes: CIG #5980; cf. A. Deissmann, Light from the Ancient East (1911), 132.

129a Youngest son becomes king

David is here said to be the youngest of *eight* brothers; so also in 17:12, 14. But in I Chron. 2:13–15, only *seven* sons of Jesse (Ishai) are mentioned, and David is the seventh. This variant may go back to the familiar folktale motif of the blessed seventh son: cf. Stith Thompson, MI, L 10.—Similarly, in the Welsh Mabinogion, Peredur is the last and sole survivor of the seven sons of the Count of York, and Peredur has much in common with David.

133 The Witch of Endor

On the basis of Sumerian, Akkadian and Hittite evidence, H. Hoffner has suggested (JBL 86 [1967], 385–401) that the Hebrew *ʼôb* really denotes the pit from which the dead were evoked.

145a Giant with extra fingers and/or toes   II Sam. 21:20

Folklore often equips giants with extra limbs. Thus, "Italian writers of the sixteenth century often call giants *quatromani* ["four-handers"]; giants with thirteen elbows [are mentioned] in Fischart's *Gargantua; Bilfinger* in Swabia are families with twelve fingers and twelve toes": Grimm-Stallybrass, TM 1440.—On the motif in general, cf. Stith Thompson, MI, F 551.2.—For a Celtic parallel, cf. J. A. McCulloch, Celtic Mythology (1918), 143.

150 The Judgment of Solomon

For Indic parallels, cf. W. Kirfel, in Saeculum 7 (1956), 369–84.

157 "Measuring" the sick

The practice seems to be mentioned also in an ancient Mesopotamian text: R. C. Thompson, Devils, ii.56 (*qa-nu-u el-lu lu-qi-e-ma a-me-lu šu(!)-a-tim šum-di-id-ma*, "take a clean rod and measure that man"); cf. K. Frank, Bab. Beschwörungsreliefs (1908), 69.—Cf. also: R. Killan, in BZ, N.F. 10 (1966), 44–56.

158 Elijah on Carmel

The "calling with a loud voice" is a common device in magic, in order to gain the deity's attention: cf. A. Dieterich, Mithrasliturgie[2] (1910), 41.—On the other hand, it may have been designed originally to produce rain by imitating thunder: cf. Frazer-Gaster, NGB, §41. The Zuñis of Mexico use bull-roarers and whips for this purpose: E. O. James, in ERE x.562[b]. The Navahos use a "groaning stick": W. Matthews, in Fifth Annual Report of the Am. Bureau of Ethnology (1887), 435 f. At Dorpat, Estonia, hammers and kettles are so used: W. Mannhardt, Antike Wald- und Feldkulte (1877), 342n.—Orgiastic rites and noise (pandemonium) are often employed to imitate the actions of demons: O Gruppe, Griechische Mythologie (1906), 906.

171 Whistling in charms

For an example of this practice from Mahuran, Iran, cf. Percy Sykes, Ten Thousand Miles in Persia (1902), 115.

193a The combat against the Dragon

The description of the dragon as "riddled" (Heb.: *ḥ-l-l*) accords with the fact that the determinative use in writing the name of his Egyptian counterpart Apepi (who, however, is celestial) indicates that he was "sword-smitten," and the epithet "transpierced" (*mdś*) is sometimes applied to him: P. le Page Renouf, in PSBA 1894.295.—In Mandaean lore, Leviathan personifies the submarine monster who will swallow all sinners and demons at the end of the present era: Ginza r., 293.20. (For the netherworld as a fish in Jewish lore, cf. I. Scheftelowitz, Altpers. Rel. und d. Judentum [1920], 198 ff.).—The *seven* heads of Leviathan are mentioned already in the Ugaritic text, I*AB, i. 1 ff. Cf. also the pseudepigraphic Odes of Solomon, 22:5.—G. R. Driver, in Studi Levi della Vida (1956), 238 ff., says that Leviathan is simply "any large serpent."

194 The Suffering Servant

Cf. also: L. Waterman, in JBL 56 (1937), 27–34.

203 The ritual lament

It has been asserted that the figure of Adonis is a Hellenistic creation. To be sure, the so-called "mysteries of Adonis" are known to us only from texts of that age and of the subsequent Roman period, but it should be noted that the wailing for Adonis is attested already by Sappho. What this means is, in a nutshell, that the familiar myth is late, but some earlier story, by means of which the Semitic Adon in the ritual cry was thus transmogrified, must indeed have existed.

209 The righteous Daniel

Cf. also: B. Mariani, Daniel il patriarche sapiente (Rome, Pontificium Athenaeum Antonianum 1945).

211 Salting newborn children

The text mentions not only salting, but also anointing. The latter is a worldwide practice; cf. F. Ratzel, The History of Mankind, English translation (1896), iii.286; A. E. Crawley, in ERE i.522a. It is common among primitive as well as civilized peoples: cf. W. E. Roth, Ethnological Studies among the North-West-Central Queensland Aborigines (1897), 183; T. Williams and J. Calvert, Fiji and the Fijians (1858), i.125; F. Caron, "Account of Japan," in Pinkerton's Voyages and Travels, vii (1811), 635; A. B. Ellis, The Yoruba-speaking People of the Slave Coast of West Africa (1894), 141.

212 Crossroads

For crossroads in ancient Mesopotamian magic, cf. R. C. Thompson, Devils, ii.1, 5; 4.16 (suq irbitti).

213 The fallen paragon

Cf. H. G. May in Muilenburg Festschrift (1962), 166–76; G. Widengren, in Myth, Ritual and Kingship, ed. S. H. Hooke (1958), 165 ff. (I find Widengren's interpretation strained and far-fetched.)

224 Stripping a divorcee

A curious parallel to the Babylonian custom whereby a husband who divorces his wife tears the fringe of her garment is afforded by modern Gypsy usage. A Gypsy is outlawed for marrying a non-Gypsy woman. The latter is required to tear a piece of cloth from her dress and throw it at the head of the Rom, after he has been formally condemned by his kinsmen. He is then expelled. Cf. Jean-Paul Clébert, The Gypsies, tr. C. Duff (1967), 160 (on the authority of the Gypsy novelist, Mateo Maximoff).

241 The prayer of Habakkuk

Concerning Resheph, cf. also: F. Vattioni, in Annali dell'Istituto Univ. Orientale di Napoli, N.S. 15 (1965), 39–74.—n.77. The Hebrew expression 'eryah te'ôr qaštēka (lit.: "Thy bow is utterly naked"), which has given trouble to commentators, is admirably illustrated by the Greek γυμνὸν τόξον in Odyssey 11.607 and γυμνὸς οἴστος, ib., 21.417.—A text from Nuzu indicates that a quiver might contain some thirty arrows: Y. Yadin, The Art of Warfare in Biblical Lands (1963), i.82.

259 Paradisal bliss

The phrase, "In thy light do we see light," is usually explained as an imitation of one used conventionally in addressing kings, e.g., in the Tell Amarna Letters, 190.9; 214.11 ff.; 239, 8 ff., Winckler. The Egyptian pharaoh was commonly regarded as an embodiment of Horus, son of the sun-god Re': cf. H. Ranke, Aegypten (1923), 60. Similarly, in Hittite hieroglyphic script, the sign for "sun" appears in the name of kings: cf. E. F. Weidner, in AfO 1 (1927), 135–37; A. Goetze, Kleinasien[1] (1933), 82 f.—Similarly, among the Natchez of Mississippi, the culture-hero is a sun-child, and his offspring are called "suns": Le Page du Praz, Histoire de la Lusiane (1758), ii.331–36. It may be suggested, however, that the expression really continues the description of paradise, or the Faery Garden. In Hebrew folklore this was located in the region of the rising sun (Gen. 2:7; see above §13), and in the Mesopotamian Epic of Gilgamesh (IX.v.45 ff.), the divine garden seems to lie at the point of sunrise.

262a "A river whose streams rejoice the city of God" Psalm 46:4

A mythological allusion. The "city of the gods" (so we should render) is the celestial city, where they dwell; the term is so used again in Ps. 87:3 (see below, §272). The river is the stream which runs through Paradise and which is sometimes identified astrally with the Milky Way (see above, §14). This pleasant, tranquil river is here contrasted with the raging seas which symbolize the turbulence of the heathen (v.7). It is the river mentioned in Rev. 22:2.—Cf. also: H. Kruse, in Verbum Domini (1949), 23–27; H. Junker, in Biblica 43 (1962), 197–201.

The immediately succeeding clause (RSV: "the holy habitation of the Most High") is somewhat difficult. The traditional text's QᵉDôŠ MiŠKᵉNê 'ELYôN involves positing an unusual masculine plural of the word miškan, paralleled only in Ezek. 25:4. Elsewhere the plural always has the feminine form miškᵉnôth. The Greek (Septuagint) Version therefore vocalizes the words, QiDDeŠ MiŠKāNô 'ELYôn, "The Most High has sanctified his habitation," and this is adopted by many modern scholars. Tentatively, I suggest that the word QDŠ should be emended to the very similar QRŠ, which, in the Canaanite texts from Ras Shamra-Ugarit, denotes a portion of the special desmene of the supreme god, El. It does not occur in this sense in the Old Testament, and therefore, being unrecognized, was misread. The correct translation would then be: "O river whose rills rejoice the City Divine, the demesne of the dwelling-place supernal!"

Some scholars have emended the word PᵉLāGāW, "its streams," to GāLāW, "its waves." This is silly. First, a river has no waves. Second, this destroys the imagery, the picture of the heavenly city—here in turn equated with the earthly Zion—being drawn from the analogy of early Mesopotamian cities built on lagoons.

265 Bottled tears

On this custom at the annual Hosein-ceremonies in Iran, cf. S. G. Wilson, Life and Customs³ (1896), 190 ff.

272 The heavenly and earthly Zion

Cf. also: H. Jefferson in VT 13 (1963), 87–91. I cannot accept the treatment of this psalm by E. Beauchamp, in Studii Biblici Franciscani Liber Annuualis 13 (1962–63), 53–75, which seems to me to involve too many arbitrary transpositions of verses.

274 The soul as bird

Cf. also Greek Apoc. Baruch, ch. 10—TB Sanhedrin 91ᵃ has the soul declare, "After I leave the body, I flutter in the air like a bird."—Abôth dᵉ-R. Nathan, Add. 2, p. 160, ed. Schechter, applies Eccles. 12:4 ("one shall rise up at the voice of a bird") to the soul.

284 The ritual of enthronement

On the ritual acclamation of the new king, cf. E. Spanheim, In Callimachi hymnos observationes (1697), 647; G. van der Leeuw, Religion in Essence and Manifestation (1963), 431.

294 Mother Earth

On the concept that earth both bears and ultimately receives all men, cf. Aeschylus, Choephoroe 120–21; Euripides, Supplices 536; Lucretius, v. 319; Pacuvius, fr. 86.—For the concept in Sanskrit literature, cf. S. L. Sütterlin, in ARW 8 (1906), 533 f.—This notion begets the custom of lifting a child from the earth immediately after birth, and of depositing the dead there immediately after death; cf. T. H. Gaster, The Holy and the Profane (1955), 163.

298a   Spirits of the field   Job 5:23

The traditional Hebrew text reads:

> For thou shalt be in league with the stones of the field,
> and the beasts of the field shall be in compact with thee.

It has been objected that there would be no point in a league with the stones of the field, since they could offer nothing as their part of the bargain: L. Köhler, in ARW 7 (1910), 75–79. Accordingly, the words, 'aBNê Ha-SaDeH ("stones of the field"), have been emended to 'aDôNê Ha-SaDeH, "lords of the field" (Rashi, Köhler) or to BeNê Ha-SaDeH, "sons of the field," i.e., field-spirits. These would be the spirits of the soil, called in Arabic ahl el-ard, "earth-folk"; cf. M. Pope, Job (1965), 46.

This seductive interpretation is, however, quite unnecessary. What the poet is saying is that God's chastisements are directed toward the correction, not the destruction, of men. If they are accepted, men can still hope for eventual good fortune. God will ransom them from death in time of famine, and from the sword in time of war. They will be kept in hiding from the scourge of slander and need have no fears when seeming disaster approaches. They can safely "laugh off" any appearance of imminent hunger or ruin, and can feel secure before savage beasts (vv. 17–22). The stony soil—known to the modern fellahin as "devil's land" (ard Iblis; cf. T. Canaan, in ZDMG 70 [1916], 168)— will not prove an obstacle to their getting earth's produce; they will be, so to speak, on friendly terms with it. Similarly, wild beasts will not assail them; they will, as it were, have come to terms with them. (Heb. hašlamah is to be understood in the sense of Akkadian šulmu, "agreement"; cf. Obad. 7).

311   The thread of life

It may be suggested that the simile is continued in the second half of the verse, "When God takes away his life," for the Hebrew word (nafšô) rendered "his life" may in fact contain a play on a word (*nefš; cf. Akkadian napšu; Aram. and Arabic n-f-s) meaning "carded wool," while that rendered "takes away" means properly "pulls off." (This interpretation has the advantage of giving special point to the rare verb, and thus of avoiding capricious emendation.)

314   Blowing kisses to the sun

Lucian says that the Greeks worshiped the sun by kissing their hands to it; cf. Grimm-Stallybrass, TM 1294.

319   Rain from bottles

Cf. Trinculo in Shakespeare's The Tempest, II.ii.20 ff.: Yond same black cloud, yond huge one, like a foul bombard that would shed his liquor. (A bombard is a leather jug or a bottle.)

319a   Numbering the clouds with wisdom   Job 38:37-38

> Who can number the clouds with wisdom,
> or tilt the waterskins of heaven,
> when the dust congeals into a mass,
> and the clods stick fast together?

The parallelism suggests that this refers specifically to measuring the due amount of rainfall, for the Mesopotamians spoke likewise of "measuring" or "weighing out" rain: Atraḫasis Epic, A 11. In omen texts, "weighed rainfall" (*zunnu šaqlu*) means scarce, or measured rainfall, in contrast to a violent downpour: cf. F. R. Kraus, in ZA 43 (1946), 109; T. Bauer, ib., 311; B. Landsberger, MSL II (1937), 228; Lassøe, in Bibliotheca Orientalis 13 (1956), 91.

An alternative suggestion might be, however, that the Hebrew word *YiSPôR*, "numbers," should be emended to *YᵉSaPpeᵃḤ*, "pours out."

ABBREVIATIONS

AAA	Annals of Archaeology and Anthropology
AASOR	Annual of the American Schools of Oriental Research
AB	The Ugaritic *Poem of Baal* (Virolleaud's numeration)
Abh.BAW	Abhandlungen der Bayerischen Akademie der Wissenschaften
Afo	Archiv für Orientforschung
AJP	American Journal of Philology
AJSL	American Journal of Semitic Languages and Literatures
ALW	Archiv für Liturgiewissenschaft
ANEP	*The Ancient Near East in Pictures,* ed. J. B. Pritchard. Princeton 1955
ANET	*Ancient Near Eastern Texts relating to the Old Testament,* ed. J. B. Pritchard. Princeton 1955
AO	Der Alte Orient
AOF	H. Winckler, *Altorientalische Forschungen*
AOr	Archiv Orientální
APAW	Abhandlungen der Preussischen Akademie der Wissenschaften
AR	*Ancient Records of Egypt,* tr. J. H. Breasted. Chicago 1906
ARAB	*Ancient Records of Assyria and Babylonia,* tr. D.D. *Luckenbill.* Chicago 1926–27
ARM	*Archives Royales de Mari,* ed. A. Parrot and G. Dossin. Paris 1940–
ARW	Archiv für Religionswissenschaft
ASAE	Annales du Service des Antiquités de l'Égypte
ASAW	Abhandlungen der Sächsischen Gesellschaft der Wissenschaften
ASKT	P. Haupt, *Akkadische und sumerische Keilschrifttexte.* Leipzig 1881
ASTI	Annual of the Swedish Theological Institute in Jerusalem
AT	Alte Testament
ATOB	H. Gressmann, ed., *Altorientalische Texte und Bilder zum Alten Testament*[2]. Berlin-Leipzig 1926–27
ÄZ	Ägyptische Zeitschrift
BA	The Biblical Archaeologist
BASOR	Bulletin of the American Schools of Oriental Research
BBAE	Bulletin of the Bureau of American Ethnology
BD	The Egyptian Book of the Dead
BEUP	The Babylonian Expedition of the University of Pennsylvania
BIFAO	Bulletin de l'Institut Français d'archéologie orientale
BJRL	Bulletin of the John Rylands Library, Manchester, England
BM	British Museum
BOr	Bibliotheca Orientalis
BoTU	E. Forrer, *Die Boghazköi-Texte in Umschrift.* Leipzig 1922, 1926
BSGW	Berichte der Sächsischen Gesellschaft der Wissenschaften
BTLVNI	Bijdragen Taal, Land– en Volkenkunde van Nederlandsch Indië

CAH	Cambridge Ancient History
CBQ	Catholic Biblical Quarterly
CIA	Corpus Inscriptionum Atticarum
CIH	Corpus Inscriptionum Himjariticarum (CIS iv)
CIS	Corpus Inscriptionum Semiticarum
CQ	Classical Quarterly
CR	Classical Review
CRAIBL	Comptes Rendus, Académie des Inscriptions et Belles Lettres, Paris
CT	Cuneiform Texts from Babylonian Tablets in the British Museum
Cult. Bib.	Cultura Bíblica, Segovia

| DB | Dictionary of the Bible, ed. J. Hastings |
| DM | J. Grimm, *Deutsche Mythologie*[4], ed. E. H. Meyer. Berlin 1875 |

EBib.	Encyclopaedia Biblica, ed. T. K. Cheyne and J. Black
EBrit.	Encyclopaedia Britannica
EEF	Egyptian Exploration Fund
EG	*Epigrammata graeca ex lapidibus collecta,* ed. G. Kaibel. Berlin 1876
ERE	Encyclopaedia of Religion and Ethics, ed. J. Hastings
ET	The Expository Times
ETL	Ephemerides Theologicae Lovanienses
EV	English Version (KJV, RV) of the Bible

| FFC | Folklore Fellowship Communications, Helsinki |
| FHG | *Fragmenta Historicorum Graecorum,* ed. K. Müller. Paris 1868–83 |

| GB | James G. Frazer, *The Golden Bough* |
| GThT | Gereformeerd Theologisch Tijdschrift |

Heb.	Hebrew
HN	Pliny, *Historia Naturalis*
HUCA	Hebrew Union College Annual, Cincinnati
HWb	Handwörterbuch
HWbDA	Handwörterbuch des deutschen Aberglaubens, ed. H. Bächtold-Staubl et al. Berlin 1927–

ICC	International Critical Commentary
IDB	Interpreters' Dictionary of the Bible
IEJ	Israel Exploration Journal
ILN	Illustrated London News

JA	Journal asiatique
JAF	Journal of American Folklore
JAI	Journal of the Anthropological Institute, London
JAOS	Journal of the American Oriental Society
JAS	Journal of the Asiatic Society
JBL	Journal of Biblical Literature and Exegesis
JCS	Journal of Cuneiform Studies
JEA	Journal of Egyptian Archaeology
JHS	Journal of Hellenic Studies
JHUC	Journal of the Hebrew Union College, Cincinnati

JJS	Journal of Jewish Studies
JMEOS	Journal of the Manchester Egyptian and Oriental Society
JQR	The Jewish Quarterly Review
JRAI	Journal of the Royal Anthropological Institute, London
JRAS	Journal of the Royal Asiatic Society
JRS	Journal of Roman Studies
JTS	Journal of Theological Studies

KARI	*Keilschrifttexte aus Assur religiösen Inhalts*, ed. E. Ebeling. Leipzig 1919–
KAT	*Die Keilinschriften und das Alte Testament*[3], ed. H. Zimmern and H. Winckler. Berlin 1903
KAVI	*Keilschrifttexte aus Assur verschiedenen Inhalts*, ed. O. Schroeder. Leipzig 1920
KB	*Keilinschriftliche Bibliothek*, ed. E. Schrader. Berlin 1889–1915
KBo	Keilschrifttexte aus Boghazköi
KJV	King James (Authorised) Version of the Bible
Kl.Forsch.	Kleinasiatische Forschungen
KUB	Keilschrifturkunden aus Boghazköi

| LSS | Leipziger semitische Studien, ed. A. Fischer and H. Zimmern |
| LXX | Septuagint (Greek) Version of the Old Testament, ed. Rahlfs |

MDOG	Mitteilungen der Deutschen Orientalistichen Gesellschaft
MeL	R. Pettazzoni, *Miti e Leggende*
MGWJ	Monatsschrift für Geschichte und Wissenschaft des Judentums
MI	Stith Thompson, *Motif-Index to Folk Literature*[1] (FFC, 106–09, 116–17; Indiana University Studies, 106–12). 6 vols. Helsinki-Bloomington 1932–36
MScRel	Melanges de Sciences Religieuses
MVAG	Mitteilungen der Vorderasiatisch-Aegyptischen Gesellschaft

N.F.	Neue Folge
NGB	J. G. Frazer—T. H. Gaster, *The New Golden Bough*. New York, Mentor Books, 1964
NTT	Norsk Teologisk Tidsskrift

OECT	Oxford Editions of Cuneiform Texts, ed. S. Langdon
OLz	Orientalistische Literaturzeitung
OT	Old Testament

PBS	Publications of the Babylonian Section of the University Museum, Pennsylvania
PE	Eusebius, *Praeparatio evengelica*
PEFQS	Quarterly Statement of the Palestine Exploration Fund
PEQ	Palestine Exploration Quarterly
PG	Patrologia Graeca, ed. Migne
PMLA	Proceedings of the Modern Language Association
PQ	Philological Quarterly
PRE	Realencyclopädie für protestantische Theologie und Kirche[3]. Leipzig 1896–1913
PSBA	Proceedings of the Society of Biblical Archaeology

P–W   Pauly-Wissowa-Kroll, Realencyclopädie der klassischen Altertums-
                    wissenschaft

R   H. C. Rawlinson, *The Cuneiform Inscriptions of Western Asia*. Lon-
                    don 1861–64
RA   Revue d'assyriologie et d'archéologie orientale
RB   Revue biblique
RBCalz   Rivista Biblica, Villa Calbada (Argentine)
Rev. Celt.   Revue celtique
RGG   Die Religion in Geschichte und Gegenwart. First ed., Tübingen,
                    1909–13; second ed., Tübingen, 1927 ff.
Rhein. Mus.   Rhienisches Museum für Philologie
RHPR   Revue d'Histoire et de Philosophie Religieuses
RHR   Revue de l'histoire des religions
RIA   Reallexicon der indogermanischen Altertumskunde[2]. Leipzig 1929
Riv. Stud. Or.   Rivista degli Studi Orientali
RR   Review of Religion
RS   Ras Shamra text
RSV   Revised Standard Version of the Bible
RV   Revised Version of the Bible
RVV   Religionsgeschichtliche Versuche und Vorarbeiten

SBE   Sacred Books of the East
SBOT   Sacred Books of the Old Testament (the "Rainbow Bible"), ed.
                    P. Haupt
SEG   *Sylloge Inscriptionum Graecarum*[2], ed. W. Dittenberger. Leipzig
                    1898–1901
SMSR   Studi e materiali di storia delle religioni
SOTS   Society for Old Testament Study (Great Britain)

TANAG   Tijdschrift v. h. Kon. Nederl. Aardr. Genootschap
TAPA   Transactions of the American Philological Association
TAPS   Transactions of the American Philosophical Society
TB   Babylonian Talmud
ThLZ (also TLZ)   Theologische Literaturzeitung
TITLV   Tijdschrift voor Indische Taal–, Land en Volkenkunde
TJ   Jerusalemitan (Palestinian) Talmud
TM   J. Grimm, *Teutonic Mythology*, tr. F. Stallybrass (reprint, New
                    York 1966)
TSBA   Transactions of the Society of Biblical Archaeology
TT   Theologisch Tijdschrift
TZ   Theologische Zeitschrift

UCP   University of California Publications in American Archeology and
                    Ethnology
UH   C. H. Gordon, *Ugaritic Handbook*. Rome 1947
UILL   University of Illinois Studies in Language and Literature

VAB   Vorderasiatische Bibliothek, ed. H. Winckler and A. Jeremias
VAT   Cuneiform tablet in the Vorderasiatische Abtheilung of the Staatliche
                    Museen, Berlin

VD	Verbum Domini
VT	Vetus Testamentum
W.A.I.	See R
WO	Die Welt des Orients
WZKM	Wiener Zeitschrift für die Kunde des Morgenlandes
ZA	Zeitschrift für Assyriologie
ZÄS	Zeitschrift für ägyptische Sprache
ZAW	Zeitschrift für die alttestamentliche Wissenschaft
ZDMG	Zeitschrift der Deutschen Morgenländischen Gesellschaft
ZE	Zeitschrift für Ethnologie
ZK	Zeitschrift für Keilschriftforschung
ZKM	Zeitschrift für die Kunde des Morgenlandes
ZNTW	Zeitschrift für die neutestamentliche Wissenschaft
ZS	Zeitschrift für Semitistik
Zs.f.V(1)k.	Zeitschrift für Völkerkunde
ZTK	Zeitschrift für Theologie und Kirche

INDEX OF MOTIFS

Numbers in the left-hand column refer to Stith Thompson's standard *Motif-Index of Folk-Literature;* those in the right-hand column refer to the sections of the present work.

Garden of gods	A 151.2; * F 111	12
Griffin guards treasure	N 575	19
Honey, rivers of	* F 162.2.3	14
Horns blow down wall	D 1562.3	104
Hunt, Wild	E 50b	71; 337
Inexhaustible cruse	* D 1652 ff.	165
Jonah, swallowed by great fish	F 911.4	236(c)
Joseph and Potiphar's wife	K 2111	76
places cup in sack	H 151.4	77
Ladder to upper world	F 52	64
Lengthening day by magic	D 2146.1.1	106
Leviathan	B 61	186
Lot's wife turned to salt	C 961.1	58
Maimed king must retire	P 16.2	
Mandrake	* D 965.1; B 754.2	67
Manna	D 1030.1.1	88
Milk and honey	F 701.1	14
Moses rescued by princess	R 131.11.1	78
Mutilations	S 161.1	107; 134
Navel of the earth	A 875.1	113
North, abode of demons	G 633	180; 233
Paradise		
on mountain	F 132.1	213
four rivers of	* F 162.2.1	14
serpent in	B 176.1	18
waters of	A 878.1	14
Password, recognition by	H18(ad.)	116
Pillar(s) of heaven	A 665.2	309
Precious stones, city of	F 761	195
Raven	A 2234.1	47, 156
Serpent, immortality of	A 1355(ad.)	18
Seven, formulistic	Z 71.5	
Seventy-seven	Z 71.15	31
Sheba, Queen of, riddles of	H 540.2.1	153
Shibboleth	H 18(ad.)	116
Solomon, judgment of	J 1171.1–2	150
Staff		
blossoming	* F 971.2; H 331.3	95
draws water from stone	D 1549.5	81
Subterranean castle	* F 721.5	321

INDEX

References are to *numbered sections,* not to pages

WILLIAM K. SANFORD TOWN LIBRARY

0000170324

WITHDRAWN

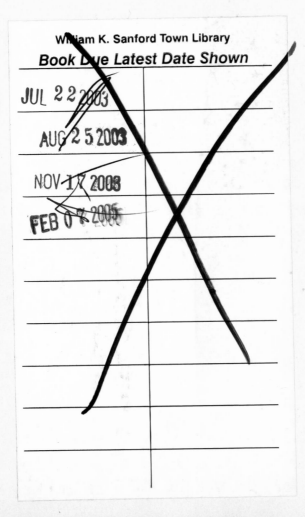

William K. Sanford Town Library
Book Due Latest Date Shown

JUL 2 2 2003

AUG 2 5 2003

NOV 1 7 2003

FEB 0 7 2005